The most you can ask of any World History program

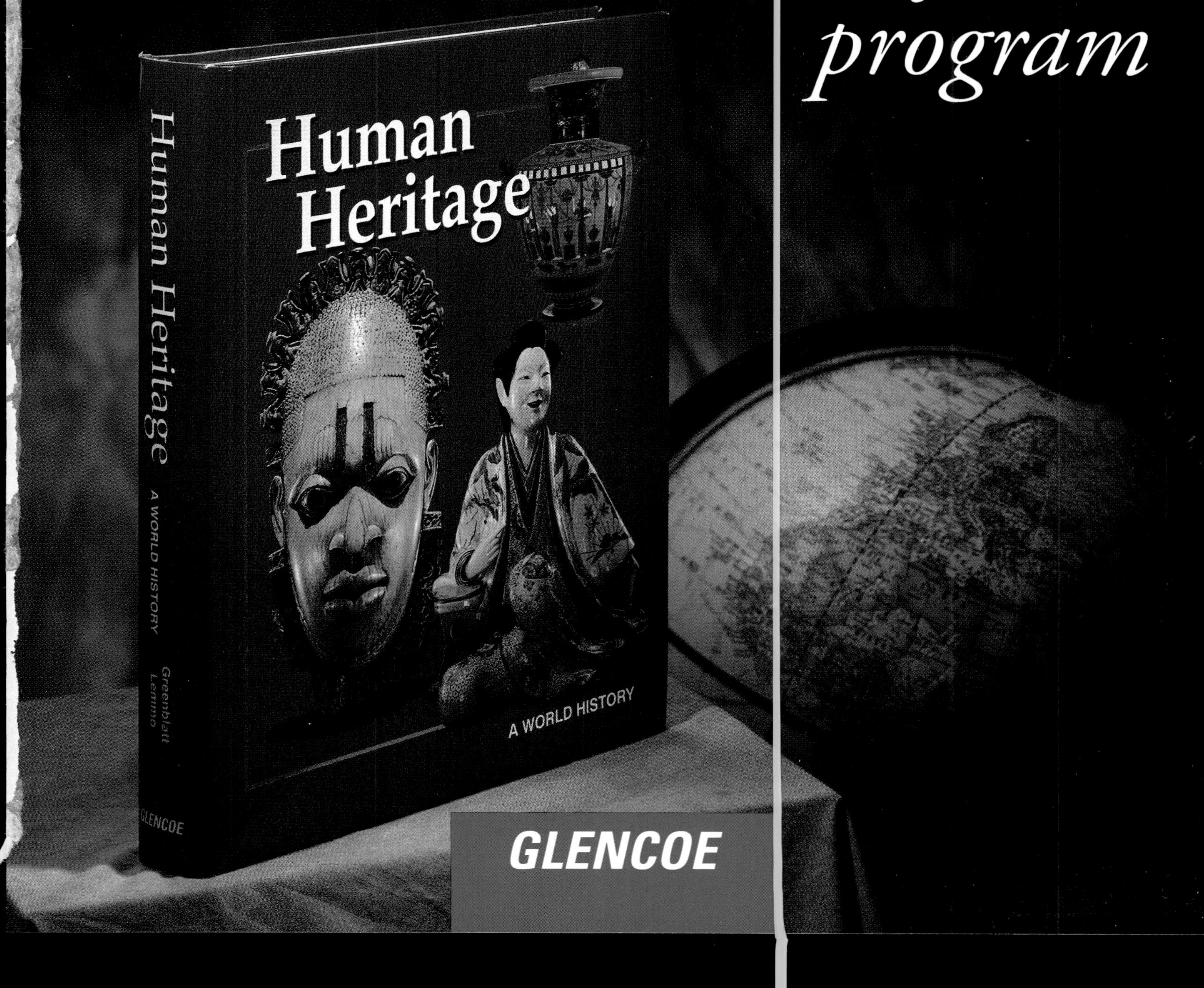

GLENCOE

STUDENT EDITION

The most popular

You've told us so, over and over again. *Human Heritage* is continually selected as the ***number one*** choice by World History teachers all over the country. And now it's completely updated and better than ever.

The most readable

It's the strong ***narrative style***, which weaves a wonderful, rich, and colorful story about people of the past and the lives they lived, that truly sets this book apart from any other. And the easy-to-follow, ***single-column format*** is another element of this book's appeal.

Only *Human Heritage* succeeds in captivating the imaginations of your students.

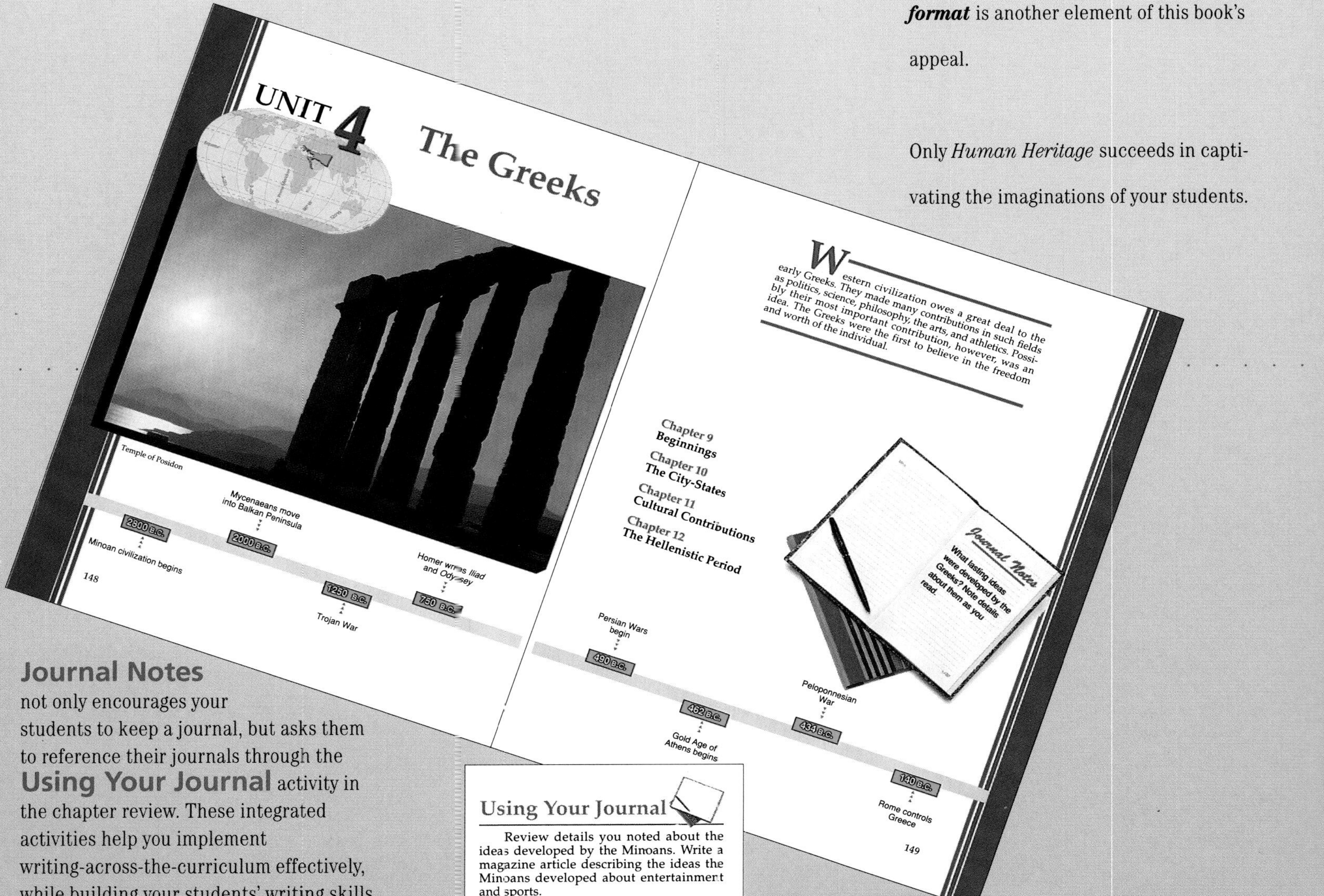

UNIT 4
The Greeks
Temple of Posidon
Mycenaeans move into Balkan Peninsula
2800 B.C.
Minoan civilization begins
2000 B.C.
1250 B.C.
Trojan War
Homer writes Iliad and Odyssey
750 B.C.
148
Western civilization owes a great deal to the early Greeks. They made many contributions in such fields as politics, science, philosophy, the arts, and athletics. Possibly their most important contribution, however, was an idea. The Greeks were the first to believe in the freedom and worth of the individual.
Chapter 9 Beginnings
Chapter 10 The City-States
Chapter 11 Cultural Contributions
Chapter 12 The Hellenistic Period
Journal Notes
What lasting ideas were developed by the Greeks? Note details about them as you read.
Persian Wars begin
490 B.C.
462 B.C.
Gold Age of Athens begins
Peloponnesian War
431 B.C.
140 B.C.
Rome controls Greece
149
Using Your Journal
Review details you noted about the ideas developed by the Minoans. Write a magazine article describing the ideas the Minoans developed about entertainment and sports.

Journal Notes not only encourages your students to keep a journal, but asks them to reference their journals through the **Using Your Journal** activity in the chapter review. These integrated activities help you implement writing-across-the-curriculum effectively, while building your students' writing skills.

The most richly illustrated

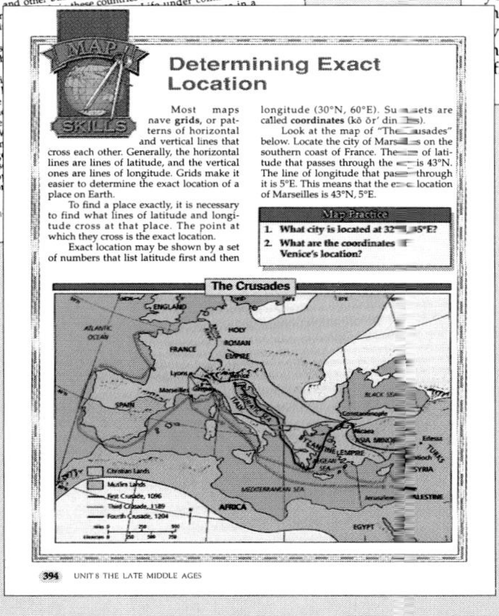

Geography in History

LOCATION Refer to the map on page 356. Imagine that the czar has asked you to choose the location of a new settlement in the area acquired by the death of Ivan IV. Where would you locate the settlement and why? What geographic features affected your decision?

Breathtaking artwork and photographs, clear and colorful maps, and dynamic special features make *Human Heritage* the one textbook your students will never put down.

Map Skills lessons in each chapter let you make the history-to-geography connection more easily–and successfully–than ever before. Combined with the **Map Study** program and the **Geography in History** activity in every chapter review, geography becomes a relevant part of every history lesson.

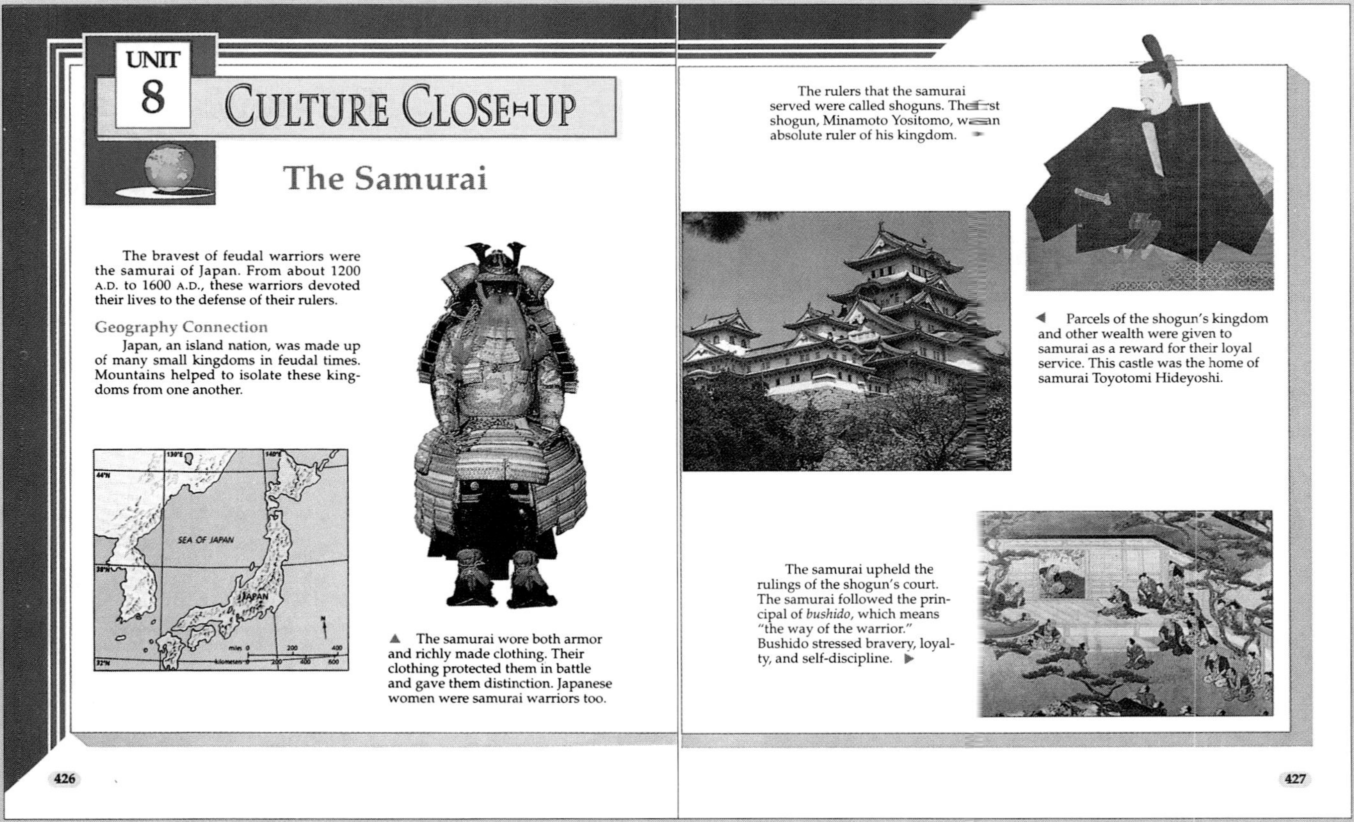

UNIT 8
CULTURE CLOSE-UP
The Samurai
The bravest of feudal warriors were the samurai of Japan. From about 1200 A.D. to 1600 A.D., these warriors devoted their lives to the defense of their rulers.
Geography Connection
Japan, an island nation, was made up of many small kingdoms in feudal times. Mountains helped to isolate these kingdoms from one another.
SEA OF JAPAN
JAPAN
The samurai wore both armor and richly made clothing. Their clothing protected them in battle and gave them distinction. Japanese women were samurai warriors too.
The rulers that the samurai served were called shoguns. The first shogun, Minamoto Yositomo, was an absolute ruler of his kingdom.
Parcels of the shogun's kingdom and other wealth were given to samurai as a reward for their loyal service. This castle was the home of samurai Toyotomi Hideyoshi.
The samurai upheld the rulings of the shogun's court. The samurai followed the principal of bushido, which means "the way of the warrior." Bushido stressed bravery, loyalty, and self-discipline.
426
427

Culture Close-Up features a high-impact, in-depth look at the art, artifacts, music, and literature of various civilizations so students actually experience the daily life of the past, rather than simply read about it.

TEACHER'S WRAPAROUND EDITION

The most manageable

The ALL-NEW Teacher's Wraparound Edition puts everything you need at the point of instruction.

The NEW **Teacher's Wraparound Edition** makes organizing your lessons easier than ever. Options for using instructional materials are cross-referenced for you, right at your fingertips. And, with the 4-step "Focus, Teach, Assess, and Close" lesson plan, you can make each lesson as thorough–and effective–as possible.

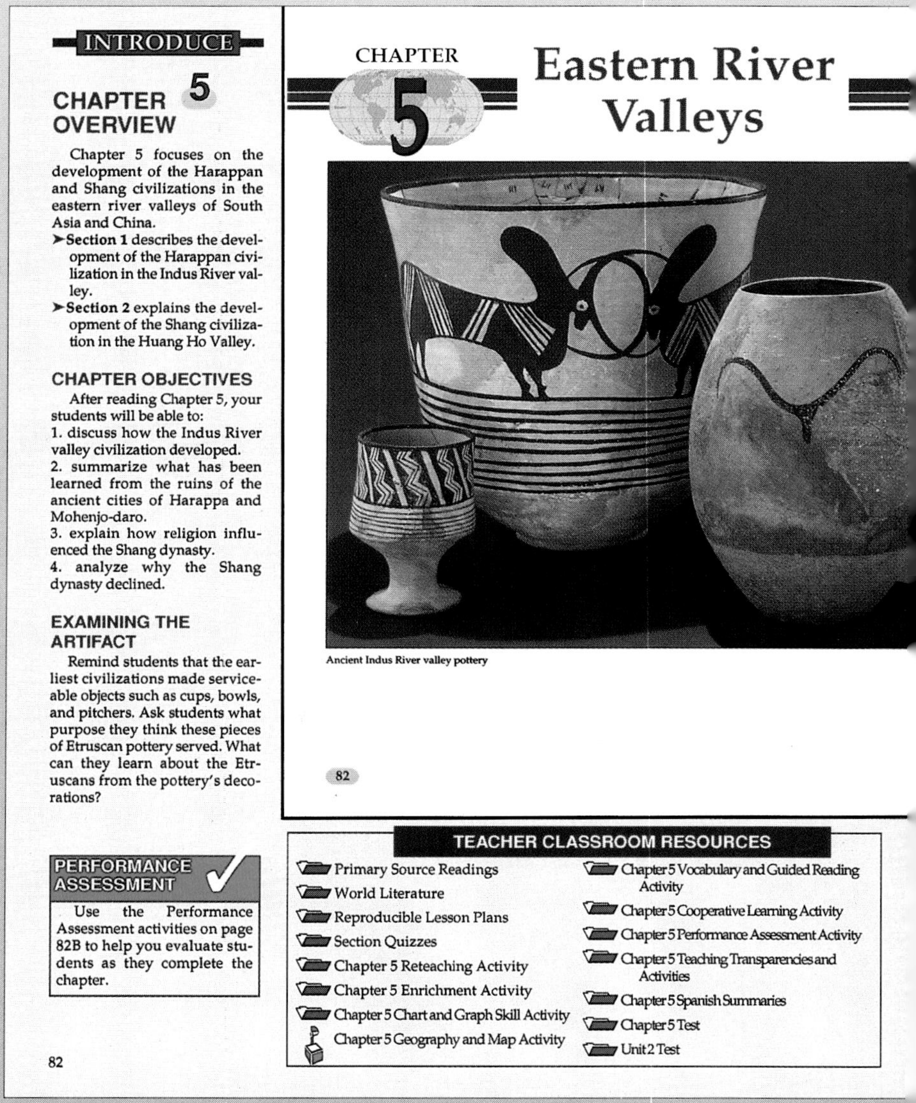
INTRODUCE

CHAPTER 5 OVERVIEW

Chapter 5 focuses on the development of the Harappan and Shang civilizations in the eastern river valleys of South Asia and China.

➤**Section 1** describes the development of the Harappan civilization in the Indus River valley.

➤**Section 2** explains the development of the Shang civilization in the Huang Ho Valley.

CHAPTER OBJECTIVES

After reading Chapter 5, your students will be able to:

1. discuss how the Indus River valley civilization developed.
2. summarize what has been learned from the ruins of the ancient cities of Harappa and Mohenjo-daro.
3. explain how religion influenced the Shang dynasty.
4. analyze why the Shang dynasty declined.

EXAMINING THE ARTIFACT

Remind students that the earliest civilizations made serviceable objects such as cups, bowls, and pitchers. Ask students what purpose they think these pieces of Etruscan pottery served. What can they learn about the Etruscans from the pottery's decorations?

PERFORMANCE ASSESSMENT

Use the Performance Assessment activities on page 82B to help you evaluate students as they complete the chapter.

82

CHAPTER 5 Eastern River Valleys

Ancient Indus River valley pottery

82

TEACHER CLASSROOM RESOURCES

- Primary Source Readings
- World Literature
- Reproducible Lesson Plans
- Section Quizzes
- Chapter 5 Reteaching Activity
- Chapter 5 Enrichment Activity
- Chapter 5 Chart and Graph Skill Activity
- Chapter 5 Geography and Map Activity
- Chapter 5 Vocabulary and Guided Reading Activity
- Chapter 5 Cooperative Learning Activity
- Chapter 5 Performance Assessment Activity
- Chapter 5 Teaching Transparencies and Activities
- Chapter 5 Spanish Summaries
- Chapter 5 Test
- Unit 2 Test

Performance Assessment Activities outline multistep, alternative-assessment activities, tied directly to chapter content. Now you can monitor your students' learning without spending excess time developing activities on your own.

Cross-Curricular Connections illustrate how history topics are integrated with the arts, science, math, and other disciplines, so students go beyond the facts to see history's "big picture."

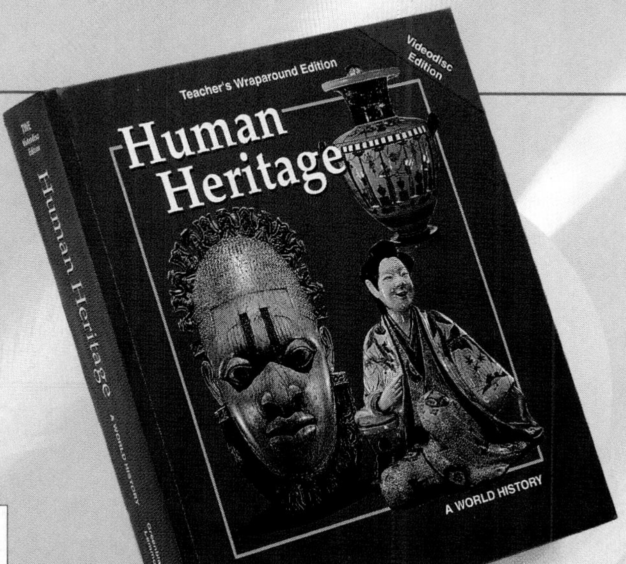

Chapter Focus

READ TO DISCOVER:

- How the Indus River valley civilization developed.
- What has been learned from the ruins of Harappa and Mohenjo-daro.
- How religion influenced the Shang dynasty.
- Why the Shang dynasty declined.

In 3500 B.C., civilization began in Sumer. Some 400 years later, it began in Egypt. Several hundred years after that, river valley civilizations began in the East. By 2500 B.C., cities started to appear in the Indus River valley of South Asia. By 2000 B.C., they were being established in the Huang Ho (Yellow River) valley of China.

More isolated than the people of Mesopotamia or Egypt, the people of eastern river valley civilizations were cut off from other parts of the world by high mountains, broad deserts, and large bodies of water. As a result, they became *self-sufficient*, or able to take care of all of their own needs. Compared to the Sumerians and the Egyptians, they did little trading with other groups of people.

Less is known about life in eastern river valley civilizations than is known about Sumerian or Egyptian life. This is because very few remains have been found. Much of what is known about ancient eastern peoples comes from legend. Until more records are found, their early life will remain in part a mystery.

2500 B.C.–1000 B.C.

KEY TERMS

planned communities
citadel
dynasty
spirits
ancestors
oracle bones
nobles

Section 1

THE INDUS RIVER VALLEY

The Indus River flows through the countries known today as Pakistan and India. About 2500 B.C., a group of people called Harappans (huh rap' uhnz) settled in the valley of the Indus River. Although others had lived there before, the Harappans

83

FOCUS

BELLRINGER

Write on the chalkboard: *How do you think mountains affected the lives of people in early civilizations?* Have students write a brief answer.

MOTIVATIONAL ACTIVITY

Have students read their thoughts about how mountains have affected civilizations. Then tell students that the early Indus River and Huang Ho Valley civilizations were isolated from other civilizations by natural barriers such as high mountains. Ask students how isolation might affect a civilization. (*It forced them to take care of all their needs. They were unable to exchange ideas or knowledge with other people.*)

VOCABULARY PRE-CHECK

Write the key terms for this chapter on the chalkboard. Ask students to use those that they know in sentences.

Assign Chapter 5 **Vocabulary and Guided Reading Activity** in the TCR.

KEY TO ABILITY LEVELS

Teaching Strategies have been coded for varying learning styles and abilities.

L1 Level 1 activities are basic activities and should be within the ability range of all students.

L2 Level 2 activities are average activities and should be within the ability range of the average to above-average students.

L3 Level 3 activities are challenging activiies designed for the ability range of above-average students.

LEP LEP activities should be within the ability range of Limited English Proficiency students.

EXTRA CREDIT PROJECT

Interested students may want to find out more about what the diet of the Shang was like. Ask them to research the grains grown and how they were grown (millet, wheat, rice) and how they were prepared. Encourage them to then find or develop a recipe for each grain they research to share with the class.

83

Videodisc Barcodes in each chapter correlate topics with the *Western Civilization Videodisc Program* and the *Non-European World History Videodisc Program*. Now you can reach today's video generation and make every lesson more dynamic, with the simple touch of a remote control.

Cooperative Learning Activities provide a broad range of strategies and activities that allow you to add the dimension of collaborative learning without adding preparation time.

Multicultural Perspectives illustrate how cultural diversity is a critical element of history, so students can develop an understanding of different cultures and their influence throughout history.

The Teacher's Wraparound Edition also includes: Geography Connections • Multimedia Resources • Historical Background Notes • Meeting Special Needs Strategies • High-Interest Biographical Sidelights • Links to the Humanities • Expanded Cultural Studies • And much more.

The most resourceful

With comprehensive new resources, you can deliver more depth...in less time.

Multimedia Resources

English and Spanish Audiocassettes with activities and tests that correspond with each chapter, to help students with limited English proficiency or reading comprehension deficiencies grasp concepts more easily.

Focus on World Art Prints includes 25 colorful, laminated fine-art posters that show students how the cultural heritage of a region is reflected through the arts.

The **Western Civilization Videodisc Program** and the **Non-European World History Videodisc Program** each feature narrative overviews of major historical periods and over 2,000 world-renowned archival images in an easy-to-access, remote-control format to help you add fascinating details to your classes.

Other video resources include:

- **Ancient Civilizations Videotape Series,** Volumes 1-6
- **Life Unworthy of Life: A Holocaust Curriculum**
- **Introduction to the Arab World**

Teaching Transparencies with Strategies and Student Activities help you introduce, reteach, and reinforce chapter concepts.

World History and Art Transparencies Package with Strategies and Student Activities provides students with a high-interest, visual record of the changes that have shaped world history.

World Music: Cultural Traditions takes your students on a musical journey around the world. This dynamic program presents the heritage of a variety of world cultures through a medium today's music-oriented students will enjoy. Available in CD and cassette formats.

Current Events Update

This reproducible resource, published in the fall and in the spring provides up-to-the-minute information on world events and issues. This valuable resource includes reproducible news stories, maps, charts and graphs to keep your classroom up-to-date.

Reproducible Activities

These valuable resources take the preparation time out of developing, expanding, and reviewing lessons.

- World Literature
- Geography and Map Activities
- Vocabulary and Guided Reading Activities
- Chart and Graph Skill Activities
- Cooperative Learning Activities
- Spanish Chapter Summaries and Glossary
- Primary Source Readings
- Enrichment Activities
- Reteaching Activities
- Reproducible Lesson Plans

Enrichment

These cross-disciplinary tools refine students' writing, social studies, and map skills, and add a cultural dimension to your World History classroom.

World History Enrichment Series:
- Map Activities
- Reinforcing Social Studies Skills
- Outline Map Resource Book
- Foods Around the World

Student Activity Book

The four activities in every chapter of this activity book emphasize culture, geography, vocabulary, and social studies skills to give students the extra practice they need to improve reading comprehension. A **Teacher's Annotated Edition** is also available.

Assessment

Performance Assessment Activities include implementation strategies, assessment activities, scoring rubrics, and more, to give you additional options and opportunities to meet your performance assessment requirements.

Additional assessment resources include:
- Chapter Tests
- Section Quizzes
- Testmaker Software
  Apple
  IBM
  Macintosh

Choose Human Heritage

It's more of what you're looking for.

Student Edition	**0-02-823187-2**
Teacher's Wraparound Edition	**0-02-823188-0**
Teacher's Classroom Resources	**0-02-823189-9**

Chapter Tests
Section Quizzes
Reteaching Activities
Enrichment Activities
Reproducible Lesson Plans
World Literature
Geography and Map Activities
Vocabulary and Guided Reading Activities
Chart and Graph Skill Activities
Cooperative Learning Activities
Performance Assessment Activities
Spanish Chapter Summaries and Glossary
Primary Source Readings
World History Enrichment Series:
- Map Activities
- Reinforcing Social Studies Skills
- Outline Map Resource Book
- Foods Around the World

Activity Book	
Student Edition	**0-02-823212-7**
Teacher's Annotated Edition	**0-02-823213-5**
Audiocassette Package	
English	**0-02-823206-2**
Spanish	**0-02-823207-0**
Teaching Transparencies	**0-02-823208-9**
World History and Art Transparencies Package	**0-02-800218-0**
Focus on World Art Prints	**0-02-823214-3**
World Music: Cultural Traditions	**0-02-823041-8**
Testmaker	
Apple (3.5" disks)	**0-02-823203-8**
IBM (3.5" and 5.25" disks)	**0-02-823204-6**
Macintosh (3.5" disks)	**0-02-823205-4**

Also ask your Glencoe representative about:

Current Events Update (Released Biannually)
World History and Cultures Videotape Library
Ancient Civilizations Videotape Series
Life Unworthy of Life: A Holocaust Curriculum
Introduction to the Arab World
The Western Civilization Videodisc Program
The Non-European World History Videodisc Program

1. Northeast Region
GLENCOE
17 Riverside Drive
Nashua, NH 03062
603-880-4701
800-424-3451

2. Mid-Atlantic Region
GLENCOE
5 Terri Lane, Suite 5
Burlington, NJ 08016
609-386-7353
800-553-7515

3. Atlantic-Southeast Region
GLENCOE
Brookside Park
One Harbison Way, Suite 101
Columbia, SC 29212
803-732-2365

4. Southeast Region
GLENCOE
6510 Jimmy Carter Boulevard
Norcross, GA 30071
404-446-7493
800-982-3992

5. Mid-America Region
GLENCOE
4635 Hilton Corporate Drive
Columbus, OH 43232
614-759-6600
800-848-1567

6. Mid-Continent Region
GLENCOE
846 East Algonquin Road
Schaumburg, IL 60173
708-397-8448
800-762-4876

7. Southwest Region
GLENCOE
320 Westway Place, Suite 550
Arlington, TX 76018
817-784-2100
800-828-5096

8. Texas Region
GLENCOE
320 Westway Place, Suite 550
Arlington, TX 76018
817-784-2100
800-828-5096

9. Western Region
GLENCOE
610 East 42nd Street, #102
Boise, ID 83714
208-378-4002
800-452-6126
Includes Alaska

10. California Region
GLENCOE
15319 Chatsworth Street
P. O. Box 9609
Mission Hills, CA 91346
818-898-1391
800-423-9534
Includes Hawaii

Glencoe Catholic School Region
GLENCOE
25 Crescent Street, 1st Floor
Stamford, CT 06906
203-964-9109
800-551-8766

Canada
Maxwell Macmillan Canada
1200 Eglinton Avenue, East
Suite 200
Don Mills, Ontario M3C 3N1
Telephone: 416-449-6030
Telefax: 416-449-0068

Overseas
Macmillan/McGraw-Hill International
10 Union Square East
New York, NY 10003
Telephone: 212-353-5700
Telefax: 212-353-5894

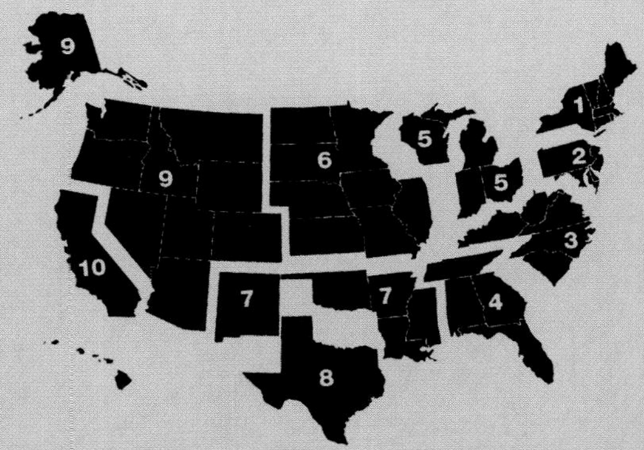

Glencoe Social Studies
Making a World of Difference

For more information contact your nearest regional office or call: 1-800-334-7344.

12/93
SS90908-2

Teacher's Wraparound Edition

VIDEODISC EDITION

Human Heritage

A World History

Human
Heritage
A WORLD HISTORY

Teacher's Wraparound Edition

VIDEODISC EDITION

Human Heritage

A World History

Miriam Greenblatt
Peter Lemmo

GLENCOE

McGraw-Hill

New York, New York   Columbus, Ohio   Mission Hills, California   Peoria, Illinois

About the Authors

Miriam Greenblatt is a writer, editor, and educational consultant who has traveled extensively in Asia, Africa, and Latin America. During the past 25 years, she has contributed to more than 40 elementary, junior high, and high school social studies texts and ancillaries. A graduate of Hunter College of the City of New York and the University of Chicago, and a former teacher, Greenblatt is listed in *Who's Who of American Women* for 1993-94, and *Who's Who of American Education* for 1993-94.

Peter S. Lemmo is a high school teacher in the New York City School System, where he has taught since 1970. A graduate of City College of New York and the City University of New York, he has trained student teachers and contributed to several books. Lemmo has been instrumental in developing pilot instructional programs and curriculum and was rated an exemplary teacher by the State Education Department of New York. He is also a member of the National Council for the Social Studies, the Association for Supervision and Curriculum Development, and other professional organizations, and has traveled extensively in more than 40 countries.

Academic Consultants

Jerrold Green, Ph.D.
Director
Middle East Studies Center
University of Arizona
Tucson, Arizona

Al Naklowycz, Ph.D.
President Ukranian-American Academic Association of California
Carmichael, California

Joseph R. Rosenbloom, Ph.D.
Professor of Classics
Washington University
St. Louis, Missouri

Sayyid M. Syeed, Ph.D.
Director
International Institute of Islamic Thought
Herndon, Virginia

Teacher Reviewers

Richard Ammentorp
Schaumburg School District
Schaumburg, Illinois

Rick Boeglin
Richardson North High School
Richardson, Texas

Margaret Gray, Ph.D.
Vigo County School Corporation
Terre Haute, Indiana

Kathleen A. Grotto
West Orange Senior High School
West Orange, New Jersey

Dianne Hill
Muskogee Public Schools
Muskogee, Oklahoma

Joseph Scheideler
Canton Junior/Senior High School
Collinsville, Connecticut

Glencoe/McGraw-Hill

A Division of The ***McGraw-Hill*** *Companies*

Send all inquires to: Glencoe/McGraw-Hill, 936 Eastwind Drive, Westerville, OH 43081

ISBN 0-02-823187-2 (Student Edition)
ISBN 0-02-823188-0 (Teachers Wraparound Edition)

Printed in the United States of America
3 4 5 6 7 8 9 10 VHJ/LHP 01 00 99 98 97 96

Table of Contents

Table of Contents

Student Edition

Unit 4 The Greeks

Unit 5 The Romans

Unit 6 The Early Middle Ages

Unit 7 Emergence of New Empires

Unit 8 The Late Middle Ages

Unit 9 Beginning of Modern Times

Unit 10 The Changing World

Unit 11 Nations and Empires

Unit 12 The Twentieth Century

Map Skills

People in History

Charts, Diagrams, and Illustrations

Maps

Fine Art Prints
World Music
Cultural Traditions
The World History Videodisc
(non-European history)
HISTORY
ART
TEACHING TRANSPARENCIES
TESTMAKER
CHAPTER DIGESTS AUDIOCASSETTES
MAP ACTIVITIES
REINFORCING SOCIAL STUDIES SKILLS
FOODS OF THE WORLD
GLENCOE SOCIAL STUDIES
OUTLINE MAP
RESOURCE BOOK
GEOGRAPHY AND MAP ACTIVITIES
WORLD LITERATURE
VOCABULARY AND GUIDED READING ACTIVITIES
SPANISH CHAPTER SUMMARIES AND GLOSSARY
REPRODUCIBLE LESSON PLANS
COOPERATIVE LEARNING ACTIVITIES
CHART AND GRAPH SKILL ACTIVITIES
PRIMARY SOURCE READINGS
CHAPTER TESTS
SECTION QUIZZES
PERFORMANCE ASSESSMENT ACTIVITIES
RETEACHING ACTIVITIES
Human Heritage
A WORLD HISTORY

Teacher's Classroom Resources

The Teacher's Classroom Resources provides you with a wide variety of supplemental materials to enhance the classroom experience. These resources meet your teaching needs and your students' abilities. Included are reinforcement and enrichment activities, geography supplements, overhead transparencies, world literature and primary source readings, social studies skills practice activities, and evaluation materials. All components have been developed to assist students in improving their reading comprehension and understanding of the text, while addressing the needs of different learning styles.

Human Heritage: A World History **components include the following titles.**

- **Reproducible Lesson Plans**
- **Vocabulary and Guided Reading Activities**
- **Cooperative Learning Activities**
- **Geography and Map Activities**
- **Chart and Graph Skill Activities**
- **Primary Source Readings**
- **World Literature**
- **Enrichment Activities**
- **Reteaching Activities**
- **Teaching Transparencies**
- **Teaching Transparency Strategies and Activities**
- **Spanish Chapter Summaries and Glossary**
- **Performance Assessment Activities**
- **Section Quizzes**
- **Chapter Tests**
- **Audiocassettes (English and Spanish)**

Additional Glencoe Social Studies Components are also correlated to the text.

VOCABULARY AND GUIDED READING ACTIVITIES

Students will find it easy to master chapter information and assimilate vocabulary words when they use the **Vocabulary and Guided Reading Activities** in conjunction with their reading.

Name ______________________ Date ____________ Class ____________

CHAPTER 1

Vocabulary and Guided Reading Activities

Vocabulary Activity

Complete the following vocabulary exercise on another sheet of paper.

Imagine that you are writing an explanation of the ways in which geography and archaeological and anthropological knowledge help us understand history. Using all of the following vocabulary words, write your explanation as clearly and as simply as you can.

elevation	**erosion**	**climate**
precipitation	**natural resources**	**minerals**
relative location	**prevailing winds**	**archaeologists**
anthropologists	**artifacts**	

Guided Reading Activity

After reading Chapter 1, you should be able to describe how the study of geography, legends, and archaeology help us understand history.

1. List the five themes of geography. ______________________

2. What surface changes are caused by forces deep within the earth? ______________________

3. Give several examples of surface changes from outside the earth helping people. ______________________

4. Give several examples of surface changes from outside the earth harming people. ______________________

COOPERATIVE LEARNING ACTIVITIES

Name ______________________ Date ____________ Class ____________

CHAPTER 1

Cooperative Learning Activity

Travel Considerations

Connection to Chapter

Chapter 1 covers the five geography themes used to tell about a place. It looks at changes in landforms and waterways and at the way climate is shaped by our natural resources. The chapter also makes a distinction between natural resources that are renewable and those that are nonrenewable. Legends and archaeological finds are important to our understanding of the world and its history. By studying our past we learn about Earth, our ancestors, and our future.

Group Directions

Imagine that everyone in your group is going to spend a year studying in a place very different from where you now live. First, you will choose a place. Then, use Chapter 1 and other resources to gather as much information as you can about the place you have chosen. Keep in mind the characteristics of the place. Split into two teams to discuss whether the group should move to the location. You may find that your opinion is different from the others in the group. Interview people who have visited this place or get some information from a travel bureau, a travel agent, or the department of tourism. Include photos and drawings as part of your argument, or include excerpts from a story set there. Then hold a debate to decide which argument is the strongest. The following questions may give you some ideas for the debate:

- **What are the climate and natural resources like?**
- **What makes this place unusual?**
- **What have I read or heard about this place?**
- **What would I like or dislike about the way people live and work there?**
- **What about its history would make me want to spend a year there?**

Cooperative Group Process

1. **Decision Making** As a group, select a place as the topic of your debate. Choose a debate leader for each side of the argument and additional people who will act as reviewers of the debate. Make a list of rules for the debate.
2. **Individual Work** Group members should research and list their own positive and negative conclusions about the place.

(continued)

Cooperative Learning Activities are designed with clear classroom management directions. Students are challenged to work together to solve problems, do research, prepare reports, or give demonstrations.

GEOGRAPHY AND MAP ACTIVITIES

Geography and Map Activities use visuals to connect the five geographic themes to chapter content, helping to make the geography to history connection. Engaging topics and creative activities make geographic learning interesting.

Name ______________________ Date ____________ Class ____________

CHAPTER 1

Geography and Map Activity

Regions: Climate Regions

The earth is divided into many different regions. People have divided it into political regions, such as cities and nations. The earth is also divided into natural regions. Some are based on landforms; others are based on climate.

Latitudes and Climate

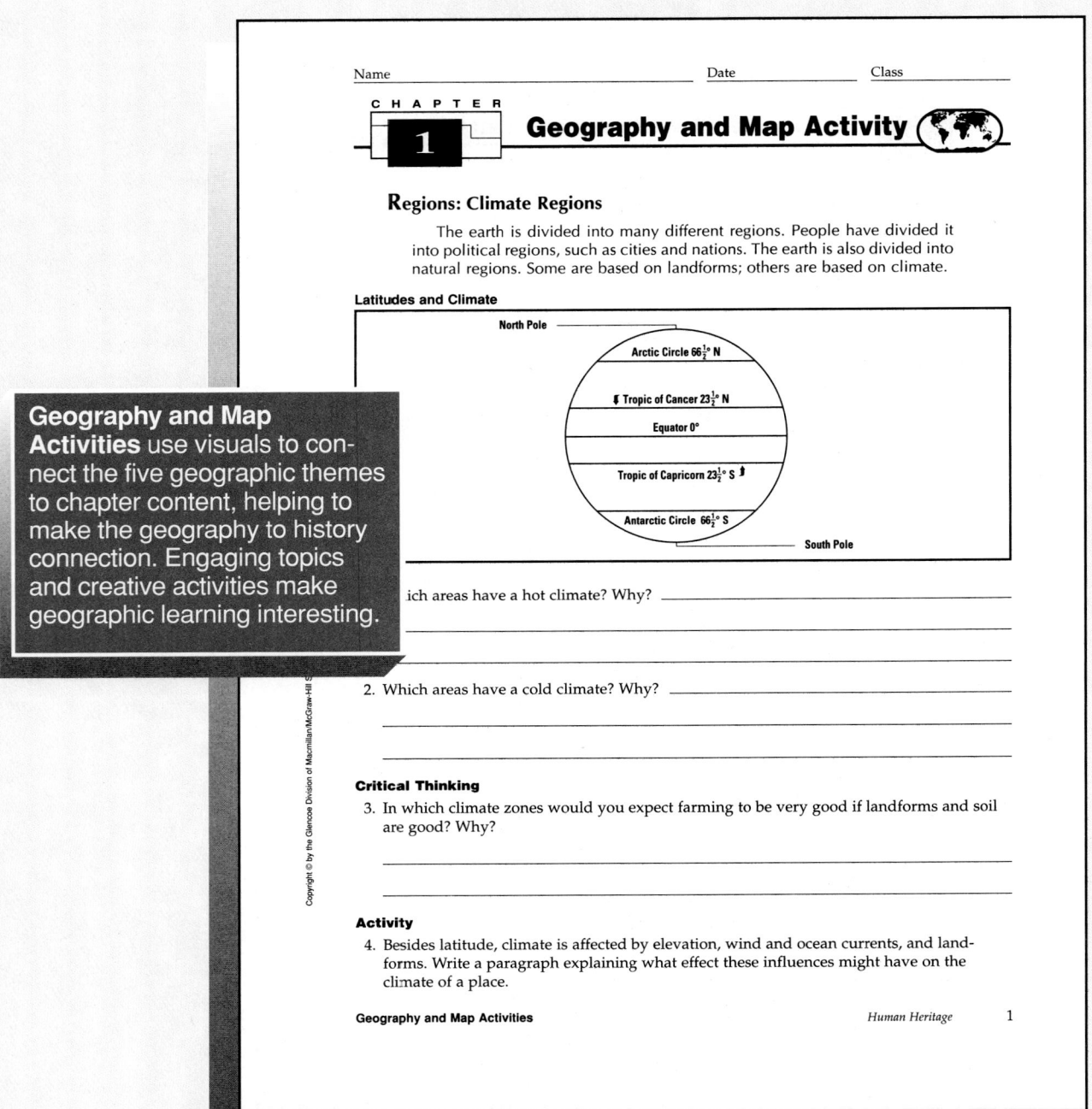

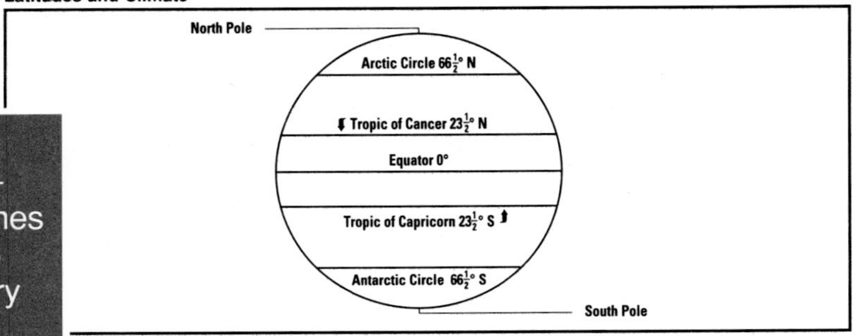

...ich areas have a hot climate? Why? ____________________

2. Which areas have a cold climate? Why? ____________________

Critical Thinking

3. In which climate zones would you expect farming to be very good if landforms and soil are good? Why?

Activity

4. Besides latitude, climate is affected by elevation, wind and ocean currents, and landforms. Write a paragraph explaining what effect these influences might have on the climate of a place.

Geography and Map Activities *Human Heritage* 1

CHART AND GRAPH SKILL ACTIVITIES

Name ______________ Date ______________ Class ______________

CHAPTER 13

Chart and Graph Skills Activity

Completing a Chart and Drawing Conclusions

Even today no one is quite sure of the origin of the Etruscans, because historians are not able to understand the small number of Etruscan writings that have been found. Etruscan contributions to the later Roman civilization, however, have been recognized.

Using Your Skills

Use your text to complete the chart and answer the following questions.

Field	Etruscan Contributions to Roman Civilization
Architecture	A. ______________
Public sanitation	B. ______________
The Forum	C. ______________
Language and writing	D. ______________
Entertainment	E. ______________
Symbol of authority	F. ______________

1. How might the Etruscan development of the arch have contributed to the building of roads by the Romans?

____

____

2. How do you think the Etruscan development in public sanitation helped Roman farming communities?

____

____

3. Why do you think entertainment was a part of most early civilizations?

____

____

Chart and Graph Skill Activities reinforce skills in using charts and graphs as quantitative and qualitative representations of information, and offer further reinforcement for the visual learner.

PRIMARY SOURCE READINGS

The **Primary Source Readings** contain introductory paragraphs that promote content reading skills and understanding.

Name ____________ Date ____________ Class ____________

UNIT 1

Primary Source Reading 1

Mary and Louis Leakey were scientists who worked in East Africa for many years. There, in a place called Olduvai Gorge, the Leakeys found some of the oldest-known evidence of human beings on earth. Not surprisingly, their son, Richard, also became an anthropologist. In this selection, Richard explains his work in Kenya's Great Rift Valley, where many fossils are found.

Directions **Read the selection below and answer the questions that follow. Use another sheet of paper if necessary.**

Fossil-hunting in East Africa

My childhood was spent in various remote areas of East Africa, in Kenya and Tanzania, where my parents were searching for evidence of our ancestors. For many months they searched the fossil sites on the islands and shores of Lake Victoria. At other times I remember chasing sheets of cellophane blowing away in the wind as my mother laboriously traced the art of our ancestors in rock shelters in Tanzania. But perhaps the most exciting times of all were at Olduvai Gorge on the Serengeti Plains, where wild animals were a natural part of our everyday life.

Since then I have continued searching for evidence of the past in my own career, and I have experienced for myself the thrill of finding a complete skull of one of our ancestors, two million years old. . . .

How to get preserved as a fossil

Unfortunately the chances of any animal becoming a fossil are not very great, and the chances of a fossil then being discovered many thousands of years later are even less. It is not surprising that of all the millions of animals that have lived in the past, we actually have fossils of only a very few.

There are several ways in which animals and plants may become fossilized. First, it is essential that the remains are buried. . . . The same chemicals which change sand and silt into hard rock will also enter the animal or plant remains and make them hard too. When this happens, we say that they have become fossilized. Usually only the bones of an animal and the toughest part of a plant are preserved.

(continued)

WORLD LITERATURE

Name ______________ Date ______________ Class ______________

UNIT 1

World Literature Reading 2

The origin myth is a kind of tale many cultures create to explain the beginnings of something. This origin myth is a traditional Zapotec tale from Mexico. The Zapotecs had a religion that focused on nature. The Zapotec civilization was eventually absorbed by the Aztec empire. Today, many Zapotecs still live in the mountainous regions of Oaxaca. No one knows exactly what their myths were like . . . because the myths were probably never written down. The ancient Zapotecs did have a hieroglyphic system of writing that has been only partially decoded by archaeologists.

World Literature offers students glimpses of history through biographies, myths, poetry, and more. Introductory paragraphs guide student reading and help develop prereading skills.

Directions **Read the selection below and answer the questions that follow. Use another sheet of paper if necessary.**

The Bat

Retold by Andrés Menestrosa

The butterflies we see today, ethereal, resting on the flowers, on the surface of the water and even on the tremulous air, are only the shadows of what the bat once was: the most beautiful bird in creation! However, there was a time when he was not.

When Light and Darkness began, the bat was just as we know him today, and was called *biguidibela* in Zapotec, from *beguidi* meaning butterfly, and *bela,* flesh: that is, a butterfly in the flesh, or bare-winged. Then the poor bat was the ugliest and the most unhappy of all creatures.

One day, tormented by the cold weather, he went up to Heaven and said to God, "I'm dying of cold: I need a few feathers." But God, although He never stops working, never revises the creatures He has finished, and so had not a single feather to offer the bat. He told the bat to go back to Earth and to beg a feather in His name from every bird. Thus God always gives more than is asked of Him.

The bat, back on Earth, sought out the birds of most colorful plumage. A green feather from the parrot's neck, a blue feather from the blue pigeon, a white feather from the dove, an iridescent feather from the humming-bird. All these and more the bat obtained. Proudly he would fly across the brow of the Morning, and all the other birds would pause in their flight to admire him. And a new glory spread over the Earth. . . . At dusk, flying with the West Wind, the bat colored the horizon. And once, coming from beyond the clouds, he left behind a rainbow as an echo of his flight.

(continued)

ENRICHMENT ACTIVITIES

Enrichment Activities extend and expand each lesson through motivating activities that engage students in meaningful analyses and interpretations of history.

Name ______________________ Date ____________ Class ____________

CHAPTER 11

Enrichment Activity

The Legacy of Pythagoras

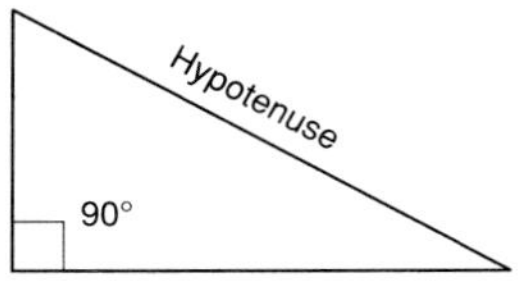

Pythagoras was a Greek philosopher who lived from 582–507 B.C. All our knowledge of Pythagoras comes from the people who followed him, who were called the Pythagoreans. The Pythagoreans believed that their souls would come back to life in another form, and they worked to purify and ready their souls. Pythagoreans were also mathematicians and scientists. They taught that the earth is a revolving sphere. They also taught that all things—from the relationships between musical notes to the concept of justice—could be expressed through numbers. Most people remember Pythagoras for the Pythagorean theorem. It states that the square of the length of the longest side (hypotenuse) of a right triangle (a triangle with a 90° angle) equals the sum of the length of the two other sides.

Directions

Write your answers on the lines provided.

1. Who was Pythagoras? Who were the Pythagoreans?

2. *Drawing Conclusions.* What do you think about the Pythagoreans' ideas? Do you agree or disagree with their ideas about numbers? Why?

3. *Making Judgments.* In what situations might you need to use the Pythagorean theorem?

Enrichment Activities *Human Heritage* 1

RETEACHING ACTIVITIES

Name ______________________ Date ____________ Class ____________

CHAPTER 7

Reteaching Activity

Military Empires

The Assyrians, the Chaldeans, and the Persians were warrior people. But they were also involved in peacetime activities, some of which influenced future civilizations, including our own.

Directions **Complete each statement that follows by choosing the correct word or phrase from the list in the box. You may want to take turns reading aloud and discussing your choices with a partner.**

Immortals	a system of roads	hanging gardens
Iran	religious leader	descendants of Hammurabi's empire
Babylonians	sundials	libraries

1. The Chaldeans called themselves Babylonians because they were ______________________.
2. King Ashurbanipal started one of the world's finest ______________________.
3. The Assyrians spoke the same language and used the same writing system as the ______________________.
4. To please his wife, Nebuchadrezzar built the legendary ______________________.
5. All Assyrian provinces were connected by ______________________.
6. The Babylonians made one of the finest ______________________.
7. Today, Persia is called ______________________.
8. The best fighters in the Persian army were called ______________________.
9. Zoroaster was a Persian ______________________.

Reteaching Activities help students focus on the main ideas and concepts in each chapter.

TEACHING TRANSPARENCIES STRATEGIES AND ACTIVITIES

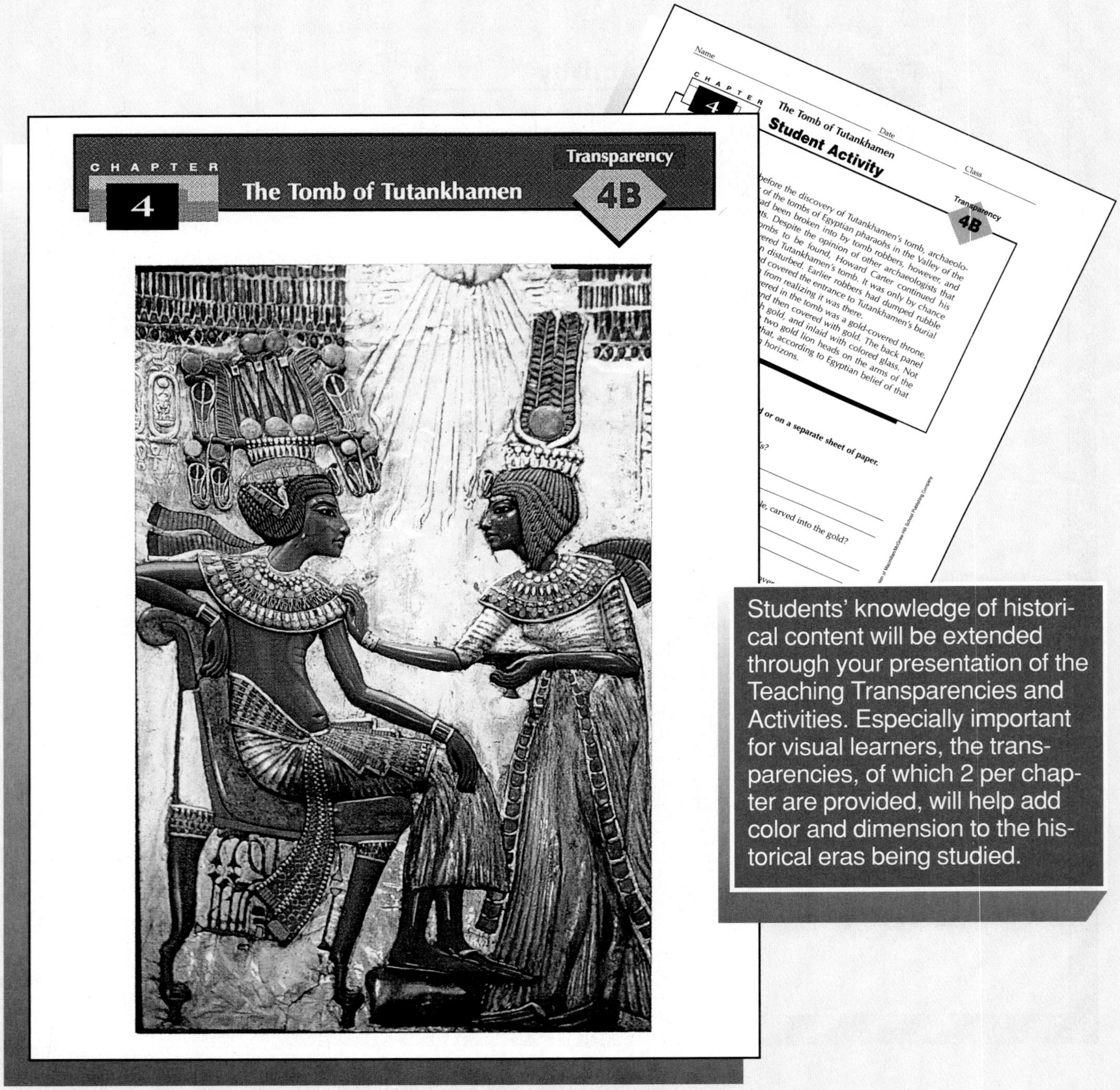

Students' knowledge of historical content will be extended through your presentation of the Teaching Transparencies and Activities. Especially important for visual learners, the transparencies, of which 2 per chapter are provided, will help add color and dimension to the historical eras being studied.

WORLD ART PRINTS

Focus on World Art Prints includes 25 display-quality posters, covering the major cultural regions from prehistoric to contemporary times.

VIDEODISCS

The World (non-European) History Videodiscs and The Western Civilization Videodiscs from Instructional Resources Corporation have been correlated specifically to *Human Heritage: A World History*. Point-of-use bar codes are included in the Teacher's Wraparound Edition to enhance presentation of historical events and locations.

The bar codes supplied are usable with Pioneer laserdisc equipment only.

AUDIOCASSETTES

Audiocassettes present chapter summaries for use with auditory learners; learning is reinforced and evaluated with special audiocassette activities and tests. Also available in Spanish.

SPANISH CHAPTER SUMMARIES AND GLOSSARY

Nombre ______________________ Fecha ____________ Clase ____________

CHAPTER 1

Resumen del Capítulo 1

1. Los geógrafos usan cinco temas para describir un lugar. Estos son la localización, la interacción humana y del medio ambiente, el movimiento y las regiones.

2. Hay cuatro tipos de formaciones terrestres—las montañas, los montes, las mesetas y los llanos—que componen un 30 por ciento de la superficie de la Tierra.

3. La superficie de la Tierra siempre está cambiando debido a fuerzas externas e internas.

4. Casi un 70 por ciento de la superficie de la Tierra está cubierta por océanos, mares, lagos y ríos.

5. Hay varios factores que afectan el clima, tales como el sol, las grandes masas de agua, los vientos y las corrientes marinas y la altitud.

6. A menudo, los geógrafos dividen la Tierra en zonas climáticas basándose en latitudes: la zona tropical, la zona templada y la zona polar.

7. Algunos de los distintos recursos naturales son el aire, el agua, la luz solar, los minerales, los combustibles de fósiles, los bosques y la fauna.

8. Los recursos renovables se pueden reemplazar. Los recursos no renovables se desaparecen para siempre al usarse.

9. Las leyendas han ayudado a la gente a explicar el pasado.

10. Los arqueólogos estudian artefactos para aprender cómo vivía la gente hace mucho tiempo.

11. Un descubrimiento arqueológico muy importante fue e Rosetta.

12. Desde el 1946 los científicos han usado el método del c desarrollado por Willard Frank Libby, para datar objet

Spanish Chapter Summaries and Glossary

Spanish Summaries and Glossary help Spanish-speaking students grasp key themes in world history.

Spanish Audiocassettes present chapter summaries for use with auditory learners and students with Limited English Proficiency. Learning is reinforced and evaluated with special audiocassette activities and tests.

PERFORMANCE ASSESSMENT ACTIVITIES

Performance Assessment Activities offer you opportunities for authentic assessment of student understanding as they go through the interactive process of learning.

Name ______ Date ______ Class ______

CHAPTER 1

Performance Assessment

Geography and History

Background

Throughout human life on Earth, geography and history, including the development of religion, tools, language, fire, clothing, art, and farming, have affected where and how people live.

Task

- ❑ You are an educational ambassador sent from your community to communities in other countries on a get-acquainted mission.
- ❑ You will draw a map of the landscape in your community to use in your presentations.

Audience

Your audience is younger students in the school.

Purpose

One purpose of your presentation is to inform students about the geography and culture of your region. Another purpose is to inform them of the ways in which geography and history have shaped life in your region.

Procedure

1. Make a map of your community that can be used to describe landforms, geographical features, and cultural life in the region.
2. Write a script for your presentation that describes the geographical conditions and the lifestyle they support.
3. Include a discussion of the ways people live that grew out of the traditions, or history, of the community.
4. Present your map of the community and your script to your classmates.
5. Maps and scripts can be presented to younger students.

Assessment

Review the classroom assessment lists for
- ✔ map
- ✔ oral presentation

SECTION QUIZZES

Name ______________________ Date ____________ Class ____________

CHAPTER 1

Section Quiz 1-1

SCORE

Matching **Match each item in the first column with the correct item in the second column. Write the correct letters in the blanks.**

____ 1. the exact location of a place

____ 2. links people and places together

____ 3. location in relation to other places

____ 4. movement of ideas and information

____ 5. used by geographers to organize the world

A. communication
B. relative location
C. absolute location
D. movement
E. regions

Multiple Choice **In the blank at the left, write the letter of the choice that best completes the statement or answers the question.**

____ 6. The movement of goods and people is known as
A. communication.
B. relative location.
C. transportation.
D. absolute location.

____ 7. Which of the following is NOT a main theme of geography?
A. place
B. movement
C. region
D. culture

____ 8. An example of a functional region is
A. a common language.
B. communication.
C. a city.
D. a culture.

____ 9. Human/environmental interaction deals with
A. how people communicate.
B. how people use products made in other countries.
C. how people adapt to or change their environment.
D. how people form a common language.

____ 10. No two places on earth have the same
A. language.
B. transportation.
C. absolute location.
D. cultural tradition.

Section Quizzes provide you with a quick, effective way to monitor the daily progress of your students.

CHAPTER TESTS

Chapter Tests evaluate student understanding of the main chapter facts, ideas, geography skills, and relationships between historical events.

Name ______________________ Date ____________ Class ____________

CHAPTER 1 **Chapter Test** SCORE

Matching **Match each item in the first column with the correct item in the second column. Write the correct letters in the blanks.**

____ 1. Exact position of a place on the earth's surface
____ 2. Sections of the earth's crust that move slowly
____ 3. Things that were made by people
____ 4. Natural features of the earth's land surface
____ 5. River plus all the streams that flow into it
____ 6. Folktale that helps explain the past
____ 7. Height above sea level
____ 8. Geographic theme that tells how all people and places are linked together

A. elevation
B. movement
C. absolute location
D. river system
E. continents
F. landforms
G. artifacts
H. legend
I. archaeology
J. tectonic plates

Multiple Choice **In the blank at the left, write the letter of the choice that best completes the statement or answers the question.**

____ 9. The middle layer of the earth, made of solid, hot rock, is the
A. mantle. C. core.
B. crust. D. tectonic plate.

____ 10. The five themes of geography help explain
A. where a place is on the earth.
B. what a place is like and why.
C. what a place is like.
D. how people and places are linked together.

____ 11. Which of the following is not a kind of major landform?
A. Mountains C. Glaciers
D. Plains

s about legends is true?
out the creation of the universe.
on stories of real people and events.
en down at first.
ed on facts or real events.

surface of the earth is made up of land?
C. 30 percent
D. 10 percent

Human Heritage 1

The ***Human Heritage: A World History*** **Testmaker** software allows you to customize section and chapter tests. Use the existing database to create tests covering one or more sections or chapters. In addition, you can edit the database questions or add your own questions. The software is available in Apple, Macintosh, or IBM formats.

Additional Components

- **World History and Art Transparencies** add visual interest to themes and concepts. The package includes teaching strategies and student activity worksheets to correspond with each transparency.
- **Introduction to the Arab World Video** lays a foundation for exploring the contemporary concerns of the Arab world. An accompanying guidebook helps you tailor the program to your needs.
- **Life Unworthy of Life: A Holocaust Curriculum Videoprogram** stimulates active student participation and guides students through both historical and modern-day ethical issues.
- **Ancient Civilizations Videotape Series** examines the remarkable civilizations of China, India, Mesopotamia, Egypt, Greece, and Rome.
- **World Music: Cultural Traditions** provides more than 14 hours of musical examples on CD to help students understand that music provides a reflection of the world's cultures.
- **Map Activities World History Enrichment Series** help you focus on specific geographic locations to help students make geographical connections.
- **Reinforcing Social Studies Skills** include activities to help students develop and reinforce Graphic, Critical Thinking, and Study and Writing Skills.
- **Outline Map Resource Book, Updated Edition,** includes a broad selection of outline maps to correspond with the text and allows students to reinforce their geography skills.
- **Foods Around the World** lets you integrate the traditional foods and recipes from various cultures into your study of different regions.

LINKING THE STUDY OF HISTORY AND THE HUMANITIES

Leaders in curriculum development have long favored integrative approaches to social instruction. Many of these experts believe that students benefit most from instructional techniques that interweave the study of the social studies with that of the humanities. Such an approach allows students to study the history of a specific period along with accompanying art, music, and literature. This integrative curriculum is particularly useful for students with special needs. For example, while studying the Jazz Age, auditory learners would benefit from listening to the music composed during the era; visual learners would grasp the concepts more easily by analyzing the paintings of the period.

As we all know, the study of history involves more than examining and understanding a series of events. History is a magnificent tale of human beings and their struggle to progress—an emo-

GLENCOE LINKS TO THE HUMANITIES

The following Glencoe products are available to assist you in teaching each chapter of *Human Heritage: A World History*	Chapter 1	2	3	4	5	6	7	8	9	10	11	12	13	14	15	16
LINKS TO READING Macmillan Literature: Discovering Literature	•	•			•			•					•	•	•	•
Macmillan Literature: Introducing Literature	•	•		•	•	•	•	•	•	•	•	•		•	•	
Macmillan Literature: Enjoying Literature	•	•	•	•	•		•	•	•	•	•	•		•	•	
LINKS TO WRITING Writer's Choice (GR 9)	•	•	•	•	•	•	•	•	•	•	•	•	•	•	•	•
Writer's Choice Fine Art Transparencies	•	•	•	•		•		•			•			•	•	
LINKS TO ART Focus on World Art Prints					•			•	•	•	•	•	•	•	•	•
World History and Art Transparencies		•		•	•			•	•						•	•
LINKS TO MUSIC World Music: Cultural Traditions			•	•	•			•				•				•
Music: Its Role and Importance in Our Lives					•			•								

Glencoe Links to the Humanities

tional process. These emotions are often represented through the art, music, literature, and architecture of a people. By studying these elements—the humanities—students are exposed to the rich diversity of the cultures of the world. *Human Heritage: A World History* examines this cultural heritage, offering students a glimpse of the past, present, and future of human expression. This story of humanity becomes a global tale that enhances students' understanding and empathy for all peoples of the world.To help you integrate the study of the humanities into your history classroom, Glencoe makes available a variety of transparencies, audiotapes, and books. These supplementary materials are correlated to the content of *Human Heritage: A World History.* For more information concerning these components, see your local Glencoe sales representative.

GLENCOE LINKS TO THE HUMANITIES

17	18	19	20	21	22	23	24	25	26	27	28	29	30	31	32	33	34	35	36	37	38	39
		•		•		•	•	•	•	•	•	•	•	•		•	•	•		•	•	•
•	•	•	•			•		•	•	•	•	•	•	•	•	•	•	•	•	•	•	•
•	•	•		•	•		•		•	•	•	•	•	•		•	•			•	•	•
•	•	•	•	•	•	•	•	•	•	•	•	•	•	•	•	•	•	•	•	•	•	•
				•	•			•	•		•	•	•	•		•	•	•	•	•	•	•
•	•	•	•	•	•		•	•	•	•	•	•	•				•	•	•	•	•	•
		•	•	•			•				•		•			•	•	•	•	•	•	•
	•	•				•		•	•	•	•	•	•			•	•	•	•	•	•	•
•	•	•	•			•					•	•	•			•	•	•	•	•	•	•

THE FIVE THEMES OF GEOGRAPHY

Knowledge of the five fundamental themes of geography as outlined by the National Council for Geographic Eduction is essential to an understanding of the essence of world history. *Human Heritage: A World History* integrates the teaching of geography with the study of history. The themes are included in every Map Skills page, and are referenced in every interactive map caption in the Student Edition, and activities in the Teacher's Wraparound Edition.

As students study **location,** they learn to describe the exact and relative position of people and places on the Earth's surface.

Students gain an awareness of the character of **places** by studying physical characteristics such as landforms, water bodies, and climate; and human characteristics such as population distribution, settlement patterns, and architectural choices.

Human/environmental interaction examines the interplay between people and their environment. This promotes an awareness of how environment has shaped human lives and how humans have shaped their environment.

The theme, **movement,** as people of the world explored and migrated from region to region and from countryside to city, adds dimension to the study of history. It is also a story of worldwide revolutions in transportation and communication methods that carried goods and ideas as well as people.

The theme of **regions** centers on where people choose to live and how these choices affect the politics, economics, and culture of regions.

MULTICULTURAL PERSPECTIVES

The interaction of different cultures and their perspective about these interactions is what makes history a fascinating study. By reading *Human Heritage: A World History* students receive a global picture of the people and events of world history. The text weaves a multicultural tapestry of the historical events, experiences, and traditions that reflect the values and beliefs of early cultures as well as those cultures of today. As the world shrinks in size because of high-speed communication and transportation, it becomes increasingly important for students to see people different from themselves as neighbors who have different ideas, customs, and languages, but who also share many of the same values. Students will read about groups of people who have been misrepresented or omitted in the past. Inclusion of these groups will help students develop more positive attitudes toward different cultural, racial, ethnic, religious, and gender groups.

The following five points have been identified as some of the major goals of multicultural education:

- Promoting the strength and value of cultural diversity
- Promoting human rights and respect for those who are different from oneself
- Promoting alternative life choices for people
- Promoting social justice and equal opportunity for all people
- Promoting equity in the distribution of power among groups

PERFORMANCE ASSESSMENT

In response to the growing demand for accountability in the classroom, many educators are advocating new approaches to assessment. One such approach is Performance Assessment, which measures student achievement in a more constructive and interactive manner than traditional tests. In general, it includes performance-based activities and portfolios.

Performance Assessment involves a way of teaching and learning that consists of both process and product. Performance Assessment tasks get students actively involved in creating a variety of products for a variety of audiences. In this process the teacher becomes a guide and resource. Performance Assessment also requires students to develop critical thinking skills that range from acquiring information to processing it and understanding it. It also allows for the most often overlooked aspect of learning—self-assessment.

Performance tests ask students to effectively and creatively apply the knowledge they have gained. These tests require the application of problem-solving skills rather than mere recall. A key element in scoring such tests is to analyze the process the students use to clarify and solve the problem. Scoring involves rating students' performance on multiple factors, resulting in a descriptive profile of performance.

The portfolio approach is often used with performance-based assessment. Portfolios contain samples of students' work collected over a period of time—an entire grading period or even a semester. Students often help choose which items will be included in their portfolios.

Portfolios allow for assessing a broader range of skills than traditional tests. Students can see how much progress they are making by comparing the work that they have completed throughout the course.

COOPERATIVE LEARNING

Cooperative Learning is a useful teaching strategy in the social studies curriculum because of its success in developing the abilities needed to work effectively in a group. Such social studies skills are beneficial for all citizens living in a democracy.

Characteristics of Cooperative Learning Cooperative Learning requires careful structuring and monitoring by the teacher if it is to be something more than a group activity. Characteristics of effective Cooperative Learning include the following:

- Students work in heterogeneous groups.
- The activity promotes positive interdependence.
- Each member of a group has individual accountability.
- The group has a common product or goal.

The Role of the Teacher Although successful Cooperative Learning groups may appear to work independently, this is no doubt due to the astute coaching of a good teacher. Students will need the teacher's help at key moments during a group project: in agreeing upon goals, in establishing a structure of accountability, and in evaluating their success.

Program Components The *Human Heritage: A World History* program provides many opportunities for Cooperative Learning. The Teacher's Wraparound Edition provides chapter cooperative learning activities designed to be completed as a chapter project. The Cooperative Learning Activities booklet offers additional activities for each chapter.

CRITICAL THINKING SKILLS

To learn about history and geography in a way that prepares students to become thoughtful participants in this world, students must learn to think critically. They need to be able to evaluate and to question the meaning of what they see, read, and hear. The teacher plays a crucial role in this development by creating a classroom climate that actively encourages critical thinking. *Human Heritage: A World History* teaches the skills used in critical thinking, such as distinguishing between fact and opinion, identifying evidence, making comparisons, and interpreting point-of-view.

The Classroom Climate The teacher can promote critical thinking in the classroom by verbalizing the inner thought processes that take place. Asking questions such as "What do I want to achieve?" and "What do I already know?" models for students the importance of setting goals and of assessing current knowledge. Asking "Have I understood what I have read?" establishes the importance of checking one's progress as one proceeds.

Critical Thinking Skills In *Human Heritage: A World History,* each Chapter Focus and Read to Discover guides student reading and requires students to apply critical thinking skills. Questions requiring critical thinking skills also appear in Section and Chapter Reviews.

AT-RISK STUDENTS

Most educators today agree that the nation's schools are facing an epidemic of students who are at risk of failure. It is difficult to define exactly what constitutes an at-risk student because being at risk is often linked to several environmental causes such as poverty, low self-esteem, substance abuse, or pregnancy. Current educational research has shown that certain teaching methods can help keep at-risk students from dropping out. One method is to maximize time-on-task to help students overcome distracting outside stimuli.

Another method is to establish high expectations and a school climate that supports learning. Many schools actively involve parents in this process so that the expectations for success are not left inside the classroom after school is out. Many teachers give positive feedback at the end of each successfully completed assignment and include awards ceremonies for students who meet expectations.

Rather than emphasizing remedial techniques, many educators believe that at-risk students need to learn at a faster rate. Instruction emphasizes assets that at-risk students often bring to the classroom—interest in oral and artistic expression and kinesthetic learning abilities. For example, at-risk students may excel at dramatizations in which they also construct the sets.

HUMAN HERITAGE

A WORLD HISTORY

MIRIAM GREENBLATT
PETER S. LEMMO

GLENCOE
McGraw-Hill
New York, New York   Columbus, Ohio   Mission Hills, California   Peoria, Illinois

AUTHORS

Miriam Greenblatt is a writer, editor, and educational consultant who has traveled extensively in Asia, Africa, and Latin America. During the past 25 years, she has contributed to more than 40 elementary, junior high, and high school social studies texts and ancillaries. A graduate of Hunter College of the City of New York and the University of Chicago, and a former teacher, Greenblatt is listed in *Who's Who of American Women for 1993-94*, and *Who's Who of American Education for 1993-94*.

Peter S. Lemmo is a high school teacher in the New York City school system, where he has taught since 1970. A graduate of the City College of New York and the City University of New York, he has trained student teachers and contributed to several books. Lemmo has been instrumental in developing pilot instructional programs and curriculums and was rated an exemplary teacher by the State Education Department of New York. He is also a member of the National Council for the Social Studies, the Association for Supervision and Curriculum Development, and other professional organizations and has traveled extensively in more than 40 countries.

Cover Photos:
Water Vase by THE GRANGER COLLECTION, New York
Nigerian Belt Mask, Laughing Porcelain, and Inca Doll by Lee Boltin

Glencoe/McGraw-Hill
*A Division of The **McGraw-Hill** Companies*

Printed in the United States of America

Send all inquiries to:

Glencoe/McGraw-Hill
936 Eastwind Drive
Westerville, Ohio 43081

ISBN 0-02-823187-2 (Student Edition)

ISBN 0-02-823188-0 (Teacher's Wraparound Edition)

5 6 7 8 9 VHJ/LH-P 00 99 98 97 96

ACADEMIC CONSULTANTS

Jerrold Green, Ph. D.
Director
Middle East Studies Center
University of Arizona
Tucson, Arizona

Al Naklowycz, Ph. D.
President Ukranian-American
Academic Association of California
Carmichael, California

Joseph R. Rosenbloom, Ph. D.
Professor of Classics
Washington University
St. Louis, Missouri

Sayyid M. Syeed, Ph. D.
Director
International Institute of
Islamic Thought
Herndon, Virginia

TEACHER REVIEWERS

Richard Ammentorp
Schaumburg School District
Schaumburg, Illinois

Rick Boeglin
Richardson North Junior High School
Richardson, Texas

Margaret Gray, Ph. D.
Vigo County School Corporation
Terre Haute, Indiana

Dianne Hill
Muskogee Public Schools
Muskogee, Oklahoma

Joseph Scheideler
Canton Junior/Senior High School
Collinsville, Connecticut

Kathleen A. Grotto
West Orange Senior High School
West Orange, New Jersey

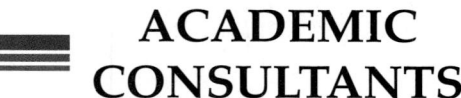

CONTENTS

Unit 1 Place and Time

Unit 2 River Valley Civilizations

Unit 3 Ideas and Armies

Unit 4 The Greeks

Unit 5 The Romans

Unit 6 The Early Middle Ages

v

Unit 7 Emergence of New Empires

Unit 8 The Late Middle Ages

Unit 9 Beginning of Modern Times

vi

Unit 10 The Changing World

Unit 11 Nations and Empires

Unit 12 The Twentieth Century

Map Skills

People in History

Charts, Diagrams, and Illustrations

Maps

INTRODUCE

UNIT 1 OVERVIEW

Unit 1 serves as an introduction to the study of world history and geography and sets the stage for the development of civilization.

- ➤ **Chapter 1** acquaints the students with the five fundamental geographic themes that geographers use to study the earth, and with geographical features. It also discusses how scientists uncover clues that help them piece together what happened in the distant past.
- ➤ **Chapter 2** deals with prehistory and the various stages of development people went through before civilization evolved.

UNIT OBJECTIVES

After reading Unit 1, students will be able to:

1. identify important geographic themes.

2. explain ways in which geography has influenced the course of history.

3. specify how scientists work together to learn about the past.

4. describe how hunters and food gatherers and food producers lived during prehistoric times.

UNIT PROJECT

Have students select five major achievements of prehistoric people that have been most important to humankind. Ask them to rank the achievements, listing the most important first. Then, working in groups, create a display of these achievements, bringing prehistoric life into the classroom. Finally, have them write a paragraph explaining the achievement and how important it was to the development of civilization.

UNIT 1 Place and Time

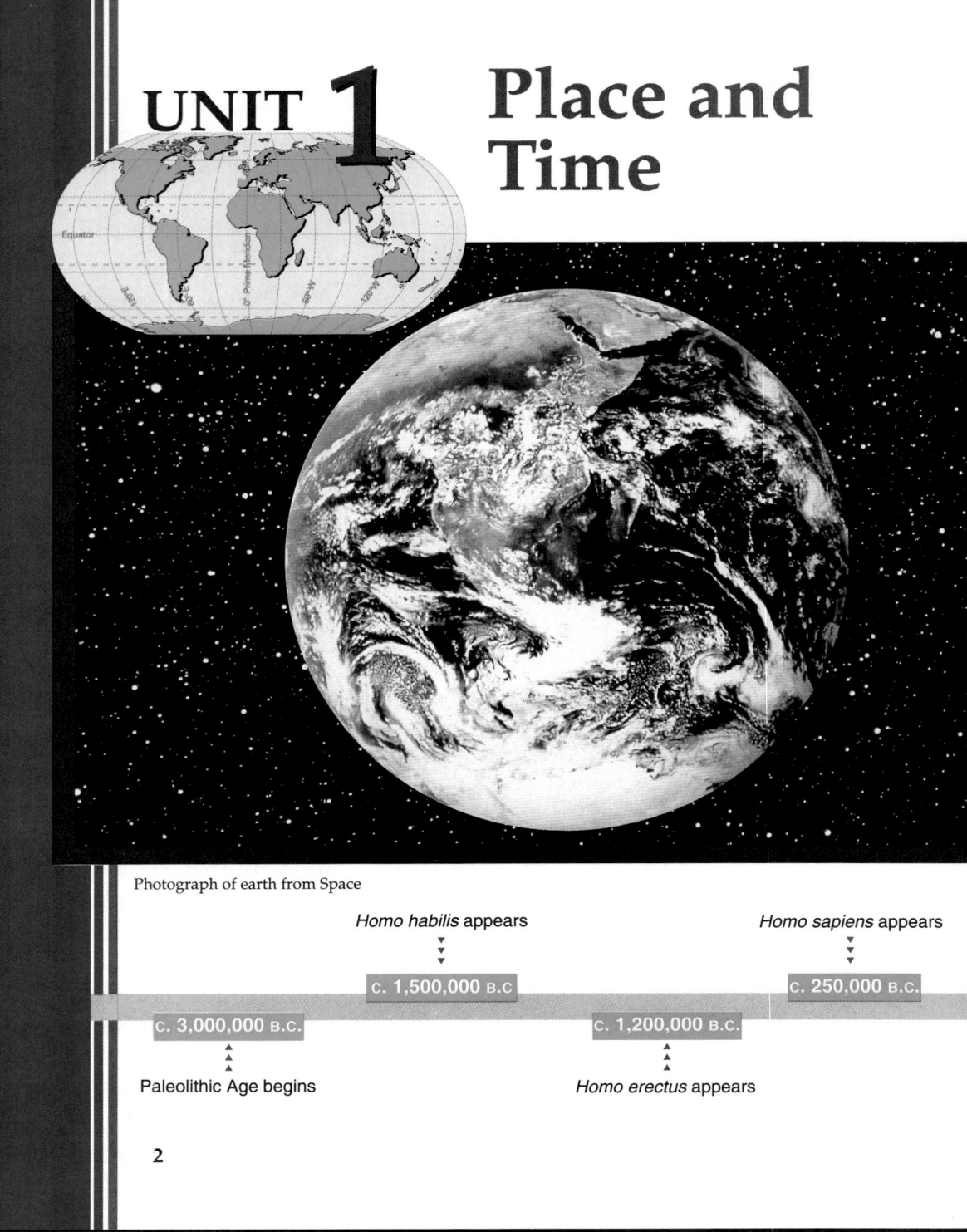

Photograph of earth from Space

- c. 3,000,000 B.C. — Paleolithic Age begins
- c. 1,500,000 B.C — *Homo habilis* appears
- c. 1,200,000 B.C. — *Homo erectus* appears
- c. 250,000 B.C. — *Homo sapiens* appears

ABOUT THE UNIT OPENING

EXAMINING THE ILLUSTRATION

Tell students the illustration shows the photograph of Earth taken from the Apollo 17 spacecraft in December 1972. The starry background has been added photographically. Ask students to identify the land masses shown in the photograph. *(Antarctica, Africa, and Arabia)* Ask students to discuss how photographs of Earth from space might help geographers study Earth.

GLOBAL CHRONOLOGY

Refer students to the unit time line above. Explain that *c.* means "about" and that B.C. means "before Christ." Ask students to explain what the time line covers. *(major events in prehistory)* About how long did the Paleolithic Age last? *(about 2,992,000 years)* About how long after the Neolithic Age began did writing develop? *(about 3,500 years)*

During the time that people have been on the Earth, geography has had an important impact on where and how people have lived. People's development of religion, tools, language, fire, clothing, art, and farming have also affected where and how people have lived.

Chapter 1
Geography and History

Chapter 2
Early People

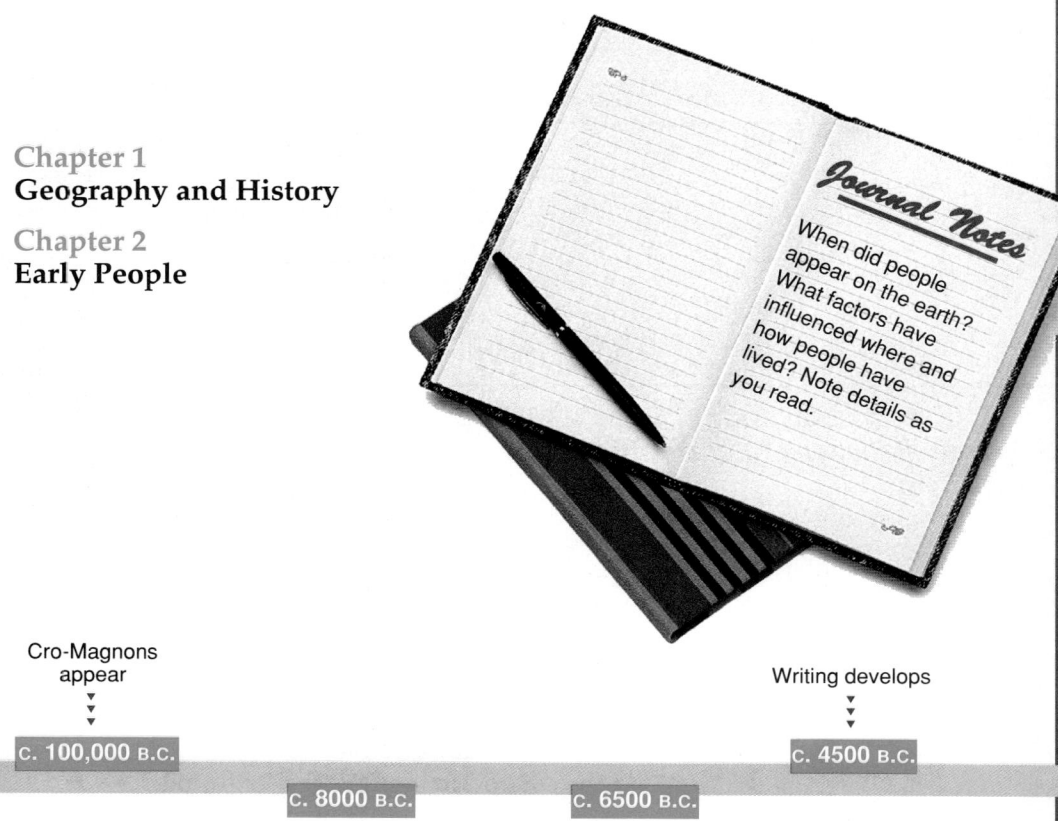

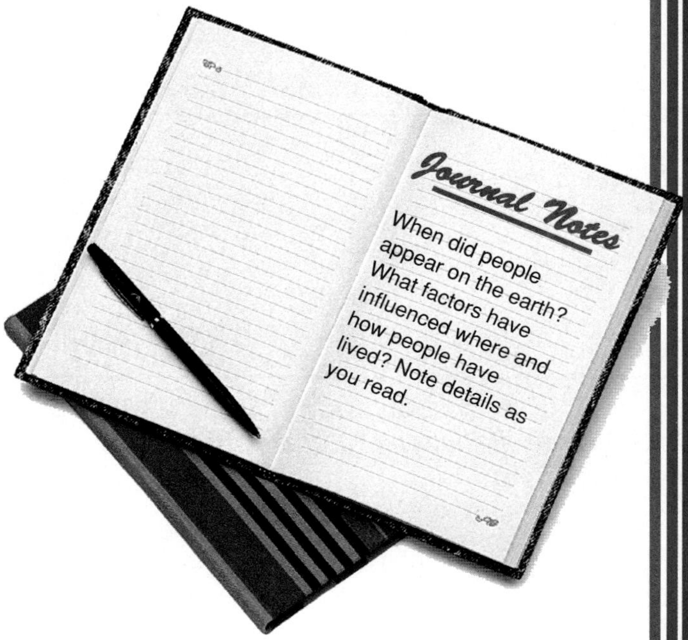
Journal Notes
When did people appear on the earth? What factors have influenced where and how people have lived? Note details as you read.

Cro-Magnons appear — c. 100,000 B.C.

Neolithic Age begins, Jericho established — c. 8000 B.C.

Catal Hüyük established — c. 6500 B.C.

Writing develops — c. 4500 B.C.

INTRODUCING THE UNIT

Write the following quotation on the chalkboard from Cicero, a Roman statesman and orator: *"Not to know what happened before one was born is to remain a child."* Have students brainstorm the meaning of the quotation. Ask them how we can overcome ignorance about our past. *(by studying history)*

Then have them discuss the meaning of history. *(a chronological record of past events and an explanation of why they happened)*

RECORDING JOURNAL NOTES

Help students begin writing in their journals by asking them to read the Unit Introduction and name the factors that have influenced where people have lived. Explain to students that details about these factors are what they want to note in their journals as they read about the first people who lived on the earth.

GEOGRAPHIC LOCATION

Unit 1 focuses mainly on the continents of Africa, Europe, and Asia where archaeologists have found the remains and artifacts of prehistoric people. However, developments here impacted the whole world.

CHAPTER 1 Geography and History

CHAPTER ORGANIZER

Objectives	Special Features	Supplemental Materials
Section 1 Five Themes of Geography Describe how the five themes of geography help explain what a place is like and why it is like that.		• Reproducible Lesson Plan • Section 1 Quiz • Testmaker • Chapter 1 Vocabulary and Guided Reading Activity • Chapter 1 Cooperative Learning Activity • Chapter 1 Activity Book Activity
Section 2 Land, Water, and Climate Explain how landforms, waterways, and climate have shaped history.	Map and Geography Skills: *Understanding a Mercator Projection,* p. 17	• Reproducible Lesson Plan • Section 2 Quiz • Testmaker • Chapter 1 Geography and Map Activity • Outline Map Resource Book, p. 39
Section 3 Natural Resources Describe how natural resources have shaped history.		• Reproducible Lesson Plan • Section 3 Quiz • Testmaker • Unit 1 Primary Source Reading
Section 4 Legends Analyze the importance of legends in the study of history.		• Reproducible Lesson Plan • Section 4 Quiz • Testmaker • Chapter 1 Teaching Transparencies and Activities
Section 5 Archaeology Summarize how archaeology helps scientists learn about ancient civilizations.	People in History: *The Leakeys,* p. 29	• Reproducible Lesson Plan • Section 5 Quiz • Testmaker • Chapter 1 Chart and Graph Skill Activity • Unit 1 World Literature
Chapter 1 Review and Evaluation		• Reteaching Activity • Enrichment Activity • Spanish Summary and Glossary • Audiocassettes (English and Spanish) • Performance Assessment Activity • Chapter 1 Test • Testmaker

If time does not permit teaching the entire chapter, use the Chapter 1 Summary on page 30 and the Chapter 1 Audiocassettes (English and Spanish) to point out the main ideas of the chapter.

Performance Assessment Activities

Posters Have students create posters that describe their community in terms of each of the five themes of geography. They might draw pictures or use pictures from magazines or newspapers. Have them label each theme that is being described. Display the posters in the classroom.

Climate Maps Have students create a simple outline map of the world showing the continents. Have them add major climate zones to their map and create a key. As they read the chapter, have them locate and mark each place they read about. Have them research more about each place's climate, weather conditions, average high and low temperatures, and so on, and summarize this data in a short paragraph. Paragraphs can be attached to the maps when they are displayed.

CHAPTER RESOURCES

LITERATURE ABOUT THE PERIOD

Bierhorst, John, ed. *The Monkey's Haircut and Other Stories told by the Mayas*. Morrow, 1986. Stories handed down through oral tradition.

Courlander, Harold. *The King's Drum, and Other African Tales.* Harcourt, 1962. Folktales from Africa south of the Sahara.

READINGS FOR THE STUDENT

Chortlon, Windsor, et al. *Ice Ages* (Planet Earth series). Time-Life Books, 1983. Looks at changes in human and animal life during the glacial ages, as well as the after-effects still apparent today.

Demko, George, Jerome Agel, and Eugene Boe. *Why in the World: Adventures in Geography.* Anchor, 1992. Multifaceted look at geography through the relationship of people and the earth.

Graves, Robert. *Greek Gods and Heroes.* Doubleday, 1960. Retelling of Greek myths.

Williams, Barbara. *Breakthrough: Women in Archaeology.* Walker & Co., 1981. Biographies of women archaeologists.

READINGS FOR THE TEACHER

Barry, Iris. *Discovering Archaeology: Stonehenge.* American Museum of Natural History, 1981. Focuses on carbon dating, the development of writing, and the decoding of artifacts from the Copper, Bronze, and Iron ages.

Leakey, Richard S. and Roger Lewen. *Origins.* E.P. Dutton, 1987. Deals with full panorama of human origins and evolution.

Natoli, Salvatore J., ed. *Strengthening Geography in the Social Studies: National Council for the Social Studies, Bulletin 81.* NCSS/SSSS. Ideas for teaching geographic concepts.

MULTIMEDIA RESOURCES

Building Map and Globe Skills. Britannica. Filmstrips (3).

Climates and the World We Live In. Coronet. Video. Explains the relationship between climate and human activity.

More than Maps: A Look at Geography. National Geographic Society. Filmstrips (3). Explains the many facets to geography.

INTRODUCE

CHAPTER 1 OVERVIEW

Chapter 1 focuses on the fundamental geographic themes in the study of the earth. It also focuses on physical geography as a basis for historical development.

- **Section 1** describes the five themes of geography.
- **Section 2** discusses the kinds of landforms, waterways, and climates found on the earth.
- **Section 3** describes the natural resources on the earth.
- **Section 4** explains how legends have been used to obtain clues to the past.
- **Section 5** examines the importance of archaeology.

CHAPTER OBJECTIVES

After reading Chapter 1, students will be able to:

1. describe how the five themes of geography help explain what a place is like and why.
2. explain how landforms, waterways, climate, and natural resources have shaped history.
3. discuss how legends have been important to the study of history.
4. summarize how archaeology helps scientists learn about ancient civilizations.

EXAMINING THE ILLUSTRATION

Geographers use aerial photographs of places as a tool to help them study the earth. Ask students to name other tools that geographers might use to help them study the earth.

PERFORMANCE ASSESSMENT

Use the Performance Assessment activities on page 4B to help you evaluate students as they complete the chapter.

CHAPTER 1 Geography and History

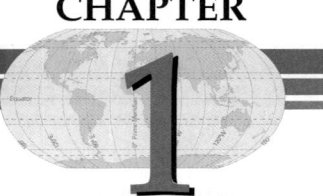

Coast of Somalia, Africa

4

TEACHER CLASSROOM RESOURCES

- Reproducible Lesson Plan
- Activity Book Activity
- Enrichment Activity
- Chart and Graph Skill Activity
- Geography and Map Activity
- Vocabulary and Guided Reading Activity
- Spanish Summary and Glossary
- Teaching Transparencies and Activities
- Cooperative Learning Activity
- Performance Assessment Activity
- Unit 1 World Literature
- Unit 1 Primary Source Reading
- Testmaker
- Audiocassettes (English and Spanish)

Chapter Focus

READ TO DISCOVER:

- How the five themes of geography help explain what a place is like and why.
- How landforms, waterways, climate, and natural resources have shaped history.
- How legends have been important to the study of history.
- How archaeology helps scientists learn about ancient civilizations.

Many scientists believe that people have been living on the earth for more than 2 million years. Where and how they lived was influenced greatly by the kind of land on which they lived. In many ways, the relationship between people and their environment has been the center of world history.

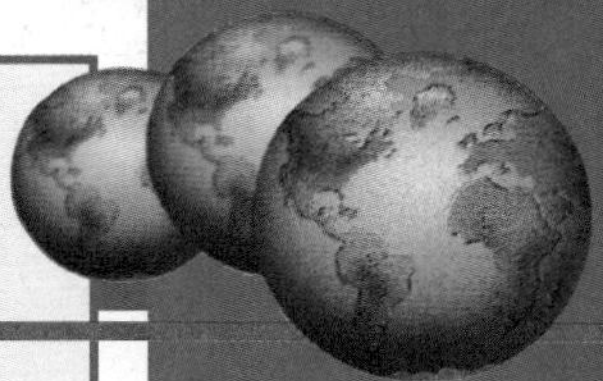

C. 3,000,000 B.C.–5000 B.C.

KEY TERMS

landforms
elevation
tectonic plates
erosion
glaciers
river system
climate
natural resources
archaeology
artifacts

Section 1

FIVE THEMES OF GEOGRAPHY

Geography is the study of the earth and of the ways people live and work on it. Geography helps explain why people live the way they do. Geography also helps explain the past by answering questions about why certain events occurred where they did. Geographers use five themes to help explain what a place is like and why it is like that.

Location The location theme helps answer the question "Where is it?" For example, where is Kenya? That question can be answered by saying that Kenya is located on the huge continent of Africa.

There are two types of location: absolute and relative. **Absolute location** refers to the exact location of a place on the earth's surface. For example, the capital of Kenya—Nairobi—is located at one place and one place only. No other place on earth has exactly the same location.

FOCUS

BELLRINGER

Write the following question on the chalkboard: *What factors have influenced the clothes you are wearing today?*

MOTIVATIONAL ACTIVITY

Ask students to share their reasons for wearing the clothes they have on today. Although many responses will focus on style, direct the responses by asking such questions as: Why are you wearing a short-sleeved shirt instead of a long-sleeved sweater? Why didn't you wear a jacket today?

VOCABULARY PRE-CHECK

Write the key terms for this chapter on the chalkboard. Ask students to use those that they know in sentences.

Assign Chapter 1 **Vocabulary and Guided Reading Activity** in the TCR.

EXTRA CREDIT PROJECT

Have students investigate career choices in the field of geography. Have them focus on one career, its required training, the scope of the job, and why they chose it as a topic. Have them present their findings about the career to the class.

KEY TO ABILITY LEVELS

Teaching strategies have been coded for varying learning styles and abilities.

L1 Level 1 activities are **basic** activities and should be within the ability range of all students.

L2 Level 2 activities are **average** activities and should be within the ability range of the average to above-average student.

L3 Level 3 activities are **challenging** activities designed for the ability range of above-average students.

LEP LEP activities should be within the ability range of Limited English Proficiency students.

TEACH

GUIDED PRACTICE

L1 **Geography** Ask students to explain the five themes of geography in their own words and use examples to clarify each. Have a volunteer chart the various examples given on the chalkboard under appropriate headings identifying the themes. LEP

DID YOU KNOW ??

The word *geography* comes from the Greek word *geographia,* which means "earth description."

CAPTION ANSWER

Answers will vary but should include details such as crowds of people, vehicles, streets, buildings, and flowers and trees.

PLACE A place such as the Moi Avenue in Mombasa, Kenya, shown here can be described easily. It is the avenue with the huge crossed elephant tusks. **What other details could be included in a description of this place?**

Relative location refers to the position of a place in relation to other places. Nairobi is located north of Mt. Kilimanjaro, west of the Indian Ocean, and southeast of Lake Turkana. Using this information, Nairobi can be found on a map of Africa if Mt. Kilimanjaro, the Indian Ocean, and Lake Turkana are located. A place may be described with many different locations.

Place The theme of place answers the question "What is the place like?" Places can be described by their physical characteristics such as climate, mountains, deserts, bodies of water, plants, and animals.

Places can also be described by their human characteristics. These characteristics tell how many people live in a place, what language they speak, and what they do for a living. Knowing about a place's soil and about how its people make a living tells more about it than just its location. The physical and human characteristics of Nairobi, for example, make it a place that is different from Tokyo.

MEETING SPECIAL NEEDS

Help Limited English Proficiency students learn the five themes of geography. Provide each student with five index cards. On one side of the cards, have students write each theme. On the other side of the cards, have students illustrate the theme written on the card. Then have students work in pairs and use the index cards like flash cards to reinforce an understanding of the themes.

Human/Environmental Interaction The theme of human/environmental interaction deals with how people use, adapt to, or change their environment. People respond to their environment in different ways. Sometimes they *adapt*, or adjust, to it. For example, people wear light clothing in a hot place and warm clothing in a cold place. At other times, people *modify*, or change, their environment. They may irrigate dry land to grow crops or build a dam to keep a river from flooding.

Ancient people adapted to their environment. They hunted animals and gathered fruit. Later, they changed the environment by farming the land and raising livestock.

Movement The theme of movement looks at how people and places are linked together. Every day you have contact with people around the world. Your breakfast may include fruit from Latin America. You may ride to school in a bus, truck, or car made in Japan or Germany.

Movement has brought the world's people closer together. Transportation—the movement of goods and people—allows people to use products made in places thousands of miles away. Modern transportation lets people themselves travel thousands of miles in a matter of hours. The movement of people has been important in world history. The bringing of ideas to a new location has changed many cultures.

INTERACTION Many acres of American forests have been cut to supply lumber products to a growing nation, as this photograph shows. Many new trees are planted to replace those removed. **What theme of geography is represented by this action?**

L2 **Geography: Human/Environmental Interaction** Have students work in small groups to create a list of ways in which their community's environment has changed as a result of human actions. Discuss each group's list. Then have students conclude whether these changes were positive or negative towards the environment. LEP

L3 **Daily Life** Have students keep a diary for a week in which they note ways in which the geographical theme of movement affects their everyday lives. Have them share their diaries and conclude whether or not this theme has much impact on their lives. LEP

CAPTION ANSWER

human/environmental interaction

COOPERATIVE LEARNING

Organize the class into five groups. Have each group prepare five questions about a particular place. Each question should be about a different theme of geography. Allow time for the group to research the place they choose in order to ask appropriate questions and to know the answers to their questions. Have the groups present their questions and quiz each other, perhaps in a competition format.

Assign the Chapter 1 **Cooperative Learning Activity** in the TCR.

L2 **Geography: Place** Have students work in pairs to write a brief description of a natural disaster and explain how it changed the earth. *(Students may describe the aftereffects of an earthquake, floods, and volcanic eruptions.)*
LEP

L1 **Critical Thinking** Ask students to explain the main characteristics of each layer of the earth's structure shown in the diagram on this page. *(The inner core is solid rock; the outer core is melted rock; the mantle is hot, solid rock; the crust is rock, sand, and soil.)*

MAKING CONNECTIONS

➤➤ **Geography** The idea of continental drift was first proposed in 1912 by Alfred Wegener. Evidence in support of his theory was found in the 1950s and 1960s, when scientists discovered a worldwide system of mountainlike ridges on the ocean floor.

Surface Changes From Inside the Earth The land surface of the earth is constantly changing. Most changes are caused by forces from deep within the earth, usually heat and pressure.

Heat and pressure are caused by the structure of the earth itself. The inside of the earth is made up of three separate layers. At the center of the earth is the **core.** The inner part of the core is solid rock, and the outer part of the core is made up of melted rock. Around the core is the **mantle,** which is made up mostly of hot, solid rock. Floating on the melted outer part of the mantle is a thin layer of rock, sand, and soil called the **crust.** The crust may be from 3 to 30 miles, or 5 to 49 kilometers, thick.

Heat from the core—the hottest part of the earth—causes the rock in the mantle to rise. This puts pressure on the crust and causes it to move. In recent years, scientists have come to believe that the crust does not move in one piece but in separate sections called **tectonic** (tek ton' ik) **plates.** These plates move very slowly, about 0.8 to 2 inches, or 2 to 5 centimeters, a year. Plates can move together, move apart, or slide past one another.

This movement of the plates explains what geographers call **continental drift.** Most geographers believe that about 220 million years ago, all the continents of the world formed one huge land mass named Pangaea (pan jē' uh). Over time, the plates

Major Landforms

The Earth's Structure

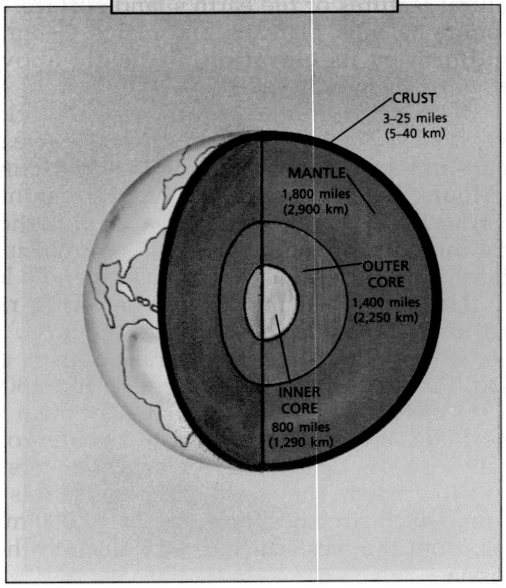

MEETING SPECIAL NEEDS

Provide students who are visual learners with an outline map of the world. Have them label the continents. Then have them cut out the continents and piece them together as they may have looked as one huge land mass named Pangea. Use this activity as a lead-in to a discussion of continental drift.

Tectonic Plates

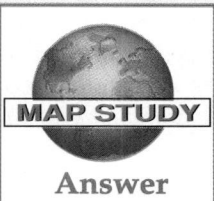

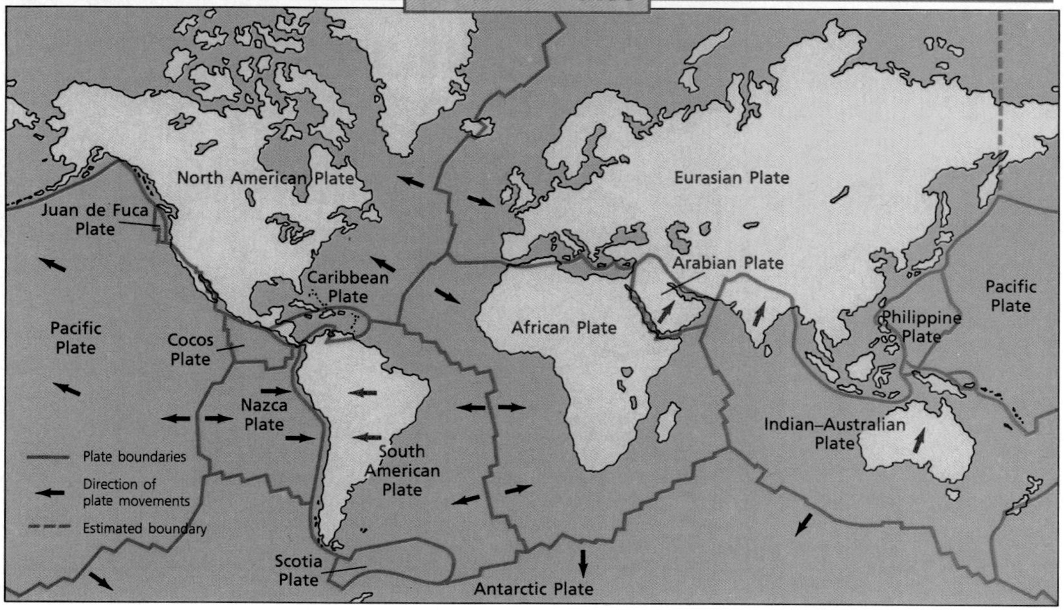

moved and Pangaea split into seven continents. Some plates, such as the ones on which Africa and South America are located, moved apart. Other plates, such as the plates on which India and most of Asia are located, collided. The crust where these two plates met was squeezed upward to form the Himalayas.

Plate movement also creates **volcanoes.** These are cone-shaped mountains made when melted rock called lava flows up from the earth's mantle, cracks the crust, and then cools into solid rock. The Hawaiian Islands, for example, were formed by volcanoes that thrust up from the ocean floor millions of years ago.

Plate movements can also cause **earthquakes**, or sudden shifts in the earth's crust. These often happen when tectonic plates slide past one another. About 800,000 earthquakes occur each year with only about 50,000 of them strong enough for people to even feel them. A strong earthquake, however, can cause loss of life and serious property damage.

Both volcanoes and earthquakes are generally found along the edges of the earth's tectonic plates. They are so common around the Pacific Ocean that geographers call one area the "Ring of Fire."

The tectonic plates are still moving. Most geographers believe that thousands of years from now, California, which is on

MAP STUDY

LOCATION The idea that the continents were once joined and then slowly drifted apart is called the continental-drift theory. **According to the plate map, which plate is colliding with the South American plate along the west coast of South America?**

DID YOU KNOW ??

Hawaii is the second largest volcanic island; Iceland is the largest. Hualalai and Mauna Loa, two of Hawaii's three active volcanoes, are among the world's highest mountains, if measured from the ocean floor.

MAP STUDY Answer

Nazca Plate

LINKING PAST TO PRESENT

There have been several serious earthquakes in the United States. In 1906, an earthquake that caused a great fire in San Francisco left more than 500 dead or missing. A 1989 earthquake in the same location killed dozens. Although this earthquake was quite strong, buildings have been constructed to withstand strong earthquakes and fireproof materials have been used in construction.

COOPERATIVE LEARNING

Organize the class into two groups. Assign volcanic eruptions to one group and earthquakes to the other group. Tell each group to make a list of natural disasters caused by these surface changes from inside the earth. Then have members work together to research information about the natural disasters on their list and to prepare an oral report and bulletin-board display of their subject.

CAPTION ANSWER

sudden shifts in the earth that happen when tectonic plates slide past one another

L3 **Critical Thinking** Have students contrast the surface changes of forces from inside the earth with the surface changes of forces from outside the earth. *(Students should note that forces from inside the earth cause sudden, drastic changes in the earth's surface and are usually destructive. Forces from outside the earth are more gradual in nature and can either help or hurt people.)*

L2 **Geography: Human/Environmental Interaction** Have a volunteer read aloud a description of the Dust Bowl in the 1930s from an encyclopedia or history book. Discuss the human/environmental interaction that contributed to this disaster as a volunteer writes the causes on the chalkboard. Have students create a graphic organizer that shows the results of your discussion.

EARTHQUAKE DISASTERS Mexico has experienced many earthquakes that have caused terrible loss of life and property. These earthquakes most often occur without warning. **What causes an earthquake?**

a different plate from most of the United States, will be located far off the west coast of Canada.

Surface Changes From Outside the Earth

Forces from outside the earth also cause changes on its surface. Three main forces are wind, water, and ice. All three reshape the land by a process called **erosion** (i rō′ zhuhn), in which rock and soil are moved from one place on the earth's surface to another. These forces can either help or hurt people.

An example of helpful wind erosion can be found in the plains of northern China, where large amounts of wheat and other food crops are grown. The plains are covered with a thick, rich, yellowish soil called *loess* (les) which was carried there by winds blowing from deserts to the west. On the other hand, during the 1930s winds blew away so much of the soil in the central part of the United States that the area became known as the Dust Bowl.

Water erosion that is helpful can be seen in the Mekong (may′ kawng) River of Southeast Asia. This river carries rich soil down from the mountains and spreads it over the lowlands, creating one of the most fertile areas in the world. Harmful water erosion occurs when the Huang Ho (hwong huh) in northern China overflows its banks and floods farms and homes.

Ice erosion has also caused changes on the earth's surface and in people's lives. Four times in the last 500,000 years, during

EXTENDING THE CONTENT

The edges of the Pacific Ocean basin (which are generally the same as the borders of the Pacific plate plus some smaller plates) have come to be called the "Ring of Fire" because most of today's active volcanoes are located here. In North America, the Ring includes Alaska's Aleutians, the Cascade Range (where Mount St. Helens erupted), and Mexico's Popocatepetl. It continues southward through Central America and down the western edge of South America into Antarctica. On the other side of the Pacific are Japan's Fujiyama, the Southern Alps of New Zealand, and mountains in the Philippines and Indonesia.

what are called the Ice Ages, great ice sheets called **glaciers** spread out from the North and South poles. The ice drove people and animals away, smoothed hills into plains, created lakes, and dug new channels for rivers.

Landforms in History All through history, landforms have played an important part in helping people decide where to live. People stayed away from mountainous areas where travel was difficult or where the air was so thin that it was hard to breathe. Instead, people settled mostly in plains and hilly areas where the soil was rich enough for crops to grow.

Landforms also have made a big difference in the political relationships of people. In ancient times the Greeks lived in many different city-states. One reason the Greeks did not join together to form a nation was that their communities were separated from one another by a landform—mountains.

Waterways About 70 percent of the earth's surface is covered with water. The largest waterways in the world are the four oceans—the Atlantic, the Pacific, the Indian, and the Arctic.

MAP STUDY

PLACE Scientists believe that in the last two million years glaciers have covered large areas of the earth's surface during the Ice Ages. **What continents were affected the most by the Ice Ages?**

Ice Ages

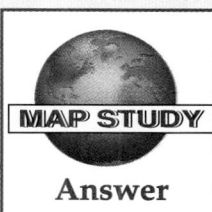

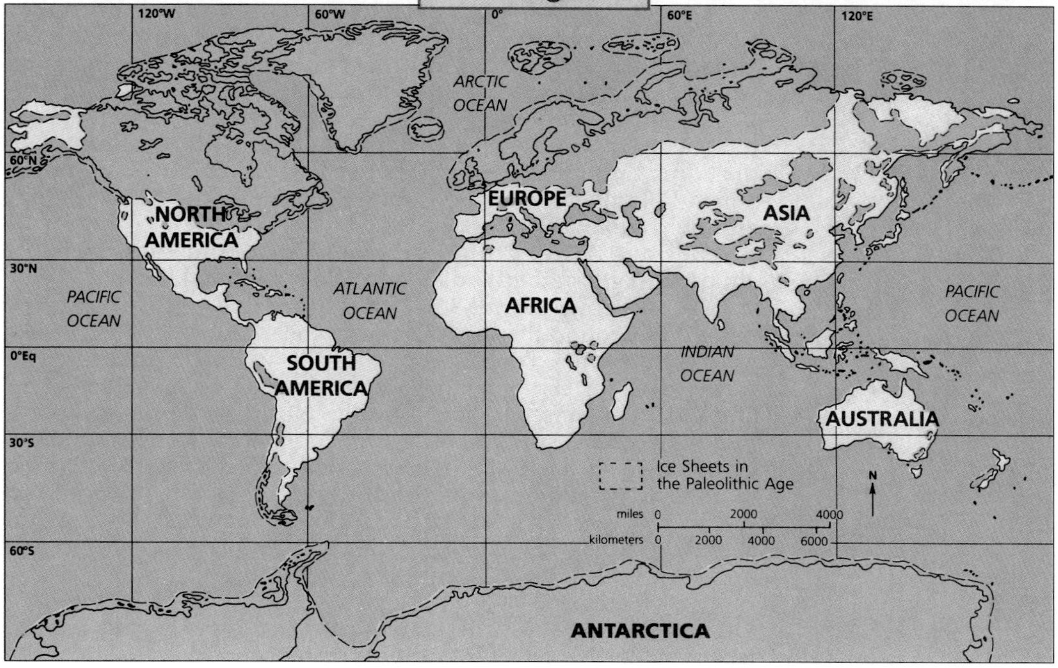

L3 **Critical Thinking** Ask students to explain the duality of the Mississippi River in bringing both prosperity and devastation to the people who live along it. Have some students research the flood of 1993 and create a graph or chart showing loss of acres of farmland, lives, and destroyed property. Have other students research the economic prosperity enjoyed by those who earn their living from the river, creating a chart or graph of dollars earned and jobs generated. Have the two groups share their charts.

DID YOU KNOW ??

The Atlantic Ocean was named by the Romans after the Atlas Mountains that rose at the western end of the Mediterranean Sea. This got its name from two Latin words meaning "in the middle of the land." The Pacific Ocean was named by Spanish explorer Ferdinand Magellan, who found it calm and peaceful after his stormy voyage around Cape Horn.

MAP STUDY Answer

North America, Europe, Asia, and Antarctica

MEETING SPECIAL NEEDS

Help students with Limited English Proficiency learn the geographical terms that are discussed in this chapter. Have the class use their textbook and geographical reference materials to create a list of geographical features. Next, ask students to group related terms into the following categories: landforms, waterways. Organize the students into two groups and assign one category to each group. Have each student in the group define and illustrate one or more terms. When all the students have finished their assignments, compile the definitions and illustrations into an illustrated dictionary to use as a class reference.

L3 **Critical Thinking** Have students research to make a list of the ten largest cities, based on population, in the United States. Using their text Atlas, have students locate each city to determine if it is near a waterway. Ask students to give reasons why so many cities are located near waterways.

MAKING CONNECTIONS

➤➤ **Geography** The Nile is not only the world's longest river, it was also the site of one of the first great cultures. Rivers are sources of fresh water and food, which makes it desirable to live along their banks. Other factors such as climate, the earth's surface changes, and certain landforms may make river areas uninhabitable. The Amazon River is the second longest river in the world, yet its course through tropical rain forests makes it undesirable to live along its banks.

L1 **Critical Thinking** Ask students to explain the differences between weather and climate. *(Weather is the conditions in the earth's atmosphere at a certain place and time. Climate is the pattern of weather over many years.)*

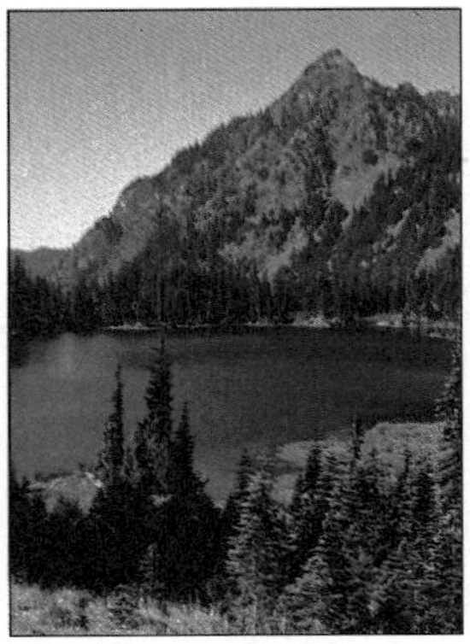

Freshwater Lake

Smaller bodies of salt water are known as seas. They are usually partly surrounded by land. Bodies of water that are completely surrounded by land are known as lakes. The world's largest freshwater lake is Lake Superior in North America. It is about 350 miles, or 563 kilometers, long and 160 miles, or 257 kilometers, wide.

Waterways that empty into another body of water are known as rivers. Most rivers begin high in mountains or hills. A river and all the streams that flow into it make up a **river system.** The longest river system in the world is the Nile, which flows about 4,160 miles, or 6,693 kilometers, from its source in the highlands of central Africa to its mouth on the Mediterranean Sea.

Waterways in History Like landforms, waterways have played an important part in helping people decide where to live. People's earliest homes were along the banks of rivers and other waterways. These bodies of water provided them with a means for travel and trade, drinking water, irrigation for crops as farming developed. Thus, river valleys were often sites for villages and cities. Animals also used waterways for food and drinking water, so the riverbanks were good hunting grounds.

Climate and the Sun The pattern of weather of a place over many years is **climate.** The most important thing that shapes climate is the sun. The sun provides the earth with heat and light. All parts of the earth, however, do not receive the same amount of sunlight.

As the earth moves through space, it *rotates,* or spins like a top. Geographers say that it spins on its *axis,* an imaginary line that runs through the earth's center from the North Pole to the South Pole. It takes one day of 24 hours for the earth to spin around completely.

Besides rotating, the earth moves around the sun in an almost circular path called an *orbit.* This motion, known as a *revolution,* takes one year of 365¼ days to complete. It is the earth's revolution around the sun that causes the seasons.

Seasons vary from one part of the world to another. The earth's axis, instead of being straight up and down, is tilted at an angle. This means that places in the Northern Hemisphere are tilted toward the sun from March to September. As a result, these places have spring and summer at that time. During these same months, however, the Southern Hemisphere is tilted away from the sun. There it is fall and winter. Six months later, from September to March, conditions reverse, and the seasons are the opposite.

New York City on the Hudson River

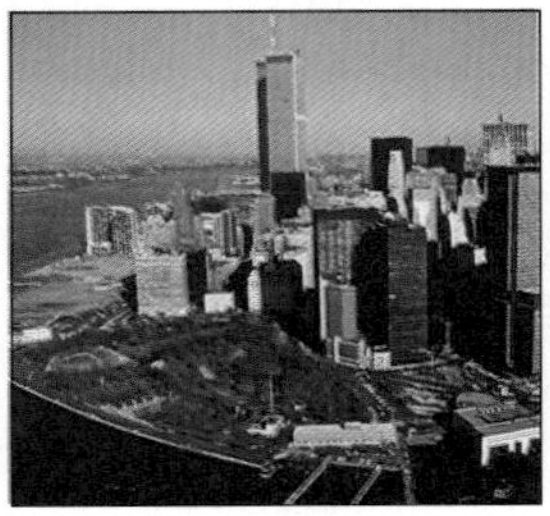

Climate Zones The amount of heat from the sun a place receives depends on its **latitude,** or distance north or south of the

EXTENDING THE CONTENT

Making a list of the world's longest rivers is not an easy task. Some references use only the length of the river itself, while others use the length of the entire river system. For example, the Mississippi River itself is 2,348 miles (or 3,779 km) long and ranks twelfth in length in the world. Some sources will rank the Mississippi the third longest river because they consider the combined Mississippi-Missouri rivers for length—3,880 miles (or 6,240 km).

The Earth's Revolution

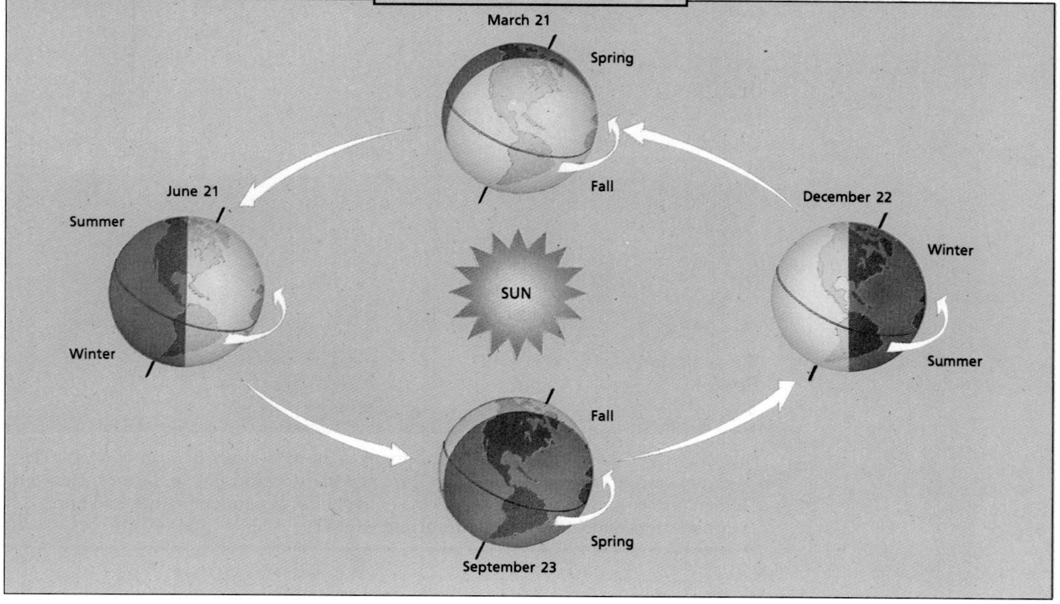

Equator. Rays from the sun are most direct at the Equator. Geographers often organize the earth into three climate zones based on latitude.

The **tropical zone,** also called the tropics, is the area between the Tropic of Cancer and the Tropic of Capricorn. The tropical zone always receives the most direct rays of the sun. Most places in the tropics are hot year-round.

The **temperate** (tem′puh ruht) **zone** is found in both the area between the Tropic of Cancer and the Arctic Circle in the Northern Hemisphere, and the area between the Tropic of Capricorn and the Antarctic Circle in the Southern Hemisphere. The sun's rays reach the temperate zone at a slant for part of the year and almost directly for the rest of the year. As a result, the weather in this zone is generally cold in winter and warm in summer.

The **polar zone** is the area north of the Arctic Circle and south of the Antarctic Circle. This area receives no sunlight at all during part of the year and only slanting rays during the rest of the year. As a result, the climate in the polar zone is very cold, and few people live there.

Climate, Water, and Wind In addition to the sun, climate is shaped by large bodies of water, which keep the temperature of a place from getting too hot or too cold. Water gains or

L1 **Science** Ask students to describe the kind of climate in which they live and the factors that affect their climate. Have them explain which of these factors has the biggest impact on their own lives.

MAKING CONNECTIONS

➤➤ **Science** Climate closely affects plant life. Hot, dry places have plants that are able to remove moisture from the air and store water in their stems. Forests flourish in areas with warm temperatures and at least moderate rainfall. When rainfall is light, vegetation consists of tall grasses. Some mosses survive in very cold places.

DID YOU KNOW ??

The sun's surface temperature is several thousand degrees and at its center, the temperature is from 10 to 20 million degrees. An object on the sun would weigh about 28 times its weight on the earth.

MEETING SPECIAL NEEDS

Help tactile/kinesthetic learners understand the earth's revolution by having them demonstrate the movement of the earth on its axis, its rotation around the sun, and its orbit around the sun. They may use a globe for the earth and a flashlight to represent the sun. Discuss how the earth's axis is always tilted in the same direction. This affects the temperature of places. Demonstrate how the earth's rotation around the sun causes day and night. Finally, demonstrate how the earth's revolution and the earth's tilt cause the changing seasons.

L2 **Science** Have students work in pairs to find examples of climate maps in newspapers and magazines and compare them to those found in geography textbooks, encyclopedias, and atlases. Have students write a summary of how these maps differ, how they are similar and what different purpose each serves. LEP

CAPTION ANSWER

Prevailing winds blow from a certain direction most of the time. Monsoon winds change direction depending on the season of the year.

MAKING CONNECTIONS

➤➤ **Science** In the days of sailing ships, experienced sea captains and navigators took advantage of their knowledge of the winds to make long voyages that seem almost unbelievable today.

MONSOON Monsoons are very important to the agriculture of southern Asia. The wet, or summer, monsoons bring moisture necessary for farming to the area. Here, an Indian farmer struggle to plow his fields in the midst of monsoon winds and rain. **How do monsoons differ from prevailing winds?**

loses heat more slowly than land. Also, air over a lake is cooler than air over the land.

Climate is also shaped by the movement of air and ocean water. Air that moves is called wind. Some winds are known as **prevailing** (pri vā' lĕng) **winds** because they blow from a certain direction almost all the time. Other winds are called monsoons because they change direction according to the season of the year. Monsoons often bring heavy rainfall. Ocean water that flows in a steady stream is called an **ocean current.** Both winds and ocean currents carry heat or cold and moisture all over the world. Ocean currents that flow from the Equator toward the poles warm the lands they pass. Currents that flow from the poles to the Equator cool the land they pass.

Climate and Altitude Climate is also shaped by altitude. The higher the altitude, the colder the climate. In the tropical zone, people often prefer living in highlands rather than lowlands because the highland temperatures are more comfortable. The ancient Incas settled in the Andes Mountains of Peru instead of along the Pacific coast for that reason. Mountains also affect **precipitation**—the falling of moisture such as rain or snow. As the air rises over mountains, it cools and drops its moisture.

EXTENDING THE CONTENT

The pattern of prevailing winds worldwide is due to temperature differences and to the earth's rotation, which deflects winds from a straight-line path. At the Equator, for instance, rising warm air causes clouds and uncertain breezes where a ship might be motionless for days. Immediately to the north and south are two bands of trade winds, cool easterly winds that blow slightly toward the Equator. In the middle latitudes, the earth's rotation makes the prevailing winds westerlies. These winds are stormier and more erratic than the trade winds. For early European explorers, though, they provided a dependable route homeward from the Americas across the Atlantic.

Understanding a Mercator Projection

Because Earth is a sphere, no flat map can show its whole surface. Mapmakers use different **projections** (pruh jek´ shuhns), or ways of representing Earth on a flat surface.

One projection used often is a Mercator (muhr kāt´ uhr) projection. Named after Gerardus Mercator, a Flemish mapmaker of the 1500s, it is made by wrapping paper around a globe. A light shining from the center of the globe projects Earth's features onto the paper. This allows the map to be traced.

The parts of the map that are most like the earth are where the paper touches the globe, such as at the Equator. The parts that are most *distorted* (dis tort´ ed), or twisted out of shape, are where the paper does not touch the globe such as near the poles.

Map Practice

1. **Which of the earth's climate zones is shown most accurately?**
2. **Which is most distorted?**
3. **Is the shape of North America more accurate on this map or on a globe? Why?**

World Climate Zones

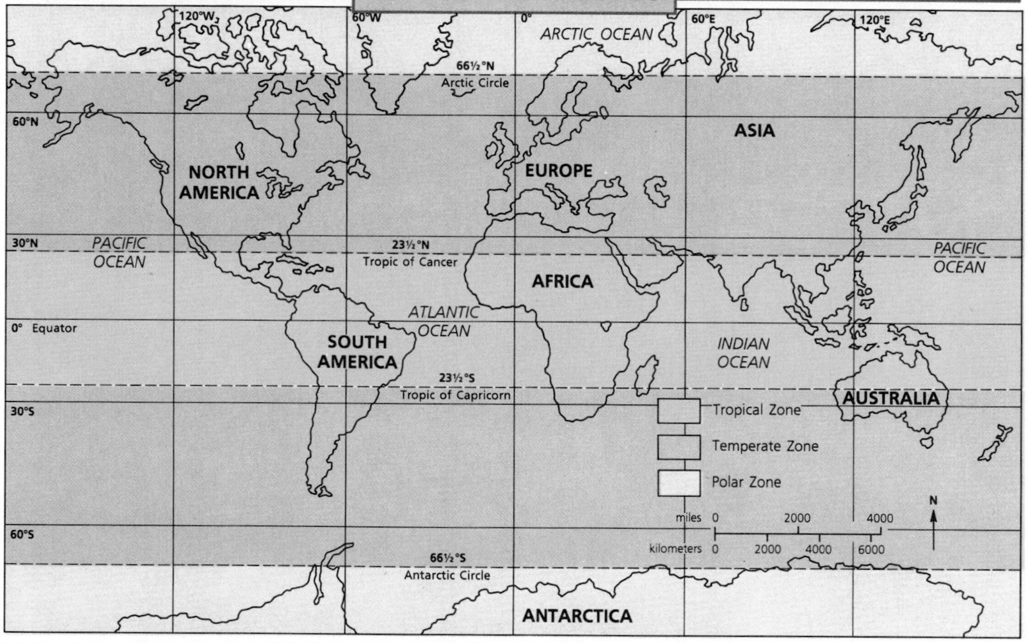

Teaching

MAP SKILLS

Understanding a Mercator Projection

Instruct the students to read the instructional part of the feature. Ask: Why can't a flat map show the whole surface of the earth? *(because the earth is a sphere)* How is a Mercator map projection made? *(by wrapping paper around a globe, shining a light from the center of the globe onto the paper, and tracing the map)* Which parts of the Mercator projection are most like the earth? *(parts where the paper touches the globe, such as at the Equator.)* Direct students to study the map. Ask: Which continent is more accurate on a Mercator projection, South America or Asia? Why? *(South America, because it is located closer to the Equator than Asia is)*

Next, have students work in small groups to study other projections of the earth. Assign each group one of the following projections: conic, sinusoidal, polar, Goode's interrupted equal-area projection, Robinson, or Gall-Peters. Then have students find an example of their projection, explain how it is made, and describe its inaccuracies and its helpfulness in studying the earth. Have a spokesperson from each group present their group's findings.

Assign the Chapter 1 **Geography and Map Activity** in the TCR.

ANSWERS to Map Practice

1. Tropical Zone
2. Polar Zone
3. The globe representation is more accurate because no flat map can accurately represent a sphere.

SPOTLIGHT ON: WORLD CLIMATE

Factors of climate can change as has been shown in recent years all over the world. Much of Africa north of the Equator receives very little rainfall. In this area is the world's largest tropical desert—the Sahara. However, at one time the Sahara was a fertile region that supported a thriving civilization. Because of a gradual lack of rainfall most of this area is now uninhabitable. On the southern border of this desert is the Sahel, which in Arabic means coastal land. Between 1968 and 1974 a drought in the Sahel destroyed livestock and caused the starvation of many West Africans.

L3 **Critical Thinking** Ask students if they think one kind of climate is more beneficial economically to a country than another. Have students explain their answers and give examples that support it.

CAPTION ANSWER

Russia has often gone to war with other countries in order to capture land for warm water ports and harbors.

Climate in History Climate, like land and waterways, plays an important part in shaping history. It helps determine where people live, what kind of clothes they wear, what kind of houses they build, and what crops they grow. It also affects the speed with which they work and the kinds of things they do for entertainment. Since climate is something humans cannot control, it has affected civilizations since prehistoric times.

Sometimes climate affects the way a country behaves towards its neighbors. Climate has also helped decide the outcomes of wars. For example, many of Russia's harbors stay frozen during much of the year. In the past, Russia has often gone to war with other countries in order to capture land for warm water ports. Climate was also one reason the Russians were able to stop the invasions of French ruler Napoleon Bonaparte (nuh pō′ lē uhn bō′ nuh part) in the 1800s and German ruler Adolf Hitler in the 1940s. The Russians were used to the bitter cold and snow of their country's winter, whereas the invaders were not.

COLD CLIMATE This buoy has become frozen in the St. Petersburg Harbor during the cold Russian winter. Such waterways have been important many times in Russia's history. **What has the lack of warm water ports and harbors caused Russia to do in the past?**

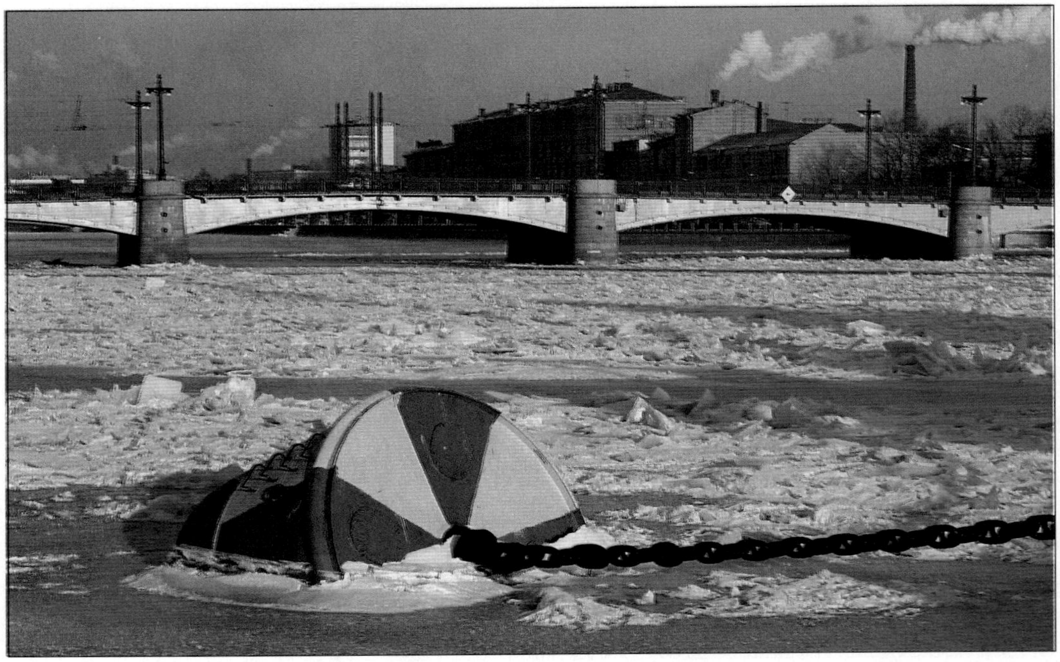

MEETING SPECIAL NEEDS

Have interested students research the affects of climate on the soldiers who fought in such wars as Vietnam and the Persian Gulf War. Encourage them to interview any participants in these wars that they happen to know. Have them explain their findings in an oral report to the class.

Section 2 Review

1. **Identify:** Himalayas, Mediterranean Sea, Lake Superior, Nile River, Tropic of Cancer, Tropic of Capricorn, Arctic Circle, Antarctic Circle
2. **Define:** landforms, elevation, relief, core, mantle, crust, tectonic plates, continental drift, erosion, glaciers, river system, climate, tropical zone, temperate zone, polar zone, ocean current, prevailing winds
3. What are some ways in which landforms and waterways have been important in history?
4. Into what climate zones do geographers often organize the earth?

Critical Thinking

5. How does climate affect the way you live?

Section 3

NATURAL RESOURCES

Natural resources are materials found in nature. Some, such as air, are found everywhere. Others, such as oil, are found only in certain areas. Some places have many natural resources, while others have few.

Kinds of Natural Resources There are different kinds of natural resources. Some resources helpful to people include air, water, soil, sunlight, minerals, fossil fuels, forests, and animal life. Some of these—air, water, soil, and sunlight—are essential for any kind of life to exist. They are the most important natural resources.

Other natural resources, while not essential for life, are important because they enable people to live better. One such resource is **minerals,** or nonliving substances found beneath the earth's surface. Throughout history, people have used such minerals as iron, copper, tin, gold, and silver to make tools, weapons, jewelry, and money. Fossil fuels, such as coal, oil, and natural gas, provide the energy needed to heat homes and power machines.

Natural resources become valuable only when people learn how to use them. For example, during the 1200s Marco Polo left his native city of Venice, in present-day Italy, and traveled to

L2 **Geography: Region** Organize students into seven groups to make natural resource maps of the continents. Assign each group one of the continents. Have a member of each group present its map to the class. Discuss which continent appears to be most abundant in resources and what implications there might be as a result. LEP

L3 **Critical Thinking** Ask students to consider why some countries think of their people as their most important natural resource. What countries would be most likely to think this way? *(China, India)* Why?

SECTION 2 ANSWERS

1. Himalayas, highest mountain range (p. 9); Mediterranean Sea, sea between southern Europe, the northern part of Africa (p. 14); Lake Superior, world's largest lake (p. 14); Nile River, longest river system (p. 14); Tropic of Cancer, 23½° N latitude (p. 15); Tropic of Capricorn, 23½° S latitude (p. 15); Arctic Circle, 66½° N longitude (p. 15); Antarctic Circle, 66½° S longitude (p. 15)
2. All terms are defined in the text Glossary.
3. Landforms and waterways played an important part in where people lived and their political relationships.
4. the tropical, temperate, and polar zones
5. Answers will vary but should give examples of the way climate affects the way they live.

Assign the Chapter 1 **Section 2 Quiz** in the TCR. Testmaker available.

CAPTION ANSWER

iron, copper, tin, gold, silver

L1 **Art** Have students find pictures in newspapers and magazines or draw illustrations of renewable resources and nonrenewable resources. Then divide a bulletin board in half. Title one side "Renewable Resources" and the other side "Nonrenewable Resources." Display pictures and illustrations on the bulletin board. Use the bulletin board to start a discussion of how the students can conserve their use of nonrenewable resources.

L3 **Geography: Human/Environmental Interaction** Have students research laws passed in their state to control the pollution of the air, soil, and water. Ask them to present their findings in an oral report to the class. Have the class decide if any additional laws are needed.

MINERALS Some natural resources are found beneath the ground and are called minerals. Oil and coal are two minerals for which people drill and mine underground. The oil well shown here (left) is in the jungles of Nigeria. Coal mining in North Dakota is also shown (right). **What are other examples of minerals?**

China. A few years after returning home, he wrote a book about the wonderful things he had seen on his journey. One of these was a black rock, now known as coal, which the Chinese dug out of the ground and burned to keep themselves warm. The Venetians (vi nē′ shuhnz) doubted Marco Polo. They had not used coal as the Chinese had. People later changed their minds about coal when they began using it as a fuel to power steam engines and to process steel.

Some resources can be replaced as they are used. These are **renewable resources.** For example, American farmers who lived in the Dust Bowl of the 1930s were able to get back their once-rich soil. To do this they used better ways of farming and planted trees to keep the soil from being blown away. Other natural resources cannot be replaced as they are used. These are **nonrenewable resources.** For example, once fossil fuels and most minerals are used up, they will be gone forever.

In recent years, people have become more and more concerned about making better use of the world's natural resources. Some countries have passed laws to slow down the pollution of the air, water, and soil. Scientists also are trying to develop new sources of energy.

COOPERATIVE LEARNING

Ask the class to name important resources that need to be conserved, as you write responses on the chalkboard. Organize the students into as many groups as there are items on the list. Have each group investigate efforts being made to conserve its resource. Have each group also brainstorm other ways in which their resource might be conserved. After each group has completed its work, ask each to participate in a round-table discussion in which group members take turns suggesting ways to conserve their assigned resource.

Natural Resources in History

Natural resources affected the location and growth of settlements all through history. The sharing of these resources has also been important. Rich soil and plenty of water made farming possible and led to the rise of cities. Asians and Europeans came into contact with one another partly because Europeans wanted the silks and spices of Asia that had been cultivated. Modern industry started in countries that had large amounts of coal and iron ore for making steel. During the 1800s, the discovery of gold in California, South Africa, Australia, and Alaska caused hundreds of thousands of people to move to those areas.

Section 3 Review

1. **Define:** natural resources, renewable resources, nonrenewable resources
2. What natural resources are needed for life to exist?
3. How are minerals important to people?
4. When do natural resources become valuable?

Critical Thinking

5. Why do you think people have become more interested in making better use of the world's natural resources?

RENEWABLE RESOURCES Soil is considered a renewable resource. Some human activities, like the strip mining of coal (left), use up the land. With careful management, however, such areas can be reclaimed, or made productive again (right). **What are some examples of nonrenewable resources?**

DID YOU KNOW ??

Oil takes millions of years to form, and the earth's supply is limited. Industrialized countries like the United States consume far more oil than they produce and must import large amounts. Many experts believe that the world's fossil fuels will be used up if steps are not taken to limit their consumption and to find alternative energy sources.

L2 **Science** Have students research to find out about alternative energy sources. Then have them make a diorama showing one of the alternative energy sources being used or applied.

CAPTION ANSWER

fossil fuels and most minerals such as copper, tin, and gold

SECTION 3 ANSWERS

1. natural resources, materials found in nature (p. 19); renewable resources, resources that can be replaced (p. 20); nonrenewable resources, resources that cannot be replaced (p. 20)
2. air, water, soil, and sunlight
3. People have used minerals to make tools, weapons, jewelry, and money and have used energy from fossil fuels.
4. when people learn how to use them
5. Answers will vary but might include that people are afraid resources will be used up, and they want to stop pollution of these resources.

Assign the Chapter 1 **Section 3 Quiz** in the TCR. Testmaker available.

L1 **Art** Discuss how legends are very descriptive and help people form pictures in their minds while they listen to the legends or while they read the legends. Ask how this might help archaeologists and anthropologists learn about early people. Have students illustrate one of the legends they read in this section.

L2 **Language Arts** Read to the students legends about the beginning of the world from the book written by Virginia Hamilton, *In the Beginning: Creation Stories from Around the World*. Harcourt, 1988. Have students compare and contrast legends from different parts of the world. What elements are similar? What seems dissimilar about these legends?

While God was weaving and shaping the earth, the mole let out the thread little by little. God was too busy to notice that at times the mole let out more thread than it should have. When God was finished, He was amazed to find that the earth was too big to fit under the heavens.

The mole, seeing what it had done, was afraid. It ran off and buried itself. God sent the bee to find the mole and ask it what should be done. But when the bee found the mole, it would not answer the question.

The bee hid in a flower, hoping the mole would think it was alone and start talking to itself. Sure enough, the mole thought out loud. It said that it would squeeze the earth so that the mountains would stick up and the valleys would sink down. Then the earth would be small enough to fit under the heavens. Upon hearing this, the bee buzzed off. The mole heard the buzzing and became angry. It put a curse on the bee, saying, "Henceforth, feed on yourself."

The bee told God what the mole had said. God squeezed the flat earth so that the mountains rose up, the valleys sank down, and the earth fit under the heavens. God then turned the mole's curse into a blessing. Ever since, the bee makes its own honey, while the mole lives underground and is afraid to come out.

Other Legends

These Chinese, African, and Rumanian legends are about the creation of the world. This is not true of all legends. Many are about the deeds of godlike men and women or about strange and wonderful lands. Other legends explain natural elements such as the placement of stars or why a maple tree has red leaves. Some even explain geographic features such as mountains and rivers.

After people developed writing more than 5,000 years ago, they wrote down their legends. Many came to be thought of as fact. In recent years, **archaeologists,** or scientists who study the remains of past human life, and **anthropologists,** or scientists who study the origin and development of humans, became curious about how much of certain legends was fiction and how much was fact. This led them to search out the truth of some of the legends.

Section 4 Review

1. **Define:** archaeologists, anthropologists
2. What are legends about?
3. How have legends helped the study of history?

Critical Thinking

4. What legends do you know? What do they try to explain?

SECTION 4 ANSWERS

1. archaeologists, scientists who study human remains (p. 24); anthropologists, scientists who study human origins (p. 24)
2. creation, the heavens, the deeds of godlike men and women, or strange and wonderful lands
3. They have caused archaeologists and anthropologists to become curious about early societies and to search out the truth of some legends.
4. Answers will vary but students should name legends they know and their themes.

Assign the Chapter 1 **Section 4 Quiz** in the TCR. Testmaker available.

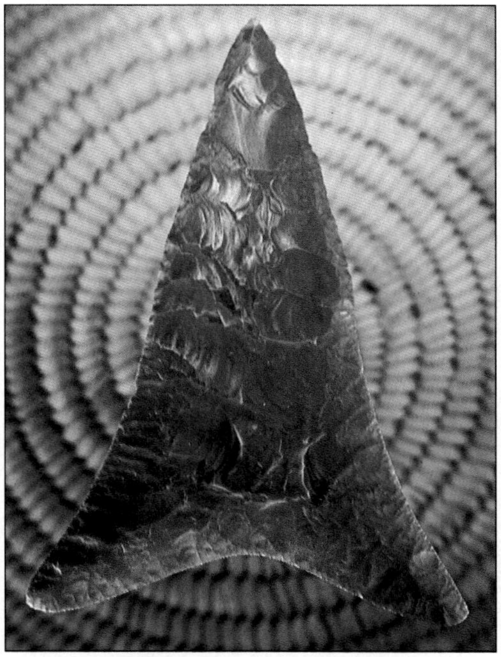

EGYPTIAN ARTIFACTS Archaeologists have uncovered many artifacts in Egypt. This spearhead (left), from about 15,000 B.C., is one of the oldest objects found in the region. The Rosetta Stone (right), from around 200 B.C., is one of the most famous archaeological finds. On it is carved a decree issued by Egyptian priests to honor a leader. **What kinds of objects can be considered artifacts?**

Section 5

ARCHAEOLOGY

Archaeology, or the study of the remains of past human life and cultures, began about 500 years ago. At that time, some Europeans dug up old marble statues and ornaments made by the ancient Greeks and Romans and sold them for a great deal of money. Scientists began to study these **artifacts,** or things made by people. They found they could learn from the artifacts how people lived long ago. People who lived in ancient times did not leave many written records.

Artifacts do not have to be works of art. They can be anything made by people such as weapons, tools, or pottery. The earliest artifacts are pieces of hard rock that were chipped into cutting or digging tools or into weapons.

CAPTION ANSWER

things made by people

L3 **Archaeology** Have students visit a local museum or library to find out what artifacts may have been uncovered in their area. Some of the oldest artifacts found in the United States have been traced to the Aanasazi people of New Mexico and Arizona. Have students research these people and their civilization and create a report on what the artifacts reveal about early inhabitants of the area. LEP

MULTICULTURAL PERSPECTIVES

In today's world, dolls are considered toys, but archaeological evidence suggests that in ancient times dolls played an important part in adult life as well. Ritual dolls, probably used in fertility rites, have been found in Europe from France to Russia, from the Aurignacian culture that existed there some 40,000 years ago.

DID YOU KNOW ??

In the summer of A.D. 79, Pompeii was a prosperous town of about 20,000. The mild, sunny climate attracted wealthy Romans to vacation there and live in the comfortable villas. Thriving vineyards (in soil rich from volcanic ash) surrounded the city. Nearby Mount Vesuvius, though unknown to be a volcano, had not erupted for centuries. Its sudden eruption one August afternoon rained hot ashes, stones, and cinders on Pompeii for a day and a half, and choked the town with deadly fumes. Only those who left the city quickly survived.

MAKING CONNECTIONS

➤➤ **History** The Rosetta Stone records a law written in 196 B.C. praising Egyptian King Ptolomy V. The Rosetta Stone is made of basalt. It was found by Jean-Francois Champollion in 1799 near Rosetta, a town 34 miles, or 54 km, east of Alexandria, Egypt.

CAPTION ANSWER

Herculaneum

Archaeological Finds About 1700, some Italian farmers discovered they were living on top of an ancient Roman city named Herculaneum (huhr kyul lā′ nē uhm) that had been buried for more than 1,000 years. In 1719 archaeologists began uncovering the city. After more than 50 years, they uncovered not only Herculaneum but also another Roman city called Pompeii (pom pā′). These cities contained, among other things, fine houses, theaters, streets, and temples. More importantly, from what they found, the archaeologists learned exactly how ancient Romans lived.

The discovery of Herculaneum and Pompeii was followed in 1799 by one of the greatest of all archaeological discoveries. This was the finding in Egypt of the Rosetta Stone, a slab of stone on which are carved ancient Egyptian picture-writing and its Greek translation. Although scholars knew the Greek language well, they had not been able to *decipher,* or explain the meaning of, the ancient Egyptian language. The Rosetta Stone was a two-

POMPEII The Roman city of Pompeii was buried under the mud and lava from a volcanic eruption in 79 A.D. Discovered in the middle 1700s, the site has provided much information on Roman life and art, such as this wall painting from a home. **What other ancient Roman city was discovered in the 1700s?**

EXTENDING THE CONTENT

When archaeologists excavated Pompeii, they found restaurants with games and wine on the table, bakeries with bread in the oven, and family pets in the houses. They found comfortable townhouses with colorful tiled floors, paintings on the walls, and elegant furnishings. Many had central gardens with pools, fountains, benches, and statues. In Pompeii's warm climate, people spent much time outside in the family garden. Less wealthy people often lived in small rooms over shops or in apartments.

Archaeological Sites

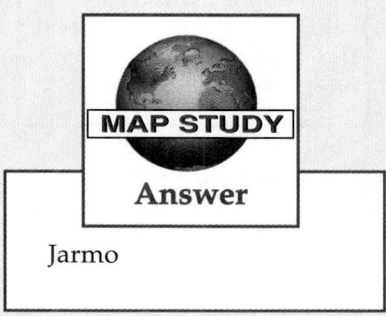

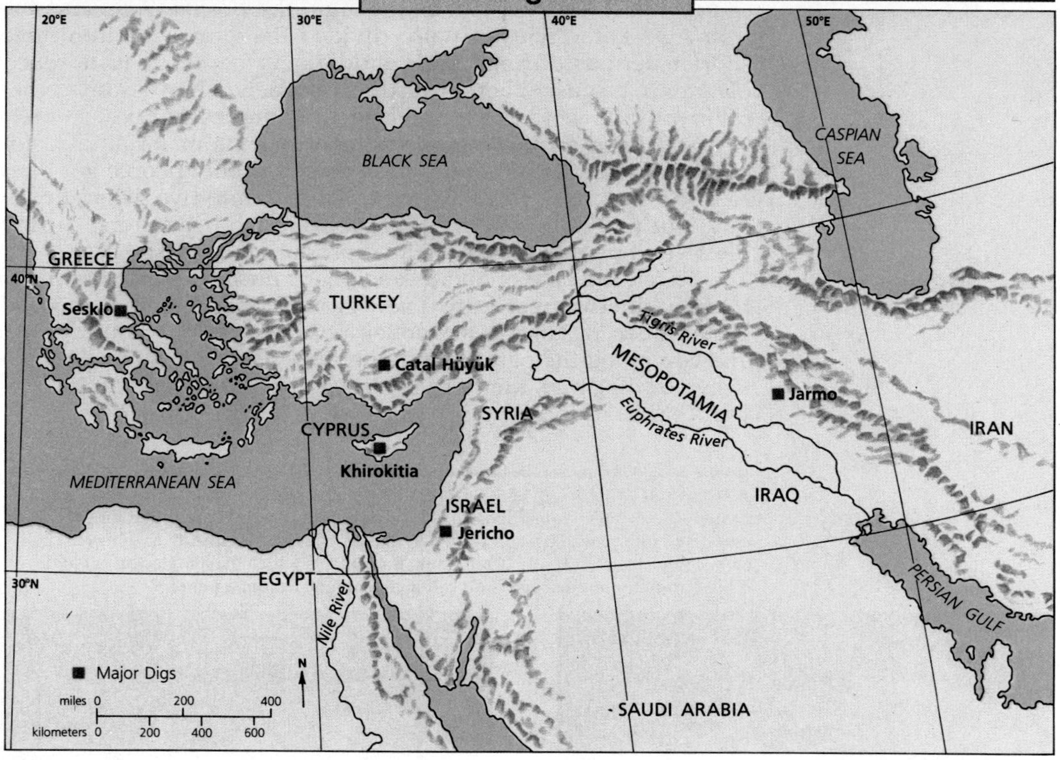

language dictionary that gave them the key to the meaning of Egyptian picture-writing. Now they could learn much more about the history of Egypt and its people.

A great many archaeological finds have been made since the discovery of the Rosetta Stone. For example, between 1850 and 1950 archaeologists uncovered five lost civilizations. In 1988 they discovered the oldest known piece of cloth, woven 9,000 years ago. Archaeologists continue to make discoveries in many parts of the world. This can be especially difficult because often only small pieces of artifacts are found. Thus archaeologists have only hints or clues about people of past civilizations.

Dating Archaeological Remains After archaeologists *excavate,* or dig into the earth, to uncover remains of the past, they have to *date,* or find the age of, the remains. In 1832 Christian J. Thomsen, a Danish archaeologist, divided early human history into three *ages,* or periods. These ages were based on the

MAP STUDY

LOCATION Archaeologists carefully piece together information gathered at archaeological sites. **What archaeological site is found near the Tigris and Euphrates rivers?**

L2 **History** Have students research the five lost civilizations uncovered by archaeologists between 1850 and 1950 and write reports about their findings to share with the class.

L2 **Daily Life** Ask students what they think archaeologists thousands of years from now would learn if life were frozen in your town today, as it was in Pompeii. What would they be able to excavate from the twentieth century? LEP

MAP STUDY

Answer

Jarmo

L3 **Critical Thinking** Have the students draw at least four conclusions about the locations of the archaeological sites shown on the map on this page. Have the students write their conclusions in statement form. For example: All the archaeological sites are located between 30° N and 40° N. Have students share their statements.

EXTENDING THE CONTENT

When people first began to investigate the past, many saw it as a "treasure house" of statues, paintings, and jewelry to be collected and sold. During this period of history, tombs were looted, temples were destroyed, and gold objects melted down. Wealthy private collectors took home objects they could find. Victorious generals systematically cleaned out the tombs and temples of conquered lands. With the development of archaeology as a science, came more responsibility and more public interest in historical findings.

DID YOU KNOW ??

Archaeologists are concerned about preserving archaeological sites that have not yet been excavated. Some of these sites are threatened by development of the land. Also, archaeologists are concerned about the illegal sale of artifacts. They are trying to create and enforce international laws to end the import of artifacts that do not have an export certificate from the country where the artifacts were discovered.

LINKING PAST TO PRESENT

Emperor Napoleon of France took scholars and scientists with him on an expedition to Egypt in 1798 to study its ancient culture. Napoleon brought boatloads of Egyptian artifacts home to Paris, but he did not keep them for himself. Instead he had a new wing built on the royal palace known as the Louvre—one of the largest art museums in the world today.

CAPTION ANSWER

Their tools tell how people got their food, what they ate, and in what time they lived.

material people used for tools and weapons during them. Thomsen named these ages the Stone Age, the Bronze Age, and the Iron Age. Later, scientists also divided the Stone Age into three shorter periods of time—old, middle, and new. Scientists relied on common sense when unearthing artifacts. They assumed that older artifacts would be found beneath more recent ones.

Still later, archaeologists realized that the material used for tools and weapons was not as important as how people got their food. So they divided early human history into two general periods. During the first period, people were food gatherers. During the second period, they were food producers.

To tell the date of an archaeological find, scientists first used trees. Each year, trees form a new growth ring. Scientists counted the number of rings in a wooden object, such as a house beam, and compared the pattern with the rings of a tree whose age they knew. In that way, they could identify dates as far back as 3,000 years earlier.

ARCHAEOLOGICAL SITES Archaeological research is a major method of learning about ancient civilizations. Specialized techniques and tools are required for successful research. This archaeological excavation (left) is at the Agora in Athens, Greece. The archaeologist shown (right) is searching for artifacts with a metal detector. **What do bones, animal remains, and tools tell archaeologists about a people?**

SPOTLIGHT ON: WILLARD FRANK LIBBY

Willard Frank Libby was born in 1908 in Grand Valley, Colorado. He taught chemistry at the University of California at Berkeley from 1933 until 1945. From 1945 until 1959, he was a member of the Institute for Nuclear Studies and the chemistry department at the University of Chicago. It was during this period that he made his famous discovery about carbon 14 dating. In 1960, in large part for this discovery, he won the Nobel Prize for chemistry.

The Leakeys

PEOPLE IN HISTORY

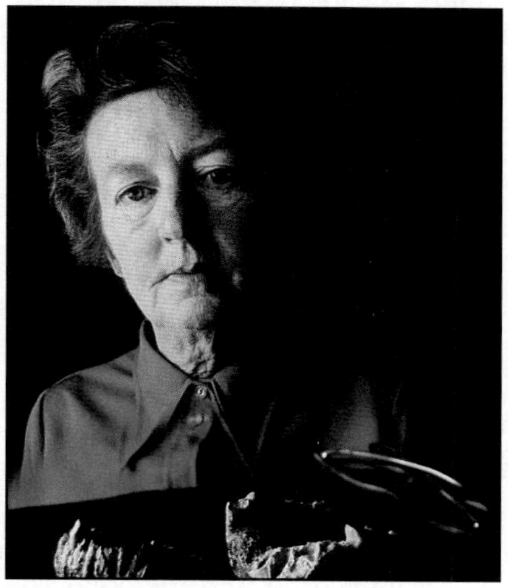

Photograph of Mary Leakey

Three members of the Leakey family—Louis, Mary, and Richard—have made exciting anthropological and archaeological discoveries in eastern Africa. They have discovered evidence of some of the earliest known humans.

Louis Leakey Louis Leakey was born in 1903 in Kenya, where his parents were missionaries. He studied anthropology in England and then returned to Africa. He spent time excavating at a place called Olduvai Gorge, in Tanzania. His fossil discoveries showed that human beings were around 2 million years old, much older than previously believed.

Mary Leakey Mary Nicol Leakey was born in England in 1913. She met Louis Leakey while preparing drawings for one of his books. They married in 1936, and she worked with her husband until his 1972 death. In 1978, Mary Leakey discovered some of the earliest evidence of prehumans. The fossilized footprints she found at Laetoli in northern Tanzania have been dated to be about 3.7 million years old.

Richard Leakey The Leakey's second son, Richard, was born in Kenya in 1944. He uncovered his first fossil bone at the age of six. Over the years, he and his fossil-hunting team have uncovered the remains of more than 200 prehumans, many near Kenya's Lake Turkana. They also found the most complete remains of an early human being discovered so far. The remains are of a 12-year-old boy who lived about 1.65 million years ago. Today, Richard Leakey is still learning more about early people.

Checking for Understanding

1. **Why were Louis Leakey's fossil discoveries important?**
2. **What did Mary Leakey discover?**
3. **How has Richard Leakey contributed to our knowledge of human history?**

SPOTLIGHT ON: THE LEAKEYS

Encourage the students to read more about the Leakey's work. Students may be interested to know, for example, that the Leakeys had worked on and off at Olduvai Gorge for 25 years before Mary made her famous discovery of two large teeth and a piece of skull in 1959. The Leakeys subsequently uncovered 400 fragments of bone and skull that enabled them to reconstruct an adult manlike skull.

Teaching

PEOPLE IN HISTORY

THE LEAKEYS

After students have read the People in History feature, describe to them how archaeologists conduct a dig. Note that archaeologists map the location and depth of each item they find, in order to evaluate the age and development of life at the site. Have the students locate the sites of the Leakeys' digs at Olduvai Gorge and at Laetoli on a map of Tanzania, and at Lake Turkana on a map of Kenya.

MAKING CONNECTIONS

➤➤ **Science** Another method of dating is by using potassium-argon to measure atomic change in rock where bones and tools are found. Dr. Leakey used this method to determine the age of his East African find.

ANSWERS to Checking for Understanding

1. They showed that human beings were around 2 million years old and that they were much older than scientists had previously believed.
2. some of the earliest evidence of prehumans
3. He discovered the most complete remains of an early human being discovered up to that time.

ASSESS

CHECK FOR UNDERSTANDING

Ask students to summarize the main points of the chapter, orally or in writing. Discuss the answers to the Section and Chapter Review questions.

EVALUATE

Assign the Chapter 1 **Performance Assessment Activity** in the TCR.

Administer the **Chapter 1 Test** found in the TCR. Testmaker available.

RETEACH

Have students work in small groups to explain what they discovered about the four "Chapter Focus" objectives on page 5.

Assign the Chapter 1 **Reteaching Activity** in the TCR.

ENRICH

Have students research and report on one of the archaeological sites on the map on page 27.

Assign Chapter 1 **Enrichment Activity** in the TCR.

CLOSE

Have the students prepare a time capsule that would include artifacts that best represent their lives and cultures today.

MEETING CHAPTER OBJECTIVES

Each objective is tested by the Review questions in parentheses.

1. **Describe** the five themes of geography. (BV; CT 1; GIH; UYJ)
2. **Explain** how landforms, waterways, climate, and natural resources have shaped history. (BV; CU 4, 6; UYJ)
3. **Discuss** how legends have been important. (CT 4)
4. **Summarize** how archaeology helps scientists. (CT 3, 4)

In 1946 an American scientist named Willard Frank Libby discovered that all living things contain a radioactive element called carbon 14. After plants, animals, and humans die, the carbon 14 gradually disappears. By measuring how much carbon 14 a skeleton or the remains of a wooden boat contain today, scientists can figure out about how old the object is as far back as about 30,000 years.

Section 5 Review

1. **Identify:** Herculaneum, Pompeii, Rosetta Stone, Willard Frank Libby
2. **Define:** archaeology, artifacts
3. Why did scientists begin to study artifacts?
4. Why was the discovery of the Rosetta Stone important?

Critical Thinking

5. What would you like about being an archaeologist? What would you dislike?

Chapter Summary

1. Geographers use five themes to describe a place. These are location, human/environmental interaction, movement, place, and regions.
2. Four major kinds of landforms—mountains, hills, plateaus, and plains—make up 30 percent of the surface of the earth.
3. The surface of the earth is constantly being changed by forces from inside it and outside it.
4. About 70 percent of the earth's surface is covered by oceans, seas, lakes, and rivers.
5. Climate is shaped by many factors, including the sun, large bodies of water, winds and ocean currents, and altitude.
6. Geographers often divide the earth into climate zones based on latitude: the tropical zone, the temperate zone, and the polar zone.
7. Some of the different kinds of natural resources include air, water, sunlight, minerals, fossil fuels, forests, and animal life.
8. Renewable resources can be replaced. Nonrenewable resources are gone forever when used up.
9. Legends have helped people explain the past.
10. Archaeologists study artifacts to learn how people lived long ago.
11. One important archaeological find was the discovery of the Rosetta Stone.
12. Since 1946, scientists have used the carbon 14 method of dating objects, which was developed by Willard Frank Libby.

SECTION 5 ANSWERS

1. Herculaneum, ancient Roman city (p. 26); Pompeii, Roman city (p. 26); Rosetta Stone, stone having carved Egyptian picture-writing and its Greek translation (p. 26); Willard Frank Libby, developed method of dating archaeological finds (p. 30)
2. archaeology, the study of human remains (p. 25); artifacts, things made by people (p. 25)
3. to learn how people lived long ago
4. It gave scholars the key to the meaning of Egyptian picture-writing.
5. Answers will vary but students should give specific examples that relate to an archaeologist's job.

Assign the Chapter 1 **Section 5 Quiz** in the TCR. Testmaker available.

Review CHAPTER 1

Building Vocabulary

Imagine you are writing an explanation of how geography has influenced history for a younger student. Use the following words to describe in a simple way how landforms, waterways, and climate have influenced history.

landforms	river system
tectonic plates	natural resources
glaciers	archaeology
climate	artifacts
elevation	erosion

Check for Understanding

1. What are the four major kinds of landforms?
2. What do many geographers believe caused Pangaea to split into seven continents?
3. How has erosion both helped and hurt people?
4. Why did early people settle along the bank of waterways?
5. Why are air, water, soil, and sunlight important natural resources?
6. How have people's views about natural resources changed in recent years?
7. How is carbon 14 used as a dating tool?

Critical Thinking

1. In which climate zone would you prefer to live? Why?
2. What is your opinion of this statement: It is important to plan the use of the world's natural resources. Explain.
3. Why is it important to identify the date of artifacts as exactly as possible?
4. How do ideas about the past change as more knowledge becomes available?

Geography in History

MOVEMENT Look at the map on page 13 that shows how far ice sheets moved during the Ice Ages. What descriptive statements could you make about the movement of ice north of the Equator compared to south of the Equator?

Using Your Journal

Review the details you have noted about the geographical factors that have influenced history. Choose three of these factors and write a short essay explaining how these factors influence your life today.

CHAPTER 1 REVIEW ANSWERS

BUILDING VOCABULARY

Explanations will vary but should include all the vocabulary words to describe how these have influenced history.

CHECK FOR UNDERSTANDING

1. mountains, the highest landforms; hills, lower than mountains; plateaus, raised areas of nearly flat land edged by steep cliffs; and plains, large areas of mostly level land with low relief
2. continental drift
3. Sometimes wind erosion contributes to making land rich for farming, as in China. Or erosion can destroy people's way of life, such as the Dust Bowl.
4. because they provided drinking water, fish and other food, good hunting grounds, rich soil for farming, water for irrigation, and easier trade and travel
5. because they are needed for any kind of life to exist
6. They are passing laws to slow down pollution and trying to develop new sources of energy.
7. Carbon 14 dating can date artifacts older than those that can be dated by using trees.

CRITICAL THINKING

1. Answers will vary, but students should provide reasons.
2. Answers will vary but should include that natural resources are necessary to maintain life.
3. Answers will vary but should include that exact dating helps reconstruct history.
4. Answers will vary.

+ BONUS +

TEST QUESTION
For Chapter 1 Test
You are living in an area where you receive no sunlight for part of the year and slanted rays the rest of the year. You see a bear. What color is it? *(white—polar bear)*

USING YOUR JOURNAL

Essays will vary but should include concrete references to modern examples. You might call on volunteers to read their essays and discuss them with the class.

GEOGRAPHY IN HISTORY

There was greater movement of ice north of the Equator than south of the Equator.

CHAPTER 2 Prehistoric People

CHAPTER ORGANIZER

Objectives	Special Features	Supplemental Materials
Section 1 The Paleolithic Age Explain how tools, language, clothing, and the discovery of fire helped early people advance, and explain what Neanderthals and Cro-Magnons were like.		• Reproducible Lesson Plan • Section 1 Quiz • Testmaker • Chapter 2 Vocabulary and Guided Reading Activity • Chapter 2 Cooperative Learning Activity • Unit 1 Primary Source Reading • World History and Art Transparency 14 • The World History Videodisc
Section 2 The Neolithic Age Discuss how people changed from food gatherers to food producers and why specialization, government, and religion were important in Neolithic societies.	Map Skills: *Determining Relative Location*, p. 44	• Reproducible Lesson Plan • Section 2 Quiz • Testmaker • Chapter 2 Geography and Map Activity • Chapter 2 Chart and Graph Skill Activity • Unit 1 World Literature • Chapter 2 Activity Book Activity • Chapter 2 Teaching Transparencies and Activities
Chapter 2 Review and Evaluation		• Chapter 2 Reteaching Activity • Chapter 2 Enrichment Activity • Spanish Summary and Glossary • Audiocassettes (English and Spanish) • Chapter 2 Performance Assessment Activity • Chapter 2 Test • Testmaker

If time does not permit teaching the entire chapter, use the Chapter 2 Summary on page 46 and the Chapter 2 Audiocassettes (English and Spanish) to point out the main ideas of the chapter.

✓ Performance Assessment Activities

Time Line Have students create an illustrated time line depicting the progression of early people from prehistory to the establishment of the first cities. The time line should depict how early people may have looked, what they wore, where they lived, and the tools they used.

Dioramas Have students make two dioramas. One diorama should show a scene of people from the Paleolithic Age. The other diorama should show a scene of people from the Neolithic Age. The dioramas should indicate the kinds of differences in the way of life of the people from each age. Display the dioramas in the classroom.

CHAPTER RESOURCES

LITERATURE ABOUT THE PERIOD

Auel, Jean M. *The Clan of the Cave Bear.* Bantam, 1984. A Cro-Magnon girl is adopted by a Neanderthal tribe.

READINGS FOR THE STUDENT

Johanson, Donald and James Shreece. *Lucy's Child: The Discovery of a Human Ancestor.* William Morrow and Company, Inc., 1989. An account of Johanson's return to Africa in 1986.

READINGS FOR THE TEACHER

Gowlett, John. *Ascent to Civilization: The Archaeology of Early Man.* Knopf, 1984. The rise and development of human culture revealed by archaeological finds.

Gregor, Arthur S. *Life Styles: An Introduction to Cultural Anthropology.* Charles Scribner's Sons, 1978. Highlights early people's family structures, values, and religion.

Pfeiffer, John. *The Emergence of Humankind.* Harper & Row, 1985. The unfolding story of human evolution and the human condition.

Wolf, Josef. *The Dawn of Man.* Harry N. Abrams, Inc., Publishers, 1978. Features illustrations of prehistory, with accompanying text.

MULTIMEDIA RESOURCES

Archaeology Search. Micromedia. Software. Apple. Simulates an archaeologist going back in history.

Early Human. Right on Program. Software. Apple. Simulates early human existence.

Mysteries of Mankind. (National Geographic) Image Entertainment. Videodisc. Uncovers clues to human origins.

Prehistory Images—The First Art of Man. Macmillan Films. Examines prehistoric cave paintings in France and Spain.

INTRODUCE

CHAPTER 2 OVERVIEW

Chapter 2 deals with the Paleolithic and Neolithic ages.

➤ **Section 1** focuses on the lifestyle of the earliest humans—the food gatherers of the Paleolithic, or Old Stone, Age.

➤ **Section 2** describes the developments of the Neolithic, or New Stone, Age—the beginning of farming, the domestication of animals, and the formation of villages.

CHAPTER OBJECTIVES

After reading Chapter 2, students will be able to:

1. explain how tools, language, clothing, and the discovery of fire helped early people advance.

2. summarize what Neanderthals and Cro-Magnons were like.

3. describe how people changed from food gatherers to food producers.

4. discuss why specialization, government, and religion were important in Neolithic societies.

EXAMINING THE ILLUSTRATION

Early artists used four basic colors: black from charcoal and manganese ore; red and yellow from red clay, animal blood, and pulverized iron compounds; and white from lime, mud, and clay. They mixed the colors in blood or animal fat and applied them by rubbing or by blowing them through a hollow bone. Ask students what information the Lascaux Cave painting imparts about prehistoric life.

PERFORMANCE ASSESSMENT ✓

Use the Performance Assessment Activities on page 32B to help you evaluate students as they complete the chapter.

CHAPTER 2 Prehistoric People

Prehistoric Cave Paintings from Lascaux, France

32

TEACHER CLASSROOM RESOURCES

- Section Quizzes/Chapter Test
- Reteaching Activity
- Enrichment Activity
- Geography and Map Activity
- Vocabulary and Guided Reading Activity
- Cooperative Learning Activity
- Performance Assessment Activity
- Teaching Transparencies and Activities
- Spanish Summary and Glossary
- Unit 1 Primary Source Reading
- Unit 1 World Literature
- Audiocassettes (English and Spanish)
- Testmaker
- The World History Videodisc

Chapter Focus

READ TO DISCOVER:

- How tools, language, clothing, and the discovery of fire helped early people advance.
- What Neanderthals and Cro-Magnons were like.
- How people changed from food gatherers to food producers.
- Why specialization, government, and religion were important in Neolithic societies.

Most archaeologists believe that there have been people on the earth for about 2.3 million years. The period beginning when people first appeared and ending when writing developed about 5,000 years ago, is called **prehistory.** The period after writing developed is called history. This was the beginning of **civilization,** or when people began to advance culturally and to live in cities.

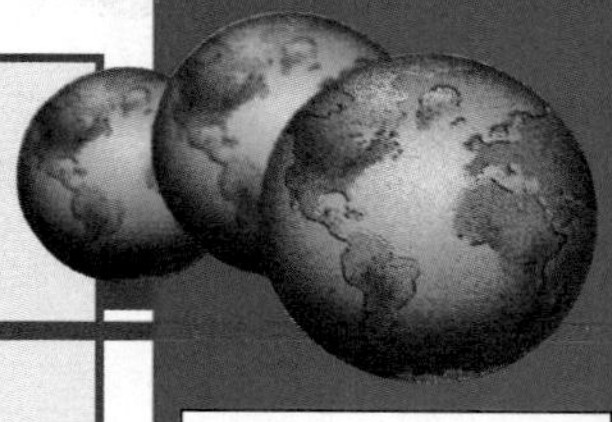

8000 B.C.–3000 B.C.

KEY TERMS

- prehistory
- civilization
- migrate
- bands
- home territory
- domesticated
- population
- specialization

Section 1 THE PALEOLITHIC AGE

Although there were no written records during prehistory, scientists have learned a great deal about prehistoric people. They have learned how early human beings lived and what important discoveries they made. Scientists also think they know why people moved out of Africa and into other parts of the world.

Many scientists believe that until about 900,000 years ago people lived only on the grasslands of eastern and southern Africa. Then the earth's climate changed—it became colder. Ocean water froze into huge glaciers that spread out from the North and South poles. As the ice sheets grew, the sea level fell and uncovered land that had been under water. Land bridges then connected Africa to both southern Europe and southwestern Asia.

FOCUS

BELLRINGER

Write the following question on the chalkboard and ask students to respond to it in writing: *If you were marooned on a desert island, what tools would you need to survive?*

MOTIVATIONAL ACTIVITY

Ask students to read their responses to what tools they would need to survive if they were marooned on a desert island. Have a volunteer list them on the chalkboard. Discuss how studying the tools left by prehistoric people can help us to understand our past.

VOCABULARY PRE-CHECK

Write the key terms for this chapter on the chalkboard. Ask volunteers to skim the chapter for these boldfaced terms and read aloud the sentences in which they are found.

Assign Chapter 2 **Vocabulary and Guided Reading Activity** in the TCR.

EXTRA CREDIT PROJECT

Have interested students investigate a particular archaeological find such as the Lindow Man discovered near Manchester, England. Have them present their findings to the class including any visuals that are available, such as photographs, sketches, or maps.

KEY TO ABILITY LEVELS

Teaching strategies have been coded for varying learning styles and abilities.

L1 Level 1 activities are **basic** activities and should be within the ability range of all students.

L2 Level 2 activities are **average** activities and should be within the ability range of the average to above-average student.

L3 Level 3 activities are **challenging** activities designed for the ability range of above-average students.

LEP LEP activities should be within the ability range of Limited English Proficiency students.

TEACH

GUIDED PRACTICE

L1 **Daily Life** Ask the students to write a short essay explaining how tools, language, clothing, and the discovery of fire helped early people advance. Have students share their essays with the class. Ask the students to rank the innovations in the order of importance. Then have students draw conclusions about the importance of tools, language, clothing, and the discovery of fire in the advancement of early people. LEP

DID YOU KNOW ??

Early people spent most of their time just trying to stay alive. Most of the larger animals could run faster, were stronger, and had better senses of smell and hearing than they did. The upright position of people, their use of their thumbs, and their larger brains and strong odor helped them to survive.

CAPTION ANSWER

the oldest or strongest men in the band

People were able to **migrate**, or make their way, around the desert of northern Africa and across the land bridges. Between about 900,000 and 700,000 years ago, people made their way into Europe and Asia. Much later, between about 40,000 and 15,000 years ago, they also migrated to the Americas.

Scientists call the first age in which people lived the Paleolithic (pā lē uh lith′ ik) Age, or Old Stone Age. It lasted from about 2.3 million years, until 10,000 years ago. During this period, people obtained their food by hunting and gathering.

Obtaining Food Paleolithic people lived in small **bands**, or groups, of about 30 members. When the food supply was good, the bands grew to about 40 or 50 members. Most of the group members lived to be no more than 20 or 25 years old. More than half of the children died from illnesses or were killed by animals before their first birthdays.

The people within a group lived and worked together and shared their food. They fed and cared for people who became injured or sick.

GROUP LIFE Experts believe that most early people lived in groups made up of several families. Here, a group of hunters use stones to sharpen tools. Two men carry a large animal killed in a hunt, as a few women tend fires near their tents. **Who were the leaders in a group of prehistoric people?**

COOPERATIVE LEARNING

Divide the class into small groups to prepare a bulletin-board display showing the history of crops such as wheat, barley, corn, rice, potatoes, yams, and cotton. Each group's contribution should graphically portray the crop, when and where it originated, and where it is grown now. Below the graphics, students should include information about the cultivation of the crop then and now, and the economic importance of the crop then and now. Each group member should have a specific task. Have each group discuss its contribution before posting it on the bulletin board.

Assign the Chapter 2 **Cooperative Learning Activity** in the TCR.

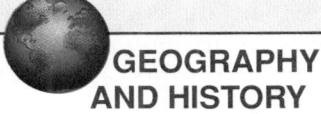

EARLY TOOLS For more than 2 million years, prehistoric people lived by hunting animals and gathering plants. They used tools made of wood and stone. The wooden tools have decayed. Archaeologists, however, have found many stone tools. **For what purposes did prehistoric people use stone tools?**

Each band searched for food within an area known as its **home territory.** This usually covered about two square miles, or five square kilometers, for every band member. There were campsites at various places throughout the home territory. The band stayed at a campsite until the available food supply was used up and then moved.

Women and children gathered berries, nuts, fruit, and eggs out of bird and turtle nests. They poked sticks into bee nests to get honey and into the ground to dig roots.

Men of the group obtained meat. They caught fish using their bare hands and hunted small animals with sticks and stones. Occasionally, they were able to kill a large animal that was too young, too old, or too badly hurt to run away. A good kill meant that the group would have enough meat to last for several days.

Making Tools

Life for hunters and gatherers became easier when they learned to make tools. At first the only tools people had were sticks and stones they found on the ground. Soon they learned to shape stones to make them more useful.

CAPTION ANSWER

to cut the meat off animals' bones, split animal bones, and chop up plants

GEOGRAPHY AND HISTORY

People in Europe, Africa, and western Asia usually made their tools of flint, a stone found on the surface of Earth. In eastern Asia, where there was not much flint, people made their tools of quartz.

EXTENDING THE CONTENT

Some scientists are predicting global warming, an increase in global average temperatures. Unlike the natural forming and melting of glaciers in prehistory, human activities are responsible for much global warming. Trapping of heat by gases in the atmosphere, such as carbon dioxide, results in a greenhouse effect. Burning fossil fuels is one human activity that releases carbon dioxide in the air.

L1 **Language Arts** Have students write a simple step-by-step set of directions for starting a fire as it was done in Paleolithic times, as if they were writing it to be used by someone who lived at that time. Have them share their directions, asking other students to judge if they were accurate. LEP

L2 **Critical Thinking** Have each student decide which advance they think was more important in the development of civilization: toolmaking or language. Have them discuss their positions.

VIDEODISC

Use the following to enrich Chapter 2.

WC A 2 9004
Stone age axes.

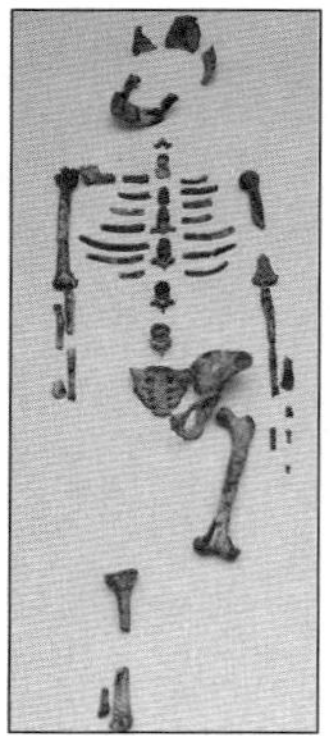

Photograph of Fossilized Skeleton

The earliest shaped stones are known as *Olduvan pebble tools*, named after the Olduvai Gorge in eastern Africa where they were first discovered. Pebble tools were made from pebbles or stones about the size of a fist. The toolmaker hit one pebble with another removing chips and creating a jagged cutting edge. This edge was sharp enough to cut the meat off of small animals' bones, split animal bones, and chop up plants.

Later people learned to knock long, sharp-edged chips called flakes from stones and use them as tools. Using flakes for knives they could butcher, or cut up, animals as big as elephants quickly and efficiently. People also used flakes to scrape one end of a wooden branch into a sharp point for a digging stick or a meat skewer.

Making Fire People also learned to make fire during the Paleolithic Age. The first fires they knew about were made by nature, such as those started by lightning. Eventually, people discovered how to make fire themselves. They created a spark by rubbing two sticks or stones together, or rapidly turning a stick in a hole in a dry log.

People used fire to keep themselves warm and dry. They also used it as a weapon, throwing burning sticks of wood at animals to drive them away. Sometimes they used fire to drive big animals into mudholes. The heavy animals would sink in the mud and people could then kill them.

People also used fire to clear out brush and undergrowth. Finally, people used fire to cook food. Cooked food was much easier to chew and digest than raw food. As a result, people spent less time eating and more time doing other things.

Seeking Shelter Early people usually camped out in the open. They protected themselves from the wind by digging pits in the ground or by crouching in dry river beds. They also took shelter under an overhanging rock or piled up brush.

At first, early people used caves only for such emergencies as escaping from a sudden storm or a large animal. By about 100,000 years ago, however, people in China, western Europe, and southwestern Asia were living in caves most of the time.

Photograph of Bone Needle and Button

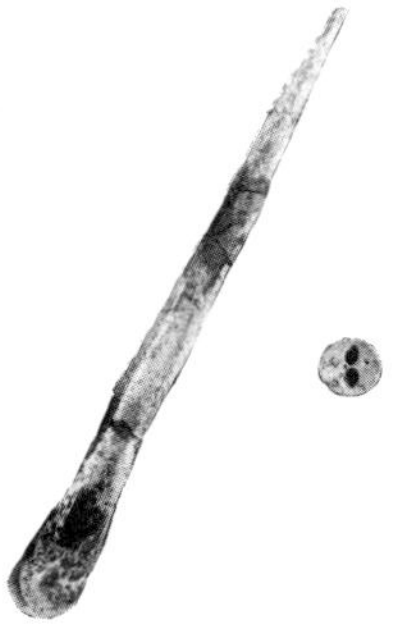

Making Clothing After hunters began killing large animals, they found that the animal skins could be used for protection and warmth. They scraped the skins clean and then laid them out in the sun to dry. Later, people discovered that pounding fat into the skin while it was drying would make it softer.

At first people wrapped the skins around themselves. Later, they learned how to fasten the skins together. Clothing made a big difference in where people lived. Before they had clothing, most people stayed in areas that were warm and dry. Once they

EXTENDING THE CONTENT

A ravine 295 feet (or 90 m) deep in northern Tanzania, known as Olduvai Gorge, is part of the Great Rift Valley, a series of valleys that extends all the way north to Syria. The sides of the ravine resemble a layer cake of different strata laid bare by the cutting action of ancient rivers. A prehistoric lake had swamped old bones with sediment and later disappeared. Through millennia, nearby volcanoes spewed ash over Olduvai, creating the distinct strata. In 1959 the Leakeys made major discoveries in the deepest and oldest layers at Olduvai.

PREHISTORIC PEOPLE There were two types of early *Homo sapiens,* Neanderthals and Cro-Magnons. From the remains of these two peoples, scientists have tried to reconstruct how they might have looked. These models show the facial features of the Neanderthal (left) and a Cro-Magnon (right). **In what areas of the world did the first people most likely live?**

had clothing to protect them from the weather, they were able to move into areas that were cooler and wetter.

Developing Language In addition to learning to make tools, fire, and clothing, early people developed language. Before they learned to talk, early people simply made sounds, or pointed to objects, to express meaning. Hand signals were probably used for common things such as water, food, animals, and weapons. Gradually because of new social needs, sounds and hand signals were no longer enough. The development of language was a great human achievement. It made it possible for people to work together, share ideas, and pass on their beliefs and stories. The younger generations could learn more easily from the older generation and greater progress was made in all areas of civilization.

The Neanderthals The first people on earth are known as *Homo habilis* (hō mō huh bil′ uhs), or "skillful man." Next came *Homo erectus* (hō′ mō ē rekt′ uhs), or "man who walks upright." Then, between about 300,000 and 200,000 years ago, came *Homo sapiens* (hō′ mō sāp′ ē uhnz), or "man who thinks."

CAPTION ANSWER

throughout Europe and in parts of Asia and Africa

LINKING PAST TO PRESENT

In 1992, a skull fragment that had been sitting in a tray at the National Museum of Kenya for 25 years was given a closer look. New dating methods reveal the fragment to be 2.4 million years old, which makes it the earliest known remains of the genus *Homo* by 500,000 years.

VIDEODISC

Use the following to enrich Chapter 2.

WC A 1 9003

Reconstructed heads of four prehistoric humans.

MULTICULTURAL PERSPECTIVES

Hadar in Ethiopia is part of the Great Rift Valley. At Hadar, sediments along shores of ancient lakes are reappearing because of earth movements and erosion. In the 1970s, Dr. Donald Johanson and a French geologist, Maurice Taieb, mounted an expedition into the area. The now world-famous fossilized skeleton "Lucy" was found in 1974. Later, other spectacular hominid finds at Hadar were made at just one site. The remains of at least 13 individuals were found jumbled together. Johanson dubbed this collection of more than 200 bones the "First Family."

L2 **Culture** Help students create a chart about what Neanderthals and Cro-Magnons were like. Divide the chalkboard into two columns, one labeled "Neanderthals" the other labeled "Cro-Magnons." Have students complete the chart with the following information: where they lived, how they got their food, kinds of tools they used, and other interesting facts. LEP

DID YOU KNOW ??

Neanderthal faces were somewhat oddly shaped, with a low, forward-sloping forehead and projecting nose and jaws, termed a muzzle shape. This shape of face, as well as the compact body, was a useful adaptation to keeping warm in the cold climate of Germany. Richard Leakey points out that people began to look "modern" in Africa at an earlier time, perhaps because they had no need to adapt to cold.

CAPTION ANSWER

to cut down trees and hollow out the logs to make canoes and to cut down stalks of bamboo to make rafts

There are two kinds of *Homo sapiens*. The first is the Neanderthal (nē an′ der tahl), named after the Neander River in Germany where their remains were first discovered in 1856. Since then, other Neanderthal remains have been found throughout Europe and in parts of Asia and Africa. Scientists estimate that about 1 million Neanderthals were living at any one time.

Neanderthal people were good hunters. They used traps to catch birds and small animals. They used *pitfalls* to catch large animals like the rhinoceros and the elephant. A pitfall was a large hole that was covered with branches, leaves, and earth. As an animal ran across this hole, it crashed through the covering and fell into the pit. The hunters would then kill the animal with spears.

Neanderthals were also builders. In northern areas, for example, they made houses by covering a framework of mammoth bones with animal skins. More bones piled on the bottoms of the skins prevented them from being blown away. As many as 30 people lived in such a house during the cold months of the year. They improved cave dwelling by digging drainage ditches in caves and designing rock protection for entrances.

According to experts, Neanderthals were also the first people to bury their dead. Archaeologists have found graves of people from this time in which they discovered the remains of flowers, tools, and food.

HAND AXE This photograph of a hand axe shows the detailed design of this tool. This axe dates from c. 200,000 B.C. **For what purposes did early human beings use a hand axe?**

MULTICULTURAL PERSPECTIVES

Most people still imagine Neanderthal people as looking like the Hollywood stereotype—stooping and gorilla-like. Actually, according to anthropologist Richard Leakey, the people of Neanderthal times could probably (with the right clothes) pass unnoticed in a modern crowd. They were fairly short, stocky, muscular, with powerful shoulders and arms, but were taller than earlier *Homo erectus* and *Homo habilis*, and walked about as upright as we do. One reason for the common stereotype is that the first, classic Neanderthal skeleton, found in 1856, was of a man whose severe arthritis had bent his neck and spine and enlarged his joints.

PREHISTORIC HORSE This prehistoric painting of a horse was found on the wall of a cave in Lascaux, France. Early art such as this always showed the animal's profile. **What can scientists learn about Cro-Magnon people from looking at their art?**

The Cro-Magnons The second kind of *Homo sapiens* is the Cro-Magnon (krō mag′ nahn), named after a rock shelter in France where their remains were first discovered in 1868. Cro-Magnons appeared in North Africa, Asia, and Europe about 100,000 years ago. Archaeologists consider them the first modern human beings.

Cro-Magnons were very skillful toolmakers. They invented the *burin,* which resembles a chisel. By using the burin, people could make other tools and objects from antler, bone, ivory, and shell, as well as stone and wood.

Using new tools made Cro-Magnons better hunters thus increasing their food supply. Points of antler or bone fastened to the end of wooden sticks could penetrate the hides of larger animals. People fashioned antler and bone into *spear throwers,* or devices that made spears fly through the air faster and farther. This allowed hunters to stay a greater distance from animals making hunting less dangerous.

LINKING PAST TO PRESENT

Ask students to name groups of people in recent history, or contemporary life, who have used bone, antler, and ivory to fashion needles, fishing hooks, combs, tools, and other items.

CAPTION ANSWER

about their ceremonies, traditions, and history

VIDEODISC

Use the following to enrich Chapter 2.

WC A 5 9007
Bison painting, Altamira.

SPOTLIGHT ON: CRO-MAGNONS

Archaeologists have unearthed evidence that prehistoric men were shaving as early as 13,000 B.C. Some Cro-Magnon cave paintings portray beardless men, and early Cro-Magnon gravesites contain sharpened shells that were the first razors. Later, people hammered razors out of bronze, and eventually, out of iron. Mirrors were first water ponds, and then highly polished metal.

DID YOU KNOW ??

The evidence for Cro-Magnon leaders consists of high-status burials. Archaeologists have discovered certain Cro-Magnons buried with ivory daggers, amber beads, and other signs of high rank.

LINKING PAST TO PRESENT

A hunter-gatherer society today lives on in Africa. The Khoisan people, who live in the Kalahari Desert region of Botswana and Namibia, hunt animals and gather wild plants, much as early peoples did.

Spear Thrower

Another important tool that Cro-Magnons invented was the axe, which they used to cut down trees and hollow out the logs to make canoes. In southeastern Asia, they cut down stalks of bamboo and tied them together with vines to make rafts. Winds or ocean currents then carried the rafts to other lands. It is likely that this is how people reached Australia about 40,000 years ago.

Cro-Magnons also fashioned bone, ivory, and shell into body ornaments, such as necklaces and rings. They decorated their clothing with bone or ivory beads. They played music on flutes carved from long, hollow bones.

Cro-Magnons were artists as well as toolmakers. They carved statues out of ivory and bone or molded them out of clay. They covered the walls of some caves in western Europe, Africa, and South America with pictures painted brightly with paints made from minerals. The pictures show mostly animals, such as horses, bulls, and deer, but also show outlines and patterns of lines, dots, and curves.

Many anthropologists think cave paintings may have had religious significance. Cro-Magnons believed that animals had spirits. They thought that painting an animal's picture gave people power over its spirit and would help them find and kill the animal. Anthropologists think the cave paintings may have been a kind of textbook about Cro-Magnon ceremonies, traditions, or history.

Cro-Magnon bands cooperated, often hunting large animals together. This required them to jointly agree on rules and the first true leaders. Every year or so, they held social gatherings, where they exchanged information about the movement of animal herds and traded materials such as amber and shells.

Section 1 Review

1. **Identify:** Paleolithic Age, *Homo habilis*, *Homo erectus*, *Homo sapiens*, Neanderthals, Cro-Magnons
2. **Define:** prehistory, civilization, bands, home territory
3. Why did early people begin to move out of Africa and into other parts of the world about 900,000 years ago?
4. How did tools change during the Paleolithic Age?
5. What hunting techniques did the Neanderthals use?
6. What was the major art form of the Cro-Magnons?

Critical Thinking

7. What do you think was the most important advancement made by the early people? Explain.

SECTION 1 ANSWERS

1. Paleolithic Age, Old Stone Age (p. 34); *Homo habilis*, first people (p. 37); *Homo erectus*, people after *Homo habilis* (p. 37); *Homo sapiens*, people from 200,000 and 300,000 years ago (p. 38); Neanderthals, *Homo sapiens* (p. 38); Cro-Magnons, *Homo sapiens* (p. 39)
2. prehistory, began when people appeared and ended when writing developed (p. 33); civilization, advanced culture (p. 33); bands, groups of about 30 members (p. 34); home territory, area bands gathered food (p. 35)
3. Climate became colder, ice sheets grew, and land bridges were created. Rain increased, changing desert to grasslands.
4. from sticks and stones to shaped tools
5. pitfalls
6. cave paintings
7. Answers will vary, but students should provide reasons for their choices.

Assign the Chapter 2 **Section 1 Quiz** in the TCR. Testmaker available.

DOMESTICATING ANIMALS Early people painted scenes of their hunting and food-producing activities. Here, a cave painting from North Africa shows cattle being herded. Some cattle are tied to a rope, while women and children do chores. **What was the importance of learning to herd animals?**

Section 2 THE NEOLITHIC AGE

In the Neolithic (nē uh lith' ik), or New Stone Age, about 8000 B.C., people changed from food gatherers to food producers. Over several thousand years they began to obtain most of their food from farming. This brought about such great changes in the way they lived that experts call the beginning of farming the Neolithic Revolution.

Farmers and Herders Two important discoveries brought on the Neolithic Revolution. One was learning to grow food. The other was learning to herd animals.

Experts believe that people discovered that seed from wild grains, such as wheat and barley, could be planted and harvested. This probably came about when they noticed that new shoots had grown from spilled grain. Scientists believe agriculture developed independently in different parts of the world. In southwestern Asia early people grew wheat and barley and in

CAPTION ANSWER

It helped people change from food gatherers to food producers.

DID YOU KNOW

The expanded food supply increased the average life expectancy of people to 30 years.

VIDEODISC

Use the following to enrich Chapter 2.

WC A 4 9006

Bison painting from the caves at Altamira, Spain.

MEETING SPECIAL NEEDS

For students who need additional reinforcement, play a "What's My Meaning?" word game. Divide the class into teams. Have each team survey the chapter and list 15 terms to be defined by another team. (These can include key terms as well as terms like *Paleolithic* and *Homo habilis.*) The first team gives a term for the second team to define or explain. The moderator assigns points—from one to five—for the answer given. The team with the most points is declared the winner.

DID YOU KNOW ??

Dogs were domesticated and used to help hunt small game. Cattle, pigs, goats, and sheep were domesticated and used for meat. Chickens provided Neolithic people with eggs and meat.

MAKING CONNECTIONS

➤➤ **History** It is believed that women remained the farmers until people learned to hitch an animal to a plow and the animal became the beast of burden on the farm. Then, men took over the farming.

CAPTION ANSWER

for carrying and storing food, and for cooking

eastern Asia they grew millet, rice, and soy beans. In Mexico they grew corn, squash, and potatoes, and they grew peanuts and a grain called sorghum in Africa.

People probably learned they could herd animals when a hunting band built fences to enclose a herd of wild animals they had chased into a ravine. The hunters killed one animal at a time, saving the rest for later. Soon captured animals began to lose their fear of people and became **domesticated,** or tamed, and the hunters became herders. In time, Neolithic people were breeding animals to improve the animals' qualities. People also began using certain animals such as donkeys, camels, and llamas as pack animals.

The Neolithic Revolution greatly increased people's food supply. With more food available, the **population**, or number of people, began to grow. Experts think there were about 5 million people in the world in 8000 B.C. Within 4,000 years the population grew to about 90 million. People were also living longer.

Early Villages Once people began to produce food, they were able to settle in one place. They built permanent shelters and formed villages of about 150 to 200 people in areas with a good soil and water supply.

POTTERY MAKING Neolithic people learned the art of baking clay pottery. Baked clay, unlike sun-dried clay, will not disintegrate in water. In this picture, men are covering the oven so that the pots inside will bake. **How did Neolithic people use pottery?**

EXTENDING THE CONTENT

Farming in the Neolithic period began at different times in different parts of the world—and the influence of crops and animals that were raised in those first centuries still can be seen in the traditional diet and cuisine in various parts of the world. In the Fertile Crescent, Mesopotamians began farming about 8,000 B.C. As in every early farming culture, the basic crop was a cereal grain. In the Middle East the original crops were wheat, barley, and other cereal grains, along with garden crops such as peas, beans, squash, and yams.

EARLY VILLAGES Archaeologists today continue to dig up artifacts of early people. These scientists have uncovered the sites of several ancient villages. **How do archaeologists know they have found the site of a prehistoric village?**

The earliest known villages in the world have been found in southwestern Asia. Two of the oldest are Jericho (jer´ uh kō) in present-day Israel (iz´rē uhl), which dates back to about 8000 B.C. and Abu Hureyra (ah bu hu rā´ rah) in present-day Syria, which was established about 500 years later. Another early village is Catal Hüyük (kat′ uhl hū´ yūk) located in present-day Turkey. People lived there from about 6500 to 5700 B.C.

Archaeologists know a great deal about Catal Hüyük because it was struck by a fire that blackened rather than destroyed wooden and cloth objects. The blackening helped preserve the objects. Evidence shows the houses in Catal Hüyük were made of sun-dried mud brick. They had flat roofs made of reeds plastered over with mud. The walls and roofs were supported by a *post-and-lintel*, or a horizontal length of wood or stone placed across two upright poles. The post-and-lintel was an important contribution to architecture because it enabled buildings to support weight above an open space.

As protection against attack, the houses in this village had two or three rooms and no doors. People went in and out of the houses through a hole in the roof by using a ladder. The houses were crowded together on the side of a hill. The floors were covered with rushes, or grasslike plants, and sleeping platforms were covered with mats.

INDEPENDENT PRACTICE

L2 **Investigate** Have students investigate the archaeological digs at Jericho, Abu Hureyra, and Catal Hüyük. Have them present their findings in a drawing or diorama.

CAPTION ANSWER

the number of artifacts found in one place; the obviously humanmade objects

GEOGRAPHY AND HISTORY

Catal Hüyük is the name archaeologists gave the village. Because of the many shrines found there, it is thought to be a religious center.

EXTENDING THE CONTENT

Based on the appearance of the first complete Neanderthal skeleton found in the mid-1800s, at La Chapelle-aux-Saints, France, the image of a clumsy Neanderthal made sense—slouching along, stooped, with bowed legs. Later physical anthropologists discovered, however, that the skeleton was of a man who had suffered from arthritis. The first researcher had not recognized the signs of the disease. Then, in 1957, archaeologists investigating a cave at Shanidar, in northern Iraq, found a skeleton of a 40-year-old Neanderthal man with a paralytic birth defect. That disabled Neanderthals survived suggests that members of the community must have taken care of one another.

Teaching

MAP SKILLS

Determining Relative Location

Have the students read the introduction to the feature. Ask: When facing the North Pole, what is the direction to the left? *(west)* What are cardinal directions? *(the four main directions of north, south, east, and west)* Why are northeast, northwest, southeast, and southwest known as intermediate directions? *(They are located between the cardinal directions.)*

Explain to students that most maps have a directional compass or an arrow on them to point north. Once north is known, the other directions can be found. Draw an arrow with an *N* above it on the chalkboard. Ask students to create a complete directional compass using the arrow and including the cardinal and intermediate directions.

Direct students to the map of "Sites of Early People." Ask: What Cro-Magnon site is northeast of Teshik-Tash? *(Malta)* In which direction is Cro-Magnon from Neanderthal? *(southwest)*

Provide students with a map of their state. Have them locate their community and ask them to determine the location of their community relative to other places shown on the map.

Assign the Chapter 2 **Geography and Map Activity** in the TCR.

ANSWERS to Map Practice

1. Cro-Magnon and Le Moustier
2. Boskop
3. southeast

MAP SKILLS

Determining Relative Location

Most maps show direction, or the line or course along which something is pointing or facing. Understanding direction makes locating places, whether on a map on in a town, much easier.

All directions heading toward the North Pole are north (abbreviated N), and all directions heading toward the South Pole are south (S). When facing the North Pole, the direction to the right is east (E) and to the left is west (W). These four main directions are called **cardinal directions.**

There are also four other directions, which are known as intermediate directions. This is because they are located between the cardinal directions. The direction between north and east is northeast (NE) and between north and west is northwest (NW). The direction between south and east is southeast (SE) and between south and west is southwest (SW).

Map Practice

1. **What sites are located southwest of Neanderthal?**
2. **Which site is south of Broken Hill?**
3. **In which direction is Lake Mungo from Ngandong?**

Sites of Early People

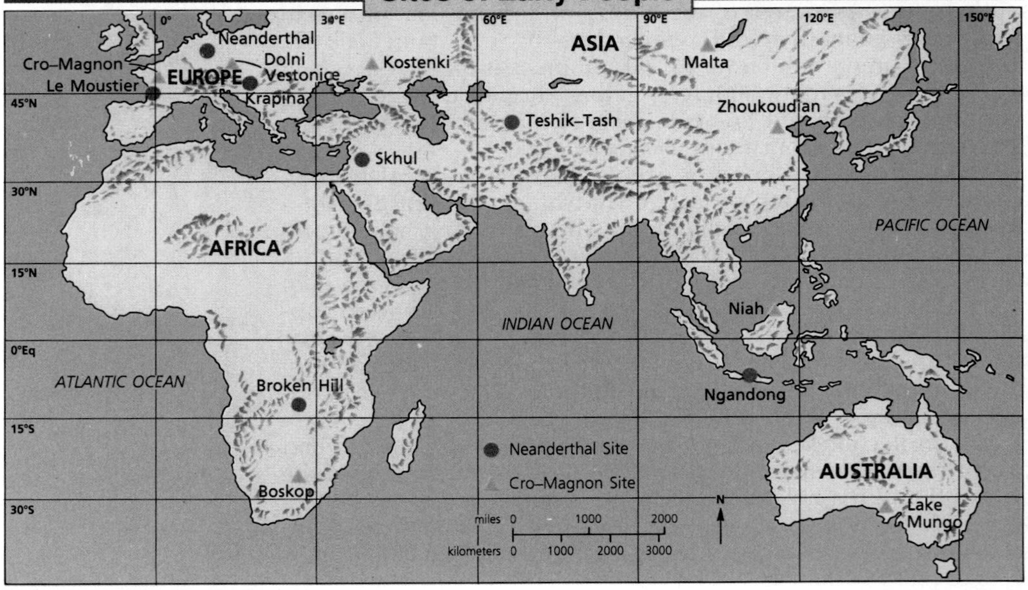

44 UNIT 1 PLACE AND TIME

SPOTLIGHT ON: EARLY PEOPLE

The fascinating prehistoric art of the Lascaux Caves was in danger of disappearing because of people entering the caves and changing the atmospheric conditions. French officials closed the caves and built an exact replica of them nearby for the public to visit.

Among the houses stood open courtyards with large ovens for baking bread. Beyond the houses were vegetable gardens, apple orchards, fields of grain, and pastures where sheep and cattle grazed.

Prehistoric Pottery

Specialization A result of increased food supplies was **specialization,** or the development of occupations. Fewer people were needed to produce food so they began to do jobs that had nothing to do with food. They became potters, weavers, and metal workers. They exchanged the things they made for grain, fruit, and meat.

Specialization was aided by a number of developments. One was that people learned to make pottery by baking clay. They used pottery for carrying and storing food, and for cooking. This enabled them to add such things as soups and stews to their diet.

In addition, people learned to weave cloth. People took wool from sheep, spun it into thread, and wove the thread into cloth on a loom, which was invented during the Neolithic Age. They dyed the cloth bright colors and used it for clothing.

Neolithic people also learned to work metals. They picked up lumps of copper, lead, gold, and silver that they found lying on the ground and hammered these metals into beads and jewelry. Soon they learned how to shape the metal into weapons. Because metals found on the ground were scarce, however, people continued to work mostly in stone, bone, and wood.

Government Another development of Neolithic times was village government. It was more complex than government in earlier times due to land ownership. People's lives depended on the use of a given piece of land. As a result, people began to protect what they had. They set boundaries and passed their land on to their children.

Even so, disputes often arose over land ownership. To keep order in Neolithic villages, a single chief was chosen. Besides settling disputes, the chief, with the help of a small group of people, directed village activities.

Religion Experts believe that the chiefs of most Neolithic villages were also priests. They handled religious duties for the village which included offering prayers for things people needed, such as rich soil, healthy animals, and water for crops.

At first, Neolithic people prayed to the forces of nature that they saw around them. After a time, they created gods and goddesses to represent these forces. The most important was the Earth Mother, the goddess of fertility. Many of the houses in Catal Hüyük, for example, had altars for this goddess.

COOPERATIVE LEARNING

Divide the class into small groups. Have each group write a short script for a play describing the importance of specialization, government, and religion in the lives of Neolithic peoples. The scripts should include a part for each member of the group. Students may supplement the text content with library research. Have groups present their plays to the class.

L2 **History** Have students look up the word *revolution* in the dictionary. Have them write a paragraph discussing whether or not the Neolithic Revolution was indeed a revolution. What other term could be applied to this era?

MAKING CONNECTIONS

➤➤ **Health** Fine-hardened pottery led to an improvement in hygiene. Cooking pots could be cleaned or thrown away when cracked. Storage pots could be covered with lids to keep out insects and rodents.

LINKING PAST TO PRESENT

Neolithic people developed special rituals called rites of passage. These marked important changes in life such as birth, puberty, marriage, parenthood, and death. These same rites are important in most societies, also.

ASSESS

CHECK FOR UNDERSTANDING

Ask students to summarize the main points of the chapter, orally or in writing. Discuss the answers to the Section and Chapter Review questions.

EVALUATE

Assign the Chapter 2 **Performance Assessment Activity** in the TCR.

Administer the **Chapter 2 Test** in the TCR. Testmaker available.

UNIT 1 CULTURE CLOSE-UP

THE ABORIGINES

FOCUS

OBJECTIVES

Identify from where the first inhabitants of Australia migrated and where they settled. Explain the cultural traits of the Aborigines.

BELLRINGER

Write the following on the chalkboard: *Write three things you know about Aborigines.*

MOTIVATIONAL ACTIVITY

Ask students to share what they know about Aborigines with the class. Ask a student to write the responses on the chalkboard. Have a student record the responses for review when they have finished reading the feature. Finally, explain to students that in this feature, they will learn about an early Australian civilization that continues to live in much the same way as it did in the past.

MAKING CONNECTIONS

➤➤ **Language** The words *kangaroo* and *koala* are Aboriginal words.

UNIT 1 CULTURE CLOSE-UP

The Aborigines

The first people to live in Australia were the Aborigines (ab uh rij' uh nēz), which means "first inhabitant." Archaeologists have found evidence, such as spearheads, that show that the first Aborigines traveled to Australia from Southeast Asia more than 40,000 years ago.

Cave paintings of the earliest people have also been found in Australia. ▼

Geography Connection

Arriving in Australia by canoe, the Aborigines settled in groups all over Australia. They discovered different kinds of vegetation such as the eucalyptus tree. ◀

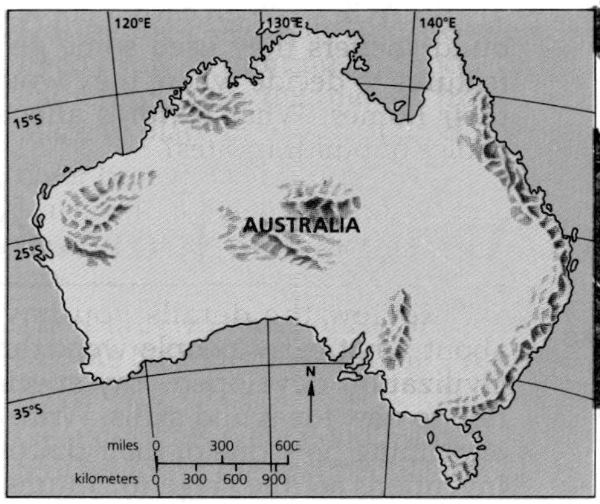

This Aboriginal art was found in a cave in Kakadu National Park, in northern Australia.

48

EXTENDING THE CONTENT

Initially, Great Britain established Australia as a penal colony to relieve overcrowding in British jails. A gold rush in 1860 lured new immigrants to the continent. When the British settlers came, they arrived in large numbers. They soon outnumbered the Aborigines. The new immigrants took the Aborigines' land. Without their land, the Aborigines could not live as they had in the past. Although few British settlers went to desert areas, ranchers and traders set up outposts there. Aborigines came to the outposts to trade. Some stayed and took jobs, mostly as ranch helpers. Religious settlers set up posts to teach the Aborigines Christianity.

Aborigines have always lived in harmony within their environment as they do today. The first Aborigines lived off the land and sea. Some fished as these men are doing. ▼

Most hunting was done by the men. Women and children gathered berries and other vegetation, and prepared the food.

Aborigines have always made tools and weapons of wood and stone. They often used a boomerang, a special hunting tool. This Aborigine man is hunting with a boomerang which he is about to throw. ▼

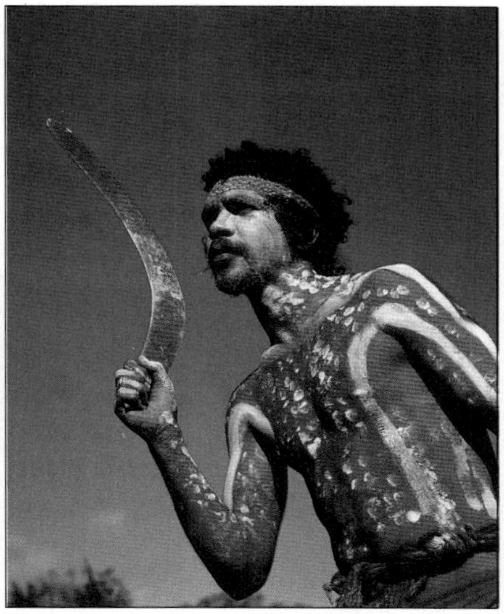

Early Aborigines hunted large animals such as kangaroo, or the ostrich-like bird, the emu (ēmyū), and smaller animals as well. ▼

TEACH

L1 **Geography: Location** On a wall map of the world, ask a volunteer to find Southeast Asia and Australia. Ask students to use the map scale to calculate the approximate distance from Southeast Asia to Australia. Discuss the kinds of difficulties that may have occurred when the Aborigines traveled from Southeast Asia to Australia 40,000 years ago. **LEP**

DID YOU KNOW ??

The word *aborigine* comes from the Latin phrase *ab origine* which means "from the beginning." About 500 tribes, with a total population of about 300,000, lived in Australia when Europeans first arrived there in 1788. Each group had its own distinct language. The Europeans took over Aboriginal land, often mistreating the Aborigines.

LINKING PAST TO PRESENT

Today the Aborigine population of Australia is about 206,000. Few of these people are direct descendants of original Aborigines. Instead, the largest percentage of them are a mix of European and Aborigine ancestry.

COOPERATIVE LEARNING

Have students work in pairs to create a relief map of Australia using whatever material they choose. Tell them to add information to the map about natural plant and animal life that inhabit different parts of the continent. Encourage them to include a legend for their map and any other explanatory material they feel is necessary. Display the finished maps in the classroom.

UNIT 1 CULTURE CLOSE-UP

L1 **Art** Ask students to describe the characteristics of Aboriginal artifacts, crafts, and musical instruments as shown in the illustrations on this page. LEP

L2 **Legends** Explain to students that Aboriginal legends told where the first Aborigines came from, how the land was formed, and how people should act. Their legends taught the difference between right and wrong. The legends helped keep the Aborigines united and helped keep peace and order. Ask students to write a legend based on one of these themes and what they know about the early Aborigines. Call on students to share their legends with the class.

GLOBAL READING FOR STUDENTS

Sociologists in your class may be interested in reading more about Aborigines. Suggest *Aborigines of Australia* by Robyn Holder, Rourke, 1985. (Average/Nonfiction)

Artifacts show the first Aborigines wore ornaments and waistbands decorted with traditional designs such as this. ▼

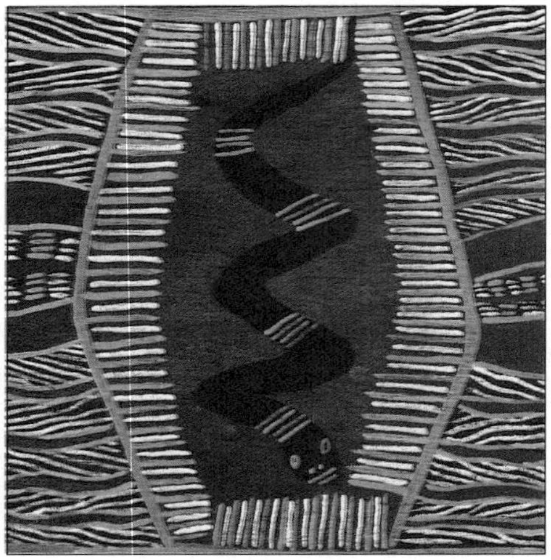

▲ Their crafts showed the Aborigines to be skilled and creative. They were known for the quality of their wood carving, basket and mat weaving, and other skilled hand crafts. This man holds an intricate woodcarving.

The music of the Aborigines, an important part of their culture, was often accompanied by a didgeridoo. This is a bamboo or wooden trumpet played by blowing into it.

Passing stories and legends down orally to younger generations was also an important part of early Aborigine culture. ▶

50

MEETING SPECIAL NEEDS

If possible, obtain Aborigine music that contains the sounds of a didgeridoo. Play the music for students who are auditory learners and have them compare and contrast the music to the kinds of music they enjoy listening to.

CULTURE CLOSE-UP

UNIT 1

Some natural features were sacred to Aborigines and were used as gathering places. Special ceremonies often took place at these sites. Ayers Rock rising out of the Australian plain is considered a holy place to the Aborigine people. ▶

The size of each Aborigine settlement depended upon the amount of food and water available in the area, and kinships.

▲ Aborigine religion was based on respect for heritage, and harmony with nature and animals, such as the Australian frilled lizard.

Taking Another Look

1. **About how long have the Aborigines been known to live in Australia?**
2. **In what parts of Australia did the Aborigine people settle?**
3. **What artifacts of early Aborigines have been found?**

Critical Thinking

4. **Why do you think the religion of a people, such as the Aborigines, is often connected to their natural surroundings?**

ASSESS

CHECK FOR UNDERSTANDING

Have students answer the questions in Taking Another Look on page 51.

ANSWERS to Taking Another Look

1. about 40,000 years
2. all parts of Australia
3. spearheads and cave paintings
4. Answers will vary. Students should explain that early peoples, such as the Aborigines, based their religions on respect for their natural surroundings because they were dependent on their environment for their survival.

ENRICH

Have students research and compare the modern Aborigine culture to the early Aborigines they have read about in this Culture Close-Up. What similarities and differences can they find?

CLOSE

Ask students to review the list of things that they said they knew about Aborigines before reading the Culture Close-Up. Ask them to identify inaccuracies and add newly learned facts to the list.

EXTENDING THE CONTENT

Around 1930, the Australian government decided to try to bring the Aborigines into mainstream society. The values of the Aborigines, however, were different from those of other Australians. The Aborigines could not understand the need for money nor the concept of owning things. As their groups were broken up, it became more difficult for them. Since the 1960s, the government has set aside land for the Aborigines and has tried to let them decide their own way of life. However, much of the land is too poor to support many people. Also, the Aborigines want to keep their old beliefs.

INTRODUCE

UNIT 2 OVERVIEW

Unit 2 describes the emergence and development of civilization in the river valleys of the Middle East, South Asia, and China.

- **Chapter 3** discusses the rise of civilization in the Tigris-Euphrates Valley of Mesopotamia, focusing on Sumer as well as later Mesopotamian empires.
- **Chapter 4** summarizes how civilization developed in the Nile Valley of Egypt and highlights the Old, Middle, and New Kingdoms.
- **Chapter 5** deals with the Harappan civilization of the Indus River valley in India and Pakistan, and the Shang civilization of the Huang Ho River valley in China.

UNIT OBJECTIVES

After reading Unit 2, your students will be able to:

1. give examples of how the environment influenced the ways in which people of the river valleys lived.

2. discuss the early civilizations of Mesopotamia, Egypt, and the eastern river valleys in terms of their similarities and differences.

3. summarize the contributions made by the river valley civilizations to other civilizations.

UNIT PROJECT

Have students create a "You Are There" display to represent what they learn about these early civilizations. After dividing them into groups, have each group choose among the Sumerians, Babylonians, Egyptians, Harappans, and Shang to display. Students can decide what and how to present their material, in written, visual, or interactive formats.

UNIT 2 River Valley Civilizations

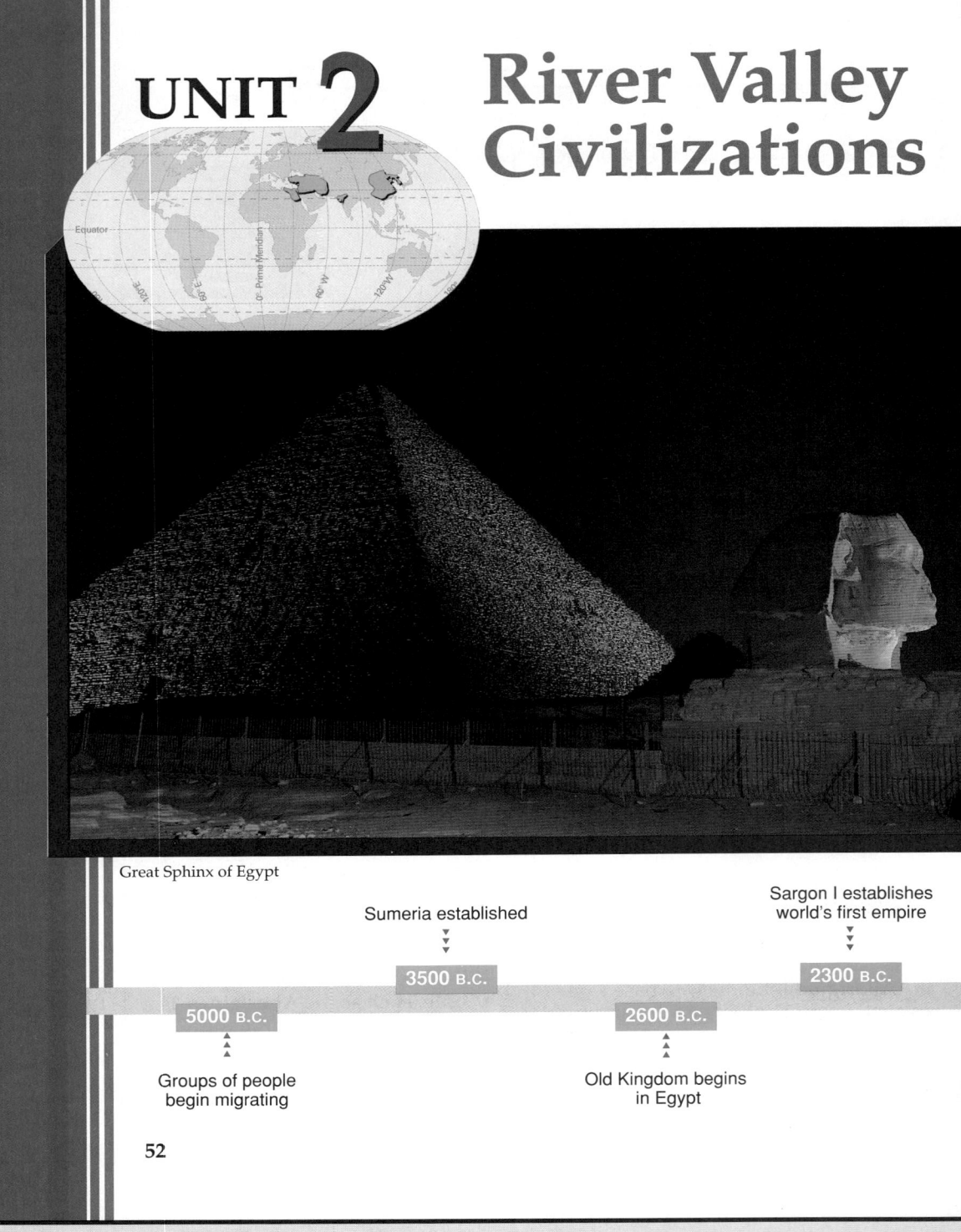

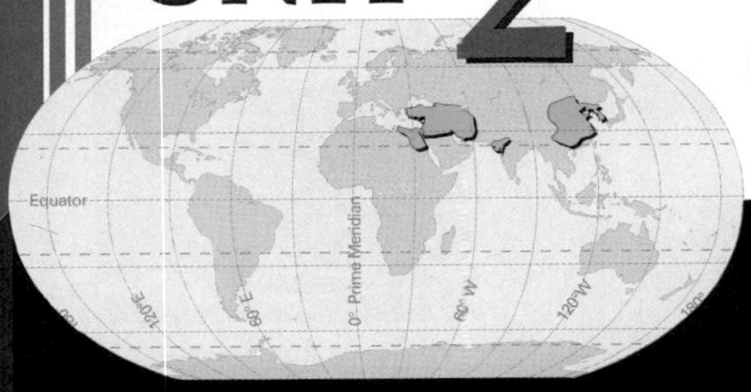

Great Sphinx of Egypt

5000 B.C. — Groups of people begin migrating

3500 B.C. — Sumeria established

2600 B.C. — Old Kingdom begins in Egypt

2300 B.C. — Sargon I establishes world's first empire

52

About the Unit Opening

EXAMINING THE ARTIFACT

Ask students to identify the material they think was used to create this statue. *(stone or clay)* Call on volunteers to describe the features of the statue. *(appears to have the face of a human)* Ask students what expression the face of the Sphinx appears to be in. *(it appears the Sphinx is standing guard over the area.)*

GLOBAL CHRONOLOGY

Refer students to the unit time line. Ask students to recall the meaning of B.C. and A.D. *(B.C. means "before Christ" and A.D. stands for* anno Domini *which means "in the year of the Lord.")* Ask students to explain what the time line covers. *(some major events in the early river valley civilizations in the Middle East, South Asia, and China)*

About 4000 B.C., civilizations began to develop in villages along the banks of rivers. These rivers provided the people with water, food, and a means of transportation and trade. Some of the earliest known villages of Mesopotamia were located along the Tigris and Euphrates rivers. From the writings and the artifacts that have been uncovered, archaeologists can conclude that these civilizations valued family, work, recreation, religion, and art. The daily lives of these early people mark the beginning of the civilization that you experience today.

Chapter 3
Mesopotamia

Chapter 4
Egypt

Chapter 5
Eastern River Valleys

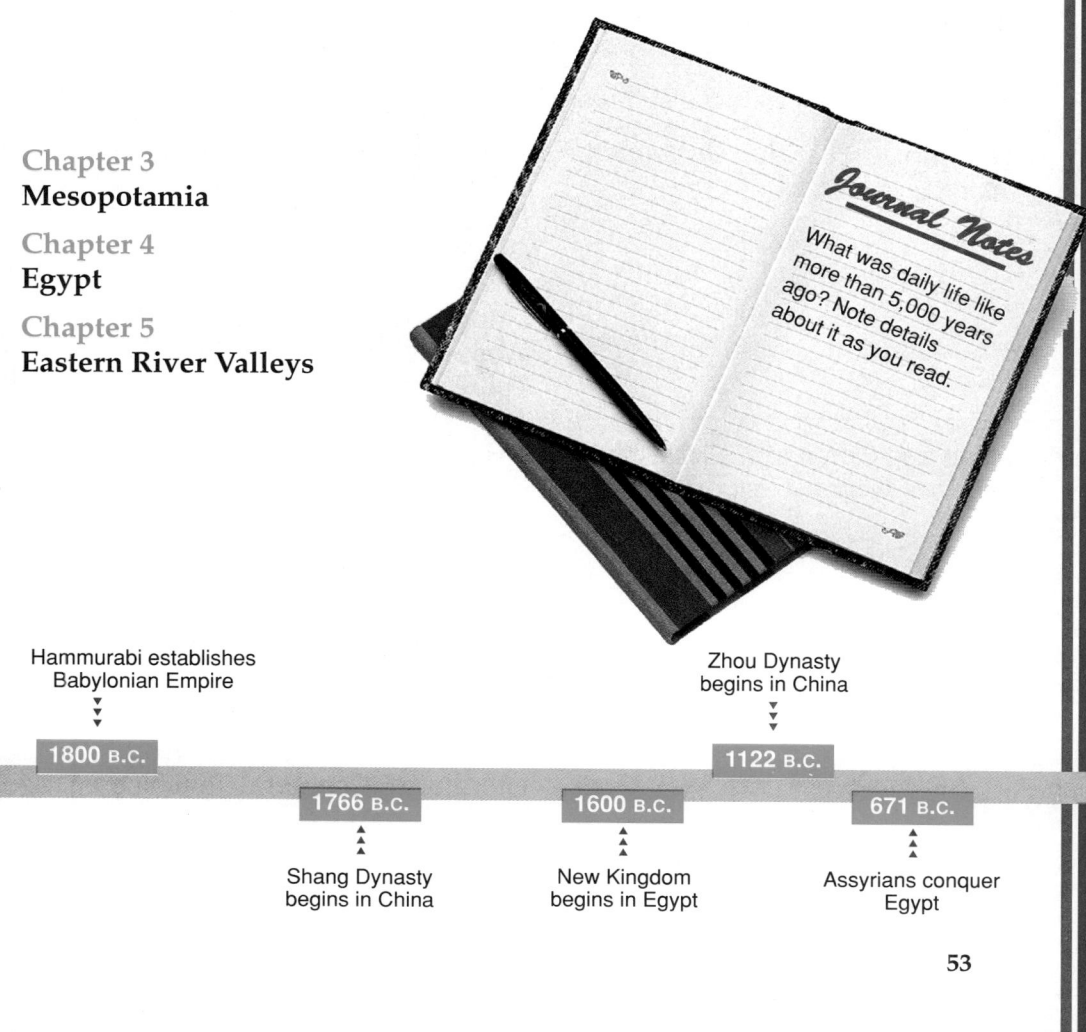

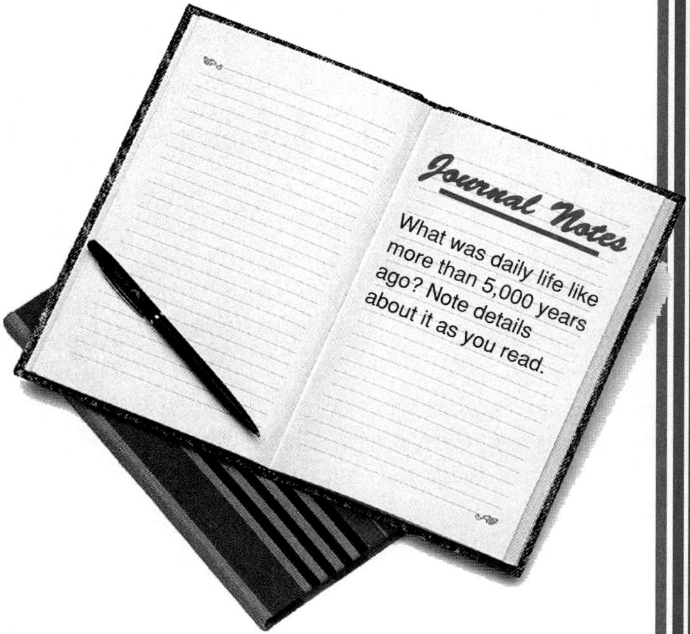

Journal Notes
What was daily life like more than 5,000 years ago? Note details about it as you read.

- 1800 B.C. — Hammurabi establishes Babylonian Empire
- 1766 B.C. — Shang Dynasty begins in China
- 1600 B.C. — New Kingdom begins in Egypt
- 1122 B.C. — Zhou Dynasty begins in China
- 671 B.C. — Assyrians conquer Egypt

INTRODUCING THE UNIT

Explain to the class that because the ancient civilizations studied in this unit developed in different parts of the world, they were different from one another. Because all the civilizations developed in river valleys, however, they were also alike in some ways. Ask students to brainstorm ways that river valley civilizations might be alike. *(They all developed ways of controlling floods, and they were able to produce a surplus of food which allowed them time to focus on other cultural endeavors.)*

RECORDING JOURNAL NOTES

Help students begin writing in their journals by suggesting they write a brief description of a typical day in their lives. Have volunteers read their descriptions. Write a few of the details on the chalkboard. Explain to students that these are the kinds of details they could note in their journals as they read about the early civilizations described in this unit.

GEOGRAPHIC LOCATION

The civilizations discussed in this unit arose along the Tigris-Euphrates, Nile, Indus, and Huang Ho river valleys. Have students locate these rivers on the appropriate maps in their text Atlas. Then have volunteers locate them on a wall map of the world.

CHAPTER

3 Mesopotamia

CHAPTER ORGANIZER

Objectives	Special Features	Supplemental Materials
Section 1 The Rise of Sumer Describe how religion, family life, and government influenced Sumerian civilization.	People in History: *Urukagina,* p. 60	• Reproducible Lesson Plan • Section 1 Quiz • Testmaker • Chapter 3 Vocabulary and Guided Reading Activity • Unit 2 Primary Source Reading • Outline Map Resource pp. 28, 39 • The Western Civilization Videodisc • The World History Videodisc
Section 2 Later Mesopotamian Empires Explain why Hammurabi and his reforms were important.	Map and Geography Skills: *Identifying Physical Features,* p. 62	• Reproducible Lesson Plan • Section 2 Quiz • Testmaker • Chapter 3 Geography and Map Activity • Chapter 3 Cooperative Learning Activity • Reinforcing Social Studies Skills, pp. 9, 13 • The World History Videodisc
Section 3 Contributions Describe how the Mesopotamian civilization contributed to other civilizations.		• Chapter 3 Chart and Graph Skill Activity • Unit 2 World Literature • Chapter 3 Teaching Transparency and Activity • Chapter 3 Activity Book Activity
Chapter 3 Review and Evaluation		• Chapter 3 Reteaching Activity • Chapter 3 Enrichment Activity • Chapter 3 Performance Assessment Activity • Chapter 3 Teaching Transparency and Activity • Chapter 3 Spanish Summary and Glossary • Audiocassettes (English and Spanish) • Chapter 3 Test • Testmaker

If time does not permit teaching the entire chapter, use the Chapter 3 Summary on page 64 and the Chapter 3 Audiocassettes (English and Spanish) to point out the main ideas of the chapter.

PERFORMANCE ASSESSMENT ACTIVITIES

Daily Life Have students work in groups to make a collage of clothing worn by people of the early civilizations covered in this chapter. Suggest students look at pictures of artifacts and read other reference materials as resources for their drawings.

Newspaper Articles Remind students that the elements of a newspaper article include who, what, where, when, and why, or how. Have students choose an event from the chapter to write about in newspaper style. Encourage them to include a headline for their articles and to do further research, if necessary. When the articles are completed, students can share them with the class.

CHAPTER RESOURCES

LITERATURE ABOUT THE PERIOD

Kramer, S.N. *History Begins at Sumer.* University of Pennsylvania Press, 1981. Focuses on various episodes in ancient history.

Oppenheim, A. Leo. *Letters from Mesopotamia.* University of Chicago Press, 1967. A translation of business and personal letters found in cuneiform.

READINGS FOR THE STUDENT

Africa and the Origin of Humans. Raintree, 1988. Easy-to-understand presentation of Africa's early history.

Bauman, Hans. *In the Land of Ur; The Discovery of Ancient Mesopotamia* (trans. by Stella Humphries). Pantheon Books, 1969. Narrative introduction to the history of Sumer and Akkad as discovered by archaeologists.

Bertman, Stephen. *Doorways Through Time: The Romance of Archaeology.* Jeremy P. Tarcher, 1986. Accounts of history and archaeology at several sites including Sumer.

Foster, Leila Merrell. *The Sumerians.* Watts, 1990. Discusses the rise and fall of the Sumerian civilization and includes several photographs of Sumerian artifacts.

Wetwood, Jennifer. *Gilgamesh, and Other Babylonian Tales.* Coward, McCann & Geoghegan, 1970. Retells ancient tales of Sumer and Babylon.

READINGS FOR THE TEACHER

Gailey, Harry A. *History of Africa Volume I: Earliest times to 1800.* Krieger, 1980. An overview of this period in African history.

Hawkes, Jacquetta, ed. *Atlas of Ancient Archaeology.* McGraw-Hill, 1974. Traces the patterns of ancient cultures and civilizations around the world.

MULTIMEDIA RESOURCES

The Ancient River Civilizations. Random House. Color filmstrips (3). Focuses on the ancient civilizations along the Tigris-Euphrates, Nile, and Indus rivers.

The Beginning is the End. Glencoe/TVOntario. Video. Describes early river valley civilizations.

The Epic of Man. Time-Life Video. Color filmstrip. Deals with Sumer and ancient Egypt.

Teaching

PEOPLE IN HISTORY

URUKAGINA

After students have read the People in History feature, have them discuss laws in the United States that protect the rights of everyone. *(Answers should include the Bill of Rights.)* Ask students to identify countries in the world today that are experiencing revolts as a result of unfair or cruel treatment by their governments. *(Answers might include South Africa.)*

ANSWERS to Checking for Understanding

1. The king before Urukagina had not cared for the people's welfare and had taxed them heavily. Urukagina removed all government inspectors, did away with most taxes, and issued laws to protect poor citizens from rich ones.
2. Answers will vary, but students should point out that most people, except those who benefitted from unfair taxes, would have liked having Urukagina as a ruler because he ended abuse and corruption in the government and cared for the welfare of his people.

PEOPLE IN HISTORY

Urukagina

All through history, people have protested against unfair or cruel behavior. To protect the rights of everyone, they have passed laws. The first known person to do this was Urukagina (ū ruk uh gē' nuh), who ruled the Sumerian city-state of Lagash (lā' gash) about 2275 B.C.

Urukagina became king as the result of a revolt. The king before Urukagina had not cared for the people's welfare. Because of abuse and corruption in the government, the people of Lagash had paid high, unfair taxes.

Unfair Taxes Citizens had to pay taxes every time they brought a sheep to the palace to be sheared. They had to pay taxes to obtain a divorce. People were taxed for burying the dead. Perfumers were taxed on every ounce of perfume they made.

Tax collectors seemed to be everywhere. Government inspectors seized boats, donkeys, sheep, cattle, and fishing businesses. The king even took the property of the temple and used it for his own. At last, the citizens of Lagash could stand it no longer. They revolted and chose a new king, Urukagina.

Urukagina became a well-liked ruler. He removed all government inspectors and did away with all taxes, except for a small burial tax. He promised Ningirsu (nin' guhr sū), the god of Lagash, that he would not allow "men of power" to take the property of widows and orphans or to harm them in any way. He issued laws to protect poor citizens against rich ones.

Reforms and Results Urukagina's reforms soon began to take effect. For example, "if a poor man's son laid out a fishing pond, no one would now steal its fish." Wealthy government workers stopped taking fruit from the orchard of a "poor man's mother."

Urukagina ruled as king of Lagash for only ten years. Then, Lagash was conquered by the neighboring city-state of Umma (uhm' uh). Urukagina's reforms, however, were written down by scribes and were not forgotten.

Checking for Understanding

1. **In what ways was Urukagina's reign different from that of the king before him?**
2. **Would you have liked to have Urukagina as a ruler? Why or why not?**

SPOTLIGHT ON: URUKAGINA

At the time Urukagina ruled Lagash, people were beginning to desire a strong government to both rule and protect them. Civilization was developing to the point that for protection from enemies, control of crime, and protection of their property, people were willing to pay taxes and fight wars.

Section 2

LATER MESOPOTAMIAN EMPIRES

About 2400 B.C., the power of Sumer started to fade. New civilizations began to develop in Mesopotamia as conquerors moved in from nearby areas.

Sargon I Sargon I (sar′ gon) was a ruler from an area in northern Mesopotamia known as Akkad (ak′ ad). About 2300 B.C., he moved his armies south and began to conquer the city-states of Sumer one by one. He united the conquered city-states with Akkad and became known as king of Sumer and Akkad. Thus, Sargon I created the world's first **empire** (em′ pīr), or group of states under one ruler. He extended this empire to include all of Mesopotamia.

Under Sargon I, Akkadian became the language of the people. Sumerian was used only for religious purposes. The Akkadians, however, worshipped the Sumerian gods. They also wrote their language in Sumerian cuneiform. Sargon I ruled his empire for more than 50 years. Shortly after his death, the empire fell.

Hammurabi of Babylon Following the death of Sargon I, the separate city-states again rose to power. Then, about 1800 B.C., a new group of people called Amorites (am′ uh rīts) entered the Tigris-Euphrates Valley and built cities of their own. One of these cities was Babylon (bab′ uh luhn). The king of Babylon, Hammurabi (ham uh rob′ ē), conquered Akkad and Sumer and became ruler of a great new empire.

The people of Babylon took as their own many parts of the **culture,** or way of life, of the people they had conquered. For example, they took over the language of the city-states. They also worshiped the same Sumerian gods that the Akkadians had worshiped, but they gave those gods Babylonian names.

Hammurabi was a great conqueror. He extended his rule to the Mediterranean Sea. As ruler, he brought about many changes. He improved irrigation systems by building and repairing canals. He changed religion by raising the god of Babylon above all other gods. When the people began to worship this god as well as their own local god, they became more united. Hammurabi also reorganized the tax system and began a government housing program.

The **reform,** or improvement, for which Hammurabi became best known was a code of law. Each city-state had its own code. Hammurabi took what he believed were the best laws from each code. He put these together and then issued one code by which everyone in the empire was to live. Hammurabi wanted to make sure that his code was carried out fairly and justly. To do this, he

A Statue of a Sumerian Woman

Statue of Sargon I

SPOTLIGHT ON: SARGON I

Sargon I tells his own story in an account found carved on a block of diorite. The story is similar to the Biblical story of Moses.

"Of my father I know only his name . . . My mother was a priestess . . . She brought me into the world secretly . . . She took a basket of reeds, placed me inside it, covered it with pitch [tar], and placed me in the Euphrates. And the river, without which the land cannot live, carried me through part of my future kingdom . . . and bore me along to Akki, who fetched water to irrigate the fields. Akki made a gardener of me. In the garden that I cultivated Inanna [chief goddess] saw me. And she turned her favor toward me and promised to make me great."

L1 **Government** Write the following sections of the *Code of Hammurabi* on the chalkboard.

1. A son who strikes his father will have his hands cut off.

2. If a man strikes and wounds another, then he will pay the physician. But, if the man puts out the eye of another, his own eye will be put out, and if he breaks another's bones, his bones will be broken.

3. If a builder has built a home for a man and has not made his work sound, so that the house he has made falls down and causes the death of the owner of the house, that builder shall be put to death.

Ask students to brainstorm reasons why Hammurabi's code is considered by historians to be a positive development in civilization. *(Hammurabi's codes were an attempt to deal fairly with people in a political state made up of former independent states with different traditions. The code set up a social order based on individual rights.)* LEP

VIDEODISC

Use the following to enrich Chapter 3.

WH E 33 14277

Hammurabi, King of Babylon.

L2 **Innovations** Ask students to name examples of Mesopotamian innovations as a volunteer writes the responses on the chalkboard. Direct students to collect pictures from magazines and newspapers or create their own drawings that illustrate objects based on inventions or ideas of the Mesopotamians. Discuss what life would be like without these objects/concepts.

Teaching

MAP SKILLS

Identifying Physical Features

Instruct the students to study the map on page 62 to answer the following questions:

What empire was located partly in the mountains? *(Hammurabi's Empire)*

What seas border Asia Minor? *(Mediterranean Sea, Black Sea)*

Have the students look at the physical map of the Middle East on pages 678-679 in the textbook Atlas. Point out to students that this map uses many colors and grades of shading to show physical features. Ask the students to identify and locate physical features of the Middle East shown on this map.

Assign Chapter 3 **Geography and Map Activity** in the TCR.

ANSWERS to Map Practice

1. Seas shown on the map in addition to the Mediterranean Sea are the Caspian Sea, the Black Sea, and the Red Sea.
2. Besides the Nile, the rivers shown on the map are the Tigris River and the Euphrates River.
3. The map and the map key indicate that there was an ancient coastline of the Persian Gulf.

Identifying Physical Features

MAP SKILLS

Different physical features making up Earth's surface are often shown on maps. They include landforms, such as mountains, hills, plateaus, and plains. Physical features also include bodies of water, such as oceans, seas, lakes, and rivers.

Most maps use black boundary lines and color to point out water and land areas. Blue is generally used to show the size and shape of large bodies of water. For example, notice the Mediterranean Sea located west of Syria on the map below. Rivers, such as the Nile River in Egypt, are often shown by black lines. To distinguish rivers from boundaries, which are also shown by black lines, rivers are usually labeled.

Maps in this textbook use earth tone colors to point out land areas. Mountains are shown by shades of black. For example, there are mountains located where the Euphrates River begins but not where the river empties into the Persian Gulf.

Look at the map below, and answer the following questions:

Map Practice

1. **In addition to the Mediterranean, what seas are shown?**
2. **Besides the Nile, what rivers are shown?**
3. **How can you tell that the Persian Gulf coastline has changed over the years?**

Mesopotamia

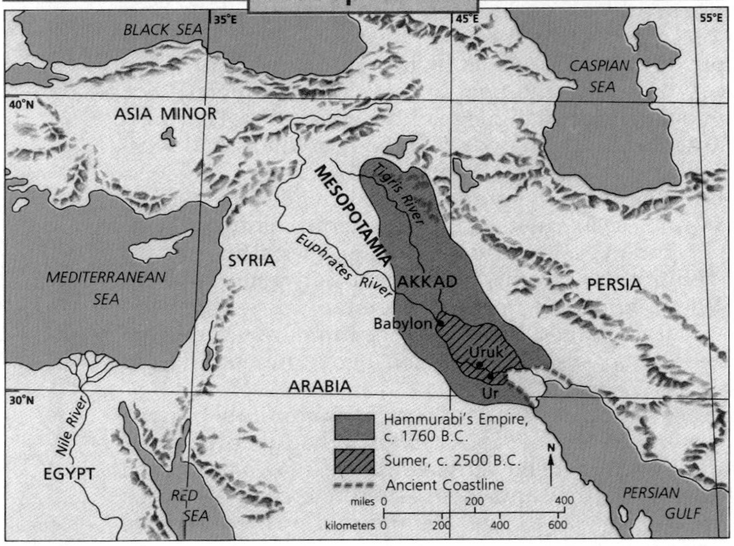

SPOTLIGHT ON: MESOPOTAMIA

The area of Mesopotamia, in addition to being known as the cradle of civilization was also known as "the fertile crescent." It was given this name because the actual area was shaped like a crescent and the land was extremely fertile. Both the climate and the silt from the Tigris and Euphrates rivers added to its richness and productivity.

appointed royal judges. Judges who were not honest and witnesses who did not tell the truth were punished.

Hammurabi's code covered almost everything in daily life. A person was believed innocent until proven guilty. Once proven guilty, a person was punished. Punishments ranged from fines to death. There were no prison sentences. Members of the upper class generally were punished more severely than members of the middle or lower classes.

During Hammurabi's rule, Babylon became an important trade center. Babylonians exchanged their *surplus*, or extra, products for money or for the goods. People from other parts of the world came to trade, some from as far away as India and China. These traders paid gold and silver for the goods made by Babylonians.

Hammurabi ruled for more than 40 years. His **reign** (rān), or period of power, is known as the Golden Age of Babylon. After his death, however, the Babylonian Empire declined, and Mesopotamia was again divided into a number of small city-states.

Sculpture of a Sumerian Chariot

Section 2 Review

1. **Identify:** Sargon I, Akkad, Babylon, Hammurabi
2. **Define:** empire, culture, reform, reign
3. What happened to Sumer under Sargon I's rule?

Critical Thinking

4. What do you think Hammurabi would say about the court system in the United States today?

Section 3 Contributions

From the beginnings of Sumer until the death of Hammurabi, the influence of Mesopotamia on other civilizations was felt in many ways. Inventions, customs, and ideas of the Sumerian and Babylonian cultures were copied and, improved upon by other peoples.

The Sumerians developed the earliest known civilization in the world and has been called "the cradle of civilization." The oldest written records known are Sumerian. The Sumerians were the first people to write down their laws. Sumerian cuneiform became the model for other people's writing.

The Sumerians also invented many things such as the wheel, which helped transportation. Another was the plow, which made

INDEPENDENT PRACTICE

L3 Mathematics Have students create illustrated time lines of Mesopotamian history from 5000 B.C. (people migrate to Mesopotamia) to 1750 B.C. (end of Hammurabi's empire). Have students plot the intervals needed and balance events. Suggest they create several mathematically based questions about their time lines for other students to answer. Display time lines in the classroom.

L2 Writing Have students research more about Sargon I or Hammurabi and write a one-page biographical sketch, including dates of birth and death, significant contributions, and other details. Have volunteers read their sketches aloud.

LINKING PAST TO PRESENT

Government officials in ancient civilizations directed and organized large construction projects that employed many people. How do the roles of these officials compare to the roles of modern government officials who oversee the expansion of cities?

ASSESS

CHECK FOR UNDERSTANDING

Ask students to summarize the main points of the chapter, orally or in writing. Discuss the answers to the Section and Chapter Review questions.

SECTION 2 ANSWERS

1. Sargon I, ruler of Akkad (p. 61); Akkad, area in Mesopotamia (p. 61); Babylon, city in Tigris-Euphrates River valley (p. 61); Hammurabi, king of Babylon (p. 61)
2. empire, states under one ruler (p. 61); culture, way of life (p. 61); reform, improvement (p. 61); reign, period of power (p. 63)
3. It was conquered and united with Akkad.
4. Answers will vary, but note that he agreed a person is believed innocent until proven guilty.

Assign Chapter 3 **Section 2 Quiz** in the TCR. Testmaker available.

EVALUATE

Assign Chapter 3 **Performance Assessment Activity** in the TCR.

Administer **Chapter 3 Test** found in the TCR. Testmaker available.

RETEACH

Organize students in small groups. Have pairs or individuals in each group outline a different section of the chapter. Have students regroup and compile the outlines into a chapter outline. Then have group members use the outline to quiz one another.

Assign Chapter 3 **Reteaching Activity** in the TCR.

ENRICH

Have students investigate Sumerian inventions and write a description of the invention and its purpose as if they were applying for a patent from Hammurabi.

Assign Chapter 3 **Enrichment Activity** in the TCR.

CLOSE

Ask students to evaluate the following statement: *"The Golden Age of Babylon" is an appropriate name for Hammurabi's reign.*

MEETING CHAPTER OBJECTIVES

Each chapter objective is tested by the Chapter Review questions that follow it in parentheses.

1. Describe how religion, family, and government influenced Sumerians. (BV; CU 2, 4; CT 2; UYJ)

2. Explain why Hammurabi and his reforms were important. (CU 7)

3. Discuss the Mesopotamian contributions to other civilizations. (BV; CU 8)

Water Clock

it possible for farmers to grow more food with less effort. Still another was the sailboat, which replaced muscle power with wind power.

The people of Mesopotamia developed a 12-month calendar based on the cycles of the moon. The calendar marked the times for religious festivals and planting.

From Mesopotamia also came contributions in the field of mathematics. The people developed a number system based on 60. From that came the 60-minute hour, 60-second minute, and 360-degree circle. The people of Mesopotamia also used a clock that was operated by controlled drops of water.

Section 3 Review

1. Why was Mesopotamia called "the cradle of civilization"?
2. What did the people of Mesopotamia contribute to the field of mathematics?

Critical Thinking

3. What things about your life today would be different if the people of Mesopotamia had not invented the things they had?

Chapter Summary

1. Civilization began in an area known as Mesopotamia, located between the Tigris and Euphrates rivers.
2. Sumer was the first known civilization in the world.
3. The Sumerians developed an irrigation system for growing crops.
4. Sumerian civilization consisted of a series of city-states, the most important of which was Ur.
5. Each Sumerian city-state had its own chief god and government.
6. Sargon I of Akkad created the world's first empire in 2300 B.C. by conquering the Sumerians.
7. About 1800 B.C., Hammurabi conquered Akkad and Sumer and established the Babylonian Empire.
8. Hammurabi unified the Babylonian Empire by setting up a single code of law and by raising the god of Babylon above all others.
9. Major contributions of the Mesopotamian civilizations include writing, the wheel, the plow, the sailboat, and a number system based on 60.

SECTION 3 ANSWERS

1. because the earliest known civilization developed there
2. a number system based on 60, which led to the 60-minute hour, 60-minute second, and 360-degree circle
3. Answers will vary, but might note that there would not be a bicycle if the wheel had not been invented.

Assign Chapter 3 **Section 3 Quiz** in the TCR. Testmaker available.

CHAPTER 3

Review

Building Vocabulary

Imagine that you are a visitor to ancient Mesopotamia. Use the following words in a letter home in which you describe what you have seen and experienced on your visit.

artisans	scribe
culture	reform
empire	cuneiform
ziggurat	city-state
priest-kings	reign

Check for Understanding

1. Why were the twin rivers important to Sumerian life?
2. Why was the ziggurat important to the Sumerians?
3. Who attended the schools in Sumer and what were the schools like?
4. Who was Gilgamesh and why was he important?
5. What did Sargon I accomplish?
6. What trading system did the people of Babylonia use?
7. What happened to the people who broke Hammurabi's laws?
8. Why was the sailboat an important invention?

Critical Thinking

1. In what ways do you think your school is similar to or different from the schools in Sumer?
2. Why do you think religion played such an important part in Sumerian life?
3. What do you think would have happened to Sumer if it had suffered ten years of drought? How would the kingdom be affected?

Geography in History

LOCATION Babylon became a major trading center. Refer to the map on page 62 and imagine that you are King Hammurabi. You must select the location for another settlement that you hope will also become a trading center. Where would you locate this settlement? Explain.

Using Your Journal

Compare the details you have noted about life in early Sumeria with details of your daily life. Write a paragraph explaining things that are similar and different as if you were explaining them to someone who lived in 2000 B.C.

65

CHAPTER 3 REVIEW ANSWERS

BUILDING VOCABULARY

Letters will vary. Students should include the terms in a letter home describing their visit to ancient Mesopotamia.

CHECK FOR UNDERSTANDING

1. They used water to irrigate crops, mud to make bricks, and fish and waterfowl for food.
2. because they were the center of Sumerian life-all great events were celebrated there
3. the sons of the rich; schools were made up of rooms off the temple courtyards; students sat in rows on brick benches and wrote on clay tablets with reeds
4. a famous priest-king; in a tale about him he learned that only the gods can live forever, and that people should take pride in what they do
5. He created the world's first empire.
6. They exchanged their surplus products for money or goods.
7. They were punished.
8. because it replaced muscle power with wind power

CRITICAL THINKING

1. Answers will vary, but could make comparisons between modern and Sumerian schools.
2. Answers will vary, but could note that Sumerians believed all forces of nature were alive, and powerful gods.
3. Answers will vary, but could note 10 years of drought could cause food and water shortages and cause Sumerians to migrate.

+ BONUS +
TEST QUESTION

For Chapter 3 Test

The Sumerians developed ways of telling time and counting. What elements of that system remain today, and what parts have disappeared? *(the 60-minute hour, 360° circle; modern numbers are based on 10.)*

USING YOUR JOURNAL

Journal entries will vary, but students should compare their way of life with that of Sumerians. You might call on volunteers to read their entries to the class.

GEOGRAPHY IN HISTORY

Answers will vary, but could mention access to transportation, central location, and balance to Babylon's location.

CHAPTER 4

Egypt

CHAPTER ORGANIZER

Objectives	Special Features	Supplemental Materials
Section 1 The Nile Analyze why the Nile River was so important to the growth of Egypt.		• Reproducible Lesson Plan • Section 1 Quiz • Testmaker • Chapter 4 Vocabulary and Guided Reading Activity • Chapter 4 Teaching Transparency and Activity
Section 2 The Old Kingdom Discuss how pharaohs, pyramids, and religious beliefs influenced the Old Kingdom of Egypt.		• Reproducible Lesson Plan • Section 2 Quiz • Outline Map Resource pp. 28, 39 • Chapter 4 Cooperative Learning Activity • The Western Civilization Videodisc • The World History Videodisc • Chapter 4 Activity Book Activity
Section 3 The Middle Kingdom Describe what happened during Egypt's Middle Kingdom.		• Reproducible Lesson Plan • Section 3 Quiz • Testmaker • Chapter 4 Teaching Transparency and Activity • Chapter 4 Chart and Graph Skill Activity • Unit 2 World Literature • World History and Art Transparency 2
Section 4 The New Kingdom Explain why Egyptian civilization grew and then declined during the New Kingdom.	Map and Geography Skills: *Reading Map Legends* , p. 75	• Reproducible Lesson Plan • Chapter 4 Geography and Map Activity • Chapter 4 Teaching Transparency and Activity • Section 4 Quiz • Testmaker
Section 5 Contributions Summarize what the Egyptians contributed to other civilizations.		• Reproducible Lesson Plan • Section 5 Quiz • Chapter 4 Reteaching Activity • Chapter 4 Enrichment Activity • The Western Civilization Videodisc • The World History Videodisc
Chapter 4 Review and Evaluation		• Chapter 4 Performance Assessment Activity• Chapter 4 Test • Testmaker.• Audiocassettes (English and Spanish)

If time does not permit teaching the entire chapter, use the Chapter 4 Summary on page 80 and the Chapter 4 Audiocassettes (English and Spanish) to point out the main ideas of the chapter.

Performance Assessment Activities

Television Newscast Have students imagine they are television journalists carried back in time to ancient Egypt. Have them write and present a newscast-style report on an object or structure to be shown on the evening news "Let's Look Back" series.

Book Review Suggest students read a book about one of the civilizations covered in this chapter and write a description of something in the civilization that appealed to them. Refer students to the books listed on this page or have them find others in the library.

CHAPTER RESOURCES

LITERATURE ABOUT THE PERIOD

Perl, Lila. *Mummies, Tombs, and Treasure: Secrets of Ancient Egypt.* Clarion Books, 1990. An account of ancient Egyptian beliefs about death and the afterlife.

READINGS FOR THE STUDENT

Macauley, David. *Pyramid.* Houghton Mifflin, 1982. Describes techniques used for building pyramids.

Morley, Jaquelin, Mark Bergin, and John James. *An Egyptian Pyramid.* Peter Bedrick, 1991. Explains how the pyramids were built and their purpose.

Romer, John. *Ancient Lives: Daily Life in Egypt of the Pharaohs.* Henry Holt, 1984. Social life and customs of ancient Egypt.

Rossini, Stephane. *Egyptian Hieroglyphics: How to Read and Write Them.* Dover, 1989. Describes the principles of Egyptian reading and writing.

READINGS FOR THE TEACHER

Bowman, Alan K. *Egypt after the Pharaohs.* Berkeley: University of California Press, 1986. History of Egypt 332 B.C.-642 A.D., portraying daily life, government, economy, architecture, and culture.

Katan, Norma J. *Hieroglyphs: The Writings of Ancient Egypt.* Athenaeum, 1981. Examines the origins, meanings, and significance of hieroglyphs.

MULTIMEDIA RESOURCES

Ancient Egypt. Coronet/SSSS. Video. Tour of Egyptian ruins with an explanation of the culture of ancient Egypt.

Balancing the Budget. Glencoe/TVOntario. Video. Describes Egyptian trade.

Egypt: Cradle of Civilization. Encyclopedia Britannica/SSSS. Video. Introduces the ancient civilization that developed along the fertile land surrounding the Nile River.

Egypt: Land of the Pharaohs. TVOntario/SSSS. Video. Survey of ancient Egyptian history and contributions made by the ancient Egyptians.

Mummies' Message: A Simulation of an Archeological Expedition into One of Man's Most Mysterious Creations, the Pyramid. Interact/SSSS. Simulation. Class is divided into camps of expeditions that compete to enter the pyramid by decoding hieroglyphs.

Mysteries of the Pyramids. Kodak/SSSS. Video. Examines the ancient structures on the Giza Plateau.

INTRODUCE

CHAPTER 4 OVERVIEW

Chapter 4 focuses on the changes in society during the Old, Middle, and New Kingdoms.

➤ **Section 1** explains the importance of the Nile River to the Egyptian civilization.

➤ **Section 2** discusses Egypt's Old Kingdom.

➤ **Section 3** describes Egypt's Middle Kingdom.

➤ **Section 4** explains the growth and decline during the New Kingdom.

➤ **Section 5** presents Egyptian contributions.

CHAPTER OBJECTIVES

After reading Chapter 4, students will be able to:

1. analyze why the Nile River was so important to the growth of Egyptian civilization.

2. discuss how pharaohs, pyramids, and religious beliefs influenced the Old Kingdom.

3. describe what happened during Egypt's Middle Kingdom.

4. explain why Egyptian civilization grew then declined during the New Kingdom.

5. summarize Egyptian contributions.

EXAMINING THE ARTIFACT

Ask students to examine the mask of King Tutankhamen and tell what strikes them the most about its appearance. Explain that this mask was found in the king's tomb. Ask students what this fact tells them about the Egyptian people.

PERFORMANCE ASSESSMENT ✓

Use the Performance Assessment activities on page 66B to help you evaluate students as they complete the chapter.

CHAPTER 4 Egypt

Mask of Tutankhamen

66

TEACHER CLASSROOM RESOURCES

- World Literature
- Reproducible Lesson Plan
- Enrichment Activity
- Chart and Graph Skill Activity
- Geography and Map Activity
- Vocabulary and Guided Reading Activity
- Cooperative Learning Activity
- Performance Assessment Activity
- Teaching Transparencies and Activities
- Spanish Summary and Glossary
- Testmaker
- The Western Civilization Videodisc
- The World History Videodisc
- Audiocassettes (English and Spanish)

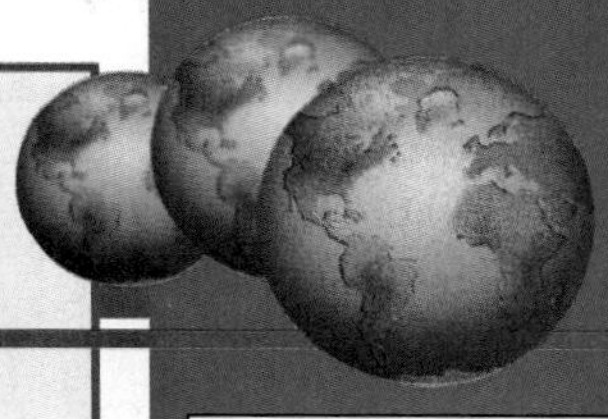

Chapter Focus

READ TO DISCOVER:

- Why the Nile River was so important to the growth of Egyptian civilization.
- How pharaohs, pyramids, and religious beliefs influenced the Old Kingdom of Egypt.
- What happened during Egypt's Middle Kingdom.
- Why Egyptian civilization grew and then declined during the New Kingdom.
- What the Egyptians contributed to other civilizations.

A people called Egyptians settled in the Nile River valley of northeast Africa. They most likely borrowed from the Sumerians the idea of farming, seeds for wheat and barley, and the idea of writing. The Egyptian civilization lasted longer than those of Mesopotamia. While the city-states of Mesopotamia fought among themselves, Egypt became a rich, powerful, and united nation. The Egyptians built a civilization that lasted for more than 2,000 years.

3100 B.C.–1100 B.C.

KEY TERMS

shadoof
pharaoh
pyramids
embalming
mummy
legend
hieroglyphic
papyrus

Section 1

The Nile

The Nile River flows north 4,145 miles, or 6,671 kilometers, from the mountains of central Africa to the Mediterranean Sea. The last 600 miles, or 960 kilometers, is in Egypt. There, the river cuts a narrow, green valley through the desert. Shortly before the Nile reaches the sea, it branches to form a fan-shaped area of fertile land called a *delta.* Most ancient Egyptians lived in this area. For a long time, they were protected from foreign invasions by the desert, the sea, and waterfalls called *cataracts* (kat' uh rakts).

FOCUS

BELLRINGER

Have students write the words *ancient Egypt* on their papers. Ask them to write words or phrases that come to mind when they think of ancient Egypt.

MOTIVATIONAL ACTIVITY

Call on volunteers to share their ideas about ancient Egypt. Write these on the chalkboard and have students notice the words and phrases that appear most often. *(Nile River, pharaohs, pyramids, fertile lands, mummies)* Have students copy any words or phrases that were not on their papers. Then tell them that they will learn the historical significance of these terms as they study the section.

VOCABULARY PRE-CHECK

Write the key terms for this chapter on the chalkboard. Ask students to list these on a sheet of paper and write the sentences in which they are found, as they encounter them in their reading.

Assign Chapter 4 **Vocabulary and Guided Reading Activity** in the TCR.

EXTRA CREDIT PROJECT

Suggest interested students develop a trivia game of interesting facts about rivers around the world. They might include the shortest, most northern, most shallow, one traveled by a famous person, one that has the most songs written about it, and other facts. Encourage the student to play the game with a partner.

KEY TO ABILITY LEVELS

Teaching strategies have been coded for varying learning styles and abilities.

L1 Level 1 activities are **basic** activities and should be within the ability range of all students.

L2 Level 2 activities are **average** activities and should be within the ability range of the average to above-average student.

L3 Level 3 activities are **challenging** activities designed for the ability range of above-average students.

LEP LEP activities should be within the ability range of Limited English Proficiency students.

TEACH

GUIDED PRACTICE

L1 **Geography: Human/Environmental Interaction** Have students locate the Nile River on the map of Africa in the text Atlas. Point out the Delta of the Nile. Next, write the following phrase on the chalkboard: *Egypt: the gift of the Nile.* Inform students that this is a phrase coined by the historian Herodotus, and elicit from them the possible meanings of the phrase. Ask students how the Egyptians made use of the Nile River.

CAPTION ANSWER

The geographical features that protected the Egyptians in the Nile River delta were the desert, the sea, and waterfalls called cataracts.

LINKING PAST TO PRESENT

The Aswan High Dam in southeastern Egypt was built in the 1960s partly to protect crops and people against seasonal flooding. The lack of this flooding, however, means that fertile soil is no longer deposited annually. Instead farmers in the area rely on chemical fertilizers to make the soil fertile. Ask students to describe how the dam has changed the environment around the Nile.

VIDEODISC

Use the following to enrich Chapter 4.

WH E 7 14251

Egyptian depiction of man grinding grain 2500 B.C.

NILE RIVER Over thousands of years, the flooding of the Nile River has left rich soil all along its banks. The Nile River valley is only 3 percent of Egypt's land, yet most Egyptians live and work in this area. **What geographical features protected the Egyptians in the Nile River delta?**

The Egyptians had an advantage over the people of the other river valley civilizations. Every year, about the middle of July, the Nile overflowed its banks. The flood waters went down but left behind large amounts of rich soil good for growing crops.

Egyptian farmers planted their fields while the soil was still wet. To water their crops during the dry season, the Egyptians dug out *basins*, or bowl-shaped holes. They used a machine called a **shadoof** (shuh dūf') to lift water from the Nile to the basins. The Egyptians raised flax, wheat, barley, and grapes.

Section 1 Review

1. **Identify:** Egyptians, Nile River
2. **Define:** shadoof
3. Where did most Egyptians live?
4. How did the Egyptians control the Nile River?

Critical Thinking

5. How did the Egyptians' use of the Nile River and its agriculture compare with the Sumerians' use of the Tigris and Euphrates rivers and their agriculture?

SECTION 1 ANSWERS

1. Egyptians, people of the Nile River valley (p. 67); Nile River, river in Africa (p. 67)
2. shadoof, machine used to lift water (p. 68)
3. in the Nile delta
4. by building a system of basins and irrigation canals
5. Answers will vary, but could note both Egyptians and Sumerians depended on the rivers for living, and both civilizations controlled their environment. The Egyptians dug out basins and built irrigation canals to the fields. The Sumerians also built irrigation canals. The Egyptians raised flax, wheat, barley, and grapes. The Sumerians grew barley, wheat, sesame, flax, fruit trees, date palms, and vegetables.

Assign Chapter 4 **Section 1 Quiz** in the TCR. Testmaker available.

Section 2

THE OLD KINGDOM

At first, Egypt was made up of two kingdoms. One was Upper Egypt, which lay in the southern part of the Nile River valley. The other was Lower Egypt, which lay in the north delta.

Narmer, also known as Menes (mē′ nēz), was a king of Upper Egypt. About 3100 B.C., he led his armies from the valley north into the delta. He conquered Lower Egypt and married one of its princesses, uniting the two kingdoms. He wore a double crown, the high white one of the south and the shallow red one of the north. Narmer had many titles. He was called "Lord of Upper and Lower Egypt," "Wearer of Both Crowns," and "Lord of the Two Lands." He set up a new capital at Memphis, a city on the border between Upper and Lower Egypt.

About 2600 B.C., the Old Kingdom started in Egypt. It lasted for nearly 500 years. During the period of the Old Kingdom, Egyptian cities became centers of religion and government. Kings, priests, government officials, and artisans lived there.

Most Egyptians, however, did not live in cities. They lived on large estates along the banks of the Nile. The rich Egyptians who owned these estates lived in wood and brick houses with beautiful gardens and pools. Walls were decorated with brightly

EGYPTIAN LIFE Paintings from tombs offer much information about everyday life in ancient Egypt. Here, a wall painting shows a man and woman plowing and planting their fields. **How did the lives of the rich differ from those of the poor in Egypt?**

GEOGRAPHY AND HISTORY

Direct students to the map of ancient Egypt on page 75. Explain that because the Nile River flows from central Africa into the Mediterranean Sea, or from south to north, the southern part of Egypt is actually Upper Egypt, and the northern half is actually Lower Egypt.

CAPTION ANSWER

The rich owned large estates and lived in elegant houses, while the poor farmed the land and lived in small mud-brick houses.

MAKING CONNECTIONS

➤➤ **Geography: Location** The Nile is the longest river in the world. Its two branches are the Blue Nile, which begins in the Ethiopian highlands, and the White Nile, which rises in Uganda and meets the Blue Nile at present-day Khartoum.

VIDEODISC

Use the following to enrich Chapter 4.

WC A 83 9085
Columns from the temple of Amon at Luxor.

EXTENDING THE CONTENT

One reason we know a great deal about homes in ancient Egypt is that small models—called soul houses—often were included in the things buried with a person to assure him or her of a pleasant afterlife. The houses of both rich and poor were comfortable in the dry, hot climate. With almost no rain, it was practical to build mud-brick walls and flat roofs with vents to catch the breeze. Egyptians had less furniture in their homes than people today have—a few brightly colored chairs and stools, small tables, oil lamps, and chests for storing clothes. Beds were like cots, with tightly stretched cord springs.

DID YOU KNOW ??

The Egyptians wore loincloths or slips of linen made from flax. The linen was strong, did not soil easily, and kept the wearer cool. On their feet, the Egyptians wore reed or leather sandals with curled-up toes, although they usually walked barefoot.

L2 **Writing** Have students imagine they are a pharaoh in ancient Egypt. Instruct them to write journal entries describing their daily responsibilities. Call on volunteers to read their journal entries to the class.

CAPTION ANSWER

The land became richer because of soil deposited by the floods. The Egyptians also used their planting time more wisely and farmed with better methods to maximize each harvest.

VIDEODISC

Use the following to enrich Chapter 4.

WH E 14 14258

A granite statue of Queen Hatshepsut.

WC A 75 9077

Egyptian pharaoh Tuthmosis III.

EGYPTIAN HARVEST Image of Egyptians preparing grain for storage (left). Rulings of the pharaohs were carved in stone (right). **How did the flooding of the Nile improve the harvest?**

colored paintings that showed scenes of daily life. A household was made up of an owner's family, servants, and artisans. The artisans were hired to build boats, weave linen, and make tools and pottery.

Most Egyptians, however, were farmers who lived in villages on the estates. At first, their houses were made of reeds and mud. Later, they were made of sun-baked mud-brick. These houses generally had only one room with a roof made of palm leaves. They were built on high ground so that they would be safe from the yearly flood. Egyptian farmers worked in the fields and took care of the cattle. When they were not farming, they built monuments, dug ditches, and repaired roads.

The Pharaoh The Egyptians believed that the strength and unity of their country came from having a strong ruler. At first, Egyptian rulers were called kings. Later, they were called **pharaoh** (fār' ō), meaning "great house." To Egyptians, the pharaoh was a ruler, a priest, and a god. He was the center of Egyptian life and ruled on Earth the way other gods ruled in heaven.

The pharaoh owned all the land in Egypt, but he gave gifts of land to rich Egyptians and priests. To make sure the land produced well, the pharaoh saw to it that dams and irrigation canals were built and repaired. The pharaoh also ordered the building of brick *granaries,* or buildings for storing grain. These were used to store grain from good harvests so people would not starve in times of bad harvests.

MULTICULTURAL PERSPECTIVES

One thing that made the position of women strong in Egypt was the economic power of inheritance. Custom dictated that property descend from mother to daughter. Thus, to keep property in the family, pharaohs often married relatives.

The pharaoh also chose all government officials. They made certain that taxes were gathered and building permits were given out. Trade with other lands was in the pharaoh's hands. The word of a pharaoh was law.

The Egyptians believed that what happened to Egypt depended on the pharaoh's actions. As chief priest, the pharaoh carried out certain rituals. For example, he made the first break in the irrigation dikes each year to open the land to the water. When the water went down, he drove a sacred bull around the capital city. The Egyptians believed this ritual would make the soil rich so they could grow good crops. The pharaoh was the first to cut the ripe grain. Egyptians believed this would bring a good harvest.

Pharaohs were treated with great respect. Whenever they appeared in public, people played music on flutes and cymbals. They also bowed and "smelled the earth" or touched their heads to the ground.

The Pyramids Another way the people of the Old Kingdom showed how they felt about the pharaohs was by building them great tombs called **pyramids** (pir' uh midz). Because the sun sank in the west, these "Houses of Eternity" were built on the west bank of the Nile. They were designed to protect the pharaohs' bodies from floods, wild animals, and robbers. The Egyptians believed the pharaohs would be happy after death if they had their personal belongings. Therefore, they placed a pharaoh's clothing; weapons, furniture, and jewelry in the pyramids.

PYRAMIDS AT GIZA The pyramids were built at Giza on the Nile River. The largest pyramid once enshrined the body of King Khufu. **What items were probably buried with the King?**

LINKING PAST TO PRESENT

Many Egyptian pyramids were built near the town of Giza, Egypt. The largest, which covers 13 acres (5.2 ha), is the Great Pyramid, built around 2600 B.C. for King Khufu. It measures 481 feet (146 m) high and 755 feet (230 m) long at each of its four bases. It is said to have taken 100,000 workers about 20 years to build. Many tourists currently travel to Egypt to see the pyramids.

L3 **Critical Thinking** Write the following criteria of a civilization on the chalkboard: *a writing system, a well-organized government, art and literature, and specialization of labor.* Ask students to write a brief explanation of how ancient Egypt met these criteria.

CAPTION ANSWER

Egyptians buried personal items, items of wealth, and any utilitarian and comfort items the person might need in the afterlife.

VIDEODISC

Use the following to enrich Chapter 4.

WH E 25 14269
An Egyptian mummy.

WC A 40 9042
Pyramids at Giza, Egypt.

COOPERATIVE LEARNING

Encourage students to study the illustrations in this chapter. Point out that ancient Egyptian paintings presented the human face and limbs in profile, while the upper torso, shoulders, and eyes were presented in front view. Suggest they find more examples of ancient Egyptian art such as in *The Atlas of Ancient Egypt* by John Baines and Jaromír Málek. Once they are familiar with this art style, have students plan and create a mural using the Egyptian style of art to illustrate a scene from Egyptian daily life.

L1 Daily Life Inform students that the organization of Egyptian society was like the structure of a pyramid. Draw a pyramid on the chalkboard and label it with Egyptian social positions as students relate them, starting with royalty at the top. Discuss the lifestyle of each.

DID YOU KNOW ??

Enslaved persons were not employed in building the pyramids. Enslavement did not become common in Egypt until the New Kingdom, when conquests in Syria and Palestine brought in prisoners of war. Then enslaved persons built monuments and temples for the pharaohs in the New Kingdom.

MAKING CONNECTIONS

➤➤ **Language Arts** The term *underworld* had a different meaning for the ancient Egyptians than it has for most people today. To the Egyptians, it meant the cool, tree-shaded land of Osiris, where even the poor could rest.

CAPTION ANSWER

They tried to lead a good life and learn certain magic spells.

VIDEODISC

Use the following to enrich Chapter 4.

WC A 43 9045

The pyramid of Chephren, and the sphinx, Giza.

It took many people and much work to build the pyramids. Farmers worked on them during the three summer months that their fields were flooded. The workers used copper tools to cut huge granite and limestone blocks from quarries across the Nile Valley or in Upper Egypt. The blocks of rock were tied with ropes onto wooden sleds, pulled to the Nile, placed on barges filled with sand, and floated across the river. Other workers then unloaded the blocks and pulled them to the place where the pyramids were being built. Huge mud and brick ramps were built beside each of the pyramids. The workers dragged the blocks up the ramps to each new layer of the pyramid.

Religious Beliefs The Egyptians believed in many gods. Two of the most important gods were the river god Hapi (hop′ ē) and the sun god Re (rā). The Egyptians depended on the river and the sun. The river brought them water and fertile soil, while the sun helped their crops to grow.

Another important god was Osiris (ō sī ris), god of the harvest and of eternal life. According to Egyptian legend, Osiris was an early pharaoh who gave his people laws and taught them farming. He and his wife Isis (ī′sis) ruled over the dead. The Egyptians believed that the souls of the dead went to the underworld. There, they were weighed on a scale. If a person had led a good life and knew certain magic spells, the scales balanced. Then, Osiris would grant the person life after death. To learn the correct magic spells, Egyptians studied a special book called the *Book of the Dead*.

EGYPTIAN GODS The god Osiris ruled over the Egyptian underworld. Here, he sits in judgment as other animal-headed gods weigh a dead man's soul and record the results. The scales have balanced, so the dead man may enter the underworld. **How did Egyptians prepare for life after death?**

MEETING SPECIAL NEEDS

Encourage students who are tactile/kinesthetic learners to make dioramas, models, or diagrams of a pyramid under construction as described in the subsection titled "The Pyramids." Display the students' creations in the classroom.

The Egyptians also used a process called **embalming** (em balm' ēng) to preserve the bodies of the dead. At first, they used the process to preserve the body of the pharaoh because they believed the soul could not live without the body. It was important for a pharaoh's soul to live after death. In that way, the pharaoh would continue to take care of Egypt.

Later, embalming was used to preserve other people as well as the pharaoh. To embalm a body, the Egyptians placed it in a wooden box and covered it with a chemical called natron. Natron dried up the water in the body, causing it to shrink. After the shrunken body had dried, it was wrapped with long strips of linen. The wrapped body was known as a **mummy.** The mummy of a poor person was often buried in a cave or in the sand. The mummy of a rich person was placed inside a special case or coffin. The coffin was then placed in a tomb.

Mummy Case

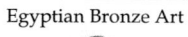

Section 2 Review

1. **Identify:** Old Kingdom, Narmer, Re, Osiris, *Book of the Dead*
2. **Define:** pharaoh, pyramids, embalming, mummy
3. What did the Egyptians believe happened to a person after death?

Critical Thinking

4. How were pharaohs similar to and different from government leaders in the United States today?

Section 3

The Middle Kingdom

About 2300 B.C., government officials, jealous of the pharaoh's power, took control of Egypt. Almost 200 years of confusion followed. Finally, new pharaohs brought peace and a new period called the Middle Kingdom.

Pharaohs had less power in the Middle Kingdom. After death, they were no longer buried in pyramids but in tombs cut into cliffs. Then the Egyptians began to trade with countries beyond the Nile Valley.

The Middle Kingdom came to an end in 1786 B.C., when Egypt was invaded by the Hyksos (hik' sōs), a people from western Asia. The Hyksos crossed the desert in horse-drawn chariots and used weapons made of bronze and iron. Egyptians had always fought on foot with weapons made of copper and stone and were defeated.

Egyptian Bronze Art

MAKING CONNECTIONS

➤➤ **Religion** Many animals were considered sacred by the Egyptians. Animals associated with gods were kept in temples, where they were pampered. When the animals died, they were mummified like human beings.

L3 **Critical Thinking** Have students locate Egypt on the map of the Middle East in the text Atlas. Ask students how Egypt's location provided opportunities for the exchange of ideas, knowledge, skills, and customs between Africa, Asia, and other civilizations.

VIDEODISC

Use the following to enrich Chapter 4.

WC A 52 9054
A cat mummy.

WH E 6 14250
Agricultural scene from ancient Egyptian tomb painting.

SECTION 2 ANSWERS

1. Old Kingdom, started about 2600 B.C. (p. 69); Narmer, king of Egypt about 3100 B.C. (p. 69); Re, sun god (p. 72); Osiris, god of the harvest (p. 72); *Book of the Dead*, book of magic spells (p. 72)
2. pharaoh, Egyptian king (p. 70); pyramids, tombs for pharaohs (p. 71); embalming, process to preserve bodies (p. 73); mummy, body wrapped with linen (p. 73)
3. Their souls went to the underworld and were weighed on a scale. If the scales balanced, Osiris granted life after death.
4. Answers will vary but could note U.S. leaders and pharaohs provide for citizens, deal with foreign trade, and are respected. Unlike the pharaohs, U.S. leaders are not considered gods.

Assign Chapter 4 **Section 2 Quiz** in the TCR. Testmaker available.

GEOGRAPHY AND HISTORY

The term *Hyksos* is believed to have come from the Egyptian words meaning "Princes from Foreign Uplands." These rulers were most likely desert warriors from the Semitic tribes of nomadic herders in nearby Palestine and Syria.

DID YOU KNOW ??

In order to show her authority and keep her name alive, Hatshepsut wore male clothes and a ceremonial false beard and built a huge temple amid the cliffs at Deir el Bahri.

The Hyksos ruled Egypt for about 150 years. They copied some Egyptian customs but most Egyptians hated them. Around 1550 B.C., an Egyptian prince named Ahmose (ah mo' suh), using Hyksos weapons, led an uprising and drove the Hyksos out of Egypt.

Section 3 Review

1. **Identify:** Middle Kingdom, Hyksos, Ahmose
2. How did the Middle Kingdom come about?
3. How did the Hyksos defeat the Egyptians?
4. What ended the Hyksos's rule?

Critical Thinking

5. Do you think the decrease in the pharaoh's power had a positive or negative effect on Egypt? Why?

Section 4 THE NEW KINGDOM

Ahmose founded another line of pharaohs and began the period known as the New Kingdom. During this time, Egypt became richer and its cities grew larger.

During the New Kingdom, most pharaohs were no longer content to remain within the Nile Valley but marched their armies into lands to the east. It was during this period that the Egyptian empire was founded. One warrior-pharaoh, Thutmose III (thūt mō' suh), with an army of 20,000 archers, spear throwers, and charioteers, extended Egyptian control into Syria (sir' ē uh) and Palestine (pal' uh stīn).

Statue of Hatshepsut

One of the few pharaohs who was not interested in war and conquest was Hatshepsut (hat shep' sūt), Thutmose III's stepmother, who had ruled Egypt before her stepson. Her chief interests were trade and the building of temples. During her rule, Egyptian traders sailed along the coast of east Africa to the land of Punt. In the land of Punt, the Egyptians traded beads and metal tools and weapons for such things as ivory, a black wood called *ebony* (eb' uh nē), monkeys, hunting dogs, leopard skins, and *incense,* or material burned for its pleasant smell. The Egyptians had never seen most of these things. They welcomed the returning traders with a huge reception.

Religion The Egyptians of the New Kingdom began to worship a new god. As the god of the city of Thebes, he had been called Amon. When Thebes became the capital of Egypt,

SECTION 3 ANSWERS

1. Middle Kingdom, period following Old Kingdom in Egyptian history (p. 73); Hyksos, people from western Asia (p. 73); Ahmose, Egyptian prince (p. 74)
2. A new line of pharaohs unified Egypt after a period of confusion.
3. by using horse-drawn chariots and bronze and iron weapons
4. Ahmose led an uprising and drove the Hyksos out of Egypt.
5. Answers will vary, but could include why the pharaoh had either a positive or a negative effect on Egypt.

Assign Chapter 4 **Section 3 Quiz** in the TCR. Testmaker available.

Reading Map Legends

In order to show information on maps, mapmakers use symbols. These are marks that stand for such things as places, directions, and features. Symbols include lines, dots, stars, and small pictures.

A list of symbols and what they stand for is called a **legend.** By reading legends, it is possible to identify empires, nations, religions, climates, and any other information that can be shown on a map.

For example, on the "Ancient Egypt" map below, notice that there are three symbols in the legend. Each symbol stands for the boundary of one of the Egyptian kingdoms. The broken line stands for the southern boundary of the Old Kingdom. The Middle Kingdom's boundary is shown by the dotted line. The area of the New Kingdom is shown in green.

Map Practice

1. **Which Egyptian kingdom included only the first cataract?**
2. **Which kingdom extended to the second cataract?**
3. **In which was Thebes located?**
4. **Of which kingdom was Phoenicia a part?**

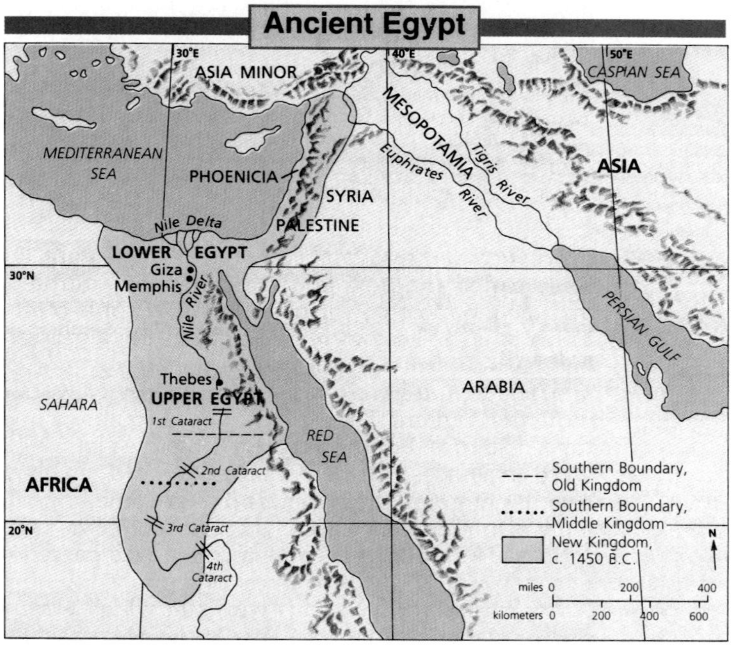

Teaching

MAP SKILLS

Reading Map Legends

Instruct the students to study the map on page 75 to answer the following questions:

What symbol should be added to the legend for cataracts? *(two short parallel lines)*

What symbol should be added to the legend for cities? *(a dot)*

Next, have the students refer to the map of Mesopotamia on page 62 to answer the following questions:

What symbol is used to show Hammurabi's Empire? *(the color brown)*

What symbol is used to show an ancient coastline? *(a dashed line)*

Assign Chapter 4 **Geography and Map Activity** in the TCR.

ANSWERS to Map Practice

1. Old Kingdom
2. Middle Kingdom
3. all three kingdoms
4. New Kingdom

SPOTLIGHT ON: ANCIENT EGYPT

Although Egypt's desert land is often thought of in connection with the camel, this animal was not actually brought to Egypt until 525 B.C. The most common beast of burden in ancient Egypt was the donkey. Lions also prowled the deserts of ancient Egypt, and cats, who were often mummified after they died, were a favorite house pet.

TEACH

GUIDED PRACTICE

L3 **Critical Thinking** Have students write letters to the editor explaining their position on this question: Did religion play a greater role in Egyptian society than it does in our society today? Ask students to respond and support their response with reasons.

CAPTION ANSWER

The temples were built by enslaved persons.

MAKING CONNECTIONS

➤➤ **Language Arts** It was difficult to become a scribe. A student enrolled in school at age 5 and attended classes from sunup to sundown until age 17. Scribes, associated with the ruling class, did not have to work in the fields and were paid more than most Egyptians.

VIDEODISC

Use the following to enrich Chapter 4.

WC A 80 9082
The Great Temple at Karnak.

WC A 55 9057
The Egyptian goddess Isis.

TEMPLE AT KOM OMBO Warring pharaohs of the New Kingdom built large temples to honor their gods. The stone block in front of this temple shows Egyptian hieroglyphs. This temple has many statues and monuments. **Who provided the labor to build temples?**

however, the Egyptians combined Amon with the sun god Re. They called the new god Amon-Re (ah′ muhn rā′). Amon-Re became the most powerful god of all. People built many temples in his honor. These were built, in part, by enslaved persons who had been captured by the warring pharaohs.

The temples were more than houses of worship. They were industrial centers. They gave work to sculptors and artisans who carved statues, built furniture, and made clothes for priests. They were treasuries, filled with copper, gold jewelry, glass bottles, bundles of grain, dried fish, and sweet-smelling oils. The temples were also schools—places where young boys were trained to be scribes. The right to become a scribe was passed on from father to son.

Scribes wrote religious works in which were spells, charms, and prayers. They kept records of the pharaohs' laws and lists of

MULTICULTURAL PERSPECTIVES

The wigs, cosmetics, and jewelry worn by the ancient Egyptians present a vivid image of these people. Generally, both men and women wore simply cut tunics and sheaths of draped, pleated, natural linen. Egyptian men and women's jewelry, wigs, and makeup, however, were elaborate and striking. They wore wigs or hairpieces with curls. Some Egyptians shaved their heads. Bold green (from powdered malachite) and black eye-liners were often worn. Red ocher was applied as lipstick and blusher. Henna colored their hair. Many Egyptians wore large necklaces that covered their chests. Earrings first became popular in the New Kingdom.

the grain and animals paid as taxes. They copied fairy tales and adventure stories and wrote down medical prescriptions.

There were several kinds of Egyptian writing. One was **hieroglyphic** (hī uhr uh glif' ik), or a kind of writing in which pictures stand for words or sounds. The Egyptians carved and painted hieroglyphs, or picture symbols, on their monuments. However, scribes needed an easier form of writing to keep records. So, they developed two other kinds of writing in which hieroglyphs were rounded off and connected.

Decline of Egypt Over time, the priests of Amon-Re gained much power and wealth. They owned one third of Egypt's land and began to play a major role in the government. As time passed, the pharaoh's power declined.

Then, about 1370 B.C., a new pharaoh named Amenhotep IV (ah muhn hō' tep) came to the throne. He did not like the priests. He did not agree with them on what was good for Egypt. He wanted to return power to the pharaohs. Amenhotep IV closed the temples of Amon-Re and fired all temple workers. He set up a new religion that was different from the old religion because only one god was worshiped. This god was called Aton (ah' tuhn). Amenhotep IV changed his name to Akhenaton (ahk nah' tuhn), which means "Spirit of Aton." Only his family and close advisers, however, accepted the new religion.

HIEROGLYPHS Ancient Egyptians viewed hieroglyphs as gifts from the gods. The pictures were first used as a way of keeping records. Later, they represented the sounds of spoken language. Here, hieroglyphs are painted on a coffin lid. **How did hieroglyphs differ from cuneiform?**

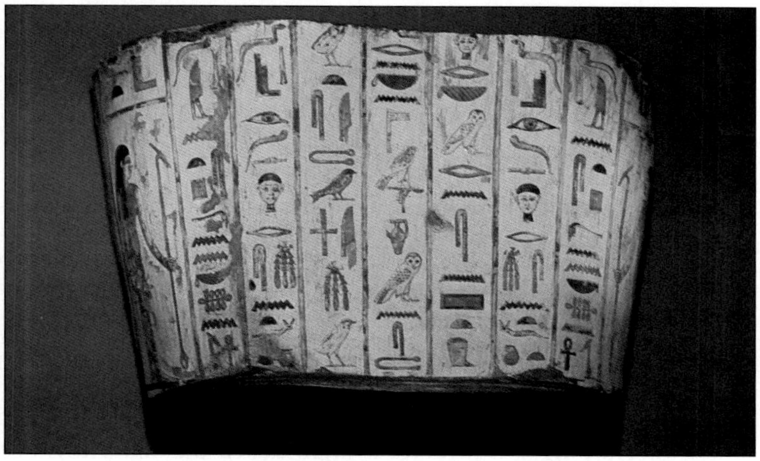

CAPTION ANSWER

Hieroglyphs were picture symbols, while cuneiform was made up of hundreds of markings shaped like wedges.

INDEPENDENT PRACTICE

L1 **Writing** Instruct students to devise a rebus writing system and to write a sample sentence or phrase. Call on volunteers to write their samples and keys on the chalkboard. Discuss similarities and differences in the rebuses used. LEP

L2 **Language Arts** Write the following scenarios on the chalkboard:

1. You are a historian studying the New Kingdom of Egypt before the reign of Amenhotep IV. Describe the main events in the growth of Egyptian civilization.

2. You are a historian studying the New Kingdom of Egypt after the reign of Amenhotep IV. Describe the most important events in the decline of Egyptian civilization.

Tell students to choose one scenario and write the description of events. Have volunteers read their histories to the class.

VIDEODISC

Use the following to enrich Chapter 4.

WH E 24 14268

Egyptian inscription from Book of Dead 13th century B.C.

COOPERATIVE LEARNING

Have the students write and perform a play about one of the people listed in the section. Divide the class into small groups. Have each group be responsible for researching the person chosen. Group members can volunteer for a specific task in the project, such as writing the script, acting, making costumes, finding props, writing and designing programs, and designing sets. At each stage of the project, all students should be given an opportunity to react to the group task. Then have the students present the play to other classes.

Assign Chapter 4 **Cooperative Learning Activity** in the TCR.

LINKING PAST TO PRESENT

Popular interest in ancient Egypt soared with the discovery in 1922 of the sealed tomb of the ruler Tutankhamen. Though "King Tut" was actually a rather minor figure in history, the discovery influenced fashion, jewelry, home decoration, and even popular music. Sensational newspapers warned of a curse on those who had opened the tomb.

The tomb was rare because it was almost untouched by vandals or grave robbers. Magnificent works of art and useful objects, rich with gold and gems were found with the young pharaoh.

The treasures of Tutankhamen, now mostly exhibited in the Egyptian Museum in Cairo, are still visited by thousands of people every year.

DID YOU KNOW ??

Egyptian ink was made from soot, glue, and water.

VIDEODISC

Use the following to enrich Chapter 4.

WC A 58 9060
Hieroglyphics on a mummy cartonnage section.

WC A 51 9053
A mummy mask portrait.

Sculpture of Akhenaton and his wife Nefertiti

After Amenhotep IV died, about 1360 B.C., his son-in-law Tutankhamen (tū tahng kah' muhn) became pharaoh. He was only nine years old. The priests made Tutankhamen return to the old religion. He died after ruling for only nine years.

Little by little, Egypt lost its power. One reason was the struggle between the priests and the pharaohs. Another was the pharaohs' attempts to keep neighboring countries under Egyptian control. Much energy and money was spent on war. Then, too, other peoples of the eastern Mediterranean were using iron weapons. Since Egypt had no iron ore, money was spent to bring in small amounts to make weapons.

By 1150 B.C., Egypt's empire was gone. Egyptian civilization kept growing weaker until Egypt was taken over by a people known as the Assyrians (uh sē' rē uhnz) in 671 B.C.

Section 4 Review

1. **Identify:** New Kingdom, Thutmose III, Hatshepsut, Puntites, Amon-Re, Amenhotep IV, Assyrians
2. **Define:** hieroglyphic
3. Why did Egypt become weak?

Critical Thinking

4. In your opinion, which of the following pharaohs contributed the most to Egyptian civilization during the New Kingdom: Thutmose III, Hatshepsut, Amenhotep IV, Tutankhamen. Explain your choice.

Section 5 CONTRIBUTIONS

The Egyptians made many contributions to other civilizations. One was a paper called **papyrus** (puh pī' ruhs). It was made from a reed also called papyrus. In order to write on papyrus, the Egyptians invented ink. The dry climate of Egypt preserved some writings so well that they can still be read today.

Papyrus had other uses. It was made into baskets and sandals. It was also tied in bundles to make columns for houses. Even rafts and riverboats were made of papyrus.

Other contributions of the Egyptians lay in the field of mathematics. They used a number system based on ten. They also

SECTION 4 ANSWERS

1. New Kingdom, period when Egypt flourished (p. 74); Thutmose III, warrior-pharaoh (p. 74); Hatshepsut, woman pharaoh (p. 74); Amon-Re, most powerful god (p. 76); Amenhotep IV, pharaoh (p. 77); Assyrians, conquerors of Egypt (p. 78)
2. hieroglyphic, a kind of writing in which pictures stand for words or sounds (p. 77)
3. because of the struggle between the priests and the pharaohs; costly attempts to keep neighboring countries under Egyptian control; and because Egypt spent money to obtain iron for weapons
4. Answers will vary, but could note one of the pharaohs and explain how each contributed to the New Kingdom.

Assign Chapter 4 **Section 4 Quiz** in the TCR. Testmaker available.

used fractions and whole numbers. They used geometry to *survey*, or measure, land. When floods washed away the boundary markers that separated one field from the next, the Egyptians surveyed the fields to see where one began and the other ended.

The Egyptians knew the Nile flooded about the same time every year. They used this knowledge to make a calendar. The calendar had three seasons of 120 days each, and 5 special feast days for the gods.

The Egyptians also made contributions in the field of medicine. As dentists, eye doctors, animal doctors, and surgeons, Egyptian doctors were the first specialists in medicine. They were

MEDICAL PRACTICE IN ANCIENT EGYPT Egyptian skill in medicine was highly valued in the Mediterranean area for 2,500 years. Here, an Egyptian doctor gives medicine to a patient. The doctor's assistant holds a scroll listing directions for treating the illness. **What kind of medical help did Egyptian doctors give their patients?**

MAKING CONNECTIONS

➤➤ **Science** There is evidence that as early as 3000 B.C. Egyptians practiced dental hygiene and probably invented the toothbrush. Called a "chew stick" and made from a twig frayed into soft strands at one end, it was rubbed against the teeth with no additional abrasive.

CAPTION ANSWER

Egyptians had dentists, eye doctors, animal doctors, and surgeons. Their physicians were the first to use splints, bandages, and compresses. They also treated such problems as indigestion and hair loss.

VIDEODISC

Use the following to enrich Chapter 4.

WH E 26 14270

Engraving from an Egyptian stele showing woman doctor.

MEETING SPECIAL NEEDS

If possible obtain a copy of the book *Ancient Lives: Daily Life in Egypt of the Pharaohs* by John Romer. (See Chapter Resources listed in the Chapter Planning Guide.) Gather students who are auditory learners and read excerpts from the book to help the students understand the social customs and daily life of Egyptians. Involve students in a discussion about how their way of life compares to the lives of ancient Egyptians.

ASSESS

CHECK FOR UNDERSTANDING

Ask students to summarize the main points of the chapter, orally or in writing. Discuss the answers to the Section and Chapter Reviews.

EVALUATE

Assign Chapter 4 **Performance Assessment Activity** in the TCR.

Administer **Chapter 4 Test** found in the TCR. Testmaker available.

RETEACH

For each section, have students write a sentence that summarizes the main concept. Call on volunteers to read their sentences. Have the class choose the best summary sentences for each section.

Assign Chapter 4 **Reteaching Activity** in the TCR.

ENRICH

Have students research one of the people mentioned in the chapter and write a biographical sketch about them.

Assign Chapter 4 **Enrichment Activity** in the TCR.

CLOSE

Have students discuss the following question: Which contribution of the Egyptians to other civilizations was the most important? Why?

MEETING CHAPTER OBJECTIVES

Each objective is tested by the Chapter Review questions in parentheses.

1. **Analyze** why the Nile River was so important to Egyptians. (CU 2; CT 1)
2. **Discuss** pharaohs, pyramids, and religion of Egypt's Old Kingdom. (BV; CU 3, 6)
3. **Describe** Egypt's Middle Kingdom. (CU 4, 5)
4. **Explain** Egyptian civilization during New Kingdom. (BV; CU 6; CT 3)
5. **Summarize** Egyptian contributions. (BV; CU 7, 8)

the first to use splints, bandages, and compresses. They were masters at sewing up cuts and at setting broken bones. The Egyptians also treated such problems as indigestion and hair loss. For indigestion, they used castor oil. For hair loss, they used a mixture of dog toes, dates, and a donkey hoof.

Section 5 Review

1. **Define:** papyrus
2. How did the Egyptians make papyrus?
3. What mathematical contributions did the Egyptians make to other civilizations?
4. What medical contributions did the Egyptians make to other civilizations?

Critical Thinking

5. Which Egyptian contribution do you think has had the greatest impact on life in the United States today?

Chapter Summary

1. Egyptian civilization began in the Nile River valley over 5,000 years ago.
2. About 3100 B.C., Narmer united Upper and Lower Egypt.
3. The Old Kingdom began about 2600 B.C. and lasted for nearly 650 years.
4. Kings of Egypt became known as pharaohs and were viewed by Egyptians as rulers, priests, and gods.
5. During the Old Kingdom, pyramids were built as tombs for pharaohs.
6. The Egyptians worshiped many gods.
7. The Egyptians placed great importance on life after death and created a process to preserve bodies as mummies.
8. The Middle Kingdom began about 1950 B.C. and lasted until the Hyksos invasion of Egypt in 1786 B.C.
9. The New Kingdom began after Ahmose, an Egyptian prince, drove the Hyksos out of Egypt about 1550 B.C.
10. During the New Kingdom, most pharaohs were interested in war and conquest.
11. During the New Kingdom, the priests of Amon-Re became very powerful.
12. Amenhotep IV, or Akhenaton, tried to establish a new religion based on one god in Egypt about 1370 B.C., but he did not succeed.
13. Toward the end of the New Kingdom, Egypt began to decline.
14. The Egyptians made several contributions to later civilizations, including surveying, certain medical treatments, and a paper known as papyrus.

SECTION 5 ANSWERS

1. papyrus, Egyptian paper (p. 78)
2. They cut the stems of the papyrus reed into thin strips that were pressed together to make a sheet and then pasted the sheets together to make a roll.
3. They used a number system based on 10, fractions and whole numbers, and geometry to survey the land.
4. They were the first to use splints, bandages, compresses, setting of broken bones, and treatment of indigestion and hair loss.
5. Answers will vary but could include the mention of any modern conveniences that were made possible by Egyptian ingenuity.

Assign Chapter 4 **Section 5 Quiz** in the TCR. Testmaker available.

CHAPTER 4

Review

Building Vocabulary

Use the following to write a newspaper article describing the contributions of the Egyptians.

shadoof
pharaoh
pyramids
embalming
mummy
hieroglyphic
papyrus

Check for Understanding

1. What did the Egyptians borrow from the Sumerians?
2. What did the Nile River give to the Egyptian people?
3. Why did the Egyptians show such great respect for a pharaoh?
4. How did the Middle Kingdom differ from the Old Kingdom?
5. What role did the Hyksos play in the development of Egyptian civilization?
6. What role did religion play in Egypt during the Old Kingdom? During the New Kingdom?
7. What kinds of writing did Egyptians have, and for what were they used?
8. How did Egyptians use the papyrus reed?

Critical Thinking

1. Why do you think some experts call Egypt "the gift of the Nile"? Do you think that is a good name? Explain.
2. How did the government of Egypt resemble that of Babylonia? In what ways was it different?
3. Do you think Akhenaton was wise to oppose the priests of Amon-Re? Give reasons for your opinion.
4. Would you have liked living in ancient Egypt? Why or why not?

Geography in History

HUMAN/ENVIRONMENTAL INTERACTION Note the area covered by ancient Egypt on the map on page 75. Why do you think the empire developed where it did rather than expanding more to the west or only to the south?

Using Your Journal

Compare the effect of government on the lives of Egyptians with the effect of government on your daily life. Write a few short paragraphs explaining elements that are similar and those that are different.

81

CHAPTER 4 REVIEW ANSWERS

BUILDING VOCABULARY

Newspaper articles will vary but should use the vocabulary words listed.

CHECK FOR UNDERSTANDING

1. farming, seeds for wheat and barley, and writing
2. water and rich soil
3. because the pharaoh was a ruler, priest, and god
4. The pharaohs had less power and the Egyptians began to trade with other countries.
5. They introduced iron and bronze weapons and a new style of fighting.
6. During both the Old and New kingdoms religious rituals were carried out by the pharaoh and brought unity. Religion during Akhenaton's rule divided the people.
7. Hieroglyphic writing used on monuments; other writing to write religious works and records.
8. for paper, baskets, sandals, columns for houses, rafts, and riverboats

CRITICAL THINKING

1. Answers will vary, but note that Egypt needed the Nile .
2. The ruler of Egypt was a god-king, while the Babylonian ruler was not.
3. Answers will vary, but could say that this helped the decline of Egypt.
4. Answers will vary, but students should give explanations.

+ BONUS +

TEST QUESTION

For Chapter 4 Test

The Old Kingdom began about 2600 B.C., the Middle Kingdom about 2060 B.C., and the New Kingdom about 1600 B.C. If the New Kingdom ended about 1500 years after the Old Kingdom began, in what year did it end? *(1100 B.C.)*

USING YOUR JOURNAL

Journal entries will vary, but students should compare the effects of Egyptian government on the lives of Egyptians with the effect of government on their own daily lives.

GEOGRAPHY IN HISTORY

Answers will vary, but should include reliance on the Nile River and Mediterranean; proximity to people; and natural barriers.

CHAPTER 5

Eastern River Valleys

CHAPTER ORGANIZER

Objectives	Special Features	Supplemental Materials
Section 1 The Indus River Valley Discuss how the Indus River valley civilization developed. Summarize what has been learned from the ruins of the ancient cities of Harappa and Mohenjo-daro.		• Reproducible Lesson Plan • Section 1 Quiz • Testmaker • Chapter 5 Vocabulary and Guided Reading Activity • World History and Art Transparency 3 • Chapter 5 Teaching Transparency and Activity • The World History Videodisc • Chapter 5 Activity Book Activity
Section 2 The Huang Ho Valley Explain how religion influenced the Shang dynasty. Analyze why the Shang dynasty declined.		• Reproducible Lesson Plan • Section 2 Quiz • Testmaker • Chapter 5 Geography and Map Activity • Chapter 5 Teaching Transparency and Activity • Chapter 5 Cooperative Learning Activity • Chapter 5 Chart and Graph Skill Activity • Unit 2 World Literature • Unit 2 Primary Source Reading • The World History Videodisc
Chapter 5 Review and Evaluation		• Chapter 5 Reteaching Activity • Chapter 5 Enrichment Activity • Chapter 5 Performance Assessment Activity • Spanish Summary and Glossary • Chapter 5 Test • Testmaker • Audiocassettes (English and Spanish)

If time does not permit teaching the entire chapter, use the Chapter 5 Summary on page 92 and the Chapter 5 Audiocassettes (English and Spanish) to point out the main ideas of the chapter.

✓ Performance Assessment Activities

Daily Life Organize students into groups of four. Suggest that students imagine that they are living during the time of the Shang dynasty. Have students in each group choose one of the following roles: a Shang ruler, a noble, a farmer, and a married women. Have the group members each describe their daily lives in each role. Then ask students to make a chart comparing each person's way of life.

Models and Dioramas Have students work together in small groups to create a diagram, model, or diorama of a community in one of the civilizations discussed in the chapter. Display the students' work in the classroom.

CHAPTER RESOURCES

LITERATURE ABOUT THE PERIOD

Chang, Richard F. *Chinese Mythical Stories*. Yale Far Eastern Publications, 1990. Legends and myths of China.

READINGS FOR THE STUDENT

Munro, Eleanor C. *Through the Vermilion Gates: A Journey into China's Past.* Pantheon Books, 1971. An art historian's look at Chinese thought and art, focusing on the Tang Dynasty but tracing earlier roots.

National Geographic Society (Special Publications Division). *Mysteries of the Ancient World.* National Geographic Society, 1979. A collection of articles with photographs of ancient sites, including Harappa and Mohenjo-daro.

Oliphant, Margaret. *Atlas of the Ancient World.* Simon and Schuster, 1992. Survey of the ancient world cultures including those of India and China.

READINGS FOR THE TEACHER

Basham, A.L. *The Wonder That Was India.* Taplinger, 1967. A survey of the history and culture of ancient India.

Blunden, Caroline and Mark Elvin. *Cultural Atlas of China.* Facts on File, 1983. Surveys China's geography, history, and culture through maps and texts.

MULTIMEDIA RESOURCES

Ancient Civilizations Keyword. Focus Media. Software. Reinforces knowledge of the prehistoric era and Egypt, Asia, India, the Middle East, and the Americas during ancient times.

China: The Beginnings. International Film Foundation. Film. Discusses the history and culture of China from ancient times to the 1100s.

India, Early Civilization. Coronet Films. Film. Surveys civilization in ancient India.

Rivers and Ancient Cultures. Computer Software Associates. Software. Simulates early civilizations and the rivers near where they flourished.

CHAPTER 5 OVERVIEW

Chapter 5 focuses on the development of the Harappan and Shang civilizations in the eastern river valleys of South Asia and China.

➤ **Section 1** describes the Harappan civilization in the Indus River valley.

➤ **Section 2** explains the development of the Shang civilization in the Huang Ho Valley.

CHAPTER OBJECTIVES

After reading Chapter 5, students will be able to:

1. discuss how the Indus River valley civilization developed.

2. summarize what has been learned from the ruins of the ancient cities of Harappa and Mohenjo-daro.

3. explain how religion influenced the Shang dynasty.

4. analyze why the Shang dynasty declined.

EXAMINING THE ARTIFACT

Remind students that the earliest civilizations made serviceable objects such as cups, bowls, and pitchers. Ask students what purpose they think these pieces of Etruscan pottery served. What can they learn about the Etruscans from the pottery's decorations?

PERFORMANCE ASSESSMENT ✓

Use the Performance Assessment activities on page 82B to help you evaluate students as they complete the chapter.

CHAPTER 5 Eastern River Valleys

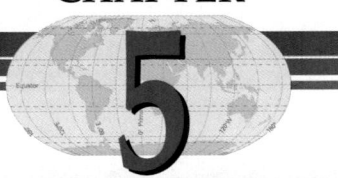

Ancient Indus River Valley Pottery

82

TEACHER CLASSROOM RESOURCES

- 📁 Primary Source Reading
- 📁 Reproducible Lesson Plan
- 📁 Section Quizzes/Chapter Test
- 📁 Reteaching Activity
- 📁 Enrichment Activity
- 📁 Chart and Graph Skill Activity
- 📁 Geography and Map Activity
- 📁 Vocabulary and Guided Reading Activity

- 📁 Cooperative Learning Activity
- 📁 Performance Assessment Activity
- 🖨 Teaching Transparencies and Activities
- 📁 Spanish Summary and Glossary
- 💿 Testmaker
- 💿 The World History Videodisc
- 🎧 Audiocassettes (English and Spanish)

Chapter Focus

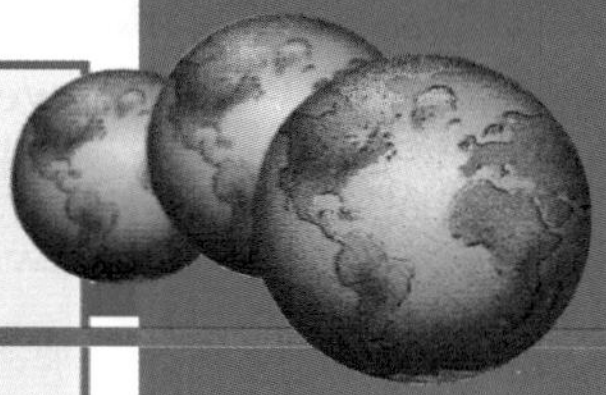

READ TO DISCOVER:

- How the Indus River valley civilization developed.
- What has been learned from the ruins of Harappa and Mohenjo-daro.
- How religion influenced the Shang dynasty.
- Why the Shang dynasty declined.

In 3500 B.C., civilization began in Sumer. Some 400 years later, it began in Egypt. Several hundred years after that, river valley civilizations began in the East. By 2500 B.C., cities started to appear in the Indus River valley of South Asia. By 2000 B.C., they were being established in the Huang Ho (Yellow River) valley of China.

More isolated than the people of Mesopotamia or Egypt, the people of eastern river valley civilizations were cut off from other parts of the world by high mountains, broad deserts, and large bodies of water. As a result, they became *self-sufficient*, or able to take care of all of their own needs. Compared to the Sumerians and the Egyptians, they did little trading with other groups of people.

Less is known about life in eastern river valley civilizations than is known about Sumerian or Egyptian life. This is because very few remains have been found. Much of what is known about ancient eastern peoples comes from legend. Until more records are found, their early life will remain in part a mystery.

2500 B.C.–1000 B.C.

KEY TERMS

- planned communities
- citadel
- dynasty
- spirits
- ancestors
- oracle bones
- nobles

Section 1

THE INDUS RIVER VALLEY

The Indus River flows through the countries known today as Pakistan and India. About 2500 B.C., a group of people called Harappans (huh rap′ uhnz) settled in the valley of the Indus River. Although others had lived there before, the Harappans

FOCUS

BELLRINGER

Write on the chalkboard: *How do you think mountains affected the lives of people in early civilizations?* Have students write a brief answer.

MOTIVATIONAL ACTIVITY

Have students read their thoughts about how mountains have affected civilizations. Then tell students that the early Indus River and Huang Ho valley civilizations were isolated from other civilizations by natural barriers such as high mountains. Ask students how isolation might affect a civilization. *(It forced them to take care of all their needs. They were unable to exchange ideas or knowledge with other people.)*

VOCABULARY PRE-CHECK

Write the key terms for this chapter on the chalkboard. Ask students to use those that they know in sentences.

Assign Chapter 5 **Vocabulary and Guided Reading Activity** in the TCR.

EXTRA CREDIT PROJECT

Interested students may want to find out more about what the diet of the Shang was like. Ask them to research the grains grown *(millet, wheat, rice)* and how they were grown and how they were prepared. Encourage them to then find or develop a recipe for each grain they research to share with the class.

KEY TO ABILITY LEVELS

Teaching strategies have been coded for varying learning styles and abilities.

L1 Level 1 activities are **basic** activities and should be within the ability range of all students.

L2 Level 2 activities are **average** activities and should be within the ability range of the average to above-average student.

L3 Level 3 activities are **challenging** activities designed for the ability range of above-average students.

LEP LEP activities should be within the ability range of Limited English Proficiency students.

GEOGRAPHY AND HISTORY

The sites of Harappa and Mohenjo-daro are located in present-day Pakistan. As civilizations collapsed in Harappa and Mohenjo-daro, some scholars believe that many people fled southward from the Indus Valley to the tip of the Indian Peninsula. Known there as Dravidians, they re-established their culture, which has remained distinct from the rest of India. Connections between Tamil—a Dravidian language currently spoken in Sri Lanka—and the scattered samples of Harappan writing that are found on Harappan seals have been made.

L1 **Critical Thinking** Ask students to give possible reasons why most Harappan gods were female. LEP

VIDEODISC

Use the following to enrich Chapter 5.

WH U 2 34608

Terra cotta toy cow, with movable head, from Mohenjodaro.

the Great Bath stood a huge granary. Traders from other areas who stopped at Mohenjo-daro most likely left their goods there.

Harappa also had a series of huge granaries. The floor of each granary was supported on low walls. In the walls were air holes that allowed air to move around in the granary. This kept the grain dry and prevented it from spoiling. Nearby were circular brick platforms. Each had a scooped-out area in the center where grain could be pounded.

Decline of the Harappans No one knows for certain how Harappan civilization came to an end. One reason may have been that the Harappans used up their natural resources. For example, the Harappan farmers may have tried to raise more and more crops on the same plots. This would have robbed the soil of nutrients needed to make it fertile enough to produce well. Without good harvests, there would not have been enough food to feed everyone, especially if the Harappan population was increasing.

Another reason may have been that the Harappans cut down too many trees to fuel their ovens. Without tree cover, floods would have swept away the soil and forced people to leave their cities and farming villages. It is known that parts of Mohenjo-daro had to be rebuilt several times because of floods. At first, the city was rebuilt carefully. As time went on, however, new buildings were not made as well, and older ones were patched up. Then, too, the Harappans may have gotten tired of rebuilding and decided to move somewhere else.

A third reason may have been that the Indus River valley was invaded and all the Harappans were killed. Unburied skeletons of groups of men, women, and children have been found in the streets of Mohenjo-daro's ruins. Every skeleton showed some kind of injury.

Sculpture of Harappan Priest-King

All that is certain is that Harappan civilization began to change about 1700 B.C. Not only were homes no longer built as well, but pottery was no longer made as carefully. By 1200 B.C., a group of people called Aryans (ār′ ē uhnz) had taken over the Indus River valley. Harappan civilization ceased to be.

Evidence of a Lost Civilization Very little is known about the Harappan people and their civilization. As yet, no one has been able to read Harappan writing. There is no record of the civilization's political history. No royal tombs have been discovered. All that is known about Harappan religion is that there was more than one god, and most Harappan gods were female.

Much of what is known comes from the ruins of Harappa and Mohenjo-daro. There, archaeologists have found jewelry made of gold and a blue stone called lapis lazuli (lap′ uhs laz′ uh lē), as

EXTENDING THE CONTENT

The Aryans were an Indo-European group who seem to have migrated to the south and east from southern Russia. Nomadic herdsmen, they had horse-driven chariots, bronze axes, and bows and arrows. Their distinctive language persisted wherever they conquered. Indo-European is the language family name given to the Aryans' language—an ancestor to almost every European language. The Aryans had no artistic tradition and no written language, but they had a rich oral tradition of songs, proverbs, hymns, and rituals. These were later collected as the four religious books called the Vedas.

HARAPPAN SEAL This Harappan seal is 1 inch, or 2.5 centimeters, square. It shows a bull facing an incense burner. In eastern civilizations, the bull was a symbol of strength. The seal also shows Harappan writing. **What is unusual about Harappan writing?**

well as tools and weapons of stone, copper, and bronze. They have also found clay models of animals, rattles, dice, and toy carts with movable wheels.

One of the most important finds was a series of tiny seals made of soapstone. An animal and a line of writing were carved on each seal. The animals included tigers, elephants, rhinoceri, and crocodiles. This suggests that at one time much of the area was jungle. Most of the seals had a small hole in them and could be worn as necklaces or bracelets. The seals may have stated the names, titles, or trades of a person, family, or business. Experts believe the seals were used to stamp the wet clay that sealed packages of goods. Some Harappan seals have been found as far away as Sumer.

Section 1 Review

1. **Identify:** Indus River, Harappans, Harappa, Mohenjo-daro, Great Bath, Aryans
2. **Define:** planned communities, citadel
3. How did the Indus River influence the Harappans?
4. What were some of the outstanding features of Harappa and Mohenjo-daro?

Critical Thinking

5. What do you think archaeologists would learn about the Harappans if they could read Harappan writing?

CAPTION ANSWER

No one has been able to decipher Harappan writing.

DID YOU KNOW ??

Soapstone is a soft stone composed mainly of talc and chlorite that has a soapy feel.

LINKING PAST TO PRESENT

Some Harappan seals had as their central figure the god Shiva, who later became a principal Hindu god.

INDEPENDENT PRACTICE

L1 **History** Have students research the excavation of Harappa or Mohenjo-daro and write a one-page journal entry from the viewpoint of an archaeologist at the site.

SECTION 1 ANSWERS

1. Indus River, flows through India and Pakistan (p. 83); Harappans, civilization in the Indus River valley (p. 83); Harappa, one capital of Harappans (p. 85); Mohenjo-daro, one capital of Harappans (p. 85); Great Bath, bath in Mohenjo-daro (p. 85); Aryans, people in Indus River valley by 1200 B.C. (p. 86)
2. planned communities, cities built by design (p. 85); citadel, fortress (p. 85)
3. in the building of dikes and dams, cities, houses, and public buildings; and in farming and irrigation
4. planned street grids, a sanitation system, citadels, and huge granaries; Mohenjo-daro also had a Great Bath
5. Answers will vary, but students might suggest that archaeologists would learn about the daily life of the Harappans.

Assign Chapter 5 **Section 1 Quiz** in the TCR. Testmaker available.

MAKING CONNECTIONS

➤➤ **Legends** Over the centuries the Chinese have developed many myths and legends. One myth tells how the universe was created from the body of a giant named Pan Gu, who hatched from an egg. Other legends celebrate the deeds of hero-kings including Yao, a person in the form of a mountain and Shun, the master of elephants.

CAPTION ANSWER

Legends are important to historians studying early China because there are no records of China's beginnings, and no remains have been found.

VIDEODISC

Use the following to enrich Chapter 5.

WH P 8 30409

Pan Gu (P'an-ku), from Chinese mythology.

WH P 13 30414

Yu (Yü) the Great, legendary founder of Xia dynasty.

Section 2

THE HUANG HO VALLEY

About 2000 B.C., or 500 years after the Harappans settled in the Indus River valley, a civilization developed in the Huang Ho valley of northern China. There are no records of its beginnings, and no remains have been found. For this reason, much of what happened comes from legend.

According to Chinese legend, a man-god named Yü the Great drove out the serpents and dragons that lived along the Huang Ho. He drained the land so that people could live there and grow crops. Yü founded a kingdom called Xia (shē′ ah) and united most of northern China under his rule.

Many experts believe that the early settlers of China chose the Huang Ho valley for their home because it was fertile. The river flooded every year, bringing rich soil with it.

The valley was cut off from other civilizations. The people there developed their culture without borrowing from other civilizations. By 1800 B.C., there were villages and farms all along the river. The people farmed the land and used the river for travel and trade. They made clay ovens, cupboards, benches, and pottery. They built small round clay houses with thatched roofs.

Cities of the Shang

The first records of Chinese civilization come from a **dynasty** (dī′ nuh stē), or ruling family, called Shang. The Shang came to power in 1766 B.C. They built the first Chinese

THE WISE MAN FU HSI Chinese legends tell the stories of Yü and another man-god, Fu Hsi. Here, Fu Hsi points to eight geometric designs used to tell the future. **Why are legends important to historians studying early China?**

EXTENDING THE CONTENT

China's Huang Ho—formerly the Yellow River—took its name from the great amounts of yellow-brown silt, or loess, that it carries downstream. Through the years the river has been given other names. Its frequent disastrous floods have led people to call it "China's Sorrow," while the rich soil it deposits in the river valley has made it known as "China's Joy." The river flows about 3,000 miles eastward to empty into the Yellow Sea. It begins in the mountains of western China and makes a large loop northward in the middle of its course. The river's course has changed many times, creating the broad, fertile North China Plain.

Shang China

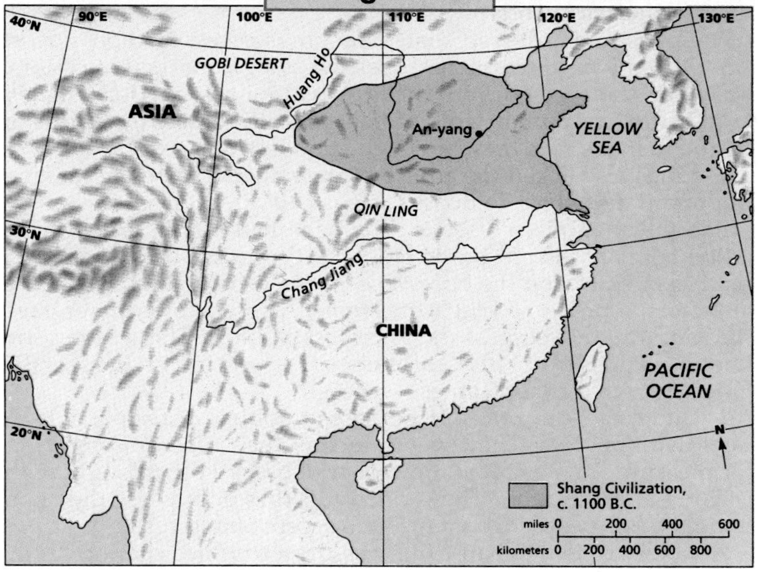

cities. Most were designed in the same way. At the center stood a palace and a temple. Public buildings and the homes of high government officials were built around the palace. Within an outer district were workshops, burial grounds, and the homes of the workers.

Most of the Shang people, however, did not live in the city. The city was the home of the rich, the learned, and the skilled. Poorer people lived in the countryside. They were farmers, who grew such grains as millet, wheat, and rice and raised cattle, sheep, and chickens. The farmers also produced silk, which was used to make clothes for the very rich. The Chinese produced silk hundreds of years before anyone else.

Spirits, Ancestors, and Kings The Shang worshiped **spirits,** or supernatural beings, which they believed lived in mountains, rivers, and seas. The people believed they had to please the spirits. If the spirits became angry or unhappy, the people might suffer a poor harvest or lose a battle.

The Shang believed that **ancestors,** or those from whom one is descended, also influenced people's fortunes. So, they offered their ancestors food, wine, and special prayers. They hoped their ancestors would help them in time of need and bring them good fortune. Because of this respect for ancestors, family ties were very important to the Shang. They had rules about how family members should act toward one another. Children were taught to

MAP STUDY

MOVEMENT The landforms of China contributed to the early isolation of the Chinese. **What geographical features would have discouraged the Shang people from movement to other lands or their contact with other people?**

MAP STUDY Answers

The geographical features that would have stopped the Shang people from movement to other lands include the mountains to the west, the Gobi, the Yellow Sea, and the Pacific Ocean.

DID YOU KNOW ??

The buildings of the Shang people faced south to get as much sun as possible during the cold winter months.

VIDEODISC

Use the following to enrich Chapter 5.

WH P 20 30421

Excavation of site of "legendary" Xia capital, Yangcheng.

WH P 27 30428

A Shang bronze with an animal motif.

MEETING SPECIAL NEEDS

Encourage students who are tactile/kinesthetic learners to prepare a bulletin board depicting the early history of China. Have the students discuss what should be included in the display. Some suggestions are maps showing what crops were grown, drawings of artifacts, and illustrations of the layout of an excavated city. Assign small groups to research and prepare each topic with individuals assuming responsibility for a specific task. Have the class design the bulletin-board display and assemble it.

MAKING CONNECTIONS

➤➤ **Language Arts** The Chinese writing system helped to hold the Chinese people together through the centuries. Although spoken language changed from place to place, the written language stayed the same.

DID YOU KNOW

The Shang oracle bones carry between 2,500 and 3,000 different syllabic characters. In order to write in Chinese, a writer had to memorize each character. Because it was so difficult to master all the characters, only a few people in ancient China could read and write.

CAPTION ANSWER

They used oracle bones before making important decisions.

VIDEODISC

Use the following to enrich Chapter 5.

WH P 24 30425

Shang oracle bone inscription of an eclipse and a nova.

obey their parents and to honor older people. Wives were trained to obey their husbands.

The Shang believed that their kings received their power from the spirits of nature and their wisdom from their ancestors. For this reason, religion and government were tied closely together. An important duty of kings was to contact the spirits of nature to make sure they provided enough water for farming.

Kings also asked the advice of their ancestors before making important decisions. To do this, kings had questions scratched on a flat, polished piece of bone. The bone had a hole drilled in it, and a hot bar was put in the hole. Heat from the bar produced a pattern of cracks on the bone. The cracks were believed to be the ancestors' replies to a king's questions. A special interpreter gave the king the meaning of the ancestors' replies. These bones are known as **oracle** (ōr′ uh kuhl) **bones.** The writing on them is the oldest known form of Chinese writing.

Under the king was a large class of **nobles,** or people of high rank in a kingdom. They spent much of their time hunting, both for pleasure and as preparation for war. Nobles often fought with each other about land. They joined together only when they had to fight other people who refused to accept Shang rule.

Nobles rode into battle in horse-drawn bronze chariots. They wore bronze helmets and armor made of buffalo or rhinoceros hide. They were skilled in the use of the bow and arrow. Their

ORACLE BONES Shang rulers tried to learn the future by using oracle bones. Here, a turtle shell used for this purpose shows an early form of Chinese writing. **When did Shang rulers use oracle bones?**

EXTENDING THE CONTENT

In addition to producing fine bronze objects, the people of the Shang dynasty carved beautiful ivory and jade statues. They wove silk into elegantly colored cloth for the upper class and fashioned pottery from kaolin, a fine white clay.

SHANG BRONZES Bronze artwork from the Shang dynasty is considered some of the finest in history. This mask (left) and vessel (right) show the high quality of Shang art. **For what other purposes did the Shang use items of bronze?**

arrows had sharp points of bone or bronze. Soldiers marched on foot behind nobles' chariots. These soldiers generally were poor peasants whom the nobles had forced to leave their farms and join the army.

Decline of the Shang There was a great gap between rich and poor during the rule of the Shang. Rich Shang lived in the cities in wooden houses. They owned bronze weapons and ornaments and wore linen, wool, fur, and silk clothes. Poor Shang lived in the countryside and worked with wooden or stone tools. Their houses were thatched or mud huts or caves scooped out of the ground. Neither group felt any loyalty toward the other.

Many experts believe that this gap between rich and poor weakened the Shang civilization. In 1122 B.C., a people known as Zhou (jō) invaded the Shang kingdom. The Shang were not united enough to hold off the invaders, and their civilization came to an end.

CAPTION ANSWER

The Shang used bronze to make chariots, helmets, arrow points, sculptures, cups, vases, and other religious items.

L1 **Daily Life** Ask students to imagine themselves as a king, noble, soldier, or farmer during the Shang dynasty in ancient China. Have students write a diary entry describing a day in the life of the person they have chosen. Call on volunteers to read their diary entries to the class.

L3 **Critical Thinking** Have students research the decline of the Shang dynasty. Then ask students to brainstorm changes the Shang could have made that might have helped them prevent the decline of their civilization.

ASSESS

CHECK FOR UNDERSTANDING

Ask students to summarize the main points of the chapter, orally or in writing. Discuss the answers to the Section and Chapter Review questions.

EVALUATE

Assign Chapter 5 **Performance Assessment Activity** in the TCR.

Administer **Chapter 5 Test** in the TCR. Testmaker available.

MULTICULTURAL PERSPECTIVES

The people of the Chinese dynasties believed that their rulers governed according to a principle known as a Mandate from Heaven. If rulers were just and effective, they received a mandate. If rulers did not govern properly—as indicated by poor crops or losses in battle—they lost the mandate to someone else who then started a new dynasty. This principle started with the Zhou dynasty.

RETEACH

Have students survey the chapter and make a list of questions to test their knowledge of the chapter. Working in pairs, students can quiz each other.

Assign Chapter 5 **Reteaching Activity** in the TCR.

ENRICH

Ask students to bring to class illustrations of bronze objects made by the Shang and other dynasties. Allow students to discuss and list similarities and differences in the art.

Assign Chapter 5 **Enrichment Activity** in the TCR.

CLOSE

Have students write a paragraph describing the features of the Harappan civilization or the Shang dynasty that made them attractive to invaders.

MEETING CHAPTER OBJECTIVES

Each objective is tested by the Chapter Review questions in parentheses.

1. **Discuss** the Indus River valley civilization. (BV; CT 1; UYJ; GIH)
2. **Summarize** what has been learned from ruins of Harappa and Mohenjo-daro. (BV; CU 4; UYJ)
3. **Explain** how religion influenced the Shang dynasty. (BV; CU 5)
4. **Analyze** why the Shang dynasty declined. (BV; CU 7; CT 2, 3)

The Shang left behind a great gift to the world in their works of bronze. These include sculptures, cups, vases, fancy vessels, and other items used for religious purposes. Art experts believe these are the finest works of bronze ever made.

Section 2 Review

1. **Identify:** Huang Ho valley, Yü the Great, Shang, Zhou
2. **Define:** dynasty, spirits, ancestors, oracle bones, nobles
3. How did the Shang people feel about nature spirits? About their ancestors?
4. What may have been one reason for the decline of the Shang civilization?

Critical Thinking

5. If world leaders today could use oracle bones, what questions might they want answered before making decisions?

Chapter Summary

1. Eastern river valley civilizations began in the Indus River valley about 2500 B.C. and began in the Huang Ho valley about 2000 B.C.
2. The first people to establish a civilization in the Indus River valley were called Harappans.
3. Like other river valley peoples, the Harappans learned to control the river.
4. The Harappans are believed to have been the first people to produce cotton cloth, bake bricks in ovens, and build sanitation systems.
5. The Harappan cities of Harappa and Mohenjo-daro are the oldest known planned communities.
6. No one knows for certain how Harappan civilization came to an end, but about 1200 B.C., Aryans moved into and took over the Indus River valley.
7. The legendary kingdom of Xia probably came into being in China about 2000 B.C.
8. The first recorded Chinese dynasty, the Shang, came to power in 1766 B.C.
9. The Shang believed that their lives were influenced by spirits and ancestors.
10. The oldest known form of Chinese writing is found on Shang oracle bones.
11. The Shang produced many fine works of art made from bronze.
12. Shang civilization ended with the Zhou invasion in 1122 B.C.

SECTION 2 ANSWERS

1. Huang Ho Valley, valley in northern China (p. 88); Yü the Great, a Chinese man-god (p. 88); Shang, first recorded Chinese civilization (p. 88); Zhou, invaders of Shang dynasty (p. 91)
2. dynasty, ruling family in China (p. 88); spirits, supernatural beings (p. 89); ancestors, those from whom one is descended (p. 89); oracle bones, bones to receive messages from ancestors (p. 90); nobles, people of high rank (p. 90)
3. They had to please the spirits to have good harvests and win battles. Their ancestors influenced people's fortunes, so they were offered food, wine, and special prayers.
4. the distance between the rich and poor
5. Answers will vary but should include questions about current affairs.

Assign Chapter 5 **Section 2 Quiz** in the TCR. Testmaker available.

CHAPTER 5 Review

Building Vocabulary

Imagine you are preparing a feature film about the civilizations in the Indus River and Huang Ho valleys. Use the following words in a brief summary you write describing the facts about this area you want to present in your film.

planned communities
citadel
dynasty
spirits
ancestors
oracle bones
nobles

Check for Understanding

1. Why is so little known about the early life of people in the Indus River and Huang Ho valleys?
2. Why were Harappa and Mohenjo-daro healthy places in which to live?
3. What are three possible reasons for the decline of the Harappans?
4. What evidence suggests there was trade between Harappa and Sumer?
5. Why were family ties important to the Shang people?
6. How did kings of the Shang use oracle bones?
7. Why was the gap between rich and poor a disadvantage to the Shang?
8. What cultural contribution did the Shang leave to the world?

Critical Thinking

1. Why did people of eastern river valleys develop their ways of life without borrowing from other civilizations?
2. What do you think may happen to a civilization if it uses up its natural resources? Why?
3. What may happen to a civilization if different classes are not loyal to each other?
4. Ancestors were important to the Shang people. Do you think ancestors are important to people today? Explain your answer.

Geography in History

PLACE Refer to the map on page 84 of early India. Note the location of the Indus civilizations and the geographic features that may have affected its development. Describe what other area of this region that is a likely place for other civilizations to develop. Explain why.

Using Your Journal

Compare the details you have noted about planned communities in Harappa and Mohenjo-daro with details about your own community. Create a chart illustrating the ways in which your community is similar and different.

CHAPTER 5 REVIEW ANSWERS

BUILDING VOCABULARY

Summaries will vary. Students should use the words and terms to prepare a summary of a feature film about the civilizations in the Indus River and Huang Ho valleys.

CHECK FOR UNDERSTANDING

1. because very few remains have been found
2. because they had sanitation systems
3. They may have used up their natural resources, or may have been invaded and killed.
4. Some Harappan seals have been found in Sumer.
5. because they respected their ancestors and believed they would bring them good fortune
6. Questions were scratched on bone. Cracks on the bone were believed to be the ancestors' replies.
7. because it prevented them from uniting to hold off invaders
8. works of bronze

CRITICAL THINKING

1. because they were cut off from other parts of the world by mountains, deserts, and water
2. Answers will vary, but should include that a civilization may die out or its people may move elsewhere.
3. Answers will vary but should include that they may die out if the classes fight or are not united enough to hold off invaders.
4. Answers will vary but should explain students' reasons.

GEOGRAPHY IN HISTORY

A likely place would be along the eastern coast and Bay of Bengal, and along the Ganges River. Students should note access to water.

+ BONUS +
TEST QUESTION
For Chapter 5 Test

The geographic locations of the Harrapan and Shang affected their quality of life. Which civilization would have been most affected by a monsoon that blew from the southwest? Explain. *(The Harrapans with coastal areas would be hit first and hardest. Shang might get rains.)*

USING YOUR JOURNAL

Charts will vary but should include information that explains ways in which students' communities are similar to and different from the planned communities in Harappa and Mohenjo-daro.

UNIT 2 CULTURE CLOSE-UP

THE NOK

FOCUS

OBJECTIVE

After reading the Culture Close-Up students will be able to identify the time period of the Nok culture and describe what is known about the culture based on its artifacts.

BELLRINGER

Ask students to list the kinds of materials used to make sculptures.

MOTIVATIONAL ACTIVITY

Conduct a class discussion based on students' responses to the bellringer. Ask students to describe any particular sculpture they have seen and explain why they think that sculpture was created. Discuss the general themes often depicted in sculpture. Tell students they will learn about an early African civilization that created some of the oldest sculptures ever discovered.

DID YOU KNOW ??

The details of Nok sculptures are seen in the art of the later Ibo people and other African groups.

UNIT 2 CULTURE CLOSE-UP

The Nok

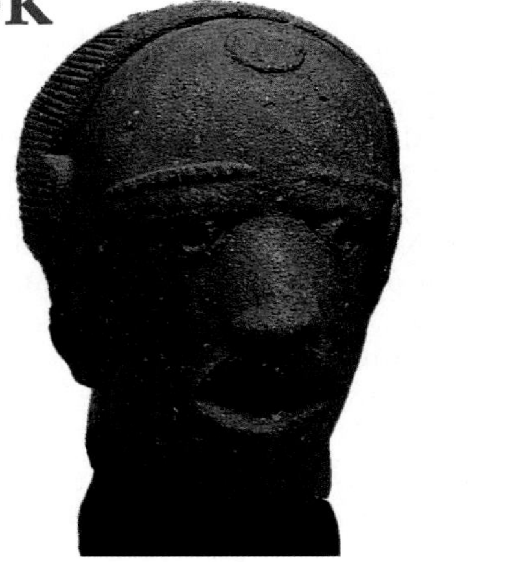

The Nok culture was one of Africa's earliest civilizations. Africans today know traditional songs, dances, art, and storytelling that date back to these early people.

Geography Connection

The Noks are thought to have lived in what is now Nigeria, from about 500 B.C. to 200 A.D. Nok sculptures were discovered in the area where the Niger and Benue Rivers meet.

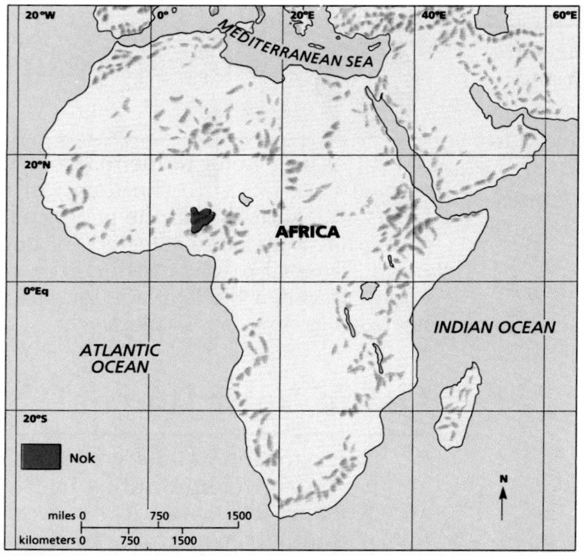

▲ The Jemaa Head and other Nok sculptures found in Nigeria are the most well-known and oldest Nok artifacts. ▼

94

EXTENDING THE CONTENT

Since there are no written records, legends, or myths about the Nok people, historians can only make educated guesses about their culture. Some historians believe the Nok lived in family clans which formed into villages governed by a strong ruler or king. They probably came into contact with the people of the city of Merö because of their ironworking. Some of the oldest artifacts found, many in the Jos tin fields, are terra cotta heads, stylized figures, animals, stone tools, ornaments, and iron tools.

◀ Cave paintings predated most art figures made by the Nok. This wall painting of animals shows how ancient people often painted over past art work.

Nok sculptures of animal and human figures are made of terra cotta, or clay. They range in size from one inch high to life size. This foot is thought to be part of a full-figure sculpture. ▶

TEACH

L2 **Geography: Place** The present-day country of Nigeria has varied landforms, climate, and resources. Encourage students to find out as much about this country as they can. Tell them to write the script for an informational video about Nigeria. Their script should include not only dialogue, but also a complete description of what the video images would be.

L2 **Mathematics** The length of time the Nok civilization flourished spanned the beginning of A.D. *(anno Domini)* time. Ask students to first compute the length of time the civilization existed. *(approximately 700 years)* Then suggest students write their own mathematical story problems about the Nok, such as: If a Nok woman were born 20 years after the civilization began and died 33 years later, what years did her life span? (480 B.C. to 447 B.C.)

VIDEODISK

Use the following to enrich Unit 2.

WH A 17 10017

A terracotta head from the Nok culture.

EXTENDING THE CONTENT

Nok sculptures show great detail of hairstyles, jewelry, and clothing. The hair on many Nok heads was intricately styled with topknots, braids, and layering. Facial hair on men often depicted knotted beards. Beaded jewelry and decorative neckbands were shown also.

DID YOU KNOW ??

The pierced ears and noses, the hollowed out eyes, and the opened mouths of the Nok sculptures may have been methods used by sculptors to create air vents in order to prevent the soft clay from cracking as it was fired, or baked.

L1 **Language Arts** Archaeologists learn a great deal by studying what different cultures choose to depict in their art. Suggest to students that they have been asked to choose only two things to depict in art that represents their own culture. Tell them to write an explanation of the two things they would choose and why.

L3 **Culture** There are many different groups that live in modern Nigeria. Suggest students research the different groups that are citizens of this country and draw a map indicating where each generally lives. Suggest students try to add at least one symbol or illustration to their map to represent each group.

GLOBAL READING FOR STUDENTS

Archaeologists in your class may be interested in reading more about ancient discoveries in *Science in Ancient Mesopotamia* by Carol Moss, Watts, 1988. (Challenging/Nonfiction)

▲ Researchers believe the Nok respected certain animals.

Daily Life

What were the Nok people like? Archaeologists think :

- they were probably farmers, but they also hunted and fished;
- they lived in homes built in the lowlands of river valleys;
- the Nok probably practiced ancestor worship, believed in an afterlife, and had many gods;
- they wore beaded jewelry and decorative neck bands;
- the Nok appear to have developed a form of iron smelting, although many of their tools and weapons were made out of stone.

Details show the people had specific hairstyles, jewelry, and clothing styles. ▶

96

MEETING SPECIAL NEEDS

If possible, to encourage tactile/kinesthetic learners, provide sculpting material of different kinds and suggest they create a bust of themselves or another student. Students may want to try to copy the Nok style of art or create a style of their own. Display completed sculptures and encourage students to explain the style they were using.

UNIT 2

CULTURE CLOSE-UP

Experts are not sure what all Nok sculptures mean. This head with its puffed cheeks suggests a musician blowing on a musical instrument. ▶

In Nok figures, all human heads have pierced ears and eyes that are hollowed out as on these two pieces. The same details are found in the art of the Ibo and other African people. ▼

No one is sure what happened to the Nok people after 200 A.D., at which time they seemed to disappear.

Taking Another Look

1. **Where and when did the Nok people live?**
2. **How did the Nok obtain food?**
3. **How do archaeologists know these people had tools and were skilled at using them?**

Critical Thinking

4. **What do you think happened to the Nok people after 200 A.D.?**

97

SPOTLIGHT ON: AFRICAN ART

African art, from whatever part of the continent it originates, reflects certain aspects of the lives of the people who created it. Social class has impacted the content and style of art in many African countries. Art pieces from many cultures reserve certain styles and materials for upper classes and others for lower classes. Religion also dominates African art, as people portray various ceremonial and ideological elements of their culture in their art. Another strong influence on African art is environment and lifestyle. Much of each group's art depicts the world around them and the way each group interacts with that environment.

ASSESS

CHECK FOR UNDERSTANDING

Have students complete the Taking Another Look questions on page 97.

ANSWERS to Taking Another Look

1. The Nok lived in present-day Nigeria, Africa, from about 500 B.C. to 200 A.D.
2. The Nok probably were farmers, and hunted wild animals and fished.
3. Tools and art of the Nok have been found that are finely made and show a great deal of use.
4. Answers will vary but could include reference to climactic disaster such as flooding, or disease, or being killed by another civilization.

ENRICH

Have students research and write a description of the area of Nigeria where the Nok are believed to have lived. Suggest they include all geographic features, plant life, animal life, and climate.

CLOSE

Ask students to work with a partner to create a dialogue as if they were two Nok young people talking about a day they have spent together. Suggest they include as many details of what their daily life might have involved. Ask pairs of students to share their dialogues with the class.

INTRODUCE

UNIT 3 OVERVIEW

Unit 3 surveys the rise and fall of important kingdoms and empires in the ancient Middle East, Africa, and the Americas to 1500 A.D.

- **Chapter 6** describes the Phoenicians and the Hebrews and their interest in trade and religion, and their contributions to later civilizations.
- **Chapter 7** discusses the contributions of the Assyrians, Chaldeans, and Persians, examines how their empires were forged and maintained, and how their ideas spread through conquest and trade.
- **Chapter 8** explains the development of civilization in sub-Saharan Africa and the Americas, and how ideas spread through trade and through conquest of these civilizations.

UNIT OBJECTIVES

After reading Unit 3, your students will be able to:

1. give examples of the important cultural and religious contributions of the Phoenicians and the Hebrews.
2. explain how the rise of empires affected the early peoples of the Middle East.
3. characterize the kinds of empires that developed in Africa and the Americas.

UNIT PROJECT

Have students create a monument to one of the kingdoms and civilizations studied in Unit 3. Their goal is to research their civilization and devise and create a monument that represents the people and/or their achievements. Monuments can take any form students choose, such as an object, videotape, story, or other form to show the achievement.

UNIT 3 Ideas and Armies

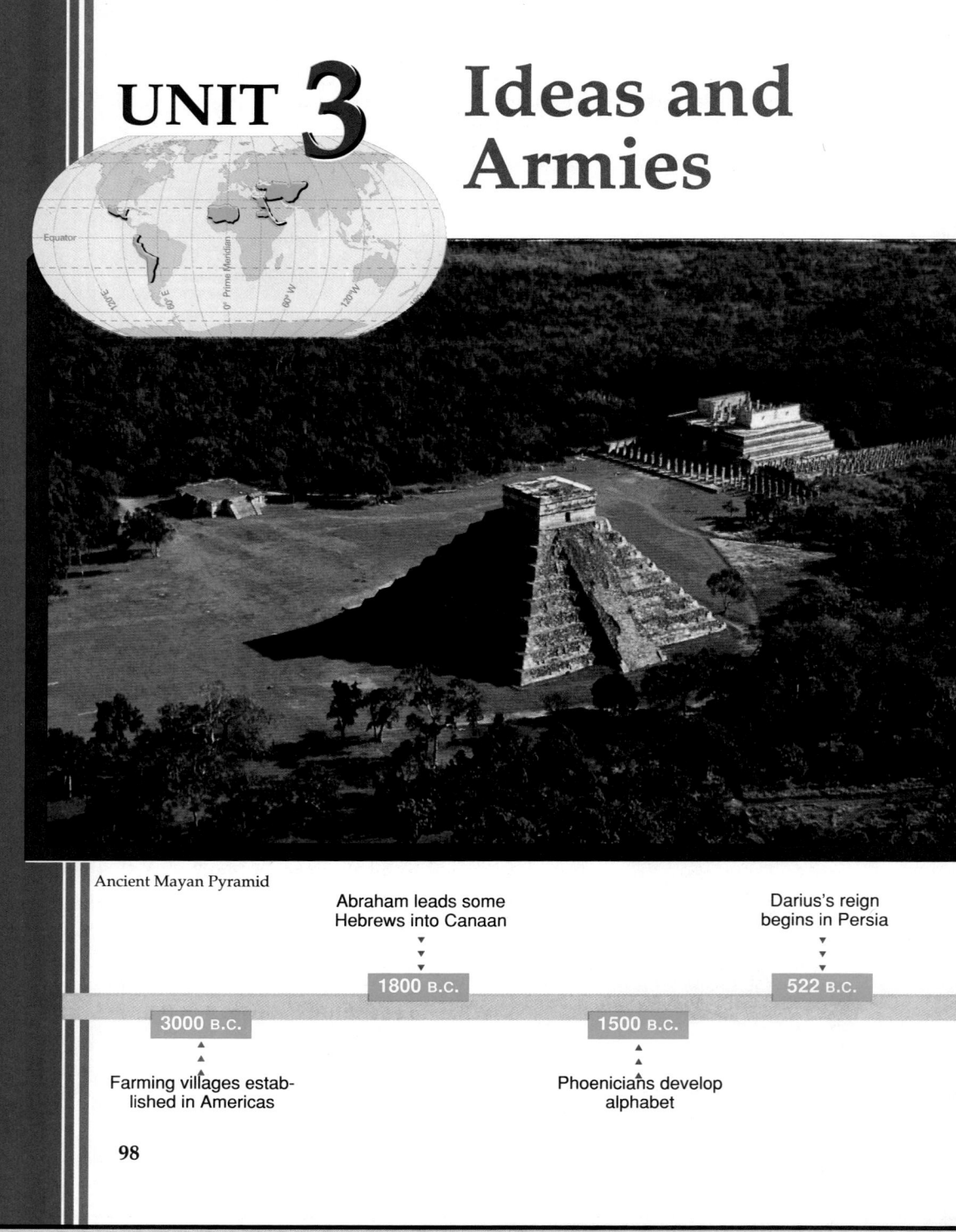

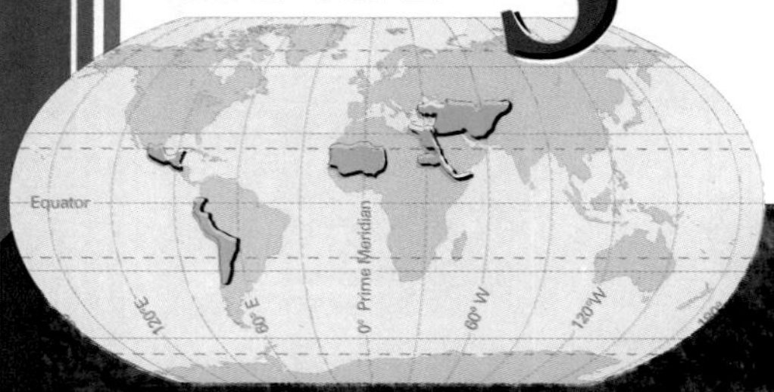

Ancient Mayan Pyramid

- **3000 B.C.** Farming villages established in Americas
- **1800 B.C.** Abraham leads some Hebrews into Canaan
- **1500 B.C.** Phoenicians develop alphabet
- **522 B.C.** Darius's reign begins in Persia

About the Unit Opening

EXAMINING THE ARTIFACT

Explain to students that often historians have to obtain information and draw conclusions about past civilizations from artifacts alone. Ask students what information they obtain or conclusions they can draw from the ancient Mayan temple shown.

GLOBAL CHRONOLOGY

Refer students to the unit time line above. Ask students about what year farming villages were established throughout the Americas. *(3000 B.C.)* Ask students what contribution the Phoenicians made to civilization in 1500 B.C. *(developed the alphabet)*

After many hundreds of years, civilizations developed in places other than river valleys. These newer civilizations arose in the Middle East, in Africa, and in the Americas. Some were interested mostly in new ideas, trade, and religion. Others were mostly interested in war. All, however, contributed important cultural and religious ideas to later civilizations.

Journal Notes

What contributions to the modern world were made by civilizations more than 3,000 years ago? Note details about them as you read.

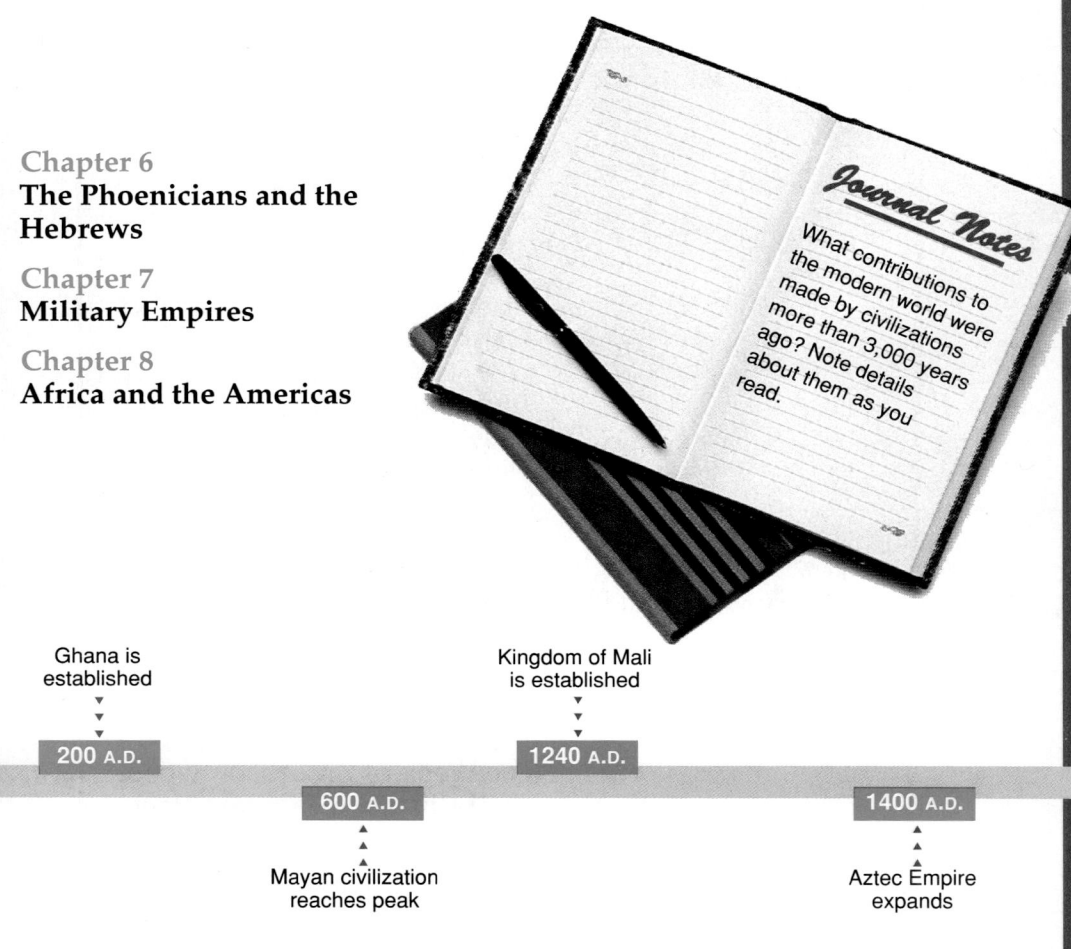

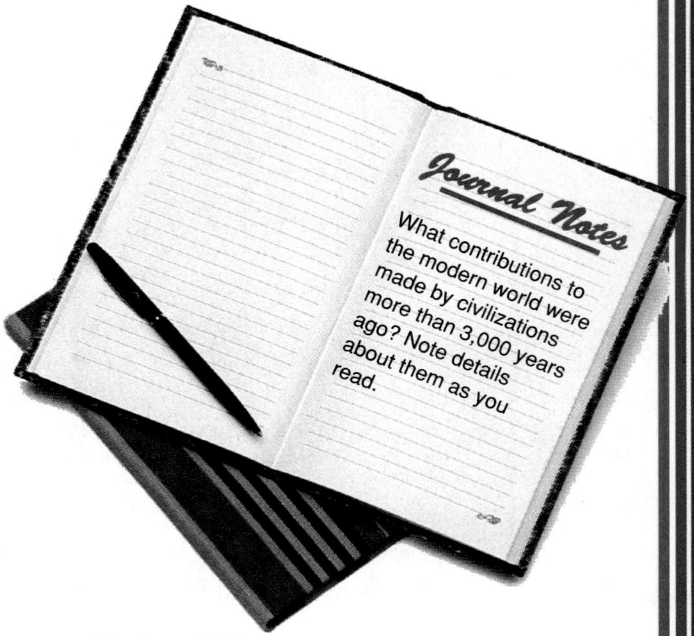

Ghana is established	Kingdom of Mali is established
▼	▼
200 A.D.	**1240** A.D.

600 A.D.	**1400** A.D.
▲	▲
Mayan civilization reaches peak	Aztec Empire expands

99

The civilizations discussed in this unit were located in the Middle East; in northeastern, eastern, and western Africa; and in Central America and South America along the Andes Mountains. Have students locate these places in their text Atlas. Then have volunteers locate them on a wall map of the world.

INTRODUCING THE UNIT

Refer the students to the unit's title—"Ideas and Armies." Point out that many ideas that have had a profound influence on world history have been transmitted peacefully through trade or forcefully through conquest. Ask students which ideas would probably be accepted more easily into a society. *(Ideas transmitted peacefully through trade would most likely be accepted rather than ideas that are forced upon a society as a result of conquest.)* Direct students to note in what ways ideas were exchanged as they read Unit 3.

RECORDING JOURNAL NOTES

Help students begin writing in their journals by suggesting they make a list of recent inventions that 3,000 years from now might be considered important contributions to society. Call on volunteers to read their lists as you write responses on the chalkboard. Explain to students that as they read they should note in their journal details about the contributions to the modern world made by civilizations more than 3,000 years ago.

 VIDEODISC

Use the following to introduce or enrich Unit 3.

WC A 32 9034
Ashurbanipal, the Assyrian king, on horseback.

CHAPTER 6

The Phoenicians and the Hebrews

CHAPTER ORGANIZER

Objectives	Special Features	Supplemental Materials
Section 1 The Phoenicians Discuss the Phoenicians and their role in the growth of Mediterranean commerce and the development of the alphabet.		• Reproducible Lesson Plan • Section 1 Quiz • Testmaker • Chapter 6 Chart and Graph Skill Activity • Chapter 6 Cooperative Learning Activity • Chapter 6 Teaching Transparency and Activity • The World History Videodisc
Section 2 The Hebrews Summarize the Hebrews and their development of new ideas, such as the belief in one god and social justice.	Map and Geography Skills: *Reading a Map Scale,* p. 108; People in History: *ar-Rāzi*, p. 111	• Reproducible Lesson Plan • Section 2 Quiz • Testmaker • Chapter 6 Geography and Map Activity • Chapter 6 Vocabulary and Guided Reading Activity • Outline Map Resource p. 28 • The World History Videodisc • The Western Civilization Videodisc • Chapter 6 Teaching Transparency and Activity • Chapter 6 Activity Book Activity
Chapter 6 Review and Evaluation		• Reinforcing Social Studies Skills pp. 9, 13, 23 • Chapter 6 Reteaching Activity • Chapter 6 Enrichment Activity • Chapter 6 Performance Assessment Activity • Spanish Summary and Glossary • Audiocassettes (English and Spanish) • Chapter 6 Test • Testmaker

If time does not permit teaching the entire chapter, use the Chapter 6 Summary on page 114 and the Chapter 6 Audiocassettes (English and Spanish) to point out the main ideas of the chapter.

✓ PERFORMANCE ASSESSMENT ACTIVITIES

Poster Have students make an illustrated map poster with key, for one civilization studied. Each poster should contain a map that shows the continent where the civilizations existed, the cities that were the centers of the civilizations, and major geographic features of the area. Map details can be shown visually in any way students choose. Farm products, wildlife, and other characteristics of the area can be shown on the maps, also. Have students decide what other information to include. Display completed posters.

Graphic Organizers: Topic Webs Ask students to keep a notebook for comparing the governing, legal, or economic structures of each civilization studied in this chapter. For example, students might compare the Persian and the Hebrew governments. Using their notes, have students construct a topic web for one civilization's governing or economic structure. Post topic webs and have students identify how these structures differed or were similar.

CHAPTER RESOURCES

LITERATURE ABOUT THE PERIOD

Herrmann, Siegfried. *A History of Israel in Old Testament Times*. Fortress Press, 1975. Focuses on the Old Testament as a history of early Israel, with additional evidence from sources other than the Bible.

The Holy Scriptures. Jewish Publication Society, 1977. New translation according to Masoretic text.

READINGS FOR THE STUDENT

Asimov, Isaac. *The Land of Canaan*. Houghton Mifflin, 1971. Popularly written history of this small area and the different peoples who have occupied it since ancient times.

Chu, Daniel and Eliott Skinner. *A Glorious Age in Africa: The Story of Three Great African Empires.* Africa World, 1990. An illustrated review of the three earliest empires of West Africa.

Edey, Maitland E., et al. *The Sea Traders* (Emergence of Man series). Time-Life Books, 1974. Thorough, well-illustrated account of Phoenician history and culture, bringing together modern knowledge about these influential but little-known explorers and traders.

Synge, Ursula. *The People and the Promise.* S.G. Phillips, 1974. The exodus of the Hebrews from Egypt as viewed through the eyes of Leah as she experiences it from childhood to old age.

READINGS FOR THE TEACHER

Davidson, Basil. *A History of West Africa, One Thousand to Eighteen Hundred.* Longman, 1978. An illustrated early history of West Africa.

De Lange, N.R.M. *Atlas of the Jewish World.* Phaidon Press, 1984. Chronicles the history of the Jewish people.

Eban, Abba. *Heritage: Civilization and the Jews.* Summit Books, 1984. Describes the 5,000-year-old Jewish civilization from its birth in the Mesopotamian desert to the modern state of Israel.

Grant, Michael. *The History of Ancient Israel.* Weidenfeld and Nicholson, 1984. Presents the social, economic, political, and religious life of ancient Israel.

Herm, Gerhard. *The Phoenicians.* William Morrow, 1975. Summarizes the history of the Phoenicians during ancient times.

MULTIMEDIA RESOURCES

Jerusalem Within These Walls. National Geographic. Views Jerusalem's 3,000-year history, its diverse mix of people, and the three major religions it embraces.

Africa: A Voyage of Discovery, "Caravans of Gold" or "Kings and Cities," by Basil Davidson. Video. RM Arts, 1984. Presents early African history.

INTRODUCE

CHAPTER 6 OVERVIEW

Chapter 6 focuses on the cultures of the Phoenicians and the Hebrews in the ancient Middle East.

- **Section 1** discusses the Phoenicians and their role in the growth of Mediterranean commerce and the development of the alphabet.
- **Section 2** summarizes the Hebrews and their development of new ideas and the impact of religious beliefs on the development of civilizations.

CHAPTER OBJECTIVES

After reading Chapter 6, students will be able to:

1. explain how trade helped the Phoenicians and the Hebrews build their civilizations.
2. identify the important cultural contributions made by the Phoenicians and the Hebrews.
3. describe the religious beliefs held by the Hebrews.

EXAMINING THE ARTIFACT

Ask students what is the first thing they notice about the Phoenician ship. What conclusions can they draw from what they see? Tell them they will discover the validity of their conclusions as they read more about the Phoenicians in this chapter.

PERFORMANCE ASSESSMENT

Use the Performance Assessment activities on page 100B to help you evaluate students as they complete the chapter.

CHAPTER 6 The Phoenicians and the Hebrews

Relief of Ancient Phoenician Ship

100

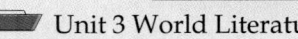

TEACHER CLASSROOM RESOURCES

- Unit 3 World Literature
- Reproducible Lesson Plan
- Section Quizzes/Chapter Test
- Enrichment Activity
- Chart and Graph Skill Activity
- Geography and Map Activity
- Vocabulary and Guided Reading Activity
- Teaching Transparencies and Activities
- Cooperative Learning Activity
- Performance Assessment Activity
- Spanish Summary and Glossary
- Audiocassettes (English and Spanish)
- Unit 3 Primary Source Reading
- Testmaker

Chapter Focus

READ TO DISCOVER:

- How trade helped the Phoenicians and the Hebrews build their civilizations.
- What important cultural contributions were made by the Phoenicians and the Hebrews.
- What religious beliefs were held by the Hebrews.

At the eastern end of the Mediterranean Sea lies a piece of land shared today by Lebanon (leb' uh nuhn) and Israel. In ancient times, it was the bridge that connected Egypt and Mesopotamia, and it was known as Canaan (kā' nuhn). Soldiers, shepherds, and merchants who passed through Canaan carried new ideas and goods between Egypt and Mesopotamia.

Two groups—the Phoenicians and the Hebrews—settled in Canaan and formed small kingdoms. Each group was interested in trade and in learning. Through these peaceful activities, they made important contributions to later civilizations.

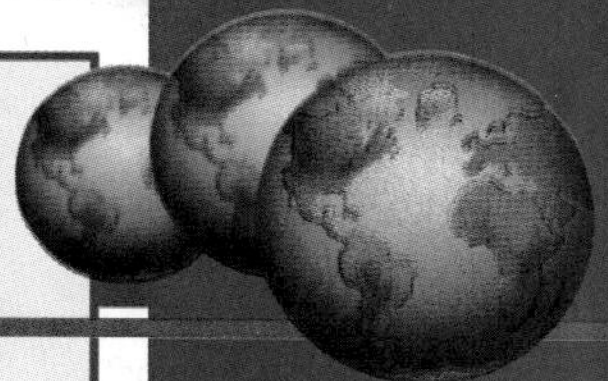

1200 B.C.–510 B.C.

KEY TERMS

- treaties
- holy of holies
- colonies
- descendants
- social justice
- judge
- psalms
- prophets
- sabbath

Section 1 THE PHOENICIANS

The Phoenicians lived in the northern part of Canaan. Most of what is known about them comes from the Bible, the writings of other ancient peoples, and the ruins of their cities and ships.

Two different groups formed the Phoenician people. One was the Canaanites (kā' nuh nīts), who came from the desert south and east of Canaan. The Canaanites were herders who wandered from pasture to pasture. The second group was the Philistines (fil' uh stēnz), who came from the eastern Mediterranean near Greece. The Philistines were traders and shipbuilders.

101

FOCUS

BELLRINGER

Ask students to solve the following money problem: What combination of 3 coins equals 20 cents if one of the coins is not a dime? *(see Motivational Activity)*

MOTIVATIONAL ACTIVITY

Ask students for the answer to the coin problem *(one of the coins is a dime so the correct combination is a dime and two nickels)* and poll how many students had the correct answer. Suggest that these students might have made good Phoenician traders. Explain to students that in this chapter they will learn about the Phoenician civilization who developed an elaborate and successful system of trade.

VOCABULARY PRE-CHECK

Write the key terms for this chapter on the chalkboard. Ask students which ones they could predict the meanings of, and suggest they write their predictions down. Ask students to review their predictions as they encounter each word in their reading.

Assign Chapter 6 **Vocabulary and Guided Reading Activity** in the TCR.

EXTRA CREDIT PROJECT

Remind students that the Hebrews were one of the first people to cultivate olives, which became an extremely important product in the future economy of the region. Suggest interested students research and prepare a report on the multiple uses of olives and why they were so important in the Mediterranean region.

KEY TO ABILITY LEVELS

Teaching strategies have been coded for varying learning styles and abilities.

L1 Level 1 activities are **basic** activities and should be within the ability range of all students.

L2 Level 2 activities are **average** activities and should be within the ability range of the average to above-average student.

L3 Level 3 activities are **challenging** activities designed for the ability range of above-average students.

LEP LEP activities should be within the ability range of Limited English Proficiency students.

CAPTION ANSWER

It was believed that sacrifices strengthened the power of the gods and kept them friendly toward the people.

L2 **Science** Ask students why they think the Phoenicians believed in many gods that were closely tied to nature. What characteristics of the different forces of nature makes this seem logical? LEP

PHOENICIAN TOMB The Phoenicians offered human sacrifices to please their gods. Inside this underground burial chamber at Carthage are clay urns that hold the ashes of victims who were sacrificed. **Why were human rather than animal sacrifices made to the Phoenician gods?**

Melqart (mel′ kart) was walking along the seashore with his girlfriend Tyrus (tī′ rus) and a dog. When the dog picked up a shellfish called *murex* (myuhr′ eks) and bit into it, the dog's mouth turned purple. Tyrus liked the color so much that she said she would not marry Melqart unless he gave her a gown of that color. Melqart gave her the gown and started the dye-making trade in Phoenicia.

Gods and Goddesses The Phoenicians believed in many gods who were closely tied to nature. Since they thought the gods met people only on hills and under trees, they worshiped only in these places at first. Later, they built temples. Each had an entrance hall, a main hall, and a **holy of holies,** or most sacred chamber, where the image or sacred stone of the god was kept. Sacrifices of wine, perfume, animals, and humans were made on a nearby stone altar. Only priests could offer these sacrifices. It was thought that this strengthened the power of the gods and kept them friendly toward people.

The Phoenicians believed in a life after death. At first, they buried their dead in clay *urns* (ernz), or ornamental vases. Later, influenced by Egyptian customs, they embalmed the bodies, wrapped them in linen, and placed them in stone coffins in hillside cemeteries.

EXTENDING THE CONTENT

The murex is a small edible sea snail common in the eastern Mediterranean. Its famous purple dye comes from a liquid produced by a small gland. Each snail produces only a few drops, which at one time were boiled down and concentrated to create a dye. One pound of dye required about 60,000 snails. Even today, huge mounds of shells can be seen piled near the ruins of ancient dye works.

Because of the smell from the snail shells, the dye "factories" were located some distances outside of town, downwind.

Carthage Some Phoenician sailors and traders set up trading posts along the coast of North Africa. Other Phoenicians built **colonies,** or permanent settlements, in these areas. These colonies soon turned into cities.

The most famous of these cities was Carthage (kar′ thij), founded in 814 B.C. in present-day Tunisia (tū nē′ zhē uh). Legend states the city was founded by a Phoenician princess named Dido (dī′ dō). At first Dido ruled the city of Tyre. Her brother, however, thought that he should rule Tyre. So, he killed Dido's husband and overthrew Dido. She fled to North Africa where she and her followers built Carthage.

Carthage soon became a Mediterranean power. It was a great trading city. Ships from Carthage may have traveled to the British Isles in search of tin, a metal highly valued by merchants.

The Alphabet Through trade, the Phoenicians spread ideas as well as goods. Their most important gift was the idea of an alphabet. The Phoenicians did not invent the alphabet. They did, however, pass it on to other cultures.

At first, the Phoenicians used a system of picture writing. However, it was difficult to keep trade records this way. So, they looked for an easier writing system. They borrowed a simple version of Egyptian hieroglyphs from the people of the Canaanite towns that lay to the south. By the time the Canaanite system of writing reached Phoenicia, it had become an alphabet.

ALPHABETS This chart shows how different alphabets developed from the Phoenician alphabet. The characters of the alphabets closely resemble each other. **On whose system of writing did the Phoenicians base their alphabet?**

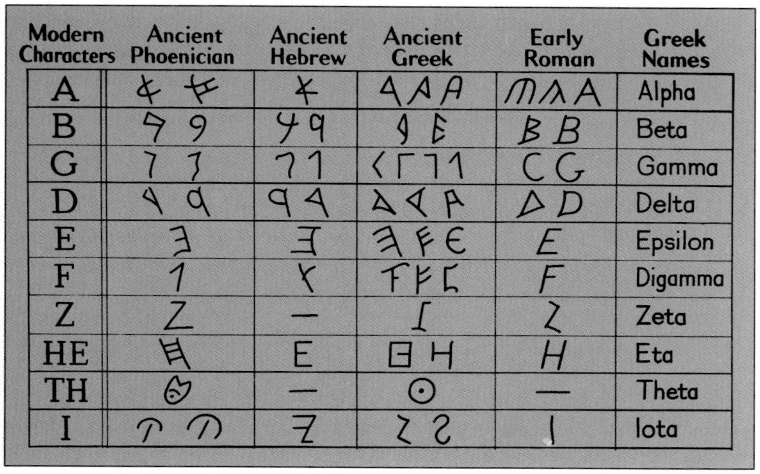

Modern Characters
Ancient Phoenician
Ancient Hebrew
Ancient Greek
Early Roman
Greek Names
A
B
G
D
E
F
Z
HE
TH
I
Alpha
Beta
Gamma
Delta
Epsilon
Digamma
Zeta
Eta
Theta
Iota

L3 **Mathematics** Have students locate the present-day Tunisian city of Carthage on a map of Africa. Point out that Carthage was once a colony of Phoenicia. Have students calculate the approximate distance between Carthage and Phoenicia and show the route that Phoenicians might have taken to travel from one to the other.

CAPTION ANSWER

the Canaanites to the south

MEETING SPECIAL NEEDS

Have interested students use the alphabet chart on this page to write the following words using each alphabet shown: *bed, bad, fade, death.* Then have them choose their own word to write using one of the alphabets. Have students exchange and decipher each other's new words.

MAKING CONNECTIONS

➤➤ **Language** The Phoenician alphabet had 22 letters, all consonants, that were written from left to right. The Phoenicians gave each letter a name. The first letter was the picture of an ox, or *aleph*. The second letter was the picture of a house, or *beth*.

L2 **Culture** Remind students that the way of life of a group of people is referred to as its culture. Divide the class into two groups. Assign one group the Phoenicians and the other group the Hebrews. Direct each group to create a chart to show examples of the following information about their assigned culture group: beliefs, language, the arts, buildings, clothing, and law. Encourage students to use the textbook and other reference books. After the groups have completed their charts, create a master chart on the chalkboard. Discuss how the cultural contributions of the Phoenicians and the Hebrews may have influenced students' lives.

The Canaanite system of writing had 22 symbols, or letters, from which any number of words could be formed. Since it was easy to use, the Canaanite system provided the writing system Phoenician traders needed for keeping records.

The Phoenicians made the Canaanite alphabet their own. They carried it to Europe, where the Greeks borrowed it and made a few changes. Later, the Romans borrowed it from the Greeks. Most western alphabets, including the English, are based on the Roman alphabet.

Section 1 Review

1. **Identify:** Canaan, Phoenicians, Canaanites, Philistines, Tyre, Carthage
2. **Define:** treaties, holy of holies, colonies
3. Why did the Phoenicians turn to trade to make a living?
4. How did the Phoenicians view their gods?

Critical Thinking

5. Why is an alphabet a major contribution to civilization?

Section 2 THE HEBREWS

Like the Phoenicians, the Hebrews were a small group among the peoples of the ancient Middle East. Because of their religion, however, they have had a great influence on the world's civilizations. Their religion still exists today. It is called Judaism (jū' dē iz uhm).

Most early Hebrews were *nomadic* (nō mad' ik), or wandering, herders; some were traveling merchants. Leading long trains of donkeys loaded with goods, these merchants walked from one trading post to the next. The Hebrews followed a route that started from the city of Ur on the Euphrates River. There, Hebrew artisans made goods from gold, copper, and ivory. Hebrew merchants then stuffed the goods into bags, loaded them on donkeys, and started up the valley of the Tigris and Euphrates. At Harran (hah rahn'), a city near the Turkish mountains, they exchanged their goods for silver. Sometimes, merchants continued west and then south along the Mediterranean coast to trade with Egyptian, Phoenician, and Cretan (krēt' uhn) merchants.

Hebrew Ivory Box

SECTION 1 ANSWERS

1. Canaan, ancient Mediterranean land (p. 101); Phoenicians, eastern Mediterranean people (p. 101); Canaanites, civilization of farmers and herders, (p. 101); Philistines, traders and ship builders (p. 101); Tyre, a city in Phoenicia (p. 103); Carthage, large city in Phoenicia (p. 105)
2. treaties, agreements between states or countries (p. 103); holy of holies, most sacred chamber (p. 104); colonies, permanent settlements (p. 105)
3. because there was not enough land to grow food
4. as closely tied to nature
5. Answers will vary but should include that the spread of an alphabet provided an easy-to-use writing system. This increased trade because records could be kept, which increased contact with other civilizations.

Assign Chapter 6 **Section 1 Quiz** in the TCR. Testmaker available.

ABRAHAM Abraham taught the Hebrews to worship Yahweh. Here, Abraham is shown beside his father, leading the Hebrews on their journey from Ur to Canaan. **Why did the Hebrews eventually leave Canaan?**

The God of Abraham The story of the Hebrews and their god is written in the Bible. It states that Yahweh (yah' wā), or God, made an agreement with Abraham. Abraham and his followers were to leave Ur and go to Canaan. There, they were to worship and obey Yahweh as the one true god. In exchange, Yahweh promised that they and their **descendants,** or offspring such as children, grandchildren, great-grandchildren, and so on, could always live in Canaan.

During ancient times, most people believed in many gods. These gods behaved like humans but were more powerful. The Hebrews, however, believed that Yahweh was different from humans. He did not get hungry or thirsty, marry, or have children. According to the Hebrews, Yahweh did only what was just and right, even though He was powerful and could do whatever He wanted.

Abraham and members of his household settled in Canaan around 1800 B.C. In Canaan, they raised flocks of sheep and grew wheat, figs, and olives. Abraham's grandson, Jacob, had 12 sons. Each son led a separate family group. These Hebrew groups later formed 12 Hebrew tribes. The Hebrews stayed in Canaan for about 100 years. Then, a drought came, and they went to Egypt where they could get food.

CAPTION ANSWER

A drought came, and they went to Egypt to get food.

DID YOU KNOW ??

In many cases, Hebrew words are written without vowels. The Israelites wrote YHVH as the name of God. Because later Israelites chose not to speak the name of God, the identity of the vowels and the correct pronunciation of the name is uncertain.

GEOGRAPHY AND HISTORY

By 3000 B.C. the Sumerians had established 12 city-states in the Tigris-Euphrates river valley, including Ur, Uruk, and Eridu. The Fertile Crescent, as the area is often called because of its relatively rich topsoil and its curved shape, was able to support city-state populations ranging from 20,000 to 250,000.

MULTICULTURAL PERSPECTIVES

According to the Book of Genesis 22:17-18 (RSV), God made the following promise to Abraham and his descendants if they would worship and obey him:

I will indeed bless you, and I will multiply your descendants as the stars of heaven and as the sand which is on the seashore. And your descendants shall possess the gate of their enemies, and by your descendants shall all the nations of the earth bless themselves, because you have obeyed my voice.

Teaching

MAP SKILLS

Reading a Map Scale

Instruct the students to read the map on page 108 to answer the following questions:

From north to south, how long is the Phoenician kingdom? *(approximately 175 miles, or 281 km)*

What is the distance from Tyre to Jerusalem? *(approximately 100 miles, or 161 km)*

Have students use the map of the Middle East and its map scale in the text Atlas to find the distances between five different places shown on the map. Ask volunteers to relate the distances.

Assign Chapter 6 **Geography and Map Activity** in the TCR.

ANSWERS to Map Practice

1. approximately 60 miles, (96 km)
2. approximately 50 miles, (80 km)
3. approximately 150 miles, (241 km)

Reading A Map Scale

Maps provide many kinds of information. One thing maps can show is distance, or how far one point on a map is from another. To do this, most maps have scale.

A map scale shows the relationship between the distances on the map and the actual distances on Earth. The length of a scale represents a certain number of miles or kilometers on Earth. Using this scale, it is possible to figure actual distances between any two points on this map.

For example, to figure the distance between the cities of Beirut and Tyre, use a ruler to measure how far apart they are. Now, compare this length with the map scale. Since Beirut and Tyre are about one-half inch, or 1.3 centimeters, apart on the map, the actual distance between them on Earth is about 50 miles, or 80 kilometers.

Map Practice

1. **What is the distance between Sidon and Damascus?**
2. **From north to south, how long is the Dead Sea?**
3. **How far is it from Jerusalem to Beirut?**

Phoenicia and the Hebrew Kingdoms

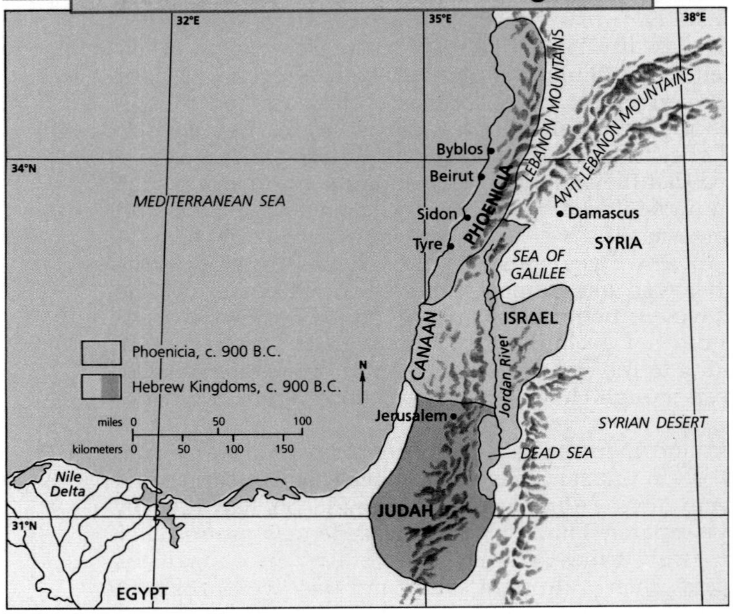

SPOTLIGHT ON: HEBREW KINGDOMS

According to the Old Testament, Moses led the Hebrew people to Palestine, the land of "milk and honey," but died before entering the area himself. Scripture states he was actually forbidden to enter Palestine as punishment because he had doubted God's word.

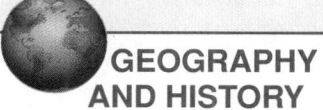

MOSES According to the Bible, Yahweh allowed Moses and the Hebrews to pass through the Red Sea. The waters then closed again, drowning the pharaoh and his army. **What important set of laws did God give Moses on Mount Sinai?**

Moses and the Ten Commandments After the Hebrews settled in Egypt, they were enslaved. About 600 years later, Moses, the Hebrew leader at the time, appeared before the pharaoh and told him to end Hebrew enslavement and let the Hebrews leave Egypt. The pharaoh at first refused but later agreed. Moses then led the Hebrews out of Egypt. The pharaoh again changed his mind and led his army in pursuit. According to the Bible, Yahweh parted the Red Sea to allow the Hebrews to cross and they escaped into the Sinai (sī′ nī) Desert. They called their escape the *Exodus* (ek′ suh duhs).

Life in the desert was hard, but Moses told the Hebrews not to give up. Moses led them to Mount Sinai. There, he climbed to the top of the mountain to receive a message from God. The Bible states that Yahweh told Moses that He would protect the Hebrews and lead them back to Canaan. In return, they were to renew the *covenant* (kuv′ uh nuhnt), or agreement, with Him. They were to promise to obey certain laws, the most important of which became the Ten Commandments.

The Ten Commandments stated that the Hebrews were to give their loyalty only to Yahweh. They were not to worship other gods or idols (ī′ dls). The Ten Commandments also taught that it was wrong to lie, steal, or murder, and that people should honor their parents and respect other people's property.

The Hebrews believed God was just, and they too should be just. They used laws to influence the way people behaved. Their

CAPTION ANSWER

the Ten Commandments

GEOGRAPHY AND HISTORY

Explain to the students that present-day Jews commemorate the Exodus from Egypt and rededicate themselves to freedom each year during an eight-day celebration called Passover. Ask volunteers to research and trace the Hebrew's Exodus on a map of the Middle East for the rest of the class.

INDEPENDENT PRACTICE

L3 **Critical Thinking** Ask students to respond to the following: Many people accept the Bible as a collection of sacred writings. How might it also be a historical document?

VIDEODISC

Use the following to enrich Chapter 6.

WH E 53 14297

Moses and the Ten Commandments.

EXTENDING THE CONTENT

According to Exodus 20:2-14, in one version of the Bible, the Ten Commandments are:

You shall have no other gods beside me.

You shall not make for yourself a sculptured image. . . .

You shall not swear falsely by the name of the Lord your God. . . .

Remember the sabbath day and keep it holy. . . .

Honor your father and your mother. . . .

You shall not murder.

You shall not commit adultery.

You shall not steal.

You shall not bear false witness against your neighbor.

You shall not covet . . . anything that is your neighbor's.

L2 **Economics** Ask students to research the Hebrew's trading practices and compare them with those of the Phoenicians. Suggest they draw conclusions about which people were the better traders and relate this in a paragraph summary.

DID YOU KNOW

For the Hebrews, Canaan was the Promised Land, a land they thought was flowing with milk and honey. To give thanks for the richness of the land, they celebrated the festival of Savouth, which began with a pilgrimage in the early spring and continued for seven weeks.

CAPTION ANSWER

olives, flax, barley, wheat, and grapes

laws affected not only individuals but the whole community. The Hebrews believed in **social justice.** Everyone had a right to be treated fairly.

The Promised Land Moses died shortly before the Hebrews reached Canaan. The Hebrews were afraid that without a strong leader they would not be able to enter Canaan. The people who already lived there had built many walled cities on hilltops. Soldiers in lookout towers guarded the cities against enemy attack. However, Joshua, a new leader and a good general, brought the Hebrews safely into the promised land.

Once they had settled in Canaan, the Hebrews became farmers and shepherds. They copied the Canaanites' tools and borrowed their alphabet. Canaan was rocky and dry. There was little water. So, during the two months of the rainy season, farmers collected and stored water in small caves or underground basins. During the dry season, they used what they had stored to irrigate their crops of olives, flax, barley, wheat, and grapes.

Most Hebrews lived in one-room houses. The room was divided in two, with one section slightly higher than the other. During the day, people cooked and did other household chores in the lower level. At night, donkeys and goats bedded down there, while the family slept on the upper level. The walls of the houses

HARVEST IN ANCIENT ISRAEL Hebrew writers called Canaan "a land flowing with milk and honey." This area, however, had a dry climate and little water. The Hebrews had to work hard to farm the land. Hebrew farmers and their workers gathering the harvest are shown in this painting. **What crops did the Hebrews grow in Canaan?**

COOPERATIVE LEARNING

Organize the class into small groups. Suggest to each group that they are members of a school (or city) "commandment committee." It is their task to write a list of commandments to guide school behavior that they think will cover all necessary considerations and possibilities. Encourage groups to list commandments by priority.

Regroup the students and allow each group to share their commandments and poll their consensus.

Ar-Rāzi

PEOPLE IN HISTORY

The Metropolitan Museum of Art, Rogers Fund, 1913

Many people throughout history have contributed to the practice of medicine. One such person was ar-Rāzi, one of the first scientists to study and describe how to identify smallpox. Ar-Rāzi was born around 865 A.D. in Rayy, Persia, which was once part of the Persian Empire. In his early years ar-Rāzi was interested in music. He became an accomplished musician and organized and wrote a music encyclopedia.

In Baghdad Ar-Rāzi went to a city called Baghdad. There he learned about medicine by studying. When he finished his studies, he returned to Rayy and was appointed the head of the community hospital. Soon he was offered the position of chief doctor in a Baghdad hospital.

Ar-Rāzi's services as a doctor were always in demand. He traveled from city to city, attending to the wealthy nobles as well as to the poor people.

Ar-Rāzi had different ideas about the role of a doctor. He believed that a good relationship between doctors and their patients was important. He urged patients to choose doctors in whom they had confidence.

Medical author Ar-Rāzi wrote many books on medicine. He studied the disease of smallpox. Ar-Rāzi then wrote a description of the disease's symptoms to help doctors diagnose the disease. His book titled *Treatise on the Small Pox and Measles*, was translated into many languages. His handbook of medicine was highly regarded and for hundreds of years later was used as a text in the teaching of medicine in European universities.

Ar-Rāzi's work was hampered in later years when his sight began to fail. He died in Rayy around 925 A.D.

Checking for Understanding

1. **What interest did ar-Rāzi have during his early years?**
2. **What were some ideas that ar-Rāzi had about the relationship between doctors and their patients?**
3. **How did ar-Rāzi's work influence other cultures?**

Teaching

PEOPLE IN HISTORY

AR-RĀZI

After students have read the People in History feature, have them discuss why they think ar-Rāzi was always in demand as a doctor. *(his medical expertise and his belief that a good relationship between doctors and their patients is important)*

ANSWERS to Checking for Understanding

1. an interest in music
2. He believed that a good relationship between doctors and their patients was important. He urged patients to choose doctors in whom they had confidence.
3. His handbook of medicine became a necessary text in the teaching of medicine in European universities; his *Treatise on the Small Pox and Measles* was translated into many languages.

SPOTLIGHT ON: AR-RĀZI

It was the custom during ar-Rāzi's time for rulers to provide for the special needs and wants of intellectuals invited to live at the court. As a result, ar-Rāzi lived at various small courts. Ar-Rāzi often referred to the Greek intellectuals and thought of himself as an Islamic Socrates in philosophy and an Islamic Hippocrates in medicine. During the 1900s ar-Rāzi's philosophical writings were reexamined and he was once again acknowledged for his contributions to society.

L3 **Language Arts** Have students write a paragraph explaining the importance of prophets in Hebrew history. Students may wish to read the writings of the prophets in the Jewish Bible or Old Testament to gain more insight into the prophet's influence on Hebrew history.

DID YOU KNOW ??

King David has been traditionally identified as the author of 150 devotional psalms that make up the Book of Psalms. Some of the psalms have titles that indicate the circumstances under which they were written. For example, the third psalm is titled: *A psalm of David, when he fled from Absalom his son.*

VIDEODISC

Use the following to enrich Chapter 6.

WC A 37 9039

A reconstruction of Solomon's temple, Jerusalem.

Painting of Joshua

were made of mud-brick or stone plastered with mud and whitewashed. Floors were made of beaten clay. Wooden beams supported a flat, thatched roof, which was covered with clay.

Kings After Joshua died the 12 Hebrew tribes split apart. Each tribe was led by a council of elders. In times of crisis, a temporary leader called a **judge** settled disputes and led troops into battle.

In time, the Hebrews decided they needed a king to unite them. A warrior-farmer named Saul became their first king. He ruled well for several years. Toward the end of his reign, however, he lost the people's support. When Saul died in battle, David became the new king.

David reunited the Hebrews and defeated the Canaanites. He captured a Canaanite fortress and on that site established Jerusalem (juh rū′ suh luhm), the capital of the Hebrew kingdom. A fine musician, David wrote many of the **psalms** (sahms), or sacred songs, found in the Bible.

After David died, his son Solomon (sahl′ uh muhn) became king. Through trade and treaties with other lands, Solomon brought peace and made the Hebrew kingdom more powerful. He built a huge temple in Jerusalem out of limestone, cedar wood, and gold. It was designed and built by artisans from Phoenicia.

Solomon's wealth and wisdom became known all through the Middle East. Many Hebrews, however, were not happy with Solomon. They did not like working on his building projects or paying the high taxes he demanded. After Solomon died, the Hebrews in the northern part of the country set up their own separate kingdom called Israel. A southern kingdom, which was ruled from Jerusalem, became known as Judah. For nearly 200 years, the two kingdoms fought each other off and on. Gradually, both became weak enough for others to conquer.

Stained-glass Window Showing David

The Prophets **Prophets,** or persons claiming to have messages from God, appeared in the Hebrew kingdoms. They came from cities and villages. They were teachers, farmers, and shepherds. They criticized the way the Hebrews were living. The rich were mistreating the poor, and government officials were accepting bribes. The prophets reminded the Hebrews of their duty to God and to one another. They warned the Hebrews that Yahweh would punish them if they did not return to His ways.

Some prophets added a new meaning to the laws of Moses. They taught that Yahweh was the god not only of Hebrews, but of everyone.

The people refused to listen to the prophets' warnings. Then, it was too late. Powerful neighbors took over the Hebrew kingdoms. After 722 B.C., the Israelites, the people of the northern kingdom, disappeared. Although the Judeans survived, most were forced to move to Babylonia in 586 B.C.

EXTENDING THE CONTENT

Solomon's Temple, though destroyed more than 2,500 years ago, is one of the best-known buildings of ancient times. From the description given in the First Book of Kings, we know even the names of artisans who worked on it. The temple had three rooms in a row, all 33 feet (11 m) wide; the outer porch, 16 feet (5 m) wide; the central hall or holy place, 66 feet (21 m) long; and steps leading up to the square inner chamber, or holy of holies, which was kept totally dark. The Ark of the Covenant was in the center of the holy of holies.

While in Babylonia, the Judeans, or Jews, made changes in their religion. Having lost the great temple at Jerusalem, they had to find some other way to worship God. They began meeting in small groups on the **sabbath,** or day of rest. The groups would pray and talk about their religion and history. The Jews wrote down their laws, sayings, and stories of the past on scrolls. The study of these writings led the Jews to value learning, and their teachers became important leaders.

The Jews spent 70 years in Babylonia before they were allowed to return to their homeland. They rebuilt Jerusalem and the temple. Under a scribe named Ezra, they wrote down the laws of Moses in five books called the *Torah* (tor' uh). Other writings were added later to make the Old Testament of the Bible.

HEBREW PROPHETS

Name	Teachings
Elijah *c. 850 B.C.*	Everyone should behave in a moral way.
Amos *c. 755 B.C.*	Prayers and sacrifices do not make up for bad deeds.
	Behaving justly is much more important than ritual.
Hosea *745-730 B.C.*	God is a god of love and compassion who loves His people the way a father loves his children.
	God suffers when people turn from Him and do not follow His commandments.
Isaiah of Jerusalem *740-701 B.C.*	People can have peace and prosperity only if they carry out God's will.
	The future depends on how justly one behaves in the present.
Micah *714-700 B.C.*	Both rich and poor have to obey God's laws.
	It is important to "do justly, love mercy, and walk humbly with thy God."
Jeremiah *626-587 B.C.*	Suffering is the result of wickedness.
	God will make a new covenant with the Jews in the future.
Ezekiel *593-571 B.C.*	People are responsible for their own behavior.
Isaiah of	God is the god of all people.
Babylon *c. 545 B.C.*	God will free Israel and lead it back to the promised land

LINKING PAST TO PRESENT

The earliest known copies of Old Testament texts make up part of the Dead Sea Scrolls. The scrolls were found in 1947 by a young Bedouin chasing a stray goat near the Dead Sea. Modern scholars continue to study these scrolls today.

L1 **Critical Thinking** Direct students to choose one of the teachings by a Hebrew prophet on the chart on page 113. Then have them explain the teaching in their own words. Ask volunteers to read their chosen teaching and interpretation.

VIDEODISC

Use the following to enrich Chapter 6.

WH E 57 14301

A Torah scroll in a synagogue in northern Israel.

ASSESS

CHECK FOR UNDERSTANDING

Ask students to summarize the main points of the chapter, orally or in writing. Discuss the answers to the Section and Chapter Review questions.

EVALUATE

Assign Chapter 6 **Performance Assessment Activity** in the TCR.

Administer **Chapter 6 Test** in the TCR. Testmaker available.

MEETING SPECIAL NEEDS

Discuss with students who are auditory learners what questions they would ask a rabbi about Judaism, if they had the opportunity. Ask a volunteer to record the questions.

If possible, arrange for a rabbi or religious resource person to speak to students, answering their questions in person. If a personal visit is not possible, ask the speaker to record the answers to the questions on tape. Play the recording for students.

RETEACH

Have students work in groups to outline different subsections. Then have groups exchange their outlines and use them to quiz other members of their group.

Assign Chapter 6 **Reteaching Activity** in the TCR.

ENRICH

Suggest students compare a psalm from the Book of Psalms to the lyrics of a modern song they know that also has a theme or message. Which is more understandable?

Assign Chapter 6 **Enrichment Activity** in the TCR.

CLOSE

Ask students to list places where people have historically practiced their religion such as temples, churches. Then have them describe how Jews changed their rituals when they no longer had the Jerusalem Temple.

MEETING CHAPTER OBJECTIVES

Each objective is tested by the Review questions in parentheses.

1. **Explain** how trade helped the Phoenicians and the Hebrews build their civilizations. (CU 2, 3; CT 1)
2. **Identify** the important cultural contributions made by the Phoenicians and the Hebrews. (BV; CU 1; UYJ)
3. **Describe** the religious beliefs held by the Hebrews. (CU 5, 6, 7; CT 3, 4)

Major Contributions The Hebrews were the first people to believe in one god. At first, they believed God was concerned only about them. They expected other people to worship many gods. Later, some prophets said God cared about all peoples and all nations.

The Hebrews were the first to believe in a just god. They believed individuals and society should likewise be just. Their laws were designed to teach people to treat one another fairly.

Section 2 Review

1. **Identify:** Hebrews, Judaism, Yahweh, Abraham, Moses, Saul, David, Jerusalem, Solomon, Israel, Judah, Jews, *Torah*
2. **Define:** Nomadic descendants, social justice, judge, psalms, prophets, sabbath
3. Where did early Hebrews trade? What goods did they trade?
4. What new ideas did Hebrews develop and contribute to later civilizations?

Critical Thinking

5. How was the Hebrew belief in one god significant to civilization?

Chapter Summary

1. Phoenician civilization began to develop about 1830 B.C.
2. Because Phoenicia's farmland was limited, many Phoenicians earned a living from the sea.
3. Phoenicia became well known for its cedar and purple dye.
4. The Phoenicians had many gods.
5. One of the most important Phoenician contributions to later civilizations is the spread of an alphabet.
6. The Phoenicians established many colonies along the North African coast, the most important of which was Carthage, founded in 814 B.C.
7. According to the Bible, God made an agreement with Abraham whereby the Hebrews could always live in Canaan if they would worship Him alone.
8. After a drought hit Canaan around 1700 B.C., the Hebrews moved to Egypt.
9. About 1200 B.C. , the Hebrews, who had been enslaved by the Egyptians, escaped and, under Moses' leadership, made a new covenant with God, promising to obey the Ten Commandments.
10. An important Hebrew contribution to later civilizations was the belief in one, just god and a just society.

SECTION 2 ANSWERS

1. Hebrews, followers of Judaism (p. 106); Judaism, ancient religion (p. 106); Yahweh, God (p. 107); Abraham, Hebrew leader (p. 107); Moses, led Hebrews (p. 109); Saul, first Hebrew king (p. 112); David, Hebrew king (p, 112); Jerusalem, Hebrew capital (p. 112); Solomon, David's son (p. 112); Israel, northern kingdom (p. 112); Judah, southern kingdom (p. 112); Jews, Judeans; *Torah*, the laws of Moses (p. 113)
2. nomadic, moving from place to place (p. 106); descendants, offspring (p. 107); social justice, equal treatment (p. 110); judge, settled disputes (p. 112); psalms, sacred songs (p. 112); prophets, had messages from God (p. 112); sabbath, day of rest (p. 113)
3. from Ur to Harran and along the Mediterranean coast; gold, copper, and ivory goods
4. the belief in a single god and a just society
5. Answers will vary.

Assign Chapter 6 **Section 2 Quiz** in the TCR. Testmaker available.

CHAPTER

Review 6

Building Vocabulary

Imagine that you are a traveler to Canaan. Use the following words to write a letter home explaining the new ideas that you have learned about in your visit.

treaties
holy of holies
colonies
descendants
social justice
judge
psalms
prophets
sabbath

Check for Understanding

1. Why were Phoenicians successful long-distance sailors?
2. How did the Phoenicians keep peace with their powerful neighbors?
3. What were some features of a Phoenician city-state?
4. What burial process did the Phoenicians learn from the Egyptians?
5. According to the Bible, what agreement did God make with Abraham?
6. Why did the Hebrews believe in social justice?
7. Why did the Jews make changes in their religion while living in Babylonia?
8. What did the Hebrews believe was the purpose of laws?

Critical Thinking

1. How can people who have very limited natural resources still manage to earn a living?
2. Why were language and religion by themselves not enough to unify the Phoenician people?
3. How does the idea that God is just affect the way in which people behave?
4. Explain the phrase, "do justly, love mercy, and walk humbly with thy God."
5. Why do you think many people during this time did not think people should listen to prophets?

Geography in History

PLACE The Hebrews moved from place to place within the same region along the Mediterranean Sea. Choose one of their migrations and describe the geography and features of the land through which they passed.

Using Your Journal

Review the details you have noted about the contributions of the Phoenicians and the Hebrews. Write a paragraph explaining how these contributions have affected your life.

CHAPTER 6 REVIEW ANSWERS

BUILDING VOCABULARY

Letters will vary but should include that these are new ideas they have learned in Canaan.

CHECK FOR UNDERSTANDING

1. because of strong, fast ships, and plotted courses
2. by signing peace treaties promising to supply free shipments of goods
3. Most were crowded, had stone walls around them for protection, with shops behind. The port lay outside the walls.
4. how to embalm bodies, wrap them in linen, and place them in stone coffins
5. that if Abraham and his followers were to go to Canaan and obey Yahweh they could always live there
6. because they should be like God who was just
7. because they had lost the great temple at Jerusalem
8. to teach people to treat one another fairly

CRITICAL THINKING

1. Answers will vary but should include through trade.
2. because mountains separated groups of Phoenicians
3. Answers will vary but should include that if people believe God is just, they will behave justly.
4. Answers will vary but should include that justice should be tempered with love and mercy.
5. Answers will vary but could refer to the power the prophets had to incite the people.

GEOGRAPHY IN HISTORY

Depending upon which migration students choose to describe, they should include arid, dry land; sand, mountains; little vegetation; rivers and/or Mediterranean Sea.

✚ BONUS ✚

TEST QUESTION

For Chapter 6 Test

Who would be more likely to win achievement awards in the following—a Canaanite or Aegean: agriculture, mathematics, wool weaving, map making, desert survival, astronomy. *(probable answers: Canaanites, Aegeans, Canaanites, both, Canaanites, Aegeans)*

USING YOUR JOURNAL

Paragraphs will vary but students might include the ways that the alphabet, the idea of treaties, the idea of one god, and the idea of social justice affect them.

CHAPTER

7 Military Empires

CHAPTER ORGANIZER

Objectives	Special Features	Supplemental Materials
Section 1 The Assyrians Discuss how the Assyrian civilization rose in Mesopotamia and expanded into neighboring lands.		• Reproducible Lesson Plan • Section 1 Quiz • Testmaker • Chapter 7 Vocabulary and Guided Reading Activity • Chapter 7 Teaching Transparency and Activity.•.Chapter 7 Activity Book Activity • The Western Civilization Videodisc • The World History Videodisc
Section 2 The Chaldeans Summarize the Chaldeans and their methods of ruling and increasing trade.		• Reproducible Lesson Plan • Section 2 Quiz • Testmaker • Reinforcing Social Studies Skills, pp.11, 28 • Chapter 7 Teaching Transparency and Activity • The Western Civilization Videodisc • The World History Videodisc
Section 3 The Persians Explain how Persian ideas spread through the forging of large empires, and how their social and religious life helped create a stable society.		• Reproducible Lesson Plan • Section 3 Quiz • Testmaker • Unit 3 Primary Source Reading • Chapter 7 Geography and Map Activity • Outline Map Resource p 32 • Chapter 7 Chart and Graph Skill Activity • Chapter 7 Cooperative Learning Activity • The World History Videodisc
Chapter 7 Review and Evaluation		• Chapter 7 Reteaching Activity • Chapter 7 Enrichment Activity • Chapter 7 Performance Assessment Activity • Spanish Summary and Glossary • Audiocassettes (English and Spanish) • Chapter 7 Test • Testmaker

If time does not permit teaching the entire chapter, use the Chapter 7 Summary on page 126 and the Chapter 7 Audiocassettes (English and Spanish) to point out the main ideas of the chapter.

✓ Performance Assessment Activities

Art Display The different cultures studied in this chapter were known for art forms of one kind or another. Have students create a visual record of the art forms and objects for each culture by modeling similar works of art. Suggest students consider a variety of media and substitute difficult-to-obtain materials with what is accessible. Display the finished projects.

Friendly Letters Instruct students to imagine that they are teenagers living in one of the civilizations described in the chapter. Tell them to write a letter to a friend in a neighboring city describing a day in their lives. Ask volunteers to share their letters with the class.

CHAPTER RESOURCES

READINGS FOR THE STUDENT

Jameson, Cynthia. *The Secret of the Royal Mounds: Henry Layard and the First Cities of Assyria.* Coward, McCann & Geoghegan, 1980. An illustrated account of the career of Layard, the discoverer of ancient Nineveh and one of the first scientific archaeologists.

Saggs, H.W. *Everyday Life in Babylonia and Assyria.* Dorset Press, 1987. Describes the life and customs of ancient Babylonians and Assyrians.

READINGS FOR THE TEACHER

Ceram, C.W. *The Secret of the Hittites.* Alfred Knopf, 1956. Discusses the role of the Hittites in ancient history.

Collins, Robert. *The Medes and the Persians: Conquerors and Diplomats.* McGraw-Hill, 1975. Recounts the daily lives, beliefs, and government of the ancient Persians.

MULTIMEDIA RESOURCES

The Rise of the West. Scholastic World History Filmstrip series. 4 Filmstrips. Discusses the origins of ancient civilizations of the Mediterranean region.

The Seven Wonders of the Ancient World. Questar. Video. Investigates the mysteries of each wonder of the world.

INTRODUCE

CHAPTER 7 OVERVIEW

Chapter 7 focuses on the Assyrian, Chaldean, and Persian empires and their contributions to the ancient Middle East.

- **Section 1** discusses the Assyrian civilization and its empire in Mesopotamia.
- **Section 2** explains the features of the Chaldean civilization and its city of Babylon.
- **Section 3** describes the contributions made by Persians to other civilizations.

CHAPTER OBJECTIVES

After reading Chapter 7, students will be able to:

1. explain how the Assyrians established and maintained an empire in Mesopotamia.
2. describe what the Chaldean city of Babylon was like.
3. discuss how the Persians were able to rule an empire that stretched from Egypt to India.

EXAMINING THE ILLUSTRATION

Ask students what form of transportation is shown. *(chariot)* Ask students to tell what they think of when they see chariots. Suggest that they decide why the chariot appropriately represents the Assyrian people, as they read the chapter.

PERFORMANCE ASSESSMENT

Use the Performance Assessment activities on page 116B to help you evaluate students as they complete the chapter.

CHAPTER 7 Military Empires

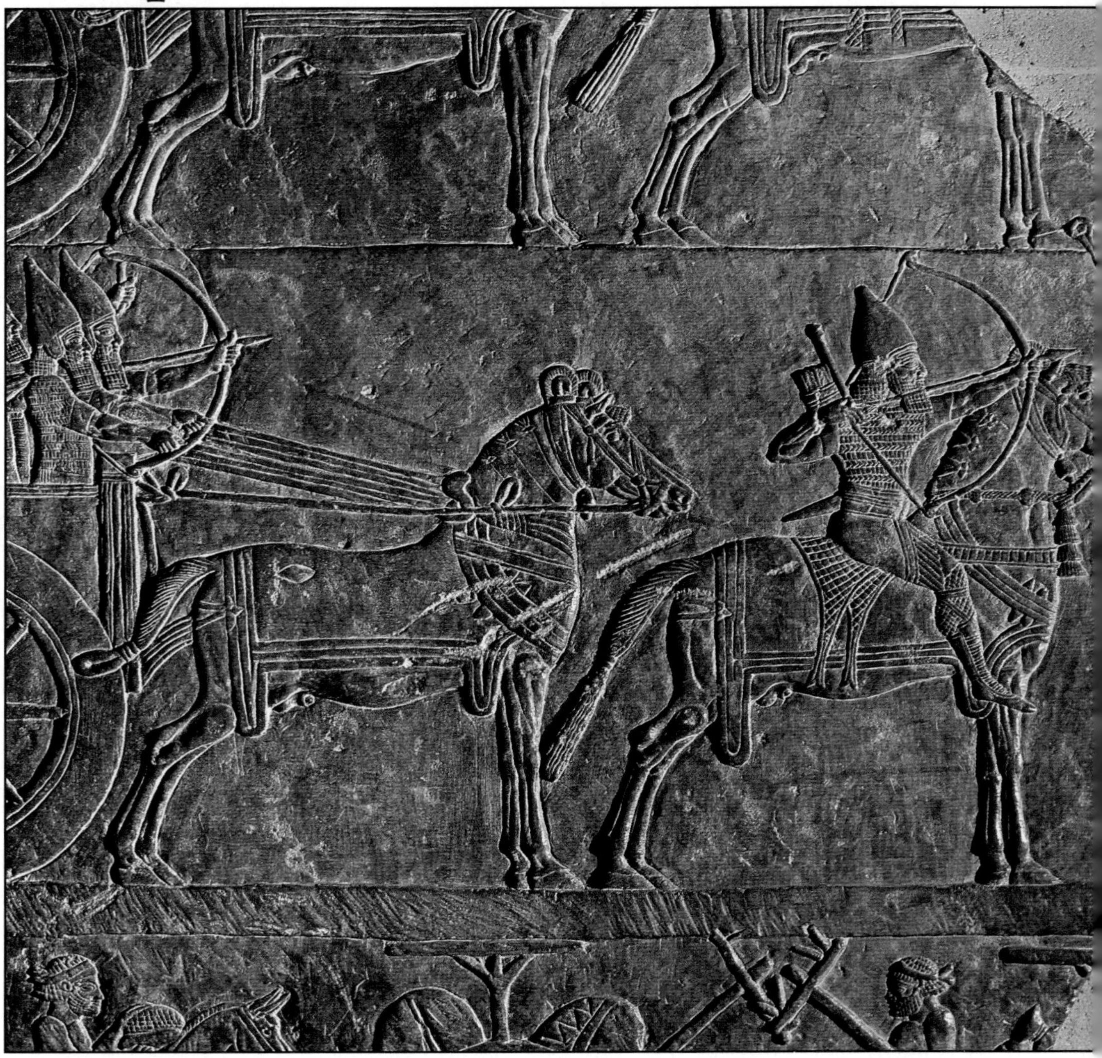

Relief Sculpture of Assyrian Chariot

116

TEACHER CLASSROOM RESOURCES

- Unit 3 Primary Source Reading
- Reproducible Lesson Plan
- Section Quizzes/Chapter Test
- Enrichment Activity
- Chart and Graph Skill Activity
- Geography and Map Activity
- Vocabulary and Guided Reading Activity
- Teaching Transparencies and Activities
- Cooperative Learning Activity
- Performance Assessment Activity
- Spanish Summary and Glossary
- Audiocassettes (English and Spanish)
- World History and Art Transparencies
- The World History Videodisc

Chapter Focus

READ TO DISCOVER:

- How the Assyrians established and maintained an empire in Mesopotamia.
- What the Chaldean city of Babylon was like.
- How the Persians were able to rule an empire that stretched from Egypt to India.

While the Phoenicians and the Hebrews were developing their civilizations, empires rose and fell in Mesopotamia. These empires were established by the Assyrians, the Chaldeans (kal dē′ uhns), and the Persians. None of these peoples were content to stay where their civilizations began. They raised powerful armies and expanded into neighboring lands. They developed new ways of ruling and increased trade. As a result, their ideas and customs spread.

1100 B.C.–570 B.C.

KEY TERMS
- smelting
- provinces
- caravans
- astronomers

Section 1

THE ASSYRIANS

About 1,000 years after Hammurabi ruled, a people called Assyrians rose to power in Mesopotamia. Their country, Assyria, lay in the upper part of the Tigris River valley. The Assyrians spoke the same language and used the same writing system as the Babylonians.

The Assyrians were warriors. Experts believe their liking for war was influenced by geography. Assyria's rolling hills and rain-watered valleys did not provide protection against invaders. Assyrian shepherds and farmers had to learn to fight to survive. In time, fighting became a way of life.

The Assyrians built a powerful army. By 1100 B.C., they had defeated their neighboring enemies. By 800 B.C., they were strong enough to take over cities, trading routes, and fortresses throughout Mesopotamia.

117

FOCUS

BELLRINGER

Write this saying on the chalkboard: *So passes away the glory of the world.* Ask students to write a sentence that explains the meaning of the word *glory* in this statement.

MOTIVATIONAL ACTIVITY

Discuss students' explanations of *glory*. Then ask the students to think about the world today and find examples of countries that are declining from a position of earlier glory.

VOCABULARY PRE-CHECK

Write the key terms for this chapter on the chalkboard. Ask students to skim the chapter for these boldfaced words and read aloud the sentences in which they are found. Ask if students can then find the meaning of the word in context.

Assign Chapter 7 **Vocabulary and Guided Reading Activity** in the TCR.

EXTRA CREDIT PROJECT

Wealthy Persian women, and sometimes men, rode in litters. Ask interested students to find out more about litters and other Persian methods of transportation. Suggest they draw illustrations or build simple models of the methods to share with the class.

KEY TO ABILITY LEVELS

Teaching strategies have been coded for varying learning styles and abilities.

L1 Level 1 activities are **basic** activities and should be within the ability range of all students.

L2 Level 2 activities are **average** activities and should be within the ability range of the average to above-average student.

L3 Level 3 activities are **challenging** activities designed for the ability range of above-average students.

LEP LEP activities should be within the ability range of Limited English Proficiency students.

CAPTION ANSWER

into units of foot soldiers, charioteers, calvary, and archers

MAKING CONNECTIONS

➤➤ **Daily Life** Many Assyrians lived in small villages in the midst of fields. Traders, government officers, and artisans lived in the cities in flat-roofed brick houses, some of which had bathrooms with asphalt floors and drains to carry away water. Most clothing was made of wool.

VIDEODISC

Use the following to enrich Chapter 7.

WC A 28 9030

Assyrian archers and slingers in battle.

ASSYRIAN SOLDIERS Assyrian kings often celebrated their victories by decorating palaces and temples with scenes of warfare. Here, a wall painting shows Assyrian soldiers killing enemy captives. **How was the Assyrian army organized?**

The Assyrian Army The Assyrian army was well-organized. It was divided into groups of foot soldiers armed with shields, helmets, spears, and daggers. It also had units of charioteers, cavalry, and archers.

At first, the Assyrians fought only during summer when they did not have to be concerned about planting or harvesting crops. Later, as they took over more land, soldiering became a year-round job. When the Assyrians needed more soldiers, they hired them from other places or forced the people they had conquered to serve.

Assyrian power was due partly to their weapons, which were made of iron. Iron weapons are harder and stronger than weapons made of copper or tin. Iron had been used in the Middle East for many centuries. Until about 1400 B.C., however, it was too soft to be made into weapons. Then, a people called Hittites (hi' tītz) developed a process of **smelting.** They heated iron ore, hammered out its impurities, and rapidly cooled it. The Assyrians borrowed the skill of smelting from the Hittites.

The Assyrians were cruel warriors. For several hundred years, their armies spread death and destruction throughout the Middle East. They were especially skilled in attacking cities. They tunneled under walls or climbed over them on ladders. They used beams mounted on movable platforms to ram holes through city gates. Once they captured a city, they set fire to its buildings and carried away its citizens and goods.

Anyone who resisted Assyrian rule was punished. Those who did not resist had to pay heavy taxes. The Assyrians also

MULTICULTURAL PERSPECTIVES

Assyrians were the first hairstylists. They refined this styling so much that hairstyles became a major part of the culture. Assyrians even had laws specifying the hairstyles of people in certain jobs. They cut short hair into graduated tiers and arranged long hair in ringlets and curls. They oiled, perfumed, and tinted hair. They even curled hair with a fire-heated iron bar, the first known curling iron.

found a way to conquer people without fighting. They spread stories of their cruelty. Other people were so frightened by the stories that they would simply surrender.

Kings and Government

Assyria's kings were strong leaders. They had to be to rule an empire that extended from the Persian Gulf in the east to the Nile Valley in the west. Assyrian kings spent much of their time fighting battles and punishing enemies. However, they were also involved in peaceful activities. A great Assyrian king, Ashurbanipal (osh uhr bon' uh pol), started one of the world's first libraries. It held 25,000 tablets of hymns, stories, and biographies.

Assyrian kings had to control many peoples spread over a large area. To do this, they divided their empire into **provinces,** or political districts. They then chose officials to govern each province. The officials collected taxes and made certain the king's laws were obeyed.

All provinces were connected by a system of roads. Although only roads near major cities were paved, all were level enough for carts and chariots to travel on. Over the roads moved the trade of the empire. Government soldiers were posted at stations along the

The Assyrian and Chaldean Empires

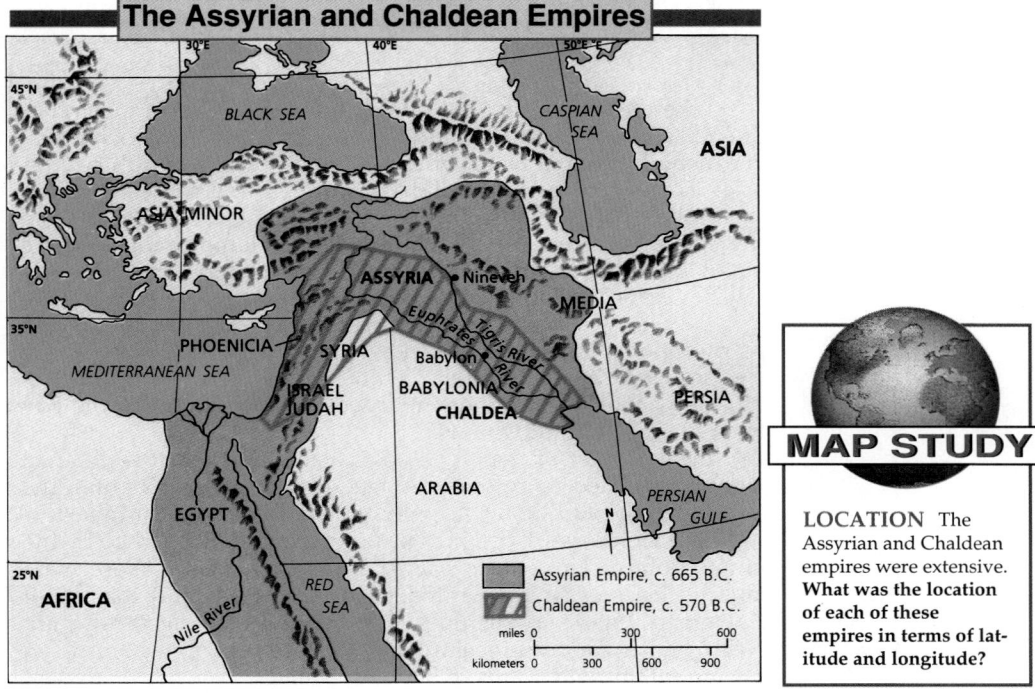

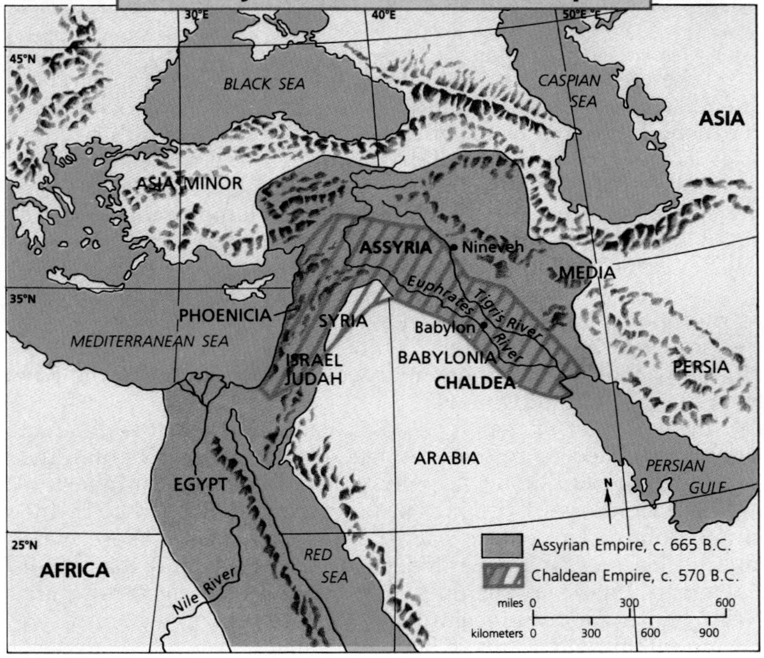

MAP STUDY

LOCATION The Assyrian and Chaldean empires were extensive. **What was the location of each of these empires in terms of latitude and longitude?**

TEACH

L1 **Map Reading** Ask the students to study the map on page 119 to answer the following questions: Which empire was larger, Chaldean or Assyrian? *(Assyrian Empire)* Which empire was located in the Tigris-Euphrates Valley? *(both)* What is the distance from Nineveh to Babylon? *(approximately 300 miles, or 483 km)* What part of the Chaldean Empire was not part of the Assyrian Empire? How can you tell? *(area in Arabia, between the Euphrates River and the Mediterranean Sea; This part has a yellow background.)*

MAKING CONNECTIONS

➤➤ **Culture** Assyrian kings were regarded as gods and as such had to follow certain religious customs. Five days a month they had to fast, and on the first day of the new year, they went without food and water until the moon came out. The king's presence at a battle was required to bring good fortune in war.

MAP STUDY Answers

approximately between 40° N and 20° N latitude and between 29° E and 50° E longitude

VIDEODISC

Use the following to enrich Chapter 7.

WH E 38 14282

Sennacherib laying seige to the city of Lachish.

SPOTLIGHT ON: ASHURBANIPAL

Ashurbanipal was both a brutal Assyrian king and a scholar. Since he was able to read and write Assyria's cuneiform writing, he collected every cuneiform tablet in the kingdom that he felt was worth saving. His collection was stored in his library at Nineveh. The collection included 22,000 tablets written in Sumerian, Babylonian, and Assyrian. These tablets represented 2,500 years of Mesopotamian written history and included letters, official documents, and dictionaries and studies of mathematics, astronomy, and botany.

GUIDED PRACTICE

L2 Geography: Movement Have students make travel plans for an ancient Greek who is planning to visit one of the empires discussed in this chapter. In a letter to the traveler, have students give detailed information, including a travel route and list of sites to visit.

VIDEODISC

Use the following to enrich Chapter 7.

WH E 40 14284

The famous Hanging Gardens of Babylon.

DID YOU KNOW ??

The ziggurat in Babylon is thought to be the Tower of Babel mentioned in the Book of Genesis, Chapter 11 of the Old Testament.

roads to protect traders from bandits. Messengers on government business used the stations to rest and to change horses.

In time, the empire became too large to govern. After Ashurbanipal died, various conquered peoples worked to end Assyrian rule. One group was the Chaldeans. In 612 B.C., they captured Nineveh (nin' uh vuh), the Assyrian capital. The Assyrian Empire crumbled shortly after.

Section 1 Review

1. **Identify:** Assyria, Hittites, Ashurbanipal, Nineveh
2. **Define:** smelting, provinces
3. How was Assyria governed?
4. Why did the Assyrian Empire fall?

Critical Thinking

5. Do you think ruling by fear is an effective way of governing people? Why or why not?

Section 2 THE CHALDEANS

Like the Assyrians, the Chaldeans were warriors who conquered many different peoples. Under their king Nebuchadrezzar (neb uh kuhd nez' uhr), they extended their empire's boundaries as far west as Syria and Palestine. The Chaldeans called themselves Babylonians. This was because most Chaldeans were descendants of the people who made up Hammurabi's empire about 1,200 years earlier. They built a new capital at Babylon in which nearly 1 million people lived.

Babylon was the world's richest city up to that time. It had its own police force and postal system. Huge brick walls encircled the city. The walls were so wide that two chariots could pass on the road on top. Archers guarded the approaches to the city from towers built into the walls.

In the center of the city stood palaces and temples. A huge ziggurat reached more than 300 feet, or over 90 meters, into the sky. When the sun shone, its gold roof could be seen for miles.

The richness of the ziggurat was equaled by that of the king's palace. The palace had "hanging gardens." These were layered beds of earth planted with large trees and masses of flowering vines and shrubs. They seemed to hang in mid-air. Nebuchadrezzar built the gardens to please his wife, who missed the mountains and plants of her native land.

Painting of Babylon's Hanging Gardens

SECTION 1 ANSWERS

1. Assyria, country in Tigris River valley (p. 117); Hittites, first to use smelting (p. 118); Ashurbanipal, Assyrian king (p. 119); Nineveh, Assyrian capital (p. 120)
2. smelting, process of heating iron ore, hammering it, and rapidly cooling it (p. 118); provinces, political districts (p. 119)
3. Assyrian kings divided their empire into provinces and then chose officials to govern each. The officials collected taxes and enforced laws.
4. because it became too large to govern and had many enemies
5. Answers will vary but students must give reasons to support their opinions. Characteristics of good leadership may be added.

Assign Chapter 7 **Section 1 Quiz** in the TCR. Testmaker available.

To please the people, Nebuchadrezzar built a beautiful street near the palace. It was paved with limestone and marble and lined by walls of blue glazed tile. Each spring, thousands of pilgrims crowded into Babylon to watch a gold statue of the god Marduk (mar' duhk) being wheeled along this street. The Chaldeans believed that the procession would make their crops grow. They also believed it would help keep peace in the empire.

Outside the center of Babylon stood houses and marketplaces. There, artisans made pottery, cloth, and baskets. These were sold to passing **caravans,** or groups of traveling merchants. Traders came to Babylon from as far away as India and Egypt. Trade helped make Babylon rich.

ENTRANCE TO BABYLON The Ishtar Gate was ancient Babylon's main entrance. It honored the goddess Ishtar and was covered with images of wild animals. **Why was Babylon surrounded by walls with gates?**

L1 **Daily Life** Provide students with an index card and suggest they imagine they are visitors in ancient Babylonia. They are to make a postcard to send to their families back in America. On one side of the postcard, students should draw an illustration of an area or a feature of the city of Babylon. On the other side of the postcard, students should write a note to their families giving their impressions of the city's appearance and the achievements and daily life of its people. Display the completed postcards on the bulletin board.

CAPTION ANSWER

because Babylon was one of the world's richest cities and it needed protection

VIDEODISC

Use the following to enrich Chapter 7.

WC A 33 9035

Ruins of of Nebuchadnezzar's palace in Babylon.

COOPERATIVE LEARNING

Have students use reference books in order to make a list of the Seven Wonders of the Ancient World. Then divide the class into seven groups. Assign each group a wonder of the ancient world to research and report on. Ask students to also list what they consider to be the Seven Wonders of the Modern World. Discuss their choices and compare them to the ancient wonders.

Assign Chapter 7 **Cooperative Learning Activity** in the TCR.

INDEPENDENT PRACTICE

L3 **Environment** In the Hanging Gardens, Nebuchadrezzar put plants that would remind his wife of her home in the mountains of Media (northern Iran). Have students research and make a catalog of plants that might have been planted in the Hanging Gardens.

L1 **Language Arts** Suggest students read more about the Assyrian cuneiform writing. Have them make a chart of some of its symbols and their meanings. Display the charts and have students explain whether or not they think cuneiform writing would be easier to learn and use than our writing. LEP

VIDEODISC

Use the following to enrich Chapter 7.

WH E 41 14285

A panorama of Persepolis, a palace built by Darius I.

Babylon was also a center of science. Chaldean **astronomers,** or people who collect, study, and explain facts about the heavenly bodies, believed that changes in the sky revealed the plans of the gods. So, they studied the stars, planets, and moon. Once they knew the movement of heavenly bodies, they made maps that showed the positions of the planets and the phases of the moon. Babylonian astronomers made one of the first sundials. They also were the first to have a seven-day week.

Babylon was the center of a great civilization for many years. As time passed, though, the Chaldeans began to lose their power. They found it hard to control the peoples they had conquered. Then, in 539 B.C., Persians from the mountains to the northeast captured Babylon. Mesopotamia became just another part of the Persian Empire.

Section 2 Review

1. **Identify:** Chaldeans, Nebuchadrezzar, Babylon, Marduk
2. **Define:** caravans, astronomers
3. What did the Chaldean astronomers contribute to science?
4. What led to the fall of the Chaldean Empire?

Critical Thinking

5. Under whose rule—the Assyrian or the Chaldean—would you have preferred to live? Give reasons for your choice.

Painting of an Immortal

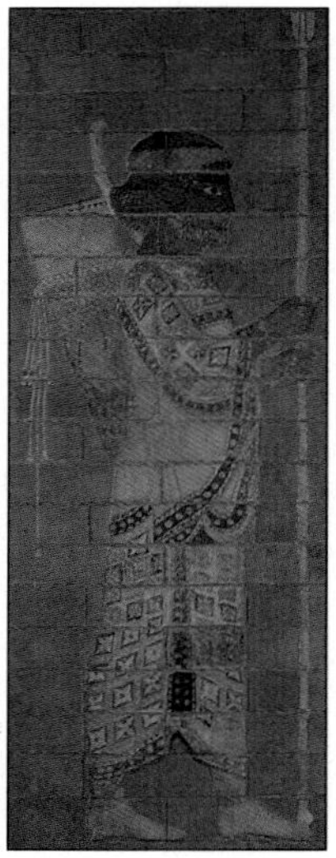

Section 3 THE PERSIANS

Originally, the Persians were part of the people known as Aryans. The Aryans were cattle herders from the grasslands of central Asia. About 2000 B.C., however, the Persians began to separate from other Aryans. They finally settled on a high plain between the Persian Gulf and the Caspian Sea, where they established Persia. Today, this region is called Iran (i ran'), or "the land of the Aryans." Modern Persians are Iranians (ir ā' nē uhnz).

The Persians lived peacefully in the highlands for over 1,000 years. They divided most of the country into large farms owned by nobles. The nobles spent most of their time riding horses and practicing archery. Their farms were worked by laborers.

There was little water on the hot plain. Farmers depended on streams that came down from the mountains. They dug underground tunnels from the springs to the fields. With water, farm-

SECTION 2 ANSWERS

1. Chaldeans, warrior people (p. 120); Nebuchadrezzar, king of Babylonians (p. 120); Babylon, capital of Babylonia (p. 120); Marduk, a Babylonian god (p. 121)
2. caravans, groups of traveling merchants (p. 121); astronomers, scholars who study the stars and planets (p. 122)
3. They made maps that showed the positions of the planets and the phases of the moon, made one of the first sundials, and were the first to use the seven-day week.
4. The Chaldeans found it hard to control the peoples they had conquered; some years, crops were poor and trade was slow; and in 539 B.C., the Persians captured Babylon.
5. Answers will vary but students must give reasons to support their opinions.

Assign Chapter 7 **Section 2 Quiz** in the TCR. Testmaker available.

PERSEPOLIS The grand city of Persepolis was built by the Persian king Darius. Here, the ruins of the royal palace at Persepolis are shown. Its walls are covered with carvings of soldiers and of conquered peoples bringing gifts to the Persian king. **Why did Darius build Persepolis?**

farmers were able to grow wheat and barley and to pasture flocks of fat-tailed sheep.

Army and Empire About 600 B.C., the Persians were conquered by the Medes (mēdz), a neighboring people. The Medes, however, were soon overthrown by the Persians under King Cyrus (sī′ ruhs). Cyrus then organized an army to conquer new territory. The army grew until it numbered in the hundreds of thousands. Its officers were Persians, while its soldiers were either Persians or conquered peoples.

The best fighters in the Persian army were the Immortals. They earned this name because their number never fell below 10,000. When an Immortal became sick, was wounded, or died, another soldier took his place. The Immortals had the honor of leading the Persian army into battle.

Within a short time, the Persians ruled an empire that stretched from Egypt to India. The Persians were mild rulers who allowed their subjects to keep their own language, religion, and laws. The Persians believed loyalty could be won more easily with fairness than with fear or force. They wanted their subjects to pay taxes and to produce goods for trade. They felt these things would not be done if those under their rule were treated badly.

One of the strongest Persian kings was Darius (duh rī′ uhs). He wanted a monument to honor his military victories. So, he brought artisans from many lands to build a grand palace-fortress-treasury in the capital city of Persepolis (puhr sep′ uh luhs). Buildings with many columns were constructed on giant stone

L2 **Critical Thinking** Have students compare the photograph on this page with the photograph of the Egyptian temple at Kom Ombo on page 76. Ask students how the buildings are alike and how they differ, and have them give reasons for their similarities and differences.

CAPTION ANSWER

He wanted a monument to honor his military victories.

MAKING CONNECTIONS

➤➤ **Language Arts** Many English words come from Iran, or ancient Persia, by way of the Greek language. There are flower names such as *rose, jasmine, lilac,* and *narcissus*. There are food names, such as *asparagus, orange, peach, rice,* and *spinach*. Other words include *peacock, tapestry, tiara,* and *tiger*.

VIDEODISC

Use the following to enrich Chapter 7.

WH E 44 14288

A carved stone archer at Susa in southwestern Iran.

MEETING SPECIAL NEEDS

Have students who are auditory learners debate the following topic: *Conquerors should maintain tight control over conquered peoples in order to keep their empires together.* Form two teams, one to defend the idea that conquerors should maintain tight control and the other to defend the idea that conquered peoples should be treated fairly. After giving each team time to research and develop its arguments, have each team present their views.

DID YOU KNOW ??

Most wealthy Persian men traveled on horseback or in a litter. They thought that only the lower class should be seen walking. Men wore their beards long and curled. They used makeup on their faces, colored their eyelids, and perfumed themselves.

LINKING PAST TO PRESENT

Zoroaster taught that one could love God only by loving humanity. In Zoroastrianism, the sun was considered the great cleansing power and fire, a symbol of purity. Today most followers of the religion live in India and are called Parsees, which means Persians.

VIDEODISC

Use the following to enrich Chapter 7.

WH E 49 14293

A silver head of woman from Persia, 1st century B.C.

Relief Sculpture of Persian Winged God

platforms. In the gateways, workers carved figures that were half human and half beast. Persepolis became the most magnificent city in the empire.

Government Officials The king did not govern alone. There were many officials to carry out his orders. They all spoke Aramaic (ar uh mā′ ik). This was the language used by Middle Eastern merchants.

The king chose a governor, a secretary, and a general for each of the 20 provinces of the empire. These officials collected taxes of gold, silver, sheep, horses, wheat, and spices and sent them to the royal treasury in Persepolis. These officials also settled local quarrels and protected the people against bandits. Each reported separately to the king. This helped keep them honest. If one was stealing tax money, for example, the others were sure to report it. The king would then remove the dishonest official from office.

Another group of officials was the inspectors. Called "the Eyes and Ears of the King," they traveled throughout the empire. They decided whether people were able to pay their taxes. They also checked on rumors of possible rebellion. The inspectors never warned provincial officials they were coming. This made provincial officials careful about doing a good job.

The last group of officials was the judges. They made sure that the king's laws were carried out properly.

Family Life The Persians lived in houses with pointed roofs and porches that faced the sun. Poor families had one-room houses. Noble families had houses with one set of rooms for men and another for women and children.

Persian families were large. Fathers ruled their families in much the same way the king ruled the empire. A father's word was law. Poor children worked with their parents. The children of nobles, however, were cared for by their mothers until they were five years old. Then, they were raised by enslaved people. Often, they did not see their fathers until they reached adulthood. Boys were trained to ride horses and draw a bow. Girls were trained to run households and raise children.

Rich women lived very sheltered lives. They spent most of their time at home apart from the men. If they had to leave the house, they stepped into a closed *litter,* or a carriage without wheels that was carried by servants. Poor women had more freedom, but they had to work hard.

Religion At first, the Persians worshiped many gods. Then, about 570 B.C., a religious leader named Zoroaster (zōr′ uh was tuhr) told the Persians about two gods. One god, Ahura Mazda (uh hūr′ uh maz′ duh), was wise and truthful. He created all good things in the world. The other god, Ahriman (ar′ i muhn),

EXTENDING THE CONTENT

Kings Cyrus and Darius are given credit for setting up a postal system that served the main part of the Persian Empire. Along the Royal Road from Sardis in Asia Minor to Susa near the Persian Gulf, there were more than a hundred relay stations where mounted messengers could change horses. The Persian postal service was described by the Greek historian Herodotus in the following way: *Neither snow, nor rain, nor heat, nor gloom of night stays these couriers from the swift completion of their appointed rounds.*

made all evil things in the world. Ahura Mazda and Ahriman were at war with each other all of the time.

Zoroaster said human beings had to decide which god they would support. Zoroaster then listed the good and bad deeds a person performed. Good deeds were keeping one's word, giving to the poor, working the land, obeying the king, and treating others well. Bad deeds included being lazy, proud, or greedy. Zoroaster could tell from the list which god a person had chosen. He believed that in the end Ahura Mazda would defeat Ahriman. People who supported Ahura Mazda would enjoy happiness after death. Those who supported Ahriman would be punished.

Trade The Persians thought they should be warriors, farmers, or shepherds. They refused to become traders. They believed that trade forced people to lie, cheat, and be greedy. They did, however, encourage trade among all peoples they conquered.

The Persians improved and expanded the system of roads begun by the Assyrians. One road, the Royal Road, ran more than 1,600 miles, or more than 2,560 kilometers. A journey that took three months before the Royal Road was built took only 15 days after it was completed. The Persians also opened a caravan route to China. Silk was first brought west along this route.

MAP STUDY

REGIONS The Persian Empire stretched from the Nile River to the Indus River, a distance of 3,000 miles, or 4,800 kilometers. Within this empire, the Persians ruled more than 50 million people. **Into what continents did the Persian Empire extend?**

The Persian Empire

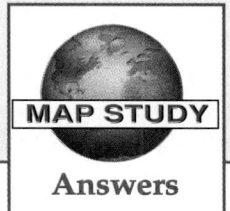

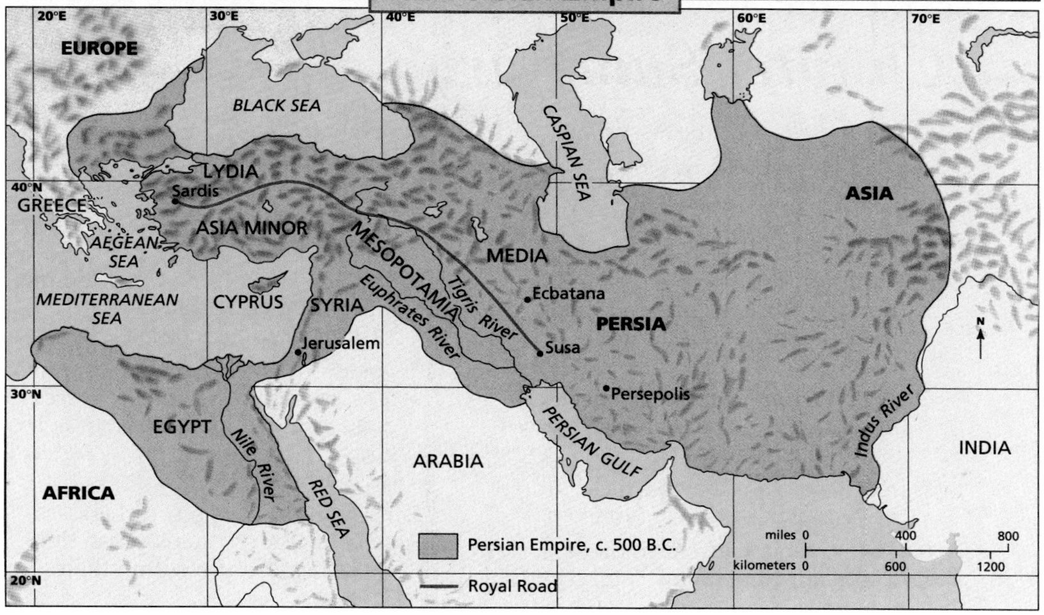

L2 **Map Scale** Have students use the map of the Persian Empire to find the distances between the following places: Susa and Sardi along the Royal Road *(approximately 2,400 miles or 3,862 km)*, Susa and Jerusalem *(approximately 750 miles or 1,206 km)*, Ecbatana and Jerusalem *(approximately 700 miles or 1,126 km)*, Persepolis and Sardis *(approximately 1,350 miles or 2,173 km)*. LEP

MAP STUDY

Answers

Europe, Asia, and Africa

ASSESS

CHECK FOR UNDERSTANDING

Ask students to summarize the main points of the chapter, orally or in writing. Discuss the answers to the Section and Chapter Review questions.

EVALUATE

Assign Chapter 7 **Performance Assessment Activity** in the TCR.

Administer **Chapter 7 Test** in the TCR. Testmaker available.

MEETING SPECIAL NEEDS

Divide students with Limited English Proficiency into three groups. Have each group prepare a travel poster on one of the empires discussed in the chapter. Explain that their poster should try to sell their assigned empire as a vacation destination. Have students work together on a format for presenting the information on the poster. Encourage students to include points of interest. Display completed posters.

RETEACH

Organize students into small groups to compose a song or rap that expresses the main ideas of one section in the chapter.

Assign Chapter 7 **Reteaching Activity** in the TCR.

ENRICH

Have students investigate one of the people discussed in the chapter and write a biographical sketch of the person. Suggest authors present the biographical sketch to the class as if they are that person.

Assign Chapter 7 **Enrichment Activity** in the TCR.

CLOSE

Have students discuss this question: *Based on your reading of the chapter—which is more likely to bring about change in a culture—an idea brought to people through peaceful means or an idea forced on them?*

MEETING CHAPTER OBJECTIVES

Each objective is tested by the Review questions in parentheses.

1. **Explain** how the Assyrians established an empire in Mesopotamia. (CU 1, 2; CT 1)
2. **Describe** what the Chaldean city of Babylon was like. (CU 3)
3. **Discuss** how the Persians ruled an empire that stretched from Egypt to India. (BV; CU 5, 6, CT 3; GIH)

Persian Coin

The Persians spread the idea of using coins for money. The first known coins had been made in Lydia (lid' ē uh), a tiny kingdom in Asia Minor bordering on the Aegean Sea. After conquering Lydia, the Persian king decided to use gold coins in his empire. This helped to increase trade. It also changed the nature of trade. Merchants who had sold only costly goods began to sell everyday, cheaper things as well. They sold chickens, dried fish, furniture, clothing, and pots and pans. Since people could get more goods, they began to live better than they had before.

Section 3 Review

1. **Identify**: Persians, Medes, Cyrus, Immortals, Darius, Persepolis, Aramaic, Lydia
2. How did the Persians treat the people they conquered?
3. What religious ideas did Zoroaster introduce to Persia?
4. In what ways did the Persians contribute to the growth of trade within their empire?

Critical Thinking

5. How do the roles of government officials in the United States today compare with the roles of the government officials in Persia?

Chapter Summary

1. Around 800 B.C., the Assyrians established an empire in Mesopotamia.
2. The Assyrians developed a well-organized, full-time army.
3. The Assyrians borrowed smelting from the Hittites and used this process to make strong iron weapons.
4. The Assyrian Empire was divided into provinces that were linked by a system of roads.
5. In 612 B.C., the Chaldeans captured the Assyrian capital of Nineveh.
6. Under Nebuchadrezzar, the Chaldeans built a new capital at Babylon.
7. Babylon was a center of trade and science for many years.
8. In 539 B.C., Babylon was captured by the Persians, and Mesopotamia became part of the Persian Empire.
9. The Persians divided their empire into provinces, each governed by various groups of officials.
10. About 570 B.C., Zoroaster taught a new religion in which the forces of good and evil took the form of two gods who were constantly fighting each other.
11. Though the Persians did not become traders themselves, they encouraged trade within their empire.

SECTION 3 ANSWERS

1. Persians, cattle herders (p. 122); Medes, conquerors of Persians (p. 123); Cyrus, king of Persians (p. 123); Immortals, best fighters (p. 123); Darius, Persian king (p. 123); Persepolis, capital of Persia (p. 123); Aramaic, language of Middle East (p. 124); Lydia, small kingdom (p. 126)
2. The Persians let them keep their own language, religion, and laws.
3. one good and one bad god, choosing a. god, and punishment after death
4. They improved the system of Assyrian roads, opened a caravan route to China, and spread coins.
5. Answers will vary but may include Persian officials were appointed, whereas U.S. officials are elected; both Persian and U.S. officials dealt with taxation, and in providing protection.

Assign Chapter 7 **Section 3 Quiz** in the TCR. Testmaker available.

CHAPTER

Review 7

Building Vocabulary

Imagine you are writing a feature magazine article about the Assyrian and Chaldean empires. Use the following words in your article to describe some of the achievements made in these two empires.

smelting
provinces
caravans
astronomers

Check for Understanding

1. What do experts believe influenced the Assyrians to become warriors?
2. What made the Assyrians such feared fighters?
3. Why did the Chaldeans call themselves Babylonians?
4. What was the importance of the god Marduk to the Babylonians?
5. What was the relationship between the Persians and the Aryans?
6. In Persian government, who were "the Eyes and Ears of the King" and what did they do?
7. How was family life in Persia alike for both rich and poor?
8. Why did the Persians refuse to become traders?

Critical Thinking

1. How can the reputation of a group like the Assyrians affect how others act toward that group?
2. How did the introduction of coins influence trade?
3. How would you describe the Persian attitude toward trade and how wise was this attitude?
4. In which of the empires discussed in this chapter would you have most enjoyed living? Why?

Geography in History

HUMAN/ENVIRONMENTAL INTERACTION What changes in their environment did the Persians make that extended ideas started by the Assyrians and Chaldeans?

Using Your Journal

Review the details you have noted about the contributions made by the people you studied in this chapter. Choose one of the contributions and in a short paragraph explain how it has been expanded and advanced.

✚ BONUS ✚

TEST QUESTION

For Chapter 7 Test

What is smelting and why was this technology important to the development of a system of roads by the Assyrians? *(Smelting, the process of heating and cooling metal to form it, allowed the Assyrians to make weapons that made them successful conquerors. The Assyrians accumulated a huge kingdom and needed a system of roads.)*

USING YOUR JOURNAL

Paragraphs will vary but should explain how the contribution has been expanded and advanced. You might call on volunteers to share their paragraphs with the class.

CHAPTER 7 REVIEW ANSWERS

BUILDING VOCABULARY

Articles will vary but students should use the words to describe some Assyrian and Chaldean achievements.

CHECK FOR UNDERSTANDING

1. Assyria's geography
2. They were cruel warriors, burned cities, and carried away its citizens and goods.
3. because most were descendants of the people who made up Hammurabi's empire about 1,200 years earlier
4. They believed Marduk would make their crops grow and help keep peace.
5. The Persians were originally part of the Aryan people.
6. They were government officials who traveled throughout the empire to assess taxes and check on rumors of rebellion.
7. Both lived in houses with pointed roofs and porches that faced the sun, and both had large families ruled by the father.
8. because they believed that trade forced people to lie, cheat, and be greedy

CRITICAL THINKING

1. Answers will vary but should include a reputation of strength or cruelty will cause fear.
2. It increased trade and the types of goods sold.
3. Answers will vary but should include Persians' aversion to trade that later changed.
4. Answers will vary.

GEOGRAPHY IN HISTORY

The Persians extended roads started by the Assyrians and maintained the division into provinces. Farming methods including irrigation canals were borrowed from the Chaldeans.

PLANNING GUIDE

CHAPTER 8

Africa and the Americas

CHAPTER ORGANIZER

Objectives	Special Features	Supplemental Materials
Section 1 Ancient African Kingdoms Discuss how the ancient African civilizations of Kush and Aksum passed along elements of their culture.		• Reproducible Lesson Plan • Section 1 Quiz • Testmaker • Chapter 8 Vocabulary and Guided Reading Activity • Chapter 8 Cooperative Learning Activity • The World History Videodisc
Section 2 The Middle Kingdoms Identify how West African kingdoms grew and developed.	Map and Geography Skills: *Reading Latitude,* p. 135	• Reproducible Lesson Plan • Section 2 Quiz • Testmaker • Primary Source Reading • Chapter 8 Geography and Map Activity • • The World History Videodisc
Section 3 East African Civilizations Summarize how East African civilizations developed as trading regions.		• Reproducible Lesson Plan • Section 3 Quiz • Testmaker • Chapter 8 Chart and Graph Skill Activity • Unit 3 Primary Source Reading • Unit 3 World Literature
Section 4 Path to the Americas Explain why bands of people crossed into the Americas from Asia.		• Reproducible Lesson Plan • Section 4 Quiz • Testmaker • The World History Videodisc
Section 5 Mesoamerica Describe the kinds of civilizations that developed in Mesoamerica.		• Reproducible Lesson Plan • Teaching Transparencies and Activities • Section 5 Quiz • Testmaker • The World History Videodisc
Section 6 The Incas Characterize what life was like for the Incas of South America.		• Reproducible Lesson Plan • World Art and History Transparency 14 • Section 6 Quiz
Chapter 8 Review and Evaluation		• Chapter 8 Reteaching Activity • Chapter 8 Enrichment Activity • Chapter 8 Performance Assessment Activity • Spanish Summary and Glossary • Audiocassettes (English and Spanish) • Chapter 8 Test • Testmaker

If time does not permit teaching the entire chapter, use the Chapter 8 Summary on page 142 and the Chapter 8 Audiocassettes (English and Spanish) to point out the main ideas of the chapter.

Performance Assessment Activities

A Geographical Journal Have students keep a geographical journal of the continents they will study in this chapter (Africa, North America, South America). Instruct them to sketch an outline map of each continent on which to locate each empire or civilization as it is studied and any other information they choose. Maps should include a title and a legend. Display the maps in the classroom.

Charting Trade Instruct students to make a trading chart that shows the products or goods each African or American culture produced and those items that each culture needed to acquire from other people. Encourage students to bring in one or two products on their charts, if possible.

CHAPTER RESOURCES

LITERATURE ABOUT THE PERIOD

Bierhorst, John, ed. *The Hungry Woman: Myths and Legends of the Aztecs.* William Morrow, 1984. New versions of traditional tales, with illustrations by Aztec artists.

Courlander, Harold. *A Treasury of African Folklore.* Crown Publishers, 1975. Collection of the oral literature, traditions, myths, and legends of Africa.

Drachler, Jacob, ed. *African Heritage.* Collier Books, 1969. Stories, poems, songs, folktales, and essays about African history.

READINGS FOR THE STUDENT

Brooks, Lester. *Great Civilizations of Ancient Africa.* Four Winds Press, 1971. Comprehensive study of the ancient empires of Africa.

Chu, Daniel, and Elliot Skinner. *A Glorious Age in Africa; the Story of Three Great African Empires.* Doubleday (Zenith Books), 1990. Illustrated account of Ghana, Mali, and Songhai.

Stuart, Gene S. *America's Ancient Cities.* National Geographic Society, 1988. Illustrated collection of essays on cultures of North America and Mesoamerica.

READINGS FOR THE TEACHER

Davidson, Basil. *African Kingdoms.* Time-Life Books, 1971. History of the early African kingdoms.

Gallenkamp, Charles. *Maya: The Riddle and Rediscovery of a Lost Civilization.* Viking, 1985. Detailed account of the Mayas.

Gardner, John L., ed. *Mysteries of the Ancient Americas.* Reader's Digest Association, 1986. Reveals new facts about the ancient American civilizations.

MULTIMEDIA RESOURCES

Africa. Opportunities for Learning Inc. Software. Simulates African history and geography.

Ancient Africans. International Film Foundation. Video. Survey of early African history.

The Ancient New World. Churchill Films. Film. Describes the early cultures of Mesoamerica.

INTRODUCE

CHAPTER 8 OVERVIEW

Chapter 8 focuses on the development of civilization in Africa and the Americas.

- **Section 1** discusses the Kush and Aksum civilizations.
- **Section 2** explains West African kingdoms and contributions.
- **Section 3** describes the contributions of the East African civilizations.
- **Section 4** explains why people migrated to the Americas .
- **Section 5** summarizes the civilizations of Mesoamerica.
- **Section 6** analyzes the Inca civilization of South America.

CHAPTER OBJECTIVES

After reading Chapter 8, students will be able to:

1. discuss how the ancient civilizations of Kush and Aksum passed along their culture.
2. summarize how West African and East African kingdoms developed because of trade.
3. explain why bands of people crossed into the Americas from Asia.
4. describe the civilizations that developed in Mesoamerica.
5. discuss life of the Incas of South America.

EXAMINING THE ARTIFACT

Ask students how they can recognize when a person holds a particular position or office. *(wearing a crown, uniform, badge)* These gold discs showed the high office of rulers in ancient Ghana.

PERFORMANCE ASSESSMENT

Use the Performance Assessment activities on page 128B to help you evaluate students as they complete the chapter.

CHAPTER 8 Africa and the Americas

Ghanan Gold Disks of Office

TEACHER CLASSROOM RESOURCES

- Unit 3 Primary Source Reading
- Unit 3 World Literature
- Reproducible Lesson Plan
- Section Quizzes/Chapter Test
- Reteaching Activity
- Enrichment Activity
- Geography and Map Activity
- Vocabulary and Guided Reading Activity
- Teaching Transparencies and Activities
- Cooperative Learning Activity
- Performance Assessment Activity
- Spanish Summary and Glossary
- Audiocassettes (English and Spanish)
- Testmaker
- World History Videodisc

Chapter Focus

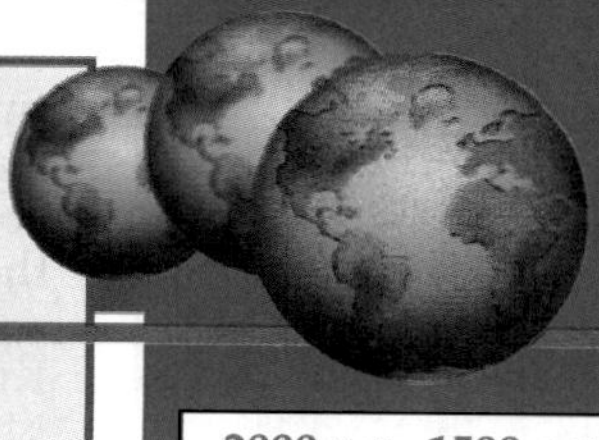

READ TO DISCOVER:

- How the ancient African civilizations of Kush and Aksum passed along elements of their culture.
- How West African kingdoms and East African civilizations grew because of trade.
- Why bands of people crossed into the Americas from Asia.
- What kinds of civilizations developed in Mesoamerica.
- What life was like for the Incas of South America.

Some civilizations developed in the Middle East. Others developed in Africa south of the Sahara and in the Americas. Like the Middle Eastern civilizations, those of sub-Saharan Africa and the Americas were of two kinds. One kind was interested in trade and ideas. The other was interested in war.

2000 B.C.–1500 A.D.

KEY TERMS

silent barter
pilgrimage
population explosion
quipus

Section 1

ANCIENT AFRICAN KINGDOMS

Other civilizations besides Egypt flourished in ancient Africa. Less is known about them than about Egypt. However, archaeologists have discovered enough remains to be able to tell what African civilizations were like.

Kush The first of these African civilizations was Kush. It lay south of Egypt on the Nile River in present-day Sudan (sū dan'). Its history began about 2000 B.C. At that time, the Kushites were nomadic cattle herders. They grazed long-horned cattle on a *savannah* (suh van' uh), or grassy plain.

During the New Kingdom, Egyptian armies conquered Kush. Kush remained part of Egypt for almost 500 years. Over

FOCUS

BELLRINGER

Ask students to estimate what percentage of time they spend each day eating and sleeping—the basic functions of living.

MOTIVATIONAL ACTIVITY

Ask students to share their time estimates. Discuss how the ability to take care of basic needs influences the kind of life people can lead. Suggest that students recall this discussion as they study the empires and civilizations in this chapter.

VOCABULARY PRE-CHECK

Write the key terms for this chapter on the chalkboard. Before students read the chapter ask students to skim the chapter for these boldfaced words and read the sentences in which they are found.

Assign Chapter 8 **Vocabulary and Guided Reading Activity** in the TCR.

EXTRA CREDIT PROJECT

What's so important about salt? Ask interested students to research to find the answer to that question and others as they relate to the people of ancient West Africa. How could salt be as valuable to people as gold? How was salt mined then? How is it mined today? Encourage students to share what they learn in a report or visual presentation.

KEY TO ABILITY LEVELS

Teaching strategies have been coded for varying learning styles and abilities.

L1 Level 1 activities are **basic** activities and should be within the ability range of all students.

L2 Level 2 activities are **average** activities and should be within the ability range of the average to above-average student.

L3 Level 3 activities are **challenging** activities designed for the ability range of above-average students.

LEP LEP activities should be within the ability range of Limited English Proficiency students.

TEACH

L2 **Communication** Have two students act out a silent barter, using modern objects and ask why this technique was used in Africa. *(to eliminate language problems, to show trust and good will)* Ask students how difficult or simple their simulated barter was. Would this be successful in modern times? Have the class discuss why effective trade was important to the growth of African kingdoms.

LINKING PAST TO PRESENT

The present nation of Ghana is not located in the same area of West Africa as the empire of Ghana was located in the mid-1000s. The early empire of Ghana is now occupied by the countries of Mauritania and Mali.

DID YOU KNOW ??

Ancient Ghana's capital consisted of two cities connected by a road lined with houses. The king and soldiers lived in one city; Arab traders lived in the second city.

VIDEODISC

Use the following to enrich Chapter 8.

WH A 36 10036
Map, caravans, gold and salt mining, Ghana.

WH A 37 10037
A salt caravan arriving at Timbuktu.

Section 2

THE MIDDLE KINGDOMS

Several large trading kingdoms arose in West Africa after 400 A.D. Their rise was aided by the knowledge of iron-smelting. This was most likely brought to West Africa by *refugees*, or people who flee for safety, from Kush.

Ghana The first of these trading kingdoms was Ghana (gah' nuh). Legend has it that Ghana was founded about 200 A.D. Around 350 A.D., the Ghanians learned how to smelt iron. With iron swords and lances, Ghanian warriors expanded the boundaries of their country. They also gained control over West Africa's major trade routes.

Along these trade routes, goods were carried by caravans of camels or donkeys. The most important goods were salt and gold. Caravans carried salt south from Taghaza (tuh gah' zuh) in present-day Algeria (al jir' ē uh). They returned north with gold from Wangara (wahn gar' uh), an area southwest of Ghana.

Ghanian merchants and Wangara gold miners used a trading technique called **silent barter.** Ghanian merchants would travel to a trading site along a river in Wangara. They would place salt and other goods on the ground and beat drums to signal the gold miners. Then, they would withdraw. Next, the gold miners would appear, look at the goods, and leave some gold. Then, they would withdraw. If the Ghanians thought they had received enough gold, they would take it and leave. If not, they would withdraw and wait for the miners to leave more gold. When the exchange was over, the Ghanians would trade the gold to merchants from North Africa. Often, the gold was shipped to Europe and Asia for sale.

Photograph of Camel Caravan

Only gold dust could be used in trade. Nuggets became the property of the king, who controlled the economy. Legend has it that one nugget was so heavy that it served as a hitching post for the king's horses.

In 1042 A.D., Arabs from North Africa started a war against Ghana. They destroyed the capital and made the Ghanians give them tribute. Ghana managed to regain its independence but was not strong enough to survive.

Mali By 1240 A.D., Ghana was a part of Mali (mah' lē), the second large trading kingdom in West Africa. The king of Mali, whose army had conquered Ghana, was Sundiata Keita (sūn dē ah' tuh kī ' tuh), or "Hungering Lion."

EXTENDING THE CONTENT

For years historians thought that the technology for making steel was first created in Europe, and that Wilhelm Siemans built the first steel-making furnace in Germany. Recently, however, 13 steel-making furnaces have been discovered on the shores of Lake Victoria in Africa. Early Africans had the technology for making steel tools before 400 A.D. and possibly as early as 100 B.C.

L1 ***Daily Life*** *Have students imagine they are Arab traders traveling to Ghana, Mali, or Songhai.* Ask the "traders" to make a list of the goods they are bringing to trade and the goods they will be trading for. Suggest students also include the means by which they are traveling. Ask students which kingdom they would most like to trade with and why.

MAKING CONNECTIONS

➤➤ **Agriculture** The people of Mali grew such crops as sorghum, rice, yams, beans, and onions. They also grew cotton, which they made into cloth.

CAPTION ANSWER

The kings or rulers controlled the gold in ancient Africa.

VIDEODISC

Use the following to enrich Chapter 8.

WH A 30 10030
Cattle and herders near Timbuktu, Mali.

WH A 38 10038
A West African king holding a gold nugget.

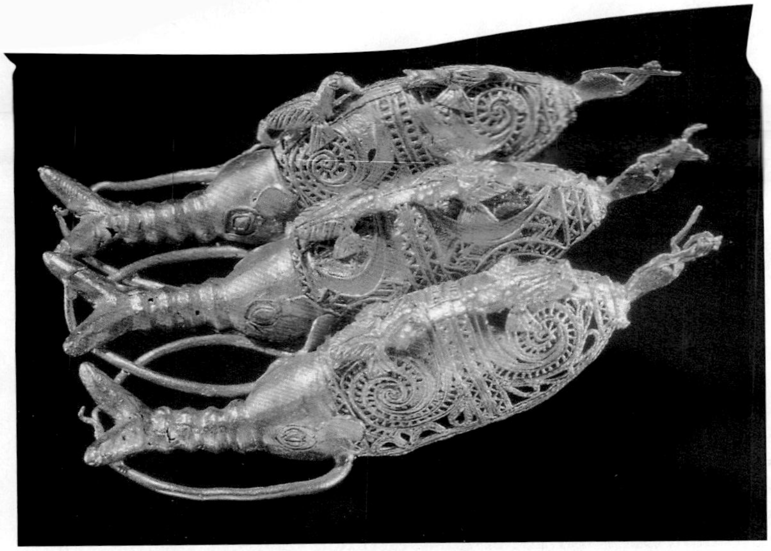

GOLD DESIGNS The gold mined in ancient Africa was often formed into intricate designs on jewelry and ceremonial ornaments. These pieces are elephant charms. **Who controlled most of the gold supply in ancient Ghana?**

Sundiata Keita did several things to make his kingdom strong. He reestablished the salt—gold trade, which the Arabs had disrupted. He organized a permanent army. He divided the kingdom into provinces, each headed by a general. The generals kept the peace and saw that there was enough food for the people. To strengthen ties with different groups in the kingdom, Sundiata Keita moved his capital from place to place.

Sundiata Keita wanted to impress the people with his power. When he appeared in public, trumpeters announced his arrival. He sat on an ebony throne under an arch made from large elephant tusks. He never spoke directly to people. Instead, requests were answered by servants standing at the foot of the stairs leading to the throne.

One of the most famous kings of Mali was Mansa Musa I (mahn' sah mū' sah), or King Moses I. One reason Mansa Musa was famous was because of a **pilgrimage** (pil' gruh mij), or religious journey, he made to Arabia in 1324–25. It took more than 14 months to cover the 3,000 miles, or 4,800 kilometers. Some 12,000 servants traveled with the king. Each carried a 4-pound, or 1.8-kilogram, gold bar. Mansa Musa gave many of these bars to poor

SPOTLIGHT ON: MANSA MUSA I

One of the most celebrated travelers of the Middle Ages was Mansa Musa I, ruler of Mali in the 1300s. Europeans who learned of his *hajj* included pictures of him holding a gold nugget on their maps of Africa. On his holy pilgrimage to Makkah, Musa stopped in Cairo where he visited the local sultan. Mansa Musa who had brought a great deal of gold with him, gave it freely to needy people in Egypt and other places he traveled. When Mansa Musa and his entourage returned to Mali, he brought with him some of the brightest and most talented scholars and architects. His dream was to build great cities in Mali to be centers of learning. Mansa Musa's sharing of wealth created aftereffects on the Egyptian economy. So much gold was in circulation that it was devalued.

LINKING PAST TO PRESENT

During the Songhai Empire, Timbuktu was a major center for trade in gold, enslaved people, and salt. Merchants, religious divines, and scholars mingled in this Muslim city. Today Timbuktu is a smaller city but retains visible remnants of its past in mosques and monuments.

GEOGRAPHY AND HISTORY

The people of Songhai used the Niger River for military transportation and trade. They also built dikes and canals along the river.

L2 **Economics** Africa's early kingdoms became wealthy from the development of trade of natural resources. Ask students to read and report on current newspaper or magazine articles discussing how African nations today are working to increase trade or development of their natural resources.

VIDEODISC

Use the following to enrich Chapter 8.

WH A 40 10040

The Sankore Mosque at Timbuktu, Mali.

WH A 51 10051

Kano, Nigeria.

people he met along the way. As a result of this trip, news of Mansa Musa and Mali reached as far as Europe.

In Arabia, Mansa Musa met a Spanish architect whom he brought back to Mali. There, the architect built a university in the trading city of Timbuktu (tim buhk tū'). It became a great center of learning and drew students from Europe, Asia, and Africa.

After 25 years, Mansa Musa's reign ended. The rulers who followed him were weak. Within 100 years after Mansa Musa's death, Mali lost its land to others.

Songhai The kingdom that replaced Mali as the most powerful in West Africa was Songhai (song' hī). By the late 1400s, it controlled almost all the land that had been part of Mali. Songhai also conquered other lands and became the largest of the three trading kingdoms.

The Sultan Sunni Ali, in 1464, ruled Songhai from the city of Gao. He maintained a huge army equipped with armor, camels and horses. He also had a large navy that patrolled the Niger River. Following Sunni Ali's death, Askia Muhammad came to power in Songhai. He extended the empire even more and culture flourished. Sultan Askia welcomed teachers, doctors, poets, students, and religious leaders from Asia and Europe.

Songhai was more organized than the other two kingdoms. It was divided into provinces and with a governor for each. Everyone used the same weights and measures and followed the same legal system. Only members of the ruling Songhai could become political leaders or join the cavalry. Other groups had special jobs, such as caring for the army's horses or serving at the royal court. Most enslaved people, often prisoners of war, worked as farmers.

Despite its power, Songhai lasted only 100 years. In 1591 A.D., the ruler of Morocco sent an army across the Sahara to seize Songhai's gold mines. Though only half of the Moroccan soldiers survived the trip, they had guns. They defeated Songhai's soldiers, who were armed only with swords and spears.

Section 2 Review

1. **Identify:** Wangara, Sundiata Keita, Mansa Musa I, Timbuktu
2. **Define:** silent barter, pilgrimage
3. What were two important trade goods in West Africa?
4. In what ways was Songhai organized?

Critical Thinking

5. Why do you think Ghanian merchants set up a system called silent barter?

SECTION 2 ANSWERS

1. Wangara, area in southwest Ghana (p. 132); Sundiata Keita, king of Mali (p. 132); Mansa Musa I, king of Mali (p. 133); Timbuktu, trading city of Mali (p. 133)
2. silent barter, system of trade in ancient Ghana (p. 132); pilgrimage, a religious journey (p. 134)
3. salt and gold
4. The ruler divided it into provinces, named governors, judges, and tax collectors. Everyone used the same weights, measures, and legal system.
5. Answers will vary but might include that Ghanian merchants might have been dealing with people who did not speak their language.

Assign Chapter 8 **Section 2 Quiz** in the TCR. Testmaker available.

Reading Latitude

To measure distances north and south, mapmakers use imaginary lines on maps and globes. These are called lines of latitude and they run east and west around Earth. Lines of latitude are often called parallels because they never meet and remain the same distance from each other all the way around Earth.

Latitude is measured in degrees, as shown by the symbol °. The Equator, which is a line of latitude, is marked 0° because all other lines of latitude are measured from it. Each line is one degree from the line next to it. One degree of latitude equals about 69 miles, or 110 kilometers.

There are 90 lines of latitude from the Equator to each pole. Those lines north of the Equator are marked with an **N**. Those lines south of the Equator are marked with an **S**.

Map Practice

1. **Which civilization was located closest to the Equator?**
2. **Which city, Timbuktu or Napata, was located closest to the 20°N line of latitude?**
3. **Which line of latitude runs through the center of the great trading civilization of Zimbabwe?**

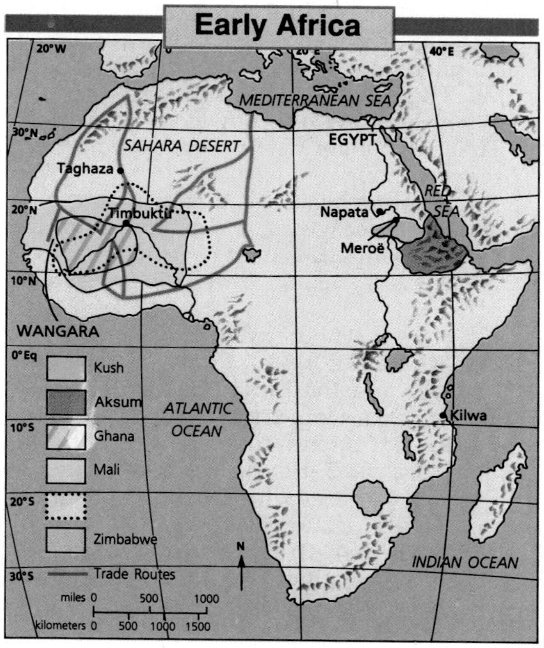

Teaching

MAP SKILLS

Reading Latitude

Instruct students to study the map on page 135 to answer the following questions:

Which city was located close to the 10° S line of latitude? *(Kilwa)*

Which city lies almost halfway between 20° N and 30° N lines of latitude? *(Taghaza)*

Between what two lines of latitude do most of the early empires and civilizations of Africa lie? *(10° N and 20° N)*

Ask students to make a generalization about early civilizations of Africa based on their latitude. *(Students' generalizations might include that the climate between 10° N and 20° N was conducive to farming and trade for early African civilizations.)*

ANSWERS to Map Practice

1. Mali
2. Napata
3. 20° S

SPOTLIGHT ON: EARLY AFRICA

As trading grew in ancient Africa, so did the need for some form of currency or money. Paper currency and coins did not yet exist. Until the mid-fifteenth century, cowrie shells and trading beads were used as currency. Among some West African people, iron chains and spearheads were also used as money. Then, in the mid-1400s, while the Songhai Empire was rising, coins became popular. As always, gold nuggets were considered to be of great value by almost all peoples.

LINKING PAST TO PRESENT

Swahili was originally a convenient language of trade or *lingua franca.* Today Swahili (or Kiswahili) is the most widely spoken language in modern East Africa. It is an official language in both Kenya and Tanzania. It has many words borrowed from Arabic, including the word *swahili* from a word meaning "of the coast."

L1 Geography: Movement Ask students to brainstorm the reasons why people today move from one geographic area to another. *(better climate, education, job opportunities, and religious or political freedom)* Ask students to compare these reasons for migration with those of early peoples.

VIDEODISC

Use the following to enrich Chapter 8.

WH A 89 10089

The conical tower at Great Zimbabwe.

Section 3

EAST AFRICAN CIVILIZATIONS

The growth of trading kingdoms in West Africa was matched by the rise of trading kingdoms and city-states in East Africa. Goods moved from the interior of East Africa to coastal markets, which, in time, became large city-states. Each of these had its own ruler and government.

Zimbabwe One of the best-known trading kingdoms was Zimbabwe (zim bah' bwā). The people of Zimbabwe speak a language known as Bantu (ban' tū). Their ancestors, the Shona (shō' nuh), once lived in present-day Nigeria (nū jir' ē uh) in West Africa. About 100 A.D., a **population explosion,** or a large and sudden growth in population, took place. Since the land could not support the increased number of people, many Shona began to leave their homeland to look for new homes.

The Shona settled in Zimbabwe in East Africa about 700 A.D. There, they built towns using stones that were cut in such a way that they fitted together without mortar. The capital had houses, a fort, and a temple. The fort stood on top of a hill and was surrounded by a huge wall. Besides the temple, the enclosed area contained the houses of the chief and his officials.

The people of Zimbabwe viewed their chief as a god-king. They approached him by crawling on their stomachs. Officials imitated him. If he coughed, they coughed. When he ate, they ate. The chief kept his throne as long as he was in good health. When he grew old, however, he was expected to take poison. Then, a younger man would become chief, and Zimbabwe could remain strong.

Zimbabwe Ruins

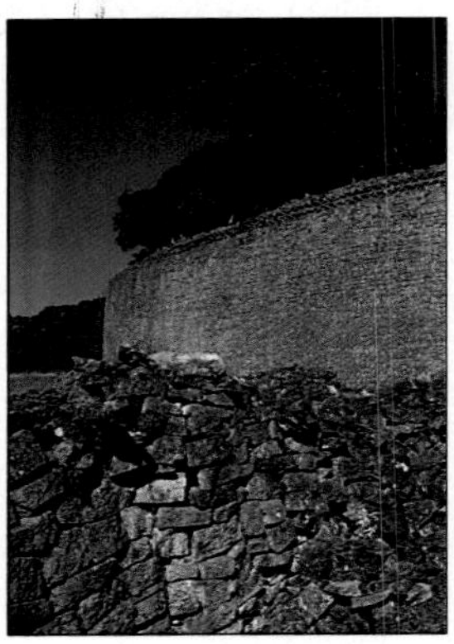

Another reason Zimbabwe remained strong was trade. Its people traded gold, copper, and ivory from the interior to merchants from cities along Africa's east coast. From these cities, trade was carried on with Arabia, Persia, India, and China.

Kilwa Another important trading city-state in East Africa was Kilwa (kil' wuh). From Kilwa, merchants sailed across the Red Sea and the Indian Ocean. The people of Kilwa collected heavy taxes from traders of other countries. They used their wealth to extend their power over neighboring city-states. They also used it to dress in fine cotton and silk and to fill their four-story houses with vases and hangings from India and China.

A culture known as Swahili (swah hē' lē) developed in Kilwa and other East African city-states. Many Arab traders had settled in the coastal cities. For this reason, Swahili culture is a mix of

EXTENDING THE CONTENT

Bantu is a language spoken over a very large area of Africa, from the fifth parallel of north latitude to the Republic of South Africa. A subgroup of the Benue-Congo group of Niger-Congo language family, Bantu includes the languages of Rwanda, Makua, Xhosa, and Zulu. Most Bantu languages are tonal, which means they use pitch to differentiate words that might be pronounced in the same way.

Arabic and African cultures. The Swahili language is a combination of Bantu and Arabic.

Section 3 Review

1. **Identify:** Bantu, Shona, Swahili
2. **Define:** population explosion
3. How did the people of Zimbabwe view their chief?
4. How did the people of Kilwa use their wealth?

Critical Thinking

5. A population explosion among the Shona resulted in many of these people leaving their homeland. What are some of the reasons people might leave their homelands today?

Zimbabwe Figurine

Section 4

Path to the Americas

Until about 25,000 years ago, there were no people in the Americas. Then, hunting-and-food-gathering bands began to cross into the Americas from Asia over a land bridge. This land bridge was formed during the last Ice Age. At that time, large amounts of ocean water were frozen into huge glaciers, and sea levels dropped. Today, this bridge is covered by the waters of the Bering Strait.

The bands came in search of food, following grass-grazing animals that had crossed earlier. The bands lived off their kill and also gathered wild plants. Over time, they spread all through the Americas. Experts believe people reached the southern tip of South America by about 9000 B.C.

About 7000 B.C., the last Ice Age ended. The climate became hotter and drier, and in many areas deserts took the place of grasslands. Large game almost disappeared. So, people had to find other ways of getting food.

By 6000 B.C., people in the Tehuacán (tā wah kahn') Valley south of present-day Mexico City had developed farming. By 3000 B.C., there were thousands of small farming villages all through the Americas. The most important crop was *maize* (māz), or corn.

Between 3000 B.C. and 1000 B.C., people developed such skills as weaving and pottery making. They grew peanuts, tomatoes, and potatoes. In a few areas, they built irrigation systems that helped support a growing population.

DID YOU KNOW ??

The earliest hunting-and-food-gathering bands had fire and cooked their food, but had not domesticated the dog. The people wore hides and furs. Their weapons were wooden spears tipped with sharpened stones.

L2 **Culture** Organize tactile/kinesthetic learners into three groups. Assign each group one of the following Mesoamerican groups: the Olmecs, the Mayas, or the Aztecs. Each group should create a simple board game involving the history and people of their chosen civilization. Suggest they design a gameboard and basic rules for playing the game. Suggest each group invite other students to play their game.

SECTION 3 ANSWERS

1. Bantu, language of Zimbabwe (p. 136); Shona, ancient people of Zimbabwe (p. 136); Swahili, culture in Kilwa (p. 136)
2. population explosion, large and sudden growth in population (p. 136)
3. as a god-king
4. to extend their power over neighboring city-states, to dress in fine cotton and silk, and to fill their houses with riches from India and China
5. Answers will vary but might include that people leave their homes because of war, famine, disease, religious persecution, or simply hope of a better life.

Assign Chapter 8 **Section 3 Quiz** in the TCR. Testmaker available.

DID YOU KNOW ??

The Mayan counting system based on 20 included concepts of zero and place value. A stylized shell was the symbol for zero, a dot stood for each unit 1-4, and the symbol for 5 was a bar.

INDEPENDENT PRACTICE

L3 **Critical Thinking** Ask students to name the characteristics of a centralized government, as you write responses on the chalkboard. Have students form groups to describe what must happen in a civilization before a centralized government can form. Suggest they make a flow chart to show how the government develops. *(division of labor—one group producing enough food, housing, and other necessities for the entire community; establishment of military or political force to maintain peace)*

GEOGRAPHY AND HISTORY

The migrating Aztecs settled on the site of Tenochtitlán (present-day Mexico City). Faced with the problems of farming in a swamp and feeding a fast-growing population, the Aztec's talents produced the unique *chinampas*, or floating gardens, useful and decorative answers to both problems.

VIDEODISC

Use the following to enrich Chapter 8.

WH H 12 18692

The Wrestler, Olmec civilization, ca. 150 B.C.

Olmec Art

Section 4 Review

1. **Identify:** Bering Strait, Tehuacán
2. How long did it take people to spread out over the Americas?
3. What caused hunting-and-food-gathering bands to develop farming?
4. What was the most important crop grown by people in the Americas?

Critical Thinking

5. What reasons do you think hunting-and-food-gathering bands from Asia might have had for crossing into the Americas?

Section 5 MESOAMERICA

As the number of people grew, societies became more complex. Several great civilizations rose in Mesoamerica, or Middle America, before 900 A.D. and others later.

The Olmecs One of the earliest civilizations in Mesoamerica was that of the Olmecs (ōl' meks). It came into being around 1000 B.C. About 900 years later, it disappeared mysteriously. The Olmecs had a great influence on other peoples of the area and was called the "mother culture." They developed planned cities, hieroglyphic writing, and a calendar.

The Olmecs lived along the southern coast of the Gulf of Mexico. Part of the year, the people farmed. The rest of the year they built stone cities, which were chiefly religious centers. The cities stood on top of huge hills. They had temples; sacred pools; and houses for priests, artists, and architects. The people lived in nearby villages. They visited the cities on festival and market days.

Mayan Figure

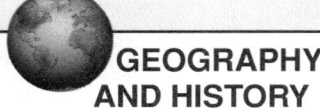

The Mayas Another great civilization, that of the Mayas (mī' uhz), began in Mesoamerica about 500 B.C. It reached its peak between 300 and 900 A.D. The Mayas lived in present-day southeast Mexico, Belize (buh lēz'), and Guatemala (gwah tuh mah' luh). Like the Olmecs, the Mayas lived in farming villages that surrounded religious cities. Mayan cities had temples and houses for priests and nobles.

The Mayas were great traders. Their cities, linked by roads paved with white cement, had busy marketplaces. Canoes handled trade along the coasts. These people were generally criminals. The

SECTION 4 ANSWERS

1. Bering Strait, water channel between Asia and America (p. 137); Tehuacán, valley south of present-day Mexico City (p. 137)
2. from 23,000 B.C. to 9000 B.C., or about 14,000 years
3. The climate became hotter and drier, and large game almost disappeared.
4. maize, or corn
5. Answers will vary but could include the need for food, safety from attack, weather, or curiosity.

Assign Chapter 8 **Section 4 Quiz** in the TCR. Testmaker available.

MAYAN MURAL Mayan artists decorated walls with brightly colored murals. This painting is of warriors in animal headpieces returning from a raiding party with their frightened captives. **Where was the Mayan Empire located?**

Mayas had no jails. They punished people by selling them into slavery.

The Mayas, however, had many accomplishments. They adapted their own hieroglyphs from the Olmecs. Mayan mathematicians came up with the idea of zero and a counting system based on 20. Mayan astronomers were able to predict when eclipses of the sun and the moon would take place. They developed a calendar, based on that of the Olmecs, with a year of 365 days. They also made cotton cloth and paper.

About 900 A.D., most Mayas abandoned their cities and disappeared. No one knows why. A plague may have broken out. Perhaps the soil could no longer produce enough food. War may have interfered with trade.

The Aztecs Later, a third great civilization, that of the Aztecs, rose in Mesoamerica. About 1200 A.D., the Aztecs began moving south into the central valley of Mexico. Through military conquest, they expanded their empire to include all of central Mexico. By 1400 A.D., the Aztec Empire had 5 million people.

The Aztecs made the people they conquered pay tribute. This took the form of corn, clothing, rubber, and wood. It is believed that each year 2 million cotton cloaks alone were sent to the capital, Tenochtitlán (tā noch tē tláhn′).

Tenochtitlán was built on an island in Lake Texcoco (teks kō′ kō). *Causeways,* or paved roads, connected the island to the mainland. The city had pyramid-temples, palaces, gardens, zoos, schools, and markets. About 300,000 people lived there. Some dressed in feathered capes and cloaks of many colors. Women wore flowers and feathers in their hair.

L1 **Art** Have students work together to create murals depicting scenes from one of the empires or civilizations described in the chapter. Murals should focus on an important aspect of the empire or civilization such as government, religion, trade, or farming.

CAPTION ANSWER

in present-day southeastern Mexico, Belize, and Guatemala

LINKING PAST TO PRESENT

Tenochtitlán means "near the cactus." Legend has it that Huitzilopochli, the god of sun and war, told the Aztecs to build their city in the place where they found an eagle with a snake in its beak perched on a cactus. The eagle-snake cactus symbol appears on the modern Mexican flag.

VIDEODISC

Use the following to enrich Chapter 8.

WH H 16 18696

A celestial bird god, Kaminaljuyú, Guatemala.

WH H 31 18711

The Castle at Chichén Itzá, Yucatan, Mexico.

MULTICULTURAL PERSPECTIVES

Olmec priests wore jaguar skins, bright red robes, bird feathers, and flower-topped headdresses. They also filed their teeth and put semi-precious stones in them. Some nobles placed splint-like boards on their children's heads and wrapped them with cloth to create elongated skulls, which they thought were beautiful.

L2 **Critical Thinking** Ask students to consider and compare the religious beliefs of the civilizations studied in this chapter. On a sheet of paper students should each write one "What if. . ." type question relating to one of the religions and have in mind what might happen "if" what they describe comes about. Collect all papers, mix, and have students each draw one, giving their opinion of the question they draw.

MAKING CONNECTIONS

➤➤ **Religion** Religion was central to Inca life. The Incas had many gods. The most important was Inti, the sun god. Because of this, the Incas called themselves the "Children of the Sun."

VIDEODISC

Use the following to enrich chapter 8.

WH H 33 18713
The founding of Tenochtitlán, ca. 1369.

WH H 37 18717
An Aztec obsidian mask.

Painting of Aztec Farmer

To feed the people, the Aztecs had to create more farmland. They filled in parts of the lake and dug drainage canals. They planted crops in soil-filled reed baskets anchored in the lake. They also built *aqueducts* (ak' wuh dukts), or water channels, to bring fresh water to the city's reservoirs from mainland springs. Canoes delivered the water from the reservoirs to people's houses.

The Aztecs were a warlike people. War and religion were closely connected. The people worshiped two major gods. One was the rain god who stood for the peaceful life of farming. The other was the sun god who stood for war and expanding empire. The Aztecs believed that the sun god needed human sacrifices. They felt that if they did not make them, the sun would not rise in the morning. Victims were generally prisoners of war.

The Aztec Empire reached its height in the early 1500s under Montezuma II (mahn tuh zū' muh). During his reign, however, Spaniards, who had guns and horses, attacked the Aztecs. Easily defeated by the Spaniards, the Aztecs lost their empire.

Section 5 Review

1. **Identify:** Tenochtitlán, Montezuma II
2. What were some accomplishments of the Mayas?
3. How did the Aztec Empire come to an end?

Critical Thinking

4. Why do you think the Mayan civilization ended?

Section 6 THE INCAS

About the same time the Aztecs moved south into central Mexico, the Incas moved out from Peru. They established an empire that stretched along the west coast of South America for about 2,500 miles, or 4,000 kilometers. By the 1500s, there were 12 million people in the Inca Empire.

History The Incas started out as farmers and shepherds. They built villages on the rocky slopes of the Andes Mountains. In the fertile valley below, they grew corn, potatoes, and other crops. On pastures above, they grazed alpacas (al pak' uhz) and llamas (lah' muhs).

In 1438, the Inca ruler Pachacuti (pah chuh kū' tē) conquered several neighboring peoples and founded the Inca Empire. He used several techniques to hold it together. He ordered

SECTION 5 ANSWERS

1. Tenochtitlán, Aztec capital (p. 139); Montezuma II, Aztec king (p. 140)
2. farming and building stone cities
3. the Spaniards, who had guns and horses, defeated the Aztecs
4. Answers will vary but could include disease, conquering army, poor farming, and bad weather conditions.

Assign Chapter 8 **Section 5 Quiz** in the TCR. Testmaker available.

conquered peoples to worship the Inca sun god in addition to their own gods. He made the Inca language of Quechua (kech' wuh) the official language. He moved people who had been living under Inca rule into newly conquered lands. They helped spread Inca culture and watched for signs of rebellion.

Pachacuti also had a huge system of stone-paved roads built. Rope suspension bridges crossed canyons and rivers. Way stations with food, weapons, and other supplies needed by the Inca army were set up on the roads. Only soldiers and government officials were allowed to use the roads.

Inca Way of Life A ruler, known as the Inca, determined the way of life. Land belonged to the ruler and not to the people who worked it. Villagers paid taxes to the empire in two ways.

Early American Empires

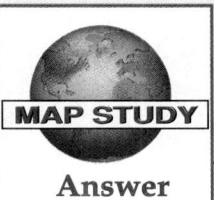

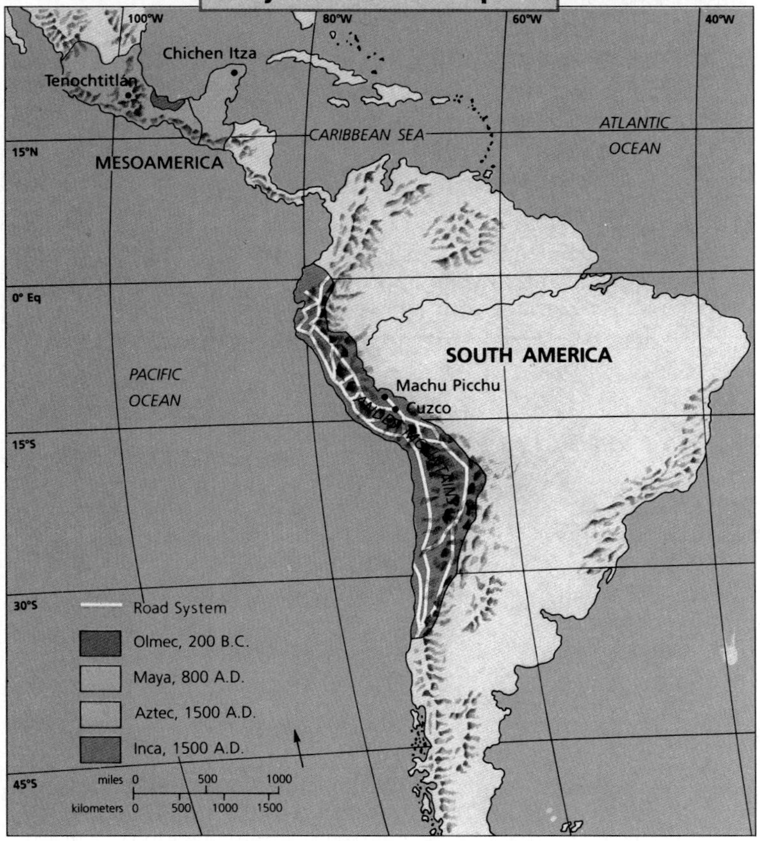

MAP STUDY

HUMAN/ ENVIRONMENTAL INTERACTION The Incas developed engineering skills that enabled them to build a large network of roads. **How did the environment of the Incas make road building more difficult?**

MAP STUDY

Answer

The Incas had to build roads through mountainous areas.

L1 **Geography: Location** Have students write five questions about the locations and relationships of places shown on the map of early American empires. Have students ask their questions to the class. LEP

VIDEODISC

Use the following to enrich Chapter 8.

WH H 40 18720
Terracing at Machu Picchu, Peru.

WH H 41 18721
A Quipu of the Inca civilization, Peru.

ASSESS

CHECK FOR UNDERSTANDING

Ask students to summarize the main points of the chapter, orally or in writing. Discuss the answers to the Section and Chapter Review questions.

EVALUATE

Assign Chapter 8 **Performance Assessment Activity** in the TCR.

Administer **Chapter 8 Test** in the TCR. Testmaker available.

EXTENDING THE CONTENT

Sometimes called the "lost city of the Andes," the Incas' startling mountain fortress of Machu Picchu had never been seen except by local Native Americans until 1911. It was discovered by a Yale University expedition led by Hiram Bingham. The ruined city perches dramatically 8,000 feet (2,438 m), high in the mountains on lush green ridge between two steep rocky peaks, about 50 miles or (80 km) from Cuzco, Peru. It has a temple and citadel as well as the ruins of many small stone houses. Thousands of worn stone steps connect the remains of farming terraces, squares, fountains, and aqueducts.

RETEACH

Ask students to retell in their own words an important event or idea of one of these early civilizations.

Assign Chapter 8 **Reteaching Activity** in the TCR.

ENRICH

Have students investigate the way in which the Mayas and Aztecs processed and prepared chocolate. If possible, encourage students to demonstrate the methods for the class.

Assign Chapter 8 **Enrichment Activity** in the TCR.

CLOSE

Hold a class discussion about why the kingdoms and civilizations described in this chapter declined.

MEETING CHAPTER OBJECTIVES

Each objective is tested by the Review questions in parentheses.

1. Discuss the ancient Kush and Aksum (BV; CT 1, 2; UYJ)

2. Summarize how West African kingdoms grew (BV; CU 1; CT 2)

3. Explain why people crossed into the Americas from Asia. (UYJ)

4. Describe the civilizations of Mesoamerica. (CU 4, 5, 6, 7; CT 3; UYJ)

5. Discuss the Incas of South America. (CU 8)

Inca Silver Llama

They paid through their labor. This involved not only farming land, but also building roads and mining gold. In addition, they paid taxes in kind.

The Inca had to keep track of people and goods. Because there was no written language, special accountants used quipus (kē′ pūz), or counting devices, to do this. Quipus were made up of knotted strings of different colors. Each color represented a different item. The knots in each string stood for tens, hundreds, and so on. The spaces between the knots stood for zero.

The wealth of the Inca Empire was shown in the way the ruler lived. His palace was the size of a town. There were hundreds of rooms and thousands of servants. The Inca's bodyguards wore gold armor. The poles of the litter in which he was carried were covered with gold. A desire for this wealth was part of the reason the Spaniards destroyed the Inca Empire in the early 1500s.

Section 6 Review

1. **Identify:** Pachacuti, Quechua
2. **Define:** quipus
3. How did Pachacuti hold the Inca Empire together?

Critical Thinking

4. How do you think the Incas would have answered if they had been asked to keep Pachacuti as their leader, or elect a new one? Explain your answer.

Chapter Summary

1. For about 500 years, Kush was ruled by Egypt. Later, a Kushite dynasty ruled Egypt.
2. The Aksumites destroyed Kush and then developed a powerful trading empire themselves.
3. The kingdoms of Ghana, Mali, and Songhai developed trading empires in West Africa based on gold, salt, and other goods.
4. Bantu-speaking Shona set up a trading kingdom at Zimbabwe.
5. Kilwa and other coastal cities handled trade between Africa and Arabia, Persia, India, and China.
6. The Olmecs developed cities, hieroglyphic writing, and a calendar.
7. The Mayas were great traders, mathematicians, and astronomers.
8. The Aztecs built Tenochtitlán, from which they ruled central Mexico.
9. The Incas controlled their empire through a common religion, language, and a system of roads.

SECTION 6 ANSWERS

1. Pachacuti, Inca ruler in 1438 (p. 140); Quechua, language of Incas (p. 141)
2. quipus, Inca counting devices (p. 142)
3. He ordered conquered peoples to worship the Inca sun god, made Quechua the official language, and moved people who had been living under Inca rule into newly conquered lands.
4. Answers will vary but should include that some people would rather replace him with a less strict, less dictatorial leader. Others may want to keep him as a leader since he provided well for them.

Assign Chapter 8 **Section 6 Quiz** in the TCR. Testmaker available.

CHAPTER

Review 8

Building Vocabulary

Imagine that you are putting together a photo display about ancient civilizations. You have found a photo showing each of the following:

silent barter
pilgrimage
population explosion
quipus

Write one sentence for each photo describing it and what it shows.

Check for Understanding

1. How did Ghana get control over West Africa's trade routes?
2. Why did Mansa Musa's pilgrimage gain fame for Mali?
3. Why did the kingdom of Zimbabwe remain strong?
4. What was the main difference between the Mesoamerican civilizations that developed before and after 900 A.D.?
5. What did Olmecs contribute to other civilizations?
6. What was the role of enslaved people in Mayan society?
7. How did the Aztecs treat the people they conquered?
8. Who directed and controlled the Inca way of life?

Critical Thinking

1. How do you think the development of African civilization would have been different if the Kushites had not learned the secret of iron-smelting? Explain.
2. Why was trade important to the growth of African civilization?
3. Which Mesoamerican civilization would you choose to live in? Why?
4. What contributions did early American civilizations make to present-day life in the United States?

Geography in History

LOCATION Compare the maps of early empires found on pages 135 and 141. What similarities in location of these civilizations can you find? What differences in location are there between the two areas?

Using Your Journal

Review the details you have noted about contributions made by the early civilizations in Africa and in the Americas. Choose an interesting contribution and imagine you are a young person living in the empire responsible for the contribution. Write an imaginary diary entry explaining its importance.

143

CHAPTER 8 REVIEW ANSWERS

BUILDING VOCABULARY

Captions will vary but should include a descriptive sentence for the scene where each could be happening.

CHECK FOR UNDERSTANDING

1. by the use of iron swords and lances
2. it took more than 14 months to cover the 3,000 miles (4,800 km) 12,000 people traveled with the king, and he gave away gold bars
3. the chief was always young and it was part of a great trading network
4. The earlier civilizations were peaceful, had rulers interested in learning, religion and trade; later civilizations were warlike, with religions marked by human sacrifice.
5. planned cities, hieroglyphic writing, a calendar
6. They ground corn, paddled canoes, and carried goods.
7. The Aztecs made them pay tribute and sacrificed some of them to the sun god.
8. the ruler

CRITICAL THINKING

1. Answers will vary but should include lack of progress.
2. Answers will vary but should include that without trade, African civilizations would not have interacted.
3. Answers will vary but should include specific reasons.
4. Answers will vary.

✚ BONUS ✚ TEST QUESTION

For Chapter 8 Test

You dig up a piece of pottery from a past civilization. You know immediately that it was made by the Olmecs. What evidence helped you reach your conclusion? *(Answers could include the pottery is adobe clay, shows a jaguar, was found on the top of a hill near the ruins of a city, contained kernels of corn.)*

GEOGRAPHY IN HISTORY

Similarities might be both are contiguous, are close to the Equator, are coastal; differences might be Mesoamerican empires stretched farther north and bordered the Pacific Ocean; African kingdoms stretched farther east and bordered the Atlantic and Indian oceans.

USING YOUR JOURNAL

Diary entries will vary. You might call on volunteers to read their entries to the class.

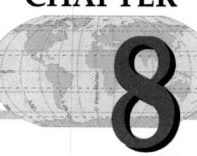

UNIT 3 CULTURE CLOSE-UP

ZHOU DYNASTY

FOCUS

OBJECTIVES

Locate the extent of the Zhou dynasty. Describe the culture of China during the Zhou dynasty.

BELLRINGER

Write the following on the chalkboard: *What do you think the phrase "mandate from heaven" means?*

MOTIVATIONAL ACTIVITY

Ask students to explain what they think is the meaning of the phrase "mandate from heaven." Explain to students that in early China, the Chinese regarded their ruler as the Son of Heaven. According to tradition, the Son of Heaven ruled on the basis of a principle known as the Mandate from Heaven. If he were just, the Son received a mandate, or the right to rule, from Heaven, the supreme ruler. If he did not rule properly, he lost the mandate, and someone else became the Son of Heaven. As a result of this tradition, China was governed by a series of 24 dynasties before the dynastic system came to an end in 1912. Tell the students that in this feature, they will learn about the Zhou dynasty and its culture.

UNIT 3 CULTURE CLOSE-UP

Zhou Dynasty

The year is 1028 B.C. in ancient China. The fierce Zhou warriors have conquered the Shang and founded the Zhou dynasty. They claimed they had a "mandate from heaven" to do so.

Geography Connection

The Zhou dynasty covered a vast area from the east coast of China westward to the central mountains.

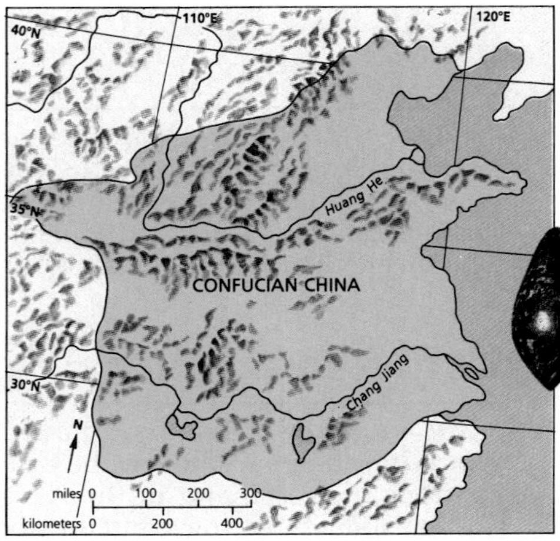

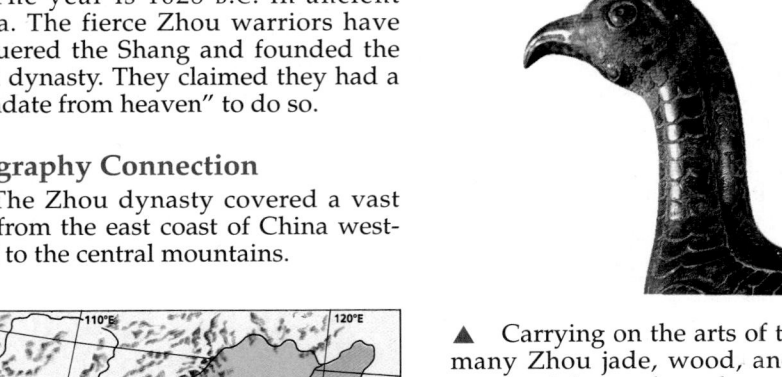

▲ Carrying on the arts of the Shang, many Zhou jade, wood, and bronze, ceremonial vessels took on the shape of animals. ▼

MEETING SPECIAL NEEDS

If possible, arrange a field trip to an art museum or a history museum to view some of the artifacts from the Shang and Zhou dynasties. Have students who are tactile/kinesthetic or visual learners bring along a drawing pad and pencils to make sketches of the artwork and to jot down notes about the kinds of themes and mediums used by the Chinese people during these dynasties. Have students share their sketches and notes with the class.

The Zhou also fashioned elaborate jewelry in the shape of animals. This jade piece was carved as a pendant. ▶

Dragons appeared on many Zhou art pieces. The Zhou were the first Chinese dynasty to work with bronze to any great extent.

The Zhou were an educated people. They further developed the Shang writing system. ◀

Confucianism

Confucius, one of the greatest Chinese philosophers, lived during the Zhou dynasty.

> *Do not do to others what you would not want others to do to you.*

This was one of the teachings of Confucius who believed in a peaceful world and respect for the family. His philosophy, Confucianism, set up a code of ethics that is still followed today. ▶

TEACH

L1 **Location** Compare a physical map of China with the map on page 144. Ask students to name the physical features located in the area ruled by the Zhou dynasty. Ask them to name the major river that flows through the middle of the dynasty. *(Huang Ho)*

DID YOU KNOW ??

The Zhou dynasty ruled for nearly nine centuries—the longest ruling dynasty in Chinese history. For the last 500 years of their rule, however, the Zhou kings were little more than figureheads as several states led by ambitious nobles rose to power and fell in succession.

VIDEODISC

Use the following to enrich Unit 3.

WH P 31 30432
Zhou Wen Wang, father of Wu Wang, leader of Zhou dynasty.

WH P 36 30437
Zhou coinage shaped as miniature spades and knives.

SPOTLIGHT ON: CONFUCIUS

Confucius was born about 551 B.C. to an upper-class family that had lost its money during the Zhou dynasty. Confucius' parents died when he was young, forcing him to make his own way in the world. He was a bright student. During his life powerful leaders fought one another for control of land in China. Poor farmers worked hard, but received little reward and were forced to pay high taxes. Confucius thought that if people were taught to behave properly, it would help to end China's troubles. He said that there were Five Relationships that were most important—ruler and ruled, father and son, husband and wife, older brother and younger brother, friend and friend.

INTRODUCE

UNIT 4 OVERVIEW

Unit 4 examines the history of the ancient Greeks from the rise of the Aegean civilizations to the conquest of Greece by the Romans.

- **Chapter 9** describes the Minoan and Mycenaean civilizations out of which Hellenic civilization grew.
- **Chapter 10** discusses the evolution of the polis as the political and geographic center of Greek life and examines in detail the city-states of Athens and Sparta.
- **Chapter 11** explains the major contributions made to western civilization by the Greeks of the Classical Age.
- **Chapter 12** summarizes the Hellenistic period from the Macedonian conquest to the coming of the Romans.

UNIT OBJECTIVES

After reading Unit 4, students will be able to:

1. discuss how the Greek culture developed.
2. describe how Greek culture spread.
3. summarize Greek contributions to western civilizations.

UNIT PROJECT

Have students imagine that they are one of the following: a Minoan priest-king, a Mycenaean seafarer, a Spartan warrior, an Athenian citizen, an Olympic athlete, Socrates, Plato, Aristotle, a Greek wife of Philip of Macedonia, Alexander the Great. Tell students that in these roles they maintained diaries. Have them write several diary entries describing special events in their lives. Ask students to make an oral presentation of their entries to the class.

UNIT 4 The Greeks

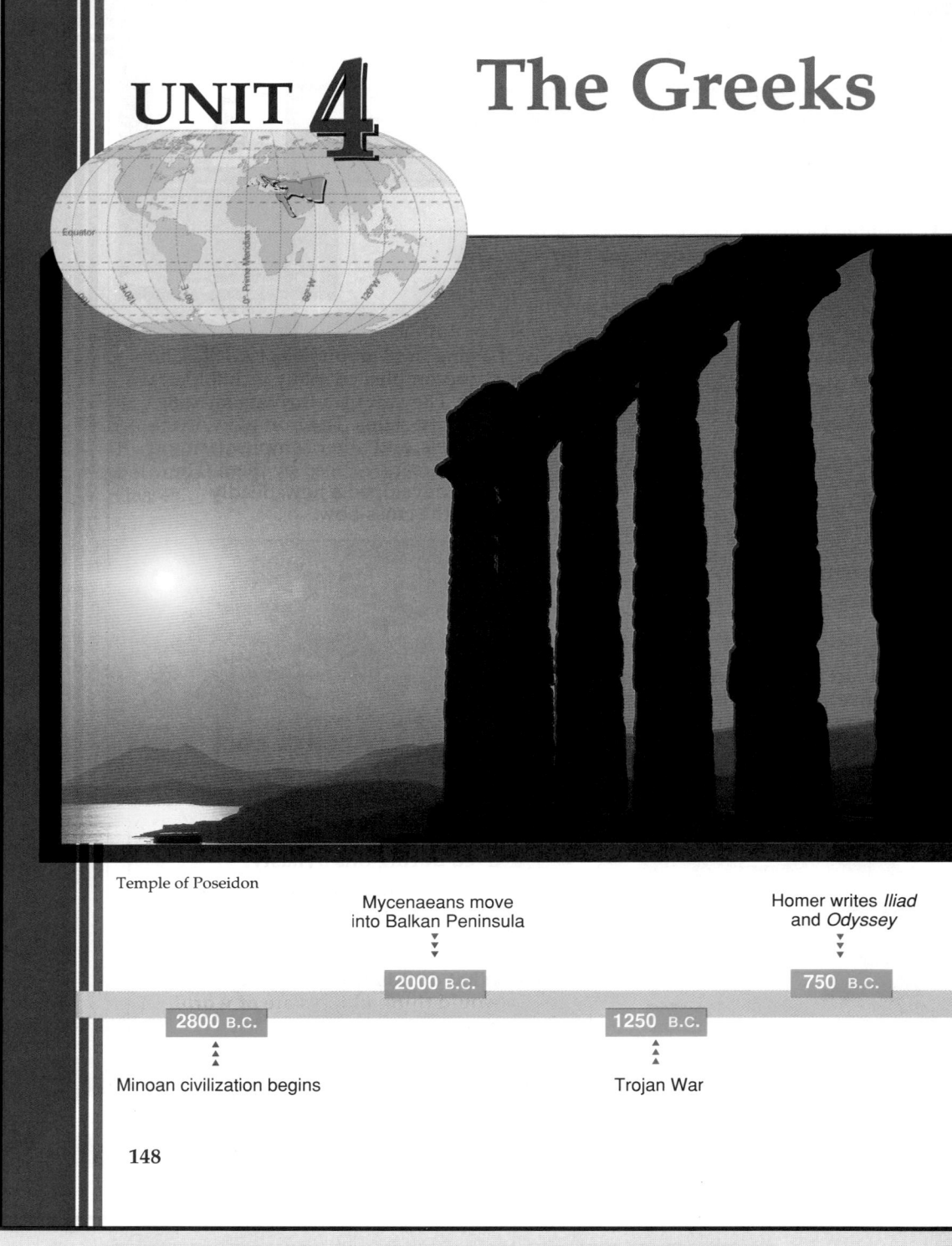

Temple of Poseidon

- 2800 B.C. — Minoan civilization begins
- 2000 B.C. — Mycenaeans move into Balkan Peninsula
- 1250 B.C. — Trojan War
- 750 B.C. — Homer writes *Iliad* and *Odyssey*

148

ABOUT THE UNIT OPENING

EXAMINING THE ARTIFACT

Ask students if they recognize the name *Poseidon*. For those who make modern references, ask if they know the name's origin. *(Greek god of the sea)* Explain this temple was built in ancient Greece to honor the god Poseidon whom they will learn more about in this unit.

GLOBAL CHRONOLOGY

Ask students to name time line entries that indicate this time period was turbulent. *(Trojan War, Persian Wars begin, Peloponnesian War)* Ask students to name time line entries that indicate culture flourished during this time. *(Homer writes* Iliad *and* Odyssey, *Golden Age of Athens begins)*

Western civilization owes a great deal to the early Greeks. They made many contributions in such fields as politics, science, philosophy, the arts, and athletics. Possibly their most important contribution, however, was an idea. The Greeks were the first to believe in the freedom and worth of the individual.

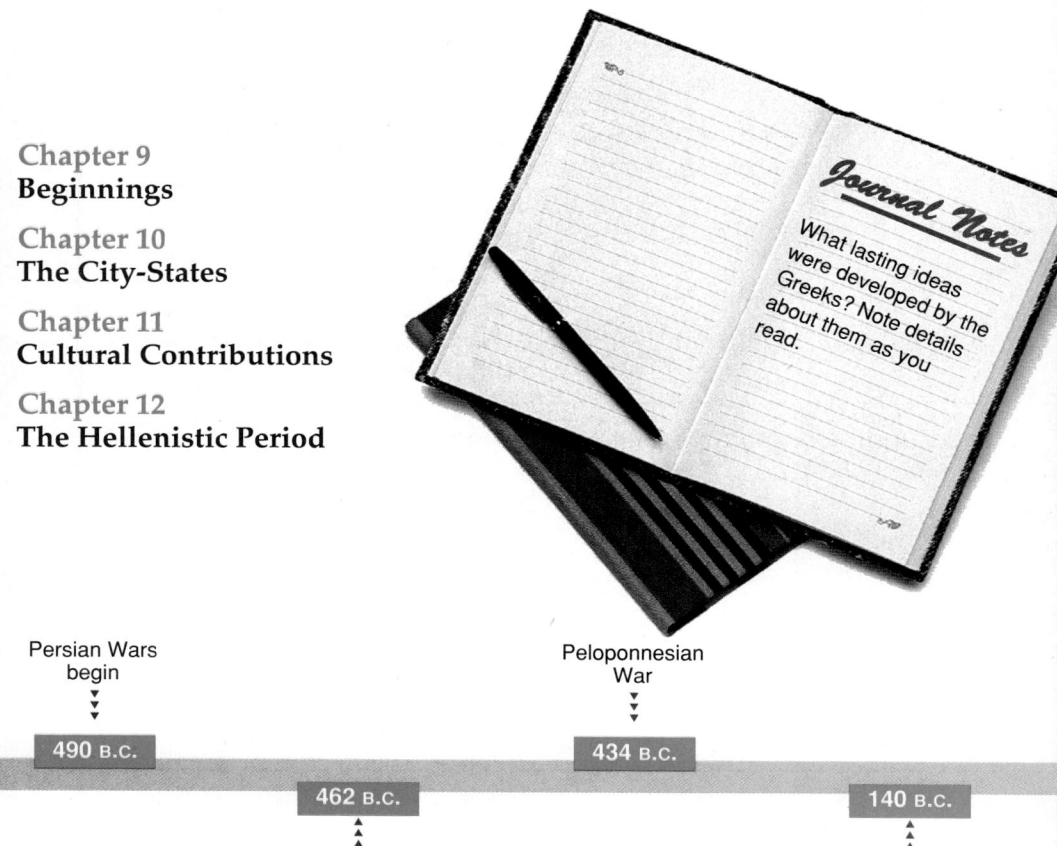

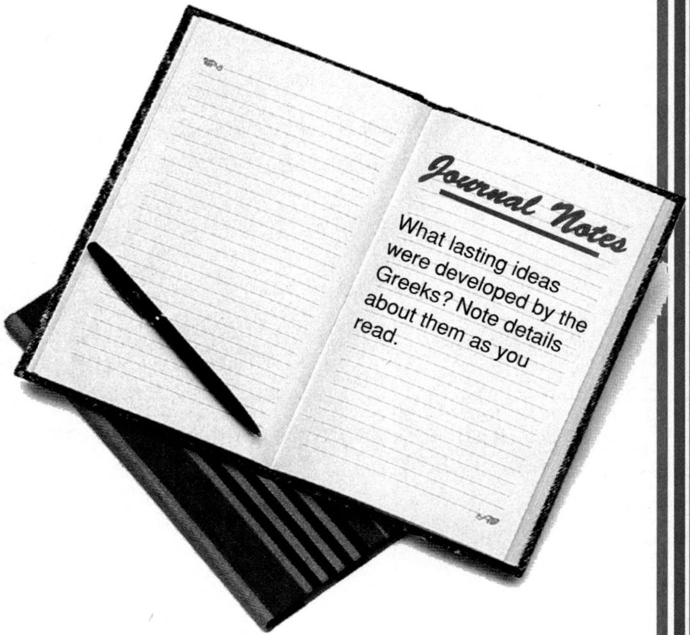

Journal Notes
What lasting ideas were developed by the Greeks? Note details about them as you read.

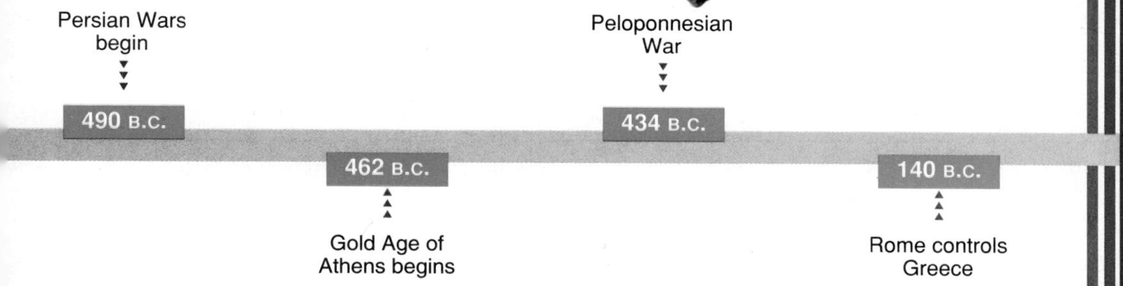

INTRODUCING THE UNIT

Construct a wheel graphic organizer on the chalkboard using Greece as the hub and the following headings on spokes coming out from the hub: *Geography, Culture, Important People, Lasting Contributions.* Have students call out ideas as you write responses on the wheel attached to the appropriate topic. Have students create another wheel about a topic of their choice as they read. Display wheels at the end of the unit.

RECORDING JOURNAL NOTES

Help students begin writing in their journals by suggesting they make a list of ideas they can think of that were developed by the Greeks. Write responses on the chalkboard. Have students note in their journal details about the contributions to the modern world that were developed by the Greeks.

GEOGRAPHIC LOCATION

The Greek civilizations discussed in this unit were located from the Mediterranean Sea eastward to the Indus Valley. Have students locate these places in their text Atlas and name the continents that this area includes. *(Europe, Africa, and Asia)*

PLANNING GUIDE

CHAPTER 9 Beginnings

CHAPTER ORGANIZER

Objectives	Special Features	Supplemental Materials
Section 1 The Minoans Discuss the way of life of the Minoans and how geography influenced the early peoples who lived on Crete and the Balkan Peninsula.		• Reproducible Lesson Plan • Section 1 Quiz • Testmaker • Chapter 9 Vocabulary and Guided Reading Activity • Chapter 9 Teaching Transparencies and Activities • World Art and History Transparency 4 • The Western Civilization Videodisc
Section 2 The Mycenaeans Summarize the way of life of the Mycenaeans and how the Dark Age affected the Aegean world.	Map and Geography Skills: *Reading Longitude*, p. 156	• Reproducible Lesson Plan • Section 2 Quiz • Testmaker • Chapter 9 Cooperative Learning Activity • Unit 4 World Literature • Chapter 9 Geography and Map Activity • Chapter 9 Chart and Graph Skill Activity • Outline Map Resource pp. 28, 29, 30, 39 • Chapter 9 Activity Book Activity • The Western Civilization Videodisc
Chapter 9 Review and Evaluation		• Chapter 9 Reteaching Activity • Chapter 9 Enrichment Activity • Spanish Summary and Glossary • Audiocassettes (English and Spanish) • Chapter 9 Performance Assessment Activity • Chapter 9 Test • Testmaker

If time does not permit teaching the entire chapter, use the Chapter 9 Summary on page 160 and the Chapter 9 Audiocassettes (English and Spanish) to point out the main ideas of the chapter.

✓ Performance Assessment Activities

Art Have students prepare a class notebook about Minoan and Mycenaean culture, each student contributing a page on some aspect of either culture: art, artifacts, clothing, food, transportation, religion, government, and so on. Have students illustrate the book and design a cover. Display the book in the classroom.

Writing Have students write their own version of the *Iliad* using prose or poetry. Have them imagine they are one of the soldiers hidden inside the Trojan horse. They should describe their feelings as the horse is pulled into Troy by the Trojans, the ensuing battle, their escape from Troy, and their adventures on their way home.

CHAPTER RESOURCES

LITERATURE ABOUT THE PERIOD

Renault, Mary. *The King Must Die.* Random House, 1988. Retells the legend of Theseus's struggle with the Minotaur.

READINGS FOR THE STUDENT

Evslin, Bernard. *Heroes and Monsters of Greek Myth.* Scholastic, 1988. Retells many Greek myths.

READINGS FOR THE TEACHER

Cotterell, Arthur. *The Minoan World.* Charles Scribner's Sons, 1979. Surveys Minoan civilization.

Cotterell, Leonard. *The Mystery of Minoan Civilization.* World Publishing, 1971. Account of Minoan civilization.

Fine, John V. A. *The Ancient Greeks.* Belknap Press, 1983. Surveys the Greek world up to the accession of Alexander the Great.

Wood, Michael. *In Search of the Trojan War.* Facts on File Publications, 1985. A study of archaeological, literary, and historical records behind the tale of Troy.

MULTIMEDIA RESOURCES

Aegean Age. Coronet Films. Film. Describes Minoan and Mycenaean civilizations.

Ancient Civilization: The End is the Beginning. TVOntario. Video. Gives possible explanations for the decline of early civilizations including the Minoans and the Mycenaeans.

The Fall of Troy. Phoenix/BFA Films and Videos. Film or video. Reveals the background and meaning of the Trojan War.

The Greeks. International Film Bureau. Film. Traces Greek culture and history from the early Aegean civilizations to the conquests of Alexander the Great.

INTRODUCE

CHAPTER 9 OVERVIEW

Chapter 9 introduces Minoan and Mycenaean cultures as forerunners of classical Greek civilization.

➤ **Section 1** discusses the way of life of the Minoans.

➤ **Section 2** explains the culture of the Mycenaeans.

CHAPTER OBJECTIVES

After reading Chapter 9, students will be able to:

1. describe what life was like for the Minoans.

2. discuss how geography influenced the early people who lived on Crete and the Balkan Peninsula.

3. summarize what life was like for the Mycenaeans.

4. explain how the Dark Age affected the Aegean world.

EXAMINING THE ILLUSTRATION

Ask students if they have ever painted a room or wall. Then ask if they have ever thought of painting a picture that covered a whole wall. Explain the Minoans were famous for the frescoes, or wall paintings they made, from which we have learned much about their civilization. Ask students what they can conclude about the Minoan civilization from this fresco. *(They were sailors and traders.)*

CHAPTER 9 Beginnings

Fresco of Minoan Ship

150

PERFORMANCE ASSESSMENT ✓

Use the Performance Assessment activities on page 150B to help you evaluate students as they complete the chapter.

TEACHER CLASSROOM RESOURCES

- Unit 4 Primary Source Readings
- Unit 4 World Literature
- Section Quizzes/Chapter Test
- Reteaching Activity
- Enrichment Activity
- Chart and Graph Skill Activity
- Geography and Map Activity
- Cooperative Learning Activity
- Performance Assessment Activity
- Teaching Transparencies and Activities
- Spanish Summary and Glossary
- The Western Civilization Videodisc
- Audiocassettes (English and Spanish)
- Testmaker

Chapter Focus

READ TO DISCOVER:

- What life was like for the Minoans.
- How geography influenced the early peoples who lived on Crete and the Balkan Peninsula.
- What life was like for the Mycenaeans.
- How the "Dark Age" affected the Aegean world.

Greek civilization grew out of a combination of two earlier civilizations, Minoan (muh nō' uhn) and Mycenaean (mīsuh nē' uhn). Due to the geography of the land, both became great sea powers. Although their power was eventually destroyed, the Minoans and the Mycenaeans left an important *legacy* (leg' uh sē), or gift from the past, to the Greeks.

2800 B.C.–800 B.C.

KEY TERMS

- bull leaping
- labyrinth
- parchment
- shrines
- megaron
- tenants
- civil wars

Section 1 THE MINOANS

Minoan civilization rose around 2800 B.C. on Crete (krēt), an island in the Mediterranean Sea. The Minoans, who were also known as Cretans, grew wheat, barley, grapes, and olives. When the olive groves and vineyards produced more than was needed, the Minoans traded the surplus for goods they could not grow or make on Crete.

Since there were many forests on Crete, the Minoans learned to work with wood and became good carpenters. They also learned to work with metal. They used their metalworking and carpentry skills to build ships and began to earn a living from trade instead of farming.

When pirates threatened them, the Minoans changed the way they built their ships so the ships could go faster. They made them slimmer, with two or three masts instead of one. The Minoans also put a deck over the heads of rowers to protect them.

KEY TO ABILITY LEVELS

Teaching strategies have been coded for varying learning styles and abilities.

L1 Level 1 activities are **basic** activities and should be within the ability range of all students.

L2 Level 2 activities are **average** activities and should be within the ability range of the average to above-average student.

L3 Level 3 activities are **challenging** activities designed for the ability range of above-average students.

LEP LEP activities should be within the ability range of Limited English Proficiency students.

FOCUS

BELLRINGER

Ask students to write their favorite commercial jingle or slogan.

MOTIVATIONAL ACTIVITY

Discuss students' favorite jingles and ask volunteers to recite them. Ask students why some commercials are remembered. *(People usually remember things they hear, especially if it rhymes or is put to music.)* Tell students that in this chapter they will learn about a world-famous poet who wrote about the songs and legends that he had heard.

VOCABULARY PRE-CHECK

Write the key terms for this chapter on the chalkboard. Ask students to use those that they know in sentences.

Assign Chapter 9 **Vocabulary and Guided Reading Activity** in the TCR.

EXTRA CREDIT PROJECT

Suggest interested students read some examples of poetry or parts of the *Iliad* written by Homer. Ask them to choose a passage to rewrite in modern English. Have students share the original passage and their translation with the class.

VIDEODISC

Use the following to enrich Chapter 9.

WC B 5 11721

The palace of Minos at Knossos, Crete.

WC B 8 11724

The "partridge fresco," Minoan palace, Knossos.

MAKING CONNECTIONS

➤➤ **Daily Life** Minoan women enjoyed a higher status than women in other civilizations. For example, they were permitted to attend sporting events. Also, Minoan religion had more goddesses than gods.

DID YOU KNOW ??

Minoan writing, which is known as Linear A, has not been deciphered.

CAPTION ANSWER

They believed she made plants grow and brought children into the world.

Rulers and Religion The rulers of Crete were priest-kings. They made the laws and represented the gods on Earth. The priest-kings would climb to the top of Mount Juktas (yūk' tuhs) to look for a sign from heaven that would tell them the will of the gods. Then, they would tell their people what the gods wanted them to do.

The Minoans had many gods. The main god was the Great Goddess, Mother Earth. She made plants grow and brought children into the world. To honor her, the Minoans built **shrines,** or sacred places to worship, in palaces, on housetops, on hilltops, and in caves. The people believed that hilltops led to heaven, and caves led to the underworld.

Sacred horns made of clay and covered with stucco rested against the back wall of each shrine. A hole between the horns held a bronze double ax. Around the horns were clay models of animals. People left offerings of human hair, fruit, flowers, jewels, and gold at the shrines.

The Minoans believed that certain things were sacred. The lily was their sacred flower. The king wore a plumed crown of lilies and a lily necklace. The double ax was sacred. It stood for the power of Mother Earth and the authority of the king. The dove was sacred because it flew to the heavens.

MINOAN RELIGION This Minoan fresco shows a religious ceremony. As a musician plays the harp, two women and a man carry offerings to a shrine. The double axes with birds sitting on them (left) are symbols of the Great Goddess. **What did Minoans believe about the Great Goddess?**

MEETING SPECIAL NEEDS

Have auditory learners view the film *Ancient Civilization: The End is the Beginning*. (See Chapter Resources in the Chapter 9 Planning Guide.) Then hold a discussion about the possible reasons for the decline of early civilizations including the Minoans and the Mycenaeans.

The Fall of the Minoans No one is certain why Minoan civilization came to an end. What is certain is that about 1400 B.C., control of the sea and of Crete passed to the Mycenaeans.

Legend explains the fall of the Minoans with the story of Theseus (thex' sex uhs) and the Minotaur (min' uh tauhr). A young Greek prince named Theseus was brought to Knossos. He was to be sacrificed to the Minotaur, a huge monster the king kept in the palace labyrinth. The Minotaur had the body of a man and the head of a bull and lived on human flesh. Theseus was put into the labyrinth. He fought the monster with a magical sword and killed it. When the Minotaur died, the power of the Minoans died too.

Relief Sculpture of Minotaur.

Section 1 Review

1. **Identify:** Minoans, Crete, Knossos, "House of the Double Ax," Mother Earth, Theseus, Minotaur
2. **Define:** bull leaping, labyrinth, parchment, shrines
3. How did the Minoans earn a living?
4. What made cities in Crete different from those of other ancient civilizations?

Critical Thinking

5. How did geography influence the development of the Minoan civilization?

Section 2

The Mycenaeans

The Mycenaeans came from the grasslands of southern Russia. Around 2000 B.C., small groups started making their way west into Europe and then south through the Balkan (bol' kuhn) Peninsula. Finally, they settled in the lowlands of Greece.

The Mycenaean kings built fortress-palaces on hilltops. In times of danger or attack, the people in the villages outside the palace walls took shelter within the palace. Its chief feature was the **megaron** (meg' uh ron), or a square room with a fireplace in its center. The king held council meetings and entertained in the megaron.

Land was divided into estates that were farmed either by enslaved people or by **tenants,** or people who live on and work another person's land. Landowners gave the king horses, chariots, weapons, wheat, farm animals, honey, and hides in exchange for protection. Tenants labored to supply many of these items.

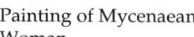

Painting of Mycenaean Woman

L3 **Critical Thinking** Ask students to explain what purpose myths and legends about monsters might have served the Minoans. *(They might have provided supernatural explanations of actual events.)*

MAKING CONNECTIONS

>> **Folklore** According to legend, Ariadne, the Minoan king's daughter, gave Theseus the clue of unwinding a ball of thread to help him find his way out of the labyrinth. After killing the Minotaur, Theseus escaped from Crete with Ariadne.

DID YOU KNOW ??

The Mycenaeans got their name from their chief fortress-palace of Mycenae, which was excavated in 1876-1877 by a German amateur archaeologist named Heinrich Schliemann.

SECTION 1 ANSWERS

1. Minoans, people of Crete (p. 151); Crete, island in Mediterranean (p. 151); Knossos, largest city on Crete (p. 152); "House of the Double Ax," Minoan king's palace (p. 153); Mother Earth, main god of Minoans (p. 154); Theseus, legendary Greek prince (p. 155); Minotaur, monster (p. 155)
2. bull leaping, Minoan sport (p. 152); labyrinth, path network (p. 153); parchment, thin animal skin (p. 153); shrines, sacred places (p. 154)
3. from trade
4. At the heart of each city stood a palace, and cities did not have walls around them.
5. Answers will vary, but due to geography the Minoans became a sea power. Because of forests on Crete, the Minoans worked with wood. Because Minoan cities were near the sea, they did not have walls.

Assign Chapter 9 **Section 1 Quiz** in the TCR. Testmaker available.

Teaching

MAP SKILLS

Reading Longitude

Ask students to study the map to answer the following questions:

Along which line of longitude is Mount Juktas located? *(25° E)*

Between which two lines of longitude is Cyprus located? *(30° E and 35° E)*

Along what approximate line of longitude is Mycenae located? *(23° E)*

Between which lines of longitude was the Minoan culture located? *(20° E and 35° E)*

Have students use the map of Western Europe in the text Atlas to create questions about the locations of places based on longitude. Have students ask a partner their questions.

ANSWERS to Map Practice

1. 25° E
2. Mycenae

Reading Longitude

To measure distances east and west on Earth, mapmakers use imaginary lines on maps and globes. These are called lines of **longitude,** or **meridians** (muh rid′ ē uhnz), and they run from the North Pole to the South Pole.

Like lines of latitude, meridians are measured in degrees. All meridians are measured from the Prime Meridian, a line of longitude that runs through Greenwich, England. The Prime Meridian is marked 0°. Those lines east of the Prime Meridian are marked with an E, from 1°E to 180°E. Those lines west of the Prime Meridian are marked with a W, from 1°W to 180°W.

Unlike lines of latitude, meridians are not always the same distance from one another. They are farthest apart at the Equator, and closest together at the poles.

Lines of longitude are often used to help specify location. For example, it is much easier to find Troy on the map below if one knows that it is located at about 26°E.

Map Practice

1. **Along which line of longitude was Knossos located?**
2. **Which early Aegean City was located closest to the Prime Meridian?**

The Early Aegean World

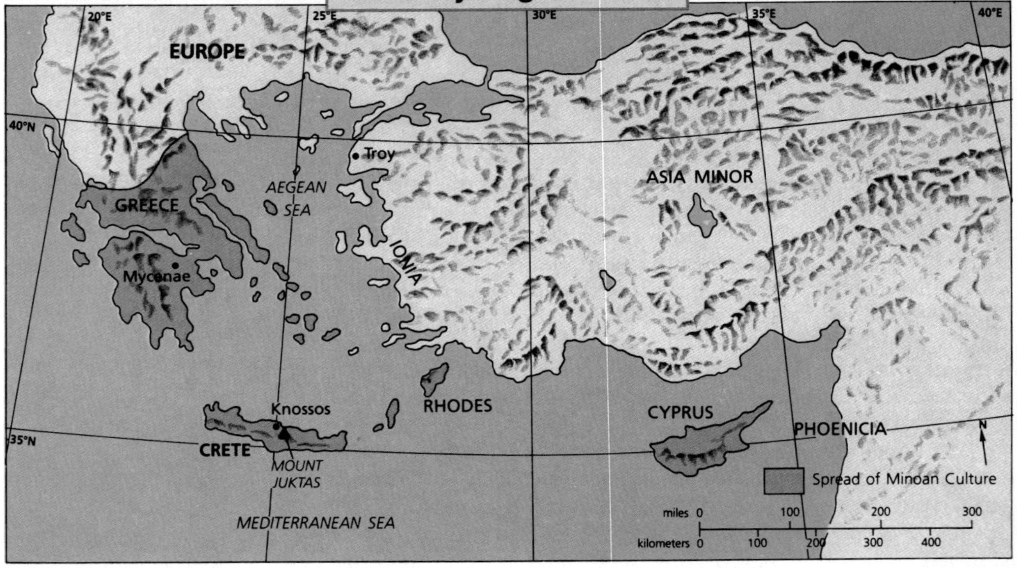

SPOTLIGHT ON: THE AEGEAN WORLD

Archaeologists have unearthed relics of the Greek civilization by digging throughout the Aegean area. Artifacts have also been found in another treasury of sorts—the Mediterranean Sea. Many important and interesting relics have been found in the waters near Crete and Cyprus. Students may enjoy reading more about these discoveries in *Diving to the Past: Recovering Ancient Wrecks* by W. John Hackwell.

MYCENAEAN SEASCAPE The Mycenaeans were great seafarers and traders. They built many settlements along the rugged coastlines of Greece and the Aegean islands. **What was the main item of Mycenaean trade?**

Although they kept large herds of cattle, the Mycenaeans relied on hunting to get more meat. They hunted rabbit, deer, boar, wild bulls, and game birds. Women rode with the men in chariots during the hunt. When hunters were after big game, they used greyhounds. The game was captured with nets or killed with spears, slings, or bows and arrows.

Traders and Pirates Shortly after the Mycenaeans settled in the lowlands of Greece, they were visited by Minoan traders from Crete. The Mycenaeans began to imitate Minoan gold and bronze work. They adapted Cretan script to their own language. They copied Minoan fashions. Most important of all, they learned how to build ships and how to navigate.

The Mycenaeans also began to grow olives. They made presses to squeeze oil from the olives. They used the oil for cooking, as fuel for lamps, and to rub on their bodies. They sold plain oil in large clay jars and perfumed oil in painted vases. Sale of the oil made the Mycenaeans rich. It also led to the founding of trading stations and settlements on nearby islands.

CAPTION ANSWER

olive oil

INDEPENDENT PRACTICE

L2 **Daily Life** Ask students to research and make a chart comparing the chief agricultural crops and occupations of the Mycenaeans to those of present-day Greeks.

DID YOU KNOW ??

Troy was discovered and excavated by Heinrich Schliemann in 1870. As he dug, Schliemann found nine cities at the site. The seventh city down is presumed to be Troy of the Trojan War period.

EXTENDING THE CONTENT

Gold was not a metal native to Mycenaean lands, but has been found in Mycenaean tombs and shaft graves. Historians believe that Mycenaean rulers either traded or fought to acquire gold and other riches. During this period, Egypt was the leading source of gold in the Mediterranean. It seems possible that mercenaries, or paid warriors, from Mycenae may have fought for the Egyptians and were paid in gold.

L1 **Writing** Have students imagine that they are traders who come to do business with the Mycenaeans. Tell them to write letters home describing Mycenaean fortress-palaces, land, occupations, and lifestyles. Have students share their letters.

LINKING PAST TO PRESENT

The events and heroes of the Trojan War, along with their later fates, became the subjects of the greatest Greek tragedies. For example, Euripedes' *Trojan Women* looks at the human aftermath of war in the fallen city. Aeschylus's *Oresteia*, a trilogy of poetic dramas about the ill-fated House of Atreus, begins with Agamemnon's homecoming from victory at Troy. Later writers throughout the world have also drawn on this famous story.

CAPTION ANSWER

from songs and legends that had been handed down by word of mouth

VIDEODISC

Use the following to enrich Chapter 9.

WC B 10 11726

A brown ceramic goblet found at Troy.

Despite their success in trade, the Mycenaeans were warriors at heart. In battle, they used large hide shields with wooden frames, and fought with spears and swords. Their leaders wore fancy bronze armor. At first, the Mycenaeans fought one another. After they learned about shipbuilding and navigation, they outfitted pirate fleets and began to raid nearby lands. By about 1400 B.C., they had replaced the Minoans as the chief power of the Aegean world.

The Trojan War The Mycenaeans are famous for their attack on Troy, a major trading city in Asia Minor. This attack probably took place during the middle 1200s B.C. At the time, the Trojans (trō′ juhns) controlled the trade routes to the Black Sea. They made money by taxing the ships that carried grain and gold from southern Russia to Greece.

About 500 years after the Mycenaeans attacked Troy, a blind Greek poet named Homer (hō′ muhr) composed a long poem about the event. He called his poem the *Iliad* (il′ ē uhd). Homer also composed a poem called the *Odyssey* (ahd′ uh sē), which tells about the wanderings of Odysseus (ō dis′ ē uhs), a Mycenaean hero of the Trojan War. Homer drew his material for the two

THE TROJAN HORSE The first Greek myths came from the Mycenaeans. Later, the poet Homer gathered these legends and used them to write his works. Here, a painting of the Trojan horse from Homer's poem the *Iliad* is shown. **Where did Homer get his material for the *Iliad* and the *Odyssey*?**

MULTICULTURAL PERSPECTIVES

Literature, sculpture, music, and even everyday speech still reflect the incidents and characters of the Trojan War. People who have never read a line of Homer's *Iliad* or Virgil's *Aeneid*, which finishes the story of Troy, are familiar with the story of the Trojan Horse. Some quotes from the story are familiar phrases, such as the reference to Helen: "Was this the face that launched a thousand ships?"

poems from songs and legends that had been handed down by word of mouth. He then added his own descriptions and details of everyday life.

According to Homer's account in the *Iliad*, the Trojan War was fought over a woman. The king of Troy had a son named Paris, who fell in love with Helen, the wife of a Mycenaean king. When Paris took Helen to Troy, her husband became angry. He formed an army and sailed after them. However, the walls of Troy were so tall, thick, and strong that the Mycenaeans could not get into the city. They had to camp on the plain outside the city walls.

After ten years of fighting, the Mycenaeans still had not taken Troy. Then, Odysseus suggested a way they could capture the city. He had the soldiers build a huge, hollow wooden horse. The best soldiers hid inside the horse, while the rest boarded their ships and sailed away.

The Trojans saw the ships leave and thought they had won the war. They did not know the Mycenaean ships would return after dark. The Trojans tied ropes to the wooden horse and pulled it into the city as a victory prize. When they fell asleep, the Mycenaean soldiers hidden inside the horse came out. They opened the city gates and let in the rest of the Mycenaean army. The Mycenaeans killed the king of Troy and burned the city. Then, with Helen, they returned to their homes.

Mycenaean Goldwork

A "Dark Age" The Mycenaeans did not return to peaceful ways after crushing Troy. Instead, a series of **civil wars,** or wars between opposing groups of citizens, broke out. Within 100 years after the end of the Trojan War, almost no Mycenaean fortress-palaces were left. Soon after, a people called Dorians (dōr′ ē uhns) entered Greece and conquered the Mycenaeans. Their iron swords were not as well made as Mycenaean bronze swords. Nevertheless, Dorian swords were stronger. Thousands of Mycenaeans fled the Greek mainland and settled in Aegean islands and on the western shore of Asia Minor. These settlements later became known as Ionia (ī ō′ nē uh).

As a result of the civil wars and the Dorian invasion, the Aegean world entered a "Dark Age," which lasted until about 800 B.C. It was a time of wandering and killing. Overseas trade stopped. The people of the Aegean region forgot how to write and keep records. The skills of fresco painting and working with ivory and gold disappeared. The Aegean world was cut off from the Middle East, and the people had to create a new civilization on their own.

The people started over. Once again, herding and farming became the main ways of life. Local leaders ruled small areas. These leaders called themselves kings, but they were little more than chiefs. At first, the borders of the areas they ruled kept

DID YOU KNOW ??

Odysseus was later called Ulysses by the Romans.

L1 **History** Have students imagine they were Mycenaeans who lived before and after the Dorian invasion. Tell them that they are responsible for writing two journal entries. In the first entry they should describe Mycenaean life before the Dorian invasion. In the second entry they should describe how their lives have changed.

ASSESS

CHECK FOR UNDERSTANDING

Ask students to summarize orally or in writing the main points of the chapter. Discuss the answers to the Section and Chapter Review questions.

EVALUATE

Assign Chapter 9 **Performance Assessment Activity** in the TCR.

Administer **Chapter 9 Test** in the TCR. Testmaker available.

COOPERATIVE LEARNING

Organize the class into small groups and have each group find additional information about a Greek hero or heroine—either from the *Iliad* or *Odyssey* or from Greek myths. Each group should then write their own adventure involving their subject, and decide how it will be presented to the class. Some suggestions include acting out a myth, making a videotape, or presenting a choral reading.

Assign Chapter 9 **Cooperative Learning Activity** in the TCR.

RETEACH

Have students use the key terms to describe the main concepts of the chapter.

Assign Chapter 9 **Reteaching Activity** in the TCR.

ENRICH

Have students take turns reading aloud passages from the *Iliad* and the *Odyssey*. What do they like most and least about what they hear?

Assign Chapter 9 **Enrichment Activity** in the TCR.

CLOSE

Ask students to discuss which of the following statements is most true: *The early Greek people shaped their environment* OR *The early Greek people were shaped by their environment.*

MEETING CHAPTER OBJECTIVES

Each objective is tested by the Review questions in parentheses.

1. Describe what Minoan life was like. (BV; CT 1, 2; UYJ)

2. Discuss how geography influenced the early people on Crete and the Balkan Peninsula. (BV; CU 1, 2, 4, 6; CT 1, 2; GIH)

3. Summarize what life was like for the Mycenaeans. (BV; CU 6; CT 4)

4. Explain how the Dark Age affected the Aegean world. (CU 8; GIH)

changing. In time, however, the borders became fixed, and each area became an independent community. The people of these communities began calling themselves Hellenes (hel′ ēns), or Greeks.

Section 2 Review

1. **Identify:** Mycenaeans, Troy, Homer, Dorians, Ionia, Hellenes
2. **Define:** megaron, tenants, civil wars
3. In what ways were the Mycenaeans influenced by Minoan culture?
4. What happened in the Aegean world during the "Dark Age"?

Critical Thinking

5. Why was the growing of olives such an important development for the Aegean world?

Chapter Summary

1. Minoan civilization began to develop on the Mediterranean island of Crete about 2800 B.C.
2. At first, the Minoans were farmers, but eventually most turned to trade to earn a living.
3. The Minoans were very fond of sports, especially bull leaping.
4. Since the Minoans depended on the sea and their ships for protection, their cities were not walled.
5. The Minoans worshiped many gods, the most important of which was the Great Goddess, Mother Earth.
6. About 1400 B.C., the control of the Mediterranean passed to the Mycenaeans, who came to Greece from southern Rus states.
7. Instead of cities, the Mycenaeans built fortress-palaces on hilltops.
8. The Mycenaeans learned many things from the Minoans, including a writing script and the skills of shipbuilding and navigation.
9. The Mycenaeans fought a lengthy war against Troy.
10. The Trojan War and its results are described in two long poems, the *Iliad* and the *Odyssey*, composed by the blind Greek poet Homer.
11. After years of civil war, the Mycenaeans were conquered by the Dorians.
12. During the 300 years of the "Dark Age," the people of the Aegean area lost many of their skills and had to create a new civilization.

SECTION 2 ANSWERS

1. Mycenaeans, people from southern Russia (p. 155); Troy, major trading city in Asia Minor (p. 158); Homer, Greek poet (p. 158); Dorians, fighters who conquered Mycenaeans (p. 159); Ionia, Aegean island (p. 159); Hellenes, Greek people (p. 160)

2. megaron, palace room with a center fireplace (p. 155); tenants, people who work another person's land (p. 155); civil wars, wars between opposing groups (p. 159)

3. They copied Minoan metal work, adapted Cretan script, copied Minoan fashions, and learned how to build and navigate ships.

4. It was a time of wandering and killing, overseas trade stopped, people forgot how to write, and artistic skills disappeared.

5. Answers will vary but could include the many uses of oil developed and the trade and the wealth it brought.

Assign Chapter 9 **Section 2 Quiz** in the TCR. Testmaker available.

CHAPTER 9

Review

Building Vocabulary

Imagine that you are living among the early Greeks. Use the following words to write a paragraph describing the life of the Minoans and the Mycenaeans.

bull leaping	megaron
labyrinth	tenants
parchment	civil wars
shrines	

Check for Understanding

1. What civilizations combined to form Greek civilization?
2. In what ways were the Minoan people able to gain control of the Mediterranean Sea?
3. What do experts believe about the sport of bull leaping?
4. Why didn't Minoan cities have walls around them?
5. What were some features of the palace at Knossos?
6. What did the Mycenaeans build instead of cities?
7. How was the Trojan War described in the *Iliad?*
8. Why did the people of Greece have to create a new civilization?

Critical Thinking

1. How well did the Minoans use their natural resources? Explain.
2. What effect did being an island civilization have on the Minoans?
3. What role did religion play in Minoan daily life?
4. In what ways would the Mycenaean civilization have been different if the people had not learned to build and sail ships?

Geography in History

REGIONS Refer to the map on page 156 as you think about the "Dark Age" of the Aegean region. What human actions and geographic factors made it possible for this period of history to happen and last for 300 years?

Using Your Journal

Review details you noted about the ideas developed by the Minoans. Write a magazine article describing the ideas the Minoans developed about entertainment and sports.

CHAPTER 9 REVIEW ANSWERS

BUILDING VOCABULARY

Paragraphs will vary but should include some comparisons and contrasts.

CHECK FOR UNDERSTANDING

1. the Minoan and Mycenaean civilizations
2. They built faster ships with a large wooden beam in the prow to smash and sink enemy ships.
3. that it was a religious ceremony as well as a sport
4. the people depended on the sea and navy for protection
5. It was five stories high, built of stone, framed with wood, and decorated with frescoes. It had bathrooms, several entrances, and labyrinths.
6. fortress-palaces
7. Paris took Helen to Troy. The Mycenaeans attacked Troy; later built a huge wooden horse with soldiers hidden inside which was pulled into Troy. The Mycenaeans burned the city.
8. because their civilization was destroyed during the Dark Age

CRITICAL THINKING

1. Answers will vary but the Minoans used resources wisely.
2. It provided natural protection, and also made travel and trade easier.
3. Answers will vary, but religion gave the Minoan kings power.
4. Answers will vary but could include lack of development.

✚ BONUS ✚

TEST QUESTION
For Chapter 9 Test

Imagine you are an archaeologist who has dug up artifacts you believe are Mycenaean. Describe two artifacts you have found and what each was used for. *(Answers will vary but should be supported by explanation.)*

USING YOUR JOURNAL

Magazine articles will vary but should include the fact that Minoans changed the way ships were made so that they could go faster. The Minoans loved sports and built what was probably the world's first arena.

GEOGRAPHY IN HISTORY

Answers will vary but should include references to the isolation caused by the sea, mountains, migrations, and civil wars.

PLANNING GUIDE

CHAPTER 10 The City-States

CHAPTER ORGANIZER

Objectives	Special Features	Supplemental Materials
Section 1 The Polis Explain why the polis was the geographic and political center of Greek life.		• Reproducible Lesson Plan • Section 1 Quiz • Testmaker • Chapter 10 Vocabulary and Guided Reading Activity
Section 2 Sparta Describe life in Sparta.	Map and Geography Skills: *Reading Physical Maps,* p. 165	• Reproducible Lesson Plan • Section 2 Quiz • Testmaker • Chapter 10 Geography and Map Activity • Chapter 10 Cooperative Learning Activity • Chapter 10 Teaching Transparencies and Activities • The Western Civilization Videodisc
Section 3 Athens Discuss life in Athens, summarize how the Persian War affected Greece, and describe how Athens controlled other city-states.	People in History: *Buddha,* p. 170	• Reproducible Lesson Plan • Section 3 Quiz • Testmaker • Unit 4 World Literature • Reinforcing Social Studies Skills, pp. 26, 27 • The Western Civilization Videodisc • Chapter 10 Activity Book Activity
Section 4 Decline of the City-States Explain why Athens and the other Greek city-states declined.		• Reproducible Lesson Plan • Section 4 Quiz • Testmaker • Chapter 10 Chart and Graph Skill Activity • The Western Civilization Videodisc
Chapter 10 Review and Evaluation		• Chapter 10 Reteaching Activity • Chapter 10 Enrichment Activity • Spanish Summary and Glossary • Audiocassettes (English and Spanish) • Chapter 10 Performance Assessment Activity • Chapter 10 Test • Testmaker

If time does not permit teaching the entire chapter, use the Chapter 10 Summary on page 176 and the Chapter 10 Audiocassettes (English and Spanish) to point out the main ideas of the chapter.

✓ Performance Assessment Activities

Biography Have students research the life of Pericles, and make a time line of important events in his life. Then have them repeat that process for a modern politician of their choice. Suggest they then compare the two to decide who made the larger contribution to their civilizations, writing a summary statement of their conclusion.

Model Have students work in small groups to create a model of a Greek city-state. Have students use the information from their textbook or from other reference books and materials of their choice. The models should include the following: farming villages, fields, orchards, acropolis and its temple, and an agora. Display models in the classroom.

CHAPTER RESOURCES

LITERATURE ABOUT THE PERIOD

Renault, Mary. *The Last of the Wine.* Random House, 1975. A novel about Athens during the Peloponnesian War.

READINGS FOR THE STUDENT

Burrell, Roy. *The Greeks: Rebuilding the Past Series.* Oxford University Press, 1990.

Hamilton, Edith. *The Greek Way.* Norton, 1983. Story of the Greek spirit and mind told by great writers.

READINGS FOR THE TEACHER

Grant, Michael. *The Rise of the Greeks.* Scribner's, 1988. An examination of Greek civilization from the collapse of Mycenae to the Peloponnesian War.

MULTIMEDIA RESOURCES

Ancient Civilization: Safekeeping. Glencoe TVOntario. Video. Explains features of civilization that helped make people feel secure, with a focus on Greek civilization.

Athens: Birthplace for Democracy. Mar/Chuck Film Industries. Film or Video. Stresses Athens' historical and cultural importance.

Our Heritage from Ancient Greece. Guidance Associates/SSSS. Video. A brief history of ancient Greece and an overview of its culture.

INTRODUCE

CHAPTER 10 OVERVIEW

Chapter 10 discusses the Greek polis, with particular attention given to the city-states of Sparta and Athens.

- **Section 1** discusses the independent development of Greek city-states and contrasts the types of societies that evolved.
- **Section 2** summarizes the way of life in Sparta.
- **Section 3** describes the growth of democracy in Athens and its dominance in the Delian League.
- **Section 4** analyzes the geographic and political divisions that eventually led to the decline of the Greek city-states.

CHAPTER OBJECTIVES

After reading Chapter 10, students will be able to:

1. explain why the polis was the geographic and political center of Greek life.
2. describe what life was like in the city-states of Sparta and Athens.
3. summarize how the Persian Wars affected Greece.
4. discuss how Athens controlled the other city-states.
5. explain why Athens and the other city-states declined.

EXAMINING THE ARTIFACT

Explain to students that this carved stone is a grave marker called a stele. Steles were common in Greece at this time. Ask students what they can tell about the woman whose grave was marked by this stele?

PERFORMANCE ASSESSMENT

Use the Performance Assessment activities on page 162B to help you evaluate students as they complete the chapter.

CHAPTER 10 The City-States

Relief of Greek Woman and Servant

162

TEACHER CLASSROOM RESOURCES

- Reproducible Lesson Plan
- Section Quizzes/Chapter Test
- Activity Book Activity
- Enrichment Activity
- Chart and Graph Skill Activity
- Geography and Map Activity
- Vocabulary and Guided Reading Activity
- Cooperative Learning Activity
- Performance Assessment Activity
- Spanish Summary and Glossary
- Teaching Transparencies and Activities
- Audiocassettes (English and Spanish)
- The Western Civilization Videodisc
- Testmaker

Chapter Focus

READ TO DISCOVER:

- Why the polis was the geographic and political center of Greek life.
- What life was like in the city-states of Sparta and Athens.
- How the Persian Wars affected Greece.
- How Athens controlled other city-states.
- Why the Greek city-states declined.

The Hellenes of different communities shared a common language and many customs and beliefs. They did not have much to do with one another, however. Their communities were separated by mountains and by the sea. Because of this, no single community had power over the others. Instead, each controlled its own affairs. However, a sense of unity began to develop among the people within each community. By 750 B.C., the outlines of Greek civilization were formed.

700 B.C.–335 B.C.

KEY TERMS

polis
acropolis
agora
aristocrats
perioeci
oligarchy
democratic
meditate
enlightenment
triremes
mercenaries

Section 1 The Polis

The **polis** (pah' lis), or city-state, was the geographic and political center of Greek life. At first, each polis was made up of farming villages, fields, and orchards grouped around a fortified hill called an **acropolis** (uh krop' uh lis). At the top of the acropolis stood the temple of the local god. At the foot was the **agora** (ag' uh ruh). This was an open area used as a marketplace. As time passed, artisans, traders, and members of the upper class settled near the agora. By 700 B.C., this inner part of the polis had become a city. Together with the villages and farmland around it, it formed a city-state.

Each city-state had its own government and laws. The average city-state contained between 5,000 and 10,000 citizens. Workers born outside Greece, as well as women, children, and to

163

FOCUS

BELLRINGER

Ask each student to list two advantages and two disadvantages of living in a modern city.

MOTIVATIONAL ACTIVITY

Discuss students' lists of advantages and disadvantages of living in a modern city. Tell students that Greeks lived in city-states. Ask them to look for the advantages and disadvantages of life in the Greek city-states as they read the chapter.

VOCABULARY PRE-CHECK

Write the key terms for this chapter on the chalkboard. Ask students to list these on a sheet of paper and write the sentence in which they are found in the text as they encounter each.

Assign Chapter 10 **Vocabulary and Guided Reading Activity** in the TCR.

EXTRA CREDIT PROJECT

Ask interested students to identify the latitude along which modern Athens is located. Then tell them to locate two other cities, in countries other than Greece, that lie along the same latitude and list them on a chart. Ask students to compare selected characteristics of all three cities, such as: size, industry, climate, and ethnic groups, and chart them.

KEY TO ABILITY LEVELS

Teaching strategies have been coded for varying learning styles and abilities.

L1 Level 1 activities are **basic** activities and should be within the ability range of all students.

L2 Level 2 activities are **average** activities and should be within the ability range of the average to above-average student.

L3 Level 3 activities are **challenging** activities designed for the ability range of above-average students.

LEP LEP activities should be within the ability range of Limited English Proficiency students.

TEACH

GUIDED PRACTICE

L2 **Critical Thinking** Ask students to name the characteristics of Sumerian city-states discussed in Chapter 3. Write student responses on the chalkboard. *(Each had its own god and government; included the city—surrounded by a brick wall—and farmland around it; houses surrounding courtyards; ziggurat surrounded by courts.)* Ask students how Greek city-states were similar to or different from Sumerian city-states.

MAKING CONNECTIONS

➤➤ **Language Arts** The *polis* of ancient Greece is the ancestor of modern democratic government, although the meaning of the term *democracy* has changed greatly since Greek times. Nonetheless, much of the vocabulary of modern government derives from Greek ideas—*politics, political, police,* and *policy* comes from *polis*.

DID YOU KNOW ??

A person could walk from one end of a city-state to the other in two or three days. The Greeks believed that a city-state should be small enough so that citizens would know one another and be able to carry on public business.

Painting of Greek Woman

enslaved people, were not citizens. Only citizens could vote, own property, hold public office, and speak for themselves in court. In return, they were expected to take part in government and to defend their polis in time of war or conflict.

For Greek citizens in ancient times, civic and personal honor were one and the same. The polis gave them a sense of belonging. They put the good of the polis above everything else.

Two of the greatest Greek city-states were Sparta and Athens. Sparta had the strongest army in Greece, while Athens had the strongest navy. However, each developed differently with a different kind of government and a different way of life.

Section 1 Review

1. **Identify:** Sparta, Athens
2. **Define:** polis, acropolis, agora
3. What rights and duties did Greek citizens have?

Critical Thinking

4. Which of the requirements for citizenship in early Greece do you think were fair and which were not? Explain.

Section 2 SPARTA

Sparta was in the south-central region of Greece, in an area known as the Peloponnesus (pel ō puh nē′ sus). By 500 B.C., it had become the greatest military power in Greece.

At first, Sparta was ruled by a king. About 800 B.C., **aristocrats** (uh rist′ ō kratz), or nobles, took over the government. From that time on, Sparta had two kings who ruled jointly. Although they kept the title of king, they had little power. Their only duties were to lead the army and conduct religious services.

Only aristocrats could be Spartan citizens. All citizens over 20 years old were members of the Assembly, which passed laws and decided questions of war and peace. Each year, the Assembly chose five managers, known as *ephors* (ef′ uhrs), to take charge of public affairs and guide the education of young Spartans. The Council of Elders helped the ephors. The Council was made up of men over 60 years old who were chosen for life. It suggested laws to the Assembly and also served as a high court.

Aristocrats, Helots, and Perioeci The Spartans had little interest in farming. The land was worked by **helots** (hel′ uhtz), or

SECTION 1 ANSWERS

1. Sparta, strong Greek city-state in 500 B.C. (p. 164); Athens, another strong Greek city-state in 500 B.C. (p. 164)
2. polis, city-state (p. 163); acropolis, fortified hill (p. 163); agora, open marketplace (p. 163)
3. rights—they could vote, own property, hold public office, and speak for themselves in court; duties—they were expected to take part in government and to defend their polis
4. Answers will vary but could include references to discrimination by birth.

Assign Chapter 10 **Section 1 Quiz** in the TCR. Testmaker available.

Reading Physical Maps

Physical maps are used to show something about the surface of Earth. The colors used on physical maps may show the rainfall of a certain area. They may also be used to show an area's temperatures or elevations. In the physical map below, the colors indicate elevation. Colors ranging from green to brown are used. The meaning of each color is explained in the legend.

Look at the map "Elevation of Ancient Greece" shown below. The legend says that light brown means above 5,000 feet, or above 1,500 meters. This means that any area on the map that is shaded light brown is at least 5,000 feet, or 1,500 meters, above sea level. Remember that having an elevation of above 5,000 feet does not necessarily mean that an area is covered with mountains. The area may actually be a plateau.

Map Practice

1. **What color shows an elevation of 1,000 to 2,000 feet, or 300 to 600 meters?**
2. **What elevation is shown by the color dark green?**
3. **What generalization can you make about the elevation of ancient Greece?**

Elevation of Ancient Greece

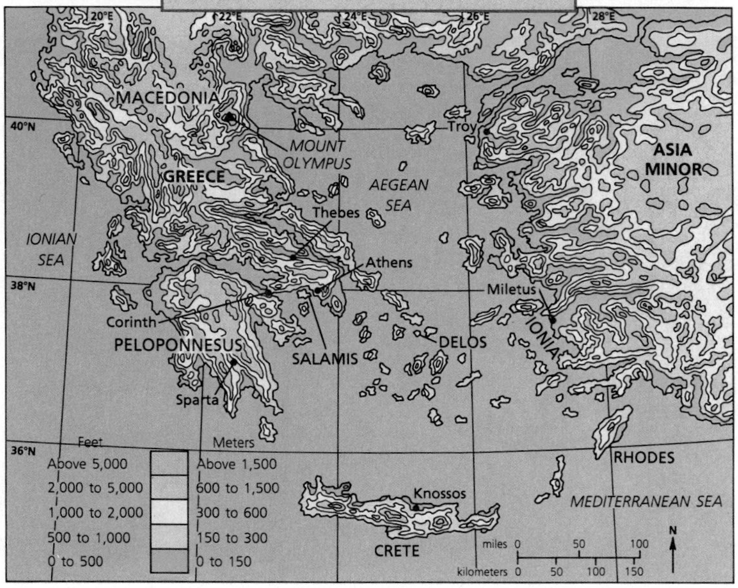

SPOTLIGHT ON: ANCIENT GREECE

The Mediterranean climate of ancient Greece made it an optimum place for growing olives, a crop that was as good as gold to the Greeks. Finding the olive growing wild, the Greeks cultivated it. Olive oil went into almost every dish prepared in Greek homes as well as in other ancient lands. Bread was dipped in oil as many people spread bread with butter today. Greek bathers used oil as soap and olive oil was burned for fuel.

Teaching

MAP SKILLS

Reading Physical Maps

Have students read the introductory section of the skill on page 165. Ask what they think colors can be used to show on maps? *(rainfall, temperatures, or elevations)* What does light brown shading on the map "Elevation of Ancient Greece" mean? *(the area is at least 5,000 feet, or 1,500 m, above sea level)* Direct students' attention to the map on the skill page. Ask students at what elevation most of the city-states are located? *(Most range from 0 to 1,000 feet, or 0 to 300 m, above sea level.)*

ANSWERS to Map Practice

1. yellow
2. dark green shows 0 to 500 feet, or 0 to 150 m
3. It has steep mountains and small, narrow plains.

VIDEODISC

Use the following to enrich Chapter 10.

WC B 22 11738
The Athenian Agora.

DID YOU KNOW ??

The helots revolted twice against the Spartan citizens. Both helots and perioeci were sometimes drafted into military service.

MAKING CONNECTIONS

➤➤ **Civics** Young Spartan boys were trained to steal to survive. If they were caught, however, they were severely punished.

CAPTION ANSWER

They were left on a hillside to die.

enslaved people owned by the city-states. Helots had to turn over one half of their crops to the aristocrats who owned the land but lived in the center of the polis.

The Spartans were not interested in business or trade either. They left those to the **perioeci** (pār ē ē' sī), or merchants and artisans who lived in the villages. The perioeci were neither enslaved people nor citizens. Helots and perioeci worked, while aristocrats trained for the army and war.

By about 750 B.C., there were 20 times as many helots and perioeci as there were aristocrats. The aristocrats were now faced with a choice. They could make life better for their workers by letting them share in the government, or they could allow things to stay the way they were. To do that meant keeping the workers down by force. Since the aristocrats were afraid that any change would destroy their way of life, they chose to keep things the way they were.

Spartan Way of Life The Spartans tried to become the strongest people in Greece. Newborn babies were examined to see if they were healthy. If they were, they were allowed to live. If they were not, they were left on a hillside to die.

THE SPARTAN WAY OF LIFE The life of a Spartan male centered on military training and physical fitness from the time he was seven years old. Here, a group of young warriors performs exercises on a Spartan racecourse. **What happened to unhealthy Spartan babies?**

MULTICULTURAL PERSPECTIVES

Many of the words in the English language came from the Spartans. The word *spartan* means "avoiding luxury and comfort" and "being as simple and frugal as possible." Another English word that came from the Spartans is *laconic*. Laconia was the plain in the southwestern part of the Peloponnesus where Sparta was situated. The Spartans were not impressed by oratory. They trained their young men to walk in silence and to say only what was absolutely necessary. The English word *laconic* refers to a person whose speaking style is short, sharp, and to the point.

When Spartan boys turned seven, they were sent to live in military camps. There, they were trained in groups under teenage leaders. They learned to read, write, and use weapons. The boys received only small amounts of food. They had to go barefoot and were given only one cloak to wear. They walked in silence, with their eyes to the ground, and spoke only when necessary. They slept outdoors without cover. Every ten days they were lined up and examined to make sure they were not getting fat.

Spartan men were expected to marry at 20 years of age. However, they could not have a household of their own. They had to live and eat in military barracks, where they shared expenses with other soldiers. They could retire from the army when they were 60 years old.

Spartan women had more freedom than the women of other Greek city-states. In the other city-states, women spent most of their time at home performing household duties. They did not go out without a chaperone. Then, they went out only to visit other women or attend religious festivals. They never spoke to men on the street or entertained their husbands' friends.

Spartan women, on the other hand, mixed freely with men. They enjoyed sports such as wrestling and racing. When Spartan women sent their men into battle, they told the men to come home with their shields or on them. If the men brought their shields home with them, it meant they had won the battle. Dead warriors were carried home on their shields.

The Spartans believed new ideas would weaken their way of life. Because of this, they tried to prevent change. When people of other Greek city-states began to use coins as money, for example, the Spartans kept using iron rods. Other city-states developed literature and art. Other city-states built up business and trade and improved their standard of living. Sparta remained a poor farming society that depended on the labor of slaves.

From its beginnings until its defeat in 371 B.C., Sparta had only one goal—to be militarily strong.

Sculpture of Spartan Girl

Section 2 Review

1. **Identify:** Peloponnesus, Assembly, Council of Elders
2. **Define:** aristocrats, helots, perioeci
3. How was the lifestyle of Spartan women different from that of other Greek women?
4. How was Sparta different from other Greek city-states?

Critical Thinking

5. What parts of Spartan life would you have enjoyed and what would you have wanted to change? Explain.

L1 **Daily Life** Divide the class into two groups, but have them work individually within their group. Assign one group to imagine they are Spartan teenagers and the other Athenian teenagers. Have students in each group write a letter to someone in the other group describing their schooling and how they feel about it. Have the groups exchange letters and have each student write a letter of response.

DID YOU KNOW ??

Women in Greek city-states could be prominent and influential in religion as priestesses.

SECTION 2 ANSWERS

1. Peloponnesus, south-central region of Greece (p. 164); Assembly, law-making group of citizens (p. 164); Council of Elders, Greek men chosen as advisors (p. 164)
2. aristocrats, Greek nobles (p. 164); helots, enslaved people (p. 164); perioeci, Greek merchants and artisans (p. 166)
3. Spartan women had more freedom, mixed freely with their husbands' friends, enjoyed sports, and encouraged their men in battle.
4. It tried to prevent change, spent its energy on war, and remained a poor farming society dependent on enslaved people.
5. Answers will vary but could include references to harsh training and physical lifestyle.

Assign Chapter 10 **Section 2 Quiz** in the TCR. Testmaker available.

TEACH

L1 **Critical Thinking** Ask students why they think Solon ordered every father to teach his son a trade. *(Answers will vary but students may say that he wanted to strengthen industry in Athens.)*

DID YOU KNOW

Draco's laws were so strict that a person could be put to death for stealing an apple. The word *draconian* comes from *Draco* and means "extremely harsh or cruel."

CAPTION ANSWER

It was important to the town's economy and was a meeting place of the people.

VIDEODISC

Use the following to enrich Chapter 10.

WC B 11 11727

Solon (ca. 639-ca. 559 B.C.).

Section 3

ATHENS

Northeast of Sparta, another city-state developed that had a very different philosophy about living than the Spartans. This polis located on the Aegean coast was Athens. Like Sparta, the location of Athens was strategic. Like all the other Greek city-states, Athens was first ruled by kings. However, about 750 B.C., some Athenian nobles, merchants, and manufacturers took over

ATHENS MARKET PLACE The agora of Athens was a favorite meeting place of the people. These ruins show archaeologists the importance of this community area. **Why would the agora be located near the center of Athens?**

MEETING SPECIAL NEEDS

Organize auditory learners into two groups. Direct one group to imagine they are Athenians defending the idea that a woman's place is in the home. Direct the other group to imagine they are Spartans defending the idea that women should be free to mix with their husband's friends and attend sporting events. Give each group time to research and develop its arguments. Hold a debate over the issues.

the government. They set up an **oligarchy** (ol' uh gahr kē), or form of government in which a few people have the ruling power. Fights broke out between them and the farmers and artisans over land ownership. The upper-class Athenians did not want these fights to turn into an uprising against the government, they agreed to make reforms. To do this, they had to change the government.

The first attempt to change the government was made by Draco (drā' kō), a noble. Draco, however, failed because his punishments were too harsh. Then, in 594 B.C., a rich merchant named Solon (sah' lon) was chosen to undertake the task.

Solon prepared a **constitution,** or a set of principles and rules for governing. This constitution broke the political power of the rich. Solon set a limit on how much land a person could own and gave landowners the right to vote in the Assembly. The Assembly was given the power to pass laws. Solon erased all debts. He freed all the people who had been forced into enslavement because of debt. Solon offered citizenship to artisans who were not Athenians, and he ordered every father to teach his son a trade.

Under Solon, more Athenians began to take part in government. Trade also increased. Still, many people were not happy. The rich thought Solon had gone too far, while the poor thought he had not gone far enough. By the time Solon had left office, he had lost much of his original popularity.

About 560 B.C., the government was taken over by another Athenian named Peisistratus (pī sis' trah tus). Peisistratus was supported by the lower classes. He divided large estates among farmers who owned no land. He stated that a person no longer had to own land to be a citizen. He also encouraged sculpture and other arts.

A Democratic Constitution When Peisistratus died, his sons took over as leaders of the Athenian government. Not long after that, their government was overthrown by the Spartans.

In 508 B.C., the Spartans themselves were overthrown by a noble named Cleisthenes (klīs' thuh nēz). A year later, Cleisthenes put into effect the world's first constitution that was **democratic,** or favoring the equality of all people. For example, it gave Athenians the right of freedom of speech. The political reforms made by Cleisthenes lasted until the fall of Greece almost 300 years later.

Cleisthenes opened the Assembly to all males over 20 years old. Each year, the Assembly elected ten generals to run the Athenian army and navy and to serve as chief *magistrates* (maj' uh strātz), or judges. One of the generals was named commander-in-chief.

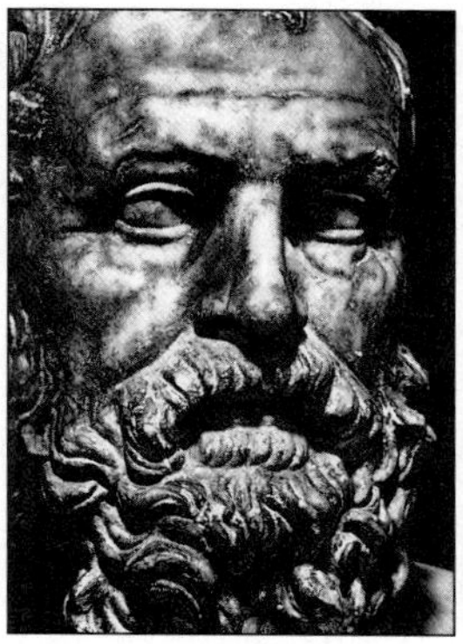

Image of Solon

MAKING CONNECTIONS

➤➤ **Language Arts** The word *solon,* updated from the name of the Greek leader Solon, is used to describe a wise legislator.

DID YOU KNOW ??

Athenian women did not receive the same education or training as men. Political activity and intellectual pursuits were not encouraged among women, whose lives focused on caring for the home and children. Few Athenian women went out at night. Those who went out during the day were accompanied by a female friend and usually were veiled. Shopping was done by the men.

VIDEODISC

Use the following to enrich Chapter 10.

WC B 13 11729

The Athenian Acropolis.

COOPERATIVE LEARNING

Organize the class into groups of seven or eight. Have four or five in each group role-play residents of Athens and the remaining group members role-play newspaper reporters who interview the residents. Have the groups research to find out about an Athenian merchant, a member of the Council of Five Hundred, an upper-class woman, a priestess to Athena, or an enslaved person. Have each group write questions the reporter might ask and answers that might be given. Each group should hold their interviews for the class.

Assign Chapter 10 **Cooperative Learning Activity** in the TCR.

Teaching

PEOPLE IN HISTORY

BUDDHA

Direct students to read the People in History feature. Ask students when Buddhism was developing. *(while Greek civilization was developing)* What did Gautama do to seek truth and wisdom? *(He left his wife and newborn son, lived as a monk, starved himself, read the holy books of Hinduism, and meditated until he gained enlightenment.)* What does Buddha mean? *(Enlightened One)*

ANSWERS to Checking for Understanding

1. He went outside his palace grounds and learned about aging, sickness, and death. He also met a poor but happy man, and realized that there was more to happiness than possessions.
2. that people could find peace by not being greedy and by living correctly, which included telling the truth, giving charity, and never harming a person or an animal

VIDEODISC

Use the following to enrich Chapter 10.

WH U 15 34621
Gautama Buddha with devotees.

WH U 24 34630
Buddhist scroll painting from China, of Song period.

PEOPLE IN HISTORY

Buddha

While Greek civilization was developing in western Europe, a new religion was growing in the East. This religion was founded by Siddhartha Gautama (si dahr′ tuh gowt′ uh muh), who was born in the foothills of the Himalayas about 563 B.C. The son of a king, he grew up shielded from unpleasant sights. He lived in luxury and was followed by servants wherever he went.

When Gautama was about 30 years old, he took a trip outside his palace grounds. For the first time, Gautama learned about aging, sickness, and death. He was troubled with the fact that humans had to suffer such tragedies.

Seeker of Truth On his way back to his palace, Gautama met a holy man. This man had nothing but a bowl for begging and a single yellow garment. Even so, he looked very happy. Gautama realized that there was more to happiness than possessions. He decided to leave his wife and newborn son and to seek truth and wisdom.

For several years, Gautama lived as a wandering monk. He starved himself and read the holy books of Hinduism, the religion of his birth. However, he could not find an answer to freedom from life's suffering.

Finally, Gautama decided to find life's answers through his own thinking. One day, he wandered into a village and sat down under a tree. He decided to **meditate,** or think, until he gained **enlightenment,** or understanding. At last, enlightenment came.

Powerful Teacher Gautama decided that people were unhappy because they wanted things they could not have. Thus, he taught that they could find peace by not being greedy and by living correctly. This included telling the truth, giving charity, and never harming a person or an animal.

Others learned of Gautama's experience and began to call him Buddha, which means "Enlightened One." His teachings became a new religion called Buddhism (bū′ diz uhm).

Checking for Understanding

1. **What led Siddhartha Gautama to change his way of life?**
2. **What did Buddha teach?**

SPOTLIGHT ON: BUDDHA

Buddha spent the remainder of his life spreading the message that people could find peace by not being greedy and by living correctly. He outlined his main ideas in the Four Noble Truths: All people suffer and know sorrow. People suffer because their desires bind them to the cycle of rebirth. People could end their suffering by eliminating their desires. One could eliminate desire by following the Eightfold Path. The Eightfold Paths are: know the truth, resist evil, say nothing to hurt others, respect life, work for the good of others, free their minds of evil, control their thoughts, and practice meditation.

The Council of Five Hundred handled the daily business of Athens. Members were chosen each year by lot. The names of 500 citizens were drawn from a large pot. No one could serve on the Council for more than two terms. Thus, every citizen had a chance to be a Council member.

There were two reasons why the Athenians preferred choosing council members by lot rather than by voting. First, they believed that in an election, people who had money or who could speak well would have an unfair advantage. Second, the Athenians believed that every citizen was smart enough to hold public office. The only exception was in times of war. Then, a skillful general was needed on the Council.

Under Cleisthenes, citizens were required to educate their sons. Since there were no public schools, boys either had a tutor or attended a private school. Starting when they were seven years old, boys studied writing, mathematics, and music. They also practiced sports and memorized the works of Homer and other noted Greek poets.

When they turned 18 years old, Athenian males became citizens. They went to the temple of the god Zeus (zūs) and took an oath of citizenship in front of their family and friends. In the oath, they promised to help make Athens a better place in which to live. They also promised to be honorable in battle, follow the constitution, and respect their religion.

Sculpture of Homer

The Persian Wars About the time Athens was going through government changes, the Persians ruled the largest and most powerful empire in the western world. In 545 B.C., the Persians conquered Ionia—the Greek city-states in Asia Minor and on the Aegean islands. About 20 years later, the Ionians revolted. They asked the city-states on the Greek mainland for help. Athens and another polis responded by sending a few warships. After five years of fighting, however, the Persians put down the revolt. Although the Ionians were defeated, Darius, the Persian king, was not satisfied. He wanted to punish the mainland Greeks for helping the Ionians.

In 490 B.C., Darius sent a fleet of 600 ships and a well-equipped army to Greece. The Persians landed on the plain of Marathon about 26 miles, or 41 kilometers, northeast of Athens. After several days, the Persians decided to sail directly to Athens and attack it by sea. They began loading their ships. As soon as most of the Persian soldiers were aboard, Greek soldiers ran down in close order from the hills around Marathon. The remaining Persian troops were not prepared to meet this kind of attack and were defeated. A runner set off for Athens with news of the victory. Upon reaching Athens, he cried out *Nike!*, the Greek goddess of victory, and then died of exhaustion. Winning the Battle of Marathon gave the Greeks a great sense of confidence.

Greek Helmet

L1 **Chronology** As a class, develop a time line depicting the historical events of Greece dating from 545 B.C., the defeat of the Ionians, to 404 B.C., the defeat of the Athenians. Lead the class in a discussion of the causes of the events listed on the time line and what effect each event had on the Greek city-states. LEP

LINKING PAST TO PRESENT

The present-day marathon is a race named after the Athenian victory over the Persians. The Greek runner who died bringing the victory news from Marathon to Athens was a well-known professional athlete named Phidippides. His run from Marathon to the agora in Athens—about 26 miles, or 42 km—was the inspiration for the modern marathon race. This race was part of the first modern Olympic Games in 1896.

MULTICULTURAL PERSPECTIVES

Have interested students research information about Greek city-states other than Athens and Sparta and report their findings to the class. The city-states of Argos, Corinth, Sicyon, Olympia, Delphi, Thessaly, Thebes, Miletus, and Ehesus are possible choices. Have students discuss the similarities and differences among the city-states.

L2 **Writing** Have students imagine they witnessed the Battle of Salamis. Have them write a letter to the editor of an Athenian newspaper describing the battle.

DID YOU KNOW ??

The Greeks trireme was about 125 feet (or 38 m) long and 20 feet (or 6 m) wide with a square sail on its mast. In battle, all three levels of 174 oarsmen rowed while a flutist piped the stroke.

CAPTION ANSWER

Xerxes returned to Asia; the remaining Persian troops were defeated by the Greeks in the Battle of Plataea; then the Persian navy was destroyed, ending the Persian War.

Shortly after the Battle of Marathon, rich silver mines were found near Athens. The Athenians spent their new wealth on **triremes** (trī′ rēmz), or warships that had three levels of rowers on each side, one above the other. Soon, Athens had the largest navy in Greece. The Athenians planned to be prepared if the Persians returned.

The Persians did return. In 480 B.C., Darius's son Xerxes (zerk′ sēz) sent 250,000 soldiers across the Aegean and conquered northern Greece. In order to stop the Persians from taking all of Greece, 20 Greek city-states banded together. The Spartans led the army, while the Athenians led the navy.

First, 7,000 Greek soldiers headed for the narrow pass of Thermopylae (ther mop′ uh lē), about 100 miles, or 160 kilometers, from Athens. There, they held off the Persian army for three days. This gave the people of Athens time to flee to the island of Salamis (sal′ uh muhs). Meanwhile, all but 300 Spartans and 700 other Greeks withdrew from Thermopylae. The Persians, helped by a traitor, found a way around the pass. They killed every soldier guarding the pass and then marched on Athens. Finding the city almost deserted, they set it on fire.

BATTLE OF SALAMIS The Greek fleet, led by the Athenians, defeated the Persian navy in the Bay of Salamis. The faster Greek triremes were able to sail close to the Persian ships and attack with spears and arrows. **What happened to the Persians after the Battle of Salamis?**

SPOTLIGHT ON: LEONIDAS

King Leonidas of Sparta stayed with the 300 Spartans at the narrow pass of Thermopylae to stand against the Persian army. He wanted to remain obedient to the law of Sparta—never surrender on the battlefield but fight until victory or death.

Ancient Greece

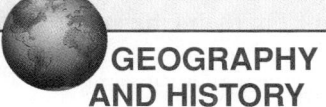

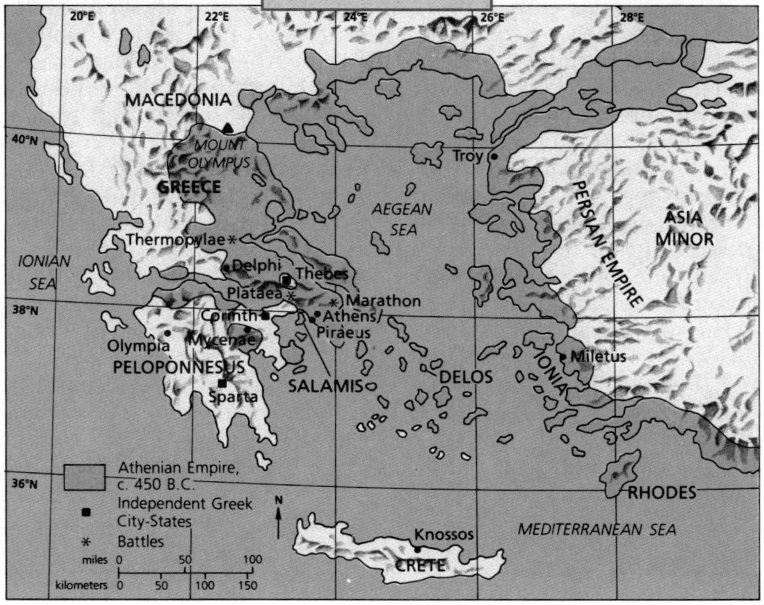

MAP STUDY

LOCATION The Persians wanted to extend their empire into Europe. **How did the location of Greece make it a likely place for a Persian attack?**

Then, the Greeks tricked the Persian fleet into sailing into the strait between Athens and Salamis. Since the strait was too narrow for all the Persian ships to enter at once, the Greeks could take them on a few at a time. Also, once the Persian ships were in the strait, their large size made them difficult to handle. With their lighter, faster ships, the Greeks defeated the Persian fleet.

Following the defeat, Xerxes returned to Asia. However, he left some troops behind. In 479 B.C., they were defeated by the Greeks in the Battle of Plataea (pluh tē′ uh). A few days later, Greek ships destroyed what was left of the Persian navy. The Persian Wars were over.

The Delian League and the Athenian Empire The Persians had been driven from Greece, but they still ruled Ionia. Because of this, the Athenians suggested that the Greek city-states form a **defensive league,** or protective group. Since the league had its headquarters on the island of Delos, it was called the Delian (dē′ lē uhn) League. Sparta was one of the few Greek city-states that did not join the League.

Once a city-state became a League member, it could not withdraw unless all the other members agreed. The League had a common navy. Its ships were usually built and crewed by Athenians, but the other city-states paid the costs.

MAP STUDY Answer

because Persia would have needed to conquer Greece in order to reach the European mainland

GEOGRAPHY AND HISTORY

Direct the students to use the map on this page. Have them locate the battle sites of the Persian War. Ask students what the location of the battle sites suggests about the probable outcome of the Persian War? *(The battles were fought on territory of Greek city-states instead of territory on the Persian Empire; therefore, the Greek soldiers knew the geography of the area better than the Persian soldiers, which gave them a great advantage toward winning.)*

VIDEODISC

Use the following to enrich Chapter 10.

WC B 12 11728
Pericles of Athens.

WC B 20 11736
The temple of Athena Nike, on the Acropolis.

MULTICULTURAL PERSPECTIVES

Pericles expressed his ideas about the importance of democracy in a funeral speech when he said democracy must be controlled by many and not a few people. He also said:

When it is a question of putting one person before another in positions of public responsibility, what counts is not membership of a particular class, but the actual ability which the man possesses.

The League worked well for a while. As time passed, though, Athens gained more and more power. Other city-states had to ask Athens for permission to sail or to trade. Criminal cases were brought to Athens for trial. Athenian coins replaced other Greek money. Athenian soldiers interfered in the politics of other Greek city-states. In short, the Delian League had turned into the Athenian Empire.

The main leader of Athens at the time was a general named Pericles (per′ uh klēz). Pericles was known as the "first citizen" of Athens. He had a dream of Athens as the most beautiful and perfect city of the time. To help make this dream come true, he rebuilt the palaces and temples on the Acropolis. It took 11 years to build the Parthenon (par′ thuh non), the temple of the goddess Athena. Much of this building was done with money that belonged to the Delian League.

Pericles also built the Long Walls. These were two parallel, fortified walls with tile roofs. The Long Walls connected Athens with its seaport of Piraeus (pī rē′ uhs) some five miles, or eight kilometers, away. Having the Long Walls meant Athens could get supplies even in times of war.

THE ACROPOLIS The Acropolis in Athens was devoted to religious purposes, rather than defensive purposes as in other Greek cities. The largest building there was the Parthenon, a temple dedicated to the goddess Athena. Here, a model shows the Acropolis. **Where did the money to rebuild the temples on the Acropolis come from?**

LINKING PAST TO PRESENT

Male citizens were expected to participate in government and to defend the polis in time of war. As Pericles said, "We do not say that a man who takes no interest in politics minds his own business. We say he has no business here at all."

Many countries today expect the same participation from their citizens, both male and female.

MAKING CONNECTIONS

➤➤ **Geography: Region** At the beginning of the Peloponnesian War, Pericles planned Athenian strategy. To avoid a direct battle with the well-trained Spartan troops, he moved the rural population of Athens behind the city walls. He ordered the Athenian navy to attack the Spartan coast and to keep the sea lanes open for supplies.

CAPTION ANSWER

the Delian League

VIDEODISC

Use the following to enrich Chapter 10.

WC B 16 11732

A three-quarter view of the Parthenon.

WC B 18 11734

Parthenon frieze, showing horsemen.

COOPERATIVE LEARNING

Organize the class into two groups. Assign one group the Persian Wars and the other group the Peloponnesian War. Each group should prepare an oral and visual presentation about their assigned war. Divide each group into subgroups to research facets of the topic, such as the impact of geography on the battles and the leaders involved. Visuals might include drawings of soldiers, weapons, battle formations, fortifications, and ships. Each group should prepare a large time line of the events.

Pericles led Athens for almost 30 years. During this period, art, philosophy, and literature reached new heights. Many people who came to Athens from other city-states settled there.

Sculpture of Pericles

Decline of Athens The more powerful Athens became, the more resentful other Greek city-states grew. Anti-Athenian feelings soon spread throughout Greece. When the Athenians attacked one of Sparta's allies, a group of city-states led by Sparta declared war on Athens. The war, which was called the Peloponnesian (pel uh puh nē′ zhuhn) War, lasted almost 30 years. It ended in 404 B.C. when Athens surrendered to Sparta.

Between the war and a plague that struck during the war, Athens also lost more than one quarter of its people. Much of its land was ruined. Thousands of young Athenian men left home and became **mercenaries** (mer′ suh nār ēz), or hired soldiers, in the Persian army.

When the Spartans took control of Athens in 404 B.C., they set up an oligarchy and chose 30 Athenian aristocrats to rule there. Not long after that, the Athenians successfully revolted and once more set up a democracy. However, Athens was never again as powerful as it had been before the Peloponnesian War.

Section 3 Review

1. **Identify:** Solon, Cleisthenes, Marathon, Xerxes, Delian League, Pericles, Long Walls, Peloponnesian War
2. **Define:** oligarchy, constitution, democratic, triremes, defensive league, mercenaries
3. What political reforms did Cleisthenes make in Athens?
4. What happened to the Athenians as a result of the Peloponnesian War?

Critical Thinking

5. In what ways is the United Nations today similar to the Delian League? Explain your answer.

Section 4 Decline of the City-States

After the Peloponnesian War, most Greeks began to lose their sense of community. The war had lasted a long time and had cost a great deal of money. People became more interested in making money and having a good time. Soon, bitterness developed between the upper and lower classes within each polis.

INDEPENDENT PRACTICE

L2 Critical Thinking Ask students to brainstorm measures that could have been taken to help prevent the decline of Athens and other Greek city-states. Ask students to share their ideas.

L2 Debate Have students orally defend this statement: Everybody lost the Peloponnesian War. *(All participants suffered disastrously from the war—lost crops, unemployment, social unrest, decline in democracy, and military weakness)*

DID YOU KNOW ??

It is generally believed that the plague was either typhus or a highly malignant form of scarlet fever, which appeared in the Mediterranean area for the first time. Among those who died in the plague were Pericles and his family.

VIDEODISC

Use the following to enrich Chapter 10.

WC C 12 14614

Lothair I, German King & Holy Roman Emperor.

SECTION 3 ANSWERS

1. Solon, Athens merchant (p. 169); Cleisthenes, Spartan noble (p. 169); Marathon, plain near Athens (p. 171); Xerxes, Persian king (p. 172); Delian League, protection group (p. 173); Pericles, Athenian general (p. 174); Long Walls, connected Athens and Piraeus (p. 174); Peloponnesian War, between Sparta and Athens (p. 175)
2. oligarchy, rule by a few (p. 169); constitution, principles for governing (p. 169); democratic, rule by people (p. 169); triremes, warships (p. 172); defensive league, protective group (p. 173); mercenaries, hired soldiers (p. 175)
3. set the first democratic constitution, opened the Assembly to males over 20, and the council to all citizens.
4. The Athenians lost their navy, their power, and their confidence.
5. Answers will vary but might include shared protection.

Assign Chapter 10 **Section 3 Quiz** in the TCR. Testmaker available.

ASSESS

CHECK FOR UNDERSTANDING

Ask students to summarize orally or in writing the main points of the chapter. Discuss the answers to the Section and Chapter Review questions.

EVALUATE

Assign Chapter 10 **Performance Assessment Activity** in the TCR.

Administer **Chapter 10 Test** in the TCR. Testmaker available.

RETEACH

Help students chart the main ideas and events described in the chapter.

Assign Chapter 10 **Reteaching Activity** in the TCR.

ENRICH

Have students present to the class illustrations of Greek vase painting, and describe the details shown on the paintings.

Assign Chapter 10 **Enrichment Activity** in the TCR.

CLOSE

Ask students to compare the advantages and disadvantages of living in a Greek-city state with those they listed for modern city life in the Bellringer activity.

MEETING CHAPTER OBJECTIVES

Each objective is tested by the Review questions in parentheses.

1. **Explain** why the polis was the center of Greek life. (BV; CU 1, 2; GIH)
2. **Describe** what life was like in the city-states of Sparta and Athens. (BV; CU 4, 5; CT 1)
3. **Summarize** how the Persian Wars affected Greece and its people. (BV; CT 1)
4. **Discuss** how Athens controlled the other city-states. (CU 8)
5. **Explain** why Athens and the other city-states declined. (CT 4)

After the war, Sparta ruled Greece. The Spartans were harsh rulers who angered the other Greeks. As a result, in 371 B.C., a group of city-states led by Thebes (thēbz) overthrew Spartan rule. The rule of Thebes, however, was no better than that of Sparta. It weakened the city-states even more. The Greeks were no longer strong enough or united enough to fight off invaders. In 338 B.C., Philip II of Macedonia (mas uh dō' nē uh) conquered Greece.

Section 4 Review

1. **Identify:** Thebes, Philip II
2. How did the Peloponnesian War help destroy the sense of community of the Greek city-states?
3. What were some other reasons for the decline of the Greek city-states?

Critical Thinking

4. Why might Greeks have become more interested in making money for themselves rather than for the city-state after the Peloponnesian War?

Chapter Summary

1. Around 700 B.C., the geographic and political center of Greek life was the polis, or city-state.
2. The two greatest Greek city-states were Sparta and Athens.
3. Since Sparta's main goal was to be militarily strong, much time and energy were spent training its citizens for war.
4. Spartan women had more freedom than the women of other Greek city-states.
5. Since they believed new ideas would weaken their way of life, the Spartans tried to prevent change.
6. Between 750 and 507 B.C., Athens went through a series of government reorganizations and reforms that changed the qualifications for Greek citizenship.
7. In 507 B.C., Cleisthenes put into effect the world's first generally democratic constitution.
8. Between 490 and 479 B.C., the Greek city-states fought several wars with the Persian Empire.
9. After the defeat of the Persians, Athens became Greece's leading polis.
10. Sparta defeated Athens in the Peloponnesian War, which was fought between 431 and 404 B.C.
11. As a result of the Peloponnesian War, the Greek city-states lost their sense of community and were no longer united enough to fight off invaders.
12. Greece was conquered by Philip II of Macedonia in 338 B.C.

SECTION 4 ANSWERS

1. Thebes, leader of group of city-states that overthrew Spartan rule in 371 B.C. (p. 176); Philip II, ruler of Macedonia in 338 B.C. (p. 176)
2. The war lasted a long time, was costly; people were discouraged and they began to lose interest in what was good for their city-state.
3. Bitterness developed between the upper and lower classes within each polis, the rule of Thebes weakened the city-states, and the Greeks could no longer fight off invaders.
4. Answers will vary but might include the idea that they were tired of being involved in war and decided to pay attention to themselves.

Assign Chapter 10 **Section 4 Quiz** in the TCR. Testmaker available.

CHAPTER 10 Review

Building Vocabulary

Imagine you are living in Greece during the time of the Persian Wars. Use the following words to write a letter to a friend describing the organization and government of Sparta and Athens at that time.

polis	oligarchy
acropolis	enlightenment
agora	democratic
aristocrats	triremes
meditate	mercenaries
perioeci	

Check for Understanding

1. Why did Greek communities have little contact with one another?
2. What did the citizens of a polis consider most important?
3. Why were Sparta's aristocrats afraid of change?
4. Why was it important for Spartan women to be healthy?
5. Why did Sparta remain a poor farming society?
6. Why was the Battle of Marathon important for the Greeks?
7. How did the Greek navy defeat the Persian fleet?
8. How did the Delian League become the Athenian Empire?

Critical Thinking

1. Do you think the Spartan way of training men benefited Sparta? Why or why not?
2. What method of choosing members of the Athenian Council of Five Hundred would you have suggested? Explain.
3. Why do you think some people in Athens might not have thought Pericles deserved the title of "first citizen" of Athens? Explain.
4. What may happen to a community as a result of a long war?

Geography in History

PLACE Note the location of the Greek city-states on the map on page 173. Why do you think these city-states developed in the places that they did and what geographic features might have affected this development?

Using Your Journal

Review the details you have noted about the ideas developed by the Greeks. Write a paragraph describing how the ideas of Solon and Cleisthenes affect you today.

CHAPTER 10 REVIEW ANSWERS

BUILDING VOCABULARY

Letters will vary but should include several points of comparison and contrast.

CHECK FOR UNDERSTANDING

1. because they were separated by mountains and by the sea
2. the good of the polis
3. because they thought it would destroy their way of life
4. so they would bear healthy male warriors
5. because it spent its time and energy only on the art of war
6. because it gave the Greeks a great sense of confidence
7. It tricked the Persian fleet into sailing into the strait between Athens and Salamis.
8. Athens gained more power, it controlled sailing and trade, and interfered in the politics of other city-states.

CRITICAL THINKING

1. Answers will vary.
2. Answers will vary but could include the blind drawing being more fair, but less qualitative than an election.
3. Answers will vary but could include reference to his good and bad qualities.
4. Answers will vary but should include that people may become discouraged, fight among themselves, and lose their sense of community.

+ BONUS +

TEST QUESTION

For Chapter 10 Test

What would Cleisthenes say about a city-state ruled by one woman who served for life, a council elected by voting, no organized army, but public schools for all citizens? *He believed in rule by men with limited terms; restricted voting; an army; and educating males.*

USING YOUR JOURNAL

Paragraphs will vary but should include the idea that constitutions are part of the U.S. government as well as many local governments; the U.S. Constitution is democratic, it includes freedom of speech; the House of Representatives, like the Assembly, has the power to make laws.

GEOGRAPHY IN HISTORY

Answers may vary but could include references to good farming land, optimum location for trade and/or sea access, the safety of highlands or islands, and heritage.

PLANNING GUIDE

CHAPTER 11 Cultural Contributions

CHAPTER ORGANIZER

Objectives	Special Features	Supplemental Materials
Section 1 Religious Practices Describe how the Greeks honored their gods and goddesses and summarize what contributions were made in athletics and the arts during the Golden Age of Greek culture.		• Reproducible Lesson Plan • Section 1 Quiz • Testmaker • Chapter 11 Vocabulary and Guided Reading Activity • Chapter 11 Cooperative Learning Activity • Unit 4 Primary Source Reading • Chapter 11 Activity Book Activity • The Western Civilization Videodisc
Section 2 Science Discuss how Socrates, Plato, Aristotle, and other Greek thinkers influenced the development of western civilization.		• Reproducible Lesson Plan • Section 2 Quiz • Testmaker • Chapter 11 Geography and Map Activity • Chapter 11 Chart and Graph Skill Activity • Chapter 11 Teaching Transparencies and Activities • The Western Civilization Videodisc • Unit 4 World Literature
Chapter 11 Review and Evaluation		• Chapter 11 Reteaching Activity • Chapter 11 Enrichment Activity • Reinforcing Social Studies Skills, pp. 20, 22 • Spanish Summary and Glossary • Audiocassettes (English and Spanish) • Chapter 11 Performance Assessment Activity • Chapter 11 Test • Testmaker

If time does not permit teaching the entire chapter, use the Chapter 11 Summary on page 190 and the Chapter 11 Audiocassettes (English and Spanish) to point out the main ideas of the chapter.

✓ Performance Assessment Activities

Bulletin Board Have students contribute to a "Golden Age of Greece" time capsule. Ask each student to research and write about one of the following aspects of Greek culture they think would be a good representation of the Greeks to be opened 100 years from now: architecture, art, history, literature, science, mathematics, philosophy, or law. Suggest students explain why each is an important contribution to western civilization. Encourage students to create a visual representation of their subject to post with their writing.

Political Cartoons Have students find political cartoons in newspapers and magazines that they think make a good point. Then have them prepare their own cartoons to illustrate the political philosophy of Plato or Aristotle, or to illustrate political issues from the days of ancient Greece.

CHAPTER RESOURCES

LITERATURE ABOUT THE PERIOD

Fagles, Robert, trans. *Sophocles: The Three Theban Plays.* Penguin, 1984. Included are *Oedipus the King, Antigone,* and *Oedipus at Colonus.*

Hamilton, Edith, trans. *Three Greek Plays.* Norton, 1958. Included are the *Trojan Woman* of Euripedes, *Prometheus Bound,* and *Agamemnon* of Aeschylus.

Jowett, Benjamin, trans. *The Dialogues of Plato.* Random House, 1920. The definitive translation, including *The Republic.*

READINGS FOR THE STUDENT

Boyer, Sophia A., and Winifred Lubell. *Gifts from the Greeks, Alpha to Omega.* Rand McNally, 1970. Descriptions of areas of Greek life illustrated with drawings of Greek art.

D'Aulaire, Ingri and Edgar. *Book of Greek Myths.* Doubleday, 1962. Collection of Greek myths.

READINGS FOR THE TEACHER

Grant, Michael. *The Classical Greeks.* Scribner, 1989. Connects culture with historical events. Spans art, architecture, philosophy, and drama.

MULTIMEDIA RESOURCES

Ancient Civilizations: Legacies. Glencoe TVOntario. Video. Describes innovations of early civilizations with an emphasis on the Greeks and Romans.

The Greek Beginning. Films for the Humanities, Inc. Film. Introduction to Greek literature, politics, and philosophy from 1300 to 323 B.C.

INTRODUCE

CHAPTER 11 OVERVIEW

Chapter 11 describes the many cultural contributions made by the Greeks during the Golden Age.

➤ **Section 1** discusses Greek creativity and the people's attempt to honor their gods and goddesses especially in athletics and theater.

➤ **Section 2** explains the roles that Socrates, Plato, and Aristotle played in the development of philosophy and political science.

CHAPTER OBJECTIVES

After reading Chapter 11, students will be able to:

1. describe how the Greeks honored their gods and goddesses.

2. summarize what contributions were made in athletics and the arts during the Golden Age of Greek culture.

3. discuss how Greek thinkers influenced the development of western civilization.

EXAMINING THE ILLUSTRATION

Ask students what sport they see depicted. *(wrestling)* Point out that they probably were able to draw this conclusion because modern wrestling, with which they are more familiar, is not much different than the wrestling of Ancient Greece.

PERFORMANCE ASSESSMENT ✓

Use the Performance Assessment activities on page 178B to help you evaluate students as they complete the chapter.

CHAPTER 11 Cultural Contributions

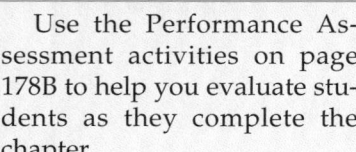

Wrestlers of Ancient Greece

178

TEACHER CLASSROOM RESOURCES

- Reproducible Lesson Plan
- Section Quizzes/Chapter Test
- Reteaching Activity
- Enrichment Activity
- Unit 4 Primary Source Reading
- Geography and Map Activity
- Vocabulary and Guided Reading Activity
- Cooperative Learning Activity
- Performance Assessment Activity
- Spanish Summary and Glossary
- Teaching Transparencies and Activities
- Testmaker
- Audiocassettes (English and Spanish)
- The Western Civilization Videodisc

Chapter Focus

READ TO DISCOVER:

- How the Greeks honored their gods and goddesses.
- What contributions in athletics and the arts were made during the "Golden Age" of Greek culture.
- How Socrates, Plato, Aristotle, and other Greek thinkers influenced the development of Western civilization.

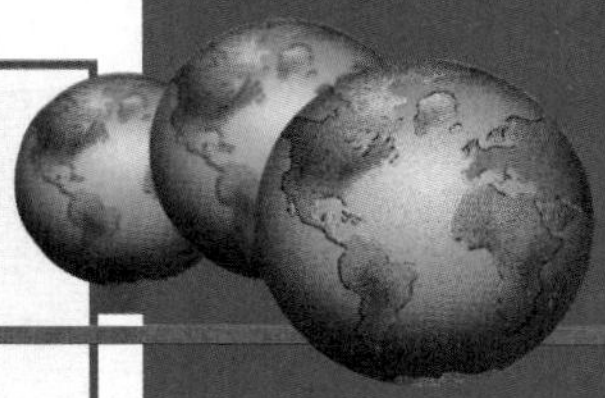

775 B.C.–338 B.C.

The Greeks made many contributions to the arts and sciences of western civilization. A great deal of this came about because of what the Greeks believed about their gods. They saw their gods as the source of all power.

The Greeks believed they could honor their gods by imitating them. This meant being the best they could be in everything they did. The greater the skill the Greeks showed in thinking, athletic games, or the arts, the more the gods were honored. The result was the "Golden Age" of Greek culture, also known as the "Classical Age of Greece."

KEY TERMS

- oracles
- pancratium
- pentathlon
- *philosophia*
- Socratic method
- political science
- scientific method
- hypothesis
- syllogism

Section 1

RELIGIOUS PRACTICES

Although most Greeks held similar religious beliefs, there was no single Greek religion. Each city-state worshiped its own gods. Officials in each polis were in charge of public feasts and sacrifices. In their own homes, heads of families prayed and offered sacrifices to the gods.

Greek priests and priestesses often served as **oracles,** or persons who, it was believed, could speak with the gods. Many Greeks went to oracles for advice. The advice was generally given in the form of a *prophecy* (prof' uh sē), or a statement of what might

179

FOCUS

BELLRINGER

Write the following quotation from the English poet John Keats on the chalkboard: *A thing of beauty is a joy forever*. Have students write a few sentences telling whether they agree or disagree with the quotation.

MOTIVATIONAL ACTIVITY

Discuss students' opinions of Keats's quotation and what might constitute a "thing of beauty" in modern times. Ask students what things from more than 2,000 years ago might be considered "a joy forever."

VOCABULARY PRE-CHECK

Write the key terms for this chapter on the chalkboard. Ask students to skim the chapter for these boldfaced words and read the sentences in which each is found. Ask students to explain the word from this context.

Assign Chapter 11 **Vocabulary and Guided Reading Activity** in the TCR.

EXTRA CREDIT PROJECT

Suggest that interested students learn more about the phenomenon of optical illusions by researching the art of M.C. Escher or Georges Suerat. Encourage students to bring examples of illusions with an explanation to class to share with other students.

KEY TO ABILITY LEVELS

Teaching strategies have been coded for varying learning styles and abilities.

L1 Level 1 activities are **basic** activities and should be within the ability range of all students.

L2 Level 2 activities are **average** activities and should be within the ability range of the average to above-average student.

L3 Level 3 activities are **challenging** activities designed for the ability range of above-average students.

LEP LEP activities should be within the ability range of Limited English Proficiency students.

VIDEODISC

Use the following to enrich Chapter 11.

WC B 50 11766
Athena as the goddess of war.

TEACH

GUIDED PRACTICE

L2 **Religion** Write the following scenario on the chalkboard: *You are a scholar with an interest in religions, living across the sea from the Greeks during the Classical Age. Your society has heard rumors that the Greeks approach their gods and goddesses differently than people have in the past. Your superiors have expressed great interest in these new religious beliefs, and have sent you to gather information on the Greek gods and goddesses.* Then tell students to write an account of their findings to be presented to their superiors upon their return home.

CAPTION ANSWER

Often a prophecy could mean more than one thing. People seeking advice had to decide what they believed to be the true meaning of the prophecy.

VIDEODISC

Use the following to enrich Chapter 11.

WC B 44 11760
Poseidon.

WC B 62 11778
The Temple of Hera II.

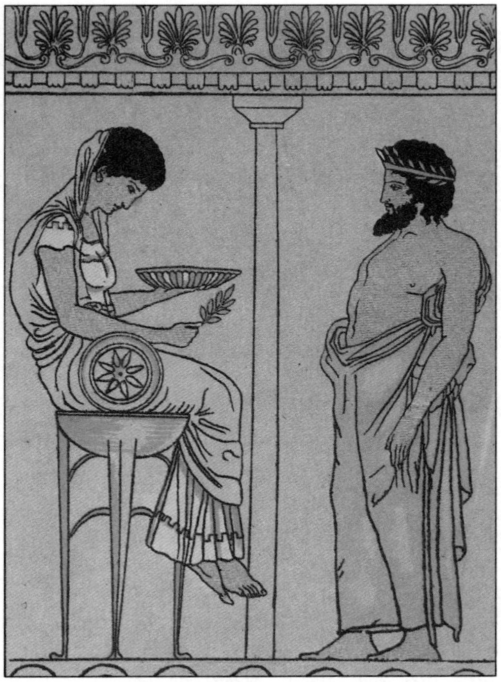

THE DELPHIC ORACLE The most popular oracle was a priestess in the temple at Delphi. The Greeks believed that Delphi was the center of the world, and they built many temples and other public buildings there (right). The painting of the Delphic oracle (left) shows offering a prophecy to a Greek man. **Why was a prophecy from an oracle often confusing?**

happen in the future. Often, a prophecy could mean more than one thing. The person seeking advice had to decide what he or she believed to be the true meaning of the prophecy.

Gods and Goddesses of Mount Olympus During the Golden Age, the Greeks worshiped the gods of Mount Olympus (ō lim′ puhs). There were 12 major gods and goddesses. Each had specific duties to carry out.

Most ancient peoples feared their gods. They believed that people were put on Earth only to obey and serve the gods. The Greeks were the first people to feel differently. They placed importance on the worth of the individual. Because they believed in their own value, the Greeks had a great deal of self-respect. This allowed them to approach their gods with dignity.

The Greeks built temples to honor their gods. Inside each temple stood a statue of the god being honored. In front of the

EXTENDING THE CONTENT

The architects of the Parthenon—the temple to Athena—understood perspective and optical illusions. Thus they made the temple's columns thicker in the middle and thinner at the top so that the columns appeared straight when viewed from a distance. The steps leading up to the Parthenon, actually lower in the center than at either end, likewise appear straight.

statue was an altar. Because the Greeks believed the temple was the god's home, they did not enter it. They worshiped outside, as a sign of respect.

Another way the Greeks honored their gods was with different kinds of festivals. Each showed the power of the god in whose honor it was given. Out of the festivals came two important contributions to western culture. These were the Olympic Games and the theater.

The Olympic Games

Every four years, in the middle of summer, a festival was held in Olympia (ō lim′ pē uh) to honor the god Zeus. Olympia was not really a town. It was a group of

OLYMPIAN GODS AND GODDESSES

Name	Realm
Zeus	ruler of Mount Olympus, king of the gods, god of the weather
Aphrodite	goddess of love and beauty
Apollo	god of the sun; patron of truth, archery, music, medicine, and prophecy
Ares	god of war
Artemis	goddess of the moon; mighty huntress and "rainer of arrows"; guardian of cities, young animals, and women; twin sister of Apollo
Athena	goddess of wisdom; city god of Athens; patron of household crafts; protectress in war of those who worshipped her; daughter of Zeus
Demeter	goddess of crops, giver of grain and fruit
Dionysus	god of fertility, of joyous life and hospitality, and of wild things
Hephaestus	god of fire and artisans; maker of Pandora, the first mortal woman; husband of Aphrodite
Hera	protectress of marriage, children, and the home; wife of Zeus
Hermes	god of orators, writers, and commerce; protector of thieves and mischief-makers; guardian of wayfarers; messenger to mortals; son of Zeus
Poseidon	god of the sea and earthquakes, giver of horses to mortals

DID YOU KNOW ??

At first, the Greeks identified their gods with the forces of nature. Later, they were given more human qualities but remained immortal. In Greek legend, gods often disguised themselves as humans and visited people.

L2 **Language Arts** Have students choose a god or goddess from the chart on this page and read a myth about them. Students might refer to *Book of Greek Myths* by Ingri and Edgar D'Aulaire. (See Readings for the Student in the Chapter Planning Guide.) Then have students give oral-reading reviews of the myths and their opinion of the worthiness of their deity.

VIDEODISC

Use the following to enrich Chapter 11.

WC B 26 11742
A Greek discus thrower.

WC B 27 11743
A Greek athlete participating in the "long jump."

MEETING SPECIAL NEEDS

Help students who need to review the vocabulary and concepts in this chapter by having them create a crossword puzzle on a large sheet of butcher paper or on the chalkboard. Have a volunteer find a word or term in the chapter and write it on the paper horizontally or vertically. Have another student write a clue that defines that word, and then add a word to the paper crossing the previous word in crossword puzzle fashion. Have students continue composing the puzzle as long as they can fit words, adding numbered clues as they go. After compiling 10 words or more, have students create a blank puzzle, using squares or blanks for each letter, and the list of numbered clues to challenge another class.

L1 **History** Ask students to compare the events of the ancient Olympic Games with those of the present-day Olympics. Have interested students investigate when and where the next modern summer and winter Olympics will be held. LEP

DID YOU KNOW ??

Although women were not allowed to take part in the Olympics, they could own the chariot teams that competed in the races.

CAPTION ANSWER

chariot race, boxing, the pancratium, and the pentathlon

temples and arenas built in fields. A 40-foot, or 12-meter, gold and ivory statue of Zeus stood in one of the temples.

The festival was known as the Olympic Games. It was the most important sporting event in Greece. While the games were going on, the Greeks would stop fighting any war in which they were involved. When the Spartans refused to call a truce during the Peloponnesian War to compete in the games, they had to pay a fine.

Athletes came from all over Greece and from Greek colonies in Africa, Italy, and Asia Minor to take part in the games. Individuals, rather than teams, competed. Only men were allowed to take part. Women were not even allowed to watch. Each athlete had to swear on the sacred boar of Zeus that he would follow the rules of the games. Those who broke the rules were fined.

The Olympics were made up of many events. One of the most exciting was the chariot race. It was held in the Hippodrome (hip' uh drōm), which was an oval track with grandstands around it. The chariots had small wheels and were open in the back. At first, they were pulled by four horses. Later, only two horses were used. About 40 chariots started the race, but only a few could finish the 9 miles, or 14.4 kilometers. The driver of the winning chariot received a crown made from olive leaves.

WARRIOR'S RACE The first Olympic Games were mainly simple foot races. Later, other events were added. One of these additions was the warrior's race. In it, runners competed wearing full armor and carrying a shield. **What were some other events in the early Olympics?**

MULTICULTURAL PERSPECTIVES

Though the Olympic Games were the oldest and most prestigious athletic event in Greece, they were not unique. There were three other major sports festivals held at two- or four-year intervals: the Pythian Games honoring Apollo at Delphi, the Nemean Games for Zeus, and the Isthmian Games held at Corinth to honor Poseidon. Games alternated so there was at least one major event a year. All of these games were "Panhellenic," drawing from all of Greece and its colonies.

Another major event was boxing. Boxers did not use their fists. They wrapped their hands with strips of ox hide and slapped one another with the flat of the hand. There were no set rounds or points. A match between two boxers went on until one raised a finger in the air as a sign of defeat.

Another fighting event was the **pancratium** (pan krā' shē uhm). This was a combination of boxing and wrestling in which no holds were barred between the two fighters. The only two things a fighter could not do were gouge an opponent's eyes or bite.

The winner of the **pentathlon** (pen tath' luhn) was considered the best all-around athlete. The pentathlon itself was made up of five events. Those who took part had to run, jump, throw the discus (dis' kuhs), wrestle, and hurl the javelin (jav' luhn). Like other winners, the winner of the pentathlon was crowned with an olive-leaf wreath.

Sculpture of Euripides

Olympic winners were heroes. Poets wrote about them. City-states held parades for them. Some city-states even gave them free meals for a year.

Between the different events at the games, poets read their works aloud. Herodotus (hi rahd' uh tuhs), the "Father of History," first read his account of the Persian Wars at the Olympics. Greek historians even dated events by Olympiads (ō lim' pē ads), or the four-year periods between games. The first recorded date in Greek history is the date of the first Olympic Games, which occurred in 776 B.C.

The Theater The theater grew out of festivals given in honor of the god Dionysus (dī uh nī' suhs). About 600 B.C., the Ionians began telling stories about Dionysus at festivals. A chorus chanted and danced each story to the music of a flute. At certain points, the chorus fell silent. The chorus leader then gave a *soliloquy* (suh lil' uh kwē), or talk in which personal thoughts and feelings are expressed to the audience.

In time, the chorus became shorter and the soliloquies longer. Stories were then told about other gods and heroes. About the time of the Persian Wars, a Greek poet named Aeschylus (es' kuh luhs) added an additional character to each story. Now, instead of singing or telling a story, it was acted out. Thus, Aeschylus created what came to be known as a play.

The first Greek plays were *tragedies* (traj' uh dēz), or stories about suffering. All dealt with the past and with the relationships between people and gods. Not all of them had unhappy endings. Still, they all pointed out that though people suffered, most individuals were able to carry on despite their suffering.

Three of the great writers of tragedy were Aeschylus, Sophocles (sahf' uh klēz), and Euripides (yū rip' uh dēz). All three lived in Athens during its Golden Age. Aeschylus wrote about power and its effect on people. Sophocles showed that people

L3 **Critical Thinking** Have students compare the ancient Greek treatment of Olympic athletes with the treatment of professional athletes in the United States today. *(Olympic winners were given hero status; U.S. professional athletes often are looked upon as heroes and sometimes make huge salaries.)*

MAKING CONNECTIONS

➤➤ **Drama** The Greek playwrights differed with each other on important issues. For example, Aeschylus, who had fought at Marathon and Salamis, was proud of Athens' military accomplishments and said so in his plays. Euripedes, on the other hand, condemned the suffering caused by war.

DID YOU KNOW ??

Sophocles's most famous play, *Oedipus Rex*, deals with the plight of Oedipus, a king who unknowingly kills his father and marries his mother. Oedipus uses all his powers to solve the crime of murder, only to discover that he is the murderer.

VIDEODISC

Use the following to enrich Chapter 11.

WC B 21 11737
The Odeum in Athens.

COOPERATIVE LEARNING

Have students plan and execute a Greek Heritage Day. Divide the class into groups. Assign each group an ancient Greek achievement to demonstrate to the class, such as drama, painting, sculpture, and architecture. The groups should decide what form their demonstration will take. Make sure that each member of the group has a specific assignment. The demonstrations could include a performance of part of a drama, a model of a vase, or a model of a building.

Assign Chapter 11 **Cooperative Learning Activity** in the TCR.

MAKING CONNECTIONS

➤➤ **Ideas** Plato rejected the senses—seeing, hearing, touch, smell, and taste—as a source of truth, believing that the many things that could be perceived by these senses were only "appearances." Reality, the "real" world, was constructed from ideas, or ideal "forms," which could be understood through logical thought and reasoning.

DID YOU KNOW ??

Aristotle's school was called the Lyceum. Because he taught while walking with his students, he and his followers were called "peripatetic," which comes from a Greek word meaning "to walk around."

Sculpture of Plato

(dī′ uh logs), he showed how difficult it is to discover truth. *The Dialogues* consists of a series of discussions in which different people talk about such things as truth and loyalty. Socrates is the leading speaker in many discussions. Through these discussions, Plato brings out the self-questioning that goes on within a person troubled by such issues.

Aristotle One of Plato's brightest pupils was Aristotle (ār′ uh stot l). Aristotle came to the Academy when he was 17 years old and stayed for 20 years. Before he died in 322 B.C., he founded his own school in Athens and wrote more than 200 books.

Aristotle was known as "the master of them that know." He believed in using one's senses to discover the laws that govern the physical world. He was the first to *classify*, or group together, plants and animals that resemble each other. His system, with some changes, is still used today. It has helped scientists handle a great amount of information in an orderly way.

Aristotle also added to the ideas of an earlier Greek scientist named Thales (thā′ lēz) of Miletus (mi let′ uhs). Thales developed the first two steps of what is known today as the **scientific method.** This is the process used by scientists to study something. First, Thales collected information. Then, based on what he observed, he formed a **hypothesis** (hī poth′ uh sis), or possible explanation. Aristotle provided a third step in the scientific method when he said that a hypothesis must be tested to see if it is correct.

Another important contribution Aristotle made was in *logic* (loj′ ik), or the science of reasoning. He developed the **syllogism** (sil′ uh jiz uhm). This is a method of reasoning that uses three related statements. The third statement is a conclusion based on the information given in the first two. For example:

Athenians are Greeks.
Socrates is an Athenian.
Therefore, Socrates is Greek.

Sculpture of Aristotle

Discoveries and Inventions Greek scientists were not looking for ways to make life easier or better. They were trying to add to their store of knowledge. They had none of the tools scientists have today. There were no telescopes, microscopes, or scales that weigh small amounts. Even without these, however, the Greeks made important discoveries.

Their curiosity led Greek scientists to discover that natural events are not caused by the way gods behave. They also learned that the world is governed by natural laws that people can discover and understand.

There were many Greek scientists. The first was Thales of Miletus, who came from Ionia. Thales not only developed the first two steps of the scientific method, but he also correctly predicted

SPOTLIGHT ON: ARISTOTLE

If the term *Renaissance man* had been coined 1800 years earlier, it would have been the perfect description of Aristotle—an inventive, curious thinker who succeeded brilliantly in every field he explored. Aristotle set standards and methods for analyzing areas of study—politics, rhetoric, drama, poetry, aesthetics, ethics, and logic. He was one of the few Classical authors whose works affected every subsequent era. Even today, we use his terms for kinds of government and apply some of his ideas of structure to plays and poetry.

GREEK SCIENTISTS

Name	Field	Accomplishments
Archimedes	*Mathematics*	explained principle of lever
Aristarchus	*Astronomy*	concluded that Earth revolves around the sun
Anaximander	*Astronomy*	pioneered concept of Earth as a body suspended in space
Eratosthenes	*Geography*	figured Earth's circumference within 200 miles, or 320 kilometers; made map complete with longitude and latitude of Asia, Africa, and Europe that accurately showed the three continents forming single landmass
Euclid	*Mathematics*	collected and organized all existing knowledge about geometry; developed axioms, or fundamental rules, used in modern geometry
Hipparchus	*Astronomy*	created system of celestial mechanics to explain how heavenly bodies move
Hippocrates	*Medicine*	founder of scientific medicine
Ptolemy	*Astronomy*	developed mathematical model of Hipparchus' system of celestial mechanics
Pythagoras	*Mathematics*	sought to explain the nature of all things in mathematical terms
Thales of Miletus	*Science*	first known Greek scientist; using Chaldean observations of stars, planets, and moon, predicted solar eclipse of 585 B.C.; developed theory about basic substance common to matter; developed first two steps of scientific method

L2 **Science** Have students research the accomplishments of a Greek scientist listed in the chart. Then hold a science fair and have students role-play their chosen scientist and explain accomplishments or discoveries using visuals or other means.

DID YOU KNOW ??

Being a doctor in Greece was often an occupation that was passed from father to son. Many doctors ran clinics near the marketplace where they bandaged wounds or bled patients to draw out diseases.

ASSESS

CHECK FOR UNDERSTANDING

Ask students to summarize orally or in writing the main points of the chapter. Discuss the answers to the Section and Chapter Review questions.

EVALUATE

Assign Chapter 11 **Performance Assessment Activity** in the TCR.

Administer **Chapter 11 Test** in the TCR. Testmaker available.

EXTENDING THE CONTENT

The ancient Greeks were heir to all the mathematical knowledge of the Mesopotamian and Egyptian civilizations. They built upon that inheritance by using their sense of reason to pursue the "Why?" and "What does it mean?" questions of mathematics. Thales of Miletus began the mathematical revolution. He laid the foundation that is still part of introductory courses in geometry. The followers of Pythagoras advanced mathematics into a quasi-religion. Euclid simplified and organized the new knowledge. Apollonius explored the aspects of conic sections. Archimedes is the father of scientific notation.

RETEACH

Divide the class into teams to try and guess a term defined in the chapter or the name of a person described in the chapter from clues given by other team members.

Assign Chapter 11 **Reteaching Activity** in the TCR.

ENRICH

Have students write syllogisms and share them with one another.

Assign Chapter 11 **Enrichment Activity** in the TCR.

CLOSE

Ask students to compare the role religion played in the lives of ancient Greeks to the role it plays in modern American society. Encourage them to note both similarities and differences.

MEETING CHAPTER OBJECTIVES

Each objective is tested by the Review questions in parentheses.

1. Describe how the Greeks honored their gods and goddesses. (CU 1; CT 1)

2. Summarize what contributions were made in athletics and the arts during the "Golden Age" of Greek culture. (BV; CU 2, 3, 4; GIH)

3. Discuss how well-known Greek thinkers influenced the development of western civilization. (BV; CU 5, 6, 7, 8, 9; CT 2, 3, 4; UYJ)

an eclipse of the sun in 585 B.C. The contributions made by Thales and other Greek scientists were important to the growth of scientific thought.

Greek scientists also contributed to the field of medicine. The "Father of Scientific Medicine" was Hippocrates (hi pok' ruh tēz). Hippocrates was considered the perfect physician. He traveled throughout Greece diagnosing illnesses and curing sick people. He believed diseases came from natural causes. At the time, most other doctors thought diseases were caused by evil spirits entering the body.

Hippocrates drew up a list of rules about how doctors should use their skills to help their patients. His rules are known as the Hippocratic (hip uh krat' ik) Oath. The oath says that doctors should honor their teachers, do their best for the sick, never give poisons, and keep the secrets of their patients. Doctors all over the world still promise to honor the Hippocratic Oath.

Section 2 Review

1. **Identify:** Socrates, Plato, *The Republic, The Dialogues*, Aristotle, Thales of Miletus, Hippocrates, Hippocratic Oath
2. **Define:** *philosophia*, Socratic method, political science, scientific method, hypothesis, syllogism
3. What were Plato's beliefs about government?
4. What two major discoveries did Greek scientists make?

Critical Thinking

5. Review the syllogism on page 188. Write a syllogism of your own for one of the Greek people you have read about.

Chapter Summary

1. During the "Golden Age," the Greeks made many contributions in thinking, athletics, and the arts.
2. The Olympic Games, held every four years in honor of the Greek god Zeus, was the most important sporting event in Greece.
3. The theater, and eventually the play, developed out of a festival given in honor of the Greek god Dionysus.
4. Socrates, in his search for truth, developed a form of questioning known as the Socratic method.
5. Plato, who was one of Socrates's pupils, founded a school and wrote the first book on political science.
6. Aristotle developed a system of classification and provided a third step in the scientific method begun by Thales of Miletus.
7. Greek scientists learned that the world is governed by natural laws that humans can discover and understand.

SECTION 2 ANSWERS

1. Socrates, philosopher (p. 185); Plato, philosopher, (p. 187); *The Republic*, Plato's ideal state (p. 187); *The Dialogues*, Plato's discussions (p. 187); Aristotle, scholar (p. 188); Thales of Miletus, scientist (p. 188); Hippocrates, "Father of Medicine" (p. 190); Hippocratic Oath, ethics for doctors (p. 190)
2. *philosophia*, studying loving wisdom (p. 185); Socratic method, way of questioning (p. 186); political science, study of government (p. 187); scientific method, studying science (p. 188); hypothesis, possible explanation (p. 188); syllogism, three-statement reasoning (p. 188)
3. order, no political liberty, and wise and good rulers
4. Natural events are not caused by the gods but by natural laws.
5. Syllogisms will vary.

Assign Chapter 11 **Section 2 Quiz** in the TCR. Testmaker available.

CHAPTER

Review 11

Building Vocabulary

Use the following words to make a chart that explains the contributions made by ancient Greeks.

oracles
pancratium
pentathlon
philosophia
Socratic method
political science
scientific method
hypothesis
syllogism

Check for Understanding

1. What was the role of oracles in Greek religion?
2. What role did women play in the Olympic Games?
3. What relationship was there between historians and the Olympic Games?
4. In what ways were tragedies and comedies different from one another?
5. How did the Athenians react to Socrates's teachings?
6. For what reason did Plato set up the Academy?
7. What are three steps in the scientific method?
8. In what were Greek scientists most interested?
9. For what achievement is Euclid most remembered?

Critical Thinking

1. How important was religion in ancient Greek civilization? Explain your answer.
2. Would you like being taught through the Socratic method? Why or why not?
3. What would you have done if it had been your decision whether or not to put Socrates on trial?
4. Why is the scientific method important to modern science?

Geography in History

MOVEMENT The Olympic Games drew contestants from all the areas under Greek control. The first games were held in 776 B.C. and they continued for more than the next thousand years. What different methods of travel were used to reach Olympia where the games were held?

Using Your Journal

Review details you noted about the ideas developed by the Greeks. Imagine that you have an opportunity to interview one of the people whose ideas you noted. Write a list of questions that you might like to ask the person.

+ BONUS +

TEST QUESTION

For Chapter 11 Test

The Greek oracles often spoke in riddles. Solve the following riddle: Your mother has received some sad news. Your mother's father's daughter has called to say your brother's grandfather's son's wife's son has died. Who called? *(your aunt)* Who died? *(your cousin)*

USING YOUR JOURNAL

Questions will vary but should include major points significant to the person's achievement. You could have students role-play the interview, one assuming the part of the Greek historical figure.

CHAPTER 11 REVIEW ANSWERS

BUILDING VOCABULARY

Charts will vary but should explain the contributions made by ancient Greeks.

CHECK FOR UNDERSTANDING

1. They spoke to the gods and gave advice and prophecies to the Greek people.
2. They were not allowed to take part in or watch the games.
3. Historians read their works aloud at the games and dated historical events by the Olympiads.
4. Tragedies told about suffering and relationships between people and the gods. Comedies were humorous, and poked fun at people.
5. Some were pleased but others saw Socrates's ideas as very dangerous.
6. because he hoped to train government leaders
7. collecting information, and forming and testing a hypothesis
8. adding to their knowledge
9. advances in mathematics

CRITICAL THINKING

1. Answers will vary but should include that religion and their gods were very important.
2. Answers will vary.
3. Answers will vary but could include the reasons for and against this decision.
4. Answers will vary but include that it provides a consistent way for scientists to do research.

GEOGRAPHY IN HISTORY

Answers may vary but should include major forms of transportation such as by foot, cart, horse, and the proximity of the sea.

CHAPTER 12

The Hellenistic Period

CHAPTER ORGANIZER

Objectives	Special Features	Supplemental Materials
Section 1 Philip II of Macedonia Summarize how the spread of Greek culture influenced people from Gibraltar to India and explain how Philip II of Macedonia gained control of Greece.		• Reproducible Lesson Plan • Section 1 Quiz • Testmaker • Chapter 12 Vocabulary and Guided Reading Activity • Teaching Transparencies and Activities • Unit 4 Primary Source Reading • Chapter 12 Activity Book Activity • The Western Civilization Videodisc
Section 2 Alexander the Great Discuss how Alexander attempted to bring unity to his empire and describe how Alexander's empire changed after his death.		• Reproducible Lesson Plan • Section 2 Quiz • Testmaker • Chapter 12 Cooperative Learning Activity • Unit 4 Primary Source Reading • Chapter 12 Geography and Map Activity • Chapter 12 Chart and Graph Skill Activity • The Western Civilization Videodisc
Chapter 12 Review and Evaluation		• Chapter 12 Reteaching Activity • Chapter 12 Enrichment Activity • Spanish Summary and Glossary • Chapter 12 Performance Assessment Activity • Audiocassettes (English and Spanish) • Chapter 12 Test • Testmaker

If time does not permit teaching the entire chapter, use the Chapter 12 Summary on page 200 and the Chapter 12 Audiocassettes (English and Spanish) to point out the main ideas of the chapter.

✓ Performance Assessment Activities

Time Line Have students work in small groups to construct a time line that illustrates the Hellenistic era. Assign each group a specific date or event to illustrate. Have students work on poster-sized paper. Have volunteers compile the time line entries. Display the time line in the classroom.

Geography Have students draw a base map showing the empire of Alexander the Great and the growth of the Greek influence. (See the map on page 196.) Then have students research to find the route of Alexander's conquest and add the route to the base map of the empire of Alexander the Great. Students' maps should include legends.

CHAPTER RESOURCES

LITERATURE ABOUT THE PERIOD

Easterling, P.E. and B. M. W. Knox, eds. *The Cambridge History of Classical Literature, Vol. 1, Greek Literature.* Cambridge, 1985. Collection of ancient Greek literature.

READINGS FOR THE STUDENT

Harris, Nathaniel. *Alexander the Great and the Greeks.* Bookwright Press, 1986. Details about the contributions Alexander made to the Greeks.

Renault, Mary. *The Persian Boy.* Bantam, 1988. The second of three novels about Alexander the Great.

READINGS FOR THE TEACHER

Grant, Michael. *From Alexander to Cleopatra: The Hellenistic World.* Weidenfield and Nicholson, 1982. Focuses on all aspects of the Hellenistic Age.

Green, Peter. *Ancient Greece.* Thames & Hudson, 1979. Presents the history and culture of Hellenistic Greece from prehistoric times through the death of Alexander the Great.

Nichols, Roger and Kenneth McLeish. *Through Greek Eyes.* Cambridge University Press, 1991. Integrates excerpts from primary sources in discussions of ancient Greek history including war, the search for knowledge, ships and the sea, daily life, the theater, leisure, and religion.

MULTIMEDIA RESOURCES

Alexander the Great & the Hellenistic Age. Coronet Films. Film. Focuses on the life of Alexander the Great.

Ancient Greece. Clearvue/SSSS. Video or filmstrip. Describes ancient Greece from the polis to its decline.

Greek Art and Architecture. Alarion. 2 Videos. Explores the culture of ancient Greece through its art and architecture.

The Great World History Knowledge Race: Ancient/Medieval. Focus Media. Apple software. A game format focusing mainly on Greece, Rome, and the Middle Ages.

INTRODUCE

CHAPTER 12 OVERVIEW

Chapter 12 describes the accomplishments of Philip of Macedonia and Alexander the Great in building an empire and spreading aspects of Greek civilization.

➤ **Section 1** analyzes the political and military strategies that enabled Philip to conquer the Greek city-states.

➤ **Section 2** describes the personality, military conquests, and political objectives of Alexander the Great and why the empire depended on strong leadership for its existence.

CHAPTER OBJECTIVES

After reading Chapter 12, students will be able to:

1. summarize how the spread of Greek culture influenced people from Gibraltar to India.

2. explain how Philip II of Macedonia gained control of Greece.

3. discuss how Alexander attempted to bring unity to his empire.

4. describe how Alexander's empire changed after his death.

EXAMINING THE ILLUSTRATION

Tell students this is a representation of a famous historical figure, Alexander the Great. Ask them what actions they might expect from a person with such a name? Suggest they will find out if their expectations are true as they read the chapter.

PERFORMANCE ASSESSMENT

Use the Performance Assessment activities on page 192B to help you evaluate students as they complete the chapter.

CHAPTER 12 The Hellenistic Period

Alexander the Great

192

TEACHER CLASSROOM RESOURCES

- Reproducible Lesson Plan
- Section Quizzes/Chapter Test
- Unit 4 Primary Source Reading
- Reteaching Activity
- Enrichment Activity
- Chart and Graph Skill Activity
- Geography and Map Activity
- Vocabulary and Guided Reading Activity
- Cooperative Learning Activity
- Performance Assessment Activity
- Spanish Summary and Glossary
- Teaching Transparencies and Activities
- Testmaker
- Audiocassettes (English and Spanish)
- The Western Civilization Videodisc

Chapter Focus

READ TO DISCOVER:

- How the spread of Greek culture influenced people from Gibraltar to India.
- How Philip II of Macedonia gained control of Greece.
- How Alexander attempted to bring unity to his empire.
- How Alexander's empire changed after his death.

After the Greek city-states lost their independence, many changes took place. The new rulers of Greece built empires and increased trade. At the same time, they spread Greek culture and customs. Before long, Greek ideas were influencing people from Gibraltar (juh brol' tuhr) to India.

The Greek language came to be spoken by many people. Greek architecture was copied for new buildings. Students studied Greek literature in school. People used Greek furniture in their homes. Greek plays became a popular form of entertainment. Business people took up Greek ways of banking.

The period in which all this took place has come to be called the Hellenistic (hel uh nis' tik) Age. The term "Hellenistic" means "like the Hellenes, or the Greeks."

335 B.C.–145 B.C.

KEY TERMS

hostage
phalanx
alliances
orator
barbaroi
factories
emigrated

Section 1

PHILIP II OF MACEDONIA

By 338 B.C., Greece had a new ruler, Philip II of Macedonia. Macedonia was a small, mountainous country north of Greece. Most Macedonians were farmers. They cared little for the Greeks and had fought them in the Persian Wars. Macedonian kings, however, were of Greek descent and admired Greek culture.

Philip became ruler of Macedonia in 359 B.C. During his youth, he was a **hostage** (hos' tij), or a person held by an enemy until certain promises are carried out, for three years in Thebes. In those

FOCUS

BELLRINGER

Have each student list three accomplishments of the ancient Greeks they have studied so far.

MOTIVATIONAL ACTIVITY

Discuss students' lists and write accomplishments on the chalkboard. Have students copy the list and then survey the chapter to add Hellenistic accomplishments.

VOCABULARY PRE-CHECK

Write the key terms for this chapter on the chalkboard. To access prior knowledge, ask students what they think of when they hear each word. Ask them to assess how accurate their association to the words were as they read the chapter.

Assign Chapter 12 **Vocabulary and Guided Reading Activity** in the TCR.

EXTRA CREDIT PROJECT

Suggest that interested students create a recruitment poster for Alexander the Great's army that might have been posted at that time. Tell them to include all pertinent information, and make the army sound like a great organization.

KEY TO ABILITY LEVELS

Teaching strategies have been coded for varying learning styles and abilities.

L1 Level 1 activities are **basic** activities and should be within the ability range of all students.

L2 Level 2 activities are **average** activities and should be within the ability range of the average to above-average student.

L3 Level 3 activities are **challenging** activities designed for the ability range of above-average students.

LEP LEP activities should be within the ability range of Limited English Proficiency students.

TEACH

GUIDED PRACTICE

L2 **History** Have students work in pairs to create a dialogue for an interview between Philip of Macedonia and a newspaper reporter from the *Macedonian Times*. Tell students to focus the dialogue on Philip's campaign to unify the Greek city-states and spread the Greek culture. Have pairs read the dialogue to the class, with one student playing the role of the reporter and the other, the role of Philip.

LINKING PAST TO PRESENT

Demosthenes's first speech in the public assembly was a dismal failure because of his weak voice and delivery, according to Plutarch. Demosthenes put pebbles in his mouth to work on his enunciation and also sought the help of an actor to improve his gestures and expression.

CAPTION ANSWER

He tried to warn them that Philip was dangerous.

VIDEODISC

Use the following to enrich Chaper 12.

WC B 29 11745
Philip V, King of Macedon from 221 to 179 B.C.

years, he learned to love Greek culture. However, he learned to dislike the weaknesses of the Greek form of government.

Philip believed it was his destiny to unify the Greek city-states and spread Greek culture. As soon as he became ruler of Macedonia, he set out to fulfill that destiny. It took him a little over 20 years.

Philip went about reaching his goal in many ways. For example, until his time, the Macedonian army was made up of volunteers, who fought only in summer. Philip turned this part-time volunteer army into a year-round, well-organized, professional one.

Philip developed an infantry formation called a **phalanx** (fā' langks). Foot soldiers formed a solid body some 16 rows deep. Those in each line stayed so close together that their shields overlapped. This gave them added protection. The phalanx charged as a group, which gave it more striking power.

Philip also armed his soldiers with spears that were 14 feet, or over 4 meters, long. This was twice as long as ordinary spears. He

DEMOSTHENES Demosthenes worked to preserve the freedom of the Greek city-states. He was known for his ability as a public speaker. It is said he trained himself by shouting above the roar of the ocean waves with his mouth full of pebbles. **What did Demosthenes try to tell the Greeks about Philip of Macedonia?**

SPOTLIGHT ON: DEMOSTHENES

Demosthenes, born in 384 B.C., was the son of the owner of a sword-making factory. He was orphaned at age 7, and his guardians squandered his inheritance so that he did not have a good education. At 22, he sued them and won, which encouraged his driving ambition to be a great orator. According to Plutarch, a first-century Greek biographer and essayist, Demosthenes studied with a well-known actor for help with gestures and expression. He practiced his gestures in front of a large mirror. Demosthenes's fervor and skill won admiration from Philip, even though Demosthenes angrily spoke against Philip.

added soldiers trained in the use of slingshots and bows and arrows. These soldiers could fight in hilly areas where the phalanx was not able to go.

Philip flattered local Greek officials and gave them gold. He found ways to cause disagreements among Greek city-states. Then, when city-states were weak from fighting each other, his army moved in and conquered them.

Philip made treaties with Greek leaders only to break them when the Greeks let down their guard. He saw marriage as a way of forming political **alliances** (uh lī′ uhn siz), or partnerships. He married six or seven times for this reason.

Demosthenes (di mahs′ thuh nēz), an Athenian **orator** (ōr′ uh ter), or public speaker, tried to warn the Greeks that Philip was dangerous, but most would not listen. They were unhappy with their local governments and thought Philip would improve things.

When Philip led his soldiers into central Greece in 338 B.C., Thebes and Athens raised a small army to stop the invasion. The Greek army, however, was not strong enough and was defeated at the Battle of Chaeronea (ker uh nē′ uh). Having gained control of Greece, Philip began preparing for a campaign against Persia. However, in 336 B.C., in the middle of his preparations, he was killed, and his son Alexander took over the throne.

Painting of Philip II

Section 1 Review

1. **Identify:** Hellenistic Age, Philip II, Macedonia, Demosthenes
2. **Define:** hostage, phalanx, alliances, orator
3. Why was Philip II able to defeat the Greek city-states?

Critical Thinking

4. How do you think a Greek citizen living under the rule of Philip II would describe him as a ruler?

MAKING CONNECTIONS

➤➤ **Civics** Demosthenes was the leader of the anti-Macedonian party and did succeed in persuading some city-states to make alliances against Philip. His speeches are known as Philippic Orations.

DID YOU KNOW ??

Alexander and his men carried Greek art with them as they traveled into the East. After Asian Buddhists saw Greek statues, they portrayed Buddha in painting and sculpture for the first time.

VIDEODISC

Use the following to enrich Chapter 12.

WC B 30 11746
Alexander the Great (356-323 B.C.).

Section 2
ALEXANDER THE GREAT

Alexander took over Philip's throne at the age of 20. He had been a commander in the army since he was 16. Upon becoming a commander he cut his shoulder-length hair and ordered his soldiers to shave their beards. This, he said, would keep enemy soldiers from grabbing them in close combat.

Alexander was physically strong and good-looking. He also had developed his mind. For three years, Aristotle had taught him literature, political science, geography, and biology. Because of this, Alexander included philosophers and scientists in his army.

Painting of Soldier

SECTION 1 ANSWERS

1. Hellenistic Age, Greek Age (p. 193); Philip II, ruler of Macedonia (p. 193); Macedonia, small country north of Greece (p. 193); Demosthenes, Athenian statesman (p. 195)
2. hostage, a person held by an enemy until promises are carried out (p. 193); phalanx, infantry formation of foot soldiers (p. 194); alliances, political partnerships (p. 195); orator, public speaker (p. 195)
3. because he encouraged them to fight each other until they became weak and disunited, and because the Greek army was small
4. Answers will vary but could include a supply of Philip's good and bad points as they related to the people.

Assign Chapter 12 **Section 1 Quiz** in the TCR. Testmaker available.

The scientists collected plant and animal samples from newly conquered lands and sent them to Aristotle for examination.

Alexander was a great general who feared nothing. He crushed the Persian Empire and then marched as far east as northern India. He would have gone farther, but his troops refused. In the course of his conquests, Alexander covered more than 22,000 miles, or over 35,200 kilometers, from the Nile to the Indus rivers. Through all that territory, he never lost a battle.

Alexander's Empire Alexander had a dream of a worldwide state in which all people would live together in peace. He wanted to bring unity and justice to his empire.

Alexander believed the only way to achieve his goal was to unite the Macedonians, the Greeks, and the Persians. He began by taking Persian soldiers into his army. Next, he married a Persian woman and had 80 of his leading army officers marry Persian women, too. Then, he began to dress in Persian fashion and to follow some Persian customs.

One custom was for rulers to claim they were gods. So, Alexander claimed he was a god and insisted that people treat him that way. The Macedonians and Greeks, however, refused to do so. The Greeks also objected to equal treatment for the Persians. They looked down on all people who did not speak Greek or

MAP STUDY

LOCATION At the time of his death, Alexander the Great ruled over much of the classical world. **Why do you think Alexander founded his capital where he did?**

The Empire of Alexander the Great

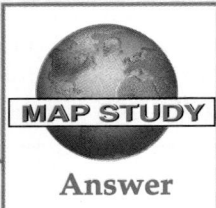

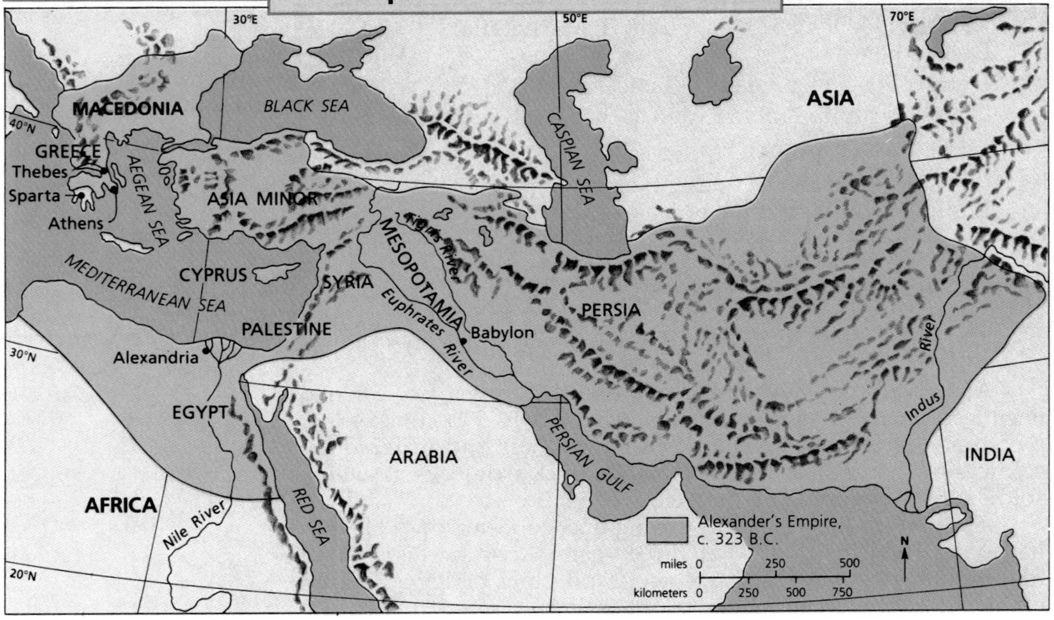

GEOGRAPHY AND HISTORY

Alexander had his first major encounter with the Persians at the Granicus River in western Asia Minor. After his victory there, he sent 300 coats of Persian armor to Athens as a thanksgiving offering to the goddess Athena. Other conquests include the Battle of Issus, the seaports of Phoenicia, the port city of Tyre, Egypt, Babylon, and Persepolis.

MAP STUDY

Answer

because it was located in a rich area, on a river where trade was an important way of blending the cultures of Greece and Asia [trade routes were most likely established throughout the empire]

DID YOU KNOW

The Greeks thought the Macedonians were barbarians because they had produced no famous writers, philosophers, or artists.

MULTICULTURAL PERSPECTIVES

Alexander the Great, like many ancient Greeks, spent much of his time reading books. According to Plutarch, a first-century Greek biographer, Alexander's favorite books were Homer's *Iliad* and *Anabasis* by Xenophon. Alexander had a copy of the *Iliad* that Aristotle had edited. It was one of the books that he took everywhere, keeping it with his dagger and pillow at night. According to Plutarch, as Alexander set off to lead his troops into Asia, he first went straight to the ruins of Troy as a kind of pilgrimage. He made a sacrifice to the goddess Athena and honored the grave of the hero Achilles.

LIGHTHOUSE OF ALEXANDRIA The lighthouse of Alexandria was one of the Seven Wonders of the Ancient World. It towered over Alexandria's two excellent harbors. A fire on top provided light to guide ships into port. **Why was Alexandria also considered a center for learning?**

follow Greek customs. They called such people ***barbaroi,*** (bar' buh roi) from which the word "barbarians" comes. Because of such feelings, Alexander's attempt to achieve unity among the people in his empire was not successful.

Alexandria During his rule, Alexander founded about 70 cities, 16 of which were named Alexandria (al ig zan' drē uh) after himself. He encouraged Greeks and Macedonians to settle in the new cities, which were scattered throughout the empire.

The most noted Alexandria was in Egypt. Within 70 years after its founding, it had become a center of trade and learning. Greeks from throughout the eastern Mediterranean came there. They wanted to make the most of its economic opportunities and to be a part of its intellectual and social life.

Alexandria had two great harbors. They were protected by *breakwaters,* or barriers that break the force of waves. A lighthouse 400 feet, or about 122 meters, tall dominated the harbors. It is considered one of the Seven Wonders of the Ancient World.

Looking out over the chief harbor was a palace and a school with a library. The school was known as the Museum. It became a center for poets, writers, philosophers, and scientists. The library had the largest collection of books in ancient times. There, Euclid (ū' kluhd) wrote his geometry book. There, Eratosthenes (er uh

CAPTION ANSWER

because of its school and library

L1 **The Arts** Prepare the class to view the film *Alexander the Great & the Hellenistic Age.* (See Chapter Resources in the Chapter 12 Planning Guide.) After viewing the film ask: *What are some examples of how Alexander tried to bring unity to his empire? Was Alexander successful in achieving this goal? Was his goal realistic? Why or why not? Could such a goal be realized today? Is such a goal desirable?*

L2 **Geography: Location** Have students research the other 15 cities named after Alexander the Great and locate them on a map. LEP

DID YOU KNOW ??

Alexander probably built the world's first zoo. It featured lions, leopards, bears, and most of the other major species known to the world at the time.

COOPERATIVE LEARNING

Divide the class into groups to prepare a class book that illustrates the exploits of Alexander. Assign each group an area of conquest to work on including Thebes, Granicus River, Issus, Egypt, Guagamela, and Indus River valley. Each group's contribution should include a description of the geographic area, what happened there and when, and a map of the region. Groups could include drawings such as costumes, weapons, and buildings. Have members agree upon individual tasks and manner of presentation.

Assign Chapter 12 **Cooperative Learning Activity** in the TCR.

INDEPENDENT PRACTICE

L1 **Daily Life** Show students examples of advertisements for cities or regions from business or travel magazines. Have them write advertisement copy for a magazine to be distributed throughout the Hellenistic world that extols the virtues of living in Alexandria, Egypt.

L1 **History** Have students use the map on page 196 to identify and locate the three divisions of Alexander's empire following his death. LEP

CAPTION ANSWER

because his troops refused to go any farther

MAKING CONNECTIONS

➤➤ **The Arts** Arrian, a Roman general, used the eyewitness accounts of Alexander's generals to write a thorough, unbiased biography of Alexander the Great. In describing the retreat from India, Arrian told the story of Alexander that reveals his leadership qualities. Marching through the hot sands toward water, Alexander led his men on foot. A party he had sent ahead to search for water returned with a helmut full. Although thirsty, Alexander took the water and poured it on the ground. This action, and that of walking when he could ride, showed the soldiers that he did not expect them to endure hardships that he wasn't willing to endure himself.

ALEXANDER THE GREAT Alexander conquered tremendous amounts of territory. His empire stretched from Greece to northern India. This painting of Alexander shows him leading his army ashore in Asia Minor and claiming all lands to the east as his own. **Why was Alexander unable to continue his conquests beyond India?**

tahs' thuh nēz) reasoned that a ship could reach India by sailing west from Spain. There, Archimedes (ar kuh mēd' ēz) and Hero (hē' rō) invented several machines.

End of the Empire In 323 B.C., when Alexander was in Babylon, he became ill and died. He was 33 years old and had ruled for 13 years. His body was wrapped in gold and placed in a glass coffin in the Royal Tombs of Alexandria, Egypt. After his death, Alexander became a romantic legend. More than 80 versions of his life have been written in more than 20 languages.

After Alexander's death, fights broke out over who was to rule the empire. The areas Alexander had conquered in India returned to their original rulers. Three of Alexander's generals divided the rest of the empire among themselves. Antigonus (an tig' uh nuhs) became king of Macedonia. Ptolemy (tahl' uh mē) established the dynasty of the Ptolemies in Egypt. Seleucus (suh lū' kuhs) formed the Seleucid Empire in Persia. Athens and

EXTENDING THE CONTENT

People in the Hellenistic world admired the Hellenic style of art and architecture and enthusiastically imitated it in temples and other public buildings that adorned their thriving cities. Greek style inspired architects and sculptors in Roman times, and later, during the Renaissance, European humanists revived the Classical style of art and architecture. The Greek Revival, or neoclassical, style of architecture arose in the late 1700s and lasted into the early 1800s. Buildings in the Greek style are still being built.

Sparta again became independent city-states. Most other Greek city-states banded together into one of two leagues, but neither league had much power or importance.

Greek cultural influence, however, became stronger than ever after Alexander's death. The rulers who took Alexander's place adopted Greek as their language and used Alexander's titles. They even used his portrait on their coins.

Trade grew. From Africa and Asia came spices, ivory, incense, pearls, and rare woods. From Syria and Egypt came glass, metals, and linen. From Greece came olive oil, wine, and pottery. From Sicily and Egypt came wheat.

The cities that had been part of Alexander's empire now existed chiefly for trade and grew along with it. City officials made their law, language, calendar, and coins Greek. Teachers brought Greek customs and ideas into schools. Merchants and bankers used Greek methods to run their businesses.

HELLENISTIC ART Hellenistic artists showed action and realism in their works. Subjects often included everyday themes, such as the sculpture of the woman playing a harp (left). Some pieces tried to show forceful movement, such as the statue of the winged goddess of victory (right), who is leading a warship into battle. **What happened to Greek culture after Alexander the Great's death?**

L1 **Geography: Human/Environmental Interaction** Have students imagine that they are African merchants who have been coming to Alexandria, Egypt, for 20 years to buy and sell goods. For the first 8 of those 20 years, Alexander the Great ruled his empire. In the 12 years since his death, they have seen many changes. Tell students to write two or three paragraphs detailing the changes that have taken place in the city that would have affected the merchants' lives since the death of Alexander. Details could include the language they use for business dealings, the availability and variety of goods to trade, the kind of money and banking procedures they use, and so on. Have volunteers share their accounts with the class.

DID YOU KNOW ??

Alexander's profile was the first portrait of a real person to be used on coins.

CAPTION ANSWER

Its influence became stronger than ever.

ASSESS

CHECK FOR UNDERSTANDING

Ask students to summarize the main points of the chapter, orally or in writing. Discuss the answers to the Section and Chapter Review questions.

EVALUATE

Assign Chapter 12 **Performance Assessment Activity** in the TCR.

Administer **Chapter 12 Test** in the TCR. Testmaker available.

MEETING SPECIAL NEEDS

Arrange for visual or tactile/kinesthetic learners to visit an art or history museum and view examples of ancient Greek art and architecture. If this is not possible enlist the help of an art teacher or local artist to bring examples of sculptures to class, and to speak to the students about the influence of Greek art on others. Encourage student participation in questioning by helping students prepare questions ahead of time.

RETEACH

Have volunteers read each heading in the chapter. After each is read, have other volunteers tell the main ideas covered under the heading.

Assign Chapter 12 **Reteaching Activity** in the TCR.

ENRICH

Have students compare the extent of Alexander's empire with other empires of the ancient Middle East and orally report their findings using maps as visual effects.

Assign Chapter 12 **Enrichment Activity** in the TCR.

CLOSE

Ask students to discuss whether they agree or disagree with the following statement: *Might makes right.*

MEETING CHAPTER OBJECTIVES

Each objective is tested by the Review questions in parentheses.

1. **Summarize** how the spread of Greek culture influenced people from Gibraltar to India. (UYJ)
2. **Explain** how Philip II of Macedonia gained control of Greece. (BV; CU 1, 2, 3)
3. **Discuss** how Alexander attempted to bring unity to his empire. (CU 5; CT 2, 3; UYJ)
4. **Describe** how Alexander's empire changed after his death. (CU 8)

Greek Coins

The Greek city-states, however, were never the same again. Although they kept their political independence, they could not gain back the power of the past. In time, economic conditions grew worse. Great **factories,** or places where goods are made, had been built in the new Hellenistic cities. Greek manufacturers now found they could not compete with these factories. Because of this, more and more young Greeks **emigrated** (em' uh grāt ed), or left one place to settle in another. Population in the Greek city-states fell. There were not enough people to work the land, and many farms once again became wilderness. By 146 B.C., most of the Greek city-states were under Roman control.

Section 2 Review

1. **Identify:** Alexander the Great, Alexandria, Antigonus, Ptolemy, Seleucus
2. **Define:** *barbaroi*, factories, emigrated
3. What conquests did Alexander make?
4. How did Greek influence continue to grow and spread after Alexander's death?

Critical Thinking

5. How successful would Alexander's dream of uniting the world in peace be today? Explain.

Chapter Summary

1. Philip II, ruler of Macedonia, believed it was his destiny to unify the Greek city-states and spread Greek culture.
2. Philip II was able to conquer Greece in 338 B.C.
3. When Philip II died in 336 B.C., his son Alexander took over the throne.
4. Alexander was a great general who never lost a battle and whose conquests stretched from the Nile to the Indus.
5. Alexander tried without success to bring the Macedonians, the Greeks, and the Persians together.
6. The most famous city founded by Alexander was Alexandria, Egypt.
7. After Alexander died in 323 B.C., his empire was divided among three of his generals.
8. After Alexander's death, Greek cultural influence became stronger than ever.
9. Although the Greek city-states again became independent following Alexander's death, economic conditions in Greece grew worse.
10. Most Greek city-states were under Roman control by 146 B.C.

SECTION 2 ANSWERS

1. Alexander the Great, Greek emperor (p. 195); Alexandria, capital of Alexander's Empire (p. 197); Antigonus, Alexander's general (p. 198); Ptolemy, Egyptian pharaoh (p. 198); Seleucus, Persian ruler (p. 198)
2. *barbaroi*, non-Greeks (p. 197); factories, places where goods were made (p. 200); emigrated, left one place to settle in another (p. 200)
3. a union among the Macedonians, the Greeks, and the Persians
4. later rulers adopted Greek language and titles; law, language, calendar, and coins; teachers used Greek ideas in schools; and merchants used Greek methods.
5. Answers will vary but could include world conflicts are difficult to end, and efforts by the United Nations.

Assign Chapter 12 **Section 2 Quiz** in the TCR. Testmaker available.

CHAPTER 12 Review

Building Vocabulary

Use the following words to write a short paragraph about the way Philip II gained control of Greece. Then write a paragraph about what helped cause the end of city-states in Greece.

hostage
phalanx
alliances
orator
barbaroi
factories
emigrated

Check for Understanding

1. What changes did Philip II make in his army?
2. How did Philip II view marriage?
3. Why would the Greeks not listen to Demosthenes's warnings?
4. What did Aristotle teach Alexander?
5. Why was Alexander unable to achieve unity among the people of his empire?
6. Why did many Greeks go to Alexandria, Egypt?
7. How did the physical features of Alexandria, Egypt, help trade?
8. What happened to the Greek city-states by 146 B.C.?

Critical Thinking

1. Why do you think many people did not listen to Demosthenes's warnings?
2. What other names did Alexander deserve to be called besides "the Great"?
3. What do you think Alexander could have done differently to achieve unity among the people in his empire? Explain.
4. In what ways can customs be spread without conquest?

Geography in History

HUMAN/ENVIRONMENTAL INTERACTION What geographical features had an impact on the Greek economy, especially their development of manufacturing over farming, and their constant trade and travel.

Using Your Journal

Review the details you noted about the ideas developed during the Hellenistic period. Imagine you are living in Greece during Alexander's rule. Write a letter to a friend of yours in another part of the world describing your hopes for the future of your country.

CHAPTER 12 REVIEW ANSWERS

BUILDING VOCABULARY

Paragraphs will vary but should include specific references to Philip's methods.

CHECK FOR UNDERSTANDING

1. He made a professional army armed with long spears, slingshots, and bows and arrows, and he developed the phalanx.
2. as a way of forming political alliances
3. because they were unhappy with their local governments
4. literature, political science, geography, and biology
5. because they refused to treat Alexander as a god, and the Greeks looked down on all non-Greeks
6. its economic opportunities and intellectual and social life
7. It had two great harbors that were protected by breakwaters.
8. Most came under Roman control.

CRITICAL THINKING

1. Answers will vary but include the powers of a crowd mentality.
2. Answers will vary but could include aspects of Alexander's character.
3. Answers will vary. Students may explain that Alexander should not have tried to force a different way of life on the people.
4. Answers will vary but might include through trade, learning, traveling missionaries and merchants, marriage, and alliances.

+ BONUS +

TEST QUESTION

For Chapter 12 Test

Alexander was a very practical, clear-thinking leader. If he were to write a handbook of rules on how to organize an army, what do you think would be the first three suggestions in his book? *(Answers will vary.)*

USING YOUR JOURNAL

Letters will vary but might include the idea that Greek culture and people would flourish and leaders would settle disagreements among Greek city-states, and form political alliances.

GEOGRAPHY IN HISTORY

Answers will vary but should include the accessibility of the sea for trade and for obtaining raw materials, lack of good farmland, and the mountains.

UNIT 4 CULTURE CLOSE-UP

THE MAURYAS

FOCUS

OBJECTIVES

Locate the Mauryan Empire and discuss its geographic significance. Describe the cultural development and the government of the Mauryas.

BELLRINGER

Write the following on the chalkboard: *What symbols are used for national emblems?*

MOTIVATIONAL ACTIVITY

Ask students to read their list of symbols used for national emblems. Discuss what the symbols stand for. Then explain that in this Culture Close-Up they will learn about an early culture in India that used the symbol of a lion and a wheel for its empire's emblem. Ask students what these symbols may have stood for.

DID YOU KNOW ??

The Mauryan Empire was supported by a large army of 650,000 men divided into groups of cavalry, charioteers, foot soldiers, and elephanteers. The elephants were protected by leather armor and wore metal spikes on their tusks. The elephants, however, panicked at the sight of fire and were often ineffective.

UNIT 4

CULTURE CLOSE-UP

The Mauryas

The Maurya (mah' ur yah) Empire, the first true empire in India, was established in 321 B.C. It's cultural developments and unified government were models for civilizations that followed.

Geography Connection

The empire of the Mauryas spread over much of northern and central India, including the rich lands of the Ganges River valley.

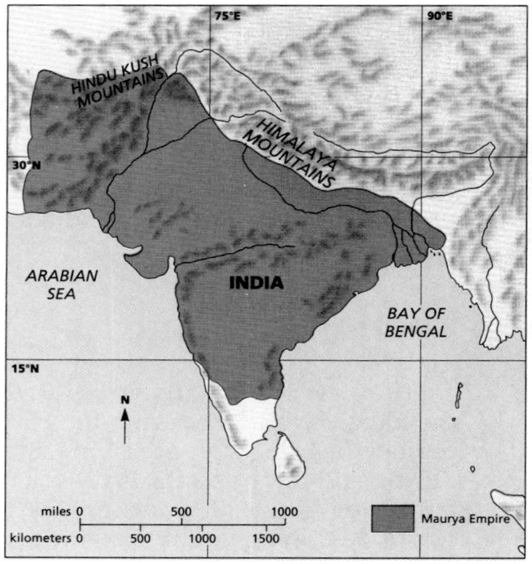

▲ The Ganges Valley has grown to be one of the most heavily populated in the world.

▲ Legends tell of the first Mauryan ruler, Chandragupta I, who defeated a great Indian king. Chandragupta gave the king 500 elephants to marry the king's daughter.

EXTENDING THE CONTENT

Chandragupta established a highly centralized and structured form of government. In this government, the empire was divided into provinces. The provinces were subdivided into districts. Chandragupta placed provincial governors over district governors and made district governors responsible for the actions of the village headmen. He also established specialized departments to handle agriculture, forestry, foreign trade, and public works.

The wealth of Chandragupta I's empire was detailed in later Indian art and sculpture. ▶

▲ Chandragupta set up a strong government and public works system. He continued already established trade with other Asian countries. Members of the lavish Mauryan court wore rich fabrics, gold, and pearls. ▼

Royal celebrations often included a hunt and the fighting of wild animals such as trotter oxen, relative of India's water buffalo, rhinoceroses, and elephants. ▶

TEACH

L1 **Location** Compare a physical map of India with the map of the Mauryan Empire on page 202. Ask students to name the physical features located in the Mauryan Empire. Ask: What major river flows through the empire? *(Ganges River)* What natural features form the northern boundary of the empire? *(Hindu Kush Mountains, Himalaya Mountains)* **LEP**

DID YOU KNOW ??

Chandragupta I was able to maintain a strong unified government partly because of the efficient postal system that he developed and the extensive spy network that he used.

MEETING SPECIAL NEEDS

Have interested students research the Ajanta Caves and write a report that answers the following questions: Who built the Ajanta Caves? How and why did they build them? How were the cave walls prepared for painting? What subjects do the sculptures and paintings show? Students might also draw sketches of the subjects shown in the sculptures and paintings. Have them share their reports with the class.

L2 **Critical Thinking** Explain to students that Asoka publicized his edicts, or laws, by having them carved on stone pillars for all to see. Ask the students to discuss why publicizing the laws might help make the government stronger. LEP

MAKING CONNECTIONS

➤➤ **History** During the first part of Asoka's rule, he expanded the Mauryan Empire to its greatest extent through violence and war. Asoka realized that his conquests had killed millions of his subjects and he turned from violence and became a Buddhist and a lover of peace. Asoka devoted the rest of his life to improving the lives of his people. He improved medical services, irrigation systems, and the lives of travelers in his empire.

GLOBAL READING FOR STUDENTS

Students in your class may be interested in reading about fables told by the Buddha. Suggest *Jataka Tales: Fables from the Buddha* edited by Nancy DeRoin, Houghton Mifflin, 1975. (Average/Fiction)

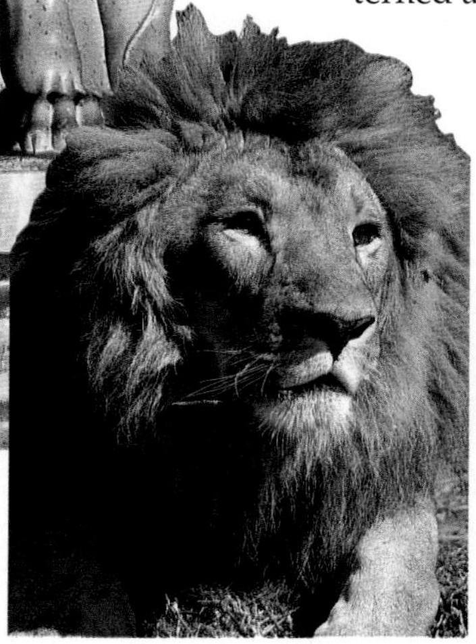

Chandragupta's grandson Asoka was the next great Mauryan ruler. Asoka, who governed from 269 to 232 B.C., treated his people with fairness and kindness.

◀ His emblem, four lions, was put atop large pillars all over his kingdom. Asoka's edicts, or rulings, were carved on these pillars. India's national emblem was patterned after Asoka's lions.

Asoka is considered one of India's greatest rulers. He ordered rest inns be built beneath tall banyan trees for religious pilgrims. Travellers, human or animal, were welcome. He ordered wells to be dug and mango orchards also to be planted for his citizens. ▶

204

COOPERATIVE LEARNING

Have students form two groups, one to support Asoka and his followers, who opposed war, and the other to defend the Indian rulers and warriors, who wanted to conquer more land. Have each group break into smaller teams to research and discuss such issues as politics, law, religion, and economics. Then have students rejoin the larger groups to discuss findings. Key ideas should be written down and presented to the class in oral arguments by one or two spokespersons.

CULTURE CLOSE-UP

UNIT 4

◀ Asoka had been influenced by his belief in the philosophy of Buddha. A great number of Maurya people shared this belief.

Buddha's philosophy dictated that all living things should live in harmony, without hurting one another. ▼

▲ The Maurya Empire declined in 185 A.D. Paintings from following civilizations depicted the grandeur of the Mauryas.

Taking Another Look

1. **How many years did the Mauryan Empire last?**
2. **In what major river valley did the Maurya live?**
3. **What philosophy had a great influence on Asoka?**

Critical Thinking

4. **Why do you think modern Indian leaders admire Asoka?**

MULTICULTURAL PERSPECTIVES

Asoka's support of Buddhism began to transform Buddhism from a local faith into a world religion. Asoka helped spread Buddhism by sending Buddhist missionaries to other Asian lands. Some crossed mountains to bring Buddhism to China; others traveled by sea to convert people in Southeast Asia. Among the missionaries was Asoka's own brother, who was sent to Sri Lanka where he converted the leader.

ASSESS

CHECK FOR UNDERSTANDING

Have students answer the questions in Taking Another Look on page 205.

ANSWERS to Taking Another Look

1. about 506 years
2. Ganges River valley
3. the philosophy of Buddha that dictated that all living things should live in harmony, without hurting one another
4. Answers will vary. Students should give reasons why they think modern Indian leaders admire Asoka.

ENRICH

Have students brainstorm a list of ideas of why the Mauryan Empire declined. Encourage them to take into account the era, geography, and conditions in the empire itself.

CLOSE

Ask students to discuss how Asoka's religious beliefs were reflected in the way he governed his people.

VIDEODISC

Use the following to enrich Unit 4.

WH U 18 34624

A Lion Capital of Emperor Asoka.

WH U 19 34625

A map of Asoka's empire.

INTRODUCE

UNIT 5 OVERVIEW

Unit 5 surveys the history of Rome from its beginnings as a small city-state to the decline of its powerful empire.

- **Chapter 13** discusses the settlement of Italy, focusing on the Etruscans.
- **Chapter 14** analyzes the history of the Roman Republic from the sixth century B.C. to the establishment of the Roman Empire and its decline.
- **Chapter 15** explains the development of the Roman Empire from its founding in 31 B.C. to its fall in A.D. 476, focusing on the *Pax Romana*.
- **Chapter 16** summarizes the rise of Christianity to become a major influence on Western civilization.

UNIT OBJECTIVES

After reading Unit 5, students will be able to:

1. explain how the city of Rome became a great empire.

2. summarize what contributions the Romans made to Western civilization.

3. discuss the relationship between the Roman Empire and Christianity.

UNIT PROJECT

Organize students into three groups. Assign each group one of the following topics: Etruria, the Roman Republic, or the Roman Empire. Tell groups to create a chart about their topic using the following headings: *Government, Religion, Daily Life, Contributions, Famous Rulers.* Compile the three charts into a master chart titled *The Romans.*

UNIT 5 The Romans

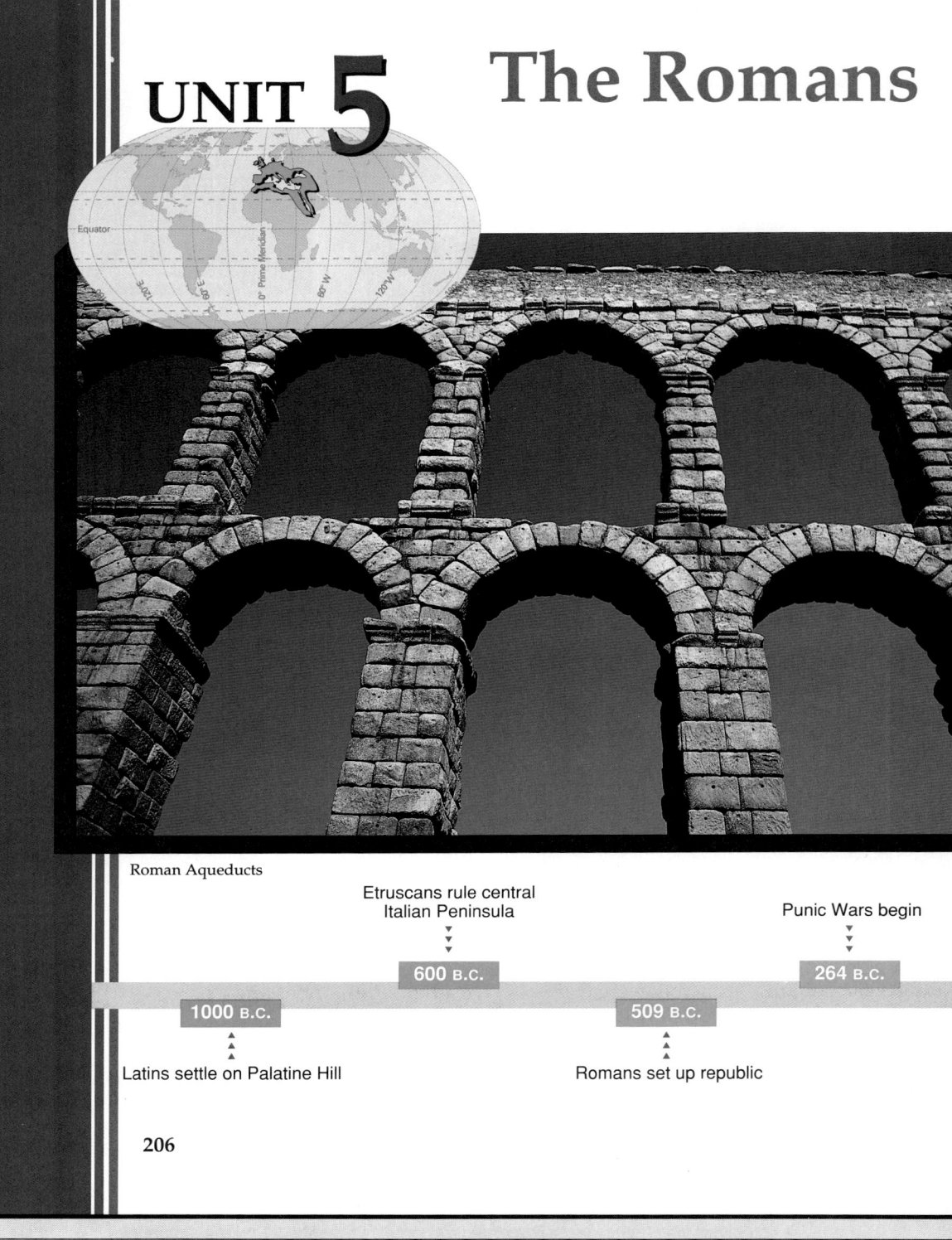

Roman Aqueducts

1000 B.C. — Latins settle on Palatine Hill

600 B.C. — Etruscans rule central Italian Peninsula

509 B.C. — Romans set up republic

264 B.C. — Punic Wars begin

206

ABOUT THE UNIT OPENING

EXAMINING THE ILLUSTRATION

Tell students this photograph shows a structure that was built in Roman times. Ask students to tell what they think an aqueduct is or is used for. Explain it is one of the more ingenious Roman constructions that they will be learning about in this unit.

GLOBAL CHRONOLOGY

Ask students to explain what the time line covers. *(major events in the history of Rome)* Ask students to name time line entries that indicate that Rome had an organized government. *(Romans set up a republic; Julius Caesar is appointed dictator of Rome)*

Much of western civilization comes from the Romans. The tradition of "equal justice for all" comes from Roman law. Many English, Spanish, French, and Italian words come from the Latin language the Romans spoke. Dozens of European cities began as Roman army camps. Christianity grew and spread in the Roman Empire.

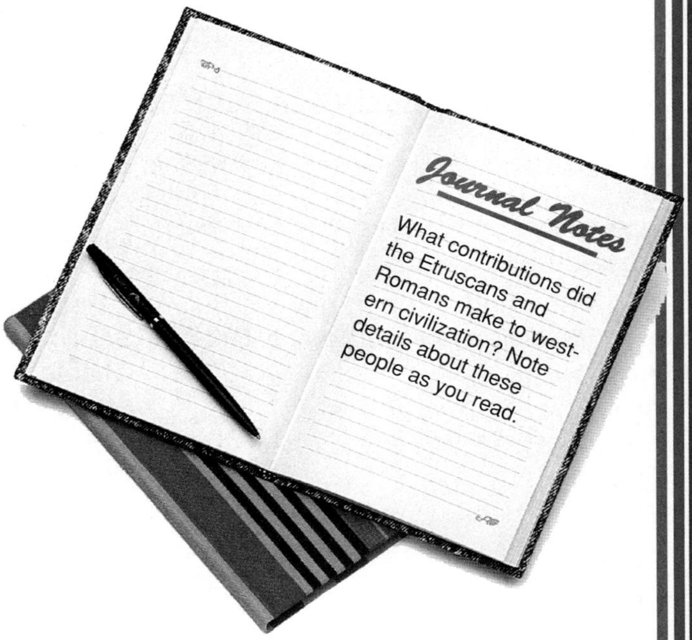
Journal Notes
What contributions did the Etruscans and Romans make to western civilization? Note details about these people as you read.

Christianity becomes official religion of Roman Empire — **392 A.D.**

46 B.C. — Julius Caesar is appointed dictator of Rome

27 B.C. — *Pax Romana* begins

476 A.D. — Roman Empire ends in West

INTRODUCING THE UNIT

Write one of the following statements on the chalkboard: *"Where there is life there is hope." "The people's good is the highest law."* (Cicero, c. 50 B.C.) *"Divine nature made the country, human art built the cities."* (Marcus Terentius Varro, c. 40 B.C.) *"It is sweet and beautiful to die for your country."* (Horace, 30 B.C.) Ask students what they think each statement means. Ask them the following questions: How did the Romans view themselves? What was important to them, and how did they regard life?

RECORDING JOURNAL NOTES

Help students begin writing in their journals by suggesting they make a list of contributions to western civilization by the Romans. Write responses on the chalkboard. Have students note in their journals details about the contributions to the modern world that were developed by the Etruscans and the Romans.

GEOGRAPHIC LOCATION

At its peak, the Roman Empire extended into the following regions: the Mediterranean, North Africa, and the Middle East. Have students locate these places in their text Atlas and name the continents that this area includes. *(Europe, Africa, and Asia)* Ask students what problems might arise in governing such a vast area. *(delays in communication, need to provide defense against invaders and rebellions, tax collection, law enforcement)*

PLANNING GUIDE

CHAPTER 13 Beginnings

CHAPTER ORGANIZER

Objectives	Special Features	Supplemental Materials
Section 1 Founding of Rome Describe how Rome was founded.		• Reproducible Lesson Plan • Section 1 Quiz • Testmaker • Chapter 13 Vocabulary and Guided Reading Activity
Section 2 The Etruscans Describe what daily life was like for the Etruscans and identify their religious beliefs.	Map and Geography Skills: *Reading a Political Map,* p. 211	• Reproducible Lesson Plan • Section 2 Quiz • Testmaker • Chapter 13 Geography and Map Activity • Chapter 13 Cooperative Learning Activity • Outline Map Resource, pp. 27, 28, 30, 39 • Chapter 13 Activity Book Activity • Foods Around the World
Section 3 Etruscans and Romans Identify how the Etruscans contributed to Roman civilization.		• Reproducible Lesson Plan • Section 3 Quiz • Testmaker • Chapter 13 Chart and Graph Skill Activity • Chapter 13 Teaching Transparencies and Activities
Chapter 13 Review and Evaluation		• Chapter 13 Reteaching Activity • Chapter 13 Enrichment Activity • Spanish Summary and Glossary • Audiocassettes (English and Spanish) • Chapter 13 Performance Assessment Activity • Chapter 13 Test • Testmaker

If time does not permit teaching the entire chapter, use the Chapter 13 Summary on page 216 and the Chapter 13 Audiocassettes (English and Spanish) to point out the main ideas of the chapter.

✓ Performance Assessment Activities

Burial Customs The Etruscans had very specific practices and traditions they followed when a person died. Organize students into groups to investigate and compare burial customs of the ancient Etruscans and those followed in the United States today. They could research beliefs about the afterlife, styles of burials, burial techniques, and so on. Suggest students choose a way to present their research findings.

Legends Have students create their own legends about the founding of their community. Students might use the name of their community, its geographic location, or its main economic activity as inspiration for their legend. Have volunteers read their legends to the class.

CHAPTER RESOURCES

LITERATURE ABOUT THE PERIOD

Virgil. *Aeneid*. Translated by John Dryden. Heritage, 1944. The national epic of Rome.

READINGS FOR THE STUDENT

Hamblin, Dora Jane. *The Etruscans* (Emergence of Man series). Time-Life Books, 1975. History of Etruscan people.

Vaughan, Agnes Carr. *Those Mysterious Etruscans*. Doubleday, 1964. History of the Etruscan culture through their art and artifacts.

READINGS FOR THE TEACHER

Grant, Michael. *The Etruscans*. Scribner's Sons, 1980. Describes the political, cultural, and social developments of Etruscan civilization.

Sprenger, Maja and Gilda Bartolini. *The Etruscans: Their History, Art, and Architecture*. Abrams, 1983. Analyzes the history of the Etruscans through their art and architecture.

MULTIMEDIA RESOURCES

Ancient Civilizations and the Middle Ages. Social Studies School Service. Software. Focuses on government and cultural development in ancient Greece and Rome, the ancient Middle East, and the Middle Ages.

The Etruscans. Educational Video Network. 2 videos. Surveys the Etruscan civilization and reconstructs daily life using information from archaeological work done on Etruscan sites.

The Etruscans. Vedo Films. Filmstrip. Tells the story of the Etruscan civilization with maps and photographs.

The Roman Empire and Its Civilization. Listening Library. 4 filmstrips. Surveys Roman history from the founding of Rome to the end of the Roman Empire.

INTRODUCE

CHAPTER 13 OVERVIEW

Chapter 13 describes the beginnings of civilization in Italy.

➤ **Section 1** describes the legendary and historical accounts of the founding of Rome.

➤ **Section 2** discusses the rise of the Etruscans, their daily life, and their religious beliefs.

➤ **Section 3** summarizes the contributions the Etruscans made to Roman civilization.

CHAPTER OBJECTIVES

After reading Chapter 13, students will be able to:

1. explain how Rome was founded.

2. describe what daily life was like for the Etruscans.

3. identify the religious beliefs held by the Etruscans.

4. discuss how the Etruscans contributed to Roman civilization.

EXAMINING THE ILLUSTRATION

Ask students if this is what they expect the interior of a burial chamber to look like. Discuss their responses and explain they will learn more about Etruscan burial customs as they read the chapter.

PERFORMANCE ASSESSMENT ✓

Use the Performance Assessment activities on page 208B to help you evaluate students as they complete the chapter.

CHAPTER 13 Beginnings

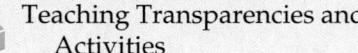

Etruscan Burial Chamber

TEACHER CLASSROOM RESOURCES

- Reproducible Lesson Plan
- Section Quizzes/Chapter Test
- Reteaching Activity
- Enrichment Activity
- Chart and Graph Skill Activity
- Geography and Map Activity
- Vocabulary and Guided Reading Activity
- Cooperative Learning Activity
- Teaching Transparencies and Activities
- Performance Assessment Activity
- Spanish Summary and Glossary
- Testmaker
- Audiocassettes (English and Spanish)

Chapter Focus

READ TO DISCOVER:

- How Rome was founded.
- What daily life was like for the Etruscans.
- What religious beliefs were held by the Etruscans.
- How the Etruscans contributed to Roman civilization.

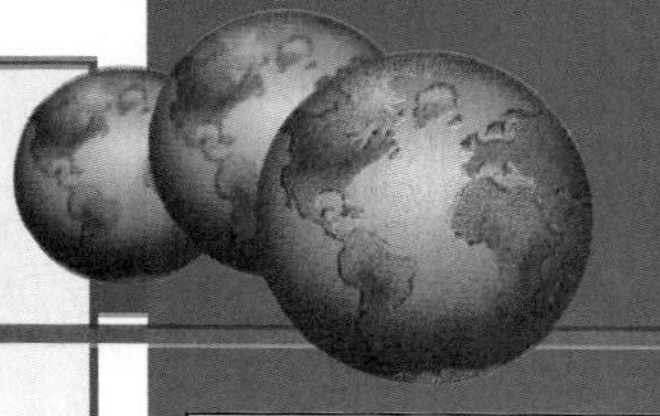

800 B.C.–500 B.C.

Italy is a boot-shaped peninsula that extends south from Europe into the Mediterranean Sea. On the west coast of the peninsula is the mouth of the Tiber (tī′ buhr) River. Fifteen miles, or 24 kilometers, upstream, the river is shallow. There stands a group of seven hills. On the hill known as the Palatine (pal′ uh tīn), a settlement was founded that came to be known as Rome.

KEY TERMS

social order
soothsayers
omens
catacombs
necropolis
Forum
fasces
municipal
mundus

Section 1

FOUNDING OF ROME

Romans have a legend about the founding of their city. After the fall of Troy, the gods ordered a Trojan prince called Aeneas (uh nē′ uhs) to lead his people to a promised land in the West. When Aeneas's group reached Italy, they joined forces with a people known as Latins (lat′ nz).

About 800 B.C., a Latin princess gave birth to twin sons fathered by the god Mars. The princess had taken an oath never to have children. Because she broke her word, she was punished. Her sons, Romulus (rom′ ū luhs) and Remus (rē′ muhs), were taken from her and left to die on the bank of the flooding Tiber.

Romulus and Remus were found by a she-wolf, which fed and cared for them. One day a shepherd killed the she-wolf and discovered the babies. He took them to his home.

When the boys grew older, they decided to build a city on the Tiber. The brothers, however, could not agree on which one should rule the city. They decided to let the gods choose between them.

209

FOCUS

BELLRINGER

Have students complete the following statement: *People made up legends to ________.*

MOTIVATIONAL ACTIVITY

Call on students to read their completed statements. *(Students' statements should include that legends often were created to explain mysterious or unknown happenings.)* Tell students that in this chapter they will learn about a legend that explains the founding of Rome.

VOCABULARY PRE-CHECK

Write the key terms for this chapter on the chalkboard. To access prior knowledge, ask students what they think of when they hear each word. Then ask them to assess how accurate their associations to the words were as they read the chapter.

Assign Chapter 13 **Vocabulary and Guided Reading Activity** in the TCR.

EXTRA CREDIT PROJECT

The Etruscans loved music and dancing. Suggest students research the double flute, the stringed lyre, or other ancient musical instruments the Etruscans might have used. Have students write a description of these instruments and the sounds they make, possibly including illustrations, to share with the class. Some students may want to make an audio component to their report.

KEY TO ABILITY LEVELS

Teaching strategies have been coded for varying learning styles and abilities.

L1 Level 1 activities are **basic** activities and should be within the ability range of all students.

L2 Level 2 activities are **average** activities and should be within the ability range of the average to above-average student.

L3 Level 3 activities are **challenging** activities designed for the ability range of above-average students.

LEP LEP activities should be within the ability range of Limited English Proficiency students.

TEACH

GUIDED PRACTICE

L2 **Language Arts** Have students work in small groups to write a script for the legend about the founding of Rome. Encourage them to include a list of characters and a setting description. Have groups present their scripts to the class.

L1 **Geography: Location** Have a student locate Italy on a wall map. Note its location in relation to the Mediterranean world. Discuss why Italy was a good place for an important civilization to develop. *(The country's central location helped the Romans assert their control over the Mediterranean world.)* LEP

LINKING PAST TO PRESENT

Scholars are still trying to translate the inscriptions found in Etruscan tombs and temple ruins.

Sculpture of Romulus and Remus

Each brother climbed to the top of a different hill to watch for a sign from the gods. Then 12 vultures flew over the Palatine. Since Romulus stood atop the Palatine, he claimed to be king. He and Remus then fought, and Remus was killed. Romulus became king of the city, which he named Rome.

Experts have learned that about 1000 B.C, groups of people with iron weapons began invading the lands around the Mediterranean. One group invaded Egypt and brought down the New Kingdom. Another group moved into the Balkan Peninsula. A third group, the Latins, settled on the Palatine. Romans belonged to this group.

The area where the Latins settled had a pleasant climate and fertile soil. Nearby were dense forests that supplied the Latins with timber. They built gravel roads to bring salt and other items from the coast.

By 776 B.C., the settlement on the Palatine had become a village of about 1,000 people. Most of the people were farmers who lived in wooden huts and worked the land. Their main crops were wheat and barley.

Section 1 Review

1. **Identify:** Palatine, Aeneas, Latins, Romulus, Remus
2. According to legend, how was Rome founded?
3. How did the Latins live?

Critical Thinking

4. How true do you think the legend of how Rome was founded is? Explain your answer.

Section 2 THE ETRUSCANS

Etruscan Jewelry

Around 800 B.C., a people called Etruscans (ē truhs' kuhnz) settled in Etruria (ē trur' ē uh), the rolling hill country north of the Latin village on the Palatine. The Etruscans wrote in an alphabet borrowed from the Greeks. They spoke a language different from any other in the ancient world. Many historians believe they came from the kingdom of Lydia in Asia Minor.

The Etruscans dug tunnels and built dams to drain their marshy fields. High on hilltops, they built a number of cities, each surrounded by a thick wall.

The Etruscans were Italy's first highly civilized people. They were known as "the people of the sea." As pirates, they were

SECTION 1 ANSWERS

1. Palatine, hill of Rome (p. 209); Aeneas, Trojan prince (p. 209); Latins, early people in Italy (p. 209); Romulus and Remus, brothers and legendary founders of Rome (p. 209)
2. About 800 B.C., a Latin princess gave birth to twin sons fathered by a god. As punishment, her sons, Romulus and Remus, were taken from her and raised by a she-wolf and then a shepherd and his wife. Later the brothers built a city on the Tiber and let the gods choose the city's ruler. The two fought, Remus was killed, and Romulus became king of Rome.
3. Most were farmers who lived in wooden huts.
4. Answers will vary. Students should give reasons why they think the legend does or does not have some validity.

Assign Chapter 13 **Section 1 Quiz** in the TCR. Testmaker available.

Reading A Political Map

In all parts of the world, people have created governments in order to live together. Maps that show areas ruled by particular governments are called **political maps.** Most people use political maps to find cities and countries.

Political maps use symbols to show the location of capitals and other cities. A star is usually used to show the capital of a country or state, and a dot is used to show other cities. Boundary lines mark where a country or state begins and ends. Boundaries may be shown by solid, dashed, or dotted lines. Colors often show the size and shape of countries and states. All these symbols, lines, and colors are not really on Earth's surface, but what they show exists.

On the map of "Early Italy" below, the three colors show the particular areas ruled by three peoples.

MAP SKILLS

Map Practice

1. **Who controlled the southernmost part of Italy?**
2. **What two cities are shown?**
3. **What people controlled the smallest area?**

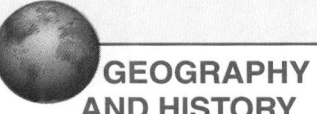

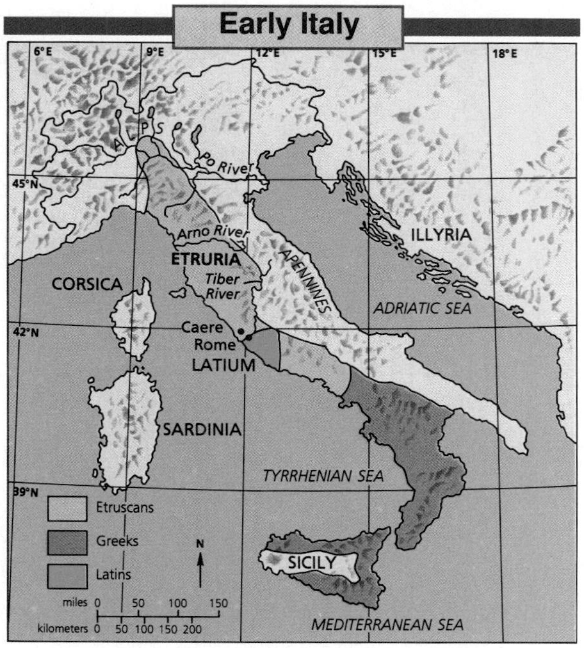

SPOTLIGHT ON: EARLY ITALY

The Tiber River was a dominant influence on Etruria. Some historians believe this 252-mile (405 km) river was known originally as Albulla—referring to the whiteness of its waters—and was later changed to the name Tiber for Tiberius, a king of Alba Lunga (an area south of Rome) who drowned in it.

Teaching

MAP SKILLS

Reading a Political Map

Have students read the introductory section of the skill on page 211. Ask students what they think most people use political maps for. *(to find cities and countries)* What are three ways boundaries may be shown on maps? *(by solid, dashed, or dotted lines)* What are often used on political maps to show the size and shape of countries and states? *(colors)* Direct students' attention to the map on the skill page. Ask them what is used to show boundary lines on this map of early Italy. *(solid lines)* What people controlled the Arno River? *(Etruscans)* What city was ruled by the Etruscans? *(Caere)*

ANSWERS to Map Practice

1. Greeks
2. Caere and Rome
3. Latins

GEOGRAPHY AND HISTORY

Why do you think the Etruscans became "the people of the sea"? *(Their extensive coastline would have encouraged the people to become dependent on the sea for their livelihood.)*

Assign Chapter 13 **Geography and Map Activity** in the TCR.

L3 **Critical Thinking** Point out that most civilizations borrow from other culture groups. For example, the Etruscans borrowed the Greek alphabet and some Greek gods. Have students brainstorm a list of some things American culture has borrowed from other cultures. *(Examples: words from Latin, French, Greek, or Spanish; foods from Italy, China, or Mexico; holiday traditions such as the Christmas tree from Germany)*

DID YOU KNOW ??

Each Etruscan city specialized in a craft or product. Veli, for example, was known for its sculpture, and Caere for its pottery and metalworks.

CAPTION ANSWER

Etruscan women enjoyed many freedoms. They took part in public celebrations, ate and drank with their husbands in public, and owned property.

feared and envied throughout the Mediterranean. As traders, they were admired and respected.

Etruscan farmers used mostly iron tools to grow barley, millet, wheat, grapes, and other fruits. They raised pigs, goats, sheep, ducks, chickens, and cattle. The farmers used cattle for food and to pull plows and wagons.

Etruscan miners dug copper, lead, iron, and tin. Etruscan metalworkers and sculptors turned these metals into weapons, utensils, and jewelry. Etruscan merchants exchanged both metals and finished goods for luxury items of gold, silver, and ivory from Syria, Greece, and other eastern Mediterranean countries.

The Etruscans had a strong army. The soldiers learned much about weapons and battle techniques from the Greeks. Their infantry formed a phalanx much like the one used by the Greeks. However, the Etruscans had one "weapon" no one else

ETRUSCAN COUPLE The Etruscans' love of art, music, and food can be clearly seen in their artwork. Here, a tomb sculpture shows an Etruscan noble and his wife. The Etruscans rested on couches while eating or listening to music. **How were Etruscan women regarded?**

COOPERATIVE LEARNING

The Romans borrowed extensively from other cultures. Provide students with a wall-sized sheet of paper on which to show a composite of what Romans borrowed with a graphic organizer of their own design. Assign students to small groups. Have each group research one major topic and then complete one portion of the wall diagram. *(Romans adapted Etruscan rituals, Etruscan and Greek gods, Greek styles of architecture and sculpture, Greek medicine and science, and Egyptian astronomy.)* Each group should divide among its members the tasks of researching, obtaining pictures, drawing illustrations, and writing captions.

Assign Chapter 13 **Cooperative Learning Activity** in the TCR.

had—their shoes. They wore heavy leather shoes that laced firmly around the ankle. This gave them better footing than their enemies on rough or hilly ground.

Over time, the Etruscan cities grew in size and power. The Etruscans became rich. By 600 B.C., they dominated all of northern Italy, including the Latin village on the Palatine.

Sculpture of Etruscan Warrior

Daily Life

The Etruscans enjoyed bright colors, riches, and a good time. They gambled with ivory dice or played games similar to chess and backgammon. They often watched or took part in such sports as wrestling, running, boxing, and horse racing.

Most of all, the Etruscans loved music and dancing. Sounds from a double flute or a stringed lyre (līr) accompanied most of their activities. Much of their dancing was connected to religion. Dances were done to gain favor from the gods.

Both Etruscan men and women danced. Dancing was just one of the freedoms enjoyed by Etruscan women. Unlike Greek or Latin women, Etruscan women took part in public celebrations. They could also own property.

The Etruscans had a strong sense of **social order,** or the way groups of people are classed. At first, there were no great class differences among them. Only acrobats and enslaved people, who were captives of war, were thought inferior. Later, people were divided into three classes. The upper class consisted of wealthy landowners, nobles, and priests. The middle class had farmers, traders, and city workers. The lower class was enslaved people.

A few wealthy families owned most of the land. They also owned most of the enslaved people, who tended the land and did other work. The rich lived in rectangular, one-story homes made of sun-dried brick on a frame of heavy timbers. A pitched roof covered with clay tiles extended beyond the house. Stone-lined drains led from each house into the main drains that ran along the pebble-paved streets. Most homes also had broad, walled courtyards open to the sky. During the day, the center room was often used for talking about business. At night, it was the scene of entertainment.

Sculpture of Etruscan Woman

Religious Beliefs

The Etruscans had many gods, most of whom were modeled after those of the Greeks. At first, the Etruscans worshiped their gods outdoors on platforms of stone or earth. Later, they built temples of wood, mud-brick, and clay on stone foundations. The temples had peaked, tiled roofs adorned with sculptures.

The Etruscans believed the universe was divided into provinces. Each province was ruled by different gods. Humans lived in the center of the universe, facing south towards the gods of nature and Earth. To the right lay the West, which was ruled by the gods of death and of the underworld. To the left lay the East,

L2 **Daily Life** Ask students to imagine they are Etruscan teenagers. Ask them to write a diary entry describing a day in their life. They might include information about their home, leisure activities, social class, and religious beliefs. Have volunteers read their entries.

DID YOU KNOW ??

Wealthy Etruscans wore a great many jewels, especially ornaments of gold.

MULTICULTURAL PERSPECTIVES

The Etruscans believed that a person was destined to live 70 years. By reading omens correctly and making the proper sacrifices to the gods, a person might live 84 years. Then, even if the body survived, the soul would be taken away.

L1 **Culture** Organize the class into five groups. Explain that each group is responsible for doing one section of a bulletin board that will show the religious beliefs of the Etruscans. Assign each group one of the following topics: temples, provinces of the universe, soothsayers, catacombs, and necropolises. Have each group illustrate its topic and write a caption below the illustration describing its role in Etruscan religious life. Have a representative from each group present and explain the group's illustration. Display the illustrations on the bulletin board. LEP

LINKING PAST TO PRESENT

The three main Etruscan gods were Tinia, ruler of the heavens and of the other gods; Uni, Tinia's wife and goddess of love and the well-being of women; and Minerva, goddess of wisdom and the arts. The names of these gods have become components of modern English.

Etruscan Religious Figure

which was ruled by the gods of the heavens. Because of this, Etruscans planned their cities and built their temples to face east.

The Etruscans also believed humans were powerless before the gods. More than anything else, the Etruscans wanted to please their gods. First, however, they had to discover what their gods willed. They did this through a priestly group of aristocrats called **soothsayers** (sūth′ sā uhrz), or people who can predict events.

Soothsayers read certain **omens** (ō′ muhnz), or signs of what is to happen. One group of soothsayers read omens from the livers of sacrificed animals. Another group of soothsayers explained the will of the gods by studying the direction and sounds of thunder and lightning and the flights of birds.

Tombs of Gold When an Etruscan noble died, a great banquet was held. At the banquet, two of the noble's slaves fought one another to the death. The spirit of the slave who was killed went with the noble's spirit to the underworld.

The dead were buried in tombs beneath the ground called **catacombs** (kat′ uh kōmz). Much of what is known about Etruscan life comes from such tombs, whose inside walls were brightly painted with pictures of daily life. The tombs had chairs and beds. The bodies of the dead rested on the beds.

The Etruscans believed that life after death lasted longer and was more important than life on Earth. So, they carved their tombs out of natural rock, which would last for a long time. They filled the tombs with works of art and treasures of gold, silver, bronze, and ivory. Because of this, Etruscan tombs are known as "tombs of gold."

Outside each Etruscan city was a **necropolis** (nek rop′ uh luhs), or cemetery, made up of acres of these tombs. The necropolis outside the city of Caere (sir′ ē) is one of the largest Etruscan cemeteries. There, great mounds of soil are piled in the shape of a dome on top of a base. Some of the mounds measure 100 feet, or 30 meters, across.

Section 2 Review

1. **Identify:** Etruscans, Etruria, Lydia, "tombs of gold"
2. **Define:** social order, soothsayers, omens, catacombs, necropolis
3. How was Etruscan society divided?
4. What was the Etruscan view of the universe?

Critical Thinking

5. What similarities are there between the way Etruscans treated their dead and the way modern people do?

SECTION 2 ANSWERS

1. Etruscans, people in Etruria (p. 210); Etruria, country north of Palatine (p. 210); Lydia, kingdom in Asia Minor (p. 210); tombs of gold, Etruscan tombs (p. 214)
2. social order, classes of people (p. 213); soothsayers, people who predict (p. 214); omens, signs of the future (p. 214); catacombs, underground tombs (p. 214); necropolis, cemetery (p. 214)
3. into an upper class of wealthy landowners, nobles, and priests; a middle class of farmers, traders, and city workers; and a lower class of enslaved people
4. They believed it was divided into three provinces, each ruled by different gods.
5. Answers will vary but could note Etruscan burial tombs, practices, and cemeteries.

Assign the Chapter 13 **Section 2 Quiz** in the TCR. Testmaker available.

Section 3

Etruscans and Romans

In 616 B.C., Lucius Tarquinius (lū′ shuhs tar kwin′ ē uhs) became the first Etruscan ruler of Rome. No one is certain whether Tarquinius took the throne from the Latin king by force or by cleverness. Nevertheless, his dynasty ruled Rome for more than 100 years.

The Etruscans were more culturally advanced than the Latins. They made many contributions to Roman civilization. In the area of architecture, the Etruscans taught the Latins how to use the arch in building bridges. The Etruscans also laid the foundations of Rome's first sewer system. They drained the swamp at the foot of the Palatine. This later became the place where Rome's **Forum** (fōr′ uhm), or the public square, was built. The Forum housed a palace, government buildings, and law courts.

The Etruscans made a contribution in the area of language as well. They borrowed the Greek alphabet and made some changes in it. The Romans, in turn, borrowed the Etruscan alphabet.

The Romans also borrowed some Etruscan customs. One was the fights of enslaved people held at Etruscan funerals. These were models for the **gladiatorial** (glad′ ē uh tōr ē uhl) **games** with which the Romans amused themselves. These games were fights between armed men, between men and animals, between women and dwarfs, and between animals. Another custom borrowed from the Etruscans was the **triumph** (trī′ uhmf), or the parade-like welcome given a Roman hero returning from battle.

In addition, the Romans borrowed Etruscan symbols of authority. One of these was the **fasces** (fas′ ēz), or a bundle of rods bound around an ax. It became the symbol of a Roman ruler's power to beat or execute other people.

The Etruscans also introduced the Romans to certain religious beliefs. These included soothsayers and gods with human forms. The Etruscans built the first temple on the Capitoline (kap′ uh tuh līn), one of the seven hills of Rome. Today, it is the center of Rome's **municipal** (myū nis′ uh puhl), or city, government.

The Romans founded their cities according to a ritual borrowed from the Etruscans. Soothsayers read omens that told where the city's boundaries should be. A ditch was dug to mark the boundaries. The plow used to dig the ditch had a bronze blade and was pulled by a white bull and cow yoked together. Workers then dug a trench at the center of the city. After each of the city's founders had tossed a handful of earth into the trench, the priests took over. They laid out the main street and determined the principal cross street. The place where the two streets met was marked by a stone.

Etruscan Gold Clasp

INDEPENDENT PRACTICE

L2 **Culture** Have students make charts showing the Etruscan contributions to Roman civilization in the following areas: architecture, language, customs, and religion.

L3 **Language Arts** Have students research and compare the letters of the Greek, Etruscan, and Roman alphabets. Suggest students should organize their findings in a table. Encourage them to try to write the same one or two words using each of the alphabets.

MAKING CONNECTIONS

>> **Language Arts** The word *temple* is of Etruscan origin. Originally it referred to the part of heaven from which soothsayers gathered their omens.

DID YOU KNOW

The Capitoline later became the religious and political heart of Rome.

ASSESS

CHECK FOR UNDERSTANDING

Ask students to summarize the main points of the chapter, orally or in writing. Discuss the answers to the Section and Chapter Review questions.

EXTENDING THE CONTENT

Mussolini's Fascist party, organized after World War I with the goal of restoring Italy's national pride and prosperity, adopted symbols from ancient Rome that they admired. The party's name and symbol was an ancient Roman-Etruscan symbol—the fasces. This symbol of the power to punish was originally a bundle of elm or birch rods tied tightly around an ax with a red strap.

EVALUATE

Assign Chapter 13 **Performance Assessment Activity** in the TCR.

Administer the **Chapter 13** Test in the TCR. Testmaker available.

RETEACH

Organize the class into three groups and assign each group a section. Have the groups write questions about the main concepts in the sections. Have groups exchange questions and answer them.

Assign Chapter 13 **Reteaching Activity** in the TCR.

ENRICH

Have students research and report on the Roman poet Virgil, and on the influence of Homer's *Iliad* and *Odyssey* on Virgil's epic poem, the *Aeneid.*

Assign Chapter 13 **Enrichment Activity** in the TCR.

CLOSE

Ask students to discuss how the information historians know about Etruscan culture might be distorted since they are able only to find artifacts of the very wealthy Etruscans.

MEETING CHAPTER OBJECTIVES

Each objective is tested by the Review questions that follow it in parenthesis.

1. Explain how Rome was founded. (CU 1)

2. Describe Etruscan daily life. (BV; CU 2, 3, 5, 7, 8; CT 1, 2)

3. Identify Etruscan religious beliefs. (BV; CU 4,8; CT 2)

4. Discuss how the Etruscans contributed to Roman civilization. (CU 7, 8; CT 3; UYJ)

The Etruscans believed that the stone covered a shaft leading to the underworld. Three times a year, an Etruscan priest lifted the stone to allow the souls of the dead to return to Earth. The Romans believed the place where the two streets met was the **mundus** (muhn' duhs), or the meeting point for the worlds of the living and the dead.

Etruscans were not the first to develop or use many of the ideas and practices the Romans borrowed from them. They were, however, the people who brought these ideas to the notice of the Romans. Thus, they played an important role in the development of Roman civilization.

Section 3 Review

1. **Identify:** Lucius Tarquinius, Capitoline
2. **Define:** Forum, gladiatorial games, triumph, fasces, municipal, mundus
3. What contributions did the Etruscans make to the Roman language?
4. How did the Etruscans and the Romans establish their cities?

Critical Thinking

5. What contribution to the Romans by the Etruscans do you think was the most important? Explain.

Chapter Summary

1. Rome, founded about 800 B.C., was a settlement on the Palatine.
2. Rome's first settlers were Latins who invaded the Mediterranean region.
3. The main occupation of the Latins was farming.
4. North of the Latins lived the Etruscans, who conquered Rome in 616 B.C.
5. The Etruscans were noted throughout the Mediterranean world as traders and pirates.
6. The Etruscans enjoyed life and had a strong sense of social order.
7. The Etruscans worshiped many gods and used soothsayers to learn what the gods wanted.
8. The Etruscans placed importance on life after death and built elaborate tombs.
9. The Etruscans taught the Romans many things, including the use of the arch in building, an alphabet, and a ritual for establishing cities.

SECTION 3 ANSWERS

1. Lucius Tarquinius, first Etruscan ruler of Rome (p. 215); Capitoline, one of Rome's hills (p. 215)
2. Forum, public square (p. 215); gladiatorial games; public fights (p. 215); triumph, parade-like welcome (p. 215); fasces, symbol of Roman power (p. 215); municipal, city (p. 215); mundus, meeting points for the living and the dead (p. 216)
3. They borrowed the Greek alphabet, changed it, and passed it on to the Romans.
4. Soothsayers told where a city's boundaries should be, and a ditch was dug to mark them. Then the priests laid out the main street and cross streets and marked the intersection with a stone.
5. Answers will vary but students should support their choice with reasons.

Assign Chapter 13 **Section 3 Quiz** in the TCR. Testmaker available.

CHAPTER

Review 13

Building Vocabulary

Imagine you are writing a travel brochure titled "Come to Etruria." Use the following words to write the brochure, which encourages people to visit Etruria.

social order	Forum
soothsayers	fasces
omens	municipal
catacombs	mundus
necropolis	

Check for Understanding

1. Who were the first highly civilized people of the Italian Peninsula?
2. How did the kind of shoes the Etruscans wore help them in battle?
3. What group of people owned most of the land in Etruria?
4. Why did the Etruscans build their temples to face east?
5. How have experts learned much of what they know about Etruscan life?
6. Who was the first Etruscan ruler of Rome?
7. What customs did the Romans borrow from the Etruscans?
8. What religious beliefs did the Etruscans introduce to the Romans?

Critical Thinking

1. Compare the role of women in Etruria with their role in Greek civilization.
2. What part did religion play in Etruscan life? How did Etruscan religious ideas differ from the religious ideas of the Greeks?
3. Was the Etruscan conquest of Rome good for the Romans? Explain why or why not.
4. What would you have enjoyed most about living in Etruria? Explain.

Geography in History

LOCATION Look at the map on page 211. If the people of Etruria were attacked by another empire, from what direction and by what means would the attack come? What geographical feature might protect Etruria?

Using Your Journal

Review the details you have noted about contributions made by the Etruscans to western civilization. Prepare an illustrated chart showing some of the contributions of Etruscan architecture in the area where you live.

CHAPTER 13 REVIEW ANSWERS

BUILDING VOCABULARY

Brochure copy will vary but students should use all the vocabulary words in their brochure titled "Come to Etruria."

CHECK FOR UNDERSTANDING

1. the Etruscans
2. They gave them better footing on rough or hilly ground.
3. a few wealthy families
4. because the Etruscans believed the east and the left were lucky
5. from Etruscan tombs
6. Lucius Tarquinius
7. gladiatorial games, the triumph, and the fasces
8. soothsayers and gods with human forms

CRITICAL THINKING

1. Etruscan women danced, took part in public celebrations, and could own property. Greek women could not attend the Olympic Games, or go out without a chaperon.
2. Religion influenced Etruscan building of temples and cities, and ceremonies, songs, and dances. The Greeks were not afraid of their gods, as Etruscans were.
3. Answers will vary but Etruscans made contributions to Roman architecture, language, customs, and religious beliefs.
4. Answers will vary but students should provide reasons for their conclusions.

+ BONUS +

TEST QUESTION

For Chapter 13 Test

You are a stranger leaving an Etruscan city with one of its citizens. Outside the city you stop and ask the citizen if what you see is an outer city. The citizen says no—that you are looking at a *necropolis*. Describe what you see. *(rows of mounds of earth piled above tombs, wide streets that open into plazas)*

USING YOUR JOURNAL

Charts will vary but students might include the arch, bridges, sewer systems, and the public square.

GEOGRAPHY IN HISTORY

Answers will vary but should include attacks coming from the sea, down rivers, or overland from north or south. Protection came from two mountain ranges.

CHAPTER 14

The Roman Republic

CHAPTER ORGANIZER

Objectives	Special Features	Supplemental Materials
Section 1 The Government Describe how the government of the Roman Republic was formed.		• Reproducible Lesson Plan • Section 1 Quiz • Testmaker • Chapter 14 Vocabulary and Guided Reading Activity
Section 2 Roman Expansion Explain how the Roman Republic was able to expand and protect its territory.		• Reproducible Lesson Plan • Section 2 Quiz • Testmaker • Unit 5 World Literature • The Western Civilization Videodisc
Section 3 The Punic Wars Describe the Punic Wars and their effect on the Roman Republic.		• Reproducible Lesson Plan • Foods Around the World • Chapter 14 Activity Book Activity • Section 3 Quiz • Testmaker
Section 4 Effects of Conquest Discuss how the effects of conquest changed the Roman economy and government.		• Reproducible Lesson Plan • Chapter 14 Teaching Transparencies and Activities • The World History Videodisc • Section 4 Quiz • Testmaker • Unit 5 Primary Source Reading
Section 5 Roman Leadership Analyze how reformers and generals attempted to save the Roman Republic.		• Reproducible Lesson Plan • Section 5 Quiz • Testmaker • Chapter 14 Chart and Graph Skill Activity • Chapter 14 Geography and Map Activity • Chapter 14 Cooperative Learning Activity
Chapter 14 Review and Evaluation		• Chapter 14 Reteaching Activity • Chapter 14 Enrichment Activity • Chapter 14 Performance Assessment Activity • Spanish Summary and Glossary • Audiocassettes (English and Spanish) • Chapter 14 Test • Testmaker

If time does not permit teaching the entire chapter, use the Chapter 14 Summary on page 230 and the Chapter 14 Audiocassettes (English and Spanish) to point out the main ideas of the chapter.

✓ Performance Assessment Activities

The Arts Have students prepare a visual "tour" of modern Rome and the remnants of the ancient Roman civilization. They should present illustrations, diagrams, and pictures of some of the most important Roman structures from various periods while providing the information and explanation as "tour guides."

Biographical Sketch Have students keep brief notes on each person mentioned in this chapter. Then have them prepare a list of "Who's Who in the Roman Empire"—those they believe were the 10 most important Romans. Students should briefly explain why they have chosen each person.

CHAPTER RESOURCES

LITERATURE ABOUT THE PERIOD

Ovid. *Metamorphoses.* Translated by Rolfe Humphries. Indiana University Press, 1955. Collection of stories from Greek and Roman mythology.

READINGS FOR THE STUDENT

Burrell, Roy. *The Romans: Rebuilding the Past.* Oxford University Press, 1991. Historical outline of ancient Rome.

Hughes, Jill. *Imperial Rome.* Gloucester Press, 1985. An introduction to Rome using illustrations and diagrams.

May, Robin. *Julius Caesar and the Romans.* Bookwright Press, 1985. Historical details about Rome during Julius Caesar's rule.

Tingay, Graham. *Julius Caesar.* Cambridge University Press, 1991. Account of the life and achievements of Julius Caesar.

Windrow, Martin. *The Roman Legionary.* Franklin Watts, 1984. Historical background and detailed information on the Roman soldier's training and duties, weapons, armor, equipment, and daily life.

READINGS FOR THE TEACHER

Asimov, Isaac. *The Roman Republic.* Houghton Mifflin, 1966. Focuses on Rome's rise to power from the founding of the city.

Connolly, Peter. *Hannibal and the Enemies of Rome.* Silver Burdett, 1980. Deals with Rome's struggles with invaders.

Miguel, Pierre. *Life in Ancient Rome.* Silver Burdett. Includes interesting and hard-to-find facts on ancient Rome.

MULTIMEDIA RESOURCES

Ancient Civilizations. Sliwa Enterprises. Software, Apple. Diskette and documentation on Greece and Rome.

Ancient Rome. Britannica Films. 5 filmstrips. Focuses on daily life, major Roman achievements, and the rise of Julius Caesar.

INTRODUCE

CHAPTER 14 OVERVIEW

Chapter 14 traces Rome's development from 509 B.C. to 31 B.C. under a republican form of government.

- **Section 1** summarizes the evolution of Roman government toward democracy.
- **Section 2** describes the army's role in the Roman Republic.
- **Section 3** discusses Rome's rise to power in the Mediterranean region.
- **Section 4** analyzes the effects of foreign conquests on the Roman Republic.
- **Section 5** examines the attempts to solve the Republic's problems.

CHAPTER OBJECTIVES

After reading Chapter 14, students will be able to:

1. describe how the Roman government was organized.

2. explain how the Roman Republic was able to expand and protect its territory.

3. summarize how the effects of conquest changed the Roman economy and government.

4. discuss how reformers and generals attempted to save the Roman Republic.

EXAMINING THE ILLUSTRATION

Ask students where in their town people gather to discuss news and business. Explain the Romans had such a place called the Forum, which they see pictured here.

PERFORMANCE ASSESSMENT

Use the Performance Assessment activities on page 218B to help you evaluate students as they complete the chapter.

CHAPTER 14 The Roman Republic

Sculpture of Julius Caesar

218

TEACHER CLASSROOM RESOURCES

- Reproducible Lesson Plan
- Section Quizzes/Chapter Test
- Enrichment Activity
- Geography and Map Activity
- Vocabulary and Guided Reading Activity
- Teaching Transparencies and Activities
- Cooperative Learning Activity
- Performance Assessment Activity
- Spanish Summary and Glossary
- Unit 5 Primary Source Reading
- Unit 5 World Literature
- Testmaker
- Audiocassettes (English and Spanish)
- The World History Videodisc
- The Western Civilization Videodisc

Chapter Focus

READ TO DISCOVER:

- How the government of the Roman Republic was organized.
- How the Roman Republic was able to expand and protect its territory.
- How the effects of conquest changed the Roman economy and government.
- How reformers and generals attempted to save the Roman Republic.

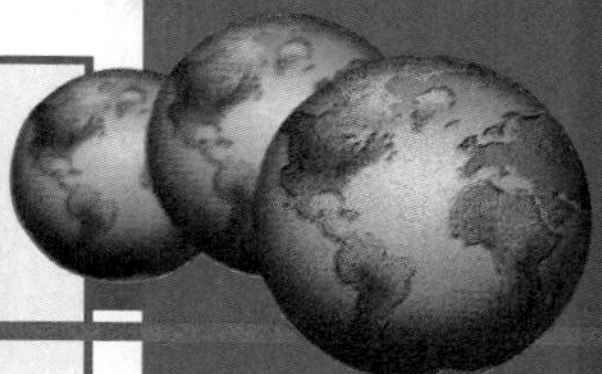

509 B.C.–30 B.C.

KEY TERMS
- republic
- patricians
- plebeians
- consuls
- veto
- tribunes
- legions
- legionaries
- latifundias
- publicans
- dictator
- triumvirate

In 509 B.C., the Romans overthrew Tarquin (tar′ kwin) the Proud, their Etruscan king. They then set up a **republic,** or a form of government in which the people choose their rulers.

The Roman people were divided into two classes, **patricians** (puh trish′ uhnz) and **plebeians** (pli bē′ uhnz). Patricians were members of the oldest and richest families. Plebeians were poorer people, such as farmers and artisans.

Patricians made up about 10 percent of the population. They had the real say in government because they were the only ones allowed to perform the religious rituals required or to hold public office.

Plebeians were citizens. They paid taxes and served in the army. However, they could not marry patricians or serve in the government. If they got into debt, they could be sold into slavery.

Section 1

THE GOVERNMENT

At the head of the Roman Republic were two **consuls** (kon′ suhlz) who were chosen each year. They were administrators and military leaders. Each had the power to **veto,** or say no to, the acts of the other. Both had to agree before any law was passed.

Next in importance was the Senate. It was made up of 300 men called senators who were chosen for life. The Senate handled the daily problems of government. It advised the consuls.

FOCUS

BELLRINGER

Ask students to write what first comes to their minds when they hear this phrase: *fields upon fields of Roman legions.*

MOTIVATIONAL ACTIVITY

Call on students to read their responses to the phrase about Roman legions. Tell students that the Roman armies, or legions, were extraordinarily disciplined fighting forces. Ask students what the implications are of keeping a standing army. *(Students may mention the need for defense or the use of armies for aggression and conquest.)* Then tell them they will learn about the Roman legions in this chapter.

VOCABULARY PRE-CHECK

Write the key terms for this chapter on the chalkboard. Ask students to predict what each term means by looking at its root word, prefixes, and suffixes.

Assign Chapter 14 **Vocabulary and Guided Reading Activity** in the TCR.

EXTRA CREDIT PROJECT

Suggest that interested students, as they read, choose one of the controversial subjects, such as a new law or planned invasion, that came before the Roman Senate during Caesar's rule. Have students write a script of the Senate debate that might have gone on over this issue. The debate should involve Caesar and at least one other Senator who opposed his viewpoint.

KEY TO ABILITY LEVELS

Teaching strategies have been coded for varying learning styles and abilities.

L1 Level 1 activities are **basic** activities and should be within the ability range of all students.

L2 Level 2 activities are **average** activities and should be within the ability range of the average to above-average student.

L3 Level 3 activities are **challenging** activities designed for the ability range of above-average students.

LEP LEP activities should be within the ability range of Limited English Proficiency students.

TEACH

GUIDED PRACTICE

L2 **Civics** Have students research and create a diagram of the republican government in Rome showing consuls, Senate, judges, assemblies, and tribunes. Discuss the diagram focusing on the special powers of consuls and tribunes. LEP

L3 **Language Arts** Have students imagine they are well-educated plebeians in the early days of the Roman Republic. Have them write letters to the Roman Senate demanding representation, written laws, and other issues. The letters should outline specific demands. Have volunteers read their letters.

CAPTION ANSWER

The Senate handled the daily problems of government. It advised the consuls, discussed ways to deal with other countries, proposed laws, and approved public contracts for building roads and temples.

DID YOU KNOW ??

The consuls were in charge of the state treasury, were judges in all law cases, and were commanders in chief of the army during wars.

MAKING CONNECTIONS

➤➤ **Citizenship** The Twelve Tables outlined how Roman citizens were to act in public. The Roman people considered knowledge of the law so important that Roman schoolboys had to learn the laws of the Twelve Tables by heart.

ROMAN SENATE This painting shows the famous orator Cicero making a speech attacking a political opponent. **What duties did the Senate perform in the Roman Republic?**

It discussed ways to deal with other countries, proposed laws, and approved public contracts for building roads and temples.

Judges, assemblies, and **tribunes** (trib′ yūnz), or government officials who protected the rights of plebeians, were also part of the Roman government. All Roman citizens belonged to the assemblies, which could declare war or agree to peace terms.

Until about 450 B.C., Roman laws were not written down. In that year laws were carved on 12 bronze tablets known as the Twelve Tables. These were placed in the Forum. The laws applied to both patricians and plebeians. Most were about wills, property rights, and court actions. The laws on the Twelve Tables became the foundation for all future Roman law.

The election of tribunes and recording of laws were the first steps to a more democratic government. Later, more plebeian demands were met. By about 250 B.C., no one could be sold into slavery because of debt. Plebeians could hold public office.

Section 1 Review

1. **Identify:** Tarquin the Proud, Senate, Twelve Tables
2. **Define:** republic, patricians, plebeians, consuls, veto, tribunes
3. What were some restrictions placed on the plebeians during the early years of the Roman Republic?
4. Who belonged to the Roman assemblies?

Critical Thinking

5. Why do you think it was important for the Romans to have laws written down?

SECTION 1 ANSWERS

1. Tarquin, Etruscan king (p. 219); Senate, part of Roman government (p. 220); Twelve Tables, tablets of Roman laws (p. 220)
2. republic, government where people choose their rulers (p. 219); patricians, the oldest and richest Roman families (p. 219); plebeians, poorer people of Rome (p. 219); consuls, heads of the Roman Republic (p. 219); veto, to say no to (p. 219); tribunes, Roman officials elected to protect the lower class (p. 220)
3. They could not marry patricians or serve in the government, and if they got into debt, they could be enslaved.
4. they could declare war or agree to peace terms; all Roman citizens
5. Answers will vary but could note that recording laws makes them more enforceable.

Assign the Chapter 14 **Section 1 Quiz** in the TCR. Testmaker available.

Section 2

Roman Expansion

Once the Romans had set up a republic, they worked to protect it. They were afraid that the Etruscans would try to get back control of Rome. To prevent this, the Romans crossed the Tiber River and conquered several Etruscan cities. Roman land now bordered that of other Italian people. To protect their new boundaries, the Romans either conquered their neighbors or made alliances with them. By 290 B.C., Rome was the leading power in central Italy. By 275 B.C., it ruled the whole peninsula. By 146 B.C., Rome ruled most of the Mediterranean world.

The Romans were able to gain territory because they had a strong army that was organized into **legions** (lē' juhnz). Each legion contained some 5,000 soldiers called **legionaries** (lē' juh ner ēz) and was divided into groups of 60 to 120 soldiers.

The legion had several advantages over the phalanx. The legion was smaller and could move faster. Soldiers in a phalanx fought as a group and attacked from only one direction. Each legionary depended on his own fighting ability. The groups within a legion could split off from the main body and attack from the sides and the rear as well as the front.

ROMAN LEGION The legions provided the military strength that made Rome great. They conquered new territories and guarded the frontiers of the expanding Republic. In this painting, legionaries armed with short swords attack an enemy army. **How was a Roman legion organized?**

MULTICULTURAL PERSPECTIVES

Although the idea of popular democracy began in the city-states of Greece, our government today is the direct heir of many things in the Roman Republic. The founders of the United States and the writers of the Constitution all had sound classical educations, knew Latin and (in many cases) Greek, and greatly admired Roman republican principles. They preferred the term *republic,* which means representative government, for the new nation, for to them *democracy* meant direct, unruly popular rule.

L1 **Critical Thinking** Lead a class discussion of how the Roman Republic was able to expand and protect its territory. Ask students what they think the role of the army was during the Roman Republic. What made the Roman army so powerful? What kind of rulers were the Romans? How did the Romans compare with the Persians in their treatment of conquered peoples? *(A well-trained, well-organized army coupled with mild rule fostered the expansion of the Roman Republic. They were fair and mild rulers to conquered people.)*

GEOGRAPHY AND HISTORY

The Romans established military settlements—called *coloniae*—throughout Italy to defend strategic heights over river crossings. To link these *coloniae,* the legions forged a chain of roads up and down the Italian peninsula. As war yielded gradually to peace, some of these roads became major trade routes.

CAPTION ANSWER

Each legion contained some 5,000 soldiers and was divided into groups of 60 to 120 soldiers.

VIDEODISC

Use the following to enrich Chapter 14.

WC B 89 11805

A Roman legionary wearing plated armor.

MAKING CONNECTIONS

➤➤ **Language Arts** *Punic* is the Latin word for *Phoenician*. The Punic Wars were so named because Carthage was a colony founded by the Phoenicians.

DID YOU KNOW ??

To frighten their enemies, Roman legionaries often carried dragon flags—said to have originated in China. Dragon flags were long pieces of cloth that, when attached to a pole and held in the wind, gave the terrifying appearance of a writhing dragon.

VIDEODISC

Use the following to enrich Chapter 14.

WC B 76 11792

Gaius Marius (157-86 B.C.).

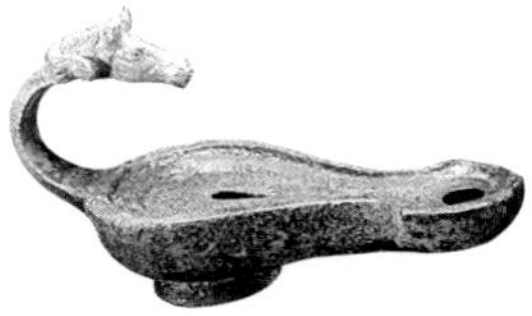

Roman Bronze Lamp

Legionaries were well trained. They spent hours practicing with their double-edged iron swords. They went on long marches every day. Before going to sleep, they had to build complete fortified camps, even when the legion would stay in an area only one night. They built roads out of lava blocks so soldiers and supplies could move forward more rapidly.

The Romans were mild rulers. At first, they did not tax the people they conquered. They let the conquered people keep their own governments and take care of their own affairs. Some were even allowed to become Roman citizens. In return, the conquered people were expected to serve in the Roman army and to support Rome's foreign policy. As a result, many enemies of Rome became loyal Roman allies.

Section 2 Review

1. **Define:** legions, legionaries
2. Why did the Romans conquer Etruscan cities?
3. Why were the Romans able to gain territory?
4. What kind of rulers were the Romans?

Critical Thinking

5. How would you describe the way the Romans treated people they conquered, and do you think this was wise?

Painting of Legionary

Section 3 THE PUNIC WARS

By 264 B.C., the Romans had conquered some Greek city-states in southern Italy. This brought them into contact with the Phoenician city of Carthage. Carthage controlled most of North and West Africa, most of what is now Spain, and some islands off the coast of Italy. Carthage also ruled the western half of Sicily (sis' uh lē), a large island at the toe of the Italian "boot." The Romans felt threatened by the Carthaginians (kar thuh jin' ē uhnz). They also wanted Sicily's granaries.

The First Punic War In 264 B.C., the Romans and Carthaginians clashed. The war that broke out lasted for 23 years. It was the first of three wars between Rome and Carthage that came to be known as the Punic (pyū' nik) Wars.

Carthage's military strength lay in its navy, while Rome's lay in its army. At first, the Romans had no navy. They built

SECTION 2 ANSWERS

1. legions, divisions of Roman soldiers (p. 221); legionaries, Roman soldiers (p. 221)
2. because they were afraid the Etruscans would try to regain control of Rome
3. because they had a strong army that was organized into legions
4. They were mild rulers who let conquered people keep their own governments.
5. Answers will vary but could note that by treating the people mildly Romans gained their loyalty.

Assign Chapter 14 **Section 2 Quiz** in the TCR. Testmaker available.

their first fleet to fight the Carthaginians. The Romans modeled their ships after a Carthaginian warship they found abandoned on a beach. They made one improvement on the Carthaginian model. They added a *corvus* (kor′ vuhs), or a kind of movable bridge, to the front of each ship. The Romans knew they could not outsail the Carthaginians, but believed they could outfight them. The corvus allowed soldiers to board an enemy ship and fight hand-to-hand on its decks. In a sense, it changed a sea war into a land war.

The Romans lost many ships and men in storms during the First Punic War. Yet, in the end, they defeated the Carthaginians. In 241 B.C., the Carthaginians agreed to make peace and left Sicily.

Hannibal and the Second Punic War In 218 B.C., the Second Punic War began. At that time, the Carthaginians, led by General Hannibal Barca (han′ uh buhl bar′ ka), attacked the Roman army by land from the north. Hannibal and his troops surprised the Roman army by marching from Spain through southern Gaul (gol), or present-day France, and then crossing the Alps into Italy. They brought elephants with them across the snow-covered mountains to help break through the Roman lines.

Winning victory after victory, Hannibal's army fought its way to the gates of Rome. When the Carthaginian army got to Rome, however, it did not have the heavy equipment needed to

HANNIBAL Hannibal's army, with elephants, faced many dangers in its attack on Rome. The elephants had to be floated on barges across rivers and brought over the snow-capped Alps. **Why did Hannibal's attack on the city of Rome fail?**

L1 **Geography: Region** Suggest students work together to develop a chart on the chalkboard or posterboard summarizing the three Punic Wars. For each war, include the dates, the areas where the war was fought, the locations of major battles, and the final outcome. LEP

MAKING CONNECTIONS

➤➤ **History** Hannibal's father was a Carthaginian general during the first Punic War. He made Hannibal take an oath to never be friends with the Romans. Hannibal was commander in chief of the Carthaginian army by age 26.

CAPTION ANSWER

because Hannibal's army did not have the heavy equipment needed to break down Rome's walls, and it was short on supplies and soldiers

VIDEODISC

Use the following to enrich Chapter 14.

WC B 80 11796
Augustus Caesar (27 B.C. - 14 A.D.).

WH E 67 14311
Ruins of Timgad, a Roman garrison.

MEETING SPECIAL NEEDS

Have gifted learners debate the following topic: *The wars between Rome and Carthage were worth the short-term and long-term costs for Rome.* Half of the group should defend the statement, the other half should argue against the statement. The rest of the class can act as the audience and decide which side presented the most persuasive arguments.

batter down the city's walls. It could not get more supplies because the Roman navy controlled the sea.

Unable to capture Rome, Hannibal and his troops roamed the countryside of southern Italy for 15 years. They raided and burned towns and destroyed crops. Then, the Romans attacked Carthage, and Hannibal was called home to defend it. Hannibal lost his first battle—and the war—at the town of Zama (zā' muh). The power of Carthage was broken.

In 201 B.C., Carthage agreed to pay Rome a huge sum of money and to give up all its territories, including Spain. The Spanish resources of copper, gold, lead, and iron now belonged to the Romans.

The Third Punic War Following the Second Punic War, there was peace for about 50 years. Then, Carthage began to show signs of regaining power. To prevent this, the Romans attacked in 149 B.C., the Third Punic War. They burned Carthage and plowed salt into its fields so nothing would grow. They killed the Carthaginians or sold them into slavery.

That same year, 146 B.C., the Greek city-state of Corinth (kor' inth) and some of its allies refused to obey a Roman order. The Romans attacked Corinth and burned it to the ground. Rome already controlled Macedonia and Syria. Now, it added Greece to the areas under its rule. Thus, Rome became the leading power of the Mediterranean world.

DID YOU KNOW ??

Under the terms of surrender, the Carthaginians also had to destroy all but 10 of their warships and promise not to make war again without Rome's permission.

LINKING PAST TO PRESENT

Speakers of English are often speakers of Latin without knowing it. Everyday terms like "A.M." and "P.M." are short for the Latin *ante meridiem* and *post meridiem*—"before noon" and "after noon." The *Exit* sign over a door is Latin for "he (she, it) goes out." Anyone who has joined an *ad hoc* committee, gone to an *alumni* reunion, figured something *per capita,* or added *P.S. (post scriptum)* to a letter, has used Latin.

Section 3 Review

1. **Identify:** Carthage, Punic Wars, Hannibal Barca, Zama
2. What territory did Carthage control in 264 B.C.?
3. What happened to Carthage in the Third Punic War?
4. How did Rome become the leading power of the Mediterranean world?

Critical Thinking

5. What might have happened to Rome if they had lost the Punic Wars?

MAKING CONNECTIONS

➤➤ **History** One of Rome's opponents, King Pyrrhus of Epirus, won two difficult victories over the Romans in 280 and 279 B.C. He sustained such great losses, however, that he reportedly exclaimed, "Another such victory and we are lost."

Painting of Roman Farmer

Section 4 EFFECTS OF CONQUEST

The conquests and the wealth that came with them changed Rome's economy and government. Among the changes were the replacement of small farms by large estates, the coming of slavery, a movement from farms to cities, and the decline of the Roman Republic.

SECTION 3 ANSWERS

1. Carthage, Phoenician city (p. 222); Punic Wars, wars between Rome and Carthage (p. 222); Hannibal Barca, Carthaginian general (p. 223); Zama, battle lost by Hannibal (p. 224)
2. all of North Africa, most of Spain, some islands off the coast of Italy, and the western half of Sicily
3. The city was burned, its land was destroyed by plowing salt into the fields, and its people were killed or sold into enslavement.
4. by destroying Corinth and adding Greece to the areas under its rule
5. Answers will vary but students might indicate that Rome would not have been able to expand its republic or might have been taken over by the Carthaginians.

Assign Chapter 14 **Section 3 Quiz** in the TCR. Testmaker available.

Agricultural Changes Rome's conquests brought changes in agriculture. One change was in the size and purpose of farms. Most Romans had been small farmers who believed in hard work and service to Rome. Now, the small farms were replaced by large estates called **latifundias** (lat uh fuhn' dē uhs). The small farms had grown wheat for food. Latifundias, on the other hand, produced crops, sheep, and cattle for sale at market. Some contained olive groves and vineyards. Because they no longer grew their own wheat, the Romans began to import wheat from such conquered areas as Sicily and North Africa.

The main reason for this change in Roman agriculture was Hannibal's invasion. While his soldiers were in Italy, they lived off the land. To prevent them from getting food, Roman farmers burned their fields and crops. By the time the Second Punic War was over, much of the land was ruined. Most Roman farmers did not have money to fix up their farms or restore the land. Only patricians and rich business people had that kind of money. They bought the small farms and combined them to make latifundias.

Another change in agriculture was in who worked the land. When Rome first began expanding, the Romans did not enslave the people they conquered. By 146 B.C., that was no longer true. The Romans were impressed by the wealth of Greece, Syria, and Carthage. Since those areas had widespread slavery, the Romans sent thousands of prisoners to Rome as enslaved people. Most lived and worked on latifundias.

Roman Grain Mill

From Farm to City The farmers who had sold their land had little choice. They could stay and work the land for the new owners or move to the city. Almost all of them moved to Rome.

There the farmers crowded into wooden apartment buildings six or more stories high. Living conditions were terrible. The aqueducts that brought water to the city were not connected to apartment buildings. Neither were the sewers that carried away waste. Buildings often caught fire or collapsed. Such diseases as typhus (tī' fuhs) were common.

Most farmers could not earn a living in the city. Except for construction, Rome had almost no industry. Most businesses were staffed by enslaved people from Greece. About the only way the farmers could get money was by selling their votes to politicians.

Decline of the Roman Republic As Rome's rule spread beyond Italy, the Romans began to demand taxes, as well as enslaved people, from the areas they conquered. Tax contracts were sold to people called **publicans** (pub' luh kuhnz). They paid Rome ahead of time for the contracts. Then, they collected taxes from the conquered people. The amount of taxes collected was supposed to be no more than 10 percent above the price paid for the contract. Most publicans, however, made extra money.

Sculpture of Roman Consul

L2 Critical Thinking Write two columns on the chalkboard headed *Economic Changes*, and *Political Changes*. Ask students to take turns writing their ideas of these changes that took place during the Roman expansion in the appropriate columns. Tell students to choose one of the changes that occurred and write a newspaper editorial giving their opinion about it. Encourage volunteers to share their editorials with the class.

GEOGRAPHY AND HISTORY

The technique of people burning their own fields and crops in the path of an invading army is known as a scorched-earth policy. It has been used for centuries by many societies.

DID YOU KNOW

In the ancient Roman apartment buildings, five or six people lived in one room.

VIDEODISC

Use the following to enrich Chapter 14.

WH E 70 14314

Mosaic depicting Roman plantation life in North Africa.

EXTENDING THE CONTENT

Enslaved persons' lives varied dramatically in the Roman Republic.

Those who worked in mines or quarries, or who rowed in the galleys of the navy, lived under brutal conditions. In contrast, educated Greeks taken prisoner might become tutors or stewards in wealthy households, leading lives more comfortable than those of free peasants. One estimate places the number of enslaved persons at one-fourth of the Italian population during Augustus's time.

CAPTION ANSWER

in wooden apartment buildings six or more stories high

MAKING CONNECTIONS

➤➤ **Economics** The provinces rebelled against high taxes causing Roman legions to be permanently stationed in most provinces. Because putting down revolts cost Rome troops and money, the provinces began to strain Rome's resources.

DID YOU KNOW ??

Roman camps were almost always rectangular with an entrance gate on each of the four sides. Tents were set up in street-like rows that were laid out in straight lines and crossed each other at right angles. At the signal of a trumpet, the camps could be broken up quickly.

ROMAN APARTMENTS Wealthy Romans built brick and stone apartments. They decorated the floors with mosaics and the walls with paintings. These apartment dwellers owned only a few pieces of furniture, most of which were simple in design. **What sort of buildings did poor Romans live in during the Republic?**

By about 135 B.C., Rome was in a great deal of trouble. Because farmers had lost their land, they had also lost their economic and political independence. Merchants had become poorer because rich Romans could get luxuries elsewhere. Artisans had lost business because rich Romans wanted goods from Greece and Syria. Government officials were too busy getting rich to worry about solving the republic's problems.

The gap between rich and poor grew greater. The poor hated the rich for what the rich had done to them. The rich hated and feared the poor. Rome was no longer politically stable.

Section 4 Review

1. **Define:** latifundias, publicans
2. How was Roman agriculture influenced by Hannibal?
3. What problems faced Roman farmers in the city?
4. What was life like in Rome during the decline of the Republic?

Critical Thinking

5. Why might a large gap between rich and poor present problems for an empire?

SECTION 4 ANSWERS

1. latifundias, large estates (p. 225); publicans, Roman tax collectors (p. 226)
2. Roman farmers burned their fields and crops. After the Second Punic War, most farmers did not have money to restore the land, so latifundias appeared, which produced cash crops. Farmers were replaced by enslaved people.
3. crowded apartment buildings without water or sewer connections, diseases, and few jobs
4. Life was hard for most farmers, merchants, and artisans. Government officials became rich and the gap between rich and poor grew greater.
5. Answers will vary but students might indicate that when the gap becomes large there is less chance of unity in a civilization.

Assign Chapter 14 **Section 4 Quiz** in the TCR. Testmaker available.

Section 5

ROMAN LEADERSHIP

Over the next 100 years, many different popular leaders tried to improve conditions in Rome. Some were reformers, while others were generals.

The Reformers Tiberius Sempronius Gracchus (tī bir' ē uhs sem prō nē uhs grak' uhs) was the first reformer. He thought making small farmers leave their land had caused Rome's troubles.

When he became a tribune in 133 B.C., Tiberius Gracchus wanted to limit the amount of land a person could own. He wanted to divide up public lands and give them to the poor. Another tribune vetoed his idea. Tiberius Gracchus then talked the assembly into putting his idea into effect and getting rid of that tribune.

Tiberius Gracchus ran for a second term as tribune, although it was against the law. To stop him, the Senate staged a riot and had him and hundreds of his followers killed.

In 123 B.C., Tiberius Gracchus's younger brother Gaius (gī' yuhs) Sempronius Gracchus was elected tribune. He thought moving the poor from the city back to the countryside was the answer to Rome's troubles.

Gaius Gracchus improved and extended the reforms of his brother. He had the government take over the sale of wheat and sell it to the poor below market price. Soon, however, wheat was being given away rather than sold. Nearly one out of every three Romans was receiving free wheat. Meanwhile, the Senate began to feel threatened by some of Gaius Gracchus's ideas and in 121 B.C. had him killed.

Sculpture of Tiberius Gracchus

The Generals After the reformers came the generals. In 107 B.C., General Gaius Marius (mar' ē uhs), a military hero, became consul. The son of a day laborer, Marius was the first lower-class Roman to be elected to such a high office. He was supported by many ex-soldiers who felt the rich and the government had taken advantage of them. Many of the ex-soldiers had been farmers who had lost their farms when they left to serve in the army.

Marius thought he could end Rome's troubles by setting up a professional army. Until this time, only property owners could become legionaries. Marius opened the army to everyone. He convinced the poor to join by offering them pay, land, pensions, and *booty,* or things taken from the enemy in war. Marius's plan helped Rome by providing jobs for many out-of-work Romans. At the same time, it hurt the Roman Republic. Instead of giving loyalty to the government, the soldiers gave it to the general who hired and paid them.

Painting of Gaius Marius

L1 **Critical Thinking** Help students create cause-event-effects graphic organizers on the chalkboard showing the attempts made by reformers and generals to improve conditions in Rome. Create an organizer for each reformer or general. LEP

DID YOU KNOW ??

During their terms of office, tribunes could not be away from the city for even one night. They also had to always keep their doors open so that citizens could come to them for help.

COOPERATIVE LEARNING

Organize the class into eight groups. Assign each group one of the following Roman leaders: Tiberius Gracchus, Gaius Marius, Lucius Cornelius Sulla, Pompey, Julius Caesar, Mark Antony, and Octavian.

Tell each group to research its assigned leader and write a list of five or six questions, along with the leader's responses, to be used in an interview for a talk show titled "Roman Forum." Then have two members of each group role-play the part of their group's leader and the part of the talk show host of "Roman Forum."

Assign Chapter 14 **Cooperative Learning Activity** in the TCR.

MAKING CONNECTIONS

➤➤ **History** Before he became dictator, Sulla began a reign of terror in Rome. He killed everyone in Rome who had opposed—either directly or indirectly—his entrance.

INDEPENDENT PRACTICE

L2 **Critical Thinking** Have students write two problem-solving questions about the map "The Expansion of the Roman Empire." Then have students work in pairs to exchange and answer one another's questions.

Assign Chapter 14 **Geography and Map Activity** in the TCR.

MAP STUDY

Answer

44 B.C.

Marius was opposed by another general, Lucius Cornelius Sulla (kor nēl' yuhs suhl' uh). Sulla had been given a military command that Marius wanted. Marius tried to get the assembly to take the command away from Sulla and give it to him. An angry Sulla marched his army on Rome and seized the city. It was the first time a Roman commander had led his soldiers against the capital.

Civil war broke out. When it was over, Sulla made himself **dictator** (dik' tā tuhr), or absolute ruler, of Rome. Sulla believed the way to end Rome's troubles was to increase the power of the Senate. So, he doubled the Senate's size. He gave the senators more duties and weakened the power of the tribunes. At the same time, he stopped generals from holding the same army command for more than one year at a time.

MAP STUDY

REGION Rome gained control of the Italian Peninsula in 275 B.C. **By what year did the Roman Republic expand to include Gaul?**

Julius Caesar

When Sulla retired, a new group of generals fought for control of Rome. In 60 B.C., political power passed to a **triumvirate** (trī um' vuhr it), or a group of three persons with equal power. This First Triumvirate was made up of Marcus

The Expansion of the Roman Republic

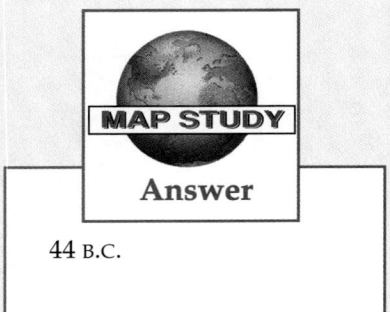

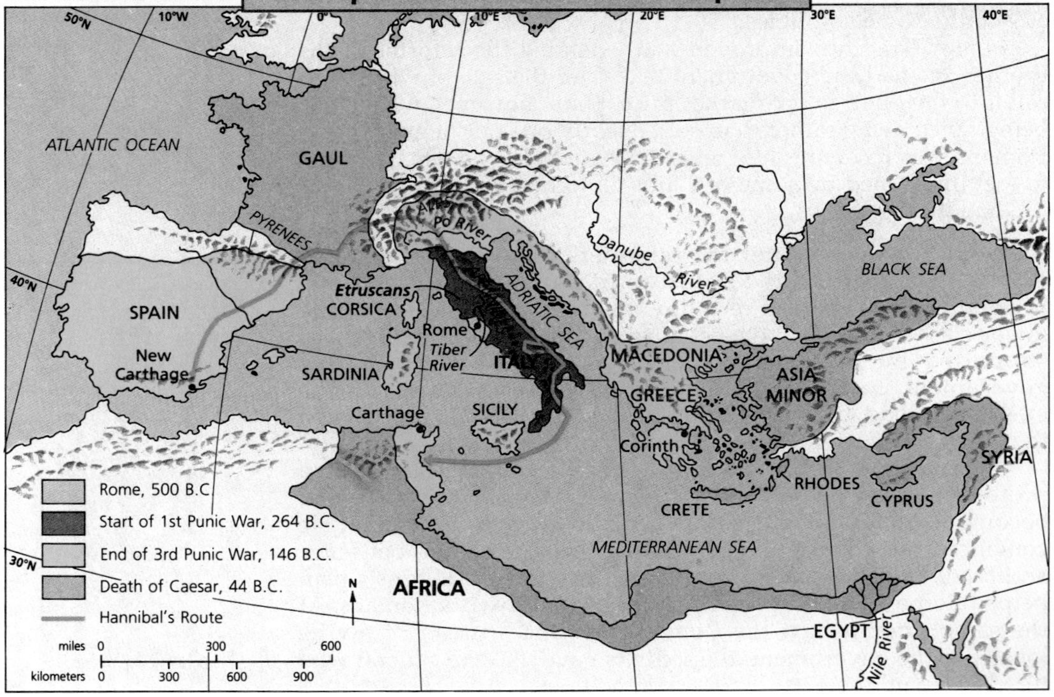

MULTICULTURAL PERSPECTIVES

The writers of *The Federalists,* a series of articles published in the 1780s supporting the U.S. Constitution, admired Roman republican principles. They considered a single executive officer—a president—as preferable to the "instances of mischief to the republic" such as had been caused by disagreements between consuls and tribunes in ancient Rome.

Licinius Crassus (mar' kus luh sin' ē uhs kras' us), Gnaeus Pompeius (guh nā' uhs pom pē' uhs), and Julius Caesar (jūl' yuhs sē' zuhr). Pompeius, who was also known as Pompey (pom' pē), and Caesar had different ideas about how Rome should be ruled. Pompey believed in a republic that was ruled by upper-class senators. Caesar believed in one-man rule.

After Crassus's death, the two remaining rulers fought for power. Caesar finally gained control after Pompey was murdered in 48 B.C. Caesar was a well-educated politician who had become a soldier. He had both military strength and strong family alliances to back him.

Painting of Julius Caesar

In 58 B.C., Caesar was named governor of a Roman province. There, he built up a large, strong army that was loyal to him. Within seven years, he conquered what is now northern France and Belgium (bel' juhm) and invaded Britain. The Senate began to fear he was growing too strong. So, in 50 B.C., it ordered Caesar to break up his legions and return to Rome. Instead, Caesar entered the city at the head of his troops. By 46 B.C., he was dictator of Rome.

Caesar brought about many reforms. He redistributed state lands in Italy and founded new colonies overseas. This gave land to thousands of ex-soldiers who had none. He began such public works projects as building roads and buildings and draining the marshes around Rome. This gave jobs to thousands of Romans who had not been able to find work. He planned and paid for gladiatorial games that were free to the public. This kept the poor and the idle from turning into unhappy and angry mobs. He doubled the size of the Senate. Although this made each senator less powerful, it gave business people a chance to become senators. He cut back the activities of the publicans. He gave Roman citizenship to Greeks, Spaniards, and Gauls. He adopted a new calendar based on the Egyptian calendar. Called the Julian (jūl' yuhn) calendar, a form of it is still in use today.

Caesar did a great deal for Rome and its people. Still, some Romans were afraid that Caesar planned to make himself king. About 60 men, most of them senators, worked out a plan to kill him. As he entered the Senate on the Ides (ī dz) of March, or March 15, 44 B.C., Caesar was stabbed to death.

End of the Republic Angered by Caesar's death, the Roman people turned against those who had killed him. Political power passed to another triumvirate. Marcus Antonius (an tō' nē uhs), or Mark Antony, Caesar's closest follower and a popular general, took command of Rome's territories in the East. Octavian (ok tā' vē uhn), Caesar's grand-nephew and adopted son, took charge of the West. Marcus Aemilius Lepidus (uh mēl' ē uhs lep'uhd uhs), one of Caesar's top officers, took over the rule of Africa. All three shared control of the Italian homeland.

Sculpture of Octavian

L3 **Language Arts** Have students research the meaning and significance of Caesar's remark, *"Veni, vidi, vici," (I came, I saw, I conquered.)* concerning one of his campaigns against Pompey. Then have them write a brief explanation of what this tells them about Caesar's personality.

MAKING CONNECTIONS

➤➤ **History** Caesar followed Pompey to Egypt where he met Cleopatra, the sister of the Egyptian king and co-ruler of Egypt. Caesar helped Cleopatra take full control of the Egyptian throne.

LINKING PAST TO PRESENT

Probably the most widely read Latin work in modern times is Julius Caesar's Commentaries on the Gallic Wars—*Commentarii de Bello Gallico.* Many first- or second-year Latin students today read at least part of this Latin classic.

MEETING SPECIAL NEEDS

Read brief portions of Shakespeare's *Julius Caesar* to auditory learners. Have students work as individuals or in small groups to present dramatic readings of *Julius Caesar* to the class.

ASSESS

CHECK FOR UNDERSTANDING

Ask students to summarize the main points of the chapter, orally or in writing. Discuss the answers to the Section and Chapter Review questions.

EVALUATE

Assign Chapter 14 **Performance Assessment Activity** in the TCR.

Administer **Chapter 14 Test** in the TCR. Testmaker available.

CHAPTER 15 The Roman Empire

CHAPTER ORGANIZER

Objectives	Special Features	Supplemental Materials
Section 1 The Rule of Augustus Explain how Augustus ruled the Roman Empire.		• Reproducible Lesson Plan • Section 1 Quiz • Testmaker • Chapter 15 Vocabulary and Guided Reading Activity • World Art and History Transparency 6
Section 2 Pax Romana Analyze what happened to trade and law during the *Pax Romana.*		• Reproducible Lesson Plan • Section 2 Quiz • Testmaker • Chapter 15 Cooperative Learning Activity • Chapter 15 Geography and Map Activity • Chapter 15 Activity Book Activity
Section 3 Daily Life Describe what daily life was like during the *Pax Romana.*		• Reproducible Lesson Plan • Section 3 Quiz • Testmaker • Unit 5 Primary Source Reading • Foods Around the World • Chapter 15 Teaching Transparencies and Activities • The Western Civilization Videodisc
Section 4 Fall of the Empire Summarize why the Roman Empire declined and what attempts were made to save the empire from collapse.	People in History: *Lady Murasaki,* p. 242	• Reproducible Lesson Plan • Section 4 Quiz • Testmaker • Chapter 15 Chart and Graph Skill Activity • Reinforcing Social Studies Skills, pp. 17, 20, 22 • The Western Civilization Videodisc
Chapter 15 Review and Evaluation		• Chapter 15 Reteaching Activity • Chapter 15 Enrichment Activity • Spanish Summary and Glossary • Audiocassettes (English and Spanish) • Chapter 15 Performance Assessment Activity • Chapter 15 Test • Testmaker

If time does not permit teaching the entire chapter, use the Chapter 15 Summary on page 244 and the Chapter 15 Audiocassettes (English and Spanish) to point out the main ideas of the chapter.

✓ Performance Assessment Activities

Daily Life The public bath was central to Roman life. Remains of Roman baths can be found throughout Europe. Have students research and prepare a presentation on one of the most elaborate public baths, the Baths of Caracalla. Students should write a detailed description and include information on what part the baths played in Roman life. Encourage them to provide illustrations or diagrams.

Mathematics Have students prepare a chart of Arabic numerals (1 through 15, then 20, 30, 40, 50, 60, 70, 80, 90, 100, 500, and 1,000), the corresponding Roman numerals, and the Latin names for the numerals. Have students research how Romans performed mathematical calculations using their numerals, and write a few problems for other students to solve.

CHAPTER RESOURCES

LITERATURE ABOUT THE PERIOD

Grant, Michael. *Greek and Latin Authors, 800 B.C.-A.D. 1000.* H.W. Wilson Co., 1980. Biographical sketches of Greek and Latin authors and bibliographies of their works from 800 B.C.-A.D. 1000.

Payne, Robert. *Ancient Rome.* American Heritage, 1970. History from the Etruscans to A.D. 476, with a chapter on the legacy of Rome.

READINGS FOR THE STUDENT

Dillon, Eilis. *Rome Under the Emperors.* Thomas Nelson, 1975. Views of Roman society and family life in the time of Trajan, as seen by young people of four different families and social classes—a patrician senator, a newly rich businessman, a prosperous farmer, and a stallholder in the Roman marketplace.

Foster, Genevieve. *Augustus Caesar's World.* Scribner's Sons, 1947. Classic history of Augustus's time.

READINGS FOR THE TEACHER

Carcopino, Jerome. *Daily Life in Ancient Rome.* Yale University Press, 1940. Discusses social conditions in Roman society.

Fagg, Christopher. *Ancient Rome.* Warwick Press, 1978. Examines the Roman Empire from its beginnings through its decline.

Gibbon, Edward. *The Portable Gibbon: The Decline and Fall of the Roman Empire.* Viking, 1965. Consists of a reading of the work on the decline of the Roman Empire.

MULTIMEDIA RESOURCES

Ancient Rome. Society for Visual Education. 4 filmstrips. Discusses Rome's historical developments, political events, leaders, and culture.

The Romans. Interact/SSSS. Simulation. Cooperative exercises on Roman daily life.

The Romans. International Film Bureau. Film. Discusses the origins, growth, and eventual fall of the Roman Empire.

The Romans: Life, Laughter, and the Law. Learning Corporation of America/SSSS. Video. Dramatizations explain the legal system of the Roman Empire.

INTRODUCE

CHAPTER 15 OVERVIEW

Chapter 15 describes the history of the Roman Empire from the rule of Augustus to the fall of Rome.

➤ **Section 1** summarizes the rule of Augustus.
➤ **Section 2** describes Roman contributions to trade and law during the *Pax Romana.*
➤ **Section 3** discusses the daily life of Romans during the *Pax Romana.*
➤ **Section 4** analyzes the political, economic, and social factors behind the fall of the Roman Empire.

CHAPTER OBJECTIVES

After reading Chapter 15, your students will be able to:

1. explain how Augustus ruled the Roman Empire.
2. analyze what happened to trade and law during the *Pax Romana.*
3. describe what daily life was like during the *Pax Romana.*
4. summarize why the Roman Empire declined.
5. discuss what attempts were made to save the Roman Empire from collapse.

EXAMINING THE ILLUSTRATION

Ask students where they go to watch their favorite sporting event? Ask if they know what sports the ancient Romans enjoyed watching? Explain many Roman sports events, which they will be reading more about, were held in the Colosseum shown here.

PERFORMANCE ASSESSMENT ✓

Use the Performance Assessment activities on page 232B to help you evaluate students as they complete the chapter.

CHAPTER 15 The Roman Empire

Roman Colosseum

232

TEACHER CLASSROOM RESOURCES

- Reproducible Lesson Plan
- Section Quizzes/Chapter Test
- Activity Book Activity
- Enrichment Activity
- Chart and Graph Skill Activity
- Geography and Map Activity
- Vocabulary and Guided Reading Activity
- Cooperative Learning Activity
- Unit 5 Primary Source Reading
- Performance Assessment Activity
- Teaching Transparencies and Activities
- Spanish Summary and Glossary
- Testmaker
- Audiocassettes (English and Spanish)
- The Western Civilization Videodisc

Chapter Focus

READ TO DISCOVER:

- How Augustus ruled the Roman Empire.
- What happened to trade and law during the *Pax Romana.*
- What daily life was like during the *Pax Romana.*
- Why the Roman Empire declined.
- What attempts were made to save the empire from collapse.

27 B.C.–410 A.D.

KEY TERMS

- emperor
- freedmen
- census
- tariffs
- *juris prudentes*
- *domus*
- gladiators
- inflation
- barter

In 27 B.C., Octavian told the Senate that he had restored the republic. When he offered to give up his job, the Senate gave him several offices. It named him *princeps* (prin' sepz), or "first citizen." It also called him *Pater Patriae* (pah' tuhr pah' trē ī), the "Father of the Country." He took for himself the title of Augustus (ah guhs' tuhs), or "revered one." That is what he is generally called in history books. In practice, Octavian then became the first Roman **emperor,** or absolute ruler of an empire.

Section 1

THE RULE OF AUGUSTUS

Augustus was a clever politician. He held the offices of consul, tribune, high priest, and senator all at the same time. However, he refused to be crowned emperor. Augustus knew that most Romans would not accept one-person rule unless it took the form of a republic.

Augustus kept the assemblies and government officials of the republic. He was careful to make senators feel honored. He talked of tradition and the need to bring back "old Roman virtues." He made the official religion important once again.

At the same time, Augustus strengthened his authority in two ways. First, he had every soldier swear allegiance to him personally. This gave him control of the armies. Second, he built up his imperial household to take charge of the daily business of

FOCUS

BELLRINGER

Write the following on the chalkboard: *"All roads lead to Rome."* Ask students to write a few sentences explaining what they think the quote means.

MOTIVATIONAL ACTIVITY

Discuss student's responses to the quote, *"All roads lead to Rome." (Rome was the center of the empire.)* Then read the following quotation from *Concerning the Soul,* c. A.D. 180, by the Latin author Tertullian who lived during the *Pax Romana: "Everywhere roads are built . . . Wherever there is a trace of life, there are houses and human inhabitants, well-ordered governments, and civilized life."* Focus discussion on what kind of empire the quote describes. Tell students that they will learn more about the Roman Empire in this chapter.

VOCABULARY PRE-CHECK

Write the key terms for this chapter on the chalkboard. Ask a volunteer to read each aloud as other students predict their meanings and use the words in a sentence.

Assign Chapter 15 **Vocabulary and Guided Reading Activity** in the TCR.

EXTRA CREDIT PROJECT

Suggest interested students research and collect information about the eruption of Mt. Vesuvius. Have students prepare a news report broadcast of the eruption as if they were present in Pompeii that day, but escaped. Encourage students to include a visual component to their news report and share their presentation with the class.

KEY TO ABILITY LEVELS

Teaching strategies have been coded for varying learning styles and abilities.

L1 Level 1 activities are **basic** activities and should be within the ability range of all students.

L2 Level 2 activities are **average** activities and should be within the ability range of the average to above-average student.

L3 Level 3 activities are **challenging** activities designed for the ability range of above-average students.

LEP LEP activities should be within the ability range of Limited English Proficiency students.

TEACH

GUIDED PRACTICE

L1 **Geography: Place** Display a wall map of Western Europe and North Africa to point out the natural barriers that Augustus used to round out the Roman Empire—the Rhine and Danube rivers, the Atlantic Ocean, and the Sahara. Discuss why these barriers made the empire easy to defend. LEP

L3 **Critical Thinking** Work with students to create a graphic organizer of contributions to the Roman Empire by Augustus Caesar. Discuss how these interrelated contributions helped to establish the *Pax Romana.*

DID YOU KNOW ??

According to the New Testament, it was during the census ordered by Augustus Caesar that Joseph and Mary, the mother and father of Jesus on whom Christianity is based, traveled to Nazareth.

LINKING PAST TO PRESENT

The dome of the Pantheon was the largest built in ancient times. It has been copied for many public buildings throughout the world, including the Capitol in Washington, D.C.

VIDEODISC

Use the following to enrich Chapter 15.

WC B 136 11852
The Via Appia (Appian Way) just outside Rome.

Sculpture of Caesar Augustus

government. He chose people because of their talent rather than their birth. This gave enslaved people and **freedmen,** or former enslaved people, a chance to be part of the government.

Augustus wanted boundaries that would be easy to defend. So, he rounded out the empire to natural frontiers—the Rhine (rīn) and Danube (dan′ yūb) rivers in the north, the Atlantic Ocean in the west, and the Sahara in the south—and stationed soldiers there.

Augustus was not interested in gaining new territory for Rome. Instead, he worked on governing the existing empire. He gave provincial governors long terms of office. This allowed them to gain experience in their jobs. He also paid them large salaries. In this way, they would not feel the need to overtax the people or keep public money for themselves. To make sure that people did not pay too little or too much tax, Augustus ordered a **census** (sen′ suhs), or population count, to be taken from time to time.

Augustus also made Rome more beautiful. He wrote strict laws to govern the way people behaved in public. He protected the city by setting up a fire brigade and a police force. He encouraged learning by building Rome's first library.

Augustus ruled for 41 years. During that time, he brought peace to Rome. He also gave the Romans a new sense of patriotism and pride. He made Roman citizenship available to people in the provinces. Most important, however, he reorganized the government of Rome so that it ran well for more than 200 years.

Section 1 Review

1. **Identify:** Augustus
2. **Define:** emperor, freedmen, census
3. Why did Augustus refuse to be crowned emperor?
4. How did Augustus make Rome like a republic?

Critical Thinking

5. Which of Augustus's improvements of Rome do you think was most important? Explain.

Section 2 PAX ROMANA

The peace that Augustus brought to Rome was called the *Pax Romana* (pahks rō mah′ nah). It lasted for 200 years. Of course, revolts and other problems were not unknown during this time. For the most part, however, Rome and its people prospered. Civilization spread, and cultures mixed.

SECTION 1 ANSWERS

1. Augustus, first Roman emperor (p. 233)
2. emperor, absolute ruler (p. 233); freedmen, former enslaved people (p. 234); census, population count (p. 234)
3. He knew most Romans would not accept one-person rule unless it was in a republic.
4. He kept the assemblies and government officials, made senators feel honored, talked of tradition and the need to bring back "old Roman virtues," and made the official religion important again.
5. Answers will vary but students should explain their choices.

Assign Chapter 15 **Section 1 Quiz** in the TCR. Testmaker available.

Trade With peace came increased trade. The same coins were used throughout the empire. There were no **tariffs** (tar′ ifz), or taxes placed on goods brought into the country. Goods and money moved freely along the trade routes. The Mediterranean was cleared of pirates, making it safe for trade and travel. Shipping became a big business. Every summer, hundreds of ships carried grain from North Africa to Italy. Other ships bound for Rome were loaded with cargoes of brick, marble, granite, and wood to be used for building. Luxury items, such as amber from the north and silk from China, passed overland across Roman roads.

Increased trade meant more business for Romans. The city hummed. Shopkeepers grew richer. Wine and olive oil were the main items bought by other countries. Italy became a manufacturing center for pottery, bronze, and woolen cloth.

Law During the *Pax Romana,* Roman law went through major changes. Because the times were different, the laws first set down

MAP STUDY

PLACE The Roman Empire had been divided into the Western Roman Empire and the Eastern Roman Empire. **What empire did Italy belong to? What empire did Greece belong to?**

The Expansion of the Roman Empire

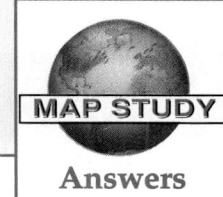

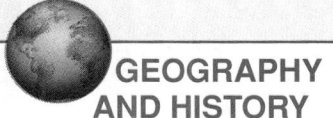

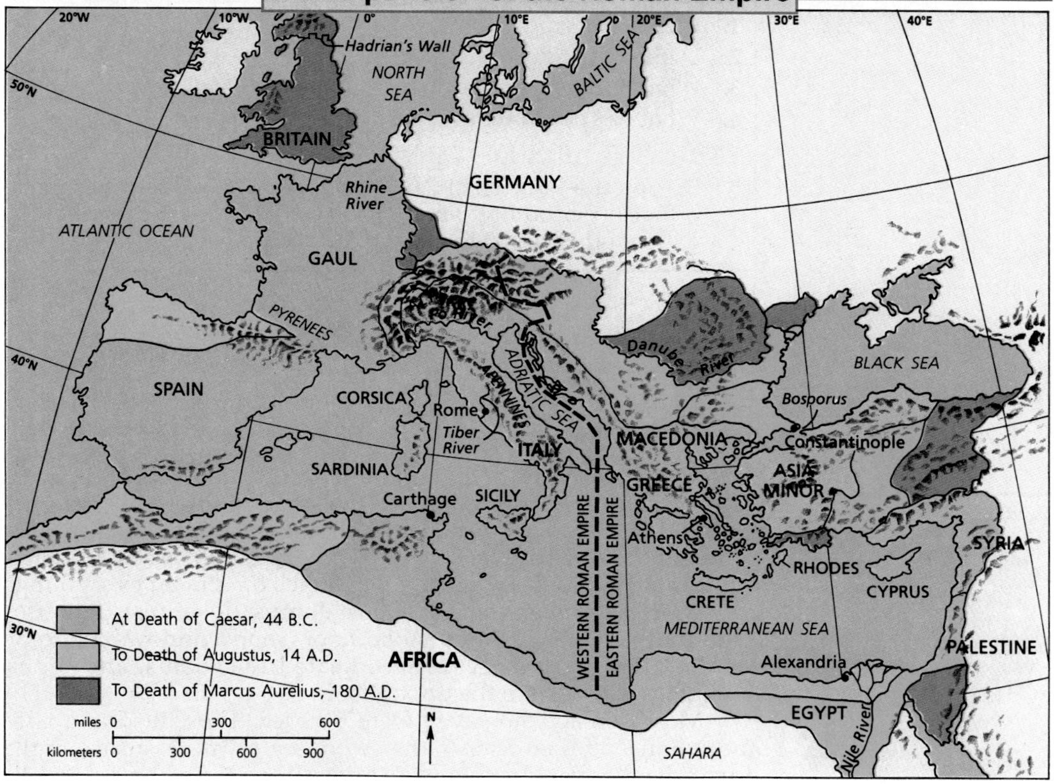

L2 **Map Skills** Have students refer to the map on this page to identify the regions in which the empire expanded. *(Western Europe, Middle East, North Africa)* What sea did most Roman land border? *(Mediterranean)* Have students use the map scale to calculate the distance of the farthest point of the empire from the city of Rome. *(about 1,800 miles, or 2,896 km)*

Assign the Chapter 15 **Geography and Map Activity** in the TCR.

MAP STUDY Answers

Western Roman Empire; Eastern Roman Empire

MAKING CONNECTIONS

➤➤ **Architecture** Augustus supported the construction of so many public buildings that it is said "he found Rome a city of brick and left it a city of marble."

GEOGRAPHY AND HISTORY

The voyage between North Africa and Rome took about two months. Grain ships also carried passengers, sometimes as many as 600.

COOPERATIVE LEARNING

Assign students to groups to research specific areas of culture during the *Pax Romana.* Divide each topic into smaller areas to be covered by individuals in each group. Groups should decide how to organize their reports into coordinated presentations. The following topics might be suggested: Roman daily life (food, housing, amusements, household duties, women's lives, education); philosophy (ideas of citizenship, justice, religion); language and literature (Romance languages, specific poets or historians); or architecture (Roman roads, the arch in architecture).

Assign Chapter 15 **Cooperative Learning Activity** in the TCR.

L1 **Economics** During the *Pax Romana* many changes took place in trade in the Roman Empire. This affected more people than those who actually carried goods to other markets. Using student volunteers, ask students to list on the chalkboard all people and/or occupations that were affected by the increase in Roman trade.

L3 **Critical Thinking** Ask students why they think a period of peace and stability, such as the *Pax Romana* would encourage great achievements.

MAKING CONNECTIONS

➤➤ **Civics** Under the *Pax Romana,* the law considered everyone who lived within the empire as Roman, and therefore equal, without regard to nationality or race.

LINKING PAST TO PRESENT

Roman law influenced law in Europe and the Americas in both principles and language. For hundreds of years, Latin was used in law courts even though it was no longer everyday speech. Today, nearly all the words relating to legal matters are Latin or Latin derivatives.

on the Twelve Tables were changed. When Rome conquered a new territory, Roman merchants had to do business with non-Romans. Roman judges had to write new laws that would be as fair to non-Romans as to Romans. The Roman judges were helped by special lawyers and legal writers called ***juris prudentes*** (jū' ruhs prū' duhntz).

After a while, the judges and their helpers developed certain principles of law that were fair to everyone. A law was believed to be just because it was reasonable, not because the government had the power to make people obey it. Everyone was considered equal before the law. A person was innocent until proven guilty.

By about 125 A.D., Roman law was *standardized.* This meant that legal procedures were the same in all parts of the empire. This helped Rome govern a large area successfully. In later years, Roman legal principles formed the basis for the laws of most western countries and of the Christian church.

Section 2 Review

1. **Identify**: *Pax Romana*
2. **Define:** tariffs, *juris prudentes*
3. What happened to trade during the *Pax Romana?*
4. What happened to law during the *Pax Romana?*

Critical Thinking

5. Do you think the term *Pax Romana* was a good term for this 200-year period in Roman history or would you describe it with another term? Explain.

Section 3 DAILY LIFE

Painting of Roman Couple

In the early years of the empire, about 1 million people lived in Rome. It suffered from many of the same problems as cities of today. There was too little housing. The air was polluted. There was crime in the streets. The cost of living was high. Many Romans could not find jobs and had to pay taxes on almost everything.

A rich person in Rome lived in a **domus** (dō' muhs), or house, with marble walls, colored stone floors, and windows made of small panes of glass. A furnace heated the rooms, and pipes brought water even to the upper floors.

Most Romans, however, were not rich. They lived in apartment houses called *islands* that were six or more stories high. Each island covered an entire block. At one time, there were 26

SECTION 2 ANSWERS

1. *Pax Romana,* time of peace (p. 234)
2. tariffs, taxes placed on goods brought into the country (p. 235), *juris prudentes*, special lawyers (p. 236)
3. It increased.
4. Certain principles of fairness were developed including that everyone is equal before the law and that a person is considered innocent until proven guilty. By about A.D. 125 the law was standardized.
5. Answers will vary but could note because it was a time that Rome prospered, few battles took place, civilization spread, and cultures mixed.

Assign Chapter 15 **Section 2 Quiz** in the TCR. Testmaker available.

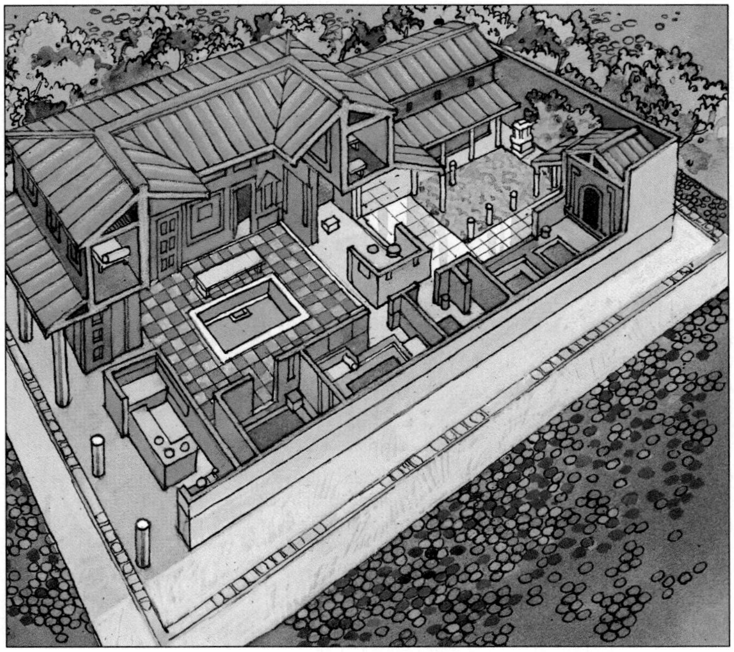

This is a typical floor plan of a *domus.* **What class of Romans would live in a house such as this?**

blocks of islands for every private house in Rome. The ground floor of most islands was given over to shops. These opened onto the street from large arched doorways.

Rents were high in Rome. They varied according to the apartment floor—the higher up the apartment, the lower the rent.

The Family In Rome, the family was all-important. The father was head of the household. His word was law. He arranged the children's marriages to improve social position or to increase wealth. Cousins were expected to help one another politically.

Until they were 12 years old, most Roman boys and girls went to school together. Then, the sons of poor families went to work, while the sons of rich families began their formal education. They studied reading, grammar, writing, music, geometry, commercial arithmetic, and shorthand. When they were 15 years old, they entered a school of *rhetoric* (ret' uhr ik), or speech and writing, to prepare for a political career. Some went to schools in Athens or Alexandria for philosophy or medicine.

Girls received a different kind of education. When they were 12 years old, their formal education stopped. Instead of going to school, the daughters of the rich were given private lessons at

L2 **Daily Life** Have students assume the role of one ancient Roman and write a first-person narrative of a typical day. Students might choose to be a Roman legionary, a shopkeeper, a senator, a public official in the provinces, an enslaved person, or a gladiator. After researching, students should relate details of the person's occupational functions and responsibilities, together with details of his or her family and social life.

CAPTION ANSWER

wealthy people

LINKING PAST TO PRESENT

In 46 B.C. Julius Caesar ordered the calendar revised. His so-called Julian calendar fixed the length of the year at 365 days with 12 months of 30 or 31 days except for February (29 days). He named one of the months Julius (now July) after himself. Later, Augustus lengthened his month, August, to 31 days by taking one day from February (leaving it 28 days). In A.D. 1582 Pope Gregory XIII formalized the system of leap years we know today.

MEETING SPECIAL NEEDS

Have students who are visual learners work in small groups to write the front page of a Roman newspaper reporting the fall of the Roman Empire. The front pages should include headlines, illustrations, and three or more articles. The political and economic reasons for the empire's decline, and the impact of foreign enemies on the empire are possible story topics. Each member of the group should be given a specific task in completing the newspaper page.

VIDEODISC

Use the following to enrich Chapter 15.

WC B 128 11844

Roman women athletes.

MAKING CONNECTIONS

➤➤ **Daily Life** The father of a Roman household conducted religious rituals in the home, controlled property, and had the power to sell family members into enslavement or kill them.

CAPTION ANSWER

the Roman government

DID YOU KNOW ??

In ancient Rome the handkerchief was a status symbol, since only wealthy Romans could afford the precious white linen. Originally the handkerchief was used to wipe away perspiration, but later it was used to wave as a way of voting life or death for a defeated gladiator.

VIDEODISC

Use the following to enrich Chapter 15.

WC B 120 11836
Three gladiators.

WC B 127 11843
Roman baths at Bath, Somerset, England.

CHARIOT RACE A favorite entertainment of the Romans was chariot racing. Thousands of spectators would gather to watch the chariots race around an oval track. **Who staged the public games during the empire?**

home. As a result, many Roman women were as well as or better informed than Roman men. Some women worked in or owned small shops. Wealthy women had enslaved people to do their housework. This left them free to study the arts, literature, and fashions, or to ride chariots in the countryside for a day's *pig-sticking,* or a type of hunt.

At Leisure At home, the Romans enjoyed gambling with dice. They met friends at public bathhouses where they could take warm, cold, or steam baths. The bathhouses of Rome, however, provided more than baths. Some had gymnasiums, sports stadiums, and libraries. There, the Romans could watch or play games. They also could listen to lectures, see musical shows, exercise, or just sit and talk.

The Romans had no team sports to watch. Instead, they flocked to see free public games, which often ran from dawn to dusk. Under the republic, the games had generally been staged by politicians who were looking for votes. Under the empire, the games were staged by the government. The games included circuses, chariot races, and gladiatorial games. The most exciting chariot races were held at the Circus Maximus, an oval arena that could seat more than 200,000 people.

The people who fought animals and one another in arenas were called **gladiators** (glad′ ē ā tuhrz). Most were enslaved people, prisoners of war, criminals, or poor people. They were

MULTICULTURAL PERSPECTIVES

Most men in Rome had three names. The middle name told from which clan a man was descended. The last name told to which branch of the clan he belonged. The first name identified the person. Thus, Caius Julius Caesar was a member of the Caesarian branch of the Julian clan. His personal name was Caius. Unmarried women had two names—the feminine form of their father's middle name, and a last name that indicated chronological rank among the girls of the family. For example, if Caesar had fathered two daughters, the older would have been called Julia Prima and the other Julia Secunda. When a woman married, a form of her husband's last name was added to her other two names.

trained by managers who hired them out. A few gladiators were upper-class Romans who wanted excitement and public attention.

The night before they were to fight, gladiators would appear at a feast. There, they could be looked over by fans and gamblers who wanted to bet on the outcome of a match. When the gladiators entered the arena on the day of the games, they would walk past the emperor's box and say, "Hail Emperor, those who are about to die salute you."

Many gladiators did die. Those whose fighting pleased the crowd became idols of the people. A few won their freedom. Those who gave a poor performance were killed, even if they survived the fight.

All kinds of animals were used in the public games. Some animals pulled chariots or performed tricks. Most, however, fought one another or gladiators. Sometimes, as many as 5,000 wild animals were killed in a single day. In some cases, such as that of the Mesopotamian lion and the North African elephant, whole species were eventually wiped out.

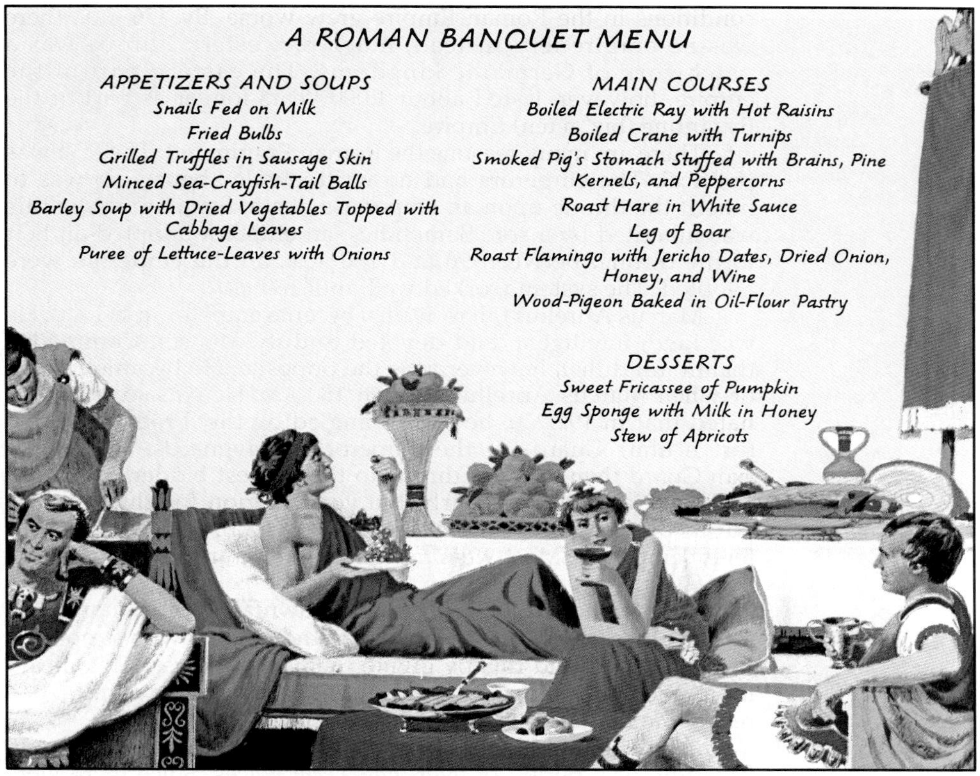

A ROMAN BANQUET MENU

APPETIZERS AND SOUPS
Snails Fed on Milk
Fried Bulbs
Grilled Truffles in Sausage Skin
Minced Sea-Crayfish-Tail Balls
Barley Soup with Dried Vegetables Topped with
Cabbage Leaves
Puree of Lettuce-Leaves with Onions

MAIN COURSES
Boiled Electric Ray with Hot Raisins
Boiled Crane with Turnips
Smoked Pig's Stomach Stuffed with Brains, Pine
Kernels, and Peppercorns
Roast Hare in White Sauce
Leg of Boar
Roast Flamingo with Jericho Dates, Dried Onion,
Honey, and Wine
Wood-Pigeon Baked in Oil-Flour Pastry

DESSERTS
Sweet Fricassee of Pumpkin
Egg Sponge with Milk in Honey
Stew of Apricots

CHAPTER 15 THE ROMAN EMPIRE **239**

DID YOU KNOW

Gladiators who were killed during combat were dragged from the arena by men wearing the mask of an Etruscan demon of the underworld. Those who were victorious fought again, some winning their freedom.

MAKING CONNECTIONS

➤➤ **Culture** All Roman households had a central place to honor the spirits of the hearth and household. The hearth of the home was watched over by the goddess Vesta (or Hestia), spirit of the home fire. Family meals began and ended with thanks to her. A newborn child was carried around the hearth to symbolize becoming part of the family. Lares and Penates were the Roman spirits of everyday things. They came from ancient times when the Romans were mostly farmers. Each family had its own Lar, perhaps the spirit of an ancestor, to guide it. A household had several Penates representing prosperity.

MEETING SPECIAL NEEDS

Have interested students research and present an oral report on Hadrian's Wall built by Romans in northern Britain in the A.D. 120s. Ask students to indicate the location of the wall on a map of Britain.

 VIDEODISC

Use the following to enrich Chapter 15.

WC B 123 11839

A bronze model of a Roman racing chariot.

Teaching

PEOPLE IN HISTORY

LADY MURASAKI

After students have read the People in History feature, ask: For what is Lady Murasaki famous? *(writing the first true novel)* In which country did she live? *(Japan)* How did historians learn so much about Lady Murasaki? *(her own diaries)* How many characters there are in Murasaki's novel, *The Tale of Genji? (around 400)* Around what does Murasaki's novel, *The Tale of Genji* center? *(Prince Genji and the women in his life)*

ANSWERS to Checking for Understanding

1. Chinese and Buddhist writings and Japanese literature
2. from one of the characters in her novel, *The Tale of Genji*
3. because it is an enormous work, divided into 54 episodes; it includes around 400 characters and spans 4 generations of people; the novel deals with the lives and accomplishments of aristocrats; it is beautifully written, using descriptions of nature and human feelings

PEOPLE IN HISTORY

Lady Murasaki

Who was Lady Murasaki? To this day her true identity is not known, but her accomplishment is. It is believed that this lady who lived in Japan during the Roman Empire, wrote the world's first true novel. The people of Japan at this time respected the imperial court of Kyoto with its elaborate rituals. Many were Buddhists.

Born in Japan Lady Murasaki, born in Japan around 976 A.D., was educated in Chinese and Buddhist writings and Japanese literature. Her real name is unknown although it is believed her father was a government official and a poet. The name Murasaki probably came from one of the major characters in her novel, *The Tale of Genji* (jen je).

Much of what is known about Lady Murasaki comes from her own diaries, which she wrote while she served in the court of the empress of Japan. She had been recently widowed when she became a royal lady-in-waiting. Her diaries are included in the book *Diaries of Court Ladies.*

First Known Novel People believe that *The Tale of Genji,* an extremely long tale, was written between the years 1001 and 1010. The novel is divided into 54 episodes, includes around 400 characters, and spans 4 generations. The novel deals with the lives and accomplishments of a group of aristocrats. Specifically, Lady Murasaki's novel centers around Prince Genji and the different women in his life.

The novel is beautifully written, using descriptions of nature and human feelings. This was a new kind of writing for ancient times. Most writing before this dealt with teaching or presenting factual information. *The Tale of Genji* is considered one of the greatest works of Japanese literature.

Checking for Understanding

1. **What did Lady Murasaki's education include?**
2. **Where does Lady Murasaki's name most likely come from?**
3. **Why is *The Tale of Genji* considered to be one of the greatest works of Japanese literature?**

SPOTLIGHT ON: LADY MURASAKI

Murasaki's novel, *The Tale of Genji,* starts with the adventures of Prince Genji and his romances. Genji is gallant and in touch with nature. As the book progresses, Genji's descendants do not follow his sensitive ways and the themes of unrequited love, death, and destruction begin to take over the story. This novel is an example of characters who are portrayed with psychological realism. It wasn't until hundreds of years later that psychological realism was used in western literature.

Diocletian, who was the son of a freedman, ruled from 284 to 305 A.D. He made many changes as emperor. He fortified the frontiers to stop invasions. He reorganized the state and provincial governments to make them work better. To keep prices from rising, he set maximum prices for wages and goods. To make sure goods were produced, he ordered workers to stay in the same jobs until they died. He also made city officials personally responsible for the taxes their communities had to pay.

One of the most important changes Diocletian made concerned the position of the emperor. Diocletian established the official policy of **rule by divine right.** This meant the emperor's powers and right to rule came not from the people but from the gods.

Relief of Diocletian

Diocletian realized the Roman Empire covered too much area for one person to rule well. So, he divided it into two parts. He allowed someone else to govern the western provinces, while he ruled the richer eastern provinces.

In 312 A.D., Constantine I became emperor. He ruled until 337 A.D. Constantine took even firmer control of the empire than Diocletian. To keep people from leaving their jobs when things got bad, he issued several orders. The sons of workers had to follow their fathers' trades. The sons of farmers had to stay and work the land their fathers worked. The sons of ex-soldiers had to serve in the army.

To escape government pressure and control, wealthy landowners moved to their *villas,* or country estates. Most villas were like small, independent cities or kingdoms. Each produced enough food and goods to meet the needs of everyone who lived on the estate.

Despite the changes made by Diocletian and Constantine, the Roman Empire continued to decline in the west. In 330 A.D., Constantine moved the capital from a dying Rome east to the newly built city of Constantinople (kon stan tuh nō′ puhl) in present-day Turkey.

Sculpture of Constantine I

End of the Empire Both Diocletian and Constantine I worked hard to save the Roman Empire. However, neither emperor succeeded in the end.

German attacks increased, especially in western Europe. There, the Germans crossed the Danube River in order to escape from the Huns, nomadic herders who had wandered west from Outer Mongolia in Asia. In 378 A.D., a Germanic group defeated Roman legions at the Battle of Adrianople (ā drē uh nō′ puhl). One reason the Germans were able to defeat the Romans was because of an invention they borrowed from the Huns. This invention was the *iron stirrup.* Using iron stirrups made cavalry stronger than infantry, even the powerful Roman legions. This was because the force of the charging horse was added to the force of the weapon.

L1 **Geography: Human/Environmental Interaction** Have students trace a map of Italy. Ask them to research the Appian Way and other Roman roads and draw these on their maps. Have students include the names of towns or cities connected by the Appian Way and the other Roman roads. LEP

MAKING CONNECTIONS

➤➤ **History** Diocletian hired Germanic soldiers to fill the ranks of the Roman army which had been depleted by plagues and war. As a result, the army no longer was the loyal citizen's army it had been in earlier Roman days.

GEOGRAPHY AND HISTORY

One reason the Huns moved westward into Europe was that the Great Wall, which had been completed by the Chinese emperor Shi Huangdi, prevented the Huns from entering China.

VIDEODISC

Use the following to enrich Chapter 15.

WC B 85 11801
The Emperor Constantine.

WC B 93 11809
A German warrior on horseback.

EXTENDING THE CONTENT

The German invaders did not intend to destroy the Roman Empire. Rather they sought safety from the Huns and a share of farmlands and prosperity within the empire. The Germans included many different groups. The Visigoths crossed the Danube into Romania and won at Adrianople (now Turkey). Thirty years later, the Visigoths asked the Romans for land in Austria. When this was refused, Alaric, their leader, sacked Rome. As the Roman Empire in the West declined, other Germanic groups and kingdoms gained control. They included the Ostrogoths (East Goths), Burgundians, Franks, and Vandals.

ASSESS

CHECK FOR UNDERSTANDING

Ask students to summarize the main points of the chapter. Discuss the answers to Section and Chapter Review questions.

EVALUATE

Assign Chapter 15 **Performance Assessment Activity** in the TCR.

Administer the **Chapter 15 Test** in the TCR. Testmaker available.

RETEACH

Have students work in small groups to list the Roman emperors and their accomplishments.

Assign the Chapter 15 **Reteaching Activity** in the TCR.

ENRICH

Have students imagine they are a friend of a Roman emperor and write a feature describing the most difficult problems that this emperor faced.

Assign Chapter 15 **Enrichment Activity** in the TCR.

CLOSE

Write these headings on the chalkboard: *Trade, Science, Literature, Government, Law, Religion, Entertainment, Military, Architecture.* Have students describe the characteristics of each of these aspects of the *Pax Romana*.

MEETING CHAPTER OBJECTIVES

Each objective is tested by the Review questions in parentheses.

1. Explain Augustus's rule of Rome. (CU 1; CT 1)
2. Analyze trade and law during *Pax Romana*. (CU 2, 3, 4; CT 2)
3. Describe daily life during the *Pax Romana*. (CU 2; CT 3)
4. Summarize why the Roman Empire declined. (BV; CU 6, 7, 8; CT 4)
5. Discuss attempts to save the Empire. (BV; CU 7, 8)

By about 400 A.D., Rome had grown quite weak. In the winter of 406 A.D., the Rhine River froze. Groups of Germans crossed the frozen river and entered Gaul. The Romans were not able to force them back across the border.

In 410 A.D., the Germanic chief Alaric (al' uhr ik) and his soldiers invaded Rome. They burned records and looted the treasury. The Roman Senate told the people, "You can no longer rely on Rome for finance or direction. You are on your own."

Section 4 Review

1. **Identify:** Marcus Aurelius, Praetorian Guard, Diocletian, Constantine I, Adrianople, Alaric
2. **Define:** inflation, barter, rule by divine right
3. What were three major reasons for the fall of the Roman Empire?
4. How did the Germans gain control of the empire?

Critical Thinking

5. What do you think could have been done by either Diocletian or Constantine to save the Roman Empire?

Chapter Summary

1. Octavian, better known as Augustus, became the first emperor of the Roman Empire in 27 B.C.
2. Augustus reorganized the Roman government so well that a period of peace known as the *Pax Romana* existed for more than 200 years.
3. Trade within the empire increased during the *Pax Romana.*
4. During the *Pax Romana*, Roman law had many changes until it was standardized about 125 A.D.
5. During the *Pax Romana,* about one million people lived in Rome, where they suffered from such problems as overcrowding, pollution, crime, and unemployment.
6. Whether rich or poor, most Roman children went to school until they were at least 12 years old.
7. The Roman government staged free public games, such as gladiator fights, to entertain the people.
8. The major reasons for the fall of the Roman Empire were the lack of a formal rule concerning who was to inherit the throne, inflation, and attacks by Germanic invaders.
9. Two emperors, Diocletian and Constantine I, tried to save the Roman Empire from collapse, but neither succeeded in the end.
10. In 410 A.D., Rome fell to Germanic invaders.

SECTION 4 ANSWERS

1. Marcus Aurelius, emperor (p. 240); Praetorian Guard, emperor's bodyguards (p. 240); Diocletian, emperor (p. 241); Constantine I, (p. 241); Adrianople, battle site (p. 243); Alaric, Germanic chief (p. 244)
2. inflation, increasing prices (p. 240); barter, exchange goods without using money (p. 241); rule by divine right, emperor's right to rule from the gods (p. 243)
3. There was no written inheritance rule about the throne , there were high taxes and inflation, and the Germans began raiding the frontiers.
4. They defeated Roman legions at the Battle of Adrianople with the help of the iron stirrup, crossed the frozen Rhine River and entered Gaul, and invaded Rome.
5. Answers will vary. Students should explain their ideas.

Assign Chapter 15 **Section 4 Quiz** in the TCR. Testmaker available.

CHAPTER 15 Review

Building Vocabulary

Imagine you are living in Rome around 400 A.D. Use the following words to write a letter to a friend explaining some of the reasons for the end of the Roman Empire that you have witnessed.

census	inflation
domus	barter
emperor	*juris prudentes*
gladiators	tariffs
freedmen	

Check for Understanding

1. How did Augustus make life in Rome safer for its people?
2. How did increased trade during the *Pax Romana* affect Rome and its people?
3. Why did the Romans change the laws set down on the Twelve Tables?
4. Why was it important to make Roman law standard across the empire?
5. What happened to some animal species as a result of the public games?
6. What did the Praetorian Guard have to do with the fall of the Roman Empire?
7. Why did Diocletian divide the Roman Empire in two?
8. What were the major reasons for the final fall of Rome?

Critical Thinking

1. What do you think was Augustus's strongest skill and his weakest skill as a ruler?
2. Why would the absence of tariffs increase trade?
3. Would you have enjoyed living in Rome during the *Pax Romana*? Explain.
4. What happens to a government if it does not have rules for passing on power from leader to leader?

Geography in History

LOCATION Refer to the map on page 235. Describe the general location of the Roman Empire according to its longitude and latitude. Also identify the location of the imaginary dividing line between the Western and Eastern Empires.

Using Your Journal

Review the details that you have noted about the contributions of the Romans to western civilization. Write a newspaper article explaining the contributions of the Romans to the ideas about law in the United States today.

CHAPTER 15 REVIEW ANSWERS

BUILDING VOCABULARY

Letters will vary but should include all the vocabulary words and an explanation for the end of the Roman Empire.

CHECK FOR UNDERSTANDING

1. by setting up a fire brigade and a police force
2. It brought more business, and wealth and turned Italy into a manufacturing center.
3. because the times were different and the old laws did not apply to conquered territories
4. It helped Rome successfully govern a large area.
5. They were eventually wiped out.
6. They weakened Rome by murdering the emperor and selling the throne .
7. He realized the Roman Empire covered too much area for one person to rule well.
8. the absence of a written rule for inheriting the throne, high taxes and inflation, and the Germanic invasions

CRITICAL THINKING

1. Answers will vary but should be explained.
2. Answers will vary but without tariffs, the prices of goods are lower.
3. Answers will vary but students should provide reasons.
4. Answers will vary.

✚ BONUS ✚ TEST QUESTION

For Chapter 15 Test

The Roman Empire's employment office has published a list of job openings, and announces all people are invited to apply. During the rule of which later Roman emperor, Marcus Aurelius or Diocletian, might this have occurred? *(probably Marcus Aurelius; Diocletian gave people lifetime jobs often the job their father's had)*

USING YOUR JOURNAL

Newspaper articles will vary but might include changing laws to correspond with the times; making laws fair to everyone; considering a person innocent until proven guilty; having the accuser not the accused have to prove his or her case; standardizing legal procedures.

GEOGRAPHY IN HISTORY

The empire stretched from about 10° W longitude to 45° E longitude, and north and south from 25° N latitude to 40° N latitude. The division between empires approximately paralleled 20° E longitude.

CHAPTER 16 Christianity

CHAPTER ORGANIZER

Objectives	Special Features	Supplemental Materials
Section 1 The Beginnings Explain how Jesus' life and teachings formed the basis of Christianity.		• Reproducible Lesson Plan • Section 1 Quiz • Testmaker • Chapter 16 Vocabulary and Guided Reading Activity • World Art and History Transparency 11 • The Western Civilization Videodisc
Section 2 Christianity and Rome Summarize how Christianity spread throughout the Roman Empire.		• Reproducible Lesson Plan • Section 2 Quiz • Testmaker • Chapter 16 Geography and Map Activity • Chapter 16 Cooperative Learning Activity • Chapter 16 Teaching Transparencies and Activities
Section 3 The Church Explain how the early Christian church was organized and what relationship existed between Christianity and Roman society before and after the time of Constantine I.		• Reproducible Lesson Plan • Section 3 Quiz • Testmaker • Chapter 16 Chart and Graph Skill Activity • Unit 5 World Literature • Reinforcing Social Studies Skills, pp. 13, 16 • Chapter 16 Activity Book Activity
Chapter 16 Review and Evaluation		• Chapter 16 Reteaching Activity • Chapter 16 Enrichment Activity • Chapter 16 Performance Assessment Activity • Spanish Summary and Glossary • Audiocassettes (English and Spanish) • Chapter 16 Test • Testmaker

If time does not permit teaching the entire chapter, use the Chapter 16 Summary on page 256 and the Chapter 16 Audiocassettes (English and Spanish) to point out the main ideas of the chapter.

✓ Performance Assessment Activities

Time Line Have students create time lines that show the development of the Christian church up to the point when the Roman Catholic and Eastern Orthodox churches were formed. Students may wish to illustrate their time lines. Display the time lines in the classroom.

Religion Have students imagine that they are Constantine I. Have them write a dialogue in which Constantine explains to his soldiers that he has converted to Christianity. Students could also write dialogue reflecting the soldiers' attitudes and responses. Have students read their dialogues to the class.

CHAPTER RESOURCES

LITERATURE ABOUT THE PERIOD

Comte, Fernand. *Sacred Writings of World Religions.* Chambers, 1992. Examines the history, beliefs, and major figures of more than 20 religions, among them Judaism, Islam, Christianity, Sikhism, Confucianism, Shinto, and Hinduism.

READINGS FOR THE STUDENT

Connolly, Peter. *A History of the Jewish People in the Time of Jesus; From Herod the Great to Masada.* Peter Bedrick Books, 1983. Background information illustrated with drawings and tools as well as everyday objects.

Rice, Edward. *The Early Christians: A Young People's Pictorial History of the Church.* Farrar Straus, 1963. An adaptation (by Blanche Jennings) of a well-known Roman Catholic scholar's history of the early Church.

READINGS FOR THE TEACHER

Benko, Stephen. *Pagan Rome and the Early Christians.* Indiana University Press, 1986. History of early Christianity in Rome.

Chadwick, Henry and G. R. Evans, eds. *Atlas of the Christian Church.* Facts on File, 1987. Offers an authoritative survey of Christian tradition and discusses the impact of the Christian Church on Western civilization.

Gager, John G. *Kingdom & Community: The Social World of Early Christianity.* Prentice Hall, 1986. Describes the social life of followers of early Christians.

Gibbon, Edward. *The Early Growth of Christianity & the History of the First Christians.* American Classical College Press, 1986. Discusses the history of the first Christians.

MULTIMEDIA RESOURCES

Catholicism: Rome, Leeds, and the Desert. Time/Life. Video. The Catholic Church is explored in visits to the Vatican and to Spain.

Jesus. Blackbox. Video. Scholar Edward de Bono examines Christ's teachings on the rewards of heaven.

Religion in Roman Life. Projected Learning Programs. 2 filmstrips. Deals with the development of religion during the Roman Republic and the Roman Empire.

INTRODUCE

CHAPTER 16 OVERVIEW

Chapter 16 describes the rise of Christianity and its impact on the Roman Empire.

- **Section 1** discusses the origins of Christianity and the life of Jesus.
- **Section 2** describes the difficulties Christianity faced in a hostile Roman society.
- **Section 3** explains the organization of the Roman Catholic church and its relationship to the Roman government.

CHAPTER OBJECTIVES

After reading Chapter 16, students will be able to:

1. explain how Jesus' life and teachings formed the basis of Christianity.
2. summarize how Christianity spread throughout the Roman Empire.
3. explain how the early Christian church was organized.
4. discuss what relationship existed between Christianity and Roman society before and after the time of Constantine I.
5. describe what life was like for early monks and nuns.

EXAMINING THE ILLUSTRATION

Ask students if they know on whose teachings Christianity is based. Tell them Jesus, shown here, lived during ancient Roman times, and the origin of Christianity dates from this time.

PERFORMANCE ASSESSMENT

Use the Performance Assessment activities on page 246B to help you evaluate students as they complete the chapter.

CHAPTER 16 Christianity

Image of Jesus

246

TEACHER CLASSROOM RESOURCES

- Reproducible Lesson Plan
- Section Quizzes/Chapter Test
- Reteaching Activity
- Enrichment Activity
- Chart and Graph Skill Activity
- Geography and Map Activity
- Activity Book Activity
- Unit 5 World Literature
- Cooperative Learning Activity
- Performance Assessment Activity
- Spanish Summary and Glossary
- Teaching Transparencies and Activities
- Testmaker
- Audiocassettes (English and Spanish)
- The Western Civilization Videodisc

Chapter Focus

READ TO DISCOVER:

- How Jesus' life and teachings formed the basis of Christianity.
- How Christianity spread throughout the Roman Empire.
- How the early Christian church was organized.
- What relationship existed between Christianity and Roman society before and after the time of Constantine I.
- What life was like for early monks and nuns.

Just as the Romans influenced the lives of people they conquered, those people influenced the lives of the Romans. Among those who brought new ideas and important changes to Rome were the Christians. Their religion, Christianity, started in Palestine among the Jews.

At first, most Romans either did not pay any attention to Christianity or made fun of it. Some emperors treated Christians cruelly. By 400 A.D., however, most Romans had changed their way of thinking. Christianity had become the official religion of the Roman Empire.

1 B.C.–800 A.D.

KEY TERMS

scriptures
messiah
gentiles
missionary
apostles
parish
priest
diocese
bishop
archbishops
patriarchs
heresy
monasteries
convents

Section 1

THE BEGINNINGS

Christianity is based on the life and teachings of Jesus (jē' zuhs), who lived in Palestine during the reign of Augustus. After Jesus died, his teachings were spread by his followers. Christianity survived the fall of Rome and grew to be one of the major influences on western civilization.

The Life of Jesus Jesus, born a Jew in the town of Bethlehem (beth' luh hem), grew up in Nazareth (naz' uhr uhth). There, he received a Jewish education. He studied the **scriptures**

247

FOCUS

BELLRINGER

Write the following unfinished statement on the chalkboard for students to fill in the blank: *"When I hear the word Christianity the first thing I think of is _____ ."* Ask students to fill in the blank with one or more responses.

MOTIVATIONAL ACTIVITY

Discuss student responses to the unfinished statement as you list them on the chalkboard. Encourage students to add to the list. Ask students why so many people know at least one or two things about this religion. Explain that in this chapter they will learn about the teachings of Jesus and the religion, which eventually became Christianity, that he helped establish in the Roman Empire.

VOCABULARY PRE-CHECK

Ask a volunteer to write the key terms for this chapter on the chalkboard as other students identify them by skimming the material for the boldfaced words.

Assign Chapter 16 **Vocabulary and Guided Reading Activity** in the TCR.

EXTRA CREDIT PROJECT

Explain to students that most Christians are part of one of three religious groups: Roman Catholic, Protestant, and Eastern Orthodox. Have students research and create a world map showing where each of these Christian religions are mostly practiced.

KEY TO ABILITY LEVELS

Teaching strategies have been coded for varying learning styles and abilities.

L1 Level 1 activities are **basic** activities and should be within the ability range of all students.

L2 Level 2 activities are **average** activities and should be within the ability range of the average to above-average student.

L3 Level 3 activities are **challenging** activities designed for the ability range of above-average students.

LEP LEP activities should be within the ability range of Limited English Proficiency students.

TEACH

GUIDED PRACTICE

L1 **Writing** Ask the students to rewrite the parable of the man from Samaria (the Good Samaritan) as if the story took place in modern times. Have students read their parables to the class and explain any changes in the meaning from the original that occurred in modernizing it.

DID YOU KNOW ??

During the time that Jesus preached, there were about 2½ million Jews in Palestine and another 4 million elsewhere in the Roman Empire.

MAKING CONNECTIONS

➤➤ **Government** Since the political situation in the Roman Empire was so unstable, anyone who drew crowds or attracted public attention was considered a threat to the Roman government. Roman officials feared that Jesus wanted to be king.

Painting of Christian Symbol

(skrip' churz), or sacred writings, and learned prayers in the Hebrew language. Later, he went to work as a carpenter.

When he was about 30 years old, Jesus began to travel around Palestine preaching to people. Men and women came in large numbers from all over the country to see and hear him. Jesus taught that God created all people and loves them the way a father loves his children. Therefore, people should behave like God's children and love God and one another. Jesus said that God loves even people who have sinned. Jesus told people that if they were truly sorry and placed their trust in God, they would be forgiven.

Jesus spoke in the everyday language of the people. He presented his teachings in *parables* (par' uh buhlz), or stories, about persons and things that were familiar to his listeners. In this way, they could better understand the religious principles he was trying to teach. For example, in the parable of the Good Samaritan (suh mar' uh tuhn), Jesus told about a man from Jerusalem who was attacked by robbers. They beat the man severely and left him lying in the road. Two passers-by from Jerusalem saw him there but did nothing. Then came a man from the city of Samaria (suh mar' ē uh). He stopped, washed the man's wounds, and carried him to a nearby inn. The parable taught that people should not ignore wrong but should do something about it. The parable also taught that people should help everyone, not just those from their own community.

In 30 A.D., after about three years of preaching, Jesus and 12 of his disciples went to Jerusalem to celebrate Passover, the holiday that marks the exodus of the Jews from Egypt. At the time, there was much unrest in the city. Many Romans were angry because the Jews refused to worship statues of the Roman emperor. The Jews were tired of the high taxes they had to pay and of the pressure put on them by the Romans. They hoped and waited for a **messiah** (muh sī' uh), or someone who would save them.

When Jesus arrived in Jerusalem, many Jews greeted him as the messiah. This worried other Jews and Romans alike. Jesus was convicted of treason under Roman law and was *crucified* (krū' suh fīd), or executed on a cross, outside Jerusalem. Usually, only lower-class criminals were killed in this way.

Painting of Jesus' Disciples

The loss of their leader greatly saddened Jesus' disciples. Then, according to Christian tradition, Jesus rose from the dead. He remained on Earth for 40 days before going directly to heaven. His *resurrection* (rez uh rek' shuhn), or rising from the dead, convinced his disciples that Jesus was the Son of God who had become man. They believed that because Jesus had suffered death and had risen to life, he could forgive the sins of all people. They thought that anyone who believed in Jesus and lived by his teachings would know eternal life after death. From then on, the disciples called him Christ, after the Greek word *Christos* (khrēs tōs'), meaning "messiah."

MEETING SPECIAL NEEDS

Have auditory learners interview a Christian minister, a priest, or a Jewish rabbi about the Jewish roots of Christianity. Students should prepare a list of questions in advance of their interview, and then they should tape record their interviews. Have students report orally on their interviews.

THE LAST SUPPER The night before he was crucified, Jesus met with his closest disciples for the meal that marks the start of Passover. At this meal, known as the Last Supper, Jesus set the guidelines for later Christian ceremonies. **Why did Jesus and his disciples go to Jerusalem?**

Paul The disciples were among the first people to become Christians. After Jesus died, they tried to spread his *gospel,* or teachings, among the Jews in Palestine. They had little success, however. Most Palestinian Jews wanted a political messiah. They were not interested in a religious one. The disciples then began to spread their message to Jews who lived outside Palestine. Soon, small groups of people who believed in Christ were meeting in Antioch (ant' ē ahk), Corinth, Rome, and other trading cities of the Mediterranean area.

At about the same time, a Jew named Paul decided to teach Christianity to **gentiles** (jen' tīls), or non-Jews, as well as to Jews. Paul had once been a close follower of Judaism. Then, according to Christian tradition, while he was traveling on the road to Damascus (duh mas' kuhs), Paul was blinded by a bright light and heard Christ's voice. After he was able to see again, Paul became a Christian. He spent the rest of his life spreading the Christian message throughout the Roman world.

CAPTION ANSWER

to celebrate the Jewish holiday of Passover

LINKING PAST TO PRESENT

About 1497, Italian Leonardo da Vinci painted the scene "The Last Supper" on a monastery wall. Soon after he finished the scene, the paint began to peel. Today the painting, although still greatly admired and considered a masterpiece, is in poor condition.

MAKING CONNECTIONS

➤➤ **Religion** The Roman governor of Bithynia, Pliny the Younger, explained the official Roman attitude toward Christianity when he said, "Great numbers of all ranks, ages and of both sexes were liable to be involved [in Christianity], for this contagious superstition is not confined to the cities but has spread its infection in the villages and country."

VIDEODISC

Use the following to enrich Chapter 16.

WC B 163 11879

St. Paul.

MULTICULTURAL PERSPECTIVES

Messiah comes from a Hebrew word that means "the anointed one." The term derives from an ancient but widespread custom of using sacred oil in certain kinds of religious ceremonies. A priest might, for instance, place holy oil on the head of a new ruler to indicate God's approval. Anointing was also used in times of danger to give symbolic protection. Sometimes objects (even weapons) were anointed. The Greek word *Christos* also means "anointed one."

MAKING CONNECTIONS

>> **History** The last Roman emperor to persecute large numbers of Christians was Diocletian. In A.D. 311, Galerius, ruler of the Eastern Roman Empire, permitted freedom of worship.

DID YOU KNOW ??

According to traditional legend, the emperor Nero sat in his palace and "fiddled" while Rome burned. In reality there were no fiddles at the time; Nero played a harp. One story hinted that Nero himself set fire to the city so he could admire the sight of Rome in flames.

Painting of Paul

In each city where Paul preached, new Christian communities formed. Paul wrote letters to these groups to help guide the members. In his letters, he stated that gentiles who became Christians did not have to follow Jewish rituals and laws. All they needed was to have faith in Jesus. This appealed to many people.

Paul was very important to the growth of Christianity. He was its first **missionary** (mish' uh ner ē), or person who spreads religious beliefs to those who do not believe. After Paul's death, other Christian missionaries continued his work.

Section 1 Review

1. **Identify:** Jesus, Bethlehem, Nazareth, Good Samaritan, Jerusalem, Paul
2. **Define:** scriptures, messiah, gentiles, missionary
3. What change did Paul make in the Christian message?

Critical Thinking

4. Who that you know of today could be called a Good Samaritan? Give examples.

Section 2 CHRISTIANITY AND ROME

The Roman Empire helped Christianity spread. The *Pax Romana* allowed missionaries to move across Roman lands in safety. The Roman system of roads helped them go from one place to another quickly. Since most people spoke either Latin or Greek, the missionaries could talk with them directly.

Political Conditions Political conditions did not favor the spread of Christianity, however. Although all people in the Roman Empire were generally allowed to worship freely, the Romans expected everyone to honor the emperor as a god. The Christians, like the Jews, refused to do this. They claimed that only God could be worshiped. This made the Romans angry.

The Romans also did not like other Christian ideas. For example, Christians did not want to serve in the army or hold public office. They often criticized Roman festivals and games. They taught that all people would be equal in heaven if they followed Jesus' teachings.

Because of these differences, the Romans blamed and punished Christians for all kinds of disasters, such as plagues and famines (fam' uhnz). In 64 A.D., the Romans accused the Chris-

SECTION 1 ANSWERS

1. Jesus, person upon whom Christianity is based(p. 247); Bethlehem, town of Jesus' birth (p. 247); Nazareth, town where Jesus grew up (p. 247); Good Samaritan, one of Jesus' parables (p. 248); Jerusalem, city where Jesus celebrated the Passover (p. 248); Paul, taught Christianity to gentiles (p. 249)
2. scriptures, sacred writings (p. 247); messiah, Savior (p. 248); gentiles, non-Jews (p. 249); missionary, person who spreads religious beliefs to nonbelievers (p. 250)
3. that gentiles who became Christians did not have to follow Jewish rituals and laws but needed only to have faith in Jesus
4. Answers will vary but should be examples of situations in which a person came to the help of another person.

Assign Chapter 16 **Section 1 Quiz** in the TCR. Testmaker available.

tians of starting a fire that burned much of Rome. Christianity was then made illegal, and many Christians were killed.

Some officials paid no attention to the law that made Christianity illegal. However, Christians still had a hard time in most areas. In Rome, they were not allowed to use Roman burial places. They had to bury their dead in crowded catacombs.

The Spread of Christianity Even with all of the hardships, Christianity spread. It was of more interest to the poor workers and enslaved people in the cities. They led very hard lives. They liked a religion that promised a happier life after death.

Over time, however, Christianity began to draw people from all classes. After 250 A.D., many Romans grew tired of war and

MAP STUDY

MOVEMENT By 1100 Christianity had spread throughout most of Europe and parts of Asia and North Africa. **How did Paul's journeys help the spread of Christianity?**

The Spread of Christianity

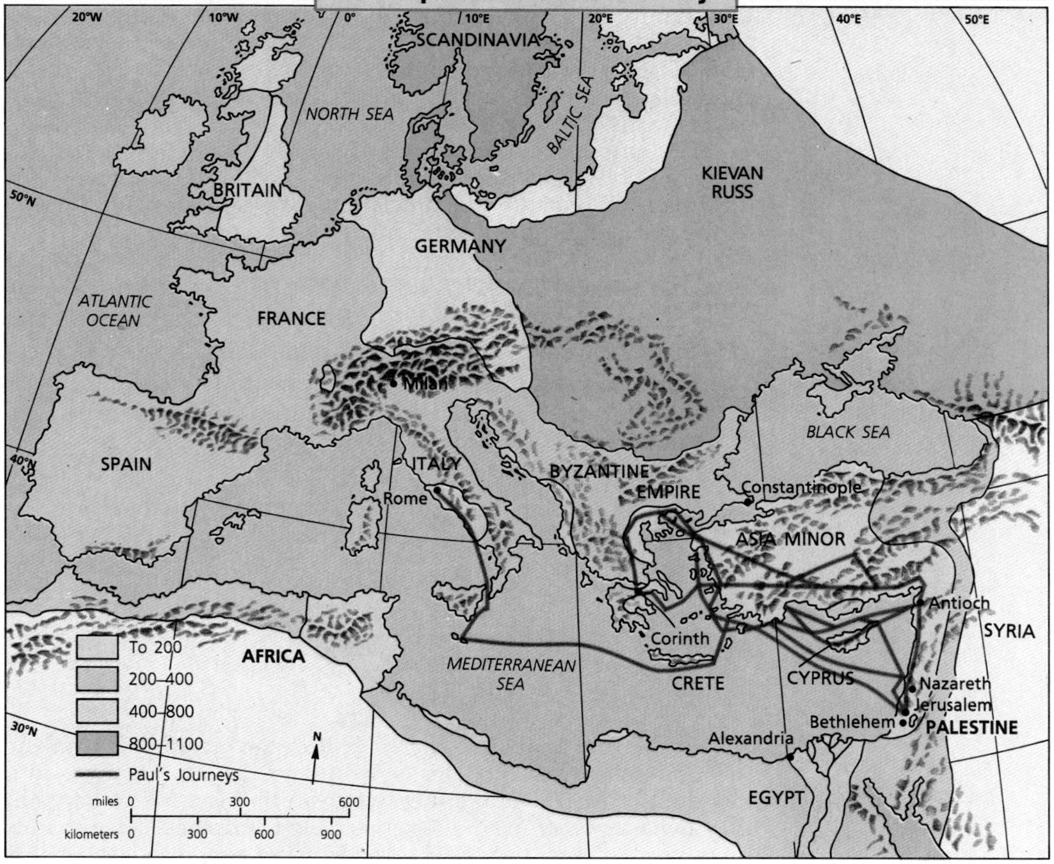

L3 **Geography: Region** Have students refer to the map of the "Spread of Christianity." Have them discuss the difference in size of the religion's area of influence from 200 to 1100, and the pattern, if any, that it followed. Then have students use the map scale to calculate the approximate length of the empire, from west to east, by the year 1100.

L2 **Critical Thinking** Have students discuss the major differences in attitudes that existed between some Roman non-Christians and Christians. Have students list these differences in two columns under the headings *Christian* and *non-Christian*. *(Students should mention differences over army service, and who should be honored as a god, hold public office, and be blamed for disasters.)*

LEP

MAP STUDY

Answer

Paul traveled extensively throughout the Mediterranean region spreading the ideas of Christianity.

Assign Chapter 16 **Geography and Map Activity** in the TCR.

COOPERATIVE LEARNING

Divide students into several groups. Have each group research one of the various religions practiced in the Roman Empire. Make sure each group member is responsible for either research, compiling information, providing illustrations, preparing answers for possible questions, or presenting to the class. Religions to be researched include the official religion of Rome, Judaism, Christianity, and the Persian and Egyptian mystery religions, such as Mithraism and the cult of Isis. Have the groups act as a panel, answering questions from the class about the religion it studied.

Assign Chapter 16 **Cooperative Learning Activity** in the TCR.

DID YOU KNOW ??

Early Christians tried to escape Roman persecution by worshiping in catacombs—underground passages dug by the Christians.

L3 **Culture** Write the following headings on the chalkboard: *Roman Soldiers, Wealthy Landowners, Farming Families.* Ask the class to discuss what each group might say about the spread of Christianity if interviewed. List student suggested responses under the appropriate headings. Then ask students to explain reasons for their answers. LEP

DID YOU KNOW ??

In ancient times, Christianity competed with various Middle Eastern mystery religions, especially Mithraism. (This was an ancient Persian religion in which followers worshiped the god Mithras.) Unlike Mithraism, however, Christianity welcomed both men and women.

MAKING CONNECTIONS

➤➤ **Language** The word *church* means "belonging to the Lord."

Christian Inscription

feared the end of the empire. They began to admire the certainty and courage of the Christian missionaries. They wanted the love, kindness, and feeling of safety that Christianity offered. At the same time, many Christians started to accept the empire.

Constantine I and Theodosius In 312 A.D., Constantine I, who was a general at the time, accepted Christianity. Legend says that as he was about to go into battle, Constantine saw a flaming cross in the sky. Written beneath the cross were the Latin words *in hoc signo vinces* (in hok sig' nō win' kās). This means, "In this sign thou shalt conquer." Constantine won the battle and with it the throne of the Roman Empire. Constantine believed God had helped him gain his victory. Because of this, he ordered his soldiers to paint crosses on their shields.

The following year, the Edict (ē' dikt) of Milan (mi lan') was issued. It gave religious freedom to all people. It also made Christianity legal. Constantine I did many other things to help Christianity grow. He had churches built in Rome and Jerusalem. He used government money to pay for Christian schools. He let church leaders enter government service and excused them from paying taxes.

The emperor who followed Constantine I continued pro-Christian policies. In 392 A.D., Emperor Theodosius (thē uh dō' shē uhs) made Christianity the official religion of the Roman Empire. At the same time, he outlawed all other religions.

Section 2 Review

1. **Identify:** Constantine I, Edict of Milan, Theodosius
2. How did the Roman Empire help Christianity spread?
3. What factors brought about a change in attitude between Romans and Christians?

Critical Thinking

4. Why do you think the hardships put on Christians by Romans could not stop the spread of Christianity?

Section 3 THE CHURCH

Early Christians thought the end of the world was near. At the time, they believed Jesus would return to set up God's kingdom on Earth. While they were waiting for this to happen, they lived together in small groups called **churches.** They shared their possessions and took turns leading worship services in

SECTION 2 ANSWERS

1. Constantine I, emperor who accepted Christianity (p. 252); Edict of Milan, gave religious freedom to all people (p. 252); Theodosius, Roman emperor (p. 252)
2. The *Pax Romana* allowed missionaries to move safely across Roman lands; the Roman system of roads allowed travel; and since most people spoke either Latin or Greek, the missionaries could talk with them directly.
3. The Romans grew tired of war and began to admire the courage of Christian missionaries and Christian values. Many Christians started to accept the empire.
4. Answers will vary but could note that people were tired of the Roman Empire and its decline. Christianity was appealing.

Assign Chapter 16 **Section 2 Quiz** in the TCR. Testmaker available.

homes and outdoors. Each group was in charge of its own affairs. **Apostles** (uh pos' uhls), or those people Jesus chose to teach his gospel, visited the different groups. The apostles taught and gave advice. They also provided a sense of unity.

Painting of Matthew

Church Structure After the apostles died, Christians realized that Jesus was not going to return to Earth as quickly as they had expected. They looked for ways to hold their churches together. One way was by organizing the churches. They used the Roman Empire's structure of government as a model for this organization.

By 300 A.D., each church was called a **parish** (par' ish). Each had a leader known as a **priest.** Several parishes were put together into larger groups. Each group was called a **diocese** (dī' uh sis), a word that originally meant a Roman military district. A **bishop** headed each diocese. The most important bishops were called **archbishops.** They governed churches in larger cities. The five leading archbishops were called **patriarchs** (pā' trē arks).

As time went on, the archbishop of Rome began to claim power over the other archbishops. By 600 A.D., he was called Pope. This comes from a Latin word meaning "father." Christians who spoke Latin saw him as the head of all the churches. Christians who spoke Greek, however, would not accept him as the leader of their churches. They turned instead to the archbishop of Constantinople. In 1054 A.D., the two church groups separated. The Latin churches as a group became known as the Roman Catholic Church. The Greek churches became known as the Eastern Orthodox Church.

The New Testament At the same time Christians were developing a church organization, they were deciding what writings to put into the New Testament, or Christian scriptures. Jesus had left no written records. However, after his death, others wrote about Jesus' life and teachings.

Toward the end of the 300s A.D., four accounts were accepted as part of the New Testament. The accounts were believed to have been written by Matthew, Mark, Luke, and John. These men were four of Jesus' early followers. A number of letters written by Paul and other disciples were also accepted as part of the New Testament.

At about the same time, bishops met to discuss questions about Christian thinking. Decisions they reached at these meetings came to be accepted as official *doctrine* (dok' truhn), or statements of faith. The points of view the bishops did not accept were declared to be **heresy** (her' uh sē), or false doctrines.

Painting of Jerome

Fathers of the Church Between 100 and 500 A.D., different scholars wrote works that greatly influenced later Christians. These scholars became known as the "Fathers of the Church."

INDEPENDENT PRACTICE

L3 **Critical Thinking** Ask students to write a brief description of everything they can remember that happened in class the day before. Have students read descriptions aloud to compare details. After students conclude that some differences are bound to appear in four accounts of their report, ask students why they think the same events are retold in different chapters of the New Testament.

L1 **Art** Have students research the meaning of the anchor and fish symbols found on many early Christian tombs. Ask them to draw the symbols and write an explanation of their meaning. LEP

MAKING CONNECTIONS

➤➤ **History** In the following parable, Jesus urged his followers to give up everything so that they would be ready for God's kingdom: *The kingdom of heaven is like treasure lying buried in a field. The man who found it, buried it again; and for sheer joy went and sold everything he had, and bought that field.*
—Matthew 13:44-46

MULTICULTURAL PERSPECTIVES

The Bible is the most sacred book to Christians. They consider the Bible to be the word of God. The word *Bible* comes from a Greek word that means "books." The Bible is not one book but actually a collection of books, or sections. The number of books in the Bible depends on the Christian group. The Roman Catholic Bible includes 73 books, while most Protestant groups include 66 books in their Bible. It is the most-read book in history.

CAPTION ANSWER

They wanted to grow closer to God and be protected from the evils of the world.

DID YOU KNOW ??

St. Augustine was born a Christian but left Christianity at age 17. In A.D. 387, he met St. Ambrose, the bishop of Milan, who influenced him to return to Christianity.

L1 **The Arts** Many movies have been made about the life of Jesus or the impact of Christianity on the people of ancient Rome. Have students view a videotape of *The Robe, Ben Hur, The Silver Chalice,* or *The Greatest Story Ever Told* and then write a review of the film. Tell them to include descriptions of details they learned about life under *Pax Romana* (for example, in *Ben Hur,* the chariot races; in *The Silver Chalice,* the Greek artisan and enslaved person; *The Robe,* the Roman legionaries). LEP

MONASTERIES Early Christian monasteries were often built into the sides of mountains. The rocky cliffs offered isolation. **Why did the people at these monasteries want to be cut off from the world?**

One such scholar was Jerome (juh rōm'). He translated the Old and New Testaments into Latin. His translation was called the *Vulgate* (vul' gāt). It became the official Bible used by the Roman Catholic Church.

Augustine (o' guh stēn) was an important leader of Christian thought. His best-known work was *City of God.* In it, he defended Christianity against those who said that Rome would not have fallen if it had not accepted Christianity. Augustine said that Rome fell because it became rich and corrupt and persecuted Christians.

Monasteries In the early years of Christianity, thousands of Christians left the cities to live and pray alone in isolated areas. Such people were known as *hermits.* In Egypt and Syria especially, thousands of hermits lived in the desert. They believed that this would help them grow closer to Christ.

A hermit was protected from the temptations of daily life. At the same time, however, such a person was not doing anything to improve the world. Near the end of the 300s A.D., a bishop named Basil (baz' uhl) suggested a different way of life. He said that Christians should form religious settlements near cities. In this way, they would be protected from the evils of the world. At the same time, they could help other people by doing good deeds and

EXTENDING THE CONTENT

The first significant translation of the scriptures was by St. Jerome, which he began in about 383 at the request of the Pope. Jerome first translated the Gospels. They came from several sources, mainly Greek. The scholarly Jerome then decided the standard Greek translation of the Old Testament would not do. He went back to Hebrew sources and made a new translation. His work completed in about 405, was called *Vulgate,* from the Latin word meaning popular.

by setting an example of Christian living. Many Christians took Basil's advice.

Christian men who did as Basil suggested were called **monks.** Their settlements, or communities, were known as **monasteries** (mon' uh ster ēz). Christian women who did the same were called **nuns.** They lived in quarters of their own called **convents** (kon' vents). Basil drew up a list of rules for these religious communities. This list, which is known as the Basilian (buh zil' ē uhn) Rule, became the model for Eastern Orthodox religious life.

In the West, another set of rules called the Benedictine (ben uh dik' tuhn) Rule was followed. It was drawn up about 529 A.D. by an Italian named Benedict (ben' uh dikt). The monks who followed Benedict's rule promised to give up all their possessions before entering a monastery. They agreed to wear simple clothes and eat only certain foods. They could not marry. They had to obey without question the orders of the **abbot** (ab' uht), or leader of the monastery. They had to attend religious services seven times during the day and once at midnight. They also were expected to work six or seven hours a day in the fields around the monastery. When they grew older, they did clerical work or worked as carpenters and weavers. They spent their whole lives serving Christ.

EARLY CHRISTIANS Church leaders often dictated their thoughts as Pope Gregory is shown (left) doing. Those thoughts were studied by a church monk shown here (right) in order to improve his knowledge of Christianity. **Where did monks at this time live?**

L1 **Daily Life** Have students imagine that they are early monks or nuns. Have them write informative letters to someone who is thinking about becoming a monk or a nun. Students' letters should include information on their beliefs and lifestyles.

MAKING CONNECTIONS

➤➤ Geography: Movement The first monasteries were founded in India by Siddhartha Guatama, or Buddha. From India, the custom spread through the Middle East and then into Europe.

VIDEODISC

Use the following to enrich Chapter 16.

WH E 82 14326

The Monastery of St. Catherine.

ASSESS

CHECK FOR UNDERSTANDING

Ask students to summarize the main points of the chapter, orally or in writing. Discuss the answers to the Section and Chapter Review questions.

EVALUATE

Assign Chapter 16 **Performance Assessment Activity** in the TCR.

Administer **Chapter 16 Test** in the TCR. Testmaker available.

EXTENDING THE CONTENT

Many monks copied ancient manuscripts. Without their efforts many literature classics would have been lost. Nuns taught needlework and the medicinal use of herbs to the daughters of nobles.

RETEACH

Help students create an outline of the chapter on the chalkboard. Have students work in pairs to ask one another questions using the outline.

Assign Chapter 16 **Reteaching Activity** in the TCR.

ENRICH

Have students research the parables told by Jesus. Have students retell a parable to the class and explain its meaning.

Assign Chapter 16 **Enrichment Activity** in the TCR.

CLOSE

Ask students to discuss what Jesus meant when he said that he would make his disciples "fishers of men." *(He would teach them to convert others to Christianity.)* Ask students if they think Jesus succeeded in making his disciples "fishers of men."

MEETING CHAPTER OBJECTIVES

Each objective is tested by the Review questions in parentheses.

1. **Explain** how Jesus' teachings formed Christianity. (BV; CU 1, 2; CT 1)
2. **Summarize** how Christianity spread throughout the Roman Empire. (BV; CU 4, 5)
3. **Explain** how the early Christian church was organized. (CU 6; CT 4)
4. **Discuss** the relationship between Christianity and Roman society before and after Constantine I. (BV; CU 3; UYJ)
5. **Describe** what life was like for early monks and nuns. (BV; CU 8; CT 4)

By 800 A.D., monks were playing an important role in spreading Christianity throughout Europe. By preserving old Roman and Greek writings, they helped western civilization survive and progress.

Section 3 Review

1. **Identify:** Roman Catholic Church, Eastern Orthodox Church, New Testament, Jerome, *Vulgate,* Augustine, *City of God,* Basil, Benedictine Rule
2. **Define:** churches, apostles, parish, priest, diocese, bishop, archbishops, patriarchs, heresy, monks, monasteries, nuns, convents, abbot
3. How was the early Christian church organized?
4. How did monks help western civilization survive?

Critical Thinking

5. How were the lives of hermits and monks and nuns similar? How were they different?

Chapter Summary

1. When Jesus was about 30, he began to preach about God's love for all people.
2. In 30 A.D., Jesus was convicted of treason and was crucified.
3. Paul preached Christianity to non-Jews and Jews alike, helping to make Christianity a world religion.
4. Some Christian ideas, such as their refusal to honor the emperor as a god, made the Romans angry.
5. In 313 A.D., the Edict of Milan made Christianity legal in the Roman Empire.
6. In 392 A.D., Christianity became the official religion of the empire.
7. By the end of the 500s A.D., Christians had organized a church, decided what writings would be included in the New Testament, and developed an official doctrine.
8. By 600 A.D., the archbishop of Rome was called Pope and was looked upon by Latin-speaking Christians as head of the Church.
9. In 1054 A.D., most Greek-speaking Christians split from the Latin churches and formed the Eastern Orthodox Church.
10. Between 100 and 500 A.D., scholars, such as Jerome and Augustine, wrote works that greatly influenced later Christian thinkers.
11. Western monks lived according to the set of rules drawn up by Benedict about 529 A.D.

SECTION 3 ANSWERS

1. Roman Catholic Church, Latin church ; Eastern Orthodox Church, Greek church; New Testament, scriptures; Jerome, Father of the Church (p. 253); *Vulgate,* Latin translation ; Augustine, scholar; *City of God,* work of Augustine ; Basil, a bishop (p. 254); Benedictine Rule, rules for monks and nuns (p. 255)
2. All terms are defined in the text Glossary.
3. It was modeled after the Roman government. Each church, or parish was led by a priest. Several parishes formed a diocese headed by a bishop. The archbishops led city churches.
4. by preserving old Roman and Greek writings
5. Answers will vary.

Assign Chapter 16 **Section 3 Quiz** in the TCR. Testmaker available.

CHAPTER

Review 16

Building Vocabulary

Sort the following words into the categories: *people, places,* and *other,* as they apply to the beginning of Christianity. Then write one sentence explaining each term you classified as *other.*

scriptures	monasteries
parish	missionary
heresy	bishop
messiah	archbishops
priest	convents
gentiles	apostles
diocese	patriarchs

Check for Understanding

1. Where did Christianity start?
2. Why did Jesus teach in parables?
3. Why did the Romans blame and punish the Christians for all kinds of disasters, such as plagues and famines?
4. What groups of people were first attracted to Christianity?
5. What legend is told about Constantine I?
6. Why did Christians develop a church organization?
7. Why did the Latin and Greek churches split?
8. What kinds of work did monks do?

Critical Thinking

1. Why do you think people seemed to remember Jesus' teaching more when he used parables?
2. Do you think citizens should have religious freedom or be required to follow one official religion? Explain your answer.
3. What do you think could have been done to prevent the split between the Latin and Greek churches? Explain.
4. Would you have become a monk or nun in 600 A.D.? Why or why not?

Geography in History

PLACE Refer to the map on page 251, noting Paul's journeys. Describe what geographic features and landscape Paul would have seen as he traveled from Antioch to Corinth.

Using Your Journal

Review the details that you have noted about Roman contributions to western civilization. Write a short explanation of how Roman ideas about religion have affected western thoughts, beliefs, and ideas.

CHAPTER 16 REVIEW ANSWERS

BUILDING VOCABULARY

People
messiah
gentiles
missionary
apostles
priest
bishop
archbishop
patriarchs

Places
parish
diocese
monasteries
convents

Other
scriptures
heresy

CHECK FOR UNDERSTANDING

1. in Palestine among the Jews
2. so listeners could better understand his religious principles
3. because the Romans did not like Christian ideas
4. the poor and enslaved people in cities
5. he saw a flaming cross in the sky with the words in *hoc signo vinces* written beneath it
6. to hold their churches together while they waited for Jesus to return to Earth
7. because the Greek Christians would not accept the Pope
8. They attended religious services, worked in the fields, did clerical work, carpentry, and weaving.

CRITICAL THINKING

1. Answers will vary, but students could note stories are easy to remember.
2. Answers will vary, but students should explain.
3. Answers will vary, but students should give reasons.
4. Answers will vary, but students should explain.

+ BONUS +

TEST QUESTION

For Chapter 16 Test

Two Romans are talking. Roman 1. states "If the winter of 406 had been milder the empire would not have fallen." Roman 2. claims, "No. The winter had no effect. The empire was doomed." With whom do you agree? Why? *(The harsh winter of 406 did allow the invasion of the Huns.)*

GEOGRAPHY IN HISTORY

As Paul traveled from Antioch to Corinth overland he would encounter arid land, seacoast, mountains, islands, and a peninsula. Traveling by sea, he would have viewed the same features.

USING YOUR JOURNAL

Essays will vary but should include the idea that Christianity is a strong religious force in Western civilization today.

THE MAYAS

FOCUS

OBJECTIVES

Identify the location of the Mayan civilization. Describe the cultural traits of the Mayas.

BELLRINGER

Write the following on the chalkboard: *What civilization do you think of when you hear the words* hieroglyphs *and* pyramids?

MOTIVATIONAL ACTIVITY

Ask students what civilization they think of when the hear the words *hieroglyphs* and *pyramids.* *(Many will respond, Egypt.)* Then explain that in this Culture Close-Up they will learn about an ancient civilization in Central America that used hieroglyphs and built pyramids.

UNIT 5

CULTURE CLOSE-UP

The Mayas

The Mayas, a group of Native American people, rose to greatness in Central America between 300 and 800 A.D., long before European explorers arrived.

Geography Connection

The steamy forests of Guatemala, on the narrow length of land that connects North America and South America, hide the remains of Mayan cities.

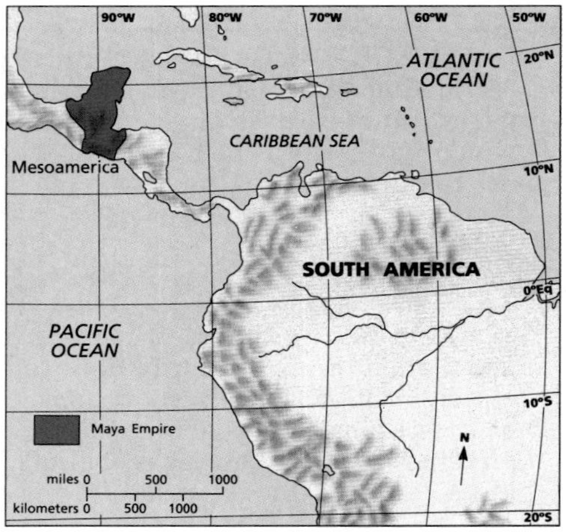

The Mayas were extraordinary architects and scientists. The ruins at a city called Palenque include a towering temple ▲ whose topmost level was used as an observatory of the stars.

258

MEETING SPECIAL NEEDS

Have students who are visual learners research to find out about the major accomplishments of the Maya civilization. Then have them choose one of the accomplishments and illustrate it. Have students show their illustration of the accomplishment to the class. After all students have shared their illustrations, ask the class to rank the accomplishments in the order of most important to least important. Have them read their rankings and give explanations for them.

Mayan priests developed a calendar and hieroglyphs with which to keep records. The calendars helped predict eclipses, and times to plant and harvest. Hieroglyphs often decorated pottery. ▶

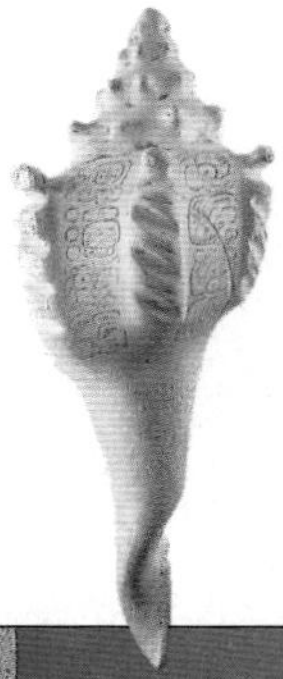

◀ Mayas were excellent sailors and traded throughout Mexico and Central America. Mayan farmers traded maize for cotton cloth, pottery, jade ornaments, fish, and salt at city markets. ▼

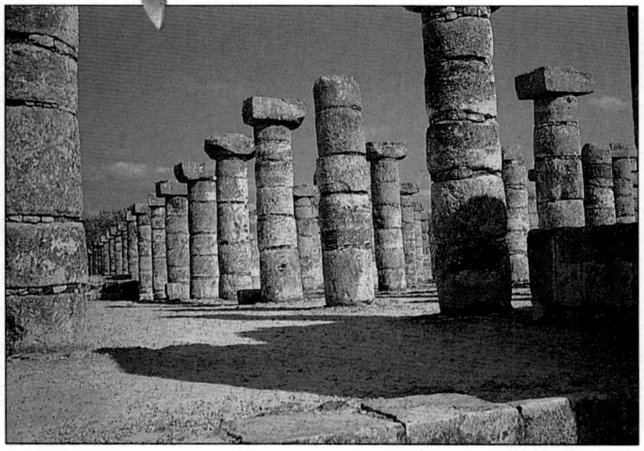

Although warriors were shown in Mayan art, wars did not happen very often. War chiefs did not hold a very high social position. ▶

TEACH

L1 Geography: Location
Compare a political map of Central America with the map of the Mayan Empire on page 258. Ask students to name the present-day countries that were once part of the Mayan Empire. *(Mexico, Belize, Guatemala, Honduras, and El Salvador)* LEP

MAKING CONNECTIONS

➤➤ **Science** Like the ancient Greeks, the Mayas believed that the movements of the sun, moon, and planets were the journeys of their gods across the sky. Since these gods controlled nature—including harvests—charting the movements of the sun and moon was an essential religious duty. Thus the religious leaders, the priests, developed an understanding of astronomy and mathematics.

EXTENDING THE CONTENT

The Mayas developed the concept of zero hundreds of years before mathematicians in India did. The Mayas also developed a numbering system with place value similar to the decimal system except that it had a base of 20 rather than a base of 10. Dots and dashes alone or in combinations were used to stand for numbers. The symbol of a shell stood for zero.

UNIT 5 CULTURE CLOSE-UP

L2 **Critical Thinking** Ask the students why they think the sun god was the most powerful god of the Mayas. LEP

DID YOU KNOW ??

Some scientists believe that the Mayan civilization collapsed partly because they managed their soil poorly. As the Mayan population increased, slash-and-burn agriculture no longer provided enough food. The Mayas tried to increase the productivity of their farms by fertilizing the soil, building drainage and irrigation ditches, and other similar techniques. They did not know, as modern agriculturalists do, that what rain-forest soil needs is a rotation system that allows it to lie fallow for 10 years after being cropped for five years.

GLOBAL READING FOR STUDENTS

Historians in your class may be interested in reading more about the Mayas. Suggest *The Ancient Maya* by Barbara L. Beck and Lorna Greenberg, Watts, 1983. (Average/Nonfiction)

Mayan life centered on religion. Cities were really religious centers with houses, courtyards, and plazas built around huge pyramid-style temples. The tallest pyramids reached 212 feet (65 meters) high. ▼

◀ The Mayas believed that their gods controlled all parts of their lives. The sun god, pictured here, was the most powerful.

Other Mayan gods represented the forces of nature. The Mayas carved the faces of their gods on many natural objects such as seashell. ▶

260

COOPERATIVE LEARNING

Organize the students into small groups. Have each group research and create a model of a Mayan city. Groups should approach the task as if they were a city-planning committee playing the roles of administrators, architects, construction teams, artisans, and researchers. Have groups make a decision on what they want to include in their models. Advise groups to assign a task to each member. When all models are completed, discuss the difficulties the Mayas may have encountered in building their cities.

CULTURE CLOSE-UP

UNIT 5

◀ On religious festival days, the cities drew large crowds. There was music, dancing, and religious ceremonies presided over by priests. A ceremonial ball game called *poke-tko* was played on a court.

Historians are not sure why the Mayan civilization ended. Famine, civil war, or disease could have been the cause.

Taking Another Look

1. **What was the center of Mayan life?**
2. **What contact with other civilizations did the Mayas have?**
3. **What activities took place at Mayan religious festivals?**

Critical Thinking

4. **What parts of Mayan life would have been affected if they had not developed a calendar?**

MULTICULTURAL PERSPECTIVES

The Mayas played a game much like soccer. They batted a rubber ball back and forth by hitting it with their bodies. The players wore protective gear such as thigh guards and heavy belts. Archaeologists believe that the game had some religious meaning with the outcome being a message from the gods that would foretell the future.

ASSESS

CHECK FOR UNDERSTANDING

Have students answer the questions in Taking Another Look on page 261.

ANSWERS to Taking Another Look

1. religion
2. They traded throughout Mexico and Central America.
3. music, dancing, religious ceremonies, and often a ball game called *poke-tko*
4. Answers will vary, however, students should note that farming would be affected since the Mayas used the calendars to predict times to plant and harvest.

ENRICH

Have students speculate as to which accomplishment of the Mayas has made the greatest contribution to modern society. Students may want to research more about some of these contributions that have been mentioned in the Culture Close-Up.

CLOSE

Ask students to discuss a possible connection between the geography of the area where the Mayas lived and the fact that wars were infrequent.

INTRODUCE

UNIT 6 OVERVIEW

Unit 6 discusses the early Middle Ages, which began in western Europe after the fall of Rome and lasted until about A.D. 1000.

- **Chapter 17** describes how Germanic peoples replaced the Roman Empire with their own kingdoms.
- **Chapter 18** analyzes the rise of the Franks.
- **Chapter 19** describes the civilizations that emerged in the British Isles after the fall of the Roman Empire.
- **Chapter 20** summarizes the Viking expansion and how they influenced other people.

UNIT OBJECTIVES

After reading Unit 6, students will be able to:

1. explain why the early Middle Ages is an important period in European history.
2. describe changes in government, economy, and learning in the early Middle Ages.
3. analyze what role religion played in the lives of the people during the early Middle Ages.

UNIT PROJECT

Organize students into five groups. Assign each group one of the following peoples: the Germans (500s), the Franks (800s), the Irish (400s), the Anglo-Saxons (600s), or the Vikings (1000s). Have each group create a newspaper about their assigned people during the given period of time. The newspaper should include headlines, articles, ads, editorials, and an entertainment section.

UNIT 6 The Early Middle Ages

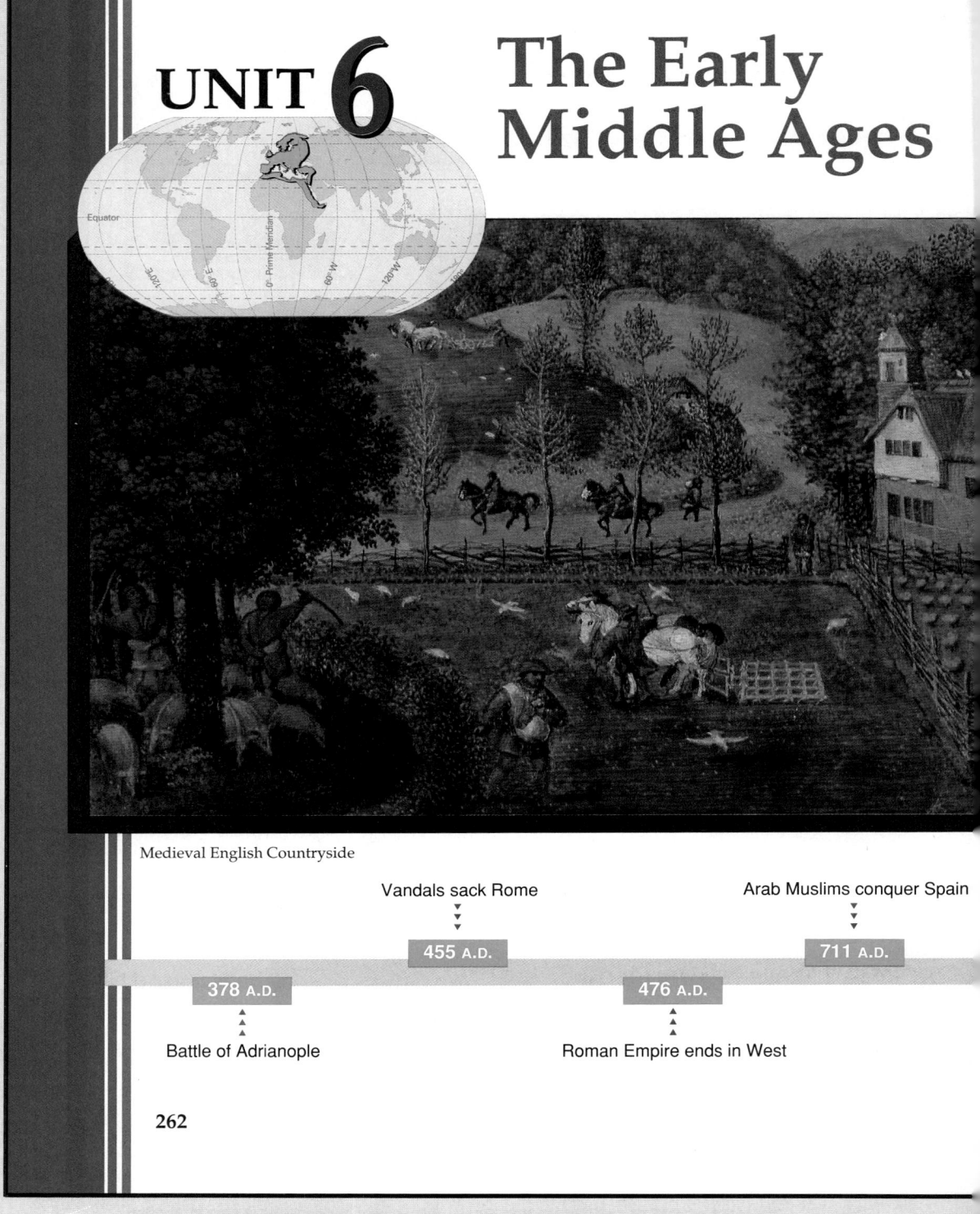

Medieval English Countryside

378 A.D. — Battle of Adrianople
455 A.D. — Vandals sack Rome
476 A.D. — Roman Empire ends in West
711 A.D. — Arab Muslims conquer Spain

262

ABOUT THE UNIT OPENING

EXAMINING THE ILLUSTRATION

Ask students to study the painting and decide if the people in it seem happy or unhappy. Ask students for their opinions and have them explain on what they based their conclusions. Point out that the early Middle Ages were a time of change and growth and many people's lives improved.

GLOBAL CHRONOLOGY

Ask students to explain what the time line covers. *(major events during the early Middle Ages in Europe)* Ask students to explain the major themes of the time line entries from A.D. 378-732. *(battles and conquering)* Where did the Vikings explore in 1000? *(north Atlantic)*

The period from the fall of the Roman Empire in the West to the beginning of modern times is called the Middle Ages. It lasted from about 500 to about 1500 A.D. The years from 500 to 1000 are known as the early Middle Ages. Some historians also called this period the Dark Ages because civilization declined after the fall of the Roman Empire. During this time, however, western Europe developed a new civilization based on Greek and Roman cultures, Christian faith, and Germanic practices.

Chapter 17
The Germans

Chapter 18
The Franks

Chapter 19
The Irish and the Anglo-Saxons

Chapter 20
The Vikings

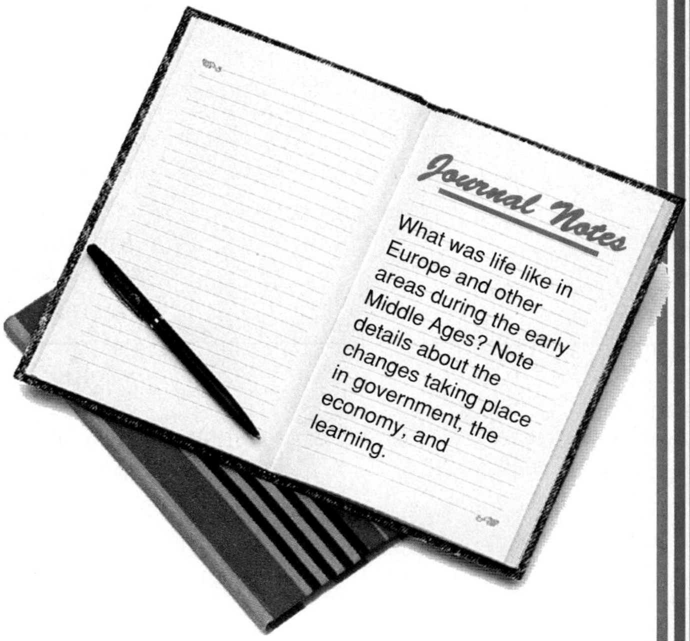
Journal Notes
What was life like in Europe and other areas during the early Middle Ages? Note details about the changes taking place in government, the economy, and learning.

732 A.D. — Battle of Tours

800 A.D. — Charlemagne is crowned emperor

911 A.D. — Normans settle in Normandy

1000 A.D. — Vikings explore north Atlantic

INTRODUCING THE UNIT

Point out to students that during the early Middle Ages western Europe was developing a new civilization to which the Germans, the Franks, the Irish, the Anglo-Saxons, and the Vikings contributed. Explain that all cultures have certain fundamental things in common. Ask students to name some of these things. *(government, religion, customs, leaders, achievements)* Tell students that in Unit 6 they will learn about the civilization that was developing in Europe and other areas during the early Middle Ages.

RECORDING JOURNAL NOTES

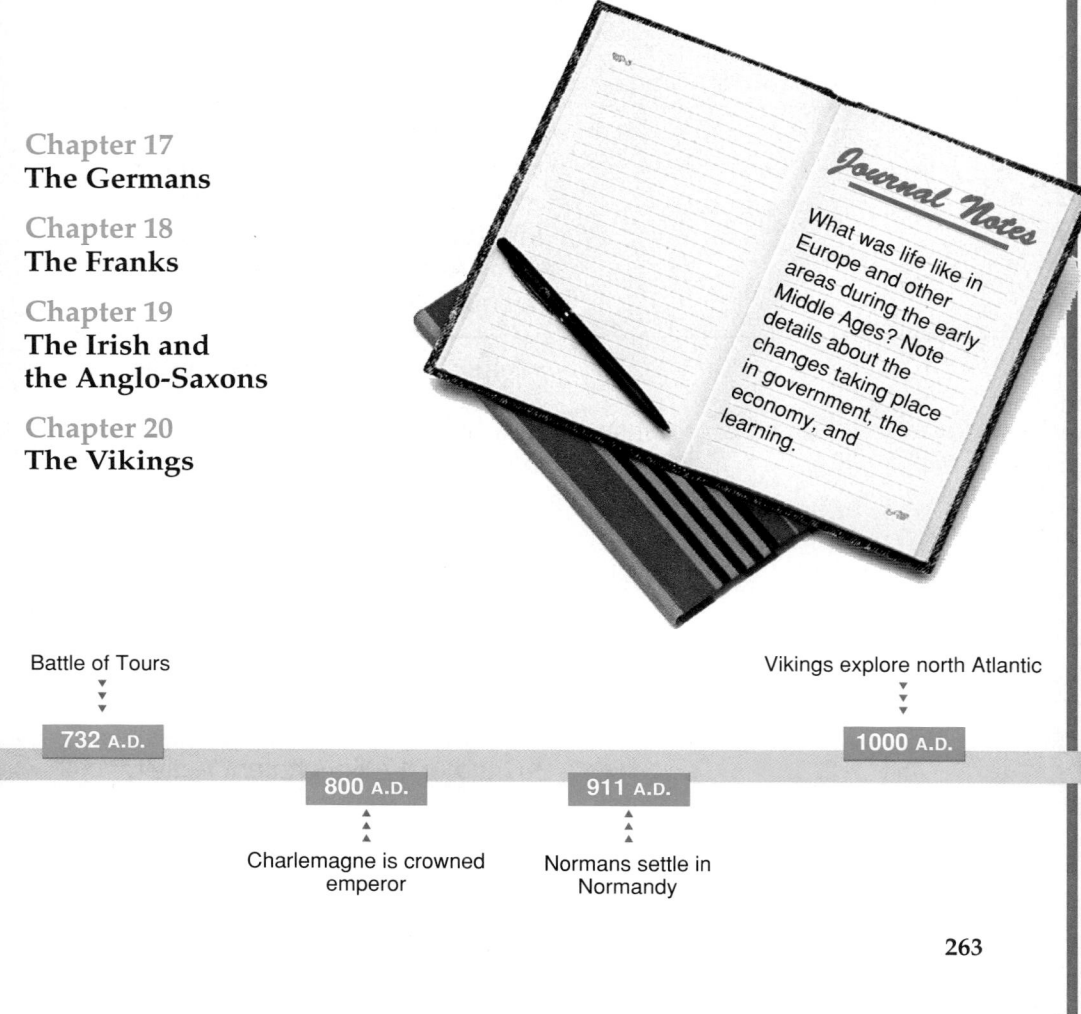

Help students begin writing in their journals by having them list major changes that have taken place in the world in their lifetimes. As they read the text, have students note in their journal details about the changes that took place in government, the economy, and learning in Europe and other areas during the early Middle Ages.

GEOGRAPHIC LOCATION

Have students use their text Atlas to locate the places in this unit that are in western Europe. *(England, Ireland, France, Spain, Italy, Germany, Denmark, Sweden, and Norway)* Ask them to locate Paris, Cluny, Canossa, Worms, and other cities in which important events in this unit take place.

PLANNING GUIDE

CHAPTER 17 The Germans

CHAPTER ORGANIZER

Objectives	Special Features	Supplemental Materials
Section 1 Village Life Characterize family life in German villages and analyze Germans' love of battle and how their laws influenced their lives.		• Reproducible Lesson Plan • Section 1 Quiz • Testmaker • Chapter 17 Vocabulary and Guided Reading Activity • Chapter 17 Activity Book Activity • Foods Around the World
Section 2 The Conquerors Discuss what role the Goths and the Vandals played in the decline of the Roman Empire, and describe what replaced the Roman Empire in the West.		• Reproducible Lesson Plan • Section 2 Quiz • Chapter 17 Geography and Map Activity • Outline Resource Maps, pp. 27, 28, 29, 30, 39 • Chapter 17 Cooperative Learning Activity • Chapter 17 Chart and Graph Skill Activity • Chapter 17 Teaching Transparencies and Activities • The Western Civilization Videodisc
Chapter 17 Review and Evaluation		• Chapter 17 Reteaching Activity • Chapter 17 Enrichment Activity • Spanish Summary and Glossary • Audiocassettes (English and Spanish) • Chapter 17 Performance Assessment Activity • Chapter 17 Test • Testmaker

If time does not permit teaching the entire chapter, use the Chapter 17 Summary on page 272 and the Chapter 17 Audiocassettes (English and Spanish) to point out the main ideas of the chapter.

✓ PERFORMANCE ASSESSMENT ACTIVITIES

Personality Sketches Have students choose one of the following Germanic leaders to research: Alaric, Odoacer, or Theodoric. Have students prepare a report of their own design that includes the personal characteristics of these leaders and their roles in the decline of the Roman Empire in the West. Suggest students may want to write a monologue or a play that involves other students, or create a visual presentation, and so on. Have students share their reports with the class.

Laws Remind students that German laws during the early Middle Ages were not written down, but instead were passed on by word of mouth. Have students imagine that they have been assigned the task of writing down the German laws. Have them write a German Law Book based on the information in the textbook and in other reference sources. Have students read their laws to the class.

CHAPTER RESOURCES

LITERATURE ABOUT THE PERIOD

Newark, Tim. *The Barbarians: Warriors and Wars of the Dark Ages.* Poole (Sterling), 1985. Account by a military historian of the medieval period.

READINGS FOR THE STUDENT

Cunliffe, Barry. *Rome and the Barbarians.* Henry Z. Walck, 1975. Description of settlements on the edges of the later Roman Empire and the mixing of Roman and barbarian cultures.

Lyttle, Richard B. *Land Beyond the River: Europe in the Age of Migration.* Atheneum, 1986. Overview of the second through ninth centuries and the customs and characters of the various peoples on the move in Europe, including Germans, Huns, Mongols, and Gypsies.

Simon, Gerald, et al. *Barbarian Europe (Great Ages of Man series).* Time-Life Books, 1968. Description of the period from the decline of Rome through the early Middle Ages.

READINGS FOR THE TEACHER

Barbor, Richard. *The Penguin Guide to Medieval Europe.* Penguin Books, 1984. Describes the political and intellectual climate of Europe from A.D. 800 to A.D. 1400.

Burns, Thomas S. *A History of the Ostro-Goths.* Indiana University Press, 1984. Highlights the history of the Ostrogoths.

Kotker, Norman. *The Horizon Book of the Middle Ages.* Bonanza Books, 1984. Surveys the thousand years from Rome's fall to the dawning of the Renaissance.

Simons, George E., gen. ed. *Barbarian Europe.* Time-Life Books, 1968. Surveys the history of Europe from A.D. 406 to A.D. 1200.

MULTIMEDIA RESOURCES

Faith and Fear. CRM/McGraw-Hill. Film. Examines medieval attitudes, arts, and architecture.

The Middle Ages. International Film Bureau. Film. Presents the economic, social, and cultural history of western Europe during the Middle Ages.

INTRODUCE

CHAPTER 17 OVERVIEW

Chapter 17 discusses the Germanic invasions of western Europe and their impact on Roman civilization.

➤ **Section 1** compares the cultures of the Romans and the Germans.

➤ **Section 2** describes the Germanic invasions and the end of the Roman Empire.

CHAPTER OBJECTIVES

After reading Chapter 17, students will be able to:

1. describe family life in German villages.

2. analyze how the love of battle and their laws influenced the Germans.

3. discuss what role the Goths and the Vandals played in the decline of the Roman Empire.

4. describe what replaced the Roman Empire in the West.

EXAMINING THE ILLUSTRATION

In this painting of Odocer receiving a blessing from the monk, Severin, characteristic dress of the Germans can be seen. Ask students what they can conclude about Odocer from this art. Ask volunteers to explain their conclusions.

PERFORMANCE ASSESSMENT

Use the Performance Assessment activities on page 264B to help you evaluate students as they complete the chapter.

CHAPTER 17 The Germans

Odoacer Receives a Blessing From the Monk, Severin

264

TEACHER CLASSROOM RESOURCES

- Reproducible Lesson Plan
- Section Quizzes/Chapter Test
- Activity Book Activity
- Enrichment Activity
- Chart and Graph Skill Activity
- Geography and Map Activity
- Vocabulary and Guided Reading Activity
- Cooperative Learning Activity
- Performance Assessment Activity
- Spanish Summary and Glossary
- Testmaker
- The Western Civilization Videodisc
- Audiocassettes (English and Spanish)
- Teaching Transparencies and Activities

Chapter Focus

READ TO DISCOVER:

- What life was like in German villages.
- How their love of battle and their laws influenced the Germans.
- What role the Goths and the Vandals played in the decline of the Roman Empire.
- What replaced the Roman Empire in the West.

During the first 400 years after the birth of Christ, a tall, fair-haired people called Germans left the forests and marshes of northern Europe. Looking for a warmer climate and new grazing land for their cattle, they slowly moved south toward the Roman Empire. They were also attracted to Rome by its wealth and culture. The Germans hoped to live peacefully within the borders of the empire.

At first, the Romans did not want to let the Germans enter their territory. They considered the Germans their enemies. By about the year 300, however, the Romans realized they were not strong enough to keep them out. So, they then began to let the Germans cross the border in small groups.

Many Germans moved into the Danube River valley. They settled there, became farmers, and gradually adopted Roman ways. They traded with Roman merchants and joined the Roman army. Some Germans became Christians.

300 A.D.–550 A.D

KEY TERMS

clans
chieftain
blood feuds
oath-helpers
ordeal
wergeld

Section 1

VILLAGE LIFE

Although the Germans took part in Roman life, they also kept much of their own culture. They lived in villages surrounded by farmlands and pastures. Most of the homes were long thatched-roof huts with an open space around them. The family lived in one end of the hut and divided the other end into animal stalls.

FOCUS

BELLRINGER

Write on the chalkboard the following: *What caused the fall of the Roman Empire?* Ask students to write a few major causes.

MOTIVATIONAL ACTIVITY

Discuss students' responses about the causes of the fall of the Roman Empire. Then read the following quote written by a Christian bishop of the A.D. 400s as his province was being overrun by barbarians: *We have planted our crops only for the enemy to burn. All our resources are gone—the flocks of sheep, the herds of camels and horses. I am writing this behind walls, under siege.* Tell students that in this chapter they will learn more about the Germanic groups who helped cause the end of the Roman Empire.

VOCABULARY PRE-CHECK

Write the key terms for this chapter on the chalkboard. Ask students to use those that they know in sentences.

Assign Chapter 17 **Vocabulary and Guided Reading Activity** in the TCR.

EXTRA CREDIT PROJECT

The modern country of Germany has undergone many organizational and governmental changes since the time of the medieval Germans. Suggest students create a time line of major events in Germany's history up to the present time.

KEY TO ABILITY LEVELS

Teaching strategies have been coded for varying learning styles and abilities.

L1 Level 1 activities are **basic** activities and should be within the ability range of all students.

L2 Level 2 activities are **average** activities and should be within the ability range of the average to above-average student.

L3 Level 3 activities are **challenging** activities designed for the ability range of above-average students.

LEP LEP activities should be within the ability range of Limited English Proficiency students.

TEACH

GUIDED PRACTICE

L1 **Daily Life** Ask the students to imagine they are teenagers living in a German village during the Roman Empire and have them write a diary entry describing a day in their lives. Ask students to share their entries with the class. LEP

CAPTION ANSWER

Most homes were long, thatched-roof huts with an open space around them. Families lived in one end of the hut and divided the other end into animal stalls. Wooden tables and benches were the only furniture.

DID YOU KNOW ??

The Germans were divided into groups that ranged in size from about 10,000 individuals to as many as 300,000.

GERMAN VILLAGE The Germans built their villages just within the borders of the Roman Empire. There they became farmers. They lived in family groups that included parents, children, grandparents, aunts, uncles, and cousins. **What was a German home like?**

The body heat of the animals helped to warm the hut during the cold winters. Wooden tables and benches placed along the walls of the hut were the only furniture. A few wealthier villagers added wall hangings or carpets.

German villagers made their living herding cattle, which provided food and clothing. They also traded cattle for Roman glass vessels, table articles, and jewelry. The Germans farmed as well. They grew barley, rye, wheat, beans, and peas. Most farm work was done by women, children, and enslaved people. When the women were not working in the fields or cooking, they spun wool and wove cloth on upright looms.

German dress was simple. The women wore long skirts made of different yarns, or one-piece sack-like dresses that extended from the shoulders to the feet. Sometimes, they wore scarves or shawls fastened with a bone pin. The men wore short woolen *tunics*, or coat-like garments, and close-fitting trousers. They covered the tunics with cloaks fastened on the right shoulder with a brooch.

SPOTLIGHT ON: TACTICUS

Most of what modern historians know about the customs, appearance, and beliefs of the Germanic tribes comes from a Roman—not a Germanic—historian. Cornelius Tacticus, a Roman lawyer, official, and historian, wrote about people in two distant parts of the Roman Empire in the A.D. 100's and early A.D. 200's. His book *Germania*, written in A.D. 98, describes the Germans along the Rhine River frontier of the empire. He uses the Germanic tribes as moral examples of upright, if primitive, people who still hold on to the simple virtues that many Romans have forgotten. He also writes about the laws, customs, and fighting methods of the Germans that developed from nearly 100 years of Roman wars and other contacts.

The Germans believed in hospitality. So strong was this belief that it was against the law to turn away anyone who came to the door. Invited guests and strangers alike were welcomed, fed, and entertained. Feasting, drinking, and dancing were favorite German pastimes. Men also enjoyed gambling with dice. Sometimes, they took part in such organized sports as boxing and wrestling. In winter, they skated on frozen ponds and lakes using skates made of flat bone.

The Germans spoke a language that later became modern German. At first, they could not read or write, because their language had no alphabet. However, some learned to speak and write Latin. Gradually, they began to use Roman letters to write their own language.

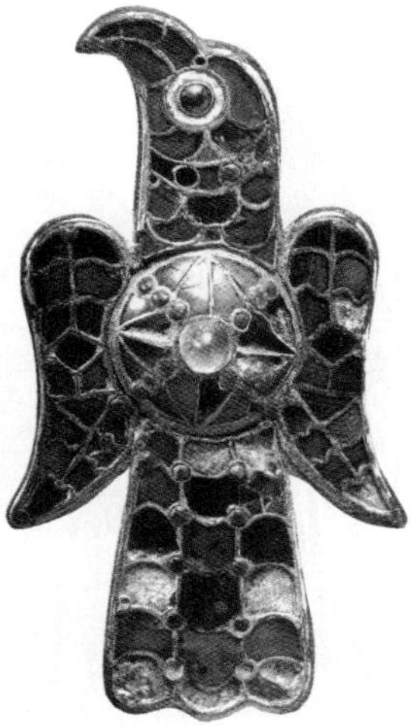

German Brooch

Warriors German men were warriors. They spent most of their time fighting, hunting, or making weapons. They began training for war when they were young boys. When a male reached manhood, he was brought before a special gathering held in a sacred grove under a full moon. There, he received a shield and a spear, which he had to carry with him at all times. The loss of the shield and spear meant loss of honor.

The Germans were divided into **clans,** or groups based on family ties. At first, the Germans gave their greatest loyalty to their clan. After a while, however, they developed a strong feeling of loyalty toward a military leader called a **chieftain** (chēf′ tuhn). A man had to fight well to become a chieftain. In the beginning, a chieftain was elected by a band of warriors. Later, this office became hereditary.

Chieftains gave their men leadership, weapons, and a chance for wealth and adventure. They also kept peace among their warriors. In some cases, they gave their warriors food and shelter. In return, warriors gave their chieftains complete loyalty. Some even gave their chieftains credit for the brave deeds they themselves did. In battle, chieftains fought for victory and warriors fought for their chieftains.

German warrior bands did not have fixed plans of fighting. Each band was small and usually fought on its own, apart from other bands. The bands made surprise raids against their enemies. Warriors on foot and on horseback would charge wildly, yelling in loud voices to frighten their foes. They fought with daggers, short swords, and heavy axes made of metal and stone. They carried light wooden shields and wore suits of leather. A successful attack provided warriors with enslaved people, cattle, and other treasures.

The Germans' love of battle was closely linked to their religion. Germans had many gods who liked to fight and to hunt. The chief god, Wodan (wōd′ n), was the god of war, poetry, learning, and magic. Another god of war was Wodan's

German Shield

L2 **Critical Thinking** Have students work in pairs to learn more about the German belief in hospitality. Have them create a presentation that compares and contrasts German hospitality in the 400s to that of today. Suggest they share their presentations with the class. LEP

MAKING CONNECTIONS

➤➤ **Religion** The warlike Wodan became the chief god of German warriors and chieftains. Earlier, these people held beliefs that centered on Mother Earth—Erce or Nerthus. Even after the Germans adopted Christianity, they kept some old beliefs in the spirits of the earth and forest. Customs such as the Yule log and the lighted Christmas tree, for instance, derive from rituals of the Germanic forest tribes.

MULTICULTURAL PERSPECTIVES

While the months on our calendar come from Roman gods and emperors, the days of the week come mainly from Germanic mythology, which is closely related to Norse myths. The dedication of days of the week to certain gods and goddesses is a good indication that they were important in everyday life. Sunday and Monday belong to the sun and moon. Tuesday belongs to the war god Tiw or Tyr, a hero-god. Wednesday is "Wodan's Day," and Thursday is for Thor or Thunor, the god of thunder. Experts disagree about Friday, but some think it is named after Frigga, goddess of fertility and wife of Wodan. Saturday is the only day of the week named after a Roman god—Saturn.

L3 **History** Have students imagine they are anchorpersons for the Rome Evening News in August, A.D. 410. The Visigoths, led by Alaric, are camped outside the walls ready to attack. Have students write news reports, including background information on Alaric and the Goths, and present their newscasts to the class. **LEP**

MAKING CONNECTIONS

➤➤ **Religion** Attila's attacks also inspired terror among the Christians of Europe. They believed he was sent by God to punish them for their sins and called him the "Scourge of God."

GEOGRAPHY AND HISTORY

Have students trace the path of each invader shown on the map of Germanic Invasions. Ask: Why do you think most of the Germanic tribes focused their attacks on the Western Roman Empire and not on the Eastern Roman Empire?

MAP STUDY

Answer

from the north and the east

Assign the Chapter 17 **Geography and Map Activity** in the TCR.

MAP STUDY

MOVEMENT In 472 A.D. Germanic people controlled about 20 percent of the western Roman Empire. **From which general directions did most of the Germanic people invade the western Roman Empire?**

Section **2**

The Conquerors

The Goths (gahths) were a Germanic people who lived in the Balkan Peninsula of Europe. They were divided into two groups called Ostrogoths (ahs' truh gahths), or East Goths, and Visigoths (viz' uh gahths), or West Goths.

In the late 300s, both groups were attacked by the Huns led by Attila (at' uhl uh), or "Little Daddy." The Huns conquered the East Goths. The West Goths feared they would be next. So, they asked the Roman emperor for protection. He let them settle just inside the empire's frontier. In return, they gave up their weapons and promised to be loyal to Rome.

Before long, trouble broke out between the West Goths and Roman officials. The West Goths had to buy the empire's food at very high prices. The Romans also kidnapped many young West Goths and enslaved them.

Germanic Invasions

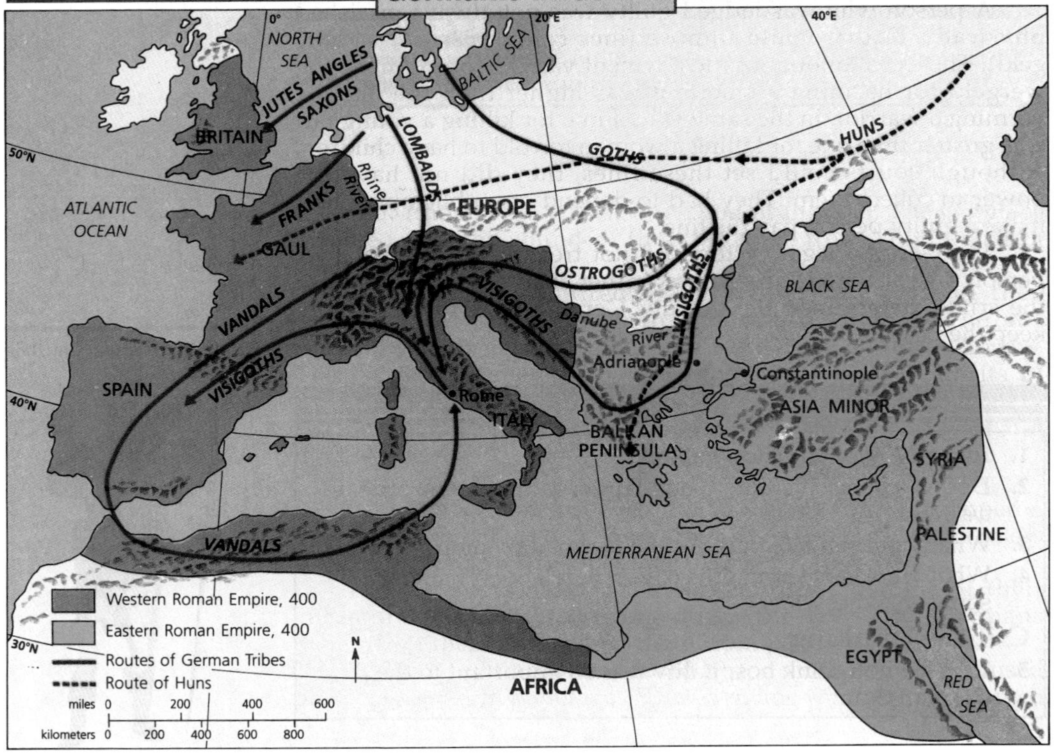

EXTENDING THE CONTENT

In 472 Germanic tribes controlled only about 20 percent of the territory that had belonged to the Roman Empire. The Huns so thoroughly devastated the western Roman Empire, however, that by 476 these Germanic tribes were able to take over the remaining 80 percent of the weakened empire.

The Germanic Kingdoms

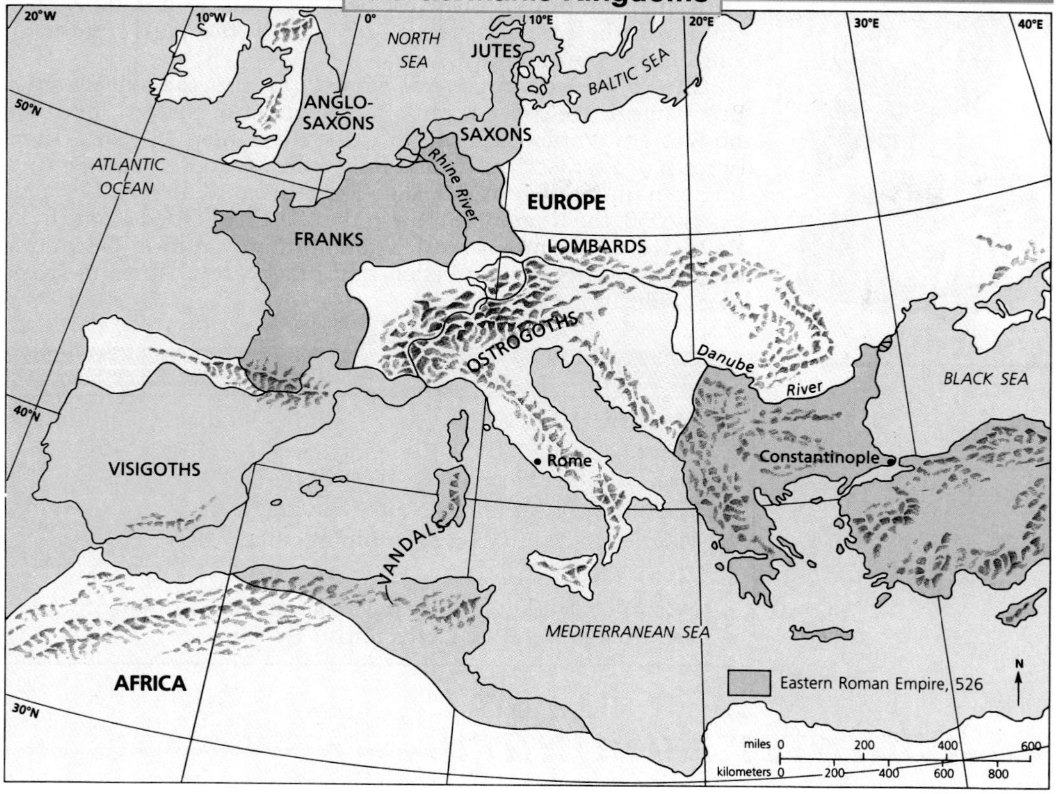

Finally, the West Goths rebelled against the Romans and defeated them at the Battle of Adrianople in 378. Then, in 410, led by the chieftain Alaric, they captured and looted Rome.

After the capture of Rome, the West Goths continued on to Gaul. Then, they moved into Spain, which was occupied by Romans and another Germanic group called Vandals (van' duhlz). The West Goths ended Roman rule in Spain, drove out the Vandals, and set up their own kingdom.

The Vandals in turn crossed the Mediterranean to North Africa. They became pirates and attacked cities along the Mediterranean coast. From these attacks came the English word *"vandalism,"* meaning the willful destruction of property.

In 455, the Vandals attacked and burned Rome. They did, however, spare the lives of the Romans. Afterwards, the Vandals returned to North Africa. Like Rome's capture in 410 by the West Goths, this event shook the Roman world.

MAP STUDY

REGIONS The Visigoths defeated the Vandals whom they forced to settle in North Africa. **What advantage did the Vandals have because of their new location in the region?**

INDEPENDENT PRACTICE

L1 **Map Skills** Have students work in pairs to write two questions based on the map on page 271. Collect the questions and ask the class to respond. LEP

L3 **Critical Thinking** Ask students why they think the German generals usually chose a Roman citizen to serve as emperor of the Roman Empire. Would the students have done the same? Why or why not?

MAP STUDY Answer

They were able to control large areas of the Mediterranean Sea.

DID YOU KNOW ??

Theodoric's kingdom included people of different races and religions, all of whom were allowed to live according to their own customs and to worship their own gods.

VIDEODISC

Use the following to enrich Chapter 17.

WC B 165 11881
Attila, Khan (king) of the Huns.

COOPERATIVE LEARNING

Many people in the United States today are of German, other European, or non-European descent. Have the class do an "Ancestor Hunt" of your class. Have them devise a way to chart or graph the ancestral background of each student. Suggest they also display their information with charts and visual representations from the countries of heritage of your students. Interested students may want to read *The Great Ancestor Hunt* by Lila Perl.

Assign Chapter 17 **Cooperative Learning Activity** in the TCR.

ASSESS

CHECK FOR UNDERSTANDING

Ask students to summarize the main points of the chapter. Discuss the answers to the Section and Chapter Review questions.

EVALUATE

Assign Chapter 17 **Performance Assessment Activity** in the TCR.

Administer **Chapter 17 Test** in the TCR. Testmaker available.

RETEACH

Have students summarize factors that led to the fall of Rome and their importance.

Assign Chapter 17 **Reteaching Activity** in the TCR.

ENRICH

Have students research Germanic mythology and report on the gods and goddesses that were worshiped in the early Middle Ages.

Assign the Chapter 17 **Enrichment Activity** in the TCR.

CLOSE

Ask students to discuss whether they think the Western Roman Empire would have fallen even if the Germanic tribes had not invaded the empire.

MEETING CHAPTER OBJECTIVES

Each objective is tested by the Review questions in parentheses.

1. **Describe** German family life (BV; CT 1, 3)
2. **Analyze** how the Germans' love of battle and their laws. (CU 3, 5; UYJ)
3. **Discuss** the Goths and the Vandals in the decline of the Roman Empire. (CU 7)
4. **Describe** what replaced the Roman Empire in the West. (CU 8)

Illustration of Attila

The Germanic invasions were one of the three main reasons the Roman Empire in the West began to fall. While the Roman Empire in the East prospered, generals in the West fought for control of Rome and Italy.

In 476, a German general named Odoacer (ŏd′ uh wā suhr) took control. He did not appoint an emperor. Instead, he ruled the western empire in his own name for almost 15 years. Then, a group of East Goths invaded Italy, killed Odoacer, and set up a kingdom under their leader Theodoric (thē ahd′ uh rik).

By 550, the Roman Empire in the West had faded away. In its place were six major and a great many minor Germanic kingdoms. Many Roman beliefs and practices remained to shape later civilizations.

Section 2 Review

1. **Identify:** Huns, Attila, Alaric, Vandals, Odoacer, Theodoric
2. What happened to the East Goths in the late 300s? What effect did this have on the West Goths?
3. What did the Vandals do after leaving Spain?
4. What replaced the Roman Empire in the West?

Critical Thinking

5. What do you think might have happened if Roman officials had treated the West Goths fairly? Explain.

Chapter Summary

1. About 300, groups of Germans began settling in the Roman Empire.
2. German warriors were organized into bands headed by military chieftains, to whom the warriors gave their complete loyalty.
3. The Germans' love of battle was closely linked to their religion.
4. The Germans determined one's guilt or innocence by oath-taking or by ordeal.
5. German courts often imposed fines called *wergeld* on the guilty.
6. The penalty for a crime depended on a person's wealth or importance.
7. The Germans believed that law came from the people and that a ruler could not change a law.
8. In 378, the West Goths defeated the Romans at the Battle of Adrianople.
9. In 410, the West Goths captured and robbed Rome and then went on to set up their own kingdom in Spain.
10. The Vandals, who were driven out of Spain by the West Goths, moved to North Africa and began to raid cities along the Mediterranean coast.
11. By 550, the Roman Empire had been replaced by six major and many minor kingdoms.

SECTION 2 ANSWERS

1. Huns, Asian people who conquered the East Goths (p. 270); Attila, leader of the Huns (p. 270); Alaric, chieftain of the West Goths (p. 271); Vandals, Germanic group (p. 271); Odoacer, German general (p. 272); Theodoric, leader of the East Goths (p. 272)
2. They were conquered by the Huns. It led them to ask the Roman emperor for protection.
3. They crossed the Mediterranean to North Africa, became pirates, and attacked and burned Rome.
4. six major and a great many minor Germanic kingdoms
5. Answers will vary but will probably mention that the West Goths might not have rebelled.

Assign Chapter 17 **Section 2 Quiz** in the TCR. Testmaker available.

CHAPTER
Review 17

Building Vocabulary

Write a short story describing the daily life of a person in one of the early Germanic groups. Use the following words in your story.

clans
blood feuds
ordeal
chieftain
oath-helpers
wergeld

Check for Understanding

1. Why did the Germans begin to move south toward the Roman Empire?
2. Why were the Germans allowed to cross the borders of the Roman Empire?
3. How did warriors show their loyalty to their chieftain?
4. What did the Germans believe the afterlife would be like for warriors?
5. According to German beliefs, from what source did law come?
6. What was the reason for the German ordeal by water?
7. Why did the West Goths want to enter the Roman Empire?
8. What did the West Goths do after they captured Rome?

Critical Thinking

1. What parts of Roman culture did the Germans adopt? What parts of their own culture did they keep?
2. Imagine that you are soon to become the chieftain of a Germanic warrior band. Explain what you would provide for your warriors.
3. What would you have liked and disliked about living in a German village?
4. Do you believe the penalty for a crime should depend on a person's wealth or importance? If not, on what should it depend? Explain.

Geography in History

PLACE Refer to the map on page 271. Access to the sea played an important role in the economy of each Germanic kingdom. Which kingdom had the longest seacoast? About how many miles (Km) long was it?

Using Your Journal

Review the details you have noted about the changes that took place during the early Middle Ages. Imagine you are in a German village at that time. Write a letter to a friend explaining how the German idea of law compares to the idea of law that you know today.

+ BONUS +

TEST QUESTION

For Chapter 17 Test

"If I may join your army I swear on our god of war, Zeus, I will fight hard. I have a letter from my chieftain saying I am a good warrior." Why would this warrior speaking to a Roman not be considered a true German? *(he named wrong god of war; could not have a letter since Germans did not yet write; showed disloyalty)*

USING YOUR JOURNAL

Letters will vary but should compare and contrast the ideas of German law with ideas of law today.

CHAPTER 17 REVIEW ANSWERS

BUILDING VOCABULARY

Short stories will vary but should include a description of daily activities and use all the vocabulary words.

CHECK FOR UNDERSTANDING

1. They were looking for a warmer climate, new grazing land, and wealth and culture.
2. because the Romans realized they were not strong enough to keep them out
3. They obeyed in battle and some gave their chieftains credit for their own brave deeds.
4. It would be spent in Valhalla, where they would feast and fight forever.
5. from the people
6. They believed water would accept anyone who was pure and reject anyone who was not pure.
7. because they were afraid they would be conquered by the Huns
8. They continued on to Gaul, ended Roman rule in Spain, drove out the Vandals, and set up their own kingdom.

CRITICAL THINKING

1. They became farmers, traded with Romans, and joined the Roman army. Some became Christians. They lived in villages, believed in hospitality, and spoke what later became modern German.
2. Answers will vary but should include some responsibilities of chieftains.
3. Answers will vary but should include specific details.
4. Answers will vary.

GEOGRAPHY IN HISTORY

Ostrogoth; about 2,000 miles (or 3,226 km)

CHAPTER 18
The Franks

CHAPTER ORGANIZER

Objectives	Special Features	Supplemental Materials
Section 1 Clovis Explain how Clovis united the Franks and brought them Christianity.	People in History: *Tunka Manin,* p. 276	• Reproducible Lesson Plan • Section 1 Quiz • Testmaker • Chapter 18 Vocabulary and Guided Reading Activity • Unit 6 World Literature • Chapter 18 Teaching Transparencies and Activities
Section 2 Charles the Hammer Describe how Charles Martel's defeat of the Arabs kept western Europe Christian.		• Reproducible Lesson Plan • Section 2 Quiz • Testmaker • Reinforcing Social Studies Skills, pp. 8, 17 • Chapter 18 Activity Book Activity
Section 3 Charlemagne Discuss how Charlemagne brought all of western Europe under his rule, what daily life was like in Charlemagne's empire, and why Charlemagne's empire collapsed.	Map and Geography Skills: *Understanding Inset Maps,* p. 284	• Reproducible Lesson Plan • Section 3 Quiz • Testmaker • Chapter 18 Geography and Map Activity • Chapter 18 Cooperative Learning Activity • Chapter 18 Chart and Graph Skill Activity • World Art and History Transparency 7 • The Western Civilization Videodisc
Chapter 18 Review and Evaluation		• Chapter 18 Reteaching Activity • Chapter 18 Enrichment Activity • Spanish Summary and Glossary • Audiocassettes (English and Spanish) • Chapter 18 Performance Assessment Activity • Chapter 18 Test • Testmaker

If time does not permit teaching the entire chapter, use the Chapter 18 Summary on page 286 and the Chapter 18 Audiocassettes (English and Spanish) to point out the main ideas of the chapter.

Performance Assessment Activities

Education Have students compile a list of the advances Charlemagne made in education during his reign. Then have students conduct a survey of students and teachers, asking what improvements they would make in the education system today if they could. Have students list those suggestions and post them next to Charlemagne's for comparison.

Writing Have students research the many inventions from the Middle Ages. Then have them create advertisements for some of these inventions, using both text and drawings. Some possibilities are portable clocks (the first watches), pies, fireplaces for warming drafty castles, improved farming equipment such as wheelbarrows and plows, and buttons and buttonholes. Display the advertisements in the classroom.

CHAPTER RESOURCES

LITERATURE ABOUT THE PERIOD

Almedingen, E.M. *A Candle at Dusk*. Farrar, Straus & Giroux, 1969. Historical novel set at the time of the Battle of Tours (732) and centering on a student in a Frankish monastery.

Sayers, Dorothy, trans. *The Song of Roland*. Penguin, 1957. Chronicles the events and legends in Charlemagne's career and the career of his young nephew Roland.

READINGS FOR THE STUDENT

Heer, Friedrich. *Charlemagne and His World*. Macmillan, 1975. Large, lavishly illustrated description of the period.

Munz, Peter. *Life in the Age of Charlemagne* (European Life Series). G.P. Putnam's Sons, 1969. Part of a classic series, illustrated with small, detailed drawings of everyday scenes and objects.

READINGS FOR THE TEACHER

Asimov, Isaac. *The Dark Ages*. Houghton Mifflin, 1968. Focuses on the Dark Ages, covering the Germanic tribes, the Gothic kingdoms, and the rise of the Merovingian and Carolingian dynasties.

Mills, Dorothy. *The Middle Ages*. Putnam, 1935. Deals with the period between 300 and 1500 covering the church, Charlemagne, the Norsemen, monasteries, chivalry, the crusaders, medieval towns, trade, travel, education, and government.

MULTIMEDIA RESOURCES

Charlemagne: Holy Barbarian. Learning Corporation of America. Film. Describes Charlemagne's attempt to Christianize and civilize his empire.

Charlemagne: Unifier of Europe. CRM/McGraw-Hill. Film. Highlights Charlemagne's ideas concerning government and education.

World History Adventure. Intellectual Software. Software, Apple and IBM. Simulates events in world history, including the Middle Ages.

INTRODUCE

CHAPTER 18 OVERVIEW

Chapter 18 discusses the Franks, who established the first strong kingdom of medieval Europe.

- **Section 1** discusses the goals of Clovis and the role of the Catholic Church in the political affairs of the Franks.
- **Section 2** describes the rule of Charles Martel and the Battle of Tours.
- **Section 3** explains the cultural and political developments during the reign of Charlemagne.

CHAPTER OBJECTIVES

After reading Chapter 18, students will be able to:

1. explain how Clovis united the Franks under Christianity.
2. describe how Charles Martel's defeat of the Arabs kept western Europe Christian.
3. discuss how Charlemagne brought all of western Europe under his rule.
4. characterize what life was like in Charlemagne's empire.
5. summarize how and why Charlemagne's empire collapsed.

EXAMINING THE ILLUSTRATION

Ask students what they notice about the warriors surrounding Charlemagne in this relief. Why do the knights wear so much armor? Suggest they will learn more about this leader and his warriors as they read the chapter.

PERFORMANCE ASSESSMENT

Use the Performance Assessment activities on page 274B to help you evaluate students as they complete the chapter.

CHAPTER 18 The Franks

Charlemagne and His Army

274

TEACHER CLASSROOM RESOURCES

- Reproducible Lesson Plan
- Reteaching Activity
- Enrichment Activity
- Chart and Graph Skill Activity
- Geography and Map Activity
- Vocabulary and Guided Reading Activity
- Cooperative Learning Activity
- Performance Assessment Activity
- Spanish Summary and Glossary
- Testmaker
- World History and Art Transparencies
- The Western Civilization Videodisc
- Audiocassettes (English and Spanish)
- Teaching Transparencies and Activities

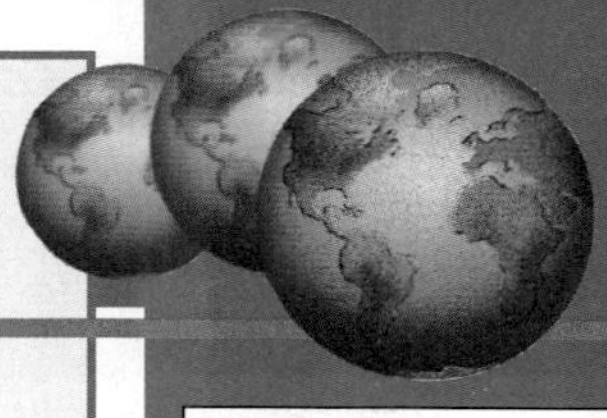

Chapter Focus

READ TO DISCOVER:

- How Clovis united the Franks and brought them Christianity.
- How Charles Martel's defeat of the Arabs kept western Europe Christian.
- How Charlemagne brought all of western Europe under his rule.
- What life was like in Charlemagne's empire.
- Why Charlemagne's empire collapsed.

The decline of the Roman Empire led to disorder everywhere in western Europe. Many of the Germanic invaders were too weak to govern well. As a result, towns and villages fell into ruin. Roads and bridges were not repaired. Robbers roamed the countryside, making it unsafe for travelers. Trading and business slowed down, and there were shortages of food and other goods. People were no longer interested in learning, and many books and works of art were damaged or lost.

480 A.D.–843 A.D.

KEY TERMS

- converted
- anointed
- counts
- lords
- serfs
- minstrels

Section 1

CLOVIS

During this period, a Germanic people called Franks became very important. They began to build a new civilization, one that later developed into modern France and Germany. The Franks lived along the Rhine River in what is now Germany. They were more successful in governing than other Germans. One reason for this was that the area in which they lived was close to their homeland, and they felt fairly secure. Also, unlike the Goths and Vandals, the Franks did more than just fight and rule. They became farmers.

At first, the Franks were divided into separate groups without a common ruler. In 481, one Frankish group chose a man named

FOCUS

BELLRINGER

Ask students to respond in writing to the term *Dark Ages.*

MOTIVATIONAL ACTIVITY

Discuss students' responses to the term *Dark Ages.* Tell students that by A.D. 500 western Europe was so backward compared to other contemporary societies that scholars once called the early part of the Middle Ages the Dark Ages. Tell students that in this chapter they will learn about events that helped move western Europe out of the Dark Ages and into an age of enlightenment.

VOCABULARY PRE-CHECK

Write the key terms for this chapter on the chalkboard. Ask volunteers to skim the chapter for the boldfaced words and read aloud the sentences in which they find them.

Assign Chapter 18 **Vocabulary and Guided Reading Activity** in the TCR.

EXTRA CREDIT PROJECT

The Franks came into conflict with the people of the Pyrenees Mountains, the Basques. Suggest interested students learn more about the Basque people and their culture. Encourage them to choose a form of presentation to share their research with the rest of the class.

KEY TO ABILITY LEVELS

Teaching strategies have been coded for varying learning styles and abilities.

L1 Level 1 activities are **basic** activities and should be within the ability range of all students.

L2 Level 2 activities are **average** activities and should be within the ability range of the average to above-average student.

L3 Level 3 activities are **challenging** activities designed for the ability range of above-average students.

LEP LEP activities should be within the ability range of Limited English Proficiency students.

Teaching

PEOPLE IN HISTORY

TUNKA MANIN

After students have read the People in History feature have them locate the Niger and Senegal rivers on a map of Africa. Tell them that the kingdom of Ghana in West Africa was northeast of the Senegal River and northwest of the Niger River. Point out that present-day Ghana is southeast of this location. Then ask: Why was Tunka Manin considered a wise leader? *(He encouraged learning and built economic stability for his people. He listened to the problems of his people and settled disputes fairly.)*

ANSWERS to Checking for Understanding

1. Ghana was the word for "warrior king."
2. to preserve their foods and to help keep moisture in their bodies in the desert heat
3. He allowed people from the north and south of Ghana to trade in his kingdom. He placed a tax on all goods bought or sold in the kingdom.

PEOPLE IN HISTORY

Tunka Manin

The Franks and other Germanic groups ruled western Europe during the Dark Ages and later. At the same time, kingdoms in other parts of the world, especially in Africa, were thriving. One of these great kingdoms—Ghana—existed in West Africa. In its later period, this kingdom was ruled by Tunka Manin.

Tunka Manin's kingdom was very wealthy. It was so wealthy that Tunka Manin was called the lord of the gold. The warriors in his kingdom were very powerful—so much so that Tunka Manin was also known as the warrior king, or *Ghana,* and his kingdom became known as Ghana.

Wise Ruler Tunka Manin was a wise leader. He encouraged learning and individual choice of religion for his people. He listened to the problems of his people and settled disputes fairly. The kingdom of Tunka Manin prospered.

One of the major reasons the kingdom was so wealthy was due to the riches brought in from the trade routes that Tunka Manin controlled. He knew that the people in his kingdom needed salt. They needed it to preserve their foods and to help keep moisture in their bodies.

Salt for Gold Ghana did not have a large supply of salt. However, the lands to the north of Ghana were abundant in salt mines and the lands to the south of Ghana were rich in gold. So Tunka Manin allowed the people of the north and the south to meet in Ghana to trade gold for salt.

Merchants from the north and south traveled to Ghana to trade their goods. The northern traders brought salt, cloths, and other goods. They traded these goods for the gold that the southern traders brought. Tunka Manin charged a tax on any goods traded in Ghana, making Ghana a very wealthy kingdom.

Tunka Manin also controlled the amount of gold that was circulating in his kingdom. The largest nuggets were kept in his own personal treasury. In this way he helped Ghana keep a balanced economy.

Checking for Understanding

1. **How did Ghana get its name?**
2. **Why did the people of Ghana need salt?**
3. **How did Tunka Manin make Ghana wealthy?**

SPOTLIGHT ON: GHANA

By the eleventh century, Ghana was a powerful empire in the western part of Africa. People who visited Ghana at that time were often dazzled by the glittering wealth of Ghana's kings. In 1067, an Arab named Abdullah al Bekri visited the ancient empire and wrote about his impressions. According to al Bekri, "When he [the king] gives audience to his people, to listen to their complaints and set them to rights, he sits in a pavilion [large tent] around which stand ten pages [young attendants] holding shields and gold mounted swords."

Clovis (klō′ vis) as king. Although he was cruel and greedy, Clovis was a good general and an able king. He eventually brought all the Franks under one rule. Part of Clovis's kingdom later became France, which took its name from the Franks.

Clovis was the first Germanic king to accept the Catholic religion. Clovis was not happy with the Frankish gods. Although he prayed to them faithfully, they failed to help him win battles. Clovis decided that if he defeated the enemy, he would become a Christian. Clovis's army won its next battle. Clovis and some 3,000 Frankish soldiers, still in full battle dress, immediately **converted** (kuhn ver′ tuhd), or changed religion, to Christianity. It was not long before all the Franks followed his example.

When Clovis became a Christian, he gained the support of the Romans in his kingdom. Before long, the Franks began speaking a form of Latin that later became the modern French language. Now, all the people in Clovis's kingdom practiced the same religion, spoke the same language, and felt united.

The Pope and other church officials gave Clovis their support. Priests served in his government. In return for the Church's help, Clovis was expected to protect the Church against all non-believers.

Clovis extended his rule over what is now France and western Germany and set up his capital in Paris. He admired the Roman Empire. He wore purple robes similar to those of the Roman emperors, and made Latin the official language of the court.

Painting of Frankish Warrior

Section 1 Review

1. **Identify:** Franks, Clovis
2. **Define:** converted
3. Why were the Franks more successful at governing than other Germanic peoples?

Critical Thinking

4. Why was it important for Clovis to have the Pope's blessing and the support of the church?

Painting of Clovis

Section 2 CHARLES THE HAMMER

The Frankish kings who followed Clovis were weak rulers. Instead of keeping the kingdom united, they divided it among their sons. The sons often fought over their shares of land. They

TEACH

GUIDED PRACTICE

L1 **Government** Write the following question on the chalkboard: *How was Clovis able to unify the Franks?* Lead a discussion in which students answer this question. Direct the discussion with the following questions: Why did Clovis's conversion to Christianity gain the support of the Romans in his kingdom? Do you think Clovis would have had a united kingdom if he had not become a Christian and adopted the Latin language? Why or why not?

DID YOU KNOW ??

Clovis began the Merovingian line of kings. Clovis's sister was married to Theodoric, the leader of the East Goths who invaded Italy and set up a kingdom there.

VIDEODISC

Use the following to enrich Chapter 18.

WC C 2 14604
Clovis, king of the Franks (466?-511).

SECTION 1 ANSWERS

1. Franks, Germanic people (p. 275); Clovis, king of the Franks (p. 277)
2. converted, changed religion (p. 277)
3. because the area in which they lived was close to their homeland, and they felt fairly secure; also, they became farmers instead of just fighting and ruling
4. Answers will vary but might include that through this, Clovis gained the support of the Romans in his kingdom.

Assign Chapter 18 **Section 1 Quiz** in the TCR. Testmaker available.

L2 **History** Ask the students to imagine that they are Charles Martel after his defeat of the Arabs and Berbers at the Battle of Tours in 732. Tell them that they are to write a letter to the Pope presenting an eyewitness account of what has taken place and giving reasons why the event is certain to be of great significance for Christianity and western Europe. Then have students imagine that they are the Pope and have them write a response to Charles Martel's letter. Have students read their letters to the class.

L2 **Critical Thinking** Remind students they have read about several rulers who were given nicknames in addition to their given names. Ask students to name a few. *(Charles the Hammer, Alexander the Great)* Ask students to explain why they think many rulers were given nicknames. LEP

CAPTION ANSWER

They hoped to spread their religion of Islam throughout Europe.

spent so much time and energy fighting that they lost much of their power to local nobles.

It was not long before the Franks began to accept the leadership of a government official known as the "Mayor of the Palace." The Mayor was a noble and the most important official in the king's household. As the Frankish kings grew weaker, the Mayors took over many of their duties. In time, the Mayors were conducting wars, giving out land, and settling disputes. Of all the Mayors, the most powerful was Charles Martel (mahr tel'). He wanted to reunite all the Frankish nobles under his rule. Before long, Charles Martel had gained the support of the Church.

Charles Martel became known as "The Hammer" because of his strength in battle. In 732, he led the Franks in the Battle of

BATTLE OF TOURS Charles Martel (shown center in this painting) leads his army against the Muslims at the Battle of Tours. The Frankish victory halted the Muslim advance into western Europe. It also helped the Frankish rulers to build a strong kingdom. **Why were the Muslims invading western Europe?**

EXTENDING THE CONTENT

Charles Martel, who held power effectively from about 720 until his death in 741, depended in part on having the backing of the Church. In return, and to help unify the empire, he encouraged Christianity and protected missionaries from the pagan Germans across the Rhine River. The most famous missionary was St. Boniface, an Anglo-Saxon priest from England.

Tours (tūrz), one of the most important battles in European history. The Franks defeated an army of Arabs and Berbers who had conquered Spain in 711. The Arabs and Berbers were Muslims, who hoped to spread their religion of Islam everywhere. The Franks' victory at the Battle of Tours enabled Christianity to survive in western Europe.

When Charles Martel died, his son Pepin (pep' in) became Mayor of the Palace. With the help of the Pope and most Frankish nobles, Pepin removed the king and started a new dynasty. Pepin was the first Frankish king to be **anointed** (uh noin' tuhd), or blessed with holy oil, by the Pope. In return for the Church's support, Pepin helped the Pope when he was threatened by a group of Germans known as Lombards (lahm' bahrdz). Pepin led an army into Italy, defeated the Lombards, and gave the land they held in central Italy to the Pope. This gift made the Pope the political ruler of much of the Italian Peninsula.

Frankish Goldwork

MAKING CONNECTIONS

➤➤ **History** Pepin, known as "Pepin the Short," began the Carolingian line of kings in 751.

Section 2 Review

1. **Identify:** Mayor of the Palace, Charles Martel, Battle of Tours, Pepin, Lombards
2. **Define:** anointed
3. Why was the Battle of Tours important?
4. How did Pepin help the Pope?

Critical Thinking

5. What might western Europe have been like if the Arabs and Berbers had won the Battle of Tours?

DID YOU KNOW ??

Charlemagne married at least four times. His sons and daughters often accompanied him as he traveled from palace to palace around the empire. He stayed fit by riding, swimming, and hunting. At Aachen (Aix-la-Chapelle), probably Charlemagne's favorite palace, there was a spring-fed swimming pool. Charlemagne liked to entertain there.

Section 3

CHARLEMAGNE

When Pepin died in 768, his kingdom was divided between his two sons. His son Carloman died within a few years. Pepin's other son Charles then became king of the Franks. He is best known by his French name Charlemagne (shar' luh mān), which means "Charles the Great."

A powerful leader, Charlemagne wanted to bring all of western Europe under his rule. He also wanted all the Germanic people to become Christian. To achieve these goals, he waged a series of wars.

First, Charlemagne went to Italy and defeated the Lombards. Next, Charlemagne attacked Saxons (sak' suhnz), who lived in what is now northern Germany. For years, the Saxons had been raiding towns and monasteries inside the Frankish border. He

VIDEODISC

Use the following to enrich Chapter 18.

WC C 8 14610

Charlemagne (742-814).

SECTION 2 ANSWERS

1. Mayor of the Palace, government official (p. 278); Charles Martel, a powerful Mayor of the Palace (p. 278); Battle of Tours, battle between the Franks and Arabs and Berbers (p. 279); Pepin, son of Charles Martel (p. 279); Lombards, Germanic group (p. 279)
2. anointed, blessed with holy oil (p. 279)
3. It enabled Christianity to survive in western Europe.
4. He led an army into Italy, defeated the Lombards, and gave the land they held in central Italy to the Pope.
5. Answers will vary but could include the idea that it might have meant the end of Christianity as the major religion of western Europe.

Assign the Chapter 18 **Section 2 Quiz** in the TCR. Testmaker available.

MAKING CONNECTIONS

➤➤ **Literature** *The Song of Roland* is not a true account of the warrior Roland's feats, but one based on legend that grew up about Roland. For example, in the poem, Roland fights Muslims rather than Basques.

CAPTION ANSWER

He appointed bishops and regarded any act against the Church as a sign of disloyalty to him.

VIDEODISC

Use the following to enrich Chapter 18.

WC C 9 14611

Archbishop Turpin and Charlemagne.

sent thousands of captured Saxons into Frankish territory and then moved many Franks onto Saxon lands. Eventually, the Saxons accepted Christianity.

Charlemagne also led his armies in several campaigns across the Pyrenees (pēr′ uh nēz) Mountains to fight the Muslims in Spain. A mountain people known as Basques (basks) did not want the Frankish armies to cross their territory. When Charlemagne was returning home from one of his Spanish campaigns, Basque warriors attacked the rear guard of his army in a narrow mountain pass. The rear guard was led by Roland, a fine warrior. Since Roland had far fewer soldiers than the Basques, he lost the battle. Even so, the fight was remembered, told, and retold throughout Europe. Over time, it became legend and was written down in French as a poem called *The Song of Roland.*

By 800, Charlemagne had created a large empire. It included most of the Germanic peoples who had settled in Europe since the early 400s. Charlemagne also fought against non-Germanic peoples in northern and eastern Europe. Although they managed to keep their freedom, they agreed to respect Charlemagne's power and not fight against his army.

CROWNING OF CHARLEMAGNE In 800, Charlemagne became emperor of a new Christian Roman Empire. Here, Charlemagne is crowned "Emperor of the Romans" by the Pope. **How did Charlemagne aid the Church?**

SPOTLIGHT ON: CHARLEMAGNE

Charlemagne's secretary—a monk named Einhard—wrote the following description of Charlemagne: "Bodily Charles was well-built, strong and noble in height, measuring seven times his own foot. His head was round, his eyes large and lively, his nose a little larger than the mean, his hair in his later years a brilliant white, his expression calm and cheerful, his bearing full of majesty, his tread firm, his carriage erect, his voice high."

A Christian Empire Charlemagne became the most powerful leader in western Europe. The people considered him as important as any Roman emperor. Charlemagne wanted to keep close ties between the Church and the government. Church officials kept records and helped Charlemagne run the country. In turn, he appointed the bishops and regarded any act against the Church as a sign of disloyalty to him.

Both Charlemagne and the Pope wanted a new Christian Roman Empire in western Europe. Charlemagne's conquests had brought him closer to their goal. On Christmas day in 800, Charlemagne was worshiping in St. Peter's Church in Rome. When the religious ceremony was over, the Pope placed a crown on Charlemagne's head. The Pope then declared that Charlemagne was the new Roman emperor. Although Charlemagne accepted the title, he was not pleased that the Pope had crowned him. This made it seem as if the emperor's right to rule came from the Pope rather than directly from God.

Charlemagne was a wise and just ruler who issued many laws. To make sure these laws were obeyed, he set up law courts all through the empire. Charlemagne chose officials called **counts** to run the courts. The counts took care of local problems, stopped feuds, protected the poor and weak, and raised armies for Charlemagne.

Charlemagne often had trouble keeping the counts under his control because of poor transportation and communication. So, he sent royal messengers all through the empire to check on them. These messengers reported to Charlemagne how well the counts were doing their jobs. Once a year, Charlemagne called his counts and warriors together. They reported troubles and talked over new laws for the empire. The final decision on what new laws to issue, however, was made by Charlemagne.

Charlemagne ruled his empire from Aachen (ah' kuhn), known today as Aix-la-Chapelle (āks' lah shah pel'). However, he did not always stay in the capital. He journeyed throughout the empire with his advisers and servants. The royal party would stop and rest at different palaces or homes. Wherever the king and his officials went, they were given food and entertained by the people. Such royal visits ensured the loyalty of local officials and people to Charlemagne's government.

Education Most people in Charlemagne's empire could neither read nor write. Charlemagne, however, appreciated learning. Unlike earlier Frankish rulers, he believed in education and was proud of his own ability to read Latin. He kept a slate and copybook next to his bed so that he could practice writing.

Charlemagne wanted his people to be educated also. He worked hard to push back the darkness that had followed the fall of the Roman Empire. He encouraged churches and monasteries

L1 **Education** Organize students into small groups. Tell students to imagine they are graduates of Charlemagne's school. The school's director, the monk Alcuin, has asked them to write a short catalog about the school that will be sent to prospective students. Each group should make a catalog that includes the following topics: the school's faculty, the courses offered, the achievements of the school, and the role of Charlemagne. Have each group present its catalog to the class. Then have the class vote on which catalog would most motivate them to enter Charlemagne's school.

DID YOU KNOW

Much of what is known about Charlemagne and the lands he ruled comes from a biography written by Einhard, his personal secretary.

VIDEODISC

Use the following to enrich Chapter 18.

WC C 10 14612

Palace Chapel of Charlemagne, Aachen.

MULTICULTURAL PERSPECTIVES

Charlemagne and his court seemed to have lived well and vigorously. The king liked good food, especially roast venison. He encouraged minstrels, jugglers, and other traveling entertainers, who would tell others about the comforts of the king's court. Sometimes there were lively discussions about theology, poetry, science, or military strategy. Charlemagne also liked to have someone read to him as he ate, preferring stories or works like St. Augustine's *City of God*.

L2 **Critical Thinking** Explain that medieval people considered their achievements a continuation of Rome's glories. Invasions and raids, however, led to a decline in learning. At the same time, a wish to preserve classical texts and religious documents was also influential. Ask students why there was a negative influence from the invasions. Ask whether the Middle Ages can be considered a bridge to the modern world. Have them explain how western European society was clinging to the past but also moving slowly toward an age of great learning and enlightenment.

CAPTION ANSWER

He wanted to push back the darkness that followed the fall of the Roman Empire by educating his people.

INDEPENDENT PRACTICE

L2 **History** Have students research and write a biographical sketch of the life and work of Alcuin. Encourage students who wish to illustrate their writing.

VIDEODISC

Use the following to enrich Chapter 18.

WC C 11 14613

Alcuin of York (735-804).

CHARLEMAGNE'S SCHOOL Charlemagne often visited his palace school, which was attended by children of the court. Directed by the monk Alcuin, the school also provided a place where scholars could gather to share their knowledge and to inspire one another. **Why was Charlemagne interested in learning?**

to found schools. He had a scholar named Alcuin (al' kwin) start a school in one of the palaces to train the children of government officials to serve in the Church or in the royal household. The children studied such subjects as religion, Latin, music, literature, and arithmetic.

Scholars came from all over Europe to teach in Charlemagne's school. One of their many tasks was to copy manuscripts. This led to the development of a new form of writing. The Roman writing the scholars used contained only capital letters. These letters took up a lot of space on a page. So, the scholars began to write with small letters instead of capital ones. The new letters not only took up less space, but they were also easier to read. The new letters became the model for the lower-case letters used today.

Under Charlemagne, the arts began to flower again. Painters, sculptors, and metalworkers developed their talents. They built palaces and churches around a large courtyard as the Romans did. Artists covered palace and church walls with pictures showing stories from the Bible. They made book covers and ornamental weapons, and they decorated the manuscripts copied by scholars.

MEETING SPECIAL NEEDS

Ask students with strong organizational skills to work in small groups with students who are having difficulty accessing the material in the chapter. Ask the groups to create descriptive outlines that show the movement of power from Clovis to the heirs of Charlemagne. Have students include biographical details and important events for each ruler. Students might also add relationships to other rulers, and major accomplishments. Have the groups compare their information in a class discussion. Create a master descriptive outline on the chalkboard. Let students decide what information is most important and should be included in the master outline.

Estate Life **Lords,** or nobles, were the most powerful people in Charlemagne's empire. They were the descendants of Frankish warriors and Roman landowners. Most of the lords' wealth came from goods grown or made on their estates. As there was little trade in Charlemagne's empire, each estate took care of its own needs. There were shoemakers, carpenters, and blacksmiths on each estate. There were also artisans who made weapons, cooking vessels, and jewelry.

Lords lived in stone farmhouses. Wooden *stockades* (stah kādz'), or fences, often were built around the houses. Each farmhouse had a banquet hall, sleeping quarters, cellars, stables, storage places, and a small chapel.

Farmers lived in simple wooden houses in small villages on the estates. They worked in the fields, vineyards, orchards, and forests around their villages. The fields were owned by the lords, but the farmers worked them three days a week. The rest of the time they worked small pieces of land the lords had given them.

ART DURING CHARLEMAGNE'S REIGN Charlemagne's desire to bring back the glory of the Roman Empire led to a new interest in art and architecture. Bibles from the period were often decorated with covers of gold and jewels (left). Charlemagne had his palace at Aachen (right) built to resemble Roman architecture. **What improvement to writing was made during Charlemagne's reign?**

GEOGRAPHY AND HISTORY

Long-distance trade with the near East improved during the reign of Charlemagne. Items traded consisted mostly of spices and silks. The trade was carried on by Jewish merchants, who were acceptable to both Christians and Muslims. Charlemagne's protection of the Jewish merchants led to the rise of the new middle class in the later Middle Ages.

DID YOU KNOW

The emperor Charlemagne admired and encouraged learning, although he could not even write his own name. He reportedly slept with a slate beneath his pillow every night so that if he awoke he might practice his writing. Unfortunately, he never mastered the art of writing that he so admired.

CAPTION ANSWER

Scholars began to write with lowercase letters as well as capital letters.

COOPERATIVE LEARNING

Have students work in small groups to create diagrams, dioramas, or models of estates in Charlemagne's empire. Students can use the information in the textbook and in reference books to create their estates. Each member of the group should be assigned a particular task in order to complete the assignment. Display students' work in the classroom.

Assign the Chapter 18 **Cooperative Learning Activity** in the TCR.

Teaching

MAP SKILLS

Understanding Inset Maps

Have students read the instructional part of the feature to answer the following questions: What are inset maps? *(small maps that are set within larger ones)* What are two reasons that inset maps are used? *(to show parts of the main map enlarged and in greater detail; to show in a different way an area on the main map)* Direct students to study the map to answer the following questions: What kingdom did the Saxons become part of after the Treaty of Verdun? *(Kingdom of Louis)* What kingdom did most Lombards become part of after the Treaty of Verdun? *(Kingdom of Lothair)*

Assign the Chapter 18 **Geography and Map Activity** in the TCR.

ANSWERS to Map Practice

1. Paris and Tours
2. Lothair
3. Kingdom of Louis

Understanding Inset Maps

Sometimes, there is not enough space on a map for information to be shown clearly. Mapmakers have solved this problem by using **inset maps,** or small maps that are set within larger ones. Often placed in a corner of the main map, inset maps may have their own scales and legends.

Inset maps are used for two reasons. One is to show parts of the main map enlarged and in greater detail. Maps of countries or states often include inset maps showing individual cities.

Another reason inset maps are used is to show in a different way an area on the main map. For example, on the map below, the main map shows the Frankish Empire from Clovis through Charlemagne. The inset map in the upper right shows what happened to the same territory after the death of Charlemagne.

Map Practice

1. **What two cities were in the kingdom of Charles?**
2. **Who controlled Rome after the Treaty of Verdun?**
3. **Through which kingdom did the Danube River flow?**

The Frankish Empire

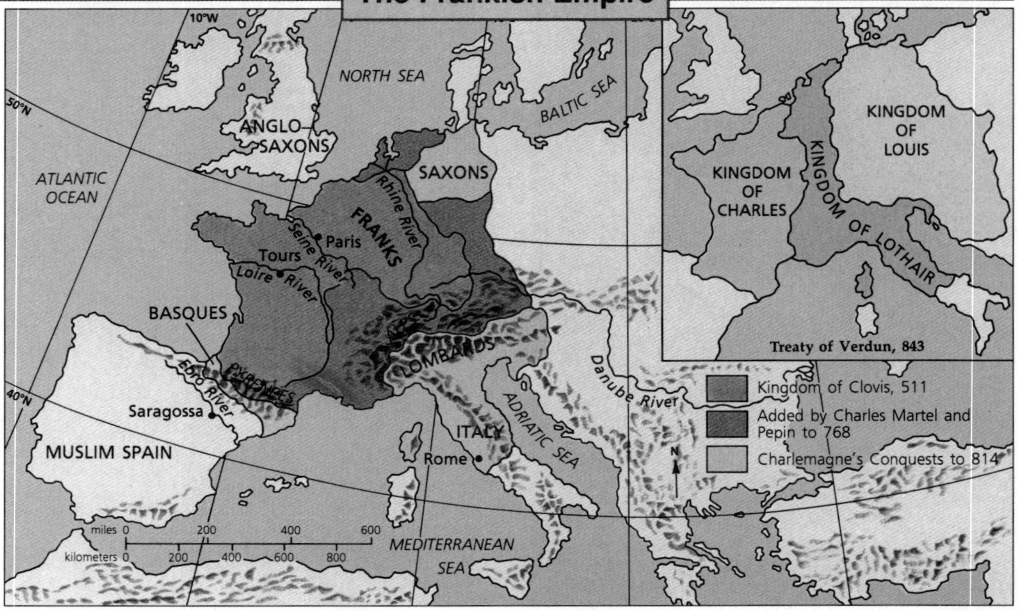

SPOTLIGHT ON: THE FRANKISH EMPIRE

A large part of the central Frankish Empire was made up by the extremely fertile North European Plain which has fed many nations for centuries. This area of western Europe, also known as the heartland, is today occupied by seven countries: France, Luxembourg, Switzerland, Germany, Belgium, Austria, and the Netherlands.

The farmers divided the land into three sections. They let one section lie *fallow* (fal' ō), or not planted. On the other two sections, they used heavy metal plows to prepare the hard but fertile soil. In autumn, they planted wheat or rye in one section. In spring, they planted oats or barley in the other section. Each year, the farmers *rotated* (rō' tā tuhd), or changed by turns, the kind of crops they grew in each section. They also let a different section lie fallow. These changes helped them grow larger crops.

Besides working the land, the farmers had to give the nobles food and animals. The farmers had to perform many services for the nobles, too. Men repaired buildings on the estates, cut down trees, carried loads, gathered fruits, and served in the army. Women worked as hard as men. They looked after the children and small animals, wove cloth, and sewed clothing copied from earlier Roman styles. The farmers gradually did more for the nobles and less for themselves. They were becoming **serfs,** or people bound to the land.

Neither the nobles nor the farmers had much time to learn to read or write or to think about religion. Both groups accepted Christianity, but the new religion had little to do with their daily lives. However, on religious holidays, both rich and poor sang, danced, and feasted. They listened to traveling musicians called **minstrels** (min' struhlz). The minstrels journeyed from place to place singing the praises of Charlemagne and his empire.

Painting of Minstrel

The Collapse of the Empire The glory of the empire did not last long after Charlemagne's death in 814. The empire needed a strong and able ruler. Charlemagne's heirs were neither. Many counts and lords became increasingly independent. They cared more about their own estates than about the good of the empire. They refused to obey Louis the Pious (pī' uhs), Charlemagne's son.

Louis the Pious unknowingly weakened the empire further when he divided it among his three sons. After he died, they began fighting among themselves over their shares. Lothair (lō thahr'), Louis's oldest son, received the title of emperor. His younger brothers, Charles and Louis, were jealous of Lothair.

In 843, the brothers agreed to a new and different division of the empire. Under the Treaty of Verdun (ver duhn'), Lothair kept the title of emperor, but he ruled only a narrow strip of land that stretched from the North Sea to the Italian Peninsula. Louis received the area to the east. Called the East Frankish Kingdom, it later became the nation of Germany. Charles received the area to the west. Called the West Frankish Kingdom, it later became France.

The brothers were weak rulers who allowed the counts and nobles to have most of the power. Once again, a united western Europe was divided into smaller territories.

Painting of Lothair

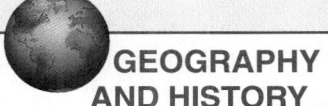

L3 **Literature** Have students read *The Song of Roland* and write a report on the characters and personalities of Charlemagne and Roland as presented in the poem. Ask students to comment on their reports on the mythical and legendary quality given to historical figures in poems.

GEOGRAPHY AND HISTORY

Lothair's "Middle Kingdom" had no natural boundaries that could be easily defended. This part of Europe has been fought over many times since the Treaty of Verdun. Have students compare the map on page 284 with a current map of Western Europe and identify the countries that are now located where the Kingdom of Lothair was located.

ASSESS

CHECK FOR UNDERSTANDING

Ask students to summarize orally or in writing the main points of the chapter. Discuss the answers to the Section and Chapter Review questions.

EVALUATE

Assign the Chapter 18 **Performance Assessment Activity** in the TCR.

Administer the **Chapter 18 Test**. Testmaker available.

MEETING SPECIAL NEEDS

Have auditory learners or gifted learners debate the following topic: *The collapse of Charlemagne's empire was inevitable.* Form two teams, one to defend the idea that the collapse of the empire was inevitable and one to defend the idea that the collapse of the empire could have been prevented. Allow each team enough time to research and develop its arguments before beginning the debate.

RETEACH

Ask students to explain how each of the following influenced the early Middle Ages: Germanic invasions, the donation of the land held by the Lombards to the Pope, and Charlemagne's dedication to education.

Assign the Chapter 18 **Reteaching Activity** in the TCR.

ENRICH

Have students research and share with the class illustrations of Charlemagne's tomb and/or manuscripts of the period.

Assign the Chapter 18 **Enrichment Activity** in the TCR.

CLOSE

Ask students to explain how during the early Middle Ages, western Europe was in a dark age, and how it was moving toward an age of enlightenment—creating a bridge between an old world and a new one.

MEETING CHAPTER OBJECTIVES

Each objective is tested by the Review questions in parentheses.

1. **Explain** how Clovis united the Franks and brought them Christianity. (BV; CU 2, 3)
2. **Describe** how Charles Martel kept western Europe Christian. (BV)
3. **Discuss** how Charlemagne conquered all of western Europe. (BV; CU 5, 6, 7; CT 1, 2)
4. **Characterize** what life was like in Charlemagne's empire. (BV; CT 3; UYJ)
5. **Summarize** why Charlemagne's empire collapsed. (BV; CU 8; CT 4)

Section 3 Review

1. **Identify:** Charlemagne, Saxons, Roland, Aachen, Alcuin, Louis the Pious, Treaty of Verdun
2. **Define:** counts, lords, serfs, minstrels
3. Why did Charlemagne object to the Pope crowning him emperor?
4. What did Charlemagne do to encourage learning?

Critical Thinking

5. What might have prevented the collapse of Charlemagne's empire?

Chapter Summary

1. During the late 400s, a Germanic people called Franks began to build a new civilization that was to develop into the modern countries of France and Germany.
2. Clovis united the Franks and set up a capital in Paris.
3. Clovis was the first Germanic king to accept the Catholic religion.
4. Clovis gained the support of the Romans in his kingdom and made Latin the official language of the royal court.
5. The Frankish kings who followed Clovis were weak rulers who lost much of their power to local nobles.
6. Frankish leadership gradually came into the hands of a government official who was known as the "Mayor of the Palace."
7. In 732, a Mayor of the Palace called Charles Martel led the Frankish army that defeated the Muslim army in the Battle of Tours. This kept western Europe Christian.
8. Charles Martel's son Pepin, who removed the king and started a new dynasty, was the first Frankish king to be anointed by the Pope.
9. Pepin's son Charlemagne brought all of western Europe under his rule.
10. In 800, the Pope crowned Charlemagne the new Roman emperor.
11. Charlemagne was a wise and just ruler who issued many laws.
12. Charlemagne was very interested in learning and encouraged the founding of schools in his empire.
13. During the rule of Charlemagne, powerful lords grew wealthy from goods grown or made on their estates.
14. Louis the Pious divided the Frankish Empire among his three sons, which led to the final collapse of Charlemagne's empire.

SECTION 3 ANSWERS

1. Charlemagne, king of the Franks (p. 279); Saxons, Germanic group (p. 279); Roland, a warrior (p. 280); Aachen, Charlemagne's ruling city (p. 281); Alcuin, a scholar (p. 282); Louis the Pious, Charlemagne's son (p. 285); Treaty of Verdun, agreement that divided Charlemagne's empire (p. 285)
2. counts, court officials (p. 281); lords, nobles (p. 283); serfs, people bound to the land (p. 285); minstrels, traveling musicians (p. 285)
3. It seemed the emperor's right to rule came from the Pope rather than from God.
4. He encouraged churches and monasteries to found schools, and had Alcuin teach the children of government officials.
5. Answers will vary but could include that Charlemagne might have planned on who was to succeed him after his death.

Assign the Chapter 18 **Section 3 Quiz** in the TCR. Testmaker available.

CHAPTER

Review 18

Building Vocabulary

Write a paragraph about the Franks and their rule in western Europe. Highlight one of the people mentioned in the chapter in your paragraph. Use the following words.

converted	lords
anointed	serfs
counts	minstrels

Check for Understanding

1. What happened in western Europe after the decline of the Roman Empire?
2. What helped the people of Clovis's empire feel united?
3. What was the relationship between the Church and Clovis?
4. Why did the Mayor of the Palace become important?
5. What were Charlemagne's main goals when he became king of the Franks?
6. How did church officials help Charlemagne's government?
7. What purpose did Charlemagne's travels throughout the empire serve?
8. How did Frankish farmers become serfs?
9. What happened to western Europe after Charlemagne's heirs came to power?

Critical Thinking

1. How wise do you think Charlemagne's traveling all over his empire was?
2. Why was the title "the Great" good for Charlemagne? What other title might have been better?
3. What parts of life in Charlemagne's empire would you have liked? What parts would you have disliked?
4. What do you think Louis the Pious could have done with the Frankish Empire instead of dividing the land among his three sons?

Geography in History

PLACE Refer to the map on p. 284 and compare the locations of Saragossa, Paris, and Rome. Each of these was an important city in the Frankish Empire. What geographic similarities can you see in these places and what differences are there?

Using Your Journal

Review the details you have noted about the changes that took place during Charlemagne's empire. Write a diary entry describing how some of these changes can still be seen today.

CHAPTER 18 REVIEW ANSWERS

BUILDING VOCABULARY

Paragraphs will vary but should include specific details and use all the vocabulary words.

CHECK FOR UNDERSTANDING

1. There was disorder, towns and roads fell into ruin, the countryside was unsafe, trading slowed, and there were shortages of food.
2. They all had the same religion and language.
3. The Pope and other Church officials supported Clovis's government. In return, Clovis was expected to protect the Church.
4. because he took over many of the king's duties
5. to rule all of western Europe and to have all Germanic peoples become Christian
6. They kept records and helped him run the country.
7. They insured the loyalty of local officials and his people.
8. They began to work more for the nobles on estates.
9. It was divided into smaller territories.

CRITICAL THINKING

1. Answers will vary but might include that it was wise because it made him appear strong and in control.
2. Answers will vary but might include that Charlemagne unified his empire.
3. Answers will vary but should include examples.
4. Answers will vary.

GEOGRAPHY IN HISTORY

Paris and Saragossa are both located on rivers; all three cities lie on flat lands somewhat near a seacoast; Paris is centrally located while Saragossa and Rome are not.

+ BONUS +

TEST QUESTION

For Chapter 18 Test

A historian has incorrectly reported several facts about Charlemagne. What are they?—Scholars from Europe and the Americas came to teach in Charlemagne's school. Most people could not read or write. Religion, however, was not taught. *(Scholars did not come from the Americas; religion was a major topic in education.)*

USING YOUR JOURNAL

Diary entries will vary. Possible changes might include the practice of heads of government to keep in touch with the people they govern, the use of lowercase letters, and the importance of art in public buildings.

CHAPTER 19

The Irish and the Anglo-Saxons

CHAPTER ORGANIZER

Objectives	Special Features	Supplemental Materials
Section 1 Celtic Ireland Discuss Rome's influence on the area known today as the British Isles and what life was like in Celtic Ireland.		• Reproducible Lesson Plan • Section 1 Quiz • Testmaker • Chapter 19 Vocabulary and Guided Reading Activity • Unit 6 Primary Source Reading • The Western Civilization Videodisc • Chapter 19 Activity Book Activity • Chapter 19 Teaching Transparencies and Activities
Section 2 Christianity Explain how Christianity developed in Ireland and England and why the Anglo-Saxons united under Alfred the Great.		• Reproducible Lesson Plan • Section 2 Quiz • Testmaker • Chapter 19 Geography and Map Activity • Chapter 19 Cooperative Learning Activity • Chapter 19 Chart and Graph Skill Activity • World Art and History Transparency 8 • The Western Civilization Videodisc
Chapter 19 Review and Evaluation		• Chapter 19 Reteaching Activity • Chapter 19 Enrichment Activity • Spanish Summary and Glossary • Audiocassettes (English and Spanish) • Chapter 19 Performance Assessment Activity • Chapter 19 Test • Testmaker

If time does not permit teaching the entire chapter, use the Chapter 19 Summary on page 296 and the Chapter 19 Audiocassettes (English and Spanish) to point out the main ideas of the chapter.

✓ Performance Assessment Activities

Filmstrip/Videotape As students read the chapter, have them keep brief notes on each important person mentioned. In groups have them prepare a biographical filmstrip that portrays one of the people and their achievements. Students may illustrate, use still photographs, or videotape a reenactment of each person's life. Have them present their biographical filmstrips to the class.

Travel Journals Have students imagine they are Romans traveling through the British Isles in the year A.D. 250. On their trip, they are able to see many sights and talk with many people. Tell students that they are to write a travel journal describing the Roman influences they have noticed in the region and the different people they have encountered. Encourage volunteers to read their diary entries for the class.

CHAPTER RESOURCES

LITERATURE ABOUT THE PERIOD

Guerber, H.A., ed. *Middle Ages*. Avenel Books, 1985. From the *Myths and Legends Series*, covers Beowulf, Charlemagne, Arthur and his knights, and other tales of the Middle Ages.

READINGS FOR THE STUDENT

Corfe, Tom. *St. Patrick and Irish Christianity* (A Cambridge Topic Book). Lerner Publications, 1979. Brief overview with interesting, detailed illustrations.

Crossley-Holland, Kevin. *Green Blades Rising: The Anglo-Saxons.* Seabury Press, 1976 (A Clarion Book). An introduction to Anglo-Saxon culture through artifacts and literature; part of a series on British history.

Mapp, Alf J., Jr. *The Golden Dragon: Alfred the Great and His Times.* Open Court, 1974. A detailed look at the period.

Quennell, Marjorie and C.H.Quennell. *Everyday Life in Roman and Anglo-Saxon Times.* B.T. Batsford; G.P. Putnam, rev. ed., 1959. Updating of one volume in a classic series in print since the 1920s, distinctive for its many details and sketches of everyday tools, household objects, clothing, and the like.

READINGS FOR THE TEACHER

Cruise O'Brien, Marie. *The Story of Ireland.* Viking, 1972. Examines the turbulent political and religious conflicts of the Irish people.

Cunliffe, Barry. *The Celtic World.* McGraw-Hill, 1979. Portrays the civilization of the Celts from prehistoric Europe to present-day Ireland.

Morgan, Kenneth O., ed. *The Oxford Illustrated History of Britain.* Oxford University Press, 1984. Summarizes the political, economic, social, and cultural events in Great Britain from Roman times to the present.

Thompson, E.A. *Who Was St. Patrick?* St. Martin's Press, 1985. Focuses on the writings of St. Patrick.

MULTIMEDIA RESOURCES

Anglo-Saxon England. International Film Bureau. Film. Presents the history of England from the end of the Roman rule in 410 to the Norman Conquest in 1066.

Anglo-Saxons in England. McIntyre Visual Publications. Filmstrip. Depicts life in an early English village.

INTRODUCE

CHAPTER 19 OVERVIEW

Chapter 19 discusses the development of civilization in the British Isles from the Roman conquests to the reign of Alfred the Great.

➤ **Section 1** describes the development of an independent Celtic culture in Ireland.

➤ **Section 2** explains the development of English government and society under the Anglo-Saxon monarchy.

CHAPTER OBJECTIVES

After reading Chapter 19, students will be able to:

1. discuss how Rome influenced the area known today as the British Isles.

2. summarize what life was like in Celtic Ireland.

3. describe how Christianity developed in both Ireland and England.

4. explain why the Anglo-Saxons united under Alfred the Great.

5. describe what life was like in Anglo-Saxon England.

EXAMINING THE ARTIFACT

Ask students who they think might wear a helmet such as the one pictured. After sharing their responses tell students this particular helmet was worn by an early Anglo-Saxon king about whom they will be reading in this chapter.

PERFORMANCE ASSESSMENT ✓

Use the Performance Assessment activities on page 288B to help you evaluate students as they complete the chapter.

CHAPTER 19

The Irish and The Anglo-Saxons

Helmet of Anglo-Saxon King

288

TEACHER CLASSROOM RESOURCES

- Section Quizzes/Chapter Test
- Reteaching Activity
- Enrichment Activity
- Chart and Graph Skill Activity
- Geography and Map Activity
- Activity Book Activity
- Cooperative Learning Activity
- Unit 6 Primary Source Reading
- Performance Assessment Activity
- Spanish Summary and Glossary
- Teaching Transparencies and Activities
- World Art and History Transparency
- Testmaker
- Audiocassettes (English and Spanish)
- The Western Civilization Videodisc

Chapter Focus

READ TO DISCOVER:

- How Rome influenced the area known today as the British Isles.
- What life was like in Celtic Ireland.
- How Christianity developed in Ireland and England.
- Why the Anglo-Saxons united under Alfred the Great.
- What life was like in Anglo-Saxon England.

Off the west coast of Europe lies a group of islands that never became part of Charlemagne's empire. Known today as the British Isles, they consist of Great Britain, Ireland, and many smaller islands.

This area was influenced by the Romans. Roman legions led by Julius Caesar invaded Britain in 55 B.C. The Romans eventually conquered much of the island and ruled it for almost 400 years. The Romans had difficulties ruling some of the area. A conquered people called Celts (kelts) were not interested in or influenced by Roman culture.

Roman rule in Britain began to crumble during the 300s A.D. Roman soldiers had been called home to defend the empire's borders against the Germanic invasions. After the last legions left Britain in 410 A.D., the island was gradually overrun by groups from northern Germany and Denmark, called Angles (ang'guhlz), Saxons, and Jutes (jūts). The Angles, Saxons, and Jutes united to become the Anglo-Saxons. They built settlements and set up several small kingdoms. The southern part of Britain soon became known as Angleland (ang'guhl land), or England. The people became known as the English.

55 B.C.–911 A.D.

KEY TERMS

- coracles
- shires
- sheriff
- king's peace
- witenagemot
- witan

Section 1

CELTIC IRELAND

With the coming of the Anglo-Saxons, most of the Celts who lived in Britain fled to Ireland. In time, Ireland became the major center of Celtic culture. Ireland had no cities. The people were divided into clans that lived in small villages. Most farmed and

FOCUS

BELLRINGER

Write on the chalkboard the following: *Who was Saint Patrick?*

Ask students to write a sentence or two answering this question.

MOTIVATIONAL ACTIVITY

Have students read their sentences about Saint Patrick. Explain that Saint Patrick brought Christianity to Ireland. Tell students that in this chapter they will learn more about Saint Patrick and the importance of Christianity in Ireland and England in the early Middle Ages.

VOCABULARY PRE-CHECK

Write the key terms for this chapter on the chalkboard. Ask students to use those that they know in sentences.

Assign Chapter 19 **Vocabulary and Guided Reading Activity** in the TCR.

EXTRA CREDIT PROJECT

The epic poem *Beowulf* was originally written in Old English. Encourage interested students to obtain the original version and practice reading the introduction, or memorize it, to present to the rest of the class in the original version.

VIDEODISC

Use the following to enrich Chapter 19.

WC C 5 14607

A gold belt buckle of an Anglo-Saxon king.

KEY TO ABILITY LEVELS

Teaching strategies have been coded for varying learning styles and abilities.

L1 Level 1 activities are **basic** activities and should be within the ability range of all students.

L2 Level 2 activities are **average** activities and should be within the ability range of the average to above-average student.

L3 Level 3 activities are **challenging** activities designed for the ability range of above-average students.

LEP LEP activities should be within the ability range of Limited English Proficiency students.

TEACH

GUIDED PRACTICE

L1 **Legends** Point out to students that during the early Anglo-Saxon and Jute raids of Britain, a legend grew about a king named Arthur and his Knights of the Round Table. Obtain a copy of this legend and read excerpts to your students. LEP

GEOGRAPHY AND HISTORY

The Anglos, Saxons, and Jutes were seafaring peoples who traveled across the North Sea to Britain in long, open boats. They were strong warriors and controlled most of the land by the A.D. 600s.

MAKING CONNECTIONS

➤➤ **History** Early Celts were divided into clans. Since they never became a united nation, the Romans had a difficult time trying to control them.

VIDEODISC

Use the following to enrich Chapter 19.

WC C 6 14608

Anglo-Saxon glass drinking-horn, ca. 5th c.

Irish Cross

raised cattle. The more cattle a person owned, the wealthier that person was considered to be.

The Irish were a seafaring people, too. They made boats called **coracles** (kor' uh kuhls) by stretching cow hides over a wooden frame. Some coracles were large enough to hold as many as 30 people. The boats handled well at sea and were used for travel, trade, and fishing.

The Irish were able to remain free of Germanic attacks because their island was located farther out in the Atlantic Ocean than Britain. Scholars, artists, merchants, and monks from many parts of Europe came to Ireland because of its peace and safety.

Irish scholars and artists were influenced by Christianity. The Irish Church was founded by Saint Patrick. Born in Britain in the 400s A.D., Saint Patrick was kidnapped when he was young and taken to Ireland by Irish pirates. Later, he escaped to Europe, where he studied to be a priest. After becoming a bishop, he returned to Ireland and converted the people to Christianity. He spread his message all through the island and set up many new churches.

Ireland lost contact with Rome during the Germanic invasions of the Roman Empire. This meant the Pope could no longer lead the Irish Church. So, the Church turned to its abbots. Many were related to the heads of the different clans. Each clan supported its own monastery.

The monasteries became centers of Irish life although many were in places that were not accessible—on rocky coasts or steep hills. Most monasteries were made up of a group of huts with a wooden stockade around them. Later, some monasteries were built of stone. Because of poor transportation and communication, church organization was weak. So, each monastery took charge of its own affairs. Irish monks soon began to follow practices different from those of the Roman Church. They wore their hair in a different way and celebrated Easter on a different day. Their rituals were not the same as those of the Romans.

Irish monasteries set down few rules. A monk was free to move from one monastery to another. Many monks chose to be hermits. Others set up schools to teach Christianity. Still others became missionaries. They sailed the North Atlantic and the Irish Sea seeking new converts and looking for islands on which to build new monasteries.

Irish Bowl

One of the best-known monks was Saint Columba (kuh luhm' buh). He set up a monastery on Iona (ī ō' nuh), an island off the west coast of Scotland. From his base on Iona, Saint Columba did missionary work among the many non-Christian Celts along the coast.

Monks from Iona went to northern England to preach to the Anglo-Saxons. Other Irish monks went to northern Europe,

EXTENDING THE CONTENT

In Celtic Britain and Ireland, distinctive styles of arts and crafts developed. Celtic bronzeworkers in southern Britain, for example, made mirrors engraved with intricate curving designs. Metalworkers also worked in gold and silver, making jewelry, armlets, and a neck ornament called a torc. Christian Celtic art developed using Christian symbols. The objects were mainly religious such as stone crosses, chalices, and intricately illuminated manuscripts.

IRISH MONASTERY Irish Christian monks established monasteries throughout the British Isles and Europe. Many of their stone living quarters, like the ones shown here, still stand today along the rocky coast of western Ireland. **What attracted monks to Ireland?**

where they built monasteries and churches. Many Irish scholars became part of Charlemagne's palace school. They helped spread Christianity and learning throughout his empire.

Section 1 Review

1. **Identify:** British Isles, Celts, Anglo-Saxons, England, Saint Patrick, Saint Columba
2. **Define:** coracles
3. How did the Irish earn a living?
4. How did the Germanic invasions of the Roman Empire affect the Irish church?

Critical Thinking

5. What might have happened in Britain if the Romans had not left in 410 A.D.

CAPTION ANSWER

Ireland's peace and safety

DID YOU KNOW ??

The Celts, skilled warriors and metalworkers, created Europe's first civilization north of the Alps. The Celts had many gods and goddesses. Priests known as Druids offered sacrifices to the gods, settled disputes, and educated the young.

LINKING PAST TO PRESENT

The Celts of medieval England and Ireland were descendants of people from the eastern part of central Europe who migrated throughout Europe. The Celts settled in Gaul and northern Spain and then crossed over to the British Isles by about 800 B.C. Celtic culture still is part of the modern cultures and languages of Ireland, Scotland, Wales, and Cornwall.

SECTION 1 ANSWERS

1. British Isles, Great Britain, Ireland, and smaller islands (p. 289); Celts, people in what is now Ireland (p. 289); Anglo-Saxons, Angles, Saxons, and Jutes (p. 289); England, land settled by Anglo-Saxons (p. 289); Saint Patrick, founder of Irish Church (p. 290); Saint Columba, a missionary monk (p. 290)
2. coracles, Irish boats (p. 290)
3. most farmed, raised cattle, traded, and fished
4. They cut off its contact with Rome and the Pope, so the Church had abbots for leadership.
5. Answers will vary but could include the idea that the Romans might have defeated the Angles, Saxons, and Jutes when they crossed over to Britain, and Roman culture would have remained.

Assign Chapter 19 **Section 1 Quiz** in the TCR. Testmaker available.

L2 **Culture** Tell the students to imagine that a group of English travelers during the early Middle Ages are interested in seeing different cultures. Ask the students to prepare travel brochures that will encourage them to visit Celtic Ireland. The brochures should contain the following information: landscape, points of interest, occupations, religion, and Celtic art. Display the brochures on a bulletin board.

MAKING CONNECTIONS

➤➤ **Religion** Because Augustine had converted King Ethelbert and thousands of his subjects to Catholicism, Pope Gregory made him the first archbishop of Canterbury in 601. The archbishop was soon recognized as the most important church leader in England.

VIDEODISC

Use the following to enrich Chapter 19.

WC C 7 14609

"Carpet page" from Lindisfarne Gospels ca. 700.

Painting of Pope Gregory I

Section 2

CHRISTIANITY

Ireland was Christian, but the Anglo-Saxon kingdoms of Britain were not. They followed the Germanic religions. Then, Pope Gregory I decided to convert the Anglo-Saxons to Christianity. Legend has it that he saw some Anglo-Saxon boys waiting in the marketplace of Rome to be sold into slavery. Gregory noticed their light skin, handsome faces, and blonde hair and asked where their home was. When he learned that the boys were Angles, he said they had the faces of angels and should be Christians.

Therefore, in 597 A.D., Pope Gregory sent a mission of 41 monks from Rome to England under the leadership of Augustine. The missionaries landed in the small kingdom of Kent in southern England. Kent's queen, Bertha, was already a Christian, but its king, Ethelbert (eth' uhl bert), was not. At first, Ethelbert was very suspicious of Augustine and the other monks. He would meet with them only in the open air where their "magic" could not hurt him. Within a year, however, Ethelbert became a Christian. He allowed Augustine to build a church in the town of Canterbury (kant' uhr ber ē) and to teach the people about Christianity.

The Anglo-Saxons were quick to accept the new religion, and by 700 A.D. all England was Christian. The Pope was head of the Church. Monasteries were built throughout England. As in Ireland, they became centers of religion and culture.

One monk, Bede (bēd), was a great scholar. He wrote the first history of the English people. He also brought to England the Christian way of dating events from the year of Jesus' birth.

Painting of Augustine

Although they accepted Christianity, the Anglo-Saxons kept much of their old culture. They told old legends about brave warriors fighting monsters and dragons. One such legend was about a warrior named Beowulf (bā' uh wulf). *Beowulf,* one of the earliest known tales, is an epic poem of almost 3,200 lines. Written by an unknown poet in about 700, it was passed along by oral tradition for two centuries. Finally, in the 900s, the work was written down. In colorful verses it describes how the hero warrior Beowulf goes from place to place fighting wicked people and ferocious animals. His greatest battle is when he defeats a horrible monster named Grindel. The language in which *Beowulf* was written is a form of English called Old English. This poem is one of the most important works of Anglo-Saxon literature.

During this time, stories, tales, and historical events were told orally, sung or recited. *Beowulf* and other early literature became the source of later Anglo-Saxon poetry and music. With the increased influence of the Christian Church in western

MULTICULTURAL PERSPECTIVES

Many legends developed about the saints. A legend about Saint Patrick stated that his fervent preaching drove the snakes out of Ireland. A legend about a seafaring monk, Saint Brendan, claimed that he sailed a coracle to new lands across the ocean, perhaps to America.

Europe, religion would also provide the subjects for much early literature. This literature reflected the lives of the people of the time and their culture.

Alfred the Great About 835 A.D., bands of Danes began attacking the coast of England. Before long, they were making permanent settlements in conquered areas. The English kingdoms decided to resist the invaders. They chose as their leader Alfred, King of Wessex (wes' iks). Alfred later became known as Alfred the Great, one of England's best-loved rulers.

Alfred knew the Anglo-Saxons were not yet strong enough to drive out the Danes. To gain time to build a stronger army, he paid the Danes a sum of money each year to leave England alone. When he felt his army was strong enough, he refused to make any more payments. The Danes invaded England and defeated the

DANES RAIDING THE ENGLISH COAST The Danes regularly raided the English coast, and some even settled in England. English villagers in this painting seek safety behind stone walls as Danish ships are spotted off the coast. **How did Alfred the Great finally make peace with the Danes?**

L3 **Writing** Remind students that a common element in Anglo-Saxon folklore is the slaying of a monster or dragon, such as in *Beowulf*. Ask students to write their own folktale that involves a similar situation of a hero or heroine destroying a monster or evil force. Encourage students to share their folktales.

DID YOU KNOW ??

Alfred the Great's united kingdom became known as "Angleland" or England.

CAPTION ANSWER

He signed a treaty with the Danes that recognized their right to rule the Danelaw.

SPOTLIGHT ON: ALFRED THE GREAT

Alfred the Great encouraged a revival of English culture and learning. He wrote, "So completely had learning decayed in the English nation that there were very few from here to the Humber [River] who could understand their mass-books in English . . . and I think there were not many beyond the Humber." Alfred learned Latin so he could make his own Old English translations, including comments, of classic works that he thought people ought to be able to read in their own language.

INDEPENDENT PRACTICE

L3 **Religion** Have students research one of the following saints: Saint Patrick, Saint Augustine, or Saint Columba. Students should investigate why the saint was important and how he contributed to the spread of Christianity in Ireland or England.

MAKING CONNECTIONS

➤➤ **History** Alfred risked his life many times for his country. Legend states that he once disguised himself as a minstrel to go into the Danes' camp to find out their plan of attack. The next day, he and his army ambushed and defeated them.

MAP STUDY Answers

the North Sea and the Irish Sea; London, Canterbury

Assign the Chapter 19 **Geography and Map Activity** in the TCR.

Anglo-Saxons. The next year, Alfred again gathered his army and met the Danes in battle. This time, the Danes were defeated.

Alfred continued to strengthen his army. He built the first English fighting ships and constructed fortresses throughout England. The entire country rallied behind him. He was no longer just King of Wessex but King of England.

Alfred never became strong enough to drive the Danes completely out of England. So, he signed a treaty with them. The treaty recognized the right of the Danes to rule the northeast part of England, an area that became known as the Danelaw (dān' lah). In return, the Danes promised to remain inside the Danelaw and not try to conquer more English land. In later years, the English took control of the Danelaw and made it part of their kingdom.

The Danes had destroyed part of the English city of London. Alfred had it rebuilt. Before long, it became the country's leading city. To gain the continued loyalty and obedience of the people, Alfred set forth new laws based on old Anglo-Saxon customs. These customs protected the weak against the strong and stressed honesty in making agreements.

England and the Danelaw

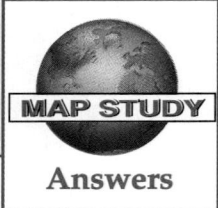

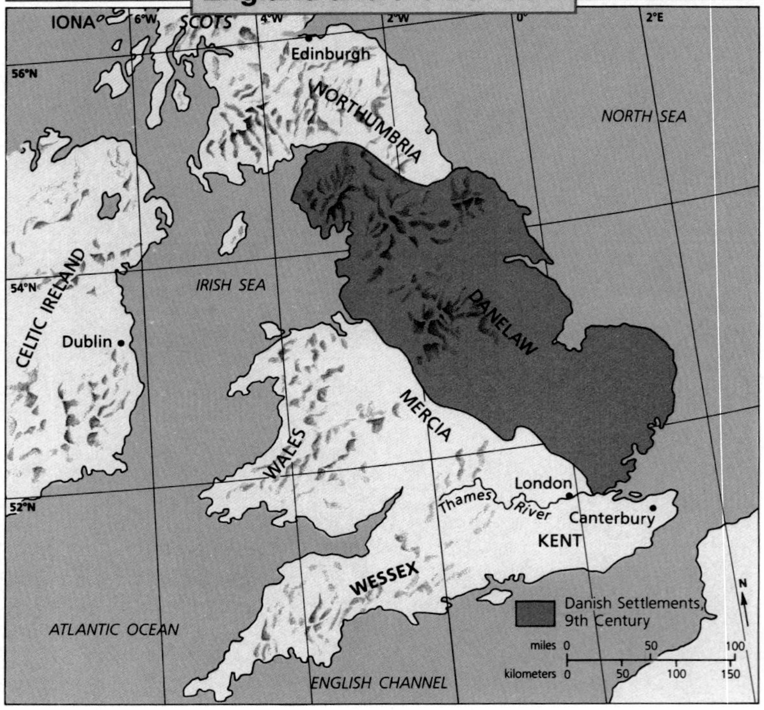

MAP STUDY

LOCATION The Danes had conquered an area north of the Thames River and established permanent settlements there. **What bodies of water border Danelaw? What two cities were located south of Danelaw?**

MEETING SPECIAL NEEDS

Have visual learners create murals or wall hangings to illustrate what life was like in Anglo-Saxon England. Divide the group in two. Have one group illustrate what life was like for nobles, and the other group illustrate what life was like for the peasants. The murals should feature the dress, housing, and activities of the nobles or peasants.

Alfred was well-educated and interested in learning. He did much to educate the English. Like Charlemagne, Alfred started a palace school to train nobles' sons for government posts. At that time, books were generally written in Latin, a language most English church and government officials did not know. Alfred's scholars translated the books into English. So that the people would become familiar with their history, Alfred had monks begin a record of English history starting with Roman times.

Sketch of English Sheriff

The Government The government of Anglo-Saxon England centered on the king. A council of lords generally elected kings from among members of the royal family. After 700 A.D., the Church usually crowned the new rulers. The king directed the central government, which was made up of royal servants and advisers. They handled the king's needs and wishes.

The central government, however, was too weak to govern the whole country. So, the king set up local governments. England was divided into districts called **shires** (shīrz). Each was run by a **sheriff,** who was a local noble chosen by the king. The sheriff collected money, enforced the law, called out soldiers when needed, and told the king what was happening in the shire.

The king and his household moved around instead of remaining in a capital city. Whatever area the royal household was in was under the **king's peace,** or royal protection. Lawless acts were not allowed. Anyone who committed a crime was punished under the king's laws rather than local laws. In time, the king's peace spread to all areas of the kingdom, whether the king was there or not. This helped unite Anglo-Saxon England.

Nobles and church officials gave the king advice on how to run the country. They could not, however, order a king to act against his will. A group of nobles and church leaders, known as the **witenagemot** (wit uhn uh' guh mōt), met with the king to talk over problems. Each member of the group was known as a **witan** (wi' tuhn), or wiseman. The group approved laws drawn up by the king and his household. It also acted as a court.

The People The people in Anglo-Saxon England were generally divided into two classes. One was the nobles. An Anglo-Saxon became a noble by birth or as a reward for special service to the king. Nobles had to attend the witenagemot, keep peace in local areas, and serve the king in war. Noblemen wore pants and tunics covered by silk or fur cloaks. Noblewomen wore tunics and long cloaks held in place on each shoulder by a brooch.

The king rewarded many nobles with gifts of gold, silver, horses, and weapons. He also gave them estates throughout the kingdom. As a result, nobles spent a great deal of time moving from place to place with their families and servants. A noble's house had a large hall where meals were served and guests

MAKING CONNECTIONS

➤➤ **Literature** The record of English history that Alfred commissioned monks to write was called the *Anglo-Saxon Chronicle.* It provides an accurate account of the events of Alfred's time and was the first historical record ever attempted in England. Its style is simple and straightforward and reveals many of the outlooks and superstitions of the time. It may have been planned as a way to raise Anglo-Saxon's pride in their history.

L1 **Writing** Have students imagine that they are monks assigned the task of recording English history. Have them choose an event from early English history and write an account for the *Anglo-Saxon Chronicle.*

ASSESS

CHECK FOR UNDERSTANDING

Ask students to summarize orally or in writing the main points of the chapter. Discuss the answers to the Section and Chapter Review questions.

EVALUATE

Assign Chapter 19 **Performance Assessment Activity** in the TCR.

Administer **Chapter 19 Test** in the TCR. Testmaker available.

COOPERATIVE LEARNING

Have students choose a historical event presented in this chapter and plan the presentation of a pictorial record. Divide the class into three groups. One group will determine the style and nature of the record and how it will be produced, choose particular scenes to present, and make recommendations during its execution. Another group will be responsible for the actual production. The third group will be responsible for creating a narrative to accompany the record. Have a class presentation when the record is finished.

Assign the Chapter 19 **Cooperative Learning Activity** in the TCR.

RETEACH

Have students work in small groups to write a sentence that summarizes each subsection in the chapter.

Assign the Chapter 19 **Reteaching Activity** in the TCR.

ENRICH

Have students role-play a scene from one of the many legends of King Arthur and the Knights of the Round Table.

Assign the Chapter 19 **Enrichment Activity** in the TCR.

CLOSE

Have students discuss how the settlements in the British Isles during the early Middle Ages might have been different if Christianity had not been an important part of everyday life.

MEETING CHAPTER OBJECTIVES

Each objective is tested by the Review questions in parentheses.

1. **Discuss** how the Roman Empire influenced the British Isles. (CU 1, 2, 3)
2. **Summarize** what life was like for people in Celtic Ireland. (BV; CT 2)
3. **Describe** how Christianity developed in Ireland and England. (BV; CU 5)
4. **Explain** why the Anglo-Saxons united under Alfred the Great. (CU 6, 7)
5. **Describe** what life was like in Anglo-Saxon England. (BV; CT 3, 4)

entertained. Its walls were covered with *tapestries* (tap' uh strēz), or woven hangings with pictures on them. Tables and benches were the hall's only furniture. The bedrooms of nobles and their families were next to the hall or in a separate building.

The other class of people in Anglo-Saxon England was the peasants. They lived in small villages on or near a noble's estate and led a hard life. Most did not own their own land but worked fields belonging to the noble. Every year, the noble redivided the land, and each peasant received different strips. This was done to make sure that peasants would be treated equally. They helped each other farm the land by sharing tools and oxen. The peasants kept part of the crop for food and gave part to the noble. In return, the noble protected his peasants from enemy attacks.

Peasants lived in one-room wood and plaster huts. Both the family and the animals shared the same room. An open fireplace, which provided heat during winter, stood in the center. Smoke from the fire escaped through a hole in the straw roof.

Section 2 Review

1. **Identify:** Pope Gregory I, Ethelbert, Bede, *Beowulf*, Alfred the Great, Danelaw
2. **Define:** shires, sheriff, king's peace, witenagemot, witan
3. What did Alfred do to unite Anglo-Saxon England?
4. What was the life of an Anglo-Saxon peasant like?

Critical Thinking

5. Why do you think Alfred was given the title "the Great"?

Chapter Summary

1. The Romans ruled most of Britain for about 400 years, but they were unable to gain the loyalty of the conquered Celts.
2. After Roman legions left Britain in 410 A.D., it was gradually overrun by the Angles, Saxons, and Jutes, who united to become the Anglo-Saxons.
3. After the Anglo-Saxons drove most of the Celts from Britain, Ireland became the major center of Celtic culture.
4. Monasteries became centers of Irish life.
5. In 597 A.D., Pope Gregory sent a mission of monks led by Augustine to England, and by 700 A.D., England had become Christian.
6. Around 835 A.D., bands of Danes began raiding England.
7. The Anglo-Saxons united behind Alfred the Great to keep the Danes from spreading their control.
8. The king of England was assisted by a central government as well as local governments.

SECTION 2 ANSWERS

1. Pope Gregory I, sent monks to England (p. 292); Ethelbert, king of Kent (p. 292); Bede, monk (p. 292); *Beowulf*, important Anglo-Saxon literature (p. 292); Alfred the Great, English ruler (p. 293); Danelaw, part of England ruled by Danes (p. 294)
2. shires, districts (p. 295); sheriff, noble who ran a district (p. 295); king's peace, royal protection (p. 295); witenagemot, group of nobles and Church leaders (p. 295); witan, wise man (p. 295)
3. He defeated the Danes, built ships, constructed fortresses, and set forth new laws.
4. He or she lived in a one-room hut shared with animals, and usually worked fields belonging to a noble.
5. Answers will vary, but students will most likely point to his achievements.

Assign the Chapter 19 **Section 2 Quiz** in the TCR. Testmaker available.

CHAPTER Review 19

Building Vocabulary

Write a paragraph to be used in a book on the Celts and Anglo-Saxons describing one part of their lives. Use the following words in your paragraph.

coracles	king's peace
shires	witenagemot
sheriff	witan

Check for Understanding

1. Why did the Romans have difficulty ruling Britain?
2. Why did Roman rule in Britain crumble during the 300s A.D.?
3. What happened to Britain when the Roman legions left?
4. What country became the major center of Celtic culture?
5. Why did the Irish church turn to its abbots for leadership?
6. Why did Alfred pay the Danes to leave England alone?
7. Why did the king divide England into shires?
8. What were the duties of nobles?

Critical Thinking

1. What effect did the Germanic invasions of the Roman Empire have on the development of England?
2. How did Ireland's location affect the development of Celtic culture?
3. Would you agree or disagree with the following: The king had too much power in Anglo-Saxon England? Explain.
4. What parts of an Anglo-Saxon noble's life would you have liked? What parts would you have not liked?

Geography in History

MOVEMENT Refer to the map on page 294. What distance would a person traveling from Edinburgh to London by the most direct route, have to travel? How much farther would that person have to travel to meet with priests of the church in Canterbury?

Using Your Journal

Review the details you have noted about the changes that took place during the early Middle Ages. Review the role of a witan in the Anglo-Saxon government. Imagine you are a witan today working with the President of the United States. Write a letter to the President suggesting the problems in the country that you think should be solved. Include any specific solutions you have for these problems.

CHAPTER 19 REVIEW ANSWERS

BUILDING VOCABULARY

Paragraphs describing the lives of the Celts and Saxons will vary but should include all the vocabulary words.

CHECK FOR UNDERSTANDING

1. They could not win over the Celts.
2. because Roman soldiers were called home to defend the empire's borders against the Germanic invasions
3. It was gradually overrun by Angles, Saxons, and Jutes.
4. Ireland
5. because Ireland lost contact with Rome and the Pope during the Germanic invasions
6. to gain time to build a stronger army
7. because the central government was too weak to govern the whole country
8. He had to attend the witenagemot, keep peace, and serve the king in war.

CRITICAL THINKING

1. They forced Roman soldiers to be called home, which allowed Angles, Saxons, and Jutes to overrun the island.
2. Its isolation allowed it to remain free of Germanic attacks. This allowed Celtic culture to develop.
3. Answers will vary, but students should support their reaction with examples.
4. Answers will vary but should include specific examples.

GEOGRAPHY IN HISTORY

About 310 miles (or 500 km); about 55 miles (or 85 km)

+ BONUS +

TEST QUESTION

For Chapter 19 Test

Two Anglo-Saxon people were arguing. One person said, "My family has been here since the Romans left the British Isles. That makes my family the oldest." The other person replied, "My family has been here since the Celts fled to Ireland." Whose family history is the oldest? *(neither—both began at about the same time)*

USING YOUR JOURNAL

Letters will vary but should include specific problems. You might call on volunteers to read their letters to the class.

PLANNING GUIDE

CHAPTER 20 The Vikings

CHAPTER ORGANIZER

Objectives	Special Features	Supplemental Materials
Section 1 The Land Describe the effects of climate and environment in the development of the Vikings as seafaring people.		• Reproducible Lesson Plan • Section 1 Quiz • Testmaker • Chapter 20 Vocabulary and Guided Reading Activity • Unit 6 World Literature
Section 2 Daily Life Summarize the daily life and culture of the Vikings in their towns and villages.		• Reproducible Lesson Plan • Section 2 Quiz • Testmaker • Chapter 20 Cooperative Learning Activity • Chapter 20 Activity Book Activity• Chapter 20 Transparencies and Activities
Section 3 Raiders and Adventurers Explain the extent of Viking influence in shaping the cultures of England, France, Russia, and lands in the North Atlantic.	Map and Geography Skills, *Tracing Historical Routes,* p. 306	• Reproducible Lesson Plan • Foods Around the World • Section 3 Quiz • Testmaker • Chapter 20 Geography and Map Activity • Chapter 20 Chart and Graph Skill Activity • Reinforcing Social Studies Skills, pp. 9, 13 • The Western Civilization Videodisc
Chapter 20 Review and Evaluation		• Chapter 20 Reteaching Activity • Chapter 20 Enrichment Activity • Spanish Summary and Glossary • Audiocassettes (English and Spanish) • Chapter 20 Performance Assessment Activity • Chapter 20 Test • Testmaker

If time does not permit teaching the entire chapter, use the Chapter 20 Summary on page 308 and the Chapter 20 Audiocassettes (English and Spanish) to point out the main ideas of the chapter.

✓ Performance Assessment Activities

Making Maps Provide students with outline maps of the world. Have them draw the routes taken by the Danish, Swedish, and Norwegian Vikings during the A.D. 800s, 900s, and 1000s. Students should label each route or include a map key that explains each route. Suggest students add other information such as an indication of products traded. Display the maps on a bulletin board.

Re-creations Have students research and draw illustrations of Viking ships or make models of them. These creations should be accompanied by explanations of ship construction, parts, and functions. Students should research to find details about the kinds of ships the Vikings used. Display the illustrations and models in the classroom.

CHAPTER RESOURCES

LITERATURE ABOUT THE PERIOD

Gibson, Michael. *The Vikings.* G.P. Putnam's Sons, 1972. Based on sagas and other sources, describes the Vikings as farmers, artisans, traders, storytellers, and warriors.

Treece, Henry. *The Invaders.* Crowell, 1972. Three stories about the Vikings.

READINGS FOR THE STUDENT

Chubb, Thomas Caldecott. *The Northmen.* World Publishing, 1964. An account of Viking culture.

Kirkby, Michael Haslock. *The Vikings.* Dutton, 1977. A look at Vikings throughout Europe, including striking photography.

Wernick, Robert. *The Vikings: The Seafarers.* Time-Life Books, 1979. An in-depth look at the Viking traders, raiders, and conquerors.

READINGS FOR THE TEACHER

Ehrenreich, Barbara and Deirdre English. *Witches, Midwives, and Nurses: A History of Women Healers.* Feminist Press, 1972. Describes the role of women in medicine during the Middle Ages.

Graham-Campbell, James. *The Viking World.* Frances Lincoln Publishers Limited, 1980. Features various aspects of Viking life, including photographs and illustrations of art, housing, and artifacts.

Jones, Gwyn. *A History of the Vikings.* Oxford University Press, 1984. Surveys the Viking world, including archaeological findings.

Power, Eileen. *Medieval People.* Barnes and Noble, 1963. Includes detailed portraits of medieval people from different social classes, including peasants, merchants, and clergy.

MULTIMEDIA RESOURCES

Vikings and Their Explorations. Coronet Films. Film. Describes the travels and discoveries of the Vikings.

The Vikings. Interact/SSSS. Simulation. Through simulation, students become members of either Swedish, Danish, or Norwegian clans.

TEACH

GUIDED PRACTICE

L1 **Daily Life** Have students help complete an informational bulletin board about the daily life of the Vikings. Ask them to make illustrations about one of the following areas of Viking life: family life, occupations, or religion. Have them write captions to explain their illustrations. Display the illustrations and captions on the bulletin board. LEP

MAKING CONNECTIONS

➤➤ **Language** The word *Viking* comes from the word *vik* which means "creek" in all the Scandinavian languages. *Vik* was also the name of a pirate lair in southern Norway. The phrase *to go a Viking* meant "to fight as a pirate."

CAPTION ANSWER

silk, wine, and wheat

Ships and Trade The Vikings built ships with timber from the dense forests. These ships were large and well suited for long voyages. The bodies were long and narrow. The sides, where a single row of 16 oars was placed, were usually decorated with black or yellow shields. The tall bows were carved in the shape of a dragon's head. This was supposed to frighten both enemies and the evil spirits of the ocean. The strongly sewn sails were square and often striped red and yellow. The ships bore names like "Snake of the Sea," "Raven of the Wind," and "Lion of the Waves."

An awning in the forepart of the ship protected sailors from bad weather. They slept in leather sleeping bags and carried bronze pots in which to cook meals. Whenever possible, they cooked meals ashore to avoid the danger of a fire on board ship.

The Vikings plotted their courses by the positions of the sun and the stars. They sailed far out into the North Sea and the Atlantic Ocean in search of good fishing areas and trade. They did most of their traveling and trading in spring after their fields were sown or in fall after their crops were harvested. They spent the long winters repairing their boats and weapons.

The Vikings were as successful in trade as the Phoenicians. Viking traders carried furs, hides, fish, and enslaved people to western Europe and the Mediterranean. They returned from these areas with silk, wine, wheat, and silver.

VIKING TRADE The Vikings traveled very far in order to trade. They sailed to the Mediterranean and traded for Arabic silver coins. The Vikings then melted down the coins and used the silver to make jewelry. **What other items did the Vikings trade for?**

MULTICULTURAL PERSPECTIVES

Perhaps one of the best indications of how important the ship was in Viking life is the custom of ship burials. Sometimes the body of a dead chief or hero was set adrift on his boat. Sometimes the entire ship was buried on land, richly equipped for the afterlife much as an Egyptian pyramid was. Archaeologists have discovered many interesting and beautiful Viking artifacts in ship burials, including solid gold jewelry and ornaments. Two of the most famous ship burials are at Sutton Hoo in England and Gokstad in Norway.

Towns, Villages, and Jarls Trade led to the growth of market towns in Scandinavia. These towns generally had two main streets that ran along the water's edge. Buyers and sellers set up booths along these streets where they showed their wares. The towns were protected on their land side by mounds of earth surrounded by wooden walls with towers.

Most Vikings lived in villages scattered all through the country. Their houses were made of logs or boards. The roofs, which were made of sod-covered wood, slanted deeply to shed the heavy winter snows. Carved dragons decorated the roofs at either end. Each house had a small porch at its front that was held up by carved pillars.

Distance and the cold winters isolated the people of one village from those of another. Because of this, there was no central government. The people were divided into groups ruled by military chiefs called ***jarls*** (yahrlz). Some jarls were elected, while others inherited their position. Sometimes, a jarl became strong enough to take over neighboring lands. When a jarl had enough land under his rule, he was looked upon as a king.

Dragon Carving

Section 1 Review

1. **Identify:** Vikings, Scandinavia, Jutland
2. **Define:** *jarls*
3. How did people in Scandinavia make a living?
4. What were some features of Viking towns?

Critical Thinking

5. How did the Vikings use their natural resources?

Section 2

DAILY LIFE

Family life was important to the Vikings. Most households had 20 to 30 members, including parents, grandparents, married children, and grandchildren. Families often fought bloody feuds to defend their honor. The payment of fines later ended such feuds.

The People Viking warriors were called ***berserkers*** (ber zerk' erz). They believed in a life of action and valued deeds that called for strength and courage. They fought to gain wealth, honor, and fame. They believed that a liking for war brought special honors from the gods.

To call their warriors to battle, the Vikings lit bonfires on the tops of mountains. Those who saw a fire would light a new one to

Viking Sword Hilt

GEOGRAPHY AND HISTORY

Viking boats were sturdy enough to cross the Atlantic Ocean, shallow enough to navigate Europe's rivers, and light enough to be carried past fortified bridges. The Vikings became known for surprise attacks and speedy retreats. What they could not steal, they burned.

MAKING CONNECTIONS

➤➤ **Language** The word *berserk* comes from the Viking term *berserkers* and is used to describe a person who acts wildly.

DID YOU KNOW ??

When the Vikings arrived at a town or city to trade, they displayed white shields to indicate that they meant no harm.

SECTION 1 ANSWERS

1. Vikings, Norsemen (p. 299); Scandinavia, far northern part of Europe (p. 299); Jutland, Denmark (p. 299)
2. *jarls,* Viking military chiefs (p. 301)
3. by farming, fishing, and trading
4. They generally had two main streets that ran along the water's edge and were lined with booths. They were protected on their land side by mounds of earth surrounded by wooden walls with towers.
5. The Vikings built ships and houses with timber from the dense forests, turned to the sea to make a living, and grew herbs that were used as medicines.

Assign the Chapter 20 **Section 1 Quiz** in the TCR. Testmaker available.

L3 **Critical Thinking** Ask students to examine the role women played in Viking society. Ask why they think the position of Viking women was quite high.

DID YOU KNOW ??

Some Viking swords were handed down from father to son. The weapons bore fanciful names, such as Thorn of the Shields, Fire of the Sea Kings, and Serpent of the Wound.

CAPTION ANSWER

so the evil spirits would be scared away and the Vikings would appear fierce

spread the message. Warriors fought with battle axes, swords, and spears. Metal helmets decorated with animal figures protected their heads. Shirts made of iron rings and covered by a large cloth protected their bodies. Warriors preferred to die by their own hand rather than give their enemies the satisfaction of capturing or killing them.

The women encouraged their men to fight. A Viking groom bought his wife from her family on their wedding day. If he was not pleased with her, he could sell her. Yet, the position of Viking women was quite high. They took complete charge of the home. They could attend public meetings and talk with men other than their husbands. They could own property and get a divorce. Many Viking women grew herbs that were used as medicine.

Both men and women liked fine clothes. Men usually dressed in trousers and woolen shirts covered by knee-length tunics. Broad leather belts held the clothing in place. Sheepskin hoods and caps kept their heads warm. For special events, men wore red cloaks with brooches and carried decorated swords and daggers. Women also wore tunics held in place by a belt. They covered their heads with woolen or linen caps and wore large brooches, pins, and bracelets. Both men and women wore their hair long. The men took great pride in their mustaches and beards. Calling a

VIKING ADVENTURES This painting of Leif Ericksson, one of the most adventuresome Vikings, shows the detail and decoration these north people put into their ships. The bows of their ships were usually elaborately carved. **Why did many Viking ships display the head of a dragon on the bow?**

COOPERATIVE LEARNING

Have students create a historical account of a medieval village under Viking attack. Some students will take on the roles of Vikings, who keep a record of their voyage, their intentions, and their strategies for attack. Other students can assume the roles of clergy members, who keep the official records of the village. Still others can represent the villagers who record the raid with drawings of the long ships as they approach. Some of the few villagers who could read and write might keep journal accounts of their fate. Students should be encouraged to do outside research and to include vivid details in their drawings and writing projects.

Assign the Chapter 20 **Cooperative Learning Activity** in the TCR.

Viking man "beardless" was an insult that could be wiped out only by death.

The Vikings had no schools. Girls were taught household skills, such as spinning, weaving, and sewing, by their mothers. Boys were taught to use the bow and arrow and to be good fighters by their fathers. Boys also memorized tales of heroes and gods and competed in games that tested their strength and endurance.

Viking Rune Stone

Religion The Vikings worshiped many gods that at first were similar to the Germanic gods. Over time, they changed their gods to suit the hard life of Scandinavia. The Vikings believed that the gods were responsible for the weather and for the growth of crops. Since the gods liked to hunt, fish, and play tricks on one another, the Vikings viewed them as extra-powerful humans.

The Vikings bargained with their gods to get what they wanted. Priests offered sacrifices of crops and animals for the whole village. Most Vikings also had small shrines in their homes where they could pray or offer sacrifices.

The Vikings were proud of their gods and told stories of the gods' great deeds. These stories later became written poems called ***Eddas*** (ed' uhz). The Vikings also made up *sagas* (sah' guhz), or long tales. At first, storytellers used to recite them at special feasts. One such tale took 12 days to recite. After 1100, the Vikings wrote down their sagas. With the coming of Christianity, however, the people lost interest in them. Many were forgotten or were forbidden by the Church. Only the people on the isolated island of Iceland passed on the old tales.

Early on, the Vikings spoke a language similar to that of the Germans. In time, the one language developed into four—Danish, Norwegian (nor wē' juhn), Swedish, and Icelandic. These languages were written with letters called ***runes*** (rūnz), which few people except priests could understand or use. The Vikings used the runes as magic charms. They wrote the runes in metal and carved them in bone in the hope that they would bring good luck. When the Vikings accepted Christianity, they began to write their languages with Roman letters.

Section 2 Review

1. **Define:** *berserkers, Eddas, runes*
2. What kind of education did Viking children receive?
3. In what way did the Viking gods change over time?
4. How did the Vikings view their gods?

Critical Thinking

5. How was the role of Viking women similar to the role of women today? How was it different?

MAKING CONNECTIONS

➤➤ **History** The Vikings believed in a heaven called Asgard, which contained 12 great halls. Warriors wanted to go to the Hall of the slain, called Valhalla. There, the chief Viking god, Odin, held court.

DID YOU KNOW ??

Christian missionaries to the Germanic peoples in northwest Europe were so eager to wipe out all traces of pagan religion that very little survived in the way of songs, stories, or other traditions. Besides the Icelandic Eddas, there are only *Beowulf* in England, the *Song of the Nibelung* in Germany, and some shorter pieces.

SECTION 2 ANSWERS

1. berserkers, Viking warriors (p. 301); Eddas, Viking poems (p. 303); runes, Viking letters (p. 303)
2. Girls were taught household skills. Boys were taught to use the bow and arrow, to be good fighters, and memorized tales of heroes and gods and competed in games.
3. They were changed to suit the hard life of Scandinavia and were believed to be responsible for the weather and for the growth of crops.
4. as extra-powerful humans
5. Answers will vary but might include the idea that in both cases women can take charge of the home, attend public meetings, talk to men, own property, and get a divorce. Women today, however, have equal rights. Unlike Viking women, they are not bought from the husband's family and cannot be sold by their husbands.

Assign the Chapter 20 **Section 2 Quiz** in the TCR. Testmaker available.

L2 **Myths and Legends** Have students write a list of the Norse gods and goddesses and their realms. Then have them brainstorm a list of where these names are used in modern times. For example, names are used as calendar items, in advertising, in city names, and so on. LEP

LINKING PAST TO PRESENT

In 1991, 3 authentically built Viking ships retraced early Norse exploration routes, sailing from Norway to L'Anse aux Meadows, Newfoundland, Canada. The trip, lasting 3 months, was made to honor the Vikings who sailed to America 1,000 years before.

L1 **Geography: Movement** Refer students to the map of "Viking Trade and Expansion" on page 306 to trace the routes that the Vikings traveled to raid places. LEP

VIDEODISC

Use the following to enrich Chapter 20.

WC M 137 41467
A Norse ship, from about 1000 A.D.

NORSE GODS

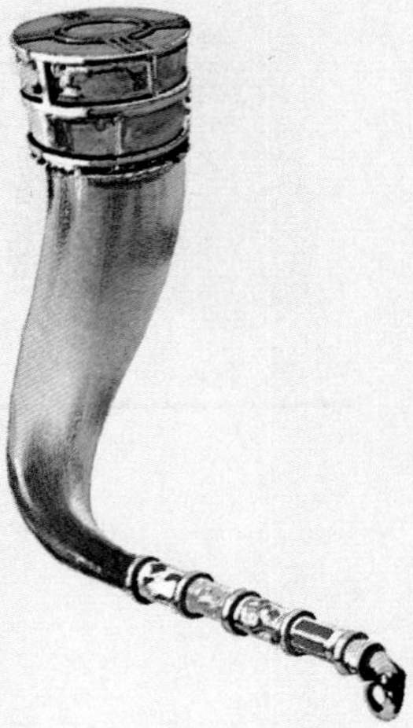

Name	Realm
Odin (or Wodan)	king of the gods; sky god; god of war and wisdom, *Wodan's day became Wednesday.*
Balder	god of light, joy, and spring
Bragi	god of poetry and stories
Freya	goddess of love and beauty
Freyr	god of rain, sunshine, and the harvest
Frigg	goddess of earth, marriages, and motherly love; Odin's wife; *Frigg's day became Friday.*
Hel (or Hela)	goddess of the dead
Idun	goddess of youth
Loki	god of fire; the mischief-maker
Njord	god of the sea
Thor	god of thunder, lightning, and the tides; *Thor's day became Thursday.*
Tyr	god of legal contracts and of truth; *Tyr's day became Tuesday.*

Section 3

RAIDERS AND ADVENTURERS

Scandinavia's population kept increasing. By the end of the 800s, many Viking villages were overcrowded, and there was not enough food for everyone. Since there was no central government, the kings constantly fought one another and made life difficult for their enemies. Before long, many Viking warriors began to seek their fortunes in other lands. They set sail on their long, deckless ships that were propelled through the water with oars. On them, the Vikings could safely sail the deep water of the Atlantic Ocean or the shallow rivers of Europe.

From East Europe to North America Viking adventurers traveled to and raided areas from east Europe to North America. Swedish Vikings crossed the Baltic Sea and traveled down the rivers toward what is now Belarus, Ukraine, and Russia. They established a trade water route from the Baltic to the

MEETING SPECIAL NEEDS

Help students who are having difficulty accessing the information in the chapter by creating cause-and-effect graphic organizers of the major events in the chapter on the chalkboard.

Black Sea and on to the wealthy city of Byzantium (bi zan' tē uhm). This water route became known as the Varangian (vah rahng ē'uhn) Route. In 862, a Swedish chief named Rurik (rū' rik) founded a Viking settlement that became the Kievan Rus state.

Norwegian Vikings set up trading towns in Ireland, explored the North Atlantic, and founded a colony on Iceland. Led by an adventurer named Erik the Red, they founded a colony on the island of Greenland in 986. Then, Erik's son, Leif Eriksson (lēf er' ik suhn), landed on the northeast coast of North America. He and his followers named the spot where they landed Vinland because of the wild grapes they found growing there. Today, the area is called Newfoundland (nū' fuhn luhnd). The Vikings did not set up a colony in Vinland because it was so far away from home and because they were repeatedly attacked by Native Americans.

Most Viking adventurers, however, went to western and southern Europe in search of food and valuables. They disguised their ships to look like wooded islands by covering them with tree branches. Then, they traveled far up the rivers to make surprise

VIKING BURIAL SITE Viking graves throughout Scandinavia were sometimes marked by stones set in the form of a ship. The dead Viking warrior then had a symbolic ship in which to sail to the afterlife. **To whose gods were the Vikings' gods similar?**

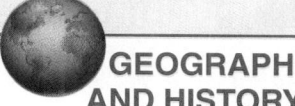

GEOGRAPHY AND HISTORY

Some historians believe that Viking sailors first spotted the North American continent in 986 when Bjarni Herjulfsson was blown off course on a trip to the Greenland settlement. Leif Eriksson's voyage included stops at what he called "Helluland" (perhaps Baffin Island), "Markland" (Labrador), and "Vinland" (Newfoundland), so called because of the grapes that grew there. After Leif's stay in Vinland, his brother Thorvald made the trip. Several other Greenlanders also took expeditions to the settlement.

CAPTION ANSWER

They were similar to Germanic gods.

SPOTLIGHT ON: VIKINGS

Viking adventurers made many voyages across the Northern Atlantic. One such Viking believed the first to set eyes on North America was Bjarni Herjulfsson. Bjarni, living in Iceland, set sail for Greenland in search of his father. Following the North Star, he reached the coast of Labrador, Canada, instead. According to Norse sagas, it was his course that Leif Eriksson and his men followed years later to reach Vinland.

Teaching

MAP SKILLS

Tracing Historical Routes

Have students read the introductory section of the skill on page 306. Ask: Why are historical routes often colored? *(to show information more clearly and to make the map easier to read)* Why do historical routes on maps often have arrows at their beginning or several arrows along its length? *(to point out the directions taken by people or goods)* Where should you look to find out the meaning of the different lines and colors on a map? *(in the legend or key)* Direct students' attention to the map on the skill page. Ask: What rivers and seas did the Viking Invasion Routes follow? *(Volga River, Dnieper River, Caspian Sea)* What bodies of water did the Vikings cross on their trade routes? *(North Sea, Baltic Sea, Mediterranean Sea, Atlantic Ocean)*

Assign the Chapter 20 **Geography and Map Activity** in the TCR.

ANSWERS to Map Practice

1. England, Ireland, Iceland, Greenland, Vinland, France, Spain, Italy, Norway, Sweden, and Denmark
2. invasion routes and the Varangian Route
3. Kiev and Baghdad

Tracing Historical Routes

Lines on maps generally show boundaries or rivers. On some maps, however, lines may show other things, such as **historical routes.** These are roads or courses over which people or goods have traveled all through history.

Such routes are often colored to make the map easier to read. A colored line may have arrows to point out the direction taken by people or goods. If there is a legend on the map, it may provide clues to the meaning of the different lines and colors.

For example, on the map of "Viking Trade and Expansion" below, the legend shows that the brown line is the Varangian Route. The two arrows along the line point out that the route began in Sweden and ended in Byzantium.

Map Practice

1. **What were some places visited by Vikings along their trade routes?**
2. **Which routes ran through the largest area of Viking settlement?**
3. **What two cities lay along Viking invasion routes?**

Viking Trade and Expansion

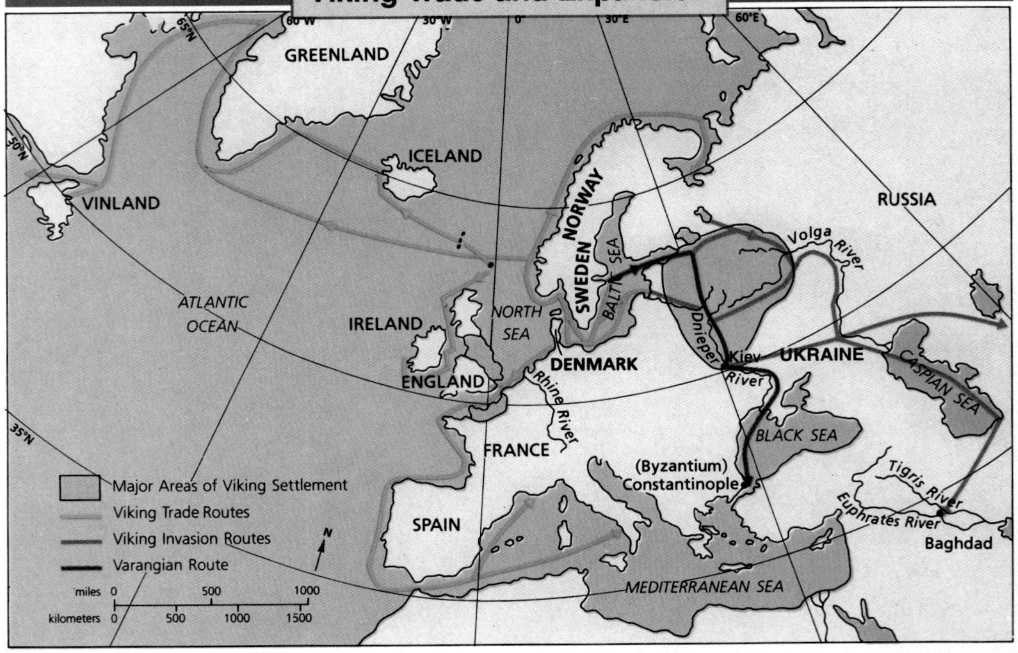

COOPERATIVE LEARNING

Divide the class into five groups. Have each group do research and prepare a report on one of the following Viking leaders: Eric the Red, Leif Eriksson, Rurik, Canute, or Rollo. Each report should describe the Viking leader's life and achievements. Have students illustrate their reports. Each member of the group should be assigned a specific task in preparing the report. Have a spokesperson from each group read its report to the class.

VIKING SHIPS The Vikings were among the best shipbuilders of their time. At sea, the Vikings depended on the wind and sails for power. On a river, rowers powered the ship. The Viking ships in this painting pursue enemy trading ships. **How did Vikings disguise their ships on rivers?**

attacks. They stole goods, destroyed homes, burned churches, and killed or enslaved people they captured. All Europe feared the Vikings. In their churches, the people prayed, "From the fury of the Norsemen, Good Lord, deliver us!"

The Danes The Danes were among those Vikings who raided western and southern Europe. One group invaded England and set up settlements there in the Danelaw. Their right to rule this area had been recognized by Alfred the Great. In 954, an heir of Alfred the Great forced the Danes to leave. In 978, Ethelred (eth' uhl red), nicknamed the Unready, became king of England. The Danes saw their chance and began raiding England again. At first, Ethelred was able to buy them off with silver. In 1016, however, a Danish king called Knut, or Canute (kuh nūt'), conquered England and made it part of his North Sea Empire. Canute was a powerful and just ruler. He converted to Christianity and brought peace and prosperity to England. Soon after his death in 1035, however, Danish control of the country came to an end. Some Danes left England. Those who remained became a part of the English people and culture.

Another group of Danes tried to take the city of Paris in France, but the French managed to fight them off. In 885, the

INDEPENDENT PRACTICE

L2 **Time Line** Have students make a time line of events in the chapter. Have students draw conclusions about the possible similarities among events on their time lines; explain the causes and effects of the events; and summarize the Vikings by describing them with no more than two adjectives. LEP

L3 **Critical Thinking** Ask students to write a paragraph comparing the importance of Christianity in the everyday lives of the Celts and the Anglo-Saxons during the Middle Ages with the importance of Christianity in the everyday life of the Vikings.

LINKING PAST TO PRESENT

A Viking settlement called *L'Anse aux Meadows* on the northern tip of Newfoundland has been carefully studied and is believed to be the probable site of Vinland. Archaeologists have excavated the remains of several houses with turf walls. One was a Norse "longhouse" with a great hall and other rooms. This and other houses resembled those in Greenland. A soapstone spindle that was found is believed to be evidence that the settlers included both women and men.

SPOTLIGHT ON: CANUTE

Canute was the first Danish king of England. Legend states that he wanted to end the flattery of his nobles, who declared that he was all-powerful. To teach the nobles a lesson, he took them to the edge of the sea, where he commanded the incoming tide to come no further. His failure to stop the water proved to his nobles that a king's power was limited.

ASSESS

CHECK FOR UNDERSTANDING

Ask students to summarize the main points of the chapter. Discuss answers to the Section and Chapter Review questions.

EVALUATE

Assign the Chapter 20 **Performance Assessment Activity** in the TCR.

Administer the **Chapter 20 Test** in the TCR. Testmaker available.

RETEACH

Have students work in small groups to outline the chapter. Have them use the outline to quiz one another.

Assign Chapter 20 **Reteaching Activity** in the TCR.

ENRICH

Have students research illustrations of runes and rune stones to present to the class.

Assign the Chapter 20 **Enrichment Activity** in the TCR.

CLOSE

Have students discuss the importance of poems, myths, legends, and sagas in the everyday life of the Vikings.

MEETING CHAPTER OBJECTIVES

Each objective is tested by the Review questions in parentheses.

1. Explain how the Vikings earned a living. (CU 1)

2. Summarize daily life of the Vikings. (BV; CU 3, 4, 6, 8; CT 1, 2)

3. Describe Viking warriors and adventurers. (BV; CT 3, 4)

4. Explain the role of Vikings in the history of England and France. (CT 4)

Danes tried again. The people of Paris held them off for ten months. Finally, the French king paid the Danes gold to abandon their attack.

Led by a warrior named Rollo (rahl' ō), the Danes began settling along the French coast opposite England. In 911, the French king signed a treaty with Rollo. He gave the Danes this land. In return, the Danes became Christians and promised to be loyal to the French king. The region in which the Danes settled became known first as the Norselaw and then as Normandy (nōr' muhn dē). The people became known as Normans.

Section 3 Review

1. **Identify:** Varangian route, Rurik, Erik the Red, Leif Eriksson, Vinland, Canute, Rollo, Norselaw
2. Why did many Vikings leave Scandinavia?
3. Why did Europeans fear the Vikings?
4. What happened to the Danes who settled in England?

Critical Thinking

5. How might life have been different for the Vikings if there had been a central government in Scandinavia?

Chapter Summary

1. The Vikings lived in northern Europe in an area now called Scandinavia.
2. The Vikings were excellent warriors, sailors, and navigators who earned their living mainly by fishing and by trading with other European regions.
3. The Vikings lived in villages that were isolated from one another.
4. The Vikings worshiped many gods and often told stories about them.
5. Early on, the Vikings spoke one language, but over time, it developed into four separate languages.
6. When the Vikings accepted Christianity, they stopped writing their languages in runes and began to write with Roman letters.
7. By the 800s, Scandinavia was overpopulated, and many Viking warriors traveled to other lands.
8. In 862, a Swedish Viking named Rurik established a settlement that later became Kievan Rus.
9. In 986, Norwegian Vikings founded a colony on Greenland and then sailed as far west as the northeast coast of North America.
10. In 1016, a Danish king called Canute conquered England, but after his death, Danish control of the country came to an end.
11. Other Danish Vikings, after besieging Paris, settled along the French coast in an area known as the Norselaw.

SECTION 3 ANSWERS

1. Varangian route, from the Baltic to the Black Sea (p. 304); Rurik, a Swedish chief (p. 305); Erik the Red, Viking leader (p. 305); Leif Eriksson, Viking adventurer (p. 305); Vinland, Newfoundland (p. 305); Canute, Danish king (p. 307); Rollo, Danish warrior (p. 308); Norselaw, region where Danes first settled (p. 308)

2. Viking villages were overcrowded and had food shortages, and the kings constantly fought one another.

3. because they stole, destroyed homes, and killed or enslaved people

4. Danes in England lost control of England after Canute died. Danes in France settled in Normandy, and became Christians.

5. Answers will vary but could include that life might have been more stable.

Assign the Chapter 20 **Section 3 Quiz** in the TCR. Testmaker available.

CHAPTER Review 20

Building Vocabulary

Imagine you are a journalist writing a magazine article about Scandinavia. Use the following words to write a paragraph describing the Viking way of life.

jarls
Eddas
runes
berserkers

Check for Understanding

1. Why did many Vikings turn to the sea to make a living?
2. How did the Vikings plot their sailing courses?
3. How were Viking houses protected from the winter?
4. Why was there no central government in Scandinavia?
5. How did a *jarl* become a king?
6. What position in society did Viking women hold?
7. What were Viking stories about?
8. How did the Vikings use *runes?*
9. What effect did the Vikings have on Kievan Rus?
10. Why did the Vikings decide not to set up a colony in North America?

Critical Thinking

1. How did Christianity affect Viking life?
2. What would you have liked about being a Viking? What would you have disliked?
3. What do you think might have happened in Scandinavia if many Viking warriors had not left during the 800s?
4. What effect did the Vikings have on the development of Europe during the early Middle Ages?

Geography in History

REGION The Vikings settled in areas beyond the Scandinavian region. What geographic features of Scandinavia may have contributed to the Viking's expansion and movement?

Using Your Journal

Review the details you have noted about Viking explorations that took place in Europe in the early Middle Ages. Imagine you are a Viking adventurer landing on the northeast coast of North America. Write a diary entry describing your first impression of North America.

CHAPTER 20 REVIEW ANSWERS

BUILDING VOCABULARY

Paragraphs will vary but should use all the vocabulary words to describe the Vikings.

CHECK FOR UNDERSTANDING

1. because the land was not suited to farming
2. by the positions of the sun and the stars
3. Their roofs slanted deeply to shed the heavy winter snows.
4. because distance and the cold winters isolated the people
5. by taking over neighboring lands
6. They took charge of the home and could attend public meetings, talk with all men, own property, and get a divorce.
7. the gods' great deeds
8. as magic charms
9. They founded a settlement that became the Russian nation.
10. because it was so far from home, and Native Americans attacked them

CRITICAL THINKING

1. It caused the people to lose interest in their sagas and to write with Roman letters.
2. Answers will vary but should include examples.
3. Answers will vary but could include that there might not have been any explorations to North America.
4. They spread fear but also opened up new trade routes and taught seafaring skills.

✚ BONUS ✚

TEST QUESTION
For Chapter 20 Test

If the Vikings had sailed directly from Norway to Newfoundland, they could have covered the approximately 2,500-mile distance in under 20 days. About how many miles per hour would their speed have to be to make the trip in under 20 days. *(slightly over 5 miles [3 km] per hour)*

USING YOUR JOURNAL

Diary entries will vary but could include a description of their emotional reactions. You might ask volunteers to read their entries to the class.

GEOGRAPHY IN HISTORY

Viking expansion was caused by limited space and mountains on their peninsula, and their access to the Baltic Sea and the Atlantic Ocean.

UNIT 6 CULTURE CLOSE-UP

THE GUPTAS

FOCUS

OBJECTIVES

Locate the Gupta Empire. Identify the time period of the Gupta Empire. Describe India's Golden Age under the Guptas.

BELLRINGER

Write the following on the chalkboard: *What is the meaning of* infinity *and who developed the concept?*

MOTIVATIONAL ACTIVITY

Ask students to read their definitions of infinity *(unlimited expanse of time, space, or quantity)* and who developed the concept *(the Guptas)*. Discuss with those who guessed the idea came from the Greeks or Romans why they assumed that. Then explain that in this Culture Close-Up they will learn about the Guptas and their other accomplishments during the Golden Age of India.

UNIT 6

CULTURE CLOSE-UP

The Guptas

The Gupta (gup' tuh) Empire was called India's Golden Age. Lasting for about 800 years, it began in 320 A.D.

Geography Connection

The Gupta Empire, covering much of India and parts of southwest Asia, was a peaceful civilization. Travel was common as the empire expanded. ▶

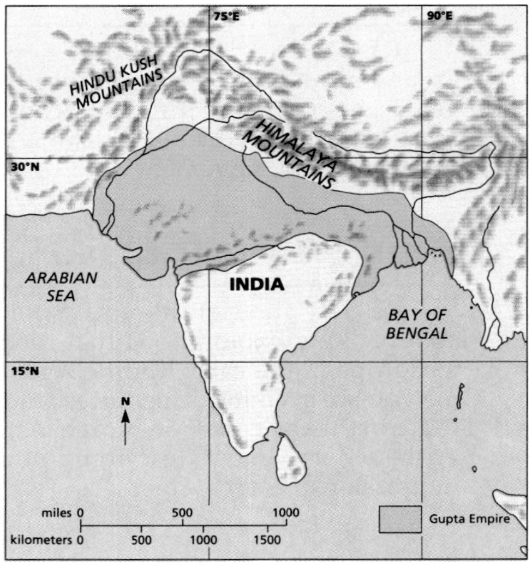

Gupta people loved learning—literature, science, and mathematics. They developed a system of numbers that was later adopted by Arabs. Today it is a number system used all over the world. ▶

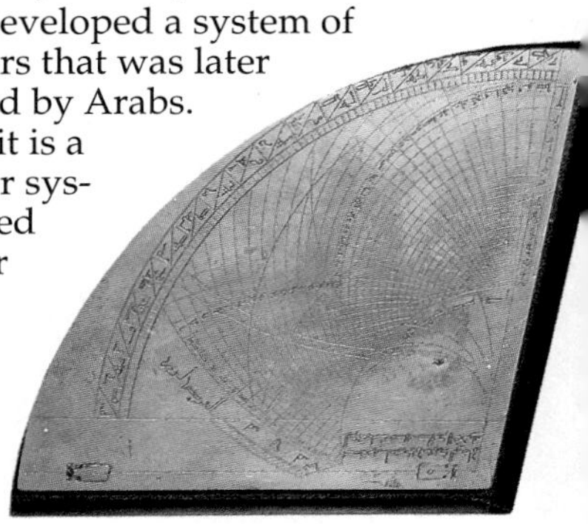

310

MULTICULTURAL PERSPECTIVES

A Buddhist monk from China named Faxian traveled to the Gupta Empire during Chandragupta II's rule. He recorded the following observation in his diary: "*In the Gupta Empire, people are numerous and happy, only those who cultivate the royal land have to pay* [in] *grain. . . . If they want to go, they go; if they want to stay, they stay. The king governs without decapitation* [cutting off heads] *or corporal* [bodily] *punishment. . . . The leaders of Vaisya families have houses in the cities for dispensing charity and medicine.*

◀ Art and sculpture flourished under Gupta rulers. Great detail was used to decorate buildings.

Women and men were glorified in sculpture and in literature. Gupta writers brought back the classical writing of India—Sanskrit. Plays, poetry, and fables were part of the Gupta literature. ▶

One ruler, Chandragupta II, minted his own gold coins. ▼

TEACH

L1 **Geography: Location** Have students compare the map of the Maurya Empire on page 202 with the map of the Gupta Empire on page 310. Ask: Which empire was larger? *(the Maurya)* What physical features were part of both empires? *(Ganges River, Himalaya Mountains, Vindyha range)* What pre-sent-day country contained both of these empires? *(India)* LEP

L2 **Mathematics** Form teams to solve a series of math problems on the chalkboard. Assign one team to work the problem using Roman numerals, the other with Arabic numerals. Halfway through the exercise, have teams switch so each team can use both types of numerals. Discuss with the class why Arabic numerals are easier to work with than Roman numerals. Also discuss why the concept of zero and the symbol *0,* developed by Gupta mathematicians, are important. Remind the students that Arabic numerals were first developed by the Guptas and then adopted and used by the Arabs, hence the name Arabic numerals. LEP

L3 **Religion** Have interested students research and write a report about the most dominant Hindu gods and what each represents.

MEETING SPECIAL NEEDS

Read aloud some tales from the *Panchatantra* to students who are auditory learners. Explain that stories from this collection have been passed down through Persian, Arabic, Greek, Hebrew, Latin, and German to the English language. Have students compare these Indian tales with those of other countries about which they may have read or heard.

MAKING CONNECTIONS

➤➤ **Religion** Hinduism was not founded on the teachings of one person, nor did it have one holy book. Instead it was based on different beliefs and practices, many of which had their roots in the Vedas and the Indian epics. Other ideas that became part of Hinduism came from religious thinkers who had grown discontented with complex Vedic rituals. Between 800 and 400 B.C., their search for wisdom and truth was reflected in the religious writings known as *Upanishads,* which tell of a universal spirit, or soul, present within all life. Thus Hindus came to regard animals as sacred and forbade killing them.

L1 **Critical Thinking** Have students discuss what the effects might be on future civilizations if the developments of the Guptas, such as in mathematics, had not been made. Suggest students rate the Guptas, on a scale of 1 to 10, on their impact on the future.

GLOBAL READING FOR STUDENTS

Suggest students read a collection of ancient Hindu scriptures, epic tales, and contemporary poems. Suggest *Poems from India* compiled by Daisy Aldan, Crowell, 1969. (Average/Fiction)

◀ The entrance to the Ajanta (uh jan´ tuh) caves in southern India is ornate. It is where much Gupta art has been found.

▼ Details such as figures dancing or playing musical instruments show the influence of music in the Gupta culture.

◀ The Guptas replaced the philosophy of Buddhism with Hinduism as their primary religion. Many Hindu gods, such as Ganesh, were sculpted by them.

312

COOPERATIVE LEARNING

Organize the students into four groups. Assign each group one of the following Hindu beliefs to research and explain to the class: reincarnation, karma, ahisma, moksha. Allow students within each group to decide how they will present their research and what role each will play.

UNIT 6

CULTURE CLOSE-UP

The disc of Vishnu is another Hindu piece crafted by Guptas. This god adorned some of the earliest free-standing Hindu temples in India. ▶

▼ Kings, queens, and other wealthy Guptas benefitted from medical advances of the civilization. Plastic and corrective surgery was commonly practiced.

Taking Another Look

1. **During what years did the Guptas flourish?**
2. **What arts grew during the Gupta empire?**
3. **What religion replaced Buddhism as the leading religion?**

Critical Thinking

4. **What uses do you think the Guptas had for their numbering system?**

ASSESS

CHECK FOR UNDERSTANDING

Have students answer the questions in Taking Another Look on page 313.

ANSWERS to Taking Another Look

1. about A.D. 320–1120
2. literature, sculpture, cave drawings, music, and architecture
3. Hinduism
4. Answers will vary. Students should list uses the Guptas had for their numbering system, such as for use in trade and predicting the seasons, eclipses, and other events.

ENRICH

Have students research more about the medical advancements of the Gupta, especially in the areas of plastic surgery. Have students compare and contrast the reasons why such surgery was performed by the Guptas and why it is performed today.

CLOSE

Ask students to discuss the following Hindu philosophy and its possible affect on the Golden Age of India, "By good deeds a man becomes what is good, and by evil deeds what is bad."

EXTENDING THE CONTENT

Many Gupta developments and achievements had lasting effects and showed they were an advanced civilization.

Doctors who practiced during India's Golden Age developed plastic surgery. They rebuilt ears and noses and removed scars. Metallurgists made iron columns that are still free from rust after more than 1500 years.

INTRODUCE

UNIT 7 OVERVIEW

Unit 7 discusses the emergence of new empires in the Middle East and eastern Europe from the fall of Rome to A.D. 1600, focusing on the Byzantines, the Arabs, and the Eastern Slavs and the emergence of Russia.

- **Chapter 21** describes how the Byzantines forged an empire based on Greco-Roman culture and the Eastern Orthodox Church.
- **Chapter 22** analyzes the role of Muhammad in the emergence and spread of Islam and the creation of the Arab Empire.
- **Chapter 23** discusses the Eastern Slavic civilization from the founding of their early settlements to the establishment of a powerful Rus state centered around Moscow that later developed as modern Russia.

UNIT OBJECTIVES

After reading Unit 7, students will be able to:

1. discuss how religion influenced the growth and development of the Middle East and eastern Europe from 500 to the 1500s.

2. analyze how the Arabs influenced the civilization of western Europe.

3. explain how the Byzantines influenced Russia.

UNIT PROJECT

Divide the class into three groups. Assign each group one of the following leaders: Justinian, Muhammad, or Ivan the Great. Tell each group that it will be responsible for writing and performing a short play based on the life of their assigned leader.

UNIT 7 Emergence of New Empires

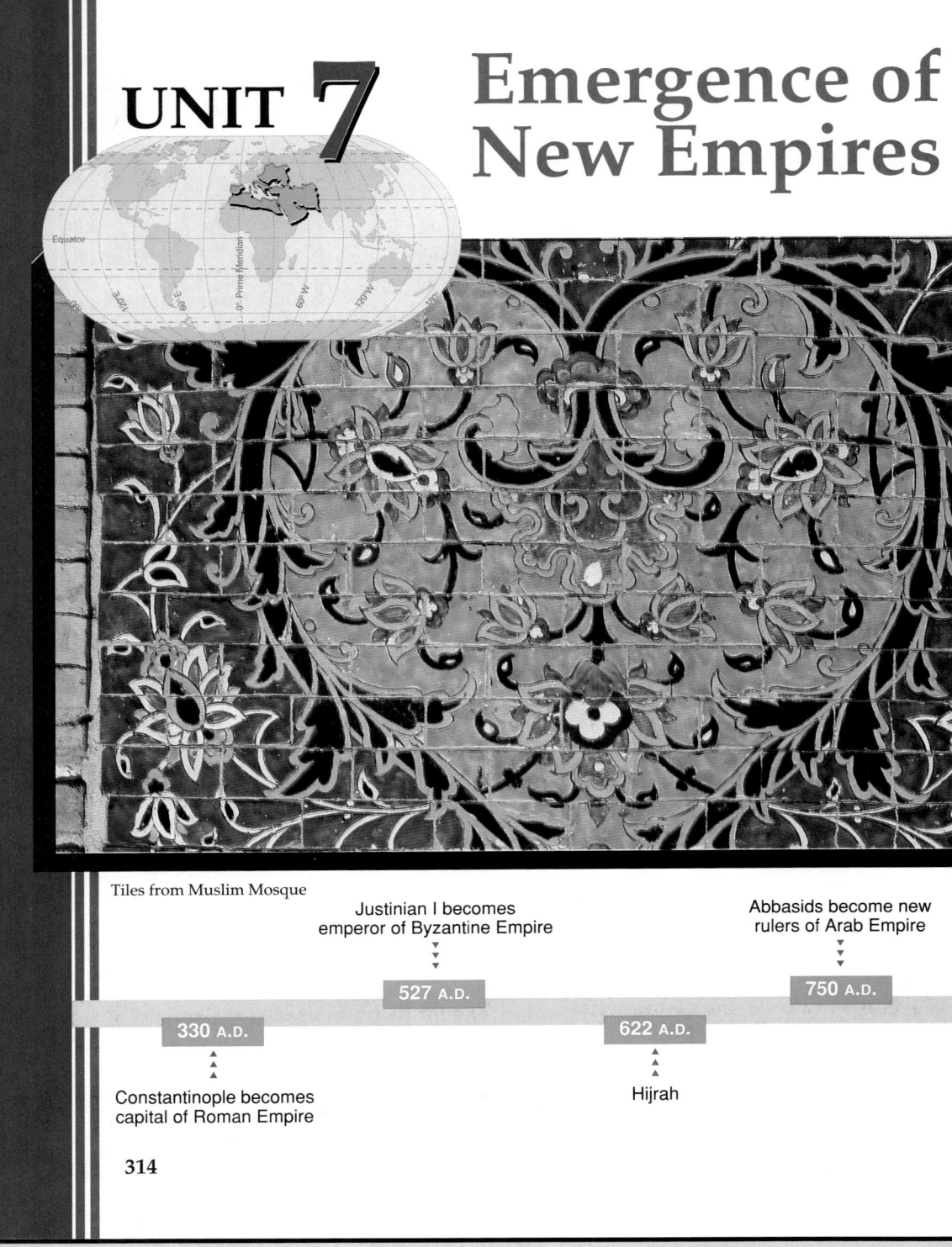

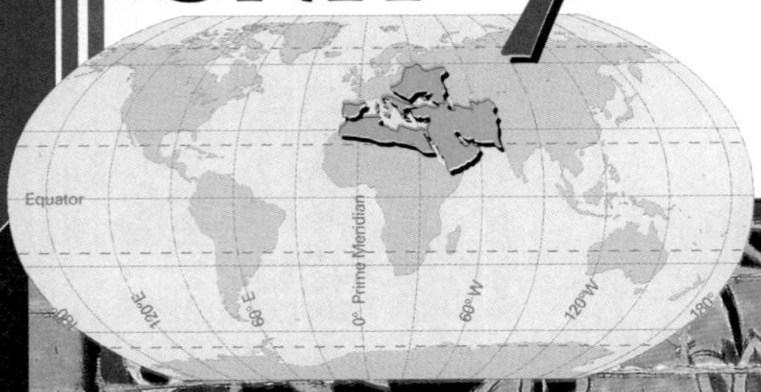

Tiles from Muslim Mosque

330 A.D. — Constantinople becomes capital of Roman Empire

527 A.D. — Justinian I becomes emperor of Byzantine Empire

622 A.D. — Hijrah

750 A.D. — Abbasids become new rulers of Arab Empire

314

ABOUT THE UNIT OPENING

EXAMINING THE ARTIFACT

Ask students to explain what a mosque is. *(Muslim place of worship)* Explain that these tiles that decorate a mosque are a sample of the beautiful art of the Middle East. This is a part of the world they will be reading more about in this unit.

GLOBAL CHRONOLOGY

Ask students to explain what time period the time line covers. *(330 to 1547)* According to the time line, what cities became political centers during this time in the Middle East and the eastern part of Europe? *(Constantinople, Moscow)* What empires existed during this time period? *(Roman, Byzantine, Arab empires)*

From about 500 to about 1500, there was a flowering of civilization in what is today the eastern part of Europe and the Middle East. Two groups of people, the Byzantines and the Arabs, built large empires during this time. A third group, the Eastern Slavs, developed a civilization modeled on that of the Byzantines. For most of the period, the Byzantine and Arab civilizations were more advanced than those of western Europe.

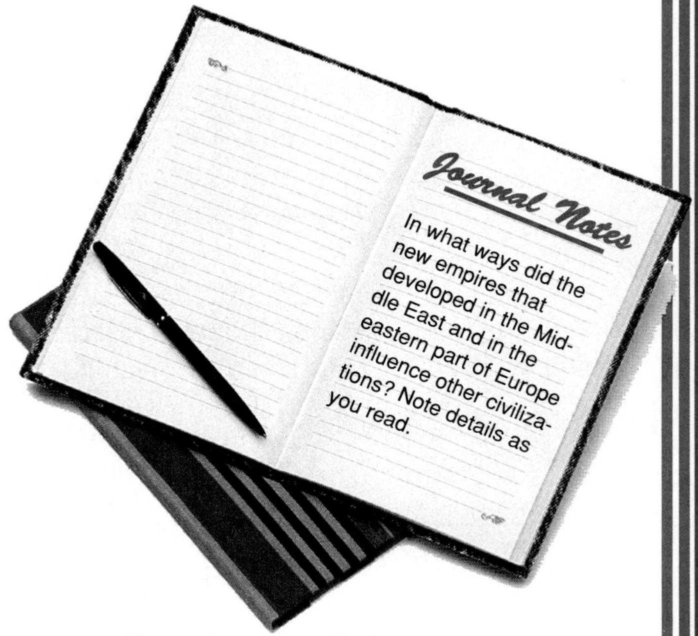

Journal Notes
In what ways did the new empires that developed in the Middle East and in the eastern part of Europe influence other civilizations? Note details as you read.

1243 A.D. — Mongols defeat Seljuq Turks

1453 A.D. — Ottoman Turks capture Constantinople

1500 A.D. — Moscow becomes political center of Rus

1547 A.D. — Ivan IV is crowned czar of Russia

INTRODUCING THE UNIT

Ask students to consider the cultural changes they have witnessed during their lives. Guide a discussion in which students identify specific achievements that have affected their culture. *(Answers can include technological advances, medical breakthroughs.)* Point out that each civilization in this unit changed throughout its history. Each culture also produced significant achievements. Ask students to express their thoughts about how achievements can change a culture.

RECORDING JOURNAL NOTES

Help students get started writing in their journals by having them list ways in which other cultures have influenced the culture of the United States in their lifetimes. Have students note in their journal details about the ways the empires that developed in the Middle East and in eastern Europe influenced other civilizations.

VIDEODISC

Use the following to enrich Unit 7.

WC C 41 14643
An exterior view of Hagia Sophia.

GEOGRAPHIC LOCATION

Have students use their text Atlas to locate the places in this unit that are in the Mediterranean area, identifying the Balkan Peninsula and the waterways from the Mediterranean Sea to the Black Sea and up to Russia. Then have students locate the Arabian Peninsula—the area where Islam originated—and identify the areas to its north, west, and east where Islam spread.

PLANNING GUIDE

CHAPTER 21

The Byzantine Empire

CHAPTER ORGANIZER

Objectives	Special Features	Supplemental Materials
Section 1 Constantinople Explain why the Byzantine Empire survived and prospered for 1,000 years.		• Reproducible Lesson Plan • Section 1 Quiz • Testmaker • Chapter 21 Vocabulary and Guided Reading Activity • The Western Civilization Videodisc
Section 2 Justinian I Discuss why Constantinople was important to the empire.	People in History: *Anna Comnena,* p. 321	• Reproducible Lesson Plan • Section 2 Quiz • Testmaker • Chapter 21 Cooperative Learning Activity • Chapter 21 Geography and Map Activity • Chapter 21 Teaching Transparencies and Activities
Section 3 The Church Analyze what the practices of the Eastern Orthodox Church were and what role they played in the Byzantine Empire.		• Reproducible Lesson Plan • Section 3 Quiz • Testmaker • World History and Art Transparency 9 • The Western Civilization Videodisc
Section 4 Decline of the Empire Summarize what helped bring about the decline of the Byzantine Empire.		• Reproducible Lesson Plan • Section 4 Quiz • Testmaker • Chapter 21 Chart and Graph Skill Activity • Chapter 21 Activity Book Activity
Chapter 21 Review and Evaluation		• Chapter 21 Reteaching Activity • Chapter 21 Enrichment Activity • Spanish Summary and Glossary • Audiocassettes (English and Spanish) • Chapter 21 Performance Assessment Activity • Chapter 21 Test • Testmaker

If time does not permit teaching the entire chapter, use the Chapter 21 Summary on page 328 and the Chapter 21 Audiocassettes (English and Spanish) to point out the main ideas of the chapter.

✓ Performance Assessment Activities

Word Puzzles Have students create a list of important people, places, buildings, or religious terms mentioned in this chapter. Have students use these lists to create a crossword puzzle. Have them prepare a blank puzzle with numbered clues for another student to solve.

Friendly Letters Have students imagine that they are Byzantine farmers who are visiting Constantinople for the first time. Have them write letters home describing the impressive sights in Constantinople.

CHAPTER RESOURCES

LITERATURE ABOUT THE PERIOD

Dickinson, Peter. *The Dancing Bear.* Dell, 1972. Tells an adventure story that takes place during the time of the Byzantine Empire.

READINGS FOR THE STUDENT

Browning, Robert. *The Byzantine Empire*. Charles Scribner's Sons, 1980. Byzantine world from A.D. 500 to fall of Constantinople in 1453.

Lamb, Harold. *Constantinople*. Alfred A. Knopf, 1957. A historical narrative about the birth of the Byzantine Empire.

READINGS FOR THE TEACHER

Bridge, Antony. *Theodora.* Academy Chicago Publishers, 1978. Biography of Theodora with accounts of history during her lifetime.

Browning, Robert. *Justinian and Theodora: The Byzantine Recovery.* Thames & Hudson, 1987. Explores the relationship between Justinian and Theodora and focuses on the Byzantine emperor's attempt to recreate the Christian Roman Empire of Constantine.

Mango, Cyril. *Byzantium: The Empire of New Rome.* Charles Scribner's Sons, 1980. Considers Byzantine life from a thematic perspective, focusing on people and languages, society and the economy, the disappearance and revival of cities, monasticism, education, and culture.

MULTIMEDIA RESOURCES

The Byzantine Empire. Coronet Films. Film. Major events and achievements of Byzantine civilization.

The Fall of Constantinople. Time-Life Film and Video. Film. History of city told with pictures of sites in modern Istanbul.

INTRODUCE

CHAPTER 21 OVERVIEW

Chapter 21 describes the major features of the Byzantine Empire from the founding of Constantinople to the Turkish conquest.

- ➤ **Section 1** summarizes Constantinople's role as the "New Rome."
- ➤ **Section 2** discusses the Byzantine contributions to government and law.
- ➤ **Section 3** discusses the effects of Orthodox Christianity on Byzantine and eastern European culture.
- ➤ **Section 4** analyzes the causes for the decline of the Byzantine Empire.

CHAPTER OBJECTIVES

After reading Chapter 21, students will be able to:

1. explain why the Byzantine Empire survived and prospered for 1,000 years.

2. discuss why Constantinople was important to the empire.

3. analyze what the practices of the Eastern Orthodox Church were and what role it played in the Byzantine Empire.

4. summarize what helped bring about the decline of the Byzantine Empire.

EXAMINING THE ILLUSTRATION

Ask students to speculate where the Hagia Sophia is located. *(Constantinople, now Istanbul, Turkey)* Explain that this city is important in the following chapter.

PERFORMANCE ASSESSMENT

Use the Performance Assessment activities on page 316B to help you evaluate students as they complete the chapter.

CHAPTER 21 The Byzantine Empire

Interior of Hagia Sophia

TEACHER CLASSROOM RESOURCES

- Reproducible Lesson Plan
- Activity Book Activity
- Enrichment Activity
- Geography and Map Activity
- Vocabulary and Guided Reading Activity
- Cooperative Learning Activity
- Spanish Summary and Glossary
- Performance Assessment Activity
- Teaching Transparencies and Activities
- World History and Art Transparency 9
- Testmaker
- Audiocassettes (English and Spanish)
- The Western Civilization Videodisc

Chapter Focus

READ TO DISCOVER:

- Why the Byzantine Empire survived and prospered for 1,000 years.
- Why Constantinople was important to the empire.
- What role the Eastern Orthodox Church played in the Byzantine Empire.
- What forces helped bring about the decline of the Byzantine Empire.

Emperor Constantine I moved the capital of the Roman Empire from Rome to Constantinople about 330. About 100 years later, the Roman Empire in the West fell. The Roman Empire in the East, however, survived and prospered. It became known as the Byzantine Empire. Its people were called Byzantines. The Byzantines built a civilization based on a blend of Greek, Roman, and Christian ideas.

The empire in the East survived for several reasons. Most of its people were Christians and their religion united them. Also, Constantinople was a mighty fortress that needed few soldiers to defend it. This freed soldiers to protect other areas of the empire. In addition, the empire's wealth was used to support a large army and to pay invaders to move farther and farther west.

330 A.D.–1455 A.D.

KEY TERMS

relics
theology
dowry
mosaics
Greek fire
metropolitans
icons

Section 1 CONSTANTINOPLE

When Constantine first chose the old Greek city of Byzantium as the place for his new capital, he was aware of its advantages. The Roman Empire depended on trade, and the great centers of trade lay to the east. Byzantium was on the waterway between the Black and Aegean seas. Its harbor offered a safe haven for fishing boats, merchant ships, and warships. The city sat at the crossroads of the trading routes between Europe and Asia. Its location gave it control of the sea trade between Kievan Rus and the Mediterranean area. One of the most important east-west land routes passed through the city, too.

FOCUS

BELLRINGER

Write the following on the chalkboard: *Make a list of some things you know about the country of Turkey.*

MOTIVATIONAL ACTIVITY

Discuss students' lists of what they know about Turkey. Ask them if they realize that Istanbul is the ancient city of Constantinople. Explain that they will learn about the importance of this city in history.

VOCABULARY PRE-CHECK

Write the key terms for this chapter on the chalkboard. Ask students to use those that they know in sentences.

Assign Chapter 21 **Vocabulary and Guided Reading Activity** in the TCR.

EXTRA CREDIT PROJECT

Each important historical city had a distinct personality, but not all had flags. Encourage interested students to create a flag and a motto for Constantinople that symbolizes the strongest parts of that city's personality. Have them include a brief explanation of their flag design and then post the finished products.

KEY TO ABILITY LEVELS

Teaching strategies have been coded for varying learning styles and abilities.

L1 Level 1 activities are **basic** activities and should be within the ability range of all students.

L2 Level 2 activities are **average** activities and should be within the ability range of the average to above-average student.

L3 Level 3 activities are **challenging** activities designed for the ability range of above-average students.

LEP LEP activities should be within the ability range of Limited English Proficiency students.

TEACH

GUIDED PRACTICE

L1 **Geography: Location** Ask students to make an outline map of Europe, the Middle East, and North Africa similar to the one on page 323. Have them locate and label Rome, Constantinople, Athens, the Mediterranean and Black seas, the Bosphorus, Asia Minor, Syria, Egypt, Italy, Greece, and the Balkan Peninsula. Explain that the boundaries of the Byzantine Empire varied over time, but that it remained a geographic crossroads of sea and land travel. LEP

DID YOU KNOW ??

Constantinople's oval arena was called the Hippodrome.

CAPTION ANSWER

because it was modeled after Rome

VIDEODISC

Use the following to enrich Chapter 21.

WC C 42 14644
4th c. Byzantine mosaic, Salonika, Greece.

WC C 43 14645
Emperor Constantine VII (912-959).

The location also favored the city's defense. The sea protected it on three sides, and a huge wall protected it on the fourth side. Later, a huge chain was even strung across the city's north harbor for greater protection. Invaders would not easily take the new capital, which was renamed Constantinople.

It took more than four years to build Constantinople. Constantine modeled it after Rome. The city stood on seven hills. Government buildings and palaces were designed in the Roman style. Streets were narrow and apartment houses crowded. Constantinople even had an oval arena like the Circus Maximus where races and other events were held.

The city's political and social life was patterned on that of Rome, too. The emperor operated under Roman laws and ruled with the help of highly trained officials, who took charge of building roads, bridges, wells, and caravan shelters. The army followed Roman military customs. The poor people of Constantinople received free bread and enjoyed circuses and chariot races put on by the government. The wealthy people lived in town or on large farming estates. In fact, Constantine convinced many of the wealthy Romans to move to Constantinople by offering to build them palaces.

CONSTANTINOPLE Constantinople's location made it an important center for trade. The wealth from this trade was used to make Constantinople an ornate and beautiful city. Citizens shown in this painting gather to watch a royal procession. **Why was Constantinople called the "new Rome"?**

MULTICULTURAL PERSPECTIVES

A contemporary historian points out that a modern-day time traveler would feel more at home in the Byzantine world of Constantinople than in any of the depressed, dangerous countries of the early medieval western Europe. The city had shops, factories, and banking houses. It had a well-educated population who were curious and informed about current events, politics, and literature. The Byzantines were enthusiastic sports fans at games and chariot races. They loved ornamentation and rich colors especially in their illuminated manuscripts and stained-glass windows.

The family was the center of social life for most Byzantines. The majority of them made their living through farming, herding, or working as laborers. There was, however, one important difference between Constantinople and Rome. From the beginning, Constantinople was a Christian city. It had been dedicated to God by Constantine, who viewed it as the center of a great Christian empire. Church leaders were consulted about all important events of everyday life and had great influence over the people. For a young man of Constantinople, a career in the church was considered a very high goal.

Constantinople had many Christian churches. Constantine saw to it that they were the most magnificent buildings in the city. Government and church leaders gathered **relics** (rel′ iks), or valued holy objects from the past, from throughout the Christian world. These were placed in public monuments, palaces, and churches. The bodies of saints rested in beautiful shrines. Thousands of people came to these shrines to pray to God for cures for their ills.

The city's Christian values could be seen in the way needy people were treated. The Byzantines believed that each Christian was responsible for the well-being of other Christians. Wealthy Byzantines formed organizations to care for the poor, the aged, and the blind. Even members of the emperor's household took great pride in founding and supporting good causes.

About 600,000 people lived in Constantinople during Constantine's rule. There were Greeks, Turks, Italians, Slavs, Persians, Armenians, and Jews. They spoke Greek among themselves but used Latin, the official language, for government business. Most people became Christians, and all called themselves Romans. Byzantine nobles and rulers continued to boast of their ties to Rome for the next 1,100 years.

Two Byzantine Coins

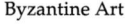

Section 1 Review

1. **Identify:** Constantinople, Byzantine Empire, Byzantium
2. **Define:** relics
3. Why did Constantine choose Byzantium as the site for the empire's new capital?
4. In what ways was Constantinople like Rome? In what ways was it different?

Critical Thinking

5. What, in your opinion, were some good things about living in Constantinople?

Byzantine Art

L3 **Critical Thinking** Have students create a chart comparing the elements of the Old Rome to the New Rome on the chalkboard. They can title the columns *Rome* and *New Rome (Constantinople)*. Under each title have them list elements that show contrasts, such as language, people, and architecture.

MAKING CONNECTIONS

➤➤ **Daily Life** Most of Constantinople was a complex maze of about 3,000 narrow streets, many of which were jammed with caravan traffic, peddlers, and porters. In spite of its many benefits, Constantinople had its share of problems. As a result of refuse-filled streets, disease spread rapidly. Living conditions worsened during times when the city was under siege.

LINKING PAST TO PRESENT

Trade and industry in Constantinople were strictly controlled by the government. The main industry was textiles. About 550, silkworms smuggled out of China were brought to Constantinople, where beautiful fabrics and clothes were made from raw silk. Silkworms are still raised today to commercially produce this fine fabric.

SECTION 1 ANSWERS

1. Constantinople, capital of Byzantine Empire (p. 317); Byzantine Empire, the Roman Empire in the East (p. 317); Byzantium, later became known as Constantinople (p. 317)
2. relics, holy objects (p. 319)
3. because it lay at the crossroads of the trading routes between Europe and Asia
4. It stood on seven hills; buildings were designed in Roman style; streets were narrow and crowded; sporting events were held in an oval arena; political and social life and army were patterned on Rome's. Unlike Rome, Constantinople was a Christian city from the beginning.
5. Answers will vary but students should include examples from the information in the section.

Assign Chapter 21 **Section 1 Quiz** in the TCR. Testmaker available.

L3 **Critical Thinking** Ask students to pretend that they are public relations advisers to Justinian I and have been asked to write a speech for the emperor to deliver to the people of the Byzantine Empire. The purpose of the speech is to improve the people's level of satisfaction with their lives under Justinian rule. Speeches should include references to Justinian's life and work, accomplishments, and influence on the daily life of the people. The speech should be based on factual information. Have volunteers share their speeches with the class.

MAKING CONNECTIONS

➤➤ **History** Justinian was the son of a prosperous peasant family. Peasants in the Byzantine Empire could rise to high positions, including emperor.

CAPTION ANSWER

Theodora was an actress, and there was a law forbidding marriages between actresses and high government officials. After Justinian became emperor, he abolished the law.

Section 2

JUSTINIAN I

After Constantine died, his sons ruled the empire. They were followed first by a general named Julian and then by a series of other emperors. Finally, in 527, a Macedonian named Justinian (juh stin' ē uhn) came to the throne. He was a strong ruler who came to be considered the greatest Byzantine emperor.

Justinian had served in the army and was a good general. He was well trained in law, music, architecture, and **theology** (thē ol' uh jē), or the study of religion. The people who served him were chosen for their ability rather than wealth or social position.

As emperor, Justinian controlled the army and navy, made the laws, headed the Church and the government, and was supreme judge. He could declare war or make peace. The Church taught that the emperor's acts were inspired by God. Therefore, what Justinian did could not be questioned. Those who came into contact with him were expected to bow down before him and kiss his feet and hands.

Theodora Justinian's wife, the empress Theodora (thē uh dor' uh), was a great help to him. Theodora's family had been poor, and she had worked as an actress before meeting Justinian.

JUSTINIAN AND THEODORA Theodora had a much greater influence on Byzantine government than other empresses. In this painting she urges Justinian to take action against a revolt. **What problems did Justinian face in marrying Theodora?**

COOPERATIVE LEARNING

Organize a travel agency in which teams will assume responsibility for providing information to people traveling to Constantinople during Justinian's rule. One team will plan the important stops, another will give information on climate and food, and another group will prepare one or two travel posters. The team that plans the stops will provide a map showing the route. Each team should research the various points of interest and be able to contribute to the packet of information.

Assign Chapter 21 **Cooperative Learning Activity** in the TCR.

Anna Comnena

PEOPLE IN HISTORY

The Byzantines believed that to be uneducated was a disgrace. This was especially true for both men and women of the upper class.

Well Educated Woman One of the best-educated upperclass Byzantine women was Anna Comnena (kahm nē′ nuh). Born in 1083, she was the elder daughter of Emperor Alexius I Comnenus (uh lek′ sē uhs kahm nē′ nuhs) shown in the painting above. Alexius was a fine scholar and taught Anna to love books. All of the upper-class Byzantines studied Latin, Greek, history, and classical literature. Anna also studied geography, medicine, and nursing.

When she was fourteen years old, Anna married Nicephorus Bryennius (nī sef′ ō rus brī en′ ē us), the son of another noble family. Although the marriage had been arranged, it turned out to be a love match. Anna plotted to have her father disinherit his own son and put Nicephorus on the throne. Her plot failed. After Alexius I died, he was succeeded by Anna's brother, John II Comnenus.

This failure did not stop Anna's plotting. Less than a year after her brother took the throne, Anna led an unsuccessful conspiracy to assassinate him. Finally, John II became so angry that he banished his sister from the royal court.

A Historian Anna then retired to a convent. There, she became a historian and wrote the *Alexiad* (uh lek′ sē ad). This is a history of the reign of her father. It tells about events at court and about the important role Byzantine women played in politics. Its accounts of Byzantine weapons and battle tactics are detailed and full of action.

Anna Comnena finished the *Alexiad* in 1148 and died that same year. Anna was one of the earliest, and some say the greatest, female historian.

Checking for Understanding

1. **Why did Anna Comnena retire to a convent?**
2. **What can people learn about Byzantine history from the *Alexiad*?**

Teaching

PEOPLE IN HISTORY

ANNA COMNENA

After students have read the People in History Feature, ask: Why do some people think of Anna Comnena as the world's greatest female historian? *(She wrote the* Alexiad.*)* Point out to students that some people think Anna Comnena's work is biased. They say she wrote too favorably about her father.

ANSWERS to Checking for Understanding

1. because her brother banished her from the royal court

2. about the reign of Emperor Alexius I Comnenus, events at the court, the role of Byzantine women in politics, and weapons and battle tactics

SPOTLIGHT ON: ANNA COMNENA

In 1097 Anna Comnena married Nicephorus Bryennius, the leader of Bryennium. While her father the emperor was on his death bed, Anna and her mother Irene, tried to talk him into disinheriting his son John II Comnenus in favor of Nicephorus. They were unsuccessful. Anna later tried to depose her brother, but Nicephorus refused to go along with her plot and she was forced to give up her property and move to a convent.

DID YOU KNOW ??

Theodora built many hospitals for the poor and established a home for destitute actresses.

LINKING PAST TO PRESENT

Constantinople is now called Istanbul, part of Muslim Turkey. After the Muslims captured Constantinople in 1453, they decided that Hagia Sophia, with some changes, could be as beautiful a mosque as it was a church. All the Christian symbols were removed or hidden. Whitewash covered over mosaics and murals. Some new wings were built off the huge central dome. Tall, tapering minarets now stand at the four corners of the building. The Turkish government declared the building a national museum in 1935. They restored many of the original mosaics and other Byzantine decorations.

The people of the empire had a low opinion of actresses. There was even a law forbidding marriages between them and high government officials. Justinian, however, wanted to marry Theodora. After he became emperor, he abolished the law and made Theodora his empress.

At first, Theodora only entertained guests and attended palace ceremonies. Gradually, however, she began to take an interest in politics. Soon she was helping Justinian fill government and church offices. She also convinced Justinian to allow women more rights. For the first time, a Byzantine wife could own land equal in value to her **dowry** (dow′ rē), or the wealth she brought with her when she married. A widow could raise and support her young children without government interference.

In 532, Theodora made her most important contribution. A group of senators had organized a revolt to protest high taxes. They were able to gain much support from both the poor and the rich. The poor were angry because they were receiving less free food and entertainment. The rich were angry because, for the first time, they had to pay taxes. The leaders of the revolt were prepared to crown a new emperor. Justinian's advisers urged him to leave the city. Theodora, however, urged him to stay and fight. Justinian and his supporters took Theodora's advice. They stayed in Constantinople, trapped the rebels, killed 300,000 of them, and crushed the uprising. As a result, Justinian kept control of the government and became an even stronger ruler.

Law and Public Works Justinian was very interested in law and spent much time reading the laws made by other emperors. He decided that the old legal system was too complicated and disorganized. He chose ten men to work out a simpler and better system. This group was headed by a legal scholar named Tribonian (tri bō′ nē ahn).

Tribonian and the others studied the existing laws. They did away with those that were no longer needed. They organized and rewrote those laws that remained. In six years, they had developed a legal code that became the law of the land.

This code came to be known as the Justinian Code. It is considered one of Justinian's greatest achievements. It provided a summary of Roman legal thinking. It also gave later generations insight into the basic ideas of Roman law. It has had a great influence on the legal systems of almost every western country.

Justinian was as interested in public works as he was in law. He was almost always busy with some building program. He built churches, bridges, monasteries, and forums. He also built a system of forts connected by a large network of roads. When an earthquake destroyed Antioch, he had the whole city rebuilt.

One of Justinian's greatest accomplishments was the church called Hagia Sophia (hag′ē ī sō fē′ uh), or "Holy Wisdom."

EXTENDING THE CONTENT

In May 542 a plague struck Constantinople and raged for four months. The Greek historian Procopius witnessed the epidemic and wrote detailed accounts. At its height, the disease killed 10,000 people a day. By the end of that summer 300,000 people had died. Justinian contracted the plague, which caused serious political concern because he and Theodora had no children and a successor had yet to be named. Theodora called a secret meeting with her ministers to plan for her husband's nephew to succeed him. Justinian survived the plague. During the months when he was sick, Theodora was in charge and dealt with the plague's devastation.

Nearly 10,000 workers, watched over by 200 supervisors, labored in shifts to build the church. It was built exactly as Justinian planned. The church had a gold altar and walls of polished marble. Gold and silver ornaments, woven cloth, and colorful **mosaics** (mō zā′ iks), or pictures made up of many bits of colored glass or stone, were everywhere. Figures of Justinian and Theodora were among the angels and saints that lined the walls.

Most impressive was the huge dome that rose high over the central part of the church. It was the first time such a huge circular dome had been set atop a rectangular opening. During the day, sunlight poured through the many windows in the dome. At night, thousands of oil lamps turned the building into a beacon that could be seen for miles.

Hagia Sophia was later called St. Sophia. For more than 900 years, it served as the religious center of the Byzantine Empire. It still stands today.

Conquest Justinian wanted to reunite the eastern and western parts of the empire and restore the glory and power that was Rome's. To do this, he needed to conquer the German kingdoms in western Europe and North Africa. He appointed an officer named Belisarius (bel uh sar′ ē uhs) to reorganize and lead the Byzantine army.

MAP STUDY

PLACE Justinian conquered parts of Italy, North Africa, and Spain. **About how many miles (km) did the Byzantine Empire under Justinian extend from its most eastern to its most western points?**

The Byzantine Empire Under Justinian

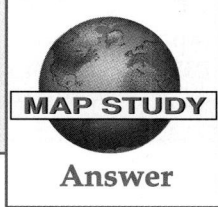

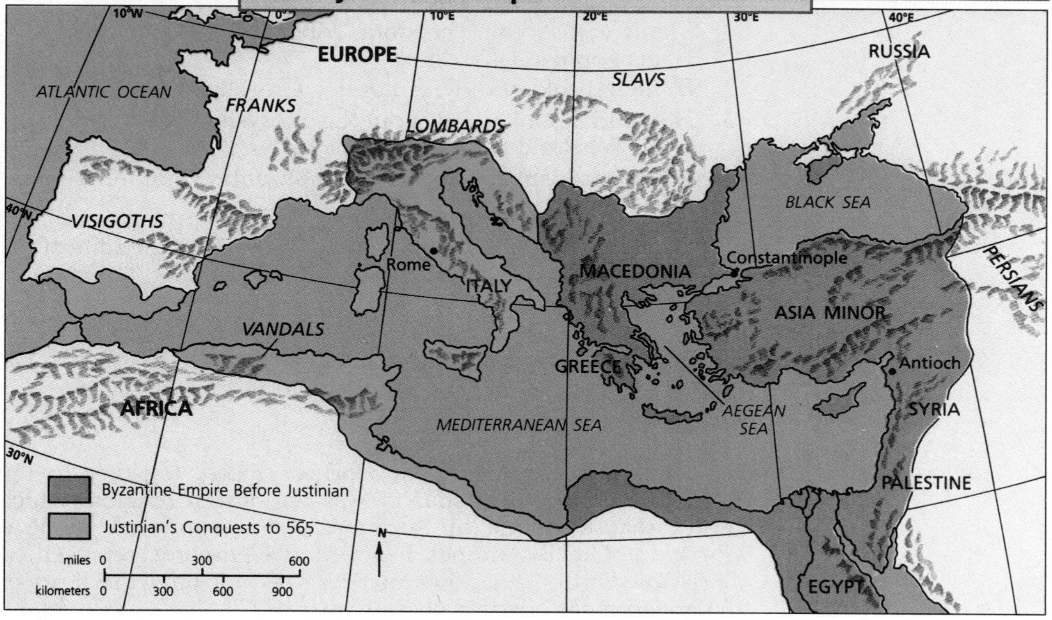

MAKING CONNECTIONS

➤➤ **Government** The Justinian Code consisted of four parts: the *Digest*, the decisions of the great Roman jurists; the *Institutes*, a textbook for law students; the *Novels*, the actual edicts issued by Justinian; and the *Codex*, a collection of statutes and principles.

LINKING PAST TO PRESENT

Modern-day art historians rank the Hagia Sophia with the Parthenon and with St. Peter's cathedral in Rome as one of the most important buildings in European history.

MAP STUDY

Answer

2,850 miles (or 4,585 km)

Assign the Chapter 21 **Geography and Map Activity** in the TCR.

SPOTLIGHT ON: THEODORA

Theodora was considered a feminist in her time. She was determined to improve the status of women in the Byzantine patriarchal society. Changes and improvements for which Theodora is credited include equal inheritance rights for daughters and sons. Another social reform provided that children of female slaves did not automatically become slaves. Theodora also converted a palace on the Bosporus into a convent where young girls could begin a new life.

MAKING CONNECTIONS

➤➤ **Government** Military expeditions took on the nature of sacred wars. When an emperor returned triumphant from battle, he would ride his white horse over flower-strewn streets to the city's center. There, after all the prisoners of war had been paraded before the court, the emperor would put his red boot on the shaved head of the chief prisoner, while courtiers sang: "Who is great like our God? You are the God who performs miracles."

DID YOU KNOW ??

Since there was no legal succession to the throne, Byzantine politics often were violent. Of the 107 emperors who ruled from 395 to 1453, only 40 died a natural death.

Until that time, the cavalry had been divided into groups of private soldiers hired by landowning nobles. Each group had its own commanders. Foot soldiers, who made up the largest part of the army, were called up when needed and then sent back to their homes. As a result, they felt little loyalty toward their officers.

When Belisarius took command, he set up a basic group of loyal and heavily armed cavalry soldiers. The group was so strong that the other soldiers willingly obeyed its orders. Then, Belisarius developed a series of battle moves that greatly strengthened the army's striking power.

During this time, the Byzantine navy was also improved and the first secret weapon in history was developed. It was called **Greek fire,** a chemical mixture that ignited when it came into contact with water. Greek fire burned a person's skin and was hard to put out. The Byzantines guarded their secret so carefully that its exact formula is still unknown.

With these improvements, the Byzantines were able to control more of the Mediterranean. They were also able to win back much of Italy and North Africa. They defeated the Persians, and ensured the security of the empire's eastern borders. Most of the western provinces Justinian regained, however, were lost again a generation or so after his death.

Section 2 Review

1. **Identify:** Justinian, Theodora, Tribonian, Justinian Code, Hagia Sophia, Belisarius
2. **Define:** theology, dowry, mosaics, Greek fire
3. How did Justinian feel about the old system of Roman laws? What did he do about it?
4. What was Justinian's goal for the Byzantine Empire?

Critical Thinking

5. What do you think Justinian would say about the state of the American legal system today?

Section 3 THE CHURCH

Church and government worked closely together in the Byzantine Empire. Christianity was the official religion, which meant that everyone in the empire was supposed to be a Christian. The Byzantines believed the emperor represented Christ on Earth. Thus, the emperor was not only the head of the government but also of the Church.

SECTION 2 ANSWERS

1. Justinian, Byzantine emperor (p. 320); Theodora, Byzantine empress (p. 320); Tribonian, scholar (p. 322); Justinian Code, a legal code (p. 322); Hagia Sophia, Byzantine church (p. 322); Belisarius, Byzantine army officer (p. 323)

2. theology, the study of religion (p. 320); dowry, the wealth a woman brought when married (p. 322); mosaics, pictures made of bits of glass or stone (p. 323); Greek fire, chemical mixture that ignited when it touched water (p. 324)

3. that it was too complicated and disorganized; he chose 10 men to work out a better system

4. to reunite its eastern and western parts and restore Rome's glory and power

5. Answers will vary but might include that modern laws are somewhat based on previous laws.

Assign Chapter 21 **Section 2 Quiz** in the TCR. Testmaker available.

BYZANTINE ICON The Byzantine people paid respect to icons in their homes and churches. Icons were often masterful works of art. The ornately decorated dome of a Byzantine church with the image of the enthroned Christ at center is shown here. **Why did the Byzantines argue over the use of icons?**

The leader of the Church in Constantinople was called the Patriarch. He was chosen by the emperor. Under him were the **metropolitans** (met ruh pol′ uh tuhns), or church officials in charge of the empire's important areas. Under them were the bishops and priests. Most priests were married. All higher Church officials, however, came from monasteries and were not married.

The monasteries played an important role in the Byzantine Empire. They helped the poor and ran hospitals and schools for needy children. They sent missionaries to neighboring lands to help keep the peace. These missionaries translated parts of the Bible and some religious services into several eastern European languages. They believed more people would become Christians if the Bible and Church ceremonies were in their own language.

Some missionaries, including a man named Cyril (sir′ uhl), traveled among the Slavs, a people who had settled in eastern Europe. These missionaries gave the Slavs a new alphabet. It was based on the Greek alphabet and was called the Cyrillic (suh ril′ ik) alphabet in honor of the man who had helped create it.

Religion was very important to the Byzantines. They often argued about religious matters. One point divided the Byzantines for more than 100 years. It centered on whether or not **icons** (ī′ konz), or religious images, should be used in worship.

Many Byzantines honored icons. They covered the walls of their churches with them. Monasteries owned icons that were

L2 **Religion** Have students draw an icon. They should choose a subject from one of the illustrations in the text, or from another source, and copy it in the Byzantine style. Students should try to color the drawing using colors similar to the examples. Ask students to observe the motionless aspect of the faces and the symmetry. LEP

CAPTION ANSWER

Some thought the icons were an aid to worship. Others believed that devotion to icons was a form of idol worship forbidden by God.

MAKING CONNECTIONS

➤➤ **Language** The Cyrillic alphabet has 33 letters and is based largely on the Greek alphabet.

VIDEODISC

Use the following to enrich Chapter 21.

WC C 40 14642

An interior view of Hagia Sophia, Constantinople.

MEETING SPECIAL NEEDS

To help auditory learners understand the role of the Eastern Orthodox Church in the Byzantine Empire, invite a resource person to speak to the students. The speaker might be a member of the Eastern Orthodox Church, a professor of theology or history, or someone else well versed in Byzantine history. Ask the speaker to examine the role of the emperor and the importance of monasteries and to show illustrations or examples of Byzantine art and architecture. Ask the speaker to explain that much of what we know about the early Eastern Orthodox Church is the result of the striking artwork that has survived from that period.

L2 **Debate** To illustrate the influence of religious conflict in the Byzantine Empire, divide the class into two teams—one favoring icons, the other opposing. Have students present an opening statement about their team's position, then open the floor to discussion.

MAKING CONNECTIONS

>> **Economics** While money was scarce in the West, the Byzantines had a strong monetary system based on gold. Their gold *bezant* became an important means of exchange throughout Europe and the Mediterranean area.

INDEPENDENT PRACTICE

L2 **Religion** Have students research Byzantine art to make lists of specific examples of how religion is revealed in Byzantine art and architecture. Have students write short essays explaining the relationship. Students may also wish to make drawings or sketches of some examples. Have students share their work with the class. LEP

Painting of Cyril

believed to work miracles. Some Byzantines, however, wanted an end to the use of icons. They thought honoring them was a form of idol worship forbidden by God.

In 726, Emperor Leo III ordered a stop to the use of icons in religious worship. He did not approve of icons and he wanted to keep church officials who favored them from gaining too much power. Leo and the church leaders argued over this. Most people refused to give up their icons. In 843, the emperor realized the cause was lost and once again allowed their use.

The fight over icons damaged the empire's relations with western Europe. Because so few people in the West could read, church leaders there used images instead of the written word to explain Christian teachings. When Leo decided to do away with icons, the Pope called a council of bishops. The council declared that Leo and his supporters were no longer Church members.

An argument also developed between the Pope and the Patriarch. The Patriarch would not recognize the Pope as head of the Church. The Pope broke his ties with the Byzantine emperor and turned to the Frankish kings for military protection. When the Pope crowned Charlemagne "Emperor of the Romans" in 800, the Byzantines were very angry. They believed this title belonged only to their emperor. These disputes helped pave the way for the break between Western and Eastern Christianity in 1054.

Section 3 Review

1. **Identify:** Patriarch, Cyrillic alphabet, Leo III
2. **Define:** metropolitans, icons
3. What role did Christianity play in the Byzantine Empire?
4. What caused the dispute between the Pope of Rome and the Patriarch of Constantinople?

Critical Thinking

5. Why do you think the Slavs needed an alphabet that was different from the one used in the Byzantine Empire?

Section 4 DECLINE OF THE EMPIRE

The Byzantine Empire lasted for about 1,100 years. Its capital was the largest, richest, and most beautiful city in Europe. Its people were among the most educated and creative of that time. They preserved Greek culture and Roman law for other civilizations. They also spread Christianity to peoples in the East. The empire did much to help the growth of trade. It also gave the

SECTION 3 ANSWERS

1. Patriarch, leader of the Church (p. 325); Cyrillic alphabet, based on the Greek alphabet (p. 325); Leo III, Byzantine emperor (p. 326)
2. metropolitans, church officials (p. 325); icons, religious images (p. 325)
3. It was the official religion, and the emperor was the head of the Church as well as the government.
4. The Patriarch would not recognize the Pope as head of the Church.
5. Answers will vary but might include that the missionaries would convert Slavs more easily if they were not associated with the Byzantine Empire.

Assign Chapter 21 **Section 3 Quiz** in the TCR. Testmaker available.

world new techniques in the fine arts. Even with all of these achievements, however, forces from both inside and outside the empire weakened it and led to its downfall.

Early Byzantine emperors had counted on farmers to make up the army. In return for their services, these farmers were given land. By the 1100s, however, the empire's borders were safe, and not as many soldiers were needed. The emperor decided to cut costs by changing the policy toward the farmers. Once they had lost their land, the farmers found little reason to remain loyal to the empire.

The empire also began to have problems with trade. When the Vikings conquered Byzantine lands in southern Italy in 1080, they threatened to attack Constantinople. The Byzantines no longer had enough soldiers to fight them. So, they turned for help to the Italian city-state of Venice. The Venetians defeated the Vikings. In return, the Byzantine emperor gave them the right to do business tax-free in all the empire's cities. Venetian ships and merchants soon controlled most of the empire's trade. This meant a great loss of income for the Byzantines.

Meanwhile, Christians from the West and Muslims from the East attacked the empire. Asia Minor was lost to these invaders. This greatly weakened the empire, which had depended on Asia Minor for food and materials as well as soldiers. One by one, the invaders took over more lands. Before long, the Byzantine Empire was reduced to a small area around Constantinople.

The End of the Byzantine Empire

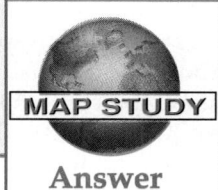

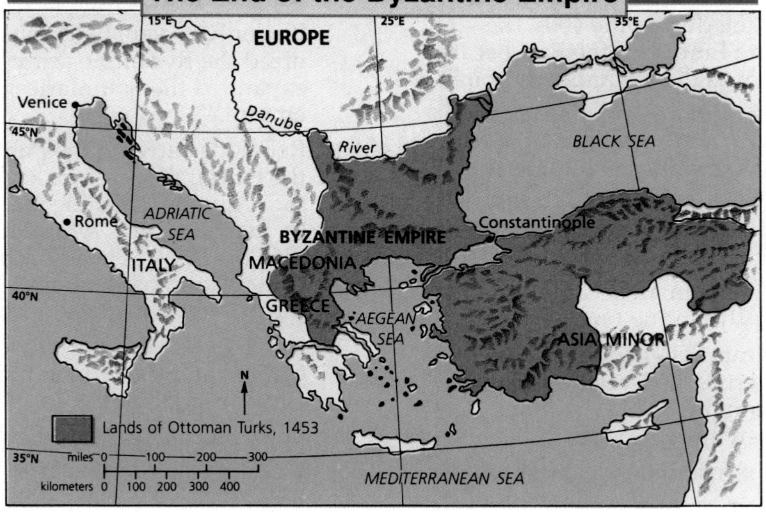

MAP STUDY

REGION The Byzantine Empire was frequently attacked by invading armies. Compare this map with the map on page 323. **What territory did the Byzantine Empire lose between 565 and 1453?**

L2 **Sports** Have students research Constantinople's oval arena, called the Hippodrome, and compare its architecture and the events held there to modern arenas such as the Astrodome in Houston, Texas, the Forum in Los Angeles, California, and the SkyDome in Toronto, Canada. LEP

MAKING CONNECTIONS

➤➤ **History** The Byzantine court became so poor as the empire declined that at the marriage feast of Emperor John V, food was served in clay vessels. No gold or silver items appeared on the table.

MAP STUDY

Answer

parts of Spain, North Africa, Italy, Macedonia, and Egypt

GEOGRAPHY AND HISTORY

By A.D. 700 the Byzantine Empire was reduced to the territories that were primarily Greek. The loss of the non-Greek lands actually helped strengthen the empire because it now had one religion, one language, and one culture.

EXTENDING THE CONTENT

The Church of Holy Wisdom, or Hagia Sophia, was such a miracle of architecture that legend said an angel had given Justinian directions for building it. Its architects were actually two Greeks from Asia Minor. The remarkable engineering of the broad central dome and the brilliant reds, blues, and greens of the interior are still amazing nearly 1,500 years after their construction. The floor mosaics are rich marble and the wall mosaics are glittering glass.

ASSESS

CHECK FOR UNDERSTANDING

Ask students to summarize the main points of the chapter. Discuss the answers to the Section and Chapter Review questions.

EVALUATE

Assign Chapter 21 **Performance Assessment Activity** in the TCR.

Administer **Chapter 21 Test** in the TCR. Testmaker available.

RETEACH

Ask students to make lists of the key elements of Byzantine culture during Emperor Justinian's rule.

Assign Chapter 21 **Reteaching Activity** in the TCR.

ENRICH

Have students prepare a report about the Turkish attack on Constantinople in 1453.

Assign Chapter 21 **Enrichment Activity** in the TCR.

CLOSE

Have students list the achievements of the Byzantine Empire and rank them in order of importance. Have students explain their rankings.

MEETING CHAPTER OBJECTIVES

Each objective is tested by the Review questions in parentheses.

1. Explain why the Byzantine Empire survived for 1,000 years. (CU 1)

2. Discuss why Constantinople was important to the empire. (CU 2; CT 1)

3. Analyze the role the Eastern Orthodox Church played in the Byzantine Empire. (BV; CU 3; CT 2)

4. Summarize the decline of the Byzantine Empire. (CU 7, 8; CT 3)

The population dropped to less than 100,000. Docks marketplaces stood empty. Even the emperors were poor. W Turkish armies with guns and gunpowder attacked Constant ple in 1453, they easily conquered the Byzantines.

Section 4 Review

1. **Identify:** Venetians
2. What were some contributions to civilization made by th Byzantine Empire?
3. What problems within the empire helped bring about its decline?
4. What outside forces helped cause the empire's downfall?

Critical Thinking

5. Write your opinion about the following statement: The Byzantine emperor was wise in asking Venice for help against the Vikings.

Chapter Summary

1. About 330, the emperor Constantine moved the capital of the Roman Empire from Rome to Constantinople, the site of the old Greek city of Byzantium.
2. After the Roman Empire in the West fell during the 400s, the Roman Empire in the East became known as the Byzantine Empire.
3. Constantinople's buildings and political and social life were patterned after those of Rome.
4. Constantinople was a Christian city, with many churches, shrines, and charitable people.
5. In 527, Justinian became emperor of the Byzantine Empire.
6. The empress Theodora helped Justinian rule the Byzantine Empire and convinced him to allow women more rights.
7. One of Justinian's greatest achievements was the development of the Justinian Code, which has influ enced the legal systems of almo every western country.
8. Another of Justinian's achievements was Hagia Sophia, which still stands today.
9. Under Justinian, Belisarius reor nized the Byzantine army and expanded the boundaries of the empire.
10. Relations between the Pope and the Patriarch were weakened by the argument over the use of ic by the Patriarch's refusal to rec nize the Pope as head of the Church, and by the Pope's crow ing of Charlemagne as emperor.
11. In 1054, the Eastern Orthodox Church and the Roman Catholi Church split apart.
12. Both internal problems and out forces weakened the Byzantine Empire and led to its downfall.

SECTION 4 ANSWERS

1. Venetians, defeated the Vikings (p. 327)

2. It preserved Greek culture and Roman law, spread Christianity, and created new art techniques.

3. Emperor stopped protecting farmers from rich landlords; aristocrats then took over the farmers' properties, and the farmers lost their loyalty.

4. Venetian merchants gained control of most of the empire's trade, and the empire was attacked by Christians and Muslims.

5. Answers will vary but could include that it was wise because the Byzantine Empire couldn't defend itself against the Vikings; or that it was unwise because it led to the Venetian control of most of the empire's trade.

Assign Chapter 21 **Section 4 Quiz** in the TCR. Testmaker available.

CHAPTER

Review 21

Building Vocabulary

You live in ancient Byzantium and are asked to write a paragraph describing your culture. Your paragraph is to be put in a time capsule to be opened by a future generation. Write your paragraph, including the following words.

relics	Greek fire
theology	metropolitans
dowry	icons
mosaics	

Check for Understanding

1. Why did the Roman Empire in the East survive after the Roman Empire in the West fell?
2. How did its location help Constantinople become a great trading center?
3. How did Christianity affect the way the Byzantines took care of needy people?
4. How did Theodora help women in the Byzantine Empire?
5. Why is the Justinian Code considered a great achievement?
6. Why did the Byzantine emperor change the law in 843 to permit the use of icons again?
7. Why did Byzantine farmers gradually lose their loyalty to the empire?
8. Who conquered the Byzantine Empire in 1453?

Critical Thinking

1. What is your opinion of the following statement: Constantine was wise to model Constantinople after Rome?
2. What are the advantages for a government to have an official religion? What are the disadvantages?
3. What force do you think had the most to do with the decline of the Byzantine Empire? Explain.
4. What contribution made by the Byzantines do you think was most important? Explain.

Geography in History

MOVEMENT Justinian expanded his empire greatly. Refer to the map on page 323. If you had been Justinian, in which direction would you have sent troops next to gain new territory? Why?

Using Your Journal

Review the details about the ways the Byzantine Empire influenced other civilizations. Compare the Justinian Code to modern laws in America. Write an essay explaining which set of laws seems better or more just. Include specific examples of when the laws might apply in real life situations.

CHAPTER 21 REVIEW ANSWERS

BUILDING VOCABULARY

Paragraphs will vary, but should use descriptive phrases and all the vocabulary words.

CHECK FOR UNDERSTANDING

1. Most Christians were united; Constantinople was strong and supported a large army and paid invaders.
2. Its location gave Constantinople control of the sea trade to the Mediterranean and an important land route.
3. The Byzantines formed organizations to care for the poor.
4. She convinced Justinian to allow a wife to own land and widows to raise children.
5. It provided a summary of Roman legal thinking, influenced the legal systems of almost every Western country
6. He saw that most people refused to give them up.
7. because the emperor no longer helped protect them
8. Turkish armies

CRITICAL THINKING

1. Answers will vary but students should support their opinions.
2. Answers will vary. Advantages might be it would end conflict. A disadvantage is it would end freedom of religion.
3. Answers will vary but could explain loss of trade and invasions.
4. Answers will vary.

+ BONUS +

TEST QUESTION

For Chapter 21 Test

Imagine you were a citizen of Constantinople during the Byzantine Empire and you met a man named Cyril, about whom everyone was talking. What were people saying about this man? *(He was a missionary, an educator, and helped to develop the Cyrillic alphabet.)*

USING YOUR JOURNAL

Essays will vary but should include references to specific laws. You might call on volunteers to read their essays to the class and have the class weigh the comparison.

GEOGRAPHY IN HISTORY

Answers will vary but should reflect a logical plan for avoiding geographical features that might make an invasion difficult.

CHAPTER 22 The Spread of Islam

CHAPTER ORGANIZER

Objectives	Special Features	Supplemental Materials
Section 1 Islam Explain how Islam developed around the teachings of Muhammad and the religious beliefs held by Muslims.		• Reproducible Lesson Plan • Section 1 Quiz • Testmaker • Chapter 22 Vocabulary and Guided Reading Activity • Chapter 22 Geography and Map Activity • Unit 7 Primary Source Reading • The Western Civilization Videodisc
Section 2 The Arab Empire Describe how Islam spread beyond the Arabian Peninsula and what Islamic life was like.		• Reproducible Lesson Plan • Section 2 Quiz • Testmaker • Chapter 22 Cooperative Learning Activity • Chapter 22 Teaching Transparencies and Activities • Unit 7 World Literature
Section 3 Arab Contributions Discuss what the Arab Empire contributed to science, mathematics, medicine, and the arts.		• Reproducible Lesson Plan • Section 3 Quiz • Testmaker • Chapter 22 Chart and Graph Skill Activity • The World History Videodisc
Chapter 22 Review and Evaluation		• Chapter 22 Reteaching Activity • Chapter 22 Enrichment Activity • Chapter 22 Performance Assessment Activity • Spanish Summary and Glossary • Chapter 22 Test • Testmaker • Audiocassettes (English and Spanish)

If time does not permit teaching the entire chapter, use the Chapter 22 Summary on page 344 and the Chapter 22 Audiocassettes (English and Spanish) to point out the main ideas of the chapter.

✓ PERFORMANCE ASSESSMENT ACTIVITIES

Geography: Region Have students make a relief map of the Islamic state at its peak. The map should include enough surrounding territory to show the extent of the Islamic state and its landforms, bodies of water, and elevation. Suggest students choose the materials for their map and label all places. Display the maps in the classroom.

Sharing Religion Have students research Muslim celebrations other than Ramadan. Suggest they choose one—either religious or national holiday of an area where Muslims live—to describe in an oral presentation to the class. Encourage students to include visuals in their presentation.

CHAPTER RESOURCES

LITERATURE ABOUT THE PERIOD

Arnold, T.W. and A. Guillame. *The Legacy of Islam.* Gordon Press, 1976.

READINGS FOR THE STUDENT

Goldston, Robert. *The Sword of the Prophet.* Fawcett/Crest, 1982. A history of the Arab world beginning with the time of Muhammad.

Powell, Anton. *The Rise of Islam.* Warwick Press, 1980. An overview of Islamic culture.

READINGS FOR THE TEACHER

Hitti, Philip. *History of the Arabs.* St. Martin's Press, 1970. A comprehensive study of Islamic civilization.

Mahmud, S.F. *A Short History of Islam.* Oxford University Press, 1989. A study of Islamic civilization and a history of the Islamic Empire.

MULTIMEDIA RESOURCES

The Five Pillars of Islam. Films for the Humanities. Video. Places the principles of Islam in historical perspective.

Islam, 600-1200. Landmark Films. Video. Reveals how Islam kept the flame of civilization burning for five centuries.

Middle Eastern Series: 2. Encyclopedia Britannica Educational Corp. Videodisc. *Bridging the Dark Ages.* Shows how Islam helped bridge the 800-year gap between the fall of Rome and the onset of the European Renaissance.

INTRODUCE

CHAPTER 22 OVERVIEW

Chapter 22 discusses the rise of Islam and its central role in the creation of the Arab Empire.

- ➤ **Section 1** describes the influence of Muhammad on religious, social, and political life in the empire.
- ➤ **Section 2** discusses the formation of the Arab Empire and the spread of Islam.
- ➤ **Section 3** describes the Arab contributions to science, medicine, commerce, and scholarship that later influenced Western civilizations.

CHAPTER OBJECTIVES

After reading Chapter 22, students will be able to:

1. explain how Islam developed around the teachings of Muhammad.

2. discuss what religious beliefs are held by Muslims.

3. describe how Islam spread beyond the Arabian Peninsula.

4. summarize what Islamic life was like.

5. describe what the Arabs contributed to science, mathematics, medicine, and the arts.

EXAMINING THE ILLUSTRATION

Ask students why they think a mosque would be built with such attention to beauty and richness. Explain that in the Muslim religion, which they will be learning more about in this chapter, the mosque is a very holy place.

PERFORMANCE ASSESSMENT ✓

Use the Performance Assessment activities on page 330B to help you evaluate students as they complete the chapter.

CHAPTER 22 The Spread of Islam

Golden Domed Mosque

TEACHER CLASSROOM RESOURCES

- Reproducible Lesson Plan
- Geography and Map Activity
- Vocabulary and Guided Reading Activity
- Unit 7 Primary Source Reading
- Unit 7 World Literature
- Cooperative Learning Activity
- Performance Assessment Activity
- Spanish Summary and Glossary
- The Western Civilization Videodisc
- The World History Videodisc
- Testmaker
- Audiocassettes (English and Spanish)
- Teaching Transparencies and Activities

Chapter Focus

READ TO DISCOVER:

- How Islam developed around the teachings of Muhammad.
- What religious beliefs are held by Muslims.
- How Islam spread beyond the Arabian Peninsula.
- What early Islamic life was like.
- What the Arab Empire contributed to science, mathematics, medicine, and the arts.

Between the northeast coast of Africa and central Asia lies the Arabian Peninsula. The people who live there are known as Arabs. At one time, most were Bedouins (bed' uh wuhnz). They were herders who roamed the desert in search of grass and water for their camels, goats, and sheep. They lived in tents woven from camel or goat hair.

Bedouin warriors during the 600s raided other peoples and fought one another over pastures and springs. They valued their camels and swords above all else. They enjoyed poetry and music. They believed in many gods. They worshiped stones, trees, and pieces of wood that they believed were the homes of spirits with supernatural powers.

In the 600s, a new religion called Islam (is' luhm) began in the mountainous area of western Arabia known as the Hejaz (hej az'). Within 100 years, an Arab empire based on Islamic beliefs had developed. It controlled an area larger than that of the Roman Empire.

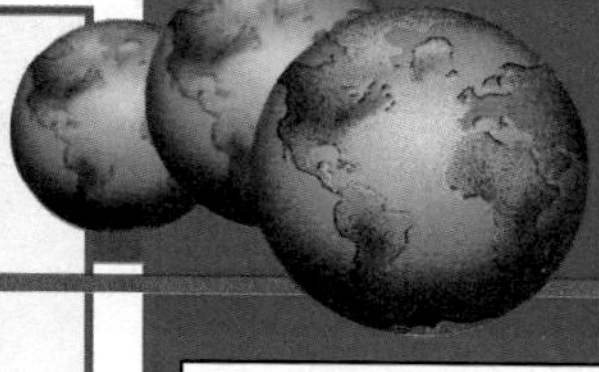

500 A.D.–1300 A.D.

KEY TERMS

pilgrims
pillars of faith
mosque
imam
zakah
hajj
caliph
vizier
alchemists

Section 1

ISLAM

The word "Islam" is an Arabic word. It means "the act of *submitting*, or giving oneself over, to the will of God." The Islamic faith was founded by an Arab merchant named Muhammad (mō ham' id). Muhammad came to be known as the prophet of Allah (ahl' uh). The word "Allah" is an Arabic word meaning

FOCUS

BELLRINGER

Write this sentence on the chalkboard: *The Islamic civilization of A.D. 600 to 1300 has had a great influence on present-day civilizations.* Have students respond to the sentence by writing *true* or *false* and giving a reason for their choice.

MOTIVATIONAL ACTIVITY

Have students read their responses to the sentence regarding whether the Islamic civilization of A.D. 600 to 1300 influenced present-day civilizations. Tell students that during this time period Islam experienced its Golden Age. Tell students that they will learn about the many things in our culture today that were contributed by this Islamic civilization.

VOCABULARY PRE-CHECK

Write the key terms for this chapter on the chalkboard. Ask volunteers to skim the chapter for the boldfaced terms and read aloud the sentences in which they are found.

Assign Chapter 22 **Vocabulary and Guided Reading Activity** in the TCR.

EXTRA CREDIT PROJECT

Suggest interested students find out more about how the Muslim faith is practiced in the modern world. Have them create a presentation to share with the class about it, using any format they choose. Suggest they include a description of: basic beliefs, ceremonies, religious leaders, and architecture in their information.

KEY TO ABILITY LEVELS

Teaching strategies have been coded for varying learning styles and abilities.

L1 Level 1 activities are **basic** activities and should be within the ability range of all students.

L2 Level 2 activities are **average** activities and should be within the ability range of the average to above-average student.

L3 Level 3 activities are **challenging** activities designed for the ability range of above-average students.

LEP LEP activities should be within the ability range of Limited English Proficiency students.

TEACH

GUIDED PRACTICE

L1 **Geography: Place** On a physical wall map of the world point out the Arabian Peninsula to the students. Explain that it is the largest peninsula in the world. Ask students to name the physical features on the Arabian Peninsula. *(deserts and mountains)* Explain that although this peninsula is part of Asia it is usually referred to as part of a region called the Middle East. LEP

L1 **History** Have students make a time line that shows important events in Muhammad's life. Display the time lines in the classroom. LEP

MAKING CONNECTIONS

➤➤ **Religion** Muslims believe that Arabs are descendants of Abraham's son Ishmael and that Jews are descendants of Abraham's son Isaac.

DID YOU KNOW ??

It was not unusual during Muhammad's time for a person to retreat somewhere to solve problems. Both Moses and Jesus had done the same thing many hundreds of years earlier.

"the God." Muhammad called those who followed his faith Muslims, which means "followers of Islam."

Islam shook the foundations of Byzantium and Persia, the two most powerful civilizations of the time. It brought into its fold people from different races and continents. It came to shape a way of life for one of every seven persons on Earth.

Makkah (Mecca) By the middle of the 500s, three major towns had developed in the Hejaz. They were Yathrib (yath' ruhb), Ta' if (tah' if), and Makkah (mak' uh). Of the three, Makkah was the largest and the richest.

Makkah was supported by trade and religion. Traders stopped there for food and water on their way north to Constantinople. Arab **pilgrims,** or travelers to a religious shrine, came there to worship. Arabia's holiest shrine, the *Ka'bah* (kah' buh), stood in the center of Makkah. It was a low, cube-shaped building surrounded by 360 idols. A black stone believed to have fallen from paradise was set in one of its walls. Nearby was a holy well.

Muslims believe that the Ka'bah was first built by Adam. Later, Abraham and his son, Ishmael, together rebuilt it. They had dedicated it to the worship of the one God. Later, however, people filled it with idols that represented the gods and goddesses of different tribes.

Muhammad In 570, Muhammad was born to a widow of a respectable clan in Makkah. When he was six years old, his mother died, and he went to live with an uncle. When he reached his teens, he began working as a business person. At the age of 25, he married a rich 40-year-old widow named Khad'juh (kahd' yuh).

Muhammad was very successful in the caravan business. He was troubled, however, by the drinking, gambling, and corruption in Makkah. He began spending much time alone in a cave on a hillside outside the city. There, he thought and fasted. He decided that the people of Makkah had been led into evil by their belief in false gods. He concluded that there was only one God, Allah, the same god as the God of the Jews and the Christians.

In 610, Muhammad had a *revelation,* or vision. It is said that, when he was meditating in the cave, an angel appeared and ordered him to read some writing. According to Muslim tradition, he heard the voice of the angel Gabriel (gā' brē uhl) telling him to preach about God. Muhammad told Khad'juh what had happened. She went to see a holy man, hoping he could explain the meaning of Muhammad's story. The holy man told her that the heavenly visitor was the same one who had visited Moses and other prophets and that Muhammad was to be the prophet of his people.

MULTICULTURAL PERSPECTIVES

Before the founding of Islam, some Arabs followed the two earlier monotheistic religions, Judaism and Christianity. Most, however, carried idols of wood or stone with them and also traveled to worship at holy places or caves or wells. Makkah, a crossroads for caravans from Egypt, Palestine, and the Persian Gulf, had holy places and many idols. Traders stopped there to pray for safe journey or to give thanks for having reached the city safe from robbers or desert storms.

KA' BAH SHRINE Modern Muslim pilgrims travel to Makkah to pray facing the shrine called the Ka' bah. It is considered a very holy place. **Who do Muslims believe first built the Ka' bah?**

In 613, Muhammad began to preach to the people of Makkah. He told them that there is only one God, Allah, before whom all believers are equal. He urged the rich to share with the poor. Muhammad saw life as a preparation for the Day of Judgment, or the day on which people would rise from the dead to be judged for their actions on Earth.

At first, the rich leaders of Makkah laughed at Muhammad. As he continued to preach, however, they began to feel threatened. They were afraid that people would stop coming to Makkah to worship at the Ka'bah. When pilgrims visited Makkah, they spent money on meals and clothing. The leaders thought that if fewer pilgrims came to Makkah, the city's economy would be ruined. Then, the leaders would no longer be rich. Because of this fear, they started persecuting Muhammad and his followers.

In 620, Muhammad preached to a group of pilgrims from Yathrib. They invited him to come there and be their leader. During the summer of 622, he and several hundred of his followers fled from Makkah to Yathrib. The year 622, called *Anno Hijrah* (an' ō hi jī' ruh), or "Year of the Migration," became the first year of the Muslim calendar. The city of Yathrib was renamed Madinat al-Nabi, "the city of the prophet," or Madina.

In Madina, Muhammad proved himself an able leader. He gave the people a government that united them and made them

L2 **History** Have students find more information about an event in Muhammad's life such as the *Hijrah.* Have them use the information to write a one-page first-person account of the event. Have students share their narratives with the class.

CAPTION ANSWER

It was built by Adam and then rebuilt by Abraham and Ishmael.

LINKING PAST TO PRESENT

A *Kiswah* is the black cloth that covers *Ka'bah.* It is embroidered in gold thread with verses from the Quran and is replaced each year. Formerly made in Egypt and carried by pilgrims to Makkah, the *Kiswah* is now made in a special Saudi Arabian government factory in Makkah.

VIDEODISC

Use the following to enrich Chapter 22.

WH E 91 14335

Pilgrims en route to Mecca.

EXTENDING THE CONTENT

The black rock housed in the *Ka'bah* was, most likely, a meteorite. Arabs believed that Abraham had built the first temple around the rock. Similarly, Makkah's holy spring or well, called Zamzam, was associated with the flight into the desert of Hagar, Abraham's handmaiden, and their son Ishmael. The well's miraculous appearance (perhaps with the aid of the angel Gabriel) saved their lives and allowed Ishmael to find the Arabic peoples. These legends gave the Arabs and the Jews a common ancestor, Abraham.

L2 Geography: Human/Environmental Interaction Have students locate the cities of Makkah, Yathrib, and Ta'if on the map of Muhammad's Arabia. Have them use the map scale to calculate the approximate distances between these cities. LEP

MAP STUDY

Answer

50 miles (or 80.45 km)

DID YOU KNOW ??

Muhammad's tomb is located in the Prophet's Mosque in Madina.

MAKING CONNECTIONS

➤➤ **Language** *Quran* means the reading, or that which is to be read. Its final version, put together in 655, contains 144 *suras*, or chapters.

VIDEODISC

Use the following to enrich Chapter 22.

WC C 48 14650

The Great Mosque at Mecca.

MAP STUDY

LOCATION Yathrib was an oasis of farms, Ta' if was a mountain refuge, and Makkah was a crossroads for trade. **About how many miles (km) inland from the Red Sea was Makkah located?**

Muhammad's Arabia

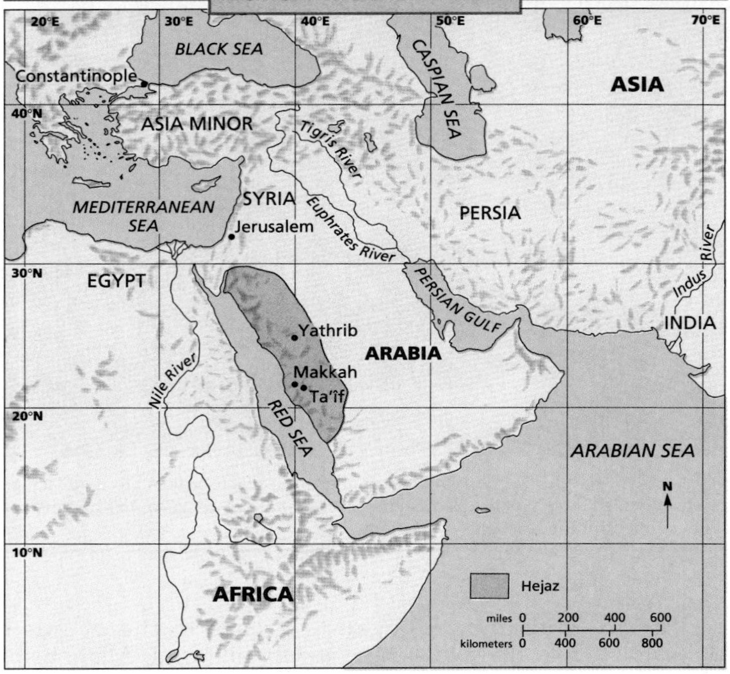

proud of their new faith. The people of Makkah were very angry with Muhammad's success in Madina. With far superior armies, they invaded Madina several times to crush the newly established Muslim community. The Muslims defended their city with great courage every time. In 628, Muhammad signed a peace treaty with the people of Makkah, which they violated in 630. It was in that year that Muhammad and his companions triumphantly entered their home city, Makkah. Their conquest was peaceful. Muhammad issued general forgiveness to all who had persecuted and opposed him. Within two years, all the tribes of Arabia declared their faith in Islam and their loyalty to Muhammad. In 632 Muhammad died.

The Quran At the heart of Islam is the Quran (ko ran'), or Muslim scriptures. Muslims believe it is the direct word of God as revealed to Muhammad. For this reason, they feel they should follow it exactly.

The Quran is written in Arabic. It tells how good Muslims should live. They should not eat pork, drink liquor, or gamble. The Quran also gives advice on marriage, divorce, inheritance, and business.

EXTENDING THE CONTENT

According to Muslim tradition, the angel Gabriel revealed divine messages to Muhammad over a 22-year period. Faithful Muslims wrote down or memorized these messages, but they were not compiled into one written collection until after Muhammad died. Then his successor, Abu Bakr, ordered Muslims to retrieve these messages from wherever they could be found, from the "ribs of palm-leaves and tablets of white stone and from the breasts of men." It took 20 years before the messages were compiled into the Quran.

The Quran describes the **pillars of faith,** or the five duties all Muslims must fulfill. The first duty is the confession of faith. All Muslims must recite the Islamic creed that states, "There is no God but Allah, and Muhammad is his prophet."

The second duty deals with prayer. Muslims must pray five times a day, facing Makkah each time. The prayers are said at dawn, noon, late afternoon, sunset, and evening. The prayers can be said anywhere. The only exception is the Friday noon prayer. It is usually recited at a ***mosque*** (mosk), or Muslim house of worship. There, believers are led by an ***imam*** (i mam'), or prayer leader.

The third duty has to do with the giving of ***zakah,*** or charity. This is a donation that every Muslim has to give at the rate of 2.5 percent of his or her annual savings. It can be given to needy people or to institutions that are involved in education and social services.

ISLAMIC FAITH Muslims learn the teachings of the Quran at an early age. A child in the photograph (left) studies passages from the Quran. From the prayer tower (right) of each mosque, announcers call the people to prayer. **What are the five duties that all Muslims must fulfill, called?**

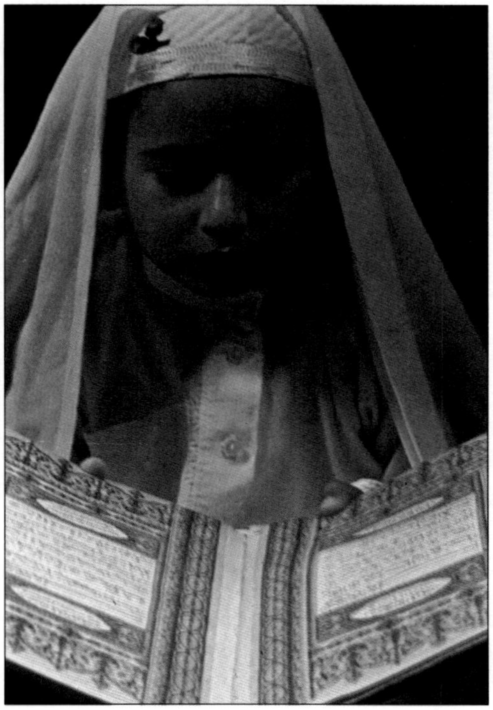

MAKING CONNECTIONS

➤➤ **Religion** Until the Muslims took Makkah and made it their holy city, prayers were said facing Jerusalem. To offer a prayer, a Muslim kneels, bows, and touches the forehead to the ground as a symbol of submitting to God.

CAPTION ANSWER

the pillars of faith

VIDEODISC

Use the following to enrich Chapter 22.

WH E 90 14334

Pilgrims arriving at Mecca to perform the hajj.

DID YOU KNOW ??

Arabic, the language of the Quran, belongs to the Semitic language group. Although no one knows for sure when the language developed, it is known from poets writing before the time of Muhammad that it had reached its present stage 100 years before the prophet was born.

MULTICULTURAL PERSPECTIVES

Up until the 1800s, there were three main caravans to Makkah. One caravan formed in Damascus, Syria, and moved south by way of Madina, and reached Makkah in about 30 days. When Constantinople was captured by the Ottoman Turks in 1453, this caravan started in Constantinople and then went through Damascus to Makkah. Along the way, pilgrims throughout Asia Minor joined the caravan. A second caravan assembled in Cairo and crossed the Sinai Peninsula following the coastal plain of western Arabia to Makkah. This journey took from 30 to 45 days and included pilgrims from North Africa. A third much more sizable caravan crossed the peninsula from Baghdad.

MAKING CONNECTIONS

>> **Religion** The purpose of fasting is to remind Muslims about spiritual values. Ramadan is the ninth month in the Islamic calendar, the month in which the Quran was first revealed to Muhammad.

DID YOU KNOW ??

Most of the great Muslim expansion outside of Arabia came between 634 and 644 during the reign of Umar I, the second Rightly Guided Caliph.

L2 **Geography: Movement** Discuss the spread of Islamic influence beyond the Arabian Peninsula. Have students use the map on page 337 and a map of the world to identify the modern countries that were partially or totally included in the Arab Empire. LEP

VIDEODISC

Use the following to enrich Chapter 22.

WH E 95 14339
Page from the Quran dating from the 8th-9th century A.D.

WH E 96 14340
The Dome of the Rock in Jerusalem.

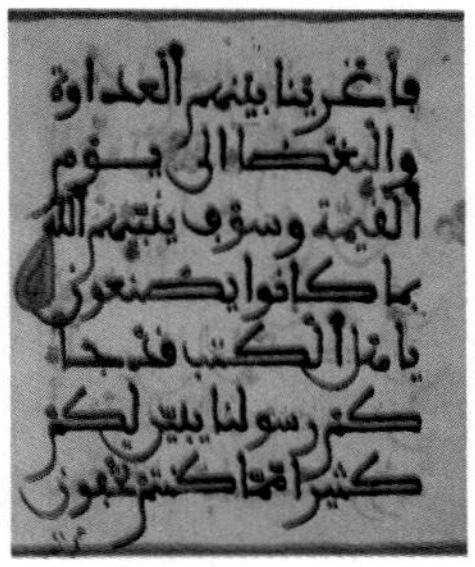

Picture of Page from the Quran

The fourth duty deals with fasting. The young, sick people, pregnant women, and travelers do not have to fast. Everyone else, however, must fast each year during the daylight hours of the holy month of Ramadan (ram' uh dahn).

The fifth duty involves a pilgrimage. Each able Muslim, at least once in his or her lifetime, must travel to Makkah two months after Ramadan. The journey is called the ***hajj*** (haj). For three days, Muslims from all over the world come together for ceremonies and sacrifice.

The Quran promises that all believers who fulfill their duties will go to Paradise, which has shade, fruit trees, beautiful flower gardens, cold springs, and singing birds. Hell is a flame-filled pit where drinking water comes from a salty well and where food is a strong-smelling plant that causes hunger.

Section 1 Review

1. **Identify:** Arabs, Bedouins, Islam, Hejaz, Muhammad, Allah, Muslims, Makkah, *Ka'bah,* Day of Judgment, *Anno Hijrah,* Madina (Yathrib), Quran
2. **Define:** pilgrims, pillars of faith, *mosque, imam, zakah, hajj*
3. According to Muslim tradition, what caused Muhammad to begin to preach?
4. What does the Quran say will happen after death?

Critical Thinking

5. What effect did the rise of Islam have on Byzantium and Persia?

Section 2

THE ARAB EMPIRE

When Muhammad died in 632, his followers needed a new leader. Without someone to guide them, the community could have broken up, and the faith could have been lost. A group of Muslims chose a new leader whom they called *khalifa,* or **caliph** (kā'lif), which means "successor."

The Rightly Guided Caliphs The first caliph was Abu Bakr (uh bū' bak' uhr), Muhammad's father-in-law and close friend. Bakr and the next three caliphs were elected for life. These caliphs ruled from Madina. They kept in close touch with the people and asked advice of their most trusted friends. For this reason, they were called the Rightly Guided Caliphs.

SECTION 1 ANSWERS

1. Arabs, people in Arabia (p. 331); Bedouins, herders (p. 331); Islam, religion (p. 331); Hejaz, area of Arabia (p. 331); Muhammad, founder of Islam (p. 331); Allah, God (p. 332); Muslims, followers of Islam (p. 332); Makkah, holy city (p. 332); *Ka'bah,* holy shrine (p. 332); Day of Judgment, when all rise to be judged (p. 333); *Anno Hijrah,* first Muslim year (p. 333); Madina, city (p. 334); Quran, Muslim scriptures (p. 334)

2. pilgrims, travelers to a shrine (p. 332); pillars of faith, five Muslim duties (p. 335); *mosque,* house of worship (p. 335); *imam,* prayer leader (p. 335); *zakah,* charity (p. 335); *hajj,* journey to Makkah (p. 336)

3. The angel Gabriel told him to.

4. All who fulfill their duties will go to Paradise.

5. It shook their foundations.

Assign the Chapter 22 **Section 1 Quiz** in the TCR. Testmaker available.

The Rightly Guided Caliphs honored Muhammad's wish to carry Islam to other peoples. They sent warriors into Palestine, Syria, Iraq, Persia, Egypt, and North Africa. Throughout all these places, the Arabs were victorious.

The Arabs were successful for many reasons. Islam held them together. They were united in striving for a common goal which they considered holy—to carry Islam to other people. This helped them to fight against tyranny and oppression. It also helped them earn an eternal place in Paradise after death. It helped them to fight against tyranny and oppression. Arab leaders were mentally and physically tough. They planned and carried out attacks. They also handled their camels and horses with great skill.

The Arab way of treating the people they conquered also contributed to their success. Those who gave in without a fight had to pay taxes. In return, the Arabs protected them and allowed them to keep their land. Those who fought and were defeated not only had to pay taxes, but also lost their land.

The Umayyads Ali, Muhammad's son-in-law and the last of the Rightly Guided Caliphs, was killed in 661. Mu'awiya (mū uh' wi yuh), the new caliph, moved the capital from Madina to Damascus and founded the Umayyad (ū mī' yuhd) Dynasty. From that time on, the title of caliph was hereditary.

MAP STUDY

MOVEMENT By 750 the Muslims ruled a vast empire that extended from the Atlantic Ocean to the Indus River. **Which caliphs added most of the territory in Asia?**

The Expansion of Islam

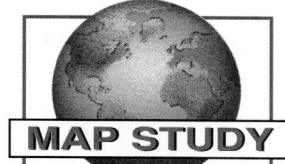

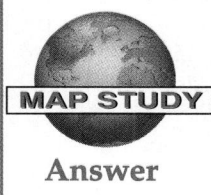

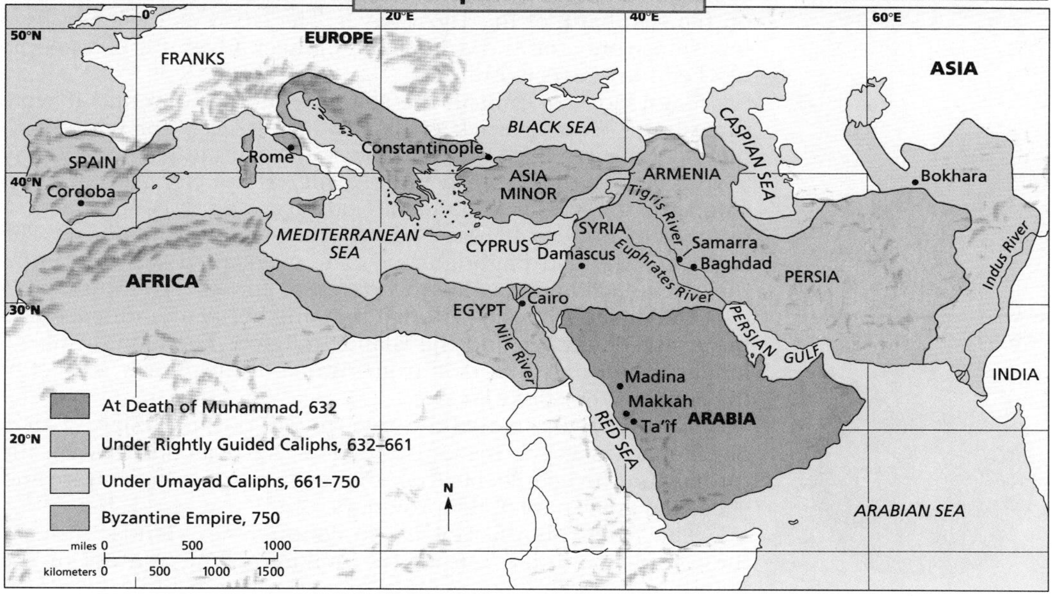

L1 **History** Have students discuss why choosing a successor to Muhammad became a problem for the Arab Empire. Help them understand that the question of succession led to the division of Islam into a Sunni majority and a Shi'ite minority, which weakened the Arab Empire. LEP

LINKING PAST TO PRESENT

The schism that developed in Islam in the A.D. 600s persists today. It was seen in the war between Iran and Iraq that began in 1980. Then many Westerners heard the term *jihad* for the first time.

MAP STUDY Answer

the Rightly Guided Caliphs

Assign Chapter 22 **Geography and Map Activity** in the TCR.

VIDEODISC

Use the following to enrich Chapter 22.

WH E 97 14341

A gold dinar coin from the reign of Hisham.

MEETING SPECIAL NEEDS

Ask students with strong organizational skills to work in small groups with students who are having difficulty tracking the expansion of Islam. Ask the groups to create descriptive outlines that show the spread of this religion. Remind students to include the succession of leaders of the Arab Empire that coincided with major events.

L3 **Critical Thinking** Have students list reasons that the first hundred years of Abbasids' rule became known as the Golden Age of Islam. Have them choose the reason they think is most important and defend it by writing a paragraph or discussing it in class.

LINKING PAST TO PRESENT

Shi'ite means party or faction in Arabic. The Shi'ites form the largest sect of the Islamic religion, numbering about 20 million. Most of them live in Iran.

L1 **Language Arts** Tell students that many words of Arabic origin have become part of the English language and usage. Have students find the following words in the dictionary, write the definition, and write the Arabic word from which it was derived: orange *(naranj)*, giraffe *(zirafah)*, syrup *(sharab)*, sofa *(suffah)*, and muslin *(mawsiliy)*.

VIDEODISC

Use the following to enrich Chapter 22.

WH E 98 14342
Silver dirhem from the reign of Abbasid Caliph Muhammad.

WH E 128 14372
Painting depicting the capture of Baghdad by invaders.

The Umayyads ruled more like kings than religious leaders. They reorganized the government and made Arabic the official language. They minted the first Arab money. They set up horseback postal routes. They repaired and maintained irrigation canals. They also built beautiful mosques and encouraged the arts.

Many of these changes helped the people of the empire. However, the Umayyads had social and economic troubles that, in the end, led to their downfall. The conquered people who became Muslim complained that they were not treated the same as those who were born Muslim. They received less money for serving in the army. They also had to pay higher taxes.

The Muslims themselves divided into two groups. The smaller group was called the Shi'ah (shē' ah). Its followers, called Shi'ites (shē' īts), believed the office of caliph should be held only by descendants of Ali. The larger group, called the Sunni (sūn' nē), followed the Rightly Guided Caliphs and the caliphs after them. After a while, war broke out between the Umayyads and a group of Muslims called Abbasids (uh' bas uhdz). In 750, the Abbasids defeated the Umayyads. They then became the new rulers of the Arab Empire.

The Abbasids

The Abbasids ruled the Arab Empire from 750 to 1258. Their first 100 years in power was known as the Golden Age of Islam.

The Abbasids built a new capital called Baghdad (bag' dad) on the east bank of the Tigris River. The city was designed by a Jewish astronomer and a Persian engineer. Over 100,000 people worked four years to build it.

Baghdad was built in the shape of a circle. Around it were three huge, sloping brick walls and a deep *moat,* or wide ditch filled with water. Each wall had four large gates linked together by two highways that crossed in the center of the city. At that point stood the great mosque and the caliph's magnificent palace. A number of public officials had luxurious homes there also. The highways divided Baghdad into four pie-shaped sections. From the gates, each highway led to a different part of the empire.

Abbasid Art

Under the Abbasids, all that remained of Arab influence was the Arabic language and the Islamic religion. The name Arab no longer meant only a person from Arabia. It meant any subject of the empire who spoke Arabic.

The Abbasids created the government post of **vizier** (vi zir'), or chief adviser. The person serving as vizier stood between the throne and the people. He took charge of running the empire and chose the governors of the provinces.

The Abbasids did not try to conquer new lands. Instead, they made Baghdad one of the major trading centers of the world. Improved trade between countries led to a fresh

EXTENDING THE CONTENT

Once a part of ancient Babylon, the area known as Baghdad has been inhabited since 4000 B.C. In A.D. 762 Baghdad was a small village when the headquarters of the Arab Empire were located nearby. Thereafter, Baghdad experienced rapid growth under Abbasid rule, with a population of more than one million people by the A.D. 800s. The Abbasid Empire declined, however, from the A.D. 800s to the A.D. 1200s. In ending the empire, Mongols from Central Asia nearly destroyed Baghdad. In 1638 it became part of the Ottoman Empire. Baghdad's population was reduced to only 15,000 people by the 1700s as a result of wars, floods, and fires.

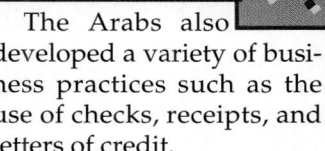

BAGHDAD Trade and science flourished in the Abbasid capital city of Baghdad. The first privately owned drug stores in the world were established in Baghdad. In this painting, a drug store owner examines logs of sandalwood, while boys chew sugarcane. **Why did Baghdad become a major trading center?**

exchange of ideas. Many writers and philosophers flocked to Baghdad. The Syrian Christians and Jews were instructed by the caliph to translate Greek writings into Arabic. Other scholars translated Indian literature into Arabic. The world's store of knowledge advanced greatly. Mathematical and scientific achievements were recorded. Mathematicians adapted numeric systems developed by the Guptas of India which are still in use today. Practical applications of this mathematics were used.

Life in the empire changed. Advanced farming methods were used to produce wheat, rice, beans, melons, cucumbers, celery, and mint. Orchards provided almonds and olives. Trade made many Arabs rich. They desired so many luxury goods that Arab artisans began producing some themselves. As trade

CAPTION ANSWER

because the Abbasids did not try to conquer new lands and concentrated on trade

MAKING CONNECTIONS

➤➤ **Government** The Arabs got their idea for the office of vizier from the Persians. Many of the government officials under the Abbasids were Persians.

DID YOU KNOW ??

The Arabs also developed a variety of business practices such as the use of checks, receipts, and letters of credit.

COOPERATIVE LEARNING

Have students research and organize an informational presentation of Arab contributions. Suggest students work in groups to decide what areas they will research such as: science, mathematics, medicine, philosophy, or the arts. Students should decide what form their presentation will take and what role each student will take. Other topics might be education, religion, or business activities. Ask students to include the impact of these contributions on their own lives.

Assign Chapter 22 **Cooperative Learning Activity** in the TCR.

L3 **Economics** Have students discuss how they think the spread of Islam enriched the Arab Empire. Discuss new taxes, trading opportunities, artisans, and natural resources. Explain that the Arabs also absorbed the traditions of the conquered peoples and synthesized them into a unique culture.

CAPTION ANSWER

the Moors

MAKING CONNECTIONS

➤➤ **Science** The Jewish physician Moses Maimonides fled from Spain after the Berber conquest in 1145, and became court physician to Saladin. He wrote extensively on diet and personal hygiene. He also wrote *Guide for the Perplexed*, showing how religion and Aristotle's scientific thinking could work together.

VIDEODISC

Use the following to enrich Chapter 22.

WC C 51 14653
The Battle of Poitiers, 732.

WC C 52 14654
The Lion's Court, the Alhambra, Granada, Spain.

grew, more records had to be kept. This led to the opening of banks. People had time to play games like polo and chess. Men stopped wearing the traditional Arab robe and began wearing pants. Meals were now served on tables instead of on the floor.

The empire soon became too large for one caliph to control. It began to break up into independent kingdoms. In 836, the caliph moved to a new capital city called Samarra. He returned to Baghdad in 892 and tried to regain power. By then, however, it was too late. In 945, the Persians took control of Baghdad.

The Golden Age of Muslim Spain The Muslim Arabs who conquered North Africa intermarried with the Berbers and became known as Moors (mūrz). In 710, they invaded Spain. With the help of Spanish Jews, they defeated the West Goths, who had taken the country from the Romans. Then, the Moors set up a kingdom that allowed religious freedom.

For the next 400 years, a rich culture flourished in Spain. Many beautiful buildings, such as the Alhambra (al ham′ bruh) in Granada, were built all through the country. Schools were founded in which Muslims, Jews, and Christians studied medicine and philosophy together.

During this time, Jews traveled to and traded in every part of the Arab Empire and beyond. In southeastern Rus, they met the Khazars (kuh zarz′), a half-Mongolian people who had converted to Judaism. From India and China, they brought back spices and silks to Spain.

THE ALHAMBRA Under Islamic rule, many beautiful buildings were built in Spain. The Alhambra, a palace in Granada, is considered the finest example of Islamic architecture in Europe. **What Islamic group invaded Spain in 710?**

MULTICULTURAL PERSPECTIVES

During Abbasid rule, Islamic philosophers translated Aristotle from Greek to Arabic. Since Islamic philosophers had no philosophical system of their own, they turned to the system that was within their reach, classical Greek. Their goal, like that of early Christian thinkers, was to solve the apparent contradiction between a perfect God and an imperfect world.

EASTERN CONQUERORS

Seljuq Turks *c. 900-1258*

Seljuq *c. 900*	chief from central Asia; settled with a group of followers near city of Bokhara and became Muslim
Toghril *c. 1055*	grandson of Seljuq, conquered Baghdad; took title al-sultan, meaning "he with authority"; set up Muslim kingdom in western Asia

Mongols *c. 1206-1300*

Genghis Khan *c. 1220*	united central Asian nomads; conquered Arab territory and created empire that covered most of Asia and eastern Europe
Hulagu *c. 1258*	grandson of Genghis Khan; led attack on Baghdad in 1258; became first khan, or overlord, of a kingdom that stretched from Syria to India

Mamelukes *c. 1250-1517*

Shajar *c. 1250*	freed slave who became first Mameluke ruler of Egypt; only Muslim woman to rule a country
Baybars *c. 1260*	seized throne of Egypt; restored caliphate in Cairo; created Mameluke dynasty

Ottoman Turks *c. 1290-1922*

Osman *c. 1290-1326*	founded Ottoman dynasty in Asia Minor
Muhammad II *c. 1451-1481*	captured Constantinople in 1453; established Ottoman Empire

Genghis Khan

Muhammad II

L2 **History** Have students make a crossword puzzle by using the Eastern Conquerors on this page. Students should construct a grid for their puzzle and write short clues for the conquerors. Have students exchange and solve each others' puzzles. LEP

INDEPENDENT PRACTICE

L1 **Religion** Ask students to imagine that they are followers of Muhammad in Madina during his lifetime. Have them write what they would say on a flier or poster to be put in the town to announce the next time Muhammad would be speaking. Remind them to include all necessary information and encouragement for people to attend. LEP

VIDEODISC

Use the following to enrich Chapter 22.

WC C 53 14655

Columns of the Alhambra, Granada, Spain.

MEETING SPECIAL NEEDS

Have students who are having difficulty understanding the main concepts in the chapter and students who are visual learners, create charts showing the Arab contributions to modern civilization.

LINKING PAST TO PRESENT

The Islamic calendar was instituted in A.D. 622 and is still used today by Muslims. The calendar is a lunar one containing 354 days. It contains 12 months that alternate between 30 and 29 days. Time is divided into 30-year cycles—9 years of 354 days and 11 years of 355 days.

L2 **Science and Technology** Have students find out more about Arab contributions to other civilizations such as astrolabe, alchemy, optics, calligraphy, mosques, or Islamic literature. Students should choose a topic of interest and then write a report or prepare a demonstration to present to the class.

VIDEODISC

Use the following to enrich Chapter 22.

WH E 136 14380
An astrolabe.

WH E 137 14381
Detail from a page from Ibn Sina's Canon of Medicine.

Islamic Jug

Islamic Life Islam was born in a society where men could have unlimited numbers of wives and the killing of female children was common. Islam attempted to correct this situation.

Muhammad taught that raising a female child guaranteed a reward in Paradise for her parents. Before Islam, women could not inherit property from their parents. Islam, however, entitled them to half the share of their husband's wealth. Islam recognized a woman's right to an inheritance. In Islam only under extreme circumstances is a man allowed to have up to four wives. One condition of this is the man could afford and could deal fairly with more than one wife.

Both men and women were obligated to seek knowledge. Islamic society produced some women of great knowledge and power. At the time of the birth of a Muslim baby, the call for prayer was recited into the baby's ears. By doing this, the child was brought into a life of Islamic culture. Reciting and memorizing the Quran was an important requirement in education. The mosques served as neighborhood schools. The boys were sent for higher education to institutions in major cities. People would travel from country to country within the Muslim world seeking more knowledge. There was tremendous interest in traveling and exploration.

Section 2 Review

1. **Identify:** Rightly Guided Caliphs, Umayyad Dynasty, Abbasids, Baghdad, Moors
2. **Define:** caliph, vizier
3. What were some accomplishments of the Umayyads?
4. How did the Arab Empire change under the Abbasids?

Critical Thinking

5. Why were the years from 710 called the Golden Age of Muslim Spain?

Section 3

ARAB CONTRIBUTIONS

Between the 770s and the 1300s, Arab scholars helped preserve much of the learning of the ancient world that otherwise would have been lost. They also made many other contributions to the modern world. The use of Arabic as a common language helped unite scholars and promote the sharing of knowledge. The Quran being written in Arabic contributed to this advancement.

SECTION 2 ANSWERS

1. Rightly Guided Caliphs, ruled from Madina (p. 336); Umayyad Dynasty, founded by Mu'awiya (p. 337); Abbasids, rulers of Arab Empire (p. 338); Baghdad, Arabian capital (p. 338); Moors, Arabs with Berber ancestry (p. 340)
2. caliph, Muslim leader (p. 336); vizier, chief adviser (p. 338)
3. They reorganized the government, minted money, set up postal routes, repaired irrigation canals, and encouraged arts.
4. Baghdad was built, post of vizier was created, trade developed, and interest in Greek science and philosophy grew. Arab artisans produced luxury goods.
5. Answers will vary but should include that a rich culture flourished.

Assign Chapter 22 **Section 2 Quiz** in the TCR. Testmaker available.

Many Arab scientists tried to turn base metals, such as tin, iron, and lead, into gold and silver. These scientists, called **alchemists** (al' kuh mists), used both chemistry and magic in their work. The word "chemistry" comes from the Arabic word "Al-Chemist." Alchemists never were able to turn base metals into gold and silver. However, their work led to the practice of making experiments and keeping records of the results. The Arabs are considered the founders of modern chemistry.

Arab astronomers studied the heavens. They gave many stars the names they still carry today. They correctly described the eclipses of the sun. They also proved that the moon affects the *tides,* or the rise and fall of the oceans. The astronomers worked with Arab geographers to determine the size of Earth and the distance around it. From their studies, they decided that Earth might be round. The astronomer-geographer al-Idrisi (al i drē' si) drew the first accurate map of the world.

Arab mathematicians invented algebra and taught it to Europeans. Arab mathematicians also borrowed the numerals 0-9 from Gupta mathematicians and passed them to Europeans.

The Arabs gave much to the field of medicine. Unlike doctors in most other countries, Arab doctors had to pass a test before they could practice medicine. The Arabs set up the world's first school of pharmacy. They also opened the world's first drugstores. They organized medical clinics that traveled all through the empire giving care and medicines to the sick.

Arab doctors were the first to discover that blood *circulates,* or moves, to and from the heart. They were the first to diagnose certain diseases. The Persian doctor ar-Razi (al rā sē') discovered differences between measles and smallpox. Another Persian, Avicenna (ä vä sēn ä), was the first to understand that tuberculosis is *contagious,* or could be passed from person to person.

Arab doctors informed the scientific community about their discoveries by publishing their findings. Avicenna's *Canon of Medicine,* an encyclopedia of medicine, was used in European medical schools for 500 years.

The Arabs also made many contributions to the arts. One of their best known writings is *The Arabian Nights,* a collection of tales put together from Persian stories. The tales paint an exciting picture of Islamic life at the height of the empire. The Persian poet Omar Khayyám's (ō' mahr kī yahm') *Rubáiyát* (rū' bē aht) has been translated into many languages. It is considered one of the finest poems ever written.

Islamic art is distinct and full of color. It is used on walls, books, rugs, and buildings. It differs from most other art because of the Muslim belief that Allah created all living creatures. Islamic artists think it is a sin to make pictures of Allah's creations. As a result, most of their art is made up of geometric designs entwined with flowers, leaves, and stars.

Islamic Medical Diagram

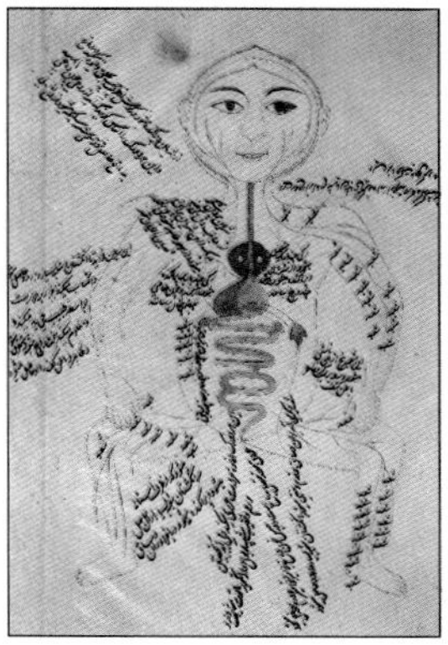

L1 **Culture** Ask students to discuss how a religion moves from one region to another. Have them brainstorm a list of ways as a volunteer records their responses on the chalkboard. When their list is compiled have them rank these ways religion moves, from most important or most effective, to least effective. LEP

DID YOU KNOW ??

The symbol of Islam, the crescent and star, appears on the flags of several nations whose population has a Muslim majority.

VIDEODISC

Use the following to enrich Chapter 22.

WH E 141 14385

A doctor performing surgery on a patient.

WH E 140 14384

An anatomical sketch , 1396.

ASSESS

CHECK FOR UNDERSTANDING

Ask students to summarize orally or in writing the main points of the chapter. Discuss the answers to the Section and Chapter Review questions.

EVALUATE

Assign Chapter 22 **Performance Assessment Activity** in the TCR.

Administer the **Chapter 22 Test** in the TCR. Testmaker available.

EXTENDING THE CONTENT

Carpets made by craftspeople in the Islamic world are famous for their glowing colors and intricate designs of interwoven leaves and flowers, geometric figures, and in some rugs, animal figures. From the silk rugs that adorned the caliph's palaces to the carpets of sheep's wool that served as walls between different sections of a tent, carpets have always been far more than floor coverings in this culture. Most Muslims owned small rugs that they used in daily prayer. Today, carpets from Iran, Afghanistan, and other parts of the Islamic world are prized.

RETEACH

Have students review the chapter sections and list the main ideas in each part. Discuss the lists in class.

Assign Chapter 22 **Reteaching Activity** in the TCR.

ENRICH

Have students research caravans in the Middle East during this time period. Have them write a description of a typical caravan and the importance of oases to the caravans.

Assign the Chapter 22 **Enrichment Activity** in the TCR.

CLOSE

Write these names on the chalkboard: *Abu Bakr, Ali, Umayyads,* and *Abbasids*. Have students identify the names and explain the importance of each in the history of Islam and the expansion of the Arab Empire.

MEETING CHAPTER OBJECTIVES

Each objective is tested by the Review questions in parentheses.

1. **Explain** how Islam developed around the teachings of Muhammad. (CU 2, 3)
2. **Discuss** what religious beliefs are held by Muslims. (BV; CU 4, 5; CT 1)
3. **Describe** how Islam spread beyond the Arabian Peninsula. (CU 6; CT 2, 3; UYJ)
4. **Summarize** what Islamic life was like. (BV; CT 4; UYJ)
5. **Describe** the Arab contributions in science, mathematics, medicine, and the arts. (BV; CU 9; CT 3; UYJ)

Much of what is known about this time comes from Arabs who wrote down the history of Islam. They began to write about events centered around rulers and peoples. This is how most historians present history today. The Muslim historian Ibn Khaldun (ib' uhn kal dun') wrote about the Arabs, the Berbers, and the Persians. His writings were the first to take into account the influence of geography and climate on people.

Section 3 Review

1. **Identify:** al-Idrisi, ar-Razi, Avicenna, Ibn Khaldun
2. **Define:** alchemists
3. What are some Arab contributions to science? To mathematics?
4. What are two of the best-known Arab writings?

Critical Thinking

5. Do you think the numerals 0-9 should be called Arabic or Gupta numerals? Why?

Chapter Summary

1. Makkah had a holy shrine to which Arab pilgrims came to worship.
2. Muhammad was born in Makkah in 570.
3. In 613, Muhammad began to preach that the only god is Allah. This was the beginning of the Islamic religion.
4. In 622, Muhammad and his followers went from Makkah to Yathrib, where Muhammad changed the city's name to Madina, organized the city's government, and army.
5. In 630, Muhammad led his followers into Makkah and dedicated the Ka'bah to Allah.
6. In 631, delegates throughout Arabia declared their faith in Allah and their loyalty to Muhammad.
7. The Quran describes the five pillars of Muslim faith.
8. After Muhammad's death in 632, his followers chose a new leader, known as a caliph.
9. The Arabs succeeded in creating a huge empire.
10. In 661, the capital of the Arab Empire was moved to Damascus and the Umayyad Dynasty began.
11. In 750, the Abbasids took control of the Arab Empire and concentrated on trade rather than warfare.
12. The Moors in Spain combined the Arab and Jewish cultures and allowed religious freedom.
13. The Arabs made many contributions to modern civilization, especially in the fields of chemistry, astronomy, geography, mathematics, medicine, and the arts.

SECTION 3 ANSWERS

1. al-Idrisi, astronomer-geographer (p. 343); ar-Razi, doctor (p. 343); Avicenna, Persian doctor (p. 343); Ibn Khaldun, Muslim historian (p. 344)
2. alchemists, Arab scientists (p. 343)
3. science—keeping records of experiment; the names of stars; eclipses; the moon's effect on tides; the earth's size; and the first accurate map of the world; mathematics—the invention of algebra, passing on the numerals 0-9 from Guptas in India to Europeans
4. *The Arabian Nights* and *Rubáiyát*
5. Answers will vary, but students should support their opinions about the development of numbering systems with reasons.

Assign Chapter 22 **Section 3 Quiz** in the TCR. Testmaker available.

CHAPTER 22 Review

Building Vocabulary

Imagine you are a traveler in the Arab Empire. Use the following words to write a journal entry describing your impressions of the empire.

pilgrims	*hajj*
pillars of faith	caliph
mosque	vizier
imam	alchemists
zakah	

Check for Understanding

1. How did Bedouins earn a living?
2. Why did Muhammad begin to spend time alone in a cave outside Makkah?
3. Why did Makkah's leaders persecute Muhammad and his followers?
4. What is the Islamic Creed?
5. In what direction do Muslims face when they pray?
6. What does the Quran promise all believers who fulfill their duties?
7. What brought about the downfall of the Umayyad Dynasty?
8. What did the name "Arab" mean under the Abbasids?
9. What discoveries did Arab doctors make?

Critical Thinking

1. What role did religion play in Arab life?
2. How did the Moorish kingdom in Spain show that it had been influenced by different cultures?
3. Which Arab contribution do you think has most affected other civilizations? Explain your choice.
4. What parts of life in the Arab Empire would you have liked? What parts would you have disliked?

Geography in History

LOCATION Islam spread across a wide area, as seen on the map on page 337. It included most area from the western edge of the Mediterranean Sea to the eastern shores of the Arabian Sea. What longitude and latitude lines mark the approximate location of this area?

Using Your Journal

Review the details about the ways the Arabs influenced other civilizations. Choose three contributions made by the Arabs that you see in your everyday life. Write a paragraph explaining how these contributions affect you.

CHAPTER 22 REVIEW ANSWERS

BUILDING VOCABULARY

Journal entries will vary but should include all vocabulary words.

CHECK FOR UNDERSTANDING

1. as herders and traders
2. because he was troubled by the corruption in Makkah
3. because they were afraid that fewer pilgrims would come to Makkah and they would no longer be rich
4. a confession of faith stating "There is no God but Allah, and Muhammad is His prophet."
5. toward Makkah
6. They will go to Paradise.
7. that conquered people who became Muslim felt that they were treated unfairly, and the division of Muslims into two groups, the Shi'ah and the Sunni
8. any subject of the empire who spoke Arabic
9. the circulation of the blood, the differences between measles and smallpox, and that tuberculosis is contagious

CRITICAL THINKING

1. It brought pilgrims to Makkah, which helped its economy; it united the Muslims; and it set the guidelines for the way Muslims lived.
2. Many groups lived there; and Muslims, Jews, and Christians studied medicine and philosophy together.
3. Answers will vary, but students should provide reasons.
4. Answers will vary, but students should cite specific examples of likes and dislikes.

GEOGRAPHY IN HISTORY

The area spanned from about 45° N to 25° N and 5° W to 65° E.

+ BONUS +

TEST QUESTION
For Chapter 22 Test

What is false about the following: A man and woman move to Madina in 613, the year Muhammad began preaching. That year, called the *Anno Hijrah*, they joined the thousands who supported Muhammad. *(Muhammad began preaching in 613, when the city was still named Yathrib; the Anno Hijrah was 620.)*

USING YOUR JOURNAL

Paragraphs will vary but should include three specific examples. You might ask volunteers to read their paragraphs to the class.

CHAPTER 23

The Eastern Slavs

CHAPTER ORGANIZER

Objectives	Special Features	Supplemental Materials
Section 1 Early Eastern Slavs Describe what life and economic development was like for the earliest Eastern Slavs.		• Reproducible Lesson Plan • Section 1 Quiz • Testmaker • Chapter 23 Vocabulary and Guided Reading Activity
Section 2 Kievan Rus Summarize how early Rus states developed around Kiev.		• Reproducible Lesson Plan • Section 2 Quiz • Testmaker • Unit 7 Primary Source Reading • Chapter 23 Cooperative Learning Activity
Section 3 The Mongol Conquest Analyze how the Mongol invasion influenced internal developments and foreign relations of Rus states.		• Reproducible Lesson Plan • Section 3 Quiz • Testmaker • Chapter 23 Chart and Graph Skill Activity • Unit 7 Primary Source Reading • Teaching Transparencies • Unit 7 World Literature • The World History Videodisc
Section 4 The Rise of Moscow Discuss how Moscow became powerful and how the czars affected life in Rus states.	Map and Geography Skills: *Analyzing Historical Maps*, p. 356	• Reproducible Lesson Plan • Section 4 Quiz • Testmaker • Chapter 23 Geography and Map Activity • Foods Around the World
Chapter 23 Review and Evaluation		Chapter 23 Reteaching Activity • Chapter 23 Enrichment Activity • Chapter 23 Performance Assessment Activity • Spanish Summary and Glossary • Audiocassettes (English and Spanish) • Chapter 23 Test • Testmaker

If time does not permit teaching the entire chapter, use the Chapter 23 Summary on page 358 and the Chapter 23 Audiocassettes (English and Spanish) to point out the main ideas of the chapter.

✓ Performance Assessment Activities

Multicultural Day Have students research to learn about the foods popular in or dishes originating in the Slavic area. They might select recipes, show sample menus, or even prepare food for the class. The significance of dishes served at holidays could also be reported to the rest of the class.

Newspaper Articles Have students write five newspaper headlines about major events in the life of Ivan the Great or one of the other czars of the early Rus states. Then have the students choose one of the headlines and write a newspaper article explaining the details of the headline. Have students read their headlines and articles to the class.

CHAPTER RESOURCES

LITERATURE ABOUT THE PERIOD

Kimmel, Eric A. *Mishka, Pishka, and Fishka*. Coward, McCann & Geoghan, 1976. English translations of folktales from Ukraine.

READINGS FOR THE STUDENT

Sutcliff, Rosemary. *Blood Feud*. E.P. Dutton, 1977. Young adult novel about an English boy sold as an enslaved person to Varangian traders; set in early Kiev and Constantinople.

Ustinov, Peter. *My Russia*. Little, Brown, 1983. The span of Russian history from earliest times.

READINGS FOR THE TEACHER

Cherniavsky, Michael, ed. *Structure of Russia*. Random House, 1970. Surveys the broad scope of Russian history.

Klein, Mina C. *The Kremlin: Citadel of History*. Macmillan, 1973. Describes the origin and growth of the Kremlin from the ninth century to modern times.

Riasanovsky, Nicholas V. *A History of Russia*. Oxford University Press, 1984. Surveys the history of Russia beginning with Kievan Rus.

Wallace, Robert. *Rise of Russia*. Time-Life Books, 1967. Presents the history of Russia from the ninth century through the reign of Peter the Great.

MULTIMEDIA RESOURCES

Early Russia. Random House. Filmstrips. Depicts Russia from earliest times to reign of Peter the Great.

INTRODUCE

CHAPTER 23 OVERVIEW

Chapter 23 discusses the Eastern Slav civilization from A.D. 500 to 1600.

- ➤ **Section 1** describes the influences that transformed the early Slav agricultural settlements into trading centers.
- ➤ **Section 2** discusses the emergence of a Rus state.
- ➤ **Section 3** describes the effects of the Mongol invasions on the Rus states.
- ➤ **Section 4** discusses the rules of Ivan the Great and Ivan the Terrible and the rise of Muscovy.

CHAPTER OBJECTIVES

After reading Chapter 23, students will be able to:

1. describe what life was like for the earliest Eastern Slavs.
2. summarize how early Rus states developed around Kiev.
3. analyze how Eastern Christianity influenced the Rus.
4. explain changes the Mongols brought about in Rus life.
5. discuss how Muscovy became powerful Moscow.
6. examine how the czars affected life in Rus states.

EXAMINING THE ILLUSTRATION

Ask students how they know this icon has religious importance. *(the cross, men in religious robes, church-like buildings)* Suggest they will be reading more about the early Eastern Christian Church and icons in this chapter.

PERFORMANCE ASSESSMENT

Use the Performance Assessment activities on page 346B to help you evaluate students as they complete the chapter.

CHAPTER 23 The Eastern Slavs

Russian Icon

346

TEACHER CLASSROOM RESOURCES

- Reproducible Lesson Plan
- Enrichment Activity
- Unit 7 World Literature
- Geography and Map Activity
- Vocabulary and Guided Reading Activity
- Cooperative Learning Activity
- Foods Around the World
- Teaching Transparencies and Activities
- Performance Assessment Activity
- Unit 7 Primary Source Reading
- The World History Videodisc
- Testmaker
- Audiocassettes (English and Spanish)

Chapter Focus

READ TO DISCOVER:

- What life was like for the earliest Eastern Slavs.
- How early Rus states developed around Kiev.
- How Eastern Christianity influenced the people of Rus.
- What changes the Mongols brought about in Rus life.
- How Moscow became powerful.
- How the czars affected life in Muscovy.

North of the Byzantine Empire lived a people that historians today call Slavs. All that is known about their origins is that they were Indo-Europeans, like the Aryans who entered the Indus Valley and the Dorians who conquered the Mycenaeans. About 500 B.C., the Slavs began to develop well-organized settlements in eastern Europe in the areas now known as eastern Poland and western Ukraine.

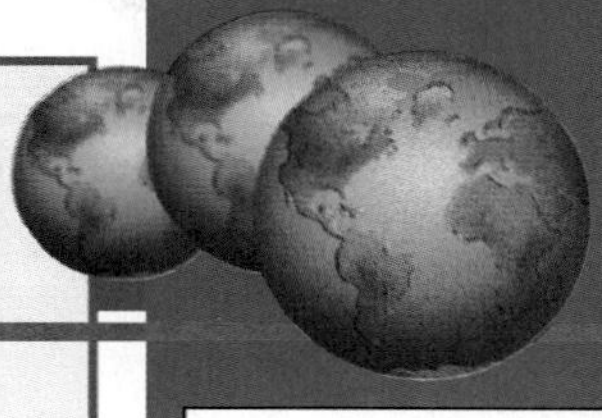

500 A.D.–1035 A.D.

KEY TERMS

izbas
boyars
veche
khan
kremlin
czar
historical maps

Section 1 Early Eastern Slavs

About 500 A.D., a group of Eastern Slavs began to move eastward toward the Volga (vol′ guh) River. They were hunters and farmers who were the ancestors of Ukrainians, Belarussians, and Russians. They settled in villages made up of about 25 related families. Each family owned a house that was built partly underground to provide warmth during the cold winter months. The house had low walls and an earth-covered roof. The land, animals, tools, and seed belonged to the village rather than to individuals. Around each village was a wall of earth and a wooden stockade for protection.

The oldest male governed the village with the help of a council. He assigned villagers different farming tasks and judged quarrels. During attacks, he acted as military leader.

By the 600s, the Eastern Slavs controlled all the land as far east as the Volga River. To clear this heavily forested land for farming, farmers used a method called *slash-and-burn.* They cut

347

FOCUS

BELLRINGER

Write this direction on the chalkboard: *List as many cities of the Commonwealth of Independent States as you can.*

MOTIVATIONAL ACTIVITY

Have students share their lists of cities of the Commonwealth of Independent States. One city likely to be on their lists is Moscow. Ask students if they realize that Russia still exists as a republic in the Commonwealth of Independent States. Ask students to look in their text Atlas to find the names of the other republics. Then tell students that they will learn about the early history of these republics and their cities.

VOCABULARY PRE-CHECK

Write the key terms for this chapter on the chalkboard. Ask a volunteer to record responses as you ask students what each word makes them think of. Tell students they will be able to assess the accuracy of their associations as they read the chapter.

Assign Chapter 23 **Vocabulary and Guided Reading Activity** in the TCR.

EXTRA CREDIT PROJECT

As students read they will become aware that the names of cities, including many they have learned about, were chosen for specific reasons, and sometimes were changed. Suggest that interested students choose three or four major cities in their state and research how they got their names. Then suggest that students write a brief explanation of this naming, and also what they might have named the city if it had been their choice, and why. Encourage students to share their research with the class.

KEY TO ABILITY LEVELS

Teaching strategies have been coded for varying learning styles and abilities.

L1 Level 1 activities are **basic** activities and should be within the ability range of all students.

L2 Level 2 activities are **average** activities and should be within the ability range of the average to above-average student.

L3 Level 3 activities are **challenging** activities designed for the ability range of above-average students.

LEP LEP activities should be within the ability range of Limited English Proficiency students.

TEACH

GUIDED PRACTICE

L1 **Daily Life** Have students imagine they are members of the early Eastern Slavs and they are to write an entry in their diaries describing a day in their lives. Have students share their entries with the class. LEP

LINKING PAST TO PRESENT

The slash-and-burn method is common today in developing countries throughout the world. After the trees are cut and the logs hauled away, remaining stumps and brush are set on fire. The ashes are used as fertilizer.

GEOGRAPHY AND HISTORY

Russia's rivers form a unique network of navigable waterways. Although all the major rivers run north-south, their lateral branches provide east-west access to land. This helped increase trade for the early Eastern Slavs.

CAPTION ANSWER

It was only one room. Although each *izba* had a fireplace, some did not have chimneys, and smoke had to escape through the shutters that covered the windows.

down trees, which they burned for fertilizer. On the cleared land, they planted such crops as barley, rye, and flax. After a few years, when the wood fertilizer in the soil had been used up, the farmers moved to a new place. There, they repeated the process.

The forests provided the East Slavs with all the timber they needed. The East Slavs soon became skilled in building with wood. They made musical instruments out of wood and used logs to make boats and *izbas* (uhz bahs'). An izba was a one-room log cabin with a gabled roof and wooden window frames. The whole family lived, worked, ate, and slept in the single room. Although each izba had a fireplace, some did not have a chimney. Smoke from fires had to escape through shutters that covered the windows.

The villagers worshipped many gods and honored nature, spirits, and ancestors. The most popular gods were Volos (vō' lōs), who protected cattle and sheep; Perun (pār' uhn), the god of thunder and lightning; and the Great Mother, the goddess of the land and harvest. The people built wooden images of their favorite gods on the highest ground outside the villages.

There were many slow-moving rivers in the area west of the Volga. At first, the East Slavs used them as roads between their villages. Before long, they began using them for trade as well. They set up a trade route that ran from the Baltic Sea in the north to the Caspian in the south.

RUS CABIN Houses in early Rus towns and villages were made of wood from the surrounding thick forests. Here, a modern Russian cabin is shown that is a good example of decorative styles passed on from early Rus artisans. **What was the inside of an izba, or Rus log cabin, like?**

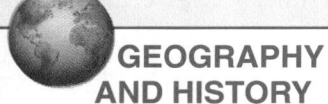

MEETING SPECIAL NEEDS

Have students who are tactile/kinesthetic learners make models or dioramas of early Russian towns or villages. Students can use the information in the textbook and in other resources. Display the models or dioramas in the classroom.

By the end of the 800s, the East Slavs had built many trading towns along the riverbanks. During the five months of winter, merchants who lived in the towns gathered furs, honey, and other forest products from the people in neighboring villages. In spring, when the ice on the rivers had melted, the merchants loaded their goods on boats and floated south to Byzantium. There, they traded their goods for cloth, wine, weapons, and jewelry. Trade helped the East Slavs to live more comfortably and to develop their civilization.

Drawing of Rus Sled

The Eastern Slavs, to protect their trade route, relied on Viking warriors from Scandinavia. These men were known as Varangians, and the route was called the Varangian Route or the route from the Varangians to the Greeks. Eventually, the Varangians became part of the larger Slav population.

Section 1 Review

1. **Identify:** Eastern Slavs, Volga River, Varangians
2. **Define:** *izbas*
3. How were early villages governed?
4. Why were rivers important to the Eastern Slavs?

Critical Thinking

5. Why do you think the Eastern Slavs chose Vikings to protect their trade route?

Section 2
Kievan Rus

In 862, a Varangian named Rurik became the prince of Novgorod (nahv′ guh rahd), a northern town on the East Slav trading route. About 20 years later, Rurik's Varangian friend Oleg (ō′ leg) established the state of Kievan Rus. The term "Rus" meant "warrior band." He set up his capital at Kiev (kē ev′).

Kiev stood on a group of hills overlooking the main bend in the Dnieper (nē′ puhr) River. It was the southernmost town on the Varangian trading route. Whoever ruled Kiev controlled trade with Byzantium. Kiev also lay close to where the Ukraine forest turned into a *steppe* (step), or grassland. For hundreds of years, this steppe had served central Asian warriors as a highway into Europe. Because of this, Kiev was in a good location to protect merchant ships from attack.

Painting of Eastern Slav Warriors

The Kievan Rus state that Oleg established was really a group of small territories. The main ruler was the Grand Prince of Kiev. He was helped by local princes, rich merchants, and

L2 **Culture** Discuss the influences from the Byzantines on early Slav people (*trade items such as silk, jewels, food; the Cyrillic alphabet; and Christianity*). Ask students to consider how they think the early Eastern Slavs might have felt about these influences on their traditional culture and practices. Suggest they write a description of what their feelings might be as if they were an Eastern Slav.

MAKING CONNECTIONS

➤➤ **History** Around A.D. 1100 Slavic traditions were written down in the *Primary Chronicle,* a record that combines legends and facts. According to the *Primary Chronicle,* in about A.D. 860 the Slavic people from the northern forest village of Novgorod asked Vikings from Scandinavia for aid: "Our land is great and rich, but there is no order in it. Come to rule and reign over us." The Viking leader Rurik accepted the invitation.

SECTION 1 ANSWERS

1. Eastern Slavs, lived north of the Byzantine Empire (p. 347); Volga River, runs from the Baltic to the Caspian Sea (p. 347); Varangians, Vikings (p. 349)
2. *izbas,* one-room log cabins (p. 348)
3. by the oldest male with the help of a council
4. because they were used as roads between the Rus villages and for trade
5. Answers will vary but might include that they needed people to protect their trade route.

Assign Chapter 23 **Section 1 Quiz** in the TCR. Testmaker available.

L1 **Geography: Movement** Have students trace an outline map of eastern Europe and draw and label the following on the map: Dnieper, Don, and Volga rivers; Novgorod, Smolensk, Moscow, Kiev, and Constantinople; the Black and Baltic seas. Then have students draw and label the Varangian Route. Point out the openness of the land to attackers. LEP

L2 **Geography: Movement** Refer students to the map, "Kievan Rus" on page 350, and have them trace the Varangian Route. Ask students to identify the part of the route that did not follow a river or body of water. *(the north central part of Kievan Rus)*

MAP STUDY

Answer

Baltic Sea, Dnieper River, Black Sea (to Mediterranean Sea)

Assign the Chapter 23 **Geography and Map Activity** in the TCR.

DID YOU KNOW

Tribute usually consisted of one animal skin—black marten, fox, or squirrel—per year from each household.

VIDEODISC

Use the following to enrich Chapter 23.

WH W 39 38407

Mt. Elbrus in the Caucasus.

Kievan Rus

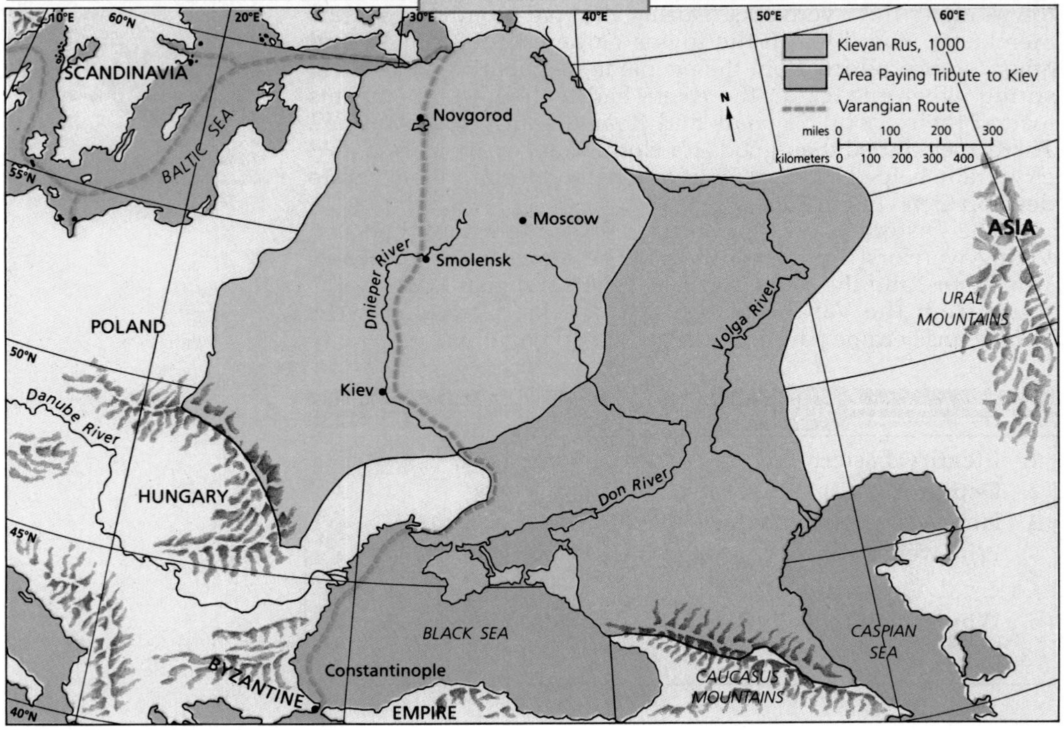

MAP STUDY

PLACE Rivers that flow north to south such as the Dnieper and the Volga provided an easy means of transportation in early Rus. **Along what bodies of water did the Varangian Route extend?**

boyars (bō yahrs'), or landowning nobles. The Grand Prince collected tribute from the local princes who in turn collected it from the people in their territory.

A ***veche*** (ve' chuh), or assembly, handled the daily matters of the towns. It did everything from settling business differences to accepting or removing a prince. Any free man could call a meeting of the veche by ringing the town bell.

Vladimir I and the Eastern Orthodox Church One of the most important princes of Kiev was Vladimir I (vlad' uh mēr), a good soldier and a strong ruler. He spent the early years of his reign expanding Kievan Rus territory. His armies pushed the country's borders west into Poland and north along the stormy Baltic coast.

In 988, Vladimir chose Eastern or Byzantine Christianity as the country's official religion. The story is told about Vladimir's long search for a new faith that would unite the people. Vladimir sent a number of people to other countries to observe different

MEETING SPECIAL NEEDS

Students with any hearing impairment will need extra visual help with learning the material in this chapter. Select an advanced student to prepare a simple graphic organizer of key events of the chapter. Have students list key terms under appropriate events once organizers are complete. Encourage students to share organizers with the class as a whole, since this is an effective study method for all students.

religions. Those sent were not impressed with what they saw in Islamic, Jewish, or Roman Catholic worship. Then, in Byzantium's Hagia Sophia, they saw Eastern Orthodox worship. They were stunned by its beauty. When they returned to Kievan Rus, Vladimir accepted Eastern Orthodoxy as the official religion.

The Eastern Orthodox Church brought Byzantine culture to Kievan Rus. Priests from Byzantium taught the people religious rituals and the art of painting icons. They learned to write their language in the Cyrillic alphabet. Sons of boyars and priests were sent to newly built schools. The look of Kievan Rus towns changed as stone churches with domes and arches rose among the wooden buildings. Monasteries appeared.

Eastern Orthodoxy gave the Kievan Rus people a sense of belonging to the civilized world. However, it separated them

RELIGIOUS LIFE Eastern Orthodoxy inspired art and architecture in Kievan Rus. These later Russian icons (left) closely resembled Byzantine examples. Stone churches with ornate, tiled domes (right) were built in Rus towns. **How did Eastern Orthodoxy separate Kievan Rus from the culture of western Europe?**

L2 **Daily Life** Direct students to imagine they are going to be exchange students from Kiev to another country. Have them write letters to their host families describing their own city, home, and family.

MAKING CONNECTIONS

➤➤ **Language** The Kievan Rus people told stories about Vladimir and the *bogatyrs*, or knights, that are similar to western European tales about King Arthur and his Knights of the Round Table.

CAPTION ANSWER

Since Russian scholars had books in their own language, they developed their own body of learning separate from that of the West.

VIDEODISC

Use the following to enrich Chapter 23.

WH W 40 38408

The ancient Georgian capital of Mtskhet.

MULTICULTURAL PERSPECTIVES

Just as Greeks and Romans influenced churches and government buildings in western Europe, the architectural style of Constantinople had a lasting effect in Russia and eastern Europe. Most influential was Hagia Sophia in Constantinople. Later churches in Eastern Christian countries followed similar designs. These churches took the shape of a Greek cross, with four equal arms and a square open area in the center topped by a dome.

L1 **History** Have students write a personality sketch about the life and achievements of one of the following: Oleg, Vladimir I, Yaroslav the Wise. Have students share their personality sketches with the class.

L3 **The Arts** Have students find examples of Eastern Slavic folktales or legends, music, or art. Traditional musical instruments, art tools, or popular art media could also be included. They should give a brief presentation to the class on the subject of the research including any examples they found.

MAKING CONNECTIONS

>> **History** The marriages of Yaroslav's sister to the king of Poland and his daughters to the kings of France, Hungary, and Norway indicated Yaroslav's prestige among European rulers.

Fur-lined Crown

from western Europe. Since Kievan scholars had books in their own language, they had developed their own body of learning separate from that of the West.

Yaroslav the Wise Another important ruler of early Rus was Yaroslav (yuh ruh slahf'), son of Vladimir I. Yaroslav became the Grand Prince of Kiev in 1019, after a long struggle with his brothers. Yaroslav was very interested in learning. He invited scholars from Byzantium to live in Kiev and he was called Yaroslav the Wise.

Yaroslav encouraged artisans to practice their skills. The artisans built magnificent brick churches covered with white plaster and decorated with gold. Artists covered the walls of Yaroslav's palace in Kiev with scenes of music and hunting.

Under Yaroslav's rule, Kievan Rus enjoyed a golden age of peace and prosperity. Kiev grew until the city was larger than either Paris or London. Yaroslav developed closer ties with western Europe by family marriages.

Yaroslav also organized Kievan Rus laws based on old Slavic customs and Byzantine law. Under Yaroslav's code, crimes against property were thought to be more serious than those against people. There was no death penalty. In fact, criminals usually were not punished physically but had to pay a fine.

Decline of Kievan Rus Kievan Rus began to decline around 1054. After Yaroslav's death, the princes of Kiev began to fight over the throne. People from the steppe took advantage of this fighting and attacked Kievan Rus's frontiers. This upset the trade flow which meant the loss of Kiev's major source of wealth. Kievan Rus became more isolated. In 1169 Kiev was attacked and plundered by Andrei Bogoliubsky who wanted Kiev destroyed. The area never recovered.

Gradually, Kievan Rus changed from a trading land of towns into a farming land of peasants. To escape the invaders from the steppe, many of its people fled to the north and settled in the dense forests along the upper Volga.

Section 2 Review

1. **Identify:** Oleg, Kiev, Dnieper River, Grand Prince of Kiev, Vladimir I, Yaroslav the Wise
2. **Define:** boyars, *veche*
3. How did the decline of Kiev affect the area and people?

Critical Thinking

4. How would you have felt about Yaroslav's code of law and his ways to punish criminals?

SECTION 2 ANSWERS

1. Oleg, Rus ruler (p. 349); Kiev, Rus capital (p. 349); Dnieper River, river near Kiev (p. 349); Grand Prince of Kiev, ruler of Rus state (p. 349); Vladimir I, prince of Kiev (p. 350); Yaroslav the Wise, Grand Prince of Kiev (p. 352)
2. boyars, landowning nobles (p. 350); *veche*, Rus assembly (p. 350)
3. It changed Rus states into a farming land of peasants, and more people fled north.
4. Answers will vary, but students should include reasons for their feelings about the punishments.

Assign Chapter 23 **Section 2 Quiz** in the TCR. Testmaker available.

Section 3

THE MONGOL CONQUEST

About 1240, a group of different but united tribes known as Mongols (mon′ guhls) swept out of central Asia and took control of Rus principalities, or states. They destroyed villages and towns and killed many people. They made the Rus people pay tribute to the **khan** (kahn), or Mongol leader. They also made the Rus citizens serve in the Mongol armies.

The Church The Eastern Orthodox Church remained strong during the Mongol invasion. Priests continued to preach and to write. They encouraged the people to love their land and their religion.

During this time, monks began to found monasteries deep in the northern forests. They were followed by Rus farmers searching for new land. Soon, towns and villages began to grow up around the monasteries. Although the Mongol rule caused Rus people to cling more to their religion, it also made them distrustful of ideas and practices from other countries.

THE MONGOLS The Mongols were chiefly interested in controlling and collecting taxes from Rus. This painting shows the Rus people paying tribute to a Mongol leader. **What were Mongol leaders called?**

DID YOU KNOW ??

The Mongols were also known as Tartars and the Golden Horde. They were led by Genghis Khan's grandson Batu Khan.

CAPTION ANSWER

Khan

VIDEODISC

Use the following to enrich Chapter 23.

WH R 68 30566

Genghis Khan.

EXTENDING THE CONTENT

Mongols were not the only invaders of the Rus states in the thirteenth century. Although the northerly town of Novgorod was out of the direct wave of Mongol destruction, it still had to contend with invaders from the west. Its leader, Prince Alexander, was an outstanding military leader who became one of the great heroes of Rus history.

INDEPENDENT PRACTICE

L2 **Daily Life** Have students prepare a report with illustrations or a fashion show on some traditional Russian dress for both the wealthy and the peasants. Encourage students to include what influence this dress has had on modern fashion styles. LEP

LINKING PAST TO PRESENT

From a small unimportant town on the Moskva River, Muscovy grew to be a center of the Soviet Empire. Troikas, or sleighs, guided by horses, still glide over snowy trails on the city's outskirts. Today the golden-domed Kremlin has walls of brick and stone instead of the wooden ones of the thirteenth century.

VIDEODISC

Use the following to enrich Chapter 23.

WH R 70 30568

Kublai Khan (1215-1294).

Church Vestment

The Mongol conquest somewhat isolated the Rus Church from other Christian churches. Because of this, the Church developed local rituals and practices. This united the people and made them proud of their own culture.

Daily Life Even under Mongol rule, differences between the lives of the rich in Rus and the lives of peasants remained. The wealthy sometimes entertained guests with feasts of deer and wild pig. Peasants, on the other hand, rarely ate meat. Instead, they ate dark rye bread, cabbage, salted fish, and mushrooms.

The few pleasures the peasants had were visiting one another. They told stories that praised the brave deeds of their warriors and other heroes. The stories were passed from old to young and became part of the Rus heritage.

Common dress for peasant men was white tunics, wide linen trousers, and heavy shoes woven from long strips of tree bark. They tied rags around their legs and feet instead of stockings to keep out the cold. Rich merchants and boyars wore tall fur hats and *caftans* (kaf' tanz), or long robes tied at the waist with a sash.

Rus women of all classes wore blouses or smocks, skirts, and long shawls. On holidays, they added headdresses with decorations that indicated the region from which a woman came and if she was married.

Section 3 Review

1. **Identify:** Mongols
2. What did the Mongols do to the Rus people when the Mongols invaded Rus lands?
3. How was the Eastern Church affected by Mongol rule?

Critical Thinking

4. How might life have been different in the Rus states if the Mongols had not conquered these lands?

Section 4 THE RISE OF MOSCOW

At the time of the Mongol conquest, Moscow (mos' kō), or Muscovy, founded in 1147, was a small trading post on the road from Kiev to the forests in the north. As more Rus people moved north to escape the Mongols, many artisans settled in or near Moscow's **kremlin** (krem' luhn), or fortress.

SECTION 3 ANSWERS

1. Mongols, people from central Asia (p. 353)
2. They murdered people and destroyed villages, made Rus people pay tribute and serve in the Mongol armies.
3. It was isolated from other Christian churches and developed local rituals and practices.
4. Answers will vary but could include that if the Mongols had not conquered Rus, these states might have been less isolated.

Assign Chapter 23 **Section 3 Quiz** in the TCR. Testmaker available.

The princes of Moscow were bold and ambitious. They learned to cooperate with the Mongols and even recruited Muscovy soldiers for the Mongol army. In return, the Mongols gave the princes of Moscow the power to collect taxes throughout the country. If a Rus territory could not provide soldiers or tax money for the Mongols, Moscow's princes took it over. In this way, Moscow, the principality of Muscovy, began to expand.

As Moscow grew in size, it became stronger. The princes passed their thrones from father to son. Thus, there was no fighting over who the next ruler would be, and the people remained united.

The Muscovite metropolitan lived in Moscow. This created a second center for the Eastern Orthodox Church outside of Kiev. The metropolitan blessed the princes for their efforts to make Moscow a great city. The people obeyed the prince as a ruler chosen and protected by God.

Meanwhile, Mongol chiefs started fighting among themselves. As a result, they grew weaker, while Moscow grew stronger. In 1380, an army formed by Dmitry (duh mē′ trē), the prince of Moscow, attacked and defeated the Mongols. The Mongols still remained powerful but no longer were feared or obeyed as they had been in the past.

Ivan the Great

In 1462, Ivan III (ī′ vuhn), known as Ivan the Great, became prince of Moscow. In 1480, he ended Mongol control of Muscovy. He also expanded its boundaries to the north and west.

A few years before Mongol rule ended, Ivan married Sophia, a niece of the last Byzantine emperor. The Muscovite people felt this marriage gave Ivan all the glory of past Byzantine emperors. The Church believed it meant that Moscow had taken Byzantium's place as the center of Christianity.

Ivan began living in the style of the Byzantine emperors. He used the two-headed eagle of Byzantium on his royal seal. He brought Italian architects to Moscow to build fine palaces and large cathedrals in the kremlin. He raised the huge walls that still guard the kremlin. He called himself **czar** (zahr), or emperor. This later became the official title of the emperor.

Ivan died in 1505. By then, the people were convinced that their ruler should have full and unquestioned power over both Church and state.

Painting of Ivan the Great

Ivan the Terrible

In 1533, Ivan IV, the three-year-old grandson of Ivan III, became czar of Muscovy. He was not crowned until 1547, however. While he was growing up, a council of boyars governed the country for him. The boyars, however, wanted more power. To frighten Ivan into obeying

L3 **Editorial Cartoons** Have the students write an editorial cartoon concerning one of the following events: Ivan the Great's marriage to Sophia, Ivan the Great's end of Mongol control of Rus, Ivan the Terrible's order to peasants not to leave their land, Ivan the Terrible's move to a monastery, Ivan the Terrible's takeover of boyar lands. Display cartoons on a bulletin board.

MAKING CONNECTIONS

➤➤ **History** In 1395, Tamelane, also called Timur the Lame, led a group of Muslim Mongols that sacked Muscovy in revenge for Dmitry's actions.

EXTENDING THE CONTENT

Moscow was first settled on a trail by a river where people built a blockhouse as a place to stop on the way to Kiev. The site—a hill of pines—was chosen because it offered protection and provided a good observation point. Around A.D. 1155, a log stockade was built to protect against raiders. Huts and storehouses were later added, and eventually the area became known as the *kremlin*, or fort. The heart of today's Moscow is still the Kremlin, although Moscow has spread and grown since then. The "new" Kremlin has a massive red brick wall surrounding a medieval fortress that was built in the fifteenth century.

Teaching

MAP SKILLS

Analyzing Historical Maps

Have students read the introductory section of the skill on page 356. Ask: What do historical maps show? *(boundary changes over time)* Direct students' attention to the map on the skill page. Ask: In what year was Muscovy smallest? *(1300)* In what year did Moscow first acquire part of the Volga River. *(1462)* Under which czar did Moscow gain control of Novgorod? *(Ivan III)*

Next, have students refer to a current map of the area shown on the map "The Growth of Moscow" and name the countries that were once controlled by Moscow.

ANSWERS to Map Practice

1. 1462
2. 1505
3. Ivan IV

MAP SKILLS

Analyzing Historical Maps

Some maps show how a certain country expanded and changed its boundaries over time. Maps that show boundary changes are called **historical maps.**

The map of "The Growth of Moscow" below shows the changes in Moscow's borders from 1300 to 1584. The color used to shade a certain area shows when that land became part of Moscow. It also shows the exact location of the land that was added. For example, green is the color used to show the land acquired by the time of Ivan IV's death. The shading on the map indicates that this land extended to the Caspian Sea in the southeast and to the Black Sea in the southwest.

Map Practice

1. **By what year did Moscow include part of the Don River?**
2. **By what year had Moscow acquired territory bordering on the Arctic Ocean?**
3. **Under which czar did Moscow control the largest amount of territory?**

The Growth of Moscow

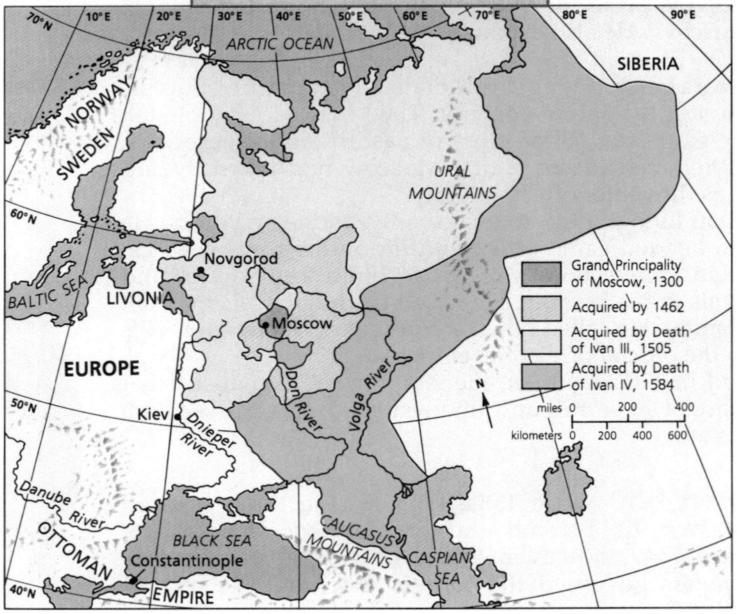

SPOTLIGHT ON: MOSCOW

The area around Moscow was dependent on both the Don and Volga rivers. The Volga is Europe's largest river, being comprised of 151,000 rivers, streams, and temporary streams, and having a length of 357,000 miles (or 574,000 km). The Volga River basin occupies a huge area stretching from the Valdi and Central Russian hills on the west to the Ural Mountains in the east, to the Caspian Sea in the south. Snow accounts for 60 percent of the river's annual drainage.

them, they began to mistreat him. Ivan came to hate the boyars. He did, however, adopt their cruel habits. By the time he was a teenager, he was killing people just for going against his wishes.

When Ivan IV was 16 years old, he was crowned czar and began to rule in his own right. He ignored the boyars and turned to merchants and close friends for advice. He gave his advisers gifts of land and jobs as officials. To make sure that the officials' country estates were farmed while the officials themselves were in Moscow with him, Ivan ordered peasants not to leave their land. In this way, he took the first step in turning free peasants into serfs.

Painting of Ivan the Terrible

In 1552, Ivan led his armies against Mongol territories on the Volga. By this time, the Muscovites had learned the use of gunpowder from western Europe. The Mongols, however, still depended on bows and arrows. Within six years, Ivan conquered most of the Mongol territories. Muscovites settlers began to move east. Some, called Cossacks (kos' aks), began to farm along the Volga.

In 1558, Muscovite armies attacked Livonia (luh vō' nē uh), a land on the Baltic Sea. Livonia's neighbors sent troops to fight the Muscovite armies. In 1562, these troops defeated the Muscovite soldiers and took over much of their Baltic territory. Ivan blamed the boyars for his terrible defeat.

In 1564, Ivan suddenly left Moscow and went to live in a small monastery in the country. A month later, he announced that he was giving up the throne because of the boyars. Afraid that without Ivan the empire would fall, the people begged him to change his mind. They told Ivan that if he came back, he could have full authority to punish traitors and to take over their lands.

Ivan returned to Moscow, took over boyar lands, and gave the land to 5,000 of his most loyal supporters. In return, they formed the *Oprichnina* (ah prich' nē nuh), or secret police or soldiers of terror. Members of the Oprichnina dressed in black and rode black horses through the countryside. They scared the czar's enemies and carried a broom to show their desire to sweep treason from the land. They killed thousands of people. Finally, when the Oprichnina had defeated the boyars and returned control of the empire to Ivan, he broke up the group.

Ivan came to be called Ivan the Terrible. This is because the English translated the word meaning "awesome" as "terrible." To the Muscovites, however, Ivan was a great ruler who protected their country from enemies.

Ivan encouraged art and learning. He brought artists, scholars, and engineers from western Europe to teach the Muscovites new skills. He established a link between Moscow and England and Holland. He also increased the czar's power.

GEOGRAPHY AND HISTORY

Under Ivan's rule, the first Rus settlers began to move eastward into Siberia.

MAKING CONNECTIONS

➤➤ **History** Ivan introduced printing in Russia and allowed English traders to enter the country. He was so fascinated with the West and its culture that he considered marrying one of the ladies of Queen Elizabeth's court.

DID YOU KNOW ??

The Cossacks were rebellious pioneers against medieval Rus's established order. They generally included bands of runaway peasants, serfs, farmers, and adventurers who moved to the frontier, along the Dnieper and Don rivers in the sixteenth century.

ASSESS

CHECK FOR UNDERSTANDING

Ask students to summarize orally or in writing the main points of the chapter. Discuss the answers to the Section and Chapter Review questions.

COOPERATIVE LEARNING

Divide the class into six groups. Assign each group one of the following characters: Rus peasant, prince of Moscow, Rus soldier, Rus church leader, the khan, or Ivan the Great. Inform students that they will role-play these characters in a panel discussion based on the question, "Is Mongol rule good for Moscow?" Ask each group to decide how Mongol rule affected their assigned character and prepare a note card containing approximately five points to be brought out in the discussion. Have each group select a representative to role-play their character.

Assign Chapter 23 **Cooperative Learning Activity** in the TCR.

EVALUATE

Assign the Chapter 23 **Performance Assessment Activity** in the TCR.

Administer **Chapter 23 Test** in the TCR. Testmaker available.

RETEACH

Have students explain the significance of waterways and mobility in early Rus.

Assign Chapter 23 **Reteaching Activity** in the TCR.

ENRICH

Have students read Russian folktales and write reports about their themes.

Assign Chapter 23 **Enrichment Activity** in the TCR.

CLOSE

Have students evaluate the declaration by Ivan the Terrible that Rus was the third Rome.

MEETING CHAPTER OBJECTIVES

Each chapter objective is tested by the Chapter Review questions that follow it in parentheses.

1. **Describe** what life was like for the earliest Eastern Slavs. (CU 1; UYJ)
2. **Summarize** how early Rus states developed around Kiev. (CT 1)
3. **Analyze** how Eastern Christianity influenced the people of Rus. (CU 4; UYJ)
4. **Explain** what changes the Mongols brought to Rus. (BV; UYJ)
5. **Discuss** how Moscow became powerful. (CU 6, 7)
6. **Examine** how the czars affected Rus states. (BV; CU 7, 8; CT 2, 3)

When he died in 1584, however, Ivan left no suitable heir. He had killed the oldest of his three sons in a fit of rage. His middle son was feeble-minded, and his youngest son was still a baby. As a result, for some 25 years after Ivan's death, the Muscovy was in confusion and disorder.

Section 4 Review

1. **Identify:** Moscow, Dmitry, Ivan the Great, Sophia, Ivan the Terrible, Cossacks, *Oprichnina*
2. **Define:** kremlin, czar
3. Why did Moscow become powerful?
4. What happened to Muscovy after Ivan the Terrible's death?

Critical Thinking

5. Which of the three rulers—Dmitry, Ivan the Great, or Ivan the Terrible—do you think contributed most to the development of the Muscovy? Explain.

Chapter Summary

1. Between 500 and 800 A.D., a group of Eastern Slavs settled the forested land west of the Volga River.
2. By the end of the 800s, the Kievan Rus had established a trade route that ran from the Baltic Sea in the north to the Caspian Sea in the south.
3. The early East Slavs relied on Viking warriors known as Varangians to protect their trade route.
4. In 882, the Viking warrior Oleg established the first Kievan Rus state, with its capital at Kiev.
5. In 988, Eastern Orthodox Christianity became the official religion of Kievan Rus.
6. The Byzantine Orthodox Church brought Byzantine culture, including the Cyrillic alphabet, to Kievan Rus.
7. Yaroslav the Wise supported learning, encouraged artisans, and organized Rus laws.
8. After 1054, Rus trade declined and people shifted to farming.
9. About 1240, Rus was conquered by the Mongols, and many more Rus people fled north to settle in or near Moscow. Others fled west.
10. Moscow gradually became the center of economic and religious life.
11. In the late 1400s, Ivan the Great ended Mongol control of Muscovy and took the title of czar.
12. Beginning in 1552, Ivan the Terrible conquered most of the Mongol territories, and many Muscovites began moving eastward.
13. In 1584, when Ivan the Terrible died with no suitable heir, Muscovy entered a time of disorder that lasted for 25 years.

SECTION 4 ANSWERS

1. Moscow, Rus city (p. 354); Dmitry, prince of Moscow (p. 355); Ivan the Great, prince of Moscow (p. 355); Sophia, wife of Ivan III (p. 355); Ivan the Terrible, czar of Muscovy (p. 355); Cossacks, Rus settlers (p. 357); *Oprichnina*, secret police (p. 357)
2. kremlin, fortress (p. 354); czar, emperor (p. 355)
3. because its princes cooperated with the Mongols who took over territories that were not wealthy; and because the princes passed their thrones from father to son, which eliminated fighting
4. It was in a state of confusion and disorder because he left no suitable heir.
5. Answers will vary, but students should give reasons for their choice of the best leader.

Assign Chapter 23 **Section 4 Quiz** in the TCR. Testmaker available.

CHAPTER

Review 23

Building Vocabulary

Imagine what a photograph showing what each of the words below would look like. Write a sentence describing each picture, using the vocabulary word.

izbas	khan
boyars	kremlin
veche	czar

Check for Understanding

1. How did the houses of Eastern Slavs provide warmth?
2. Why did the Eastern Slavs invite the Varangians to enter their territory?
3. How was the first Rus state that Oleg established organized?
4. Why did Vladimir I choose the Eastern Orthodox Church as the official church of his state?
5. How did Yaroslav develop closer ties with western Europe?
6. How did the people view the princes of Moscow?
7. What did Ivan III do for the Rus states?
8. Why did the people think Ivan the Terrible was a great ruler?
9. Between what European countries and Moscow did Ivan IV develop a link?

Critical Thinking

1. Why do you think trade with other cities is one of the first activities of a successful city such as Kiev?
2. What do you think are the advantages of rule passing from father to son, as it did during the time of the czars? What are the disadvantages of this method?
3. Do you think the word "terrible" or the word "awesome" better describes Ivan IV? Explain.

Geography in History

LOCATION Refer to the map on page 356. Imagine that the czar has asked you to choose the location of a new settlement in the area acquired by the death of Ivan IV. Where would you locate the settlement and why? What geographic features affected your decision?

Using Your Journal

Review the details you have noted about the ways the people of Rus states were influenced by other civilizations. Write a magazine article explaining how the Eastern Orthodox Church affected the culture of this area.

359

CHAPTER 23 REVIEW ANSWERS

BUILDING VOCABULARY

Sentences will vary, but students should use all the vocabulary words in their descriptions.

CHECK FOR UNDERSTANDING

1. They were built partly underground.
2. to protect their trade route to Byzantium
3. as a group of small territories ruled by the Grand Prince of Kiev; a *veche* handled the daily matters of towns
4. because observers had been stunned by the beauty of Eastern Orthodox worship
5. by having family members marry into other European royal families
6. as rulers protected by God
7. He ended Mongol rule, expanded Muscovy, built palaces and cathedrals and walls around the Kremlin.
8. because he protected their country, encouraged art and learning, and created a Rus empire
9. between Moscow, and England and Holland

CRITICAL THINKING

1. Answers will vary but might include that successful cities needed industries, and isolated cities do not grow.
2. Answers will vary, but students should explain the advantages and disadvantages.
3. Answers will vary, but students should refer to the ruler's deeds and explain their choices.

+ BONUS +

TEST QUESTION

For the Chapter 23 Test

The distance between Novgorod and Kiev along the Varangian Route was approximately 600 miles (966 km). The town of Smolensk was halfway between them. Traveling by sled at 3 miles per hour (5 kmph) how many days would it take to go from Kiev to Smolensk, traveling only during daylight hours? *(about 10 days)*

USING YOUR JOURNAL

Articles will vary but should indicate that the Eastern Orthodox Church brought Byzantine culture to Rus states. Priests taught rituals and the art of painting icons. The Church brought the Cyrillic alphabet to Russia and unity to the people of Rus during the Mongol invasion.

GEOGRAPHY IN HISTORY

Answers will vary but should include an explanation of why they would locate the settlement where they did.

THE MONGOLS

FOCUS

OBJECTIVES

Locate the Mongol Empire. Identify the time period of the Mongol Empire. Describe the cultural traits of the Mongols.

BELLRINGER

Write the following on the chalkboard: *List the adjectives you think of when you hear the name Ghengis Khan.*

MOTIVATIONAL ACTIVITY

Ask students to read their adjectives that describe the name Ghengis Khan. *(Some adjectives might be fierce, ferocious, strong, and mighty.)* Then explain that in this Culture Close-Up they will learn about the Mongol ruler, Ghengis Khan, and the reasons he became famous.

UNIT 7

CULTURE CLOSE-UP

The Mongols

During the 1200s, the Mongol people created the greatest land empire the world has ever known. They ruled for 200 years.

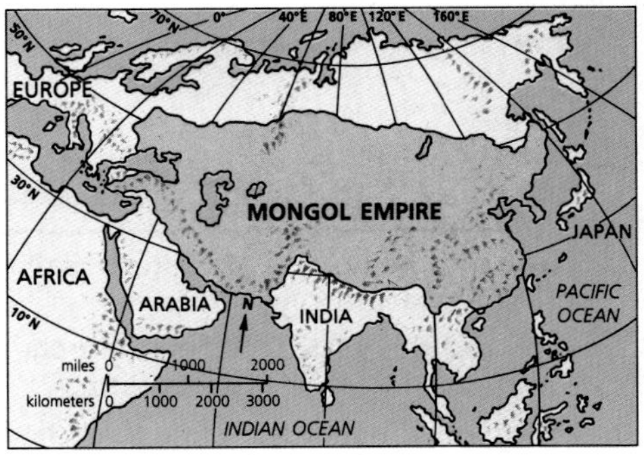

Geography Connection

The frosty steppes of central Asia were home to these fierce warrior people. The Mongol Empire at one time included China, Persia, Mesopotamia, Afghanistan, Poland, and Hungary.

◀ Being nomads, the Mongols moved from place to place, herding their livestock as they went. They put up their yurts, or tents, wherever they found good grazing for their horses, sheep, camels, oxen, and goats.

MULTICULTURAL PERSPECTIVES

The Mongols, who ruled Russia for more than 200 years, came from the steppes of central Asia, which has a very cold climate in winter. Both men and women Mongols wore felt trousers and leather coats lined with fur. They covered their feet with thick felt boots. The Mongols were short, broad, and black-haired. Mongol men shaved the tops of their heads and wore the rest of their hair in long braids. The hairstyles of the women showed whether they were married, single, or widowed.

One of the greatest Mongol leaders was Ghengis Khan. His name meant " Supreme Ruler." His invasions of China have been often reflected in art. ▶

▲ A Mongol's most prized possession was a horse. Horses, symbols of social standing, served as transportation as well as food. When Mongols conquered other people they first chose horses to take rather than gold or silver.

◀ Here Ghengis Khan leads followers in a prayer to the sun. The appearance of the Mongol people in their felt and leather dress was impressive. Both men and women wore distinctive hairstyles.

361

TEACH

L1 Geography: Location Have students compare the map of the Mongol Empire on page 360 with a physical/political map of Europe and Asia. Ask: On what continents was the Mongol Empire located? (Europe and Asia) What major physical features were part of the Mongol Empire? (Huang Ho, Gobi, Hindu Kush Mountains, Caucasus Mountains, Caspian Sea, Tian Shan, Mongolian Plateau) What physical feature prevented the Mongol invasion of southern Asia? (Himalaya Mountains) LEP

DID YOU KNOW ??

Mongol boys began learning how to ride horseback and shoot arrows when they were 3 years old. When they grew up, they spent their time herding, hunting, and fighting. Women milked the animals and made camel's hair and sheep's wool into felt. They also traded with traveling merchants.

VIDEODISC

Use the following to enrich Unit 7.

WH R 71 30569

Mongol horsemen hunting with leader Kublai Khan.

EXTENDING THE CONTENT

Genghis Khan was a great military organizer. He chose officers on merit and organized his troops as units instead of tribes. He used a signaling system of flags by day and torches by night so he could stay in constant communication with his soldiers. He had his soldiers wear silk shirts under their oxhide armor so that if a soldier was cut or shot, the weapon could push the silk into the wound and help keep infections from settling in. Genghis Khan also had Chinese and Persian doctors accompany his soldiers so that the wounded could be cared for near the battlefield.

UNIT 7 CULTURE CLOSE-UP

L2 **Critical Thinking** Mongols gained control of China by superior military strength. Ask students if they think that Mongol rule during Kublai Khan's time benefitted China. With students volunteering ideas, list on the chalkboard some of the benefits the Chinese gained from Mongol rule. *(Great architecture and literature flourished. Many areas were rebuilt.)* LEP

MAKING CONNECTIONS

➤➤ **Government** Kublai Khan was tolerant of many religions, which encouraged outsiders to come to China. He understood the important contributions Muslims made to China through their occupations—craftspeople, merchants, and architects. Therefore, Kublai exempted Muslims from paying taxes. He respected the property of the people he conquered. He also gave women equal rights with men.

GLOBAL READING FOR STUDENTS

Historians in your class may be interested in reading a biography about Genghis Khan. Suggest *Genghis Khan* by Judy Humphrey, Chelsea House, 1987. (Average/Biography)

◀ The reputation of Ghengis Khan spread as he continued to conquer much of Asia. He improved many areas.

During the Mongol rule, great architecture and literature flourished. In China, Ghengis Khan rebuilt many areas including the Grand Canal.

The Mongol passage of power, by male family member, followed a very strict code. Thus, the power of Ghengis Khan passed to his grandson Kublai Khan. ▼

◀ Kublai Khan used advanced methods of fighting. Here his men cross a river on a pontoon boat.

362

MEETING SPECIAL NEEDS

Have interested students research and write a report about Marco Polo's friendship with Kublai Khan and Polo's service to the Khan as a government official in China. Have students share their reports with the class.

CULTURE CLOSE-UP

UNIT 7

▲ The grand courts of Kublai Khan were described in the literature of the time. He set up a code of laws. Like his grandfather, Kublai Khan built orphanages, schools, and hospitals.

The Mongolian Empire spread to the far eastern shores of China. Kublai Khan tried to invade Japan, but failed.

Taking Another Look

1. On what continent was the Mongol Empire located?

2. What was the most important possession of a Mongol?

3. How did most Mongols make a living?

Critical Thinking

4. Why do you think the Mongols were such successful invaders during this time?

COOPERATIVE LEARNING

Have students work in small groups to write scripts about life in the areas conquered by the Mongols. Encourage students to include eyewitness reports of how the native people viewed the Mongols. Students should use the information in the text and in other resources to help them with their scripts. The scripts should contain a part for each member of the group. Have students read their scripts to the class.

ASSESS

CHECK FOR UNDERSTANDING

Have students answer the questions in Taking Another Look on page 363.

ANSWERS to Taking Another Look

1. Europe and Asia
2. horses
3. herding
4. They used advanced methods of fighting and were very aggressive.

ENRICH

Have students discuss the importance of horses in the Mongol culture. What impact did they have on the successes of this civilization? What might the history of the Mongols been like without the horse?

VIDEODISC

Use the following to enrich Unit 7.

WH R 72 30570

Bronze cannon, believed the oldest yet discovered.

CLOSE

Ask students to discuss why they think Kublai Khan's invasion of Japan was unsuccessful.

INTRODUCE

UNIT 8 OVERVIEW

Unit 8 discusses the changes that took place in western Europe during the late Middle Ages.

- **Chapter 24** describes feudalism.
- **Chapter 25** discusses the role of the Roman Catholic Church in medieval life.
- **Chapter 26** describes how the growth of trade during the Middle Ages led to the rise of towns in western Europe.
- **Chapter 27** examines the development of strong national governments under monarchs in France, England, Germany, and Spain.

UNIT OBJECTIVES

After reading Unit 8, students will be able to:

1. discuss what roles the clergy, nobles, and peasants played during the late Middle Ages.
2. explain what led to the growth of trade and towns in western Europe.
3. describe how kings in western Europe built strong nations during the late Middle Ages.

UNIT PROJECT

Organize the class into four teams to play "The Late Middle Ages Quiz Bowl." Assign each team one chapter from this unit. Have the teams each prepare strips of paper with the names of important people, places, events, and themes discussed in their chapter, and place them in a large container. Have a moderator select a paper and read it aloud. The first team member must explain, define, or give information about the topic. If the team member is unable to do so, the question passes to the next team.

UNIT 8 The Late Middle Ages

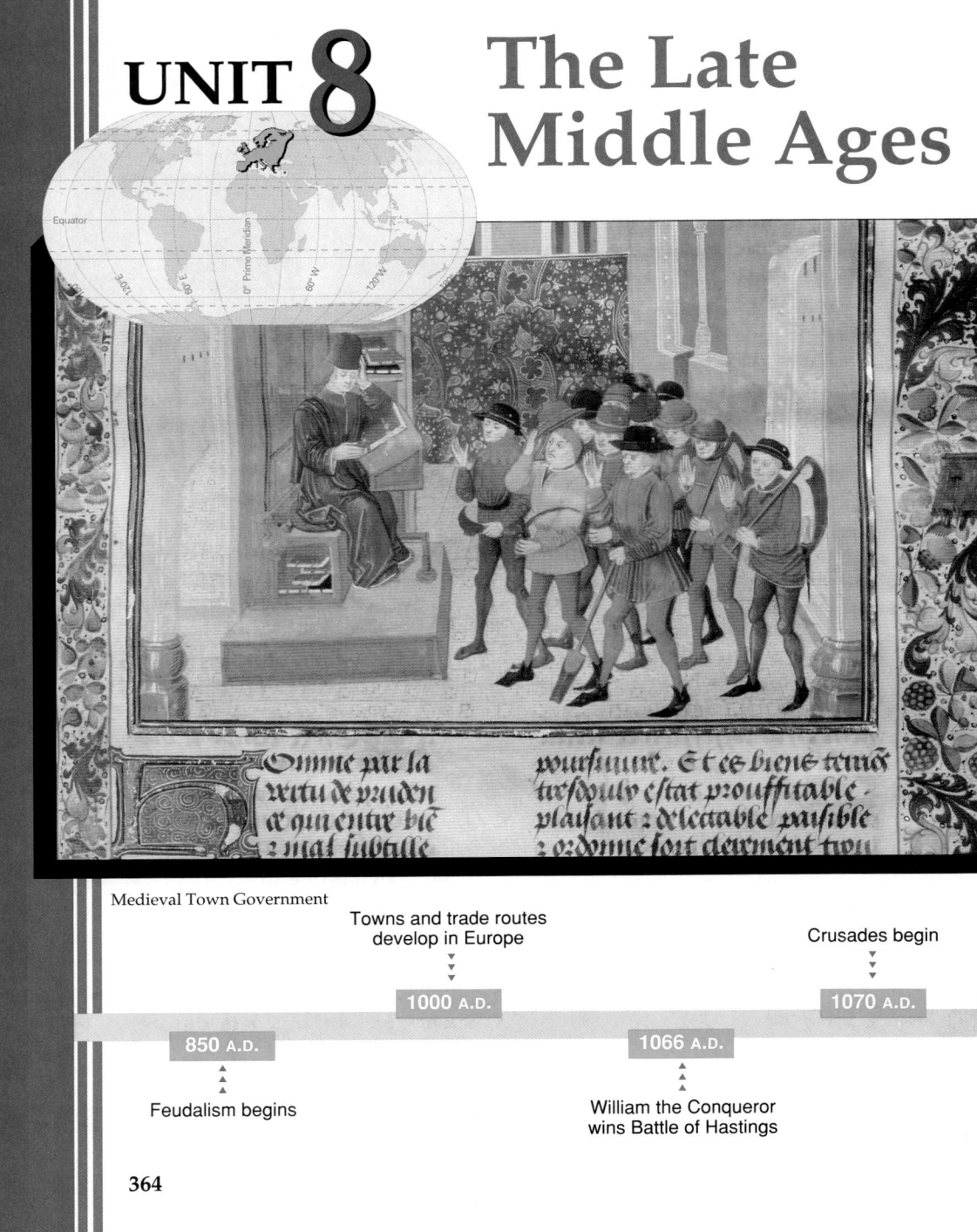

Medieval Town Government

- 850 A.D. — Feudalism begins
- 1000 A.D. — Towns and trade routes develop in Europe
- 1066 A.D. — William the Conqueror wins Battle of Hastings
- 1070 A.D. — Crusades begin

364

ABOUT THE UNIT OPENING

EXAMINING THE ILLUSTRATION

Ask students how old they will be when they are first allowed to vote. Ask how they feel about not being able to vote before then. Tell them the beginning of government on which our democracy is based, took place during the late Middle Ages.

GLOBAL CHRONOLOGY

Ask students to explain what time period the time line covers. *(850 to 1500)* How many years passed between the beginning of feudalism and the development of towns and trade routes? *(150 years)* When did the Hundred Years' War begin? *(1337)* Who were some important people during this time? *(William the Conqueror, Frederick I, Ferdinand and Isabella)*

During the late Middle Ages, from about 1000 to about 1500, many changes took place in western Europe. At first, people were ruled by landowning warrior-nobles, almost everyone lived in farming communities, and there was little trade. The Crusades helped break down feudalism. Trade expanded, towns grew, kings increased their authority, and nations began to develop.

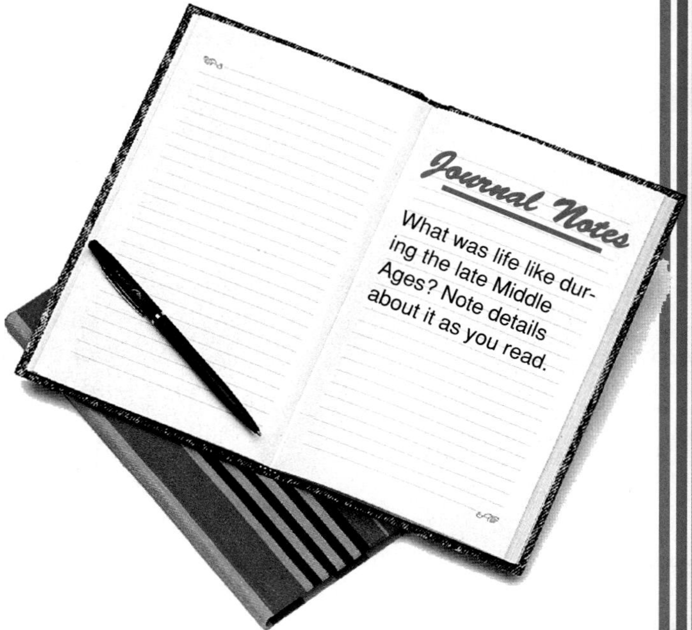

Journal Notes
What was life like during the late Middle Ages? Note details about it as you read.

Hundred Years' War begins — 1337 A.D.

1152 A.D. — Frederick I becomes Holy Roman Emperor

1215 A.D. — Magna Carta is signed

1492 A.D. — Ferdinand and Isabella unite Spain

INTRODUCING THE UNIT

Help students create a list of topics they associate with the Middle Ages such as the Crusades, the Black Death, feudalism, cathedrals, guilds, castles, etc. Ask students what it might have been like in the Middle Ages—exciting, frightening, dangerous, dull. Point out that the late Middle Ages was a time of turbulent change, and that many of the institutions and ideas in existence today had their origins in the late Middle Ages.

RECORDING JOURNAL NOTES

Set aside time for the students to record details about life in the late Middle Ages after reading each chapter in the unit. Have students read their journal entries after each recording.

VIDEODISC

Use the following to enrich Unit 8.

WC O 3 46825
"The Village Fête."

GEOGRAPHIC LOCATION

Have students look at their text Atlas to find the city of Jerusalem. *(located in the present state of Israel)* Have students discuss some of the difficulties an army in the Middle Ages might encounter traveling from Europe to Jerusalem. *(crossing mountains, crossing or going around the Black Sea, or crossing the Mediterranean Sea)*

CHAPTER 24

Feudal Society

CHAPTER ORGANIZER

Objectives	Special Features	Supplemental Materials
Section 1 Land and Government Explain why feudalism developed in western Europe.		• Reproducible Lesson Plan • Section 1 Quiz • Testmaker • Chapter 24 Vocabulary and Guided Reading Activity • The World History Videodisc
Section 2 The Nobility Describe what roles were played by lords and vassals.		• Reproducible Lesson Plan • Section 2 Quiz • Testmaker • Chapter 24 Cooperative Learning Activity • World History and Art Transparency 12 • Foods Around the World • Chapter 24 Teaching Transparencies and Activities
Section 3 Knighthood Discuss what a knight's duties were.		• Reproducible Lesson Plan • Section 3 Quiz • Testmaker • Unit 8 World Literature • Chapter 24 Activity Book Activity
Section 4 The Manor Characterize what life was like on a manor.		• Reproducible Lesson Plan • Section 4 Quiz • Testmaker • Chapter 24 Chart and Graph Skill Activity • Chapter 24 Geography and Map Activity • Outline Resource Maps, pp. 28, 29, 30,
Chapter 24 Review and Evaluation		• Chapter 24 Reteaching Activity • Chapter 24 Enrichment Activity • Spanish Summary and Glossary • Audiocassettes (English and Spanish) • Chapter 24 Performance Assessment Activity • Chapter 24 Test • Testmaker

If time does not permit teaching the entire chapter, use the Chapter 24 Summary on page 378 and the Chapter 24 Audiocassettes (English and Spanish) to point out the main ideas of the chapter.

✓ Performance Assessment Activities

Tapestry Mural Have the students create murals in the fashion of tapestry made during the Middle Ages such as the Bayeux Tapestry. (This tapestry included 72 embroidered scenes depicting the Norman Conquest of England by William I in 1066.) Have them include in the tapestry mural portraits of people from the chapter, including details of their dress and objects that symbolize their station in life. For instance, students might depict a knight in full armor with a shield showing his coat of arms. Display the murals in the classroom.

Daily Life Charts Have students make charts comparing the lives of a lord, a serf, and a monk. Include information about the home, clothing, food, daily activities, and education of each. Encourage interested students to illustrate their charts, also. Display the charts on a bulletin board.

CHAPTER RESOURCES

LITERATURE ABOUT THE PERIOD

Sancha, Sheila. *Walter Dragun's Town.* Harper Collins, 1989. Daily life in a medieval town told through the eyes of a teenage boy.

Scott, Sir Walter. *Ivanhoe.* Longmans, Green, and Co., 1897. Twelfth-century story of hidden identity, intrigue, and romance among the English nobility.

READINGS FOR THE STUDENT

Holme, Bryan. *Medieval Pageant.* Thames & Hudson, 1987. Looks at the pageantry of the Middle Ages, as shown in paintings and illuminated manuscripts reproduced in full color and gold.

McEvedy, Colin. *The New Penguin Atlas of Medieval History.* Penguin, 1992. Details the medieval history of the Mediterranean, Europe, and the nomad steppelands. Details enhanced with 45 maps.

Morgan, Gwyneth. *Life in a Medieval Village* (A Cambridge Topic Book). Lerner Publications, 1982. Interesting details and diagrams showing the everyday life and real people in medieval society.

Unstead, Robert J. *Living in a Castle.* Addison-Wesley, 1973. Description of everyday life in a medieval castle.

READINGS FOR THE TEACHER

Duby, George. *William Marshal: The Flower of Chivalry.* Pantheon, 1985. Chronicles the life of one knight during the time of the Plantagenets in England.

Gies, Frances, and Joseph Gies. *Marriage and the Family in the Middle Ages.* Harper and Row, 1987. Summarizes family history during the medieval period.

Holmes, George, ed. *The Oxford Illustrated History of Medieval Europe.* Account of 1,000 years in western European history from the fall of the Roman Empire through the onset of the Renaissance.

Sancha, Sheila. *The Castle Story.* Crowell, 1982. Covers English castle construction and life.

Turnbull, Stephen. *The Book of the Medieval Knight.* Crown, 1985. Describes knighthood during the late Middle Ages.

MULTIMEDIA RESOURCES

Castle. Social Studies School Services. Video. Tour of 13th-century British castles.

The Middle Ages. Right On Programs. Software, Apple and Pet. Game format covering basic historical facts.

Medieval Europe. Britannica Films. 4 filmstrips. Emphasizes the highly organized life of medieval times.

Medieval Society: The Nobility. Coronet Films. Film. Describes the daily life of the clergy and nobility.

INTRODUCE

CHAPTER 24 OVERVIEW

Chapter 24 discusses the development of feudal society in western Europe after the collapse of Charlemagne's empire.

- **Section 1** describes the origins of feudalism in western Europe.
- **Section 2** discusses the hierarchical structure of feudal society.
- **Section 3** describes the duties of knights in feudal society.
- **Section 4** explains the lifestyles of the people in feudal society and the organization of the manors.

CHAPTER OBJECTIVES

After reading Chapter 24, students will be able to:

1. explain why feudalism developed in western Europe.
2. describe what roles were played by lords and vassals.
3. discuss what a knight's duties were.
4. explain what life was like on a manor.

EXAMINING THE ILLUSTRATION

Ask students to identify details in the painting that tell them about the daily life of these people. Explain that they will learn about the daily activities of all levels of medieval society in this chapter.

PERFORMANCE ASSESSMENT

Use the Performance Assessment Activities on page 366A to help you evaluate your students as they complete the chapter.

CHAPTER 24 Feudal Society

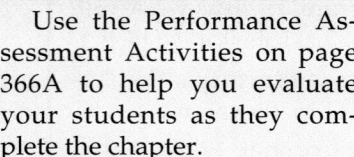

Feudal Estate

366

TEACHER CLASSROOM RESOURCES

- Reproducible Lesson Plan
- Cooperative Learning Activity
- Reteaching Activity
- Enrichment Activity
- Chart and Graph Skill Activity
- Geography and Map Activity
- Vocabulary and Guided Reading Activity
- Activity Book Activity
- Performance Assessment Activity
- Spanish Summary and Glossary
- Audiocassettes (English and Spanish)
- Testmaker
- Teaching Transparencies and Activities
- The World History Videodisc
- World History and Art Transparency

Chapter Focus

READ TO DISCOVER:

- Why feudalism developed in western Europe.
- What roles were played by lords and vassals.
- What a knight's duties were.
- What life was like on a manor.

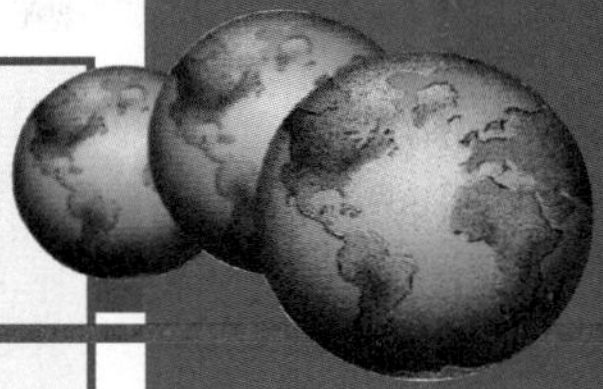

700 A.D.–1200 A.D.

KEY TERMS

feudalism
clergy
vassal
act of homage
knight
castles
code of chivalry
tournaments
joust
manors
seneschal
bailiff

After the Viking attacks, the people of western Europe wanted security and protection. Western Europe, however, had no central government to keep the peace. Real power had passed from kings to local lords. To protect their property, the nobles raised their own armies. They also developed **feudalism** (fyū′ dl iz uhm), or government by landowning nobles.

Under feudalism, the people of western Europe were divided into groups. One group was the **clergy** (kler′ jē), or religious leaders. Their duty was to teach Christianity and to help the poor and the sick. A second group was the nobles. Their duty was to govern, enforce laws, and protect the people. The third group included the peasants and townspeople. Their duty was to support the clergy and nobles by farming the land and providing services.

Section 1

LAND AND GOVERNMENT

During feudal times, power was based on the ownership of land. Before feudalism, kings owned all the land within their territories. Then Charles Martel the Frankish leader began giving his soldiers **fiefs** (fēfs), or estates, as a reward for their service and loyalty. From their fiefs, the soldiers got the income they needed to buy horses and battle equipment. After 800, the kings of Europe followed Martel's example. From that time on, land ownership was tied to military service. With land ownership went power and wealth, giving soldiers a base from which to rule Europe.

367

FOCUS

BELLRINGER

Ask students to write a one-sentence description of the following: a knight, a squire, a page, a noblewoman, and a serf.

MOTIVATIONAL ACTIVITY

Have students read their sentences describing a knight, a squire, a page, a noblewoman, and a serf. Discuss the misconceptions they might have about people and everyday life in the Middle Ages. Then tell students that they will learn about the lives of these people in this chapter.

VOCABULARY PRE-CHECK

Write the key terms for this chapter on the chalkboard. Ask students to use those that they know in sentences.

Assign Chapter 24 **Vocabulary and Guided Reading Activity** in the TCR.

EXTRA CREDIT PROJECT

Explain to students that once knights began to wear helmets, it was impossible to tell one knight from another. To identify themselves, knights had individual designs, called coats of arms, painted on their shields. These designs revealed their family and heritage. Have students design a coat of arms to identify themselves.

KEY TO ABILITY LEVELS

Teaching strategies have been coded for varying learning styles and abilities.

L1 Level 1 activities are **basic** activities and should be within the ability range of all students.

L2 Level 2 activities are **average** activities and should be within the ability range of the average to above-average student.

L3 Level 3 activities are **challenging** activities designed for the ability range of above-average students.

LEP LEP activities should be within the ability range of Limited English Proficiency students.

TEACH

GUIDED PRACTICE

L1 **Daily Life** Draw a simple figure to represent the human body on the chalkboard and label its parts as you explain the following comparison made by one medieval scholar who compared feudal society to the human body. He saw: priests and clerks, as spiritual guides, or the head and eyes; nobles, as protectors and defenders, or the arms and hands; and peasants, the workers on whose labor all society was based, as the legs and feet. LEP

L2 **Critical Thinking** Ask: *Was feudalism an effective system of government? Why or why not?* Have students write a list of recommendations of changes they would submit to improve government.

DID YOU KNOW ??

The basic philosophy of feudalism was that the man on horseback was a natural leader. Physical strength was considered intrinsically good, and it was only right that the stronger should rule the weaker.

VIDEODISC

Use the following to enrich Chapter 24.

WC C 88 14690

Medieval hierarchy: monk, knight, and peasant.

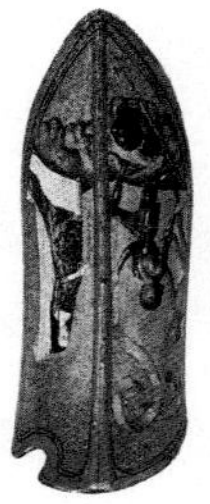

Feudal Shield

The Rise of Feudal Territories After Charlemagne's death in 814, Europe had no central government. The kings who followed Charlemagne were so weak they could not even rule their own kingdoms well. They ignored their responsibilities and spent most of their time traveling from one royal estate to another. Before long, they began to depend on the nobles for food, horses, and soldiers. Some nobles grew more powerful than the king and became independent rulers. They gained the right to collect taxes and to enforce the law in their areas. Many nobles raised armies and coined their own money.

Around 900, the nobles took on the duty of protecting their lands and people from the Vikings. They built fortresses on hilltops and fenced their lands. The peasants asked these powerful nobles to protect them. In return, the peasants gave their lands to nobles and promised to work for them in the fields. However, most peasants ended up giving the nobles not only their land but also their freedom.

By 1000, the kingdoms of western Europe were divided into thousands of feudal territories. Each was about the size of an ancient Greek city-state. Unlike the polis, however, a feudal territory had no central city. The noble who owned the land also had the political power. He made the laws for his fief, and the people obeyed them. Peasants, unlike Greek citizens, had no say in the government.

Although the peasants and townspeople made up the largest group, they had fewer rights than the clergy and nobles. Almost everyone believed that God wanted it that way. As a result, few people tried to improve society or change their own way of life. Most people remained in the group into which they were born.

Painting of an Act of Homage

Lord and Vassal Feudalism was based on ties of loyalty and duty among nobles. Nobles were both lords and vassals. A **vassal** (vas' uhl) was a noble who served a lord of higher rank and gave him loyalty. In return, the lord protected the vassal. All nobles were ultimately vassals of the king, who might even be the vassal of another king.

The tie between lord and vassal was made official in a special ceremony known as the **act of homage** (om' ij). The vassal, his head bare to show respect, knelt on one knee and placed his hands between those of the lord. He promised to serve the lord and to help him in battle. The lord accepted the promise, helped the vassal to his feet, and kissed him.

In return for the promise of loyalty and service, the lord gave his vassal a fief. Since there were few written agreements in the Middle Ages, the lord gave his vassal a glove, a stick, or a stone. This was to show that the lord's word could be trusted. He also gave the vassal the right to govern the people who lived on the

EXTENDING THE CONTENT

The basic structure of feudalism looks like a simple pyramid, but in fact sometimes grew very complicated. Many lords, of course, simply had peasants or very minor knights as their vassals. On the other hand, in the higher ranks of feudalism, lords and vassals often were social equals. Even a poor knight with a rundown manor house might come from a family as proud as that of his overlord. At several times in history, the kings of England were vassals of the kings of France for territories such as Anjou and Aquitaine.

fief. The lord promised to protect his vassal from enemy attacks. If the lord failed in this, the vassal no longer owed him loyalty.

Vassals had certain duties to perform. Their most important duty was to help the lord in battle. Vassals had to bring their own knights with them. They themselves were expected to take part in military service 40 to 60 days a year.

Vassals had to make payments to their lord. When a lord's daughter married, or his son became a **knight,** or warrior on horseback, his vassals had to give the lord money. If a lord were captured in battle, his vassals either became prisoners in his place or paid his *ransom.* This is a sum of money given in exchange for a person's release.

Another duty of vassals was to attend the lord's court. Vassals were also expected to provide food and entertainment when their lord visited them. If a vassal failed in his duties to his lord, the lord had the right to take away the vassal's fief. When a vassal died, his fief usually passed on to his oldest son. The son then performed the act of homage.

Painting of Peasant Farmer

Section 1 Review

1. **Define:** feudalism, clergy, fiefs, vassal, act of homage, knight
2. How did land ownership become tied to military service?
3. How did nobles become so powerful?
4. What were some duties of a vassal?

Critical Thinking

5. What do you think were the advantages of being a vassal? The disadvantages?

Section 2

The Nobility

Life was not always easy or pleasant for nobles during feudal times. They did, however, enjoy more benefits than the common people.

From the 800s to the 1000s, nobles and their families lived in wooden houses surrounded by *palisades* (pal uh sāds'), or high wooden fences built for protection. In case of attack, people from nearby villages sought shelter inside the palisade.

The house consisted of one room with a high ceiling and a straw-covered floor. All activity took place in that one room. There, nobles met with vassals, carried out the laws, and said their prayers. The nobles, their families, servants, and warriors

Photograph of Feudal Fortress

L2 **Culture** Have students explain the importance of cooperation and interdependency among kings, lords, vassals, knights, and peasants in maintaining the feudal society. Suggest they devise their own graphic organizer to show these relationships.

L1 **Critical Thinking** Ask students to create lists of the responsibilities of lords and vassals. Then create two columns on the chalkboard headed, "Lords" and "Vassals." Have students write their ideas in the appropriate column. Then ask students to explain why the relationship between the lords and vassals developed and whether they think it was a fair one. LEP

MAKING CONNECTIONS

➤➤ **History** The ties between lord and vassal could be confusing because a vassal could owe loyalty to several lords at once in times of war. In such cases, the vassal chose one lord to whom he was the most loyal. Some vassals simply supported the side most likely to win.

DID YOU KNOW ??

In the Middle Ages, the castle's main meal was served at 10:00 in the morning. King Richard II of England was renowned for the meals he served at court. He was said to sometimes dine with 10,000 guests fed by 300 cooks.

SECTION 1 ANSWERS

1. feudalism, government by land-owning nobles (p. 367); clergy, religious leaders (p. 367); fiefs, estates (p. 367); vassal, a noble who served a lord (p. 368); act of homage, ceremony tying a lord and his vassal (p. 368); knight, warrior on horseback (p. 369)
2. Fiefs were given to soldiers as a reward.
3. Kings depended on nobles for food, horses, soldiers, and taxes.
4. to serve the lord in battle, make payments to the lord, become a prisoner in his place or pay his ransom, and entertain him when the lord visited him
5. Answers will vary. Advantages might include that the vassal was protected from enemies and gained land. Disadvantages might include that the vassal's life was completely tied to the lord.

Assign the Chapter 24 **Section 1 Quiz** in the TCR. Testmaker available.

L2 **Daily Life** Ask students to imagine they are cooks during the Middle Ages. Tell them that they are to prepare a banquet for the king and his court. What foods would they serve? How would they be cooked? Encourage students to research the menu of such a meal and share their research with the class.

CAPTION ANSWER

Wooden tables were set up in the castle's main room where all people gathered.

VIDEODISC

Use the following to enrich Chapter 24.

WC C 91 14693

A medieval dinner scene.

NOBLE'S FEAST Nobles celebrated special occasions with elaborate feasts. Such meals often included many courses of meats, fruits, and vegetables. In this painting a noble sits down to dinner while his many servants bring out more food. **Where were meals for nobles held?**

also ate and slept in that room. At mealtime, wooden tables were set up and piled high with meat, fish, vegetables, fruits, and honey. People ate with their fingers and threw scraps of food on the floor for the dogs. The straw got so dirty with mud, bones, and food that every few months it had to be swept outdoors and burned.

The fires that cooked the meals were also used to heat the house. Actually, the fires did little to keep out the cold. Smoke from them often stung the eyes and darkened the walls and ceiling.

The Castle By the 1100s, nobles were living in stone houses called **castles.** Because they were designed as fortresses, the castles made nobles secure and independent. Castles had thick stone walls, one within another. Each corner had its own lookout tower with archers in it. Some castles were further protected by a moat with a soft and muddy bottom that stopped attackers from using ladders to climb over the outer walls. To cross the moat, a

MULTICULTURAL PERSPECTIVES

During the Middle Ages, several books on courtesy were written to teach the nobility table manners. Since fingers were used to transport food from large platters to individual trenchers, and from there to one's mouth, the cleanliness of one's fingers was a matter of concern for all the diners. One author wrote, "Thou must not put thy fingers into thine ears." Other writers asked their readers not to blow their noses with their fingers or scratch their heads, especially since fleas and lice were common.

person had to use the castle's drawbridge, which could be raised to prevent entry. The drawbridge led to the *portcullis* (pōrt kul' is), an iron gate that often served as the entrance to the castle.

Within the castle walls was a large open area. In the middle of this area was a **keep,** or tall tower with thick walls. It contained a great hall, many rooms, and a dungeon. The people of the household lived in the keep, which could be defended even if the rest of the castle fell to attackers. Shops, kitchens, stables, and rooms for troops and guests were also built inside the castle walls.

Many people, including the noble's servants and officials, lived in the castle. Since the noble was away fighting most of the time, the servants and officials were responsible for the castle's care and defense. Most castles had enough space to store a large supply of food and drink. As a result, people inside a castle could hold out against attackers for as long as six months.

CASTLE A castle was both a noble's home and a military fortress. During enemy attack, people from the surrounding area sought protection within the castle walls. Here, the moat and entrance of an English castle are shown. **Who was responsible for a castle's care and defense?**

DID YOU KNOW ??

Early stone castles had square towers that were easily damaged by large siege-cannons. The towers were later rounded off so they could withstand a direct hit from the cannons.

CAPTION ANSWER

servants and officials

GEOGRAPHY AND HISTORY

Castles were often built on top of hills or mounds so sentries could easily spot attackers. Castles had their own wells so that defenders would have water if the castle came under attack.

VIDEODISC

Use the following to enrich Chapter 24.

WC C 105 14707
Caernarvon Castle, Wales.

WC C 107 14709
Bodiam Castle, Sussex.

COOPERATIVE LEARNING

Have the class work in small groups to create plans for a medieval castle like the one described in this section. Refer to David Macaulay's book *Castle* and the videocassette that accompanies it. Tasks may be divided in several ways: researching medieval architecture, organizing data, writing plans, and illustrating the finished design by blueprint and sketch on poster board. Another group can present the finished project, describing various aspects of the castle and explaining the rationale.

L3 **Critical Thinking** Ask students why they think chess was a favorite game in the Middle Ages. Then ask them how the game pieces relate to feudal society. Students may wish to research the history of chess and present an oral report to the class.

MAKING CONNECTIONS

➤➤**The Arts** Many ladies of the Middle Ages could read and were interested in music and poetry. They also spent time riding, hunting, and doing hard exercise.

CAPTION ANSWER

by 12 years old

DID YOU KNOW ??

Some knights attacked and robbed passersby, especially traveling merchants, and raided their neighbors' lands for sheep and cattle.

Castle Life When nobles were at home, they looked after their estates, went hunting and fishing, and held court. During long winter evenings, they often played chess with family members. Wandering minstrels sometimes came to entertain the nobles and their guests by singing songs and playing stringed instruments.

Noblewomen were called **ladies.** Once they married, their husbands had complete authority over them. Most marriages were planned to unite important families, and a woman had little say about who was chosen for her. The bride's family gave the groom a dowry. Most nobles looked for wives with large dowries. Women were often married by the time they were 12 years old. Those who were not married by the time they were 21 could expect to stay single for the rest of their lives.

Wives helped their husbands run their estates. When the men were away, the women had to defend the castle. The main duties of a wife, however, were to have and raise children and to

CASTLE LIFE Women played an important part in the running of a feudal estate. Women in this painting are shown defending a castle against an attack (left). Other duties, such as weaving silk cloth (right), were more commonplace. **By what age were women often married during feudal times?**

SPOTLIGHT ON: NOBLEWOMEN

The noblewoman was technically under her husband's control, although she could exert power both inside and outside of the castle. If her dowry included lands and manors or abbeys, they remained under her control. When the lord was away or at war—sometimes a matter of many years—the lady was in charge of the castle. If necessary, she organized its defenses. Some women actually led the castle troops into battle.

take care of the household. She was also expected to train young girls from other castles in household duties and to supervise the making of cloth and fine embroidery. Another duty was to use her knowledge of plants and herbs to care for the poor and sick on her husband's fief.

Photo of Castle Gate

Section 2 Review

1. **Define:** castles, keep, ladies
2. What activities took place in the noble's house?
3. How did a castle protect people?
4. What were the duties of a feudal noblewoman?

Critical Thinking

5. What parts of castle life would you have liked? What parts would you have disliked?

Section 3

KNIGHTHOOD

Almost all nobles were knights. However, knighthood had to be earned. Knights were expected to follow certain rules known as the **code of chivalry** (kōd of shiv' uhl rē). These rules stated that a knight was to obey his lord, show bravery, respect women of noble birth, honor the Church, and help people. A knight was also expected to be honest and to fight fairly against his enemies. The code of chivalry became the guide to behavior from which the western idea of good manners developed.

Training A noble began training to be a knight when he was seven years old. He was sent away from his family to the castle of another lord. There, he learned to be a **page,** or a person who helped the knights of the castle care for their *destriers* (dā trē' uhrs), or war-horses. Pages also polished the knights' armor, some of which weighed up to 80 pounds, or 36 kilograms.

A page learned good manners and ran errands for the ladies. He was taught to ride and fight. By the age of 14, he could handle a lance and sword while on horseback.

When he was 15 years old, a page became a **squire.** Each squire was put under the care and training of one knight. The squire's duty was to go into battle with his knight. He was expected to rescue the knight if he was wounded or fell off his horse.

If the squire proved to be a good fighter, he was rewarded by being made a knight. This was done in a special ceremony

Painting of Mounted Knight

L3 **Language Arts** Have students read one of the following selections and present an oral report to the class: *Ivanhoe* by Sir Walter Scott, the Arthur legends (several appropriate translations and editions exist), *A Medieval Castle* by Fiona Macdonald (Peter Bedrick, 1990), or *Arms and Armor of the Medieval Knight* (Crescent/Crown, 1988).

MAKING CONNECTIONS

➤➤ **Daily Life** Books of etiquette with instructions for the behavior of children were common during this period. A book of medieval conduct called *Babees Book* details the rules of conduct for a page: *When you enter your lord's place, say "God Speed" and with humble cheer greet all who are there present. Do not rush in rudely, but enter with head up and at an easy pace and kneel on only one knee only to your lord. . . . Make obeisance* [bow with obedience] *to your lord always when you answer, otherwise stand still as a stone unless he speaks.*

VIDEODISC

Use the following to enrich Chapter 24.

WC C 116 14718

Jousting: Nicholas Clifford vs. John Boucmel.

SECTION 2 ANSWERS

1. castles, stone houses of nobles (p. 370); keep, tall tower (p. 371); ladies, noblewomen (p. 372)
2. Nobles met with vassals, carried out laws, and said their prayers; people slept there; meals were cooked there and people ate there.
3. It had thick stone walls, one within another, and each corner had its own lookout tower with archers in it. Some castles had a moat, drawbridge, and portcullis and a keep, which could be defended if the rest of the castle fell.
4. She helped her husband run their estates, defended the castle when the men were away, raised children, took care of the household, supervised sewing, and cared for the poor and sick.
5. Answers will vary, but students should provide specific examples of castle life.

Assign the Chapter 24 **Section 2 Quiz** in the TCR. Testmaker available.

L1 **Language Arts** Divide students into teams of two. Have each team write an interview between a squire and a knight on how nobles achieved knighthood and what a knight's duties were. Then have each team read the dialogue to the rest of the class, with one student playing the role of the knight and the other, the role of the squire. Ask students to critique the interviews.

CAPTION ANSWER

because men and horses might be killed, equipment damaged, and all the people who attended had to be fed

DID YOU KNOW ??

There were two types of medieval jousts. One was held for pleasure or exercise, and the knights used lances with blunt tips and swords that were not pointed. The other was a fight to the death in which sharp weapons were used. The arms of a defeated man belonged to the victor and could be ransomed for money. Because of this, tournaments were a way for poor but powerful fighters to earn a living.

VIDEODISC

Use the following to enrich Chapter 24.

WC C 117 14719

A medieval tournament.

MEDIEVAL TOURNAMENT In this painting knights on horseback joust during a tournament. Even the king is attending this match. **Why were medieval tournaments costly events?**

known as **dubbing.** The squire knelt before his lord with his sword suspended from his neck. He then promised to defend the Church, his lord, and to protect the weak. Then, the lord tapped the squire on his shoulder with the blade of a sword and pronounced him a knight. The knight's sword was placed in a *scabbard,* or sword holder, at the knight's side. This showed that the knight would fight by the side of his lord.

Tournaments Knights trained for war by fighting each other in **tournaments,** or special contests that test strength, skill, and endurance. Tournaments were held in large fields. They were exciting gatherings that brought in lords, ladies, and knights who watched the events from stands. The most popular event was the **joust** (jowst). Two armored knights on horseback carrying dull lances galloped towards each other from opposite ends of the field. Each tried with all his strength and skill to knock the other to the ground with his lance.

The cost of tournaments was high. Men and horses were killed and wounded. Lances, swords, and suits of armor were damaged. The noble who gave the tournament had to feed hundreds of people. In spite of the cost, however, tournaments remained popular. In fact, it was believed that a knight who had not learned to fight in one could not fight well in battle.

MEETING SPECIAL NEEDS

Have tactile/kinesthetic or gifted learners research the styles of armor worn by knights in the various regions of western Europe. Then have students make armor and model it or draw pictures of its various styles and designs. Students may wish to write a report explaining their findings.

Section 3 Review

1. **Define:** code of chivalry, page, squire, dubbing, tournament, joust
2. How did a squire become a knight?
3. What was the purpose of tournaments?

Critical Thinking

4. How were tournaments similar to the Olympic Games in ancient Greece? How were they different?

Section 4

THE MANOR

Nobles, knights, and peasants all depended on the land for everything they needed. The land was divided into **manors,** or farming communities. Manors were found on fiefs and were owned by nobles.

Daily Life The noble chose a number of officials to run his manor. They were loyal to the noble and made sure his orders were carried out. One official was the **seneschal** (sen' uh shuhl).

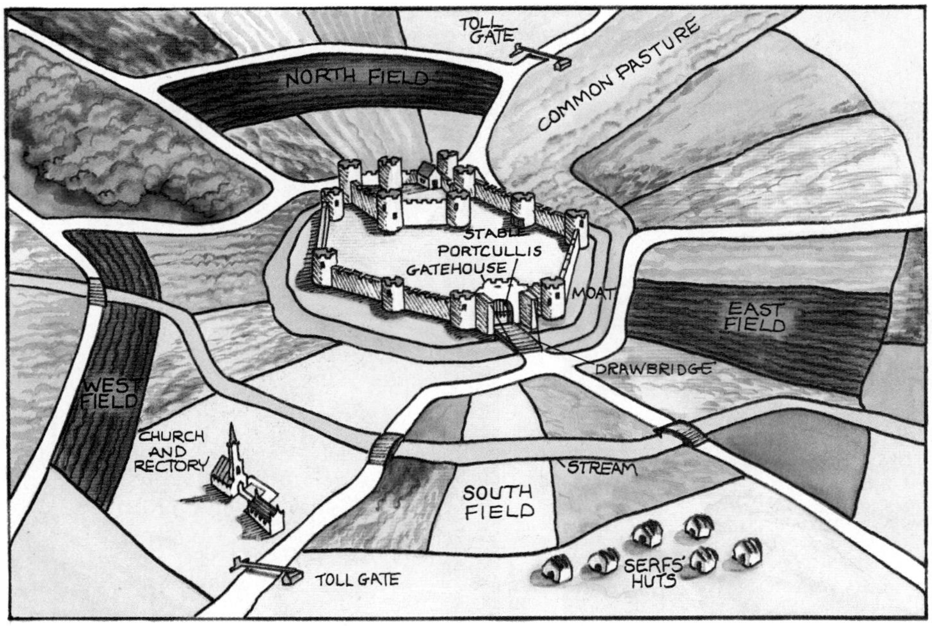

INDEPENDENT PRACTICE

L3 **Science** There were many diseases and medical problems during the Middle Ages. Ask students to research and present information about the following to the class: Who would treat peasants' diseases? Who did a king go to for medical problems? What kinds of treatments were commonly used?

MAKING CONNECTIONS

➤➤ **History** Manors formed the basis of the medieval agricultural system known as manorialism. While feudalism involved ties among nobles, manorialism concerned agreements between the nobles and peasants.

VIDEODISC

Use the following to enrich Chapter 24.

WC C 89 14691
Life on a medieval manor.

WC O 2 46824
Harvesting wheat with a sickle.

SECTION 3 ANSWERS

1. code of chivalry, rules for knights (p. 373); page, person who helped the knights (p. 373); squire, second step in becoming a knight (p. 373); dubbing, ceremony in which a squire became a knight (p. 373); tournament, contests for knights (p. 374); joust, an event in a tournament (p. 374)
2. He helped the knights care for their warhorses, cleaned and polished the armor, learned good manners, ran errands for the ladies, and was taught to ride and fight.
3. to train knights for war
4. Like the Olympics, the tournaments had many events watched by many people outside. The tournaments were designed to prepare knights for war. The Olympic Games, however, were held to honor the gods. Unlike the Olympic Games, women were allowed to view the tournaments.

Assign the Chapter 24 **Section 3 Quiz** in the TCR. Testmaker available.

L3 **Daily Life** Have students research the roles of women from different classes (nobility, clergy, common people, merchants). Have them report on what they discover and include a comparison of the roles, goals, and beliefs of medieval women with those of women today.

DID YOU KNOW ??

The roofs of the cottages were thatched with bundles of straw fastened on a wood frame. The thick thatch kept the cottage warm in winter and cool in summer.

CAPTION ANSWER

whatever the noble asked of them in maintaining the manor

VIDEODISC

Use the following to enrich Chapter 24.

WC C 93 14695

A medieval dance, the Carole.

He looked after the noble's fiefs by visiting each fief regularly. Another official was the **bailiff** (bā' lif). He made sure the peasants worked hard in the fields. Every manor had its own court of law. The court settled differences, gave out fines and punishments, and discussed manor business.

Poor transportation and frequent fighting isolated manors from one another. The men and women of each manor produced food, clothing, and shelter for themselves and the noble. They raised sheep for wool and cattle for meat and milk. They also grew grain and vegetables, made cloth, built homes, and fashioned tools.

The noble of each manor lived in a wooden house or a castle. Nearby stood a small village of cottages in which the peasants lived. Most villages also had a church, a mill, a bread oven, and a wine press. Around the village were forests, meadows, pastures, and fields.

The cottages were crowded around an open area called the village green. They were made of wood and earth and had thatched roofs. Most had only one room. At night, family members slept there on piles of straw or on the dirt floor. Three-legged stools and a table were the only furniture. Diseases and fleas from the animals that also slept in the cottage often sickened the people.

PEASANTS AT WORK Peasants spent long hours working in the fields of a manor. In this painting, a group of peasants is shown mowing and binding sheaves of wheat (left). Another group of peasants is shown shearing sheep (right). **What other work did the peasants do?**

MULTICULTURAL PERSPECTIVES

Commercial fairs served as centers of trade for medieval Europe. These fairs were great annual events that attracted merchants from all over Europe, and brought many people from different cultures together.

PEASANT CELEBRATION Although peasants' lives were mostly long hours of hard work, there were times for celebration. Peasants celebrated special occasions with music, dancing, and feasting. Here, the festivities at a peasant wedding are shown. **What sports did peasants enjoy?**

Freemen and Serfs Two groups of peasants worked on a manor. One was the **freemen,** or peasants who paid the noble for the right to farm land. They worked only on their own strips of land and had rights under the law. They moved wherever and whenever they wished. The noble, however, had the right to throw them off the manor without warning.

The other group was the serfs. Serfs and their descendants were a noble's property. They could not move to another area, own their own property, or marry without the noble's permission. Serfs, however, could not be driven off the land and did not have to serve in the army.

It was not easy for serfs to gain their freedom. One way was to escape to the towns. If a serf was not caught and remained in town for more than a year, he or she was considered free. By the end of the Middle Ages, serfs were allowed to buy their freedom.

As in Charlemagne's time, the serfs worked long hours in the fields and performed many services for the nobles. Serfs spent three days of the week working the lord's strips of land and the rest of the week caring for their own strips. However, they had to give part of their own crops to the noble. They also paid him for the use of the village's mill, bread oven, and wine press.

In spite of the difficulties, a serf's life had some bright moments. Sunday was a day of rest from work. At Christmas, the

CAPTION ANSWER

wrestling, archery, soccer

GEOGRAPHY AND HISTORY

In the three-field system of planting, one field might be planted with winter wheat, a second with spring wheat and vegetables, and a third left fallow. The next year, different crops were planted in the fallow field. One of the two remaining fields was planted and the other one was left fallow until the next year.

LINKING PAST TO PRESENT

A serf and his family could be sold as part of the property on which they lived and worked. This made the serf different from an enslaved person, whose family could be sold separately to anyone. The idea of enslavement, originally started by Greeks and Romans, prepared people's minds for the eventual enslavement of other peoples, such as Africans, when Europe later expanded its empires.

EXTENDING THE CONTENT

Peasant meals varied from country to country, just as basic cuisines do today. Bread—whole wheat, rye, or barley—was basic, along with several kinds of pasta in Italy. Porridges and oatmeal made of grain with peas or beans were common everywhere. In France, peasants ate hearty soups, stews, and vegetables and drank wine or cider. They grew apples and grapes and stored them over the winter by drying or cooking them in honey. The English had several kinds of cheese and curds. They made ale, cider, and mead—a fermented honey drink. Germans made lentils, sauerkraut, cabbage, peas, and turnips.

VIDEODISC

Use the following to enrich Chapter 24.

WC C 104 14706

A medieval marriage ceremony.

ASSESS

CHECK FOR UNDERSTANDING

Ask students to summarize the main points of the chapter, orally or in writing. Discuss the answers to the Section and Chapter Review questions.

EVALUATE

Assign the Chapter 24 **Performance Assessment Activity** in the TCR. Administer the **Chapter 24 Test.** Testmaker available.

RETEACH

Divide the class into small groups. Have each group summarize a particular part of the chapter.

Assign the Chapter 24 **Reteaching Activity** in the TCR.

ENRICH

Have students research the kinds of "mystery plays" that serfs attended for amusement. Students may perform a skit similar to one of the plays.

Assign the Chapter 24 **Enrichment Activity** in the TCR.

CLOSE

Ask students to share their opinions of people in the Middle Ages. If students had to travel back in time to medieval England, what kind of life would they choose? Why?

MEETING CHAPTER OBJECTIVES

Each objective is tested by the Review questions in parentheses.

1. Explain why feudalism developed in western Europe. (BV; CU 1, 2)

2. Describe what roles were played by lords and vassals. (BV; CU 3; CT 1)

3. Discuss what a knight's duties were. (BV; CU 4; CT 3)

4. Explain life on a manor. (BV; CU 6; CT 2; UYJ)

lord paid for a great feast and entertainment. Certain holidays were celebrated with singing and dancing on the village green. When they could, serfs took part in such sports as wrestling, archery, and soccer.

By the 1200s, peasants began to learn better farming methods. They used the three-field system of farming and started to use a heavy iron plow. The horse collar was invented, allowing horses instead of slow-moving oxen to plow fields. All of this enabled the peasants to grow more food.

Section 4 Review

1. **Define:** manors, seneschal, bailiff, freemen
2. What were some features of a manor village?
3. What rights did freemen have?
4. What did serfs contribute to a manor?

Critical Thinking

5. What interests did nobles and serfs have in common?

Chapter Summary

1. Charles Martel tied land ownership to military service when he gave his soldiers fiefs.
2. Following Charlemagne's rule, kings began to depend on nobles for food, horses, and soldiers.
3. Some nobles grew more powerful than the king, and they began to collect their own taxes, run their own courts, raise their own armies, and coin their own money.
4. The nobles agreed to protect people from Viking attacks in exchange for land and labor.
5. By 1000, the kingdoms of western Europe were divided into thousands of feudal territories.
6. Lords gave their vassals land in exchange for loyalty and military service.
7. Nobles lived in wooden houses until the 1100s, when stone castles were built.
8. Young nobles spent eight or nine years training to become knights.
9. Knights followed rules of behavior known as the code of chivalry.
10. Knights trained for war by fighting in tournaments.
11. Land was divided into manors owned by nobles and worked by peasants.
12. There were two groups of peasants on a manor—freemen and serfs.
13. Freemen could come and go as they wished, while serfs were considered a noble's property.
14. By the 1200s, changes were taking place in peasant life.

SECTION 4 ANSWERS

1. manors, farming communities (p. 375); seneschal, overseer of a noble's fief (p. 375); bailiff, official who supervised peasants (p. 376); freemen, peasants who paid for the right to farm land (p. 377)

2. It was made up of peasant cottages and was surrounded by forests, meadows, pastures, and fields. Most had a church, mill, bread oven, and wine press.

3. to move wherever and whenever they wished

4. They worked long hours in the fields, obeyed nobles' wishes, and had to give the noble part of their crops.

5. Answers will vary but might include that nobles and serfs had the land in common. Without the serfs, the land was useless to the noble. Without the noble's protection from enemies, the serfs could not survive.

Assign the Chapter 24 **Section 4 Quiz** in the TCR. Testmaker available.

CHAPTER

Review 24

Building Vocabulary

Imagine you are living in the late Middle Ages. Write an interview with a noble and a serf in which they describe their lives. Use the following words in your interview.

feudalism	code of chivalry
clergy	tournaments
vassal	joust
act of homage	manors
knight	seneschal
castles	bailiff

Check for Understanding

1. Into what three groups were people divided under feudalism?
2. Who held the political power within a feudal territory?
3. Who usually received a vassal's fief when the vassal died?
4. What was expected of a knight?
5. Why was it necessary for the people on a manor to produce everything they needed?
6. In what two ways could serfs obtain their freedom?
7. What changes had taken place in farming by the 1200s?

Critical Thinking

1. What advantages would there be to being a vassal rather than a lord?
2. Why do you think women provided the medical care in a fief?
3. What would you have enjoyed about being a knight? What would you have disliked?
4. How do you think a serf's life would be affected by improved farming methods?

Geography in History

HUMAN/ENVIRONMENTAL INTERACTION The people of the manor made good use of their natural resources to support themselves. Predict and describe how you think manor life would have changed if disease had gone through the area killing all the trees.

Using Your Journal

Compare the details you have noted about the lives of women in the late Middle Ages with the lives of women today. Write a paragraph explaining the similarities and differences as if you were explaining them to someone who lived on a European manor.

379

✚ BONUS ✚

TEST QUESTION

For Chapter 24 Test

Identify the liar in the following exchange between two nobles. Noble 1. "The king gave this manor to my mother. Here is the paper to prove it." Noble 2. "This is my land. I served the king in battle, was held hostage in his place, and he awarded it to me." *(Noble 1 is the liar. Land (fief) was awarded to men. Also, it is unlikely there would be a written agreement.)*

USING YOUR JOURNAL

Paragraphs will vary but may include issues of basic human freedoms. You might ask volunteers to read their paragraphs to the class.

CHAPTER 24 REVIEW ANSWERS

BUILDING VOCABULARY

Interviews will vary, but students should use all the vocabulary words.

CHECK FOR UNDERSTANDING

1. the clergy, the nobles, and the peasants and townspeople
2. the noble who owned the land
3. his oldest son
4. to follow the code of chivalry
5. because the manors were isolated from one another
6. by escaping to the towns for more than a year or by buying their freedom
7. Peasants began to learn better farming methods, used the heavy iron plow, and used horses instead of slow-moving oxen to plow their fields.

CRITICAL THINKING

1. Answers will vary but should include that vassals had fewer responsibilities, received a fief, and had the protection of a noble.
2. Answers will vary but might include that she was usually there, and medical care was considered a domestic concern.
3. Answers will vary but students should give some specific examples.
4. Answers will vary, but might include that serfs would have more time for themselves. With more food grown, they would be healthier.

GEOGRAPHY IN HISTORY

Answers will vary but should reflect the uses of wood in the lives of serfs and the impact of the loss of trees. Students may also suggest other plants may be affected by the same disease.

PLANNING GUIDE

CHAPTER 25 The Church

CHAPTER ORGANIZER

Objectives	Special Features	Supplemental Materials
Section 1 Catholic Influence Discuss how the Roman Catholic Church influenced life during the Middle Ages.		• Reproducible Lesson Plan • Section 1 Quiz • Testmaker • Chapter 25 Vocabulary and Guided Reading Activity • The World History Videodisc
Section 2 Attempts at Reform Summarize what attempts were made to reform the Church during the Middle Ages.		• Reproducible Lesson Plan • Section 2 Quiz • Testmaker • The World History Videodisc • Chapter 25 Teaching Transparencies and Activities
Section 3 Learning Describe what learning was like during the Middle Ages.		• Reproducible Lesson Plan • Section 3 Quiz • Testmaker • Chapter 25 Cooperative Learning Activity • The World History Videodisc
Section 4 The Crusades Explain why the Crusades took place during the Middle Ages and what the effects of the Crusades were.	People in History: *Eleanor of Aquitaine,* p. 390; Map and Geography Skills: *Determining Exact Location,* p. 394	• Reproducible Lesson Plan • Section 4 Quiz • Testmaker • Chapter 25 Chart and Graph Skill Activity • Chapter 25 Geography and Map Activity • The World History Videodisc
Chapter 25 Review and Evaluation		• Chapter 25 Reteaching Activity • Chapter 25 Enrichment Activity • Spanish Summary and Glossary • Audiocassettes (English and Spanish) • Chapter 25 Performance Assessment Activity • Chapter 25 Test • Testmaker

If time does not permit teaching the entire chapter, use the Chapter 25 Summary on page 396 and the Chapter 25 Audiocassettes (English and Spanish) to point out the main ideas of the chapter.

✓ PERFORMANCE ASSESSMENT ACTIVITIES

Crusading Have students imagine they are a member of the Children's Crusade. Before they leave they must collect supplies, map out their route, and generally organize their crusade. Tell students to each prepare these trip materials: a list of what they will take with them, and a map showing their planned route. Have students share their plans with the rest of the class.

Research During the Middle Ages, for the first time family names came into widespread use in Europe. Have students research and present a report on the origin and development of the following names: Bridges, Fletcher, Ford, Masterson, Smith, Taylor, or other English names they choose from their reading.

CHAPTER RESOURCES

LITERATURE ABOUT THE PERIOD

Konisburg, E. L. *A Proud Taste for Scarlet and Miniver.* Atheneum, 1973. A biography of Eleanor of Aquitaine.

O'Dell, Scott. *The Road to Damietta.* Houghton Mifflin, 1985. Novel about Francis of Assisi, as seen through the eyes of a friend.

READINGS FOR THE STUDENT

Boyd, Anne. *Life in a 15th-Century Monastery* (A Cambridge Topic Book). Lerner Publications, 1979. An account of the daily life of monks in the monastery at Durham, England.

Macaulay, David. *Cathedral.* Houghton Mifflin, 1973. The building of a medieval cathedral, with detailed drawings and descriptions of the people who took part.

Suskind, Richard. *Cross and Crescent: The Story of the Crusades.* W. W. Norton, 1967. An account of knights and battles.

READINGS FOR THE TEACHER

Chadwick, Henry, and G. R. Evans, eds. *Atlas of the Christian Church.* Facts on File, 1987. An authoritative survey of Christian traditions and the impact of the Christian Church on the development of Western civilization.

Gies, Frances, and Joseph Gies. *Women in the Middle Ages: The Lives of Real Women in a Vibrant Age of Transition.* Barnes and Noble, 1978. Highlights women's lives in the Middle Ages.

Lyons, Malcolm, and David Jackson. *Saladin: The Politics of the Holy War.* Cambridge University Press, 1982. Historical account of the famous Islamic leader Saladin and his role in the Crusades.

MULTIMEDIA RESOURCES

The Crusades. EAV/SSSS. Video. Examines the cultural differences, religious conflicts, and political strategies of the Crusades.

The Crusades: Quest for the Holy Land. Zenger/SSSS. Video. Traces the background of events preceding Pope Urban's call for a crusade in 1095 through the last Crusade.

Crusades: Saints and Sinners. Learning Corporation of America Film. Focuses on the Crusade of 1099 and the motives behind it.

The Medieval Monument. Random House Media. 2 filmstrips. Concentrates on the cathedrals and the role of the Church in medieval times.

L2 **The Arts** Explain to students that in the Middle Ages stained glass might be one of the few means of communication some people would understand. Have students create posters in the style of stained glass windows to tell a story of something they have learned about people or events in this chapter. LEP

L3 **Culture** Ask students to imagine they are students during the Middle Ages. Divide the class into two groups: cathedral-school students and university students. Each group is responsible for preparing an advertisement that will be posted in the center of town to generate people's interest in enrolling in their school. The advertisements should focus on the school's curriculum and faculty, its environment, or any aspect that might encourage students to enroll in the school. Have representatives from each group present their advertisement to the class. LEP

VIDEODISC

Use the following to enrich Chapter 25.

WC C 73 14675

St. Francis of Assisi receives stigmata.

Painting of Francis of Assisi

Two well-known **orders,** or groups of friars, were the Franciscans (fran sis' kuhns) and Dominicans (duh min' uh kuhns). The Franciscan order was founded in 1200 by Francis of Assisi (uh sē' zē), the son of a rich Italian merchant. Franciscans were known for their cheerfulness and confidence that God would take care of them. They had a deep love of nature. They believed it was a gift of God and should be respected.

The Dominican order was started in 1216 by a Spanish monk named Dominic. Like the Franciscans, the Dominicans lived a life of poverty. They studied different languages so they could preach everywhere. Through their words and deeds, they kept many people loyal to Church teachings.

Section 2 Review

1. **Identify:** Cluny, Gregory VII, College of Cardinals, Francis of Assisi, Dominic
2. **Define:** tithes, friars, orders
3. How did the church become rich during the Middle Ages?
4. In what ways were friars different from other monks?

Critical Thinking

5. Why do you think the monks of Cluny gained the people's respect?

Section 3

Learning

During the late Middle Ages, the rise of governments brought more security, and the economy grew stronger. There was more time for learning and learning was in the hands of the Church.

Stained-glass Window

Cathedral Schools The parish clergy set up schools in **cathedrals,** or churches headed by bishops. The schools were to prepare the sons of nobles for service in the Church. Not every boy who went to school, however, wanted to be a priest or monk. So, the schools also trained students to be government workers, lawyers, and teachers. Seven subjects were taught at cathedral schools. They were grammar, rhetoric, logic, arithmetic, geometry, astronomy, and music.

Students paid a fee to attend classes held in a cold, dark hall rented by the teacher. Books were few and costly. So, students memorized the teacher's explanation.

SECTION 2 ANSWERS

1. Cluny, a monastery (p. 385); Gregory VII, pope who continued reforms (p. 385); College of Cardinals, group of bishops who helped pope rule (p. 385); Francis of Assisi, founder of Franciscan order of monks (p. 386); Dominic, founder of Dominican order of monks (p. 386)
2. tithes, Church offerings equal to 10 percent of income (p. 384); friars, preachers (p. 385); orders, groups of friars (p. 386)
3. Church members supported it by giving tithes, and rich nobles donated money and land.
4. They did not shut themselves off from the rest of the world, but lived in towns to bring Christianity to the people.
5. because they led simple lives, spending much of their time in prayer

Assign the Chapter 25 **Section 2 Quiz** in the TCR. Testmaker available.

Universities After a while, students began to complain that teachers held few classes and did not cover enough subjects. Teachers began to complain that too many untrained people were teaching. So, students and teachers decided to make some changes by forming **unions,** or groups of people joined together for a common cause. These unions became **universities,** or groups of teachers and students devoted to learning. By the 1200s, universities had spread all through Europe.

Universities were alike in many ways. A Church official called a **chancellor** (chan' suh luhr) headed each. No one could teach without his permission. All universities had well-organized classes held at set times each day. In class, students listened to lectures on a specific subject. All students had to pass special tests. Lecturers had to be at least 21 years old and had to have studied for at least 6 years.

Students from all over Europe came to the universities. At first, they lived in boarding houses. Later, rich sponsors built special buildings in which they could live. Those who missed daily mass, disturbed the peace, or took part in gambling or sword practice were punished.

MEDIEVAL CLASSROOM Dissatisfied with earlier forms of schools, teachers and students joined together to create universities as places for serious study. In this painting a teacher at the University of Paris holds a discussion with students. **What did a scholar have to do in order to become a teacher?**

MAKING CONNECTIONS

➤➤ **Daily Life** Girls did not receive the same education as boys during the Middle Ages. Girls did not attend universities. Those who entered convents and became nuns learned to read and write, sing for Church services, do needlework, care for the sick, and conduct convent business. Those who did not enter convents received much of the same training at home and learned to manage a household.

LINKING PAST TO PRESENT

The crisscross-shaped pretzels that we enjoy today were the creation of an Italian monk who baked treats for children as an incentive for memorizing their prayers. He shaped his prize to resemble the folded arms of children in prayer.

CAPTION ANSWER

Each had to pass special tests, be at least 21 years old, and have studied for at least six years.

COOPERATIVE LEARNING

Have students research and then represent a person from a particular sect of the medieval clergy: Benedictine monks, abbesses and nuns, missionaries, or Fransiscan or Dominican friars. Have students work in groups to present a day in the life of someone in their order, complete with fictitious names and background history. Have them relate, for instance, how they came to enter a certain order and what their family background might have been.

Assign the Chapter 25 **Cooperative Learning Activity** in the TCR.

INDEPENDENT PRACTICE

L3 **Music** Have students research the type of music fostered by the Church during the Middle Ages—the Gregorian Chant. Encourage students to obtain records or tapes of this type of music and learn how and why it was created. Some students may also compare this music to forms of music today. Have researchers share their information with the class.

MAKING CONNECTIONS

➤➤ **History** Probably the first European universities—all in existence by the early 1200s—were at Salerno and Bologna in Italy, Paris and Montpellier in France, and Oxford and Cambridge in England. They offered the seven liberal arts—Latin grammar and rhetoric, logic, arithmetic, geometry, astronomy, and music—along with natural science taught according to Aristotle. Students could then go on to specialties such as law or medicine.

VIDEODISC

Use the following to enrich Chapter 25.

WC C 74 14676
St. Thomas Aquinas (1225?-1274).

WC C 57 14659
Crusaders besiege a castle.

Painting of Thomas Aquinas

Thomas Aquinas One noted scholar of the Middle Ages was Thomas Aquinas (uh kwī′ nuhs). Aquinas believed that both faith and reason were gifts of God. He saw no conflict between the two and tried to bring them together. He thought reason helped people know what the world was really like. It helped them lead a good life. He thought faith revealed religious truths to people. It helped them find life after death.

Aquinas wrote a book called *Summa Theologica* (sū′ muh tā ō lō′ ji kuh), or *A Summary of Religious Thought*. In it, he asked questions and presented different opinions. He then gave answers to the questions. Aquinas's teachings were later accepted and promoted by the Church.

Section 3 Review

1. **Identify:** Thomas Aquinas
2. **Define:** cathedrals, unions, universities, chancellor
3. What were classes in cathedral schools like?
4. In what ways were universities alike?

Critical Thinking

5. Why do you think that only specific subjects were taught at cathedral schools?

Section 4

THE CRUSADES

For hundreds of years, Christians from western Europe had visited shrines in Jerusalem. Then, in 1071, a people called Seljuq (sel′ juk) Turks conquered Jerusalem and took control of the Christian shrines. Traveling in Palestine became difficult for the Christians because of the trouble there.

When news of what was happening in the Holy Land reached Christians in western Europe, they were shocked and angered. The result was a series of holy wars called **crusades** (krū sāds′), which went on for about 200 years.

A Call to War Even after they had taken Palestine, Turkish armies continued to threaten the Byzantine Empire. The Byzantine emperor asked the Pope for military aid. Pope Urban II (er′ buhn) agreed to help the Byzantines. He hoped that in return, the Eastern Orthodox Church would again unite with the Roman Catholic Church and accept him as its religious leader.

In 1095, Urban spoke before a large crowd in the town of Clermont in eastern France. He told the people that Europe's

SECTION 3 ANSWERS

1. Thomas Aquinas, scholar (p. 388)
2. cathedrals, churches headed by bishops (p. 386); unions, groups of people joined by a common cause (p. 387); universities, groups of teachers and students devoted to learning (p. 387); chancellor, a church official (p. 387)
3. They were held in a cold, dark, hall; students sat on a straw-covered floor and listened and then memorized what the teacher read.
4. A chancellor headed each, all had well-organized courses of study, all students had to pass special tests, and lecturers had to be 21 years old and have studied six years.
5. Answers will vary but might include that these subjects were considered ones that would provide people with a balanced and well-rounded education.

Assign the Chapter 25 **Section 3 Quiz** in the TCR. Testmaker available.

lords should stop fighting among themselves. Instead, they should fight in a crusade against the Turks.

Urban reminded the people that Europe was not producing enough food to feed its growing population. Palestine, on the other hand, had rich, fertile land on which any knight could live in comfort. The Pope promised that those who went on a crusade would be free of debts and taxes. He also promised that God would forgive the sins of those who died in battle. He encouraged soldiers to go to Palestine wearing a red cross on their tunics as a symbol of obedience to God.

The Peasants' Crusade Urban II spent nine months journeying from one European city to another calling for a crusade. The people of Europe responded eagerly to his call. As a sign of their religious devotion, they adopted the war cry *"Deus vult"* (dā' uhs wūlt'), which means "It is the will of God." The people felt it was their duty as Christians to win back the Holy Land. They had other reasons for being willing to fight, too. Nobles hoped to gain more land for themselves in Palestine. They also wanted the fame a crusade could bring. Peasants wanted to escape from their hard work on the land.

Urban II wanted the nobles to plan and lead the crusade. While they were drawing up their plans, however, the peasants

CALL FOR A CRUSADE The conquest of Palestine and persecution of Christians by the Seljuq Turks angered western Europeans. A call went up to free the Holy Land from the Muslims. A church leader in this painting urges local knights to join the crusade. **What symbol did the crusaders wear?**

DID YOU KNOW ??

Pope Urban tried to convince all classes of people to go on a crusade. He promised that serfs and prisoners would be set free if they went along.

CAPTION ANSWER

They wore a red cross on their tunics as a symbol of obedience to God.

VIDEODISC

Use the following to enrich Chapter 25.

WC C 64 14666

Crusader fortifications in Caesarea, Palestine.

MEETING SPECIAL NEEDS

Have tactile/kinesthetic learners research and prepare historic maps of the various routes used by the crusaders to reach the Middle East. The maps should include the following information: outline map of the area from western Europe to the Middle East, topographic features in those areas, the routes used by the crusaders, and a legend explaining the routes. Display the maps in the classroom.

Teaching

PEOPLE IN HISTORY

ELEANOR OF AQUITAINE

After students have read the People in History feature, ask: Why was Eleanor of Aquitaine able to inherit Aquitaine? *(Aquitaine allowed women to inherit property.)* Why did Louis VII have his marriage to Eleanor annulled? *(because she had not given birth to a male heir)* Why do you think Eleanor set up a school of manners and a Court of Love? *(She had two husbands who did not treat her with respect. She wanted to teach men how to treat women with respect.)*

ANSWERS to Checking for Understanding

1. She was the wife of a king of France and a king of England and the mother of two English kings.
2. It had troubadours, traveling minstrels, and artists; a school of manners in which knights and pages were taught to treat women with respect; and a Court of Love in which a jury of ladies decided cases involving knights' behavior toward women.

PEOPLE IN HISTORY

Eleanor of Aquitaine

The wife of two powerful kings, and the mother of two more, Eleanor of Aquitaine (ak' wuh tān) had a great influence on the history of Europe. Born around 1122, Eleanor was a beautiful, strong-willed woman who loved music, poetry, and intelligent conversation.

Twice the Queen

Eleanor was also one of the largest landowners in Europe. When she was 15 years old, she inherited Aquitaine, a region in southern France about one-fourth the size of the present-day country. Unlike most of Europe, Aquitaine allowed women to inherit property.

Soon after she inherited Aquitaine, Eleanor married Louis VII, king of France. In 1147, she accompanied him on a crusade to Palestine. After 15 years of marriage, however, Louis had his marriage from Eleanor annulled because she had not given birth to a male heir.

A few months later, Eleanor married Henry Plantagenet (plan tahj' uh nit), who would become Henry II of England. At first, the marriage was very happy. They had nine children, five of them sons. Henry II, however, was unfaithful to his wife. So, Eleanor left him and returned to Aquitaine.

A Cultured Court

Eleanor's court at Aquitaine was cultured and glamorous. She welcomed both traveling minstrels and **troubadours,** or poets and composers who remained at court. She encouraged artists. She set up a school of manners, in which knights and pages were taught to treat women with respect. She also set up a Court of Love in which a jury of ladies decided cases involving knights' behavior toward women.

In 1173, Eleanor helped her sons in a revolt against their father. It failed, however, and Henry II shut Eleanor in her castle for 12 years. After Henry died in 1189, Eleanor's son Richard the Lionheart became king of England. Eleanor ruled England while he was on a crusade to Palestine. After Richard died in 1199, Eleanor helped her son John gain the English throne. She died in 1204 at 82.

Checking for Understanding

1. **What role did Eleanor play in the histories of France and England?**
2. **What was Eleanor's court at Aquitaine like?**

390 UNIT 8 THE LATE MIDDLE AGES

SPOTLIGHT ON: ELEANOR OF AQUITAINE

Eleanor of Aquitaine was also known as the Damsel of Brittany. Eleanor's marriage to Henry Plantagenet, who became Henry II of England, caused conflict between England and France that lasted some 400 years. She compiled and published a book of maritime laws called, *Laws of Oléron.* Ask students how Eleanor of Aquitaine might have affected attitudes toward women during the Middle Ages. *(She was a positive image of women as strong, capable, and determined.)*

grew impatient and formed their own armies. Although they lacked training in warfare, they believed God would help them.

In the spring of 1096, about 12,000 French peasants began the long journey to Palestine. At the same time, two other groups of peasants set out from Germany. As the peasant armies marched through Europe, they attacked farmers, looted cottages, and burned wheat fields. They *massacred,* or killed, all the Jews they could find. The peasants thought that since Jews were not Christians, they were enemies. Frightened villagers tried to keep the armies away from their homes. At night, the villagers often poisoned wells and attacked crusader camps.

By the time the peasant armies reached Constantinople, they had lost about one third of their number. Their clothes were in rags, and they had no money. They wandered through the streets of the city attacking passersby and stealing from markets and homes.

The Byzantine emperor had expected the Pope to send trained soldiers, not unskilled peasants. The actions of the western Europeans worried him, and he wanted to get them out of his capital. So, he gave them supplies and ships and sent them to fight the Turks in Asia Minor. There, the peasant armies were almost completely wiped out by Turkish bowmen.

The Nobles' Crusade In 1097, the nobles set out on their crusade. Great lords led each army. They brought with them their vassals, wives, children, clerks, cooks, and blacksmiths. The crusade was very costly. Each lord had to provide his own battle gear, wagons, supplies, and horses. Nobles often had to borrow money or sell their land or jewelry to cover the costs.

About 30,000 crusaders arrived in Asia Minor and defeated the Turks. From there, they moved south through the desert to Syria. However, they were not prepared for the heat and did not have enough food or water. Many died of starvation or thirst. Those who survived pushed on to Palestine, capturing Syrian cities along the way.

In 1099, the 12,000 surviving crusaders reached Jerusalem. They captured the Holy City, killing Turks, Jews, and Christians alike. Then, they looted it, taking gold, silver, horses, mules, and all kinds of goods.

The Kingdom Beyond the Sea After the crusaders captured Jerusalem, they lost much of their religious enthusiasm. Many returned to their homes in western Europe. Those who remained set up four feudal kingdoms called Outremer (ū truh mār'), or "the kingdom beyond the sea," in the areas they won.

The crusaders took over the estates of rich Turkish and Arab Muslims and divided them among themselves and their best knights. Arab peasants worked the land for them and cared for

MAKING CONNECTIONS

➤➤ **History** The Noble's Crusade is considered the First Crusade. Organized and led by four knights—Raymond of Toulouse, Godfrey of Bouillon, and Bohemond and Tancred of Sicily—it was the only successful crusade.

GEOGRAPHY AND HISTORY

The city of Jerusalem became historically important about 1000 B.C. when King David united the Israelite tribes and made Jerusalem the capital. Although Jerusalem has been under the control of many nations and groups through the centuries, today Jerusalem is once again the capital city of Israel.

VIDEODISC

Use the following to enrich Chapter 25.

WC C 56 14658
Present-day Jerusalem.

WC C 61 14663
The Church of the Holy Sepulchre.

MEETING SPECIAL NEEDS

To reinforce the ideas in this section, have students who are visual learners draw a series of illustrations depicting important events and people. Such illustrations could include Pope Urban II delivering his call for the First Crusade, a series of drawings depicting the journeys of crusaders to the Holy Land, or a portrait of King Richard I of England. Ask the artists to work with other students in creating text to accompany their drawings.

L2 **Geography: Human/Environmental Interaction** Ask students to report on how the European lifestyle of a knight differed from the lifestyle he had in the Middle East. Have students report on such things as housing, food, and clothing, and what adjustments the knight had to make in his new home. Ask students to read their reports aloud in class.

CAPTION ANSWER

They were not prepared for the desert's heat and did not have enough food or water. Many died.

GEOGRAPHY AND HISTORY

Outremer consisted of the kingdom of Jerusalem and the counties of Tripoli, Antioch, and Edessa.

VIDEODISC

Use the following to enrich Chapter 25.

WC C 63 14665
Mamurize Castle, at Anamur, Turkey.

CRUSADERS' ATTACK ON JERUSALEM After weeks of siege warfare, the crusaders were finally able to mount a successful attack on Jerusalem. The Christians, using towers and catapults, broke through the city's walls and defeated the Muslim defenders. **What hardships did the crusaders face on their way to Jerusalem?**

the orchards and vineyards. Other Arabs served as advisers and helped them manage their estates. Friendships developed between the crusaders and the Muslims. The Muslims admired the crusaders' bravery. The crusaders discovered that many Arab scholars knew more than Europeans did about medicine, science, and mathematics.

When the crusaders were not fighting Turks, they ran their estates, went hunting, and attended the local court. Each noble built a castle in Outremer more magnificent than the one he had in Europe. This castle was more than a fortress. It was a comfortable place in which to live, with a large dining hall, living room, and bedchambers. All the rooms had marble walls and painted ceilings and were decorated with silk hangings, carpets, silver and gold objects, and beautiful furnishings.

The crusaders found that their old way of living did not suit their new surroundings. It was too hot in Palestine to wear fur and woolen clothes. Men began to wear turbans and loose, flowing silk or linen robes. However, they continued to fight in armor. Women wore jeweled tunics and gowns made with gold thread. They adopted the Muslim custom of wearing veils when they were outdoors and learned to use makeup and perfume. The heat also led the westerners to develop the habit of bathing.

EXTENDING THE CONTENT

During the Crusades several military orders of monks developed. Some are still in existence. The Knights Hospitallers first formed to care for pilgrims in Jerusalem and for the sick. They were dedicated to Saint John the Baptist and were sometimes known as the Knights of Saint John. They followed Benedictine rule. In 1291 they moved to Cyprus when the Muslims took over Jerusalem. Another group, the Knights of Templars took their name from the Dome of the Rock in Jerusalem. They helped guide and protect pilgrims as well as keeping order among crusaders and Saracens. The Templars became a wealthy secret army. King Philip the Fair of France, fearing their influence, tried to destroy the group.

The crusaders changed their eating habits, too. It was too hot to eat the heavy, solid foods they were used to. They learned to have light meals with less meat and more fruit and vegetables. They also ate new foods, such as rice, oranges, figs, and melons.

The crusaders led an easier life in Palestine than they had at home. Still, they had trouble adjusting. Many died in battle against the Turks or in fights among themselves over rights and lands. Others could not survive the hot climate.

Painting of Arab Scholars

Saladin and the Crusade of Kings In 1174, a Muslim military leader named Saladin (sal' uhd uhn) became the ruler of Egypt. He united the Muslims throughout the Near East and started a war against the Christian occupation of Palestine by western Crusaders. Saladin's armies were well organized and devoted to Islam. Groups of soldiers headed by leaders called ***emirs*** (i miuhrs') made up the armies. Many emirs were known for their honesty and for the consideration they showed their captives. The emirs often were shocked by the cruelty and greed of the Christian soldiers.

Saladin's soldiers rode into battle on swift ponies. Their weapons were short bows. The crusaders found it hard to fight them. The crusaders' armor was heavy, their swords were too long to handle easily, and their horses were not protected. They had to learn to depend on a new weapon called the *crossbow,* which fired an arrow with great force and speed. In 1187, Saladin's armies took Jerusalem. When he refused to massacre the city's Christians, he won the respect of many of the crusaders.

After Saladin's victory, the Church urged another crusade. This time the western armies were led by King Richard I of England, Emperor Frederick Barbarossa (bahr buh ros' uh) of Germany, and King Philip II Augustus of France. They were the three most powerful rulers in Europe.

This Crusade of Kings, as it was called, was a failure. Frederick died in Asia Minor, and many of his troops returned home without ever having fought a battle. Richard and Philip were enemies and were always quarreling. They did take a few coastal cities in Palestine together. Then, Philip returned home. Richard and his armies had to continue the crusade alone.

Richard was a brave warrior. Because of this, he was called "the Lionheart." Nevertheless, he could not defeat Saladin. After three years, he gave up and signed a truce with the Muslim leader. Although the crusaders still controlled large areas of Palestine, Jerusalem remained in Muslim hands.

Painting of Saladin

The Loss of an Ideal In 1202, Pope Innocent III called for yet another crusade. Knights from all over Europe answered the call. They decided not to take a land route to Palestine but to go by ship from the Italian port of Venice. Rich merchants there wanted

MAKING CONNECTIONS

>> **Religion** The truce signed by King Richard and Saladin allowed both Muslims and Christians to visit the Holy Land in peace and safety.

DID YOU KNOW ??

The medieval practice of making a pilgrimage to Jerusalem began during Constantine's time and was common among all classes of people including the aristocracy. Some people made the pilgrimage as an act of piety; others went to ask for forgiveness for their sins.

VIDEODISC

Use the following to enrich Chapter 25.

WC C 59 14661

Barbarossa embarking on 2nd Crusade in 1147.

SPOTLIGHT ON: SALADIN

Saladin made the following reply to King Richard I of England after Richard wrote Saladin that he and his men would continue to fight for Jerusalem: *To us Jerusalem is as precious, aye and more precious than it is to you, in that it was the place whence our Prophet made his journey by night and is destined to be the gathering place of our nation at the last day. Do not dream that we shall give it up to you. . . . It belonged to us originally, and it is you who are the aggressors.*

Teaching

MAP SKILLS

Determining Exact Location

Have students read the introductory section of the skill on page 394. Ask: Why do most maps have grids? *(to help find different points on a map)* What do you need to find in order to know the exact location of a place? *(the line of latitude and the line of longitude that cross at that exact location)* Direct students to the map on this page. Ask: What are the coordinates of Constantinople? *(41° N, 29° E)*

Next, have students write five questions about the crusades based on the information on the map. Then collect the questions and quiz the class on the map using the questions written by the students.

Assign the Chapter 25 **Geography and Map Activity** in the TCR.

ANSWERS to Map Practice

1. Jerusalem
2. 45° N, 12° E

MAP SKILLS

Determining Exact Location

Most maps have **grids,** or patterns of horizontal and vertical lines that cross each other. Generally, the horizontal lines are lines of latitude, and the vertical ones are lines of longitude. Grids make it easier to determine the exact location of a place on Earth.

To find a place exactly, it is necessary to find what lines of latitude and longitude cross at that place. The point at which they cross is the exact location.

Exact location may be shown by a set of numbers that list latitude first and then longitude (30°N, 60°E). Such sets are called **coordinates** (kō ōr′ din uhts).

Look at the map of "The Crusades" below. Locate the city of Marseilles on the southern coast of France. The line of latitude that passes through the city is 43°N. The line of longitude that passes through it is 5°E. This means that the exact location of Marseilles is 43°N, 5°E.

Map Practice

1. **What city is located at 32°N, 35°E?**
2. **What are the coordinates of Venice's location?**

The Crusades

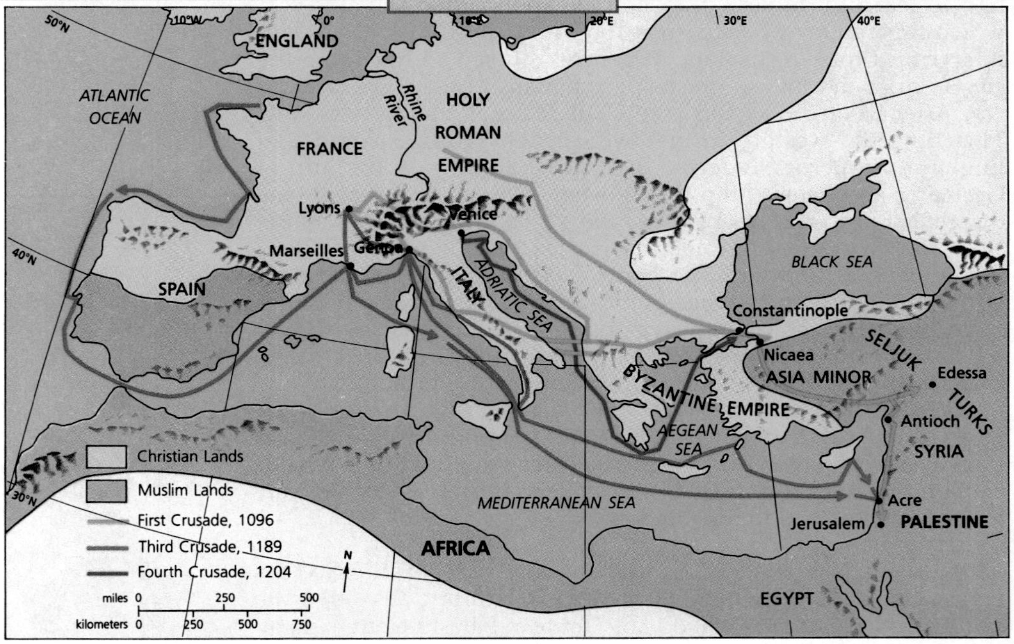

SPOTLIGHT ON: THE CRUSADES

The general climate of the area through which the Crusaders travelled was not unlike that of the western United States and Mexico—a combination of semi-desert and mediterranean climates. The average annual temperature fell in the range of 60° - 70° F (16°-21° C) which is similar to the temperatures felt throughout the southern half of the United States.

Venice to replace Constantinople as the trading center of the eastern Mediterranean. The crusaders agreed to pay these merchants a large sum of money and to share one half of all their conquests with the Venetians. In return, the Venetians agreed to supply the crusaders with ships and equipment.

When the soldiers found they could not pay all they owed, they agreed to conquer the city of Zara for the Venetians. Then, the Venetians convinced them to capture Constantinople. For three days, the crusaders and the Venetians burned and looted Constantinople. Many priceless manuscripts and works of art were either taken to Venice, lost, or destroyed.

The crusaders finally decided not to go to Palestine. Instead, they stayed in Constantinople and divided the city with the Venetians. Their conduct shocked many western Europeans, who lost respect for the crusader ideal.

Several other crusades were fought during the 1200s, but the Europeans did not win any of them. The saddest of all was the Children's Crusade. A group of French children, led by a peasant boy named Stephen of Cloyes, set sail from Marseilles (mahr sā'), France, in 1212. Most of the children never reached Palestine. Along the way they were sold into slavery by captains of the ships on which they sailed. At the same time, another group of children set forth on foot from Germany, intending to march toward Italy. Most of them, however, starved to death or died from disease.

In 1291, the Muslims took over the city of Acre (ah' kuhr), the last Christian stronghold. The Muslims had won the Crusades. They also gained back all the land in Palestine that the crusaders had taken earlier.

Jeweled Box

Effects of the Crusades The Crusades affected both the Near East and western Europe. The Byzantines were so angry at the actions of western Europeans that the split between eastern and western Christianity became permanent. At the same time, the Byzantine Empire was so weakened by the Crusades that it could no longer defend itself. This left Europe open to Turkish attack.

The Crusades helped to break down feudalism in western Europe. While feudal lords were fighting in Palestine, kings at home increased their authority. The desire for wealth, power, and land grew and began to cloud the religious ideals of many western Europeans.

The crusaders' contact with the cultured Byzantines and Muslims led western Europeans to again become interested in learning. At the same time, Europeans began to demand such luxuries as spices, sugar, lemons, rugs, tapestries, and richly woven cloth. To meet these demands, European merchants opened up new trade routes. As trade grew, so did the towns of western Europe.

L3 **Culture** Have students research and report on some of the ideas brought back by the crusaders, especially new knowledge in mathematics and the sciences, that have impacted modern society. How were medieval universities like universities today? How have medieval mathemtics impacted modern mathematics?

DID YOU KNOW ??

The children were not going to the Holy Land to fight but to convert the Muslims to Christianity.

VIDEODISC

Use the following to enrich Chapter 25.

WC C 23 14625

Pope Innocent III, one of the youngest popes.

ASSESS

CHECK FOR UNDERSTANDING

Ask students to summarize the main points of the chapter, orally or in writing. Discuss the answers to the Section and Chapter Review questions.

EVALUATE

Assign the Chapter 25 **Performance Assessment Activity** in the TCR.

Administer the **Chapter 25 Test**. Testmaker available.

MULTICULTURAL PERSPECTIVES

Have students debate the following topic: *The Crusades took place only for religious reasons and purposes.* Divide students into two groups, one group to defend the idea that the motivations of the crusaders were solely religious and the other to defend the idea that the crusaders had other reasons for going to the Holy Land. Allow each group time to research and develop their arguments. Then have each group present its views.

RETEACH

Have students work in small groups to list the important features of each crusade. Have the groups compare and discuss their lists.

Assign the Chapter 25 **Reteaching Activity** in the TCR.

ENRICH

Have students investigate accounts of Saladin and King Richard I of England during the Crusade of Kings. Ask students to give a brief oral report on the character of these two men, their motives for fighting, and how they regarded each other.

Assign the Chapter 25 **Enrichment Activity** in the TCR.

CLOSE

Discuss how the Crusades changed western civilization. Ask: *Did the crusaders help or hurt western civilization?* Have students debate the gains and losses.

MEETING CHAPTER OBJECTIVES

Each objective is tested by the Review questions in parentheses.

1. Discuss how the Roman Catholic Church influenced life during the Middle Ages. (BV; CU 1; CT 1; UYJ)
2. Summarize what attempts were made to reform the Church during the Middle Ages. (BV)
3. Describe what learning was like during the Middle Ages. (BV; CT 2; UYJ)
4. Explain why the Crusades took place during the Middle Ages. (CU 5; CT 3)
5. Explain what the effects of the Crusades were. (CU 7, 8, 9; CT 4)

Section 4 Review

1. **Identify:** Seljuq Turks, Urban II, Outremer, Saladin, Richard the Lionheart, Innocent III, Children's Crusade, Acre
2. **Define:** crusades, *emirs*
3. Why were western Europeans of all classes of society eager to go on a crusade?
4. What effect did the Crusades have on trade?

Critical Thinking

5. What do you think was the most important effect of the Crusades on the entire civilized world, and not just on western Europe? Explain.

Chapter Summary

1. The Roman Catholic Church was the center of life in Europe during the Middle Ages.
2. Increased wealth led many members of the clergy to grow careless about their religious duties.
3. Around 1000, the monks of Cluny began working to reform the Church by giving attention to Christian ideals.
4. In 1075, Pope Gregory VII issued a document stating that the Pope was above all kings and feudal lords and had the greatest power.
5. By the 1200s, universities, which developed from cathedral schools, had spread all through Europe.
6. During the Middle Ages, such scholars as Thomas Aquinas tried to bring faith and reason together.
7. In 1071, the Seljuq Turks conquered Jerusalem and took control of the Christian shrines there.
8. In 1095, Pope Urban II agreed to help the Byzantines against the Turks and called on the people of western Europe to join in a crusade.
9. In 1097, nobles set out on a well-organized and well-equipped crusade that succeeded in reaching and capturing Jerusalem.
10. Richard the Lionheart, who set out on a crusade with two other kings, could not defeat Saladin and signed a truce with him.
11. In 1202 another crusade began, but instead of going to Palestine, the crusaders, with the help of the Venetians, burned and looted Constantinople.
12. By 1291, the Muslims had regained all the land in Palestine that the crusaders had conquered earlier.
13. The Crusades made the split in the Roman Catholic Church permanent, helped break down the system of feudalism, and encouraged the growth of trade and towns in western Europe.

SECTION 4 ANSWERS

1. Seljuq Turks, people who conquered Palestine (p. 388); Urban II, pope (p. 388); Outremer, kingdoms near Jerusalem (p. 391); Saladin, Muslim ruler of Egypt (p. 393); Richard the Lionheart, British king (p. 393); Innocent III, pope (p. 393); Children's Crusade, crusade led by children (p. 395); Acre, Christian stronghold (p. 395)
2. crusades, a series of holy wars (p. 388); *emirs*, Muslim military leaders (p. 393)
3. They felt it was their duty as Christians to win back the Holy Land; nobles hoped to acquire more land and gain glory; and peasants wanted to escape hard work.
4. They led to the opening up of new trade routes and an increase in trade.
5. Answers will vary, but students should provide reasons for their choices.

Assign the Chapter 25 **Section 4 Quiz** in the TCR. Testmaker available.

CHAPTER

Review 25

Building Vocabulary

Imagine that you are a traveler in Europe during the Middle Ages. Write an article for a travel magazine describing what you see that shows you the importance of the Roman Catholic Church. Use the following words.

mass	cathedrals
canon laws	unions
excommunicated	chancellor
tithes	crusades
friars	*emirs*
orders	troubadours

Check for Understanding

1. What role did Church officials play in the political life of the Middle Ages?
2. Why did many monks grow careless about carrying out religious duties?
3. Why were universities started?
4. How did Urban II encourage people to go on a crusade?
5. What effect did the climate in Palestine have on the crusaders?
6. What happened during the Children's Crusade?
7. Why did the split in the Roman Catholic Church become permanent?
8. How did the Crusades affect the power of western Europe's kings?

Critical Thinking

1. What were advantages and disadvantages in having Church leaders run the government during the Middle Ages?
2. What would have been enjoyable about being a student in a medieval university?
3. How would you respond to Urban II's speech about going on a crusade?
4. How do you think crusaders felt about settling in Palestine? Explain.

Geography in History

MOVEMENT The Fourth Crusaders sailed from Venice to Constantinople. About how many miles long was their voyage? Was their voyage longer or shorter than if they had sailed to Jerusalem as planned?

Using Your Journal

Review the details you have noted about how the Church influenced daily life, government, and education during the late Middle Ages. Write a paragraph comparing the role of the Church then with the role of churches in the lives of people today.

397

CHAPTER 25 REVIEW ANSWERS

BUILDING VOCABULARY

Articles will vary but should describe highlights of the area and dominance of the Church.

CHECK FOR UNDERSTANDING

1. They served as advisers, and kept records for illiterate kings.
2. because they became wealthy
3. because students complained that teachers were poor and held few classes, and untrained people were teaching
4. He told them about Palestine's rich land, promised that crusaders would be free of debts and taxes, and that God would forgive their sins.
5. They were not accustomed to the heat and lack of water. Many died of thirst.
6. Many of the children were sold into enslavement, starved to death, or died from disease.
7. because the Byzantines were so angry at the actions of western Europeans in burning and looting Constantinople
8. They increased the kings' authority.

CRITICAL THINKING

1. Answers will vary, but one advantage was the Church was a unifying force. The disadvantage was Church officials became wealthy and corrupt.
2. Answers will vary but should include examples.
3. Answers will vary.
4. Answers will vary, but students should indicate why they would have or would not have liked to settle there.

+ BONUS +

TEST QUESTION

For Chapter 25 Test

You are a Monk of Cluny faced by an angry bishop who resents your activities. Explain your beliefs and convince the bishop to work with you. *(Answers may vary, but students should indicate they know the Cluny monks were trying to reform the Church and end corruption, to which the bishop should agree.)*

USING YOUR JOURNAL

Paragraphs will vary but might indicate that churches have a more personal effect on people today rather than the all-encompassing effect the Church had in the Middle Ages.

GEOGRAPHY IN HISTORY

about 1,400 miles (or 2,250 km); shorter

CHAPTER
26 Rise of Trade and Towns

CHAPTER ORGANIZER

Objectives	Special Features	Supplemental Materials
Section 1 Trading Centers Analyze how the growth of trade led to the rise of towns in the Middle Ages.		• Reproducible Lesson Plan • Section 1 Quiz • Testmaker • Chapter 26 Vocabulary and Guided Reading Activity • Chapter 26 Geography and Map Activity
Section 2 Merchants Summarize how merchants became an important part of European life.		• Reproducible Lesson Plan • Section 2 Quiz • Testmaker
Section 3 Living Conditions Describe what living conditions were like in medieval towns.		• Reproducible Lesson Plan • Section 3 Quiz • Chapter 26 Cooperative Learning Activity • Unit 8 Primary Source Reading
Section 4 The Rise of Guilds Explain why guilds were formed and why they were later opposed.		• Reproducible Lesson Plan • Section 4 Quiz • Testmaker
Section 5 Cultural Changes Summarize what cultural changes took place in Europe during the 1400s.		• Reproducible Lesson Plan • Section 5 Quiz • Testmaker • Chapter 26 Chart and Graph Skill Activity • Unit 8 World Literature
Chapter 26 Review and Evaluation		• Chapter 26 Reteaching Activity • Chapter 26 Enrichment Activity • Spanish Summary and Glossary • Audiocassettes (English and Spanish) • Chapter 26 Performance Assessment Activity • Chapter 26 Test • Testmaker

If time does not permit teaching the entire chapter, use the Chapter 26 Summary on page 408 and the Chapter 26 Audiocassettes (English and Spanish) to point out the main ideas of the chapter.

✓ Performance Assessment Activities

Literature Collages As students study the people of the Middle Ages in this chapter, read portraits from Chaucer's Prologue to *The Canterbury Tales* aloud to them. Read about the following characters: the Knight, the Wife of Bath, the Squire, the Monk, the Friar, the Parson, the Prioress. Have students create collages to represent the people as described by Chaucer. Encourage them to use a variety of materials and write a short explanation of their collage.

Diorama Have students create dioramas or three-dimensional miniature scenes of a medieval trade fair or burg. Encourage students to include as many details as possible. Have them write a paragraph about their diorama to attach to it. Display the dioramas or scenes in the classroom.

CHAPTER RESOURCES

LITERATURE ABOUT THE PERIOD

Chaucer, Geoffrey. *The Canterbury Tales.* In *The Complete Poetry and Prose of Geoffrey Chaucer.* Holt, Rhinehart and Winston, 1977. This masterpiece of English literature gives insight into the character of the Middle Ages.

Dante. *The Divine Comedy.* Holt, Rhinehart and Winston, 1954. The epic poem by the prominent poet of the Middle Ages.

READINGS FOR THE STUDENT

Clarke, Charles Cowden. *Tales from Chaucer.* The Heritage Press, 1947. A selection of nine tales (and the Prologue) retold in prose for young readers, with colorful illustrations.

Macdonald, Fiona. *The Middle Ages: Everyday Life.* Silver Burdett Co., 1984. Describes how people lived and worked during the time between the 1200s and 1500s.

READINGS FOR THE TEACHER

Huisman, M. and G. *Stories of the Middle Ages.* (trans. and ed. by Patricia Crampton). Burke Books, 1983. A variety of popular tales, hero stories, and fables (translated from the French classic, *Contes et Legendes du Moyen Age).*

Tuchman, Barbara W. *A Distant Mirror.* Ballantine Books, 1978. Examines life problems of the fourteenth century.

MULTIMEDIA RESOURCES

Guilds and Trades. Coronet. Video. A view of the growth of merchant and craft guilds throughout Europe.

Medieval Society: the Villagers. Coronet Films. Film. Highlights the daily life of a typical village in the Middle Ages.

The Medieval World. Coronet. Video. Dramatization of medieval times in Europe from the rise of the feudal system to the development of urban societies.

The Middle Ages. National Geographic Society. 3 filmstrips. Focuses on aspects of everyday life in medieval times and on the development of towns.

INTRODUCE

CHAPTER 26 OVERVIEW

Chapter 26 examines the rise of towns in western Europe during the Middle Ages.

- **Section 1** describes the growth of trade and rise of towns.
- **Section 2** discusses the merchant class in western Europe during the Middle Ages.
- **Section 3** describes the living conditions in the towns.
- **Section 4** explains guilds and their importance.
- **Section 5** summarizes the cultural developments in medieval towns.

CHAPTER OBJECTIVES

After reading Chapter 26, students will be able to:

1. analyze how the growth of trade led to the rise of towns in the Middle Ages.
2. summarize how merchants became an important part of European life.
3. describe living conditions in medieval towns.
4. explain why guilds were formed and were later opposed.
5. summarize what cultural changes took place in Europe during the 1400s.

EXAMINING THE ILLUSTRATION

Ask students what skilled trades they see depicted in this painting. Point out that the painting seems to show a town being built all at once, when in fact towns would have developed more slowly and been built gradually.

PERFORMANCE ASSESSMENT

Use the Performance Assessment activities on page 398B to help you evaluate students as they complete the chapter.

CHAPTER 26 Rise of Trade and Towns

Medieval Builders

398

TEACHER CLASSROOM RESOURCES

- Reproducible Lesson Plan
- Section Quizzes/Chapter Test
- Reteaching Activity
- Chart and Graph Skill Activity
- Geography and Map Activity
- Vocabulary and Guided Reading Activity
- Cooperative Learning Activity
- Performance Assessment Activity
- Spanish Summary and Glossary
- Unit 8 Primary Source Reading
- Testmaker
- Audiocassettes (English and Spanish)
- Teaching Transparencies and Activities
- The Western Civilization Videodisc

Chapter Focus

READ TO DISCOVER:

- How the growth of trade led to the rise of towns in the Middle Ages.
- How merchants became an important part of European life and development.
- What living conditions were like in medieval towns.
- Why guilds were formed and why they were later opposed.
- What cultural changes to civilization took place in Europe during the 1400s.

500 A.D.–1400 A.D.

KEY TERMS

fairs
burgs
burghers
communes
charters
guilds
apprentice
masters
journeyman

During the 1000s and 1100s, things went well for the people of western Europe. For the first time since the fall of Rome, there were more births than deaths. Better ways of farming helped farmers grow enough food for the people. Many peasants left the fields to work in mines or village workshops. They became skilled artisans and began to turn out cloth and metal products.

Western nobles, however, wanted such luxury items as sugar, spices, silks, and dyes. These goods came from the Near East. So, European merchants carried western products to the Near East to exchange for luxury goods. The increased trade had a major effect on western European life.

Section 1

TRADING CENTERS

The growth of trade led to the rise of the first large trading centers of the later Middle Ages. They were located on the important sea routes that connected western Europe with the Mediterranean Sea, Russia, and Scandinavia. Two of the earliest and most important trading centers were Venice and Flanders (flan' duhrz).

Venice Venice was an island port in the Adriatic (ādrēat' ik) Sea close to the coast of Italy. It was founded in the 500s by people fleeing from the Germans.

399

FOCUS

BELLRINGER

Write the following on the chalkboard for students' written responses: *What if there were no place to take the garbage?*

MOTIVATIONAL ACTIVITY

Have students suggest what would happen if there were no place to take garbage. Explain that during the Middle Ages, peasants began moving to towns from the old manorial estates. Although the towns were safer and offered more freedom, they were also dirty, noisy, and crowded. Garbage as well as raw sewage was thrown into the streets, and houses of wood with thatch roofs were a constant fire hazard. Tell students that in this chapter they will learn more about the advantages and disadvantages of living in towns in the Middle Ages.

VOCABULARY PRE-CHECK

Write the key terms for this chapter on the chalkboard. Ask students to use those that they know in sentences.

Assign Chapter 26 **Vocabulary and Guided Reading Activity** in the TCR.

EXTRA CREDIT PROJECT

Have students read an English translation of Dante's *Divine Comedy.* Have them write a script about the medieval ideas of life after death using this epic poem as the basis. Students may wish to act out the scripts. Students who are not advanced readers may benefit from reading *The Stones of Green Knowe* by L. M. Boston (Atheneum, 1977), a story about a twelfth-century lord who travels through time.

KEY TO ABILITY LEVELS

Teaching strategies have been coded for varying learning styles and abilities.

L1 Level 1 activities are **basic** activities and should be within the ability range of all students.

L2 Level 2 activities are **average** activities and should be within the ability range of the average to above-average student.

L3 Level 3 activities are **challenging** activities designed for the ability range of above-average students.

LEP LEP activities should be within the ability range of Limited English Proficiency students.

TEACH

GUIDED PRACTICE

L1 **Discussion** Lead a discussion on how the growth of trade led to the rise of towns in western Europe during the Middle Ages. Ask: *What effect did increased trade have on western European life? Where were some of the most important trading centers located? What did these centers have in common?* LEP

GEOGRAPHY AND HISTORY

Two reasons for the population growth during the 1000s and 1100s were the decline of foreign invasions and good weather, caused by a retreat of polar ice.

MAKING CONNECTIONS

➤➤ **Economics** Italian merchants loaned money to the kings of France and England. In return, the merchants were allowed to conduct trade and collect taxes there. As a result, French and English townspeople often disliked the merchants.

MAP STUDY Answer

a land route to Genoa and then a water route to Alexandria

Assign the Chapter 26 **Geography and Map** Activity in the TCR.

Since the land was not very fertile, the early Venetians had to depend on the sea for a living. They fished in the Adriatic and produced salt from the seawater. They exchanged their products for wheat from towns on the mainland of Italy. They also traded wheat, wine, and slaves to the Byzantines for fabrics and spices.

During the 1100s, Venice became a leading port and many of its citizens became fulltime merchants. Venetian merchants learned to read and write, use money, and keep records. In time, they developed an effective banking system.

Venice's prosperity soon spread to other parts of Italy. Towns on the Italian mainland began to make cloth, which they sent to Venice to be shipped to other areas. Before long, other Italian towns along the seacoast became shipping centers.

The navies of the Italian trading towns drove the Muslims from the Mediterranean, making it safe for Italian seafarers. As a result, the Italians opened the Near East to Europeans.

However, the Italian trading towns quarreled among themselves over profits and trade routes. While they were quarreling,

MAP STUDY

MOVEMENT Trade routes tied all parts of western Europe together. **What was the most direct route merchants could take from Milan to Alexandria?**

Medieval Towns and Trade Routes

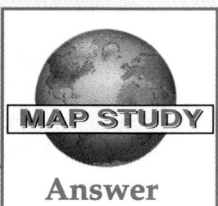

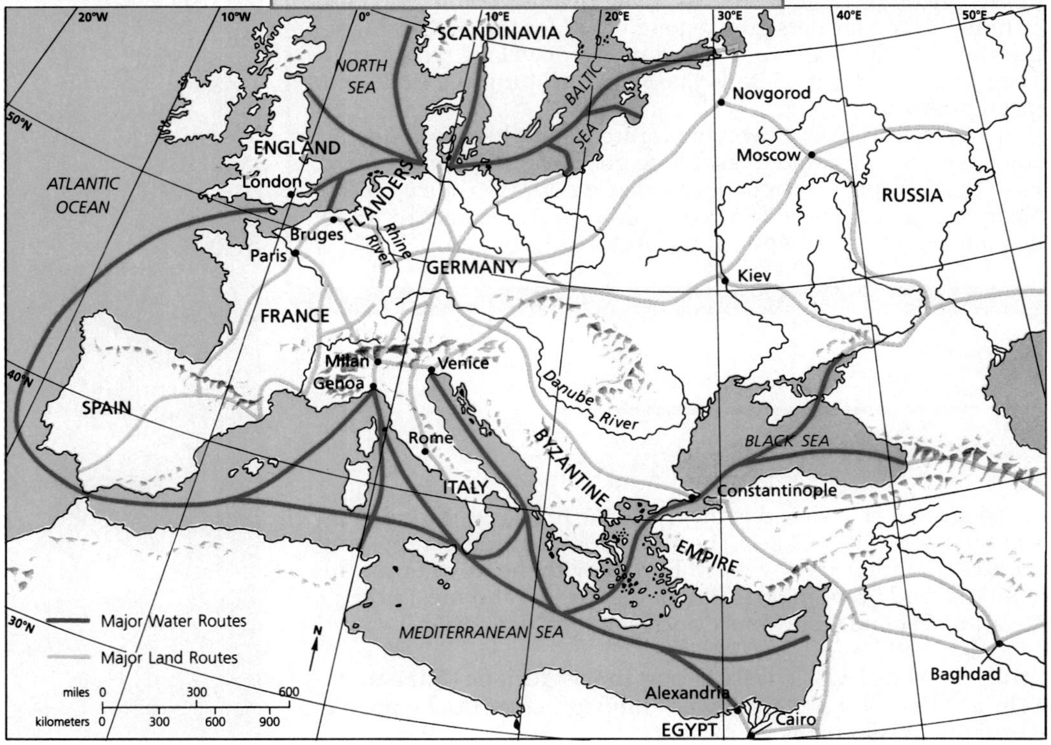

EXTENDING THE CONTENT

The most famous Venetian traveler is Marco Polo who wrote a colorful journal of his adventures in Mongol China. Marco's father and uncle were wealthy jewel merchants and the first Polos to trade in Asia. In about 1260, they traded in central Asia with the Khan of the Golden Horde and then went on to the court of Kublai Khan, emperor of China. On their second trip in 1271, the Polos took Marco, then about 17. They traveled overland through Tibet on the Silk Road. Marco had a flair for languages and a gift for diplomacy, which allowed him to become a trusted official for the Khan.

towns along Europe's Atlantic coast developed trade routes. By 1500, these towns had become more powerful than those in Italy.

Flanders Flanders, which today is part of Belgium, was an area of small towns on the northwest coast of Europe. The Flemish (flem' ish) people raised sheep and used the wool to develop a weaving industry. The cloth they produced became famous for its quality and soon was in heavy demand.

Flanders became the earliest Atlantic trading center. Its rivers joined together before they emptied into the North Sea. Where the rivers met, the Flemish built harbors. From these harbors, they shipped their valuable woolen cloth to other lands.

Flanders became an important stopping place for ships traveling along the Atlantic coast from Scandinavia to the Mediterranean. It also became an important link in the trade route between Constantinople and the North Sea.

By 1300, the most important trading partner of Flanders was England. Flemish traders set up shop in the dockyards of London. They relied on English shepherds to supply them with wool to be made into cloth. The finished cloth was then shipped back to England. In this way, the Flemish developed an international industry.

Painting of Money Changers

Section 1 Review

1. **Identify:** Venice, Flanders
2. What led to the growth and development of Venice's trade?
3. How did the location of Flanders help it become an important trading center?
4. How did the Flemish develop an international industry?

Critical Thinking

5. What do you think would be attractive about living in a trading town during the Middle Ages?

Section 2 MERCHANTS

As sea trade grew, so did overland trade. Italian towns began sending goods across the Alps to areas in the north. Soon, an overland trade route connected Italy and Flanders. From this route, other routes developed and spread across Europe.

Merchants became an important part of European life during the late Middle Ages. The first merchants were mostly adventurers who traveled from place to place. As protection

Painting of Medieval Merchant

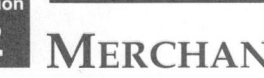

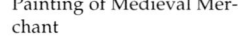

MAKING CONNECTIONS

➤➤ **History** Flanders was a member of the Hansa, or Hanseatic League, a trading league formed during the 1100s and 1200s by northern German trading towns.

DID YOU KNOW ??

Medieval fairs were much more than a chance to buy goods from faraway places, though that was rare and exciting. They also broadened the world of the medieval townspeople. Though they might never have traveled more than a few miles from home, the fair drew travelers with exciting stories and visitors from distant places. Merchant caravans might also bring news or letters from friends or relatives who had left home.

VIDEODISC

Use the following to enrich Chapter 26.

WC C 17 14619

The Tower of London.

SECTION 1 ANSWERS

1. Venice, trading center in Italy (p. 399); Flanders, trading center in Belgium (p. 401)
2. Because the land was not very fertile, the early Venetians had to depend on the sea for a living. Venice became a leading port, and its merchants learned to read and write, use money, keep records, and develop a banking system.
3. It had many rivers, a seacoast, and water deep enough for harbors.
4. Flemish traders relied on English shepherds for wool, which they sent to Flanders to be made into cloth. The finished cloth was then shipped back to England.
5. Answers will vary, but students should provide specific examples of life in medieval towns.

Assign the Chapter 26 **Section 1 Quiz** in the TCR. Testmaker available.

L1 **Trade** Play the following game called "Merchant" with the students. Divide the class into two teams. Read true-false statements to the class. Call on the first student who raises his or her hand to answer each statement. Give teams two points for correct answers, and subtract two points for each incorrect answer. Some sample statements: Merchants engaged in only sea trade. *(F)* The first merchants set up marketplaces in towns. *(F)* Fairs enabled merchants to trade with one another. *(T)* Fairs attracted merchants from faraway places. *(T)* LEP

DID YOU KNOW ??

Most of the important fairs were held on saint's days. Before a fair could be held, a charter had to be obtained from the lord or bishop who owned the land on which the fair was to be held. Usually, no two fairs could be set up within 7 miles (or 11 km) of each other. Fairs were often specialized—a week-long leather and fur fair, a 10-day cloth fair, and so on. Entertainers, food merchants, and wine sellers, as well as moneylenders and bankers set up temporary quarters to make a profit from the crowds.

CAPTION ANSWER

to help protect themselves from robbers and fights between nobles

against robbers, they traveled in armed groups. They carried their goods in open wagons pulled by horses.

Fairs Merchants traveling along the chief route through eastern France stopped to trade with each other at special gatherings called **fairs.** The fairs were sponsored by nobles who collected taxes on sales. Fairs were held once a year for a few weeks at selected places. Over time, they attracted merchants from as far away as England and Egypt.

At the fairs, merchants could buy and sell goods or settle debts. They set up booths to show such *wares,* or things for sale, as pots, swords, armor, and clothing. Before long, merchants began to pay for goods with precious metals instead of bartering. Italian money changers tested and weighed coins from many different lands to determine their value. From the *banc,* or bench, at which the money changers sat comes the English word "bank."

The Growth of Towns After awhile, merchants grew tired of moving around. They began to look for places where they could settle permanently and store their goods. They generally chose places along a trade route near waterways or road crossings. They also tried to settle close to a castle or monastery. This helped protect them from robbers and fights between nobles. The merchants surrounded their settlements with pal-

MEDIEVAL MARKETPLACE During the Middle Ages merchants set up permanent shops that eventually developed into towns. Medieval merchants in this painting sell shoes, cloth, and tableware. **Why did merchants try to settle near castles or monasteries?**

MEETING SPECIAL NEEDS

Have interested students research and create a medieval fair or marketplace. Have students set up several booths with wares that would have been sold at the time. Include moneychangers. Invite other classes to the fair or marketplace.

isades and moats. Most towns of the Middle Ages developed from these merchant settlements.

The towns came to be called **burgs** (bergs) because they were often near castles, which the Germans called *burgs*. The new towns grew steadily and attracted people from the surrounding countryside. Markets became centers of business and social life. Once a week, nobles and peasants sold food for goods they could not make on the manor. Artisans came from the villages to find work. Often they brought their families with them. Over time, the towns became more than just centers of trade. They became communities in which people lived.

Painting of Medieval Family

Section 2 Review

1. **Define:** fairs, burgs
2. Why did the nobles sponsor fairs?
3. Where did merchants set up their marketplaces?
4. How did merchants contribute to the growth of towns?

Critical Thinking

5. What types of activities at fairs today are similar to those of the fairs of the Middle Ages?

Section 3

Living Conditions

By the 1200s, many towns were wealthy and large enough to have their palisades replaced by walls and towers. Inside the walls, public buildings of stone and houses of wood were jammed close together. To save even more space, the houses had extra stories that extended over crooked narrow alleys.

The crowded conditions often made towns unhealthy places in which to live. Sewers were open, and there was little concern for cleanliness. People threw garbage out of windows onto the streets below. Rats were everywhere.

During the 1300s, diseased rats came to Europe on trading ships from the Middle East. They carried with them a plague called the "Black Death." This disease swept through Europe, killing millions of people. Experts think that one out of three Europeans died in the plague. To escape it, people fled from the towns and settled in the countryside. Trading, farming, and war came to a temporary halt.

Burgher Life Merchants and artisans controlled a town's business and trade. They hired workers from the countryside to

L2 **Environment** Have students discuss the garbage problem that faced medieval towns. Encourage them to brainstorm solutions to the problem. Then have them devise the best way to inform the people of what they must do to achieve "garbage control." LEP

LINKING PAST TO PRESENT

The term *burg* originally meant a fortified town or castle. As part of town names, it appeared in the Germanic *-burg*, the French *-bourg*, and the English *-borough* and *-bury*. Today, in Europe, we find Hamburg, Strasbourg, Edinburgh, and Canterbury; in the United States, Pittsburgh, Harrisburg, and Salisbury.

DID YOU KNOW ??

People living during the plague known as the Black Death, did not know that the plague came from rats and was contagious. The Crusades were responsible for carrying the disease to western Europe.

GEOGRAPHY AND HISTORY

In Switzerland and western Germany, the Jews were blamed for the Black Death, and thousands were burned to death or hanged. As a result, there was a movement of Jews into eastern Germany and Poland.

SECTION 2 ANSWERS

1. fairs, special gatherings for trade (p. 402); burgs, medieval towns (p. 403)
2. because they collected taxes on sales
3. along a trade route near waterways or road crossings, and close to a castle or monastery
4. Most of the towns developed from merchant settlements.
5. Answers will vary, but students might mention flea markets, farmers' markets, and county or state fairs.

Assign the Chapter 26 **Section 2 Quiz** in the TCR. Testmaker available.

L2 **Science** Have groups of students research and report on exactly what the Black Plague was, what effect if had on towns, what people did to combat the disease, and how it was eradicated. Suggest students work together to create a "Black Death" display on what they learn. One group could devise changes that might have been made to make the towns healthier places in which to live.

DID YOU KNOW ??

Peasants ate dark bread, broth, cheese, and curds. Other dishes of the burghers and manor nobility included miniature cod liver pastries, beef marrow fritters, a sauce of pounded crayfish tails, and other types of fish. Aristocrats ate many of the foods that the burghers ate, but in larger quantities.

CAPTION ANSWER

At first, the merchants, artisans, and workers who lived in towns were all called burghers. Later, only rich merchants used the title.

make goods for them. At first, the merchants, artisans, and workers who lived in towns were all called **burghers** (ber′ guhrz). Later the title was used to mean rich merchants.

The daily life of burghers and their families started with prayers at dawn. The burgher hurried off to the docks and market to see how his products were selling. Then, he met with his business partners.

The burgher's wife kept house, managed servants, and cared for children. The family ate two large meals a day—one at ten o'clock in the morning and another at six o'clock in the evening. A typical meal consisted of eel, roast beef, lark pastry, and curded milk. About nine o'clock in the evening, the family went to bed.

Changing Ways Under the feudal system, the land on which towns were built was owned by kings, nobles, and bishops. They taxed the people in the towns and charged them

BURGHER LIFE Meals were important events in the daily lives of burgher families. In this painting a burgher warms his hands by the fire as he rests from a hard day's work. His wife is setting the table for a roast beef dinner. **What groups of people were called burghers?**

MULTICULTURAL PERSPECTIVES

Town life in the Middle Ages gave middle-class women many new opportunities. They not only worked with their husbands or sons in family shops and businesses, but they also had the freedom to operate their own enterprises in what became known as *femme sole.* It is true that women were kept out of certain crafts and guilds unless they were a master's wife, widow, or daughter. In other guilds, however, women had equal status with men, and in some trades and businesses they had a near monopoly. Women dominated the silk-making industry in Paris and London and were important in the cloth trades such as spinning, weaving, dyeing, tailoring, and glove making. Women also worked in the medieval food industry as bakers, fishmongers, and poultry sellers.

fees to use the marketplace. The burghers did not like this or the other restrictions placed on them. They resented having to get a noble's permission to marry, move around, or own land and serving in the noble's army.

Many nobles viewed the rise of towns as a threat to their power. They resented the wealth of the burghers and began to use feudal laws to keep them in their place. The Church was also against the rise of towns. Its leaders feared that the making of profit would interfere with religion.

The burghers, however, resented feudal laws. They thought these laws were not suited to business. The burghers now had wealth and power. Thus, they began to depend less on nobles and bishops. Instead, they developed a sense of loyalty toward their town. They worked together to build schools, hospitals, and churches. They began to demand changes.

Painting of Medieval Court

Communes and Charters In the 1100s, townspeople in northern Italy formed political groups called **communes** (kom' yūnz). Their purpose was to work against the nobles and bishops and for the people by establishing local self-government. The Italian communes were successful. Soon, the idea of communes spread to the towns of northern Europe. Some kings and nobles gave the townspeople **charters,** or documents allowing towns to run their own affairs.

The charters gave the townspeople the right to elect officials to run their towns. A council collected taxes and set charges for merchants who bought and sold goods in the town market. It also repaired streets, formed citizen armies, and ran hospitals, orphanages, and special homes for the poor.

The towns enforced their own laws and special courts were set up. To reduce crime, the towns severely punished those who broke the law. Murderers were hanged. Robbers lost a hand or an arm. Those who committed minor crimes, such as disturbing the peace, were whipped or put in the *stocks,* or a wooden frame with holes in which the feet and hands were locked.

Section 3 Review

1. **Identify:** "Black Death"
2. **Define:** burghers, communes, charters
3. What were some problems faced by medieval towns?
4. What changes did burghers want to make in feudal laws?

Critical Thinking

5. What laws or regulations would you have written to further improve conditions of medieval towns?

L2 **Critical Thinking** Ask students to compare the forms of punishment for crimes committed during the Middle Ages with the forms of punishment for crimes committed today. Ask them to create a chart showing each. Then ask students to vote on which society seems more humane.

MAKING CONNECTIONS

>> **Economics** Burghers got around the Church's opposition to interest in two ways. First, they used Jews as moneylenders. Second, they lent money at no interest but charged "damages" if the loan was not repaid at once. By the 1200s, the Church changed its position, and interest became acceptable.

VIDEODISC

Use the following to enrich Chapter 26.

WC C 86 14688
Canterbury Tales, first edition, 1478.

WC C 85 14687
Geoffrey Chaucer (1343-1400).

SECTION 3 ANSWERS

1. "Black Death," plague that swept through Europe in the 1300s (p. 403)
2. burghers, rich merchants (p. 404); communes, political groups (p. 405); charters, documents allowing towns to run their own affairs (p. 405)
3. They were overcrowded, unhealthy, and dirty.
4. They wanted to run their own affairs and to have their own courts and laws.
5. Answers will vary, but students might suggest regulations to relieve overcrowding, to plan for growth, and to determine disposal of sewage.

Assign the Chapter 26 **Section 3 Quiz** in the TCR. Testmaker available.

L3 **Critical Thinking** Ask students to discuss how well the guild system would work in present-day society. Suggest they write a case study of its application in modern times.

LINKING PAST TO PRESENT

Medieval guilds controlled all the business in a town, establishing rules on prices, wages, and unemployment. In the United States today, laws prohibit price fixing and monopolies. In addition, the Taft-Hartley Act outlaws both hiring only union members and forcing employees to join unions.

DID YOU KNOW

Unlike modern trade unions that are organizations of workers only, guilds included employers, masters, and workers. Craft guilds also had religious ties and their own patron saints.

MAKING CONNECTIONS

➤➤ **History** Often, masters were required to teach their apprentices to read and write and to provide them with clothing and a salary. Masters were also responsible for the behavior of their apprentices.

VIDEODISC

Use the following to enrich Chapter 26.

WC C 95 14697

The crest of the cooper's guild ca. 1450.

Section 4

THE RISE OF GUILDS

Around the 1100s, merchants, artisans, and workers formed **guilds** (gildz). These were business groups whose purpose was to make sure that their members were treated equally. Each craft had its own guild, whose members lived and worked in the same area of town.

Craft guilds controlled the work of artisans such as carpenters, shoemakers, blacksmiths, masons, tailors, and weavers. Women working as laundresses, seamstresses, embroiderers, and maidservants had their own trade association. Guild members were not allowed to compete with one another or to advertise. Each member had to work the same number of hours, hire the same number of workers, and pay the same wages.

Guilds controlled all business and trade in a town. Only members could buy, sell, or make goods there. Outsiders who wanted to sell their goods in the town market had to get permission from the guilds. The guild decided the fair price for a product or service, and all members had to charge that price. Guild members who sold poorly made goods or cheated in business dealings had to pay large fines. They could also be expelled from the guild.

Guilds were more than business or trade groups. If members became ill, other members took care of them. If members were out of work, the guild gave them food. When members died, the other members prayed for their souls, paid for funerals, and supported the families. Guilds were also centers of social life. Holy day celebrations, processions, and outdoor plays were sponsored by the guild. Close friendships often developed among guild members.

It was not easy to become a member of a guild. A person had to be an **apprentice** (uh pren' tis), or trainee, in a trade for two to seven years. Apprentices were taught their trade by **masters,** or experts. They had to live with and obey their masters until their training was finished.

The next step was becoming a **journeyman** (jer' nē muhn), or a person who worked under a master for a daily wage. After a certain amount of time, journeymen took a test to become masters. The test was given by guild officials. Journeymen had to make and present a "masterpiece" to prove they had learned their craft. Those who passed the test were considered masters and could make their own goods. Often, they worked in the back of their houses and sold their goods in a shop in the front of the house.

By 1400, many merchants and artisans had begun challenging the control of the guilds. They felt the guilds kept them from

Stained-glass Window of Medieval Craftsmen

COOPERATIVE LEARNING

Have students work in groups to write and present a brief skit showing daily life in a medieval town. Assign small groups to research the daily work, clothing, food, and homes of townspeople. Assign each student a specific task such as selecting an event and characters, outlining and writing parts of the script, and obtaining or making props. Students can choose to portray such characters as apprentices, journeymen, masters of various guilds, university students, clergy, moneychangers, or troubadours.

Assign the Chapter 26 **Cooperative Learning Activity** in the TCR.

increasing their trade and profits. Then, too, apprentices disliked the strict rules set by guilds. It was getting harder and harder for apprentices to become masters. Many masters were grouping together and hiring unskilled workers instead of apprentices.

Section 4 Review

1. **Define:** guilds, apprentice, masters, journeyman
2. What rules did guild members have to obey?
3. Why did people begin to challenge the guilds in the 1400s?

Critical Thinking

4. Do you agree or disagree with the following statement: The steps taken to become a master were too difficult. Give reasons for your opinion.

Painting of Dante

Section 5 CULTURAL CHANGES

During the 1400s, merchants, artisans, and bankers became more important than they had been in the past. Their growing power led to the decline of feudalism.

Many townspeople were as rich as, or richer than, the nobles. Bankers lent money to kings, nobles, and church officials for wars, building repairs, and entertainment. With their new wealth, merchants turned their homes into mansions. Some even bought castles from nobles who had lost their money. They began to set fashions. Women wore furs and gowns made of *brocade* (bro kād′), or a cloth woven with raised designs on it. Men dressed in colorful jackets, stockings, and feathered caps.

The townspeople had more leisure time and money to spend on their interests. Many hired private teachers to educate their sons. The sons later went to universities to study law, religion, and medicine. There was time to enjoy art and books, so townspeople began to support the work of painters and writers.

Most townspeople used such languages as German, French, and English. A scholar named Dante (dahn′ tā) wrote the *Divine Comedy* in Italian. It is one of the most famous poems of the Middle Ages. Geoffrey Chaucer (jef′ rē cho′ suhr) wrote the *Canterbury Tales* in English. These tales are still popular today.

Townspeople began to think differently from nobles and peasants. The townspeople came to believe that they should be free to develop their talents and to improve their way of life. They wanted a strong central government. They began to look toward kings to provide leadership.

Painting showing *Canterbury Tales*

INDEPENDENT PRACTICE

L3 **Writing** Have students imagine that they are editors of a newspaper during the Middle Ages. Tell them to write two editorials, one written about 1220 titled, "Why We Need to Establish Guilds," the other one written about 1400, titled, "Why We Need to Abolish Guilds."

MAKING CONNECTIONS

➤➤ **Literature** Dante's *Divine Comedy* is divided into three parts—*Inferno* (Hell), *Purgatio* (Purgatory), and *Paradiso* (Paradise). The epic's main theme is life after death.

DID YOU KNOW ??

Chaucer was a government official who wrote poetry as an avocation. His *Canterbury Tales* is a collection of stories told by a group of pilgrims on a journey to Thomas á Becket's shrine in Canterbury.

VIDEODISC

Use the following to enrich Chapter 26.

WC C 96 14698

A guild warden judges work.

SECTION 4 ANSWERS

1. guilds, business groups organized to protect members (p. 406); apprentice, trainee (p. 406); masters, experts (p. 406); journeyman, person who worked under a master (p. 406)

2. They were not allowed to compete with one another or to advertise, and they had to work the same number of hours, hire the same number of workers, and pay the same wages.

3. because they felt the guilds kept them from increasing their trade and profits, and because apprentices found it hard to become masters

4. Answers will vary, but students should indicate why they think the steps were or were not too difficult.

Assign the Chapter 26 **Section 4 Quiz** in the TCR. Testmaker available.

ASSESS

CHECK FOR UNDERSTANDING

Ask students to summarize the main points of the chapter. Discuss the answers to the Section and Chapter Review questions.

EVALUATE

Assign the Chapter 26 **Performance Assessment Activity** in the TCR.

Administer the **Chapter 26 Test**. Testmaker available.

RETEACH

Have students in groups prepare charts of significant medieval innovations in economics, trade, literature, and art.

Assign the Chapter 26 **Reteaching Activity** in the TCR.

ENRICH

Have students investigate the death rates of western European countries during the Black Death and graph their findings.

Assign the Chapter 26 **Enrichment Activity** in the TCR.

CLOSE

Have students summarize how medieval life shifted from the feudal manor to the towns.

MEETING CHAPTER OBJECTIVES

Each objective is tested by the Review questions in parentheses.

1. Analyze the growth of trade and towns. (CU 1; UYJ)
2. Summarize how merchants became important. (CT 1)
3. Describe living conditions in medieval towns. (BV; CU 8; CT 3)
4. Explain why guilds were formed and were later opposed. (BV; CT 4)
5. Summarize cultural changes in Europe. (BV; CU 7, 8)

Section 5 Review

1. **Identify:** Dante, Geoffrey Chaucer
2. What during the 1400s led to the decline of feudalism?
3. In what ways did the cultural life of townspeople change during the 1400s?
4. What did townspeople want government to do?

Critical Thinking

5. Why might nobles have disliked the success of merchants during the Middle Ages?

Chapter Summary

1. During the 1000s and 1100s, increased trade between Europe and the Near East led to the rise of trading centers, such as Venice and Flanders.
2. Venetian traders became fulltime merchants who developed an effective banking system.
3. By 1100, the navies of the Italian trading towns had driven the Muslims from the Mediterranean.
4. Flanders was the earliest Atlantic trading center.
5. By 1300, the Flemish had developed an international industry by importing wool from England, turning it into cloth, and then shipping the finished product back to England.
6. Overland trade, as well as sea trade, developed during the 1000s and 1100s.
7. The first medieval merchants traveled overland in armed groups and stopped to trade with each other at fairs.
8. After a while, merchants began to settle in permanent places that developed into towns called burgs.
9. Most towns were overcrowded, unhealthy places in which to live.
10. Artisans and rich merchants called burghers controlled the business and trade of towns.
11. Nobles viewed the rise of towns as a threat to their power, and church officials feared that the making of profit would interfere with religion.
12. Burghers resented feudal laws and wanted to run their own affairs.
13. By the 1100s, towns in northern Italy had become independent city-states.
14. Guilds set wages, prices, and working conditions and helped members who were sick or out of work.
15. As townspeople grew richer and more powerful, they began looking to kings to provide leadership.

SECTION 5 ANSWERS

1. Dante, scholar who wrote *Divine Comedy* (p. 407); Chaucer, wrote *Canterbury Tales* (p. 407)
2. the growing power of merchants, artisans, and bankers
3. Many became as rich as landed nobles and spent their new wealth on homes and clothes. They hired private teachers for their sons and helped painters and writers.
4. to give them the peace and security they needed to reach their goals
5. Answers will vary, but students might indicate that nobles were envious and somewhat afraid of the wealth and power the merchants had developed.

Assign the Chapter 26 **Section 5 Quiz** in the TCR.

CHAPTER Review 26

Building Vocabulary

Imagine you are living in a town in western Europe during the Middle Ages. Write a diary entry describing your life there. Use the following words in your diary.

fairs	guilds
burgs	apprentice
burghers	masters
communes	journeyman
charters	

Check for Understanding

1. What led to the development of trade between Europe and the Near East during the 1000s and 1100s?
2. What led to the decline of Italian trading centers?
3. How did fairs affect the development of banking?
4. What effects did the "Black Death" have on Europe?
5. How did a person become a master in a guild?
6. Why were the nobles against the rise of towns?
7. Why was the clergy against the rise of towns?
8. How were the ideas of townspeople different from those of the nobles and peasants?

Critical Thinking

1. What would you have liked about being a merchant in the Middle Ages?
2. Would you have supported or opposed the position taken by Italian communes during the 1100s? Explain.
3. Would you have preferred to be a burgher or a noble during the Middle Ages? Explain.
4. Do you approve or disapprove of the rules established by the guilds? Explain.

Geography in History

PLACE Refer to the map on page 400. Imagine you are a pirate hoping to rob European trading ships. At what place would you wait for ships to attack? What geographic features of this place affected your choice? Explain.

Using Your Journal

Review the details you have noted about life during the late Middle Ages. Write a paragraph explaining what developments started in the towns of Europe during the Middle Ages are evident in your life today.

CHAPTER 26 REVIEW ANSWERS

BUILDING VOCABULARY

Diary entries will vary, but students should use all the vocabulary words.

CHECK FOR UNDERSTANDING

1. Western nobles wanted luxury goods that came from the Near East.
2. They quarrelled among themselves over profits and routes.
3. Merchants began to pay for goods with precious metals and coins from many different lands.
4. It killed millions of people and halted trading, farming, and war.
5. by becoming an apprentice, a journeyman, passing a master's test, and creating a masterpiece
6. They viewed towns and burghers as a threat to their power.
7. because they feared that the making of profit would interfere with religion
8. Townspeople believed they should be free to improve their way of life.

CRITICAL THINKING

1. Answers will vary, but students should include specific examples.
2. Answers will vary, but students should support their opinion with reasons.
3. Answers will vary, but students should explain their preference of burgher or noble.
4. Answers will vary.

+ BONUS +

TEST QUESTION
For Chapter 26 Test

How did the Flemish become one of the first to develop an international industry? *(They were able to create the economic bridge between the supply source, production source, and customer; became merchants of products people needed and wanted.)*

GEOGRAPHY IN HISTORY

Answers will vary but should include reference to the trade routes crossing the Mediterranean Sea. Likely spots for pirates were the passage between Spain and Africa, or near Constantinople.

USING YOUR JOURNAL

Paragraphs will vary but students might indicate commerce, fairs, banks, towns, town charters, business associations, fashion, and literature.

CHAPTER 27
Rise of Monarchies

CHAPTER ORGANIZER

Objectives	Special Features	Supplemental Materials
Section 1 France Describe how the Capetian kings strengthened the French monarchy.		• Reproducible Lesson Plan • Section 1 Quiz • Testmaker • Chapter 27 Vocabulary and Guided Reading Activity • The World History Videodisc
Section 2 England Discuss what changes took place in the English monarchy during the Middle Ages.		• Reproducible Lesson Plan • Section 2 Quiz • Testmaker • Chapter 27 Cooperative Learning Activity • Unit 8 Primary Source Reading • The World History Videodisc
Section 3 The Hundred Years' War Analyze the causes and results of the Hundred Years' War.		• Reproducible Lesson Plan • Section 3 Quiz • Testmaker • The World History Videodisc • Chapter 27 Activity Book Activity
Section 4 Germany Explain how the Holy Roman Empire was created and ruled.		• Reproducible Lesson Plan • Section 4 Quiz • Testmaker • Chapter 27 Geography and Map Activity • Chapter 27 Teaching Transparencies and Activities
Section 5 Spain Summarize how the Catholic monarchs united Spain.		• Reproducible Lesson Plan • Section 5 Quiz • Testmaker • Chapter 27 Chart and Graph Skill Activity • Unit 8 World Literature
Chapter 27 Review and Evaluation		• Chapter 27 Reteaching Activity • Spanish Summary and Glossary • Audiocassettes (English and Spanish) • Chapter 27 Performance Assessment Activity • Chapter 27 Test • Testmaker

If time does not permit teaching the entire chapter, use the Chapter 27 Summary on page 424 and the Chapter 27 Audiocassettes (English and Spanish) to point out the main ideas of the chapter.

✓ Performance Assessment Activities

Research Economic unrest, wars, and plagues led the downtrodden peasants and workers of France, Flanders, and England to unprecedented rebellions in the 1300s. One of the most famous uprisings was the 1381 Peasant's Revolt in England, led by Wat Tyler and John Ball. Have students prepare a report on the Peasant's Revolt, including details about the causes and its long-term results. Have students present their research to the class.

News Account Have students imagine that they are newspaper reporters in England in 1066, and they witnessed the Battle of Hastings. Have them create headlines and accounts of the battle. Some students may also choose to illustrate these news events with either descriptions of the events or political cartoons.

CHAPTER RESOURCES

LITERATURE ABOUT THE PERIOD

Warner, Marina. *Joan of Arc: The Image of Female Heroism.* Random House, 1982. Account of Joan of Arc.

READINGS FOR THE STUDENT

McKendrick, Melveena. *Ferdinand and Isabella.* American Heritage, 1968. Photographs and contemporary paintings help recreate the period.

READINGS FOR THE TEACHER

Brown, R. Allen. *The Normans.* St. Martin's Press, 1984. Concentrates on Norman influence on the western world.

Hallam, Elizabeth, ed. *The Plantagenet Chronicles.* Weidenfeld and Nicholson, 1986. Examines the reigns of Henry II, Richard I, and King John and discusses the Magna Carta, the Crusades, and life in England during the 1100s.

MULTIMEDIA RESOURCES

European History. Projected Learning Programs. Software, Apple and IBM. Surveys Europe from the Middle Ages to present.

Joan of Arc. Social Studies School Services. Video. Movie based on the life of Joan of Arc.

Medieval Art and Music. Educational Audio Visual. 2 filmstrips. Features the paintings, manuscripts, tapestries, sculpture, stained glass, architecture, and music of the medieval period.

Normans in England. McIntyre Visual Publications. Filmstrip. Examines the impact of the Norman conquest on England.

INTRODUCE

CHAPTER 27 OVERVIEW

Chapter 27 describes the growth of central governments in France, Germany, and Spain.

- ➤ **Section 1** discusses the powers of the French monarchy.
- ➤ **Section 2** describes the limitations placed on the English monarchy by the Magna Carta and Parliament.
- ➤ **Section 3** analyzes the causes and effects of the Hundred Years' War.
- ➤ **Section 4** explains the importance of the Holy Roman Empire .
- ➤ **Section 5** summarizes the unification of Spain.

CHAPTER OBJECTIVES

After reading Chapter 27, students will be able to:

1. describe how the Capetian kings strengthened the French monarchy.
2. discuss the English monarchy during the Middle Ages.
3. analyze the causes and results of the Hundred Years' War.
4. explain how the Holy Roman Empire was created and ruled.
5. summarize how the Catholic monarchs united Spain.

EXAMINING THE ILLUSTRATION

Ask students to determine who is in charge of this group. After discussing the king was the head of Parliament in England, tell students they will be reading about other European countries and kings.

PERFORMANCE ASSESSMENT

Use the Performance Assessment activities on page 410B to help you evaluate students as they complete the chapter.

CHAPTER 27 Rise of Monarchies

Medieval English Parliament

410

TEACHER CLASSROOM RESOURCES

- Section Quizzes/Chapter Test
- Reteaching Activity
- Enrichment Activity
- Geography and Map Activity
- Vocabulary and Guided Reading Activity
- Unit 8 Primary Source Reading
- Cooperative Learning Activity
- Activity Book Activity
- Performance Assessment Activity
- Spanish Summary and Glossary
- Testmaker
- Unit 8 World Literature Reading
- Audiocassettes (English and Spanish)
- Teaching Transparencies and Activities
- The World History Videodisc

Chapter Focus

READ TO DISCOVER:

- How the Capetian kings strengthened the French monarchy.
- What changes took place in the English monarchy during the Middle Ages.
- What were the main causes and results of the Hundred Years' War.
- How the Holy Roman Empire was created and ruled.
- How the Catholic monarchs united Spain.

The growth of trade and towns during the late Middle Ages led to many changes in western Europe. Some of these changes were political. The rise of **monarchies** (mon' uhr kēz), or countries governed by one ruler, led to the decline of feudalism. As kings gained power, the Church and the people were affected. In France, England, Germany, and Spain, things would never be the same again.

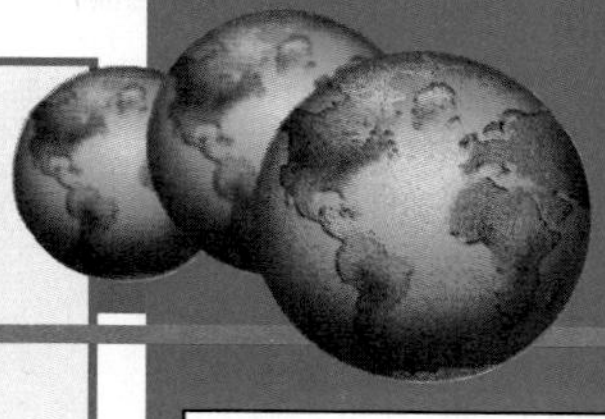

1000 A.D.–1300 A.D.

KEY TERMS

monarchies
circuit judges
grand jury
trial jury
dauphin
diet
corregidores

Section 1

FRANCE

In 987, Hugh Capet (ka pā'), a French noble, was chosen as the new king of France. At the time, France consisted of many feudal territories. As king, Capet ruled only a small area between the Seine (sān) and Loire (lwahr) rivers. Capet, who died in 996, was the first of a line of Capetian (kuh pē' shuhn) kings who ruled France for some 300 years. For 100 years after his death, however, these kings were weak and did little to increase royal power.

In 1108, Louis VI, known as "Louis the Fat," became king. He helped to increase the power of the monarchy in several ways. He got rid of nobles who did not fulfill their feudal duties and put loyal persons of lower birth in their place. He brought the people security by stopping the raids of lawless vassals. He granted charters of freedom to many towns, thus winning the loyalty of the townspeople.

The king's power was further increased under Philip II, also known as Philip Augustus. Philip, who ruled from 1179 to 1223,

FOCUS

BELLRINGER

Write the following question on the chalkboard for students' written responses: *What do you think it means to be a king?*

MOTIVATIONAL ACTIVITY

Have students read their responses explaining what they think it means to be a king. Explain that in various periods in history the power of kings has varied dramatically. Sometimes they were absolute rulers, and sometimes they were nothing more than figureheads. Ask students to discuss what problems might arise for our federal government if all the state governors and church leaders collected their own taxes and raised their own armies. Tell students that in this chapter they will learn about the struggle for power between the Church and the monarchs during the Middle Ages.

VOCABULARY PRE-CHECK

Write the key terms for this chapter on the chalkboard. Ask students to use those that they know in sentences.

Assign Chapter 27 **Vocabulary and Guided Reading Activity** in the TCR.

EXTRA CREDIT PROJECT

Have students research and write a biography of Marco Polo. Suggest they include accounts of his travels, important historical figures he met, and what impact his travels had on Europe and its development. Encourage students to share their biographies with the class.

KEY TO ABILITY LEVELS

Teaching strategies have been coded for varying learning styles and abilities.

L1 Level 1 activities are **basic** activities and should be within the ability range of all students.

L2 Level 2 activities are **average** activities and should be within the ability range of the average to above-average student.

L3 Level 3 activities are **challenging** activities designed for the ability range of above-average students.

LEP LEP activities should be within the ability range of Limited English Proficiency students.

TEACH

GUIDED PRACTICE

L2 **Panel Discussion** Organize the class into five groups. Assign each group one of the following Capetian monarchs: Hugh Capet, Louis VI, Philip Augustus, Louis IX, and Philip the Fair. Tell the students to decide how their monarch strengthened the French monarchy and prepare an index card containing at least three points to be brought out in a panel discussion of the Capetian kings.

MAKING CONNECTIONS

➤➤ **Architecture** Philip Augustus built a fortress called the Louvre, which is now France's national museum. He was also responsible for the construction of the great Cathedral of Notre Dame.

CAPTION ANSWER

the Capetians

DID YOU KNOW ??

Hugh Capet always wore beautiful capes. At first, he had no last name. He was given the name *Capet* from the French word meaning "cape."

VIDEODISC

Use the following to enrich Chapter 27.

WC C 24 14626

St. Louis buries bones of the crusaders.

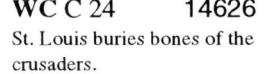

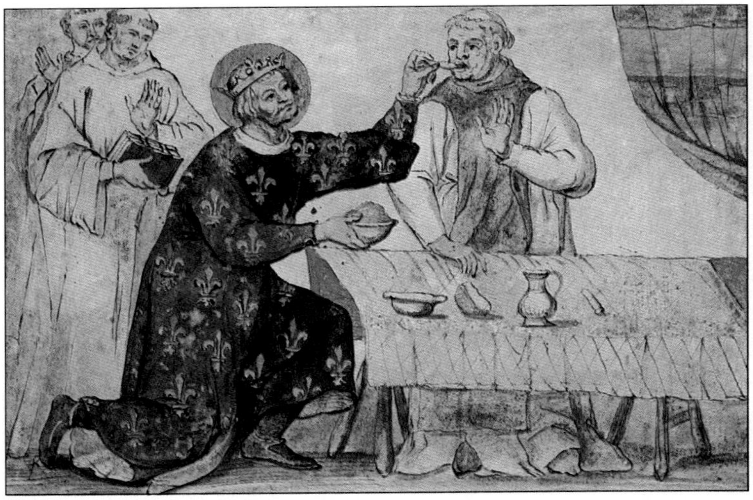

LOUIS IX King Louis IX of France was known for his honesty and just dealings. After his death, he was made a saint of the Roman Catholic Church. Louis's support of the Church is expressed in this painting of the king feeding a church official. **To what line of French kings did Louis IX belong?**

made Paris the center of government. He increased the size of his kingdom through marriage and by winning back French lands held by the English. To make sure the nobles did not become too powerful while he was fighting in the Crusades, Philip II appointed royal agents to keep a close watch on them.

In 1226, Philip's grandson became King Louis IX. He brought peace to France and helped unite the French people. He ordered the nobles to stop feuding and forbade them to settle disputes by fighting duels. Most nobles minted their own money. Louis IX made it illegal to use coins made anywhere else but the royal mint. He set up a royal court to which anyone could bring disputes.

Philip IV, Louis's grandson, ruled from 1285 to 1314. Known as "Philip the Fair," Philip IV believed the interests of the state came first. So, he seized the English fortresses in France that he felt were necessary for his kingdom's security. He also went to war with the Flemish when they refused to let France control their cloth trade. Philip believed a kingdom could not exist without taxes. So, he made sure that taxes were collected regularly. He also taxed the clergy, who had not been taxed before. To help him run the country, Philip IV formed the Estates-General, an assembly of nobles, clergy, and townspeople. This marked the beginning of a national government in France. By the time Philip IV died in 1314, France was united under one ruler.

MULTICULTURAL PERSPECTIVES

The structure of the Estates-General reflected medieval French society (and did so until the French Revolution). The First Estate was the clergy. The Second Estate was the nobility. The Third Estate was the townspeople, the *bourgeoisie*. Philip IV had the support of all three estates, including the French clergy, in his struggle for power with the Pope. Philip IV had a French Pope elected in 1305 and installed at Avignon, France, not Rome. This papacy lasted until 1378. There was a period of time in which there were two popes—one in Rome and one in Avignon.

Section 1 Review

1. **Identify:** Hugh Capet, Louis VI, Philip Augustus, Louis IX, Philip the Fair
2. **Define:** monarchies
3. How did Louis VI increase the power of the monarchy?
4. What did Louis IX and Philip the Fair do to help unite France?

Critical Thinking

5. Which French king do you think contributed the most to French unity? Explain.

Painting of Philip the Fair

Section 2

ENGLAND

In 1042, the witenagemot made Edward the Confessor, an Anglo-Saxon prince, king of England. Edward gave money to the poor and sponsored the building in London of Westminster Abbey, the church in which later English kings and queens were crowned. He spent so much time in religious work, however, that he failed to carry out his royal duties. As a result, the nobles increased their hold on the country. The most powerful noble was Harold Godwinson. When Edward died in 1066 without an heir, Harold became the new king.

William the Conqueror Harold Godwinson did not remain king for long. William, Duke of Normandy, a cousin of Edward the Confessor, claimed that before Edward died, he had promised him the English throne.

In 1066, William led an army of between 4,000 and 7,000 Norman knights across the channel to England. They met Harold's army in battle near Hastings, a town just south of London. To stop the Norman charge, English foot soldiers armed with axes formed a wall of shields on the edge of a low hill. William knew he could not break through the wall. So, he had his soldiers pretend to retreat. When the English broke formation to follow them, the Normans turned on the English. By nightfall, King Harold was dead, and the English were defeated. William the Conqueror, was crowned King William I of England.

At first, the English resisted William's rule. To crush English revolts—and to keep the Normans in line—William introduced feudalism. He seized the lands of English nobles and divided them among Norman nobles. In return, they became his vassals. They promised to be loyal and to provide him with soldiers.

L1 **Government** Each of the French kings detailed in Section 1 made reforms that made life easier for peasants. Help students make a chart that lists the kings and at least one beneficial reform they instigated. Have students decide what information should be included in the chart, and have several students put the information on a large poster board. LEP

DID YOU KNOW ??

The witenagemot was a group of church officials and nobles that advised the king.

MAKING CONNECTIONS

➤➤ **History** William's and Harold's armies were very different. William's soldiers were knights and full-time fighters. Harold's were farmers who left their fields when called to battle.

VIDEODISC

Use the following to enrich Chapter 27.

WC C 14 14616

The Bayeux Tapestry, showing Norman conquest.

SECTION 1 ANSWERS

1. Hugh Capet, French king (p. 411); Louis VI, French king (p. 411); Philip Augustus, French king (p. 411); Louis IX, French king (p. 412); Philip the Fair, French king (p. 412)
2. monarchies, countries governed by one ruler (p. 411)
3. He got rid of nobles who did not fulfill their feudal duties and put loyal persons of lower birth in their place; stopped raids of lawless vassals; and granted charters of freedom to many towns.
4. Louis IX ordered the nobles to stop feuding and fighting duels; required use of royal coins; and set up a royal court. Philip the Fair seized the English fortresses in France, went to war with the Flemish, set up a tax system, and formed the Estates-General.
5. Answers will vary but students should provide reasons for their choices.

Assign the Chapter 27 **Section 1 Quiz** in the TCR. Testmaker available.

MAKING CONNECTIONS

➤➤ **Language** The Old Saxon language continued to be spoken only by farmers and tradespeople. In time, many French words were used in common speech and greatly altered what became the English language.

LINKING PAST TO PRESENT

The Domesday Book, completed in the 1060s, was the first official record of English property owners and the amount of land they owned. The first modern census in the United States occurred in 1790. The U.S. Constitution required an official account not only for taxation but also to determine representation for each state.

CAPTION ANSWER

He became King William I of England.

VIDEODISC

Use the following to enrich Chapter 27.

WC C 18 14620

Tomb of Henry II, Fontevrault Abbey, Anjou.

William kept many English laws and government practices. He received advice from the witenagemot, now called the Great Council. He depended on such local officials as the sheriff. William also made many changes. In 1086, he took a census and a survey of the land in order to tax the people properly. This information was recorded in two huge volumes called the *Domesday Book.* The title comes from the Anglo-Saxon word *doom,* meaning "judgment."

William brought *continental,* or European mainland, ways to England. Under his rule, the English learned Norman customs and the French language. The wealthy built castles, cathedrals, and monasteries in the French style. The people learned new skills from Norman weavers and other artisans.

Henry II After William died in 1087, there was confusion in England until 1154 when William's great-grandson became King Henry II. Henry ruled England, most of Ireland, Scotland, and Wales. He was also a feudal lord in France, where he owned more land than he did in England. Some of the French lands belonged to his wife, Eleanor of Aquitaine.

BATTLE OF HASTINGS William the Conqueror took the throne of England after his army defeated the English army at the Battle of Hastings in 1066. This painting shows Norman knights on horseback attacking the English soldiers. **What title did William the Conqueror take after his victory at Hastings?**

COOPERATIVE LEARNING

Divide the class into four groups. Assign each group one of the following topics: William the Conqueror, Henry II, Magna Carta, and Parliament. Each group is responsible for researching and preparing a report explaining how these rulers and institutions brought about changes in the English monarchy during the Middle Ages. Have a spokesperson from each group present their group's report to the class.

Assign the Chapter 27 **Cooperative Learning Activity** in the TCR.

Henry II restored order and forced the nobles to give him their loyalty. He also used the law to gain more power, and he worked to reform English courts. A central royal court was set up in London with trained lawyers as judges. **Circuit judges,** or judges who travel throughout the country, brought the king's law to all parts of England. They made it the common law of the land, thus helping to unite the country.

Henry also set up juries to settle quarrels about land. After a while, two kinds of juries came into being. One was the **grand jury,** or a group of people who present to judges the names of people suspected of crimes. The other was the **trial jury,** or a group of people who decide whether a person accused of a crime is innocent or guilty. The trial jury took the place of the medieval trial by ordeal.

Painting of Henry II

Henry II believed that everyone, even church officials, should be tried in the king's courts. Thomas à Becket, Henry's close friend and the Archbishop of Canterbury, did not agree. Becket wanted Church officials to be free of royal control. The quarrel between the king and the archbishop ultimately led to the murder of Becket by four of Henry's knights. After the murder, Henry II made peace with the Church by allowing some of the clergy to be tried in church courts.

Magna Carta and Parliament When Henry II died in 1189, his oldest son Richard became king. Richard, however, was more interested in his French lands than in ruling England. He spent most of his time fighting in the Near East on the Crusades.

When Richard died in 1199, his brother John became king of England. John lost most of his lands in France to the French king. When he increased England's taxes and began to ignore the law, the country's nobles became angry. They refused to obey him unless he agreed to give them certain rights. In 1215, John met the nobles in the meadow of Runnymede (ruhn' ē mēd), where they forced him to sign the *Magna Carta* (mag' nuh kar' tuh), or Great Charter.

Stained-glass Window of Thomas à Becket

The Magna Carta took away some of the king's power and increased that of the nobles. A king could no longer collect taxes unless the Great Council agreed. Freemen accused of crimes had the right to a trial by their *peers,* or equals. The Magna Carta was viewed as an important step toward democracy. It brought to government the new idea that even a king is not above the law.

John died in 1216, and his son became King Henry III. Henry, however, was a weak ruler who allowed the feudal lords in the Great Council to rule England. In 1264, Simon de Montfort (mahnt' fuhrt), Henry's brother-in-law, came to power. He gave the people a voice in government by letting them have representatives in the Great Council.

L2 **Language Arts** Discuss the word *conflict* as it applies to the conflicts between the English monarch and the Church. Ask students for other words that could be used in place of *conflict*. List these on the chalkboard and have volunteers research their origins and meanings for comparison. LEP

DID YOU KNOW ??

Thomas à Becket was murdered in his own cathedral during Christmastime. He became an instant medieval celebrity. Within months, miracles were reported at Becket's tomb and pilgrims flocked to the site.

MAKING CONNECTIONS

➤➤ **History** During the 10 years of his rule, Richard spent less than a year in England. Most of his time was spent on the Crusades. On his way home from the Third Crusade, he was shipwrecked in the Adriatic Sea. While trying to make his way home by land, the Duke of Austria took him prisoner. He was released after the English people collected and paid a large ransom.

MEETING SPECIAL NEEDS

Have auditory learners hold a debate between representatives of the English monarchy and the Church of Rome. Divide the class into three groups. One group should gather information from the text and from other references. The second group should prepare arguments, questions and possible answers to be used during the debate. The third group should form a committee to hear the arguments from each side, weigh the merits of each argument, and determine the winning position.

VIDEODISC

Use the following to enrich Chapter 27.

WC C 19 14621
The murder of Thomas Becket, 1170.

WC C 21 14623
The Magna Carta, 1215.

CAPTION ANSWER

the idea that even the king is not above the law

L3 **Debate** Have students learn more about the importance of the Magna Carta. Form two groups of students, one to represent King John and the other to represent the nobles. Have students prepare their arguments to debate the need for the Magna Carta. Students should hold their debate, and the other students, as audience, can judge who presents the most convincing arguments.

MAKING CONNECTIONS

➤➤ **Language** The word *parliament* introduced by Simon de Montfort, comes from *parler,* the French word meaning "to talk or discuss." Because it set the precedent for the holding of future parliaments, Edward I's gathering was later called the Model Parliament.

L2 **History** Ask students to imagine that they were newspaper reporters living during the Middle Ages. They have been asked to write two articles on the Hundred Years' War. One article should discuss the causes of the war between France and England in 1339. The other should deal with the end of the war in 1453 and emphasize the results of the war. Students should write appropriate headlines for the two articles. Have students read their articles to the class.

MAGNA CARTA The Archbishop of Canterbury and merchants joined the nobles at Runnymede to force King John to sign the Magna Carta. In this painting, as the Archbishop looks on, a noble shows King John where to sign the document. **What new idea did the Magna Carta bring to government?**

Eight years later, the new king, Edward I, went even further. He called for a meeting of representatives to advise him and to help him make laws. This gathering, known as Parliament (par' luh muhnt), gave the people a greater share in the ruling of England. Parliament later broke into two separate groups. Nobles and clergy met as the House of Lords, while knights and townspeople met as the House of Commons.

Section 2 Review

1. **Identify:** William the Conqueror, *Domesday Book,* Henry II, Thomas à Becket, King John, Magna Carta, Parliament
2. **Define:** circuit judges, grand jury, trial jury
3. How did the Normans win the Battle of Hastings?
4. Why was King John forced to sign the Magna Carta?

Critical Thinking

5. Why was the idea that a king is not above the law an important step in democracy?

SECTION 2 ANSWERS

1. William the Conqueror, English king (p. 413); *Domesday Book,* English book of census (p. 414); Henry II, English king (p. 415); Thomas à Becket, Archbishop of Canterbury (p. 415); King John, English king who signed Magna Carta (p. 415); Magna Carta, Great Charter (p. 415); Parliament, representative body (p. 416)
2. circuit judges, judges who travel (p. 415); grand jury, people who judge others suspected of crimes (p. 415); trial jury, group who decides innocence or guilt (p. 415)
3. William's soldiers pretended to retreat and attacked when the English broke formation to follow after them.
4. because he had increased taxes and had begun to ignore the law
5. Answers will vary, but students could indicate that this was the beginning of equality under law.

Assign the Chapter 27 **Section 2 Quiz** in the TCR. Testmaker available.

Section 3
The Hundred Years' War

In the early 1300s, the English still held a small part of southwest France. The kings of France, who were growing more powerful, wanted to drive the English out. In 1337, the English king, Edward III, declared himself king of France. This angered the French even more. In 1337, England and France fought the first in a long series of battles known as the Hundred Years' War.

The Hundred Years' War began when the English defeated the French fleet and won control of the sea. The English then invaded France. They defeated the French at the Battle of Crécy (krā sē') in 1346 and again at the Battle of Agincourt (aj' uhn kōrt) in 1415.

The English owed their success on land mostly to a new weapon called the *longbow,* which shot steel-tipped arrows. The French still used the shorter crossbow. The crossbow could not send arrows as far as the longbow, and the French arrows were not as sharp as the steel-tipped English arrows.

At Crécy the English forces also used the first portable firearm in European warfare—a very crude cannon. This early weapon was made of a long iron tube mounted on a pole. The weapon was difficult to carry and use, but led to the development of a more refined cannon that was a major weapon in many later wars.

Joan of Arc By 1429, much of France was in English hands. Charles, the French ***dauphin*** (dō' fuhn), or eldest son of the king, was fighting the English for the French throne. Then, a 17-year-old French peasant named Jeanne d'Arc (zhahn dark'), or Joan of Arc, appeared. She said that while praying, she had heard heavenly voices telling her she must save France. She went to see Charles and told him that God had sent her to help him. She said that if she had an army she would free Orleans (or lā ahn'), a city the English had been besieging for seven months. Charles gave Joan an army, a suit of armor, and a white linen banner.

Joan led an attack against the English army at Orleans. Within ten days, the city was free, and Joan became known as the "Maid of Orleans." Shortly after, with Joan at his side, the dauphin was crowned King Charles VII of France. Joan wanted to return home, but Charles convinced her to stay with the army. A few months later, a French traitor captured her and sold her to the English. After spending a year in prison, she was tried as a witch and burned at the stake. Joan died at the age of 18, a girl who could neither read nor write but who had led an army. A trial twenty-four years later proclaimed her innocence.

Photograph of Crossbow

L2 **Religion** Ask students why Joan of Arc was successful and why French soldiers accepted her reports of hearing heavenly voices. List the reasons on the chalkboard. Remind students that religion played an important role during the Middle Ages. LEP

L3 **Research** Ask students to research and report on the life of Joan of Arc. With their report, have students prepare a scenario of what might happen if she appeared in modern times in the same kind of situation. How do students think people today would react to her and her "messages"?

MAKING CONNECTIONS

➤➤ **History** It is believed that gunpowder, invented in China, was used for the first time in European warfare at the Battle of Crécy. Its use helped bring the Middle Ages to an end by destroying the ability of castles to withstand an attack.

VIDEODISC

Use the following to enrich Chapter 27.

WC C 29 14631
The Battle of Poitiers, 1356.

WC C 30 14632
The King of France and his council.

COOPERATIVE LEARNING

Have groups of students prepare and present readings from the play *Saint Joan* by George Bernard Shaw, choosing suitable passages for presentation, assigning and reading the roles, preparing and presenting a summary of the play, and explaining scenes being presented.

LINKING PAST TO PRESENT

Today, Joan of Arc is the second patron saint of France.

MAKING CONNECTIONS

➤➤ **Government** During the Hundred Years' War, English kings depended increasingly on Parliament to raise funds in order to support the war. This reliance on Parliament by England's monarchy strengthened Parliament's power. The arrangement strengthened the king as well, giving him power to work with Parliament to raise funds and change laws. In France, the Estates-General was the king's council. Because the king retained the right to raise money and make laws, the Estates-General never assumed the same powers as the English Parliament and eventually was disbanded. Without the Estates-General, the French king was an absolute monarch.

CAPTION ANSWER

She led an attack against the English army at Orleans and freed the city.

The French continued to fight after Joan's death. By 1453, they had driven the English from all of France except the seaport of Calais (ka lā'), and the war came to an end.

Results of the War Both France and England were changed by the Hundred Years' War. By 1500, the last French feudal territories were under the king's rule, and France was unified. England, too, was unified by the war, but its monarchy was weakened. Not until 1485, when a Welshman named Henry Tudor (tū' duhr) became king, did it become strong again.

Because of the Hundred Years' War, the common people in both England and France became more important. Many peasants had died during the war from disease or fighting. Those who remained were greatly needed as workers. The peasants knew this and began to make demands. They forced the nobles to pay them wages and allow them to move outside the manors. When the nobles tried to force them back to the old ways, they revolted. Most became farmers who rented land from the nobles.

JOAN OF ARC Claiming that heavenly voices had instructed her to do so, Joan of Arc led a French army against the invading English and helped return the French king to the throne. She became a national heroine and a saint of the Roman Catholic Church. **How did Joan earn her nickname "Maid of Orleans"?**

EXTENDING THE CONTENT

One of the most famous uprisings was the 1381 Peasant's Revolt in England, led by Wat Tyler and a priest, John Ball. Three ragged peasant armies marched on London in the summer of 1381. They kidnapped several high royal officials, including the Archbishop of Canterbury, and beheaded them. They demanded freedom and an end to all class distinctions or feudal duties. King Richard II began to bargain with the rioters. His army seized and punished the leaders, and the rebellion came to an end.

Section 3 Review

1. **Identify:** Hundred Years' War, Joan of Arc, Charles VII
2. **Define:** *dauphin*
3. Why did France and England go to war?
4. How did the Hundred Years' War affect French and English peasants?

Critical Thinking

5. How did the Hundred Years' War help end feudalism?

Section 4

GERMANY

During the 900s, Germany was the most important country in western Europe. Over time, though, German kings lost much of their authority to powerful nobles who wanted to rule their own territories. The king, however, still had the right to remove lords who would not obey him.

Otto I In 936, Otto I became king of Germany. He wanted to unite the country and rule without nobles. He removed lords who would not obey him and gave their estates to his family. Then, he turned to the Roman Catholic Church for help. Its leaders wanted him to set up a Christian Roman Empire in western Europe. So, Otto made many of his loyal followers bishops and abbots and gave them government posts. In return, they supplied him with money and soldiers.

Otto began expanding Germany. In 951, he marched south into Italy, where he took over the northern Italian trading cities. In 962, he led an army to Rome to free the Pope from the control of Roman nobles. In return, the Pope crowned Otto I emperor of the Holy Roman Empire, a large new state made up of Germany and northern Italy. Otto saw himself as the heir of the Roman emperors. For the next 90 years, Otto and the emperors who followed him controlled the office of Pope.

Frederick I In 1152, Frederick I became emperor. Because of his full red beard, he was called Barbarossa, or "red beard." Frederick forced the powerful lords to promise him loyalty and to work for his government.

Frederick's attempts to control the nobles and unify the empire worked against him. The nobles grew rich from their government posts. At the same time, the Italian city-states, aided

German Crown

L1 **Discussion** Lead a discussion of the following questions as students build a cause-and-effect graphic organizer on the chalkboard. Encourage volunteers to add to the graphics as the questions are answered. Ask: *How was the Holy Roman Empire created and ruled? What was the relationship between Otto I and the Roman Catholic Church? How did Otto I become emperor of the Holy Roman Empire? What caused the Holy Roman Empire to become weaker during the rule of Frederick I? Why did the Pope call for a crusade against Frederick II? What happened as a result of Hapsburg rule?* LEP

MAKING CONNECTIONS

➤➤ **History** Otto was the son of Henry I, or Henry the Fowler, powerful German Duke of Saxony who was elected king of Germany in 919. Henry's bravery and ability won the respect of the nobles and paved the way for the rule of his son.

VIDEODISC

Use the following to enrich Chapter 27.

WC C 31 14633
Richard II gives Aquitaine to John of Gaunt.

WC C 36 14638
Joan of Arc (1412-1431).

SECTION 3 ANSWERS

1. Hundred Years' War, long war between England and France (p. 417); Joan of Arc, French peasant who attacked the English at Orleans (p. 417); Charles VII, French king (p. 417)
2. *dauphin,* eldest son of the French king (p. 417)
3. The kings of France wanted to drive the English out, and Edward III of England declared himself king of France.
4. They became more important.
5. Answers will vary but could include that kings took control of feudal territories, England and France were unified, and peasants became more important.

Assign the Chapter 27 **Section 3 Quiz** in the TCR. Testmaker available.

MAKING CONNECTIONS

➤➤ **Legends** According to legend, when Frederick Barbarossa's red beard grows long enough to wrap completely around the large table next to which he "sleeps," Barbarossa will rise and destroy Germany's enemies.

CAPTION ANSWER

He founded a university at Palermo.

by the Pope, banded together and defeated Frederick's armies. Frederick had to accept a peace that recognized the independence of the city-states.

While leading the Third Crusade in 1190, Frederick drowned in a river in Asia Minor. Later, a legend about him spread among the Germans. It stated that he was not dead but under a magic spell that had put him to sleep somewhere high in the mountains. The people believed that one day he would awake and restore the glory of Germany.

Frederick II In 1220, Frederick II, Frederick I's grandson, became emperor. Frederick II was raised in Palermo (puh luhr' mō), Sicily, which his father had made part of the Holy Roman Empire. So, he ignored Germany and concentrated on ruling the people of Sicily.

Frederick was known as the best-educated monarch of his time. He spoke several languages and enjoyed doing scientific experiments. He supported many artists and scholars. He

FREDERICK II Frederick II was greatly interested in the sciences and medicine and encouraged their study during his reign. He had a special interest in the study of birds and wrote a book on the subject. This painting of Frederick is showing him with his falcon handler. **How did Frederick II aid medieval learning?**

EXTENDING THE CONTENT

Today the Catholic Pope is elected by the College of Cardinals without interference from any political groups. The Popes have been traditionally Italian, however, in 1978 the college elected the Polish Pope John Paul II.

YOUNG SCHOLARS Scholarship was important to the Hapsburg family, which included Maximilian I. The Hapsburgs encouraged the growth of universities throughout Germany. **In what year did Maximilian I become emperor of the Holy Roman Empire?**

founded a university in Palermo so young men could study at home rather than in other countries. Although the Church was against it, Frederick even adopted many Muslim customs.

When Frederick began conquering land in Italy, the Pope became afraid that he would take over church lands around Rome. To stop Frederick, the Pope excommunicated him in 1227. He also called for a crusade against Frederick. This gave the German princes the chance for which they had been waiting. They broke away from Frederick's rule and made Germany a loose grouping of states under their control.

The Hapsburgs Whenever an emperor of the Holy Roman Empire died, the German princes met in a **diet,** or assembly. There, they elected a new emperor. In 1273, the princes elected as emperor a member of the Hapsburg (haps' berg) family named Rudolf. He and members of his family served as Holy Roman emperors for about the next 650 years.

One important Hapsburg was Maximilian I (mak suh mil' yuhn), who became emperor in 1493. He worked to extend the empire's power all through Europe. When he married Mary of Burgundy, he gained control of Flanders and other areas of what are now the Low Countries, or Belgium, the Netherlands, and Luxembourg. By marrying his children into other European

CAPTION ANSWER

1493

L2 **Culture** One of the favorite pastimes of nobles during the Middle Ages was falconry. Suggest students research this sport, its origins, and report their findings to the rest of the class. Encourage the class to discuss possible modern spin-offs of this sport.

GEOGRAPHY AND HISTORY

Maximilian's older son Philip I, married Joanna, the daughter of Ferdinand and Isabella of Spain. His second son, Ferdinand, married Anna of Bohemia and Hungary. By 1520, the Hapsburgs ruled half of Europe and most of the settled areas in the Americas.

SPOTLIGHT ON: THE HAPSBURGS

Emperor Charles V retired to a monastery in 1556 after ruling much of Europe for 37 years. The resulting division of Hapsburg lands gave the family power in parts of Europe for hundreds of years, outlasting the Holy Roman Empire. Charles' son became king of Spain as Philip II, who ruled a vast empire in the Americas. The Spanish line continued until 1700. A lack of an heir caused the War of the Spanish Succession. The Austrian Hapsburg dynasty continued under Charles' brother Ferdinand. Hapsburg emperors and an empress ruled the Holy Roman Empire until the empire was ended in the early 1800s. They then ruled Austria-Hungary. The last Hapsburg emperor of Austria had to abdicate after World War I.

INDEPENDENT PRACTICE

L1 **History** Have students work in pairs to prepare a list of questions that a news reporter might ask one of the people mentioned in this chapter. Have them role-play the interview for the class.

L2 **Geography: Region** Have the students create five geography-based questions based on the map of "Europe in the Late Middle Ages." Collect the questions and use them to quiz the students. LEP

MAP STUDY

Answer

The Holy Roman Empire was larger than the other regions.

Assign the Chapter 27 **Geography and Map Activity** in the TCR.

royal families, he brought still more countries under Hapsburg control. He could not gain complete control, however, in Germany where the princes continued to have authority over their own lands.

Section 4 Review

1. **Identify:** Otto I, Holy Roman Empire, Frederick I, Frederick II, Hapsburgs, Maximilian I
2. **Define:** diet
3. How were German emperors able to control the office of Pope in the late 900s and early 1000s?

Critical Thinking

4. Why do you think a strong rule by a king or queen did not develop in Germany?

Europe in the Late Middle Ages

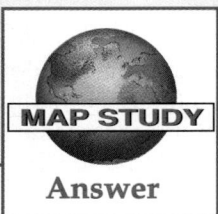

MAP STUDY

REGIONS Strong kings and queens appeared in England, France, Spain, and Portugal in the late Middle Ages. **How did the size of the Holy Roman Empire compare to other regions of western Europe during the late Middle Ages?**

SECTION 4 ANSWERS

1. Otto I, German king (p. 419); Holy Roman Empire, state of Germany and northern Italy (p. 419); Frederick I, emperor of Holy Roman Empire (p. 419); Frederick II, emperor of Holy Roman Empire (p. 420); Hapsburgs, family of Holy Roman emperors (p. 421); Maximilian I, Hapsburg (p. 421)
2. diet, assembly (p. 421)
3. Otto had freed the Pope from the control of Roman nobles. In return, the Pope crowned him Emperor of the Holy Roman Empire.
4. Answers will vary but might include the idea that Germany was a loose grouping of states under the control of German princes. Also, emperors were elected by German princes rather than inheriting the position.

Assign the Chapter 27 **Section 4 Quiz** in the TCR. Testmaker available.

Section 5

SPAIN

Painting of Spanish Hero El Cid

While the western European monarchies were increasing their power, Spain was under the control of the Moors. When the Moors conquered Spain in 711, they brought with them learning and luxury. Most Spaniards, however, were Christians and opposed Muslim rule. They banded together to drive the Moors out of the country. By the 1200s, the Moors controlled only the small southern kingdom of Granada (gruh nahd' uh).

The rest of Spain was made up of several kingdoms, the most powerful of which were Castile (kas tēl') and Aragon (ar' uh gahn). In 1469, Prince Ferdinand of Aragon married Princess Isabella of Castile. Within ten years, they became king and queen and united their kingdoms into one country.

Ferdinand and Isabella accomplished this in different ways. To control the nobles, the king and queen took away some of their privileges. To keep order in the land, they sent royal officials called ***corregidores*** (kō rā hē dō' rās) to govern the towns. They also set up special courts in the countryside.

The most important way in which they unified Spain, however, was through religion. Ferdinand and Isabella were known as the "Catholic Monarchs." They believed that to be truly united, all Spaniards should be Catholic. They turned their attention first to the Jews. The Jews had lived freely under the Moors. However, as Christians took over more of Spain, they killed thousands of Jews. To save themselves, many Jews converted.

Ferdinand and Isabella believed these new Christians were practicing their old religion in secret. So, they set up the Spanish Inquisition. The Spanish Inquisition tried and tortured thousands of people charged with heresy. More than 2,000 people were burned to death. Still, most Jews refused to change their faith. So, in 1492, Ferdinand and Isabella told the remaining Jews to convert or leave the country. Most left the country.

Next, the king and queen turned their attention to the Moors. In 1492, the last of the Moors had surrendered Granada to armies of Ferdinand and Isabella. The treaty signed at the time promised the Moors freedom of religion. Nevertheless, in 1502 the Catholic Monarchs ordered the remaining Moors to convert or leave. Most left Spain for northern Africa.

Although now a united Catholic monarchy, Spain was weaker than it had been before. This was because most of its artisans, merchants, bankers, doctors, and educators had been either Jews or Moors. After these people left, there were few trained Spaniards to take their place.

SPOTLIGHT ON: EL CID

Spain's national epic, which created a hero like England's King Arthur or France's Roland, comes out of the long period of wars between Moors and Christians known as the *Reconquista*. The Christians of the old Visigothic kingdoms had been pushed back into the Pyrenees. From there they moved southward city by city. Spanish rulers also warred against each other. In addition, Muslim kingdoms were resisting takeover by fanatic Almoravids from North Africa. The hero of the battle of Valencia in 1094 was El Cid. This was the name given to the military leader Rodrigo Díaz de Vivar who later became ruler of Valencia. More legends than facts are known about El Cid.

L2 **Language Arts** The crusades of the northern Christian kingdoms of Spain against the Moors influenced the growth of Spanish literature. Students might enjoy reading excerpts from the twelfth-century *Poem of the Cid,* which chronicles the life of Spanish soldier-hero Rodrigo Díaz.

L2 **The Arts** When Ferdinand and Isabella captured the Moorish province of Granada, they gained some remarkable examples of Moorish art and architecture, such as the Alhambra. Have students research and report on the art and architecture of the Spanish Moors. Have them give oral summaries of their reports including pictures of the art and architecture.

VIDEODISC

Use the following to enrich Chapter 27.

WC C 112 14714

Avila, a key town in the Spanish reconquista.

ASSESS

CHECK FOR UNDERSTANDING

Ask students to summarize the main points of the chapter, orally or in writing. Discuss the answers to the Section and Chapter Review questions.

EVALUATE

Assign the Chapter 27 **Performance Assessment Activity** in the TCR.

Administer the **Chapter 27 Test**. Testmaker available.

RETEACH

Have the students create a time line of events covered in this chapter.

Assign the Chapter 27 **Reteaching Activity** in the TCR.

ENRICH

The son of the English King Edward III was known as the Black Prince because he wore black armor. Have students research the Black Prince and his role in the Hundred Years' War. Ask them to imagine being Edward and write a first-person account of his career.

Assign the Chapter 27 **Enrichment Activity** in the TCR.

CLOSE

Have students debate the advantages and disadvantages of a strong monarchy during the Middle Ages.

MEETING CHAPTER OBJECTIVES

Each objective is tested by the Review questions in parentheses.

1. Describe how Capetian kings strengthened the French monarchy. (BV; CU 1)
2. Discuss changes in the English monarchy during the Middle Ages. (CU 2, 3; CT 1; UYJ)
3. Analyze the causes and results of the Hundred Years' War. (CU 4; CT 2, 3)
4. Explain how the Holy Roman Empire was ruled. (CU 5, 6)
5. Summarize how Catholic monarchs united Spain. (CU 8; CT 4)

Section 5 Review

1. **Identify:** Granada, Ferdinand and Isabella, Spanish Inquisition
2. **Define:** *corregidores*
3. How did Ferdinand and Isabella control the nobles and keep order in Spain?
4. How did Ferdinand and Isabella's religion unite Spain?

Critical Thinking

5. How might Spain have been different if the Spanish king and queen had allowed freedom of religion?

Chapter Summary

1. The rise of trade and towns in western Europe during the late Middle Ages led to the rise of strong monarchies.
2. The Capetian dynasty of France began in 987 and lasted for some 300 years.
3. Capetian kings strengthened the French monarchy by granting town charters, setting up a national court and currency, a tax system, and the Estates-General.
4. In 1066, William the Conqueror defeated the English at the Battle of Hastings.
5. William the Conqueror continued to accept advice from the witenagemot but also brought feudalism and the French language to England.
6. Henry II strengthened England by making the king's law the law of the land and by reforming courts.
7. In 1215, English nobles forced King John to sign the Magna Carta, which established the idea that even a king is not above the law.
8. In 1272, Edward I set up Parliament to advise him.
9. Between 1337 and 1453, England and France fought the Hundred Years' War.
10. In 1429, Joan of Arc succeeded in driving the English from Orleans.
11. Because of the Hundred Years' War, both France and England were unified and the common people became more important.
12. In 962, the Pope crowned Otto I emperor of the Holy Roman Empire.
13. The Hapsburg family ruled the Holy Roman Empire from 1273 until the early 1900s.
14. By 1492, Ferdinand and Isabella conquered the Moors and made Spain a united Catholic country.

SECTION 5 ANSWERS

1. Granada, kingdom of Spain (p. 423); Ferdinand and Isabella, monarchs who united kingdoms of Spain (p. 423); Spanish Inquisition, heresy court in Spain (p. 423)
2. *corregidores*, Spanish royal officials (p. 423)
3. They took away some of their privileges, sent *corregidores* to govern the towns, and set up special courts in the countryside.
4. They forced the Jews and the Moors to convert to Christianity or leave the country.
5. Answers will vary but might include that the artisans, merchants, bankers, doctors, and educators who were needed to keep the nation strong would not have left Spain.

Assign the Chapter 27 **Section 5 Quiz** in the TCR. Testmaker available.

CHAPTER Review 27

Building Vocabulary

Imagine that you are a news reporter who has a chance to interview one of the kings or queens you have read about in this chapter. Identify who you will interview and write five questions you would like to ask that person. Use the following words in your questions.

monarchies	*dauphin*
circuit judges	diet
grand jury	*corregidores*
trial jury	

Check for Understanding

1. How did the Estates-General help to strengthen the French monarchy?
2. Why did William the Conqueror take a census of the people and a survey of the land in England?
3. What changes did the Magna Carta bring about in English government?
4. Why did the position of the common people in England and France improve as a result of the Hundred Years' War?
5. How did Otto I set up a Christian Roman Empire in western Europe?
6. Why did Frederick II ignore Germany and concentrate on ruling Sicily?
7. What did the Moors bring to Spain?
8. What was the purpose of the Spanish Inquisition?

Critical Thinking

1. If you had been King John how would you have reacted to the demand that you sign the Magna Carta? Explain.
2. If you had been Joan of Arc, what decision would you have made about attacking the English at Orleans?
3. How did the Hundred Years' War both help and hurt England and France?
4. Would you have agreed or disagreed with Ferdinand and Isabella that all the people in a country should follow the same religion? Explain.

Geography in History

PLACE Refer to the map on page 422. There were several places outside the control of either the English or the Holy Roman Empire. What geographic features do these places have in common?

Using Your Journal

Review the details you have noted about life during the late Middle Ages. Imagine you have gone back in time to England during that era. Write a letter to a friend there explaining what you think of your king, John, and the new Magna Carta.

CHAPTER 27 REVIEW ANSWERS

BUILDING VOCABULARY

Questions will vary according to the king or queen selected but students should include all the vocabulary words.

CHECK FOR UNDERSTANDING

1. It united the nobles, clergy, and townspeople.
2. in order to tax the people properly
3. It increased the nobles' power, gave freemen the right to a trial, and said that the king had to obey laws.
4. because many had died, and those who remained were greatly needed as workers
5. He made his loyal followers bishops and abbots and gave them government posts.
6. because he was raised in Palermo
7. learning and luxury
8. to deal with heresy

CRITICAL THINKING

1. Answers will vary, but students might disagree with King John's acceptance.
2. Answers will vary.
3. Answers will vary, but might include that it helped by unifying them but hurt the countries by resulting in the deaths of many peasants.
4. Answers will vary, but students should explain why they agree or disagree.

✚ BONUS ✚

TEST QUESTION

For Chapter 27 Test

If medieval kings and queens had been able to access modern technology, they might have avoided some of their problems. Assume the role of one of these monarchs and name a modern invention you could have used and what problem it would have solved. *(Answers will vary.)*

USING YOUR JOURNAL

Letters will vary but students might include the idea of grand juries, trial juries, right to a trial by peers, and Parliament.

GEOGRAPHY IN HISTORY

They are on the outer fringes of Europe and are widely spaced and most often surrounded by water.

425

UNIT 8 CULTURE CLOSE-UP

THE SAMURAI

FOCUS

OBJECTIVES

Locate where the samurai lived. Identify the time period during which the samurai lived. Describe the rich tradition and culture of the samurai.

BELLRINGER

Write the following on the chalkboard: *List everything you know about the samurai.*

MOTIVATIONAL ACTIVITY

Ask students to read their responses to what they know about the samurai. Have a student record the responses on the chalkboard. Save the responses to review after the feature has been studied. Then explain to the students that in this Culture Close-Up they will learn about the samurai and their way of life.

UNIT 8 CULTURE CLOSE-UP

The Samurai

The bravest of feudal warriors were the samurai of Japan. From about 1200 A.D. to 1600 A.D., these warriors devoted their lives to the defense of their rulers.

Geography Connection

Japan, an island nation, was made up of many small kingdoms in feudal times. Mountains helped to isolate these kingdoms from one another.

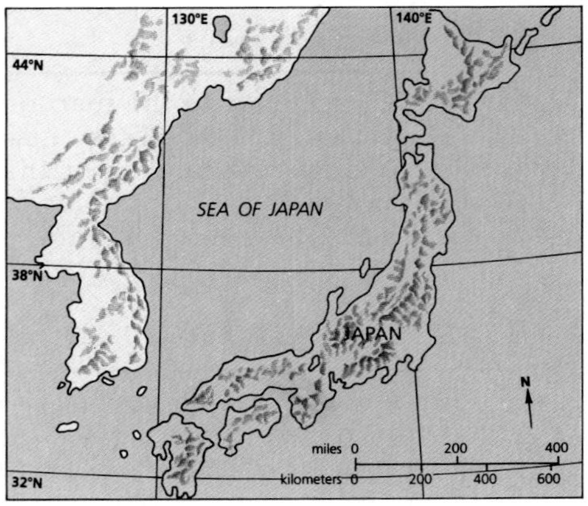

▲ The samurai wore both armor and richly made clothing. Their clothing protected them in battle and gave them distinction. Japanese women were samurai warriors too.

426

MEETING SPECIAL NEEDS

During feudal Japan, a new period in the arts was established. As a result, there are many paintings that show the samurai from this time period. Have students who are visual learners research history books and art history books to find paintings of the samurai. Have the students share the paintings with the class.

The rulers that the samurai served were called shoguns. The first shogun, Minamoto Yositomo, was an absolute ruler of his kingdom. ▶

◀ Parcels of the shogun's kingdom and other wealth were given to samurai as a reward for their loyal service. This castle was the home of samurai Toyotomi Hideyoshi.

The samurai upheld the rulings of the shogun's court. The samurai followed the principal of *bushido*, which means "the way of the warrior." Bushido stressed bravery, loyalty, and self-discipline. ▶

TEACH

L1 **Geography: Location** Have students study the map of Japan on page 426. Ask: What two physical features of Japan helped to isolate the many small kingdoms from one another? *(mountains and islands)* LEP

MAKING CONNECTIONS

➤➤ **History** In the 1000s and 1100s, the emperor of Japan was only a symbol of Japanese unity. Large clans fought one another for control of the country. In the late 1100s, one clan seized power. Its head claimed that he was protecting the emperor and ruling in his name. The emperor then gave him the title of *shogun.*

MULTICULTURAL PERSPECTIVES

A samurai dressed for battle was a colorful work of art. The samurai's armor was made of hundreds of tiny leather squares and was light and flexible, unlike that of a knight in medieval Europe whose armor was heavy and cumbersome. The squares on the samurai's armor were lacquered to steel hardness and woven together with silver thread. The swords and sword holders were finely crafted.

UNIT 8 CULTURE CLOSE-UP

L2 **Daily Life** Ask students to imagine that they are living in Japan in the 1300s and they are training to become a samurai. Have them write a letter home to a younger brother or sister explaining what their life is like. Have students share their letters with the class. LEP

DID YOU KNOW ??

Bushido taught self-discipline. The samurai were expected to put up with pain and sacrifice. A sense of pride was important. The samurai believed they had to save face, or save their honor and pride. They took offense at the smallest insult.

GLOBAL READING FOR STUDENTS

Historians in your class may be interested in reading a book about the samurai. Suggest *Samurai Warriors* by Stephen Turnbull, Blandford, 1990. (Challenging/History)

▲ Japanese Poem

Daily Life

The training and education of a samurai began early.

- You first had to be born into the samurai class.
- At a young age, you learned riding, wrestling, archery, and fencing.
- You began to learn reading and writing as soon as you could hold a writing brush.
- At age six, you began memorizing Japanese poems and classical stories.
- Young samurai were taught good manners and courtesy. They were trained in the ancient ritual of pouring tea.
- At the age of 15, you carried two heavy swords—the symbols of your station.

▲ Japanese Tea Jar

Honing a Sword ▶

428

COOPERATIVE LEARNING

Assign each group one of the following arts in which the samurai were educated: the tea ceremony, Japanese poetry, and calligraphy. Have each group research, write a report, and prepare a demonstration about their assigned topic. Remind the groups that each member is to be given a task to help complete the assignment. Have each group present their report and demonstration to the class.

UNIT 8 CULTURE CLOSE-UP

◀ Only a samurai could carry weapons. The samurai fought on foot and on horseback, with bows and arrows, and steel swords.

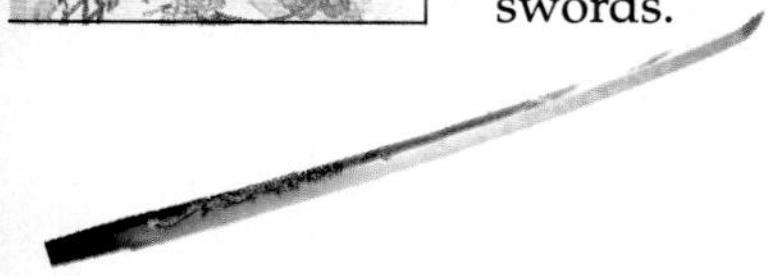

▲ The values of the samurai spread to every class of Japanese society. At this time, however, Japan was beginning to come in contact with other cultures. The samurai tradition would not last in the changing world of the eighteenth century.

Taking Another Look

1. **To whom did the samurai owe loyalty?**
2. **How did a person become a samurai?**
3. **What did *bushido* mean to a samurai?**

Critical Thinking

4. **Why do you think a samurai's education went beyond learning how to be a warrior?**

ASSESS

CHECK FOR UNDERSTANDING

Have students answer the questions in Taking Another Look on page 429.

ANSWERS to Taking Another Look

1. their rulers, or shoguns
2. You had to be born into the samurai class.
3. "the way of the warrior"
4. Answers will vary. Students may note that the samurai needed to have education to better serve their shogun and the fact that samurai came from a high class in Japan.

ENRICH

Ask students to discuss modern parallels to the samurai. What people today play a similar role in society, or seem most like the samurai of ancient times. In what ways are they similar and different from ancient samurai? Suggest students also consider people in other cultures than their own.

CLOSE

Ask students to review their responses to what they knew about the samurai previous to reading this feature. Have them correct misinformation and add new facts they have learned to their lists.

EXTENDING THE CONTENT

Along with the emergence of the samurai came an interest in literature and works of art that glorified the samurai warriors and their military values. Thus, rather than glamorize beauty, artists began to glamorize warriors and war. Poets and writers created stories and conquests in which they highlighted the prowess of samurai warriors. Artists portrayed military subjects that were infused with a great sense of action and immediacy.

INTRODUCE

UNIT 9 OVERVIEW

Unit 9 discusses the changes that took place in western Europe from the 1300s to the 1600s as the Middle Ages came to an end.

- **Chapter 28** describes the Renaissance, when western Europeans experienced new attitudes about themselves and the world around them.
- **Chapter 29** discusses the Reformation and how differences in religions led to religious wars.
- **Chapter 30** summarizes the principal European voyages of discovery from the 1400s to the 1600s.

UNIT OBJECTIVES

After reading Unit 9, students will be able to:

1. describe what changes took place in learning in western Europe during the 1300s and 1400s.
2. summarize what changes took place in religion during the 1400s and 1500s.
3. discuss what western Europeans learned about the world during the Age of Discovery.

UNIT PROJECT

Tell the students to imagine they are on an explorer's ship in the middle 1600s. Their ship has landed in an overseas port. The local ruler expresses interest in hearing about the Renaissance, the Reformation, and the Age of Discovery in western Europe. The students are asked by the captain to give a historical sketch of important events and people during this time. Have them prepare their presentations.

UNIT 9 Beginning of Modern Times

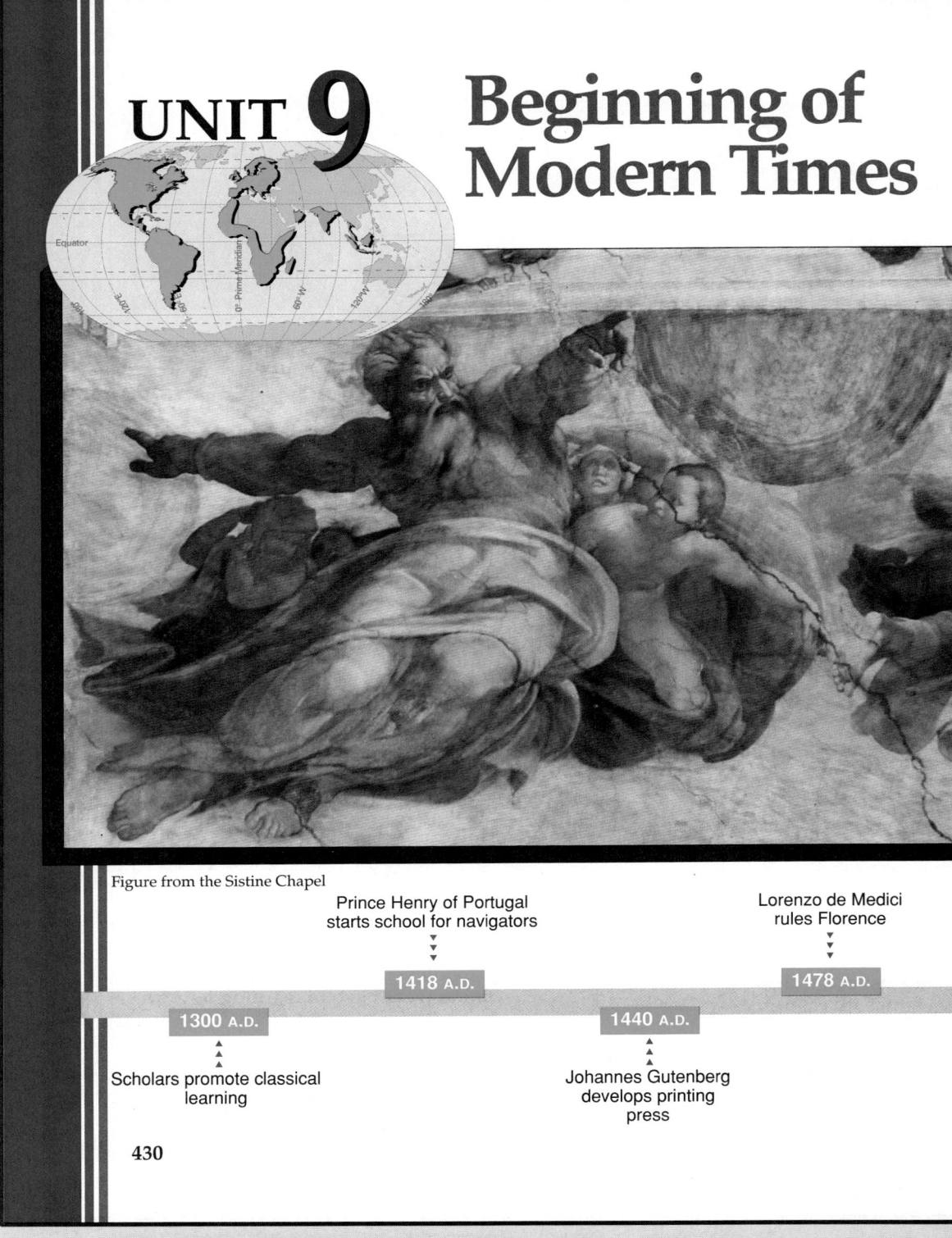

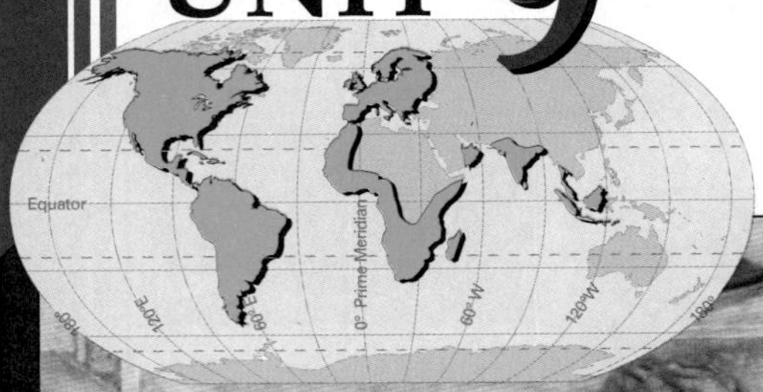

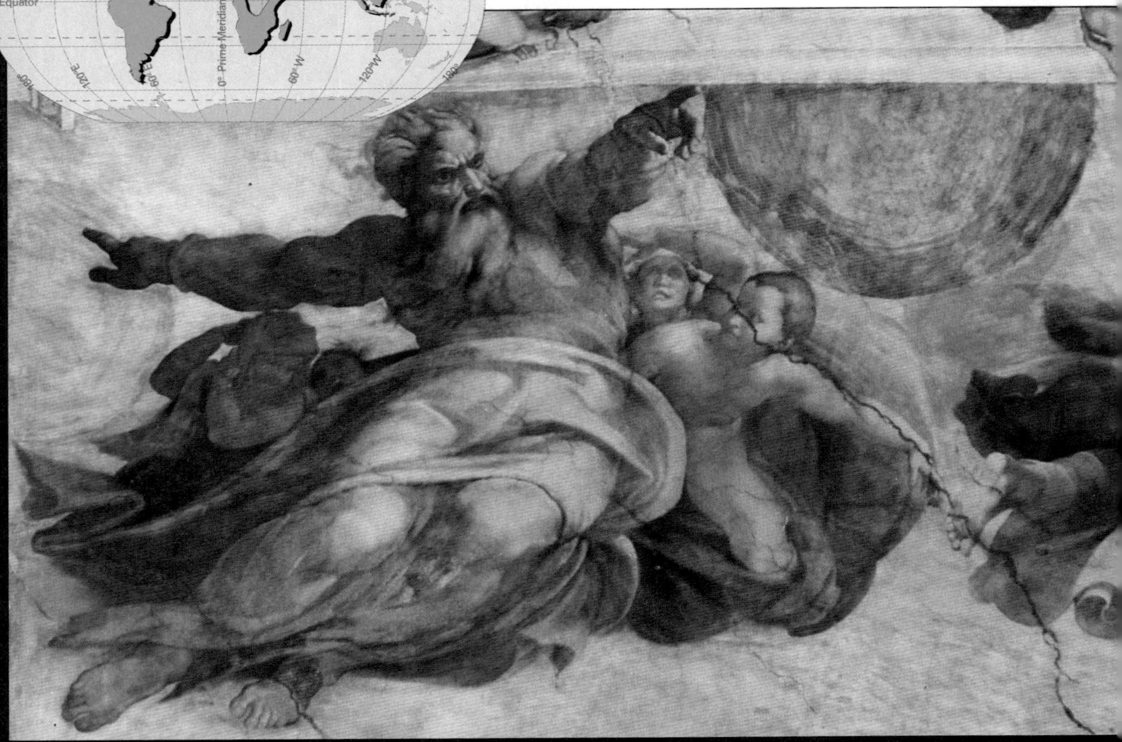

Figure from the Sistine Chapel

- **1300 A.D.** Scholars promote classical learning
- **1418 A.D.** Prince Henry of Portugal starts school for navigators
- **1440 A.D.** Johannes Gutenberg develops printing press
- **1478 A.D.** Lorenzo de Medici rules Florence

430

About the Unit Opening

EXAMINING THE ILLUSTRATION

Ask students where they would expect to see the painting shown on the unit opener. Explain that they may be surprised to learn this art was painted on the ceiling of a famous church about which they will be reading.

GLOBAL CHRONOLOGY

Ask students to explain what time period the time line covers. *(1300 to 1648)* How do they know learning was important during this time period? *(scholars promote classical learning, school for navigators started, printing press invented)* What entries indicate exploration? *(Prince Henry starts school for navigators; Columbus lands at San Salvador; Magellan begins voyage to Pacific)*

During the 1300s and 1400s, western Europe experienced many changes. People became more interested in art and learning. Some people called for a change in the way the Church taught and practiced Christianity. European explorers searched for a shorter and less costly route to the Far East. Their explorations led to the discovery of new continents and peoples. Western Europe began to enter the modern period.

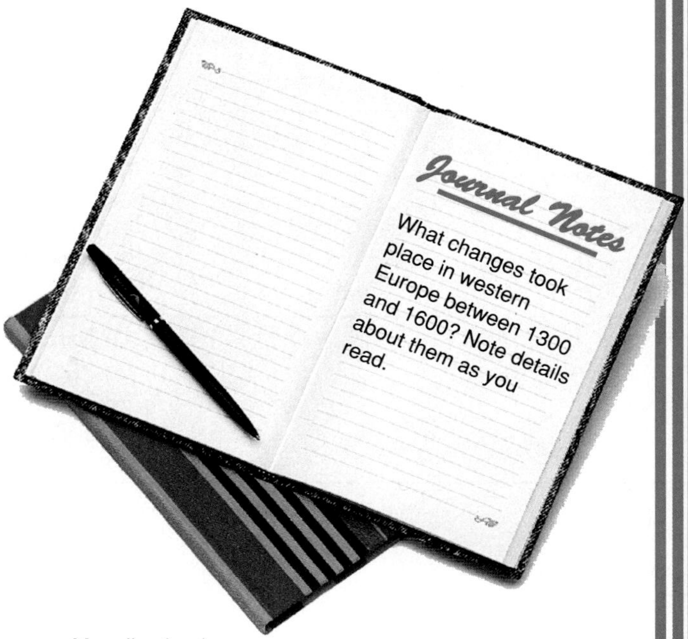

Chapter 28
The Renaissance

Chapter 29
The Reformation

Chapter 30
The Age of Discovery

Journal Notes

What changes took place in western Europe between 1300 and 1600? Note details about them as you read.

Renaissance
comes to France

Magellan begins
voyage to Pacific

1492 A.D.		1519 A.D.	

	1517 A.D.		1648 A.D.

Columbus lands at
San Salvador

Martin Luther
posts 95 theses

Peace of
Westphalia

431

INTRODUCING THE UNIT
Write the word *CHANGES* on the chalkboard. Ask students to make a list of innovations in a particular area such as communications that have occurred in recent times. *(Student lists might include CDs, portable or cellular phones, personal computers, FAX machines, video cameras and games.)* Inform students that in this unit they will learn about the changes in the arts, learning, innovations, and Christian teachings and practices that took place in western Europe during the 1300s and 1400s.

RECORDING JOURNAL NOTES

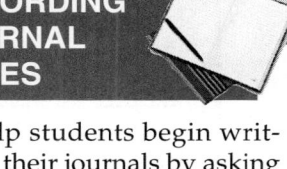

Help students begin writing in their journals by asking them to name the changes described in the unit introduction as you record their responses on the chalkboard. Tell the students that these are the kinds of changes they want to detail in their journals as they read Unit 9.

GEOGRAPHIC LOCATION
Using a world map or globe, have students locate the countries of western Europe and North and South America, the islands of the Caribbean, Africa, and the East Indies. Discuss the dangers involved in sailing from western Europe to unknown lands during the 1400s–1600.

CHAPTER 28

The Renaissance

CHAPTER ORGANIZER

Objectives	Special Features	Supplemental Materials
Section 1 The Italian City-States Explain how the Renaissance began and flourished in the Italian city-states.		• Reproducible Lesson Plan • Section 1 Quiz • Testmaker • Chapter 28 Vocabulary and Guided Reading Activity • Unit 9 Primary Source Reading • The Western Civilization Videodisc
Section 2 France Identify how France was influenced by the Italian Renaissance.		• Reproducible Lesson Plan • Section 2 Quiz • Testmaker • Chapter 28 Cooperative Learning Activity • The Western Civilization Videodisc
Section 3 Germany and Flanders Describe how the Renaissance spread to Germany and Flanders.		• Reproducible Lesson Plan • Section 3 Quiz • Testmaker • Chapter 28 Geography and Map Activity • Chapter 28 Teaching Transparencies and Activities
Section 4 Spain Discuss how the Roman Catholic Church and the government influenced the Renaissance in Spain.		• Reproducible Lesson Plan • Section 4 Quiz • Testmaker • Unit 9 World Literature • World History and Art Transparencies 15, 17 • The Western Civilization Videodisc
Section 5 England Summarize how the English monarchy promoted the Renaissance in England.		• Reproducible Lesson Plan • Section 5 Quiz • Testmaker • Chapter 28 Chart and Graph Skill Activity • Unit 9 World Literature • The Western Civilization Videodisc
Chapter 28 Review and Evaluation		• Chapter 28 Reteaching Activity • Chapter 28 Enrichment Activity • Spanish Summary and Glossary • Audiocassettes (English and Spanish) • Chapter 28 Performance Assessment Activity • Chapter 28 Test • Testmaker

If time does not permit teaching the entire chapter, use the Chapter 28 Summary on page 446 and the Chapter 28 Audiocassettes (English and Spanish) to point out the main ideas of the chapter.

Performance Assessment Activities

Art Museum Have students bring to class books with examples of Renaissance art and architecture to be used to set up their own Renaissance museum. Have them create a display on Renaissance art and architecture styles, with written descriptions of each style. Students may want to tape an audio description for each art piece as many museums do.

Architecture Ask students to decide whether the Renaissance succeeded in recreating classical architecture. Have them review Greek and Roman architecture, focusing on column styles, existing structures, and those that have been destroyed. Suggest they create a presentation of architecture of the Renaissance that reflects Greek and Roman styles. For example, they may show examples of original Greek and Roman column styles for comparison.

CHAPTER RESOURCES

LITERATURE ABOUT THE PERIOD

Castiglione, Baldassare. *The Book of the Courtier*. Translated by George Bull. Penguin, 1976. Contemporary handbook of courtly etiquette.

Chute, Marchette. *Shakespeare of London*. Dutton, 1950. Biography based on contemporary accounts.

Shakespeare, William. *The Merchant of Venice*. Scott Foresman, 1980. The moneylender Shylock demands a pound of flesh from the merchant Antonio.

Shakespeare, William. *The Riverside Shakespeare*. Houghton Mifflin, 1974. Authoritative collection of Shakespeare's complete works, including a historical background.

READINGS FOR THE STUDENT

Chamberlin, E.R. *Everyday Life in Renaissance Times*. Putnam, 1965. Portrays the social background of Europe between 1450 and 1650.

Mee, Charles L. *Daily Life in the Renaissance*. American Heritage, 1975. Illustrated with works of art showing people in their daily lives.

READINGS FOR THE TEACHER

Goodenough, Simon. *The Renaissance*. Arco, 1979. Describes life during the Renaissance period.

Lucas, Henry. *The Renaissance and the Reformation*. Harper & Bros., 1960. Historical survey of the Renaissance, Reformation, and the Counter-Reformation.

Severy, Merle, ed. *The Renaissance: Maker of Modern Man*. National Geographic, 1970. Complete history of the Renaissance period.

MULTIMEDIA RESOURCES

Leonardo da Vinci and His Art. Coronet/Social Studies School Service. Video. Examination of Da Vinci's major work and biographical information.

Michelangelo and His Art. Coronet/Social Studies School Service. Video. Examines the life and artistic career of Michelangelo.

National Gallery of Art. Videodisc Publishing Inc. Videodisc. Shows over 1,600 images, including Da Vinci.

Shakespeare Primer. Coronet/Social Studies School Service. Film. Biography of William Shakespeare along with dramatic readings from some of his major plays.

Women in Medieval Renaissance Europe. Projected Learning Programs. Software. Focuses on women in medieval and Renaissance Europe.

INTRODUCE

CHAPTER 28 OVERVIEW

Chapter 28 describes the Renaissance and the changes it brought to western Europe.

- **Section 1** discusses the ways in which Italian scholars, writers, and artists created the foundations of modern western civilization.
- **Section 2** describes the Italian Renaissance of France.
- **Section 3** analyzes the Renaissance in Germany and Flanders.
- **Section 4** explains the Renaissance in Spain.
- **Section 5** summarizes the Renaissance in England.

CHAPTER OBJECTIVES

After reading Chapter 28, students will be able to:

1. explain how the Renaissance began and flourished in the Italian city-states.
2. identify how France was influenced by the Italian Renaissance.
3. describe how the Renaissance spread to Germany and Flanders.
4. discuss how the Church and the government influenced the Renaissance in Spain.
5. summarize the Renaissance in England.

EXAMINING THE ILLUSTRATION

Ask students to describe what is happening in the painting. Explain that this style of art, among others, flourished in Europe during the arts renaissance described in this chapter.

PERFORMANCE ASSESSMENT ✓

Use the Performance Assessment activities on page 432B to help you evaluate students as they complete the chapter.

CHAPTER 28

The Renaissance

Return of the Hunters by Brughel

TEACHER CLASSROOM RESOURCES

- Section Quizzes/Chapter Test
- Enrichment Activity
- Chart and Graph Skill Activity
- Geography and Map Activity
- Vocabulary and Guided Reading Activity
- Cooperative Learning Activity
- Performance Assessment Activity
- Spanish Summary and Glossary
- Unit 9 Primary Source Reading
- Unit 9 World Literature
- World History and Art Transparencies
- Teaching Transparencies and Activities
- Audiocassettes (English and Spanish)
- The Western Civilization Videodisc

Chapter Focus

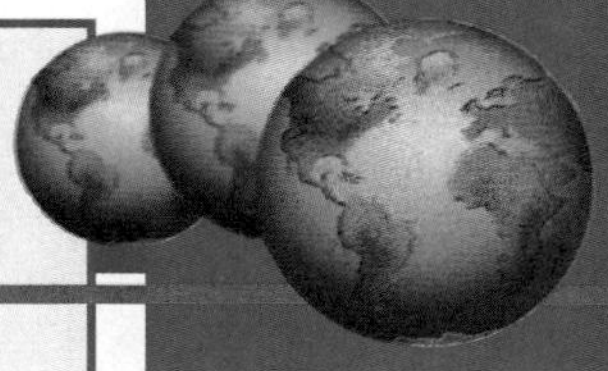

READ TO DISCOVER:

- How the Renaissance began and flourished in the Italian city-states.
- How France was influenced by the Italian Renaissance.
- How the Renaissance spread to Germany and Flanders.
- How the Roman Catholic Church and the government influenced the Renaissance in Spain.
- How the English monarchy promoted the Renaissance in England.

Around 1300, scholars in western Europe developed a new interest in **classical writings,** or the writings of the ancient Greeks and Romans. The scholars improved their knowledge of Greek and Latin, studied old manuscripts, and tried to copy the authors' manner of writing. They also began to accept some Greek and Roman ideas.

One idea that the scholars accepted was a belief in the importance of people. Because of this, the scholars were called **humanists** (hyū' muh nists). Their work caused a break with the thinking of the Middle Ages and led to a new age called the Renaissance (ren' uh sahns), a French word meaning "rebirth." During this age, people became less concerned with the mysteries of heaven and more interested in the world around them.

1300 A.D.–1600 A.D.

KEY TERMS

- classical writings
- humanists
- *piazza*
- *doge*
- *chateaux*
- printing press

Section 1

THE ITALIAN CITY-STATES

The first and leading center of the Renaissance was Italy, which consisted of small, independent city-states. The most important were Florence, Venice, and the Papal (pā' puhl) States. The Papal States were central Italian territories, including Rome, that were ruled by the Pope. All these city-states had grown wealthy from trade.

433

KEY TO ABILITY LEVELS

Teaching strategies have been coded for varying learning styles and abilities.

L1 Level 1 activities are **basic** activities and should be within the ability range of all students.

L2 Level 2 activities are **average** activities and should be within the ability range of the average to above-average student.

L3 Level 3 activities are **challenging** activities designed for the ability range of above-average students.

LEP LEP activities should be within the ability range of Limited English Proficiency students.

FOCUS

BELLRINGER

Write *Leonardo da Vinci* on the chalkboard. Have students write what they think of when they see this name.

MOTIVATIONAL ACTIVITY

Have students read their responses explaining what they think of when they see the name Leonardo da Vinci. *(They may know that Da Vinci painted the "Mona Lisa" or that he designed an early flying machine.)* Ask: What do Da Vinci's accomplishments tell you about the time in which he lived? *(Unlike medieval art, art in Da Vinci's time was no longer anonymous. Da Vinci's inventions show a renewed interest in science and technology.)* Tell students that in this chapter they will learn about the ideas that inspired a Renaissance in western Europe.

VOCABULARY PRE-CHECK

Write the key terms for this chapter on the chalkboard. Ask students to use those that they know in sentences.

Assign Chapter 28 **Vocabulary and Guided Reading Activity** in the TCR.

EXTRA CREDIT PROJECT

Have students research and write a report about the Globe Theater, how it was designed, who attended its performances, and what kinds of plays were performed there. They might also practice and deliver a dramatic reading from one of Shakespeare's plays.

TEACH

GUIDED PRACTICE

L1 **The Arts** Divide students into small groups. Have each group write brief descriptions of the visuals in this chapter. How does this art look different from the medieval art shown in Chapters 24–27? Discuss the groups' descriptions as a class. *(Students' responses might include three dimensional, less likely to have religious themes, more emotional expression.)* LEP

MAKING CONNECTIONS

>> **Daily Life** In their workshops, artists worked on dozens of projects at a time. In addition to painting and sculpting, Renaissance artists designed and carved furniture, made jewelry, painted festival cloaks and carnival masks, planned scenery for plays, molded candlesticks and chandeliers, and decorated cakes.

VIDEODISC

Use the following to enrich Chapter 28.

WC D 74 17058
"Ginevra de'Benci," by Leonardo da Vinci.

WC D 75 17059
Movement of birds, from da Vinci's notebooks.

Museum Display of da Vinci's Bicycle

At first, each city-state was ruled by guilds. Later, powerful individuals or families took control. They often fought each other for land and wealth. At times, they had difficulty gaining the people's loyalty and had to govern by force.

The leaders of the Italian city-states, however, were interested in more than power. They wanted to be remembered as wise, generous rulers. To be sure this would happen, they spent money on ceremonies and parades to impress and entertain the people. They ordered the building of churches and palaces. They also encouraged scholars, poets, and philosophers to set up palace schools to educate the sons of the rich. In these schools, pupils learned to develop their minds and make their bodies stronger. They spent part of the day studying classical writings and learning good manners. They spent the rest of the day wrestling, fencing, and swimming.

Art Art was an important part of life in Renaissance Italy. City-states were proud of their artists. In fact, the city-states often competed for the services of certain painters and sculptors. The artists knew they were important and began to seek individual honor and attention. They worked hard to develop their own distinctive style.

Renaissance artists carefully studied ancient Greek and Roman art, science, and mathematics. They began to pay close attention to the details of nature. They became interested in *perspective* (puhr spek' tiv), or a way of showing objects as they appear at different distances. Above all, the artists studied the structure of the human body to learn how to draw it accurately. They began to experiment with light, color, and shade. As a result, they painted and sculpted works that were true to life and full of color and action.

Good artists were given money by the rulers of the city-states. In return, they were expected to make paintings and sculptures for the rulers' palaces and gardens. Artists often had workshops where they trained apprentices. The apprentices added backgrounds, costumes, or hands to the artists' paintings.

Painting of Leonardo da Vinci

Many artists painted portraits for the rich. The artists tried to paint people's facial features so they showed what the people were really like. At first, portraits were painted only to honor dead or famous people. Later, any merchant with money could have a portrait painted.

One of the greatest Renaissance artists was Leonardo da Vinci (lē uh nahr' dō dah vin' chē). He is known for the *Mona Lisa,* a portrait of an Italian noblewoman. He also painted a fresco called *The Last Supper* on the wall of an Italian monastery's dining room. It shows Christ and his disciples at their last meal before Christ's death. In these works, da Vinci tried to reveal people's feelings as well as their outward appearance.

COOPERATIVE LEARNING

Divide students into groups with each group taking on the role of Da Vinci, the inventor. Tell each group they are to look around them and come up with an invention that would be helpful to them all, as Da Vinci did. Within the group, have them choose an illustrator, planner, supply manager, builder, and whatever else they need to plan and create their invention. Have groups present their inventions, with explanations, to the class.

Da Vinci was a scientist as well as an artist. He filled notebooks with drawings of inventions far ahead of the times. Da Vinci designed the first parachute and made drawings of flying machines and mechanical diggers.

Another outstanding artist was Michelangelo Buonarroti (mī kuh lan' juh lō bwah nah rō' tē). He is known for his paintings on the ceiling and altar wall of Rome's Sistine (sis' tēn) Chapel. He also sculpted the *Pietà* (pē ā' tah), which shows the dead Christ in his mother's arms. Michelangelo went farther than the ancient Greeks and Romans in presenting the human body. His figures are large and muscular, and show a sense of motion.

City Life Most Italian Renaissance cities had narrow paved streets with open sewers in the middle. Merchants and shopkeepers lived on the top floors of the buildings that housed their

RENAISSANCE ARTISTS Michelangelo Buonarroti and Leonardo da Vinci were two leading artists of the Italian Renaissance. Michelangelo carved a very large statue of Christ and his mother known as the *Pietà* (left). Da Vinci tried to capture the personality of an Italian noblewoman in the painting known as the *Mona Lisa* (right). **What did da Vinci try to reveal in his works of art?**

L3 **Language Arts** Have students research the life and works of an Italian artist mentioned in this chapter. Have them develop a dramatic monologue to present to the class portraying this artist. Encourage students to dress appropriately for their presentations.

MAKING CONNECTIONS

➤➤ **The Arts** Another influential Italian artist was Raphael, who painted historical and religious frescoes. He became known for his portraits of the Madonna, or Virgin Mary. As an architect, he helped in the construction of St. Peter's Basilica in Rome.

CAPTION ANSWER

people's thoughts and feelings as well as their outward appearances

VIDEODISC

Use the following to enrich Chapter 28.

WC M 9 41339
Posterior muscles, De Humani Corporis Fabrica.

WC D 61 17045
"Madonna and Child," by Hans Memling.

SPOTLIGHT ON: MICHELANGELO

Michelangelo was working on the sculpture of Moses for Pope Julius's tomb when the Pope asked him to paint the ceiling of the Sistine Chapel instead. Michelangelo painted scenes from the Bible on the ceiling while lying on his back on scaffolding 70 feet (or 21 m) above the floor. The Renaissance biographer Giorgio Vasari described the completion of Michelangelo's ceiling of the Sistine Chapel in the following way: *"When the work was thrown open, the whole world came running to see what Michelangelo had done; and certainly it was such as to make everyone speechless with astonishment."*

L1 **Geography: Place** Have students locate the various Italian city-states on the map on page 438 as they are mentioned in the chapter narrative. Have volunteers keep a running list of city-states on the chalkboard. Have students add one adjective to the list that describes each city. LEP

L2 **Daily Life** Ask students to create a list of manners that might appear in a modern book on etiquette. Have them compare their lists with the list on page 436. What conclusions about Renaissance manners can students draw? LEP

LINKING PAST TO PRESENT

The Renaissance revived the Greek ideal of the balanced individual who participated in a variety of activities, such as politics, art, sports, and music. Today we still admire this ideal, and we apply the term *Renaissance man* or *Renaissance woman* to someone who has wide interests and many different talents. Ask students to think of someone today whom they would describe this way.

VIDEODISC

Use the following to enrich Chapter 28.

WC D 57 17041
Lorenzo de Medici (1449-1492).

WC P 42 49701
Ponte Vecchio over the Arno River at Florence.

shops. The rich built homes in the classical style, with rooms that were large and had high ceilings. In the center of the homes stood courtyards filled with statues, fountains, and gardens. Most people in the cities, however, were poor. They worked for low wages and lived in run-down areas.

The center of city life was the ***piazza*** (pē aht' suh), or central square. There, markets were set up, and merchants traded goods. People gathered to talk to friends and to carry out business dealings. On holidays, the people often watched or took part in parades and ceremonies there.

Families were close-knit. Most family members lived and worked together in the same neighborhood. Marriages were arranged as if they were business deals. Women stayed at home, ran the household, and raised children. Men spent their days at work and talking with friends on the streets and in taverns.

Most men dressed in tights and tunics. Some also wore cloaks and caps. Women dressed in simply cut, flowing dresses with tight bodices. The rich often wore brightly colored clothing made from expensive silks and velvets and trimmed with fur.

Florence The Italian Renaissance began in Florence, which was ruled by the Medici (med' uh chē) family. One of its most

RENAISSANCE MANNERS

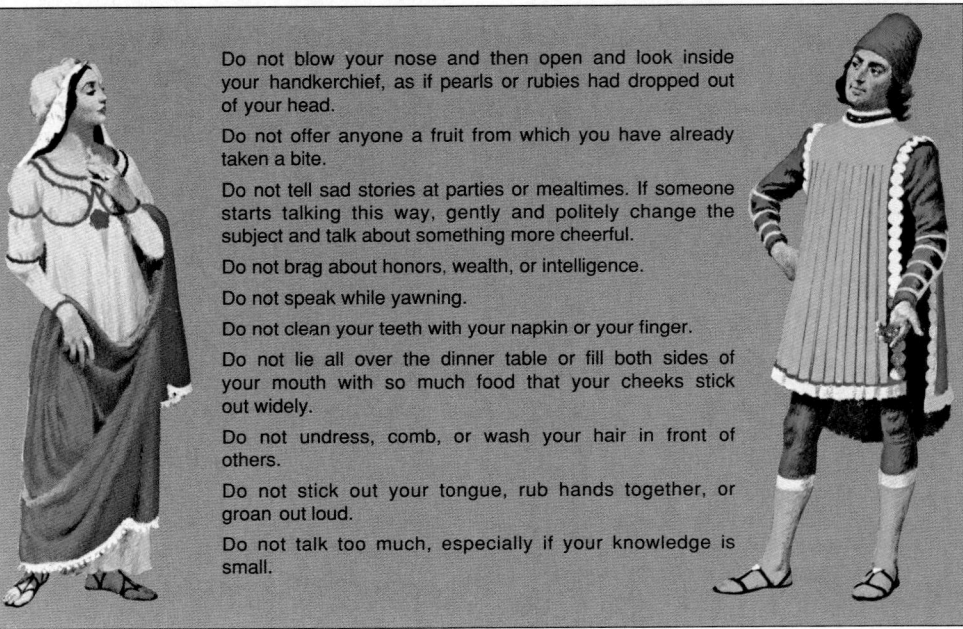

- Do not blow your nose and then open and look inside your handkerchief, as if pearls or rubies had dropped out of your head.
- Do not offer anyone a fruit from which you have already taken a bite.
- Do not tell sad stories at parties or mealtimes. If someone starts talking this way, gently and politely change the subject and talk about something more cheerful.
- Do not brag about honors, wealth, or intelligence.
- Do not speak while yawning.
- Do not clean your teeth with your napkin or your finger.
- Do not lie all over the dinner table or fill both sides of your mouth with so much food that your cheeks stick out widely.
- Do not undress, comb, or wash your hair in front of others.
- Do not stick out your tongue, rub hands together, or groan out loud.
- Do not talk too much, especially if your knowledge is small.

MULTICULTURAL PERSPECTIVES

The Renaissance revived the Greek notion that an ideal person participated in a variety of activities, including sports. Games and sports that were popular at this time included javelin hurling, chess, archery, fencing, boxing, snowfights, and gambling. Women as well as men participated in many sports, including *giuco della palla*—a game that led to the modern game of tennis.

RENAISSANCE FLORENCE Under the rule of the Medici family, Florence became known as the jewel of the Italian Renaissance. The Medicis sponsored festivals to entertain the people of Florence. The horse races shown in this painting were held every spring. **Where was the center of social life in an Italian Renaissance city?**

famous members was Lorenzo de Medici, who became the ruler of Florence in 1478. He made the city a center of art and learning. Artists, poets, and philosophers flocked there to benefit from his generous support. Because of the city's prosperity and fame, Lorenzo became known as "the Magnificent."

About 1490, Florence's trade started to decline. Merchants began to complain that Lorenzo was too strict and spent too much money. The poor in Florence began to grumble about their housing and the shortages of food.

People looked for an escape from their problems. They thought they found it in a monk named Savonarola (sav uh nuh rō′ luh). Savonarola accused the Medicis of not ruling justly. He gained the people's support and overthrew the Medicis in 1494.

Savonarola did not like the gaiety and loose life of the Renaissance. He thought Renaissance ideas were hurting Florence. On his advice, the new government did away with parties, gambling, swearing, and horse-racing. Savonarola's supporters also burned paintings, fancy clothes, musical instruments, and classical books.

By 1498, the people of Florence had tired of Savonarola's strict ways, and he was hanged for heresy. The Medicis returned to power. Florence's greatness, however, had passed.

The Papal States During the 1300s and 1400s, the power of the Popes declined. However, they wanted to show Europe's

L3 **Economics** The Medicis, who dominated the politics and culture of Florence, obtained their wealth from international banking. Have students research the Medici family and write a brief report on their role in the origins of modern banking.

CAPTION ANSWER

the *piazza,* or central square

DID YOU KNOW ??

The Medici family ruled Florence from the 1400s to the 1700s.

MAKING CONNECTIONS

➤➤ **History** Under Savonarola, children were organized into Bands of Hope. They watched for gamblers and swore to help stamp out dancing, pageants, love poems, and music schools. During Carnival Week, the bands went from house to house seeking such forbidden objects as playing cards and musical instruments to throw into a large bonfire.

VIDEODISC

Use the following to enrich Chapter 28.

WC P 17 49676
Florence, ca. 1600.

WC P 18 49677
Present-day Florence, looking north.

MEETING SPECIAL NEEDS

To help students with Limited English Proficiency, divide students into small heterogeneous groups and ask each group to discuss one section of the chapter. Have group members work together to prepare a list of the important points. Discuss each group's list in class and write major points on the chalkboard. Have students who are visual learners illustrate important events discussed in this chapter. After they present all the drawings, ask the class to identify what event was illustrated in each drawing.

L1 **Geography: Place** Have students study the map of Renaissance Italy to answer the following questions: Which Italian city-state was the largest in land size? *(Naples)* In which city-state was Rome located? *(Papal States)* Which city-states had access to both the Adriatic Sea and the Tyrrhenian Sea? *(Naples, Papal States)* LEP

MAP STUDY

Answer

Venice had easier access to the Byzantine Empire by both land and water.

Assign the Chapter 28 **Geography and Map Activity** in the TCR.

MAKING CONNECTIONS

➤➤ **Religion** Unlike today, earlier Popes had children. The actions of such church leaders as Pope Alexander VI caused many devout Catholics to favor reform of the Church.

VIDEODISC

Use the following to enrich Chapter 28.

WC D 80 17064

St. Peter's Cathedral and the Piazza, Rome.

WC D 58 17042

Pope Julius II, Renaissance prince, arts patron.

kings that the Church was still powerful. In Rome they built large churches and palaces. Piazzas and wide streets were built in areas that had been in ruins.

Most Popes were not very religious. They acted more like political rulers than church leaders. They sent representatives to other states and countries, collected taxes, minted money, raised armies, and fought wars.

In 1492, Rodrigo Borgia (rōd rē′gō bōr′ jah) became Pope Alexander VI. He did this by bribing cardinals to vote for him. Pope Alexander's goal was to make central Italy a kingdom ruled by the Borgia family. His daughter Lucretia (lū krā′ shuh) married a noble and became known for her lively parties and for poisoning her enemies.

Alexander spent a great deal of money building an army for his favorite son, Cesare (chā′ sah rā). The army marched through Italy and took control of many towns. All of this territory was lost, however, after Alexander's death in 1503. By this time, Rome had replaced Florence as the center of the Renaissance.

Renaissance Italy

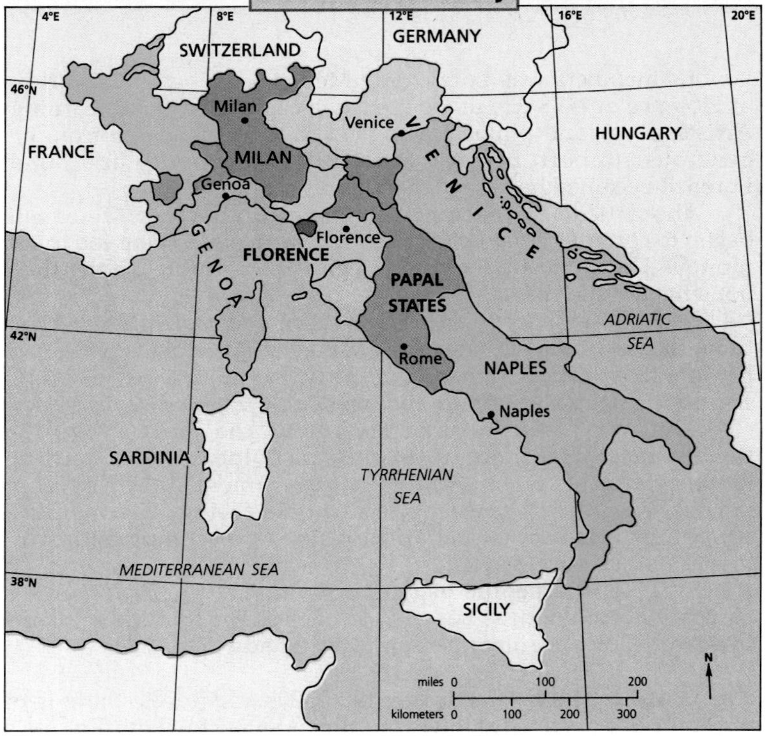

MAP STUDY

PLACE The Renaissance began in Italy partly because Italian towns were important centers of trade during the late Middle Ages. **Why did Venice trade more with the areas outside of Italy than other Italian city-states?**

COOPERATIVE LEARNING

Have students compare the Renaissance in Florence, the Papal States, and Venice. Assign students to three teams, each of which will study one city. Team members can choose topics such as architecture, government, and painting. Split teams into subgroups. The subgroups will research their topics together and bring their findings back to their whole team. Have the team then prepare a panel report on their city to be presented to the rest of the class.

Assign the Chapter 28 **Cooperative Learning Activity** in the TCR.

VENICE The city of Venice is famous for being built on 117 islands. About 150 canals, rather than streets, carry most of the city's traffic. Here, some of Venice's many bridges and grand palaces are shown. **Who ruled Renaissance Venice?**

Venice The Renaissance did not reach Venice until the late 1500s. This was because the Venetians had looked to Constantinople rather than to western Europe for art and literature.

Venice was different from most Italian city-states in other ways, too. The city, including its palaces and churches, was built on 117 islands linked by nearly 400 bridges. Instead of streets, Venice had canals. The largest and busiest was the Grand Canal, which was lined with brightly colored stone and marble palaces. The Rialto (rē ahl′ tō), or the business area of Venice, also lay along a stretch of the Grand Canal. There, traders from Europe and the East crowded the docks to buy and sell goods.

Venice was ruled by a few merchant aristocrats. They controlled the Senate and the Council of Ten. The Council passed laws and chose the ***doge*** (dōj), or official ruler. The doge had little power and had to obey the Council of Ten.

The Venetians were expected to place loyalty to their city above anything else. If a neighbor did something suspicious, a Venetian was expected to report it to the Council of Ten. Citizens who wanted to accuse someone of treason placed a letter stating the charges in special boxes located all through the city. Those charged were quickly arrested and brought before the Council. Council members then met in secret to study the evidence, listen to witnesses, and decide guilt or innocence.

MEETING SPECIAL NEEDS

Have auditory learners bring recordings of Renaissance music to class or perform a piece themselves. Before playing the piece, each students should give background information. Students who are studying foreign languages could help with translation and pronunciation of songs.

L2 **Government** Create three columns on the chalkboard, headed *Florence, Papal States,* and *Venice.* Ask students to compare the governments of these three Renaissance city-states. What did they have in common? How did they differ? LEP

CAPTION ANSWER

a few merchant aristocrats

DID YOU KNOW ??

During the 1400s the penknife was just that—a knife for trimming quilt pens, which lost their points quickly. After steel pens were invented, the term came to mean any small blade that can be carried in a pocket.

GEOGRAPHY AND HISTORY

Venice became a great naval power during the 1300s and 1400s. It controlled the trade of the eastern Mediterranean until the rise of the Ottoman Turks in the 1500s.

VIDEODISC

Use the following to enrich Chapter 28.

WC P 9 49668
Venice, ca. 1600.

WC P 11 49670
St. Mark's Cathedral, Venice.

DID YOU KNOW ??

French architects blended elements of classical and Gothic architecture to create chateaux.

MAKING CONNECTIONS

➤➤ **Literature** Marguerite of Angouleme, sister of Francis I and wife of Henry II of Navarre, wrote a collection of lively, satirical traveler's tales, the *Heptameron*, modeled after Boccaccio's *Decameron*. She also wrote poetry, much of which was not published until after her death in 1549. Marguerite welcomed artists and scholars at her court, corresponded with Eramus, and was a patron of Rabelias. She tried to protect her humanist friends from Francis I's prosecution of Huguenots.

SECTION 2 ANSWERS

1. Francis I, French king (p. 440); Rabelais, French author (p. 440)
2. chateaux, castles (p. 440)
3. He encouraged French authors to model their works on those of Italian authors.
4. that humans were not tied down by their past and could do whatever they wished
5. Answers will vary but might include that it gave people a more positive outlook on life.

Assign the Chapter 28 **Section 2 Quiz** in the TCR. Testmaker available.

Painting of Renaissance Merchant

Section 1 Review

1. **Identify:** Renaissance, Florence, Venice, Papal States, Leonardo da Vinci, Michelangelo Buonmarroti, Lorenzo de Medici, Savonarola, Pope Alexander VI, Grand Canal, Rialto, Council of Ten
2. **Define:** classical writings, humanists, *piazza, doge*
3. How important was art during the Renaissance?
4. What made Venice different from other Italian city-states?

Critical Thinking

5. Do you approve or disapprove of the system of justice in Renaissance Venice? Explain.

Section 2

FRANCE

In 1494, the French began invading Italy. French kings became fascinated by Italian architecture, art, and fashions. In the 1500s, King Francis I arranged for Italian artisans to work for him in France. He and many of his nobles hired Italian architects to design ***chateaux*** (sha tōz'), or castles, which were then built along the Loire River.

Francis I also encouraged French authors to model their works on those of Italian authors. Every evening, Francis and his family listened to readings of the latest books. Many were written by Rabelais (rahb' uh lā), a physician-monk. He believed that humans were not tied down by their past and could do whatever they wished. In his most popular book, *The Adventures of Gargantua and Pantagruel*, Rabelais's main characters were two comical giants.

Painting of Rabelais

Section 2 Review

1. **Identify:** Francis I, Rabelais
2. **Define:** *chateaux*
3. What did Francis I do to encourage Renaissance thought in French literature?
4. What did Rabelais believe?

Critical Thinking

5. How do you think people of the time reacted to Rabelais's ideas?

SECTION 1 ANSWERS

1. Renaissance, a new age (p. 433); Florence, city-state (p. 433); Venice, city-state (p. 433); Papal States, Church city-states (p. 433); Leonardo Da Vinci, artist (p. 434); Michelangelo Buonarroti, artist (p. 435); Lorenzo de Medici, ruler of Florence (p. 437); Savonarola, monk (p. 437); Pope Alexander VI, Italian pope (p. 438); Grand Canal, canal in Venice (p. 439); Rialto, business area (p. 439); Council of Ten, law making body (p. 439)
2. classical writings, of ancient Greeks and Romans (p. 433); humanists, scholars who valued people (p. 433); *piazza*, plaza (p. 436); *doge*, ruler (p. 439)
3. an important part of life
4. It copied Constantinople's for art and literature, was built on 117 islands, and had canals instead of streets.
5. Answers will vary.

Assign the Chapter 28 **Section 1 Quiz** in the TCR. Testmaker available.

Section 3 GERMANY AND FLANDERS

Photograph of Gutenberg Bible

The Renaissance also spread to the rich trading centers of Germany and Flanders. There, religious scholars learned Greek and Hebrew so they could understand the earliest versions of the Bible. The German and Flemish scholars decided that over the years many church leaders had interpreted the Bible to suit their own needs. The scholars wanted changes that would make church teachings simpler. One outspoken scholar, a Dutchman named Erasmus (i raz' muhs), made a new Latin translation of the New Testament. He also wrote *Praise of Folly,* a book that attacked corrupt church leaders and practices.

At the same time, Italian traders living in the north set an example for merchants. The German merchants began to appreciate wealth, beauty, personal improvement, and other Renaissance values. This was the beginning of a new, privileged middle class.

Northern European artisans made many discoveries during the Renaissance. About 1440, a German named Johannes Gutenberg (yō' hahn gūt' n berg) developed a **printing press.** It used carved letters that could be moved around to form words and then could be used again. As a result, books could be quickly printed by machine rather than slowly written by hand. This made many more books available to people. Since printing came at a time when many townspeople were learning to read and think for themselves, new ideas spread rapidly.

Northern European artists studied Italian works of art and then developed their own styles. They painted scenes from the Bible and daily life in sharp detail. Hubert and Jan Van Eyck (van īk'), two brothers from Flanders, discovered how to paint in oils. The colors of the oil paintings were deep and rich. Soon, other artists began to use oils also.

Section 3 Review

1. **Identify:** Erasmus, Johannes Gutenberg, Hubert and Jan Van Eyck
2. **Define:** printing press
3. What church reforms did German and Flemish scholars want to make?
4. How did the printing press change European life?

Critical Thinking

5. How might life in Europe have been different without the development of Gutenberg's printing press?

LINKING PAST TO PRESENT

The term *Middle Ages* used to describe the medieval period, was invented by Renaissance historians. They saw the preceding millennium as the *media tempora* or "middle time," which separated their glorious era from the beauty of ancient Greece and Rome. They considered their own time to be the beginning of a new period of history. Today's historians agree with them.

MAKING CONNECTIONS

>> **History** Printing was invented by the Chinese. The oldest-known printed book in the world is a Buddhist scripture dated A.D. 868. The Chinese invented movable type about A.D. 1000.

L2 **Science** Have students research the development of paper and the different materials from which it has been made. Divide students into groups and have each group outline a presentation of a different papermaking process to share with the class. If possible, encourage students to demonstrate how each process was completed.

SECTION 3 ANSWERS

1. Erasmus, Dutch scholar (p. 441); Johannes Gutenberg, invented printing press (p. 441); Hubert and Jan Van Eyck, Flemish artists (p. 441)
2. printing press, machine that used carved letters that could be reused to print (p. 441)
3. They wanted changes that would make church teachings simpler.
4. It made many more books available to people and also made them cheaper to buy.
5. Answers will vary but could include that the Renaissance ideas might not have spread as quickly throughout Europe.

Assign the Chapter 28 **Section 3 Quiz** in the TCR. Testmaker available.

VIDEODISC

Use the following to enrich Chapter 28.

WC P 25 49684
A detail of a Flemish town, 16th century.

WC D 89 17073
Erasmus of Rotterdam.

L2 **History** Have students read more about the Wars of Roses and develop a graphic organizer showing the series of events that caused, continued, and concluded these wars.

CAPTION ANSWER

He made the monarchy stronger and built up trade, which made England both peaceful and rich.

DID YOU KNOW

Elizabeth I had been educated in the tradition of the Renaissance. She spoke English, French, and Italian as well as being skilled at translating Latin and Greek.

VIDEODISC

Use the following to enrich Chapter 28.

WC D 94 17078

William Shakespeare (1564-1616).

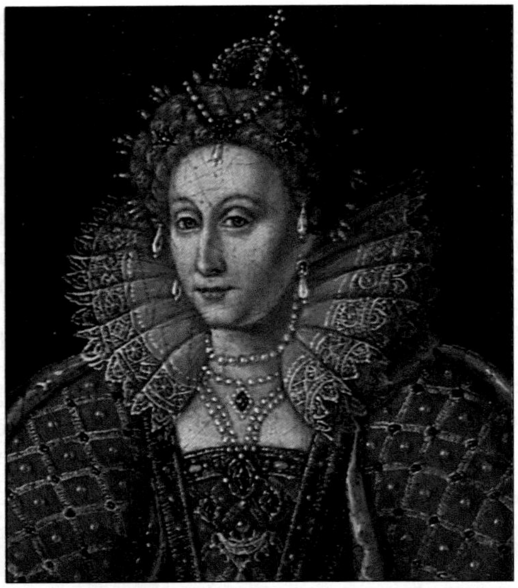

THE TUDORS These paintings of King Henry VIII of England (left) and his daughter Queen Elizabeth I (right) show members of the Tudor family, who ruled England from 1485 to 1603. Henry and Elizabeth both were strong and forceful rulers, and they were able to gain the respect and love of the English people. **How did the first Tudor king, Henry VII, pave the way for the English Renaissance?**

Henry VII's work was continued by his son, Henry VIII, who became king in 1509. He enjoyed and encouraged art, literature, hunting, and parties. He played several musical instruments and even composed his own music. Under his rule, English nobles and merchants began to look to Renaissance Italy for guidance in politics, diplomacy, and behavior.

The English Renaissance reached its height, however, during the reign of Henry VIII's daughter Elizabeth I. She became queen in 1558 when she was 25 years old. She was shrewd, and well-educated. Although she had a sharp tongue and iron will, she won the loyalty and confidence of her people.

Elizabeth often made journeys through the kingdom so that the people could see her. During her travels, she stayed at the homes of nobles who entertained her with banquets, parades, and dances. Poets and writers praised her in their writings. The sons of merchants, lawyers, and landowners copied Italian clothes and manners and came to court to capture her attention and favor.

Poetry, music, and the theater became a part of daily life. Most nobles wrote poetry. People of all classes enjoyed singing ballads and folk songs. Many played violins, guitars, and lutes.

EXTENDING THE CONTENT

Henry V died in France in 1422 leaving an infant son, Henry VI. Nobles from rival branches of the Plantagenet family (Henry II's line) began maneuvering for power, and Henry VI never gained control. When rivalry erupted into war in 1455, two parties formed around Richard, Duke of York, and Cardinal Beaufort, who backed King Henry VI. Shifting loyalties, intermittent fighting, and treachery marked the war. Over the next 30 years, four men became king of England and were deposed, murdered, or killed in battle. The young sons of Edward IV (York) were sent to the Tower of London and never seen again. The deaths of hundreds of nobles seriously weakened the English nobility.

The people of Renaissance England were especially fond of plays. Not since the days of ancient Greece had so many plays been written and performed. About 1580, the first theaters in England were built. Their stages stood in the open air. Most of the audience, however, sat under a roof or some sort of covering. Those who could not afford to pay for seats stood in the *pit,* or an open area in the front of the theater, and on the sides of the stage. Since there were no lights, plays were performed in the afternoon. They attracted large crowds.

One of the best known English *playwrights,* or authors of plays, was William Shakespeare (shāk' spir). He drew ideas for his tragedies and comedies from the histories of England and ancient Rome. He often used Italian scenes, characters, and tales in his plays. Some of his most famous works are *Romeo and Juliet, Macbeth, Hamlet, Julius Caesar,* and *A Midsummer Night's Dream.* Many experts consider Shakespeare the greatest playwright in the English language.

ENGLISH THEATER The Globe Theater (left) stood near the south bank of the Thames River in the London suburb of Southwark. The Globe Theater became the home of William Shakespeare's (right) acting company in 1599. **What kind of reputation have the plays of William Shakespeare earned for him?**

L3 **Music** Have students research the music and musical instruments of Renaissance England. Have them chart their information including the topics and uses of music, occasions where it was played, and other information they uncover. Display their charts and play recordings of music to culminate the activity.

DID YOU KNOW ??

Audiences that disliked a play would hurl insults and toss ripe fruit at the actors to drive them from the stage. Since women were not permitted on the stage, boys whose voices had not yet changed played the female roles, which were usually smaller and less important than the male roles.

CAPTION ANSWER

He is considered the greatest playwright in the English language.

VIDEODISC

Use the following to enrich Chapter 28.

WC D 95 17079

A reconstruction of Shakespeare's Globe Theater.

COOPERATIVE LEARNING

Assign students to small groups to develop a set of TV quiz-show-style questions about a Renaissance artist of their choice. Students should consult art history books and, as a group, analyze the artist's style, subjects of art, and also the facts of their lives. Each panel can present their questions in a class competition. Each member of the group should be responsible for a task: research, recording group discussion, developing questions, or acting as panel moderator in presenting the questions.

ASSESS

CHECK FOR UNDERSTANDING

Ask students to summarize the main points of the chapter, orally or in writing. Discuss the answers to the Section and Chapter Review questions.

EVALUATE

Assign the Chapter 28 **Performance Assessment Activity** in the TCR.

Administer the **Chapter 28 Test** in the TCR. Testmaker available.

RETEACH

Ask students to suggest the ways in which Italian Renaissance ideas spread to other areas of western Europe. Have volunteers write responses on the chalkboard.

Assign the Chapter 28 **Reteaching Activity** in the TCR.

ENRICH

Have students choose an influential social critic who lived during the Renaissance, such as Eramus or Rabelais, and report on the person's criticisms of the Catholic Church or Renaissance society.

Assign the Chapter 28 **Enrichment Activity** in the TCR.

CLOSE

Have students write an essay that summarizes major characteristics of the arts of the Renaissance—painting, literature, drama, and architecture.

MEETING CHAPTER OBJECTIVES

Each objective is tested by the Review questions in parentheses.

1. **Describe** the Renaissance in Italian city-states. (CU 1, 2, 3; CT 1, 2)
2. **Identify** how France was influenced by the Italian Renaissance. (CU 6)
3. **Explain** how the Renaissance spread to Germany. (CU 7)
4. **Discuss** the Church and government in Renaissance Spain. (CU 8)
5. **Summarize** how the English monarchy promoted the Renaissance. (BV; UYJ)

Section 5 Review

1. **Identify:** Wars of the Roses, Tudor, Henry VII, Henry VIII, Elizabeth I, William Shakespeare
2. What did the Tudors do to encourage the Renaissance in England?
3. What were English theaters like?
4. From where did Shakespeare draw ideas for his plays?

Critical Thinking

5. Why do you think Henry VIII and Elizabeth I were respected by the people they ruled?

Chapter Summary

1. Around 1300, certain western European scholars developed an interest in classical writings that led the Renaissance.
2. During the Renaissance, which began in the Italian city-states of Florence, Venice, and the Papal States, a great deal of importance was placed on art.
3. Leading Renaissance artists included Michelangelo Buonarroti and Leonardo da Vinci, a scientist.
4. The Italian Renaissance began in Florence, which was ruled by the Medicis until Savonarola came to power in 1494.
5. When Savonarola was overthrown in 1498, the Medicis returned to power.
6. To prove their power to European kings, the Popes rebuilt Rome, which became the center of the Italian Renaissance.
7. In the late 1500s, the Renaissance reached Venice.
8. After 1494, the Renaissance spread to France, where it was encouraged by King Francis I.
9. The Renaissance spread to Germany and Flanders, where religious scholars worked for Church reforms.
10. About 1440, Johannes Gutenberg invented a printing press, which spread new ideas.
11. In the late 1400s and early 1500s, the Renaissance spread to Spain, where it was influenced by the close ties between the Church and the government.
12. The English Renaissance reached its height during the reign of Elizabeth I, which began in 1558.
13. The people of Renaissance England were very fond of plays, especially those by William Shakespeare.

SECTION 5 ANSWERS

1. Wars of the Roses, wars between English noble families (p. 443); Tudor, English ruling family in 1485 (p. 443); Henry VII, first Tudor king (p. 443); Henry VIII, later Tudor king (p. 444); Elizabeth I, queen of England (p. 444); William Shakespeare, English playwright (p. 445)
2. They made the monarchy stronger, built up trade, and encouraged the arts.
3. open-air stages where the audience sat under a roof or stood in the pit to see afternoon plays
4. from the histories of England and ancient Rome and also from Italian tales
5. Answers will vary, but students might indicate that people in England were exposed to a variety of learning, art, and music that created more interesting lives.

Assign the Chapter 28 **Section 5 Quiz** in the TCR. Testmaker available.

CHAPTER Review 28

Building Vocabulary

Imagine you are a drama critic writing about the literature of the Renaissance. Write a short magazine article explaining the kinds of plays being written and how they reflect the life of the times. Use the following words in your article.

classical writings	*doge*
humanists	*chateaux*
piazza	printing press

Check for Understanding

1. Whose writings did the scholars of western Europe study during the Renaissance?
2. Why were Renaissance scholars called humanists?
3. What did the rulers of the Italian city-states do to encourage learning and development of art?
4. Why did the people of Florence turn to Savonarola in 1494?
5. How was France introduced to the Italian Renaissance?
6. What did Germany and Flanders contribute to the Renaissance?
7. Of what did El Escorial become a well-known symbol?
8. How did the Wars of the Roses get their name?

Critical Thinking

1. How did the Renaissance differ from the Middle Ages?
2. Why did the Renaissance start in Italy?
3. Why was Lorenzo de Medici called "the Magnificent"?
4. If you could go back in time and talk with a Renaissance artist or ruler, whom would you choose? What questions would you ask?

Geography in History

LOCATION Refer to the map of Renaissance Italy on page 438. This country is often compared to the shape of a boot. Describe the location of this country by giving its latitude and longitude.

Using Your Journal

Review the details you have noted about the changes in art and learning that took place in western Europe during the 1300s and 1400s. Write a paragraph explaining which of the changes has had the greatest impact on your life today.

CHAPTER 28 REVIEW ANSWERS

BUILDING VOCABULARY

Magazine articles will vary, but students should cite love, adventure, family conflicts, and other themes and use all the vocabulary words.

CHECK FOR UNDERSTANDING

1. those of the ancient Greeks and Romans
2. because they believed in the importance of people
3. They spent money and encouraged scholars, poets, and philosophers, and set up palace schools.
4. They thought he would stop too much government spending, and food and housing shortages.
5. through French invasions of Italy
6. Bible studies and a new Latin translation, a printing press, and the use of oils in painting
7. the power and religious devotion of Spanish rulers
8. from the symbols of the two noble families who fought

CRITICAL THINKING

1. During the Renaissance, people became more interested in art, learning, and the world around them.
2. The Italian city-states had grown wealthy from trade and spent their wealth on the arts.
3. Answers will vary, but might include that he made Florence prosper.
4. Answers will vary but students should write specific questions.

✚ BONUS ✚ TEST QUESTION

For Chapter 28 Test

Is the man charged with theft innocent or guilty? His alibi: "During the theft, at 3:00 P.M., I was at the Globe Theater watching Shakespeare's *Romeo and Juliet.* Afterward, it was so crowded along the Thames River that I didn't leave the area until after dark." *(innocent—facts are accurate)*

USING YOUR JOURNAL

Paragraphs will vary but students should explain that learning and art do have an impact on their lives. You might call on volunteers to read their paragraphs to the class.

GEOGRAPHY IN HISTORY

Italy stretched from about 48°–38° N latitude, and from about 5°–18° E longitude

CHAPTER 29 The Reformation

CHAPTER ORGANIZER

Objectives	Special Features	Supplemental Materials
Section 1 Martin Luther Explain why Martin Luther's beliefs brought him into conflict with the Roman Catholic Church.		• Reproducible Lesson Plan • Section 1 Quiz • Testmaker • Chapter 29 Vocabulary and Guided Reading Activity • Chapter 29 Cooperative Learning Activity
Section 2 A New Religion Describe how Protestantism developed.		• Reproducible Lesson Plan • Section 2 Quiz • Testmaker • The Western Civilization Videodisc • Chapter 29 Activity Book Activity
Section 3 Catholic Reform Identify how Catholic reformers worked to improve their Church.		• Reproducible Lesson Plan • Section 3 Quiz • Testmaker • The Western Civilization Videodisc
Section 4 A Middle Way Discuss how the reformation of the Church of England came about.		• Reproducible Lesson Plan • Section 4 Quiz • Testmaker • The Western Civilization Videodisc • Chapter 29 Teaching Transparencies and Activities
Section 5 Wars of Religion Explain why Europeans became involved in religious wars.	People in History: *Akbar,* p. 461	• Reproducible Lesson Plan • Section 5 Quiz • Testmaker • The World History Videodisc
Section 6 The Thirty Years' War Discuss how the Thirty Years' War affected Europe.		• Reproducible Lesson Plan • Section 6 Quiz • Testmaker • Chapter 29 Geography and Map Activity • Chapter 29 Chart and Graph Skill Activity
Chapter 29 Review and Evaluation		• Chapter 29 Reteaching Activity • Chapter 29 Enrichment Activity • Spanish Summary and Glossary • Audiocassettes (English and Spanish) • Chapter 29 Performance Assessment Activity • Chapter 29 Test • Testmaker

If time does not permit teaching the entire chapter, use the Chapter 29 Summary on page 464 and the Chapter 29 Audiocassettes (English and Spanish) to point out the main ideas of the chapter.

✓ Performance Assessment Activities

Battle Plan Have students research the battle that involved the defeat of the Spanish Armada. Tell them to present an explanation/re-creation of the event as if they were explaining the event, its causes, and its effects to a younger child. Have students share their presentations with the class.

Comparing Reformers Have students choose one of the following reformers to compare to a modern reformer of their choice whom they think has made a similar impact: Teresa of Avila, William Tyndale, Charles Borromeo, John Knox, Jan Hus, or John Wycliffe. Have students create a poster that parallels the achievements of both, and a summary statement that compares each person's overall importance to their reformation movement.

CHAPTER RESOURCES

LITERATURE ABOUT THE PERIOD

Dumas, Alexandre. *The Three Musketeers.* Translated by Henry L. Williams. Street and Smith, 1919. Exaggerated tale of four swashbucklers in France during the reign of Louis XIII.

READINGS FOR THE STUDENT

Cowie, Leonard W. *Martin Luther: Leader of the Reformation* (A Pathfinder Biography). Frederick Praeger, 1969. Detailed biography of Luther.

Cowie, Leonard W. *The Reformation* (A Young Historian Book). John Day Co., 1968. Background information about the Reformation.

O'Dell, Scott. *The Hawk that Dare Not Hunt by Day.* Houghton Mifflin, 1975. Novel about a boy who helps the reformer Tyndale smuggle his translation of the Bible into England.

Simon, Edith, et al. *The Reformation* (Great Ages of Man). Time-Life Books, 1966. Illustrations, maps, and diagrams describe religious changes and their effects on European society.

READINGS FOR THE TEACHER

Bainton, Roland H. *The Age of Reformation.* Van Nostrand Reinhold Company, 1956. Shows how the Christian faith shaped history during the Reformation.

George, Margaret. *The Autobiography of Henry VIII.* St. Martin's Press, 1986. Depicts the life of Tudor monarch Henry VIII in novel form.

Grimm, Harold J. *The Reformation Era: 1500-1650.* Macmillan, 1965. Presents a comprehensive study of the Reformation.

Simon, Edith. *The Reformation.* Time-Life Books, 1969. Emphasizes the sixteenth century movement that gave rise to Protestantism.

Williams, Jay. *The Spanish Armada.* American Heritage Publishing Co., 1966. Deals with the defeat of the Spanish Armada by England.

MULTIMEDIA RESOURCES

Martin Luther and the Reformation. Multi-Media Productions. 2 filmstrips and cassette. Luther's attack on dogma and ritual are detailed.

The Protestant Reformation. EAV. Video. Details the impact of the Protestant Reformation in European countries.

The Reformation. Coronet. Video. Overview of Germany's Protestant Reformation.

INTRODUCE

CHAPTER 29 OVERVIEW

Chapter 29 examines the main features of the Protestant and Catholic reformations.

- **Section 1** discusses Martin Luther's excommunication from the Catholic Church.
- **Section 2** describes the founding of Protestantism.
- **Section 3** explains the work of Catholic reformers.
- **Section 4** examines the Church of England's reformation.
- **Section 5** summarizes the religious wars in Europe in the late 1500s and the 1600s.
- **Section 6** discusses the Thirty Years' War.

CHAPTER OBJECTIVES

After reading Chapter 29, students will be able to:

1. explain why Luther's beliefs brought him into conflict with the Roman Catholic Church.
2. describe how Protestantism developed.
3. identify how Catholic reformers changed their Church.
4. discuss the reformation of the Church of England.
5. explain why Europeans became involved in religious wars.
6. discuss how the Thirty Years' War affected Europe.

EXAMINING THE ILLUSTRATION

Have a volunteer explain what is meant by church reformer. Explain that they will be reading about Luther and other reformers in this chapter.

PERFORMANCE ASSESSMENT

Use the Performance Assessment activities on page 448B to help you evaluate students as they complete the chapter.

CHAPTER 29

The Reformation

Martin Luther, Church Reformer

448

TEACHER CLASSROOM RESOURCES

- Reproducible Lesson Plan
- Section Quizzes/Chapter Test
- Reteaching Activity
- Enrichment Activity
- Chart and Graph Skill Activity
- Geography and Map Activity
- Vocabulary and Guided Reading Activity
- Cooperative Learning Activity
- Spanish Summary and Glossary
- Performance Assessment Activity
- The World History Videodisc
- The Western Civilization Videodisc
- Audiocassettes (English and Spanish)
- Teaching Transparencies and Activities
- Testmaker

Chapter Focus

READ TO DISCOVER:

- Why Martin Luther's beliefs brought him into conflict with the Roman Catholic Church.
- How Protestantism developed.
- How Catholic reformers worked to improve their Church.
- How and why the reformation of the Church of England came about.
- Why Europeans became involved in religious wars.
- How the Thirty Years' War affected Europe.

The Roman Catholic Church did not adjust to the many changes taking place in western Europe during the 1400s and 1500s. Many Europeans began to call for a **reformation** (ref uhr mā' shuhn), or a change, in the way the Church taught and practiced Christianity.

Church leaders, however, were too busy with their own and government affairs to make changes. They did not like the reformers' ideas, especially those that could affect their power. Because of this, the unity of the Church was threatened.

1475 A.D.–1650 A.D.

KEY TERMS

reformation
indulgences
theses
heretic
ministers
seminary
armada
galleons
civil service

Section 1

Martin Luther

One reformer who challenged the Church was a German monk named Martin Luther (mart' uhn lū thuhr). Luther, born in 1483, was the son of peasants. His family wanted him to be a lawyer. However, he later decided to become a monk.

As a monk, Luther faithfully followed Church teachings and practices. However, he could find no peace of mind. He wondered how God would judge his actions.

While studying the New Testament, Luther found the answer to the questions that had been troubling him. He decided that trusting in Jesus, rather than doing good works, would save people from their sins. Luther's ideas soon brought him into conflict with the Church. In 1517, Pope Leo X wanted money to

FOCUS

BELLRINGER

Write the following quotation on chalkboard, *"It is neither safe nor prudent to do aught against conscience. Here I stand—I cannot do otherwise. God help me."* Ask students to write down their first impressions of the person who said these words.

MOTIVATIONAL ACTIVITY

Have students share their impressions of the quotation above. Explain that the person quoted was Martin Luther who, in his speech, refused to take back his criticisms of the Catholic Church.

VOCABULARY PRE-CHECK

Write the key terms for this chapter on the chalkboard. Ask students to use those that they know in sentences.

Assign Chapter 29 **Vocabulary and Guided Reading Activity** in the TCR.

EXTRA CREDIT PROJECT

One of the more interesting European cities, Geneva, Switzerland, is important in this chapter. Have interested students research and report on both the history and modern events of this city. Suggest they prepare a presentation of their research to share with the class.

KEY TO ABILITY LEVELS

Teaching strategies have been coded for varying learning styles and abilities.

L1 Level 1 activities are **basic** activities and should be within the ability range of all students.

L2 Level 2 activities are **average** activities and should be within the ability range of the average to above-average student.

L3 Level 3 activities are **challenging** activities designed for the ability range of above-average students.

LEP LEP activities should be within the ability range of Limited English Proficiency students.

VIDEODISC

Use the following to enrich Chapter 29.

WC D 16 17000

The sale of indulgences, 1517.

TEACH

GUIDED PRACTICE

L1 **History** Have students create a time line of major events during the Reformation of western Europe discussed in this chapter. LEP

DID YOU KNOW ??

According to Roman Catholic theology, a sin merits a certain amount of punishment. This can be diminished by performing certain acts of penance. Some members of the Church believed that buying indulgences equated to a certain amount of penance.

CAPTION ANSWER

Pope Leo X wanted money to rebuild Peter's Church in Rome.

LINKING PAST TO PRESENT

Martin Luther introduced the practice of the congregational singing of hymns in the vernacular. He wrote about 37 hymns—many still sung today. His best-known composition is "A Mighty Fortress is Our God."

VIDEODISC

Use the following to enrich Chapter 29.

WC D 19 17003

Contemporary German cartoon lampoons Luther.

rebuild St. Peter's Church in Rome. He sent out monks to sell **indulgences** (in dul' juhnt sez), or documents that freed their owners from the punishment they were due to receive for their sins. Luther believed the sale of indulgences led people to think they could buy God's forgiveness for their sins.

One night Luther posted a list of 95 **theses** (thē' sēz), or statements of beliefs, on the door of the castle church in Wittenberg (wit' uhn buhrg), Germany. In the list, Luther stated that only God could forgive sins. He challenged anyone who disagreed to debate with him.

Luther began to attack other Catholic beliefs openly. He said that Popes could make mistakes; that the only true guide to religious truth was the Bible, which every Christian had the right to read; and that every Christian had the right to pray to God without the aid of a priest.

In 1520, Pope Leo condemned Luther's teachings and excommunicated him. Leo insisted that the German emperor,

SALE OF INDULGENCES Hoping to lessen God's punishment upon them, many Christians bought the indulgences offered by the Church. Here, indulgences are sold at the village marketplace. **Why was the Church selling indulgences?**

COOPERATIVE LEARNING

Divide students into two teams: one representing John Tetzel, the Church's agent for selling indulgences in northern Germany, and the other representing Martin Luther. Have students research the practice of selling indulgences and prepare arguments from the point of view of the person they represent. Have each team choose its representative to debate this proposition: *The sale of indulgences is justified by the beauty of the rebuilt St. Peter's Basilica that it helps to finance.* One student should serve as moderator. Conclude by having the entire class analyze the arguments.

Assign the Chapter 29 **Cooperative Learning Activity** in the TCR.

Charles V, try Luther as a **heretic** (her′ uh tik), or person who holds a belief that is different from the accepted belief of the Church. Charles was loyal to the Church, but he relied on German princes who supported Luther. To keep their loyalty, Charles agreed to give Luther a fair trial. At the same time, he secretly promised the Pope that Luther would be condemned. In 1521, Luther was tried by the German Diet of Worms. When he refused to give up his ideas, he was condemned for heresy.

Painting of Pope Leo X

Section 1 Review

1. **Identify:** Martin Luther, Pope Leo X, Charles V
2. **Define:** reformation, indulgences, theses, heretic
3. What happened to Luther at Worms?

Critical Thinking

4. Why might other people have agreed with Luther when he said it was wrong to sell indulgences?

Section 2 A New Religion

By 1524, most people in northern Germany supported Luther. They left the Roman Catholic Church and formed the Lutheran (lū′ thuhr uhn) Church.

The Lutheran princes of Germany had strong armies, which Charles V could not defeat. In 1555, Charles realized he could not force the people to return to the Roman Catholic Church. He then agreed to sign a treaty known as the Peace of Augsburg (ogz′ buhrg). There could be both Catholic and Lutheran churches in Germany. The Peace of Augsburg kept German Lutherans and Catholics from fighting each other for nearly 50 years.

Protestant Groups Luther's ideas soon spread to other areas of Europe. People in Scandinavia founded Lutheran churches. Preachers and merchants in Switzerland (swit′ suhr luhnd) also left the Roman Catholic Church. They set up Reformed churches. Because they protested against Catholic ideas, Lutheran and Reformed churches were called Protestant (prot′ uh stuhnt). Protestant church leaders were called **ministers.** They spent more time teaching from the Bible. They conducted services in the language of the area instead of in Latin. This made services easier for people to understand.

Painting of Catholic Saints

L2 **Critical Thinking** Have students imagine they are the editor of the Worms newspaper. Tell them to write an editorial—from the Church's point of view—about Luther's appearance before the Diet.

DID YOU KNOW ??

The word *diet* can mean "legislative body." Worms is a German city. Therefore, the Diet of Worms was "a legislative body in the city of Worms, Germany."

MAKING CONNECTIONS

➤➤ **History** Even after he posted his 95 theses, Luther still considered his activities to be directed toward reforms within the Catholic Church. It was his opponents who found his ideas heretical. After the Diet of Worms, Luther was "kidnapped" by his protector, Prince Frederick of Saxony, and hidden in his castle for a year. In 1525, Luther married Katherina con Bora, a former nun, thus emphasizing his rejection of monastic rules. He died in 1546 and was buried in the castle church in Wittenberg.

SECTION 1 ANSWERS

1. Martin Luther, German monk who founded Lutheran church (p. 449); Pope Leo X, Roman Catholic pope (p. 449); Charles V, German emperor (p. 451)
2. reformation, a change (p. 449); indulgences, documents that freed owners from punishment for their sins (p. 450); theses, statements of beliefs (p. 450); heretic, person who holds a belief different from accepted Church beliefs (p. 451)
3. He was condemned for heresy.
4. Answers will vary but might include that other people would have been opposed to the idea that only the rich would be able to buy salvation.

Assign the Chapter 29 **Section 1 Quiz** in the TCR. Testmaker available.

VIDEODISC

Use the following to enrich Chapter 29.

WC D 21 17005
The opening of the Diet of Worms in 1521.

WC D 24 17008
Freedom Flag of the Peasants' War in Germany.

LINKING PAST TO PRESENT

Luther translated the New Testament from Greek to German. Later, he translated the Old Testament. Luther's German Bible greatly influenced the development of the modern German language.

MAKING CONNECTIONS

➤➤ **History** Geneva was newly independent (from Savoy) and self-governing. Its council at first rejected Calvin and his strict ideas but later asked him back. Calvin wrote books and pamphlets on every detail of church organization, personal conduct, and doctrine. His rules for the city inns, for example, not only forbade dancing and card playing but even set bedtime at 9:00. The city government carried out church laws. Church elders inspected people's homes and monitored their behavior.

L3 **Language Arts** Ask students to choose to be a publisher of Calvin's time that either supports Calvin's rules and ideas, or disagrees with the rules Calvin has forced on the people of Geneva. Have them write a pamphlet that supports their opinions to be distributed to the people. Encourage them to be thorough and convincing in presenting their ideas.

Painting of John Calvin

Ulrich Zwingli was important in leading the Protestant movement in Switzerland. Zwingli lived from 1484 to 1531. Unlike Luther, however, he wanted to break completely from Catholic rituals. He ordered the removal of images from churches, and he wanted to close monasteries. Zwingli led a group of Protestants from Zurich, Switzerland, in a battle against Catholic forces in 1531 and was killed. After Zwingli's death the Protestant church was firmly established in Switzerland.

John Calvin The most powerful Reformed group was in the Swiss city of Geneva (juh nē′ vuh). There, John Calvin set up the first Protestant church governed by a council of ministers and elected church members. Calvin also wrote books that became a guide for Protestants throughout Europe.

Calvin believed that there was nothing in the past, present, or future that God did not know about or control. He also held that from the beginning of time, God decided who would be saved and who would not. Calvin used the scriptures to support his ideas. He believed that God's will was written in the Bible, which ministers had the right to interpret. The ministers also had the right to make sure everyone obeyed God's will. Calvin had the Geneva town council pass laws to force people to follow strict rules of behavior. They could not dance, play cards, go to the theater, or take part in drinking parties. Those who refused to obey these laws were put in prison, executed, or banished.

Calvinism taught people to work hard and to save money. For this reason, many rich merchants supported Calvin. With their help, Calvin worked to improve Geneva. Streets and buildings were kept clean. New workshops opened, providing more jobs for people. Persecuted Protestants from all over Europe found safety in Geneva. Young men came to study at the school Calvin founded to train Reformed ministers. Many of them later returned to their own countries to set up Reformed churches.

Section 2 Review

1. **Identify:** Lutheran Church, Peace of Augsburg, Reformed Church, Protestant, Geneva, John Calvin
2. **Define:** ministers
3. What were some differences between Catholic and Protestant practices?
4. What did Calvin believe?

Critical Thinking

5. What ideas of Calvinism do you agree with? What ideas do you disagree with? Explain.

SECTION 2 ANSWERS

1. Lutheran Church, German church (p. 451); Peace of Augsburg, allowed Catholic and Lutheran churches in Germany (p. 451); Reformed Church, church that left the Roman Catholic Church (p. 451); Protestant, Lutheran and Reformed churches (p. 451); Geneva, Swiss city (p. 452); John Calvin, organized Protestant church in Switzerland (p. 452)
2. ministers, Protestant leaders (p. 451)
3. Ministers were not as powerful as priests, taught more from the Bible, and used native languages.
4. God controlled all; that God decided who would be saved and who would not; and that God's will was written in the Bible, which ministers had the right to interpret.
5. Answers will vary, but students should explain their choices.

Assign the Chapter 29 **Section 2 Quiz** in the TCR. Testmaker available.

Section 3

Catholic Reform

While Protestants formed new churches, Catholic reformers worked to improve their church. Many came from Spain and Italy, the leading countries of the Catholic reform movement.

One of the best known Catholic reformers was Ignatius (ig nā' shē uhs) of Loyola (loi ō' luh). In 1521, he gave up his life as a Spanish noble to serve God and the Roman Catholic Church. In 1540, he founded the Society of Jesus. Its members were called Jesuits (jezh' ū its). This group was formed to spread Roman Catholic ideas to all parts of the world. Jesuits also worked to help the people strengthen their faith. They wore black robes and lived simple lives. They set up schools, helped the poor, and preached to the people. They also taught in universities, served as advisers in royal courts. Jesuit missionaries were the first to carry Catholic ideas to India, China, and Japan.

IGNATIUS OF LOYOLA Ignatius of Loyola was a Roman Catholic religious leader who founded the Society of Jesus. Ignatius was especially interested in setting up foreign missions and educating children. In this painting he is shown holding mass with his followers. **What were members of the Society of Jesus called?**

MAKING CONNECTIONS

➤➤ **Geography: Region** In 1549, Jesuit missionaries began preaching in Japan. They were expelled in 1638. In 1600, Jesuit missionaries established themselves at Beijing, China, where they served for 200 years as advisers to the emperor in astronomy, mathematics, translation, and other areas. Encourage students to locate this city on a map.

LINKING PAST TO PRESENT

The Catholic Reformation renewed religious enthusiasm in the arts, sparking a new style of art and music called *baroque*. Renaissance art had demonstrated symmetry, order, and restraint, but baroque art employed asymmetry and exaggeration for dramatic effect. This art style had great influence on later generations of artists.

CAPTION ANSWER

the Jesuits

VIDEODISC

Use the following to enrich Chapter 29.

WC D 28 17012

Ignatius of Loyola (1491-1556).

EXTENDING THE CONTENT

In addition to Loyola, the movement for Catholic reform (or the Counter-Reformation) produced other outstanding and unforgettable figures. Francis Xavier, an early follower of Loyola, was perhaps the most indefatigable missionary since Paul. Following closely behind Portuguese explorers who reached India, Francis Xavier brought Catholic Christianity to Asia, establishing Jesuit communities in India, Goa, Ceylon (Sri Lanka), and Hong Kong. He was one of the first Europeans in Japan (1549).

L3 **Critical Thinking** Ask: Why do you think another name for the Catholic Reformation is the Counter-Reformation? *(The Catholic Church was reacting to the Protestant Reformation.)*

GEOGRAPHY AND HISTORY

The reason masses were spoken in Latin only was to insure religious uniformity regardless of what country or area in which the service was to be held.

CAPTION ANSWER

to discuss changes in the Church and to defend Catholic teachings

LINKING PAST TO PRESENT

The Catholic Church published the *Index Librorum Prohibitorum*—Index of Prohibited Books—until 1966.

VIDEODISC

Use the following to enrich Chapter 29.

WC D 26 17010
The Council of Trent.

COUNCIL OF TRENT Meeting three times between 1545 and 1563, the Council of Trent helped to renew Catholic life and worship. In this painting bishops and other church leaders from throughout Europe debate an issue at a session of the Council. **Why did the Pope call for the Council of Trent?**

The Jesuits used reason and good deeds to defend the Roman Catholic Church against criticisms. They also tried to bring Protestants back to the Church. Because of their work, people in eastern European countries such as Poland, Bohemia (bō hē mē uh), and Hungary once again became loyal to the Roman Catholic Church.

During this time, the Pope also took steps to strengthen the Roman Catholic Church. He called a council of bishops to discuss reforms and to defend Catholic teachings. The council met at different times between 1545 and 1563 at Trent, Italy. The Council of Trent ended many Church practices that had been criticized for hundreds of years such as the sale of indulgences. Church leaders were ordered to follow strict rules. Each diocese was told to build a **seminary** (sem′ uh ner ē), or a school to train priests.

The Council of Trent also explained Catholic doctrine. It said that good works, as well as faith, helped people get to heaven. It also held that the Church alone decided how the Bible was to be interpreted and that mass would be said in Latin only. Together, the Council of Trent and the Jesuit missionaries helped the Pope reclaim Protestant areas.

SPOTLIGHT ON: HENRY VIII

Henry VIII was typical of Renaissance rulers—a king who tried to excel in many areas. As a youth he had a lean, athletic physique and a keen mind. He enjoyed tennis, jousting, music, and discussions about astronomy and geometry. He composed several pieces of music and may have even written the song "Greensleeves." He also wrote the book called *Assertions of the Seven Sacraments,* in which as a devout Catholic he attacked the views of Martin Luther.

Section 3 Review

1. **Identify:** Ignatius of Loyola, Council of Trent
2. **Define:** seminary
3. What were the leading countries of the Catholic reform movement?
4. What did the Council of Trent do?

Critical Thinking

5. What is your opinion of the following statement: The Council of Trent was important in strengthening the Roman Catholic Church.

Section 4

A Middle Way

Reformation of the Church in England was led by a monarch, not by church leaders. It started as a political quarrel between the Tudor king Henry VIII and Pope Clement VII. Religious beliefs did not play a part in the struggle until later.

HENRY VIII AND ANNE BOLEYN Henry's hopes for a son made him determined to marry Anne Boleyn and led to a political break with the Pope. In this painting Henry and Anne are shown at the home of Thomas Wolsey, the king's chief adviser. **How was Henry eventually able to marry Anne Boleyn?**

INDEPENDENT PRACTICE

L2 **Critical Thinking** Have students watch a film portraying people from the time period discussed in this chapter, such as *Anne of a Thousand Days* (Anne Boleyn) or *A Man for All Seasons* (Thomas More). Have them write notes about the presentation and decide from what point of view these people are represented. LEP

CAPTION ANSWER

Henry set up the Anglican Church and received permission from the Archbishop of Canterbury to end his marriage to Catherine of Aragon.

DID YOU KNOW ??

Henry's desire for an heir and a happy marriage led him to marry six times.

VIDEODISC

Use the following to enrich Chapter 29.

WC D 30 17014
Henry VIII of England (1491-1547).

WC D 31 17015
Pope Clement VII (1478-1534).

SECTION 3 ANSWERS

1. Ignatius of Loyola, Catholic reformer (p. 453); Council of Trent, council that ended many Church practices (p. 454)
2. seminary, school to train priests (p. 454)
3. Spain and Italy
4. It stopped the sale of indulgences, ordered Church leaders to follow strict rules of behavior, told each diocese to build a seminary, and explained Catholic doctrine more fully.
5. Answers will vary but might include that the council corrected many things in the Roman Catholic Church, although it may have been too late to strengthen the Church.

Assign the Chapter 29 **Section 3 Quiz** in the TCR. Testmaker available.

DID YOU KNOW ??

Thomas More, who served as the highest judicial official in England from 1529 to 1532, was beheaded for refusing to accept the king as the head of the English Church. The Roman Catholic Church declared More a saint in 1935.

MAKING CONNECTIONS

➤➤ **History** Lady Jane Grey was the Protestant noblewoman the council tried to put on the throne. Earlier, her guardian had tried unsuccessfully to convince Edward VI to marry her. After Edward's death, she ruled as queen for nine days before she was imprisoned in 1554. At the age of 17 she was beheaded.

VIDEODISC

Use the following to enrich Chapter 29.

WC D 35 17019

Anne Boleyn, second wife of Henry VIII.

Painting of Thomas Cranmer

The Break With Rome The trouble between Henry VIII and the Pope began in 1527. At that time, Henry was married to Catherine of Aragon, the daughter of Ferdinand and Isabella of Spain and the aunt of German emperor Charles V. Henry and Catherine had only one living child, Mary. As Catherine grew older, Henry feared she could not have any more children. This was very important to Henry because he wanted a son to succeed to the throne.

At the same time, Henry had fallen in love with Anne Boleyn (bu lin′) a young woman of the court. He wanted Pope Clement to end his marriage to Catherine so that he could marry Anne, by whom he hoped to have a son. When the Pope refused, Henry declared that the Pope no longer had power over the Church in England. Henry was then excommunicated.

In 1534, the English Parliament passed a law stating that the king was head of the Church of England. Any English church leader who did not accept the law would stand trial as a heretic. Thomas Cranmer (kran′ muhr), the Archbishop of Canterbury and the most important church leader in England, supported Henry. Cranmer helped Henry end his marriage to Catherine. Henry then married Anne Boleyn, who gave him one child, a daughter named Elizabeth. A few years later, Henry had Anne executed for treason. He then married Jane Seymour (sē′ mōuhr), who died shortly after giving Henry the son he wanted.

Edward and Mary When Henry VIII died, his nine-year-old son became King Edward VI. Since Edward was too young and sick to rule, a council of nobles governed England for him. Most of the council members were Protestants, and they brought Protestant doctrines into the English Church. Thomas Cranmer supported the council. He wanted the people to have an orderly form of Protestant worship. To help achieve this, he wrote a worship service in English called the *Book of Common Prayer.* It was used in all the churches in England.

When Edward died in 1553, the council of nobles tried to bring a Protestant noblewoman to the throne. Their attempt failed, however, because the people of England refused to accept any ruler who was not a Tudor. They wanted Henry's daughter Mary as their monarch.

Painting of Edward VI

Mary was Catholic. As soon as she became queen, she accepted the Pope as head of the English Church. She then insisted that all English men and women return to the Roman Catholic Church. Many Protestants refused and were persecuted. More than 300 of them, including Cranmer, were burned at the stake for heresy. The people turned against their queen, calling her "Bloody Mary."

Mary was married to King Philip II of Spain. The English were unhappy about the marriage because Spain was England's

MULTICULTURAL PERSPECTIVES

Anabaptists, Protestant sects in western Europe who admitted only adult members, denied the authority of local governments to direct their lives. They refused to hold office, bear arms, or swear oaths, and many lived separate from a society they saw as sinful. As a result, they were often persecuted by government officials, forcing many Anabaptists to wander from country to country seeking refuge. Many Anabaptist groups left Europe for North America during the 1600s. There they promoted the ideas of religious liberty and separation of church and state.

PHILIP II AND MARY TUDOR Queen of England from 1553 to 1558, Mary I shown in this painting (right) longed to bring England back to the Roman Catholic Church. Mary married Philip II (left) of Spain, shown here, who considered himself the champion of the Roman Catholic faith. **Why did the English people object to the marriage of Mary and Philip?**

enemy and the leading Catholic power in Europe. They feared that Philip and the Pope would become the real rulers of England. The people decided that England would remain free only if it became a Protestant country. For this reason, they wanted a Protestant ruler.

Elizabeth's Church Mary died in 1558 without a child to succeed her. Thus, her half-sister, Elizabeth, became queen. Elizabeth I was Protestant. With the help of Parliament, she ended the Pope's authority in the English Church.

Elizabeth was very popular with her subjects. She worked to set up the Church in a form that would appeal to as many people as possible. Elizabeth and Parliament decided that the Church should be Protestant. However, the Church would keep some Catholic features. The monarch would be head of the Church, which would use Cranmer's prayer book and teach Protestant beliefs.

L3 **Critical Thinking** Ask: *How did the religious turmoil in England influence the colonization of America?* Encourage students to brainstorm ideas, and then research to find how valid their ideas were. Encourage them to make a graphic organizer of their ideas.

CAPTION ANSWER

Spain was England's enemy and the leading Catholic power in Europe. The English people feared that Philip and the Pope would become the real rulers of England.

MAKING CONNECTIONS

>> **Religion** The combination of Protestant beliefs and Catholic rituals devised by Elizabeth and Parliament became known as the beliefs of Anglicanism.

VIDEODISC

Use the following to enrich Chapter 29.

WC D 6 16990
Philip II of Spain (1527-1598).

WC D 36 17020
Mary Tudor and her husband, Philip II of Spaln.

MEETING SPECIAL NEEDS

Help visual learners create an outline of Section 4 on the chalkboard. Place the following brief outline on the chalkboard. Then have students give details to complete the outline.

How the Reformation of the Church of England Came About:

I. Henry VIII
II. Edward VI
III. Mary Tudor
IV. Elizabeth I

DID YOU KNOW ??

Although Zwingli personally loved music, he outlawed its use in worship and even smashed church organs.

LINKING PAST TO PRESENT

Several new Protestant sects in western Europe, called Anabaptists, initiated the practice of baptizing only adult members. They based this practice on the belief that only people who could make a free and informed choice to become Christians should be allowed to do so. The Mennonite church originated among Anabaptists in Europe in the 1500s under the leadership of Menno Simons. Many of the Mennonites who migrated to the United States settled in Lancaster County, Pennsylvania.

CAPTION ANSWER

Italy

VIDEODISC

Use the following to enrich Chapter 29.

WC D 38 17022

Elizabeth I before Parliament.

ST. TERESA OF AVILA Another church reformer, St. Teresa of Avila, Spain lived from 1515–1582. As a nun she reformed convent life and wrote about religious life. **What other country besides Spain had many Roman Catholic reformers?**

Most of the English people were pleased with the mix of Protestant belief and Catholic practice since many Catholic rituals remained. Those who were not pleased stayed outside the church. Some Protestants also did not like Elizabeth's Church, but they did not leave it. Because these people wanted to purify the English Church of Catholic ways, they became known as Puritans (pyur' uh tuhnz).

Section 4 Review

1. **Identify:** Henry VIII, Catherine of Aragon, Anne Boleyn, Thomas Cranmer, Jane Seymour, Edward VI, *Book of Common Prayer,* Mary Tudor, Philip II, Elizabeth I, Puritans
2. What happened when Pope Leo refused to end Henry's marriage?
3. What did Mary expect the people to do as soon as she became queen? How did the people feel about this?
4. What was the Church of England like under Elizabeth I?

Critical Thinking

5. How good do you think Elizabeth I was in dealing with England's problems with establishing a church?

SECTION 4 ANSWERS

1. Henry VIII, English king (p. 455); Catherine, wife of Henry VIII (p. 456); Anne Boleyn, wife of Henry VIII (p. 456); Thomas Cranmer, Archbishop of Canterbury (p. 456); Jane Seymour, wife of Henry VIII (p. 456); Edward VI, son of Henry VIII (p. 456); *Book of Common Prayer,* worship service (p. 456); Mary Tudor, queen of England (p. 456); Philip II, king of Spain (p. 456); Elizabeth I, queen of England (p. 456); Puritans, wanted to purify English Church (p. 458)

2. Henry said he controlled the Church in England and was excommunicated.

3. return to the Roman Catholic Church; many refused and were persecuted

4. led by the monarch, used Cranmer's prayer book, and taught Protestant beliefs

5. Answers will vary but might include that Elizabeth was effective.

Assign the Chapter 29 **Section 4 Quiz** in the TCR. Testmaker available.

Section 5

Wars of Religion

By the middle 1500s, most northern Europeans were Protestants, while most southern Europeans were Catholics. European monarchs had used religion to help unite their people and to build powerful nations. The ruler and people of each country were expected to belong to the same church. Those who refused were persecuted. This led to much bitterness between people of different faiths. Differences in religion also led to wars between countries. Toward the end of the 1500s, Europe entered a period of religious wars that lasted until 1648.

The Armada Under Elizabeth I, England became the leading Protestant power in Europe. Spain, under Philip II, remained the leading Catholic power. Philip knew that if he could defeat England, Protestant Europe would be open to Catholic control. Therefore, he ordered the building of an **armada** (ar mah' duh), or a large group of warships.

After two years, the Spanish Armada, with its 130 ships, was ready. Its strength lay in its **galleons** (gal' ēuhns), or heavy ships with square-rigged sails and long, raised decks. In 1588, the Armada sailed toward England. Its main purpose was to help the Spanish armies on the continent cross over to the English shore.

SPANISH ARMADA In 1588, the English fleet faced the Spanish Armada in the English Channel. Here, English fire ships move toward the Armada. This action broke the curved formation of the Spanish ships and made possible a successful English attack. **What was the main strength of the Spanish Armada?**

MAKING CONNECTIONS

➤➤ **History** People expected that Elizabeth would marry and that her husband would rule. The common attitude of the time was that only men were fit to rule and that government matters were beyond a woman's ability. Elizabeth, however, feared that marrying a foreign prince would endanger England and that marrying an Englishman would cause jealousy among the English nobility.

DID YOU KNOW

When the Spanish Armada faced the English ships, the Spanish ships carried 1,100 cannons and about 27,000 men, half of whom were soldiers. The English ships carried about 2,000 cannons and 16,000 sailors.

CAPTION ANSWER

its galleons, or heavy ships with square-rigged sails and long, raised decks

VIDEODISC

Use the following to enrich Chapter 29.

WC D 41 17025

English defeat of the Spanish Armada, 1598.

COOPERATIVE LEARNING

Divide students into three research groups. Ask them to do research and write a report about one of the Spanish minorities during Philip's reign—Protestants, Marranos, and Moriscos. Reports should include information about daily life, professions, reasons for conversion or defiance in the face of danger, persecution during the Spanish Inquisition, and decisions people made to flee Spain or stay in spite of persecutions. Students should delegate tasks of finding information, organizing ideas, making outlines and note cards, and writing the drafts.

L2 **Geography: Region** Ask students to research and write about the Low Countries. Why were they called this? What geographical features do they have and how does this environment affect peoples' lives? Students should include basic facts about the area and its people.

GEOGRAPHY AND HISTORY

Spain and France posed the greatest naval threats to England. The attack of the Spanish Armada made England realize the dangers of an alliance between Spain and France. As a result England relied on diplomacy as well as sea power to protect its interests. During Elizabeth's reign, England worked to balance the power of European nations.

MAKING CONNECTIONS

>> **History** Henry IV founded the Bourbon dynasty, which ruled France until the early 1800s.

VIDEODISC

Use the following to enrich Chapter 29.

WC D 45 17029

Catherine de Médicis (1519-1589).

Elizabeth knew the Spanish forces were coming and prepared England for war. She had a naval commander, John Hawkins, reorganize the English fleet. He remodeled old ships and built new ones. He formed a new navy of 134 fighting ships and merchant vessels. Most of the ships were smaller than the Spanish ships, but they had larger guns and more ammunition. Expert sailors handled the English ships with much skill. One naval captain, Sir Francis Drake, was known for his overseas voyages and his capture of Spanish merchant ships.

The English knew they had to make the Spanish ships break their curved formation. Their chance came when the Spanish fleet anchored off the coast of Europe to wait for the Spanish armies to meet it. That night, the English set fire to eight small ships and sent them into the Spanish fleet. As the burning ships reached the Armada, the Spanish ships broke formation and began to drift. The English were then able to fight the Spanish ships one by one.

The Spanish naval command soon realized that the Armada was defeated. Short of food and water, it decided to return to Spain. A great storm came up, however, causing the voyage to be long and difficult. Only half the Armada reached home.

The English celebrated their victory with bonfires and parades. Although Spain was still a powerful enemy, England had shown it could defend itself. The English gained respect throughout Europe as champions of the Protestant cause. The defeat of the Armada allowed northern Europe to remain a Protestant stronghold.

The Huguenots Most people in France during the 1500s were Catholics. Many nobles, lawyers, doctors, and merchants, however, were Protestants. These French Protestants, who were called Huguenots (hyū' guh nots), followed Calvin's teachings.

In 1534, King Francis I, who was Catholic, forbade the Huguenots to worship freely. He wanted all French people to support the Roman Catholic Church. Catholics began to persecute Huguenots, and by 1562 a civil war broke out. By then, Charles IX had become king. Since he was too young to rule, his mother, Catherine de Medici, ruled for him.

Painting of Henry IV

Catherine tried to keep peace by showing favor first to one group and then to the other. She finally decided to support the Roman Catholic Church. In 1572, she allowed Catholic nobles to kill the leading Huguenots in Paris. Catholic mobs in other parts of France began to kill Protestants and burn their homes. Many Protestants left the country. The few who remained to carry on the fight were led by Henry of Navarre (nuh var'), a Huguenot prince.

In 1589, the king of France was killed. Henry of Navarre, who was next in line for the throne, became Henry IV. He wanted to gain the loyalty of the people. Since most French people were still

EXTENDING THE CONTENT

Ruling France as regent for her sons, Catherine de Medici balanced Catholic and Huguenot rivalries for many years. The leader of the Huguenots was Henry of Navarre, who was in line for the throne after Catherine's sons. On August 24, 1572—St. Bartholomew's Day—the queen's daughter Margaret of Valois was to marry Henry of Navarre in Paris. Most Protestant nobles came to the wedding, where hired assassins attacked and murdered them all except Henry and another heir to the throne. At the same time, mobs of Catholic Parisians turned on their Protestant neighbors and slaughtered thousands of them. As the killing spread to the countryside, more than 10,000 Huguenots were killed in the next six weeks.

Akbar

PEOPLE IN HISTORY

While western Europeans were busy with religious conflicts and wars, the ruler of India was trying to unify his empire by showing tolerance for all religions. The ruler's name was Akbar (ak' bahr). He was descended from Genghis Khan, the Mongol chief. Because of this, Akbar and other members of his dynasty are known as Moguls (mō' guhlz), an Indian variation of the word "Mongol."

Young Ruler Akbar ruled from 1556 to 1605. He was only 13 years old when he came to the throne. Soon, however, he conquered most of India and part of central Asia. Then, he began to strengthen his empire.

To improve government in the Mogul Empire, Akbar set up a **civil service,** or a system of appointing government workers. Under civil service, each job had a fixed salary, and each was given only to a qualified person. As a result, many able people entered government service.

To make life better for farmers, Akbar changed the tax system. At the time, each farmer was subject to the same tax rate. Under Akbar's system, land was taxed according to its ability to bear crops. This meant that taxes were lowered for farmers with less productive land.

Tolerance for Religion To unify the people, Akbar promoted religious toleration. He did away with taxes that had been levied on non-Muslims. He welcomed scholars of different faiths to his court. In addition, as a Muslim, Akbar was allowed to have four wives. So, he married women of different faiths.

Akbar showed that he cared about his people in other ways as well. When famine struck an area, he sent the people wheat from other areas. He ordered officials to treat people kindly. Akbar is considered to be one of the greatest Mogul rulers.

Checking for Understanding

1. **How did Akbar improve government in the Mogul Empire?**
2. **How did Akbar make life better for farmers?**
3. **In what ways did Akbar show tolerance for all religions?**

SPOTLIGHT ON: AKBAR

The mogul dynasty was ruled by Akbar for 49 years. Under the Moguls, the arts thrived. Such local crafts as cotton weaving became important, and luxury goods and precious metals were brought into India. Mogul rulers surrounded themselves with luxuries. Also under the Moguls, social and trade networks tied together villages, towns, and cities. A culture that was a blend of Muslim and Hindu ways developed.

Teaching

PEOPLE IN HISTORY

AKBAR

After students have read the People in History feature, ask: Why is Akbar and other members of his dynasty known as Moguls? *(He is descended from Genghis Khan, a Mongol chief. Mogul is an Indian variation of the word Mongol.)* Why is Akbar considered to be one of the greatest Mogul rulers? *(because of his wise actions and concerns for his people)* How would you compare the way Akbar ruled with the way the following European rulers ruled: Henry VIII, Mary Tudor, Elizabeth I, King Francis I, Catherine de Medici, Henry IV, Philip II? *(The rulers of Europe, except Henry IV, did not allow freedom of worship. This created great turmoil within Europe.)*

ANSWERS to Checking for Understanding

1. He set up a civil service.
2. He changed the tax system.
3. He did away with taxes that had been levied on non-Muslims, welcomed scholars of different faiths to his court, and married women of different faiths.

VIDEODISC

Use the followingf to enrich Chapter 29.

WH U 41 34647

A map of Akbar's empire (in pink, above).

DID YOU KNOW ??

Henry IV is credited with two famous statements. One, that "Paris is worth a Mass," was made when he converted to Catholicism. The other, "A chicken every Sunday in every peasant's pot," summed up his concern for the welfare of his people.

L1 **Religion** Before beginning the section on the Thirty Years' War, refer students to the map "Religions of Europe" on page 463 and have them familiarize themselves with the religions of the areas involved in the war. LEP

L2 **History** Divide the class into two groups. Have students in one group imagine they are living in France in 1648 and students in the other group imagine they are living in Germany during the same year. Tell students that the Thirty Years' War has just ended. Ask students to write an eyewitness account of how life in their country has changed since the war ended. The account should include any changes that have occurred in religion. Have volunteers read their accounts to the class.

VIDEODISC

Use the following to enrich Chapter 29.

WC E 6 19787

Initiation of the Thirty Years' War (1618-1648).

Catholic, he decided to convert. Nevertheless, Henry ended the fighting between Protestants and Catholics. Although he made Catholicism the national religion, he also made life easier for Protestants. In 1598, he signed the Edict of Nantes (nahnts), which gave Huguenots freedom of worship. France thus became the first European country to allow two Christian religions.

The Low Countries The Low Countries were part of the Spanish Empire. The people of the Low Countries were divided into Protestants and Catholics. Neither group liked Philip II's harsh rule. They did not like the heavy taxes imposed by Spain or the Spanish laws. Philip, however, made money from the wealth and trade of the Low Countries. He wanted to keep them under Spanish control.

Philip also wanted all his subjects to be Catholic. To achieve this, he set up an Inquisition in the Low Countries to stamp out Protestantism. In 1567, Protestants in the northern provinces revolted. Philip sent soldiers to restore order. They were joined by French Catholics from the southern provinces.

The fighting did not end until 1648. At that time, it was decided that the southern provinces, known today as Belgium, were to remain Catholic and continue under the rule of Spain. The northern provinces, known today as the Netherlands, were to be an independent Protestant country.

Section 5 Review

1. **Identify:** Spanish Armada, John Hawkins, Sir Francis Drake, Huguenots, Francis I, Catherine de Medici, Henry of Navarre, Edict of Nantes
2. **Define:** armada, galleons
3. How did the English defeat the Spanish Armada?
4. What led to civil war in France in 1562?

Critical Thinking

5. How do you think the religious wars in Europe in the 1500s and 1600s might have been avoided?

Section 6 THE THIRTY YEARS' WAR

During the 1590s and early 1600s, the German states began to quarrel over the terms of the Peace of Augsburg. They formed alliances based on religion. The Catholic alliance was led by the German emperor Ferdinand II.

SECTION 5 ANSWERS

1. Spanish Armada, Spanish warships (p. 459); John Hawkins, English commander (p. 460); Sir Francis Drake, English captain (p. 460); Huguenots, French Protestants (p. 460); Francis I, French king (p. 460); Catherine de Medici, French ruler (p. 460); Henry of Navarre, Huguenot prince (p. 460); Edict of Nantes, allowed two Christian religions to exist in France (p. 462)
2. armada, group of warships (p. 459); galleons, ships with square-rigged sails (p. 459)
3. by causing the Spanish ships to break formation and fighting the Spanish ships one by one
4. King Francis I forbade Huguenots to worship freely, and Catholics began to persecute Huguenots.
5. Answers will vary, but could say by allowing different religions to exist in their countries.

Assign the Chapter 29 **Section 5 Quiz** in the TCR. Testmaker available.

One Protestant state that resisted Ferdinand was Bohemia. In 1618, the Protestant nobles of Bohemia revolted. They chose a German Protestant prince as their new king. Ferdinand's armies crushed the Bohemians in a fierce battle, and Ferdinand proclaimed himself king of Bohemia. He did not allow Protestant worship. He sent Jesuits throughout the country to win the people back to the Roman Catholic Church.

The revolt in Bohemia soon grew into the Thirty Years' War. During the war, half the armies of Europe fought in Germany. First Denmark and then Sweden invaded Germany. Their kings were Protestants who wanted to stop the spread of Catholicism. They also hoped to conquer German territory. When the Swedes were finally defeated in 1634, the French became involved. Although France was a Catholic country, it entered the war on the Protestant side. This changed the nature of the war. It became

MAP STUDY

REGIONS By 1560 many Europeans were either Protestants or Catholic. **In which European countries did Calvinism take hold?**

The Religions of Europe

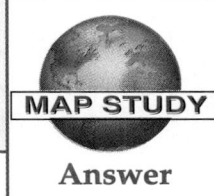

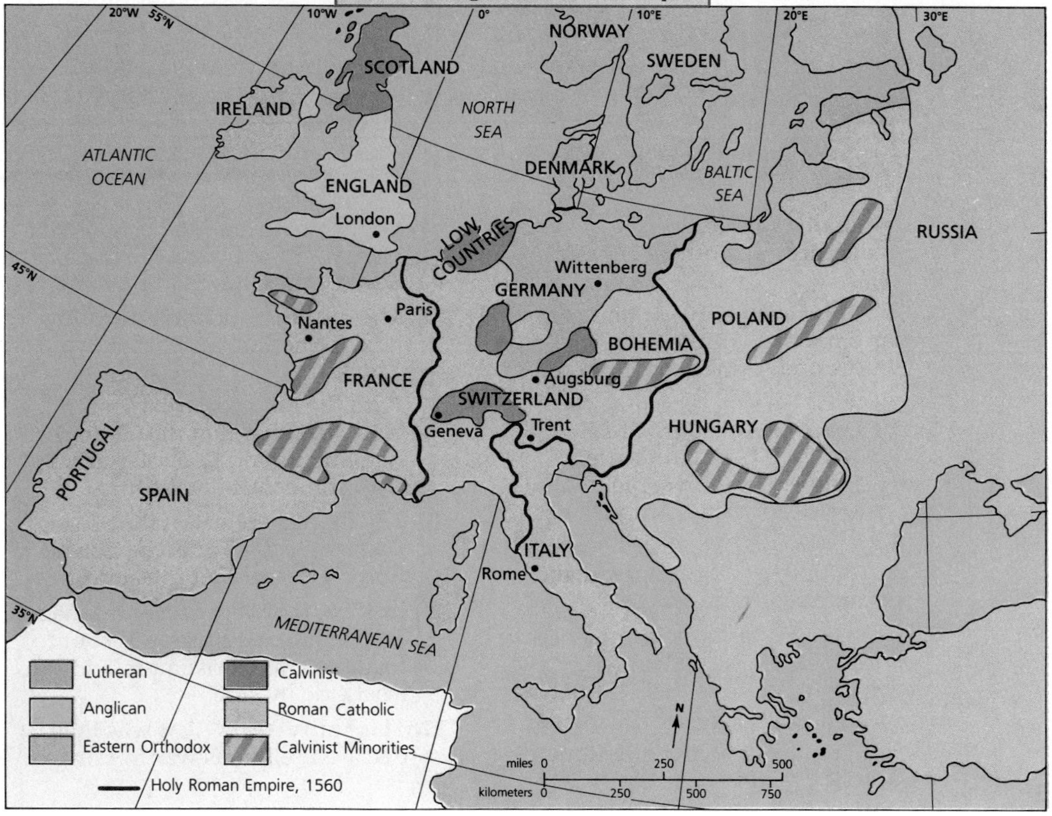

L1 **Geography: Location** Most of the Thirty Years' War took place in Germany, but soon other powers became involved. Have students list all the powers involved in the Thirty Years' War and locate them on the map on page 463.

DID YOU KNOW ??

In the midst of the brutal Thirty Years' War, traders brought tulip bulbs into Europe from Turkey. Public demand for tulips reached a peak in the 1630s. Frenzied buyers bid increasingly large sums for the flowers. Investing in tulips became big business.

MAP STUDY

Answer

Scotland, Low Countries, Germany, Switzerland

Assign the Chapter 29 **Geography and Map Activity** in the TCR.

GEOGRAPHY AND HISTORY

The splitting of the northern and southern provinces, as discussed in the section on Low Countries, was also part of the Peace of Westphalia.

EXTENDING THE CONTENT

The Thirty Years' War ended as a struggle over the balance of power in Europe. The huge landholdings and family ties between the Spanish and Austrian Hapsburgs combined to make the German Hapsburg emperors dominant, thereby upsetting the balance. France under the Bourbon kings was the only serious political rival. Sweden, Denmark, and the Netherlands entered the war for religious and political reasons. Cardinal Richelieu, Louis XIII's adviser, then brought Catholic France into the war to resist the alarming growth in Hapsburg power. The peace treaty changed the balance of power. German princes were autonomous; Bourbon France dominated western Europe; and Sweden was locally powerful in the north.

ASSESS

CHECK FOR UNDERSTANDING

Ask students to summarize the main points of the chapter. Discuss answers to the Section and Chapter Review questions.

EVALUATE

Assign the Chapter 29 **Performance Assessment Activity** in the TCR.

Administer the **Chapter 29 Test** in the TCR. Testmaker available.

RETEACH

Divide students into six groups. Assign each group a section from this chapter. Have the students write questions about the main ideas of their assigned section and quiz other groups.

Assign the Chapter 29 **Reteaching Activity** in the TCR.

ENRICH

Ask students to summarize the main reasons Luther felt he must break away from the Roman Catholic Church.

Assign the Chapter 29 **Enrichment Activity** in the TCR.

CLOSE

Have students discuss how religious wars during this time seemed to have been started by one or two people, but ended up involving whole nations.

MEETING CHAPTER OBJECTIVES

Each objective is tested by the Review questions in parentheses.

1. **Explain** how Luther's beliefs conflicted with the Church. (BV; UYJ)
2. **Describe** Protestantism. (BU; CU 1; UYJ)
3. **Identify** efforts of Catholic reformers. (BV; CU 3)
4. **Discuss** the reformation of the Church of England. (BV; CU 4; CT 2)
5. **Explain** why Europe had religious wars. (BV; CU 5, 6, 7)
6. **Discuss** the Thirty Years' War. (BV)

less a war over religion and more a struggle for territory and wealth.

The German people suffered great hardships during the war. Finally, in 1643, after a serious defeat, the German emperor asked for peace. In 1648, representatives of European nations signed the Peace of Westphalia (west fāl' yuh), which ended the war. The German emperor lost much of his power and France emerged as a strong nation. After this war, Europeans no longer fought over religion. Instead, nations tried to gain power through trade and expansion overseas.

Section 6 Review

1. Identify: Ferdinand II, Thirty Years' War, Peace of Westphalia
2. What led to the Thirty Years' War?
3. What effect did the Thirty Years' War have on Europe?

Critical Thinking

4. How well do you think friendship between countries based on religion would work today? Why do you think so?

Chapter Summary

1. Luther objected to the sale of indulgences and other Catholic beliefs.
2. By 1524, most people in northern Germany had left the Catholic Church and formed the Lutheran Church.
3. The Peace of Augsburg of 1555 allowed each German prince to decide whether the people in his territory were to be Catholic or Lutheran.
4. Martin Luther's ideas spread and became Protestantism.
5. While the Protestants formed new churches, Catholic reformers worked to improve their Church.
6. Between 1545 and 1563, the Council of Trent reformed many Roman Catholic practices.
7. English reformation began when Henry VIII removed the Pope as head of the Church of England.
8. Mary Tudor failed to return England to the Roman Catholic Church.
9. With the help of Parliament, Elizabeth I decided that the Church of England would be Protestant, but with some Catholic features.
10. The English defeat of the Spanish Armada in 1588 allowed northern Europe to remain Protestant.
11. In 1598, the Edict of Nantes made France the first European country to allow two Christian religions to exist side by side.
12. The Thirty Years' War was the last declared religious war in Europe.

SECTION 6 ANSWERS

1. Ferdinand II, German emperor (p. 462); Thirty Years' War, series of religious wars (p. 463); Peace of Westphalia, ended the Thirty Years' War (p. 464)
2. the revolt in Bohemia against the German emperor Ferdinand II
3. The German emperor lost much of his power, France emerged as a strong nation, and nations tried to gain power through trade and expansion.
4. Answers will vary but students should explain their answers. Students may make reference to recent conflicts in Ireland and the Middle East.

Assign the Chapter 29 **Section 6 Quiz** in the TCR. Testmaker available.

CHAPTER 29 Review

Building Vocabulary

Use the following words to write a paragraph explaining the conflicts over religion among European countries during the 1500s and 1600s.

reformation	ministers
indulgences	seminary
theses	armada
heretic	galleons

Check for Understanding

1. What churches were called Protestant?
2. What rules of behavior did Calvin make the people of Geneva follow?
3. What organization did Ignatius of Loyola found?
4. Why was Henry VIII excommunicated?
5. Why did Mary Tudor become known as "Bloody Mary"?
6. How did the defeat of the Spanish Armada help the Protestant cause?
7. What was the basis of the alliances formed by German states during the 1590s and early 1600s?

Critical Thinking

1. What would you have liked about living in Geneva at the time of John Calvin? What would you have disliked? Explain.
2. Do you approve or disapprove of the way Elizabeth I organized the Church of England? Explain.
3. Explain why you would or would not have converted to Catholicism if you had been Henry IV?
4. If you had been a Catholic in the middle 1500s, in which European country would you have preferred to live? Why?

Geography in History

LOCATION Refer to the location of Calvinist minorities on the map of western European religions on p. 463. What connection might there be between their locations and the fact that they are minority groups, or groups with fewer members than other religions?

Using Your Journal

Review the details you have noted about the changes in religion that took place in western Europe during the 1500s and 1600s. Review the Edict of Nantes and the importance it had at the time. Write an editorial explaining why the idea in that edict continues to be important today.

CHAPTER 29 REVIEW ANSWERS

BUILDING VOCABULARY

Paragraphs will vary but students should use all the vocabulary words.

CHECK FOR UNDERSTANDING

1. the Lutheran and Reformed churches
2. They could not dance, play cards, go to the theater, or take part in drinking parties.
3. the Society of Jesus
4. because he declared that the Pope no longer had power over the Church of England
5. because under her rule, many Protestants were persecuted or burned at the stake for heresy
6. It allowed northern Europe to remain a Protestant stronghold.
7. religion

CRITICAL THINKING

1. Answers will vary but should make reference to the agreement or disagreement with Calvinism.
2. Answers will vary but students should explain why they approve or disapprove.
3. Answers will vary but students should provide reasons for their choices.
4. Answers will vary but students should choose a specific location and explain the reasons for their choices.

+ BONUS +

TEST QUESTION

For Chapter 29 Test

How would Akbar have treated a non-Muslim farmer in his district who's crops had failed? *(Answers will vary but should include , with fairness.)*

USING YOUR JOURNAL

Editorials will vary but might include the idea that the Edict of Nantes had the beginnings of religious freedom, which is guaranteed in the U.S. today.

GEOGRAPHY IN HISTORY

The minorities were spread all over Europe in small pockets, while other religious groups lived in larger areas. Smaller groups are more apt to remain minorities if cut off from others of their beliefs.

CHAPTER 30

The Age of Discovery

CHAPTER ORGANIZER

Objectives	Special Features	Supplemental Materials
Section 1 The Portuguese Identify why Europeans searched for a direct sea route to India and the Far East and what discoveries were made by Portuguese explorers.		• Reproducible Lesson Plan • Section 1 Quiz • Testmaker • Chapter 30 Vocabulary and Guided Reading Activity • World History and Art Transparencies 13, 16 • The Western Civilization Videodisc
Section 2 The Spanish List what discoveries were made by explorers financed by Spain.	Map and Geography Skill: *Reviewing Map Legends,* p. 475	• Reproducible Lesson Plan • Section 2 Quiz • Testmaker • Chapter 30 Geography and Map Activity • Chapter 30 Cooperative Learning Activity • Foods Around the World • Chapter 30 Activity Book Activity
Section 3 Northwest Passage Discuss how the search for the northwest passage affected the Americas.		• Reproducible Lesson Plan • Section 3 Quiz • Testmaker • Chapter 30 Chart and Graph Skill Activity • Unit 9 Primary Source Reading • Foods Around the World
Chapter 30 Review and Evaluation		• Chapter 30 Reteaching Activity • Chapter 30 Enrichment Activity • Spanish Summary and Glossary • Audiocassettes (English and Spanish) • Chapter 30 Performance Assessment Activity • Chapter 30 Test • Testmaker • The World History Videodisc

If time does not permit teaching the entire chapter, use the Chapter 30 Summary on page 478 and the Chapter 30 Audiocassettes (English and Spanish) to point out the main ideas of the chapter.

✓ Performance Assessment Activities

Drama Have students write scripts for a class presentation of the first voyage of Christopher Columbus. Encourage students to include at least these scenes: (1) Columbus at the court of Ferdinand and Isabella; (2) Columbus at sea on October 12, 1492; (3) Columbus landing in the Americas.

Legends During the age of discovery, many Europeans believed in terrible sea monsters and odd beings that inhabited unknown lands. Some believed in the Seven Cities of Cíbola, fabled cities of gold in the Americas. Have students research and report on some of these legends. Students may want to prepare an oral reading, a summary report about legend themes, or an essay expressing opinions about legend themes.

Chapter Resources

LITERATURE ABOUT THE PERIOD

Cervantes, Miguel de. *The Ingenious Gentleman Don Quixote de la Mancha* in *The Portable Cervantes.* Modern Library, 1949. Translated and edited by Samuel Putnam. Translation of the adventures of Don Quixote and his sidekick Sancho Panza.

READINGS FOR THE STUDENT

Bilaug, Karla (trans. by Neil Jones). *Voyages of Discovery: Through Artists' Eyes.* St. Martin's Press, 1976. Intriguing introduction, for young readers, to art styles as they reflect world discoveries.

Hampden, John, ed. *New Worlds Ahead.* Farrar, Straus, & Giroux, 1968. Collection of exciting excerpts from first-hand accounts of Elizabethan-era voyages, taken from Hakluyt and others.

Lomask, Milton. *Exploration: Great Lives.* Scribners, 1988. Biographies of explorers.

Morison, Samuel Eliot. *Christopher Columbus, Mariner.* New American Library (Signet paperback), 1984. The well-known sailor-historian's own short version of his classic two-volume *Admiral of the Ocean Sea.*

O'Dell, Scott. *The King's Fifth.* Houghton Mifflin, 1966. Novel about a young mapmaker with Coronado's expedition in the Southwest, who unwillingly becomes caught up in the fever for gold.

READINGS FOR THE TEACHER

Blandford, Percy W. *Maps & Compasses: A User's Handbook.* TAB Books, Inc., 1984. Handbook that guides people interested in doing orienteering.

Morison, Samuel E. *The European Discovery of America: The Northern Voyages.* Oxford University Press, 1971. Focuses on the discoveries of North America.

MULTIMEDIA RESOURCES

Age of Discovery: English, French, and Dutch Explorations. Coronet Films. Film. Surveys the voyages of English, French, and Dutch explorers.

Age of Discovery: Spanish and Portuguese Explorations. Coronet Films. Film. Accounts of the explorations of Spanish and Portuguese explorers.

Christopher Columbus: Americas 1492. BBC/Time-Life. Video. Recounting of the four voyages of Christopher Columbus to the Americas.

L3 **Critical Thinking** Ask: Why do you think Columbus kept two separate logs—in one record he recorded the actual distance covered, and in the other he recorded a much shorter distance. *(He reported the shorter distance to his crew so they would not know how far they had gone.)*

GEOGRAPHY AND HISTORY

Although Columbus was one of the first to reach the Americas, it was named after the Florentine geographer Amerigo Vespucci. In 1504, Vespucci was quoted as saying that the lands across the ocean made up a new continent which "it is proper to call the new world." Martin Waldseemüller, a German publisher, was so taken with the remark that in 1507, he issued a world map that labeled the southern land "America."

CAPTION ANSWER

that the world was round, not flat, and that he could find the shortest route to Asia

VIDEODISC

Use the following to enrich Chapter 30.

WC N 6 44061
Columbus battles his Spanish colonists.

they threatened **mutiny** (myūt′ nē), or an overthrow of officers. Columbus then promised to turn back if land was not sighted within three days. The night of the second day, a lookout on the *Pinta* spotted land. In the morning, Columbus landed at an outer island in the Bahamas (buh hah′ muhs), probably Watling Island. Because he thought he had reached the Indies, Columbus called the people living on the islands Indians. For this reason, Native Americans are sometimes referred to as Indians.

Columbus spent several months sailing around the Bahamas, Cuba, and Hispaniola (his puhn yō′ luh), an island that today consists of Haiti (hā′ tē) and the Dominican Republic. In Cuba, he found Native Americans smoking cigars. This was the first European contact with tobacco.

On Christmas Eve, the *Santa Maria* ran aground on a reef and was wrecked. Columbus had his crew use the wood from the *Santa Maria* to build a fort. This was the first European settlement in the Americas.

In January 1493, Columbus boarded the *Niña* and headed back to Spain. He took with him gold, parrots, cotton, other plants and animals, and a few Native Americans. In Spain, he was

CHRISTOPHER COLUMBUS Upon his return from the Americas, Columbus was greeted as a hero. In this painting he is being received by King Ferdinand and Queen Isabella. At the bottom of the steps are Native Americans and riches from the Americas. **What did Columbus hope to prove by sailing westward to Asia?**

MULTICULTURAL PERSPECTIVES

Columbus wrote the following impression of the inhabitants of the Bahamas: *The islanders came to the ships' boats, swimming and bringing us parrots and balls of cotton thread...which they exchanged for...glass beads and bawk bells...they took and gave of what they had very willingly, but it seemed to me that they were poor in every way. They bore no weapons, nor were they acquainted with them, because when I showed them swords they seized them by the edge and so cut themselves from ignorance.*

received with great honors. Six months later, he was leading a fleet of 17 ships and 1,500 men on another search for Asia.

Columbus made four voyages in all. He explored the coasts of Venezuela and Central America. He returned from his last voyage in 1504. Two years later, he died still convinced he had found the way to Asia. He never realized he had discovered the Americas.

The Treaty of Tordesillas The Spanish monarchs were worried that Portugal might try to take from Spain the riches Columbus had discovered. So, they asked Pope Alexander VI for help.

In 1493, the Pope drew a **papal line of demarcation** (dē mahr kā' shuhn), or an imaginary line from the North Pole to the South Pole, some 300 miles, or 480 kilometers, west of the Azores Islands. Spain was to have the non-Christian lands west of the line, and Portugal the non-Christian lands east of the line.

The Portuguese, however, did not like the way the lands were divided. They protested and called for a meeting. In 1494, the Treaty of Tordesillas (tord uh sē' yuhs) was drawn up. It moved the line about 500 miles, or 800 kilometers, farther west. Because of this, Portugal was able to claim Brazil.

Other countries, like England, France, and the Netherlands, paid no attention to the Pope's rulings. They explored and claimed land where they wished.

The Conquistadores The Spanish were eager to learn more about their new possessions. Over the next few years, Spanish *conquistadores* (kon kē stuh dōr' ēz), or conquerors, set out to find the gold Columbus had talked about and to explore new lands.

In 1513, Ponce de León (pahn' suh de lē on') sailed north from the island of Puerto Rico (pwer' tō rē' kō) to explore Florida. That same year, Vasco Núñez de Balboa (vas' kō nū' nyāth dā bal bō' uh) crossed the isthmus of Panama and became the first European to see the Great South Sea. Between 1519 and 1521, Hernando Cortés (her nan' dō kōr tes') invaded Mexico. With the help of guns and the spread of smallpox, he destroyed the Native American empire ruled by the Aztec king Montezuma. Cortés and his troops took large amounts of gold from the Native Americans to send back to Spain.

In 1532, Francisco Pizarro (fran sis' kō puh zahr' ō) invaded Peru. Within five years, he conquered the Inca Empire. Like Cortés, Pizarro took great treasures of gold and silver from the Native Americans. Pizarro and his men then headed for the coast, where they built Lima (lē' muh), the "City of Kings."

In 1539, Hernando de Soto (duh sō' tō) sailed from Cuba to Florida and explored westward from there. He found no gold but explored the Mississippi River. In 1540, Francisco Coronado

Painting of Francisco Pizarro

DID YOU KNOW ??

Columbus made four voyages to the Americas, each time bringing back to Europe plants and descriptions he claimed "proved" that the land he had found was part of Asia. An inedible West Indian nut, *nogal de pais,* Columbus insisted must be the coconut that Marco Polo had described in his accounts of Cathay.

INDEPENDENT PRACTICE

L1 **Language Arts** Students may enjoy reading the diary written by Fernando, Columbus's 13-year-old son, in *The High Voyage: The Final Crossing of Christopher Columbus,* by Olga Litowinsky (Delacorte, 1991). Encourage students to share their impressions of the book with the class.

VIDEODISC

Use the following to enrich Chapter 30.

WH I 10 18736
Cortés enters Tenochtitlán.

WC N 7 44062
Vasco Nuñez de Balboa.

SPOTLIGHT ON: CORONADO

Francisco Vasquez de Coronado was a younger son who had not inherited his family estate. He went to the Americas as an aide to the viceroy of New Spain in order to seek his fortune. In 1540 he was sent on an expedition in search of the fabled Cíbola—seven cities of gold. Coronado took along about 250 horsemen, 70 Spanish foot soldiers, about 1,000 Native American allies, and numerous priests, along with baggage animals and sheep, goats, and cattle for food. According to the myth, Cíbola—located somewhere near what is now New Mexico—had rich pastures, cities with jewel-studded temples, and people riding on camels and elephants. Coronado only found barren land and pueblos of Zuni Indians.

CAPTION ANSWER

the Aztec and the Inca

L1 Geography: Movement After tracing Magellan's voyage on the map on page 475, have students locate the Strait of Magellan and notice that it is a narrow waterway that separates the islands of Tierra del Fuego from the mainland of South America.

DID YOU KNOW ??

The search for gold was heightened by stories about the Seven Cities of Cíbola and the Indian ruler called El Dorado, who was said to be so rich that he was covered daily with gold dust.

L2 Culture Explain to students that common ship supplies for voyages to the Americas were: sea biscuits, salted meat, cheese, raisins, beans, honey, water, and wine. Ask students to choose an explorer they would like to travel with and create a supply list for what they would take along if their exploratory voyage were made today. Have them share their lists with the rest of the class.

VIDEODISC

Use the following to enrich Chapter 30.

WC N 18 44073
Juan Ponce de León (1460?-1521).

WC N 17 44072
Magellan battles the inhabitants of Mactan.

PONCE DE LEÓN While governing Puerto Rico, Ponce de León heard stories of an island to the north that held great riches. Setting out to find this island, Ponce de León discovered Florida instead. He is shown in this painting landing on the Florida coast. **From which two Native American civilizations did the Spaniards acquire much gold?**

(kōr uh nahd′ ō) led an army overland from Mexico into the present-day United States. He reached the Grand Canyon but returned without finding any treasure. Thus, between 1492 and 1550, Spain explored an area from North America through Central America and the West Indies to South America.

Ferdinand Magellan In 1517, Portugal controlled the eastern route to the Indies. As a result, Portugal was growing rich. This angered the Spanish king. So, when a Portuguese explorer named Ferdinand Magellan (muh jel′ uhn) offered to find Spain a western route to the Indies, the king accepted the offer. He wanted Spain to become as wealthy as Portugal.

In 1519, Magellan set sail from Spain. He commanded a fleet of five ships and a crew of 256. In October of the following year, he sailed through a stormy strait at the tip of South America. The trip took one month. Today, the strait bears Magellan's name.

From the strait, Magellan sailed on into the Great South Sea. He renamed it the Pacific Ocean from the Spanish word *pacifico,* meaning peaceful. By this time, Magellan had lost two of his ships. He continued on, however. Conditions were terrible. The drinking water was spoiled, and the biscuits were full of worms. The crew was forced to eat rats, sawdust from ship boards, and leather soaked in the sea and grilled on wood coals. By the time the fleet reached the Mariana (mar ē an′ uh) Islands three months

COOPERATIVE LEARNING

Early Spanish and Portuguese explorers encountered many groups in the Americas (the Arawak, Carib, Maya, Aztec, Inca), each culture slightly different from the others. Divide the class into small groups and have each group research and report on one of these Native American groups. Each student should be assigned one of the following areas to research: geographic location and method of subsistence, art and decorations, religious beliefs, customs, and effect of European contact on the inhabitants.

Assign the Chapter 30 **Cooperative Learning Activity** in the TCR.

Reviewing Map Legends

Legends, as explained in the map skill on page 75, are used to identify information shown on maps. Legends provide the key to the meaning of an unlimited number of symbols and colors that can be used on maps.

Sometimes, however, one legend may be used in several ways. For example, on the "European Voyages of Discovery" map below, five colors are used in the legend. On this particular map, these colors are used to show two different things. First, they point out the five European countries that took part in the voyages of discovery. Second, the colors show the different routes taken by explorers from these countries.

For example, Portugal is shown in yellow. The routes that the Portuguese explorers took are also shown in yellow.

Map Practice

1. **What two countries had explorers sail around the world?**
2. **What country did not send any explorers south of 25°N latitude?**

European Voyages of Discovery

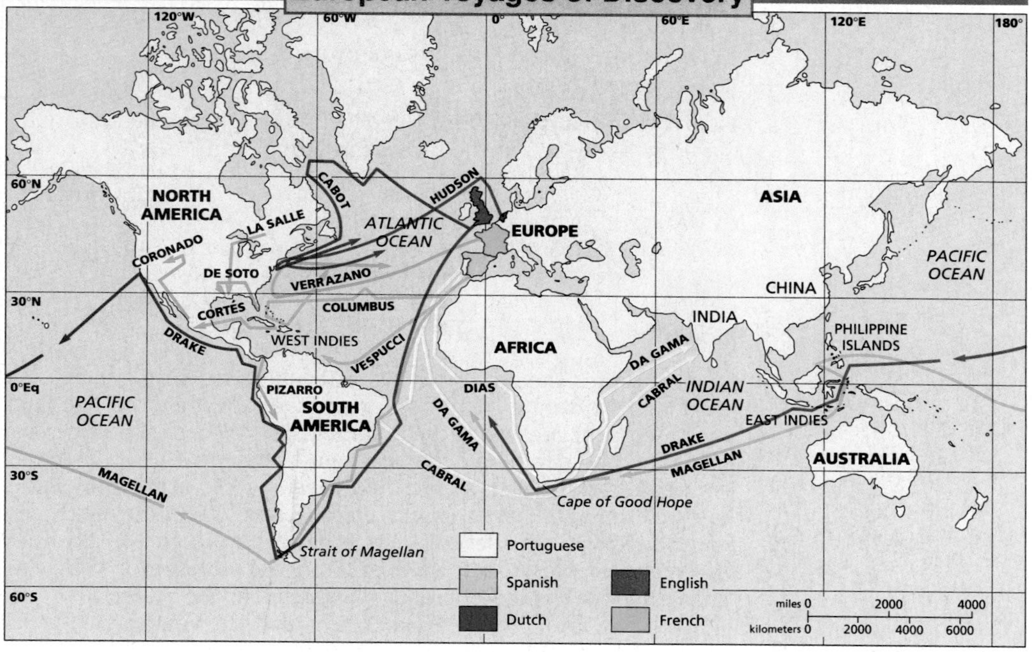

Teaching

MAP SKILLS

Reviewing Map Legends

Have the students read the instructional part of the feature and answer the following questions: What are used to identify information shown on maps? *(legends)* In what two ways are colors used on the map on this page? *(to point out the five European countries that took part in the voyages of discovery and to show the routes taken by explorers from these countries)* Next, direct the students to study the map to answer the following questions: What countries explored the coastline of South America? *(Portugal, Spain, England)* What countries explored North America? *(Spain, England, France, the Netherlands)* What countries explored the Philippine Islands and the East Indies? *(England, Spain)*

Assign the Chapter 30 **Geography and Map Activity** in the TCR.

ANSWERS to Map Practice

1. Spain and England
2. France

SPOTLIGHT ON: WORLD VOYAGES

After Spanish soldiers and explorers followed Columbus to the Americas, they returned to Europe with fantastic stories of the Seven Cities of Gold. One Spaniard, Estevanico, a black sailor shipwrecked in the Gulf of Mexico, spent many years wandering the deserts of southwest North America in search of these cities. He eventually died, unsuccessful in his quest, and the rumors of the existence of these golden cities persisted.

L3 **Language Arts** Have students select an explorer that is discussed in this chapter and write five entries in a ship's log that describes the discoveries of these explorers and the difficulties of the journeys.

L2 **Charts** Have students create charts of the following explorers who searched for the northwest passage to the Far East: John Cabot, Giovanni da Verrazano, Jacques Cartier, Martin Frobisher, and Henry Hudson. The charts should include the explorers' names, countries of origin, countries for which he explored, the date/dates of his explorations, the area explored/land claims made, and interesting facts about his explorations.

GEOGRAPHY AND HISTORY

The English also made several attempts to reach the Far East by sailing northeast. Two of their ships reached Lapland, while a third got as far as the White Sea before being stopped by ice. Its crew then traveled to Moscow by horse-drawn sleds and started a trade with the Russians for furs and tallow.

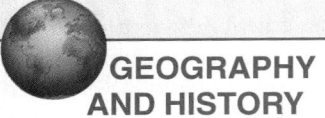

Painting of Ferdinand Magellan

later, it was almost helpless. The crew was suffering from scurvy and had no food of any kind.

After they had eaten and rested, Magellan and his crew set a southwest course for the Philippine (fil uh pēn') Islands. There, Magellan became involved in a local war and was killed. Shortly after, more crew members were killed, and two more ships were lost. The one remaining ship continued on into the Indian Ocean and around Africa. It finally arrived in Seville (suh vil'), Spain, in 1522 with 18 men and a load of spices.

The voyage was a great accomplishment. By *circumnavigating*, or sailing completely around the world, it proved that Earth is indeed round. The voyage opened the Pacific Ocean to European ships. It also proved that Columbus did not land in Asia but in the Americas.

Section 2 Review

1. **Identify:** Christopher Columbus, Treaty of Tordesillas, Ponce de León, Vasco Núñez de Balboa, Hernando Cortés, Francisco Pizarro, Hernando de Soto, Francisco Coronado, Ferdinand Magellan
2. **Define:** mutiny, papal line of demarcation, *conquistadores*
3. What were some discoveries made by the Spanish between 1513 and 1540?
4. What did Magellan's voyage prove?

Critical Thinking

5. Which Spanish exploration do you think advanced knowledge of the world the most? Explain.

Section 3 NORTHWEST PASSAGE

Even after the Americas were reached, the English, French, and Dutch continued to look for another route to the Far East. Since the Portuguese and the Spanish controlled the southern sea lanes, the others looked for a northwest passage.

English merchants persuaded their king to send John Cabot (kab' uht), an Italian navigator, to the Far East by a northwest route. In 1497, Cabot set sail with a handful of men. He explored the coasts of Newfoundland and Nova Scotia (nō' vuh skō' shuh) and established claims for England in the Americas.

In 1523, the French hired Giovanni da Verrazano (jē uh vahn' ē dah ver rah tsah' nō), another Italian navigator, to find a

SECTION 2 ANSWERS

1. Christopher Columbus, navigator who sailed for Spain (p. 471); Treaty of Tordesillas, divided non-Christian lands between Spain and Portugal (p. 473); Ponce de León, Spanish explorer (p. 473); Vasco Núñez de Balboa, Spanish explorer (p. 473); Hernando Cortés, Spanish explorer (p. 473); Francisco Pizarro, Spanish explorer (p. 473); Hernando de Soto, explored Mississippi River (p. 473); Francisco Coronado, explored Grand Canyon (p. 473); Ferdinand Magellan, sailed around the world (p. 474)
2. mutiny, an overthrow of officers (p. 472); papal line of demarcation, an imaginary line of separation (p. 473); *conquistadores*, conquerors (p. 473)
3. Florida, Mexico, Peru, Mississippi River, Grand Canyon, and Pacific Ocean
4. that the earth is round
5. Answers will vary.

Assign the Chapter 30 **Section 2 Quiz** in the TCR. Testmaker available.

northwest passage. He sailed along the Atlantic coast from North Carolina to New York. Eleven years later, Jacques Cartier (zhahk kahr tyā'), a French navigator, sailed up the St. Lawrence River as far as present-day Montreal (mahn trē ahl'). This gave the French a claim to eastern Canada.

In 1576, Sir Martin Frobisher (frō' bi shuhr), an English **sea dog,** or sea captain, sailed the coast of Greenland and fought a storm that almost wrecked one of his three ships. Frobisher finally discovered the bay that today bears his name.

In 1609, the Dutch sent Henry Hudson an English navigator to locate the passage. He explored the Hudson River and sailed to what is today Albany, New York. In 1610 he set out on a second voyage. He became lost in a storm and was never seen again. Nevertheless, his first voyage gave the Dutch their claim in the Americas.

EXPLORERS

Name	Country	Achievements
Amerigo Vespucci	*Spain Portugal*	explored Atlantic coast of South America, 1497–1504; one of first to believe he had reached a new world
Pedro Alváres Cabral	*Portugal*	discovered Brazil and sailed east to India, 1500–1501
Vasco Núñez de Balboa	*Spain*	first European to sight eastern shore of Pacific Ocean, 1513
Alvar Núñez Cabeza de Vaca	*Spain*	explored Florida and Gulf region from Texas to Mexico, 1528–36
Juan Rodríguez Cabrillo	*Spain*	explored Pacific coast to Drake's Bay near San Francisco, 1542
Richard Chancellor	*England*	reached Moscow in search of northeast passage to Asia; opened trade with Russia, 1553–54
John Davis	*England*	explored west coast of Greenland in search of northwest passage to Asia, 1585
Sir Francis Drake	*England*	first Englishman to sail around the world, 1577–80
Father Jacques Marquette Louis Jolliet	*France*	explored Mississippi Valley to mouth of Arkansas River, 1673
Vitus Bering	*Russia*	explored coasts of Alaska and northeast Asia; discovered Bering Strait and Bering Sea, 1728, 1741

LINKING PAST TO PRESENT

Vasco Núñez de Balboa led an expedition of soldiers and guides across the Isthmus of Panama in 1513 to search for a region rumored to be "flowing with golde," and to find "another sea, where they sayle with shippes as bigge as yours." Balboa's company fought rain forest undergrowth, poisonous snakes, and angry inhabitants for about 25 days as they crossed the isthmus. Today, people travel by ship through the Panama Canal completed in 1914.

DID YOU KNOW ??

It was not until 1906 that the northwest passage was successfully navigated by Roald Amundsen, a Norwegian explorer. His voyage took three years, part of which was spent at a standstill because of ice.

ASSESS

CHECK FOR UNDERSTANDING

Ask students to summarize the main points of the chapter, orally or in writing. Discuss the answers to the Section and Chapter Review questions.

EXTENDING THE CONTENT

In 1522, French pirates captured a Spanish treasure ship filled with gold, silver, and jade mosaics sent home from Mexico by Cortés. Amazed and covetous, King Francis I decided to send his own expedition to bring home wealth from the Americas. Francis chose the Italian navigator Giovanni da Verrazano to head the expedition in 1524. It was paid for by silk merchants of France who also had an interest in finding a route to China. Verrazano worked his way gradually up the coast from North Carolina to Nova Scotia. His ships sailed in and around Chesapeake Bay, the Hudson River, Cape Cod, and the Maine coast.

EVALUATE

Assign the Chapter 30 **Performance Assessment Activity** in the TCR.

Administer the **Chapter 30 Test** in the TCR. Testmaker available.

RETEACH

Organize students into two groups. Have each group develop statements about each significant person, event, or item discussed in this chapter. Have each group challenge the other group to identify the person, event, or item from the statements.

Assign the Chapter 30 **Reteaching Activity** in the TCR.

ENRICH

Have students research the expeditions of Amerigo Vespucci or Vasco Núñez de Balboa. Then have them prepare a script about the explorer's expedition.

Assign the Chapter 30 **Enrichment Activity** in the TCR.

CLOSE

Ask students to discuss the discoveries made by the explorers discussed in this chapter. Ask them to rank the discoveries in the order of importance. Then ask students to explain their rankings.

MEETING CHAPTER OBJECTIVES

Each chapter objective is tested by the Chapter Review questions that follow it in parentheses.

1. Explain why Europeans searched for a direct sea route to the Far East. (CU 1; CT 1)

2. Identify Portuguese discoveries. (BV)

3. Describe discoveries by Spanish explorers financed by Spain. (BV; CT 2, 3)

4. Discuss the search for a northwest passage. (CU 8; CT 3, 4)

All of these voyages failed in their search to find a northwest passage to the Far East. They did, however, establish claims in the Americas for England, France, and the Netherlands.

Section 3 Review

1. **Identify:** John Cabot, Giovanni da Verrazano, Jacques Cartier, Sir Martin Frobisher, Henry Hudson
2. **Define:** sea dog
3. How did English, French, and Dutch explorers plan to reach the Far East?
4. What lands in the Americas were claimed by England? By France? By the Netherlands?

Critical Thinking

5. What characteristics or kinds of personalities do you think the English, French, and Dutch explorers had to have to achieve what they did?

Chapter Summary

1. By the 1300s, Europeans began to search for a direct sea route to India and the Far East.
2. Europeans were interested in obtaining spices and precious metals and in spreading Christianity to other parts of the world.
3. The development of better maps, ships, and instruments for navigation helped Europeans in their search.
4. In the early 1400s, Prince Henry of Portugal started the first school in Europe for navigators.
5. By 1473, Portuguese ships had crossed the Equator.
6. In 1487, Bartolomeu Dias sailed around the Cape of Good Hope.
7. Between 1497 and 1499, Vasco da Gama sailed from Portugal around Africa to India and back again.
8. Between 1492 and 1504, Christopher Columbus made four voyages to what he thought was Asia but was really the Americas.
9. In 1494, the Treaty of Tordesillas divided new non-Christian lands between Spain and Portugal.
10. In the first half of the 1500s, Hernando Cortés and Francisco Pizarro conquered the Aztec and Inca empires and explored much of the Americas for Spain.
11. Between 1519 and 1522, Ferdinand Magellan's expedition sailed around the world, proving that Columbus did not land in Asia but in the Americas.
12. Between 1497 and 1609, the English, French, and Dutch sent explorers to the Americas to search for a northwest passage to the Far East.

SECTION 3 ANSWERS

1. John Cabot, English explorer who reached Newfoundland (p. 476); Giovanni da Verrazano, navigator who sailed for England to the Americas (p. 476); Jacques Cartier, French navigator who sailed up the St. Lawrence River (p. 477); Sir Martin Frobisher, English navigator who searched for a northwest passage (p. 477); Henry Hudson, explored Hudson River for the Dutch (p. 477)

2. sea dog, sea captain (p. 477)

3. by a northwest passage

4. Newfoundland, Nova Scotia; lands along the St. Lawrence River; lands along the Hudson River

5. Answers will vary but might include that these explorers were brave, adventurous, greedy, or liked traveling.

Assign the Chapter 30 **Section 3 Quiz** in the TCR. Testmaker available.

CHAPTER

Review 30

Building Vocabulary

Imagine you are writing a newspaper column titled Great Explorer Achievements. Use each of the following words in a description of what you think some of these achievements were.

compass	papal line of demarcation
astrolabe	*conquistadores*
caravel	sea dog
mutiny	

Check for Understanding

1. Why did Europeans begin to search for a direct sea route to India and countries of the Far East?
2. What three things helped European explorers in their search for new sea routes to India and the Far East?
3. What were some of the problems that European explorers faced on their voyages of discovery?
4. Why did Columbus's crew threaten mutiny?
5. What was the first European settlement in the Americas?
6. How long did it take Magellan's ship to sail around the world?
7. What are three bodies of water named after European explorers?
8. What did the European voyages in search of a northwest passage to the Far East accomplish?

Critical Thinking

1. Why do you think Queen Isabella of Spain agreed to support Columbus after others had turned him down?
2. What would you have liked about being one of the sailors on Magellan's voyage around the world? What would you have disliked?
3. How do you think Native Americans felt about the *conquistadores?*
4. How did competition between nations affect European voyages of discovery?

Geography in History

MOVEMENT The lengths of voyages made by explorers were very different. Whose voyage from Portugal to India was longer in miles (or kilometers)—da Gama's or Cabralis's? How many miles (or kilometers) longer was it?

Using Your Journal

Review the details you have noted about the changes that took place in western Europe between 1300 and 1600. Imagine you are a peasant living in London, England, in 1550. Write a diary entry describing what you have learned about the world in recent years.

CHAPTER 30 REVIEW ANSWERS

BUILDING VOCABULARY

Columns will vary, but students should include some achievements and use all the vocabulary words.

CHECK FOR UNDERSTANDING

1. to obtain spices, precious metals, and to spread Christianity
2. more accurate maps, better ships, and improved navigational instruments
3. storms, scurvy, spoiled food and water, and starvation
4. They were afraid and Columbus refused to turn back.
5. a fort built with wood from the Santa Maria
6. three years
7. Strait of Magellan, Frobisher Bay, and Hudson River
8. claims in the Americas for the countries of England, France, and the Netherlands

CRITICAL THINKING

1. Answers will vary but might include that she thought finding a new route to Asia would make Spain richer.
2. Answers will vary but students should provide specific examples.
3. Answers will vary but might include fear, dread, and sadness.
4. Each nation wanted to extend its trade and power, and to be richer than other nations. They thought they could do this by finding a new route to the Far East. The search led to the discovery of the Americas.

GEOGRAPHY IN HISTORY

da Gama's; about 2,900 miles (or 4,666 km) longer

+ BONUS +

TEST QUESTION

For Chapter 30 Test

How did discoveries by non-Europeans help Europeans begin their voyages of exploration? Make a cause-and-effect chart showing these relationships. Add a summary statement to explain your chart. *(Charts will vary.)*

USING YOUR JOURNAL

Diary entries will vary but should include major events that affected England. You might ask volunteers to read their entries to the class.

UNIT 9 CULTURE CLOSE-UP

THE KHMERS

FOCUS

OBJECTIVES

Locate where the Khmers lived. Identify the time period during which the Khmers lived. Describe the culture of the Khmers.

BELLRINGER

Ask students to list what they know about the early history of the following countries in Southeast Asia—Cambodia, South Vietnam, Thailand, and Laos.

MOTIVATIONAL ACTIVITY

Ask students to read their responses to what they know about Cambodia, South Vietnam, Thailand, and Laos. Tell students that many countries in Southeast Asia adopted cultural elements from China and India. Point out the location of these Southeast Asian countries in relation to China and India. Then explain to the students that in this Culture Close-Up they will learn about a powerful people in Southeast Asia, the Khmers.

UNIT 9

CULTURE CLOSE-UP

The Khmers

The Khmers (kuh muhrs') were a powerful people in Southeast Asia from 800 A.D. until about 1450 A.D. They founded a kingdom called Angkor (ang' kor).

Geography Connection

At the height of its power, the Khmer kingdom included the lands of present-day Thailand, Cambodia, South Vietnam, and parts of Laos.

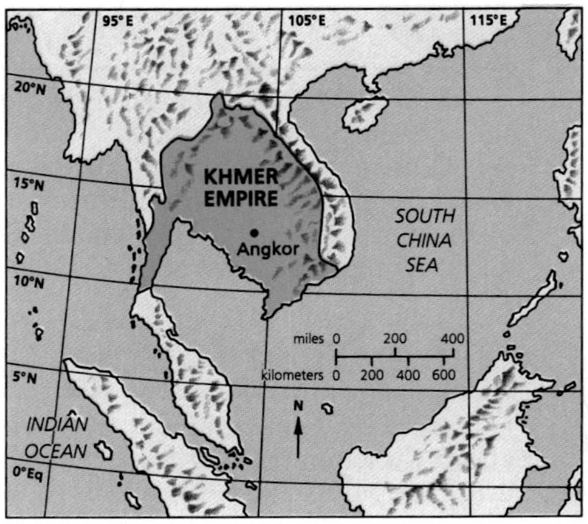

▲ The wealth of the Khmers, shown in their art, came mostly from rice production. ▼

480

SPOTLIGHT ON: KHMER WOMEN

Women were the merchants in Angkor. Every day they displayed their goods on mats from six in the morning until noon. The goods ranged from fish, clothing, and silverwork to live animals and rice wine. In addition to being merchants, Khmer women served as judges, doctors, and astronomers.

The lower classes of Khmer society were taxed to support the rulers. The highest ruler's class was followed by magistrates, teachers and priests, landowners, and then peasants and enslaved people. ▶

▲ The Khmer built great cities of temples, palaces, and waterways. Using Indian architecture as a base, they created their own distinctive architectural style.

Khmer temples were built to glorify their kings, Hindu gods, and later, Buddha. ▶

TEACH

L1 **Geography: Region** Ask students to compare a physical/political map of Southeast Asia with the map of the Khmer Empire on page 480. Ask: What major river was part of the Khmer Empire? *(Mekong River)* What physical feature made up the northeastern boundary of the Khmer Empire? *(Aninmite Mountains)* What present-day countries were part of the Khmer Empire? *(Thailand, Cambodia, South Vietnam, and parts of Laos)* LEP

DID YOU KNOW ??

The first ruler of Angkor, Jayavarman II, encouraged the belief that leaders were god-kings. As a result, each Khmer ruler had a huge temple built in which his spirit could live after death.

VIDEODISC

Use the following to enrich Unit 9.

WH X 71 42304

Cambodian sculpture, Shiva's consort.

MEETING SPECIAL NEEDS

Have students who are tactile/kinesthetic learners research the architecture of the Khmer Empire and make models of the architecture. Have them explain the architectural style of the Khmers to the class as they show their models.

UNIT 9 CULTURE CLOSE-UP

L2 **Architecture** Have students research and report on Angkor Wat, giving details about construction and wall decorations. Display pictures of the temple complex that students find.

GLOBAL READING FOR STUDENTS

Historians in your class may be interested in reading a book about the history of Cambodia. Suggest *A History of Cambodia* by David P. Chandler, Westview, 1983. (Challenging/History)

VIDEODISC

Use the following to enrich Unit 9.

WH X 72 42305

Angkor Wat, Cambodia.

◀ The most famous Khmer temple, Angkor Wat, was built in the 1100s. It was a three-level complex, surrounded by a moat, that covered 1 square mile.

Huge statues guarded the temple. ▶

◀ Sculptures found at Angkor Wat show elaborate clothing, jewelry, and rich furnishings were common for wealthy Khmer. The poorest classes lived in small villages.

482

EXTENDING THE CONTENT

The moat at Angkor Wat was supposed to represent the ocean which the Khmers believed lay around Earth. Angkor Wat was built of huge grey stone blocks, which the Khmers brought from a quarry more than 50 miles (or 80 km) away. Every block was carved. Some showed Hindu gods and smiling Buddhas. Others portrayed Khmer kings and soldiers. Still others showed scenes of everyday life, such as men fishing and women selling goods.

CULTURE CLOSE-UP

UNIT 9

◀ Caravans passed through Angkor Thom the Khmer capital. There the Khmer constructed roads, reservoirs, irrigation canals, and hospitals.

The Khmer civilization began to decline because of a series of weak kings. The people were finally defeated by the Thai (tī) people in the middle 1400s. ▼

Taking Another Look

1. **Which modern countries are part of the former Khmer kingdom?**
2. **On what did the Khmer base their architecture style?**
3. **What religious beliefs were observed by the Khmer people?**

Critical Thinking

4. **How do you think a Khmer king would respond to a suggestion that the Khmers be allowed to elect their leaders? Explain.**

483

ASSESS

CHECK FOR UNDERSTANDING

Have students answer the questions in Taking Another Look on page 483.

ANSWERS to Taking Another Look

1. Thailand, Cambodia, South Vietnam, and parts of Laos
2. Indian architecture
3. Khmer temples were built to glorify their kings, Hindu gods, and later Buddha.
4. Answers will vary. Students may note that the Khmer kings would lose their power if they allowed the Khmers to elect their leaders.

ENRICH

Have students discuss whether or not they think it was inevitable for the Khmers to eventually be overthrown by another group of people. Opinions should be supported by definite reasons.

CLOSE

Ask students to review their responses to what they knew about the early history of Cambodia, South Vietnam, Thailand, and Laos. Have them correct misinformation and add new facts they have learned to their lists.

MULTICULTURAL PERSPECTIVES

The Khmer royal court was located in the capital city of Angkor Thom. People wishing to see the king would sit in front of a closed curtain with their heads bowed to the floor. At the sound of conch horns the curtain would rise and the king could be seen through a gold-framed window. If he wanted to show special favor to someone, the king would invite that person to sit on a lion's skin next to the king's throne.

INTRODUCE

UNIT 10 OVERVIEW

Unit 10 discusses the changes that took place in the world from the time the Europeans discovered the Americas to the 1800s.

- **Chapter 31** describes the colonizing efforts of Portugal, Spain, England, the Netherlands, and France from the early 1500s to 1763.
- **Chapter 32** outlines the revolutions in England, the American colonies, and France during the 1600s and the 1700s.
- **Chapter 33** summarizes the Industrial Revolution of the 1700s and 1800s, highlighting key developments in textiles, agriculture, mining, and transportation.

UNIT OBJECTIVES

After reading Unit 10, students will be able to:

1. describe how the Americas changed during the 1500s and 1600s.

2. discuss what changes in government took place in the West during the 1600s and 1700s.

3. analyze economic changes that took place in the West during the 1700s and early 1800s.

UNIT PROJECT

Tell students to create an advertising campaign that does one of the following: encourages Europeans in the 1500s to help colonize the Americas; supports a political uprising against a monarchy in the 1700s; promotes the latest inventions and their uses and benefits. Encourage students to use whatever advertising media are available today. Have them share their campaigns with the rest of the class.

UNIT 10 The Changing World

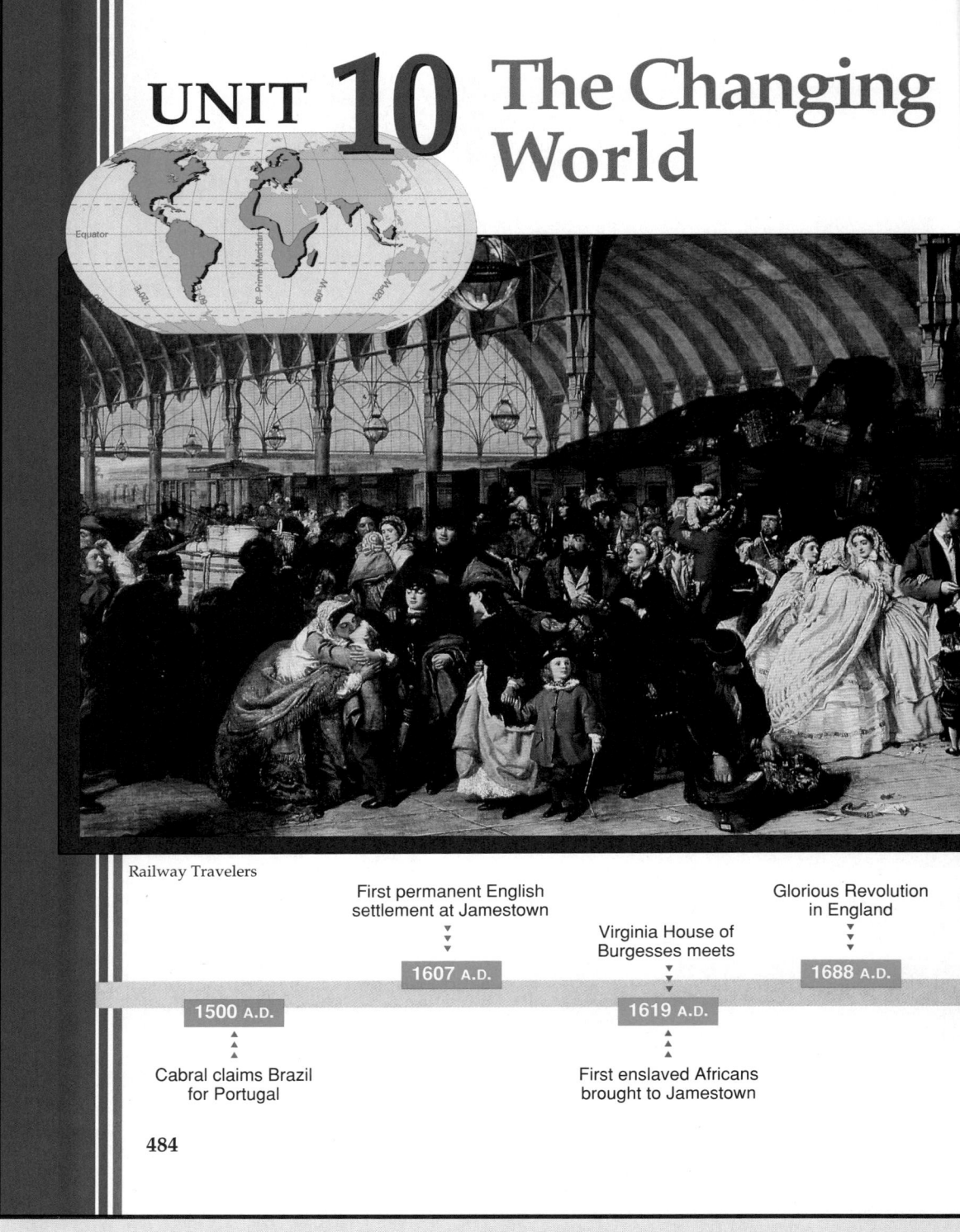

Railway Travelers

- **1500 A.D.** — Cabral claims Brazil for Portugal
- **1607 A.D.** — First permanent English settlement at Jamestown
- **1619 A.D.** — Virginia House of Burgesses meets; First enslaved Africans brought to Jamestown
- **1688 A.D.** — Glorious Revolution in England

484

ABOUT THE UNIT OPENING

EXAMINING THE ARTIFACT

Ask students what mode of travel is depicted in this painting. Have them compare it to the form of transportation they last used for a trip. Tell them they will learn how trains and ships were opening up the world as they read this chapter.

GLOBAL CHRONOLOGY

Ask students to explain what time period the time line covers. *(1500 to 1800)* What entries indicate new ideas about government were taking place? *(Virginia House of Burgesses meets, Glorious Revolution in England, Declaration of Independence, First French Republic)*

Many changes took place after the Europeans arrived in the Americas. Several western European nations established empires there. People in England, America, and France obtained greater political rights from their governments. The West shifted from a farming society using animal and human power to an industrial society using machine power.

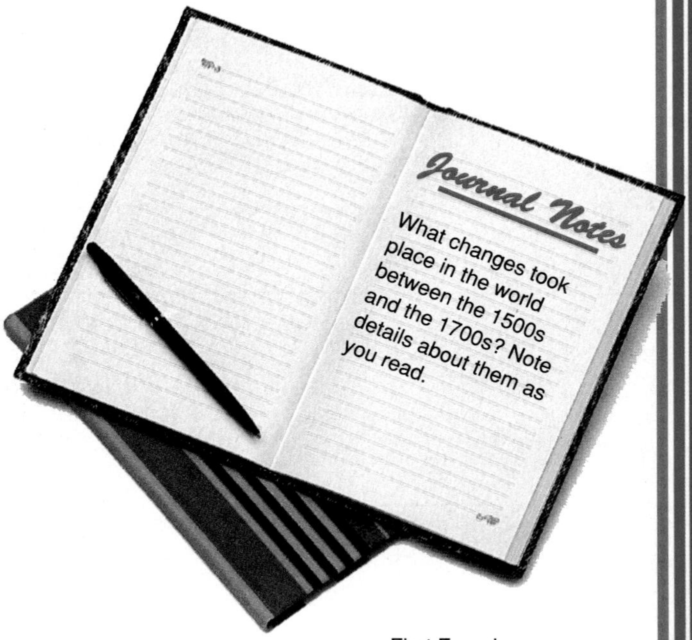

Journal Notes
What changes took place in the world between the 1500s and the 1700s? Note details about them as you read.

1763 A.D. — Treaty of Paris

1769 A.D. — James Watt perfects steam engine

1776 A.D. — U.S. Declaration of Independence

1798 A.D. — First French Republic

INTRODUCING THE UNIT

Ask students what would happen if explorers today suddenly discovered a nearby planet inhabited by intelligent life much like ourselves—a new civilization. Discuss how our civilization might react. What plans might big businesses begin to make? How would contact with this new civilization eventually change our world and our individual lives? Tell students that they will learn how people in Europe during the 1400s-1700s faced the same unanswered questions about newly reached lands.

RECORDING JOURNAL NOTES

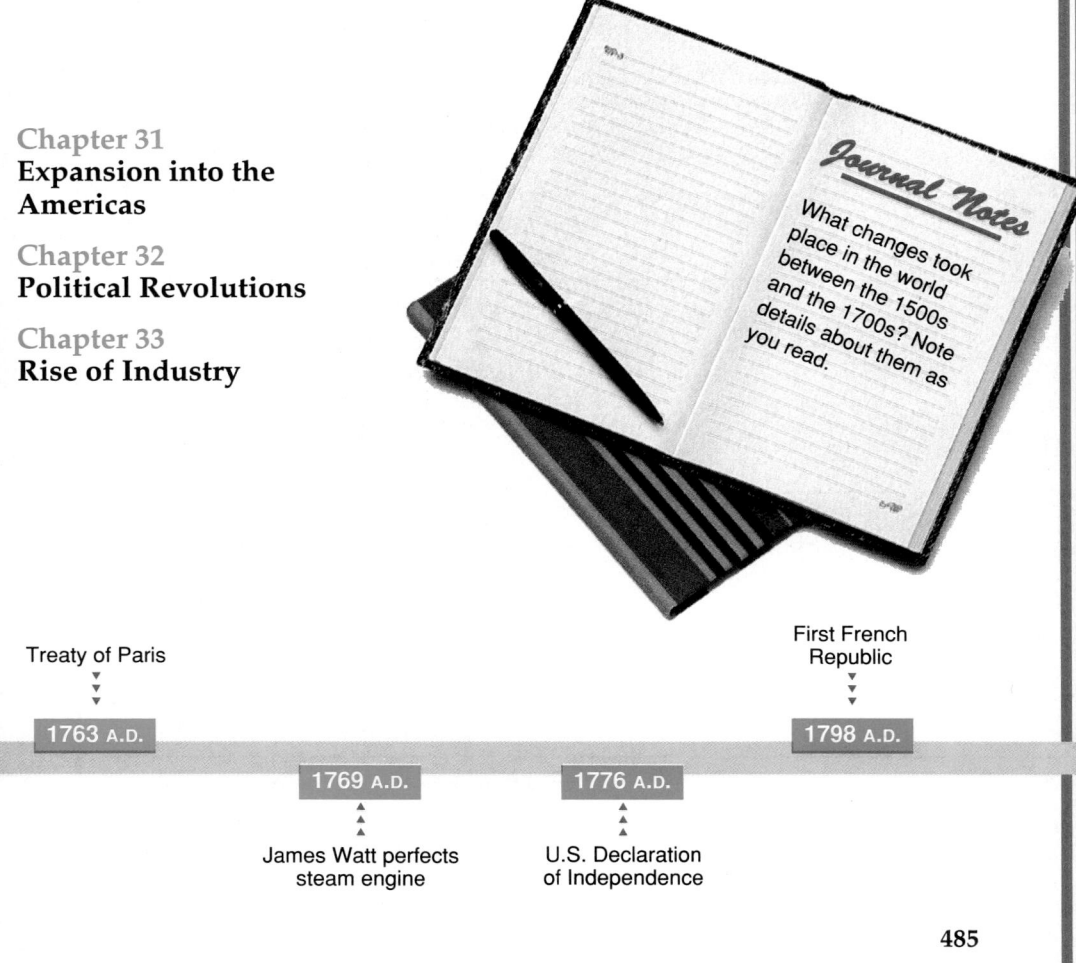

Help students begin writing in their journals by asking them to name time-line entries and information described in the unit introduction that indicate the kinds of changes that took place in the world between the 1500s and the 1700s. Record their responses on the chalkboard. Tell students that these are the kinds of changes they want to detail in their journals as they read Unit 10.

GEOGRAPHIC LOCATION

Using their text Atlas, have students locate the countries of western Europe and North and South America, the islands of the Caribbean, Africa, the Philippines, and the East Indies. Have students calculate the approximate distances from the countries in western Europe to the other continents or islands listed above. Discuss the length of time that it might have taken colonists to get to these foreign lands in the 1500s-1700s.

PLANNING GUIDE

CHAPTER 31
Expansion Into the Americas

CHAPTER ORGANIZER

Objectives	Special Features	Supplemental Materials
Section 1 Portugal Summarize the development and decline of Portugal's empire in the Americas.		• Reproducible Lesson Plan • Section 1 Quiz • Testmaker • Chapter 31 Vocabulary and Guided Reading Activity • Chapter 31 Cooperative Learning Activity
Section 2 Spain Discuss the establishment of Spain's colonial empire in the Americas and its decline.		• Reproducible Lesson Plan • Section 2 Quiz • Testmaker • Unit 10 Primary Source Reading • Reinforcing Social Studies Skills, pp. 13, 22 • The World History Videodisc
Section 3 England Describe the colonies established by the English in the Americas.		• Reproducible Lesson Plan • Section 3 Quiz • Testmaker • Chapter 31 Teaching Transparencies and Activities
Section 4 The Netherlands Discuss how the Dutch established colonies in the Americas.		• Reproducible Lesson Plan • Section 4 Quiz • Testmaker • Unit 10 World Literature
Section 5 France Explain how and where the French established settlements in the Americas.		• Reproducible Lesson Plan • Section 5 Quiz • Testmaker • Chapter 31 Geography and Map Activity
Section 6 The Influence of Empires Describe how empires in the Americas influenced Europe.		• Reproducible Lesson Plan • Section 6 Quiz • Testmaker • Chapter 31 Chart and Graph Skill • Foods Around the World
Chapter 31 Review and Evaluation		• Chapter 31 Reteaching Activity • Chapter 31 Enrichment Activity • Spanish Summary and Glossary • Audiocassettes (English and Spanish) • Chapter 31 Performance Assessment Activity • Chapter 31 Test • Testmaker

If time does not permit teaching the entire chapter, use the Chapter 31 Summary on page 500 and the Chapter 31 Audiocassettes (English and Spanish) to point out the main ideas of the chapter.

✓ Performance Assessment Activities

Mapmaking Have students research in historical atlases and create two maps of European claims in the Americas. One map should show the claims in 1650, the other map should show the claims in 1753. Then have students write five questions about the two maps. Have students exchange and answer questions.

Graphic Learning Have students make a collage of important elements from this chapter using materials of their choice. For example, students might make drawings of discoveries or innovations discussed in the chapter, encounters Europeans had with Native Americans, the settlement at Jamestown, and so on. Have students write a summary statement of what their collages shows.

CHAPTER RESOURCES

LITERATURE ABOUT THE PERIOD

Speare, Elizabeth George. *The Witch of Blackbird Pond.* Houghton Mifflin, 1958. Novel about heroine among the strict Puritans of colonial Connecticut.

READINGS FOR THE STUDENT

Davis, James E. and Sharryl Davis Hawke. *Seeds of Change: The Story of Cultural Exchange After 1492.* Addison-Wesley, 1992. An account of the exchanges made between Europe and the Americas and their effects on each region.

Foster, Genevieve. *The World of Captain John Smith (1580-1631).* Charles Scribner's Sons, 1959. A history of the American colonies and events worldwide.

Hooks, William H. *The Legend of White Doe.* Macmillan, 1988. A tale about Virginia Dare, the first child of English settlers born in the Americas.

Schouweiler, Tom. *The Lost Colony of Roanoke: Great Mysteries.* Greenhaven Press, 1991. Story of the establishment of the English settlement at Roanoke and its disappearance.

READINGS FOR THE TEACHER

Bailyn, Bernard. *Voyagers to the West: A Passage in the Peopling of America on the Eve of Revolution.* Alfred Knopf, 1986. Examines British motives for settling in America.

Díaz del Castillo, Bernal. *The Discovery and Conquest of Mexico 1517-1521.* Farrar, Straus, and Cudahy, 1956. A first-person account of the conquest and exploration of Mexico by a foot soldier who served in the army of Cortés.

Greene, Lorenzo. *The Negro in Colonial New England.* Broadside, 1975. Accounts of early life in the Americas.

Scott, John Anthony. *Settlers on the Eastern Shore: The British Colonies in North America 1607-1750.* Facts on File, 1991. Eyewitness accounts and primary sources describe the first years of British settlement in the Americas.

Wright, Esmond, general ed. *The Expanding World.* Chartwell Books Inc., 1979. Surveys the history of Europe from the 1500s to the 1700s, focusing on the birth of the modern age through European exploration and discovery.

MULTIMEDIA RESOURCES

America's Beginnings: Indians and Explorers. Encyclopedia Britannica. Video. History of early people in the Americas.

Colonial America. Video. United Learning, 1989. Informative look at life in colonial America.

Geography Search. McGraw-Hill. Software. Simulates "explorer teams" searching for the Americas while teaching navigation and record-keeping skills.

Where America Began: Colonial Williamsburg, Jamestown, Yorktown. Finley-Holiday. Video. Explains the history and culture of each colony.

INTRODUCE

CHAPTER 31 OVERVIEW

Chapter 31 outlines the expansions of Portugal, Spain, England, the Netherlands, and France to the Americas.

- **Section 1** discusses Portugal's empire in the Americas.
- **Section 2** describes the Spanish empire in the Americas, and the role the Church played in it.
- **Section 3** summarizes why, how, and where the English settled in the Americas.
- **Section 4** examines the Dutch colonies in the Americas.
- **Section 5** describes the French settlements in the Americas.
- **Section 6** discusses the effects of American colonies on European empires.

CHAPTER OBJECTIVES

After reading Chapter 31, students will be able to:

1. summarize why Europeans colonized the Americas.
2. discuss what European empires were established in the Americas.
3. explain why many colonial empires declined.
4. describe how the empires in the Americas influenced Europe.

EXAMINING THE ILLUSTRATION

Ask students what ship is depicted in this painting. What season is it? What do students already know about this ship? Explain that they will learn more about colonists coming to the Americas as they read.

PERFORMANCE ASSESSMENT

Use the Performance Assessment activities on page 486B to help you evaluate students as they complete the chapter.

CHAPTER 31 Expansion Into The Americas

The *Mayflower* in Plymouth Harbor

486

TEACHER CLASSROOM RESOURCES

- Reproducible Lesson Plan
- Section Quizzes/Chapter Test
- Foods Around the World
- Enrichment Activity
- Geography and Map Activity
- Reinforcing Social Studies Skills
- Cooperative Learning Activity
- Performance Assessment Activity
- Spanish Summary and Glossary
- Unit 10 Primary Source Reading
- Unit 10 World Literature
- Testmaker
- Audiocassettes (English and Spanish)
- The World History Videodisc
- Teaching Transparencies and Activities

Chapter Focus

READ TO DISCOVER:

- Why Europeans colonized the Americas.
- What European empires were established in the Americas.
- Why many colonial empires declined.
- How empires in the Americas influenced Europe.

From the early 1500s to the 1700s, several western European countries set out to **colonize,** or build permanent settlements in, the Americas. It was a time when the known world was expanding and exploration of it was unbounded. Europeans wanted the riches of the Americas, which they thought would bring them power. They also wanted to spread Christianity.

1500 A.D.–1700 A.D.

KEY TERMS

colonize
captaincies
viceroy
peninsulares
mestizos
balance of trade
indentured servants
burgesses

Section 1

PORTUGAL

By 1512, the Portuguese had claimed all of Brazil. They had also established trading posts in Africa, India, Southeast Asia, and the Moluccas (muh luhk' uhz), or Spice Islands. They took most of the Asian coastal cities by force. First, Portuguese warships bombarded the coast. Then soldiers went ashore.

Portugal found it difficult to rule its new territories. One reason was that it did not have a large enough population to send settlers to all its territories. Also, most of Portugal's territories already had large populations. Then, too, the hot, wet climate of the trading posts was too uncomfortable for most Portuguese. As a result, Portugal had to depend on sea power and the cooperation of defeated leaders to protect its interests.

Brazil In 1500, the Portuguese explorer Pedro Alváres Cabral (pā' drō al vuh rez' kuh brahl') claimed Brazil for Portugal. Since no precious metals were found, Portugal paid little attention to the discovery. Then, other countries started to take *brazilwood,* or a red wood used to make dyes. When the Portuguese realized the value of the wood, they became more interested in Brazil.

FOCUS

BELLRINGER

Write the following quotation on the chalkboard: *Of gold is treasure made, and with it he who has it does as he wills in the world and it even sends souls to Paradise.* Tell students that these are the words of Christopher Columbus, and have them interpret the quote.

MOTIVATIONAL ACTIVITY

Have students share their interpretations of Columbus's quote. Ask them what they think the quote had to do with the establishment of empires in the Americas. Tell the students that the desire for wealth, as well as the desire to spread Christianity, inspired European overseas empires.

VOCABULARY PRE-CHECK

Write the key terms for this chapter on the chalkboard. Ask students to use those that they know in sentences.

Assign Chapter 31 **Vocabulary and Guided Reading Activity** in the TCR.

EXTRA CREDIT PROJECT

Have interested students research and prepare a presentation on the Anasazi who lived in the southwest United States thousands of years before the Europeans arrived. Encourage students to include a time line in their presentation.

VIDEODISC

Use the following to enrich Chapter 31.

WC N 34 44089

King of the Congo receives Dutch ambassador.

KEY TO ABILITY LEVELS

Teaching strategies have been coded for varying learning styles and abilities.

L1 Level 1 activities are **basic** activities and should be within the ability range of all students.

L2 Level 2 activities are **average** activities and should be within the ability range of the average to above-average student.

L3 Level 3 activities are **challenging** activities designed for the ability range of above-average students.

LEP LEP activities should be within the ability range of Limited English Proficiency students.

TEACH

GUIDED PRACTICE

L1 **History** Show students on a wall map of the world the city of Calicut, India, located in southwestern India. Tell them that Calicut was one of the world's five great harbors in the 1500s. The city reflected elements of Muslim and Asian culture because of its location at the junction of the Arabian-Indian sea trade. Ask students why they think Portugal wanted control of this seaport. *(The Portuguese wanted control of the lucrative spice trade.)*

L1 **Geography** Have students locate Brazil on the map "European Colonies in the Americas" on page 498. LEP

DID YOU KNOW ??

One reason the Portuguese used force in order to establish trading posts in the Far East was that the Portuguese did not produce anything that the people of the Far East were willing to accept in exchange for spices.

GEOGRAPHY AND HISTORY

Cabral wanted to sail around Africa but traveled too far west and accidentally landed in Brazil. The question of when Brazil was first discovered is still argued by scholars.

Relief Sculpture of Pedro Cabral

In 1532, the Portuguese established their first permanent settlement in Brazil. The king of Portugal divided the area into 15 territorial strips called **captaincies** (kap' tuhn sēz). Each strip was given to a different Portuguese family who could establish towns, give out land, and raise armies. In return, they promised to colonize and protect their captaincies.

Portugal sent large numbers of settlers to Brazil. Portuguese sailors landed there and decided to stay. Criminals were sent to work off their sentences. Soldiers and officials came to protect royal interests. Ranchers arrived with herds of cattle. Missionaries came looking for converts to Christianity.

The Portuguese set up plantations in Brazil. Most plantations grew sugarcane, which was used to make sugar, molasses, and rum. About 2 million Native Americans were living in Brazil when Portugal claimed the land. The Portuguese settlers enslaved them to work the land. Most of the Native Americans, however, either ran away or died from diseases brought by the Europeans.

Before long, the Portuguese settlers began bringing over enslaved Africans. The number of Africans grew until, in some places, there were at least 20 enslaved Africans for each Portuguese settler. The Africans brought their religions with them. They also brought African music and dance to Brazil. They told folktales about their African history and carved wooden figures for churches. They also added many new words to the Portuguese language.

By the end of the 1600s, there was less demand for sugar. ***Bandeirantes*** (ban duh ran' tās), or fortune-hunters, looking for precious stones and escaped enslaved people, began to appear. Bandeirantes were the frontiersmen of Brazil. Traveling in bands of fifty to several thousand men, they followed the rivers into the jungle. They established Portugal's claim to the far western and southern areas of Brazil.

Early Map of Brazil

Royal interest in Brazil grew when gold was discovered in the 1690s. The king sent government clerks to check the mineral resources and make sure the monarchy received one fifth of each miner's gold. Gold brought still more people to Brazil and more wealth to Portugal. So did the growing of coffee, which was introduced in the early 1700s.

In many ways, Brazil was a tolerant society. It welcomed people of different countries and religions. Many men of part-African ancestry rose to high positions in the Church and the government. Women, however, were allowed little freedom or power, and hardly anyone knew how to read and write.

The Loss of Empire By the middle of the 1500s, Portugal began losing its empire. The colonial government was not well

MULTICULTURAL PERSPECTIVES

Jesuit missionaries to Brazil set up mission villages in remote areas along the Amazon River. There, thousands of Native Americans were baptized, gathered into fortified settlements, and taught farming. These missions provided a place of safety for the Native Americans against raiders who enslaved people. They also became outposts of Portuguese political and economic influence. At the same time, however, they disrupted the hunting and gathering life of the Native Americans.

organized and the economy was in poor shape. Another reason was that the conquered peoples of Southeast Asia disliked the Portuguese for forcing Christianity on them. By the time the Portuguese king died in 1580, Portugal was very weak. The king left no heirs, and the throne was claimed by Philip II of Spain. Portugal was ruled by Spain until 1640. Then, Portugal regained its independence. During that time, the English and the Dutch took over most of the Portuguese trading centers in Southeast Asia.

Section 1 Review

1. **Identify:** Pedro Alvárez Cabral
2. **Define:** colonize, captaincies, *bandeirantes*
3. What kept Portugal from colonizing settlements?
4. What happened to the Native Americans who lived in Brazil when the Portuguese claimed the land?

Critical Thinking

5. How do you think the Native Americans felt about the Portuguese settlement of Brazil?

BRAZILIAN PLANTATION Early Portuguese settlers established plantations in Brazil. At first, Native American populations were enslaved to provide the needed labor. Most of the Native Americans, however, proved too rebellious or too sickly to perform the hard work required. Enslaved Africans were then brought to work on the plantations. **For what was the sugarcane grown on plantations used?**

DID YOU KNOW ??

At this time, Brazil had only a few elementary schools. It lacked both a university and a printing press.

LINKING PAST TO PRESENT

The culture of modern Brazil, like its people, is a blend of Portuguese, African, and Native American influences. Although major elements—the Portuguese language, the Roman Catholic religion, and many customs—came from Portugal, a unique Brazilian blend has developed since colonial times. The Native American language Tupi is still spoken in the northern interior of Brazil. The words *cashew* and *tapioca* are Tupi words. African influences are strongest on the coast north of Rio de Janeiro. Foods and dances such as the samba and bossa nova have African influences.

CAPTION ANSWER

to make sugar, molasses, and rum

VIDEODISC

Use the following to enrich Chapter 31.

WH I 74 18800

A Brazilian native.

SECTION 1 ANSWERS

1. Pedro Alvárez Cabral, Portuguese explorer (p. 488)
2. colonize, to build permanent settlements (p. 487); captaincies, territorial strips into which the Portuguese divided Brazil (p. 488); *bandeirantes*, fortune-hunters (p. 488)
3. Portugal did not have a large enough population to send settlers to all its territories; most territories already had large populations; and the Portuguese were not accustomed to the hot, wet climate of the new colonies.
4. They were enslaved by the Portuguese.
5. Answers will vary but might include the idea that they were angry and overwhelmed.

Assign the Chapter 31 **Section 1 Quiz** in the TCR. Testmaker available.

L1 **Geography: Location** Have students locate the Spanish colonies on the map "European Colonies in the Americas" on page 498. Ask them why the Spanish colonies were difficult to govern.

L2 **Economics** Discuss the use of enslaved people in the colonies by explaining how enslaved Africans contributed to colonial economic prosperity. Ask students why enslaved people were used on sugarcane and coffee plantations. *(Growing these crops required a great deal of manual labor.)* Ask why large numbers of Africans were not imported to Europe. *(Europe did not have large plantations requiring a great deal of manual labor.)*

MAKING CONNECTIONS

➤➤ **History** The Native Americans of Peru revolted several times unsuccessfully. Conquistadore Francisco Pizzaro was especially cruel to the Incas who were ordered by him to fill a room with gold to ransom their ruler. The Incas provided the gold to the Spanish, but their ruler was murdered anyway. Peru's great mineral wealth made it one of Spain's most important possessions, and the Spaniards were determined to keep it under their control.

Colonial Vase

Section 2

SPAIN

By 1535, Spain had established the largest colonial empire in the Americas. Spain's colonies reached from southern North America through Central America and the West Indies to South America. Spain also had trade interests in the Philippines.

Unlike Portugal, Spain had a fairly large population. This allowed it to send thousands of people to its colonies in the Americas. Spain also had a strong, centralized colonial government.

Mexico and Peru In the early 1500s, Spain conquered the Native American empires of Mexico and Peru. They set the example for other Spanish colonies. They were governed by the Council of the Indies, which met at the Spanish court. This council made laws, acted as a court of final appeal, and chose officials to send to the Americas. It even took charge of religious matters.

The colonies were divided into two **viceroyalties** (vīs' roi uhl tēz), or districts—New Spain, or Mexico, and New Castile, or Peru. Each viceroyalty was ruled by a **viceroy** (vīs' roi), or person who represented the king.

The colonists in the viceroyalties sent large amounts of gold and silver back to Spain. They also ran plantations that produced cocoa, coffee, tobacco, tea, and sugar. They forced Native Americans to do all of the heavy work in mines and on plantations. Most of the Native Americans were badly treated. Many died of overwork, starvation, or such diseases as measles and smallpox.

After a time, the Spanish, like the Portuguese, brought enslaved Africans to the Americas. Most of these enslaved people worked on sugar plantations located on the islands of the Caribbean. There were still far more Portuguese-owned enslaved people in Brazil, however, than Spanish-owned enslaved people in the Caribbean.

By the middle 1500s, colonists in the Americas were divided into clear-cut social groups. At the top were ***peninsulares*** (puh nin sū la' rās), or Spaniards born in Spain. Then came Creoles (krē' ōlz), or those of Spanish descent born in the Americas. Next were ***mestizos*** (me stē' zōz), or people of mixed European and Native American ancestry. They were followed by Native Americans. At the lowest level were blacks. Each group held certain jobs. Peninsulares served as viceroys or important church leaders. Mestizos were mostly artisans and merchants.

The way in which colonial cities grew up also reflected this social structure. Most cities centered on a square. On one side of the square was the cathedral. On the other three sides stood the government headquarters and the houses of peninsulares. Farther out were the houses of Creoles and mestizos.

COOPERATIVE LEARNING

Divide the class into small groups and assign an oral report on the advantages and disadvantages of the introduction of the profit motive during the age of exploration. Each student is responsible for a specific task or area of research. Have students address these questions: *What effect did the profit motive have on European countries? What effect did the profit motive have on the inhabitants of the Americas and Africa?* One or more students in each group should compile the research and prepare the report, gather necessary supplies and visuals, and another student should present the report to the class.

Assign the Chapter 31 **Cooperative Learning Activity** in the TCR.

The Roman Catholic Church played a large role in Spanish colonization. It controlled most of the best land in the Spanish colonies. Although the Church itself did not pay taxes, it charged the people who rented or farmed its land a 10 percent income tax.

The Church worked to better conditions in the colonies. Leaders, such as Bartholomé de Las Casas (bar tol uh mā' dā lahs kah' sahs), tried to improve life for the Native Americans. The Church built schools, hospitals, and *asylums* (uh sī' luhms), or places for the mentally ill, and staffed them mostly with nuns. It established the first two universities, in the Americas. One was the University of Mexico. The other was San Marcos (mar' kuhs) University at Lima.

The Decline of an Empire Spain received a great deal of wealth from the colonies, but it did not hold on to that wealth. The Spanish Inquisition had driven out most of the Jews and Muslims who had been the backbone of Spanish industry. As a result, much of the gold and silver sent to Spain ended up going to northern Europe to pay for goods made there.

THE CATHOLIC CHURCH Spanish missions, or churches, in the Americas provided services to local people. The mission shown here (left) is in Texas, which was formerly a part of Mexico. Church leaders, such as the priest Bartholomé de Las Casas shown in this painting (right), protested against the enslavement of Native Americans and worked to help them. **How did the Church improve conditions in the colonies?**

LINKING PAST TO PRESENT

Although Peru was appealing to the Spanish in the 1500s because of its gold reserves, its real wealth was hidden. Today Peru's most valuable export is oil.

DID YOU KNOW ??

When Hernán Cortés arrived at the court of Moctezuma, he was welcomed with a chocolate drink. Cortés brought knowledge of cultivation and chocolate manufacturing to Spain.

CAPTION ANSWER

The Church built schools, hospitals, asylums, and two universities.

VIDEODISC

Use the following to enrich Chapter 31.

WH I 43 18769

Mexico City, ca. 1670.

EXTENDING THE CONTENT

Even the huge amounts of silver and gold from Mexico and Peru paid only about a quarter of the war costs that Philip II and his successors accrued. Their leaders saw themselves as the defenders of the Roman Catholic Church and went to war against Muslims, Turks, Huguenots, Calvinists, and Protestants. Little revenue from trade or industry could be had in the country because of the lack of middle class and the expulsion of non-Catholics. The Spanish people were heavily taxed, and still the government ran out of money. The high taxes caused rebellions.

MAKING CONNECTIONS

➤➤ **The Arts** Spaniards consider the 1500s and early 1600s a "Golden Century" in their culture. Spanish writers included Saavedra de Cervantes, Lope de Vega, and Calderón. In art and architecture, the early 1600s was the beginning of the baroque period, with artists such as El Greco and Diego Velázquez.

DID YOU KNOW ??

At the time England sent Sir Walter Raleigh to establish a colony in the Americas, well-established Native American civilizations existed across the continent. One of the oldest of these was the settlement of Anasazi, established in the Arizona-New Mexico area about four thousand years earlier.

L2 **Critical Thinking** Ask: How do you think Native Americans might have felt about people from foreign lands settling on their land and trying to convert the Native Americans to their religious beliefs? LEP

Painting of Sir Francis Drake

The Spanish also had trouble getting gold and silver from their colonies to Spain. Ships loaded with the precious metals were robbed at sea by English, French, and Dutch pirates. English sea dogs attacked Spanish treasure ships with the blessing of their queen, Elizabeth I. One of the most successful sea dogs was Sir Francis Drake. When the Spanish Armada was defeated by the English in 1588, Spain lost its power in the Atlantic. This opened the Americas to colonization by England, the Netherlands, and France.

Section 2 Review

1. **Identify:** Mexico, Peru, Council of the Indies, Creoles, Bartholomé de Las Casas
2. **Define:** viceroyalties, viceroy, *peninsulares, mestizos*
3. What role did the Roman Catholic Church play in the Spanish colonies?
4. Why did the Spanish have trouble transporting gold and silver from the Americas to Spain?

Critical Thinking

5. What do you think might have happened if Spain had used the gold and silver to develop industries in the Americas?

Section 3 ENGLAND

Like Portugal and Spain, England looked to the Americas for wealth. English nobles and merchants saw it as a place to get raw materials as well as gold and silver. With enough gold, silver, and raw materials, the English could establish a favorable **balance of trade.** This meant England would be able to sell more products to other countries than it would have to buy from them. The English would no longer have to depend on other countries for their needs.

The English had other reasons for wanting colonies in the Americas. England had such a large population that jobs were becoming hard to find. New colonies meant more jobs. Then, too, the Anglican (ang' gluh kuhn) Church had become England's official church and the English people were expected to follow Anglican beliefs. Because of this, Catholics and groups of Protestants called Separatists (sep' uhr uh tists) were looking for a place where they could have religious freedom. They believed that in the Americas they would be able to worship freely.

SECTION 2 ANSWERS

1. Mexico, Spanish colony (p. 490); Peru, a colony of Spain (p. 490); Council of the Indies, governed Spanish colonies (p. 490); Creoles, Spanish born in the Americas (p. 490); Bartholomé de Las Casas, church leader (p. 491)
2. viceroyalties, districts (p. 490); viceroy, king's representative (p. 490); *peninsulares,* Spaniards born in Spain (p. 490); *mestizos,* people of mixed European and Native American ancestry (p. 490)
3. It controlled the best land, taxed the people who rented or farmed its land, and built schools, hospitals, and asylums.
4. Ships loaded with the precious metals were robbed at sea by English, French, and Dutch pirates.
5. Answers will vary but might include that Spain might have become more wealthy and powerful.

Assign the Chapter 31 **Section 2 Quiz** in the TCR. Testmaker available.

In 1585, a group of colonists financed by Sir Walter Raleigh (rahl' ē) sailed for North America. There, they founded a colony on Roanoke (rō' uh nōk) Island off the coast of North Carolina. After six years, however, the colonists disappeared. No one knows for certain what happened to them. For this reason, Roanoke Island became known as the "Lost Colony."

The English did not try again to found colonies in the Americas for more than 20 years. However, in 1600 English merchants formed the East India Company to trade with the East Indies. The company set up trading posts in India, Malaya (muh lā' uh), and some islands in both the East and West Indies.

Painting of Sir Walter Raleigh

Jamestown In 1607, a group of English nobles and merchants formed the Virginia Company of London. The following year the company sent about 100 settlers to the Americas to search for gold and silver. They founded the first permanent English settlement in America. It was located near the mouth of Chesapeake (ches' uh pēk) Bay. The settlers named it Jamestown after their king, James I.

The area in which the colony was founded had long been home to Native Americans. By the time Christopher Columbus arrived in the Americas, there were more than 1 million Native Americans scattered across the North American continent. They were divided into some 500 different groups.

Each group of Native Americans had its own language, religion, and way of life. Some, like the Pima (pē' muh), Papago (pap' uh gō), Creeks, and Cherokee (cher' uh kē), were farmers. Others, like the Comanche (kuh man' chē), Blackfoot, Sioux (sū), Apache (uh pach' ē), and Navaho (nav' uh hō), were hunters and warriors who traveled in bands.

The Native Americans who lived in the area near Jamestown were the Powhatan (pau uh tan'). Their chief, whom the settlers called Powhatan, controlled 128 Native American villages.

Life in Jamestown was hard. The land was swampy and filled with mosquitoes that carried disease. Winters were colder in Jamestown than in England. The colonists burned parts of their houses as fuel. Many became sick and died.

Captain John Smith kept the settlement from total failure. He made it clear that those who did not work would not eat. He also convinced the Powhatan to supply the colonists with corn and beans. When Smith returned to England in 1609, however, many of the colonists starved to death. Those still alive a year later were ready to go back to England. When an English fleet arrived with supplies, the colonists decided to stay.

The settlers worked the land, but they did not own it. It belonged to the Virginia Company. Then, in 1618 the company began granting land to individuals. All colonists who paid their own way to America were given 50 acres, or about 20 hectares, of

Painting of John Smith

L1 **Geography: Location** Ask students to locate Jamestown on the map of "European Colonies in the Americas" on page 498. Ask them to describe its location in reference to later British colonies. LEP

MAKING CONNECTIONS

➤➤ **Literature** English interest in establishing colonies in North America was stimulated by books and pamphlets written by English nobles, clergy, and geographers who gave eyewitness accounts of voyages to North America.

DID YOU KNOW ??

On August 18, 1587, Virginia Dare was born on Roanoke Island. She was the granddaughter of the governor of the island and the first child born in America of English parents.

MEETING SPECIAL NEEDS

Help students having difficulty accessing chapter information use a kind of rapid "reading" or scanning to locate specific information in the text. Show students how to scan by sliding a finger down the middle of the column rapidly. Demonstrate finding the date 1585 on page 493. Read the event that occurred on that date. Then have students use this method to find the following dates and the events in Section 3: 1600, 1606, 1609, 1618, 1612, 1619, 1630, 1634, 1681, 1691, 1733. Create a time line of events on the chalkboard as students respond.

L2 **Geography: Region** Provide students with an outline map of North America. Help them make a map of the regions where each of the Native American culture groups listed in the chart on page 494 lived in North America. Then have them compare their maps of the Native American culture groups with a climate map of North America. Discuss how the climate where each group lived affected their way of life. LEP

MAKING CONNECTIONS

➤➤ **Culture** In 1619, 20 enslaved African Americans were brought to Jamestown colony, the first of many such shipments. This important event changed the culture and social structure of the Americas from then on.

L3 **Science** John White, a Roanoke colonist and artist, painted pictures of the animals and vegetation that he encountered in the Americas. Ask students to research and write a report explaining how these paintings affected 16th-century science. Students might share examples of White's paintings with the class. LEP

NATIVE AMERICANS

REGION	WAY OF LIFE
Arctic	fished and hunted whales, seals, walruses, and caribou; lived in wood and stone houses or igloos in winter and animal skin tents in summer
Subarctic	hunted and gathered food; built wood-frame houses; traveled by snowshoes, canoe, and toboggan
Northwest Coast	fished and hunted; built cedar wood houses and sea-going canoes; carved totem poles to honor ancestors; held potlatches, or ceremonial feasts
Plateau	hunted bison, fished, and gathered food; lived in multifamily lodges; bred the Appaloosa horse
Great Basin	hunted and gathered food; wandered over territory; wove reed baskets decorated with beads, feathers, and shells
California	hunted, fished, and gathered food; settled in communities; used acorns to make bread
Southwest	farmed corn, beans, and squash; built pueblos of stone and adobe; wove straw and reed baskets and cotton cloth
Great Plains	farmed and hunted; lived in log houses or cone-shaped tipis; communicated with other tribes by hand signals
Eastern Woodlands	fished and hunted; lived in longhouses and birch lodges; women owned property, chose chief, and passed on family name
Southeast	farmed and hunted; built towns with open squares; women owned houses and land; counted descent through mothers

EXTENDING THE CONTENT

Many historians think that American settlers were influenced in their development of a new government by the confederations they observed among the Native Americans on the east coast. According to legend, a holy man in the 1500s tried to end the constant warfare among the related Iroquois-speaking peoples of the Five Nations. A Mohawk leader, Hiawatha, brought the tribes together in a political and military alliance that came to be known as the Iroquois League. In the confederation, each tribe continued to manage its internal affairs, but they cooperated against outside enemies. The Iroquois League served as a model for the Albany Plan of Union and the Articles of Confederation.

land. In order to attract more colonists, the company began giving each settler an additional 50 acres, or 20 hectares, for each person that settler brought to the Americas. Soon, the number of people coming to the Americas increased tremendously.

Most of the newcomers were **indentured** (in den' chuhrd) **servants.** These were people who agreed to work for four to seven years after their arrival to pay for their passage. At the end of that time, they were free and could obtain land of their own.

The settlers saw the Native Americans using tobacco and began to use it themselves. People in Europe also started using tobacco. At first, they used it as a medicine. Later, they smoked it in clay pipes. About 1612, a settler named John Rolfe (rahlf) began planting tobacco. It soon became Virginia's most important crop. Most of the tobacco grown was exported to England, because people there were willing to pay a good price for it.

The settlers brought English laws and government with them to the Americas. They were far from England, however, and travel was slow. Soon, it became necessary for them to make their own laws. In 1619, they elected 22 **burgesses** (ber' jis ez), or representatives, from among landowning males over 17 years old. The burgesses met to decide laws for the colony. This House of Burgesses set an important example of self-government.

Plymouth Another company, the Virginia Company of Plymouth (plim' uhth), was formed in England in 1606. In 1620, it was reorganized as the Council for New England. It gained the right to grant land to settlers for colonies in New England.

That same year, a group of Separatists called Pilgrims sailed for Virginia on the *Mayflower.* They had received grants of land from the Virginia Company. Strong winds blew the *Mayflower* off course, causing the Pilgrims to land in New England just north of Cape Cod in present-day Massachusetts.

The lands in New England belonged to the Council for New England, and the Pilgrims had not been given the right to govern in them. Therefore, they signed an agreement to set up a civil government. This agreement was called the Mayflower Compact. The majority of free men would govern. Neither women nor indentured servants could vote.

The Pilgrims named their settlement Plymouth after the English town from which they had sailed. Their first winter in the Americas was hard. About one half of the settlers died. In the spring, those who remained cleared the fields for farming. The Native Americans taught them how to fertilize their crops, and how to hunt and fish in the wilderness.

The people of Plymouth governed themselves for 70 years with almost no outside control. Then, in 1691, Plymouth became part of the Massachusetts Bay Colony.

Painting of John Rolfe and Pocahontas

DID YOU KNOW ??

John Smith claimed he escaped death at the hands of Native Americans as a result of the pleas of Pocahontas, the daughter of a Native American chief. Pocahontas later married John Rolfe and settled in England.

MAKING CONNECTIONS

➤➤ **History** Originally, the Pilgrims set sail in two ships—the *Mayflower* and the *Speedwell.* The *Speedwell,* however, was not seaworthy and had to turn back. Many of its passengers transferred to the already overcrowded *Mayflower*.

L2 **Writing** Have students imagine they are Europeans living in one of the following countries in the 1600s: Portugal, Spain, England, the Netherlands, or France. They wish to travel to the Americas to establish colonies. They are to write letters to the ruler of their country to grant them permission to colonize the Americas.

EXTENDING THE CONTENT

France and Great Britain fought three wars in Canada and the American frontier—King William's War, 1689-1697; Queen Anne's War, 1702-1713; and King George's War 1744-1748. In America, the French had more territory, the British more people. What is called the French and Indian War broke out in 1754. This war between France and England was a struggle for control of North America. Quebec, center of New France, fell to the British in 1759. So did the island possessions of France and Spain (which had joined France's side). The 1763 Treaty of Paris ended France's empire in the Americas and was the virtual end of its empire in India.

L2 **Critical Thinking** Help students create cause-event-effect organizers of important concepts in Section 3. Write the following events on the chalkboard and ask volunteers to write in the causes and effects for each event: *a group of colonists financed by Sir Walter Raleigh sailed for North America; settlers founded the first permanent colony at Jamestown; people in Europe began smoking tobacco; English settlers in the Americas made their own laws.* LEP

LINKING PAST TO PRESENT

The plentiful harvest in the fall of 1621 led Governor William Bradford to declare a festival. The Pilgrims invited their Native American friends to a three-day feast that is now known as Thanksgiving.

Painting of Pilgrims

The Growth of Empire Jamestown and Plymouth were not the only English settlements in the Americas. In fact, by 1733 Great Britain had 13 colonies along the Atlantic coast of America. One of these colonies was founded in 1630, when a group of Puritans seeking religious freedom sailed to New England. There, they formed several settlements of the Massachusetts Bay Colony in the area around present-day Boston.

In 1634, the English settled in Maryland. King Charles I had granted the land to his friend Cecilius Calvert (se sēl′ yuhs kal′ vuhrt), the second Lord Baltimore. Calvert wanted a place in America where English Catholics could live in peace.

In 1681, William Penn, the leader of a religious group called the Quakers (kwā′ kuhrz), founded a colony in Pennsylvania. King Charles II had granted Penn the land in payment for a debt he owed Penn's father.

Section 3 Review

1. **Identify:** Anglican Church, Separatists, Sir Walter Raleigh, Roanoke Island, East India Company, Jamestown, Powhatan, John Smith, John Rolfe, Council for New England, Pilgrims, Plymouth, Cecilius Calvert, William Penn
2. **Define:** balance of trade, indentured servants, burgesses
3. Why did colonists set up the House of Burgesses?
4. What group founded the Massachusetts Bay Colony? Why did they establish it?

Critical Thinking

5. Why would the Americas be a likely place for people to settle who were unhappy in their own countries?

Painting of Lord Baltimore

Section 4 THE NETHERLANDS

The Dutch also established colonies in the Americas. In 1602, Dutch merchants founded the Dutch East India Company to trade in Africa and the East Indies. The Dutch had a fleet of more than 10,000 merchant ships. One by one, they seized Portuguese trading posts in the East Indies and soon controlled most of the East Indies. In addition, they became the first Europeans to reach Australia and New Zealand. They also founded a

SECTION 3 ANSWERS

1. Anglican Church, church of England (p. 492); Separatists, Protestants (p. 492); Sir Walter Raleigh, colonizer; Roanoke Island, North Carolina island; East India Company, English company; Jamestown, English settlement; Powhatans, Native Americans; John Smith, Jamestown leader (p. 493); John Rolfe, Jamestown settler (p. 495); Council for New England, was Virginia Company (p. 495); Pilgrims, Separatists (p. 495); Plymouth, Pilgrim settlement (p. 495); Cecilius Calvert, colonizer (p. 496); William Penn, colonizer (p. 496)
2. balance of trade, balance of imports and exports (p. 492); indentured servants, pledged labor for passage (p. 495); burgesses, representatives (p. 495)
3. to make their own laws
4. the Puritans; for religious freedom
5. Answers will vary.

Assign the Chapter 31 **Section 3 Quiz** in the TCR. Testmaker available.

colony named Capetown at the southern tip of Africa. Many Dutch colonists, called Boers (borz), settled there.

In 1621, the Dutch formed another company called the Dutch West India Company to establish colonies in the Americas. Colonists were sent first to islands in the West Indies and along the coast of South America. In 1624, the Dutch founded the city of New Amsterdam (am' stuhr dam) on the island of Manhattan (man hat' n). They bought the island from the Native Americans for goods worth about $24. The Dutch called the colonies they established in North America "New Netherlands." New Amsterdam was the capital.

Later in the 1600s, rivalry between the Dutch and the English led to a series of wars, which the Dutch lost. The English took over most of the Dutch colonies, including New Amsterdam, which they renamed New York.

Section 4 Review

1. **Identify:** Capetown, Boers, New Amsterdam, New Netherlands, New York
2. Why were the Dutch East India Company and the Dutch West India Company formed?
3. To what nation did the Dutch lose most of their colonies?

Critical Thinking

4. Do you think the Dutch purchase of Manhattan was fair or unfair to the Native Americans? Explain.

Section 5 France

In 1608, Samuel de Champlain (sham plān'), a French explorer, founded the first permanent French colony in the Americas at Quebec (kwi bek'). Soon after, the French established other settlements around the Great Lakes. They also established settlements at the northern end of the Mississippi River and along the rivers and streams that flowed into it.

Most of these settlements resembled villages in France. Houses stood side by side along a lake or river bank. Behind each house stretched a long, narrow farm. The settlements were small, because few people wanted to leave France.

Most of the French in the Americas were fur traders. On foot or by canoe, they visited various Native American tribes. They gave the Native Americans blankets, guns, knives, and wine in

Painting of French Settler

L1 Geography: Location Have students locate Quebec on the map "European Colonies in the Americas" on page 498. Ask a volunteer to explain its location geographically. Ask students why Quebec was a good location for a settlement. *(It was located along a river with an outlet to the Atlantic Ocean.)* LEP

L2 Critical Thinking Ask students to consider how the Native American belief that land belongs to everyone clashed with the European belief that land could be bought and sold and owned by individual people. Have students decide how they feel about the issue and write a position paper explaining their views. Have several volunteers representing each viewpoint read their papers aloud.

LINKING PAST TO PRESENT

The Dutch settlers' homes along the Hudson River have been restored and today serve as museums. Most of the houses are made from local stone topped with curved gambrel roofs. A split door, called a Dutch door, often divides family living quarters from a barn. The top half of the door lets air into the main house when open, while the closed bottom half of the door keeps animals and small children in their proper places. The restored Dutch houses also show evidence of Dutch culture in their furnishings.

SECTION 4 ANSWERS

1. Capetown, Dutch colony in Africa (p. 497); Boers, Dutch colonists (p. 497); New Amsterdam, capital of New Netherlands (p. 497); New Netherlands, Dutch colonies in North America (p. 497); New York, English colony (also New Amsterdam) (p. 497)
2. Dutch East India Company—to organize trade in Africa and the East Indies; Dutch West India Company—to establish colonies in the Americas
3. England
4. Answers will vary but students should provide reasons for their opinion. Realistic comparison to land values may help understanding.

Assign the Chapter 31 **Section 4 Quiz** in the TCR. Testmaker available.

INDEPENDENT PRACTICE

L2 Critical Thinking Have students make charts titled "Colonial Empires in the Americas," and use these headings to sort information: "Country," "Location of Empire," "Reason for Settlement," "Major Resources and Goods Received from Colonies," "Reasons for the Empire's Decline." Have volunteers write their charts on the chalkboard or large poster board.

GEOGRAPHY AND HISTORY

European politics and worldwide rivalry for trade and colonies were interconnected in the wars between France and Great Britain in the 18th century. By the 1750s, both had colonies in India, the West Indies, and the Americas. The general name given to the final encounter between these two European countries is the Seven Years' War (1756-1763.) Ask students to describe the British empire in the Americas after the Treaty of Paris. *(The British empire in the Americas after the Treaty of Paris included much of the eastern half of North America from the Great Plains east to the Atlantic Ocean and several Caribbean islands.)*

MAP STUDY Answer

in the northern part of North America

Assign the Chapter 31 **Geography and Map Activity** in the TCR.

European Colonies in the Americas

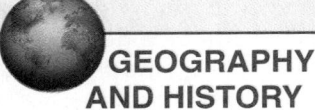

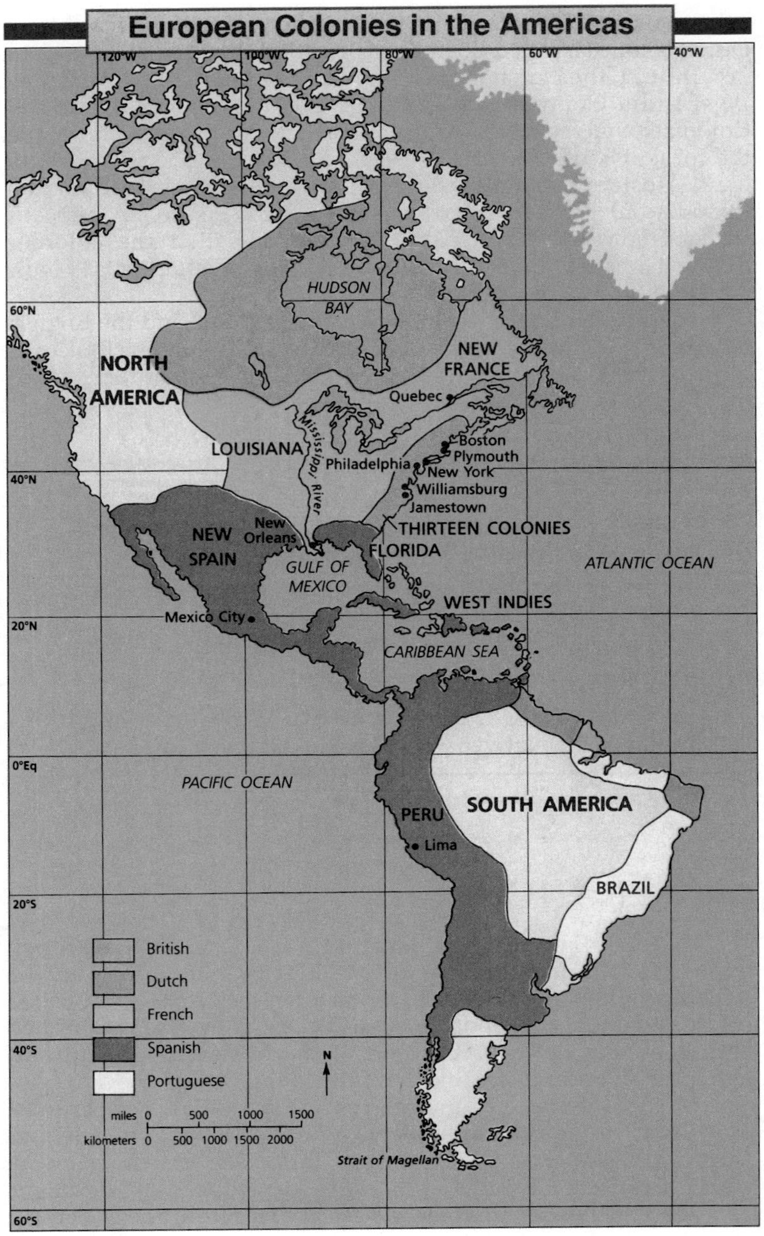

MAP STUDY

LOCATION By the mid-1700s, France, England, Portugal, and the Netherlands had extended their American claims. **In what parts of the Americas were the British claims located?**

EXTENDING THE CONTENT

Less than 50 years of Dutch occupation left some lasting reminders in the Middle Atlantic states. Besides the main settlement at New Amsterdam, the Dutch also had Fort Orange, near present-day Albany, and Fort Nassau, across the river from Philadelphia. Settlement in the Dutch colonies was slow, partly because the Dutch West India Company had strict rules for settlers and partly because life in Holland was peaceful and prosperous. To boost immigration, the Dutch tried the patron system—a semi-feudal arrangement in which large estate owners found settlers for their land and then oversaw their settlements.

exchange for beaver and other animal skins. Beaver hats for gentlemen became very fashionable in Europe, and the fur trade brought France much wealth.

In 1682, René-Robert Cavelier (ka ve lyā'), Sieur de La Salle (sjoer dā la sal), claimed the Mississippi River valley for France. He named the area Louisiana in honor of the French king, Louis XIV. The French called Louisiana and their other lands in the Americas "New France."

The French also established settlements in the West Indies and in India. In time, the French and the English became great rivals. They clashed in Europe, the Americas, and India. After a series of four wars, the French finally were defeated. In 1763, they signed the Treaty of Paris. Under the treaty, the French lost their North American colonial empire and almost all of their settlements in India.

Section 5 Review

1. **Identify:** Samuel de Champlain, René-Robert Cavelier, Louisiana, New France, Treaty of Paris
2. What was the first permanent French colony founded in the Americas?
3. Why did France's established settlements in the Americas remain small?
4. How did the French lose their lands in North America?

Critical Thinking

5. Why do you think so few French people wanted to settle in the Americas?

Section 6

THE INFLUENCE OF EMPIRES

Empires in the Americas helped make the nations of western Europe richer and more powerful. These empires also introduced western Europeans to many new foods. Among them were avocados, lima beans, peanuts, pineapples, tomatoes, and turkeys. Farmers in Spain, Portugal, and Italy began to grow corn, while farmers in Germany and Ireland started to specialize in potatoes. Both corn and potatoes were nourishing and easy to grow. As a result, fewer western Europeans died because of famine, and Europe's population increased.

Another popular product from the Americas was a drink made by roasting dry cocoa beans over a fire and pounding them into a paste. The chocolate paste was then mixed with water,

L1 **Role Play** Encourage students to learn more about the foods that were introduced to Europe by the empires. Have student pairs role-play a sea captain returning from the Americas who tries to sell some of these foods to the people of London and Paris. Have the rest of the class act as an audience, judging whether they would be willing to try the new foods from the sales pitch they hear.

MAKING CONNECTIONS

➤➤ **Religion** All the French settlers were Roman Catholic since Huguenots, or French Protestants, were not allowed in France's colonies.

DID YOU KNOW ??

The Americas provided western Europeans with tobacco. People either smoked it in clay pipes or inhaled it in a powdered form called snuff.

ASSESS

CHECK FOR UNDERSTANDING

Ask students to summarize the main points of the chapter, orally or in writing. Discuss the answers to the Section and Chapter Review questions.

EVALUATE

Assign the Chapter 31 **Performance Assessment Activity** in the TCR.

Administer the **Chapter 31 Test**. Testmaker available.

SECTION 5 ANSWERS

1. Samuel de Champlain, French explorer at Quebec (p. 497); René-Robert Cavelier, claimed the Mississippi River valley for France (p. 499); Louisiana, French territory (p. 499); New France, Louisiana and other French territory (p. 499); Treaty of Paris, lost France its North American empire (p. 499)
2. Quebec
3. because few people wanted to leave France
4. They were defeated by the English in a series of four wars.
5. Answers will vary but might include the idea that the French were satisfied and did not see opportunities in America.

Assign the Chapter 31 **Section 5 Quiz** in the TCR. Testmaker available.

RETEACH

Divide the class into five groups. Each group will represent one country: Spain, Portugal, France, England, or the Netherlands. Have the groups summarize their colonial actions.

Assign the Chapter 31 **Reteaching Activity** in the TCR.

ENRICH

Have students investigate Portuguese exploration and colonization in Asia and Africa—the trading kingdoms on Africa's east coast, Native American trading posts, and Asian cities such as Macao. Ask them to write a report describing the history of each of these settlements.

Assign the Chapter 31 **Enrichment Activity** in the TCR.

CLOSE

Ask students to discuss the empires of the five European countries in the Americas and decide which of them most influenced the histories of the following places: Canada, the United States, the Caribbean islands, Central America, South America.

MEETING CHAPTER OBJECTIVES

Each objective is tested by the Review questions in parentheses.

1. Summarize why Europeans colonized the Americas. (BV; CU 1)

2. Discuss European empires in the Americas. (BV; CU 2, 3, 7; UYJ).

3. Explain why many colonial empires declined. (UYJ)

4. Describe how American empires influenced Europe. (CU 4, 8)

sugar, vanilla, and cinnamon, and shaken up and down until it bubbled. The people in London, Paris, and other cities in western Europe became so fond of the chocolate drink that they opened cafes where they could sip the drink and talk about events of the day.

Section 6 Review

1. What did the empires in the Americas do for the nations of western Europe?
2. What were some of the new foods the empires introduced to western Europeans?
3. What crops did Germany and Ireland specialize in raising?

Critical Thinking

4. Which of the foods introduced to western Europeans from the Americas are a part of your diet today?

Chapter Summary

1. By 1532, Portugal had a colony in Brazil and posts in Africa, India, and Southeast Asia.
2. Portuguese settlers first used Native Americans to work their plantations and mines but later used enslaved Africans.
3. By 1535, Spain had the largest colonial empire in the Americas.
4. When the Spanish Armada was defeated in 1588, Spain lost its power in the Atlantic.
5. The first successful English settlement in the Americas, founded in 1607, was at Jamestown.
6. The Powhatan near Jamestown helped the settlers through the first difficult winter in the Americas.
7. In 1619, the Jamestown colonists organized the House of Burgesses, which set an example of government in the Americas.
8. Plymouth, England's second permanent settlement in the Americas, was established by the Pilgrims in New England in 1620.
9. In 1624, the Dutch founded the city of New Amsterdam, which was later taken over by the English and renamed New York.
10. The first permanent French settlement in the Americas was Quebec, which was founded in 1608.
11. Empires in the Americas gave western European nations wealth and power and introduced western Europeans to many new foods.

SECTION 6 ANSWERS

1. They helped make the nations richer and more powerful.

2. avocados, lima beans, peanuts, pineapples, tomatoes, turkeys, corn, potatoes, and chocolate

3. corn and potatoes

4. Answers will vary but should include more than one food.

Assign the Chapter 31 **Section 6 Quiz** in the TCR. Testmaker available.

CHAPTER 31 Review

Building Vocabulary

Write a paragraph as if you were a Spanish person of the 1500s who has decided to go to America. Explain what you have heard about America that has convinced you to go there. Use the following words in your paragraph.

colonize	*mestizos*
captaincies	balance of trade
viceroy	indentured servants
peninsulares	burgesses

Check for Understanding

1. Why did western European nations want to colonize the Americas?
2. Why did the Portuguese settlers in Brazil bring over enslaved Africans?
3. How were social groups within the Spanish colonies divided?
4. What happened to most of the gold and silver Spain received from its colonies in the Americas?
5. Why was the colony on Roanoke Island called the "Lost Colony"?
6. In what ways did the Native Americans help the settlers at Jamestown? At Plymouth?
7. How many colonies did England have in America by 1733?
8. What kind of trade did the French establish with the Native Americans?

Critical Thinking

1. What was the most difficult problem Europeans faced in the Americas?
2. What changes did European colonization cause in the lives of the Native Americans in the Americas?
3. What would you have liked about being a Jamestown settler? What would you have disliked?
4. What is your opinion about the following statement: Working as an indentured servant for several years to pay for the trip to the Americas was fair.

Geography in History

PLACE Refer to the map on page 498. The European colonies stretched from Hudson Bay in the north to the Strait of Magellan in the south. What is similar about the places where colonial cities were established?

Using Your Journal

Review the details you have noted about the changes that took place in the Americas in the 1500s and the 1600s. Imagine you are a news reporter in the Americas during that time. Write an editorial in which you give your impression of the effects of the colonization of the Americas on the land and its people.

CHAPTER 31 REVIEW ANSWERS

BUILDING VOCABULARY

Paragraphs will vary but students should have reasons to support emigration from Spain.

CHECKING FOR UNDERSTANDING

1. because they wanted its riches and to spread Christianity
2. because most of the Native Americans they had enslaved ran away or died from diseases
3. At the top were *peninsulares;* then came Creoles, *mestizos,* Native Americans, and blacks.
4. It ended up going to northern Europe to pay for goods made there.
5. because no one knows for certain what happened to it
6. They taught the colonists how to plant corn and beans, and how to hunt and fish.
7. thirteen
8. fur trade

CRITICAL THINKING

1. Answers will vary but should present difficulties, such as disease, wars, and starvation.
2. Many died from diseases and doing heavy work; many were moved and introduced to guns and wine.
3. Answers will vary but should give specific examples.
4. Answers will vary, but students could mention that indentured servants were often treated badly.

+ BONUS +

TEST QUESTION

For Chapter 31 Test

If you were the ruler of a viceroyalty in the early 1500s, what would your title be, where might you be living, and what major problems would you face. *(viceroy; Mexico or Peru; controlling Native Americans, making plantations profitable, and sending gold and silver back to Spain)*

USING YOUR JOURNAL

Editorials will vary. You might call on volunteers to read their editorials to the class and discuss.

GEOGRAPHY IN HISTORY

Colonial cities were located on seacoasts, often clumped in regions; the British established the most cities.

CHAPTER 32

Political Revolutions

CHAPTER ORGANIZER

Objectives	Special Features	Supplemental Materials
Section 1 Revolution in England Summarize how revolution in England began during the 1600s.		• Reproducible Lesson Plan • Section 1 Quiz • Testmaker • Chapter 32 Vocabulary and Guided Reading Activity • Chapter 32 Cooperative Learning Activity • Unit 10 World Literature • The World History Videodisc
Section 2 The American Revolution Identify what British policies led to the American Revolution of the late 1700s.	Map and Geography Skill: *Reading a Military Map,* p. 511	• Reproducible Lesson Plan • Section 2 Quiz • Testmaker • Chapter 32 Teaching Transparencies and Activities • Chapter 32 Activity Book Activity • The Western Civilization Videodisc
Section 3 The French Revolution Describe how the French Revolution came about in the late 1700s and what its results were.	People in History: *Domingo Sarmiento,* p. 516	• Reproducible Lesson Plan • Section 3 Quiz • Testmaker • Chapter 32 Geography and Map Activity • Chapter 32 Chart and Graph Skill • The Western Civilization Videodisc
Chapter 32 Review and Evaluation		• Chapter 32 Reteaching Activity • Chapter 32 Enrichment Activity • Spanish Summary and Glossary • Audiocassettes (English and Spanish) • Chapter 32 Performance Assessment Activity • Chapter 32 Test • Testmaker

If time does not permit teaching the entire chapter, use the Chapter 32 Summary on page 520 and the Chapter 32 Audiocassettes (English and Spanish) to point out the main ideas of the chapter.

✓ Performance Assessment Activities

Biography Have students write a brief biography about an individual from each revolution covered in this chapter from the viewpoint of someone living at the same time. Have students compare these people's beliefs and experiences in the revolutions.

Pictorial History Have students develop a pictorial history of one of the revolutions covered in this chapter. Tell them to illustrate the major events before, during, and after the revolution. Have students include written information that explains the events. Display the projects in the classroom.

CHAPTER RESOURCES

LITERATURE ABOUT THE PERIOD

Defoe, Daniel. *Robinson Crusoe.* Oxford University Press, 1981. The adventures of a man marooned on an island who survives through ingenuity and hard work.

Dickens, Charles. *A Tale of Two Cities.* Dutton, 1970. A romantic novel that takes place during the French Revolution.

Milton, John. *Paradise Lost.* Heritage, 1940. Poem that explores Heaven, Hell, Paradise, and Earth.

READINGS FOR THE STUDENT

Burton, Hester. *Kate Ryder* T.Y. Crowell, 1975. Novel focusing on a family's divided loyalties in the English Civil War.

Davis, Burke. *Black Heroes of the American Revolution.* Harcourt, Brace and Jovanovich, 1991. Highlights achievements of African Americans during the Revolution.

Forbes, Esther. *Johnny Tremain.* Houghton Mifflin, 1971. Novel about young boy in Boston during the American Revolution.

Foster, Genevieve. *George Washington's World.* Charles Scribner's Sons, 1944. Biography of Washington and the world events during his lifetime.

READINGS FOR THE TEACHER

Andrews, Allen. *The King Who Lost America: George III and Independence*. Jupiter Books, 1976. Emphasizes the British view of the American Revolution.

Banfield, Susan. *The Rights of Man, The Reign of Terror: The Story of the French Revolution.* Lippincott, 1989. Explores the French Revolution and the French society in turmoil.

Churchill, Winston S. *The Age of Revolution.* Bantam Books, 1963. Focuses on English, American, and French Revolutions.

Durant, Will and Ariel. *The Age of Voltaire.* Simon and Schuster, 1965. History of western Europe from 1715-1756.

Lancaster, Bruce. *The American Revolution: American Heritage Library.* Houghton Mifflin, 1987. Details the American Revolution.

MULTIMEDIA RESOURCES

The English Revolution. Random House. Filmstrips. Discusses the people and events that contributed to the British tradition of law, justice, and freedom.

French Revolution: Birth of a New France. Encyclopedia Educational Corp. Video. Dramatization of the period following the French Revolution, using pictures and art.

Prelude to Revolution: American History. Social Studies School Service. Video. Narration of events preceding the American Revolution.

Revolution—Past, Present, and Future. Focus Media, Inc., Software. Nature of political revolutions shown interactively.

INTRODUCE

CHAPTER 32 OVERVIEW

Chapter 32 examines the political revolutions that occurred during the 1600s and 1700s in England, the American colonies, and France as a result of the changes in ideas about freedom and government.

- ➤ **Section 1** discusses the reasons why revolution occurred in England in the 1600s.
- ➤ **Section 2** describes the reasons that led to the American Revolution in the late 1700s.
- ➤ **Section 3** summarizes the causes and effects of the French Revolution in the late 1700s.

CHAPTER OBJECTIVES

After reading Chapter 32, students will be able to:

1. summarize how revolution in England began during the 1600s.
2. identify what British policies led to the American Revolution of the late 1700s.
3. describe how the French Revolution came about in the late 1700s and what its results were.

EXAMINING THE ILLUSTRATION

Ask students what building they think represents the United States government. Explain that to the French, the Bastille represented the kind of government they didn't want. Ask students what the painting tells them the French people did about their government.

PERFORMANCE ASSESSMENT

Use the Performance Assessment activities on page 502B to help you evaluate students as they complete the chapter.

CHAPTER 32 Political Revolutions

Painting of Revolutionaries Storming the French Bastille

502

TEACHER CLASSROOM RESOURCES

- Section Quizzes/Chapter Test
- Reteaching Activity
- Enrichment Activity
- Chart and Graph Skill Activity
- Geography and Map Activity
- Vocabulary and Guided Reading Activity
- Cooperative Learning Activity
- Spanish Summary and Glossary
- Performance Assessment Activity
- Testmaker
- Audiocassettes (English and Spanish)
- Teaching Transparencies and Activities
- The Western Civilization Videodisc
- The World History Videodisc

Chapter Focus

READ TO DISCOVER:

- How revolution in England began during the 1600s.
- What British policies led to the American Revolution of the late 1700s.
- How the French Revolution came about in the late 1700s and what its results were.

By the 1700s, people in the western world had new ideas about government. They were less willing to be ruled without having a voice in government. They also wanted equal justice under the law. They did not believe that monarchs or the Church had the right to tell them what to do. Thinkers and writers began spreading ideas about freedom and the right of people to change the government to meet their needs. For these reasons, the 1700s came to be known in Europe and the Americas as the Age of Enlightenment, or a time of increased knowledge.

1600 A.D.–1800 A.D.

KEY TERMS

revolution
martial law
mercantilism
monopoly
direct tax
boycott
popular sovereignty
estates
bourgeoisie
tyranny
constitutional monarchy

Section 1

Revolution in England

In England, there was a struggle for power between the king and Parliament. After a civil war and a **revolution,** or an attempt to overthrow or change the government, Parliament won. From that point on, the monarch ruled in the name of the people.

Conflict with Parliament In 1603, the last Tudor monarch, Queen Elizabeth I, died. Since she had never married, the Crown, or royal power, passed to a distant relative. This was James VI of Scotland, a member of the Stuart family. He became James I of England.

The Tudors had enjoyed great power. They had been careful, however, to get Parliament's opinion on their actions. James I, on the other hand, believed in rule by divine right. When Parliament

FOCUS

BELLRINGER

Write this question on the chalkboard: *Do you think that the destruction of another person's property can ever be justified? If yes, under what circumstances?*

MOTIVATIONAL ACTIVITY

Have students share their responses to the questions of whether the destruction of another's property is ever justified. Then tell students that in this chapter they will learn about incidents such as the Boston Tea Party in which people destroyed property in order to get across their way of thinking. Ask students if they feel this justifies the actions of the protestors.

VOCABULARY PRE-CHECK

Write the key terms for this chapter on the chalkboard. Ask volunteers to skim the chapter for these boldfaced words and read aloud the sentences in which they appear.

Assign Chapter 32 **Vocabulary and Guided Reading Activity** in the TCR.

EXTRA CREDIT PROJECT

Have students research the life of Benjamin Banneker, African American colonist, inventor, scientist, and patriot. Have them create a biographical presentation of this American to share with the class.

KEY TO ABILITY LEVELS

Teaching strategies have been coded for varying learning styles and abilities.

L1 Level 1 activities are **basic** activities and should be within the ability range of all students.

L2 Level 2 activities are **average** activities and should be within the ability range of the average to above-average student.

L3 Level 3 activities are **challenging** activities designed for the ability range of above-average students.

LEP LEP activities should be within the ability range of Limited English Proficiency students.

TEACH

GUIDED PRACTICE

L1 **Civics** Point out that the English civil war was the outcome of the deep conflict between the king and Parliament. Ask students to identify the source of that conflict. *(the king's belief in the divine rights of kings and Parliament's desire to have a voice in government)* LEP

L2 **Critical Thinking** Ask students to create a list of Parliament's grievances against the king. Putting themselves in the place of members of Parliament, have students rank the grievances from most to least important.

DID YOU KNOW ??

The mother of James I was Mary Queen of Scots, who had been put to death by Elizabeth I.

MAP STUDY Answers

from the southern and eastern part of England; from the northern and western part of England

VIDEODISC

Use the following to enrich Chapter 32.

WH I 67 18793

The taking of the Bastille, July 14, 1789.

objected to some of his actions, he dismissed it and ruled without a legislature for ten years.

Religious differences also caused trouble between the king and Parliament. James I wanted to force the Anglican Church on the people. Many members of Parliament, however, were Puritans. They wanted to be able to worship as they pleased. They believed in hard work and plain living, and did not like the Crown's free-spending ways. They wanted a say in how the government raised and spent taxes. With the help of other groups, they worked against what they felt was the king's unjust power.

Although James I did not agree with many of his subjects about religion, it was his idea to have a new translation of the Bible. He appointed a committee of church officials who put together the King James version. Its style has greatly influenced English speech and literature. Many English-speaking Protestant churches today still use the King James version.

When James I died in 1625, his son became King Charles I. He held the same beliefs about the monarchy as his father.

The English Civil Wars

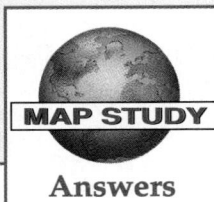

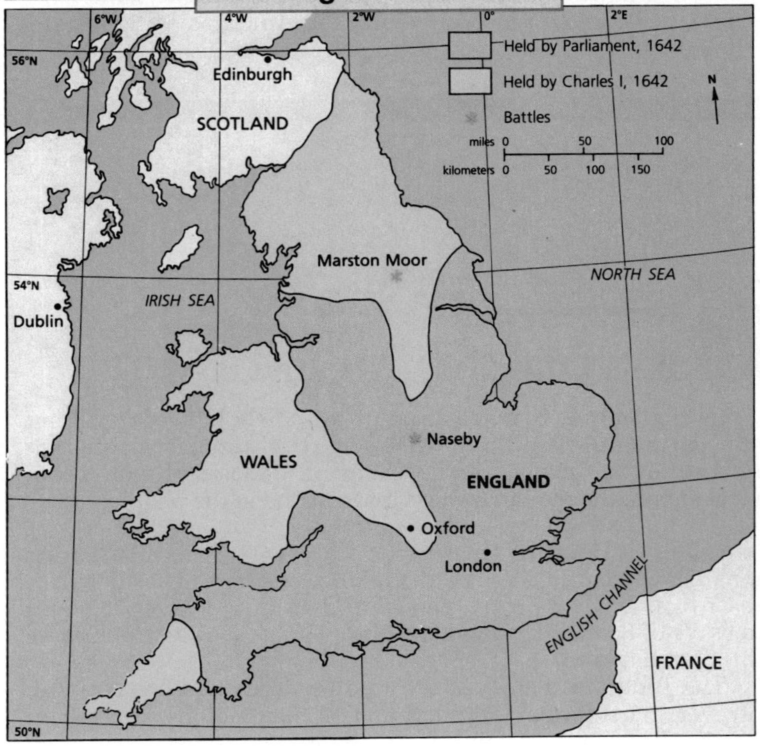

MAP STUDY

REGIONS The English civil war was both a religious and a political war. **From what part of England did Parliament draw its support? From where part did Charles I draw his support?**

MULTICULTURAL PERSPECTIVES

Many supporters of the Parliamentary cause were Puritans. Like other Protestants, Puritans believed that the Bible was the only source of religious authority. The Puritans were different from other Protestants, such as those belonging to the Church of England, in that Puritans were extremists in their religious discipline and the militancy of their beliefs. They wanted to "purify" the Church of England, which they felt retained too many vestiges of the Roman Catholic Church, and to purify the rest of society as well. Puritans considered themselves the spiritual elite, separate from the wickedness of the world.

In 1628, Charles I was forced to call a meeting of Parliament to approve new taxes to pay for wars with France and Spain. Parliament saw a chance to limit the Crown's power and gain more for itself. It drew up the Petition of Right. This said that the king could not declare **martial** (mar' shuhl) **law,** or rule by the army instead of by law. It also said that the Crown could not pass tax laws without Parliament's consent. In addition, people could not be put in prison just because the king wanted them out of the way. At first, Charles I agreed to the petition. Then, in 1629, he broke his word and dismissed Parliament.

In 1640, however, Charles I needed money to build a larger army to fight the Scots. He had tried to force the Anglican Church on the Presbyterian Scots, and they had revolted, taking over part of northern England. So, he called a meeting of Parliament.

Parliament again saw a chance to limit Charles' power. It passed a law abolishing taxes collected by the Crown without Parliament's consent. It also passed a law to set up regular meetings of Parliament and to do away with the Star Chamber. This was a royal court that tried people without a jury.

Painting of a Cavalier

Civil War Once again, Charles I at first accepted the laws Parliament passed and then disregarded them. In 1642, civil war broke out between the Crown and Parliament.

Those who backed the Crown were called Cavaliers (kav uh lirz'). They wore their hair shoulder length, often in curls. They were mostly rich Roman Catholics and Anglicans. Those who backed Parliament were called Roundheads because they wore their hair short. They were mostly middle- and lower-class Puritans and other Calvinists.

Oliver Cromwell (krahm' wel), a Puritan leader who backed Parliament, formed a New Model Army. It drilled hard and followed strict rules against drinking, swearing, and robbing. It chose its officers because they were good fighters and leaders, not because they were of high birth. In 1646, the New Model Army defeated the king's forces and ended the war.

Most English leaders still believed that monarchy was the best form of government. They did not, however, trust Charles I and were afraid to allow him to return to the throne. Cromwell and his supporters put Charles I on trial for treason. The court found him guilty, and he was beheaded in 1649.

Oliver Cromwell After the king's death, Cromwell took over the rule of England, now called the Commonwealth. The Commonwealth was overwhelmed with troubles from the start. The Irish and the Scots both looked to Charles I's son as the true ruler of England. Cromwell had to put down their rebellion. He also had trouble balancing the English who felt enough changes had been made with those who wanted more. He finally did away

L3 **History** Have students draw a political cartoon about the English civil war. For example, students might draw a cartoon that lampoons King Charles or Cromwell that expresses the ideas of the Parliamentarians or the Cavaliers, or that shows the tragedy of the civil war. LEP

DID YOU KNOW ??

The region that became the state of Maryland was named for Queen Henrietta Maria, the Catholic French wife of Charles I.

MAKING CONNECTIONS

➤➤ **History** Cromwell's New Model Army also became known for its religious devotion. Soldiers listened to sermons during their free time and often marched into battles singing psalms.

VIDEODISC

Use the following to enrich Chapter 32.

WC E 51 19832
Oliver Cromwell dissolves Parliament in 1653.

WC E 52 19833
1662 cartoon, hanging of the Long Parliament.

COOPERATIVE LEARNING

Divide students into three groups to stage the trial of King Charles. Explain that one group is to prosecute the king and one group is to defend the king. The third group is to act as witnesses for the prosecution and the defense. Make sure each student has a task to perform. Students should choose one student to role-play Charles and one to role-play Cromwell. Assign other students to research arguments for the prosecution and arguments used by the defense, and prepare dialogue for the role play. Then stage the trial.

Assign the Chapter 32 **Cooperative Learning Activity** in the TCR.

CAPTION ANSWER

The Irish and the Scots were in rebellion, and groups of English did not agree on the charges that had been made.

LINKING PAST TO PRESENT

One of the radical revolutionary factions of English society was the Levellers, who believed that every citizen had the right to vote. Although Cromwell considered this a dangerous idea and destroyed a Leveller-inspired mutiny, the ideas of the Levellers have finally been fulfilled in today's American democracy.

MAKING CONNECTIONS

➤➤ **History** Richard Cromwell did not have the support of the army, and he resigned after ruling only nine months.

VIDEODISC

Use the following to enrich Chapter 32.

WC E 55 19836

Coronation of Charles II in Westminster Abbey, 1661.

OLIVER CROMWELL AND KING CHARLES I Oliver Cromwell shown in this painting (left) organized the New Model Army that defeated the army of King Charles I shown in the painting above (right) in 1646. This ended the four-year civil war between the Crown and Parliament. After Charles was beheaded, Cromwell took over the rule of England, which was then called the Commonwealth. **What problems did Cromwell face as he came to power?**

with Parliament and governed as a military dictator for the Puritan minority.

Many Puritans were very strict. They disapproved of dancing, theater-going, sports, and other popular amusements. They believed people should spend their free time praying and reading the Bible. Despite this, Puritan rule was not completely gloomy. Cromwell himself was fond of music and horses, and allowed women to act on stage for the first time. After Cromwell died, his son Richard took over. By 1660, however, Parliament decided that England again needed a monarch.

The Return of the Stuarts Parliament's choice was Charles I's son, who became Charles II. Charles II had spent most of the previous 15 years in France. He brought French dances, food, and clothing styles with him to London. Soon, the English court was a center of gaiety and fashion. Men copied the fashions of Paris and wore silks and velvets and huge wigs. The wealthy ate large meals. One meal might include rabbit and chicken stew, a leg of mutton, a side of lamb, roasted pigeons, lobsters, tarts, anchovies, and wine. The English nobility was ready for this kind of living, and Charles II became very popular.

SPOTLIGHT ON: CHARLES II

Under the rule of Charles II, the Restoration period (1660-1685) was a brilliant time for literature, drama, music, architecture, and science. In 1662 Charles chartered the Royal Society to encourage investigations in science. The king had his own laboratory, where he performed experiments in chemistry. Charles also established the Royal Observatory at Greenwich. He hoped that discoveries in astronomy would produce better navigational instruments.

In September 1666, a great fire destroyed two-thirds of London's buildings. Charles II put Sir Christopher Wren, an architect, in charge of rebuilding the city. Wren designed St. Paul's Cathedral and 52 other churches. He also had most new houses and shops built of brick and stone instead of wood.

As king, Charles II tried to work with Parliament and not anger it. He refused, however, to consult with it about **foreign policy,** or relations with other countries. Parliament was worried by his friendship with the Roman Catholic king of France.

The Glorious Revolution In 1685, Charles II died and his brother James became king. Openly Roman Catholic, James II named many Roman Catholics to high posts in the army and the government. This went against a law passed by Parliament under Charles II. James II also tried to have the Act of Habeas Corpus (hā′ bē uhs kōr′ puhs) **repealed,** or abolished. That act had also been passed under Charles II. It stated that a person could not be put in jail unless charged with a specific crime.

The leaders of Parliament did not like James II. They did not move against him, however, until 1688 when his second wife, who was Roman Catholic, had a son. Fearing the ultimate establishment of Roman Catholic rule, they offered the throne to Mary, James's Protestant daughter by his first wife. William landed in England in 1688 with a large army, and James II fled to France. William and Mary were then named joint rulers. Because the change in monarchs took place without a shot being fired, it came to be called the "Glorious Revolution."

After becoming the new rulers of England in 1689, William and Mary accepted Parliament's Declaration of Rights. This made Parliament stronger and protected the rights of the English people. The declaration stated that the Crown could not tax people or keep an army in peacetime without Parliament's consent. Parliament had the right to debate openly, meet often, and be freely elected. People had the right to a fair and speedy trial by a jury of their peers. People could also petition the Crown without fear of being punished.

The Writings of John Locke Many of the ideas behind the Glorious Revolution were explained in a book called *Two Treatises of Government.* It was written in 1690 by an English philosopher named John Locke. He believed that people are born with certain natural rights. Among them are the right to life, liberty, and property. Locke believed that the purpose of government is to protect these rights. If it fails to do so, then the people can revolt and set up a new government. Locke thought the best kind of government was a representative one. His writings were widely read, and his ideas became a basis for the American Revolution and, later, the French Revolution.

Painting of Queen Mary II

L2 **Architecture** Ask students to present a report on the life and works of Sir Christopher Wren, architect to Charles II. The report should include illustrations of some of the buildings Wren designed.

L3 **Critical Thinking** Have students read and research more about the plague and how this medical problem was dealt with. Then ask students to suppose a similar plague swept through Washington, D.C. How would United States health-care officials deal with it today?

MAKING CONNECTIONS

➤➤ **Daily Life** In 1665, London was hit by the plague. It was carried by rats, who flourished in the filthy streets and old buildings. As many as 7,000 persons died in one week. They had to be buried in great pits because the churchyards were full. Business came to a standstill, and the royal court fled to the countryside.

VIDEODISC

Use the following to enrich Chapter 32.

WC E 93 19874

John Locke, philosopher and political theorist.

MEETING SPECIAL NEEDS

Have tactile/kinesthetic or gifted learners produce a "documentary" about the London fire of 1666. Make sure each student is assigned a specific task. Assign, or have students choose, a "producer" to coordinate the class effort. Some teams should be responsible for researching, writing, and presenting "news desk" reports about the fire. Other teams should prepare on-the-scene skits about the fire, such as interviews with local residents, fire fighters, or government officials. If possible, have students videotape their documentaries. Have students present their documentaries for the class.

L2 **Research** Have the students research and report on the beliefs of one of the political thinkers, philosophers, and writers of the revolutionary time period, such as John Locke *(Two Treatises of Government)*, Montesquieu *(The Spirit of Laws)*, Thomas Paine *(Common Sense* and *The Rights of Man)*, or Jean-Jacques Rousseau *(Social Contract)*. Have students do a dramatic reading of the writings of their chosen philosopher.

L1 **Civics** Students may understand the philosophies of Locke if they were applied to a specific situation. Ask students to select a problem facing their city or state, such as people thinking their taxes are too high, and address it as they think Locke might. LEP

MAKING CONNECTIONS

➤➤ **Economics** Mercantilists believed that a nation's strength depended on how much gold and silver it had. So, they emphasized foreign trade rather than the production of goods. Mercantilists also emphasized the role of the government in a nation's economy.

VIDEODISC

Use the following to enrich Chapter 32.

WC N 35 44090

European factories on the west coast of Africa.

WC N 36 44091

"Noble Savages" of the New World.

Section 1 Review

1. **Identify:** Age of Enlightenment, Crown, James I, Charles I, Petition of Right, Star Chamber, Cavaliers, Roundheads, Oliver Cromwell, New Model Army, Charles II, James II, William and Mary, Declaration of Rights, John Locke
2. **Define:** revolution, martial law, foreign policy, repealed
3. Why did civil war finally break out between the Crown and Parliament in 1642?
4. Why did Parliament remove James II from the throne?

Critical Thinking

5. What would it have meant to the English people if the Act of Habeas Corpus had been repealed?

Section 2

THE AMERICAN REVOLUTION

At first, England and its American colonies got along well. Over time, however, things changed. The colonists became angry over English controls. This led to revolution and the forming of a new country.

Mercantilism In 1660, when Charles II became king of England, most European leaders believed in an economic system called **mercantilism** (mer' kuhn tēl iz uhm). Under it, colonies served as a source of raw materials and as a market for finished products. England's colonies in America were supposed to send goods to England that were scarce or could not be grown there, such as furs, lumber, tobacco, and cotton. The colonists were supposed to buy only goods made in England so that English merchants could make money. These goods could be carried only in ships built in England or in the colonies. The ships also had to be sailed by English crews. This was to make the shipbuilding industry and merchant marine stronger in case of war.

Painting of Charles II

Mercantilism worked well until the 1700s. There were not enough skilled people in the American colonies to produce many goods. The colonists also enjoyed a **monopoly** (muh nop' uh lē), or sole right, on the sale of several major crops. In addition, their ships were protected against pirates by the English navy.

Then, things changed. With the population in the colonies growing, the colonists wanted to make their own manufactured goods, such as iron products and beaver hats. Also, people in northern colonies were not able to sell as much to England as

SECTION 1 ANSWERS

1. Age of Enlightenment, the 1700s (p. 503); Crown, royal power (p. 503); James I, Stuart king (p. 503); Charles I, Stuart king (p. 504); Petition of Right, restricted the king (p. 505); Star Chamber, royal court (p. 505); Cavaliers, Crown supporters (p. 505); Roundheads, supporters of Parliament (p. 505); Oliver Cromwell, English Puritan leader (p. 505); New Model Army, Cromwell's army (p. 505); Charles II, a Stuart king (p. 506); James II, a Stuart king (p. 507); William and Mary, English rulers (p. 507); Declaration of Rights, protected English rights (p. 507); John Locke, philosopher (p. 507)
2. All terms are defined in the text Glossary.
3. because Charles accepted the laws Parliament passed and then disregarded them
4. because Parliament was afraid of control by the Roman Catholic Church.
5. Answers will vary.

Assign the Chapter 32 **Section 1 Quiz** in the TCR. Testmaker available.

people in southern colonies did. Yet, they needed money to buy English goods. So, they began smuggling goods to and from the West Indies. Soon, a triangular, or three-way, trade grew up. The colonists shipped in sugar and molasses from the West Indies. They made rum and traded it for enslaved Africans. Then, they brought the enslaved Africans to the West Indies, where they traded them for sugar and molasses.

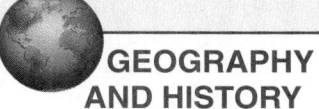

Stamp

Changes in British Policy Although England, now known as Great Britain, regulated colonial trade, the colonists handled local affairs. Their legislatures generally passed tax laws. Since colonial officials were paid out of taxes, they had to do as the colonial legislatures wished. This gave the legislatures a great deal of power.

In the middle of the 1700s, this changed. The French, who also had colonies in America, built a fort on the site of present-day Pittsburgh, Pennsylvania. The French and their Native American allies wanted to keep the British out of northern and western America. Great Britain, however, had already claimed the area for itself. The dispute led to the French and Indian War. By the time it ended in 1763, the British controlled nearly all of North America east of the Mississippi River.

The war left the British government deeply in debt. It wanted the colonies to pay a large share of the money owed. After all, the war had been fought partly to protect their western frontier. So, Great Britain moved to raise money by tightening its control over the colonies.

In 1765, Parliament passed the Stamp Act. It called for a tax on all newspapers, legal documents, calendars, and playing cards. All these items had to bear a stamp showing that the tax had been paid. This was the first **direct tax** Parliament placed on the colonies. That is, it was a tax paid directly to the government, not included in the price of the goods.

The Stamp Act hurt merchants, lawyers, and people in the newspaper business. These groups were among the most able to lead the colonists in a fight against British control. Angry mobs formed in many cities. Tax officials were threatened, and stamps were destroyed. People throughout the colonies decided to **boycott,** or refuse to buy, British goods.

In October 1765, delegates from 9 of the 13 colonies met in New York to discuss the Stamp Act. They sent a letter to the British government. It stated that the colonies had not been taxed before by anyone except their own legislatures. It also said that Parliament had no right to tax them because they did not have representatives in Parliament.

In March 1766, Parliament finally voted to repeal the Stamp Act. At the same time, however, it passed the Declaratory Act, which stated that Parliament had the right to make laws on all

L2 **History** Have students write a report about the lasting impact of the French on North America, stating when the French first came. Have them note French influences that remain, such as in the names of cities, states, and other geographical features; French customs; French foods; and so on.

GEOGRAPHY AND HISTORY

In 1707, England and Scotland united to become Great Britain. After 1707, England was referred to as Great Britain.

DID YOU KNOW

The French and Indian War is also known as the Seven Years' War. In addition to losing most of its possessions in the Americas, France was forced to leave India, which was taken over by the British East India Company.

MEETING SPECIAL NEEDS

Show students some current political cartoons from the daily newspaper or magazines. Have students who are visual learners or who have Limited English Proficiency draw a series of political cartoons depicting some of the events that led to the Revolution and how the colonists felt about the British. For example, students might draw cartoons depicting the Stamp Act, the Boston Tea Party, and the Boston Massacre. Have them write dialogue for their cartoons that explains what is being expressed.

LINKING PAST TO PRESENT

Many colonists took radical measures to rid themselves of Great Britain's political control. In every colony a volunteer army was organized and weapons collected. In New England, minutemen (so named because they could be ready for battle on a minute's notice) and state militias assembled to drill on village greens, while the town's officials stored ammunitions, weapons, and food. State militias remain in force in the United States today as National Guard troops.

MAKING CONNECTIONS

➤➤ **History** The song "Yankee Doodle" began as a song that mocked the colonists. *Macaroni* was a term used for British men who thought they were dressed in the latest styles but who actually looked ridiculous. British troops sang it as a song of ridicule. The colonists, however, loved the song and added their own verses to it. Ironically, it was to this tune that the British surrendered at Yorktown.

DID YOU KNOW ??

It is believed, yet never proven, that Samuel Adams was largely responsible for the instigation of the Boston Tea Party. The Coercive Acts, passed to punish the colonists for the Boston Tea Party, are also known as the Intolerable Acts.

Painting of British Soldier

matters concerning the colonies. This showed that Parliament was not going to give in completely to the demands of the American colonists.

The Road to Revolution In 1767, Parliament passed a series of laws known as the Townshend Acts. These acts placed a tax on such goods as paper, paint, glass, lead, and tea that were shipped to the colonies. Part of the tax money was to be used to pay colonial officials. This took away the colonial legislatures' main source of power. The following year, the British sent soldiers to Boston to make sure the colonists obeyed the new laws. The colonists called the soldiers "redcoats" because of their bright red uniforms.

The Townshend Acts made the colonists angry. Soon, there were incidents of violence. One of the worst of these took place in Boston in 1770. A crowd of colonists began insulting British soldiers and throwing stones at them. The soldiers fired into the crowd. Five people were killed. This incident came to be called the Boston Massacre. Shortly after, all the Townshend taxes were repealed except the one on tea. The Boston Massacre itself would probably have been forgotten had not some colonists used it to stir up feelings against British rule.

Three years later, Parliament passed the Tea Act. It allowed the British East India Company to sell tea directly to the colonists rather than to colonial merchants, who took part of the profits. This hurt the merchants. The act also further angered those colonists already tired of British tax policies. In Massachusetts, a group of colonists dressed as Native Americans boarded a British ship in Boston harbor and dumped its cargo of tea into the water. This event is known as the Boston Tea Party.

To punish the colonists, Parliament, in 1774, passed the Coercive (kō er' siv) Acts. These acts closed Boston harbor and put the government of Massachusetts under military rule. These acts also said that British troops in the colonies should be *quartered,* or given a place to live, in private homes. Next, Parliament passed the Quebec Act, which extended the boundaries of Quebec west of the Appalachians and north of the Ohio River. This took in land that Massachusetts, Connecticut, and Virginia claimed as their own. The colonists called these laws the Intolerable Acts, or laws they could not bear.

Painting of Boston Tea Party

The Coercive Acts only made the colonists more determined than ever to fight for their liberties. In September 1774, delegates from 12 of the colonies met in Philadelphia. They called themselves the First Continental Congress. The Congress spoke out against the Coercive Acts and called for their repeal.

Colonial leaders, however, were divided about what to do. Some, like George Washington of Virginia, hoped to settle the differences with Great Britain. Others, like Samuel Adams of

MULTICULTURAL PERSPECTIVES

As the struggle for control of the colonies began, colonial leader John Adams wrote in his diary: *The people have become more attentive to their liberties, . . . and more determined to defend them. . . . Our presses have groaned, our pulpits have thundered, our legislatures have resolved, our towns have voted; the crown officers have everywhere trembled, and all their little tools and creatures been afraid to speak and ashamed to be seen.*

Reading a Military Map

Maps that contain information about wars are called **military maps.** They show troop movements, battle sites and dates, and battle victories.

Look at the legend for the two maps below. Notice that different symbols and colors stand for American and British advances, retreats, and battle victories.

For example, the map has a solid red line to show that the British advanced to New York City, where they won a battle in August 1776. This victory is indicated by a red star. The Americans then retreated to Trenton, New Jersey, as shown by a dashed blue line.

Map Practice

1. **Which army won the battle at Saratoga, New York?**
2. **Which army advanced to Camden, South Carolina, after the Battle of Charleston?**
3. **Where did the British retreat to after the Battle of Guilford Courthouse?**

American Revolution: North **American Revolution: South**

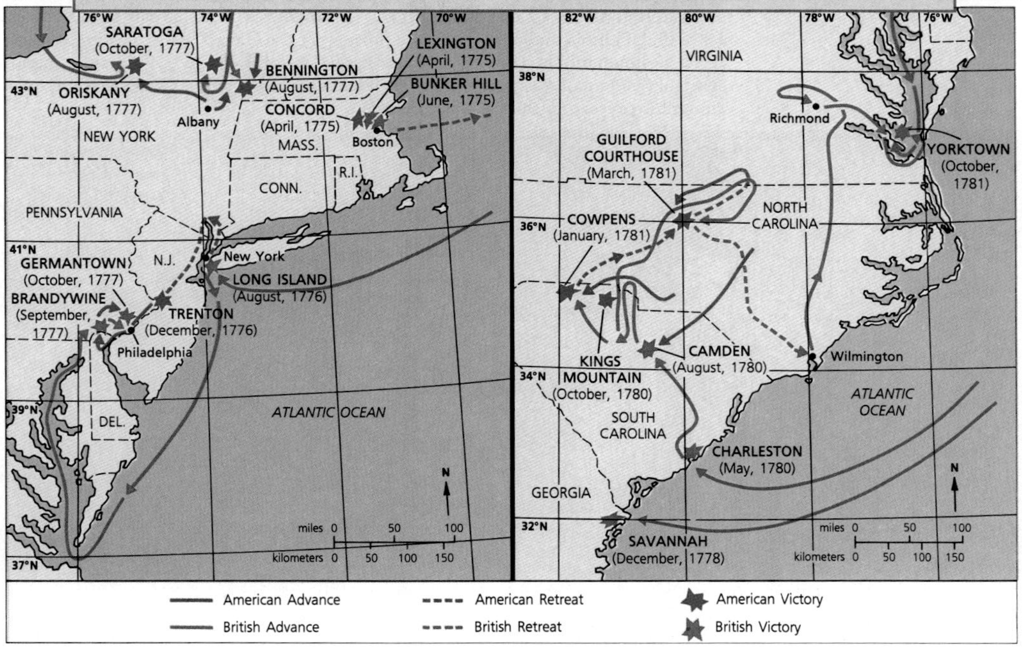

SPOTLIGHT ON: AMERICAN REVOLUTION

African Americans played an important role in the military successes that the American army was able to achieve against the British during the Revolutionary War. In 1776, Congress recruited only free African Americans. By the winter of 1777, however, General George Washington welcomed all African Americans, free or enslaved. At the time the war ended, 5,000 African Americans from all 13 states except North Carolina had served in the Continental Army. Another 2,000 had served in the colonial navy.

Teaching

MAP SKILLS

Reading a Military Map

Have the students read the instructional section of the feature. Ask: What kind of information is generally shown on a military map? *(information about wars such as troop movement, battle sites and dates, and battle victories)* Direct students to study the map. Ask: Who won most of the battles along the Atlantic coast? *(the British)* According to the maps, where did most of the fighting during the American Revolution take place, North or South? *(North)*

Next, have students use the information on the maps to create charts about the battles of the American Revolution. The charts might include the following headings: "Battles," "Dates," "Victories."

Assign the Chapter 32 **Geography and Map Activity** in the TCR.

ANSWERS to Map Practice

1. the American army
2. the British army
3. Wilmington

L3 **Critical Thinking** Help students create a chart on the chalkboard showing the similarities and differences between the English civil war and the American Revolution. Begin by posing questions such as: *What were the issues and goals of each uprising? Who were the opponents? What were the outcomes?* LEP

MAKING CONNECTIONS

History Thomas Paine had come to the American colonies from Great Britain shortly before he wrote the following thoughts in his pamphlet *Common Sense* in January 1776: *Everything that is right begs for separation from Britain. The Americans who have been killed seem to say, 'TIS TIME TO PART. England and America are located a great distance apart. That is itself strong and natural proof that God never expected one to rule over the other.*

DID YOU KNOW

When the Second Continental Congress met, Georgia was the only colony without delegates.

CAPTION ANSWER

popular sovereignty and limited government

VIDEODISC

Use the following to enrich Chapter 32.

WC E 69 19850

French vs. British fleets off Yorktown, 1781.

Massachusetts and Patrick Henry of Virginia, wanted the colonies to become independent.

The Outcome Before anything was decided, fighting broke out in Massachusetts between the colonists and British soldiers. The British set out to destroy a store of weapons at Concord. On the way there, they met the colonists at Lexington and fought the first battle of the American Revolution.

In May 1775, the Second Continental Congress met. George Washington was named head of the colonial army. The colonists then tried again to settle their differences with Great Britain. They appealed to King George III, who refused to listen.

On July 4, 1776, Congress issued the Declaration of Independence. Written mostly by Thomas Jefferson of Virginia, it stated that all men are created equal and have certain God-given rights. In the Declaration, the colonies broke away from Great Britain and declared themselves the United States of America.

War between the British and Americans dragged on. In 1778, the French, who were old enemies of Great Britain, agreed to help the Americans. In 1781, the Americans and French forced the British to surrender at Yorktown, Virginia. This ended the fighting. Two years later, the Treaty of Paris ended the war.

UNITED STATES CONSTITUTION In 1787, representatives from 12 states met in Philadelphia and drew up a constitution for the United States. George Washington is shown in this painting addressing the delegates. In 1789, Washington became the first President of the United States. **What are some principles of American government expressed in the Constitution?**

MEETING SPECIAL NEEDS

Have auditory learners debate the following topic: *The American Revolution was justified because of unfair British policies.* Divide the class into two teams, one to defend the American Revolution and the other to defend British policies. Tell students that they should base their arguments on the following: British trade laws, the Stamp Act, the Declaratory Act, the Townshend Acts, the Tea Act, the Coercive Acts, and the Quebec Acts. After giving each team time to research and develop its arguments, begin the debate and have each present its views.

In 1789, the United States adopted a constitution that set up a new form of government. The Constitution set forth certain principles of government. One of these is **popular sovereignty** (sov′ ruhn tē), or the idea that a government receives its powers from the people. Another is **limited government,** or the idea that a government may use only powers given to it by the people.

Later, ten **amendments,** or formal changes, known as the Bill of Rights, were added. The Bill of Rights guarantees all American citizens such rights as freedom of speech, press, and religion; the right to trial by jury; and freedom from unreasonable searches and seizures.

Painting of Thomas Jefferson

Section 2 Review

1. **Identify:** French and Indian War, Stamp Act, Declaratory Act, Townshend Acts, Boston Massacre, Boston Tea Party, Coercive Acts, Concord, Lexington, Declaration of Independence, Yorktown, Bill of Rights
2. **Define:** mercantilism, monopoly, direct tax, boycott, popular sovereignty, limited government, amendments
3. Why were colonial legislatures powerful?
4. How did the Townshend Acts affect the power of colonial legislatures?

Critical Thinking

5. What is your opinion of the following statement: The Bill of Rights is an important addition to the U.S. Constitution.

Section 3

THE FRENCH REVOLUTION

What happened in America influenced people in France. The American example pointed up the need for political change and helped bring about a revolution.

Old Regime During the 1600s and early 1700s—the time of the Old Regime (ri zhēm′)—France was a divine-right monarchy. French society was divided into three **estates** (e stāts′), or classes. The First Estate was the clergy. Although they made up less than 1 percent of the people, they owned 10 percent of the land. They were not only *exempt,* or free, from taxes. They also received income from church lands. Church income was not divided evenly, however. Most went to high church officials, who were generally nobles. They wore robes of purple and scarlet velvet

L1 **Government** Read the Preamble to the Declaration of Independence to the students. Discuss the certain basic rights that cannot be taken away by any government. LEP

LINKING PAST TO PRESENT

The six fundamental principles on which the U.S. Constitution was based—popular sovereignty; separation of powers among legislative, executive, and judicial branches; checks and balances; federalism; supremacy of national law; and civilian control of government—were mostly derived from English political tradition. The U.S. Constitution became a model for other later democratic constitutions.

VIDEODISC

Use the following to enrich Chapter 32.

WC E 143 19924
First estate of Orléans in assembly, 16th century.

WC E 71 19852
John Paul Jones' ship vs. H.M.S. Serapis.

SECTION 2 ANSWERS

1. French and Indian War, between Britain and France (p. 509); Stamp Act, taxed publications (p. 509); Declaratory Act, Parliament could make colonial laws (p. 509); Townshend Acts, taxed goods (p. 510); Boston Massacre, British vs. colonists (p. 510); Boston Tea Party, protest against Tea Act (p. 510); Coercive Acts, controlled Massachusetts (p. 510); Concord, city near Boston (p. 512); Lexington, city near Boston (p. 512); Declaration of Independence, formed United States (p. 512); Yorktown, city in Virginia (p. 512); Bill of Rights, amendments to the Constitution (p. 513)
2. All terms are defined in the text Glossary.
3. because they passed tax laws and controlled officials
4. took away the legislatures' main power
5. Answers will vary.

Assign the Chapter 32 **Section 2 Quiz** in the TCR. Testmaker available.

L2 **Language Arts** Ask students to brainstorm definitions of the term *revolution*. Stimulate the discussion by asking, "When are people justified in choosing revolution as a solution to political problems?" Have students write a case study of a situation they feel would justify a revolution or people taking the government into their own hands.

L3 **Daily Life** The estate into which French individuals were born was the level of society where they stayed. Have students research and write a report about other countries that had or have a similar system. The students' research might lead them to explore the class system in ancient Egypt or the caste system in India.

MAKING CONNECTIONS

➤➤ **History** From 1642 to 1715, France was ruled by Louis XIV. His was the longest rule in modern European history. Under Louis, France led Europe in the arts and had the most powerful army on the continent. After Louis, French power and influence began to decline.

VIDEODISC

Use the following to enrich Chapter 32.

WC E 164 19945
The birth of the First Republic, 1792.

WC E 145 19926
Louis XVI reigned from 1774 to 1792.

trimmed with lace. Parish priests lived simply and served people's religious needs.

The Second Estate was the nobility. They made up about 2 percent of the people and also owned large areas of land. Nobles, too, were free from taxes. They lived off grants from the royal treasury and rents paid by the peasants. Some nobles spent their time at the royal court, dancing, hunting, and gambling. Others filled the highest posts in the government and the army.

The Third Estate was everyone else in France. At the top of this class was the **bourgeoisie** (bur zhwah zē')—bankers, merchants, lawyers, doctors, manufacturers, and teachers. They controlled much of France's wealth and trade. Next were the city workers—artisans, day laborers, and servants. At the bottom were the peasants, who made up more than 80 percent of the French people.

Members of the Third Estate had no power in the government. Yet, they paid the country's taxes. They paid taxes on income, personal property, land, and crops. They paid sales taxes on salt, tobacco, and wine. Parents even paid a tax when a child was born. In addition, the peasants still paid feudal dues.

The Estates-General

By the 1780s, the French government was in trouble. Educated French writers and thinkers called ***philosophes*** (fē luh zofs'), or philosophers, wrote articles pointing out the country's political problems. One of the most widely read philosophes was Francois Marie Arouet (fran' swah muh rē' ah rwe'), known as Voltaire (vōl ter'). Voltaire favored free speech, a free press, freedom of religion, and equal justice for everyone. One of his favorite sayings was: "I do not agree with a word you say, but I will defend to the death your right to say it."

Painting of Louis XVI and Family

The major problem facing the French government, however, was a lack of money. The French government had given so much help to the colonies during the American Revolution that it was almost bankrupt. King Louis XVI and his wife added to the problem by spending money on jewels, hunting parties, horse races, and balls. In fact, Queen Marie-Antoinette (muh rē an twuh net') spent so much that France's *deficit*, or shortage of money, increased. For this reason, the French people called her Madame Deficit. The king wanted the clergy and nobles to give him money. They, however, had never paid taxes and saw no reason to start.

Finally, Louis XVI called a meeting of the French legislature to help decide how to raise money. It was the first time that this body, known as the Estates-General, had met since 1614. In the past, each of the estates had met separately, with each casting one vote. This meant the nobles and clergy together could outvote the Third Estate and protect themselves from change.

MULTICULTURAL PERSPECTIVES

Men and women were equally instrumental in spreading the Enlightenment ideas that helped to spark the French Revolution. Influential Parisian intellectuals such as Madame de Pompadour, Madame Geoffrin, and Madame du Deffand sponsored evenings of long political discussions in gatherings called salons—where writers, artists, and educated people of the middle class mingled with men and women of nobility.

Now the Third Estate wanted a bigger voice in government. "What is the Third Estate?" one of their leaders wrote in a pamphlet. "Everything. What has it been until now? Nothing. What does it demand? To become something." The members of the Third Estate wanted the Estates-General to meet as a single body with each representative having a vote. They also wanted to have the same number of representatives as the other two estates together.

In May 1789, the Estates-General met. The Third Estate was granted more representatives, but the other two estates refused to meet with it. So, the Third Estate and a small number of parish priests and nobles met as a separate body. They called themselves the National Assembly. When Louis XVI threatened to break up the National Assembly, its members swore not to do so until they had written a constitution for France. At last, the king gave in and ordered the First and Second Estates to meet with the National Assembly.

Uprisings in City and Country Meanwhile, a series of uprisings took place throughout most of France. When the Estates-General was called to meet, most French people had high hopes for change. Before long, however, they began to fear that nothing would improve. The fall harvests had been poor, and

TENNIS COURT OATH Members of the Third Estate met on a tennis court to write a new French constitution. **What was the Third Estate?**

INDEPENDENT PRACTICE

L2 **Critical Thinking** Ask students to imagine they are members of the Third Estate and to write a letter to a friend in another country expressing their thoughts in the summer of 1789.

CAPTION ANSWER

the common people of France

DID YOU KNOW ??

Francis Bacon once described philosophers as ants who are diligent but only gather useless facts. Philosophers should be like bees, he said, not ants. They should find raw materials, absorb nature's lessons, and transform these lessons into theories.

VIDEODISC

Use the following to enrich Chapter 32.

WC E 167 **19948**
The execution of Louis XVI, 1793.

WC E 169 **19950**
Marie Antoinette led to her execution.

COOPERATIVE LEARNING

Explain that during the social unrest in the United States during the 1960s, a popular slogan was "Power to the People." Ask students to debate this phrase as it might have applied to pre-revolutionary France. Organize students into two groups: one group representing the common people of the Third Estate, the other group representing the nobility and clergy of the First and Second Estates. Each group should address the statement: "More power should be given to the common people of France." Each student should have a role in preparing for or taking part in the debate.

Teaching

PEOPLE IN HISTORY

DOMINGO SARMIENTO

After students have read the People in History feature, ask: After whom did Sarmiento want to model himself? *(Benjamin Franklin)* Why was Sarmiento exiled to Chile? *(The revolution he was involved in to overthrow a local dictator failed.)*

Have students research Horace Mann, American educator, and prepare an oral report about his life and his ideas that helped reform the American school system.

ANSWERS to Checking for Understanding

1. because without it, self-government cannot work
2. He set up libraries and opened normal schools. He brought 63 teachers from the United States to train Argentinean teachers, set up evening classes for adults, and had gyms built in schools.

VIDEODISC

Use the following to enrich Chapter 32.

WH K 8 18852
Domingo Fausto Sarmiento (1811-1888).

WC E 149 19930
"The Third Estate Awakens."

PEOPLE IN HISTORY

Domingo Sarmiento

The political revolutions that took place in England, America, and France led to self-government by the people. These citizens, however, needed an education.

One of the leaders in educating people in Latin America was Domingo Sarmiento (dō mēng′ ō sahr myān′ tō). He was born in Argentina in 1811. As a child, he read Benjamin Franklin's *Autobiography* and decided to follow in Franklin's footsteps.

Exile As a teenager, Sarmiento became involved in a revolution to overthrow a local dictator. When the revolt failed, Sarmiento was **exiled** (eg′ zīld), or sent out of the country, to Chile.

In Chile, Sarmiento became a teacher. After a time, he decided to learn more about how to teach future citizens. He went to Europe to visit its schools. While in London, he read a book by Horace Mann (hor′ uhs man), an educator who had done much to reform the American school system. Sarmiento was so impressed with Mann's book that he traveled to the United States, knocked on the door of Mann's house, and started asking him questions.

Reformer Later, after returning to Chile, Sarmiento began carrying out many of the educational reforms he had seen abroad. He set up libraries and opened **normal schools,** or schools that trained teachers. He improved education in Chile so much that he was asked to come back to Argentina to do the same there.

When he returned to Argentina, Sarmiento brought 63 teachers from the United States to train Argentinian teachers. He set up evening classes for adults and built gyms in schools.

In later years, Sarmiento became the Argentinian ambassador to the United States and was elected President of Argentina. Sarmiento died in 1888, knowing that he had tried to help people become better citizens through education.

Checking for Understanding

1. **Why is it important for citizens to have an education?**
2. **What educational reforms did Sarmiento bring to Chile? To Argentina?**

SPOTLIGHT ON: DOMINGO SARMIENTO

In 1868 Domingo Sarmiento was elected president of Argentina. As president, Sarmiento encouraged and worked for public education—including libraries and museums, increased trade, increased agricultural production, and improved transportation and communication systems. He believed in and worked for democratic principles such as civil liberties.

food was scarce and expensive. A loaf of bread cost more than a day's pay. The winter was so cold that water froze in front of fireplaces. Hundreds of thousands of city workers were unemployed.

In Paris, mobs began to form. On July 14, 1789, a mob in search of weapons attacked and captured the Bastille (ba stēl'). This was an old fort used as a prison. To the mob, it was a symbol of the **tyranny** (tir' uh nē), or unjust use of power, of the monarchy. The mob then killed the mayor of Paris and set up a new city government.

News of what happened in Paris spread. In the countryside, there were rumors that the nobles were planning to hire *brigands* (brig' uhndz), or roving bandits, to destroy the peasants' homes and crops. So, the peasants attacked and burned the houses of the nobles, and destroyed all records of feudal dues.

The National Assembly

The uprisings caused the National Assembly to act. To calm the people, it did away with the privileges of the clergy and nobles.

On August 27, 1789, the Assembly issued the Declaration of the Rights of Man and the Citizen. It said that people "are born equal and remain free and equal in rights." It said that the government's right to rule came from the people, not from the

FRENCH PEASANTS Farmers of the French countryside worked hard to raise their crops. They were tired of paying most of their earnings to the nobles. **What did peasants in the countryside do to show their unhappiness when they heard about the riots in Paris?**

CAPTION ANSWER

Peasants attacked and burned the houses of nobles.

MAKING CONNECTIONS

➤➤ **History** One famous French philosopher was François Marie Arouet, whose pen name was Voltaire. He wrote poetry, plays, essays, and books in a style that was entertaining and often satirical. He served time in the Bastille for his writings that mocked the Church and the royal court of France.

LINKING PAST TO PRESENT

Bastille Day, July 14, is celebrated as a national holiday in France every year with speeches, parades, and dancing in the streets.

VIDEODISC

Use the following to enrich Chapter 32.

WC E 158 19939

"Long Live the King! Long Live the Nation!"

MULTICULTURAL PERSPECTIVES

During the late 1700s the people of the Third Estate in France grew increasingly unhappy with their country's social structure. An Englishman, Arthur Young, traveling in France in 1789, recorded the following conversation with a French peasant woman in *Travels: Walking up a long hill . . . I was joined by a poor woman who complained of the times, and that it was a sad country; . . . she said her husband had but a morsel of land, one cow, and a poor little horse, yet they had* [42 lbs.] *of wheat and three chickens to pay as rent to one* [lord], *and* [four lbs.] *of oats, one chicken and 1s.* [shilling] *to pay another, besides very heavy tailles and other taxes.*

L2 **The Arts** The Enlightenment played a great role in shaping French political thought before and during the Revolution. Have students research and write a brief biography on an artist, philosopher, or writer of the Enlightenment and that person's ideas about the French Revolution.

MAKING CONNECTIONS

➤➤ **Religion** Under freedom of religion, Huguenots had the same civil rights as Catholics. Also, for the first time, Jews were allowed to become citizens.

LINKING PAST TO PRESENT

The card game solitaire is said to have been invented by a French nobleman sentenced to solitary confinement in the Bastille.

VIDEODISC

Use the following to enrich Chapter 32.

WC E 176 19957
Assignats, currency during French Revolution.

Crown. It gave everyone freedom of speech and the right to share in government. The ideas of equal rights and individual freedoms came mostly from the philosophes and from the English and American revolutions.

For the next two years, the National Assembly worked to write a constitution. At the same time, to pay off what the government owed, it began selling church lands to peasants. Although many peasants now owned land for the first time, the Roman Catholic Church was angered. It was further angered when the National Assembly declared that the clergy should be elected and should swear an oath to the government. The Church did not like being brought under state authority.

In 1791, a constitution was finished. It established freedom of religion and made France a **constitutional monarchy.** Under this kind of government, the ruler's power is limited by written law. The Crown and the legislature would govern together. Both representatives and voters had to have a certain amount of wealth. This pleased the bourgeoisie because it gave them the power they wanted. It did not please most peasants and the ***sans-culottes*** (san skū lahts'), or city workers, because they did not have enough money to vote. (The word "sans-culottes" means "without knee breeches." Wealthy men wore knee breeches and silk stockings. Workers wore long pants.)

The End of the Monarchy

Many of the ideas of the French Revolution spread to other countries. Rulers throughout Europe were afraid that these ideas would weaken their own power. French ***émigrés*** (em' uh grāz), or political exiles, encouraged the rulers to march into France and help Louis XVI take back control of the government. Many of the French revolutionary leaders also wanted war because it would unite the French people. Before any country could act, in the spring of 1792 France declared war on Austria, where the queen's brother ruled.

Painting of Sans-culotte

At first, the war did not go well for France. By August 1792, Austrian and Prussian armies were marching toward Paris. Meanwhile, in the city, the sans-culottes took over. They set up a new government called the National Convention. It made France a republic. The following year, Louis XVI and Marie Antoinette were executed. As a result, more European countries joined the war against France.

Threats from outside and inside the country made the new French government take drastic action. Although another constitution was written, it never was put into force. Instead, the Committee of Public Safety, led by a lawyer named Maximilien de Robespierre (mak suh mil' yuhn duh rōbz' piuhr), took over the government. Thousands of people, suspected of being against the Revolution, lost their lives to the **guillotine** (gil' uh tēn). This was a machine with a heavy blade that fit between two wooden

COOPERATIVE LEARNING

Have the class work together to plan the front page of the *Revolutionary Times,* a newspaper chronicling the events of the French Revolution. The newspaper should have headlines, articles, and visuals. Divide the class into groups and have each group list the stories and visuals they would put on the front page. As a group they can decide which event gets the top headline and where the other lead articles and visuals should go. Then, as a class, the groups can decide on the final placement of stories and visuals.

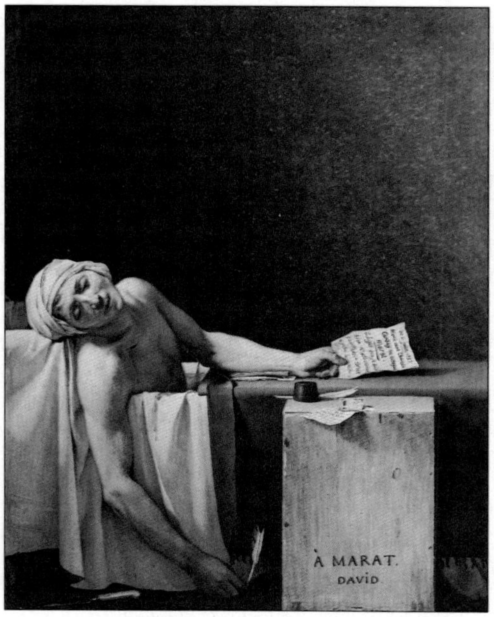

REIGN OF TERROR This is a painting of the French revolutionary leader Jean-Paul Marat who was stabbed to death in 1793 (left) by a young aristocratic woman who opposed Marat's policies. Another victim of the times was the wife of Louis XVI, Queen Marie-Antoinette shown in this painting (right). She was executed for treason in October 1793. **Why was this period known as the "Reign of Terror"?**

posts. When it was released, the blade came crashing down and cut off the victim's head. The wave of killing came to be known as the "Reign of Terror." Because of it, the people began to turn against Robespierre. In 1794, government leaders had him executed.

The following year, a third constitution was written. It set up a government known as the Directory. Besides the legislature, there was an executive branch with five directors. Only people who owned land could vote.

Under the new government, most reforms of the Revolution came to an end. The people of France had grown more conservative. The Directory spent its time trying to handle food shortages, rising prices, government bankruptcy, and attacks by other countries.

One reform that did remain was the idea that all French people had the right to choose their government. Another was a standard system of weights and measures known as the metric

CAPTION ANSWER

because of mass killings of those suspected of opposing the revolution

MAKING CONNECTIONS

>> **History** Historians estimate that about 40,000 people were executed during the Reign of Terror.

DID YOU KNOW ??

The guillotine was considered a "humane" way of execution at the time. Beheading was quick and merciful. It was the official instrument of execution in 1792 and was used until capital punishment was officially abolished in France in 1981.

MULTICULTURAL PERSPECTIVES

The French Revolution destroyed an entire society and began a new era in France. Since France led European and colonial fashion, the styles of the revolutionary period influenced the rest of Europe and America. The revolutionary fashions were simplistic, at least in comparison to the brocade gowns, embroidered waistcoats, and large powdered wigs of the previous social system of France. During the Reign of Terror, wearing the old styles became dangerous. Anyone whose clothes suggested luxury was likely to be seized as an aristocrat and sent to the guillotine. Because England represented political freedom, the new fashions imitated English country styles, with muslin and broadcloth in place of silks and satins.

ASSESS

CHECK FOR UNDERSTANDING

Ask students to summarize the main points of the chapter, orally or in writing. Discuss the answers to the Section and Chapter Review questions.

EVALUATE

Assign the Chapter 32 **Performance Assessment Activity** in the TCR.

Administer the **Chapter 32 Test**. Testmaker available.

RETEACH

Have students make time lines of the major events in the chapter.

Assign the Chapter 32 **Reteaching Activity** in the TCR.

ENRICH

Have students read a book—fiction or nonfiction—related to events of this chapter, and deliver an oral report about the book to the class.

Assign the Chapter 32 **Enrichment Activity** in the TCR.

CLOSE

Have students discuss how the following slogan would have applied in each of the revolutions in this chapter: "No taxation without representation."

MEETING CHAPTER OBJECTIVES

Each objective is tested by the Review questions in parentheses.

1. Summarize how revolution in England began. (BV; CU 1, 2, 3; CT 2)

2. Identify what British policies led to the American Revolution. (BV; CU 4, 5; CT 1)

3. Explain the French Revolution and its results. (BV; CU 7, 8; CT 1, 2, 3)

system, which the National Assembly adopted in 1791. Metrics, a system of numbers that is based on powers of ten, helped scientists carry out experiments and made international trade easier. Today, metrics are used by all major countries in the world except the United States.

Section 3 Review

1. **Identify:** Old Regime, Voltaire, Madame Deficit, National Assembly, Declaration of the Rights of Man and the Citizen, Maximilien de Robespierre, Reign of Terror, Directory
2. **Define:** estates, bourgeoisie, *philosophes,* tyranny, constitutional monarchy, *sans-culottes, émigrés,* guillotine
3. What groups made up the three French estates?
4. What did the National Assembly do about the uprisings in 1789?
5. Why did most reforms of the French Revolution come to an end under the Directory?

Critical Thinking

6. How was the Declaration of the Rights of Man and the Citizen similar to the American Declaration of Independence?

Chapter Summary

1. As a result of new ideas about freedom and government, the 1700s are known in the western world as the Age of Enlightenment.
2. England's political revolution began during the 1600s when the Crown and Parliament disagreed about rule by divine right and about religion.
3. In 1642, disagreements between the king and Parliament led to civil war and the overthrow of the rule of Charles I.
4. In 1689, Parliament passed the Declaration of Rights, which made Parliament stronger and protected the rights of the English people.
5. In 1776, disagreements between the American colonies and Great Britain led to the Declaration of Independence and a war that made the colonies an independent nation.
6. In 1789, the United States adopted a constitution that set up a new form of government in which the people have the right to govern themselves.
7. In 1789, to help decide how to raise money, the French king called a meeting of the Estates-General.
8. The French Revolution expressed the idea that people have the right to choose their own government.

SECTION 3 ANSWERS

1. Old Regime, the 1600s to early 1700s (p. 513); Voltaire, a *philosophe* (p. 514); Madame Deficit, Queen Marie-Antoinette (p. 514); National Assembly, government body (p. 515); Declaration of the Rights of Man and the Citizen, equal rights for people (p. 517); Maximilien de Robespierre, French leader (p. 518); Reign of Terror; killing in France (p. 519); Directory, French government (p. 519)
2. All terms are defined in the text Glossary.
3. the clergy, the nobility, and the bourgeoisie, city workers, and peasants
4. It ended the privileges of the clergy and nobles.
5. because the people of France had grown more conservative
6. Answers will vary but might include that both protected the rights of the people.

Assign the Chapter 32 **Section 3 Quiz** in the TCR. Testmaker available.

CHAPTER 32 Review

Building Vocabulary

Sort these words describing the revolutions in England, America, and France by the country to which each applies (words may be used more than once). Use the following words to write a sentence or two about each country's revolution.

revolution	boycott
martial law	estates
mercantilism	bourgeoisie
monopoly	tyranny
direct tax	constitutional monarchy
popular sovereignty	

Check for Understanding

1. What were some Puritan beliefs?
2. Why did Charles I dismiss Parliament?
3. Why was the Glorious Revolution called "glorious"?
4. Why did Great Britain tighten its control over the American colonies?
5. How did colonists respond to the Stamp Act?
6. What did the Declaration of Independence do?
7. Who had the most power in the French government before the French Revolution? After the Revolution?
8. Why were European rulers afraid of the ideas of the French Revolution?

Critical Thinking

1. What economic questions played a part in the American Revolution? In the French Revolution?
2. What were the most important political issues that played a part in England's Glorious Revolution?
3. Do you agree or disagree with the idea that people have a right to rule themselves? Explain.
4. Why are the 1700s known as the Age of Enlightenment?

Geography in History

MOVEMENT Look at the maps of the American Revolution on page 511. The advances and retreats of both armies are shown. About how many miles (or kilometers) did the British advance from the battle at Long Island, New York to the battle at Brandywine, Pennsylvania?

Using Your Journal

Review the details you have noted about the changes in government that took place in the 1700s. Imagine you are setting up your own country with its own government. Using ideas you have noted, write a description of what you think would be the perfect government.

CHAPTER 32 REVIEW ANSWERS

BUILDING VOCABULARY

England: revolution, martial law, mercantilism, tyranny, direct tax; America: revolution, foreign policy, monopoly, boycott, popular sovereignty; France: revolution, sans-culottes, mercantilism, tyranny, estates, bourgeoisie, constitutional monarchy. Sentences will vary.

CHECK FOR UNDERSTANDING

1. freedom of worship, hard work, and having a say in government
2. because it had limited the Crown's power
3. because the change in monarchs took place without gunfire
4. because the French and Indian War left the British government in debt
5. Angry mobs threatened tax officials, and British goods were boycotted.
6. It stated that all men are created equal with certain rights, and the colonies were an independent nation.
7. the king; the Directory
8. because these ideas would weaken their own power

CRITICAL THINKING

1. mercantilism, direct taxes, and a boycott of British goods; exemption of a few from taxes, the nation's deficit, and high food prices
2. the conflict between Parliament and the king
3. Answers will vary but students should provide reasons.
4. Answers will vary.

+ BONUS +
TEST QUESTION
For Chapter 32 Test

Choose one of the revolutions you have read about and identify one thing that could have been done to avoid that revolution. Explain. *(Answers will vary.)*

USING YOUR JOURNAL

Descriptions will vary but should include some of the governmental principles discussed. You might call on volunteers to read their letters to the class.

GEOGRAPHY IN HISTORY

about 575 miles (or 925 km)

CHAPTER 33 Rise of Industry

CHAPTER ORGANIZER

Objectives	Special Features	Supplemental Materials
Section 1 Scientific Revolution Summarize the inventions and discoveries that marked the Scientific Revolution.		• Reproducible Lesson Plan • Section 1 Quiz • Testmaker • Chapter 33 Vocabulary and Guided Reading Activity • Chapter 33 Cooperative Learning Activity • The Western Civilization Videodisc
Section 2 Agricultural Revolution Explain what the Agricultural Revolution was and how it contributed to the Industrial Revolution.		• Reproducible Lesson Plan • Section 2 Quiz • Testmaker • Chapter 33 Teaching Transparencies and Activities • Chapter 33 Activity Book Activity
Section 3 Industrial Revolution Discuss the development of the Industrial Revolution.		• Reproducible Lesson Plan • Section 3 Quiz • Testmaker • Unit 10 Primary Source Reading • Reinforcing Social Studies Skills, pp. 13, 27
Section 4 Industrial Impact Describe what the effects of industrialization were.		• Reproducible Lesson Plan • Section 4 Quiz • Testmaker • The Western Civilization Videodisc
Section 5 Spread of Industry Analyze how industrialization continued and spread.		• Reproducible Lesson Plan • Section 5 Quiz • Testmaker • Chapter 33 Geography and Map Activity • Chapter 33 Chart and Graph Skill Activity • The Western Civilization Videodisc
Chapter 33 Review and Evaluation		• Chapter 33 Reteaching Activity • Chapter 33 Enrichment Activity • Chapter 33 Performance Assessment Activity • Chapter 33 Test • Testmaker • Audiocassettes (English and Spanish)

If time does not permit teaching the entire chapter, use the Chapter 33 Summary on page 536 and the Chapter 33 Audiocassettes (English and Spanish) to point out the main ideas of the chapter.

✓ Performance Assessment Activities

Writing Commercials Ask each student to select an invention or discovery of the 1400s-1800s and write a promotional flyer or commercial promoting the product. Have students present their commercials to the class.

Essay Have students write an essay that discusses problems related to the Industrial Revolution with which we are still dealing today. Some suggestions include pollution, labor/management disputes, or urban decay. Have students suggest possible solutions that may have been overlooked.

CHAPTER RESOURCES

LITERATURE ABOUT THE PERIOD

Dickens, Charles. *Oliver Twist*. Bantam Books, 1982. The saga of an orphan's adventures in industrial London.

Twain, Mark. *Life on the Mississippi*. Harper & Bros., 1951. An autobiographical account of Twain's years as a steamboat pilot.

READINGS FOR THE STUDENT

Hart, Roger. *English Life in the Eighteenth Century*. Putnam's Sons, 1970. A look at everyday English life and culture in the 18th century.

Macaulay, David. *Mill*. Houghton Mifflin, 1983. Detailed drawings and clear descriptions of the history and construction of a typical New England mill.

READINGS FOR THE TEACHER

Avery, Gillian. *The Echoing Green: Memories of Victorian Youth*. Viking Press, 1974. Actual diaries and memories recreate life in the 1800s.

Smith, Page. *The Rise of Industrial America*. Facts on File, 1980. Examines the industrialization of the United States between the years 1876 and 1901.

Thompson, Paul. *The Edwardians: The Remaking of British Society*. Indiana University Press, 1975. Focuses on social change and class differences in Great Britain in the late 1800s.

MULTIMEDIA RESOURCES

The Industrial Revolution. International Film Bureau. Film. Features the Industrial Revolution in Great Britain.

The Industrial Revolution: Beginnings in the United States. Encyclopedia Britannica. Video. Traces the growth of the Industrial Revolution in the United States.

Industrializing America: A Game of American Industrial Development. Social Studies School Service. Software, Apple. The growth and decline of key American industries are traced in this simulation.

INTRODUCE

CHAPTER 33 OVERVIEW

Chapter 33 traces the rise of industry in Europe and North America during the 1700s and 1800s and advancements in agriculture, textile production, mining, and transportation.

- **Section 1** examines changes in scientific thinking that led to the Scientific Revolution.
- **Section 2** describes developments in farming that led to the Agricultural Revolution.
- **Section 3** summarizes the major developments that led to the Industrial Revolution.
- **Section 4** examines the effects of industrialization on the standard of living.
- **Section 5** describes how industrialization spread.

CHAPTER OBJECTIVES

After reading Chapter 33, students will be able to:

1. summarize the inventions of the Scientific Revolution.
2. explain the Agricultural Revolution.
3. discuss the development of the Industrial Revolution.
4. describe the effects of industrialization .
5. analyze how industrialization spread.

EXAMINING THE ILLUSTRATION

Ask students what a textile mill produces. Ask why such mills were often located along rivers.

PERFORMANCE ASSESSMENT

Use the Performance Assessment activities on page 522B to help you evaluate students as they complete the chapter.

CHAPTER 33 Rise of Industry

Samuel Slater's Textile Mill

TEACHER CLASSROOM RESOURCES

- Section Quizzes/Chapter Test
- Enrichment Activity
- Chart and Graph Skill Activity
- Geography and Map Activity
- Vocabulary and Guided Reading Activity
- Cooperative Learning Activity
- Performance Assessment Activity
- Spanish Summary and Glossary
- Unit 10 Primary Source Reading
- Teaching Transparencies and Activities
- Audiocassettes (English and Spanish)
- Testmaker
- The Western Civilization Videodisc

Chapter Focus

READ TO DISCOVER:

- What inventions and discoveries marked the Scientific Revolution.
- How the Agricultural Revolution contributed to the Industrial Revolution.
- How the Industrial Revolution developed.
- What the effects of industrialization were.
- How industrialization continued and spread.

By the 1700s, people in the western world not only had new ideas about government but also new ideas about science. These, in turn, led to the development of new forms of power and new ways of making goods. Industry and ways of living changed. In fact, they changed so much that historians call these changes the Industrial Revolution.

The Industrial Revolution involved the shift from animal and human power to machine power. This meant that society became less agricultural and more industrial.

During the early years of the Industrial Revolution, Great Britain took the lead. Later, other countries rose to challenge Great Britain.

1600 A.D.–1800 A.D.

KEY TERMS

enclosure
textile
domestic system
spinning jenny
factory system
interchangeable parts
automation
assembly line
open-hearth process
macadam road
trade unions
industrialized
immigrants

Section 1

SCIENTIFIC REVOLUTION

Many of the changes that occurred during the Industrial Revolution grew out of changes in scientific thinking. Beginning in the 1400s, scientists started to break away from old ideas. They used the scientific method to form and test their own hypotheses. This became known as the Scientific Revolution.

Nicolaus Copernicus (kuh per' nuh kuhs) was one of the first people to use the scientific method. Copernicus was a Polish astronomer who studied the motion of the planets. What he saw proved to him that Ptolemy was wrong and that Earth was not the center of the universe. In 1543, Copernicus published a book explaining his idea that planets revolve around the sun rather

FOCUS

BELLRINGER

Have students write the names of three appliances that they use frequently.

MOTIVATIONAL ACTIVITY

Have students share the names of appliances they use frequently. Ask students to discuss how their lives would be affected if these appliances did not exist. How important are factory-made goods in our society? Tell the students that in this chapter they will learn about inventions that led to the Industrial Revolution.

VOCABULARY PRE-CHECK

Write the key terms for this chapter on the chalkboard. Ask students to use those that they know in sentences.

Assign Chapter 33 **Vocabulary and Guided Reading Activity** in the TCR.

EXTRA CREDIT PROJECT

Have interested students research and report to the rest of the class about the patent system in the United States today. Tell them to include all details of applying for and receiving this protection. Encourage students to write a patent application for one of the inventions they learn about in this chapter as if they were the inventor.

KEY TO ABILITY LEVELS

Teaching strategies have been coded for varying learning styles and abilities.

L1 Level 1 activities are **basic** activities and should be within the ability range of all students.

L2 Level 2 activities are **average** activities and should be within the ability range of the average to above-average student.

L3 Level 3 activities are **challenging** activities designed for the ability range of above-average students.

LEP LEP activities should be within the ability range of Limited English Proficiency students.

VIDEODISC

Use the following to enrich Chapter 33.

WC M 76 41406
One of Leeuwenhoek's earliest microscopes.

TEACH

GUIDED PRACTICE

L1 **Critical Thinking** New interest in science led to discoveries and philosophies based on reason. Lead students in defining reason. *(the logical and systematic way of proving a case by supporting it with facts)*

L2 **Science** Have students choose one of the scientists discussed in the chart on this page. Have them research the inventions or discoveries of their chosen scientists, including lesser-known inventions. Then have students create a visual presentation of their inventor's achievements. Students may choose to role-play their scientist in their presentation.

MAKING CONNECTIONS

➤➤ **History** Great Britain pioneered in the Industrial Revolution because it possessed the factors of industrialization, including (1) capital, (2) a mobile labor force, (3) natural resources, (4) entrepreneurs, (5) a new technology, (6) markets, (7) a supportive government.

VIDEODISC

Use the following to enrich Chapter 33.

WC M 78 41408
Von Guericke experimented with vacuum pump.

WC M 117 41447
Tycho Brahe (1546-1601), Danish astronomer.

SCIENTISTS

NAME	FIELD	ACCOMPLISHMENTS
Johannes Kepler *Germany*	*Astronomy*	announced laws of movement of planets, 1609
William Harvey *England*	*Medicine*	published theory on human blood circulation, 1628
Sir Isaac Newton *England*	*Physics*	stated laws of motion and theory of gravitation, 1687
Antoine-Laurent Lavoisier *France*	*Chemistry*	discovered nature of combustion, 1777
John Dalton *England*	*Chemistry*	announced atomic theory, 1803
Maria Mitchell *United States*	*Astronomy*	discovered new comet, 1847
Charles Darwin *England*	*Biology*	advanced theory on development of plants and animals, 1858
Gregor Mendel *Austria*	*Botany*	discovered principles of heredity, 1866
Louis Pasteur *France*	*Medicine*	advanced germ theory of disease, 1876; successfully vaccinated against rabies, 1885
Pierre Curie **Marie Curie** *France*	*Chemistry*	discovered radium and polonium, 1898

COOPERATIVE LEARNING

Divide the class into two groups to role-play a presentation on the solar system by Galileo before a group consisting of opposing academic and Church leaders. Have the first group plan Galileo's presentation in a manner that is convincing and tactful. The second group should prepare the academic and Church leaders' rebuttal. Within each group, have students assume tasks such as conducting research, listing arguments, anticipating responses, and taking part in the role play. After the presentation and rebuttal, have the class evaluate the statements and identify which group had the most convincing argument and why.

Assign the Chapter 33 **Cooperative Learning Activity** in the TCR.

than around Earth. This book began a complete change in scientific thinking.

Another important scientist was the Italian astronomer Galileo Galilei (gal uh lē′ ō gal uh lā′ ē). He invented a telescope and began to study the stars and planets. He learned that the moon's surface is not smooth but has mountains and craters. He learned that the Milky Way holds a vast number of stars and that the sun rotates on its axis. Galileo was strongly criticized by the Roman Catholic Church for teaching that Earth revolves around the sun. Even so, Galileo's ideas spread throughout Europe.

In 1642, the same year Galileo died, another important scientist, Sir Isaac Newton (ī′ zuhk nūt′ n), was born in England. It was Newton who explained the theory of gravitation and how objects move through space. The technology for today's rockets and space satellites is based on his work.

It was at this time that scientists in Great Britain and France formed organizations in which they could discuss their ideas and research. In this way, scientific information began to spread more quickly. Soon, thousands of people were using the scientific method to add to their knowledge and improve their lives.

Painting of Copernicus

Section 1 Review

1. **Identify:** Industrial Revolution, Scientific Revolution, Nicolaus Copernicus, Galileo Galilei, Sir Isaac Newton
2. What scientific discoveries were made by Galileo Galilei?
3. Why were Sir Isaac Newton's theories important?

Critical Thinking

4. Why was the time beginning in the 1400s known as the Scientific Revolution?

Section 2 Agricultural Revolution

As changes were taking place in science, there were new developments in farming. These changes were called the Agricultural Revolution. It set the stage for the Industrial Revolution.

By the 1700s, a system of land division called **enclosure** (en klō′ zhuhr) was in use in Great Britain. Landowners combined the many small strips of land worked by tenant farmers into large areas closed in by fences, hedges, or ditches. Enclosure allowed landowners to make more money. Now, whole areas could grow the same crop. This meant larger harvests and greater profits. Landowners also needed fewer workers.

Example of Animal Power

DID YOU KNOW ??

French law outlawed the dissection of any human bodies. English law allowed the dissection of executed criminals only. These laws prevailed until the Anatomy Act of 1832. This act allowed, but regulated, anatomical studies and corpse distribution. Some physicians, wanting additional bodies, went so far as to purchase them from grave robbers.

MAKING CONNECTIONS

➤➤ **Science** Changes also took place in medicine. In 1628, Dr. William Harvey discovered that blood circulates in one direction through the body. In 1718, Lady Mary Wortley Montague brought the Chinese practice of inoculation against smallpox from Turkey to England.

VIDEODISC

Use the following to enrich Chapter 33.

WC M 179 41509

Marie Curie at the Radium Institute, 1919.

SECTION 1 ANSWERS

1. Industrial Revolution, time in which industry developed (p. 523); Scientific Revolution, time when scientific method was used (p. 523); Nicolaus Copernicus, Polish astronomer (p. 523); Galileo Galilei, Italian astronomer (p. 525); Sir Isaac Newton, English scientist (p. 525)
2. that the planets revolve around the sun
3. because his work formed the basis for today's rockets
4. This was a time when scientists broke away from old theories and used the scientific method.

Assign the Chapter 33 **Section 1 Quiz** in the TCR. Testmaker available.

L1 **Critical Thinking** Ask students to analyze the term *revolution.* What revolutions have they studied besides the Industrial Revolution? *(English, American, French political revolutions)* What changes occurred? *(changes in government and in society)* Ask if they think these changes were positive or negative. LEP

GEOGRAPHY AND HISTORY

In farming developments, Viscount Charles Townshend introduced the system of rotating crops. Instead of letting a field lie fallow for one year, Townshend planted such crops as alfalfa and clover, which restore nitrogen to the soil and make it more fertile. Townshend was nicknamed "Turnip" because he encouraged farmers to grow root crops.

DID YOU KNOW ??

The 1800s saw many innovations in Great Britain's textile industry. In 1807 the die-stamped metal button was invented. In 1820 T. Hancock invented the first elastic fabric. Called webbing, it replaced the ribbons that secured women's shoes.

VIDEODISC

Use the following to enrich Chapter 33.

WC M 98 41428

A spinning jenny.

The tenant farmers had two choices. They could stay on as paid workers, or they could look elsewhere for jobs. Most left to find work in other places. They moved to cities and became industrial workers.

Enclosure was just part of the revolution in agriculture. New ways of growing crops and breeding animals were also developed. These changes led to greater production of food. More food meant better health and longer life spans. Population increased, and the demand for manufactured goods grew.

Section 2 Review

1. **Identify:** Agricultural Revolution
2. **Define:** enclosure
3. Why did the landowners use the enclosure system?
4. How did the growth in population influence the Industrial Revolution?

Critical Thinking

5. Do you think agriculture was more or less important in the 1700s than it is today in Great Britain?

Section 3

INDUSTRIAL REVOLUTION

The Industrial Revolution began in the early 1700s. It was a long, slow process at first. However, as one development led to another, the revolution moved faster and faster. Much of the world changed. By the 1850s, the changes had become so widespread that people realized they were entering a new age.

Painting of Cottage Worker

The Textile Industry The Industrial Revolution began in Great Britain in the **textile** (tek' stuhl), or woven cloth, industry. In the 1600s and early 1700s, cloth was made by the **domestic system.** Under this system, most work was done in workers' cottages, where families worked together. Merchants went from cottage to cottage, bringing the workers raw wool and cotton. Using hand-powered spinning wheels and looms, the workers would spin the thread and weave it into wool and cotton cloth. The merchants then picked up the finished cloth to sell.

The domestic system could not meet the strong growing demand for cloth. Before long, people started looking for ways to make more cloth in less time. The first major breakthrough came in 1733 when a British inventor named John Kay invented the

SECTION 2 ANSWERS

1. Agricultural Revolution, time of change in farming (p. 525)
2. enclosure, land division (p. 525)
3. They could grow the same crop over a large area with fewer workers.
4. As the population increased, the demand for manufactured goods grew.
5. Answers will vary but might include growing organic crops and hybrid crops.

Assign the Chapter 33 **Section 2 Quiz** in the TCR. Testmaker available.

flying shuttle. It was mounted on rollers, and one weaver could send it rapidly from one side of a loom to the other. It cut in half the time needed to weave cloth. Now, however, spinners could not keep up with the weavers. Then, in 1764, James Hargreaves (hahr′ grēvz), a British carpenter, invented the **spinning jenny.** It had a number of spindles fastened to a single wheel. The jenny made it possible for one person to spin many threads at the same time.

More progress was made when ways were found to use the power of falling water instead of hand power to run textile machines. This meant, however, that the machines had to be near a large water supply. Accordingly, factories were built next to rivers that could supply the necessary water power. This was the beginning of the **factory system,** which brought workers and machines together in one place to make goods. Workers still lived in their cottages, but they came to factories to work. In time, towns grew up around these factories.

Water power did not work very well with heavy machinery. So, people began looking for still another source of power. In 1769, a Scottish mechanic named James Watt perfected the steam engine. Steam soon replaced water as the major source of power. Factories of all kinds could now be set up near raw materials and town markets.

Cotton farmers in America and in India could not supply enough raw cotton to meet the needs of British textile factories. Eli Whitney (ē′ lī hwit′ nē), an American inventor, found a way to solve this problem. While visiting a cotton plantation in Georgia, he learned that it took a great deal of time to clean the seeds out of cotton by hand. In 1793, with the help of Catherine Littlefield Greene, he invented the **cotton gin,** or cotton-cleaning machine. It could clean cotton 50 times faster than a person working by hand. If it were driven by water power, it could clean cotton 1,000 times faster.

Picture of Cotton Gin

Organizing Production

About five years later, Whitney developed a new way of organizing production. This was the system of **interchangeable parts,** which means that a certain part of a product is the same size and shape as that same part in another product. Whitney first used interchangeable parts in the making of guns. Until that time, each gun was made individually, and no two guns were alike. Broken parts had to be specially made by a skilled worker in order to fit a specific gun. Whitney's use of parts of identical size and shape made it possible for less-skilled workers to make or fix guns much faster.

Other Americans also developed new ways of organizing production. In the late 1700s, a shopkeeper-mechanic named Oliver Evans was the first to use **automation,** or the process in which machines instead of people do much of the labor. Evans'

L2 **Science** Have students research and make a flow chart showing how cloth was made using the domestic system. Encourage them to illustrate their chart and share it with the class. LEP

DID YOU KNOW ??

The technological breakthrough took place in the manufacture of cotton cloth rather than woolen cloth partly because cotton fibers are very adaptable to machinery.

MAKING CONNECTIONS

➤➤ **History** The invention of the cotton gin brought about social changes as well as economic ones. Enslavement in the southern states of the United States increased partly because of it.

VIDEODISC

Use the following to enrich Chapter 33.

WC M 85 41415
Making steel by the Bessemer process.

WC O 39 46861
Steam power applied to mining, 1835.

MEETING SPECIAL NEEDS

To help students of Limited English Proficiency organize and remember information about the people in this chapter, have them make a graphic organizer of the names of these people and their achievements. Have the students work in pairs to classify and then quiz each other; for example, "Who was Galileo Galilei?" "He was an astronomer." After the students know these facts, have pairs add another fact about each person; then have them quiz each other again.

L3 **Research** Have the students research one of the following inventors and their inventions: Samuel Crompton, Edmund Cartwright, Alessandro Volta, Richard Trevithnick, Cyrus McCormick, Charles Goodyear, Elias Howe, Zénobe T. Gramme, Christopher L. Stoles, Norbert Rillieux, Richard Arkwright. Have students recreate a model of the invention made by the inventor. Then hold an "Invention Convention" in which the students role play the inventor and explain the invention.

CAPTION ANSWER

garment makers

VIDEODISC

Use the following to enrich Chapter 33.

WC O 50 46872
Workshop of a master iron maker, 18th century.

WC O 44 46866
Cartoon, exploitation of British coal miners.

automated flour mill was water-powered, and cut by four-fifths the number of workers needed to run it.

In 1847, Samuel Colt used Whitney's idea of interchangeable parts to develop the **assembly line.** On an assembly line, each worker adds a part of the product and passes it on to the next worker, who also adds a part, until the entire product has been put together. Colt used the assembly line to produce the Colt revolver. Before assembly lines, a skilled worker had to make one product at a time from start to finish. With the assembly line, work could be divided, and many products could be put together at one time by unskilled workers. All of these discoveries and new techniques greatly increased production.

Iron, Coal, and Steel

To build machine parts, iron was needed. To fire steam engines, coal was needed. Without iron, coal, and steel, which replaced iron, the Industrial Revolution could not have continued.

By the early 1700s, ironmaking had become expensive. To smelt iron, the British used *charcoal,* a fuel that is made by burning wood. The British, however, were running out of

SEWING COMPETITION Here Elias Howe competes for sewing speed with 5 hand-sewers. He is using his invention the sewing machine. Howe's invention proves to be faster. **What industry did Howe's invention help the most?**

SPOTLIGHT ON: JOSIAH WEDGWOOD

When china clay, used for pottery and chinaware, was found in nearby Cornwall, Josiah Wedgwood took the lead in establishing the famous potteries in 18th-century Great Britain. Wedgwood learned the craft of making pottery from his family and other famous potters and opened his own factory in Etruria. His first success was a cream-colored earthenware he called Queen's ware. Wedgwood's dishes became quite popular with the prosperous middle class. Wedgwood was the first pottery maker to use steam-powered engines.

forests, which made wood scarce and costly. In 1753, a way was found to use coal instead of charcoal for smelting. As a result, iron became cheaper, iron production grew, and coal mining became a major industry.

Iron, however, was too brittle for rails, bridge supports, and heavy equipment. In 1856, a British inventor named Henry Bessemer (bes' uh muhr) found a cheap way of removing the impurities from iron to make steel, which was harder and stronger than iron. The Bessemer Process lowered the cost of making steel from $200 a ton to $4 a ton. Seven years later, in 1863, Pierre-Emile Martin of France and William Siemens of England invented the **open-hearth process,** which used a special kind of furnace to make steel. It was even cheaper than the Bessemer Process and could turn out many different kinds of steel. Soon, mining towns and steel centers grew up in areas with supplies of iron ore and coal.

Picture of Iron Furnace

Transportation

Raw materials and finished products had to be moved quickly and cheaply. Before this could happen, transportation had to be improved. Until the 1700s, the chief means of transportation over land was by horse or horse-drawn wagon. Roads were no more than rough and narrow dirt paths. Travel was slow and uncomfortable. It was even worse when rain made the roads muddy.

Late in the 1700s, the British began to improve their roads. A Scottish engineer named Thomas Telford (tel' fuhrd) designed roadbeds so that water would drain off the roads. Another Scottish engineer, John L. McAdam, developed what became known as the **macadam** (muh kad' uhm) **road.** It had a surface made of layers of crushed stone. This surface allowed horse-drawn wagons to use the roads in all kinds of weather and to travel faster.

The British also made their rivers wider and deeper and built canals to connect navigable rivers to factory and mining centers. Horses walked beside canals and pulled barges. The barges were slow but could carry 50 times the amount of goods that horse-drawn wagons could. By 1830, Great Britain had a complete system of inland waterways.

The biggest improvement in land transportation was the railroad. For years, donkeys had pulled carts over wooden rails inside coal mines. Then, the production of iron grew. The wooden rails were replaced by iron ones that could carry heavier loads. Inventors began to build locomotives to run on iron rails. In 1829, George Stephenson (stē' vuhn suhn), a British mining engineer, won a contest to see who could build the best locomotive. Stephenson's locomotive, the *Rocket,* could pull a train about 36 miles, or 58 kilometers, an hour. The *Rocket* started a railroad-building boom in Great Britain and around the world.

LINKING PAST TO PRESENT

Henry Bessemer established his steel works at Sheffield, England, a city that is still noted for its fine steel products.

DID YOU KNOW ??

In 1825, the first locomotive in the United States was built by John Stevens, but it only ran in circles around Steven's estate. The first practical locomotive, the Tom Thumb, was built five years later by Peter Cooper.

VIDEODISC

Use the following to enrich Chapter 33.

WC O 107 46929
Cotton factories in Manchester.

WC O 117 46939
Factory children attend a Sunday school.

COOPERATIVE LEARNING

Divide students into groups. Have each group research innovations in one of these areas: farming, transportation, power sources, textiles, factories. Each team member should be assigned a specific topic; students examining "power sources" could research the use of waterwheels or coal, for example. After researching, have groups share their findings. Have one member of each group orally present the group's findings.

GEOGRAPHY AND HISTORY

It took sailing ships about two months to cross the Atlantic. Steamboats made the trip in ten days.

LINKING PAST TO PRESENT

The use of tin cans for preserving food started in 1812. Originally these tin-plated containers were called *canisters.* The term *can* was used for the first time at Boston's Underwood Cannery in 1839 by bookkeepers who apparently tired of writing the longer word again and again.

INDEPENDENT PRACTICE

L2 **Literature** Have students read parts of *Life on the Mississippi* by Mark Twain, an account of the author's years as a steamboat pilot. Have students consider what functions steamboats served and how they affected life and commerce in that area. Have students conclude by discussing what the book tells about society in the Mississippi River valley at that time.

VIDEODISC

Use the following to enrich Chapter 33.

WC O 79 46901

Women workers in a paper mill, 18th century.

Painting of the *Rocket*

Railroads changed daily life as well as transportation. People started using such phrases as "keeping on track" and "tooting your own whistle." They also collected autographs of railway engineers. When American railroads adopted standard time zones in 1883, everyone else in the United States did too. The next year, time zones were established all over the world.

The biggest improvement in water transportation was the steamboat. The first practical one was developed by Robert Fulton (fūhl' tuhn), an American inventor. In 1807, Fulton's *Clermont,* powered by a British steam engine, set a record by making the trip from Albany to New York City in 32 hours. Soon, steamboats were carrying passengers and goods along the inland waterways of the United States and Europe. Steamboats, however, did not replace sailing ships in trans-oceanic travel until the late 1800s, when fuel-efficient engines were developed.

Section 3 Review

1. **Identify:** John Kay, James Hargreaves, James Watt, Eli Whitney, Oliver Evans, Samuel Colt, Bessemer Process, John L. McAdam, Robert Fulton
2. **Define:** textile, domestic system, flying shuttle, spinning jenny, factory system, cotton gin, interchangeable parts, automation, assembly line, open-hearth process, macadam road
3. What effect did the assembly line have on the type of workers needed?
4. Why did transportation have to be improved during the Industrial Revolution?

Critical Thinking

5. What are the advantages in using the assembly line to produce goods? What are the disadvantages?

Section 4 INDUSTRIAL IMPACT

The Industrial Revolution brought many changes in people's lives. These changes showed up first in Great Britain. They spread from there to other countries.

Changes in Society In England, until the Middle Ages, there had been two major social classes—the nobles, who were the upper class, and the peasants, who were the lower class. Then, a middle class of rich merchants developed.

SECTION 3 ANSWERS

1. John Kay, British inventor (p. 526); James Hargreaves, inventor (p. 527); James Watt, perfected the steam engine (p. 527); Eli Whitney, inventor (p. 527); Oliver Evans, first used automation (p. 527); Samuel Colt, developed assembly line (p. 528); Bessemer Process, process to make steel (p. 529); John L. McAdam, developed the macadam road (p. 529); Robert Fulton, developed steamboat (p. 530)
2. All terms are defined in the text Glossary.
3. It made it possible for less-skilled workers to make or fix products much faster.
4. to move raw materials and finished products quickly and cheaply
5. Answers will vary but might indicate an advantage of increased productivity and disadvantage of monotonous work.

Assign the Chapter 33 **Section 3 Quiz** in the TCR. Testmaker available.

During the Industrial Revolution, the middle class increased in numbers and grew richer. Many factory, railroad, and mine owners became as wealthy as the nobles. They began to keep servants and to dress like members of the upper class. Women wore lacy petticoats and hooped skirts with stiff linings. Men wore dark suits, with top hats in winter and *boaters,* or stiff straw hats, in summer. Members of the middle class had iron ranges for cooking and gave huge dinner parties. Middle-class families began spending their weekends at seaside resorts, which were easy to reach now that railroads were common. Middle-class children went to upper-class schools.

In time, the middle class gained political power. In Great Britain, its male members gained the right to vote and to be represented in Parliament.

The Industrial Revolution also created an industrial working class. Most members of this class were peasants who could no longer support themselves by farming. Since they had no property of their own to sell, they had to sell their labor in order to live.

Members of the working class did not benefit from the Industrial Revolution in its early years. They worked 12 to 16 hours a day, six days a week, for low wages. They had to work at the pace set by machines and factory owners and were fined or

INDUSTRIAL WORKING CLASS The Industrial Revolution required tremendous amounts of unskilled labor. Women and children were the cheapest sources of labor available. The woman in this photograph operates machinery in a cotton mill (left), and young boys are shown in this photograph working in a mine (right). **What group made up the industrial working class?**

LINKING PAST TO PRESENT

Punched cards, an early method for feeding data into computers, were first used in a loom designed in 1745 by Frenchman Jacques de Vauçanson. The punch cards "programmed" the loom to weave a pattern. An American, Herman Hollerith, adapted the cards to feed census data into calculators. He founded the Tabulating Machine Company, later called International Business Machines Corporation, or IBM.

CAPTION ANSWER

peasants who could no longer support themselves by farming

VIDEODISC

Use the following to enrich Chapter 33.

WC O 124 46946
Workers' housing in Alsace, France, 1861.

WC O 129 46951
Attack on New Union Work house, 1842.

SPOTLIGHT ON: ROBERT OWEN

Robert Owen tried to turn his mill town in New Lanark, Scotland, into an ideal community. He was a reformer who believed that better conditions would create better people and reduce crime and undesirable habits. Working hours were shortened and pay was increased at his mill. Owen built cottages for the workers. The town's stores offered affordable clothing and food. Children under ten did not work in the mill but attended free schools. Classes for older children were provided as well. By 1815, visitors from other parts of Great Britain and other countries came to observe the "ideal" town.

MAKING CONNECTIONS

➤➤ **Daily Life** In 1841 an anonymous woman who worked in the textile mill in Lowell, Massachusetts, wrote about the poor working conditions in the workers' magazine *The Lowell Offering: I am going home, where I shall not be obliged to rise so early in the morning, . . . Up before day, at the clang of the bell—and out of the mill by the clang of the bell—into the mill, and at work in obedience to that ding-dong of a bell—just as though we were so many living machines.*

L2 **Economics** Have students research and present an in-class report on the early railroad industry. Students should use the following questions to focus their reports: *How did this new means of transportation affect the economies of countries such as Great Britain and the United States? How did railroads affect markets for goods, opportunities for travel, and communication?*

L3 **Critical Thinking** Have students investigate reform movements to outlaw child labor in the United States. Who headed these movements? Were they successful?

CAPTION ANSWER

because workers had little economic power; It was against the law to form trade unions, and workers could not vote.

beaten if they did not keep up. Working conditions were difficult, dirty, and dangerous. Many people were killed or injured by unsafe machinery. The working class did not have job security. Factory and mine owners hired and fired whenever they wanted.

Most children of the working class did not have time to go to school or to play. Instead, they worked in factories and mines along with men and women. Employers often preferred to hire children. One reason was that children were paid even less than adults. Another reason was that in mines, they could crawl through narrow tunnels into which adults could not fit. Children sometimes were crippled by this difficult work.

The Growth of Cities Another change brought by the Industrial Revolution was the growth of cities. Before the Industrial Revolution, less than 10 percent of the people in Great Britain lived in cities. By 1900, the number had reached 75 percent. Indeed, 10 percent of the people in the whole country lived in the city of London.

Some cities grew up around factories or mines that had been built in rural areas. Most factories, however, were built in existing cities, which grew rapidly as people moved there to find jobs. Soon, the cities became overcrowded. Houses could not be built fast enough. Sometimes, a dozen people had to live in one room. Many moved into damp basements or rooms with no windows. Garbage floated in the streets because sewers had not yet been built. Water supplies became polluted. Epidemics of cholera (kol' uhr uh), typhoid, and tuberculosis were common. The death rate

INDUSTRIAL CITIES The development of industry in England led to the growth of large cities. English industrial cities were located near coal or iron deposits. This painting shows a nineteenth-century steel factory in the city of Sheffield. **Why could workers in the city do nothing about their working or living conditions?**

EXTENDING THE CONTENT

The city of Manchester, England, had many geographic factors that an industrial city needed for growth, such as the availability of raw materials and accessible transportation routes. Manchester lies within 25 miles (or 40 km) of two coal fields, at the meeting point of three rivers, and has a canal that connects the city to the Irish Sea. During the 1800s, Manchester grew into one of the world's centers for the production of cotton textiles. Mills and warehouses replaced private homes in many areas.

among the working class was more than twice that of the middle and upper classes.

Workers had little economic or political power. It was against the law to form **trade unions,** or workers' associations. Workers did not have the right to vote. For these reasons, they could do nothing about their working or living conditions.

Reform Most people in the middle and upper classes paid little attention to the suffering of the workers. Factory owners, for example, felt that raising wages and improving working conditions would raise the cost of goods and lower profits. Some, however, believed that higher wages and better working conditions could produce good profits. They began to work for reform.

The reformers started schools, orphanages, and hospitals for the poor. They also worked to change laws. In 1824, trade unions were made legal. During the 1830s and 1840s, children under ten years old and women were prohibited from working underground in mines. The workday was cut to ten hours.

The reformers also worked to improve living conditions. New laws required public sewer systems and the building of better houses. Every room had to have at least one window, and every house had to have piped-in water. Over time, life became better for the working class. There were fewer epidemics. Clothing, food, and other products became cheap enough for the workers to buy.

Painting of Trade Union Card

Section 4 Review

1. **Define:** trade unions
2. What happened to the middle class during the Industrial Revolution?
3. What problems were caused by the rapid growth of cities?
4. Why were some people against reform?

Critical Thinking

5. What reforms would you have worked for had you lived during the Industrial Revolution?

Section 5 SPREAD OF INDUSTRY

Meanwhile, the Industrial Revolution spread from Great Britain to other countries. These countries, aided by technology, soon **industrialized,** or built up industry. The expansion of railroads and transportation were also important factors.

L3 **History** Have students imagine they are immigrants to the United States who encounter the working and living conditions of the factory laborers for the first time. Have them write a letter home to their families that describes what they have discovered in America.

MAKING CONNECTIONS

➤➤ **History** The British laws against child labor were called the Factory Acts of 1833 and 1844. In the United States, the child labor problem was not settled until 1938, when the Fair Labor Standards Act was passed.

L1 **History** Have students investigate and present an oral report on child labor in the United States during the 1800s. Students should research the type of work young children performed, the length of their working day, and the amount they were paid. Suggest they create a list or daily schedule of what a day in the life of one of these children might have been like. What modern counterparts to these movements remain today? Have students report on their findings to the class.

SECTION 4 ANSWERS

1. trade unions, workers' associations (p. 533)
2. It grew in numbers, grew richer, and in time gained political power.
3. Overcrowding; disposing of garbage; obtaining fresh water supplies; and epidemics of cholera, typhoid, and tuberculosis were problems.
4. because they felt that raising wages and improving working conditions would raise the cost of goods and lower profits
5. Answers will vary but students should give reasons for their answers.

Assign the Chapter 33 **Section 4 Quiz** in the TCR. Testmaker available.

L1 **Geography: Human/Environmental Interaction** Have students use the world map in their text Atlas to locate the countries that were industrialized by the late 1800s.

Assign the Chapter 33 **Geography and Map Activity** in the TCR.

MAKING CONNECTIONS

>> **History** In 1789, a young British mechanic named Samuel Slater arrived in New York, bringing with him the secrets of new spinning and weaving machines built by British inventors. Slater was soon operating the first factory in the United States.

DID YOU KNOW ??

Crusader for workers' rights, especially those of African Americans, William Lloyd Garrison, published his successful newspaper, *The Liberator*, in the early 1800s.

CAPTION ANSWER

British immigrants brought industrial secrets to their new homelands.

VIDEODISC

Use the following to enrich Chapter 33.

WC M 148 41478
Advertisement for German automobiles, 1917.

WC M 168 41498
Louis Blériot in his No. XI monoplane.

Other Countries At the beginning of the Industrial Revolution, Great Britain tried to keep its inventions secret. Machines or plans for machines were forbidden to be taken out of Great Britain. Skilled workers were forbidden to leave the country. By the 1800s, however, many workers had ignored the law and left. Other nations welcomed these **immigrants,** or people who settle permanently in a different country, because they brought British industrial secrets to their new homelands.

These countries used what they learned to build their own industries. Belgium, with its rich deposits of iron and coal, was the first country after Great Britain to industrialize. The next country was France. There, the process began in the 1700s but was slowed by war and revolution. The United States, with its many natural resources, soon followed France.

Then came Germany. Although Germany was well supplied with coal and iron, it was divided into more than 30 separate states. These states were not willing to cooperate in economic matters. Germany, therefore, did not make much industrial progress until after its unification in 1871. It then matched the others as a leading industrial power.

WORLD'S FAIR In 1851, Great Britain held the first World's Fair in London to celebrate its industrial achievements. Other countries then began to hold similar fairs. This painting shows the royal family attending opening day. **How did the Industrial Revolution spread from Great Britain to other countries?**

SPOTLIGHT ON: SAMUEL SLATER

Samuel Slater was working as an engineer overseeing the machines in a British cotton mill when he heard about the rewards for textile-machine designs in the United States. Disguising himself as an apprentice, he sailed to New York. There Moses Brown, a Quaker merchant from Rhode Island, hired him. Slater re-created from memory the Arkwright-designed spinning machines that he had worked with in England. His water-powered mill was built next to the falls of the Blackstone River. Slater later built other mills in New England. The Old Slater Mill in Pawtucket, Rhode Island, has been restored as a museum.

THOMAS EDISON Although best known for the electric light, Thomas Edison had numerous other important inventions. These include the first successful phonograph, an electric railroad, and an electric battery. This photograph shows Edison in his laboratory. **What advances in communications were powered by electricity?**

Technological Advances The development of new kinds of power helped continue the Industrial Revolution. One of these was electricity. In 1837, two Americans, Samuel F. B. Morse and Alfred Vail, built the first successful electric telegraph. It made quick communication possible. Some years later, Alexander Graham Bell, also an American, invented the telephone. Communications took another step forward. In 1895, an Italian physicist, Guglielmo Marconi (gū yel' mō mahr kō' nē), built the wireless telegraph, or radio. Six years later, he was able to send a message across the Atlantic Ocean.

Meanwhile, there were other advances in electricity. By 1879, Thomas Alva Edison, an American, developed the electric light. It would soon illuminate factories and homes all over the world.

Another new source of power was the **internal combustion engine,** or an engine that is fueled by gasoline. It was invented around 1885 by German engineer Gottlieb Daimler (gōt' lēb dīm' luhr). Daimler's engine was used to drive the first automobile as well as other machines. Another German engineer, Rudolf Diesel, developed an oil-burning internal combustion engine that could run large industrial plants, locomotives, and ocean liners. These developments helped open a whole new era in transportation.

CAPTION ANSWER

the electric telegraph, the telephone, and the wireless telegraph, or radio

DID YOU KNOW

Thomas Edison held a total of 1,093 patents—a world record. Partially deaf from an early age, he was so curious as a child that his family nicknamed him "the nervous little question box." Edison was famous for his tenacity. Once, when someone called him a genius, he responded: "Genius is 1 percent inspiration, and 99 percent perspiration."

LINKING PAST TO PRESENT

The first high-speed passenger elevators were installed in 1879 at New York's Boreel Building. The elevators were built in groups of four that could be operated simultaneously. While technically it would have been possible to build skyscrapers before this time, high-speed elevators made the towering structures practical.

EXTENDING THE CONTENT

The invention of the gasoline-powered engines carried aviation technology to new levels. In the 1890s Ferdinand von Zepplin streamlined the dirigible—a balloonlike craft that could carry passengers. Wilbur and Orville Wright achieved success in 1903 with the first flight of a motorized airplane. Airplanes and other vehicles needed a steady supply of fuel for power and rubber for tires and other parts. As a result, the worldwide petroleum and rubber industries skyrocketed.

ASSESS

CHECK FOR UNDERSTANDING

Ask students to summarize the main points of the chapter, orally or in writing. Discuss the answers to the Section and Chapter Review questions.

EVALUATE

Assign the Chapter 33 **Performance Assessment Activity** in the TCR.

Administer the **Chapter 33 Test**. Testmaker available.

RETEACH

Have students create time lines that list important inventions that contributed to the Industrial Revolution.

Assign the **Chapter 33 Reteaching Activity** in the TCR.

ENRICH

Have students write scripts and perform skits showing working-class life during the Industrial Revolution.

Assign the **Chapter 33 Enrichment Activity** in the TCR.

CLOSE

Remind students that people often use the phrase, "the good old days," out of nostalgia for the past. Have them discuss what people living in the United States during the Industrial Revolution might have meant when they used this phrase with reference to preindustrial times.

MEETING CHAPTER OBJECTIVES

Each objective is tested by the Review Questions in parentheses.

1. **Examine** the inventions and discoveries of the Scientific Revolution. (BV; CU 1)
2. **Explain** the Agricultural Revolution. (CU 2; CT 1)
3. **Discuss** the development of the Industrial Revolution. (BV; CT 1, 3; UYJ)
4. **Describe** the effects of industrialization. (CU 4, 5, 6; CT 4: UYJ)
5. **Analyze** how industrialization spread. (CU 8; CT 3; GIH; UYJ)

Section 5 Review

1. **Identify:** Samuel F. B. Morse, Alexander Graham Bell, Guglielmo Marconi, Thomas Alva Edison, Gottlieb Daimler
2. **Define:** industrialized, immigrants, internal combustion engine
3. How did the Industrial Revolution spread?
4. What were the first countries after Great Britain to become industrialized?

Critical Thinking

5. Which of the advances in technology made during the Industrial Revolution do you consider the most important?

Chapter Summary

1. The revolution in scientific thinking was set off in 1543 when Copernicus said that the planets revolve around the sun, not Earth.
2. The Agricultural Revolution, a new system of land division, growing crops, and breeding animals, began during the revolution in science.
3. The Industrial Revolution began in Great Britain's textile industry.
4. Many inventions helped workers produce more in less time.
5. Factories were built near rivers in order to use the power of falling water to run machines.
6. With the steam engine in 1769, steam replaced water as the major source of power, and factories were built near raw materials.
7. Eli Whitney and Catherine Littlefield Greene invented the cotton gin in 1793. Whitney also developed a new way of organizing production in 1798.
8. Automation and the assembly line increased production.
9. The development of inexpensive ways to smelt iron and make steel provided cheaper building materials in the Industrial Revolution.
10. Transportation also improved with the development of better roads, canal systems, railroads, and steamboats.
11. The Industrial Revolution increased the size and power of the middle class and created a class of industrial workers.
12. The rapid growth of cities and the poor working and living conditions of workers during the Industrial Revolution led to reforms.
13. During the 1800s, the Industrial Revolution spread from Great Britain to Belgium, France, the United States, and Germany.
14. The development of electricity and the internal combustion engine helped the Industrial Revolution.

SECTION 5 ANSWERS

1. Samuel F. B. Morse, built electric telegraph (p. 535); Alexander Graham Bell, invented telephone (p. 535); Guglielmo Marconi, built radio (p. 535); Thomas Alva Edison, developed electric light (p. 535); Gottlieb Daimler, invented internal combustion engine (p. 535)
2. industrialized, built up industry (p. 533); immigrants, people who settle in a different country (p. 534); internal combustion engine, engine fueled by gasoline (p. 535)
3. Workers who left England brought British industrial secrets to their new homelands.
4. Belgium, France, Germany, and the United States
5. Answers will vary but students should give reasons for their choices.

Assign the Chapter 33 **Section 5 Quiz** in the TCR. Testmaker available.

CHAPTER 33 Review

Building Vocabulary

Imagine Thomas Jefferson, who lived during the 1700s, has appeared and has asked you to describe the most important details and ideas of the Industrial Revolution. Use the following words.

enclosure	assembly line
textile	open-hearth process
domestic system	macadam road
spinning jenny	trade unions
factory system	industrialized
automation	immigrants
interchangeable parts	

Check for Understanding

1. In what ways did ideas about science change in the 1400s, 1500s, and 1600s?
2. What effect did the Agricultural Revolution have on population growth?
3. How did the development of the macadam road affect transportation?
4. How did railroads change daily life?
5. What new social class developed as a result of the Industrial Revolution?
6. What benefits did people of the working class eventually receive from the Industrial Revolution?
7. How did the British try to keep their inventions secret?
8. What new sources of power helped spread the Industrial Revolution?

Critical Thinking

1. What did changes in agriculture have to do with the beginning of the Industrial Revolution?
2. Why did Great Britain want to keep its inventions secret from the rest of the world?
3. What things are necessary for a country to be able to industrialize?
4. Do you believe that the Industrial Revolution was good or bad for most of the workers? Explain the reasons for your answer.

Geography in History

HUMAN/ENVIRONMENTAL INTERACTION Progress that came about during the Industrial Revolution was caused by people interacting with their environment. What geographic features were involved in this progress? Explain.

Using Your Journal

Review the details that you have noted about the changes that took place in the world between the 1400s and the 1700s. Write a newspaper editorial in which you give your opinion about which of the developments that occurred during the Industrial Revolution that might cause problems for people in the future.

CHAPTER 33 REVIEW ANSWERS

BUILDING VOCABULARY

Paragraphs will vary but students should use all the vocabulary words.

CHECK FOR UNDERSTANDING

1. Scientists used the scientific method to test their hypotheses.
2. More food meant better health and longer life spans.
3. It allowed horse-drawn wagons to travel faster in all kinds of weather.
4. People traveled farther, faster; used railroad phrases; established world time zones.
5. the middle class
6. There were fewer epidemics, and products were cheaper.
7. by not allowing machines, plans for machines, or skilled workers to leave the country
8. electricity and the internal combustion engine

CRITICAL THINKING

1. Farmers moved to cities; population grew and demand increased for manufactured goods.
2. because it wanted to monopolize profits
3. natural resources, technology, power sources, production, transportation, and workers
4. Answers will vary but students should explain their reasons.

+ BONUS +

TEST QUESTION
For Chapter 33 Test

How did the invention of the electric light change American society forever? Explain. *(Answers will vary.)*

USING YOUR JOURNAL

Editorials will vary. You might call on volunteers to read their editorials to the class and discuss them.

GEOGRAPHY IN HISTORY

Factories were built next to rivers for water power and steam power, and near raw materials and markets. Transportation systems were improved.

UNIT 10 CULTURE CLOSE-UP

THE MAORIS

FOCUS

OBJECTIVES

Locate where the Maoris lived. Identify the time period during which the Maoris lived. Describe the culture of the Maoris.

BELLRINGER

Ask students to name and describe an action song that they know.

MOTIVATIONAL ACTIVITY

Have students name and perform the action songs that they know such as *Bingo* or *The Hokey Pokey*. Then explain to the students that in this Culture Close-Up they will learn about an early culture group who used action songs to pass down history from one generation to another.

VIDEODISC

Use the following to enrich Unit 10.

WH Z 46 50080

Maori canoes.

UNIT 10 CULTURE CLOSE-UP

The Maoris

The first people in New Zealand were the Maoris (ma orh rēs). It is believed they arrived on this island by canoe during the 900s A.D. A second Maori group is documented to have arrived around 1300 A.D.

Geography Connection

The Maoris, believed to have migrated from Polynesia, settled on the coast of New Zealand and eventually moved inland.

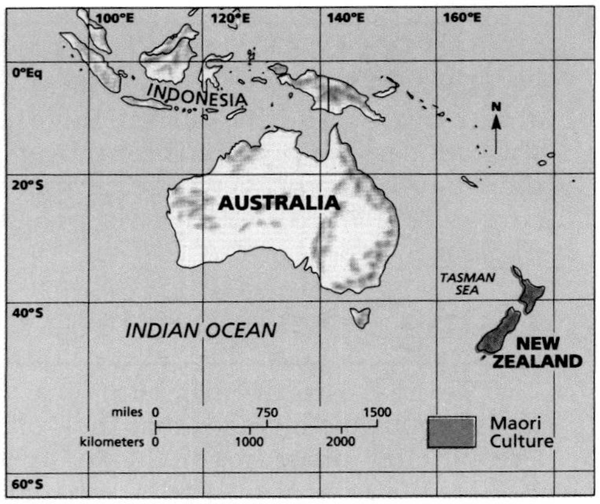

◀ Being isolated from the rest of the world until about 1640, the Maoris developed their own distinctive culture.

538

MULTICULTURAL PERSPECTIVES

Like most cultures, the Maoris have a creation myth. In this myth, the sky, called Rangi, loved the earth, called Papa. The two of them gave birth to many gods. These gods were squeezed as a result of the hugging of Rangi and Papa. In order to survive, the gods separated their parents—so that life could breathe between them.

The Maoris hunted, fished, and later farmed. Birds, snakes, and lizards served as food. Hunting tools were made from wood, stone, and seashell. This bird snare is wood inlaid with shell. ▶

These people were named the Maoris, or "the mao hunters," because they hunted the maos, a huge wingless bird. They used its feathers and those of other birds to fashion clothing. ▶

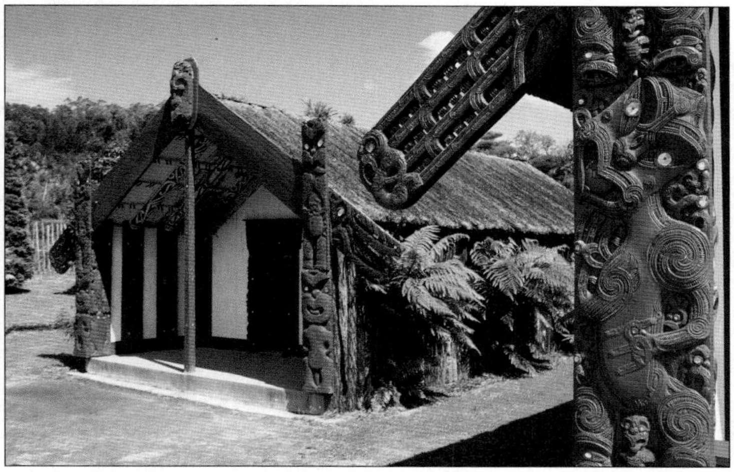

◀ Maoris became known as outstanding carvers and sculptors. They often created carved wooden doorways or sculptures for buildings.

TEACH

L1 **Geography: Human/Environmental Interaction** Have students use a wall map of the world to locate the following Pacific islands: Cook, Marquesas, and Society islands. Point out that these are the Polynesian islands that historians believe the first New Zealanders came from. Then ask the students to use the map's distance scale to measure the distance from each of these islands to New Zealand. Discuss with the students the difficulties that the first people in New Zealand may have encountered on their trip in a canoe from these islands to New Zealand. **LEP**

VIDEODISC

Use the following to enrich Unit 10.

WH Z 66 50100

A Maori mother and child.

COOPERATIVE LEARNING

Have students work in cooperative learning groups to develop a television documentary on the settlement of New Zealand. In each group, have students take on the roles of writers, researchers, on-location reporters, British settlers, Maoris, and so on. Other students can create maps and other graphic materials. Have students do research as necessary and then write and produce the documentary. If possible, record the performance on videotape.

L2 **Art** Have students study the pictures of Maori artwork shown in the illustrations in this feature. Have them list the mediums used and the subjects of the artwork. Discuss why certain mediums, such as wood, shells, and feathers were used to make their artwork. *(These items could be found in great supply in the environment.)* LEP

MAKING CONNECTIONS

➤➤ **History** The first Europeans to settle in New Zealand were from James Cook's expedition in 1770. Hunters from Great Britain and the United States set up whaling stations during the 1790s. New Zealand also attracted timber traders.

GLOBAL READING FOR STUDENTS

Students in your class may be interested in reading a book about the history of New Zealand. Suggest *The Oxford History of New Zealand* edited by William H. Oliver and B. R. Williams, Oxford, 1981. (Challenging/History)

◀ This carving decorated the interior of a Maori meeting house. Large ceremonial meetings called *hui* were held here.

◀ This detailed wooden piece is a weaver's peg, a tool used commonly by the Maoris.

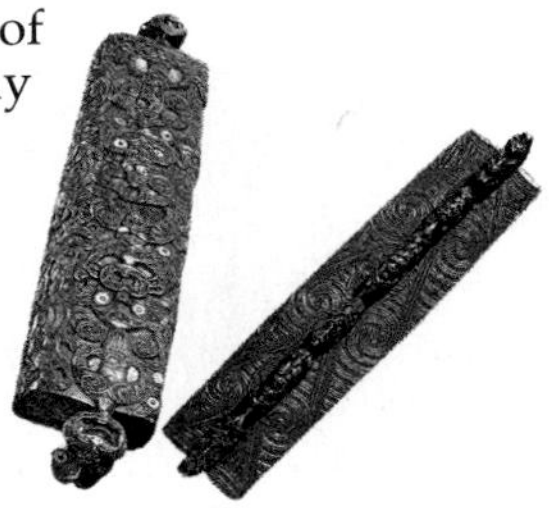

This Maori box of wood with shell inlay was used to keep feathers and other items. ▶

Outside a storehouse where supplies were kept, the Maoris displayed carvings, also. ▶

EXTENDING THE CONTENT

Foreigners brought many problems to the Maoris. Firearms, for example, increased warfare among the Maori tribes. Foreigners also brought diseases to which the Maoris had no immunity, causing an almost 50 percent reduction in Maori population in 20 years. Today Maoris make up about 9 percent of the population of New Zealand, or about 300,000 people.

CULTURE CLOSE-UP

UNIT 10

◀ This Maori treaty house was decorated with pillars of carved wood and woven designs.

Maoris today are proud of their heritage and keep many old customs in their lives. These action songs show the villagers acting out events from Maori history. ▼

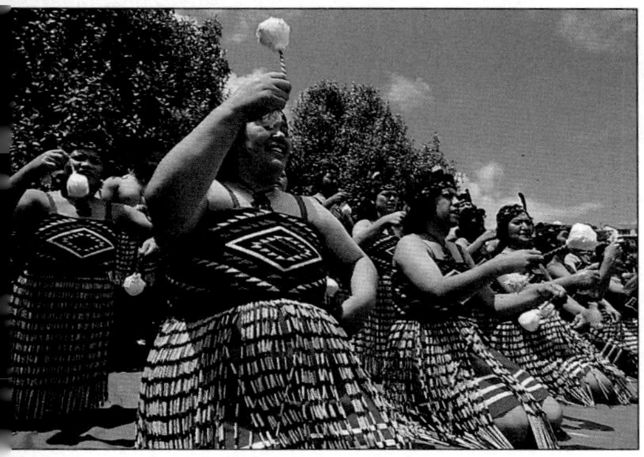

Taking Another Look

1. **From where did the Maori people originally come?**
2. **How did the Maoris receive their name?**
3. **In what ways did the early Maoris obtain food?**

Critical Thinking

4. **Do you think it is an advantage or disadvantage for a group of people to be cut off from the rest of the world as the Maoris were? Explain.**

541

ASSESS

CHECK FOR UNDERSTANDING

Have students answer the questions in Taking Another Look on page 541.

ANSWERS to Taking Another Look

1. Polynesia
2. because they hunted a bird called the maos
3. hunted, fished, and farmed
4. Answers will vary. Students should explain why it is an advantage or a disadvantage for a group of people to be cut off from the rest of the world.

ENRICH

Have students learn more about New Zealand and its geography. Suggest they create their own simple outline maps of the island nation, adding labels for cities and other features they read about.

CLOSE

Ask students to imagine being the first people to inhabit New Zealand. Have them write a poem expressing their thoughts about their new homeland.

MEETING SPECIAL NEEDS

Have interested students research to find out about the conflicts that arose between the Maori and the British settlers in the late 1700s and the 1800s and the current status of Maoris in New Zealand. Have students give an oral report to the class about their findings.

INTRODUCE

UNIT 11 OVERVIEW

Unit 11 discusses the changes in the world during the 1800s, focusing on the emergence of new nations and the building of empires in Africa and Asia.

- **Chapter 34** describes how the United States and Latin American countries developed different forms of governments and economies.
- **Chapter 35** discusses how the ideas of the French Revolution spread.
- **Chapter 36** summarizes the move toward imperialism by western European powers, the United States, and Japan.

UNIT OBJECTIVES

After reading Unit 11, students will be able to:

1. discuss how nationalism influenced the western world during the 1800s.
2. identify what economic ideas developed in Europe.
3. describe changes in Africa and Asia during the 1800s.

UNIT PROJECT

Have students choose one of the following topics: the Americas during the early 1800s; or the Americas, Europe, Africa, Asia and the Pacific, during the late 1800s. Have students write newspaper headlines and articles that characterize the assigned region's economic ideas, nationalism, and imperialism during that time. Ask volunteers to compile all the articles into a newspaper.

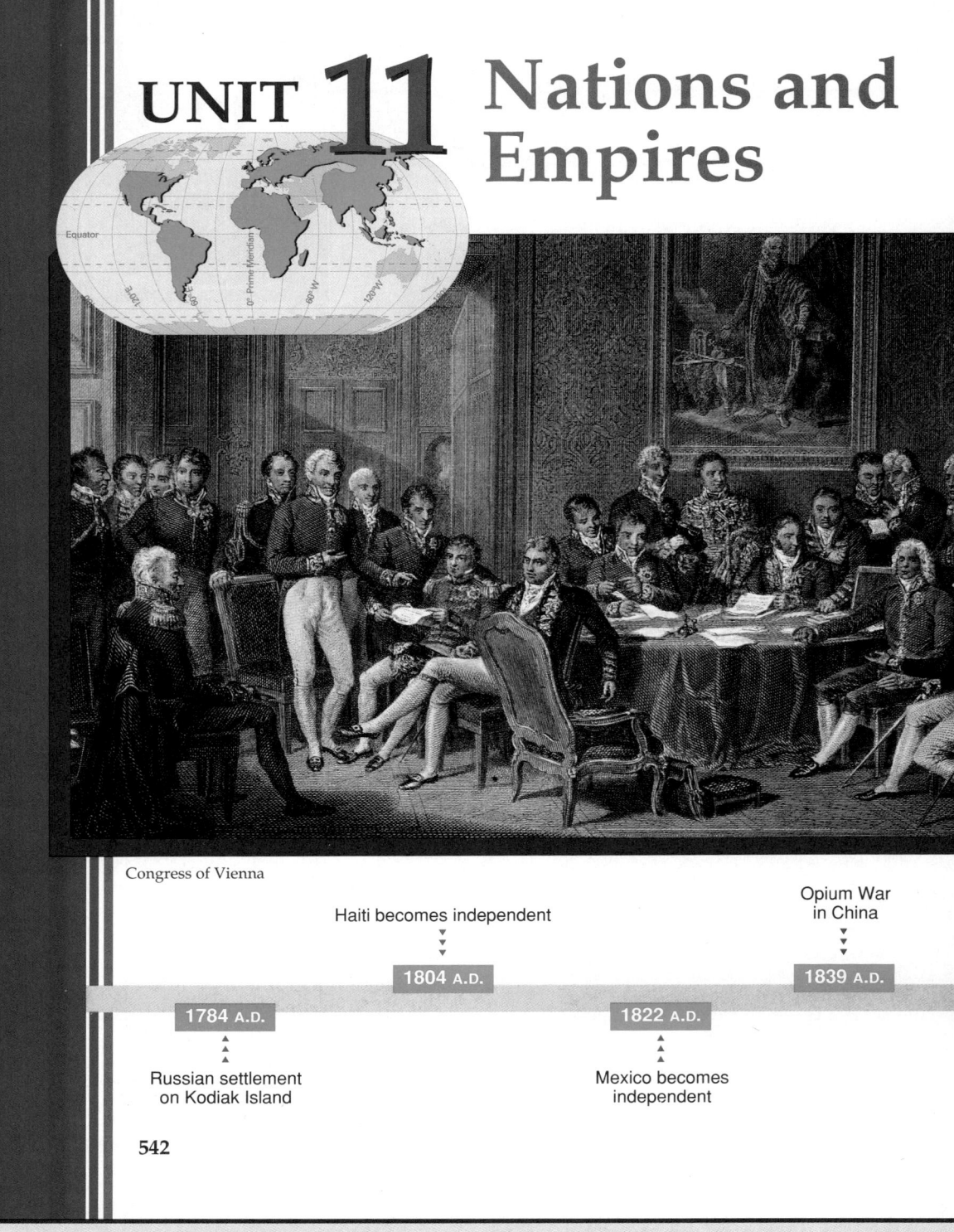

UNIT 11 Nations and Empires

Congress of Vienna

1784 A.D. — Russian settlement on Kodiak Island

1804 A.D. — Haiti becomes independent

1822 A.D. — Mexico becomes independent

1839 A.D. — Opium War in China

542

About the Unit Opening

EXAMINING THE ARTIFACT

Ask students what they think is happening in this painting. Where is it happening? What details and evidences gave them this information? Tell students this scene depicts some governmental changes they will be reading about in the unit.

GLOBAL CHRONOLOGY

Ask students to explain what time period the time line covers. *(1784 to 1914)* What countries are mentioned? *(Russia, Haiti, Mexico, China, United States, South Africa, Panama)* What do the entries in 1804 and 1822 indicate? *(Latin American countries became independent.)* What dates and events indicate that this time period was turbulent? *(the wars and rebellions in 1839, 1846, and 1900)*

The world saw many changes during the 1800s. It saw new nations emerge, grow, and become powerful. It saw the beginnings of new agricultural, scientific, and economic ideas. Events helped the development and spread of the Industrial Revolution. The world also saw the United States, Japan, and countries of western Europe establish empires in Africa and Asia.

Chapter 34
The Americas

Chapter 35
Unrest in Europe

Chapter 36
Rise of Imperialism

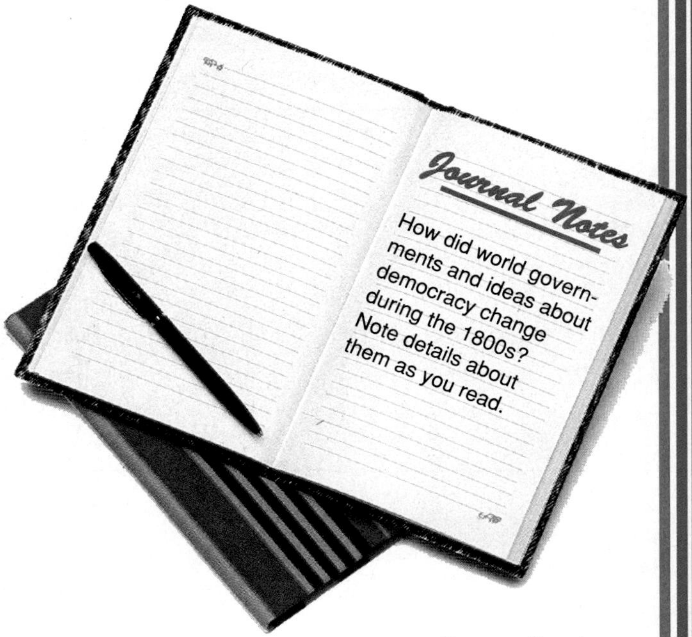

Journal Notes
How did world governments and ideas about democracy change during the 1800s? Note details about them as you read.

War between U.S. and Mexico begins — 1846 A.D.

Boxer Rebellion breaks out in China — 1900 A.D.

Union of South Africa formed — 1910 A.D.

Panama Canal opens — 1914 A.D.

INTRODUCING THE UNIT

Ask students to describe the monarchial governments of Europe before 1800. Ask what advantages these governments offered nations. Why would people become dissatisfied with such governments? Ask students whether they think it would be easy to change a system of government that had been in place for centuries and what problems would be encountered. Tell students that in this unit they will learn about the difficulties encountered by some countries in establishing new forms of government.

RECORDING JOURNAL NOTES

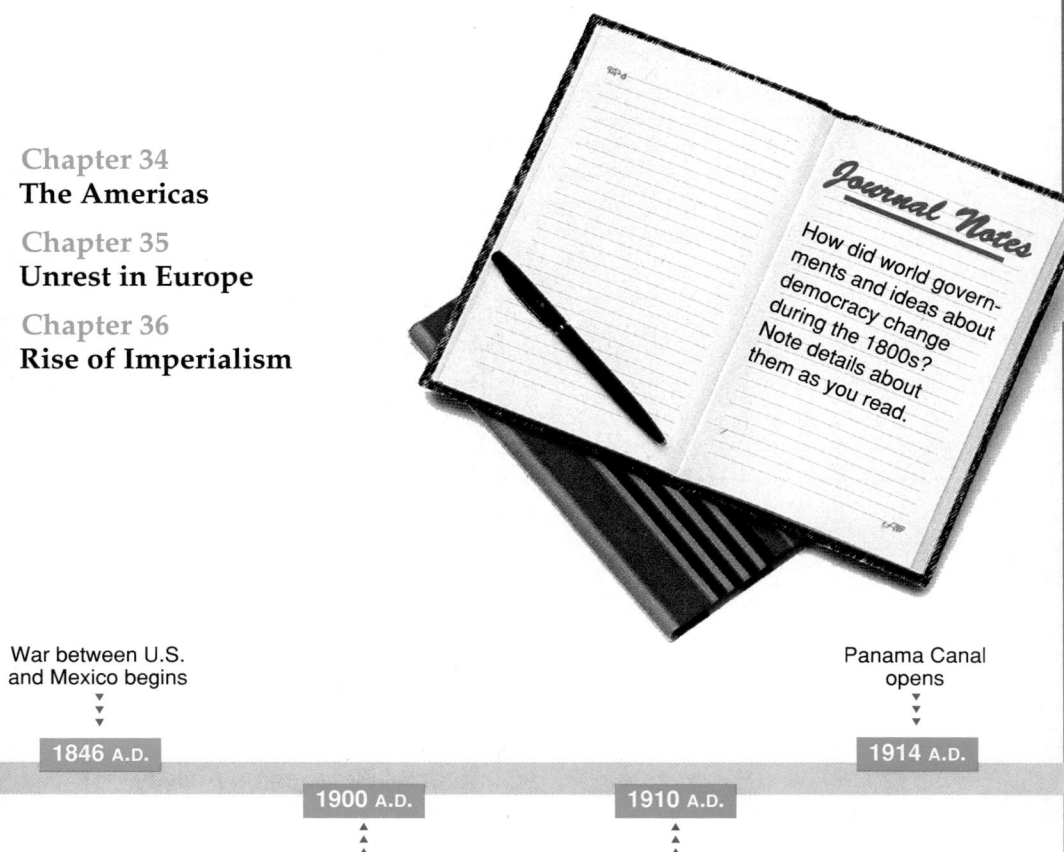

Help students begin writing in their journals by asking them to name changes, described in Unit 10, in government and ideas about democracy that occurred in England, the Americas, and France. Record their responses on the chalkboard. Tell the students that these are the kinds of changes they want to detail in their journals as they read Unit 11.

GEOGRAPHIC LOCATION

Ask students to name the continents that will be discussed in this unit. *(all except Antarctic)* Tell students that in this unit they will learn how nationalism caused independence movements in countries and how industrialization increased the interest of some nations in building empires in nonindustrialized countries.

CHAPTER 34

The Americas

CHAPTER ORGANIZER

Objectives	Special Features	Supplemental Materials
Section 1 The United States Summarize the government in the United States, westward expansion in the United States during the 1800s, and the causes of the Civil War in the United States.		• Reproducible Lesson Plan • Section 1 Quiz • Testmaker • Chapter 34 Vocabulary and Guided Reading Activity • Chapter 34 Cooperative Learning Activity • Unit 11 World Literature • World History and Art Transparency 24 • Chapter 34 Teaching Transparencies and Activities • The Western Civilization Videodisc
Section 2 Latin America Describe the independence movements in Latin America and governments that were established in Latin America in the late 1800s.		• Reproducible Lesson Plan • Section 2 Quiz • Testmaker • Chapter 34 Geography and Map Activity • Chapter 34 Chart and Graph Skill • Unit 11 Primary Source Reading • The World History Videodisc • Chapter 34 Activity Book Activity
Chapter 34 Review and Evaluation		• Chapter 34 Reteaching Activity • Chapter 34 Enrichment Activity • Spanish Summary and Glossary • Audiocassettes (English and Spanish) • Chapter 34 Performance Assessment Activity • Chapter 34 Test • Testmaker

If time does not permit teaching the entire chapter, use the Chapter 34 Summary on page 558 and the Chapter 34 Audiocassettes (English and Spanish) to point out the main ideas of the chapter.

✓ Performance Assessment Activities

Role Play Have students investigate voting-rights movements during the 1800s in some of the countries discussed in this chapter. Have students also investigate the lives of the leaders of the movements—both successful and unsuccessful—and the tactics that they used to reach their goals. After students complete their research, have them prepare scripts in which they role-play a leader of their choice, explaining their philosophies and methods.

Government Assessment The United States government made many formal agreements with various Native American groups to acquire necessary land and to try to keep conflicts to a minimum. Encourage students to choose a Native American group affected by Western expansion, and research how they were dealt with by the federal government. Students should report their findings and include their opinions of how well or how poorly the Native Americans were treated.

CHAPTER RESOURCES

LITERATURE ABOUT THE PERIOD

Keith, Harold. *Rifles for Watie.* T.Y. Crowell, 1957. Story of a teenage soldier in the West during the American Civil War.

READINGS FOR THE STUDENT

Davis, William C., ed. *Touched by Fire: A Photographic Portrait of the Civil War.* Little, Brown and Company, 1985. Portrays the tragedy of the American Civil War.

Freedman, Russell. *Lincoln: A Photobiography.* Clarion Books, 1987. Newbery Award winner that offers a photo essay of the life and times of Abraham Lincoln.

Lester, Julius. *To Be A Slave.* Scholastic, 1968. A primary source documentation of the feelings and experiences of African Americans from colonial times through the Civil War.

Rink, Paul. *Warrior Priests and Tyrant Kings: The Beginnings of Mexican Independence.* Doubleday, 1976. Story of Mexico's fight for independence, from Hidalgo through Iturbide.

READINGS FOR THE TEACHER

Bailey, Helen M. and Abraham P. Nasatir. *Latin America: The Development of Its Civilization.* Prentice Hall, 1973. Surveys the broad spectrum of historic, political, economic, and social development of the Latin American republics.

Chambers, William N. *Political Parties in a New Nation.* Oxford University Press, 1963. Describes the development of modern political parties in the United States.

Faust, Patricia, ed. *Historical Times Illustrated Encyclopedia of the Civil War.* Harper and Row Publishers, 1986. Provides a view of the American Civil War through illustrations and entries by leading historians.

Prago, Albert. *The Revolutions in Spanish America: The Independence Movements of 1808-1825.* Macmillan, 1970. Surveys the history of the independence movements in Latin America during the early 1800s.

Quarles, Benjamin. *The Negro in the Making of America.* (3rd ed.) Collier, 1987. Presents an overview of black participation in the context of American development.

MULTIMEDIA RESOURCES

Civil War: The Fiery Trial. Social Studies School Service. Video. Documentary of the American Civil War.

Latin America. Random House. 2 filmstrips. Surveys the history, geography, and economy of Latin America from the Spanish conquest to modern times.

Westward Expansion: The Pioneer Challenge. Rainbow/Social Studies School Service. Video. Examines the role of geography in the growth of America.

INTRODUCE

CHAPTER 34 OVERVIEW

Chapter 34 examines the political, economic, and cultural developments in the Western Hemisphere during the 1800s.

- **Section 1** discusses the government, the westward expansion of the United States, and the differences that led to the Civil War.
- **Section 2** describes the independence movements in Latin America.

CHAPTER OBJECTIVES

After reading Chapter 34, students will be able to:

1. describe what kind of government developed in the United States.
2. summarize how and why the United States expanded during the 1800s.
3. analyze what led to the Civil War in the United States.
4. identify cultural changes in the United States during the late 1800s and early 1900s.
5. explain how colonies in Latin America won independence.
6. discuss why democracy did not develop in Latin America.

EXAMINING THE ILLUSTRATION

Ask students what time period this painting represents. Ask what clues led them to that conclusion. Explain that this chapter will discuss the expansion of the United States.

PERFORMANCE ASSESSMENT

Use the Performance Assessment activities on page 544B to help you evaluate students as they complete the chapter.

CHAPTER 34 The Americas

Crossing the Great Plains

544

TEACHER CLASSROOM RESOURCES

- Section Quizzes/Chapter Test
- Reteaching Activity
- Enrichment Activity
- Geography and Map Activity
- Vocabulary and Guided Reading Activity
- Cooperative Learning Activity
- Performance Assessment Activity
- Unit 11 World Literature
- Unit 11 Primary Source Reading
- World History and Art Transparency
- Teaching Transparencies and Activities
- The Western Civilization Videodisc
- The World History Videodisc
- Audiocassettes (English and Spanish)
- Testmaker

Chapter Focus

READ TO DISCOVER:

- What kind of government developed in the newly formed United States.
- How and why the United States expanded its boundaries during the 1800s.
- What led to the Civil War in the United States.
- What cultural changes took place in the United States during the late 1800s and early 1900s.
- How colonies in Latin America won their independence.
- Why democracy did not develop in Latin America.

Many changes took place in the Americas from 1800 to the early 1900s. The United States more than doubled in size, and its government was set on a firm base. This allowed the country to grow industrially and to become a world power. Latin America, which is made up of Mexico, Central America, the Caribbean islands, and South America, won independence from European rule. However, colonial traditions remained strong. So, despite many efforts, democracy did not develop in most of Latin America.

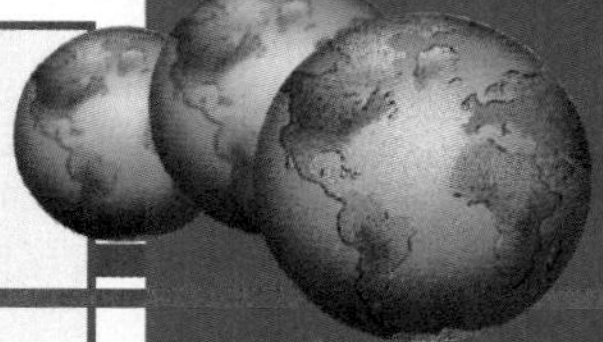

1800 A.D.–1875 A.D.

KEY TERMS

stable government
political parties
federal
representative government
manifest destiny
annexation
seceding
urbanization
tenements
slums
junta
caudillo

Section 1

The United States

In the years after winning independence, the Americans set up a democratic government and expanded the boundaries of their country. They fought each other in a civil war and then worked to reunite the nation after the war ended. Industry grew and brought about many changes in daily life. By 1900, the United States had become a powerful country.

Government One thing that helped the United States become powerful was its government. Americans developed a tradition of **stable government,** or a government that rules from year to year without great changes.

545

FOCUS

BELLRINGER

Tell students that in the 1800s many settlers wanted to expand the United States across the continent. Have students write three reasons Native Americans or Mexicans might be hostile to this attitude.

MOTIVATIONAL ACTIVITY

Have students share their reasons Native Americans or Mexicans might be hostile to settlers wanting to expand across the continent. Then tell students that in this chapter they will learn about the expansion of the United States and how this affected Native Americans and Mexicans.

VOCABULARY PRE-CHECK

Write the key terms for this chapter on the chalkboard. Ask volunteers to skim the chapter for these boldfaced words as they read aloud the sentences in which they appear.

Assign Chapter 34 **Vocabulary and Guided Reading Activity** in the TCR.

EXTRA CREDIT PROJECT

Suggest that students research one of the Latin American countries formed from the United Provinces of Central America. Have them create a time line of important events in the history of their chosen country, from its inception to current times. Encourage students to share their time lines with the class.

KEY TO ABILITY LEVELS

Teaching strategies have been coded for varying learning styles and abilities.

L1 Level 1 activities are **basic** activities and should be within the ability range of all students.

L2 Level 2 activities are **average** activities and should be within the ability range of the average to above-average student.

L3 Level 3 activities are **challenging** activities designed for the ability range of above-average students.

LEP LEP activities should be within the ability range of Limited English Proficiency students.

TEACH

GUIDED PRACTICE

L1 **History** To help students understand the swiftness of the expansion of the United States, guide them in developing a time line showing the acquisition of territory. LEP

GEOGRAPHY AND HISTORY

The Federalist party, which received much of its support in the New England and Middle Atlantic states, was formed by Alexander Hamilton and his followers. The Democratic-Republican party, popular in the southern states, was started by Thomas Jefferson and his supporters.

DID YOU KNOW

During the 1890s, four western states—Utah, Wyoming, Colorado, and Idaho—extended the right to vote to women.

Painting of Campaign Poster

By 1800, two **political parties,** or groups with different ideas about government, had come into being. One was the Federalist (fed′ uhr uh list) party. It favored a strong **federal,** or national, government. Most Federalists believed that only people of wealth and education should hold office. They thought the economy should be based more on industry than on trade or agriculture. The other political party was the Democrat-Republican party. It favored more power for the states. Most Democrat-Republicans believed that average people should lead the country. They thought the economy should be based more on agriculture than on industry or trade.

Although in other countries wars were often fought when political power changed hands, in the United States the government changed hands through peaceful elections. For example, in 1800 Thomas Jefferson, who was a Democrat-Republican, was elected President. He took the place of John Adams, who was a Federalist. This was the first peaceful passing of power from one political group to another.

The United States also had a tradition of **representative government.** This is a government in which officials are elected by the people. In 1800, however, only white males who owned property could vote. This changed over the next 30 years. New states in the West began to allow all adult white males to vote. Other states soon followed. By 1830, the number of voters had greatly increased. Although women, enslaved people, and Native Americans were not allowed to vote, the United States government was one of the most democratic in the world at the time.

With the growing number of voters, election campaigns changed. They became filled with entertainment and advertising. People sang songs and wore ribbons to show which candidates they backed. Political parties held parades, rallies, and dinners. Presidential races in particular were noted for slogans and symbols. For example, Andrew Jackson, who became President in 1829, was known as "Old Hickory." So, during his campaign, the newly formed Democratic party planted hickory trees in town squares and gave out hickory brooms and canes.

Photograph of Native American Clothing

The Westward Movement At the end of the American Revolution, the United States claimed most of the land east of the Mississippi River. Soon, thousands of Americans were putting their belongings into farm wagons and traveling across the Appalachian Mountains to find new homes. When they came to the Ohio River and other water routes, they loaded their goods and animals on flatboats and floated downstream.

The settlers were careful about choosing a spot for their new home. It had to be near a stream for water. It also had to be near a large settlement or fort for safety. After choosing a place, the settlers would clear the land of trees and build a log cabin. It

EXTENDING THE CONTENT

In the election of 1800 there was no distinction on the electoral ballot between President and vice president. Thomas Jefferson and Aaron Burr of the Democratic-Republican party ran against John Adams and Charles C. Pinckney of the Federalist party. During this election the candidate who received the most electoral votes became President. The person who won the second-largest number of votes became vice president. Since both Jefferson and Burr received the same number of electoral votes, the House of Representatives had to vote to break the tie. They voted to make Jefferson President and Burr vice president. The Twelfth Amendment was passed in 1804 to assure that an electoral tie could not happen again.

usually had one room, with a dirt-packed floor and a door made of wood planks. Each cabin had one or two tiny windows covered with deerskin. There was a fireplace that supplied heat for warmth and cooking.

The settlers' way of life was generally different from that of the Native Americans in the area. The settlers were farmers, while most Native Americans were hunters. The settlers claimed land for themselves. The Native Americans believed land belonged to everyone.

The Native Americans and the settlers did learn from one another, however. Many of the settlers wore Native American clothing, such as moccasins and deerskin leggings. They used Native American herbs as medicine and paddled Native American canoes. Many of the Native Americans used rifles, iron pots and woolen blankets that were made in Great Britain.

The Native Americans tried to defend their lands against the settlers. However, there were many more settlers than Native Americans. Also, many Native Americans died from such diseases as measles and smallpox brought by the whites. Over time, the Native Americans were slowly pushed farther and farther west. In the 1830s, the United States government forced the Native Americans to live on reservations.

Territorial Expansion Many settlers chose land newly acquired by the United States. In 1803, the United States doubled its size by buying the Louisiana Territory from France for $15 million. The Louisiana Purchase, as it was called, provided an

NATIVE AMERICAN LIFE Many Native Americans west of the Mississippi were nomadic and hunted the great migrating herds of buffalo. The Native Americans depended on the buffalo meat for food and its hide for clothing and shelter. **Why were the Native Americans unable to stop the movement of the settlers?**

L2 **Critical Thinking** Have students put themselves in the position of members of the United States Congress during the country's rapid period of expansion. Have them brainstorm the major problems these legislators would have to deal with. What new laws would be needed? What other changes would be needed? Suggest that students list these problems and then rank them from most to least important.

L3 **Geography: Movement** Suggest that students research and map the changing center of population of the United States. (*The Statistical Abstract of the United States* contains this information.) Have students prepare to lead a class discussion that covers what the center of population is, why it moves, and speculate what its next move, if any, will be. Display student maps.

CAPTION ANSWER

There were more settlers than Native Americans, many Native Americans died from diseases, and the whites were better armed and had an army.

MEETING SPECIAL NEEDS

Obtain a copy of David S. Lavender's book, *The Way to the Western Sea: Lewis and Clark Across the Continent.* Harper, 1988. Read excerpts from the book to auditory learners. Ask students to describe the journal entries of Lewis and Clark in their own words. Have students find the places described in the journal on a map of the United States.

GEOGRAPHY AND HISTORY

In 1804, American explorers Meriwether Lewis and William Clark explored the Louisiana purchase territory and traveled to the Pacific Ocean. They brought back to the East much information about the Native American way of life and the abundance of natural resources in the West.

DID YOU KNOW ??

In 1954 America's first large group of Polish immigrants landed in Galveston, Texas. The Poles called their community Panny Marie.

MAKING CONNECTIONS

➤➤ **Geography: Movement** The Spaniards had originally colonized California by establishing a series of 21 missions along the coast from San Diego to San Francisco. Each mission consisted of a central church, outlying buildings, and a fort. Father Junípero Serra was responsible for establishing the first of these missions.

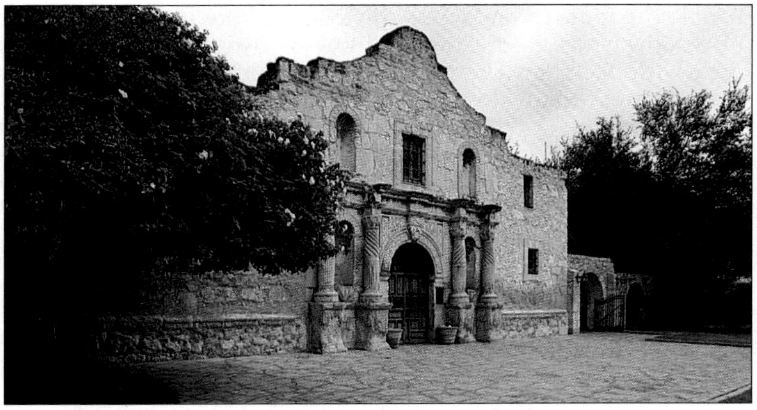

THE ALAMO The Alamo was a Catholic mission in San Antonio, Texas. In 1836, during the war for Texan independence, 187 Texans used the Alamo as a fortress and held out for several days against nearly 4,000 Mexican soldiers before being defeated. **What conditions had the Mexicans placed on Americans settling in Texas?**

area rich in farmland, minerals, and forests. It also gave the United States control of the Mississippi River and the important seaport of New Orleans.

In 1819, the United States and Spain signed a treaty. This treaty, called the Adams-Onís Treaty, gave Florida to the United States and set the boundary between the Louisiana Purchase and the Spanish lands to the south and west.

One of the Spanish lands was Mexico. It became independent in 1821. The Mexicans wanted more people to settle in their territory, especially in Texas. So, they offered people from the United States large areas of free land if they would swear loyalty to Mexico and become Catholic. By the early 1830s, there were 30,000 Americans living in Texas. Most were from the South, and many owned enslaved people.

Enslavement and other issues soon led to quarrels between the Americans who moved to Texas and the Mexican government. Mexico had outlawed enslavement in 1824, and it objected to Texans enslaving people. It also began wondering whether American settlers were loyal to Mexico or to the United States. So, the Mexican government tried to stop more Americans from entering Texas. The Texans then asked for more control over their local affairs. Finally, in 1835, the Texans revolted. The following year, they declared their independence.

Many Americans believed in the **manifest destiny** (man′ uh fest des′ tuh nē) of the United States, or the idea that it was the fate of the United States to stretch from the Atlantic Ocean to the Pacific Ocean. They wanted the federal government to allow the

EXTENDING THE CONTENT

Have interested students imagine the year is 1845 and many people want the United States to annex land from Mexico. Have students take the roles of Mexican peasants and landowners, southern plantation owners, northern industrialists, Native Americans, or others. Have students investigate the concerns of their choice of people and write speeches, articles, or posters promoting their view. Have students role-play their chosen person and share their information with the class.

annexation of Texas. **Annexation** (an ek sā′ shuhn) is the act of taking over a territory and combining it with an existing country or state. In 1845, the United States did annex Texas. This greatly angered Mexico. A dispute over the Texas-Mexico boundary caused more trouble. By the following year, the two countries were at war. American soldiers invaded California, which was part of Mexico. They also marched into Mexico City.

In 1848, Mexico signed the Treaty of Guadalupe Hidalgo (gwah dl ū′ pā huh duhl′ gō). It gave the United States almost one half of Mexico's land. It also set the Rio Grande (rē′ ō gran′ dā) as the boundary between Texas and Mexico.

Five years after the treaty, in 1853, the United States bought a piece of land from Mexico in order to build a railroad to the Pacific. This was called the Gadsden (gadz′ duhn) Purchase after James Gadsden, the American who arranged the purchase.

Meanwhile, the United States acquired the Oregon Territory. During the 1840s, thousands of American settlers made the long, hard trip over the Rocky Mountains to Oregon, which both the United States and Great Britain claimed. The presence of these settlers gave the United States control of much of the area. In 1846, the two countries agreed to divide the Oregon Territory at the 49th parallel.

MAP STUDY

LOCATION The Louisiana Purchase eventually formed parts of 13 states. **What geographic features marked the western and eastern boundaries of the Louisiana Purchase?**

The Growth of the United States

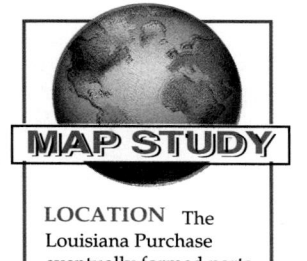

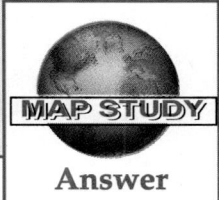

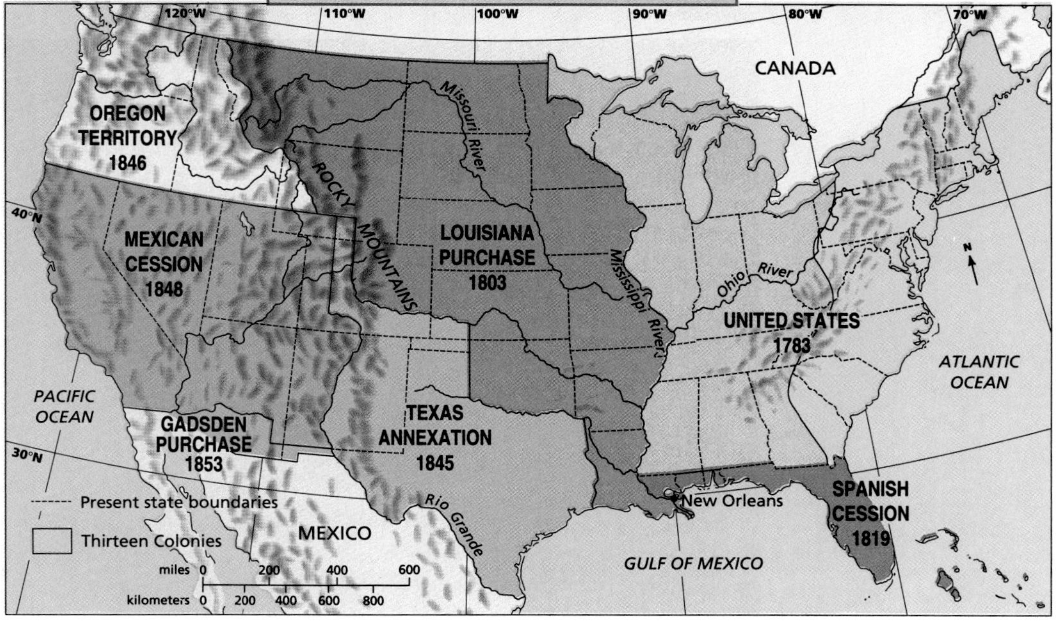

L1 **Geography: Human/Environmental Interaction** Have students use the map "The Growth of the United States" to locate the areas of territorial expansion discussed in this subsection. Have them name present states that were part of each territory. In particular, have them locate their own state and determine where it fit into the United States expansion. LEP

DID YOU KNOW ??

The locations of the first Spanish missions in California was decided according to how far and fast a priest could walk. Each mission was one week's travel time apart.

MAP STUDY

Answer

Rocky Mountains and Mississippi River

EXTENDING THE CONTENT

Explain to students that the term *Manifest Destiny* was first used in a magazine in 1845 supporting the view that the United States was given the divine right to conquer and settle new land in North America and elsewhere. The phrase soon became popular. Ask the students which acquisitions allowed the United States to reach its "Manifest Destiny" of spreading from sea to sea. *(Oregon country, 1846; Mexican Cession, 1848)*

L3 **Critical Thinking** Divide students into small groups to consider whether any state should have the right to withdraw from the United States if it feels it has just cause. Have each group draw from slips of paper on which you have written *yes* or *no* an equal number of times. Have each group gather information on their assigned side of the issue. Then have each group choose a member to participate in a panel debate on the issue.

DID YOU KNOW ??

Alaska became the 49th state of the Union in 1959.

CAPTION ANSWER

the Confederate States of America or the Confederacy

Later, another large area of land, Alaska, was added to the United States. In 1784, Russian fur hunters had established a permanent settlement at Kodiak (kōd' ē ak) Island off the Alaskan coast. From there, they set up hunting and trading settlements as far south as California. After a time, however, Russia lost interest in Alaska and sold the territory to the United States in 1867.

Civil War and Reunion

As the United States expanded westward, different ways of life developed in the northern and southern states. The northern states were industrialized. They had most of the nation's factories, railroads, and canals. Labor in the North was done by hired workers. About 20 percent of the people lived in cities. Education was widespread, and immigration brought in all different kinds of people. Northern leaders wanted a strong national government. They also wanted the government to aid industry and improve transportation. They believed that enslavement should not be allowed in new areas of the country.

The southern states depended on agriculture. Tobacco, rice, sugar cane, and especially cotton were important. These crops

ABRAHAM LINCOLN As President during the Civil War, Abraham Lincoln led the United States through one of the most critical periods in the nation's history. Lincoln was assassinated by a southern sympathizer shortly after the North and South were reunited. **What did the southern states that seceded call their new government?**

COOPERATIVE LEARNING

Organize the class into groups to discuss the ways American life might be different if the Civil War had not been fought and the country had remained divided into two separate nations. Have each group focus on a different topic, such as economy, international relations, labor, government, or culture. One person from each group should take notes on the discussion and report the group's ideas to the class. Encourage students from the other groups to ask questions after each group's presentation.

Assign the Chapter 34 **Cooperative Learning Activity** in the TCR.

were grown on large plantations that used enslaved labor. Enslaved people made up about one third of the South's population. Only 10 percent of the people lived in cities. There were few immigrants. Southern leaders believed that the rights of the states were more important than those of the federal government. They also believed that as the country grew, enslavement should be allowed in new areas.

In 1860, Abraham Lincoln was elected President. Southerners feared he would try to do away with enslavement and destroy their way of life. Seven southern states announced that they were **seceding** (si sēd' ēng), or withdrawing, from the nation. They formed a new government called the Confederate States of America or the Confederacy (kuhn fed' uhr uh sē). Soon, four more states seceded and joined the Confederacy. Northerners did not think the southern states had a right to secede. By 1861, the North and the South were fighting a civil war. In 1865, the North won, and the country was once more politically united.

The Civil War settled the question of whether or not states have the right to secede. It also led to freedom for nearly 4 million enslaved African Americans. The country began to build itself up again. By 1870, it was on its way to becoming a strong industrial country and a world power.

Cultural Changes As the United States expanded and industrialized, many cultural changes took place. The rise of industry led to **urbanization,** or the growth of cities. During the late 1800s and early 1900s, many Americans left the farm and moved to the city. At the same time, a large number of immigrants came to America. Most settled in cities. City life provided jobs, education, and new ways for people to enjoy themselves.

Not everyone lived in the same way in the cities. The lives of the lower, middle, and upper classes differed greatly from one another. One way in which people's lives differed was in housing. The lower class, which included most immigrants, lived in old houses or commercial buildings that had been made into apartments. These were called **tenements** and were generally rundown. Areas with large numbers of tenements were called **slums.**

The middle class lived in various types of housing. One was the apartment house. It was often six to eight stories high, with at least two apartments on each story. Another kind of house was the row house. It was a private house that shared its side walls with its neighbors. Some members of the middle class lived in homes built for two families or in single-family residences. The upper class generally lived in huge homes staffed with servants.

Another way in which people's lives differed was in jobs. Lower-class men, women, and children worked in factories. Middle- and upper-class men held business and professional jobs, and their wives rarely worked outside the home.

L1 **History** Tell students that they are to imagine that the United States had not expanded beyond the Appalachian Mountains. Have them work in groups and brainstorm how the world, the United States, or their own lives would be different. Have students share their ideas. LEP

MAKING CONNECTIONS

➤➤ **History** On September 22, 1862, President Lincoln issued the Emancipation Proclamation. As of January 1, 1863, if the Confederate states had not surrendered, all enslaved persons held in states that were still in rebellion would be declared free.

DID YOU KNOW ??

In 1883 African American inventor Jan Earnest Metzeliger received a patent for an invention that revolutionized the shoe-making business. His machine raised production levels to 700 shoes per day.

EXTENDING THE CONTENT

Although enslavement was one main moral issue dividing the North and the South, most white Northerners did not agree with abolitionism and viewed their efforts as a struggle to preserve the Union. In fact, many Northern Republicans supported a proposed amendment to the U.S. Constitution prohibiting the federal government from ending enslavement in any state that wanted it. Most white southerners saw the Confederate States of America as a way to keep states' rights intact.

DID YOU KNOW ??

Of the 26 million people who arrived at immigration stations in New York City between 1870 and 1920, only 2 percent were turned away.

MAKING CONNECTIONS

➤➤ **History** In towns and cities across the United States after 1890, racial segregation in housing continued. This was promoted in the South because of Jim Crow legislation, which called for separate facilities for whites and blacks. In northern cities, however, segregation was based on custom and economics rather than law.

L1 **Geography: Location** Have students use the map "Independence in Latin America" on page 555 to locate the areas of Latin America as they are discussed in this section. Have students name the present-day countries of the areas as they are discussed. LEP

VIDEODISC

Use the following to enrich Chapter 34.

WC N 39 44094

Toussaint L'Ouverture (1744?-1803).

People's lives also differed in education. By the late 1800s, there were tax-supported public schools that all children could attend. However, it was generally middle- and upper-class children who benefited. Lower-class children, who had to work, rarely went past elementary school.

Technological advances changed daily life during the late 1800s and early 1900s. For example, the invention of the refrigerator ended the need for daily shopping. Labor-saving machines gave many Americans time to read books, newspapers, and magazines. They also enjoyed music and the theater. City governments began to set aside land for parks.

Section 1 Review

1. **Identify:** Latin America, Federalist party, Democratic-Republican party, Louisiana Purchase, Treaty of Guadalupe Hidalgo, Gadsden Purchase, Confederacy
2. **Define:** stable government, political parties, federal, representative government, manifest destiny, annexation, seceding, urbanization, tenements, slums
3. How did election campaigns change by the 1830s?
4. What were two results of the United States Civil War?

Critical Thinking

5. Do you agree with the settlers' or the Native Americans' ideas about land ownership? Explain your answer.

Painting of Toussaint-L'Ouverture

Section 2 LATIN AMERICA

While the United States was expanding and settling its internal differences, the European-ruled colonies of Latin America were moving toward independence. The American and French Revolutions stirred the people of Latin America to action. Everywhere, colonists tried to take charge of their own affairs.

The First Revolt The first major successful revolt against European rule took place in the French West Indies on Saint Domingue (san duh manj'), the western part of the island of Hispaniola. There, a few French plantation owners used the labor of 500,000 enslaved African Americans to grow sugarcane, coffee, cotton, and *indigo* (in' duh gō), or a kind of plant that yields a blue dye.

SECTION 1 ANSWERS

1. Latin America, Mexico, Central America, the Caribbean islands, and South America (p. 545); Federalist party, political party favoring a national government (p. 546); Democratic-Republican party, party favoring more state power (p. 546); Louisiana Purchase, territory bought from France in 1803 (p. 547); Treaty of Guadalupe Hidalgo, gave U.S. almost one-half of Mexico's land (p. 549); Gadsden Purchase, land bought from Mexico in 1853 (p. 549); Confederacy, southern states that seceded from the United States (p. 551)
2. All terms are defined in the text Glossary.
3. They became filled with entertainment, advertising, and slogans.
4. It settled the question of whether states have the right to secede, and led to freedom for enslaved African Americans.
5. Answers will vary.

Assign the Chapter 34 **Section 1 Quiz** in the TCR. Testmaker available.

Then, Pierre Dominique Toussaint-L'Ouverture (pē auhr' dom uh nēk' tū san' lū vuh tyuhr') appeared on the scene. The grandson of an African chief, Toussaint was born enslaved in 1743. His white master, however, taught Toussaint to read and write and, in 1777, gave him his freedom. When news of the French Revolution reached Saint Domingue, Toussaint was inspired. In 1791, he led a revolt of enslaved people. In 1794, the French government agreed to abolish enslavement. Toussaint became governor-general of Saint Domingue in 1801. Two years later, he issued a constitution. The French then tried to regain control of Saint Domingue but were unsuccessful. In 1804, Saint Domingue became the first free country in Latin America. It changed its name to Haiti, a Native American word meaning "mountainous."

Painting of Simón Bolívar

Revolution Spreads The fight for independence in South America was led by the Creoles. They were well educated and had enough power to change things. The Creoles resented the peninsulares, who held the most important government posts.

Soon after the French Revolution began, a Creole named Antonio Nariño (ahn tō' nē ō nah rēn' yō), translated into Spanish the Declaration of the Rights of Man and the Citizen. This helped spread French democratic ideas throughout the Spanish colonies. Before long, the people there began to revolt.

In the northern part of South America, Simón Bolívar (sē mōn' bō lē' vahr), another Creole, led the fight for freedom. Known as "the Liberator," Bolívar was the son of a rich family in New Granada, or what is today Columbia and Venezuela. In 1805, he went to Europe. There, he learned about the French Revolution and its ideas. He then returned home, vowing to free his people.

In 1810, Bolívar and other leaders of New Granada organized a **junta** (hun' tuh), or political committee, to take over the government. Spanish officials soon crushed the movement, however. Bolívar then went into exile where he formed and trained an army. In 1817, he successfully invaded what is today Venezuela. In August 1819, he defeated the Spanish in what is today Colombia (kuh lum' bē uh). Later that year, he became the first president of Gran Colombia, Ecuador (ek' wuh dor), and Panama. In 1824, Bolívar freed Peru from Spanish rule. He also sent one of his generals to free a Spanish colony called Upper Peru. After declaring its independence in 1825, the new nation was named Bolivia (buh liv' ē uh).

While Bolívar was fighting for freedom in the north, another Creole, José de San Martín (hō sā' dā san mahr tēn'), was fighting for freedom in the south. In 1810, Creole leaders in La Plata (luh plaht' uh) organized a junta to take over the government. In 1812, San Martín joined the struggle for independence. A professional

L1 Government Review with the students the contents of the Declaration of the Rights of Man and the Citizen on pages 517-518 of Chapter 32. Ask which French democratic ideas spread throughout the Spanish colonies. LEP

L2 Critical Thinking Explain to students that Simón Bolívar is often called "the George Washington of South America." Ask students to give their opinions concerning the appropriateness of this name.

MAKING CONNECTIONS

➤➤ **Medicine** Thousands of French soldiers sent to Saint Dominque died from yellow fever, which was not eradicated from Hispaniola until the early 1900s.

DID YOU KNOW ??

Haiti was the second republic in the Western Hemisphere. The United States was the first. Its first leader, Touissant-L'Ouverture, fought for the Americans during the American Revolution.

VIDEODISC

Use the following to enrich Chapter 34.

WC N 41 44096
Detail of slave revolt in Saint Domingue, 1791.

WH J 21 18837
José San Martín and Símon Bolívar at Guayaquil, Ecuador.

MULTICULTURAL PERSPECTIVES

The class structure of Latin America was complex. In addition to peninsulares, Creoles, mestizos, and mulattoes, there were about 20 other classes including Native Americans and African Americans. With independence, this structure changed only slightly, although there was some shifting of power. African Americans gained some influence, although enslavement continued for many years in some countries. The Creoles were harsh judges of the Native American people. The Native Americans lost both power and security. For decades, the system prevailed, as Creoles ruled.

L2 **Civics** Discuss with students the definition of *nationalism. (the feelings of loyalty and pride that a people have toward their nation)* Ask students how nationalism might lead to revolution in a nation that is considered a colony of another nation. *(People revolt against foreign governments in an effort to rule themselves.)* Have students cite examples of present-day or historic struggles for nationalism. LEP

LINKING PAST TO PRESENT

On September 16, 1810, Father Hidalgo rang the bells in his small church in the village of Delores and shouted the *Grito de Dolores* (Cry of Delores) in which he demanded independence. To this day, the president of Mexico rings a bell in Mexico City each September 16 and repeats the *Grito de Dolores.*

MAKING CONNECTIONS

➤➤ **History** Father Morelos was a mestizo. A constitution he wrote gave the government the right to take land from the penisulares and other wealthy people and distribute it to the poor peasants.

VIDEODISC

Use the following to enrich Chapter 34.

WH J 12 18828

José de San Martín (1778-1850).

WH K 12 18856

Bernardo O'Higgins (1778-1842).

Painting of Bernardo O'Higgins

soldier, San Martín organized an army. He was aided by his wife, who persuaded the women of Buenos Aires (bwā' nuhs er' ēz) to give their jewels to help buy supplies for her husband's troops. He was also aided by Father Luís Beltrán (lū ēs' bel trahn'), who melted down church bells to make guns and bullets. In 1816, the part of La Plata that is now Argentina (ahr juhn tē' nuh) won its independence.

In 1817, San Martín led his army across the Andes Mountains into what is now Chile. The crossing was difficult, and many soldiers died from the cold and the lack of oxygen. Most of their horses and pack mules also died. However, San Martín was able to take the Spanish forces in Chile by surprise. He and another soldier, Bernardo O'Higgins (ber nahrd' ō ō hig' enz), defeated the Spanish. Chile became independent a year later.

Mexico, Central America, and Brazil A fight for independence went on in Mexico as well. Father Miguel Hidalgo y Costilla (mē gel' ē dahl' gō ē kahs tē' yuh) played an important part in this struggle. He had long been upset about the way the Native Americans were treated. Now, he urged his congregation not to submit any longer to Spanish rule.

Led by Hidalgo, the Native Americans revolted in 1810. Frightened by the Native Americans, the Creoles joined with the peninsulares to crush the revolt. Hidalgo himself was caught and put to death. Three years later, another priest, Father José María Morelos y Pavón (hō sā' mah rē' ah mō rā' lōs ē pah vōn'), led a second revolt. It was no more successful than the first. Morelos, like Hidalgo, was caught and put to death.

In 1820, there was a revolt in Spain. The rebels there wanted to stop forced labor in Mexico and divide the land among the peasants. This greatly upset the Creoles, church leaders, and army officers. So, they joined together and revolted against Spanish rule in Mexico. Two years later, Mexico was declared to be independent. It was ruled by Agustín de Iturbide (ah gūs tēn' dā ē tur bē' thā), a Creole army officer, who served as emperor. Iturbide, however, refused to share power with the Mexican legislature. He was also a poor administrator. The Mexicans soon tired of his rule and in 1823, they overthrew him. In 1824, after a new constitution was written, Mexico became a republic.

Painting of Father Hidalgo

Moved by what had happened in Mexico, the people of Central America also revolted. In 1821, they declared their independence and two years later joined together to form the United Provinces of Central America. Not long after, the United Provinces split into the present-day countries of Costa Rica (kos' tuh rē' kuh), El Salvador (el sal' vuh dor), Guatemala, Honduras (hon dūr' uhs), and Nicaragua (nik uh rah' gwuh).

A struggle for independence also took place in Brazil. Many Brazilians could see no reason to remain a part of the Portuguese

COOPERATIVE LEARNING

Divide students into teams: priests, peninsulares, mestizos, mulattoes, and Creoles. Tell students that their colony has just achieved independence from Spain and they now have the opportunity to form a new government. Have students research the social and economic interests and goals of their groups. Next have the groups discuss their concerns and draw up a platform stating their positions and their goals for the new government. Then have students meet in a Constitutional Convention to create the laws for their new government. Allow students to debate their needs and draw up a constitution.

Independence in Latin America

L1 Geography: Location Ask students to identify the areas ruled by European nations on the map on this page. Have students compare these maps with the map of modern Latin America in their Atlas. Help them identify present-day nations that were at one time ruled by other countries. LEP

INDEPENDENT PRACTICE

L2 Geography: Region Have students study the map on this page and draw conclusions about the difficulties early Latin Americans, especially those living in present-day Central and South America, may have had in communicating, trading, and transporting goods. Have students list their conclusions and rank them from most to least troublesome.

Assign the Chapter 34 **Geography and Map Activity** in the TCR.

L2 History Have students investigate the dictatorships of Santa Anna and Benito Juárez to compare and contrast their histories and styles of ruling. Ask students to act as historians, charting the information and writing a paragraph that summarizes what subsequent rulers could have learned from these two dictators.

MEETING SPECIAL NEEDS

Remind students that the main reason the European powers wanted colonies in the Americas was to obtain raw materials. Ask visual learners to research the natural resources of Latin America. Using a simple outline map, have them make natural resource maps of Latin America. Display the maps in the classroom.

LINKING PAST TO PRESENT

Caudillos ruled in Latin America well into the 1900s. Two latter-day examples are Rafael Trujillo of the Dominican Republic (1930-1961) and Juan Perón of Argentina (1943-1955).

CAPTION ANSWER

Brazil was the only country in South America to become a monarchy after gaining its independence.

L3 **Religion** The Roman Catholic Church was powerful in Latin America in the nineteenth century. Have students investigate the role of the Church in Latin America today and how its role has changed there in the past 150 years. Have students write a summary paragraph that tells how the Church's influence evolved and what they expect to happen concerning the Church in the future.

VIDEODISC

Use the following to enrich Chapter 34.

WC F 1 22470
The Congress of Vienna, 1814-1815.

WC F 2 22471
Prince Clemens von Metternich (1773-1859).

Empire. They were angry that Portugal tried to control their trade. They also did not like the way the Portuguese parliament treated Brazilian representatives. In 1822, the Brazilians declared their independence from Portugal. Pedro (pā' drō), their Portuguese ruler, agreed to accept a constitution and became their emperor. Brazil was the only country in South America to become a monarchy after independence.

Rule by Caudillos Most people in Latin America hoped the newly independent countries would become democratic. Spanish rule had given the people little training in self-government, however. The mestizos, Native Americans, and African Americans had received no opportunity for education. Also, the Creoles were not willing to share power with other groups.

A new kind of leader called a **caudillo** (kau thē' yō), or strong man, rose to power. Caudillos were backed by the army. Most were also backed by large landowners and church leaders, who did not want their lands divided among the peasants.

Generally, a caudillo took over a government by force. He ruled until he was overthrown by another caudillo. With each change in government, there was a violent revolution and much bloodshed. Because of this, most Latin American countries did not have a stable government.

Most caudillos ruled as dictators. They did not care about improving the lot of the people. One such caudillo was Antonio López de Santa Anna (ahn tō' nyō lō' pās da san' tuh an' uh) of Mexico, who had been a commander in Iturbide's army. One historian described Santa Anna as "a fortune hunter and a glory

BRAZILIAN INDEPENDENCE Brazil gained its independence from Portugal in 1822. Here, Pedro I, Brazil's first emperor, is shown raising his sword and crying out "Independence or death." **What was unusual about Brazil's independence?**

EXTENDING THE CONTENT

In 1808 Napoleon's French army had invaded Portugal, causing the Portuguese royal family to flee to Brazil. King João transferred his monarchy to Brazil, declaring Rio de Janiero capital of the Portuguese empire. João immediately introduced governmental reforms in Brazil. He reinstated more favorable trade laws by opening Brazil's ports to the world. João also worked to make the agriculture and mining industries more profitable. He funded public education including military academies, art school, and medical schools. João returned to Brazil in 1820 to save his throne and left Brazil to his son Pedro to rule.

EMPEROR MAXIMILIAN Maximilian was able to rule Mexico only with the aid of French troops. After the troops were withdrawn, Maximilian was captured. This painting shows Maximilian being led to his execution. **Who was elected president of Mexico after Maximilian's death?**

hound." In 1833, Santa Anna led his troops into Mexico City and had himself elected president. He ruled Mexico six times between 1833 and 1855. It was during his rule that Mexico lost almost one half of its land to the United States through the Treaty of Guadalupe Hidalgo.

A different type of caudillo eventually took Santa Anna's place. His name was Benito Juárez (ba nē' tō hwahr' ez). He proved that a caudillo could care about the needs of the people. A lawyer, Juárez was the first Native American to rule Mexico since the fall of the Aztec Empire.

Juárez was officially elected president in 1861, after several years of civil war. At the time, Mexico owed money to several foreign countries, including France. Juárez asked these countries to wait two years for their money. France refused. Instead, it sent troops and made a European prince named Maximilian (mak suh mil' yuhn) emperor. Juárez and his followers refused to give up, however, and finally defeated the French.

Juárez was again elected president in 1867. He held office until his death in 1872. As president, he worked to hold democratic elections. He reduced the power of the Roman Catholic Church by selling its land to the peasants. He started free schools to educate Native American children. This made education the responsibility of the state rather than the Church. He also reduced the size of the army.

CAPTION ANSWER

Benito Juárez

MAKING CONNECTIONS

>> **History** Mexican conservatives in exile prompted Napoleon III of France to send Maximilian of Hapsburg to restore a "Latin" empire in Mexico. In 1866 Napoleon yielded to international pressure and withdrew his support from Maximilian. Stranded and outnumbered, Maximilian tried to engineer an honorable defeat for himself. However, Juárez had Maximilian executed as a warning to European leaders. A month later the republic was restored.

VIDEODISC

Use the following to enrich Chapter 34.

WH K 31 18875

Benito Juárez (1806-1872).

SPOTLIGHT ON: BENITO JUÁREZ

Benito Juárez was born in 1806 to a Zapotec Native American family. He studied law and entered politics in Oaxaca in 1831. In a political system known for its corruption, Juárez gained a reputation for unshakable honesty. He served as a legislator, a judge, then governor of the state of Oaxaca. Land reform was one of Juárez's main goals, for most of Mexico's land belonged to the Church and a few aristocratic landowners. He believed that to prosper the country needed a middle class who owned small farms and businesses.

ASSESS

CHECK FOR UNDERSTANDING

Ask students to summarize the main points of the chapter, orally or in writing. Discuss the answers to the Section and Chapter Review questions.

EVALUATE

Assign the Chapter 34 **Performance Assessment Activity** in the TCR.

Administer the **Chapter 34 Test**. Testmaker available.

RETEACH

Have students work in pairs. Assign each pair a subsection to summarize. Have a students from each pairs read their summary to the class.

Assign the Chapter 34 **Reteaching Activity** in the TCR.

ENRICH

Have students write an essay comparing the English, American, or French revolutions with a revolutions that took place in Latin America.

Assign the Chapter 34 **Enrichment Activity** in the TCR.

CLOSE

Have students discuss the possible meanings of the following quotation by Simón Bolívar, "Those who have toiled for liberty in South America have plowed the sea."

MEETING CHAPTER OBJECTIVES

Each objective is tested by the Review questions in parentheses.

1. **Describe** the government of the United States. (BV; CU 1; CT 1)
2. **Summarize** the expansion of the United States. (BV; CU 2, 3: UYJ)
3. **Analyze** what led to the U.S. Civil War. (BV; UYJ)
4. **Identify** cultural changes in the United States. (BV; CU 4; CT 2; UYJ)
5. **Explain** how colonies in Latin American won independence. (CU 5, 6; CT 3, 4; UYJ)
6. **Discuss** why democracy did not develop in Latin America. (BV; CU 7; UYJ)

Section 2 Review

1. **Identify:** Toussaint-L'Ouverture, Haiti, Antonio Nariño, Simón Bolívar, José de San Martin, Bernardo O'Higgins, Miguel Hidalgo y Costilla, José María Morelos y Pavón, Agustín de Iturbide, Benito Juárez
2. **Define:** junta, caudillo
3. What inspired the people of Latin America to move toward independence?
4. Why did caudillos rule most of the newly independent countries of Latin America?

Critical Thinking

5. Why do you think Simón Bolívar was known as "The Liberator"?

Chapter Summary

1. Soon after the United States became an independent nation, it developed traditions of stable and representative government.
2. In 1800, political power in the United States passed from one political party to another through a peaceful election rather than through war.
3. By 1830, most adult white males in the United States were able to vote, making the government one of the most democratic in the world at the time.
4. As settlers moved westward, they came into conflict with the Native Americans. In the 1830s, many Native Americans were forced onto reservations.
5. By 1867, the United States had tripled its size by acquiring the Louisiana Territory, Florida, the Oregon Territory, almost one half of Mexico's land, and Alaska.
6. Different ways of life in the northern and southern states led to the Civil War in the United States between 1861 and 1865.
7. The Civil War led to freedom for nearly 4 million enslaved African Americans.
8. Urbanization changed life in the United States during the late 1800s and early 1900s.
9. The American and French Revolutions inspired the people of Latin America toward independence.
10. In 1804, Haiti became the first independent country in Latin America.
11. Spain's colonies in Latin America and the Portuguese colony of Brazil gained their independence in the early 1800s.
12. The newly independent Latin American countries lacked training in self-government. As a result, most were ruled by caudillos.

SECTION 2 ANSWERS

1. Toussaint-L'Ouverture, leader in Saint Domingue (p. 553); Haiti, country in Latin America (p. 553); Antonio Nariño, Creole patriot (p. 553); Simón Bolívar, freedom fighter (p. 553); José de San Martín, freedom fighter (p. 553); Bernardo O'Higgins, fought for independence of Chile (p. 554); Miguel Hidalgo y Costilla, fought for Mexican independence (p. 554); José Maria Morelos y Pavón, fought for Mexican independence (p. 554); Agustín de Iturbide, Mexican ruler (p. 554); Benito Juárez, Mexican ruler (p. 557)
2. junta, political committee (p. 553); caudillo, strong man (p. 556)
3. the American and French revolutions
4. because Spanish rule had given the people little training in self-government, and because the Creoles were aggressive
5. because he freed so many countries in Latin America

Assign the Chapter 34 **Section 2 Quiz** in the TCR. Testmaker available.

CHAPTER

Review 34

Building Vocabulary

Write a newspaper article that gives an overview or summary of the major changes in government that took place in the United States and Latin America during the 1800s. Use the following words in your article.

stable government	seceding
political parties	urbanization
federal	tenements
representative government	slums
manifest destiny	junta
annexation	caudillo

Check for Understanding

1. What was important about the American election of 1800?
2. What happened to the Native Americans east of the Mississippi River in the 1830s?
3. What did the United States gain by the Louisiana Purchase?
4. How did city life differ for lower-, middle- and upper-class Americans?
5. How did Antonio Nariño help spread French democratic ideas throughout the Spanish colonies?
6. Why did Father Hidalgo revolt against Spanish rule?
7. How was Benito Juárez different from most caudillos?

Critical Thinking

1. What are the advantages of living in a country with a stable government? What are the disadvantages?
2. What do you think are some ways the creation of public schools changed American life?
3. If you had lived in Brazil in 1822, would you have supported the Portuguese government or the monarchy? Why?
4. How did the revolution in Brazil compare to the revolution in Mexico?

Geography in History

PLACE Refer to the map of Latin America on page 555. The three battle sites marked show these were all fought near large cities. What other things do these battle sites have in common?

Using Your Journal

Review the details you have noted about changes in the United States and Latin America in the 1800s. Review the people who made some of these changes happen. Write a journal entry describing what characteristics these leaders had in common. Would these people probably be leaders if they lived today? Explain.

559

CHAPTER 34 REVIEW ANSWERS

BUILDING VOCABULARY

Newspaper articles will vary but students should include major points and all the vocabulary words.

CHECK FOR UNDERSTANDING

1. It was the first peaceful passing of power from one political group to another.
2. The government began forcing them to live on reservations west of the Mississippi.
3. It doubled its size; gained rich farmland, minerals, and forests; and gained control of the Mississippi River.
4. in housing, in jobs, and in education
5. He translated into Spanish the *Declaration of the Rights of Man and the Citizen.*
6. because he was upset about the way the Native Americans were treated
7. He cared about the needs of the people.

CRITICAL THINKING

1. Advantages are a nation can grow industrially, become powerful, and avoid internal fighting. Disadvantages could include one group becoming too powerful.
2. Answers will vary but indicate that it gave people a chance for a better life.
3. Answers will vary.
4. Answers will vary but revolution in Brazil came about more peacefully than in Mexico.

+ BONUS +

TEST QUESTION

For Chapter 34 Test

Imagine that in Latin America around 1800, no one could translate French. How would this have changed the history of the region? Explain. *(Answers will vary but refer to the* Declaration of the Rights of Man and the Citizen.*)*

USING YOUR JOURNAL

Journal entries will vary but students should describe some characteristics of good and bad leaders. If negatives are not stated, discuss how corruption in leadership can develop.

GEOGRAPHY IN HISTORY

Answers could include the three sites are in mountainous regions, located centrally, but are at opposite ends of the continent.

PLANNING GUIDE

CHAPTER 35 Unrest in Europe

CHAPTER ORGANIZER

Objectives	Special Features	Supplemental Materials
Section 1 The Age of Napoleon Discuss how Napoleon influenced France and formed the Grand Empire.		• Reproducible Lesson Plan • Section 1 Quiz • Testmaker • Chapter 35 Vocabulary and Guided Reading Activity • World History and Art Transparency 21 • The Western Civilization Videodisc
Section 2 Revolution and Reform Describe how the Congress of Vienna established a balance of power and brought peace to Europe, and analyze how liberals, nationalists, and socialists led revolutions that threatened the Congress System.	Map and Geography Skills, *Comparing Historical Maps,* p. 567; People in History, *Ci Xi,* p. 571	• Reproducible Lesson Plan • Section 2 Quiz • Testmaker • Chapter 35 Geography and Map Activity • Chapter 35 Cooperative Learning Activity • Chapter 35 Teaching Transparencies and Activities • The Western Civilization Videodisc
Section 3 Growth of Nationalism Examine what effects nationalism had on Italy, Germany, and Austria.		• Reproducible Lesson Plan • Section 3 Quiz • Testmaker • Chapter 35 Chart and Graph Skill • Unit 11 World Literature • The Western Civilization Videodisc • Chapter 35 Activity Book Activity
Chapter 35 Review and Evaluation		• Chapter 35 Reteaching Activity • Chapter 35 Enrichment Activity • Spanish Summary and Glossary • Audiocassettes (English and Spanish) • Chapter 35 Performance Assessment Activity• Chapter 35 Test • Testmaker

If time does not permit teaching the entire chapter, use the Chapter 35 Summary on page 576 and the Chapter 35 Audiocassettes (English and Spanish) to point out the main ideas of the chapter.

✓ Performance Assessment Activities

Folktales Have students research folktales by the Brothers Grimm that were first published in 1812–1815. Have them compare the original folktales with the way the same folktales have been retold in more modern versions. After reading both versions, have students write a summary that describes how the story changed in details or format and why this may have happened. Have students conclude by defending the versions they prefer.

Flow Charts Have students create a flow chart or graphic organizer of their own design that shows the major events in Napoleon's career from beginning to end. Ask students to then imagine they could change history and intervene in Napoleon's career, having it end in a different way. Have them write an explanation that tells how and when they would intervene and what the changed outcome would be.

CHAPTER RESOURCES

LITERATURE ABOUT THE PERIOD

Hugo, Victor. *Les Misérables.* New American Library, 1987. Novel about the conflicts in France in the early 1800s.

READINGS FOR THE STUDENT

Forester C.S. *Midshipman Hornblower.* Little, Brown Company, 1981. First of eleven sea stories set in the era of Napoleonic Wars.

Lengyel, Emil. *The Congress of Vienna.* Franklin Watts, 1974. Account of the Congress and its participants.

Marrin, Albert. *Napoleon and the Napoleonic Wars.* Viking, 1991. Biography of Napoleon.

READINGS FOR THE TEACHER

Cate, Curtis. *The War of the Two Emperors: The Duel Between Napoleon and Alexander, Russia, 1812.* Random House, 1985. Discusses Napoleon's invasion of Russia.

Herold, J. Christopher. *The Horizon Book of the Age of Napoleon.* Bonanza Books, 1983. Story of the Napoleonic world.

Nicolson, Harold. *The Congress of Vienna, A Study in Allied Unity: 1812-1822.* Harcourt, Brace, Jovanovich, 1965. Focuses on the Congress of Vienna and its attempts to settle the problems that arose after the defeat of Napoleon.

MULTIMEDIA RESOURCES

Bismarck: Germany from Blood and Iron. Learning Corporation of America. Video. Focuses on the unification of Germany.

Napoleon: the End of a Dictator. Learning Corporation of America. Video. Napoleon's final days.

Napoleon: The Making of a Dictator. Learning Corporation of America. Video. Study of Napoleon's rise to power.

Marxism: The Theory that Split a World. Learning Corporation of America. Video. Explains Marx's theories.

INTRODUCE

CHAPTER 35 OVERVIEW

Chapter 35 discusses the political changes and conflicts that transformed Europe during the 1800s.

- **Section 1** analyzes the effects Napoleon's reforms and the role his military conquests played in spreading French revolutionary ideas.
- **Section 2** describes the political movements that challenged the traditional European political order.
- **Section 3** discusses how each European country accepted or resisted change.

CHAPTER OBJECTIVES

After reading Chapter 35, students will be able to:

1. discuss how Napoleon influenced France and formed the Grand Empire.
2. describe how the Congress of Vienna established a balance of power and brought peace to Europe.
3. analyze how liberals, nationalists, and socialists led revolutions that threatened the Congress System.
4. examine what effects nationalism had on Italy, Germany, and Austria.

EXAMINING THE ILLUSTRATION

Ask students what they can tell about Napoleon's character from observing details in this painting. Tell them they will learn how true their assumptions are as they read the chapter.

PERFORMANCE ASSESSMENT ✓

Use the Performance Assessment activities on page 560B to help you evaluate students as they complete the chapter.

CHAPTER 35 Unrest in Europe

Coronation of Emperor Napoleon

560

TEACHER CLASSROOM RESOURCES

- Section Quizzes/Chapter Test
- Reteaching Activity
- Enrichment Activity
- Chart and Graph Skill Activity
- Geography and Map Activity
- Vocabulary and Guided Reading Activity
- Unit 11 World Literature
- Cooperative Learning Activity
- Performance Assessment Activity
- World History and Art Transparencies
- Teaching Transparencies and Activities
- Testmaker
- Audiocassettes (English and Spanish)
- The Western Civilization Videodisc
- The World History Videodisc

Chapter Focus

READ TO DISCOVER:

- How Napoleon influenced France and formed the Grand Empire.
- How the Congress of Vienna established a balance of power and brought peace to Europe.
- How liberals, nationalists, and socialists led revolutions that threatened the Congress System.
- What effects nationalism had on Italy, Germany, and Austria.

In the early 1800s, Napoleon occupied the center of the European stage. He came closer than anyone else to unifying Europe politically. In so doing, he spread revolutionary ideas. After his downfall, there was a return to the old order. However, the ideas of the Napoleonic (nuh pō lē ahn′ ik) era had taken hold, and from 1820 to 1848, revolutions took place in country after country. The years after 1848 saw the breakup of the old order and the formation of new nations.

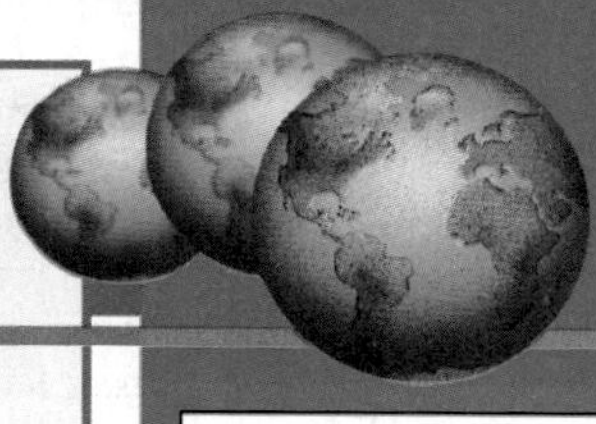

1775 A.D.–1875 A.D.

KEY TERMS

- plebiscite
- scorched-earth policy
- abdicate
- balance of power
- liberals
- proletariat
- communism
- strike
- guerrilla warfare
- kaiser

Section 1

The Age of Napoleon

By 1799, France had experienced ten years of revolution and war. The people longed for a return to peace and order. They were ready for a strong leader to take charge. It was during this time that Napoleon rose to power. His rule started a chain of events that affected not only France, but all of Europe.

Napoleon When the French Revolution began, Napoleon Bonaparte, who had come to France from Corsica (kōr′ si kuh), was a lieutenant in the French army. By the time he was 24 years old, he had become a general. He was not satisfied, however. He wanted more.

In 1796, Napoleon was chosen to lead French troops into Italy. There, the French defeated the Austrians, who ruled Italy at

561

FOCUS

BELLRINGER

Write the following on the chalkboard for students' written responses: *People have the right to overthrow a government with which they disagree.* Tell students to agree or disagree and list reasons to support their viewpoint.

MOTIVATIONAL ACTIVITY

Have students share their responses about whether or not people have the right to overthrow a government with which they disagree. Then read the following quotation to the students: "The world is always childish, and with each new gewgaw of a revolution or new constitution that it finds, thinks it shall never cry any more." Explain that Ralph Waldo Emerson wrote these words in 1847. Discuss the quote, asking students if they agree or disagree. Tell them to keep the quote in mind as they read the chapter.

VOCABULARY PRE-CHECK

Write the key terms for this chapter on the chalkboard. Ask volunteers to skim the chapter for these boldfaced words and read aloud the sentences in which they appear.

Assign Chapter 35 **Vocabulary and Guided Reading Activity** in the TCR.

KEY TO ABILITY LEVELS

Teaching strategies have been coded for varying learning styles and abilities.

L1 Level 1 activities are **basic** activities and should be within the ability range of all students.

L2 Level 2 activities are **average** activities and should be within the ability range of the average to above-average student.

L3 Level 3 activities are **challenging** activities designed for the ability range of above-average students.

LEP LEP activities should be within the ability range of Limited English Proficiency students.

EXTRA CREDIT PROJECT

Have students find examples of European art from the mid to late 1800s such as Impressionism, art nouveau, or the avant-garde in Russia. Have each student prepare a presentation of one or two of the art works to share with the class. Ask them to explain how the art reflects European society at that time.

TEACH

GUIDED PRACTICE

L1 **Chronology** Help students keep the events in this chapter in perspective by creating on the chalkboard or bulletin board a time line from 1775 to 1875. Have students record dates and events as they occur while reading the chapter. LEP

L2 **Geography: Movement** Have students create a large map of Europe on the chalkboard or a large sheet of paper, using the map in their text on page 564 as a guide. On the map, have them identify key places in Napoleon's movement through Europe.

DID YOU KNOW ??

Napoleon Bonaparte was known as "the little Corsican" because he was only 5 feet, 2 inches tall. He was a very hard worker who slept only three hours a night and often ate his meals while dictating to his secretaries.

MAKING CONNECTIONS

➤➤ **Medicine** The first ambulance was designed by Napoleon's personal surgeon, Baron Larrey, in 1792. The horse-drawn carts had special springs meant to smooth the ride over rough terrain. An ambulance division was first used in Napoleon's campaign against Italy in 1796.

that time. As a result of this victory, France acquired Belgium from Austria. France also acquired hundreds of art treasures from Italy, which were placed in the Louvre (lūv), the French national museum.

Two years later, Napoleon sailed for Egypt, where British forces were stationed. He won a great land victory there, but the British fleet destroyed the French fleet. Nevertheless, the French succeeded in establishing their influence in Egypt. Another important outcome of the French campaign was that soldiers accompanying Napoleon discovered the Rosetta Stone.

Meanwhile, Austria, Russia, and Great Britain defeated French forces in Europe. When Napoleon learned of this, he saw his chance to gain more power. He left his troops in Egypt and returned to Paris. There, he and two members of the Directory plotted to take over the government. On November 9, 1799, they put their plan into effect and met with success.

Napoleon set up a new government called the Consulate (kon′ suh luht). He placed himself at its head and took the title of First Consul. By this time, Russia was no longer at war with France. However, Austria and Great Britain were. In 1801, Napoleon led French forces to victory over Austria. In 1802, he arranged a peace treaty with Great Britain.

Affairs at Home Once France was at peace, Napoleon turned his attention to affairs at home. The Directory had been weak and in debt. Napoleon set out to make the Consulate strong and rich. He took away the people's right to choose their own local officials and gave that power to the national government. He prohibited local governments from collecting taxes and assigned all tax collection to the national government. Because Napoleon's system was better organized, the French government was able to collect more taxes. In a few years, France's debt was paid, and its economy had improved. Napoleon also used some of the tax money to set up a system of public education.

Example of Napoleonic Dress

Napoleon also set to work to bring order to the French legal system. The French Revolution had swept away most laws and the different revolutionary governments had never been able to agree on new ones. As a result, different laws were followed in different parts of the country. To correct this, Napoleon appointed a committee of lawyers and told them to write a new code of law for the whole country. The laws they wrote were divided into five parts and were called the Napoleonic Code.

The Napoleonic Code preserved the most important rights won in the French Revolution. Serfdom was ended. People were made equal before the law. Anyone charged with a crime was guaranteed a public trial by jury. Freedom of religion was also guaranteed. However, some rights the people had won in the revolution were taken away. No one was allowed to criticize the

SPOTLIGHT ON: NAPOLEON

Napoleon was born in 1769 to a noble Italian family. He studied French for a few months and at 10 entered a French military school. Napoleon wasn't a brilliant student, but he was good in mathematics and history, was extremely persistent, and believed in himself. The French Revolution began in 1789. The fall of Toulon was credited to Napoleon. Here Napoleon developed a brilliant strategy that formed the basis for all his future battles. He learned to seek an enemy's weakest point, put all his effort into breaking through, and then overwhelm the enemy.

national government. There was no freedom of speech or of the press. A large police force kept watch on anyone suspected of being against Napoleon. Many people were put in jail.

Napoleon tried to make both Paris and France more beautiful. He had a huge marble arch, called the Arc de Triomphe (ahrk deh trē ahmf'), built as a monument to his campaigns. He named Jacques-Louis David as court painter. David designed furniture that looked like that of ancient Greece and Rome. Soon, the "Empire" style spread throughout Europe. This style affected clothes as well as furniture. Women wore narrow white cotton or muslin dresses with low square necklines and short puffed sleeves. They also fixed their hair like the women of ancient Rome.

Photograph of Arc de Triomphe

Napoleon also worked to improve transportation. Under his direction, French workers dug canals and improved roads. Fourteen new bridges were built across the Seine River, which runs through Paris.

Because Napoleon brought peace and order, he was very popular. In 1802, he asked the people to elect him First Consul for life. They did so in a **plebiscite** (pleb' uh sīt), or popular vote. Two years later, the French made Napoleon emperor of France. His coronation was held in the Cathedral of Notre Dame (nō' truh dahm). The Pope came from Rome for the crowning but did not have a chance to place the crown on Napoleon's head. Instead, Napoleon took the crown from the Pope's hands and crowned himself.

The Grand Empire Being emperor of France was not enough for Napoleon. He wanted to built a Grand Empire that would take the place of the Holy Roman Empire. He had the advantage of an army whose soldiers worshiped their emperor and whose officers were chosen because they were able in battle, not just because they were aristocrats.

In 1803, Great Britain, threatened by Napoleon's actions, declared war on France. Great Britain and its allies, however, were not able to stop Napoleon and his soldiers. In 1805, Napoleon had himself crowned king of Italy. In 1806, he formed the Confederation (kuhn fed uhr ā' shuhn) of the Rhine, which consisted of a group of conquered German states. In 1808, he invaded Spain and Portugal. The following year, he made the Papal States part of France and put the Pope in prison. France's boundaries now included much of Europe.

Painting of Napoleonic Officer

The countries in Napoleon's Grand Empire were strongly influenced by France. French citizens, including relatives of Napoleon, took over the government of many conquered areas. The French rulers made the Napoleonic Code law. Thus, Napoleon's conquests helped spread the ideas of the French Revolution all through Europe.

L3 **Critical Thinking** Read aloud Napoleon's words: "I knew that I was superior to other men." Have students summarize Napoleon's strengths, such as military and administrative skills, and rank them from most to least important. Have students discuss whether or not his beliefs about himself were important to his success.

MAKING CONNECTIONS

➤➤ **Culture** Some features of the Napoleonic Code were unfavorable to women. For example, a husband had complete control over his wife's money and property, and a wife was expected to obey her husband.

DID YOU KNOW ??

In 1796, Napoleon married Josephine de Beauharnais, a Creole from the West Indies. When she failed to have children, Napoleon divorced her and married Marie Louise, daughter of the Emperor of Austria, who bore him a son.

VIDEODISC

Use the following to enrich Chapter 35.

WC E 187 19968
Napoleon, Tsar Alexander confer, Nieman River.

WC E 188 19969
Napoleon invades Russia, 1812.

EXTENDING THE CONTENT

Napoleon realized that French Catholics opposed the Civil Constitution of the Clergy—passed by the French Assembly in 1790 giving each parish the right to elect its own priests. He negotiated an agreement called the Concordat of 1801 with Pope Pius VII. In this agreement Napoleon acknowledged that Catholicism was the religion of the majority of French people but affirmed religious tolerance for all. Napoleon did retain the right to name all bishops, who had to swear allegiance to the state.

L1 **Geography: Location** Have students study the map "Napoleonic Europe" on this page to reinforce their awareness of the size and importance of Napoleon's empire in Europe. LEP

L2 **Role Play** Have students create a short skit about Napoleon's decision to march into Moscow. Students should include the invasion, the fire, the peace proposals sent to the Russians by Napoleon, and the French army's withdrawal from Moscow. LEP

MAP STUDY

Answer

the North Sea and Atlantic Ocean

VIDEODISC

Use the following to enrich Chapter 35.

WC E 195 19976
"Liberty à la Francaise!" 1803 British cartoon.

WC E 182 19963
Napoleon I, Emperor of the French 1804 to 1814.

MAP STUDY

PLACE Napoleon had power over most of the European continent in 1812. **What geographic features helped to protect Great Britain from Napoleon's armies?**

Only Great Britain and Russia remained undefeated by Napoleon. Since the French could not defeat the British navy, Napoleon tried to obtain victory in a different way. He forbade the countries in his empire to trade with Great Britain, which he called a "nation of shopkeepers." His order, however, was hard to enforce, and it proved unsuccessful.

Napoleon then decided to take on Russia. He organized a Grand Army of about 600,000 soldiers of different nationalities. It was the largest army the world had yet seen. In the summer of 1812, the Grand Army invaded Russia. Except for one battle, though, the Russians did not fight. Instead, they retreated, drawing the French deeper into Russia. As the Russians retreated, they burned their villages and food supplies, leaving nothing for the advancing French. This tactic is called a **scorched-earth policy.**

Napoleonic Europe

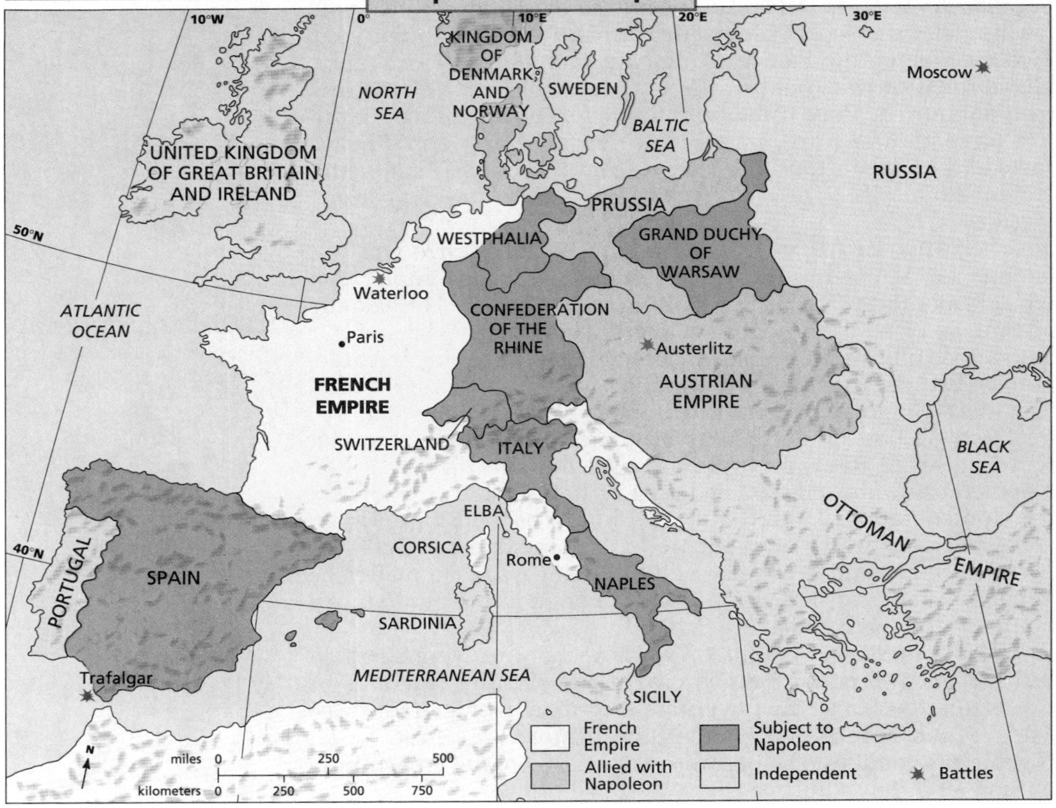

EXTENDING THE CONTENT

When Great Britain declared war on France in 1803, Napoleon had many different plans to invade England (including a fleet of hot air balloons to cross the Channel). In 1805 a combined French and Spanish navy set sail. At Trafalgar off the southern coast of Spain, they encountered the British fleet under Lord Horatio Nelson. Although Nelson was killed at Trafalgar, nearly two-thirds of the French fleet was destroyed. The British victory ended the threat of invasion. Later that same year, Napoleon recovered to win two famous battles. Splitting the Austrian and Russian forces, he beat one at Ulm, the other at Austerlitz.

In September, Napoleon reached Moscow, which had been abandoned by the Russians. Shortly after the French arrived, the city caught fire and three fourths of it was destroyed. The French army now had neither food nor shelter. Napoleon sent several peace proposals to the Russians, which they ignored. He finally gave the order to withdraw. By then the bitter Russian winter had started. Hundreds of thousands of French soldiers froze to death as temperatures fell to 40 degrees below zero. Thousands more died from disease and lack of food. In the end, fewer than 100,000 soldiers made it back to France.

Napoleon quickly raised another army, but the new soldiers were not well trained. They were defeated by the allied forces of Austria, Prussia, Russia, and Great Britain. This was the first time the four countries had joined together to fight Napoleon.

In 1814, the allies took Paris, and Napoleon was forced to **abdicate** (ab′ duh kāt), or give up the throne. He was sent into exile to the small island of Elba off the coast of Italy. He managed to escape, however, and gathered together enough troops to invade France. For 100 days, Napoleon again reigned as emperor. The allies, under the British leadership of the Duke of Wellington, finally defeated him in 1815 at the Battle of Waterloo. This time, Napoleon was sent to the island of St. Helena (huh lē′ nuh) off the west coast of Africa, where he died in 1821.

Section 1 Review

1. **Identify:** Napoleon Bonaparte, Louvre, Consulate, Napoleonic Code, Grand Empire, Grand Army, Duke of Wellington, Battle of Waterloo
2. **Define:** plebiscite, scorched-earth policy, abdicate
3. Why did Napoleon's invasion of Russia fail?

Critical Thinking

4. In your opinion, was the Napoleonic Code something that Napoleon should be proud of? Explain.

Section 2

Revolution and Reform

After Napoleon's defeat, representatives from Austria, Prussia, Russia, and Great Britain met in Vienna (vē en′ uh) to decide what to do about France and the rest of Europe. Although the settlement they agreed upon brought peace to Europe for a time, it also set the stage for revolution in many countries and reform in some.

L1 **History** Ask students to discuss some of the most important changes in Europe brought about by Napoleon's reign in France. Then ask them to predict how the European nations might react after Napoleon loses his power. LEP

L3 **Music** Have interested students research composers such as Tchaikovsky or Beethoven, who were inspired to write music about the events in France under Napoleon. Encourage students to share samples of the music, pointing out the parts that sound warlike to them.

DID YOU KNOW ??

The scorched-earth policy used by the Russians was the same policy the Romans had used against Hannibal and the Cartheginians.

VIDEODISC

Use the following to enrich Chapter 35.

WC E 202 19983
Paris celebrates the fall of Napoleon in 1814.

WC E 205 19986
The Island of St. Helena.

SECTION 1 ANSWERS

1. Napoleon Bonaparte, French emperor (p. 561); Louvre, French museum (p. 562); Consulate, Napoleon's government (p. 562); Napoleonic Code, French laws (p. 562); Grand Empire, Napoleon's empire (p. 563); Grand Army, Napoleon's army (p. 564); Duke of Wellington, leader of allies (p. 565); Battle of Waterloo, Napoleon's defeat (p. 565)
2. plebiscite, popular vote (p. 563); scorched-earth policy, retreating army burns land (p. 564); abdicate, give up the throne (p. 565)
3. because of the Russian scorched-earth policy and the bitter Russian winter
4. Answers will vary but might include that it was positive because it made laws uniform throughout the country and it protected certain rights; it was negative because it took away freedoms of speech and press.

Assign the Chapter 35 **Section 1 Quiz** in the TCR. Testmaker available.

L1 **Critical Thinking** Have students describe the goals for the Congress of Vienna and briefly explain how the members of the Congress intended to attain each goal. LEP

L2 **Government** Help students make a chart on the chalkboard of the groups who were against the Congress System. The chart should explain the grievances of each group. Then suggest students put themselves in each group and choose one grievance they would like corrected if they could choose only one. LEP

DID YOU KNOW

The French representative, Prince Charles Maurice de Talleyrand, served under Louis XVI, the various revolutionary governments, Napoleon, and the restored French king, Louis XVIII.

GEOGRAPHY AND HISTORY

The peace treaty had a significant effect on the German state of Prussia. Because its territories were divided, it became more interested in uniting the German states into a single nation.

Painting of Metternich

The Congress of Vienna

The Congress of Vienna was sometimes called the "Waltzing Congress." This was because the representatives spent much of their time at dinners, dances, and fox hunts. However, decisions were made by a few leaders. They included Prince Klemens von Metternich (met′ uhr nik), the Austrian foreign minister; Czar Alexander I of Russia; King Frederick William III of Prussia; and Viscount Castlereagh (vī′ kownt kas′ uhl rā), the British foreign secretary. Charles-Maurice de Talleyrand (tal′ ē ran) decided matters for France.

The leaders did not want to punish France too harshly. At the same time, they wanted to build a peaceful and stable Europe. They believed the best way to do this was by establishing a **balance of power,** or equal strength among countries. They hoped that a balance of power would prevent any single country from starting another war.

To accomplish this, the leaders divided Napoleon's Grand Empire. Russia got Finland and most of Poland. Sweden got Norway. Austria got part of northern Italy. Great Britain got the islands of Malta (mahl′ tuh) and Ceylon (sā lahn′), as well as the Dutch Cape Colony in South Africa. Belgium and Holland were made into a single nation. In addition, the 39 German states were combined into a loose confederation headed by Austria.

The leaders of the Congress of Vienna were against democracy. Hoping to crush revolutionary ideas, they brought back divine-right monarchy. They had already put Louis XVIII, younger brother of Louis XVI, on the French throne. Now, they brought back the monarchy in Spain and Portugal. The Pope was again made ruler of the Papal States.

Political Movements

The balance of power in Europe was maintained for a number of years. However, the revolutionary ideas that had been spread by Napoleon's Grand Empire did not die. Several groups were against the Congress System, or the political plan and division of Europe set up by the Congress of Vienna.

One group was the **liberals.** They wanted political reform based on the ideals of the French Revolution. These included individual freedom, equal rights under the law, and freedom of thought and religion. Most liberals were members of the middle class. They also wanted changes that would improve their own lives. Among these changes were voting rights for landowners and the protection of private property. Some liberals wanted a constitutional monarchy. Others wanted a republic. The liberals were strongest in Great Britain and France.

Another group that was against the Congress System was the **nationalists** (nash′ uh nuh lists). They wanted political independence for areas where people shared the same language, customs, and history. The Congress of Vienna had paid no

EXTENDING THE CONTENT

Prince Klemmens von Metternich was the dominant figure at the Congress of Vienna. As an Austrian aristocrat, he disliked and feared nationalism, for the Austrian Empire included many minorities—Magyars, Czechs, Slavs, and others. Metternich believed that any upset in the established order might bring down the whole structure. To follow up the decisions made at the Congress of Vienna, Metternich put together a series of treaties aimed at involving all monarchs in preserving the status quo against liberalism and nationalism. The treaties called for periodic conferences and for settling international crises by diplomacy, if possible.

Comparing Historical Maps

A comparison of historical maps can reveal the changes that occur in the political features of an area over time.

Look at the map on page 564. Now, look at the map below. Note that both show about the same area, but at different times. The map on page 564 shows Europe's political aspects during Napoleon's rule. The map below shows Europe after the Congress of Vienna.

To compare historical maps, first look at both maps to make sure the same region is being illustrated. Then, study the boundaries and note any changes. Study also the names of the countries to see if they have changed.

For example, note that the Grand Duchy of Warsaw was subject to Napoleon. After the Congress of Vienna, however, both its boundaries and its name changed.

Compare both maps and answer the following questions.

Map Practice

1. **How was the French Empire divided after the Congress of Vienna?**
2. **What countries were not directly affected by either Napoleon's rule or the Congress of Vienna?**

Europe After the Congress of Vienna

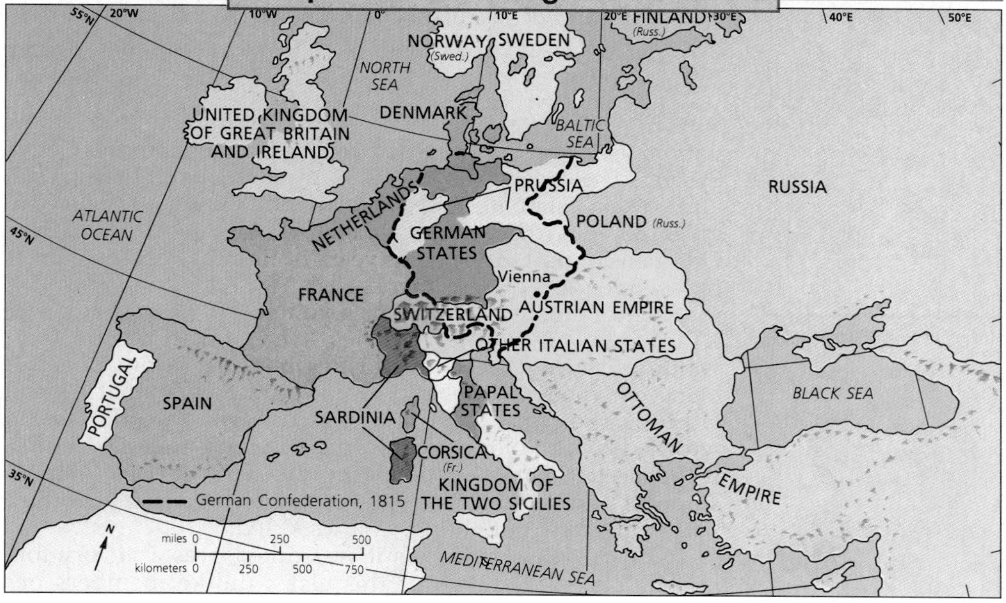

SPOTLIGHT ON: EUROPE

Several European leaders met at the Congress of Vienna to reorganize the Napoleonic lands. One leader, Alexander I of Russia, called a Holy Alliance that would let God guide the Congress and their relations. Most countries agreed to join his alliance although they doubted it could be successful. Alexander later died mysteriously in a remote part of Russia with many doubting he was really dead. He was sighted alive all over Europe.

Teaching

MAP SKILLS

Comparing Historical Maps

Have students read the instructional part of the feature. Ask: What can a comparison of historical maps of the same region show? *(the changes that occur in the political features of an area over time)* What are two things to study when comparing historical maps of the same region? *(boundaries, names of countries)*

Next, have students use the skills they have learned in this feature to compare the historical map "Europe After the Congress of Vienna" on this page with the map "Europe in the Late Middle Ages" on page 422. Ask them to write five questions that compare both maps. Then call on students to ask their questions of the class.

ANSWERS to Map Practice

1. into France; the Netherlands; Sardinia; the Papal States; and parts of Italy, Austria-Hungary, and Prussia

2. Portugal, the United Kingdom of Great Britain and Ireland, Sweden, and the Ottoman Empire were not directly affected.

INDEPENDENT PRACTICE

L3 **Debate** Have students discuss the part of Marx's philosophy that states: "In a worker's revolution all people would be equal and government would not be needed." In a blind drawing have students assigned to a team, either agreeing or disagreeing with Marx's philosophy. Have students conduct a debate with the rest of the class deciding who presents the best arguments.

GEOGRAPHY AND HISTORY

The delegates to the Congress of Vienna redrew national boundaries in Europe based on the desires of the rulers rather than those of the people they governed. The new boundaries ended the hopes of many groups. For example, the boundaries crushed the Polish people's hopes for a united nation. Instead their land was divided among Austria, Vienna, Prussia, and Russia.

Assign the Chapter 35 **Geography and Map Activity** in the TCR.

DID YOU KNOW ??

Many romantic artists and writers throughout Europe supported the Greek fight for independence. Among them was the English poet Lord Byron, who went to Greece to fight as a volunteer. He died there of a fever.

attention to nationalist feelings when it divided the Grand Empire. For example, the Belgians did not want to be part of Holland. The northern Italians did not want to be ruled by Austria.

A third group that was against the Congress System was the **socialists.** They wanted to end private ownership of land and factories. They believed the state, or the people as a whole, should own all means of production. In this way, the socialists believed, everyone would be treated fairly and the workers' lot would improve.

Some socialists tried to set up ideal communities based on economic cooperation. They thought these communities would show that theirs was a better way of life. Such socialists were known as **utopian socialists** (yū tō' pē uhn sō'shuh lists).

Other socialists believed the only way to bring about reform was by revolution. One such socialist was Karl Marx, a German. He believed the **proletariat** (prō luh tār' ē uht), or industrial working class, would rise up and take power. "The workers have nothing to lose . . . but their chains," he wrote in his book *The Communist Manifesto* (kahm' yū nist man uh fes' tō). "They have a world to gain. Workers of the world, unite!"

Marx believed that after the workers' revolution, there would be no hunger or poverty. Everyone would become equal. Governments would not even be needed. People would work because they wanted to give something to society. In return, they would be able to develop their own interests and talents. Marx called his kind of socialism **communism** (kahm' yū niz uhm). He believed the workers' revolution would be led by his new Communist party.

An Era of Revolution

Beginning in 1820, liberals, nationalists, and socialists led revolutions against the Congress System. The earliest of these took place in Spain, Portugal, Italy, and Russia. They all failed. However, Greek nationalists were given hope by these attempts. In 1821, they rebelled against the Ottoman Empire. After eight years of fighting, Greece gained its independence.

Painting of Karl Marx

In 1830, there was another revolution in France. After Louis XVIII died, his brother Charles X had taken the throne. He wanted to bring back the Old Regime. Just a few weeks after being crowned, Charles did away with the National Assembly. He took the right to vote away from the middle class and returned control of the schools to the Roman Catholic Church. In response to Charles' actions, middle-class liberals, helped by students and unemployed workers, overthrew the government. After three days of fighting, Charles X fled.

The July Revolution, as it was called, was a victory for the middle class. Members of this class, unlike members of the working class, wanted a constitutional monarchy rather than a

EXTENDING THE CONTENT

Karl Marx believed that capitalism was only a temporary phase. A crisis in one of the advanced industrial countries would cause the workers, or the proletariat, to seize control from the bourgeoisie, or middle class. The proletariat would build a society in which the people owned everything. Without private property, class distinctions would disappear, and the government would wither away. He felt that this last stage would be genuine communism. He wrote *The Communist Manifesto* along with Friedrich Engels. Marx expanded his views in *Das Kapital* written in 1867.

THE JULY REVOLUTION Charles X caused popular unrest in France when he tried to disband the National Assembly, control the press, and restrict the number of people who could vote. Mobs of French citizens took to the streets in rebellion and forced Charles to flee. **What had members of the working class wanted to accomplish from the July Revolution?**

republic. So, they gave the throne to Charles X's cousin, Louis-Philippe (lū' ē fi lēp'). Under Louis-Philippe's rule, the number of people who could vote increased. However, of the middle class, only its richest members could vote. This angered other members of the middle class. Working-class people were also angry. They had wanted not only a republic but also **universal male suffrage** (suhf' rij), or the right of all adult males to vote.

News of the July Revolution touched off rebellions in other countries. In 1831, Belgian nationalists won independence from Holland. The Poles fought against Russia, but were defeated. Uprisings in several German and Italian states also were put down and ended quickly.

In Great Britain, however, liberal reforms were made by gradual change instead of revolution. In 1832, the British government passed a law that lowered the amount of land a man had to own in order to vote. This increased by one half the number of voters. It also gave the new industrial towns more representation in Parliament. As a result, the British middle class had more say in the government.

Reforms also helped the working class. Labor unions gained the right to **strike,** or stop work, in order to obtain shorter hours,

L2 **Government** Organize the class into three groups, and assign each one of the following political groups: the liberals, the nationalists, and the socialists. Have students write a speech, the purpose of which is to gain support for his or her assigned political group in response to the Congress System. The speeches should outline the basic goals of the group's philosophy and indicate how they plan to achieve them. Have students read their speeches.

CAPTION ANSWER

They wanted a republic and universal male suffrage.

DID YOU KNOW ??

Only 3 percent of the French citizens could vote, even after the July Revolution.

VIDEODISC

Use the following to enrich Chapter 35.

WC F 17 22486
A barricade built during the July Revolution in France.

WC F 19 22488
Louis-Philippe rides into Paris,1830.

MEETING SPECIAL NEEDS

Allow time for students with learning difficulties to make charts, diagrams, time lines, or other graphic organizers for each section. These organizers will help them retain a grasp of the relationships among people, dates, and events and will help them quickly review important data.

L2 **Critical Thinking** Ask students how the events described in this section can be called a continuation of the French Revolution of 1789. Encourage students to refer to pages 513-520 to refresh their memories. Then have them write a paragraph explaining the connections, if any, that they see.

MAKING CONNECTIONS

➤➤ **History** Although workers had done most of the fighting in the 1830 revolution that put Louis-Philippe on the throne, he ignored their demands for economic reforms. Labor unions were declared illegal, and police were used to break up strikes. Napoleon III was aware of the problems of the industrial age. He favored aid for industries, banks, railroads, and the poor. He also favored nationalism and supported international conferences to settle disputes.

LINKING PAST TO PRESENT

In 1844 Antoine Joseph Sax performed in Paris on a new instrument he had invented—the saxophone—which still pleases audiences today.

VIDEODISC

Use the following to enrich Chapter 35.

WC F 51 22520

A National Workshop.

Painting of Louis-Philippe

higher wages, and better working conditions. By 1890, working-class males also obtained the right to vote.

The Revolutions of 1848 In 1848, another series of revolutions broke out. All over Europe, governments were overthrown. Once again, the rebellion started in France.

Louis-Philippe had tried to be a "citizen-king." He walked through the streets of Paris without any servants to show that he was a bourgeois rather than an aristocrat. He wore a frock coat and trousers like the men of the middle class. He was very rich himself, however, and his government served only the rich. Industrial workers and middle-class liberals became increasingly unhappy. At the same time, the economy was bad throughout Europe, including France. Many people did not have jobs. Then, in 1845 and 1846, the potato and wheat crops failed. There was not enough food to feed everyone.

In February of 1848, riots broke out in the streets of Paris. Louis-Philippe fled, and the revolutionary leaders declared the Second French Republic. They set up a temporary government to rule until a new National Assembly could be elected. Louis Blanc (lū ē blahnk), a socialist, was one of the leaders. He persuaded the other leaders to set up **national workshops**, or factories run by the workers but paid for by the government. The national workshops provided jobs for thousands of people. However, the number of people out of work grew faster than jobs could be created. Before long, the French government was supporting over 100,000 people.

When the new National Assembly was finally elected in April, it did away with the workshops. The workers revolted, fighting violently for three days. They were defeated by the army, but not before over 10,000 people were killed.

Painting of Louis-Napoleon

The National Assembly then drew up a constitution. It called for a strong president to be elected by universal male suffrage. Napoleon's nephew, Louis-Napoleon Bonaparte, was elected president of the Second French Republic. He believed, however, that he had inherited his uncle's destiny. So, in 1851 he did away with the constitution. A year later, the people voted him Emperor Napoleon III. At the same time, the Second French Republic was renamed the Second French Empire. Louis-Napoleon remained on the throne until 1870.

The revolution in France was followed by revolutions in other parts of Europe. The Hungarians (hung ger' ē uhns), the Italians, and the Germans all rebelled. Their revolts failed. Even so, the revolutions of 1848 led to some important changes. In time, universal male suffrage spread to most northern and western European countries. Workers, who felt they had been cheated, began to form political parties. Soon, there was a socialist party in almost every European country.

COOPERATIVE LEARNING

Divide students into broadcast teams to provide coverage of the revolutions in France. Each team should divide up responsibility to research and prepare stories that provide a rounded picture of events in one of the revolutions. Each team member should have a role as a news anchor, on-the-scene reporter, or subject of an interview. Have teams report on events, reactions of royalists, republicans, leaders, and the person-in-the-street. Remind students to base their reports on actual events and actual people when possible. Have students write scripts and present their broadcasts to the class.

Assign the Chapter 35 **Cooperative Learning Activity** in the TCR.

Ci Xi

PEOPLE IN HISTORY

No one could know that when Ci Xi (tsuh′ sē) was born in China on November 29, 1835, she would one day be the most powerful woman in China. During the late 1800s, when Europe was going through major changes, Empress Ci Xi came to power in China.

Royal Court Ci Xi had arrived in the court of the Chinese emperor at the age of 16. In 1856 she became the mother of the emperor's only son and heir to the throne. When the emperor died in 1861, Ci Xi's son became the emperor. Since her son was still a child, Ci Xi ruled China in his name. Her strength and intelligence allowed her to take more and more power. She often said that she considered herself to be "more clever than any other woman who had ever lived." When her son died, Ci Xi then ruled through her nephew who became emperor. She made many enemies in her country because of her power.

Foreign Relations When foreigners arrived in China, Ci Xi was against modernization and change in her country. She did not want to lose power, nor did she want her country to become westernized. Later, however, Ci Xi was wise enough to realize that if she did not allow some social and political changes, China might be completely taken over by foreign powers.

Ci Xi began making a few reforms in her government. She modernized the China's civil service whose test was still based on the ancient teachings of Confucius. She forced some Europeans who had demanded representation, out of the government.

Ci Xi also opened schools for girls and did away with the practice of binding the feet of young girls. Ci Xi was one of the first rulers in Asia to be concerned about the lives and rights of women. Three years after Ci Xi's death in 1908, the Chinese monarchy came to an end.

Checking for Understanding

1. **Why was Ci Xi able to rule China when her son was the emperor?**
2. **What reforms did Ci Xi achieve during her rule?**

Teaching

PEOPLE IN HISTORY

CI XI

After students have read the People in History feature, ask: What reforms did Ci Xi make in her government? *(She started the modernized China's civil service test and forced Europeans out of the government.)* How do you know that Ci Xi was concerned about the rights of women? *(She opened schools for girls, and ended the practice of binding the feet of young girls.)*

Have students compare the life of Eleanore of Aquitaine (see feature on page 390) with that of Ci Xi. In what ways were their lives similar? Different?

ANSWERS to Checking for Understanding

1. because the emperor was still a child

2. She established schools and reorganized the government and changed rules requiring the binding of girls' feet.

SPOTLIGHT ON: CI XI

Ci Xi retired in 1889 to a summer palace located northwest of Peking (Beijing). In 1898, however, Ci Xi and some officials loyal to her enacted a military coup against Emperor Kuang-hsü because they disliked his liberal government-reform policies. The Emperor lost his power and Ci Xi once again returned to head the Chinese monarchy. She ended the reforms Kuang-hsü had begun. The Boxer Rebellion was at its height in 1900. Foreign troops captured Peking and forced Ci Xi to leave the capital and accept their peace agreement. She returned to Peking in 1902 and put into place the reforms that she had ended a few years before.

DID YOU KNOW ??

An 1816 French law prohibited the Bonapartes from living in France, so Napoleon III grew up in Italy, Germany, and Switzerland.

LINKING PAST TO PRESENT

Another result of the fighting between Austria and Sardinia and France was the founding of the International Red Cross by a Swiss stretcher-bearer who was named Henri Dunant. He was horrified by the death of thousands of wounded soldiers from typhus and poor care. The symbol of the new organization was the Swiss flag with its colors reversed.

VIDEODISC

Use the following to enrich Chapter 35.

WC G 108 25247
Count Camillo di Cavour (1810-1861).

Section 2 Review

1. **Identify:** Congress of Vienna, Congress System, Karl Marx, July Revolution, Louis-Philippe, Louis Blanc, Napoleon III
2. **Define:** balance of power, liberals, nationalists, socialists, utopian socialists, proletariat, communism, universal male suffrage, strike, national workshops
3. What were two goals of the Congress of Vienna?
4. What were some results of the revolutions of 1848?

Critical Thinking

5. Which one of the three groups who were against the Congress System—liberals, nationalists, or socialists—would you have supported had you lived in the 1800s? Why?

Section 3 GROWTH OF NATIONALISM

After the revolutions of 1848 failed, the Congress System seemed stronger than ever. However, this was not the case. Before long, the growth of nationalism would destroy the balance of power that had been established at Vienna. Three countries that were affected by the growth of nationalism were Italy, Germany, and Austria.

Italy In 1848, eight of the nine Italian states were under Austrian control. Only Sardinia (sahr din' ē uh) was independent. Ever since Napoleon's time, the Italians had been unhappy about this state of affairs. They remembered that Rome had once ruled the ancient world and that Italian city-states had led the Renaissance. They wanted to become a unified nation.

Many nationalists in Italy looked to Sardinia to take the lead. This was because of Sardinia's prime minister, Count Camillo di Cavour (kont kuh mē' lō dē kuh vuhr'). Cavour believed in industrialization and favored a constitutional monarchy. He also realized that Sardinia needed help to drive the Austrians out of Italy. To this end, he made an agreement with Napoleon III. It stated that if the Austrians attacked Sardinia, the French would help the Sardinians. When Austria declared war on Sardinia in 1859, Napoleon III kept his word. Austria was defeated, and the Italian state of Lombardy (lahm' bahr dē) was united with Sardinia. By 1860, the other northern Italian states also revolted against Austria and united with Sardinia.

That same year, an Italian nationalist named Giuseppe Garibaldi (jū zep' ā gār uh bahl' dē) led another revolution in

SECTION 2 ANSWERS

1. Congress of Vienna, decided Europe's boundaries after Napoleon's defeat (p. 566); Congress System, political plan set up by the Congress of Vienna (p. 566); Karl Marx, German socialist (p. 568); July Revolution, French revolution (p. 568); Louis-Philippe, French king (p. 569); Louis Blanc, a socialist leader of the Second French Republic (p. 570); Napoleon III, emperor of the Second French Empire (p. 570)
2. All terms are defined in the text Glossary.
3. to build a peaceful and stable Europe and to crush revolutionary ideas
4. In time, universal male suffrage spread to most northern and western European countries, and workers began to form political parties.
5. Answers will vary but students should give reasons for their choices of one of the three groups.

Assign the Chapter 35 **Section 2 Quiz** in the TCR. Testmaker available.

GIUSEPPE GARIBALDI Giuseppe Garibaldi led the fight for Italian unification in southern Italy. He was skilled in guerilla warfare, having fought in other revolutionary wars. In this painting, Garibaldi leads his Red Shirts in an attack on troops from Naples. **Who became king of the united Italy?**

southern Italy. Garibaldi had spent much of his life in exile in Brazil and Uruguay (yūr' uh gwī). There, he had learned how to lead small bands of soldiers behind enemy lines. The bands would hide in forests and on hillsides. They would make surprise attacks on the enemy and then go back into hiding. This kind of fighting is called **guerrilla warfare** (guh ril' uh wōr fār). In guerrilla warfare, a small group of soldiers can often defeat a much larger army.

Garibaldi taught guerrilla warfare to his followers. They were called "Red Shirts" because, like their leader, most of them wore red shirts. They also wore loose grey trousers, silk handkerchiefs around their necks, grey cloaks, and black felt hats. In 1860, Garibaldi's Red Shirts conquered Sicily within three months. Then, they sailed to the Italian mainland and conquered the state of Naples.

In 1861, the northern and southern nationalist groups combined. The Kingdom of Italy was formed as a constitutional monarchy. Victor Emmanuel II (ē man' yū el) of Sardinia became king. The Pope, who wanted to keep control over the Papal

CAPTION ANSWER

Victor Emmanuel II

LINKING PAST TO PRESENT

Major wars are not generally won exclusively through guerrilla warfare, which has been used since the eighteenth century to wear down the enemy and keep opponents from winning. During the American Revolutionary War, Francis Marion, the "Swamp Fox," effectively led guerrilla groups in South Carolina against the British. Guerrilla warfare has proven effective in rough terrain, as in the rain forests of Latin America and Southeast Asia.

MAKING CONNECTIONS

➤➤ **Biography** Garibaldi's military skills were recognized worldwide. In 1861, the United States offered him command of a Union force at the outbreak of the American Civil War. Garibaldi refused the offer.

VIDEODISC

Use the following to enrich Chapter 35.

WC G 110 25249
Giuseppe Garibaldi, Italian nationalist leader.

WC G 112 25251
Neapolitan troops surprised by Garibaldi's.

MEETING SPECIAL NEEDS

Organize students who are auditory learners into small groups. Ask the students in each group to discuss all the examples they can think of—both historical and current—where regional differences have been a source of tension within a nation. Have students also include any examples of such tensions that exist in their own state. Bring the students back together and make a list on the chalkboard of each group's examples. After discussing the kinds of factors that create regional differences, ask students if they can make any generalizations about the examples they have generated.

L2 **Critical Thinking** Ask students what they think Bismarck meant when he said he would unite Germany, not "by speeches and majority votes—but by blood and iron."

MAKING CONNECTIONS

➤➤ **History** After Paris surrendered, a civil war broke out between the city's municipal government, called the Commune, and the national Assembly at Versailles. More people were killed in the civil war than during the entire French Revolution. After the Commune was defeated, some 20,000 persons were executed and another 7,000 were exiled to a penal colony on an island in the Pacific.

VIDEODISC

Use the following to enrich Chapter 35.

WC G 31 25170
Bismarck forces army budget on the Reichstag.

WC G 48 25187
Napoleon III and Bismarck at Biarritz in 1865.

States, fought against Italian unity and lost. In 1870, the Papal States became part of Italy, and Italian unification was complete. The balance of power in Europe, however, was weakened.

Germany Nationalist feelings were also strong in the 39 German states. German poets and writers, like Johann Wolfgang von Goethe (ger' tuh) and Friedrich von Schiller (shil' uhr), wrote about German nationalism. German composer Richard Wagner (vahg' nuhr) wrote operas based on German folk tales. In 1834, many of the German states signed a trade agreement. In it, they promised not to tax goods coming from other German states. Soon, the economy of these states improved. However, many of the rulers of the smaller states were not willing to give up their political power. Austria was also against any attempt to unify Germany.

These obstacles were overcome by the Kingdom of Prussia. In 1862, King William I named Count Otto von Bismarck (biz' mahrk) prime minister of Prussia. Bismarck was a **junker** (yung' kuhr), or rich landowner, who believed in divine-right monarchy. He said that he would unite Germany, not "by speeches and majority votes—but by blood and iron." He also believed that war against a common enemy would bring the German states closer together.

In 1864, Bismarck joined with Austria to defeat Denmark and to gain territory. Two years later, he used a dispute over this territory as an excuse to go to war against Austria. Prussia won the war in seven weeks. It had superior weapons, as well as an excellent railroad system that moved troops quickly from one battlefield to another. The resulting peace treaty ended the loose German Confederation. The North German Confederation, led by Prussia, was set up in its place.

In 1870, Bismarck found an excuse to go to war against France, Germany's oldest enemy. As Bismarck had hoped, the southern German states joined the northern German states in the struggle. Well-trained and well-equipped, the German army easily defeated the French army. Bismarck then laid siege to Paris. The city held out for four months. Food became so scarce that the people were forced to eat the animals in the zoo. The trees that Napoleon III had planted along the streets of Paris were cut down and used for fuel. At last, on January 28, 1871, the city surrendered.

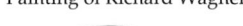

Painting of Richard Wagner

Meanwhile, at Versailles (vuhr sī'), William I of Prussia was named **kaiser** (kī' zuhr), or emperor, of the new German Empire. This included both the northern and the southern German states, as well as the rich mining and manufacturing lands of Alsace (al' sas) and Lorraine (luh rān'), which had been won from France. A unified Germany, however, meant a further weakening of the balance of power.

EXTENDING THE CONTENT

Nationalism deeply influenced European music and literature during the 1800s. It inspired widespread interest in folktales, myths, and national history. In Germany, for instance, the Brothers Grimm (Jakob and Wilhelm) collected folktales in their famous collection, first printed in 1812–1815. Following the Grimm's example, Asbjornsen and Moe made a similar collection of Norwegian folktales, including stories like "East of the Sun and West of the Moon." Romantic novelists, playwrights, and poets found themes in national history. Sir Walter Scott collected Scottish ballads and wrote about medieval England in *Ivanhoe.* In Germany, Friedrich von Schiller wrote plays based on historical fighters for liberty, such as William Tell and Joan of Arc.

THE GERMAN EMPIRE The struggle for a united Germany was led by Count Otto von Bismarck, prime minister of Prussia. In this painting, Bismarck (center) proclaims King William I of Prussia (on platform) the emperor of a new German empire. **What effect did a unified Germany have on Europe?**

Austria Nationalists in Italy and Germany wanted to unify their nations. Nationalists in Austria, on the other hand, threatened the unity of the Austrian Empire.

The Austrian Empire was made up of many nationalities. Although its emperor, Francis Joseph, was German, four out of five people were not. Other nationalities included the Czechs, the Slovaks, the Poles, the Croats, the Slovenes, and the Magyars (mag' yahrs), the largest group in Hungary. Each had its own language and history and wanted to rule itself.

By 1866, Austria had been defeated by both Sardinia and Prussia. Magyar nationalists saw their chance to become independent. They revolted. In 1867, a weakened Austria agreed to create a dual monarchy. Now, the emperor ruled over two separate kingdoms—Austria and Hungary. Each had its own official language, parliament, and laws. Although they were separate politically, the two countries needed each other economically. Austria supplied manufactured goods to Hungary. In return, Hungary supplied Austria with food products.

CAPTION ANSWER

The balance of power was weakened further.

DID YOU KNOW ??

In 1874 in Budapest, Hungary, Ehrich Weiss (later known as Harry Houdini, the world's greatest escape artist) was born.

LINKING PAST TO PRESENT

In addition to having a common ruler, Austria and Hungary had a single army and a common postal system. Systems today were modeled on these early examples.

VIDEODISC

Use the following to enrich Chapter 35.

WC G 35 25174

Francis Joseph I, Austrian Emperor 1848-1916.

MULTICULTURAL PERSPECTIVES

European composers in the 1800s were influenced by nationalism and drew on folk ballads or patriotic themes. Chopin, Liszt, and Smetana used traditional Polish, Hungarian, and Czech melodies. Folk songs came from German and Austrian composers including Beethoven, Schubert, and Schumann. In Italy, a patriotic chorus from Giuseppe Verdi's opera *Nabucco* became virtually the national anthem of the movement for unification. In 1874, Verdi wrote his "Requiem Mass" to honor the poet and nationalist patriot Alessandro Manzoni.

ASSESS

CHECK FOR UNDERSTANDING

Ask students to summarize the main points of the chapter, orally or in writing. Discuss the answers to the Section and Chapter Review questions.

EVALUATE

Assign the Chapter 35 **Performance Assessment Activity**

Administer the **Chapter 35 Test.** Testmaker available.

RETEACH

Have students work in small groups. Assign each group a section to outline. Ask a student from each group to write their outline on the chalkboard.

Assign the Chapter 35 **Reteaching Activity** in the TCR.

ENRICH

Have students choose one of the people mentioned in this chapter and write a short biographical sketch of the person.

Assign the Chapter 35 **Enrichment Activity** in the TCR.

CLOSE

Have students compare the map "Europe After the Congress of Vienna" on page 567 with a present-day map of Europe in the text Atlas. Discuss boundary and country name changes.

MEETING CHAPTER OBJECTIVES

Each objective is tested by the Review questions in parentheses.

1. Discuss how Napoleon formed the Grand Empire. (CU 1, 2; CT 1, 2)
2. Describe how the Congress of Vienna brought peace to Europe. (CU 3)
3. Analyze how revolutions threatened the Congress System. (BV; CU 4, 5; UYJ)
4. Examine nationalism in Italy, Germany, and Austria. (CU 6, 7, 8; CT 3)

The Magyars were satisfied with the situation of having separate countries, but other nationalities in Austria-Hungary were not. Their unhappiness presented a continuing threat to the dual monarchy and the peace of Europe.

Section 3 Review

1. **Identify:** Count Camillo di Cavour, Giuseppe Garibaldi, Red Shirts, Count Otto von Bismarck, Magyars
2. **Define:** guerrilla warfare, junker, kaiser
3. What did Garibaldi do to further nationalism in Italy?
4. How was Austria-Hungary formed? How did most of the citizens feel about this?

Critical Thinking

5. Why do you think the Italian city-states wanted to be a unified nation? Explain.

Chapter Summary

1. In 1799, Napoleon Bonaparte helped to overthrow the Directory and, by 1804, had become emperor of France.
2. Napoleon strengthened the central government and established a code of law for France but took certain rights away from the people.
3. After conquering most of Europe, Napoleon was defeated and exiled from France.
4. In 1814, representatives from Austria, Prussia, Russia, Great Britain, and France met at Vienna to establish a balance of power in Europe.
5. The Congress of Vienna divided Napoleon's empire and brought back divine-right monarchy in many areas.
6. Liberals, nationalists, and socialists opposed the Congress System.
7. In 1820, 1830, and 1848, political revolutions broke out in different European countries.
8. Liberal reforms were made in Great Britain without a revolution.
9. After the revolutions of 1848, universal male suffrage began to spread throughout Europe, and the working class began to turn toward socialism.
10. Between 1859 and 1870, the Italian states united to form one nation.
11. Between 1862 and 1871, the German states, led by Otto von Bismarck of Prussia, united to form one nation.
12. In 1867, the Austrian Empire became two separate kingdoms—Austria and Hungary—each of which had many different national groups that wanted independence.

SECTION 3 ANSWERS

1. Count Camillo di Cavour, prime minister of Sardinia (p. 572); Giuseppe Garibaldi, Italian nationalist (p. 572); Red Shirts, followers of Garibaldi (p. 573); Count Otto von Bismarck, prime minister of Prussia (p. 574); Magyars, group in Hungary (p. 575)
2. guerrilla warfare, a kind of fighting (p. 573); junker, rich landowner (p. 574); kaiser, emperor of German Empire (p. 574)
3. He led a revolution in southern Italy. Soon after, the northern and southern nationalist groups combined.
4. Magyar nationalists in Hungary revolted, and Austria agreed to create a dual monarchy with a common emperor but separate language, parliament, and laws.
5. They remembered ancient Rome's strength and that of Italian city-states. They wanted to be strong and dominant again.

Assign the Chapter 35 **Section 3 Quiz** in the TCR. Testmaker available.

CHAPTER

Review 35

Building Vocabulary

Imagine you are a writer in Europe in the 1800s. You're asked to write a brief introduction to a revolutionary handbook—a book telling people how to be revolutionaries. Use the following words in your introduction.

plebiscite	proletariat
scorched-earth policy	communism
abdicate	strike
balance of power	guerrilla warfare
liberals	kaiser

Check for Understanding

1. How did the Napoleonic Code change the French legal system?
2. What effects did Napoleon have on the art and fashion styles in France?
3. Why did the representatives at the Congress of Vienna try to bring back divine-right monarchy?
4. Why did the temporary French government of 1848 set up national workshops in that country?
5. How did Napoleon III help Italian nationalists?
6. How did the German states become unified?
7. What were some results of the war between Prussia and France?
8. Why were national groups in Austria-Hungary unhappy in the 1860's?

Critical Thinking

1. What did Napoleon reveal about himself at his crowning as the emperor?
2. Do you think Napoleon's conquests were good or bad for Europe? Explain.
3. How important was nationalism in Europe during the second half of the 1800s? Explain.
4. Do you agree or disagree with the following: Liberal reforms can only be made with a revolution. Why?

Geography in History

LOCATION Refer to the map on page 564. During Napoleon's time, as during other historical eras, Paris was an important city. What are the latitude and longitude coordinates of Paris?

Using Your Journal

Review the details you have noted about changes in government in European countries in the 1800s. Review the reasons the different revolutions took place. Write a brief editorial in which you give your opinion about one of these revolutions and whether or not the people had a good reason to revolt. Be sure to include reasons to support your opinions.

CHAPTER 35 REVIEW ANSWERS

BUILDING VOCABULARY

Handbook introductions will vary but students should use all the vocabulary words.

CHECK FOR UNDERSTANDING

1. It ended serfdom, made people equal before the law, and guaranteed certain freedoms.
2. Styles returned to Greek styles which Napoleon favored.
3. because they wanted to crush revolutionary ideas
4. to provide jobs for unemployed workers
5. He helped the Sardinians when Austria declared war on Sardinia.
6. by joining together to fight Denmark, Austria, and France
7. Prussia won from France the rich mining and manufacturing lands of Alsace and Lorraine.
8. because each had its own language and history and wanted to rule itself

CRITICAL THINKING

1. By crowning himself, Napoleon showed he thought he was above the Church.
2. Answers will vary but students should provide reasons for their answers.
3. very important because it led to important governmental changes in Italy, Austria, Germany, and France
4. Answers will vary, but should include the idea that Great Britain adopted reforms without a revolution.

+ BONUS +

TEST QUESTION

For Chapter 35 Test

Think about the following group of words and tell what they have in common with one another in the context of this chapter. How are they different?

liberals nationalists socialists

(*Answers will vary.*)

USING YOUR JOURNAL

Editorials will vary but students should support their choices with reasons. They might point to the conflict in the former Yugoslavia and other modern revolutions as comparisons.

GEOGRAPHY IN HISTORY

about 49° N, 2° E

PLANNING GUIDE

CHAPTER 36

Rise of Imperialism

CHAPTER ORGANIZER

Objectives	Special Features	Supplemental Materials
Section 1 Growth of Imperialism Specify causes of the move toward imperialism.		• Reproducible Lesson Plan • Section 1 Quiz • Testmaker • Chapter 36 Vocabulary and Guided Reading Activity • World History and Art Transparencies 22, 23, 24, 26 • The World History Videodisc
Section 2 Africa Discuss how Great Britain and other European powers established colonies in Africa.		• Reproducible Lesson Plan • Section 2 Quiz • Testmaker • Chapter 36 Cooperative Learning Activity • Unit 11 Primary Source Reading • The Western Civilization Videodisc
Section 3 Asia Describe how Asian countries were affected by imperialism.		• Reproducible Lesson Plan • Section 3 Quiz • Testmaker • Chapter 36 Geography and Map Activity
Section 4 Latin America Explain why the United States became involved in Latin America.		• Reproducible Lesson Plan • Section 4 Quiz • Testmaker • Reinforcing Social Studies Skills, p. 20
Section 5 Effects of Imperialism Summarize what the effects of imperialism were.		• Reproducible Lesson Plan • Section 5 Quiz • Testmaker • Chapter 36 Chart and Graph Skill • Chapter 36 Activity Book Activity
Chapter 36 Review and Evaluation		• Chapter 36 Reteaching Activity • Chapter 36 Enrichment Activity • Spanish Summary and Glossary • Audiocassettes (English and Spanish) • Chapter 36 Performance Assessment Activity • Chapter 36 Test • Testmaker

If time does not permit teaching the entire chapter, use the Chapter 36 Summary on page 594 and the Chapter 36 Audiocassettes (English and Spanish) to point out the main ideas of the chapter.

Performance Assessment Activities

Making Maps Provide the students with an outline map of the world. Have them label countries discussed in the chapter and create a key using different colors to indicate the European power that ruled each country. Then have students color their maps accordingly, creating a map titled, "Age of Imperialism."

Creating a Collage Have students gather pictures of the many products introduced to the Western world as a result of imperial expansion during the 1800s. Have them divide their collages, labeling which products came from which parts of the world.

CHAPTER RESOURCES

LITERATURE ABOUT THE PERIOD

Conrad, Joseph. *Heart of Darkness.* In *Joseph Conrad, Tales of Land and Sea.* Hanover House, 1916. Story of one man's journey up the Congo River in the 1800s.

Forster, E.M. *A Passage to India.* Harcourt Brace, 1989. A novel about life in India under British rule.

READINGS FOR THE STUDENT

Clark, Leon E. *Through African Eyes.* Center for International Training & Education, 1981. Collection of material about Africans from before the growth of enslavement to the present.

Killinggray, David. *A Plague of Europeans.* Penguin Books, 1973. History from the era of European explorers and missionaries.

Roberts, John G. *Black Ships and Rising Sun.* Julian Messner, 1971. The opening of Japan to the West and its modernization.

READINGS FOR THE TEACHER

Hobsbawm, Eric. *The Age of Empires, 1875-1914.* Pantheon, 1987. Describes the period from 1875-1914 and the empires that were formed.

Hsu, Immanuel C. *The Rise of Modern China.* Oxford Press, 1990. Focuses on major historical events in China from 1600 to present.

Pakenham, Thomas. *The Boer War.* Random House, 1979. Deals with the origins, course, and aftermath of the Boer War.

MULTIMEDIA RESOURCES

Africa: Its People and Promise. Social Studies School Service. Software. Program dealing with the people and history of Africa.

Imperialism. Video. EAV/Social Studies School Service. Study of imperialist policies and their lasting repercussions.

The Maharajas: Imperialism by Conspiracy. Centron Educational Films. Film. Describes the rise and fall of the maharajas during the British rule of India.

INTRODUCE

CHAPTER 36 OVERVIEW

Chapter 36 examines the rise of imperialism in Africa, Asia, Latin America, and the Pacific Islands during the late 1800s and early 1900s.

➤ **Section 1** analyzes the economic, religious, and political motivations of imperialism.

➤ **Section 2** describes how the European powers explored and colonized Africa.

➤ **Section 3** discusses imperialism in Asian countries.

➤ **Section 4** explains the role of the United States in the developments of Latin American nations.

➤ **Section 5** discusses the effects of imperialism.

CHAPTER OBJECTIVES

After reading Chapter 36, students will be able to:

1. specify causes of the move toward imperialism.

2. discuss how Great Britain and other European powers established colonies in Africa.

3. describe how Asian countries were affected by imperialism.

4. explain United States' involvement in Latin America.

5. summarize what the effects of imperialism were.

EXAMINING THE ILLUSTRATION

Ask students if they know the location of the Suez Canal. After establishing its geographic location *(Middle East)*, ask students to decide as they read the chapter if it was a positive or negative development for this area.

PERFORMANCE ASSESSMENT

Use the Performance Assessment activities on page 578B to help you evaluate students as they complete the chapter.

CHAPTER 36 Rise of Imperialism

Opening of the Suez Canal

578

TEACHER CLASSROOM RESOURCES

- Section Quizzes/Chapter Test
- Enrichment Activity
- Chart and Graph Skill Activity
- Geography and Map Activity
- Cooperative Learning Activity
- Performance Assessment Activity
- Spanish Summary and Glossary
- Activity Book Activity
- Unit 11 Primary Source Reading
- Teaching Transparencies and Activities
- Audiocassettes (English and Spanish)
- Testmaker
- World History and Art Transparencies
- The World History Videodisc
- The Western Civilization Videodisc

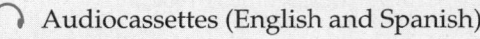

Chapter Focus

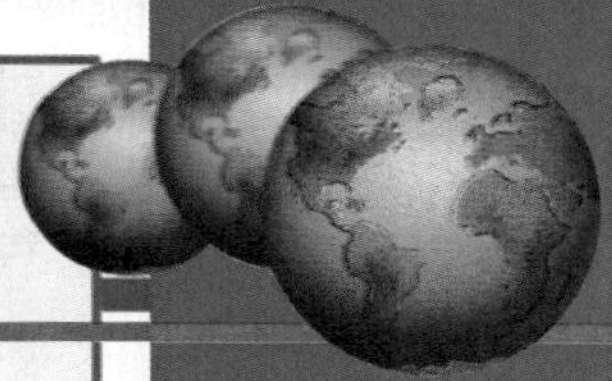

READ TO DISCOVER:

- What caused the move toward imperialism.
- How Great Britain and other European powers established colonies in Africa.
- How Asian countries were affected by imperialism.
- Why the United States became involved in Latin America.
- What the effects of imperialism were.

In the late 1800s, an interest in colonies rose again. Many countries rushed to take over parts of the world that had not been claimed during the Age of Discovery and the Expansion of the Americas. New colonial powers were added. Among these new powers were Belgium, Germany, Italy, Japan, and the United States. Those countries in Africa, Asia, and Latin America who were colonized had little choice in how their nations developed.

1840 A.D.–1916 A.D.

KEY TERMS

imperialism
protectorate
sepoys
spheres of influence
right of extraterritoriality
zaibatsu

Section 1

GROWTH OF IMPERIALISM

There were many reasons for the rise of **imperialism** (im pir′ ē uh liz uhm), or the policy of setting up colonies and building empires. One was the Industrial Revolution. Factories in the industrialized countries needed such raw materials as rubber, cotton, oil, tin, and copper. There was also a growing demand for tea, sugar, and cocoa. Both the raw materials and the food could be found in areas that were not industrially developed, such as Africa, Asia, and Latin America.

Then, too, industries needed new markets for their products. Factories were turning out more goods than people at home could afford to buy. Many industrial leaders and merchants believed new markets could be found in areas that were not industrially developed.

Also, many factory owners had grown rich during the Industrial Revolution. They could not find enough places in their

FOCUS

BELLRINGER

Write the following on the chalkboard: *The sun never sets on the British Empire.* Ask students to write a sentence explaining this statement.

MOTIVATIONAL ACTIVITY

Have students share their sentences about the statement, "The sun never sets on the British Empire." Explain that in 1900, the British Empire included one-fifth of the world's land and one-fourth of its population. Then tell students that in this chapter they will learn how Great Britain, other European powers, Japan, and the United States established colonies in Africa, Asia, Latin America, and Pacific Islands.

VOCABULARY PRE-CHECK

Write the key terms for this chapter on the chalkboard. Ask students to write a brief definition of what they think each word means. Have students check their definitions for accuracy as they read the chapter.

Assign Chapter 36 **Vocabulary and Guided Reading Activity** in the TCR.

EXTRA CREDIT PROJECT

Have students read more about Rudyard Kipling and his poetry, in particular his poem "The White Man's Burden," which was considered the anthem of imperialism. Have them interpret the poem and summarize Kipling's opinion. Have them conclude their summary with a statement of agreement or disagreement.

KEY TO ABILITY LEVELS

Teaching strategies have been coded for varying learning styles and abilities.

L1 Level 1 activities are **basic** activities and should be within the ability range of all students.

L2 Level 2 activities are **average** activities and should be within the ability range of the average to above-average student.

L3 Level 3 activities are **challenging** activities designed for the ability range of above-average students.

LEP LEP activities should be within the ability range of Limited English Proficiency students.

TEACH

GUIDED PRACTICE

L1 **Culture** Have students discuss travel during the late 1800s and early 1900s in relation to their own personal travels. How has traveling to new places changed their views of the world, of other people, and of themselves? LEP

L2 **Religion** Have students read more about Dr. David Livingstone and other missionaries who went to Africa. To what areas did they go? What religious groups sent missionaries to these areas? How successful were they in achieving their goals?

MAKING CONNECTIONS

➤➤ **History** During the 1890s and 1900s, Germany sought to replace Great Britain as the world's leading sea power and began building a large navy. Great Britain, in turn, enlarged its navy in order to keep ahead of the Germans. This build-up race, along with colonial rivalries among the European powers, led to World War I.

VIDEODISC

Use the following to enrich Chapter 36.

WH A 45 10045

A caravan approaching Timbuktu.

Photo of Cocoa Pods

own countries in which to invest. Even when they did invest, they thought the profits were too small. Investments in undeveloped areas, however, generally brought large profits.

Another reason for imperialism was nationalism. Many people thought colonies would add to their country's power. The newly formed countries of Italy and Germany wanted to catch up with Great Britain, France, and other established colonial powers. Japan and the United States wanted to become as important as the colonial powers of western Europe.

Still another reason for imperialism was the belief that western countries had a duty to "civilize" the "backward" peoples of the world. To many westerners, any people whose way of life and religion were different from their own were "backward." These westerners believed they had a mission to spread Christianity and the Industrial Revolution everywhere. The British author Rudyard Kipling (ruhd' yuhrd kip' lēng) called this mission "the white man's burden."

Section 1 Review

1. **Define:** imperialism
2. How did the Industrial Revolution lead to imperialism?
3. How did nationalism lead to imperialism?

Critical Thinking

4. If you had lived during the late 1800s, would you have supported or opposed imperialism? Why?

Section 2 AFRICA

Painting of Rudyard Kipling

Before 1870, European powers had few holdings in Africa. Those they did have were mostly seaports and trading stations along the coast. The only major exceptions were the Cape Colony at Africa's southern tip and Algeria in northern Africa. Great Britain had received the Cape Colony from the Dutch at the Congress of Vienna. Algeria was held by France. Before long, however, most of Africa belonged to European powers.

The Opening of Africa At first, most Europeans stayed along the African coast because they were safer there from tropical diseases and other dangers. Little was known about Africa's interior. Then, missionaries and explorers opened up these areas.

SECTION 1 ANSWERS

1. imperialism, having colonies and building empires (p. 579)
2. Industrialized countries needed raw materials and food such as tea, sugar, and cocoa, and new markets for their products.
3. Many people thought colonies would add to their country's power.
4. Answers will vary, but students should give reasons for their opinions about imperialism.

Assign the Chapter 36 **Section 1 Quiz** in the TCR. Testmaker available.

In 1840, a Scottish medical missionary named David Livingstone (liv' ing stuhn) went to Africa to convert the people to Christianity. During his years in Africa, Dr. Livingstone worked hard to end the Arab trade of enslaved Africans and explored much of the continent's interior. He wrote about his journeys in letters that appeared in newspapers in Great Britain and the United States. These letters aroused a great deal of interest in Africa.

Suddenly, the letters stopped. A New York newspaper decided to find out what had happened to Dr. Livingstone. It assigned reporter Henry Stanley to the story. After two years of searching, Stanley found Dr. Livingstone in a small Arab village on the shores of Lake Tanganyika (tan guhn yē' kuh). Stanley then became an explorer himself. Between 1874 and 1889, he explored the Congo and wrote about his adventures.

In 1879, Stanley was hired by King Leopold II of Belgium to obtain African lands for him. Stanley signed many treaties with African chiefs in the Congo Basin. Most of the chiefs could not

STANLEY AND LIVINGSTONE This painting shows Henry Stanley (center left) who found David Livingstone (center right) living in the tiny village of Ujiji on Lake Tanganyika. Stanley greeted him with the now famous words, "Dr. Livingstone, I presume?" **Why had Dr. Livingstone gone to Africa?**

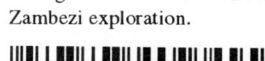

L2 **Geography: Location** For an overall introductory view of the depth and spread of imperialism, have students note the nations and areas involved on the map "Imperialism" on page 590. LEP

L3 **Economics** Discuss the close connection between the Industrial Revolution in Europe and America and the rise of imperialism. Include the idea that the colonies that provided raw materials also became new markets for mass-produced goods. LEP

CAPTION ANSWER

to convert Africans to Christianity

VIDEODISC

Use the following to enrich Chapter 36.

WH B 29 10143
Livingstone's steam launch for Zambezi exploration.

WH B 31 10145
"Dr. Livingstone, I presume."

MEETING SPECIAL NEEDS

Have students with learning problems divide into five groups and have each group concentrate on one area of Africa covered in this section: North Africa, West Africa, central Africa, East Africa, and southern Africa. Have the students in each group use the material in the chapter and an encyclopedia to prepare a brief oral or written report on the history of their region of Africa. Then ask one person in each group to present that group's oral report to the other groups.

L2 **Geography: Location** Ask students to research and report on the economic and geographic importance of the Congo River and the Congo Basin to the rest of Africa. Have them create a poster that shows data about this area, including a map showing its location in the continent.

LINKING PAST TO PRESENT

Among the ceremonies at the opening of the Suez Canal was the premiere performance of the opera *Aida,* composed by Giuseppe Verdi especially for the occasion. *Aida* is among the most popular operas in the world today.

DID YOU KNOW ??

Boer means "farmer." The average Boer farm comprised about 6,000 acres (or 2,400 hectares).

VIDEODISC

Use the following to enrich Chapter 36.

WH B 92 10206
African laborers carrying ivory and rubber.

WH F 43 14496
Egyptians and British pull steamer up Nile rapids.

read or write English and did not realize what they were signing away. In return for their lands, many of which were rich in minerals and rubber, the chiefs received cloth, beads, and sometimes guns. The signing of such treaties became a common way of gaining colonial territory.

Leopold II wanted to make a lot of money as quickly as possible. He had his soldiers force the Africans to collect rubber for him. Anyone who resisted was shot. However, missionaries and other Europeans protested so much that the king finally turned the Congo over to the Belgian government. The government did away with forced labor.

In northern Africa, the Suez (sū ez') Canal was opened in 1869. Built by Egyptian workers and paid for with French funds, it connected the Mediterranean and Red seas. The Suez Canal made possible a shorter all-water route to India and the Far East. In 1875, however, the Egyptian ruler needed money. So, he sold his shares in the canal to Great Britain. Great Britain and France then took over Egypt's finances. This made many Egyptians angry. When they rebelled in 1882, British troops moved in. Egypt became a British **protectorate** (pruh tek' tuhr it), or a country under the control and protection of a larger, stronger nation.

From the Cape to Cairo

Soon after Great Britain made Egypt a protectorate, the British began moving south. After several years of fighting, they conquered the Sudan. There, Great Britain set up a joint government with Egypt.

At the same time, the British began moving north from the Cape Colony. The Boers, or Dutch farmers in South Africa, did not like British rule. They did not want to speak English, and they disagreed with Great Britain's doing away with enslavement. In 1836, many Boers decided to leave the Cape Colony. They traveled northward and finally settled in the grasslands of the interior. There, they set up two independent states, the Transvaal (trans vahl') and the Orange Free State.

Painting of Charles G. Gordon, Military Governor of the Sudan

In the late 1800s, gold and diamonds were discovered in the Boer states. Thousands of adventurers began pouring into the area. The Boers were soon outnumbered. Afraid of losing control of their government, the Boers would not allow the newcomers, who were mostly British, to vote. However, the newcomers had to pay heavy taxes.

This angered Cecil Rhodes (rōdz), the prime minister of the Cape Colony. Rhodes had a dream of an English-speaking empire that would stretch from the Cape to Cairo (kī rō), the capital of Egypt. The British already controlled land to the south and west of the Boer states. So, Rhodes built a railway line into land to the north of the Boer states. As soon as the railroad was completed, British settlers began moving into this area, which was called Rhodesia (rō dē' zhuh).

COOPERATIVE LEARNING

Have students prepare a news report on the Boer War in the style of a prime-time television program. Divide students into groups—those who will gather information about the war and the issues surrounding it, those who will prepare written copy for the telecast, those who will represent the Boers and the British in interviews, and those who will serve as reporters and anchors for the show.

Assign the Chapter 36 **Cooperative Learning Activity** in the TCR.

BRITISH AFRICA British possessions in Africa ranged from Egypt to South Africa. Here, a late nineteenth-century cartoon (left) shows Cecil Rhodes's dream of spreading British rule in Africa. Resistance to the British by the Boers in South Africa led to the Boer War (right), fought between 1899 and 1902. **How did the British finally defeat the Boers?**

At this point, Germany, jealous of Great Britain's growing power, offered the Boers its best artillery. The Boers promptly attacked British outposts, and the Boer War began. At first the Boers defeated the British. Then, the British captured the Boer capital. The Boers, however, refused to surrender and carried on guerrilla warfare for more than two years. Finally, the British destroyed Boer farms and imprisoned Boer women and children. When that happened, the Boers gave up. In 1910, the Transvaal and the Orange Free State were joined with the Cape Colony and one other British colony to form the Union of South Africa.

The British gained other African possessions besides Egypt, the Sudan, Rhodesia, and the Union of South Africa. Between 1890 and 1914, Zanzibar (zan' zuh bahr), Uganda (yū gan' duh), British East Africa, and Nigeria all came under British control. Except for one German colony, Cecil Rhodes's plan of an English-speaking empire in Africa came true.

CAPTION ANSWER

The British destroyed Boer farms and imprisoned Boer women and children, forcing the Boers to surrender.

LINKING PAST TO PRESENT

Cecil Rhodes came to Africa at the age of 18 and made a fortune in gold and diamonds. He used his wealth to support students by setting up Rhodes scholarships at England's Oxford University. Students may be interested in discovering what requirements must be fulfilled today to obtain a Rhodes scholarship.

VIDEODISC

Use the following to enrich Chapter 36.

WH C 8 10232
The "Great Trek" of the Boers.

WH C 22 10246
"The Rhodes colossus," from Cape Town to Cairo.

MEETING SPECIAL NEEDS

Have students who are visual learners work in pairs to create posters depicting the many opportunities awaiting the bold adventurer in the far-off colonies in the 1800s. Tell them to be detailed in their designs and add a title in the style of a headline. Some examples might include: gold mining in southern Africa; exchanging Western goods for tea and silk with traders in China. Display the posters in the classroom.

L2 **History** The countries along Africa's northern coast were once known as the Barbary States. From 1550 to 1815, this area of the Mediterranean Sea was notorious for pirate raids on merchant ships. In 1815, the Barbary States promised to stop pirate attacks on U.S. ships. In 1830, France used the raids as an excuse to invade Algeria. Have students create political cartoons illustrating the Barbary States' promise to the United States to stop raids, or France's decision to invade Algeria. LEP

DID YOU KNOW

British rule in India was known as the *raj*.

VIDEODISC

Use the following to enrich Chapter 36.

WC N 65 44120
The English fort at Bombay, India, 1672.

WH B 66 10180
Map, African resistance to European rule.

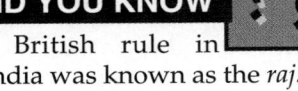

Painting of King Menelik II

Other European Empires Leopold's actions in the Congo and the British takeover of Egypt spurred other European powers into action. Over the next few years, they divided the African continent among themselves.

Spain and Portugal kept their original possessions. Angola (an gō' luh), founded in 1648 by the Portuguese, was the oldest colony in Africa. In 1885, Portugal also made Portuguese East Africa, or Mozambique, a protectorate.

The French moved out from Algeria to establish the largest European empire in Africa. This empire included Tunisia, Morocco, French West Africa, French Equatorial Africa, and Madagascar (mad uh gas' kuhr).

The Italians conquered Eritrea (er uh trē' uh), an area on the east coast, and took over part of Somaliland (sō mahl' ē land). However, when they tried to take Ethiopia in 1896, they were defeated by the troops of King Menelik II. In 1911, the Italians acquired two Turkish provinces from the Ottomans. The Italians combined the two and renamed the area Libya. The Germans set up protectorates over Togoland and the Cameroons (kam uh rūnz') in 1884. They later added German Southwest Africa and German East Africa.

By 1914, only two areas in Africa remained independent. One was Ethiopia. The other was Liberia (lī bir' ē uh), which had been founded in the 1830s by former enslaved African Americans from the United States.

Section 2 Review

1. **Identify:** David Livingstone, Henry Stanley, Leopold II, Suez Canal, Boers, Cecil Rhodes
2. **Define:** protectorate
3. Why did many Boers leave the Cape Colony?
4. What was Cecil Rhodes's plan for Africa? How successful was Great Britain in achieving this plan?

Critical Thinking

5. Why was the Suez Canal so valuable to Europe?

Section 3 ASIA

The British and the Dutch started trading with Asia in the 1600s. However, Chinese and Japanese rulers allowed only limited contact with the West. So, western European countries turned their attention to India.

SECTION 2 ANSWERS

1. Livingstone, Scottish medical missionary (p. 581); Stanley, newspaper reporter (p. 581); Leopold II, king of Belgium (p. 581); Suez Canal, connected Mediterranean and Red seas (p. 582); Boers, Dutch farmers in South Africa (p. 582); Rhodes, prime minister of the Cape Colony (p. 582)
2. protectorate, country under the control and protection of a larger nation (p. 582)
3. because they did not like British rule, abolition and enslavement, and did not want to speak English
4. He wanted an English-speaking empire that would stretch from the Cape to Cairo. Except for one German colony, it was achieved.
5. Answers will vary. Students might indicate that the canal made trade easier by providing a shorter all-water route to India and the Far East.

Assign the Chapter 36 **Section 2 Quiz** in the TCR. Testmaker available.

India By the middle 1700s, the Mogul Empire of India was breaking up. This allowed Great Britain and France to set up trading stations along the Indian coast. Then, in 1763, France lost the Seven Years' War, also known in the Americas as the French and Indian War. As a result, the French left India, and the British East India Company took over.

The British East India Company stayed in power for almost 100 years. During that time, it brought many changes to India.

Not everyone was happy with British rule, however. Many Indians felt the British were trying to change their culture. In 1857, the **sepoys** (sē' pois), or Indian soldiers in the British army, mutinied. The immediate cause was a new rifle. Its cartridges were greased, and one end had to be bitten off before loading. The Hindus thought the grease was beef fat. The Muslims thought it was pork fat. Hindus are not allowed by their religion to eat beef, while Muslims are not allowed to eat pork.

Although the Sepoy Mutiny failed, the British government realized that changes were needed. It took control of India away from the British East India Company and gave it to the Crown.

Great Britain wanted to protect its Indian empire from other countries, especially Russia. From 1865 to 1884, most of the central Asian centers of Muslim civilization fell to Russia. To guard India's northwest frontier, the British made Afghanistan (af gan' uh stan) a protectorate. In Persia, both Great Britain and Russia set up **spheres of influence,** or areas within a country in which another country has special rights.

THE BRITISH IN INDIA British settlers in India kept many Indian servants. In this painting, Indians unload a newly arrived British family and their luggage. **How did Great Britain try to protect its Indian Empire from Russia?**

L2 **Literature** Have students read a work by Rudyard Kipling, such as *The Jungle Book, Kim,* or "Gunga Din." Have them write a report on the work, concentrating on how Kipling uses India—its culture, people, and geography—in his stories.

MAKING CONNECTIONS

>> **History** Local British garrisons were unprepared for the mutiny of the sepoys. Many British regulars had been sent to duty in the Crimean War before the rebellion began.

DID YOU KNOW

The British allowed Indian princes to remain in power in many parts of India because it was easier to use them to help run the country than it was to conquer them all.

CAPTION ANSWER

To guard India's northwest frontier, the British made Afghanistan a protectorate and set up a sphere of influence in Persia.

VIDEODISC

Use the following to enrich Chapter 36.

WH S 21 30641

A view of Macao in the early 1800s.

MULTICULTURAL PERSPECTIVES

The incident that led to the Sepoy Rebellion reveals how Great Britain, like many of the imperialist powers in the 1800s, imposed its own culture and values on its colonies. Imperialists were often contemptuous of the sacred beliefs and rituals of the colonial people, often to the point of wiping out other cultures in the name of progress. Where Africans and Asians tried to resist imperialist pressures to discard traditional ways of life, as in the Sepoy Rebellion, tension—and sometimes fighting—occurred.

L1 **Economics** Discuss the importance of the Chinese opium trade to the merchants in imperialist countries. For what did the British traders exchange opium? *(tea and silk)* Why did the Chinese government want the trade of opium ended? *(They saw how much damage the drug was doing.)* How did the outcome of the Opium War affect China? *(The Chinese were forced to sign a treaty that opened more ports and gave Hong Kong to Great Britain.)*

MAKING CONNECTIONS

➤➤ **Religion** Confucius said the following about the importance of the family in society: *The superior man spreads his culture to the entire nation by remaining at home . . . . The teaching of filial piety* [children's respect for their parents] *is a preparation for serving the ruler of his state; the teaching of respect for one's elder brothers is a preparation for serving all the elders of the community; and the teaching of kindness in parents is a training for ruling over people . . . . When individual families have learned kindness, then the whole nation has learned kindness.*

CAPTION ANSWER

with the husband's parents

VIDEODISC

Use the following to enrich Chapter 36.

WH S 35 30655

Factories of the British East India Company in Canton.

China From the early 1500s, all trade between China and the West was limited to the city of Guangzhou (gwong jō′). The Chinese looked upon westerners as barbarians.

The Chinese people were divided into two classes. The upper class were mostly government officials, scholars, and landowners. They knew how to read and write, and looked down upon people who worked with their hands. The lower class were usually farmers and artisans who did not know how to read and write.

Both classes, however, had certain things in common. They followed the teachings of Confucius and believed that the family was most important. Marriages were arranged to benefit families. When a son married, he and his wife lived with his parents. The Chinese greatly respected their ancestors. On New Year's Day they would burn incense and place an offering of food on the family altar. Then they would tell the ancestors what had happened to the family in the past year.

The Chinese followed their way of life until the 1800s. Then came the Industrial Revolution. Western factory owners and merchants became interested in increasing overseas trade. They were no longer satisfied with the amount of business the Chinese allowed them.

CHINESE SOCIETY Here an upper-class Chinese family is shown receiving gifts for a wedding. **Where will the new husband and wife probably live?**

COOPERATIVE LEARNING

Organize the class into four teams. Then assign each team one of the following questions: How did imperialism affect India? How did imperialism affect China? How did imperialism affect the Pacific Islands and Southeast Asia? How did imperialism affect Japan? Have each team answer its question and select a note taker to record its answers. Encourage students to use their texts and other resources. Have the recorders present their team's findings visually. Conclude by asking students what similarities and differences they see in the effects of imperialism on these nations or areas.

OPIUM WAR The British and Chinese battled over the selling of opium in China. **From what natural source did opium come?**

About this time, British traders discovered that they could make large profits selling *opium* (ō pē uhm), or a drug made from the dried juice of certain poppies, to the Chinese. The traders took cotton cloth made in Great Britain to India, where they traded it for opium. They then took the opium to China, where it was exchanged for tea and silk to be shipped to Great Britain.

At first, the Chinese government paid little attention to the opium trade. When it saw how much damage the drug was doing, the government declared the trade illegal. When a government official in Guangzhou seized and publicly burned a large shipment of opium, British traders became angry. In 1839, what became known as the Opium War broke out between the British and the Chinese.

Although they greatly outnumbered the British, the Chinese had neither cannon nor steam-driven warships. In 1842, they were defeated and forced to sign a treaty that opened more ports and gave Great Britain the island of Hong Kong. The treaty also gave British citizens in China the **right of extraterritoriality** (rīt of ek struh ter uh tōr ē al' uh tē). This meant that British citizens accused of breaking Chinese laws could be tried only in British courts.

L1 **Geography: Movement** On an outline map of the world, have students illustrate the triangular trade that resulted from the opium trade in China. LEP

L2 **Critical Thinking** Have students brainstorm a list of laws or rules they do not like to see broken, such as laws against theft or murder, or rules against destroying school property. Ask students how they would feel about students coming into their school, breaking rules, and not being punished for it by school officials. Have them write an explanation of how that situation relates to extraterritoriality, including a statement of their opinion of that practice in China.

LINKING PAST TO PRESENT

Hong Kong is still a British colony and is one of the busiest trade and banking centers in Asia. However, Hong Kong will again be under Chinese control in 1997.

CAPTION ANSWER

the dried juice of certain poppies

VIDEODISC

Use the following to enrich Chapter 36.

WH S 43 30663

British warship Nemesis destroying Chinese war junks.

MULTICULTURAL PERSPECTIVES

The spirit of revolt, like that of western Europe, also swept through China during the 1800s. The Taiping Rebellion (1851-1864) tore the country apart. A group trying to combine Christian and ancient Chinese beliefs attempted to create a perfect society with an equal division of land among the people. Other goals of the Taipings included ridding China of both the Westerners and the Qing dynasty. Although the rebellion was a failure, it seriously weakened the Qing dynasty and the country. The cost in lives was between 20 million and 30 million. Ironically, the term *taiping* means "great peace."

MAKING CONNECTIONS

➤➤ **History** The true name of the Boxers was the Society of Harmonious Fists. Westerners called its members "Boxers" because they practiced a Chinese form of boxing. Ci Xi promoted the Boxer Rebellion by encouraging anti-foreign groups to plot ways of driving out the imperialists.

CAPTION ANSWER

China was made to pay heavy penalties, and foreign powers gained almost total control of the country.

VIDEODISC

Use the following to enrich Chapter 36.

WH S 108 30728

Chinese Christian refugees at Tianjin in Boxer Uprising.

China lost even more power in the late 1800s. In 1894, Japan and China went to war over Korea. The Japanese won easily and took Chinese territory. Great Britain, France, Germany, and Russia rushed to get *concessions* (kuhn sesh' uhns), or special rights, from the Chinese government. These included the rights to develop mineral resources and build railroads and naval bases. Several countries also got leases on Chinese port cities.

The United States did not want China divided up by foreign powers or kept from trading with American merchants. In 1899, the American government asked countries to approve the Open Door policy. This gave everyone equal trading rights in China.

The Open Door Policy did not please the Chinese because it meant that foreign powers were still trying to control them. So, the Chinese began a movement to drive all foreigners from their country. The movement was called the Boxer Rebellion because it had been started by a Chinese secret society called Boxers. In the spring of 1900, the Boxers began attacking foreigners, including

THE BOXER REBELLION The Boxers were a secret society dedicated to removing all foreign influences from China. British, French, Russian, American, German, and Japanese troops were sent to put down the revolt. In this painting foreign troops attacked the rebels in Beijing. **What was the outcome of the Boxer Rebellion?**

EXTENDING THE CONTENT

In signing the Open Door policy, China opened its ports to western trade. The U.S. business community profited greatly from this agreement. In the 1930s, as tensions leading to World War II escalated, Japan invaded China and threatened to close the open door of trade with the West. The American business community became harsh critics of Japan's aggressive expansionism, adding even more tension to a situation that would soon explode into a world war.

the diplomats at Beijing (bā jing'), the capital of China. The foreign powers joined forces and sent an army to China. In 1901, the rebellion was put down. China had to pay heavy penalties, and foreign powers gained almost total control of the country.

Painting of Matthew Perry

Japan Like China, Japan allowed only limited trade with the West at first. The Japanese government even refused to provide shelter to shipwrecked sailors. In the middle 1800s, however, this changed.

In 1853, the American government sent a naval force under Commodore Matthew Perry to Japan. Perry was able to negotiate a treaty to open up trade and to protect shipwrecked American sailors. Soon after, Japan signed similar treaties with Great Britain, France, Russia, and the Netherlands.

The military strength and industrial accomplishments of the West impressed most Japanese leaders. They felt that in order to survive, Japan must modernize. To this end, in 1868, several Japanese lords overthrew the shogun and restored the power of the emperor. The new emperor moved the capital of Japan from Kyoto (kyō' tō) to Tokyo. He called his rule Meiji (mā' jē), which means "enlightened peace." The changes that came about during this time are known as the Meiji Restoration.

The new government did away with feudalism. Common people were now allowed to take a family name. They also could live and work where they wished. The government ordered all Japanese males to cut off the topknots worn in their hair. Western-style clothing and a new calendar were introduced.

The Meiji government took away the special position of the samurai. Instead, all Japanese men were expected to serve for a certain amount of time in the armed forces. The government also set up a modern army and navy.

In 1889, Japanese leaders wrote Japan's first constitution. Public schools were opened, and education was required for all. Japanese leaders also began a push to industrialize. To help reach this goal, they gave certain privileges and protection to the **zaibatsu** (zī' bah tsū'), or the rich and powerful families who controlled many industries.

By the end of the 1800s, Japan was fully industrialized. However, Japan needed raw materials and markets for its manufactured goods. In addition, because of modern sanitation and medicine, its population was growing rapidly. Japan did not have enough fertile land to grow food for all its people.

To help find answers to these problems, the Japanese began a program of imperialism. Japan gained control of the island of Formosa (for mō' suh), or present-day Taiwan (tī wahn'), and part of Manchuria (man chūr' ē uh) after a war with China. Ten years later, Japan went to war with Russia and got control of the

INDEPENDENT PRACTICE

L1 **History** Have students research Matthew Perry's dealings with the Japanese and prepare a television interview with questions and answers for Perry and the Japanese shoguns who signed treaties with him. Have students prepare and present a news interview for U.S. citizens eager to know the outcome of Perry's dealings with the Japanese. Some students can take the role of reporters, and others can represent Perry, his crew, and the Japanese. LEP

L3 **Critical Thinking** Have students choose a topic dealing with European-Japanese or European-Chinese relations, and create a political cartoon that depicts the situation. In doing so, remind students that their opinion of the relationship also could enter into their cartoon.

DID YOU KNOW ??

Topknots were symbolic to the Japanese because the samurai had worn their hair that way. The topknots had to be cut off because western military hats could not be worn over them.

VIDEODISC

Use the following to enrich Chapter 36.

WH N 82 23427
Commodore Perry presents gifts to the Japanese.

WH N 91 23436
Emperor Meiji opens Parliament.

SPOTLIGHT ON: PERRY

Matthew Calbraith Perry was born April 10, 1794, in Newport, Rhode Island. He began his naval career early at age 15 as a midshipman on the *Revenge,* under the command of his brother, Oliver Hazard Perry. In his dealings with the Japanese, Matthew Perry arranged for the protection of American seamen and property in Japanese waters. It is said that he impressed the Japanese who were suspicious of other countries, by his forcefulness and insistence on formality. His meetings with the Japanese were conducted with elaborate ceremony, and he and his officers always wore their finest uniforms and were always accompanied by a full honor guard.

DID YOU KNOW

In addition to teaching science and other modern subjects, Japanese schools stressed such traditional values as unquestionable obedience to the emperor.

MAKING CONNECTIONS

➤➤ **History** Under Japanese rule, the Koreans lost many of their liberties and began to resist the Japanese. However, the Japanese easily crushed Korean opposition.

L1 **Geography: Human/Environmental Interaction** Have students study the map "Imperialism" and make charts showing which countries were controlled by Japan and the European countries that are listed in the map legend.

Assign the Chapter 36 **Geography and Map Activity** in the TCR.

MAP STUDY

Answer

Great Britain

VIDEODISC

Use the following to enrich Chapter 36.

WH X 39 42272

Merchant Street in Rangoon (now Yangon), ca. 1868.

southern half of the island of Sakhalin (sak' uh lēn). It also won a sphere of influence in Korea. Five years later, Japan annexed Korea.

MAP STUDY

REGIONS By the early 1900s, Europeans had spread their rule throughout the world. **Which country's empire included territories in the greatest number of continents?**

Southeast Asia and the Pacific

Europeans first entered Southeast Asia in the 1500s in search of spices. By the 1600s, Portugal, Spain, and the Netherlands all had colonies there. Although there was an active trade with the islands in the area, no one paid much attention to the mainland.

In the late 1800s, the European powers changed their minds. The mainland of Southeast Asia was a source of cash crops, such as coffee and tea. It also had raw materials, such as petroleum, rubber, and tin.

Great Britain and France competed in Southeast Asia. The British took control of Burma, Ceylon, the Malay States, and Singapore. The French set up protectorates in Cochin-China

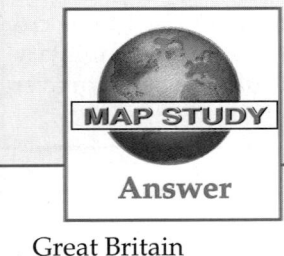

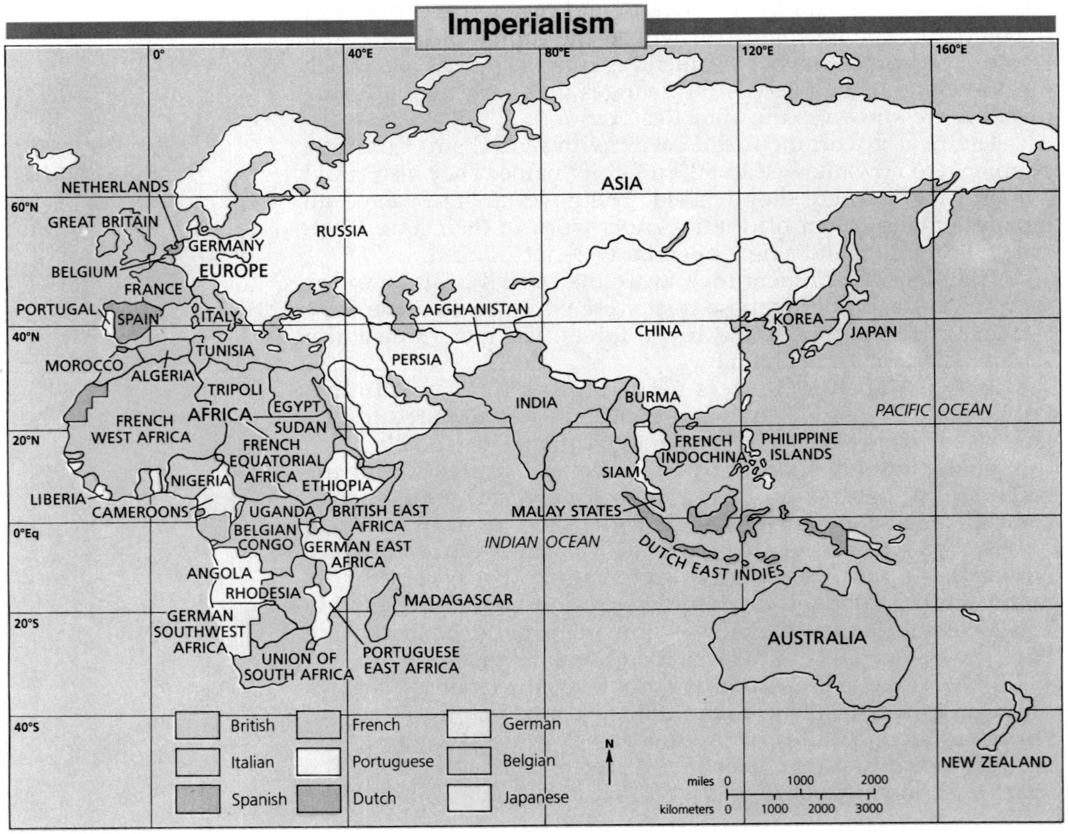

EXTENDING THE CONTENT

Liberia and Ethiopia were the only two countries in Africa that were never colonized. South Africa (1910) and Egypt (1922) gained their independence long before most other African colonies. Between 1951 and 1991, more than 50 African colonies achieved independence. Since the beginning of colonial rule, nationalist groups in Africa had resisted European control, often violently. But following World War II, these relatively small efforts for freedom swelled into powerful mass movements. Africans, many of whom served in the Allied armies, were inspired by the democratic ideals for which the Allies fought in the war—self-rule and freedom from tyranny.

(kō′ chuhn chī nuh), Kampuchea, and Annam (a nam′). They then took over Laos (lah′ ōs) and combined the four colonies into Indochina. Only Siam, or present-day Thailand, remained independent.

During this period, Great Britain, France, Germany, and the United States were also trying to win control of islands in the Pacific. Some of the islands had rich soil that could be used for sugar and pineapple plantations. Others had minerals. Still others could be used as bases for refueling and repairing ships.

Great Britain, which had the largest navy in the world, already held Australia and New Zealand. Now, it took the Fiji, Solomon, and Gilbert islands, along with parts of New Guinea (gin′ ē) and Borneo (bor′ nē ō). France claimed Tahiti, the Marquesas (mahr kā′ zuhz), and several other islands. Germany took part of New Guinea and the Marshall, Caroline, and Mariana islands. Later, Germany divided the Samoan (suh mō′ uhn) Islands with the United States. The United States also controlled the Hawaiian and Philippine islands and Guam (gwahm).

Painting of Hawaiian Queen Liliuokalani

Section 3 Review

1. **Identify:** Sepoy Mutiny, Opium War, Open Door Policy, Boxer Rebellion, Matthew Perry, Meiji Restoration
2. **Define:** sepoys, spheres of influence, right of extraterritoriality, *zaibatsu*
3. Why did the Japanese start a program of imperialism?
4. Why did many European countries in the late 1800s want to control territory in Southeast Asia?

Critical Thinking

5. If you were living in China or Japan in the 1800s, would you have agreed or disagreed with their policy of limited contact with the West? Why?

Section 4 Latin America

The imperialist powers were also interested in Latin America. The countries there that had gained their independence in the early 1800s faced many problems. Most Latin Americans were poor and had no land of their own. The new leaders had little government experience. There were many revolutions. These shaky conditions seemed to invite outside interference.

GEOGRAPHY AND HISTORY

The Pacific Islands are divided into three groups: Melanesia, Micronesia, and Polynesia. Encourage students to locate these groups in their text Atlas.

MAKING CONNECTIONS

➤➤ **Literature** The influences of various Asian cultures began to find their way into the works of Western writers and artists as a result of the increased contact brought about by imperialism. Joseph Conrad's stories, and Paul Gaugin's paintings reflect the influence of several of the cultures of Southeast Asia and the Pacific Islands.

VIDEODISC

Use the following to enrich Chapter 36.

WH X 161 42394

Palace of the Governor-General.

SECTION 3 ANSWERS

1. Sepoy Mutiny, uprising of Indian soldiers (p. 585); Opium War, war between China and Great Britain (p. 587); Open Door policy, gave equal trading rights in China (p. 588); Boxer Rebellion, to drive all foreigners from China (p. 588); Perry, American naval leader (p. 589); Meiji Restoration, changes during Meiji rule (p. 589)
2. sepoys, Indian soldiers in the British army (p. 585); spheres of influence, areas within a country in which another country has special rights (p. 585); right of extraterritoriality, right of an accused person to be tried in a court of his or her own nation (p. 587); *zaibatsu*, powerful Japanese families (p. 589)
3. to get raw materials and markets for manufactured goods, and food
4. because it was a source of coffee and tea and raw materials
5. Answers will vary.

Assign the Chapter 36 **Section 3 Quiz** in the TCR. Testmaker aavailable.

L2 **Geography: Location** Ask students to find North America and South America in the text Atlas. Have students consider the closeness of one land mass to the other. Have students write an explanation of how location explains why the United States issued the Monroe Doctrine. LEP

LINKING PAST TO PRESENT

Puerto Rico is now a commonwealth of the United States. Puerto Ricans can enter the United States without a passport. They serve in America's armed forces but do not pay federal taxes and cannot vote in national elections. The United States government handles Puerto Rico's foreign affairs. Guam is still a U.S. territory. Cuba became an independent republic in 1902.

CAPTION ANSWER

The United States supported a successful revolution by the people of Panama against Colombia and then signed a treaty with Panama.

VIDEODISC

Use the following to enrich Chapter 36.

WH L 54 18943
The wreck of the U.S.S. Maine.

WH L 55 18944
U.S. soldiers in Cuba, 1898.

To stop this, President James Monroe issued the Monroe Doctrine in 1823. It said that any attempt to gain colonies in Latin America would be considered an unfriendly act toward the United States. Most of the European powers went along with the Monroe Doctrine, largely because the British navy supported the American position. The French made Prince Maximilian of Austria the emperor of Mexico.

By the late 1800s, Spain had colonies in Cuba and Puerto Rico. The Cubans, eager to be independent, had revolted in 1868 and again in 1895. Some Americans, who had large amounts of money invested there, wanted the rebels to win. In 1898, an American battleship, the U.S.S. *Maine*, blew up in the harbor of Havana, Cuba. People in the United States blamed the Spanish. Before long, Congress declared war on Spain.

In less than a year, the United States won the Spanish-American War. The resulting peace treaty gave the United States Puerto Rico, Guam, and the Philippine Islands. Cuba became an American protectorate.

The United States was now a world power. As such, it became even more involved in Latin America.

The United States needed a way to protect its new territories. Its fleet had to be able to sail quickly between American islands in the Caribbean Sea and those in the Pacific Ocean. President

PANAMA CANAL The building of the Panama Canal took over eight years and the labor of more than 40,000 persons. About 5,600 workers died from accidents and disease. Here, the digging of the Gaillard Cut is shown. **How was the United States able to gain rights to the land for a canal?**

COOPERATIVE LEARNING

Organize students into several small groups. Have each group research U.S. relations with the Philippines during one of these time periods: immediately after the Spanish-American War; during World War I; during the World War II; during the cold war; and today. Have each group divide the tasks of gathering data, preparing summaries of the materials, providing a time line to accompany the summaries, and exhibiting the material in a class presentation.

Theodore Roosevelt wanted to build a canal across Panama, a province of Colombia. The United States, however, could not come to terms with Colombia.

In 1903, the United States supported a revolution by people in Panama against Colombia. The revolution was a success. The United States and Panama then signed a treaty in which Panama leased land to the United States to be used for building a canal. In 1914, the Panama Canal was opened. It shortened the route between the two oceans by nearly 7,000 miles, or 11,200 kilometers. The Colombians, however, were angry that the United States had interfered in their affairs.

The United States' interest in Latin America continued. Some countries there had financial and political troubles that led to riots. The United States wanted to protect its business investments. So, between 1912 and 1916, the government sent American soldiers to Nicaragua, the Dominican Republic, and Haiti to restore order.

Painting of Theodore Roosevelt

Section 4 Review

1. **Identify:** Monroe Doctrine, U.S.S. *Maine,* Panama Canal
2. Why did President Monroe issue the Monroe Doctrine?
3. Why did the United States want a canal in Panama?

Critical Thinking

4. What might have happened if most European powers had not gone along with the Monroe Doctrine?

Section 5

Effects of Imperialism

By 1914, European colonial powers, Japan, and the United States had brought about 85 percent of the world under their control. This had many benefits. Orderly governments were set up. Many local wars were stopped. Industry, agriculture, and transportation were developed. Hospitals and schools were built, and sanitation was improved. Western ideas about democracy and individual rights spread.

At the same time, however, imperialism brought about major problems. One was bitter feelings between colonists and colonizers. Most Europeans, North Americans, and Japanese thought they were better than the people in the colonies. Colonists were seldom allowed to hold high jobs in government, industry, or the armed forces. Often, they were not even allowed in city areas where Europeans and North Americans lived.

L2 **Writing** Have students study the events leading to the start of the Spanish American War. Ask them to write a paragraph about the war by answering the following questions: What reasons did some Americans have for wanting to start war with Spain? Do you think that U.S. involvement in the conflict after the sinking of the *Maine* was a rational decision, an emotional response, or a combination of both? Explain your answer.

L3 **Critical Thinking** Have students create a chart comparing and contrasting the positive effects of imperialism and the negative effects of imperialism. Suggest they include political, economic, and social factors. Then have students write a statement explaining whether they felt imperialism was justified. Encourage students to explain their charts to the class.

VIDEODISC

Use the following to enrich Chapter 36.

WH L 56 18945
Theodore Roosevelt and the Rough Riders, 1898.

WH L 62 18951
Building the Panama Canal, 1907.

SECTION 4 ANSWERS

1. Monroe Doctrine, policy limiting new colonies in Latin America by countries other than United States (p. 592); U.S.S. *Maine,* American battleship (p. 592); Panama Canal, canal across Panama (p. 593)

2. to stop outside interference in Latin American countries

3. to enable its fleet to sail quickly between the Caribbean Sea and the Pacific Ocean

4. Answers will vary, but students could indicate that these nations might have waged war to gain control of certain Latin American countries.

Assign the Chapter 36 **Section 4 Quiz** in the TCR. Testmaker available.

ASSESS

CHECK FOR UNDERSTANDING

Ask students to summarize the main points of the chapter, orally or in writing. Discuss the answers to the Section and Chapter Review questions.

EVALUATE

Assign the Chapter 36 **Performance Assessment Activity** in the TCR.

Administer the **Chapter 36 Test** in the TCR. Testmaker available.

RETEACH

Have students work in pairs to develop time lines of major events of the section.

Assign the Chapter 36 **Reteaching Activity** in the TCR.

ENRICH

Have students research political cartoons drawn during the age of imperialism. Then have students choose their favorite and share it and explain it to the class.

Assign the Chapter 36 **Enrichment Activity** in the TCR.

CLOSE

Have students comment on the meaning of the following quotation by Theodore Roosevelt in terms of imperialism: "No nation can claim rights without acknowledging the duties that go with the rights."

MEETING CHAPTER OBJECTIVES

Each objective is tested by the Review questions in parentheses.

1. **Specify** causes of imperialism. (CU 1)
2. **Discuss** how European powers established colonies in Africa. (CU 2, 3; UYJ)
3. **Describe** how imperialism affected Asian countries. (BV; CU 4, 5, 6, 7; GIH; UYJ)
4. **Explain** the United States' involvement in Latin America. (CU 8; CT 2)
5. **Summarize** the effects of imperialism. (CU 9; CT 3, 4; GIH; UYJ)

The colonists resented this. They blamed the colonial powers for the loss of their land and for being forced to work on plantations and in factories. They disliked the colonial powers for trying to change their customs, languages, and religions. These feelings helped nationalism to grow.

There was yet another problem. The scramble for colonies led to a great deal of competition among colonial powers. This, in turn, led to disputes that caused future wars.

Section 5 Review

1. What percent of the world was colonized by 1914?
2. What were some benefits of imperialism?
3. What were some problems of imperialism?

Critical Thinking

4. If you were a colonist in the early 1900s, how would you have felt towards the countries who had power over your colony? Why?

Chapter Summary

1. Imperialism in the late 1800s came about because of the need for raw materials, new markets, and investment opportunities; the growth of nationalism; and the belief that western nations had a duty to "civilize" the "backward" peoples of the world.
2. By the early 1900s, France had the largest European empire in Africa, and Britain's empire stretched from Cape Colony to Cairo.
3. By the late 1800s, Great Britain controlled India, and Russia was moving into central Asia.
4. By 1901, China was controlled by foreign powers.
5. By the early 1900s, Japan was fully industrialized and a powerful imperialist country.
6. By the end of the 1800s, Great Britain, France, Germany, and the United States controlled most of the countries in Southeast Asia and many islands in the Pacific.
7. In 1823, the United States issued the Monroe Doctrine to warn European countries not to expand their control in Latin America.
8. The United States won Puerto Rico, Guam, and the Philippine Islands from Spain in 1898, and in 1903 leased land from Panama to build the Panama Canal.
9. While imperialism led to the development of orderly governments, industry, agriculture, and social reforms, it also led to bitter feelings, nationalism, and competition among colonial powers.

SECTION 5 ANSWERS

1. about 85 percent
2. orderly governments; local wars ended; industry and agriculture developed; roads, railroads, canals, bridges, factories, hospitals, and schools were built; sanitation and communication improved; and ideas about democracy spread
3. Bitter feelings between colonists and colonizers grew over colonists not holding high jobs in government, industry, or the armed forces and for forced changes in their customs, languages, and religions. Colonists blamed colonial powers for the loss of their land and for being forced to work on plantations and in factories.
4. Answers will vary, but students should provide reasons for their feelings.

Assign the Chapter 36 **Section 5 Quiz** in the TCR. Testmaker available.

CHAPTER

Review 36

Building Vocabulary

Write a newspaper advertisement to encourage more British citizens to settle in the eastern colonies in the late 1800s. Use the following words in your ad.

imperialism	protectorate
sepoys	spheres of influence
right of extraterritoriality	*zaibatsu*

Check for Understanding

1. What were the main reasons for the rise of imperialism?
2. How did some Europeans get colonial territory from African chiefs?
3. What caused settlers to move into the Transvaal after 1885?
4. How did the British gain control of India?
5. What was the purpose of the Open Door policy?
6. Why did Commodore Perry go to Japan in 1853?
7. Why did Japan modernize and industrialize so rapidly during the second half of the 1800s?
8. Why was the United States interested in Latin American countries in the early 1900s?
9. How did imperialism lead to nationalism in the colonies?

Critical Thinking

1. Do you think countries would be as interested or less interested today in gaining control of the Suez Canal? Why?
2. If you had lived in the United States in 1823, how would you have felt about the Monroe Doctrine?
3. Do you think attitudes about imperialism have changed from the 1800s to today? Why or why not?
4. What effects of imperialism were helpful or harmful?

Geography in History

HUMAN/ENVIRONMENTAL INTERACTION Changes took place in eastern countries when colonial powers moved in. What specific changes in the growing of crops took place in India and China after they were colonized?

Using Your Journal

Review the details you have noted about changes that happened in Africa and Asia in the late 1800s. Imagine you are living then in a European colony in Africa or Asia. Write a diary entry explaining how you feel about the colonizers.

595

CHAPTER 36 REVIEW ANSWERS

BUILDING VOCABULARY

Advertisements will vary, but students should use all the vocabulary words.

CHECK FOR UNDERSTANDING

1. the Industrial Revolution, nationalism, and the idea that western countries had a duty to "civilize" the world
2. African chiefs signed treaties they could not read.
3. Gold and diamonds were discovered there.
4. The British East India Company took over from the French.
5. to give all countries equal trading rights in China
6. to negotiate a treaty to open up trade and to protect shipwrecked American sailors
7. to protect itself against the military and industrial strength of the West
8. because it needed a way to protect its new territories and American business investments
9. The colonists disliked the colonial powers for trying to change their countries.

CRITICAL THINKING

1. Answers will vary but might say less interested because of other means of transportation.
2. Answers will vary.
3. Answers will vary, but students should give reasons.
4. Answers will vary, but students should state what effects were or were not beneficial.

+ BONUS +

TEST QUESTION

For Chapter 36 Test

During which era, and in which country would the following be true: Your new emperor has called for an "enlightened peace." He has forbidden certain hairstyles, called for all men to join the new army or navy, and told peasants they can live and work where they wish. *(the Meiji Restoration; Japan)*

USING YOUR JOURNAL

Diary entries will vary. You might call on volunteers to share their diary entries with the class.

GEOGRAPHY IN HISTORY

Answers will vary but could include the increase in opium and resulting conflicts, and other crops grown to meet foreign demand.

THE ZULU

FOCUS

OBJECTIVES

Locate where the Zulu Empire existed. Identify the time period during which the Zulu Empire thrived. Describe the cultural traits of the Zulu.

BELLRINGER

Ask students: *What is a family tree?* Ask who among them has a knowledge of their family tree and if they think they could diagram it.

MOTIVATIONAL ACTIVITY

Share your own family tree with students. Then explain to the students that in this Culture Close-Up they will learn about the makeup of a traditional family from a South African culture group.

UNIT 11 CULTURE CLOSE-UP

The Zulu

The Zulu Empire was established in South Africa in 1816 and ended in 1879. The Zulu, a branch of the Bantu people, also had close cultural ties to the Swazi (swah zē) and Xhosa (zō suh).

Geography Connection

The Zulu people lived in the historic region of Zululand, in the northeast section of the present-day province of Natal, Republic of South Africa.

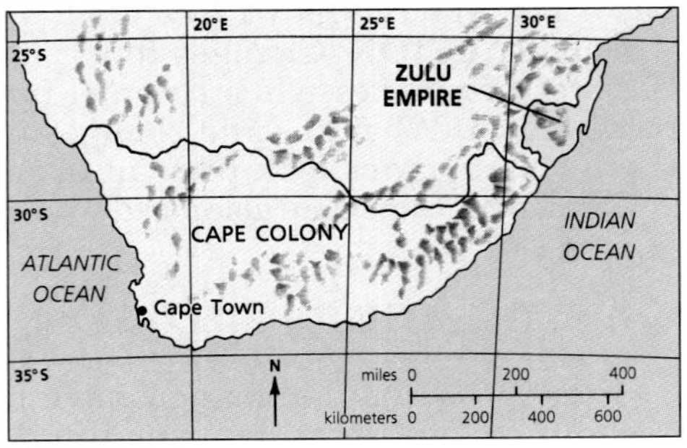

▲ The basic social group was the Zulu clan which was made up of several families. A traditional Zulu family had a man, his wives, his unmarried children, his married sons, and their wives and children. These Zulu are married women of the same clan.

MEETING SPECIAL NEEDS

Have students who are visual learners create a diagram of a Zulu clan based on the information in the text. Have them compare this organization to the standard, accepted western family organization. Ask them to note similarities and differences.

▲ Known as grain farmers, the Zulu also raised cattle. The cattle could live on the grasslands or in the more desert-like areas of South Africa.

The Zulu used all parts of the cattle. The meat was eaten, the hides became clothing and shelter, and the bones were used for utensils and tools. Even the horns of cattle could be used like a trumpet to frighten Zulu enemies. ▶

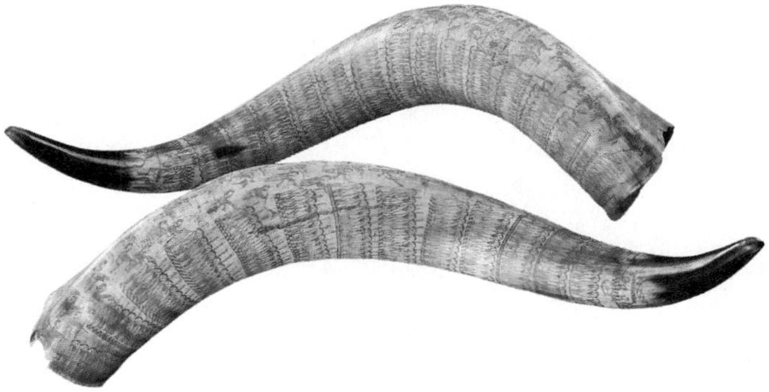

TEACH

L1 **Geography: Location** Ask students to use the map of southern Africa on page 596 to locate the Zulu Empire. Ask: What ocean borders the Zulu Empire to the east? *(Indian Ocean)* What is the approximate location of the Zulu Empire? *(28° S, 32° E)* Next, have students compare the map on page 596 with a map of present-day Africa. Ask them to name the present-day country where the Zulu Empire was located. *(Republic of South Africa)*

DID YOU KNOW ??

In modern South Africa, the Zulu and Xhosa people live on homelands, or reserves, which cover about 13 percent of the land of South Africa.

EXTENDING THE CONTENT

About 2,000 years ago the Bantu-speaking people began to gradually migrate from the present-day country of Nigeria. As the population increased in each new area, the groups divided. As generations developed, differences multiplied among the Bantu-speakers. They adapted to the environments and peoples they met, and developed new customs. Their original language split into hundreds of dialects. They began to call themselves by various names: Zulu, Swazi, Xhosa, and so on. Yet cultural traits remained, such as the importance of kinship ties. Everyone in a clan is descended from a common ancestor traced through the mother's side of the family. Bantu-speakers share the belief that their dead ancestors live among them and watch over them.

UNIT 11 CULTURE CLOSE-UP

L2 **Making Comparisons** Have students work in pairs to make charts that compare and contrast the daily life and cultural traits of the Maoris, described in the Unit 10 Culture Close-Up, and the Zulu. Have pairs share their charts with the class. LEP

GLOBAL READING FOR STUDENTS

Students in your class may be interested in reading a book about the history of South Africa. Suggest *South Africa* by Conrad R. Stein, Children's Press, 1986. (Average/History)

The Zulu shown here in an illustration from a historical book are completing some daily tasks. Their tools and pottery were all hand made. ▶

◀ The Zulu later developed a reputation as fierce warriors under the ruler Shaka.

Shaka, the greatest Zulu King, was considered a military genius. During the 1870s he led his people in wars to gain land the Zulu needed. Shaka trained his warriors, shown here, in strategic military moves.

SPOTLIGHT ON: SHAKA

Shaka trained his troops year-round. He taught his troops to move in a "cow horn" formation. The soldiers would advance in a long, close line, carrying giant cowhide shields before them. Then, the two ends of the line would move toward each other until the enemy was surrounded.

CULTURE CLOSE-UP

UNIT 11

The lightly wooded grasslands of South Africa were the home of the proud Zulu. They built their villages, usually in a circle, and raised their herds of cattle.

The king of a Zulu group was an important figure in the culture. The king guided his people to the best places to build their villages and plant their crops. The king's civil and military laws were to be obeyed without question.

Under Shaka's leadership, the Zulu Empire remained independent until they were conquered by the British in 1879.

Taking Another Look

1. **What part of Africa was home to the Zulu Empire?**
2. **How did the Zulu earn their living?**
3. **What was the leader Shaka remembered for?**

Critical Thinking

4. **What do you think are the advantages or disadvantages of living in a society made up of clans?**

599

ASSESS

CHECK FOR UNDERSTANDING

Have students answer the questions in Taking Another Look on page 599.

ANSWERS to Taking Another Look

1. the northeast section of the present-day province of Natal, Republic of South Africa
2. farming and herding
3. being a military genius
4. Answers will vary. Students should explain the advantages or the disadvantages of living in a society made up of clans.

ENRICH

Have students read current information on the Zulu that describes their involvement in South Africa's end to apartheid. Have students discuss what they think of the movement for black equality in that country.

CLOSE

Ask students to discuss the disadvantages of obeying the civil and military laws of a culture without question.

MEETING SPECIAL NEEDS

Help students who have difficulty remembering what they have learned by helping them make a chart of the daily life of the Zulu. Write *Daily Life* at the top of the chalkboard. Then write the question: *What was life like during the Zulu Empire?* Call on students to give details about daily life in the Zulu Empire as you write their responses on the chalkboard.

INTRODUCE

UNIT 12 OVERVIEW

Unit 12 discusses the major developments of the twentieth century—generally a period of turmoil marked by two global wars and the new world order.

- ➤ **Chapter 37** focuses on World War I and II, and the period between these wars.
- ➤ **Chapter 38** deals with the relationship between western countries and Communist powers after World War II and struggles in South Asia, Africa, Latin America, and the Middle East.
- ➤ **Chapter 39** describes the collapse of communism in Eastern Europe and the Soviet Union, and the challenges facing the world today and in the future.

UNIT OBJECTIVES

After reading Unit 12, your students will be able to:

1. explain how World Wars I and II changed Western Europe.
2. explain how communism came into power in Russia and China.
3. describe world events during the cold war era.
4. discuss the end of communism in major areas.
5. summarize the problems facing the world today and in the twenty-first century.

UNIT PROJECT

Have students contact recent immigrants to their community and ask them to attend a "Cultural Exchange Day" program at school. Ask guests to discuss the cultures of their home countries, emphasizing their customs, music, food, and occupations. In preparation, have students develop questions for visitors.

Have students write a summary of what they learn.

UNIT 12 The Twentieth Century

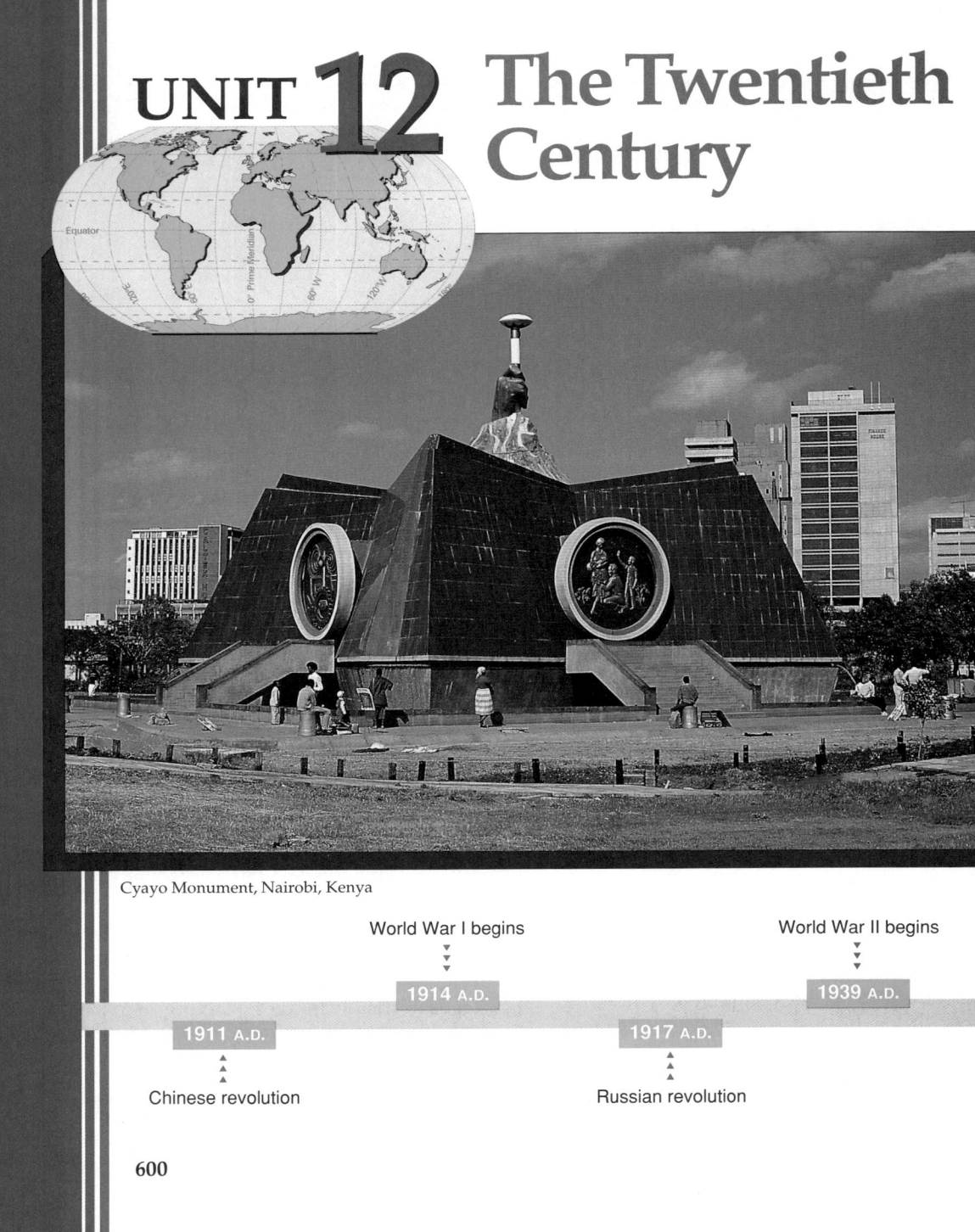

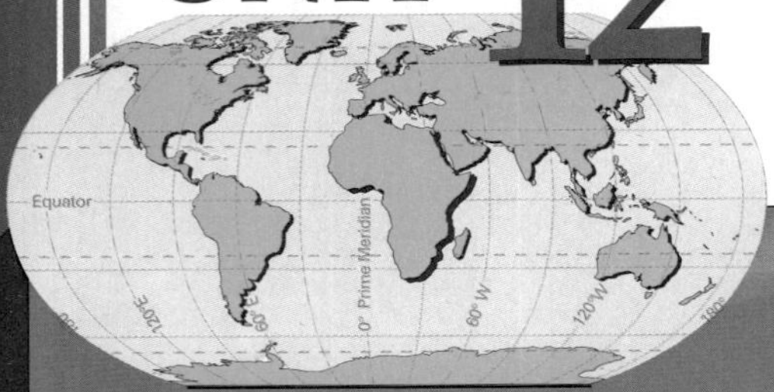

Cyayo Monument, Nairobi, Kenya

1911 A.D.	Chinese revolution
1914 A.D.	World War I begins
1917 A.D.	Russian revolution
1939 A.D.	World War II begins

600

ABOUT THE UNIT OPENING

EXAMINING THE ILLUSTRATION

Ask students if they think this photograph shows an image of Africa that most people usually think of. Tell them they will be reading more about modern Africa in this unit.

GLOBAL CHRONOLOGY

Ask students what the events on the time line suggest about the world's state during the twentieth century. *(Answers will vary but should indicate that it was a time of conflict and change.)* According to the time line, how many years after the Chinese revolution was the People's Republic of China established? *(38 years)* Ask students which year was the "Year of Africa." *(1960)*

During the 1900s, the nations of the world saw many changes. Two wars broke out in Europe that became global. Communism came into power in the Soviet Union and China, and a cold war between the Soviet Union and the United States developed. Countries in Asia, Africa, and the Middle East gained independence but continued to face such problems as overpopulation and food shortages. By the late 1980s, communism collapsed in Europe and the Soviet Union broke apart. The century was ending with the world facing the challenges of maintaining peace, protecting the environment, feeding a growing population, and improving health care.

Chapter 37
Conflict and Change

Chapter 38
The Cold War Era

Chapter 39
The World Since 1989

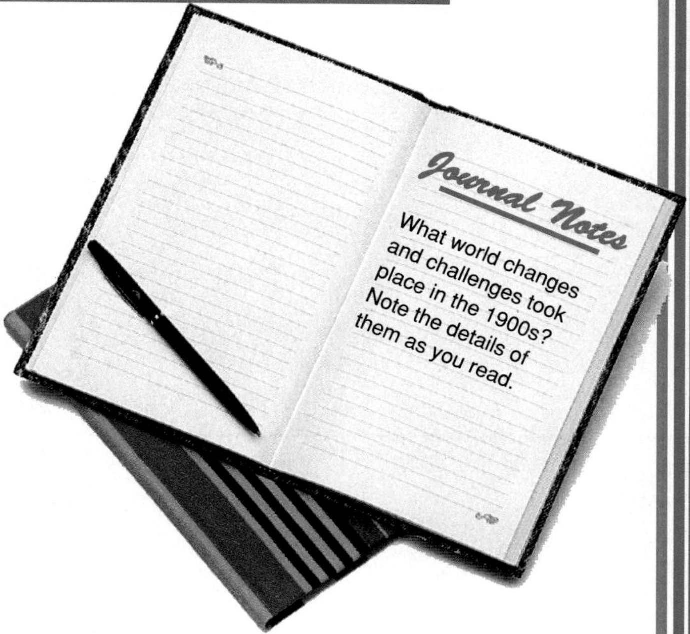

Journal Notes
What world changes and challenges took place in the 1900s? Note the details of them as you read.

1949 A.D. — People's Republic of China established

1960 A.D. — "Year of Africa"

1991 A.D. — Soviet Union breaks up

1993 A.D. — Middle East peace agreement proposed

INTRODUCING THE UNIT

Write these headings on the chalkboard and ask students to suggest changes that have occurred in these categories since 1900: Technology *(cars, airplanes, space satellites, computers)*, Economics *(international trade)*, Environment *(acid rain, greenhouse effect, ozone depletion, global warming, toxic waste)*, Culture *(cross-cultural movies and music, human-rights movements)*. Write student responses on the chalkboard. Use the responses to lead a discussion of the global aspects of these changes. Tell students that in Unit 12 they will learn how these changes and other developments have helped create a new world order in an increasingly interdependent world.

RECORDING JOURNAL NOTES

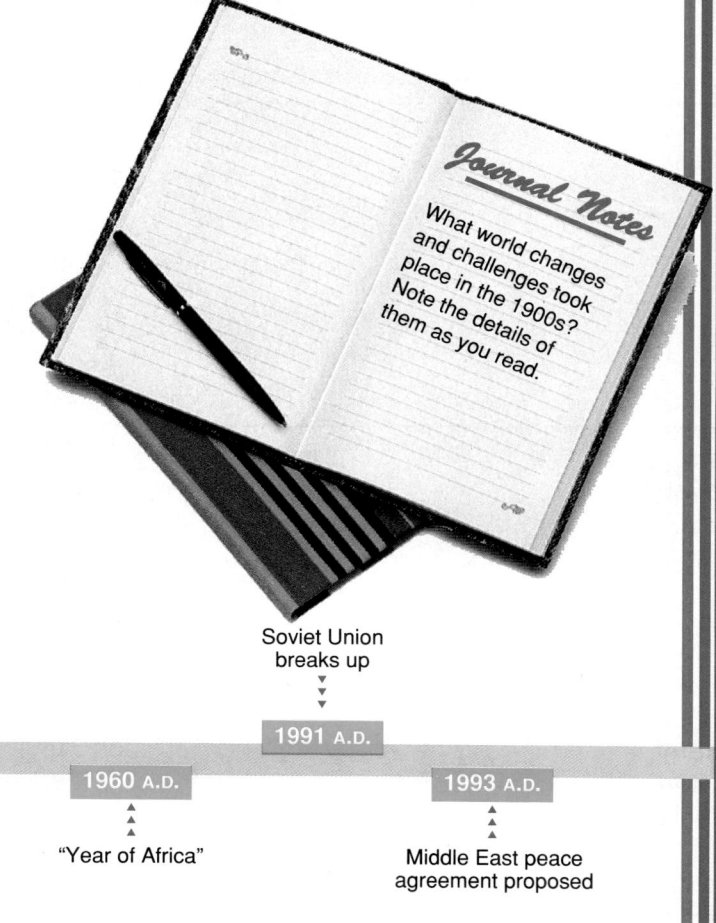

Ask students to name major changes and challenges that have occurred in the world since they were born. Write student responses on the chalkboard. Explain to students that these are the types of things they want to note in their journal as they read Unit 12.

GEOGRAPHIC LOCATION

Have students note that the geographic location of this unit encompasses all parts of the earth but will focus on the Eastern Hemisphere. Explain that the technological and economic changes that have taken place and common environmental problems that face us in the twentieth century have affected all places in the world. The world has become a global village.

CHAPTER 37

Conflict and Change

CHAPTER ORGANIZER

Objectives	Special Features	Supplemental Materials
Section 1 World War I Discuss the causes, events, and results of World War I.		• Reproducible Lesson Plan • Section 1 Quiz • Testmaker • Chapter 37 Vocabulary and Guided Reading Activity • Chapter 37 Cooperative Learning Activity • Chapter 37 Geography and Map Activity • Outline Map Resource Book, pp. 27, 28, 29, 30, 33, 34 • The Western Civilization Videodisc
Section 2 Between the Wars Describe how communism developed in Russia.		• Reproducible Lesson Plan • Section 2 Quiz • Testmaker • Reinforcing Social Studies Skills, pp. 13, 16 • World History and Art Transparencies 24, 27 • Chapter 37 Activity Book Activity • The Western Civilization Videodisc
Section 3 World War II Examine why Italy and Germany became dictatorships, and the events and results of World War II.		• Reproducible Lesson Plan • Section 3 Quiz • Testmaker • Chapter 37 Chart and Graph Skill Activity • Unit 12 World Literature • Chapter 37 Teaching Transparencies • The World History Videodisc
Chapter 37 Review and Evaluation		• Chapter 37 Reteaching Activity • Chapter 37 Enrichment Activity • Spanish Summary and Glossary • Audiocassettes (English and Spanish) • Chapter 37 Performance Assessment Activity • Chapter 37 Test • Testmaker

If time does not permit teaching the entire chapter, use the Chapter 37 Summary on page 622 and the Chapter 37 Audiocassettes (English and Spanish) to point out the main ideas of the chapter.

✓ Performance Assessment Activities

Book Review Have each student choose a fiction or nonfiction book about one of the following eras or people in it: World War I, the Russian Revolution, or World War II. You may refer them to books listed in the Chapter Resources. Have them read the book and write a book review about it concluding with an endorsement or lack of one for other students. Suggest they could include illustrations. Have students present the reviews in class.

Letters to the Editor Ask students to imagine they live in one of these countries during the post-World War I period: Italy, Germany, the Soviet Union, France, or Great Britain. Have students write a letter to the editor of their newspaper telling their thoughts and opinions about their country's post-war situation. Tell students they can represent any opinions, but must describe their identity, such as "I am a young, unmarried woman who wants a university education," or "I am a middle-aged, male farmer." Collect the letters and bind them together under a title such as "Post-war Europe Through the Eyes of its Citizens."

CHAPTER RESOURCES

LITERATURE ABOUT THE PERIOD

Hemingway, Ernest. *The Sun Also Rises.* Scribner's, 1926. A novel about English and American expatriates who roamed France and Spain after World War I.

Hilberg, Raul. *Destruction of the European Jews.* Octagon, 1978. Study of Hitler's persecution of the Jews during the 1930s and the events of the Holocaust during World War II.

Remarque, Erich Maria. *All Quiet on the Western Front.* Translated by A.W. Wheen. Fawcett, 1958. A novel about the destruction of a generation of young German soldiers during World War I.

READINGS FOR THE STUDENT

Frank, Anne. *The Diary of a Young Girl.* Doubleday, 1972. First-person account of a young Jewish girl and her family who spent years during World War II hiding from the Nazis.

Ryan, Cornelius. *The Longest Day.* Simon & Schuster Pocket Books, 1984. Detailed account of D-Day and the Normandy invasion.

Taylor, A. J. P. *Illustrated History of the First World War.* Putnam, 1964. Includes many photographs and an informative commentary about World War I.

READINGS FOR THE TEACHER

Garraty, John. *The Great Depression.* Harcourt Brace Jovanovich, 1986. Focuses on the Great Depression from a global perspective.

Toland, John. *Rising Sun.* Bantam Books, 1971. Account of the Japanese Empire and Japan's role in World War II.

Tuchman, Barbara W. *The Guns of August.* Macmillan, 1962. Account of the crucial first six weeks of World War I.

MULTIMEDIA RESOURCES

American History III. Sliwa Enterprises Inc. Software, Apple. Reviews the 1920s, World Wars I and II, and the Great Depression.

The American People in World War II. McGraw-Hill Films. Film. Influence of World War II on the quality of home life as seen in old prints, photographs, and newsreel footage.

The Tragedy of War: A Simulation. Focus Media. Software, Apple. Simulates life and battles on the Western Front during World War I.

INTRODUCE

CHAPTER 37 OVERVIEW

Chapter 37 discusses international affairs during the twentieth century from World War I to the postwar period, and then World War II.

- **Section 1** discusses World War I, focusing on its underlying causes, significant campaigns, and impact.
- **Section 2** describes the origins, beliefs, and impact of communism on the twentieth-century world, and explains the rise of dictatorships in Italy and Germany.
- **Section 3** analyzes the causes, events, and results of World War II, including the formation of the United Nations.

CHAPTER OBJECTIVES

After reading Chapter 37, students will be able to:

1. discuss what the causes, events, and results of World War I were.

2. describe how communism developed in Russia.

3. explain reasons Italy and Germany became dictatorships.

4. examine what the events and results of World War II were.

EXAMINING THE ILLUSTRATION

Ask students what they would conclude the soldiers are doing in this photo. Tell them they will learn about many important battles and soldiers in this chapter.

PERFORMANCE ASSESSMENT

Use the Performance Assessment activities on page 602B to help you to evaluate students as they complete the chapter.

CHAPTER 37 Conflict and Change

Zero Hour, WWI

602

TEACHER CLASSROOM RESOURCES

- Reproducible Lesson Plan
- Section Quizzes/Chapter Test
- Reteaching Activity
- Enrichment Activity
- Geography and Map Activity
- Vocabulary and Guided Reading Activity
- Cooperative Learning Activity
- Performance Assessment Activity
- Spanish Summary and Glossary
- Unit 12 World Literature
- Teaching Transparencies and Activities
- Audiocassettes (English and Spanish)
- The Western Civilization Videodisc
- The World History Videodisc
- Testmaker

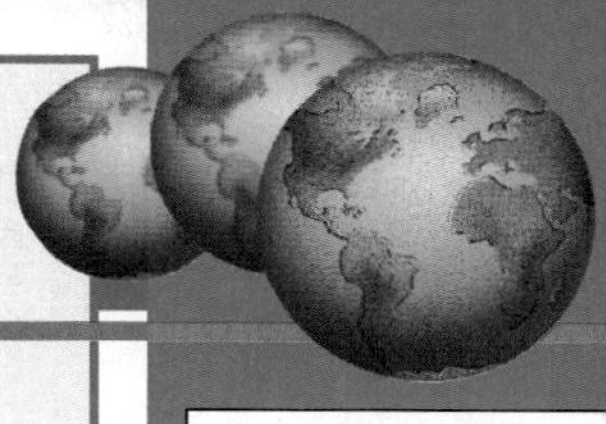

Chapter Focus

READ TO DISCOVER:

- What were the causes, events, and results of World War I.
- How communism developed in Russia.
- Why Italy and Germany became dictatorships.
- What were the events and results of World War II.

The first half of the 1900s was a period of turmoil throughout the world. In 1914, a war broke out in Europe that soon grew to be World War I. Although it ended in 1918, anger over the peace settlement and poor economic conditions following the war led to World War II. The same period also saw the rise of communism in Russia and neighboring countries.

1900–1945

KEY TERMS

mobilize
trench warfare
artillery
armistice
mandate
soviets
collectivization
dictatorship
appeasement
genocide
Holocaust

Section 1

WORLD WAR I

For almost 100 years after Napoleon's defeat, no long, general European war developed. By the early 1900s, however, rivalries among the countries of Europe were causing trouble.

Background By the early 1900s, tension grew between several countries. France was jealous of Germany because it was industrializing rapidly. Great Britain did not like Germany expanding its navy. Russia involved itself with the problems of the Slavic peoples in Austria-Hungary.

Each European country built up its armed forces and made alliances with other nations. They each promised to help the others in their alliance if they were attacked. Thus, trouble between any two nations of different alliances could draw in many countries. A small war could easily grow into a large one. All that was needed was a spark.

FOCUS

BELLRINGER

Write the following on the chalkboard for students' written response: *List two good things and two bad things about nationalism.*

MOTIVATIONAL ACTIVITY

Have students share their responses about nationalism. Point out that in the early 1900s nationalism created an atmosphere in which a simple incident could have serious consequences. Explain that the direct cause of World War I was the tension created by strong nationalist feelings in Austria-Hungary and Serbia. Tell students that in this chapter they will learn about other causes of conflicts in the first half of the 1900s.

VOCABULARY PRE-CHECK

Write the key terms for this chapter on the chalkboard. Ask students to use those that they know in sentences.

Assign Chapter 37 **Vocabulary and Guided Reading Activity** in the TCR.

EXTRA CREDIT PROJECT

Have students investigate the kinds of propaganda used during World War I and World War II by governments to promote a cause or to harm an opposing cause. Have students create examples of propaganda used during one of the World Wars in the form of posters, fliers, or leaflets for a display presentation.

KEY TO ABILITY LEVELS

Teaching strategies have been coded for varying learning styles and abilities.

L1 Level 1 activities are **basic** activities and should be within the ability range of all students.

L2 Level 2 activities are **average** activities and should be within the ability range of the average to above-average student.

L3 Level 3 activities are **challenging** activities designed for the ability range of above-average students.

LEP LEP activities should be within the ability range of Limited English Proficiency students.

TEACH

GUIDED PRACTICE

L1 **Geography: Location** Ask students to study the relative position of the Central and Allied Powers. On an outline map of the world, have students show the locations of the Central and the Allied Powers. Then ask: How did the Central Powers get their name? *(They were located between Allied countries.)* What problem did the Central Powers' location pose? *(They had to fight on two fronts: east and west.)* LEP

L2 **Geography: Region** Have students chart the European countries who became involved in World War I, including the following information for each as it was accurate for that time: population, population density, size (in sq. miles), ethnic groups, languages, religions. Encourage them to refer to these charts throughout the chapter.

GEOGRAPHY AND HISTORY

By 1910, British and French military leaders, suspicious of Germany, developed a plan to defend France against a German invasion through Belgium.

VIDEODISC

Use the following to enrich Chapter 37.

WC H 18 27985
"The lamps are going out all over Europe."

WC H 42 28009
A French soldier with a trench mortar.

Photograph of Archduke Franz Ferdinand

The spark for World War I was provided at Sarajevo (sahr uh yē vō), a small town in Austria-Hungary. There, in June 1914, a teenager named Gavrilo Princip shot and killed Archduke Franz Ferdinand, heir to the throne of Austria-Hungary. Princip belonged to a secret nationalist group called the Black Hand. This group wanted the Serbs ruled by Austria-Hungary to be ruled by Serbia (ser' bē uh).

Austria-Hungary blamed the Serbian government for the Archduke's death and declared war on Serbia. Russia, an ally of Serbia, began to **mobilize,** or call up its troops, to go to Serbia's aid. Germany then showed its support of Austria-Hungary by declaring war on Russia. Shortly after, France and Great Britain entered the war on the side of Russia. So did Japan and, later, Italy and China. The Ottoman Empire, on the other hand, decided to support Germany and Austria-Hungary. Together, Germany, Austria-Hungary, the Ottoman Empire, and Bulgaria were called the Central Powers. Russia, Serbia, France, Great Britain, Japan, Italy, and China were called the Allied Powers.

From 1914 to 1918 World War I, also called the Great War, was different from any earlier war. It was the first war where **civilians** (suh vil' yuhnz), or people who are not soldiers, were also attacked. The war grew so large that 31 countries, with 65 million soldiers, took part. Although most land fighting took place in Europe, the Middle East, and Africa, naval warfare took place all over the world.

There was also a new technology of frightening weapons. Machine guns fired bullets one after another at a rapid speed. Huge guns fired shells more than 75 miles, or 120 kilometers. Some airplanes carried bombs behind enemy lines and dropped them on enemy cities. Submarines attacked ships at sea. Poison gases were used. Tanks and flame throwers were introduced.

Painting of World War I Soldier

Much of the fighting took place on the western front, the zone between France and Germany. There, opposing armies dug themselves into the ground in trenches protected by barbed wire. This kind of fighting is called **trench warfare.** To get at the enemy, each side had to climb out of its trenches and cross open land under **artillery** (ar til' uhr ē), or mounted gun, fire. The casualties were enormous. One battle alone cost 900,000 lives. In another area, French and German soldiers engaged in trench warfare for ten months.

On the eastern front, the Russian Empire suffered heavy losses. Some 3.8 million soldiers were killed in just the first ten months of the war. In 1918, after two revolutions, Russia withdrew and signed a separate peace treaty with Germany having recognized Ukraine as an independent country. The Russians gave up huge areas of land previously conquered by them. Located

COOPERATIVE LEARNING

Have students research and report on the first six weeks of World War I. Assign each of five groups one of the following: invasion of Belgium, German sweep through France to Paris, retreat of the Allies, Russian mobilization and early victories ending at Tannenberg, and the Battle of the Marne. Students should work in pairs, each student gathering specific information on a specific topic. Then have each group present its report to create a composite picture.

Assign the Chapter 37 **Cooperative Learning Activity** in the TCR.

TRENCH WARFARE Much of the fighting of the First World War was carried out from trenches. Men had to charge across "no man's land," the open area in front of the enemy's trenches, in order to attack. Machine guns made these attacks especially dangerous. **Where was the western front located?**

to the west of Russia, these lands included one third of their farmland, one third of their population, and almost all of their resources of coal, iron, and oil.

In the meantime, German submarines tried to stop supply ships to Great Britain and France. In 1917, after the submarines sank American ships with civilians on board, the United States declared war on Germany. Until then, the United States had tried to stay out of the conflict.

The United States sent 2 million fresh troops to Europe to aid the tired Allied forces. The Americans helped to bring a quick end to the war, in favor of the Allied Powers. On November 11, 1918, Germany and its allies agreed to an **armistice** (ar' muh stis), or a stop in the fighting.

The Great War was over. It had cost the lives of over 13 million soldiers and 17 million civilians. Another 20 million soldiers had been wounded, and billions of dollars in damage to property had been done.

Making the Peace

Woodrow Wilson, the President of the United States, had drawn up a peace plan called the Fourteen Points. Wilson believed that national groups in Europe should have the right to form their own countries. He wanted to reduce **armaments** (ar' muh muhnts), or equipment for war. Above all,

L1 **History** Ask students to list the kinds of equipment and weapons they think were used for fighting before World War I. *(horses, wagons, reloadable rifles, cannons, bayonets, and swords)* Then have students make lists of the kinds of equipment and weapons that were actually used in World War I and compare their lists. LEP

CAPTION ANSWER

between France and Germany

MAKING CONNECTIONS

➤➤ **History** In May 1915, a German submarine sank the *Lusitania*, a British passenger ship. More than 1,000 people were killed including 128 Americans. As a result of President Wilson's protests, the Germans agreed to stop sinking passenger ships.

LINKING PAST TO PRESENT

The conflict from 1914 to 1918 was called at the time "The Great War" and "the war to end all wars." It is ironic that a war to end all wars was later renamed World War I.

VIDEODISC

Use the following to enrich Chapter 37.

WC H 28 27995
Inside the Krupp munitions works, November 1914.

WC H 29 27996
A German dispatch rider wearing a gas mask, 1917.

EXTENDING THE CONTENT

On the eastern front, Russia was ill-equipped and badly led. Before Lenin's new government signed the Treaty of Brest-Litovsk, more than two million Russians had been killed. In Turkey, the failing Ottoman Empire still controlled the Dardanelles. Mines in the water and on-shore artillery kept the Russians blockaded in their Black Sea ports. At Gallipoli in 1915, an Allied force failed in its attempt to land on the Turkish coast and march to Constantinople. British, New Zealand, Australian, and French troops suffered terrible losses against the Turks and Germans.

L2 **Critical Thinking** Ask students to work in small groups to list three things they would have included in the settlement for World War I. As they read "Making the Peace," have students compare their lists with Wilson's Fourteen Points and the Treaty of Versailles.

DID YOU KNOW ??

All the major powers used propaganda during World War I. In August 1918, the United States dropped leaflets behind German lines asking Germans if they were "still willing to die for a hopeless cause."

L3 **Science** Remind students World War I was the first war to employ submarines. Have students research and report on this kind of ship and the scientific principles used to control its buoyancy. Ask students to demonstrate these principles for the class.

CAPTION ANSWER

It was blamed for the war, asked to pay for war damages, and lost land in Europe and overseas.

VIDEODISC

Use the following to enrich Chapter 37.

WC H 121 28088
Refugees returning to St. Mihiel, 1918.

WC H 124 28091
Germans help wounded comrades to U.S. first aid.

he wanted a world association of nations to keep the peace. The British, French, and Italian leaders, however, had other plans. They wanted repayment for their losses during the war from the defeated countries.

The peace treaty that Germany signed after World War I was called the Treaty of Versailles (vuhr sī'). This treaty put most of the blame for the war and the financial repayment on Germany, for which the Germans were very angry. Under this treaty, Germany lost land in Europe and overseas. Alsace and Lorraine, which Germany had taken from France in 1870, were returned to France. Some of Germany's eastern territory became part of the reestablished nation of Poland. Germany's African colonies were divided between France and Great Britain, while its Pacific colonies were given to Japan.

Under the Treaty of Versailles, Russia lost even more territory than Germany did. Part of the Russian territory was lost to Poland and Romania, and part of it became the new nations of Finland, Estonia, Latvia, and Lithuania. Ukraine's desire for independence, however, was ignored.

The treaty did not deal with the needs of some other countries, however. India and people in Southeast Asia who had supported the Allied Powers wanted independence from Great Britain and France. Their wishes were ignored. Over the next 30 years, serious troubles developed in all these areas.

The other Central Powers were dealt with in separate treaties. Austria-Hungary was broken up, and four new countries—Austria,

TREATY OF VERSAILLES The Treaty of Versailles was signed in June, 1919, at the palace of Versailles outside Paris. Only the Allied Powers took part in the negotiations. Germany was not allowed to participate. Here, the Allied leaders meet in the Hall of Mirrors. **How was Germany affected by the Treaty of Versailles?**

EXTENDING THE CONTENT

The function of aircraft in World War I was at first limited to reconnaissance. Bombs were too heavy to support and were carried instead by dirigibles. Moreover, it was hard to aim heavy rifles or shotguns at anything from these "bucking machines." Roland Garros, a French pilot, was the first to have a machine gun synchronized to shoot through the propeller blades. But in 1915, Garros and his plane went down. The Germans took Garros prisoner, seized the plane, and copied and improved on the technology. Soon air fights, also called dog fights, became a glamorized aspect of war.

Hungary, Czechoslovakia, and Yugoslavia—were created. France received a **mandate** (man′dāt), or right to rule, in Syria and Lebanon. Great Britain received mandates in Iraq and Palestine.

For the most part, President Wilson's peace plan was not followed. However, one point was kept. An organization called the League of Nations was established so the countries of the world could come together to talk over their troubles. Most hoped the League could help prevent future wars. But the League had a serious weakness—it had no army of its own. If a country did not want to obey the League, it could not be forced to do so. The League was also weak because the United States refused to become a member. Many Americans disagreed with the World War I treaties. After 1919, the United States became an **isolationist** country. It decided to stay out of European affairs and world problems.

MAP STUDY

REGIONS The map of Europe changed a great deal after World War I. Some countries disappeared, while several new ones appeared. **Which part of Europe was most changed?**

Europe After World War I

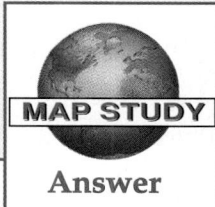

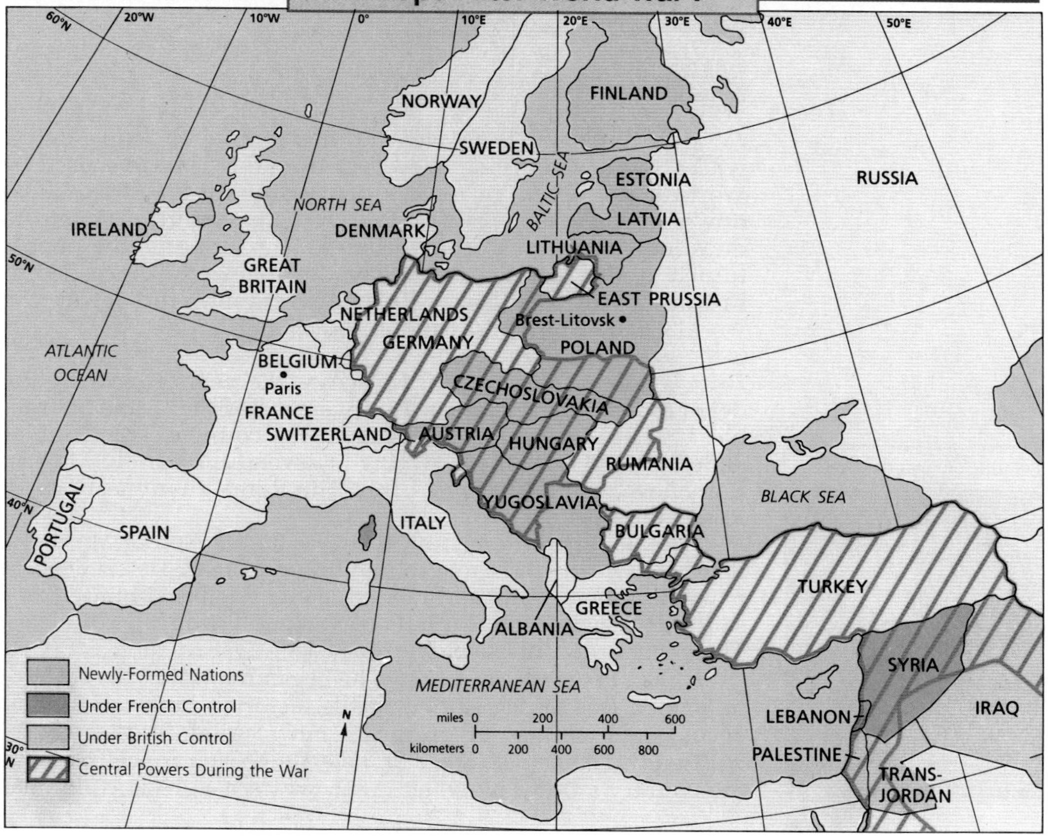

L1 **Geography: Location** Ask students to look at the map, "Europe After World War I," and locate the new nations that resulted from the war. LEP

DID YOU KNOW

After World War I, Germany's economy was especially hard-hit. High inflation caused the country's paper currency to be worthless and many people used it to light their stoves.

MAP STUDY

Answer

the eastern part

Assign the Chapter 37 **Geography and Map Activity** in the TCR.

VIDEODISC

Use the following to enrich Chapter 37.

WC H 129 28096

French troops in an Alsace town after WWI.

WC H 130 28097

German town crier reads U.S. regulations.

MEETING SPECIAL NEEDS

For those students needing extra reinforcement, encourage oral summaries of each section of the chapter. Students may be divided into small groups. Each group would then assign different sections of the chapter to pairs of students who would prepare the summaries. Have groups meet again to present the summaries.

L3 **Critical Thinking** Have students discuss the reforms brought about in Russia during the rule of Peter the Great. Ask: What reforms were made in industry, trade, the military, education, and daily life? Ask students to analyze whether each reform made was positive or negative and explain their answers in writing.

MAKING CONNECTIONS

➤➤ **History** The "Time of Troubles" in Russia included three years of famine, which led to revolt by the peasants as well as invasions by armies from Poland and Sweden. It was during the "Time of Troubles" that a system of secret police was set up in Russia.

VIDEODISC

Use the following to enrich Chapter 37.

WC E 76 19857

Peter the Great cuts the beards of the nobles.

WC E 77 19858

Peter the Great building St. Petersburg.

Section 1 Review

1. **Identify:** Sarajevo, Franz Ferdinand, Central Powers, Allied Powers, Woodrow Wilson, Fourteen Points, Treaty of Versailles, League of Nations
2. **Define:** mobilize, civilians, artillery, trench warfare, armistice, armaments, mandate, genocide
3. What made World War I different from earlier wars?
4. Why did the United States refuse to join the League of Nations?

Critical Thinking

5. Would you have supported or opposed President Wilson's League of Nations? Why?

Section 2 Between the Wars

The 1920s and 1930s were a difficult time for people everywhere. Most were trying to recover from the damage caused by World War I. Then, in 1929, a **depression,** or a sudden slowdown in business, began. People in many countries started to question their forms of government. In Germany, the people turned to a leader who would soon threaten world peace. People in Russia had overthrown their government and set up the world's first Communist nation.

Painting of Peter the Great

Emerging Russia In Muscovy, the years following the death of Ivan the Terrible in 1584 were called the "Time of Troubles." There was much disorder in the country. The troubles ended in 1613 with the crowning of seventeen-year-old Michael Romanov (rō′ muh nahf) as czar. The Romanov dynasty ruled Russia until 1917.

The first great Romanov ruler was a grandson of Michael's, Peter the Great, who came to the throne in 1682. Determined to make Muscovy strong and modern, Peter disguised himself as a sailor and visited the capitals of various European countries. There he learned all he could of western ways.

When Peter returned home, he began reforming the country he named Russia. He started textile factories, built canals, and encouraged mining. He ordered a new capital, St. Petersburg, built on the Baltic Sea. Since St. Petersburg was an ice-free port, the country's trade by water with western Europe continued

SECTION 1 ANSWERS

1. Sarajevo, town in Austria-Hungary (p. 604); Ferdinand, ruler of Austria-Hungary (p. 604); Central Powers, Germany, Austria-Hungary, Ottoman Empire, Bulgaria (p. 604); Allied Powers, Russia, Serbia, France, Great Britain, Japan, Italy, China (p. 604); Wilson, U.S. President (p. 605); Fourteen Points, Wilson's plan (p. 605); Treaty of Versailles, treaty after WWI (p. 606); League of Nations, world countries (p. 607)
2. mobilize, arm troops (p. 604); civilians, nonsoldiers (p. 604); artillery, mounted gun (p. 604); trench warfare, fighting from ditches (p. 604); armistice, end to fighting (p. 605); armaments, war equipment (p. 605); mandate, right to rule (p. 607)
3. 31 countries with 65 million soldiers took part; new weapons; civilians involved
4. Americans disagreed with the treaties.
5. Answers will vary.

Assign the Chapter 37 **Section 1 Quiz** in the TCR. Testmaker available.

even in winter. Peter revised the alphabet and set up schools for the upper class. He trained a powerful army and also built the country's first navy. He even changed people's appearance. He ordered men to shave their beards and to wear European-style short jackets instead of long coats.

The next great Romanov ruler was Catherine the Great, who came to the throne in 1762. At first Catherine wanted to improve the condition of the peasants. She even considered abolishing serfdom. Then peasants in a newly conquered area of Ukraine rebelled. Soon after, the French Revolution broke out. These two events so frightened Catherine that she gave up her ideas of reform.

Painting of Catherine the Great

Catherine did not help the peasants, but she did make Russia much larger. In a number of wars, the country's borders were pushed farther east, west, and south.

The Road to Revolution During the 1800s, there was a great deal of discontent in the Russian Empire. About 30 million serfs, one half of whom were owned by the czar, labored to support about one-half million nobles and clergy. The czar controlled what industry there was. All society suffered and students protested, peasants revolted, and workers staged strikes. In 1825 a group of army officers, inspired by the ideas of the French Revolution, rose up against the czar. The rebellion, however, was put down.

A period of strong government controls followed. Writers who ridiculed government leaders were not published. Some writers were exiled. Even so, ideas about freedom and reform spread.

In 1861 Czar Alexander II, who was trying to modernize the country and appear to be a fair ruler, freed the serfs. However, he did not give them land of their own. As a result, most became tenant farmers.

In 1905 another uprising took place. It began when thousands of workers appeared in the square before the czar's palace. They carried petitions asking for a national assembly, freedom of speech and religion, and better conditions for workers and peasants. Government soldiers fired on the crowd, killing hundreds of unarmed people. A general strike then broke out. Finally, Czar Nicholas II agreed to some of the workers' demands. He ignored the national assembly, however, and its plans for reform.

World War I only made Russia's problems worse. The country did not have enough factories to produce guns and ammunition or enough railroads to carry supplies to the front. As a result, it suffered higher casualties than any other country. Nearly 9 million soldiers were killed or wounded in battle. Civilians suffered from lack of food and fuel.

Photograph of Nicholas II

Nicholas II

L1 **Government** Have students work in small groups to chart the major leaders of Russia and their achievements and/or their acts of oppression as described in this chapter. Guide a class discussion based on their charts. LEP

MAKING CONNECTIONS

➤➤ **Economics** Russia began industrializing in the 1890s. Among its achievements was the building of the Trans-Siberian Railroad. Its 5,500 miles (or 8,800 km) make this the longest railroad in the world.

DID YOU KNOW ??

In autumn of 1917, the Bolsheviks seized Nicholas II and his family. They were reported to have been shot on July 16, 1918, although some unconfirmed reports claim that he or members of his family escaped from Russia.

VIDEODISC

Use the following to enrich Chapter 37.

WC H 138 28105
Nicholas II of Russia and the Tsarina.

WC H 139 28106
Grigori Eflmovich Rasputin (1872-1916).

COOPERATIVE LEARNING

Have students work in small groups to research and compare and contrast the daily lives of women who lived in Russia during the time of Peter the Great and Catherine the Great, and women who live in Russia today. Russian feminism of the past and feminism of the present reports could include topics such as type of work, family responsibilities, intellectual interests, and political concerns. Have groups plan how to conduct the research and report on the findings.

MAKING CONNECTIONS

➤➤ **History** Alexander Kerensky, the former minister of war and the navy in Russia, headed the temporary government after the overthrow of Nicholas II. Following Kerensky's defeat by Lenin, Kerensky fled to Paris and then to the United States, where he taught and wrote until his death in 1970.

CAPTION ANSWER

They promised land to the peasants and bread to the workers. They also promised to get Russia out of the war.

L3 **Language Arts** More adept readers may be interested in being exposted to the rich heritage of Russian literature. Poets such as Pushkin and novelists such as Tolstoy, Turgenev, and Dostoyevsky created works displaying a revolutionary style long before the Russian overthrow in 1917.

VIDEODISC

Use the following to enrich Chapter 37.

WC H 141 28108
"The days of the revolution."

WC H 146 28113
Lenin (Vladimir Ilyich Ulyanov, 1870-1924).

LENIN Lenin was a powerful speaker and was able to rally much support for the Communist cause. He ruled the Soviet Union until his death in 1924. **What did the Bolsheviks promise in order to gain support?**

At last the Russian people could stand no more. In March 1917, they revolted. Striking workers, led by women textile laborers, jammed the streets of St. Petersburg, which had been renamed Petrograd (pet' ruh grad). They demanded bread and peace. The workers were soon joined by the city's **garrison** (gar' uh suhn), or military group stationed in the area. Within a few days, the revolt spread throughout the country. Peasants took over the lands of nobles. Soldiers left the front and began walking home. The czar was forced to abdicate, and a temporary government was set up.

Lenin There was much confusion in the months following the overthrow of Nicholas II. A revolutionary group called Bolsheviks (bol' shuh viks) took advantage of this. Led by Vladimir Lenin (len' in), they gained the support of the **soviets,** or committees that represent workers and soldiers. The Bolsheviks promised land to the peasants and bread to the workers. They also promised to get Russia out of the war.

In November 1917, the Bolsheviks seized power from the temporary government. Lenin was chosen to lead the new government. Soon after, he signed a peace treaty with Germany that ended Russia's part in World War I. The treaty, however, did not end the troubles at home.

EXTENDING THE CONTENT

In their struggle for survival during the civil war in Russia in 1918, Lenin and the Bolsheviks had introduced an economic policy called war communism. Under war communism, the government carried out a policy of nationalization in which it brought under state control all major industries. Applying the principle that those who would eat must work, the government required everyone between the ages of 16 and 50 to hold a job. It also erected a huge bureaucratic administration that wielded tremendous power but was shown to be extremely inefficient.

From 1918 to 1920, Russia was divided by a civil war between the majority Bolsheviks—now known as Communists—and the minority Mensheviks (men' chuh viks), or non-Communists. The Communists were also called Reds, because red had been the color of revolution since the French Revolution. The non-Communists were called Whites.

The Whites received soldiers and supplies from other countries, including the United States. These countries were afraid that if the Reds won, communism would spread throughout Europe. The Russian people as a whole did not like the Communists. However, because they did not want to return to old ways, most of them supported the Reds and by 1921 the Whites had been defeated.

In 1922 the Union of Soviet Socialist Republics, or the Soviet Union, was formed. It was made up of four republics, the largest of which was Russia. By 1924 the Soviet Union was completely under the control of the Communist party.

Lenin died that same year. His body was embalmed and placed in a glass coffin inside a red marble tomb near the wall of Moscow's Kremlin. In his honor, Petrograd was renamed Leningrad.

Stalin After Lenin died, there was a struggle for power in the Soviet Union which lasted until 1928. In that year, Joseph Stalin (stah'lin) took control of the government. He also controlled the Communist party, which was the only political party allowed in the country.

Stalin wanted the Soviet Union to industrialize as quickly as possible. So he set up a series of Five-Year Plans. Their major goal was to build up **heavy industry,** or the manufacture of basic materials and machines. Under these plans, steel mills, power plants, oil refineries, and chemical plants were built and kept under government control. Workers were paid according to how much they produced. Factory managers had to turn out a certain quantity of goods. By 1939 the Soviet Union was a major industrial power. The people paid a price for industrialization. Workers labored long hours for low wages. Consumer goods, such as clothing and household goods, were poorly made and hard to find, and housing shortages were common.

Another goal of the Five-Year Plans was **collectivization** (kuh lek ti vuh zā' shuhn), or uniting small farms into large ones controlled by the government. On a collective, farmers were paid according to the number of days they worked. Collectivization allowed them to share tractors and other farm machinery. The government bought their crops at fixed prices and sold them abroad to buy machinery for factories.

Many peasants wanted to keep working on their own farms. They resisted collectivization by killing their horses, cows, and

Photograph of Soviet Farm Worker

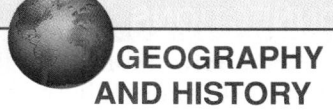

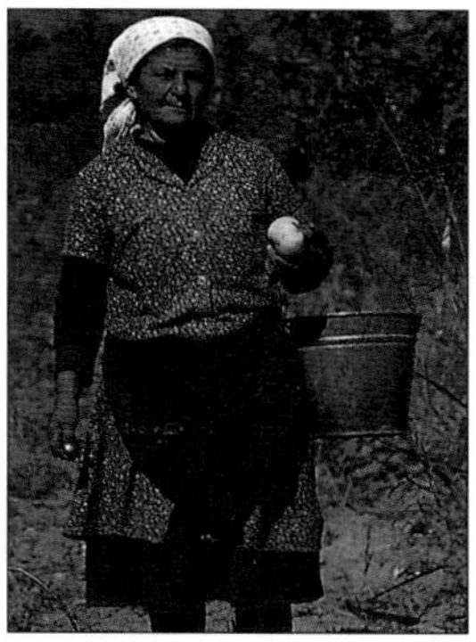

L1 **Critical Thinking** Have students create cause-event-effect graphic organizers to help them understand how communism developed in Russia. Start with the events in the subsection "The Road to Revolution" and end with events in the subsection "Lenin." LEP

L2 **Government** Have students list the changes that occurred in farming and industry in the Soviet Union under Stalin's Communist rule. Ask students to compare the benefits and costs of such government rule. LEP

GEOGRAPHY AND HISTORY

In 1922, the four republics that made up the Union of Soviet Socialist Republics included Russia, Belorussia, Transcaucasia, and Ukraine. The Russian Republic was the largest and most powerful.

VIDEODISC

Use the following to enrich Chapter 37.

WC I 95 30765

A Soviet poster, about 1925, against capitalism.

WC H 149 28116

Leon Trotsky (Lev Davidovich Bronstein).

COOPERATIVE LEARNING

Organize the class into small groups. Have the groups create advertising campaigns to promote the Five-Year Plans set up by Stalin to bring industrial and agricultural production under government control. Have each group research its topic, create a campaign, and then select a spokesperson to present the campaign.

L2 **Critical Thinking** Have students write a short essay comparing and contrasting the ways in which Hitler and Mussolini rose to power. Instruct students to include the conditions that favored each ruler.

CAPTION ANSWER

He banned all political parties except the Nazis; burned books, set up a secret police; took over media; and fought against Christian churches.

DID YOU KNOW

Hitler was a poor student who never graduated from high school. He was a good soldier, however, and a spellbinding orator.

GEOGRAPHY AND HISTORY

The First Reich was the Holy Roman Empire in the Middle Ages. The Second Reich was the German Empire from 1871 to 1918.

L2 **Geography: Region** Ask students to chart the European and Asian countries who became involved in World War II, including the following information for each at that time: population, population density, size (in sq. miles), ethnic groups, languages, and religions.

VIDEODISC

Use the following to enrich Chapter 37.

WC J 1 33353

Adolf Hitler at age 16 in 1905.

NAZI RALLY Adolf Hitler was an excellent speaker, and he used this skill to unite and gather support from the German people. The Nazis made impressive spectacles of huge rallies at which thousands of Germans would gather to listen to Hitler speak. **What political steps did Hitler take once he was in power in Germany?**

In 1933 Adolf Hitler became **chancellor,** or prime minister, of Germany. Before long, he did away with the German republic and set himself up as dictator. He called himself *Der Fuhrer* (dār fyū′ uhr), which means "the leader." He called Germany the Third Reich (rīk), which means the third empire. Hitler was supported by a violent political group called the National Socialist Party, or Nazis (nah′ tsēz). The Nazi symbol of identity was the **swastika** (swos′ tuh kuh), or hooked black cross. Many citizens of Germany were angry over the Treaty of Versailles. They saw Hitler as a leader who would make their country economically and politically strong.

Once Hitler was in power, he did away with all political parties except the Nazis. He had books about democracy burned. He took over the courts and set up a secret police. He took over the radio, the press, and abolished trade unions. He fought against the Christian churches.

Hitler blamed many of Germany's troubles on the Jews and others. The Nazis believed the Germans were a "master race." Jews were not part of the "master race." So the Nazis took away the Jews' businesses and jobs. Jews could not go to school or get medical care. They were no longer allowed to vote or to walk along the streets after eight o'clock. They had to wear a yellow six-pointed star on their clothing. This was only the beginning. Worse treatment was to come later.

EXTENDING THE CONTENT

German Jews had full rights of citizenship until the Nazis came to power. They were leaders in government, law, finance, medicine, and the arts. On November 9, 1938, however, the demonstrations against the Jews began. This night became known as *Kristallnacht,* translated "Crystal Night" or the "Night of Broken Glass." Mobs—and police—damaged Jewish shops and synagogues and sent 20,000 Jews to concentration camps. Hitler's goal was to eliminate all Jewish people in Europe. When Germany invaded the Soviet Union in 1941, the orders were to kill every Jew they could find. By the end of 1942, 2.5 million Jews had been brought to various camps and killed.

The Road to War Soon Germany and its allies, Italy and Japan, began to threaten world peace. In 1935, the Italians, bitter about not getting enough land after World War I, invaded Ethiopia. The League of Nations was not able to stop them. Hitler announced that his goal was to unite all the German people. He sent German troops into the Rhineland, a disputed area, in 1936. Then, in March 1938 his army marched into Austria. Then he demanded that the Germans living in Czechoslovakia come under German rule. The British and the French were afraid of another war. So they decided to follow a policy of **appeasement,** or giving in to demands. They did nothing while Czechoslovakia was first divided and then made a part of Hitler's Germany in March 1939.

In Japan, the military who ran the country felt that Japan needed more land and natural resources to make its economy stronger. In 1931 Japan invaded Manchuria, in northern China. In 1937 Japanese troops invaded the main part of China. That same year, Japan signed a friendship treaty with Germany and Italy.

In August 1939, Germany and the Soviet Union signed a treaty agreeing not to attack each other. Now Hitler felt safe to take more land. On September 1, 1939, the German army attacked Poland. German troops overran the western part of the country, while the Soviets occupied the rest. The British and the French realized they had made a mistake in not resisting Hitler's aggression, or attacks, earlier. Both France and Great Britain declared war on Germany.

Photograph of Adolf Hitler

Section 2 Review

1. **Identify:** Time of Troubles, Peter the Great, St. Petersburg, Catherine the Great, Alexander II, Nicholas II, Bolsheviks, Vladimir Lenin, Communists, Mensheviks, Joseph Stalin, Five-Year Plans, Great Depression, Franklin D. Roosevelt, New Deal, Adolf Hitler, Third Reich, Nazis
2. **Define:** depression, garrison, soviets, heavy industry, consumer goods, collectivization, social security laws, dictatorship, chancellor, swastika, appeasement
3. How did Peter the Great reform Russia?
4. What were the goals of Stalin's Five-Year Plans?
5. Why did Great Britain and France declare war on Germany?

Critical Thinking

6. How did the policy of appeasement contribute to the start of World War II?

L1 **Economics** Discuss specific examples of the role economics played in the events leading up to World War II. Ask students to identify any possible economic solutions that could have averted the war. LEP

L2 **Geography: Movement** Ask several students to demonstrate on a wall map of the world how Japan, Italy, and Germany moved into other countries to take them over. *(Italy: Ethiopia; Germany: Rhineland, Austria, Czechoslovakia, Poland; Japan: Manchuria, main part of China)*

LINKING PAST TO PRESENT

Many Americans thought that a dictatorship would never be possible in the United States. In 1928, however, Huey Long became the dictatorial governor of Louisiana.

VIDEODISC

Use the following to enrich Chapter 37.

WC J 19 33371
Reichstag opening the day Hitler took office.

WC J 21 33373
Students and Nazis burn "un-German" books.

SECTION 2 ANSWERS

1. Time of Troubles, 1584-1613; Peter the Great, czar; St. Petersburg, capital of Russia (p. 608); Catherine the Great, Romanov ruler; Alexander II, czar; Nicholas II, czar (p. 609); Bolsheviks, revolutionaries (p. 610); Lenin, leader of Bolsheviks (p. 610); Communists, Bolsheviks; Mensheviks, non-Communists (p. 611); Stalin, Russian leader; Five-Year Plans, Stalin's plans (p. 611); Great Depression, economic slowdown (p. 612); Roosevelt, U.S. President (p. 613); New Deal, U.S. program of relief (p. 613); Hitler, German dictator; Third Reich, Germany's third empire; Nazis, political group (p. 614)
2. All terms are defined in the text Glossary.
3. He learned modern western ways.
4. to build up heavy industry
5. the German army attacked Poland
6. Answers will vary.

Assign the Chapter 37 **Section 2 Quiz** in the TCR. Testmaker available.

L1 **History** Read, or play for the class, excerpts from President Franklin D. Roosevelt's speech asking Congress for a declaration of war.

L2 **Geography: Location** By using a text map or a projection on an overhead projector, have students create an outline map of Europe on the chalkboard and indicate the Mediterranean Sea and the northern coast of Africa. Then have students take turns filling in the names of the countries controlled by Germany in the spring of 1941. LEP

CAPTION ANSWER

British pilots and antiaircraft guns shot down so many German planes that Hitler gave up the idea of invading Great Britain.

VIDEODISC

Use the following to enrich Chapter 37.

WC K 1 35959
Hitler, calls for war against Poland.

WC K 40 35998
Air raid shelter pass used during the Blitz.

Section 3

WORLD WAR II

For the second time during the 1900s, the world was at war. World War II caught the Allied Powers—including Great Britain, France, and, later, the Soviet Union and the United States—unprepared. The Axis Powers—Germany, Italy, and, later, Japan—were prepared. The war would end with the Allied Powers victorious, but not before a terrible cost was paid.

Early Axis Victories Germany had developed a new way of fighting called **blitzkrieg** (blits' krēg), or "lightning war." German airplanes would first bomb enemy cities, roads, and airfields. Then soldiers and civilians alike would be machine-gunned from the air. Finally armored tanks would roll through the countryside, wiping out all defenses.

Using the blitzkrieg, Germany crushed Poland in three weeks. In 1940 German forces overran most of western Europe except for Great Britain. Hitler tried to bomb the British into surrendering. The British, however, under the leadership of Prime Minister Winston Churchill, fought back for 10 months. Finally, British pilots and anti-aircraft guns shot down so many German planes that Hitler gave up the idea of invading Great Britain. In the meantime, however, German and Italian troops overran much of southeastern Europe and North Africa.

BLITZKRIEG Germany's bombing of European cities was a devastating new attack in World War II. Many parts of London, as shown here, were destroyed. **Why was Germany's blitzkrieg of Great Britain unsuccessful in allowing Germany to invade that country?**

SPOTLIGHT ON: CHURCHILL

Winston Churchill became Prime Minister of Great Britain in 1940, when the country was on the brink of defeat. His eloquence and strength gave the British a renewed morale. A famous quote of Churchill's rallied his people: "We shall defend our island, whatever the cost may be. We shall fight on the beaches, we shall fight on the landing-grounds, we shall fight in the fields and in the streets, we shall fight in the hills. We shall never surrender."

At the same time, the Japanese made conquests in Asia. They took over much of China and Southeast Asia. Then they turned their attention to the United States who had military forces in the Pacific. On December 7, 1941, the Japanese made a surprise air attack on Pearl Harbor, the American naval base in the Hawaiian Islands. The United States, followed by most of Latin America, immediately entered the war on the side of the Allied Powers.

War in Europe The entry of the United States helped the Allies win the war in Europe. The United States was the greatest

Axis Expansion in Europe and Africa

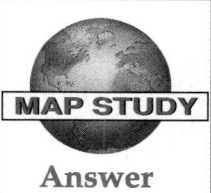

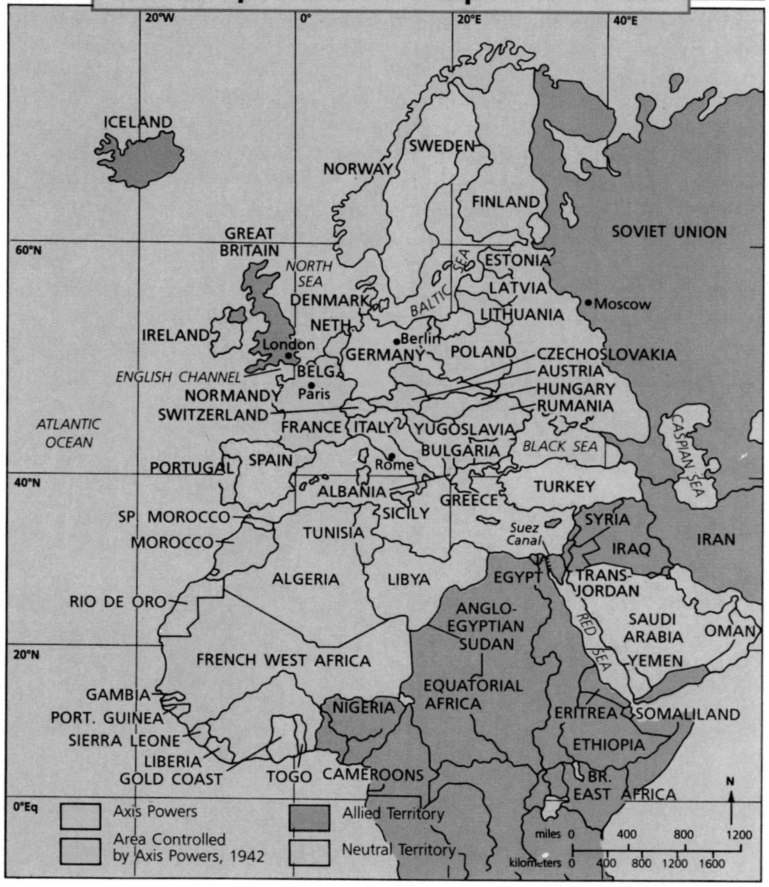

MAP STUDY

REGIONS By 1942 the Axis Powers had seized control of much of Europe and part of Africa. **Which European nations chose to be neutral during the war?**

MAKING CONNECTIONS

>> **History** Although the United States did not actually enter the war until after the attack on Pearl Harbor, in March of 1941 Congress had passed the Lend-Lease Act. It provided the enemies of the Axis powers with $50 billion in weapons, food, and other services.

DID YOU KNOW ??

Robert Watson Watts' 1935 invention of radar, an early warning system against approaching aircraft, was one factor that helped the British defeat Germany in the Battle of Britain. Another important factor in Britain's victory was the British fighter plane known as the Spitfire.

MAP STUDY

Answer

Portugal, Spain, Switzerland, Ireland, Sweden

VIDEODISC

Use the following to enrich Chapter 37.

WC K 8 35966

British troops captured at Dunkirk, 1940.

WC K 9 35967

A French World War II poster.

EXTENDING THE CONTENT

World War II created an urgent need to control the infections of thousands of wounded soldiers. In 1928 Sir Alexander Fleming had discovered an antibiotic substance in certain strains of a mold grown in glass jars. Sir H. W. Florey, E. B. Chain, and other scientists and technicians had established that this substance had antibacterial powers and was nontoxic to humans. The substance, whose name *penicillan* was taken from the name of the mold, was first used on a human in 1940. Soon the War Production Board took over the production and allocation of the drug, which was used to treat a wide range of infections in wounded soldiers.

L2 **Daily Life** Ask students what kinds of changes they think occurred in women's lives as a result of the war. Ask how they think Americans felt about those changes. *(Before the war, the majority of women were homemakers. During the war women did jobs previously done by men.)*

DID YOU KNOW

The system to quickly collect and store blood plasma was devised by African American, Dr. Charles Drew. During World War II he was called to set up the first blood donor bank in England. He later directed the American Red Cross Blood Donor project in the United States.

GEOGRAPHY AND HISTORY

Because of its far northern location, Leningrad has very short periods of daylight in winter. For about three weeks in June, it has "white nights," during which the sky is never completely black. It was more difficult for the Germans to conduct nighttime bombing missions during this month.

CAPTION ANSWER

D-day

VIDEODISC

Use the following to enrich Chapter 37.

WC K 32 35990

Winston Churchill (1874-1965).

industrial power in the world. Soon its factories were turning out thousands of planes and tanks. Ships were built in large numbers. Other supplies the Allies were lacking were provided by the United States.

Earlier, Hitler had decided that Germany needed the resources of the Soviet Union. He ignored the treaty he had signed and attacked the Soviet Union in 1941. However, Hitler had underestimated the size of the Soviet Union, the bitterness of its winters, and the Russian people's fighting spirit.

In defense, Soviet troops used a scorched-earth policy. They burned cities, destroyed their own crops, and blew up dams that produced electric power. Though the Russians sustained great losses, the tide of battle turned in 1943. The Red Army surrounded German forces at Stalingrad (stah' lin grad) and forced them to surrender. From then on, Soviet forces kept pushing the Germans back all along the eastern front. That same year, American and British armies drove the Axis forces out of North Africa and invaded Italy.

In 1944, under the command of American General Dwight D. Eisenhower, Allied troops crossed the English Channel from Great Britain and landed on the beaches of Normandy in France. About 155,000 Allied soldiers landed on the first day, June 6, known as D-day. Another 2 million landed later. By August the Allied forces had retaken Paris and were moving eastward.

German armies were now caught between the Soviets in the east and the Americans, British, French, and Canadians in the west. In April 1945, the Allied forces joined together at the Elbe

NORMANDY Landing craft and supply ships crowded the Normandy coast when Allied troops landed on June 6, 1944. **What name was given to this date?**

EXTENDING THE CONTENT

Suntan lotion got its start during World War II. American scientists invented a preparation to protect American soldiers and sailors who were constantly exposed to scorching sun. One of the earliest solutions was red petrolatum, an oil by-product with a natural red color that is very effective in blocking the sun's ultraviolet rays. When the soldiers used it, it resulted in a reddish-brown skin tone.

(el' buh) River in Germany. Hitler and the Germans realized they could not win. Hitler killed himself, and on May 7 Germany surrendered. The next day, the war in Europe was officially over.

War in Asia and the Pacific The war in Asia and the Pacific was fought at the same time as the one in Europe. At first the Japanese were victorious everywhere. They captured the Philippines and various other islands in the Pacific, including three islands off the coast of Alaska. They also captured Indochina (now Laos, Vietnam, and Cambodia), Malaya, Singapore, Hong Kong, Burma, Thailand, and the Dutch East Indies (now Indonesia). Then, in June 1942, a great sea and air battle took place at Midway Island. The battle changed the course

MAP STUDY

MOVEMENT
Between 1931 and 1942, Japan took over large areas of Southeast Asia and the Pacific. **How far east, in degrees longitude, did the Japanese extend their territory by 1942?**

Axis Expansion in the Pacific

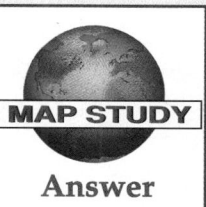

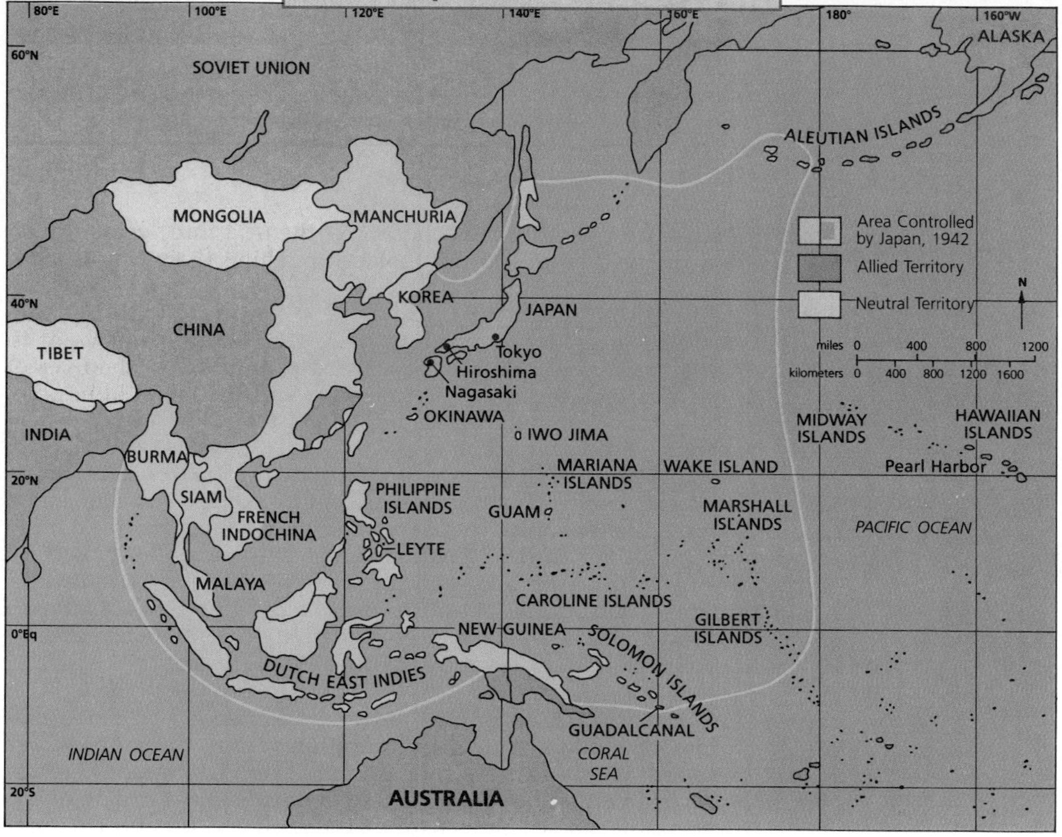

SPOTLIGHT ON: PHOTOJOURNALISTS

Robert Capa, born in 1913, was a famous combat photographer from the United States. Capa first achieved fame as a photojournalist in the Spanish Civil War. During World War II Capa covered much of the heaviest fighting in North Africa and Italy. Capa also covered the Normandy Invasion in June 1944. Margaret Bourke-White became one of the premier photojournalists in the United States during the Great Depression and after. At the end of World War II she traveled to Buchenwald, Germany, the location of a Nazi Concentration Camp and photographed the horrors faced by the Jews that had been held there.

INDEPENDENT PRACTICE

L2 **Geography: Region** Have students write five questions about the map, "Axis Expansion in the Pacific." Collect the questions and use them to lead a discussion about the war in the Pacific. LEP

MAKING CONNECTIONS

➤➤ **History** Despite the almost complete lack of weapons, some Jews organized resistance against the Germans. The most famous example took place in the Warsaw Ghetto. There, for nearly a month, about 1,000 Jews with homemade bombs held off 5,000 German soldiers armed with machine guns and tanks. There were also uprisings in several of the death camps near the end of the war.

MAP STUDY

Answer

to 180° longitude

VIDEODISC

Use the following to enrich Chapter 37.

WH N 130 23475
Japanese cruiser on fire in battle of Midway Island.

WH N 132 23477
The U.S. 3rd Amphibious Task Force off Guadalcanal.

MAKING CONNECTIONS

➤➤ **History** President Truman declared August 14, 1945, V-J (Victory over Japan) Day.

L2 **Critical Thinking** Have students brainstorm a list of pros and cons concerning the dropping of the atomic bomb on Japan, as a volunteer writes them on the chalkboard. After lists are complete, have students draw their own conclusions on whether or not to drop the bomb and write a letter to President Truman explaining their thoughts. Encourage students to share their letters with the class.

GEOGRAPHY AND HISTORY

In the years following World War II, *Western Europe* and *Eastern Europe* are capitalized. After World War II these areas became political, rather than merely geographical, divisions.

CAPTION ANSWER

He hoped for a Japanese surrender.

VIDEODISC

Use the following to enrich Chapter 37.

WC J 72 33424

German poster attempts to stimulate race hatred.

WH N 148 23493

Hiroshima after the atomic explosion.

ATOMIC BOMB The United States dropped the atomic bomb on Japan in 1945. The huge mushroom cloud from it formed over the destruction of much of Nagasaki, shown here. **Why did President Truman allow the bombing?**

of the war in favor of the Allies. Over the next three years, Allied forces moved from island to island, pushing their way toward Japan.

President Harry S Truman (tru' muhn), who became President after Roosevelt died in April 1945, did not want to invade Japan. He knew that an invasion would cost the lives of hundreds of thousands of American and British soldiers. So, hoping for a Japanese surrender, he approved the use of a new weapon — the atomic bomb.

On August 6, 1945, the bomb was dropped on Hiroshima (hir ō she' muh), Japan. It destroyed most of the city and killed about 100,000 people. Thousands more died later from radiation poisoning. When the Japanese refused to surrender, a second atomic bomb was dropped on Nagasaki (nah guh sah' kē), Japan. About 75,000 people were killed. On August 14 Japan surrendered. The peace treaty was signed on September 2 aboard the USS *Missouri* in Tokyo Bay. World War II was over.

The Aftermath of War After the war ended, Allied armies in Europe found German **concentration camps,** or camps where Germans had kept those they thought were enemies. There the Nazis had carried out a program of **genocide** (jen' uh sīd), or the mass murder of a people, against the Jews and others. This pro-

MEETING SPECIAL NEEDS

Have tactile/kinesthetic learners investigate innovations used in the invasion of Normandy. Have the students research the innovations and then recreate the invasion of Normandy showing the action unfolding in a diorama or drawing.

gram became known as the **Holocaust** (hol' uh kahst). At the start of World War II, German forces shot hundreds of thousands of Jews in Poland and the Soviet Union. However, Hitler felt that Jews were not being killed fast enough. So he ordered six concentration camps to be equipped with poison gas chambers and **cremation** (kri mā' shuhn) **ovens,** or places to burn dead bodies. The Nazis then rounded up all the Jews in the areas of Europe they controlled and shipped them in sealed cattle cars to the camps. There, most of the Jews were gassed to death. By the end of World War II, the Nazis had killed more than 6 million Jews. About 1.5 million of them were children under the age of six.

The Jews were not the only ones who died at the hands of the Nazis. The Nazis used the people they conquered as slave laborers in German factories and on German farms. Poles, Ukrainians, and Russians, gypsies, and those people considered mentally ill or whom the Germans thought were inferior, were treated worst of all. By the end of the war, about 6 million had died from starvation, overwork, and torture. More than 3 million of these were Soviet prisoners of war.

Photograph of Holocaust Victim

The Japanese, too, had killed men, women, and children in the countries they conquered. Many Allied prisoners of war both soldiers and civilians died because of poor treatment from the Japanese army.

The Allied governments felt that the cruel acts of the Nazis and the Japanese could not be excused as normal occurrences of war. So the Allied governments put German and Japanese leaders on trial for war crimes.

Making the Peace

One result of World War II was the formation of the United Nations (UN); an organization like the League of Nations. In 1945, the United Nations was approved by 50 countries. UN responsibilities were to prevent war, lend money to poor countries, and provide them with medical care and better education.

Following the war, Germany was divided into four zones. Each was occupied by one of the major Allied powers—the United States, Great Britain, France, and the Soviet Union. The German capital of Berlin, located in the Russian zone, was also divided. In addition, German territory in the east was given to Poland. This was in exchange for the Soviet Union's acquiring western Ukraine which had been occupied by Poland since 1923. In fact, the Soviet Union acquired most of the land it had lost after World War I, including Estonia, Latvia, and Lithuania.

Japan was occupied by the United States for nearly seven years. Under American General Douglas MacArthur, the Japanese military lost power in the government and Japan became a democracy. Laws were passed giving women the right to vote and allowing trade unions. The secret police was abolished.

L3 **Research** Have students research and present a report on the establishment of the United Nations and its principles. Have them include a concise list of the UN's rights and responsibilities.

LINKING PAST TO PRESENT

The new Japanese constitution was written by a group of 21 Americans. The constitution established freedom of religion and thought, and renounced warfare. Today, Japan spends almost no money for an army, navy, or air force. It relies on the United States for military protection.

MAKING CONNECTIONS

➤➤ **History** Between November 1945 and September 1946, the top surviving Nazi leaders were tried at Nuremberg, Germany. This city was chosen for the trials because, in 1935, the laws against Jewish citizenship were announced there.

VIDEODISC

Use the following to enrich Chapter 37.

WC J 76 33428
Ovens in a German concentration camp.

WC J 75 33427
Prisoners in their bunks at Dachau.

COOPERATIVE LEARNING

Have students hold a mock United Nations meeting with representatives from the five permanent members: the United States, France, Great Britain, the Commonwealth of Independent States, and China. Divide the class into five teams, one for each of these member nations. Select a current world problem for the teams to debate. First, have teams research the issue from the perspective of their nation. One member of each team will present their nation's view of the issue. The whole UN will then discuss the issue and vote on an appropriate resolution.

ASSESS

CHECK FOR UNDERSTANDING

Ask students to summarize the main points of the chapter. Discuss the answers to the Section and Chapter Review questions.

EVALUATE

Assign the Chapter 37 **Performance Assessment Activity** in the TCR.

Administer the **Chapter 37 Test** in the TCR. Testmaker available.

RETEACH

Ask students to compile a list of leaders mentioned in this chapter Have groups of students summarize the role of that leader in the two world wars.

Assign the Chapter 37 **Reteaching Activity** in the TCR.

ENRICH

Have students investigate and report on the resistance movements (organized underground groups) during World War II.

Assign the Chapter 37 **Enrichment Activity** in the TCR.

CLOSE

Ask students what leader during World War II might have said: *I cannot bear to see my innocent people suffer any longer. (Emperor Hirohito of Japan)*

MEETING CHAPTER OBJECTIVES

Each objective is tested by the Review questions in parentheses.

1. **Discuss** the causes, events, and results of World War I. (BV; CU 1, 2; CT 1; UYJ)
2. **Describe** communism in Russia. (CT 2; CU 3)
3. **Explain** dictatorship in Italy and Germany. (CU 4; CT 3)
4. **Examine** events and results of World War II. (CU, 6, 7, 8; UYJ: GH)

Large farms were divided ad sold to farm workers at low prices. Loans were made to help rebuild the economy. Japan turned its efforts to building a strong economy rather than a strong military.

Section 3 Review

1. **Identify:** Allied Powers, Axis Powers, Winston Churchill, Pearl Harbor, Dwight D. Eisenhower, Harry S Truman, Hiroshima, Nagasaki, United Nations, Douglas MacArthur
2. **Define:** blitzkrieg, concentration camps, genocide, Holocaust, cremation ovens
3. Why did Germany attack the Soviet Union in 1941?
4. Why did the United States decide to drop atomic bombs on Hiroshima and Nagasaki?

Critical Thinking

5. If you were living in 1945, would you have supported or opposed the use of the atomic bomb against Japan? Why?

Chapter Summary

1. In 1914, conflict between Serbia and Austria-Hungary sparked World War I.
2. World War I was different from earlier wars because of its size, weapons, and the number of people killed.
3. The United States entered World War I in 1917 to help to defeat Germany and its allies.
4. The Treaty of Versailles divided German lands among the Allied Powers and put the blame and financial burden for World War I on Germany.
5. Peter the Great tried to make Russia a strong, modern country.
6. After unsuccessful revolts in 1825 and 1905, the Russian people revolted again in 1917 and overthrew the czar.
7. After much confusion, a revolutionary group led by Lenin set up a Communist government, which officially formed the Soviet Union in 1922.
8. After the German invasion of Poland in 1939, France and Great Britain declared war on Germany, and World War II began in Europe.
9. The United States entered World War II in 1941 after Japan attacked the American naval base at Pearl Harbor, Hawaii.
10. Soon after the United States dropped the first atomic bombs on the Japanese cities of Hiroshima and Nagasaki in 1945, World War II came to an end.
11. After World War II, the United Nations was formed, Germany was divided into four zones, and the United States occupied Japan.

SECTION 3 ANSWERS

1. Allied Powers, France, Great Britain, Soviet Union (p. 616); Axis Powers, Germany, Italy, Japan (p. 616); Churchill, leader of Great Britain (p. 616); Pearl Harbor, American naval base (p. 617); Eisenhower, commander of Allied troops (p. 618); Truman, U.S. President (p. 620); Hiroshima, Japanese city (p. 620); Nagasaki, Japanese city (p. 620); United Nations, organization of world countries (p. 621); MacArthur, American general (p. 621)
2. blitzkrieg, lightning war (p. 616); concentration camps, for enemies of the Third Reich (p. 620); genocide, mass murder (p. 620); Holocaust, Nazi genocide (p. 621); cremation ovens, places to burn dead bodies (p. 621)
3. because Germany needed the resources of the Soviet Union
4. Truman did not want to invade Japan.
5. Answers will vary.

Assign the Chapter 37 **Section 3 Quiz** in the TCR. Testmaker available.

CHAPTER

Review 37

Building Vocabulary

Sort the following list of words into three columns under the correct heading: World War I, Between Wars, or World War II. Then write a descriptive paragraph about something in each war using all the words under that heading.

mobilize	collectivization
artillery	social security laws
trench warfare	dictatorship
armistice	appeasement
mandate	blitzkrieg
garrison	genocide
soviets	Holocaust

Check for Understanding

1. What sparked World War I?
2. How was the Treaty of Versailles different from Wilson's Fourteen Points?
3. Why were the Whites in Russia supported by other countries?
4. What happened to the world economy in 1929?
5. Why did the British and the French give in to Hitler's demand for the German rule of Czechoslovakia?
6. What major event led to the defeat of Germany in World War II?
7. What major event led to the defeat of Japan in World War II?
8. Why was the United Nations formed?

Critical Thinking

1. What do you think might have happened if the United States had not entered World War I?
2. Why do you think so many Soviet peasants resisted collectivization?
3. What do you think could have been done to stop Hitler from his invasion of neighbor countries?
4. Do you think the United States would have entered the war if the Japanese had not bombed Pearl Harbor? Explain.

Geography in History

LOCATION Refer to the map on page 619. Several small island groups in the Pacific Ocean were the sites of battles between the United States and Japan. Why do you think the battles occurred there rather than on the Japanese mainland?

Using Your Journal

Review the details you have noted about the changes that occurred in Europe in the first half of the 1900s. Review the reasons and events that led to the two world wars. Write a plan describing how you think world wars might be prevented in the future.

623

CHAPTER 37 REVIEW ANSWERS

BUILDING VOCABULARY

World War I: mobilize, artillery, trench warfare, armistice, mandate; Between Wars: garrison, soviets, collectivization, social security laws, dictatorship; World War II: appeasement, blitzkrieg, genocide, Holocaust; Paragraphs will vary, but students should include all vocabulary words.

CHECK FOR UNDERSTANDING

1. Gavrilo Princip shot Archduke Franz Ferdinand.
2. The treaty punished the nations that had lost the war.
3. because other countries were afraid that if the Reds won, communism would spread
4. a depression set in, factories closed, and banks failed
5. They feared another war.
6. Allied forces crossed the English Channel, and the Germans were caught between them and the Soviets.
7. Atomic bombs were dropped.
8. to prevent war

CRITICAL THINKING

1. Answers will vary.
2. Answers will vary but might indicate that the peasants feared losing their lands.
3. Answers will vary, but students might indicate earlier counter-aggression.
4. Answers will vary.

+ BONUS +

TEST QUESTION

For Chapter 37 Test

Evaluate this 1945 plan: WWII is dragging on. President Truman orders a full invasion of Japan to be launched from California by American land, sea, and air forces. *(poor plan; Japan too far away; troops will be intercepted)*

USING YOUR JOURNAL

Plans will vary. You might call on volunteers to read their plans to the class and discuss them. A review of world peace organizations and their current activities might also be appropriate.

GEOGRAPHY IN HISTORY

They were closer and easier to capture.

CHAPTER 38

The Cold War Era

CHAPTER ORGANIZER

Objectives	Special Features	Supplemental Materials
Section 1 An Uneasy Peace Describe how relationships between Western and Communist powers have changed since World War II.		• Reproducible Lesson Plan • Section 1 Quiz • Testmaker • Chapter 38 Vocabulary and Guided Reading Activity • Unit 12 Primary Source Reading • Chapter 38 Teaching Transparencies and Activities • The Western Civilization Videodisc • The World History Videodisc
Section 2 Communist Powers Explain what changes have occurred in the Soviet Union and what life has been like in the People's Republic of China since World War II.		• Reproducible Lesson Plan • Section 2 Quiz • Testmaker • Chapter 38 Cooperative Learning Activity • World History and Art Transparencies • Chapter 38 Activity Book Activity • The World History Videodisc
Section 3 Developing Nations Examine how countries in Africa, South Asia, and Latin America are struggling with political and economic powers.	People in History, *Albert Lutuli*, p. 636	• Reproducible Lesson Plan • Section 3 Quiz • Testmaker • Chapter 38 Geography and Map Activity • Chapter 38 Chart and Graph Skill Activity • The World History Videodisc
Chapter 38 Review and Evaluation		• Chapter 38 Reteaching Activity • Chapter 38 Enrichment Activity • Spanish Summary and Glossary • Audiocassettes (English and Spanish) • Chapter 38 Performance Assessment Activity • Chapter 38 Test • Testmaker

If time does not permit teaching the entire chapter, use the Chapter 38 Summary on page 642 and the Chapter 38 Audiocassettes (English and Spanish) to point out the main ideas of the chapter.

✓ Performance Assessment Activities

Language Arts Have students read the essay "Civil Disobedience" by Henry David Thoreau. Ask them to complete one of the following, using this essay: rewrite the essay in their words, summarizing Thoreau's ideas but putting them in modern context and language; or write a script of a conversation between Thoreau and Gandhi sharing their ideas about this topic.

Time Lines Have students choose a country mentioned in the chapter and create a time line of important events in the country's history between World War II and the present. Tell students to include political, religious, economic, and cultural events. Encourage them to include illustrations or newsphotos on their time lines.

CHAPTER RESOURCES

LITERATURE ABOUT THE PERIOD

Didion, Joan. *Salvador.* Simon and Schuster, 1983. Essays of the North American author's journey, commenting on politics and civil rights.

Paton, Alan. *Cry, the Beloved Country.* Scribner, 1948. A story of conflict between blacks and whites set in apartheid South Africa.

Soyinka, Wole. *Aké: The Years of Childhood.* Vintage Books, 1983. Autobiography by Nigerian Nobel Prize-winner.

READINGS FOR THE STUDENT

Bachelis, Faren. *The Central Americans.* Chelsea House, 1990. History and culture of Central Americans and reasons for their flight north.

Gandhi, Mohandas K. *An Autobiography: The Story of My Experiments with Truth.* Beacon Press, 1957. Explains Gandhi's arrival at his belief in civil disobedience.

Graham, Shirley. *Julius K. Nyerere: Teacher of Africa.* Messner, 1975. Describes the prominent African leader who became president of Tanzania.

Le Carre, John. *The Spy Who Came in from the Cold.* Bantam Books, 1975. Espionage fiction with the adventure leading to the Berlin Wall.

READINGS FOR THE TEACHER

Cheng, Mien. *Life and Death in Shanghai.* Grove Press, 1987. Personal account of her trials during the Cultural Revolution by an "aristocratic" Chinese woman.

Gati, Charles. *Hungary and the Soviet Bloc.* Duke University Press, 1986. Collection of essays providing a view of post-World War II developments in Eastern Europe.

Morner, Magnus. *The Andean Past: Land, Societies, and Conflicts.* Columbia University Press, 1984. Focuses on the social and physical adaptation within political and economic frameworks in Bolivia, Peru, and Ecuador.

MULTIMEDIA RESOURCES

The Aftermath of World War II: Prologue to the Cold War. McGraw-Hill. Film. Describes postwar settlements and the emergence of conflict between superpowers.

Vietnam: Ten-Thousand-Day War. Videodiscovery. Six-volume disc series chronicles history, controversy, and global effects of the Vietnam War.

INTRODUCE

CHAPTER 38 OVERVIEW

Chapter 38 discusses the cold war era (1945-1989) brought about by the growth of communism.

➤ **Section 1** explains the tension that developed between the United States and the Soviet Union following the end of World War II.

➤ **Section 2** describes changes in the kind of communism practiced in China and the Soviet Union.

➤ **Section 3** summarizes the history of developing nations and the challenges they have faced since World War II.

CHAPTER OBJECTIVES

After reading Chapter 38, students will be able to:

1. discuss how relationships between Western and Communist powers have changed since World War II.

2. describe what changes have occurred in the Soviet Union.

3. explain what life has been like in the People's Republic of China since World War II.

4. examine how countries in Africa, South Asia, and Latin America are struggling with political and economic problems.

EXAMINING THE ILLUSTRATION

The night of November 9, 1989, the famous Brandenburg Gate at the Berlin Wall was opened. Ask the students to describe the scene at the wall shown in the illustration.

PERFORMANCE ASSESSMENT

Use the Performance Assessment activities on page 624B to help you to evaluate students as they complete the chapter.

CHAPTER 38

The Cold War Era

Brandenburg Gate, Berlin, New Year's Eve 1990

624

TEACHER CLASSROOM RESOURCES

- Reteaching Activity
- Enrichment Activity
- Chart and Graph Skill Activity
- Geography and Map Activity
- Vocabulary and Guided Reading Activity
- Unit 12 Primary Source Reading
- Cooperative Learning Activity
- Performance Assessment Activity
- Spanish Summary and Glossary
- World History and Art Transparencies
- Teaching Transparencies and Activities
- Audiocassettes (English and Spanish)
- Testmaker
- The Western Civilization Videodisc
- The World History Videodisc

Chapter Focus

READ TO DISCOVER:

- How relationships between Western and Communist powers have changed since World War II.
- What changes have occurred in the Soviet Union.
- What life has been like in the People's Republic of China.
- How countries in Africa, South Asia, and Latin America have struggled with political and economic problems.

Soon after World War II ended, a split occurred among the major Allied Powers. On one side, the Soviet Union supported communism. On the other side, the democratic United States, Great Britain, and France were anti-Communist. Gradually a **cold war**, or a state of hostility without fighting, developed between the two sides.

1945–1989

KEY TERMS

cold war
satellite nations
blockaded
airlift
purges
capitalism
glasnost
perestroika
developing nations
cash crops
haciendas
campesinos

Section 1

AN UNEASY PEACE

After World War II Europe began its recovery. Tension between the United States and the Soviet Union grew over problems in Berlin, Korea, Cuba, and Vietnam (vē et nahm').

Western Europe When World War II ended, most of Western Europe was in ruins. To help rebuild areas, the United States started a loan program in 1948. It was named the Marshall Plan after George Marshall, the U.S. Secretary of State. Under the Marshall Plan, factories were rebuilt, coal mines were reopened, and roads were repaired or replaced. The economies of Western Europe soon began to grow.

In 1957 six Western European nations formed an economic union called the European Common Market. The six nations were Belgium, France, Italy, Luxembourg (luk' suhm borg), the Netherlands, and West Germany. They agreed to remove all trade barriers among them. That meant that manufacturers could sell their goods in other member nations without paying tariffs.

FOCUS

BELLRINGER

Write the following message on the chalkboard for students to decode: *Gsv xlow dzi dzh z grnv lu hkrvh zmw xlwvh.*

MOTIVATIONAL ACTIVITY

Have students share their decoded message. *(If none have solved it, tell them this is an alphabet reversal code that says: "The cold war was a time of spies and codes.")* Tell students that in this chapter they will learn about the causes and effects of the cold war after World War II.

VOCABULARY PRE-CHECK

Write the key terms for this chapter on the chalkboard. Ask volunteers to skim the chapter for these boldfaced terms and read aloud the sentences in which they are found.

Assign Chapter 38 **Vocabulary and Guided Reading Activity** in the TCR.

EXTRA CREDIT PROJECT

Have students read *One Day in the Life of Ivan Denisovich* or one of the short stories by Alexander Solzhenitsyn. This is the story of a day in the life of a Soviet prisoner during the cold war era. Have students give an oral report on the novel and the background of its author.

KEY TO ABILITY LEVELS

Teaching strategies have been coded for varying learning styles and abilities.

L1 Level 1 activities are **basic** activities and should be within the ability range of all students.

L2 Level 2 activities are **average** activities and should be within the ability range of the average to above-average student.

L3 Level 3 activities are **challenging** activities designed for the ability range of above-average students.

LEP LEP activities should be within the ability range of Limited English Proficiency students.

VIDEODISC

Use the following to enrich Chapter 38.

WC L 16 38671

Berlin divided.

AIRLIFT The children in this photograph watch as an American plane brings food to Berlin during the Soviet blockade. **Why did the Soviet Union block off access to the city of Berlin?**

Workers from one nation could take jobs in any other member nation. Between 1957 and 1986, Denmark, Great Britain, Greece, Ireland, Portugal, and Spain also joined the European Common Market. Trade among the nations increased and living conditions improved.

The Start of the Cold War Toward the end of World War II, the Soviet Union set up Communist governments in Bulgaria, Czechoslovakia, Hungary, Poland, and Romania. By 1948 these countries were Soviet **satellite nations,** or countries controlled by a stronger neighboring country. Yugoslavia, although Communist, refused to let itself be put under Soviet control.

The Soviet leader, Stalin, had originally promised the other Allies that he would allow free elections in these countries. When he broke his promise, the cold war began.

Berlin The first cold war crisis took place over Berlin. In 1948 Great Britain, France, and the United States decided to unite their zones of Germany to encourage peace. The Soviet Union disagreed. It distrusted a united Germany because that nation had invaded the Soviet Union twice in 40 years. In June 1948, the Soviets **blockaded**, or closed off, all land and water traffic into Berlin. They hoped this would force the western powers to leave the city.

In response, the United States and Great Britain began an **airlift,** or a system of carrying supplies by airplane into Berlin.

TEACH

GUIDED PRACTICE

L2 **Critical Thinking** Ask students how a "cold" war might differ from a "hot" war. *(A cold war does not involve combat, but rather diplomatic relationships.)*

CAPTION ANSWER

They hoped this would force the Western powers to leave the city.

DID YOU KNOW ??

Cryptology, the study of codes, became a full-fledged science in the late 1940s. The use of computers helped expand this science.

L1 **Geography: Location** East Berlin was the capital of East Germany. West Berlin, although surrounded by East Germany, was considered part of West Germany. Have students research a historical map of East Germany and West Germany in 1949 to realize the precarious position of West Berlin. LEP

VIDEODISC

Use the following to enrich Chapter 38.

WC L 12 38667
One of the first flights in the Berlin airlift.

WC L 36 38691
Man climbs aboard Soviet tank in East Berlin.

EXTENDING THE CONTENT

After World War II, much of Europe was a wasteland. Help came in the form of the Marshall Plan which reconstructed cities of Europe. Many cities were a leveled landscape of gutted buildings, bombed-out bridges, and twisted rail track. As many as 45 million people were homeless. Damage to transportation networks made food distribution impossible. One-fourth of the farmland was out of production. Communication lines were destroyed. The war destroyed almost every major industrial region in the world except those in North America.

Each day planes flew in tons of food, fuel, and raw materials to the city. In May 1949, the Soviets finally lifted their blockade of Berlin. That same year, two separate governments were set up—a democratic one for West Germany, and a Communist one for East Germany. East Germany became a Soviet satellite nation.

The Berlin blockade convinced the western powers that the Soviets wanted to control Europe. In 1949 the United States, Great Britain, and France joined with nine other countries to form the North Atlantic Treaty Organization (NATO). All 12 countries agreed to help one another if attacked. Six years later, the Soviet Union and its satellites formed a similar organization called the Warsaw Pact.

Meanwhile, many people in East Germany were unhappy under Communist rule. About three million fled into West Berlin in search of political freedom and better living conditions. Because many of those who fled were well-educated professionals, the East German government wanted to stop these escapes. So in August 1961, it built a wall between East and West Berlin. The Berlin Wall, with Soviet soldiers guarding it, became a symbol of the split between Communist and non-Communist Europe. Many East Berliners continued to try escaping through the wall, risking their lives.

Photograph of Fidel Castro

Korea After World War II, Korea was also geographically divided. A Communist government was set up in North Korea and a non-Communist government was organized in South Korea. In 1950 North Korea invaded South Korea in an attempt to take over that country. Both the Soviets and Chinese sent the North Koreans military aid. The United Nations sent soldiers—mostly Americans— to help South Korea.

General Douglas MacArthur, the United Nations commander, suggested that dropping atomic bombs on Chinese bases and supply lines would gain a quick victory. However, President Harry S Truman refused. Truman did not want the Korean War to turn into World War III. In 1953 North Korea and South Korea signed a truce calling for the two countries and their governments to remain separate.

Cuba In 1955 Fidel Castro (fē del′ kas trō) launched an unsuccessful revolution in Cuba against dictator Fulgencio Batista (fūl hen′ sē ō buh tēs′ tuh). In 1959 Castro tried again and finally succeeded—Batista was overthrown.

Castro at first promised free elections and social and economic reforms in Cuba. Many countries, including the United States, supported him. Most of the promises he made, however, were not kept. Cubans who had opposed Castro were jailed or executed. Thousands fled to the United States. Before long, Castro announced that his government would be Communist. He

DID YOU KNOW ??

The nine countries other than the United States that formed NATO in 1949 were Belgium, Canada, Denmark, Norway, Iceland, Italy, Luxembourg, Portugal, and the Netherlands.

MAKING CONNECTIONS

➤➤ **History** Korea had been independent until 1910, when it was annexed by Japan. The Japanese did not allow the Korean language or Korean history to be taught in the schools. Also, Koreans had to adopt Japanese names. Both Syngman Rhee, the head of South Korea, and Kim Il Sung, the head of North Korea, had fought for their country's independence during the 1930s and 1940s.

L1 **Geography: Location** Tell students that Batista was backed by the U.S. government. Next, have students locate the U.S. and Cuba on a map of North America and measure the distance between the two countries. Then ask students why the U.S. would intervene in the affairs of Cuba? *(close location)*

VIDEODISC

Use the following to enrich Chapter 38.

WC L 42 38697
The Berlin Wall at the Brandenburg Gate.

WH O 75 26504
American guards and a North Korean guard at P'anmunjom.

EXTENDING THE CONTENT

The blockade of Berlin cut off all paths of communication. In order to get food, coal, and all other important supplies into Berlin, Western forces approached by air. Between June 1948 and May 1949 British and American air forces carried more than 1.5 million tons of goods into Berlin. One day a single load exceeded 12,000 tons. In this way civilians in both western and eastern sectors were aided. To the relief of British and U.S. pilots, the Soviets did not fire at incoming planes.

MAKING CONNECTIONS

➤➤ **History** In 1960 Cuba negotiated a trade agreement with the Soviet Union that enabled the Soviets to buy Cuban sugar at low prices. Khrushchev promised Soviet protection to Cuba, claiming that the Monroe Doctrine had "outlived its time."

L2 **Culture** Discuss how opposition to U.S. foreign policies in Vietnam led to antiwar protests in the 1960s and 1970s. Ask students to name some things that people in the U.S. protest today.

LINKING PAST TO PRESENT

Helicopters in Vietnam played a part in amphibious warfare—that is, operations combining land and sea maneuvers. Amphibious warfare has been successfully conducted for centuries. The Greeks made an amphibious landing on the shores of Troy in 1200 B.C. after sailing across the Aegean Sea. The Persians crossed the Bay of Marathon to invade Greece in 490 B.C.

VIDEODISC

Use the following to enrich Chapter 38.

WH M 73 19055

Castro enters Havana, January 8, 1959.

WH X 100 42333

U.S. Special Forces in Vietnam.

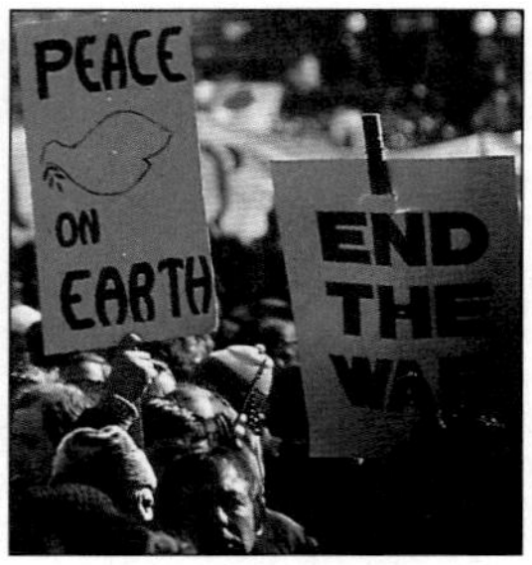

Photograph of Vietnam War Protesters

developed close ties with the Soviet Union which continued to send him economic aid.

In 1961 Cuban refugees who had been trained in the United States invaded Cuba. Their mission was to force Castro out of power. The invasion, in the area known as the Bay of Pigs, failed. Castro then asked the Soviet Union for more military aid. In 1962 Soviet nuclear missile bases were set up on the island. The United States blockaded Cuba and insisted the Soviets remove the missiles. The Soviets finally agreed and another world war was avoided.

Vietnam In 1941, Vietnam was a French colony and part of a larger region known as French Indochina. Japan invaded Vietnam in 1941 but pulled out of the country in 1945 at the end of World War II. At that time, the Vietnamese hoped to be independent but they were invaded again by the French. As a result, Communists and non-Communist Vietnamese nationalists joined together in a guerrilla war against the French. The guerrillas were led by a Communist named Ho Chi Minh (hō chē min'), a Vietnamese nationalist.

In 1954 the French were defeated and the country was temporarily divided into two parts—North and South Vietnam. North Vietnam became a Communist country headed by Ho Chi Minh. South Vietnam became a non-Communist country. A 1956 election meant to unite the two countries was never held. It was protested by the South Vietnamese government who feared it would show Ho's strength.

A war for the control of the country erupted between South Vietnam and North Vietnam. Guerrillas, known as the Vietcong, and the Soviet Union aided North Vietnam. The United States had already been sending military supplies to South Vietnam. It began sending combat troops there in 1965. Altogether, more than 3.3 million Americans fought in the Vietnam War. Eventually 58,000 of them lost their lives, and almost $200 billion was spent.

The Vietnam War deeply divided the American people. Many believed the United States should fight to help South Vietnam and prevent the spread of communism. Many others believed the fight was a civil war that the Vietnamese should settle themselves.

In 1973 an agreement between North Vietnam, South Vietnam, and the United States was reached. American troops pulled out of the country. Then, in 1975, troops from North Vietnam moved into South Vietnam and it came under Communist control.

Unmanned Satellite View of Venus

The Space Race Part of the cold war between the Soviet Union and the United States involved the race to explore space. The Soviets took the first lead. In 1957 they launched *Sputnik I*, the first spacecraft to circle the earth. Four years later Soviet

MEETING SPECIAL NEEDS

Have auditory learners listen to a record or tape of popular U.S. music from the Vietnam era—such as "The Ballad of the Green Berets" and protest songs such as "Blowin' in the Wind," "Draft Dodger Rag," or "A Hard Rain's Gonna Fall." Use these songs as a lead into a discussion of the fact that the Vietnam War created conflict among Americans since some people were in favor of the war and others opposed the war.

astronaut Yuri Gagarin (yū rē guh gahr′ uhn) became the first human being to circle the earth.

Then the United States took the lead. In 1969 American astronaut Neil Armstrong became the first person to walk on the moon. During the 1970s, the first landings on Venus and Mars were made by U.S. unmanned space vehicles. Later, these spacecraft explored Jupiter and Saturn.

Section 1 Review

1. **Identify:** Marshall Plan, European Common Market, Berlin, North Atlantic Treaty Organization (NATO), Warsaw Pact, Fidel Castro, Fulgencio Batista, Bay of Pigs, Ho Chi Minh, Yuri Gagarin, Neil Armstrong
2. **Define:** cold war, satellite nations, blockaded, airlift
3. Why did Western European nations form the European Common Market?
4. Why did East Germany build the Berlin Wall?
5. Why did Castro have the support of the United States and other nations during his revolution? Why did the United States end its support?

Critical Thinking

6. If you were living during the time of the Vietnam War, would you have supported or opposed the war? Why?

Section 2 Communist Powers

After World War II, China became a Communist nation. Later, however, both China and the Soviet Union made changes in the kind of communism they practiced.

Revolution in China While the Soviet Union and the United States were competing in the cold war, communism was gaining support in China. The conditions that led to China's acceptance of communism developed over a long time.

Before the 1900s, there had been several revolts over control of the government. All had failed. In 1911, however, a revolt led by Sun Yat-sen (sun′ yaht sen′) overturned the government. He formed the Nationalist party which wanted China to be a free, democratic republic. He was ousted and Chinese warlords divided the country.

L2 **Critical Thinking** The increased involvement in Vietnam was justified by those who believed the domino theory—the belief that if one country in a region fell to communism, its neighbors would fall as well. Ask students if they think the domino theory justified the U.S. involvement in Vietnam. Have them summarize their opinions in a written paragraph.

DID YOU KNOW ??

Within a few months after the Soviets launched *Sputnik I*, the U.S. Congress created NASA (National Aeronautics and Space Administration). The first U.S. satellite, *Explorer I*, was launched about four months after *Sputnik I* was launched.

L1 **History** Have students create a time line covering key events in Chinese history from 1919 to 1939. Have them write a summary statement describing the political situation in China in 1911 and in 1989. LEP

VIDEODISC

Use the following to enrich Chapter 38.

WH T 1 30751
Sun Yat-sen (1866-1925 "father of the Chinese revolution."

WH T 22 30772
Peasants plowing.

SECTION 1 ANSWERS

1. Marshall Plan, U.S. loans (p. 625); European Common Market, economic union (p. 625); Berlin, German capital (p. 626); NATO, organization of 12 countries (p. 627); Warsaw Pact, Soviet Union and satellites (p. 627); Castro, Cuban leader (p. 627); Batista, Cuban dictator (p. 627); Bay of Pigs, Cuban area (p. 628); Ho Chi Minh, leader of North Vietnam (p. 628); Gagarin, Soviet astronaut (p. 629); Armstrong, U.S. astronaut (p. 629)
2. cold war, nonfighting hostility (p. 625); satellite nations, countries controlled by another (p. 626); blockaded, closed (p. 626); airlift, supplies flown in (p. 626)
3. to establish an economic union
4. to stop escapes into Western Europe
5. He promised reforms; Cuba became Communist.
6. Answers will vary.

Assign the Chapter 38 **Section 1 Quiz** in the TCR. Testmaker available.

CAPTION ANSWER

the Nationalists and the Communists

LINKING PAST TO PRESENT

When the Treaty of Versailles awarded the Shandong Peninsula to the Japanese, Chinese students in Beijing came together for a mass demonstration, urging the Chinese government not to sign the treaty. Similar demonstrations throughout the country culminated in a general strike in Shanghai. Under intense pressure from the students, the government at last yielded to their demands. China's students continue to protest and demonstrate—although not always successfully—as a means of gaining their government's attention.

DID YOU KNOW ??

In 1949 Taiwan was called Formosa.

VIDEODISC

Use the following to enrich Chapter 38.

WH T 48 30798
People's Liberation Army marching in a victory parade.

WH T 50 30800
Mao Zedong, Chairman of the CCP.

INVASION Japananese troops invaded the streets of Shanghai, China. Chinese soldiers united to fight the attack. **What major Chinese parties cooperated in this effort to fight the Japanese?**

After Sun died in 1925, Chiang Kai-shek (chyang kī shek') became the leader of the Nationalist party. He tried to unite China and wipe out the Communists. However, in 1927 the Chinese Communists who opposed the Nationalists began a movement to gain control of the country. Their leader was Mao Zedong (mow' dzuh dung').

The struggle between the two parties was interrupted by the Japanese invasion of China in 1937. The Nationalists joined the Communists to fight the Japanese. After the war, however, the struggle between them continued. In 1949 the Communists gained the support of the peasants with promises of land, and forced the Nationalists to leave the Chinese mainland to go to the island of Taiwan (tī wahn'). There Chiang set up a Nationalist government claiming it ruled China. The Communists set up their own government on mainland China headed by Mao Zedong. They called it the People's Republic of China.

China Under Mao Mao's main goal was to make China a strong, modern country. In 1953 the Chinese began a series of plans to improve the country's economy. By the middle of the 1960s, the Chinese had more food and better health care. Many people had learned how to read and write. Also, under Mao the position of women in China changed. Women were now allowed to choose their own husbands, enter any occupation they chose, and receive equal pay. Men, however, continued to hold the highest positions in government and the best-paying jobs.

COOPERATIVE LEARNING

Divide the class into two groups to report on the influence of Chinese students on the politics of China. Each group should assign its members the tasks of researching, organizing, and reporting on the topic. Have one group examine the political role Chinese students played in the early part of this century. Have the other group research the role Chinese students have played in politics during the past decade. Have each group report its finding to the class. Then discuss how the Chinese student movement between 1900 and 1920 was similar to and different from the Chinese student movement of the 1980s.

Assign the Chapter 38 **Cooperative Learning Activity** in the TCR.

Then Mao began to fear that the Chinese had lost their revolutionary spirit. As a result, in 1966 he carried out **purges** (per′ juhs), or removals of undesirable members, of the Communist party. He also purged the country's *intellectuals* (in tuh lek′ chū uhls), or scholars. This purge was called the Cultural Revolution. Students and young adults known as Red Guards attacked politicians, teachers, and others accused of not supporting communism. The purge soon got out of control, however, and there were battles between Red Guards and other citizens. The Red Guards were later broken up.

China After Mao After Mao died in 1976, a group led by Deng Xiaoping (duhng′ syow ping′) came into power in China. Deng cared more about economic growth than about

CHINESE LEADERS From 1928 to 1949, General Chiang Kai-shek (shown left) was a powerful leader in China. In 1949, the Communists, led by Mao Zedong (shown right), overthrew Chiang's government. Mao proclaimed the People's Republic of China on the Chinese mainland, while Chiang set up the Nationalist government on the island of Taiwan. **Why were the Nationalists unpopular with the Chinese peasants?**

L2 **Culture** Discuss what it must have been like for the Chinese to go through the dramatic postwar changes in government policies. Ask students to imagine what would happen in the United States if the government started a Cultural Revolution. How do they think Americans would react? Which Americans would be most vulnerable in such a situation?

LINKING PAST TO PRESENT

During the Cultural Revolution, the Chinese educational system was nearly at a standstill, and the door was virtually closed to study at foreign institutions. Today, however, the Chinese constitute a majority of the foreign-student enrollment in U.S. universities.

CAPTION ANSWER

They did not make promises of bread and land, even though they wanted a democratic government.

VIDEODISC

Use the following to enrich Chapter 38.

WH T 55 30805
Young Chinese couple celebrating a "new style marriage."

WH T 97 30847
Downtown scene in Taipei, Taiwan's capital.

EXTENDING THE CONTENT

The Cultural Revolution was aimed against the bureaucracy and complacency that Mao Zedong feared had crept into the universities, the government, and the Communist Party. He thought special privileges for the educated elite worked against the ideal of a society in which everyone was equal. He wanted to purge "The Four Olds"—old thoughts, old culture, old customs, and old habits. The Cultural Revolution weakened Mao's leadership position. After Mao's death, Chinese historians began to regard the period as "the ten catastrophic years" and to view it as having been a serious setback.

DID YOU KNOW ??

Under Deng, China adopted a "one-child family" policy to try to control its population growth. Families with more than one child were fined.

L3 **Mathematics** China, the most populous country, has based its population controls on past growth and predictions of future growth. Have students research the total population of China for each decade and chart it on a bar or line graph. Using the average increase as a reference, have them add a prediction of population for the years 2000 and 2010. LEP

CAPTION ANSWER

They were protesting the political conditions.

MAKING CONNECTIONS

➤➤ **History** China exploded its first atomic bomb in 1964. It became the fifth world atomic power, following the United States, the Soviet Union, Britain, and France.

VIDEODISC

Use the following to enrich Chapter 38.

WH T 100 30850

1989 student demonstrations in Tiananmen Square.

WH T 103 30853

Man stands in front of tanks in passive resistance.

POLITICAL PROTEST As crowds of Chinese demonstrators filled Tiananmen Square in 1989, government officials decided to attack them. **What were the demonstrators protesting against?**

revolutionary spirit. He encouraged foreign countries to invest money in China. He let many factory managers decide what goods to produce and what prices to charge. As a result of such changes, economic conditions in China improved greatly.

Political conditions, however, remained the same and many people were unhappy. They wanted the same control over politics that they had been given over the economy. Then, beginning in April of 1989, a demonstration took place in Tiananmen (tyen' ahn men) Square in Beijing. For seven weeks, about one million Chinese people, mostly students, gathered in the square and demanded democracy.

The demonstration was peaceful but it frightened many Communist leaders. So Deng sent Red Army soldiers into Tiananmen Square to break up the gathering. Between 500 and 1,000 civilians were killed. Other students and labor leaders were imprisoned or executed. Since then, there have been changes in economic balance and trade in China, but not in human rights. Chinese leaders do not acknowledge that the people's human rights are being ignored.

Changes in the Soviet Union

Two groups of Communists existed in the Soviet Union after Stalin's rule. **Hard-liners,** or people who stick to the rules regardless of the circumstances, made up one group. They wanted to keep the Soviet Union as it

MULTICULTURAL PERSPECTIVES

Zhang Shuyan, a senior researcher in China's State Committee for Reforming the Chinese Written Language, has made a significant study of Chinese names. She found that during the Cultural Revolution, the single most common name was *Red.* Some people born during that time changed their revolutionary names as they entered adulthood. Since the Cultural Revolution, the most common name has been *Hua,* which means "magnificent and prosperous."

was. Reformers made up the other group of Communists. They were interested in economic growth, even if that meant introducing capitalism into the country. Under **capitalism,** most production is privately owned rather than owned by the government. After Stalin died in 1953, there was a Communist struggle for control.

In 1955 a reformer, Nikita Khrushchev (nuh kēt′ uh krūsh chof′), became the leader of the Soviet Union. The following year, he began a program of **de-Stalinization** (dē stahl uh nuh zā′ shuhn), or an attack on the policies established by Stalin. Many labor camps were shut down, and the secret police became less violent. More apartment houses were built, and consumer goods became more available.

Photograph of Mikhail S. Gorbachev

In 1964 Leonid Brezhnev (lā uh nid brezh′ nef) became the Soviet ruler. Under Brezhnev, life once again became less free for the Soviet people. In 1985, however, a reformer, Mikhail Gorbachev (mēk′ hī el gōr′ buh chahf), came to power. Gorbachev adopted two policies to try to improve the growth of the economy in the Soviet Union.

Under Gorbachev's policy of ***glasnost,*** (glaz nōst) or openness, the Soviet people could say and write what they thought without fear of being punished. Free elections were held in which many non-Communist officials gained office. Under the policy of ***perestroika,*** (per uhs troi kuh) which means restructuring, Gorbachev changed the structure of the Soviet government and moved the country's economy toward capitalism.

As the Soviet Union continued toward democracy and capitalism, tensions within the country increased. Some people thought Gorbachev was moving too quickly with reform. Others thought he was not moving fast enough. At the same time, many ethnic groups within the country were demanding independence.

Section 2 Review

1. **Identify:** Sun Yat-sen, Chiang Kai-shek, Mao Zedong, Red Guards, Cultural Revolution, Deng Xiaoping, Tiananmen Square, Nikita Khrushchev, Leonid Brezhnev, Mikhail Gorbachev
2. **Define:** purge, hard-liners, capitalism, de-Stalinization, *glasnost*, *perestroika*
3. What was Mao Zedong's main goal for China?
4. Why did some people oppose the ideas of *glasnost* and *perestroika?*

Critical Thinking

5. Do you think China will eventually become a democracy, or remain under strict Communist control? Explain.

MAKING CONNECTIONS

>> **History** Public displays of Stalin's photograph ended when Nikita Khrushchev became the Soviet leader. In his famous speech of February 1956, Khrushchev declared, "It is impermissible and foreign to the spirit of Marxism-Leninism to elevate one person and transform him into a superman with supernatural characteristics akin to those of a god." De-Stalinization included changing the name of Stalingrad to Volgograd and removing Stalin's body from its Kremlin tomb.

DID YOU KNOW ??

Gorbachev was the first Soviet leader to take full advantage of the events known by the news media as "photo opportunities." While on a tour of Washington, D.C., Gorbachev suddenly ordered his limousine to pull over. He then leaped out of the car and began shaking hands with crowds along the motorcade route, as if he were a political candidate.

VIDEODISC

Use the following to enrich Chapter 38.

WH M 77 19059

A Soviet missile base in Cuba.

SECTION 2 ANSWERS

1. Sun, Chinese leader (p. 629); Chiang Chinese leader (p. 630); Mao Chinese Communist (p. 630); Red Guards, Chinese students (p. 631); Cultural Revolution, Mao's purge (p. 631); Deng, Chinese leader (p. 631); Tiananmen Square, square in Beijing (p. 632); Khrushchev, Soviet leader (p. 633); Brezhnev, Soviet leader (p. 633); Gorbachev, Soviet leader (p. 633)
2. purge, removal of undesirables (p. 631); hard-liners, inflexible people (p. 632); capitalism, privately owned economy (p. 633); de-Stalinization, erasing Stalin (p. 633), *glasnost,* Soviet openness (p. 633), *perestroika,* Soviet restructuring (p. 633)
3. to rebuild China, making it modern
4. they thought Gorbachev was moving too quickly
5. Answers will vary.

Assign the Chapter 38 **Section 2 Quiz** in the TCR. Testmaker available.

Section 3

Developing Nations

Photograph of Mohandas Gandhi

Most of the countries in South Asia and Africa gained their independence after World War II. The majority of countries in Latin America gained independence in the early 1800s. All of these countries are considered to be **developing nations.** They generally have little industry and most of the people are poor, uneducated, and make their living from the land.

A great number of developing nations also have rapidly growing populations. They cannot produce enough food to feed their people and must buy it elsewhere. As a result, they do not have enough money to provide decent housing, health care, and education for their citizens.

India's Independence India, originally under British rule, was one of the first colonial countries of Asia in which nationalism grew. At first, several problems in India had to be dealt with. There were two major religions—Hinduism and Islam—many of whose followers did not like each other. The people also spoke hundreds of different languages. However, they had one thing in common—opposition to British rule.

In 1885 a political party called the Indian National Congress was formed. Its members called for more Indian self-government.

About that time, an Indian leader named Mohandas Gandhi (mah hahn' dahs gahn' dē) began a protest movement against British rule. Gandhi was a lawyer and a member of the upper class, but he identified himself with the common people. He went from village to village talking about self-government. The people called him Mahatma (muh haht' muh), which means Great Soul.

Photograph of Indian Villagers

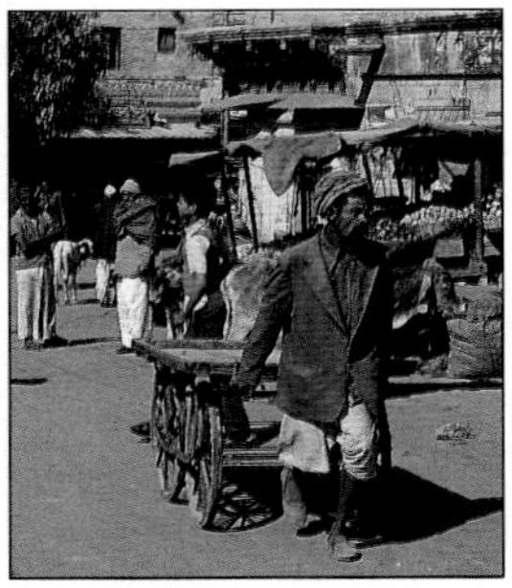

Gandhi did not believe in violence. He believed in **civil disobedience,** or refusing to obey laws considered unjust. He convinced millions of Indians to show their resistance to British rule through peaceful demonstrations and boycotts.

In 1947 Great Britain finally granted independence to its Indian colony. Instead of one country, however, two were formed. India, the larger country, had a majority of Hindus. A separate country, Pakistan, was created that had a majority of Muslims.

During the *partition,* or dividing, of India, fighting broke out between Hindus and Muslims. Many Hindus in Pakistan fled to India, while many Muslims in India fled to Pakistan. Of the more than 12 million people who changed homelands, nearly 1 million were killed in the fighting.

L1 **Geography: Location** Ask students to list the developing nations discussed in this section. Have them locate the nations on a map of the world and determine where most of the nations are located. *(Africa, Asia, and Latin America)* LEP

L2 **Critical Thinking** Ask students to list any kinds of boycotts they can think of in recent history. Ask them their views about the effectiveness of boycotts and what they can accomplish.

DID YOU KNOW ??

One important reason for the rapidly growing populations in developing nations is a drop in the death rate caused by better sanitation and by vaccinations against disease.

MAKING CONNECTIONS

➤➤ **History** Gandhi witnessed two examples of civil disobedience while he was studying law in England. One was the effort of women to obtain the right to vote. The other was the effort of trade unions to obtain the right to strike. In 1915, he returned to India, where he spent the rest of his life.

VIDEODISC

Use the following to enrich Chapter 38.

WH V 77 34748

The modernization of railroads at Allahabad in 1966.

WH V 70 34741

Gandhi's body with mourners.

SPOTLIGHT ON: GANDHI

Gandhi rejected many aspects of Western civilization, but he owed much to many Westerners. Among these were three writers of the 1800s: John Ruskin of England, Henry David Thoreau of the United States, and Leo Tolstoy of Russia. In turn, Gandhi influenced Western civilization. He served as a model for Martin Luther King, Jr., who led the African American struggle for civil rights until he was assassinated in 1968. Like Gandhi, King protested with nonviolent boycotts, court challenges, and other peaceful means.

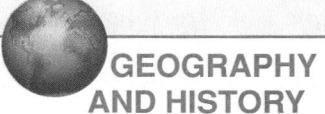

INDUSTRIAL INDIA Industry has grown rapidly in India since the nation became independent in 1947. The government has encouraged the establishment of heavy industry in hopes of improving India's economy. Here, workers are employed at an automobile plant. **How do most of India's people make their living?**

In 1971 a civil war broke out between the eastern and western parts of Pakistan. Three years later, Pakistan recognized East Pakistan as the independent nation of Bangladesh.

India Since 1947 After independence, India's leaders worked to set up a stable government. In 1950 a democratic constitution was adopted. Under prime ministers Jawaharlal Nehru (juh wu′ har lul nā′ rū) and later Indira Gandhi (in dēr′ uh gahn′ dē) democracy advanced.

Since that time the Indian government has worked to improve people's living conditions. It has encouraged such industries as electric power, iron and steel manufacturing, and textiles. About 70 percent of the Indian people, however, still make their living by farming. Although some have small farms, most work on the estates of large landowners for low pay. Families in Indian villages are generally large although the government has encouraged people to have smaller families.

Many of India's large cities have two sections. One is modern with tall apartment and office buildings. The other section has narrow, twisting, crowded streets. These narrow avenues are lined with two- and three-story, old apartment buildings and hundreds of small businesses.

L1 **Economics** Have students research a major product from one of the developing countries such as coffee or cocoa, and create a flow chart of what happens to this product as it moves from producer to consumer. Have them share their charts with the class.

GEOGRAPHY AND HISTORY

Pakistan consisted of two regions, East Pakistan and West Pakistan, separated by India. Although the people in both regions were Muslims, they spoke different languages and belonged to different ethnic groups. In 1971, a civil war broke out between the two regions. As a result, East Pakistan became the new nation of Bangladesh.

CAPTION ANSWER

by farming

MAKING CONNECTIONS

>> **History** Two years after Nehru's death his daughter, Indira Gandhi, was elected prime minister of India. She was instrumental in helping East Pakistan win its independence from West Pakistan.

MULTICULTURAL PERSPECTIVES

Indians dress according to their religion, the region in which they live, and how westernized they are. However, Indian men—except in large cities—usually wear a *dhoti*, or a white cotton garment wrapped between the legs. Most Indian women wear a sari. This is a long, straight piece of cotton or silk that is wrapped around the body and then draped over the head.

VIDEODISC

Use the following to enrich Chapter 38.

WH V 86 34757

Prime Minister Indira Gandhi.

Teaching

PEOPLE IN HISTORY

ALBERT LUTUTI

After students have read the People in History feature, ask: What kind of education did Lutuli receive? *(He learned Zulu traditions in the community of Groutville, and he graduated from a mission teacher-training college.)* Why did the government oust Lutuli as chief of Groutville? *(He encouraged people to ignore discrimination laws against blacks.)* What other famous leaders encouraged nonviolent protests? *(Gandhi and Martin Luther King, Jr.)*

ANSWERS to Checking for Understanding

1. teaching profession
2. Answers will vary, but students should indicate reasons for their positions.

VIDEODISC

Use the following to enrich Chapter 38.

WH D 46 10314
S. African policeman checks passbooks, 1963.

PEOPLE IN HISTORY

ALBERT LUTULI

In Oslo, Norway in 1961 Albert John Lutuli, black South African statesman, walked to the podium to receive the Nobel Peace Prize—the first African ever to do so. What path had Lutuli's life taken to reach this point?

Born a Leader Albert Lutuli was born in 1898 in Rhodesia. Later, Lutuli returned to South Africa, and lived with his uncle, the chief of the community of Groutville. There he learned Zulu traditions. Lutuli attended and graduated from a mission teacher-training college and began teaching there.

In 1936 Lutuli was elected chief of Groutville. He saw that the blacks faced poverty, the lack of good jobs, and no voice in the government. By 1946, Lutuli was directly involved in the black struggle against apartheid, but in a nonviolent way. In 1951 he became the president of the Natal section of the African National Congress (ANC).

A Belief in Nonviolence In 1951-1952 Lutuli led a campaign to fight certain laws allowing discrimination against blacks. His method of protesting against a law was to ignore it. That is what he encouraged others to do, also.

For this political activity, the government ousted him as chief of Groutville. His popularity had spread, however, and in 1952 Lutuli was elected president general of the ANC. The South African government then placed travel restrictions on him. Whenever possible Lutuli spoke to people about nonviolence. He continued to spread his message even after being jailed for opposition to the country's government.

The Nobel Peace Prize In 1960 Lutuli received the Nobel Peace Prize. In his acceptance speech, he asked the world to note that the blacks of South Africa were still very far from freedom. Lutuli died in 1967.

Checking for Understanding

1. **What profession did Lutuli prepare for in college?**
2. **Would you have agreed or disagreed with Lutuli's policy of nonviolent resistance? Why?**

SPOTLIGHT ON: LUTULI

Albert Lutuli held many positions in his life. Among them were secretary of the Natal African Teacher's Association, secretary of the South African Football Association, founder of the Zulu Language and Cultural Society, and member of the Institute of Race Relations in Durban. In 1946 he was elected to the Natives Representative Council, which was set up by the government as an advisory group of chiefs and intellectuals. In 1962 Lutuli wrote his autobiography called *Let My People Go.*

Malaysia Malaysia is another developing Asian country that has gone through revolution and successfully built a cooperative government since World War II. Following riots in 1969 between the Malay and the Chinese, the country has become peaceful. With a prospering economy, it lies in a major shipping crossroads of the Pacific Ocean. Muslims, Christians, Buddhists, and Hindus live together, giving Malaysia its cultural richness. The three major ethnic groups of the country—Malays, Chinese, and Indians—cooperatively share power and resources.

Independence in Africa World War II helped African nationalism grow. During the war, many Africans served in the armies of the European colonial powers. They were sent to fight in many different places around the world. The soldiers saw new sights and learned new skills. When they returned to Africa, they were not content with conditions there and wanted self-rule.

Nationalism grew quickly among educated Africans who worked for independence in different ways. They formed politi-

African Independence

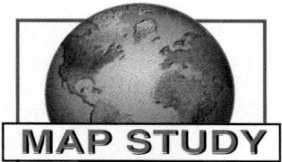

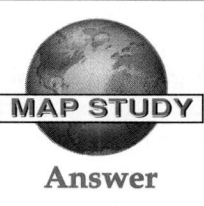

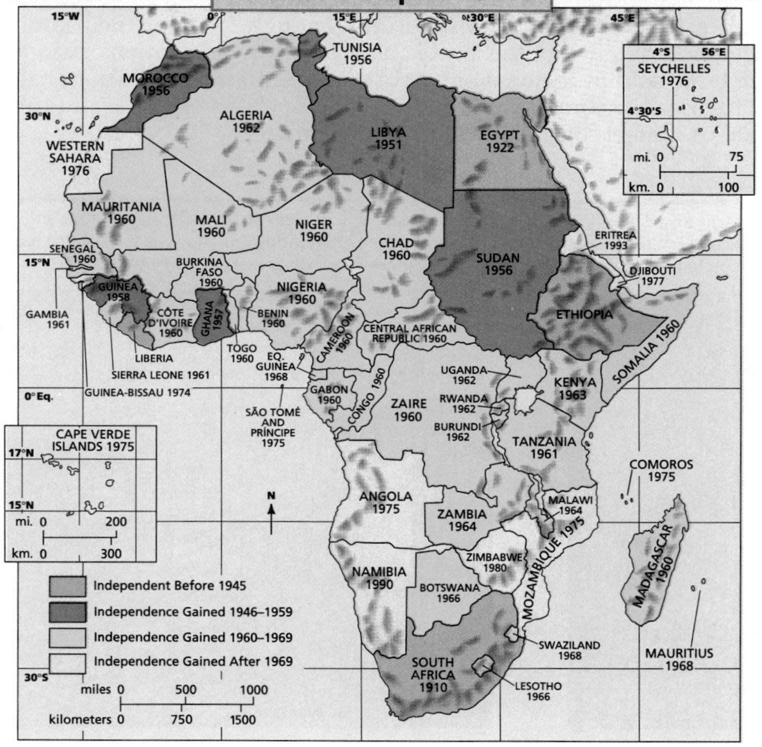

MAP STUDY

REGIONS Between 1951 and 1991, more than 50 African colonies gained independence. **Which colonies gained independence after 1969?**

INDEPENDENT PRACTICE

L1 **Geography: Region** Have students write five questions about the map "African Independence" on this page. Then have them gather in small groups and have students quiz each other with their questions. LEP

L2 **Government** Have students research more about the political history of the two countries showing no dates for independence: Ethiopia and Liberia. Have them write a report explaining what reasons there were for this situation.

MAP STUDY

Answer

Western Sahara, Guinea-Bissau, Sao Tomé and Principe, Angola, Namibia, Zimbabwe, Mozambique, Djibouti, Comoros

Assign the Chapter 38 **Geography and Map Activity** in the TCR.

VIDEODISC

Use the following to enrich Chapter 38.

WC L 40 38695

Kwame Nkrumah, President of Ghana.

WC L 41 38696

Soldiers of the UN force in the Congo in 1960.

MULTICULTURAL PERSPECTIVES

There are many results of African influence in American culture. One of these is the celebration of Kwanzaa, the African American celebration of unity that takes place at the end of December. This week-long festival that calls attention to African American achievement and creativity is based on African harvest festivals that are centuries old.

L3 **Geography: Region** Point out to students that the newly independent nations of Africa had great difficulties in forming new governments partly as a result of the way European nations had drawn colonial boundaries in Africa without regard to ethnic differences. Have students compare the map "African Independence" with African maps that show ethnic groups. Have students write a brief paragraph that compares the boundaries of the African nations with the boundaries of these groups.

DID YOU KNOW ??

Despite the cold war, both the United States and the Soviet Union supported independence for African nations.

CAPTION ANSWER

lack of education

GEOGRAPHY AND HISTORY

In recent years, such countries as Ethiopia have suffered repeatedly from drought. People from all over the world contributed money to help feed the starving Ethiopians, but the country has done little about its basic problem of deforestation.

VIDEODISC

Use the following to enrich Chapter 38.

WH D 55 10323

The Soweto demonstrations of 1976.

cal parties and bargained with government leaders. They also boycotted goods from colonial countries. In some cases, violence broke out.

In 1960, 17 African countries became independent. The year became known as the "Year of Africa." Other African colonies freed themselves from European rule in following years.

At first most newly independent African countries set up democratic governments. Many did not last, however, and today most have one-party governments or are ruled by a military leader.

Many African countries—including Angola, Ethiopia, Mozambique (mō zam beek'), Nigeria, Rwanda (roo ahn' duh), Somalia, Sudan, Zaire (zīhr), and Zimbabwe (zim bahb' wā)—have suffered from civil war since they became independent. When Europeans originally drew colonial boundaries in Africa, they often put groups that had been fighting one another for hundreds of years in the same colony. Fighting often broke out among these groups.

Farming

About 70 percent of all African workers make their living from farming. In the past, most farmers were **subsistence farmers.** They produced only enough food for their families. Today much of the land is used to grow **cash crops,** or crops that are sold in regional or world markets. In fact, more than half of Africa's income results from selling such crops as cacao (kuh kā' ō), coffee, cotton, peanuts, rubber, and tea.

Rural and Urban Africa Many Africans still live in small rural villages, such as the one in Zaire shown here (left), and hold onto their traditional ways. Africa also has many large, modern cities. **What differences face villagers who move to the city?**

MEETING SPECIAL NEEDS

Divide students with Limited English Proficiency into five groups, one group for each of the five regions of Africa. Have each group create a notebook, one page per country, for each region. Each page should consist of a map and legend, showing the major cities and geographic features. Refer students to an almanac and an atlas for other interesting statistics to include on their pages. Have them draw pictures of or list several influential people (present or past) from each country, write a brief biography, and put them on a separate page. Have students share their notebooks.

In recent years, because of poor farming methods, drought, disease, lack of fertilizer, and more cash crops being grown, there have been food shortages in Africa. Many African nations must buy food from other countries. Often this food is expensive and not plentiful. African governments have begun to teach farmers better farming methods but progress is slow. The United States has sent advisers also.

Large parts of Africa, however, are rich in energy resources. Coal, natural gas, oil, and hydroelectric power are plentiful. The continent also has large mineral deposits, such as copper, tin, iron, manganese, gold, and diamonds. To make full use of these resources, however, more money and skilled workers are needed. More roads and railroads are also needed to move the resources to market.

Photograph of African Children

Ways of Life Life has been changing in Africa since the 1960s. Most people still live in rural villages, where they belong to **extended families.** These are made up of parents, children, and other close relatives who live together in one house. Most houses in Africa consist of several buildings surrounded by a wall or fence. Rural village houses are often made of mud, clay, or tall grasses and might not have running water, electricity, or indoor plumbing. Large African cities, however, are modern active centers of growth and progress.

Children in rural areas may receive little or no formal schooling, but they have knowledge of and pride in their group's culture. Many leaders of emerging African nations have encouraged the pride each group within a nation shows in its heritage. Writers, musicians, artists, and scholars of African nations are recognized all over the world for their talent and achievements.

African heritage is also seen in the special body markings, and certain colors and kinds of clothing and jewelry African groups wear. For example, the Fulani (fū lah' nē) of West Africa wear royal blue, red, and yellow. The Masai (mah' sī) women of Kenya wear huge collars of brightly colored beads.

In recent years, many Africans have left their home villages and moved to the cities in search of jobs and better housing and education. Some high schools and colleges in the cities offer training in higher-level occupations and technology. They hope trained young people will return to the villages to improve their way of life. Lack of education, however, is a serious problem.

Photograph of Housing in Rio de Janeiro, Brazil

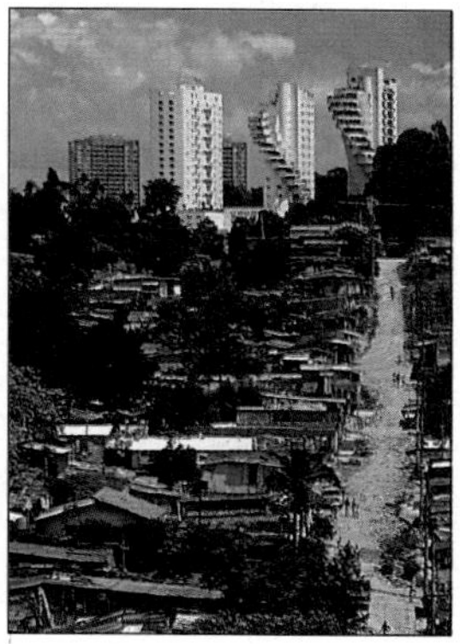

Foreign Influence in Latin America Even after gaining independence, most Latin American countries remained under foreign control. Industrial nations such as Great Britain, France, Germany, and the United States organized businesses there. They produced such goods as bananas, sugar, coffee, metals, and oil which were sold in markets overseas.

L2 **Language Arts** Have students research and create a simple outline map that shows the different languages that are spoken in Africa. Ask students to share their maps with the class and discuss the following: Do language borders follow political borders? What language is most predominant? What language(s) seems to be most widely spread out? If possible, have students learn a word or two in an African language to teach to the class.

L1 **Geography: Place** Have students research and create a chart listing Africa's top seven natural resources and in which country the largest deposit of each can be found. Have them share their charts with the class, pointing out on a wall map the countries listed. LEP

DID YOU KNOW ??

Many African nations changed their names once they gained independence. The new names had special meaningss. For example, Zimbabwe refers to the 1,000-year-old royal city of Great Zimbabwe. Massive, protective stone walls gave the city its name—*zimbabwe*—which means "stone enclosure." The city of 20,000 people contained palaces, religious buildings, markets, and the clay houses of Zimbabwe's citizens. The city declined about 1450.

EXTENDING THE CONTENT

In addition to sculpture and painting, dance is an important traditional African art form. Although it varies from area to area, traditional African dance tends to have at least two characteristics in common. First, it expresses two vital concerns of African life—religion and community relationships. There are dances to celebrate the end of harvest, to mark the beginning of puberty, to honor the village gods, and to wish for a successful hunt. Another characteristic of African dance is that it responds to polyrhythms, or complex combinations of fairly simple but different rhythms played simultaneously.

VIDEODISC

Use the following to enrich Chapter 38.

WH D 49 10317

Johannesburg.

CAPTION ANSWER

because peasant labor is cheap

L2 **Economics** Remind students that transportation is important to growing economics. Have students create a simple outline of South America and show on it where the major railway lines run. Ask them to explain, in a paragraph, any obstacles to railways that exist in undeveloped areas.

MAKING CONNECTIONS

➤➤ **History** The United States has tried to improve its relations with Latin America. When the United States took over the Panama Canal Zone in 1914, the area became rich, while the rest of Panama remained poor. This led to riots during the 1950s and 1960s, as the people of Panama demanded control over the Canal Zone. In 1977, the United States signed a treaty that will give Panama complete control over the Canal Zone in 1999.

VIDEODISC

Use the following to enrich Chapter 38.

WH H 7 18687

La Florida Street in Buenos Aires, Argentina.

LATIN AMERICAN FARMING Although Latin America is primarily an agricultural region, wealthy landowners hold much of the land in large ranches. These haciendas are worked by peasants with few modern techniques or implements. Here, a Mexican farmer plows behind a team of oxen. **Why have most hacienda owners no desire to modernize their farms?**

Latin American nations benefited from foreign investments. Wages rose, and there were more jobs. Foreign business interests also built roads, railroads, and ports. They set up telephone systems and electric plants.

Still, there were problems. The economies of most of the countries depended on only one or two products. If the price of these products dropped, their incomes did too. Also, food, clothing, household goods, and other such items had to be brought in from other countries at high cost. In addition, Latin American nationalists who wanted their countries to be free of outside influence, resented foreigners.

Domestic Changes in Latin America Since World War II, most Latin American countries have been trying to industrialize. They have greatly increased their production of such goods as steel, chemicals, oil, and automobiles. Argentina, Brazil, and Mexico are now fairly well-industrialized. Yet even they do not produce enough to meet the needs of their growing populations.

The Latin American economy depends on farming. Most land is held in ***haciendas*** (ah sē en′ duhz), or large ranches. These are owned by a few very rich families. Most work on the *haciendas* is done by peasants known as ***campesinos*** (kam puh sē′ nos).

COOPERATIVE LEARNING

Have students form five teams, each team to make a poster of one area of challenge in Latin America studied in this section: population growth, urbanization, economic development, the growth of democracy, and Latin America's international and inter-American relationships. Ask students in each group to do research, plan the poster theme, create the art, and present the poster. Tell students to focus on these areas: the background or history of the challenge, a clear statement of the issue and its current status, any key individuals or countries involved with the issue, and possible solutions to the problems. Have students research current material and consolidate information in clearly organized posters.

Campesinos usually live in villages. Their small houses are made of wood, mud, sun-dried brick, or stone. Larger villages have a church and a few stores and hold open-air markets once a week. People meet there to exchange news as well as to buy and sell food and hand-made goods.

The *campesinos* farm the land in the same way their parents and grandparents did. They are not encouraged to learn new ways. Peasant labor is cheap, so most *hacienda* owners have no wish to modernize or reform the economic system. Often the result is that the land is poorly managed and crops are small.

The *hacienda* system holds back economic progress. Many Latin Americans would like to end it. They believe that farm production will rise if *campesinos* are allowed to own land and learn new ways of farming. In recent years, peasants in several Latin American countries have started revolutions for land reform. This reform has been opposed by the governments and wealthy landowners. Some of the worst violence has taken place in El Salvador, Nicaragua, and Peru. The demand for a voice in their governments by Latin American people, however, has increased.

Latin American cities have also grown larger in recent years. Poor farming methods, drought, warfare, or drops in farm prices have forced millions throughout Latin America off the land and into the cities. There are not enough jobs in the cities to go around, however.

ELECTIONS In this photograph Oswaldo Alvarez Paz campaigns for president of his country, Venezuela. **Why are poor Latin Americans demanding free elections more than the wealthy?**

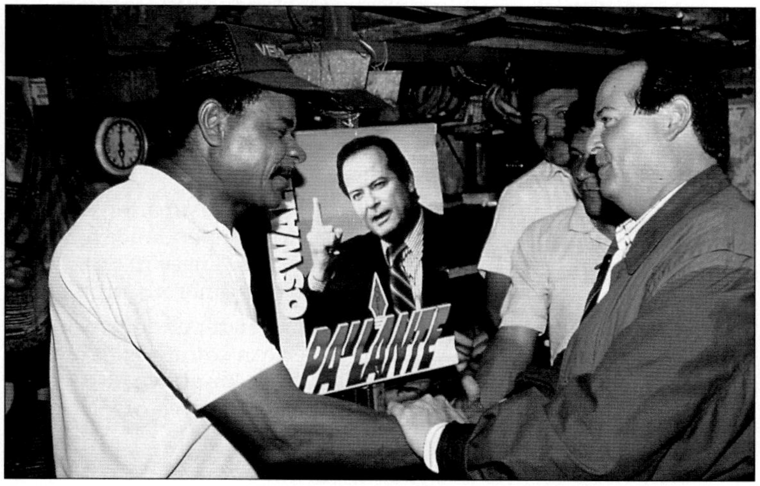

L3 **Global Issues** Have students refer to current encyclopedia yearbooks and almanacs to research the interdependent trading relationships various Latin American countries have formed with Western Europe, Asia, Africa, or Japan. They should present their findings in the forms of tables or graphs.

CAPTION ANSWER

because the wealthy control the governments and do not want the people gaining freedoms that might upset their economic dominance

VIDEODISC

Use the following to enrich Chapter 38.

WH H 6 18686

A contemporary view of Mexico City.

ASSESS

CHECK FOR UNDERSTANDING

Ask students to summarize the main points of the chapter, orally or in writing. Discuss the answers to the Section and Chapter Review questions.

EXTENDING THE CONTENT

The Organization of American States (OAS) includes every nation in the Western Hemisphere except Canada and Cuba, which was excluded in 1962. Its aims are to strengthen peace and security in the hemisphere and to encourage economic, social, and cultural cooperation. The OAS's 1948 charter states that an attack on any one member will be considered an attack on all. The three main organs of the OAS are the General Assembly, which meets annually; the Meeting of Consultation of Foreign Ministers, the emergency executive body; and the Permanent Council, consisting of an ambassador for each member state.

EVALUATE

Assign the Chapter 38 **Performance Assessment Activity** in the TCR.

Administer the **Chapter 38 Test** in TCR. Testmaker available.

RETEACH

Have students work in pairs to create crossword puzzles using key words or names of people from the chapter. Have pairs exchange and answer puzzles.

Assign the Chapter 38 **Reteaching Activity** in the TCR.

ENRICH

Have students choose a country discussed in the chapter and read current magazine and newspaper articles about the country. Have students present an oral report about their findings.

Assign the Chapter 38 **Enrichment Activity** in the TCR.

CLOSE

Have students discuss the connection between improved health care and sanitation and overpopulation that has occurred in developing nations.

MEETING CHAPTER OBJECTIVES

Each objective is tested by the Review questions in parentheses.

1. **Discuss** changed relationships between Western and Communist powers. (BV)
2. **Describe** changes in the Soviet Union. (BV; CU 6)
3. **Explain** life in the People's Republic of China. (CU 4, 5; CT 1; UYJ)
4. **Examine** developing countries. (BV; CU 7, 8; CT 3, UYJ)

Section 3 Review

1. **Identify:** Indian National Congress, Mohandas Gandhi
2. **Define:** developing nations, civil disobedience, subsistence farmers, cash crops, extended families, *haciendas*, *campesinos*
3. How did Gandhi show his resistance to British rule?
4. Why is 1960 called the "year of Africa"?
5. How does the *hacienda* system hold back economic progress in Latin America?

Critical Thinking

6. How do you think civil wars have affected African nations in recent years?

Chapter Summary

1. After World War II ended, a cold war developed between the United States and the Soviet Union.
2. The first cold war crisis took place in 1948 when the Soviet Union blockaded Berlin.
3. In 1950, a conflict broke out when North Korean soldiers invaded South Korea. The conflict ended in 1953 with a truce.
4. In 1959, a revolution in Cuba brought Fidel Castro and a communist government with close ties to the Soviet Union to power.
5. Vietnam was the site of a war between the North Vietnamese and South Vietnamese that lasted until 1975.
6. The Communists and their leader, Mao Zedong, defeated the Nationalists in 1949 and formed the People's Republic of China.
7. In 1966, Mao ordered a purge of the Communist party and China's intellectuals. This was the Cultural Revolution.
8. Deng Xiaoping relaxed some of China's economic policies. He also tightly controlled political freedoms, however.
9. Under Mikhail Gorbachev, conditions in the Soviet Union improved as he adopted the policies of *glasnost* and *perestroika.*
10. Most of the countries in South Asia, Africa, and Latin America are considered to be developing because they have little industry and many of their people are underfed and not educated.
11. Since independence, Indian leaders have worked to set up a stable government and to improve poor living conditions.
12. In Africa, nationalism after World War II led to independence for many countries. These nations, however, face numerous problems.
13. Since gaining independence, most Latin American countries have benefited from, but have also resented, foreign investors.

SECTION 3 ANSWERS

1. Indian National Congress, political party (p. 634); Gandhi, Indian leader (p. 634)
2. developing nations, nations that have little industry (p. 634); civil disobedience, refusing to obey unjust laws (p. 634); subsistence farmers, produce only food for their families (p. 638); cash crops, raised to be sold (p. 638); extended families, parents, children, and other close relatives (p. 639); *haciendas*, large ranches (p. 640); *campesinos*, peasant-farmers (p. 640)
3. through civil disobedience
4. because many African nations became independent in that year
5. farm production might rise if *campesinos* owned their own land
6. Answers will vary but civil wars empowered some African nations to develop their economies and governments.

Assign the Chapter 38 **Section 3 Quiz** in the TCR. Testmaker available.

CHAPTER

Review 38

Building Vocabulary

Imagine you are a newspaper reporter in the 1980s looking back on events in the world since World War II. Write a newspaper article describing the changes in the world since the war. Use the following words in your article.

cold war	*glasnost*	blockaded
airlift	*perestroika*	cash crops
purges	developing nations	*haciendas*
capitalism		*campesinos*

Check for Understanding

1. How did the United States propose to rebuild Western Europe following World War II?
2. Why did the Soviet Union blockade Berlin?
3. How did Castro behave once he came to power?
4. Why did Mao order the Cultural Revolution in China?
5. What were the demonstrators at Tiananmen Square demanding?
6. What two policies did Mikhail Gorbachev adopt in the Soviet Union?
7. What problems do African nations face?
8. How have Latin American nations benefited from foreign investment?

Critical Thinking

1. Why do you think Chinese leaders restricted political freedoms?
2. What do you think might have happened if the Soviet Union had not introduced the policies of *glasnost* and *perestroika*?
3. If you were the leader of a developing Latin American country, what would you do to industrialize your country?
4. What actions do you think developing countries should take to solve their food problems?

Geography in History

HUMAN/ENVIRONMENTAL INTERACTION Refer to the map of African Independence on page 637. Note the locations of countries who gained their independence before 1945. Why might you expect revolutions for freedom to develop in coastal countries?

Using Your Journal

Review the details you have noted about the challenges facing China, Latin America, and Africa. Choose one of these areas and write a paragraph describing what you think is its biggest challenge, and what could be done to answer that challenge.

CHAPTER 38 REVIEW ANSWERS

BUILDING VOCABULARY

Newspaper articles will vary but students should use all the vocabulary words and present their article in newspaper style.

CHECK FOR UNDERSTANDING

1. through the Marshall Plan
2. to try and force Western powers to leave the city
3. Cubans who opposed him were jailed or executed. Castro announced his government would be communist.
4. because he began to worry that the Chinese people were losing their revolutionary spirit
5. democracy
6. *glasnost* and *perestroika*
7. how to produce enough food, utilize natural resources, educate people, stop warring clans
8. Wages rose, there were more jobs; foreign businesses built roads, railroads, ports, and utilities.

CRITICAL THINKING

1. Answers will vary, but students could indicate that they might be afraid to give the people too much power.
2. Answers will vary but include a slower economic growth and delayed independence.
3. Answers will vary, but could include better use of resources and modernization.
4. Answers will vary, but students should provide specific solutions for the food problems.

✚ BONUS ✚

TEST QUESTION

For Chapter 38 Test

Choose one of the following countries and explain why it is considered a developing country: India, Brazil, Zimbabwe. *(Answers will vary but should offer details.)*

USING YOUR JOURNAL

Paragraphs will vary. You might call on volunteers to read their paragraphs to the class and compile the suggested challenges on the chalkboard.

GEOGRAPHY IN HISTORY

Answers will vary but, could include that coastal areas are more accessible to outside influences and new ideas.

CHAPTER 39

The World Since 1989

CHAPTER ORGANIZER

Objectives	Special Features	Supplemental Materials
Section 1 The End of the Cold War Describe the events in Eastern Europe after the collapse of communism in 1989, and how the former Soviet Union and other European countries turned toward capitalism to develop their economies.		• Reproducible Lesson Plan • Section 1 Quiz • Testmaker • Chapter 39 Vocabulary and Guided Reading Activity • Chapter 39 Geography and Map Activity • World History and Art Transparencies 32-35 • The World History Videodisc
Section 2 World Challenges Explain why tensions in other areas of the world developed after the end of the cold war.	Map Skills, *Reading a Demographic Map,* p. 657	• Reproducible Lesson Plan • Section 2 Quiz • Testmaker • Chapter 39 Cooperative Learning Activity • Unit 12 World Literature • Chapter 39 Teaching Transparencies and Activities • The Western Civilization Videodisc
Section 3 The World Today Examine the challenges the world faces in the year 2000 and beyond.		• Reproducible Lesson Plan • Section 3 Quiz • Testmaker • Chapter 39 Chart and Graph Skill Activity • Unit 12 Primary Source Reading • The Western Civilization Videodisc
Chapter 39 Review and Evaluation		• Chapter 39 Reteaching Activity • Chapter 39 Enrichment Activity • Spanish Summary and Glossary • Audiocassettes (English and Spanish) • Chapter 39 Performance Assessment Activity • Chapter 39 Test • Testmaker • Unit 12 World Literature

If time does not permit teaching the entire chapter, use the Chapter 39 Summary on page 662 and the Chapter 39 Audiocassettes (English and Spanish) to point out the main ideas of the chapter.

✓ Performance Assessment Activities

Oral Report Have students investigate the global challenge of human rights facing the world today. Have students research countries where human rights abuses have been cited, what organizations are involved in protecting these rights, and what the outcomes of world pressure on negligent nations have been. Have students create a commercial to convince people to be concerned about human rights issues. Have them record or videotape their commercials for presentation to another class.

Nationalism Have students choose a country discussed in this chapter and investigate and write a report about its inception and the story behind its national flag and national anthem. Ask students to draw the national flag and, if possible, obtain a recording of the national anthem to share with the class.

CHAPTER RESOURCES

LITERATURE ABOUT THE PERIOD

The Learning Community. *A Journey to the Heart: Capturing the Spirit of Global Education.* Rainbow Bridge/SSSS, 1991. Collection of experiences of American students who visited Kenya.

READINGS FOR THE STUDENT

Middleton, Nick. *Atlas of Environmental Issues.* New York: Facts on File, 1989. A discussion of environmental problems.

Segal, Gerald. *The World Affairs Companion.* Simon and Schuster, 1991. Overview of current international topics.

READINGS FOR THE TEACHER

Brown, Lester, ed. *The World Watch Reader: On Global Environmental Issues.* Norton, 1991. Collection of magazine articles about global issues.

Goldman, Milton F., ed. *The Commonwealth of Independent States and Central/Eastern Europe: Global Studies.* Dushkin, 1992. Explains the events as communism collapsed in the former Soviet Union.

MULTIMEDIA RESOURCES

Children of Apartheid. CBS. Video. Documentary about the effects of apartheid on the children of South Africa.

Power Up? Energy in Our Environment. Rainbow/SSSS. Video. Details the use of energy sources and their impacts on the environment.

Rain Forest (National Geographic). Image Entertainment. Videodisc. A warning about the natural wonders the world stands to lose if human encroachment on the earth's rain forests continues.

CHAPTER 39 OVERVIEW

Chapter 39 discusses the challenges facing the former Communist nations in the early 1990s and the changing global community.

- **Section 1** explains upheavals in Communist countries as communism ended.
- **Section 2** describes the tensions in the world after the end of the cold war.
- **Section 3** summarizes the challenges facing the world today and in the future.

CHAPTER OBJECTIVES

After reading Chapter 39, students will be able to:

1. discuss what happened in Eastern Europe after the collapse of communism in 1989.
2. describe how the former Soviet Union and other European countries turned toward capitalism.
3. explain why tensions in other areas of the world developed after the end of the cold war.
4. examine the challenges the world faces in the year 2000 and beyond.

EXAMINING THE ILLUSTRATION

Ask students what time is showing on the Kremlin tower. After confirming it is evening, so the 12:00 midnight time would mark the beginning of a new day, remind students they will be reading about the "new day" that is occurring in Russia.

PERFORMANCE ASSESSMENT

Use the Performance Assessment activities on page 644B to help you evaluate students as they complete the chapter.

CHAPTER 39 The World Since 1989

Clock Tower of the Kremlin, Moscow

644

TEACHER CLASSROOM RESOURCES

- Section Quizzes/Chapter Test
- Reteaching Activity
- Enrichment Activity
- Geography and Map Activity
- Vocabulary and Guided Reading Activity
- Cooperative Learning Activity
- Spanish Summary and Glossary
- Unit 12 Primary Source Reading
- Performance Assessment Activity
- Unit 12 World Literature
- Audiocassettes (English and Spanish)
- World History and Art Transparencies
- Teaching Transparencies and Activities
- The World History Videodisc
- The Western Civilization Videodisc

Chapter Focus

READ TO DISCOVER:

- What happened in Eastern Europe after the collapse of communism in 1989.
- How the former Soviet Union and other European countries turned toward capitalism to develop their economies.
- Why tensions in other areas of the world developed after the end of the cold war.
- What challenges the world faces in the year 2000 and beyond.

1945–1989

KEY TERMS

- privatize
- apartheid
- habitats
- greenhouse effect
- communicable diseases
- multinational companies

The late 1980s brought an end to the cold war. Although communism came to an end in Europe, the area still faced many political and economic problems.

Political conflicts continued in the Middle East in the 1990s. The invasion of Kuwait by Iraq resulted in a war in 1991 between Iraq and a *coalition*, or combination, of countries led by the United States. The signing of a long-awaited treaty between Israel and the Palestinian Arabs in 1993 brought an end to decades of war.

The nations of the world continued to face the issues of a growing population, a troubled environment, and a need to provide better living conditions for their people.

Section 1

THE END OF THE COLD WAR

Between 1989 and 1991, communism collapsed in Eastern Europe and the Soviet Union broke apart into independent nations. These nations faced the challenge of developing new governments and new economies.

Fall of the Berlin Wall In 1989 Mikhail Gorbachev urged Soviet satellite countries in Eastern Europe to launch reforms like the ones he had introduced in the Soviet Union. East German

FOCUS

BELLRINGER

Have students write down a recent important international event and why they feel it was important.

MOTIVATIONAL ACTIVITY

Have students share their important events and why they were important. Write student responses on the chalkboard. Have students discuss the events and agree on their order of importance. Tell students that in this chapter they will learn about recent international events and their effects on the world.

VOCABULARY PRE-CHECK

Write the key terms for this chapter on the chalkboard. Ask students to use those that they know in sentences.

Assign Chapter 39 **Vocabulary and Guided Reading Activity** in the TCR.

EXTRA CREDIT PROJECT

Have students interview family members, neighbors, or friends about important political changes the person has witnessed in his or her lifetime to ascertain what people consider to be most important. Have students write a summary of their interviews and combine their information in a poll of important events. Then ask students to write about the kinds of political breakthroughs and changes they expect to witness in their lifetimes.

KEY TO ABILITY LEVELS

Teaching strategies have been coded for varying learning styles and abilities.

L1 Level 1 activities are **basic** activities and should be within the ability range of all students.

L2 Level 2 activities are **average** activities and should be within the ability range of the average to above-average student.

L3 Level 3 activities are **challenging** activities designed for the ability range of above-average students.

LEP LEP activities should be within the ability range of Limited English Proficiency students.

TEACH

GUIDED PRACTICE

L1 **Chronology** Have students work in small groups. Assign each group a subsection of Section 1. Have the groups create illustrated time lines of the events discussed in their subsection. Display the time lines.

L2 **Critical Thinking** Ask students to explain in writing why they think the Polish labor union chose the name *Solidarity*. Have students share their conclusions.

CAPTION ANSWER

For the first time in history, a Communist government lost power as a result of an election.

VIDEODISC

Use the following to enrich Chapter 39.

WH W 51 38419

1990 rally commemorates the 1989 rally in which 20 died.

leader Erich Honecker refused. East Germans protested against Honecker's move and called for democratic reforms. During the same time, Hungary, which had been moving toward reform, opened its borders with Austria. Thousands of East Germans fled to the West through Hungary. Emigration along this route and beyond soon reached a rate of 300 people per hour. By October 1989 Honecker resigned and East Germany opened its borders.

On November 9, 1989 the main gate of the Berlin Wall between the two Germanys swung open, and cheering crowds rushed through. East and West Germans climbed on the wall and danced. The next day, soldiers began taking down the wall. Citizens joined in with hammers and axes. By December 1990, the whole wall was gone, much of it broken into chunks and sold as souvenirs.

The Reorganization of Eastern Europe East Germany was not alone in making changes. In 1989 and 1990, many Communist regimes were toppled. Gorbachev played a key role in this by not sending in Soviet troops to support the Communist governments as had been done in Hungary in 1956 and in Czechoslovakia in 1968.

In Poland the change was peaceful. In January 1989, the government agreed to lift its ban on Solidarity, a labor union that had been calling for reforms since 1980. In June, members of

DEMONSTRATIONS IN POLAND The Polish people, especially those in the labor union Solidarity, demanded free elections from the government. **What made the 1989 election in Poland so important?**

SPOTLIGHT ON: LECH WALESA

Lech Walesa, Poland's first democratically-elected president in the postwar era, started his career as an electrical worker at the Lenin Shipyard in Gdansk. He later was a founder and president of the nation's first independent trade union—Solidarity. Under Walesa's leadership, Solidarity led workers in demonstrations and strikes to demand free elections and a voice for workers in forming government policy. The Polish government outlawed Solidarity and jailed many of its leaders. Walesa and others continued their work underground and eventually were successful. The courage of the members of Solidarity inspired other people in Eastern European countries. Walesa became a symbol of freedom and an international hero. In 1983, he received the Nobel Peace Prize.

Solidarity were elected to fill two-thirds of the seats in the national legislature, putting them in charge of the Polish government. For the first time in history, a Communist government lost power as a result of an election. The following year, much the same pattern was repeated in Czechoslovakia, Hungary, and Bulgaria.

In Romania, by contrast, the overthrow of communism was violent. Here, Nicolae Ceausescu (ni′ koh lī choo shes′ kyū) and his wife had ruled as dictators for 24 years. Ceausescu's methods were brutal, and his reaction to protests for freedom in the country was violent. Hundreds of people were killed before the Romanians finally revolted and ousted Ceausescu in December 1989. The Ceausescus tried to flee the country by helicopter but were caught, tried, and executed. Crowds there celebrated the fall of the dictatorship and the end of communism.

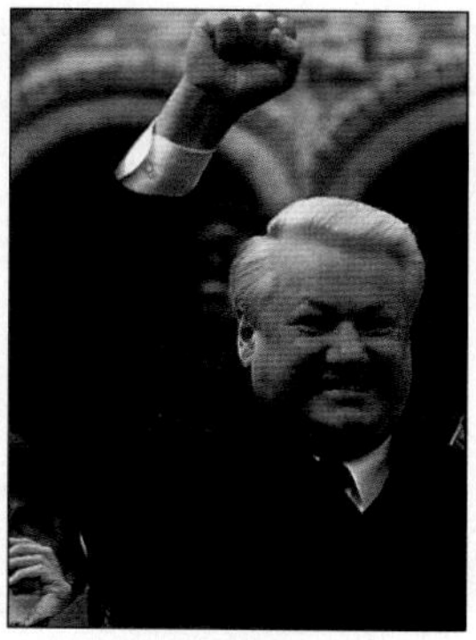

Photograph of Boris Yeltsin

Breakup of the Soviet Union In the Soviet Union, Communist hard-liners were angry with Gorbachev because the Soviet's satellite nations had collapsed. At the same time, Gorbachev was under pressure from reformers led by Boris Yeltsin who wanted quicker, deeper changes in the Soviet economy. In May 1990, Yeltsin was elected president of Russia, the first time a Russian head of state had been elected by the people. Two months later, in a dramatic televised announcement, he quit the Communist party.

Then in March 1991, Lithuania which had been under Soviet control since World War II, declared its independence. Gorbachev sent tanks to the Lithuanian capital. Instead of crushing the revolt, however, he began negotiating.

The hard-liners were outraged at this action. On August 19, they placed Gorbachev under house arrest and announced that they had taken over the Soviet government. Yeltsin immediately condemned the revolt's leaders who then lost the support of the military.

Gorbachev returned to Moscow on August 24. The next day, he shut down the Communist party, thus ending 74 years of Communist rule in the Soviet Union. At the same time, Ukraine, the largest non-Russian republic, declared total independence from the Soviet Union. The independence movement also emerged in other Soviet republics. By the end of 1991, 12 of the former Soviet republics formed the Commonwealth of Independent States (CIS), and the Soviet Union was dead. The republics within the CIS are separate, self-governing nations and have very little power together.

After the Fall The Russian Federation and other independent republics which are former satellite nations are slowly moving toward democracy. These countries are also

L2 **Religion** Explain to students that in the late 1970s the Roman Catholic Church selected its first non-Italian pope since 1523 and the first from a Communist country—John Paul II of Poland. Pope John Paul II has visited more countries than any of his predecessors. Ask students to discuss how the selection of Pope John Paul II—a staunch anti-Communist—might have affected the politics of Poland. *(He may have inspired nationalistic pride, and his anti-Communist stance may have rallied the Poles to work for independence from the Soviet Union.)*

L3 **Current Events** Have students bring in current magazine and newspaper articles about the former satellite nations of the Soviet Union and the republics that form the Commonwealth of Independent States. Have students read the articles and present oral reports about them to the class. Then on a large map of Eastern Europe and the Commonwealth of Independent States mounted on a bulletin board, have students connect each article with the country the article is about using thumb tacks and yarn.

VIDEODISC

Use the following to enrich Chapter 39.

WH W 53 38421

Yeltsin addresses crowd during coup attempt in Soviet Union.

COOPERATIVE LEARNING

Have students work in small groups to discuss the advisability of broadcasting a videotape of extreme violence, such as the execution of a dictator or atrocities committed during a war. Ask them to conduct an informal debate in which they will address such topics as freedom of the press and freedom of information versus censorship and the use of other means for communicating such information. Ask them to include current issues in their discussion, such as street violence in the United States. Have each group form an opinion and share that opinion with the class.

Assign the Chapter 39 **Cooperative Learning Activity** in the TCR.

L2 **Geography: Location** Ask students to compare a political map of the Soviet Union in the 1980s with a map of the same region today. Ask them to list and describe the political changes they see have taken place. LEP

L2 **Critical Thinking** Help students create cause-and-effect graphic organizers showing the problems that have appeared in former Communist countries as they move toward capitalism. LEP

MAP STUDY

Answer

its enormous size and central location

Assign the Chapter 39 **Geography and Map Activity** in the TCR.

VIDEODISC

Use the following to enrich Chapter 39.

WH W 54 38422

President Gorbachev on his return from Moscow 1991.

Commonwealth of Independent States

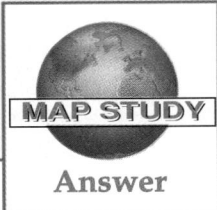

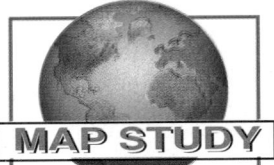

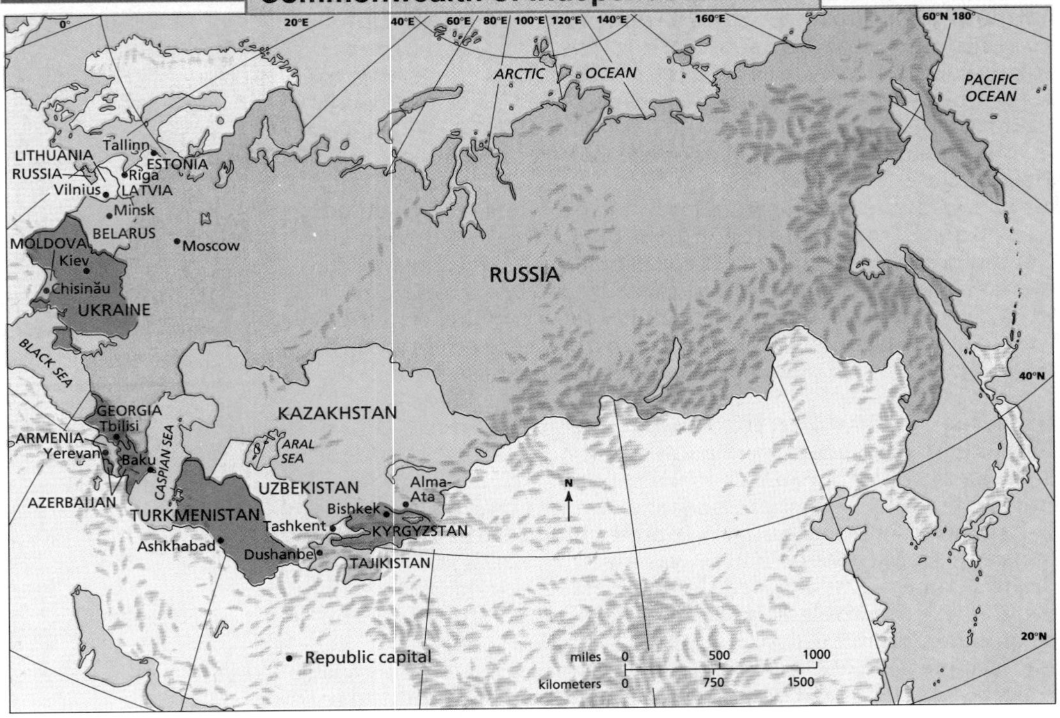

MAP STUDY

LOCATION The Commonwealth of Independent States stretches from Europe through a large part of Asia. **What geographic factors made it easier for Russia to have power over the other former republics?**

trying to **privatize,** or allow private ownership in their economies, as they adopt capitalism. State-owned stores, factories, and other businesses are being sold to private owners. However, few people in these countries have either the money or the skills to start or run businesses. Life under communism trained them to follow orders and avoid risk. Success in a capitalist economy requires just the opposite.

Other problems have appeared under capitalism. When goods are scarce, prices go up. In the former Communist countries, most goods were scarce, but the governments kept the prices low. When government controls were lifted, prices shot up. Of the former Soviet satellite nations, Poland introduced the most drastic reforms, moving directly from communism to capitalism. There, the prices on goods increased dramatically but wages did not. Workers began demanding more money, and strikes became common. The strikes resulted in the production of fewer goods, so goods became more scarce, thereby increasing the prices of these goods. This continuing cycle is a problem in Poland. Its people have shown unhappiness over the economy by electing more Communists to Parliament.

MEETING SPECIAL NEEDS

Have gifted students read and report on literature by Eastern European authors such as Václav Havel, Milovan Dijilas, Milan Kundera, or other poets, playwrites, novelists, and essayists from this region. Have students' reports include information about the authors' lives.

Czechoslovakia took a middle course in economic reforms. Some price controls were lifted and some were not. Tensions developed, however, between the country's two main ethnic groups, the Czechs and the Slovaks. Slovak leaders wanted slower economic changes because their area was less industrial. Czech leaders wanted to move quickly toward capitalism. Finally, the two groups agreed to separate. On January 1, 1993, Czechoslovakia became two countries—Slovakia and the Czech Republic.

While Czechoslovakia was dividing, Germany was reuniting. On October 3, 1990, East Germany and West Germany became a single nation again. This reunification, however, created problems. The eastern part of Germany was poor and its factories were run-down. Supporting the area with money has put a strain on the overall German economy. Many young Germans are now unemployed. This has fueled the rise of right-wing political parties. Many of these groups support the ideas of Nazism. They blame immigrants and refugees for Germany's problems and encourage violence against non-Germans.

By the early 1990s, ethnic tensions continued to rise in the former Soviet republics. For example, in Georgia more than a dozen ethnic groups wanted to govern themselves. Armenia and Azerbaijan were openly at war with one another.

ETHNIC TENSIONS Because of disagreements between European ethnic groups, fighting broke out in the early 1990's. Many civilians were forced to leave their homes as these Armenians are doing. **What former Soviet republics were openly at war with one another at this time?**

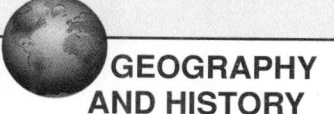

GEOGRAPHY AND HISTORY

The Czechs and the Slovaks, though ethnically similar and in close proximity for 1,000 years, were not united politically before the end of World War I. The Czechs have had close contact with Western culture since the Middle Ages. Their region experienced prosperity, urbanization, and a growing middle class because of industrialization during the Hapsburg monarchy. By contrast, the Slovaks were isolated and impoverished in rural Hungary. Their society was made up of peasants and mountain folk.

CAPTION ANSWER

Armenia and Azerbaijan

EXTENDING THE CONTENT

Since the collapse of the Soviet bloc, hundreds of thousands of refugees and immigrants seeking safety and work have flooded into Western Europe. They have joined millions of other immigrants, mainly from North Africa and the Middle East. In addition, millions of people have been displaced by the war in the former Yugoslav republics. The strain of this influx has begun to show in rising racism and xenophobia, or the fear of foreigners or strangers. Outbreaks of racist violence have occurred in France, Great Britain, and especially Germany. Austria and Switzerland have closed their borders to refugees and immigrants.

Photograph of Azerbaijanian Soldier

By 1993 the Russian economy was weak and President Yeltsin was at odds with his legislature. He wanted to move quickly to full democracy and capitalism. The legislature, which was elected before the break-up of the Soviet Union, however, was made up of many former Communists who resisted change. In October of 1993, Yeltsin dissolved the legislature, claiming it was blocking needed reforms. The legislature struck back by taking over the White House, the building where they regularly met. They also named a new president. The stand-off was broken when Yeltsin ordered the military to take back the White House by force. The troops were successful and the crisis was over for the moment. Yeltsin, however, faced more challenges from Communist leaders who gained seats in parliament in a later election.

Section 1 Review

1. **Identify:** Erich Honecker, Solidarity, Nicolae Ceausescu, Boris Yeltsin, Commonwealth of Independent States (CIS)
2. **Define:** privatize
3. How did Solidarity come to power?
4. Why did hard-liners in the Soviet Union try to take control of the government from Gorbachev in the early 1990s?
5. What problems have countries in the former Soviet Union faced?
6. What problems did the united Germany face?

Critical Thinking

7. Do you agree or disagree with the following statement: The Berlin Wall became obsolete by 1989. Explain.

Section 2 WORLD CHALLENGES

The end of the cold war relaxed many tensions around the world. Some old problems remained, however, and new tensions began to build.

The Gulf War As the cold war era was winding down, the Persian Gulf was heating up. Here, in the 1980s, Iraq and Iran had fought an eight-year-long war. Although Iraq claimed victory, it was left with a huge war debt. So Iraqi ruler Saddam Hussein (sad' dam hu sān') tried to restore his country by invading his oil-rich neighbor Kuwait (kuh wāt'). On August 2,

MAKING CONNECTIONS

➤➤ **History** Soon after Khomeini came to power in Iran, he condemned pro-Western and secular Arab leaders as enemies of Islam. Repeatedly, he urged Arab masses in other nations to join a struggle against their leaders. President Saddam Hussein of Iraq, fearful that revolution would sweep into Iraq, invaded Iran in September 1980. The eight-year war that followed is considered to be among the bloodiest wars in recent history. A UN cease-fire in 1988 ended the war, but by then the two countries had lost about 1 million people and hundreds of billions of dollars in property.

DID YOU KNOW ??

Saddam Hussein claimed that his country invaded Kuwait because it was a historic part of Iraq and that Kuwait had unfairly drilled Iraqi oil. Although Iraq is fourth in the world in the production of oil, controlling Kuwait would mean Iraq had control of over one-fifth of the world's known oil resources.

VIDEODISC

Use the following to enrich Chapter 39.

WH G 49 14571
Supertankers loading oil at pier off coast of Kuwait.

WC L 65 38720
Jiddah, Saudi Arabia's major Red Sea port.

SECTION 1 ANSWERS

1. Honecker, East German leader (p. 646); Solidarity, Polish labor union (p. 646); Ceausescu, dictator of Romania (p. 647); Yeltsin, president of Russia (p. 647); Commonwealth of Independent States, the former Soviet republics (p. 647)
2. privatize, private ownership (p. 648)
3. by winning an election
4. because they were angry that Gorbachev let Soviet satellite regimes collapse
5. ethnic tensions, weak economies, and food shortages
6. run-down factories, strained economy, unemployment, violence from right-wing groups
7. Answers will vary but with access to the West through Hungary and Austria, the Berlin Wall could not hold East Germans back.

Assign the Chapter 39 **Section 1 Quiz** in the TCR. Testmaker available.

AIR ATTACK U.S. aircraft bombed the capital city of Baghdad, Iraq, during the Gulf War. **Why did so many nations side with the United States and agree to wage war against Iraq?**

1990, Iraqi forces swept into Kuwait and looted the capital. Saddam then moved thousands of troops to the border of Saudi Arabia, source of the world's largest known oil reserves. This move alarmed industrial nations everywhere. By this time, too, Saddam had made regional enemies in the Arab world by calling for the overthrow of other Arab rulers.

United States President George Bush put together a coalition of 28 nations, some Arab, to oppose Iraq and free Kuwait. In January 1991, Bush ordered air attacks against Iraq. In February the allies attacked the Iraqi army on the ground. Within 100 hours, about 100,000 Iraqis had been killed and another 100,000 had surrendered. The remaining Iraqi troops fled Kuwait. With Kuwait freed, Bush ordered a cease-fire on February 28.

Although Iraq lost the war, Saddam Hussein remained in power. He faced opposition from the Kurds, a people in northern Iraq and other Iraqis in the south. He attacked these people and used his army to crush military and civilian resistance.

L1 **Geography: Location** Ask students to locate Kuwait and Iraq on a map of the Middle East. Ask them how Kuwait's location made it appealing to Iraq. *(Iraq has a very limited coastline. Kuwait is located next to Iraq and would allow Iraq greater access to the Persian Gulf.)* LEP

L2 **History** Have students create charts titled "World Tensions in the 1990s" of the countries discussed in this section. Have them use the following headings: "Country," "Location," "Conflicts," "Resolutions." Have students share their charts. LEP

CAPTION ANSWER

Iraq captured Kuwait and then moved thousands of soldiers to the border of Saudi Arabia. This alarmed industrial nations because of the enormous oil reserves in Saudi Arabia.

VIDEODISC

Use the following to enrich Chapter 39.

WH G 73 14595
U.N. security Council votes to remove Iraq from Kuwait.

WC L 70 38725
A drilling rig in eastern Saudi Arabia.

EXTENDING THE CONTENT

The UN set a deadline of January 15, 1991, for Iraq to withdraw from Kuwait and authorized the use of force if Iraq did not. Hussein vowed not to leave Kuwait until Israel pulled out of its occupied territories and Syria left Lebanon. He also threatened to attack Israel if Iraq were attacked. The day after the UN deadline, the U.S. bombed the Iraqi capital of Baghdad. For the next month, the coalition forces conducted a massive air war aimed at destroying Iraq's war-making ability. Hussein responded by launching missiles at Israel, hoping to draw Israel into the war and thus splinter Arab support for the coalition. Israel resisted, however, and the U.S. provided Israel with an antimissile defense system.

CAPTION ANSWER

the Serbs

DID YOU KNOW ??

Western leaders refused to supply arms and military aid to Muslims and Croats in Bosnia-Herzegovina. This helped the Serbian forces who had a stockpile of arms.

MAKING CONNECTIONS

➤➤ **History** As the civil war in Bosnia-Herzegovina escalated, Western nations airlifted supplies into and helped bus children out of the war zones. They also pressured Serbia to end the constant bombing of Sarajevo and to withdraw its support of ethnic Serbs in Bosnia-Herzegovina.

BOSNIAN CONFLICT The soldiers in this photograph are Croatian nationals who were fighting in Mostar, Bosnia. **With what other group were both the Croats and Bosnians fighting?**

Conflict in the Former Yugoslavia Yugoslavia has always been a mixture of ethnic groups. Following World War II, Yugoslavia became a union of six republics made up of ethnic groups who had a long-standing distrust of one another. This confederation was held together by the Communist leader Josip Tito (tē' toh). When Tito died in 1980, the presidents of the six republics agreed to share power. In 1991, however, the republics of Slovenia, Croatia, Bosnia-Herzegovina, and Macedonia, following a disagreement with Serbia, declared their independence from the confederation. The Serbs then fought to regain control of several areas.

Joined by Serbians who lived in the other republics, the Serbian army invaded Croatia and Bosnia-Herzegovina. A cease-fire between Serbs and Croats was established in Croatia in January 1992. The most violent fighting occurred in Bosnia-Herzegovina. Constant fighting in and around Sarajevo, Bosnian-Herzegovina's capital city, caused the United Nations to try to bring peace to the area. Many countries were concerned about the huge losses of both military and civilian lives. The Serbians, in an effort to create an all-Serbian state, had been following a

EXTENDING THE CONTENT

Yugoslavia was a federation of six republics—Bosnia, Croatia, Macedonia, Montenegro, Serbia, and Slovenia. The population included Albanians, Bulgarians, Czechs, Hungarians, Italians, Romanians, Serbs, Slovaks, and Turks. Catholics, Orthodox Christians, and Muslims all lived together in Yugoslav communities. These diverse groups had long-standing animosities that continually resurfaced. Following World War II, the republics were held together by the strong personal leadership of Josip Tito. After his death in 1980, rival communist leaders incited nationalist sympathies.

policy of "ethnic cleansing." This meant they put non-Serbians in prison camps or executed them. In late 1993 the Bosnian Serbs, Muslims, and Croats met for peace talks, but there is doubt that peace in this region will be easy to achieve.

Haiti In the early 1990s, the United Nations was also called upon to help install a democratic government in the island country of Haiti. After negotiating a peaceful exchange of power, the UN was required to send troops to enforce that exchange.

Northeast Africa Northeast Africa faced many challenges in the 1990s. Pastures turned into deserts because of drought and overgrazing. Hunger and ethnic and religious differences have caused hostilities. One African crisis centered in Somalia. This country found itself torn by hunger and civil war.

UN PEACEKEEPING Soldiers from many countries served in the UN army sent to Somalia to protect its people and food supplies. **What crisis were the people of Somalia facing?**

MAKING CONNECTIONS

➤➤ **History** Although independent since 1804, Haiti has always suffered poverty and political turmoil. From 1957 to 1971, Haiti was ruled by dictator, François Duvalier. When he died, his son, Jean-Claude took power but was overthrown by a revolution in 1986. The country was torn by political strife for 4 years. In 1990 a popular reform-minded priest, Jean-Bertrand Aristide, was elected president. A military coup forced Aristide to flee the country in 1991.

CAPTION ANSWER

hunger and civil war

MEETING SPECIAL NEEDS

Many students will benefit from a strong visual and oral presentation that reinforces what they have read. Have small groups create a brief oral summary of each country in this section. Tell strong visual learners to collect or create images—photographs, illustrations, drawings, posters, collages—of the people, places, and politics they are studying. Have students use a large wall map to trace the outline of the region on large paper. Have them paste the images on this outline map. Near the images, have them write a few key words—names, dates, or terms—to help them remember each country studied.

L2 **Critical Thinking** Ask: Are developed nations obliged to provide basic needs to people in developing nations? Why or why not? If so, to what extent should they go to provide such aid? What kind of aid should be supplied?

L3 **Current Events** Have students read current magazine and newspaper articles about the state of affairs in African nations. Have students follow the events in a particular country for a period of time. Then have students present oral reports to the class about the articles and locate the countries discussed in the articles on a wall map of Africa.

CAPTION ANSWER

Palestine Liberation Organization

DID YOU KNOW ??

During the post-war years, the unifying idea of Pan-Arabism grew. Pan-Arabism was a Mideastern political and cultural movement emphasizing ties existing among all Arab people.

VIDEODISC

Use the following to enrich Chapter 39.

WC L 23 38678
Bombed Jewish village in central Palestine.

WC L 24 38679
Palestinian refugees near Jerusalem.

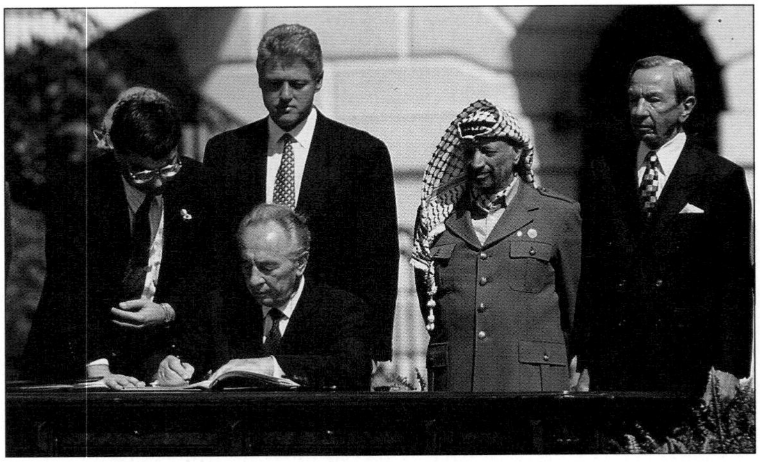

PEACE ACCORD The 1993 agreement between Israel and the PLO is being signed by Israeli leader Yitzhak Rabin as U.S. President Bill Clinton, PLO leader Yasir Arafat, and U.S. Secretary of State Warren Christopher looked on. **What is the PLO?**

In 1992, the United Nations sent about 20,000 peacekeepers to Somalia to make sure food and medicine reached needy people. The United States added several thousand soldiers to the relief effort. An unsuccessful attempt to unseat Mohammed Farah Aidid (ah dīd'), a leader of the most violent clan, caused additional problems. Eventually the United States pulled out its troops. In another crisis, at least seven million people were threatened by famine in Sudan in the early 1990s.

Some problems were resolved in Africa during this time. In 1993, Eritrea achieved independence as it broke away from Ethiopia following a civil war.

The Arab-Israeli Conflict By the end of World War I, only Saudi Arabia and Yemen were independent from European nations. An undeclared Arab war won independence for Iraq in 1932, for Lebanon in 1943, and for Syria in 1946.

In 1946, the part of Palestine east of the Jordan River became the independent country of Transjordan, now known as Jordan. The following year, the United Nations gave the part of Palestine west of the Jordan River to the Jews. They established the country of Israel in 1948. The Arabs did not accept this, and five Arab nations invaded Israel. The Israelis defeated the Arab forces. Many Arab refugees, however, remained in the West Bank of the Jordan River and in the Gaza (gahz' uh) Strip.

MEETING SPECIAL NEEDS

Explain to auditory learners that Ramadan and Yom Kippur have similar religious functions in that they are both periods of atonement. Ramadan in Islam is the holy month of fasting from dawn to dusk in obedience to God's command. Yom Kippur is the most solemn of Jewish festivals, the time when sins are confessed. On this day Jews abstain from work, food, and drink. Have students interview members ofdifferent religions to learn about periods of atonement and what customs they follow during this time.

Between 1948 and 1993, Arab nations and Israel fought four more wars over these territories and Israel's right to exist. The only Arab country that recognized Israel was Egypt. The Palestine Liberation Organization (PLO), led since 1969 by Yasir Arafat (yah´ sir ahr´ uh faht), carried out guerrilla attacks against Israel. In return, Israel bombed guerrilla bases and invaded PLO strongholds in Lebanon.

In 1987 a Palestinian uprising, known as the *intifada*, broke out in the West Bank. Workers went on strike, and street battles spread. The *intifada* focused world attention on the Palestinian issue.

Disagreements continued and the Gulf War started. Israel and several Arab countries found themselves on the same side in that war. Afterwards, Arab and Israeli negotiators agreed to talk directly with one another. In September 1993 Israel and the PLO signed an agreement that called for self-rule by Palestinian Arabs in the Gaza Strip and the West Bank city of Jericho. In the agreement, Israel and the PLO also recognized each other as

Disputed Lands, 1993

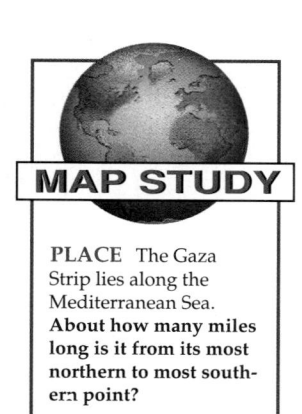

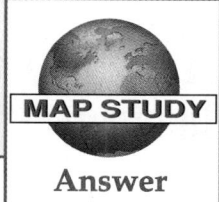

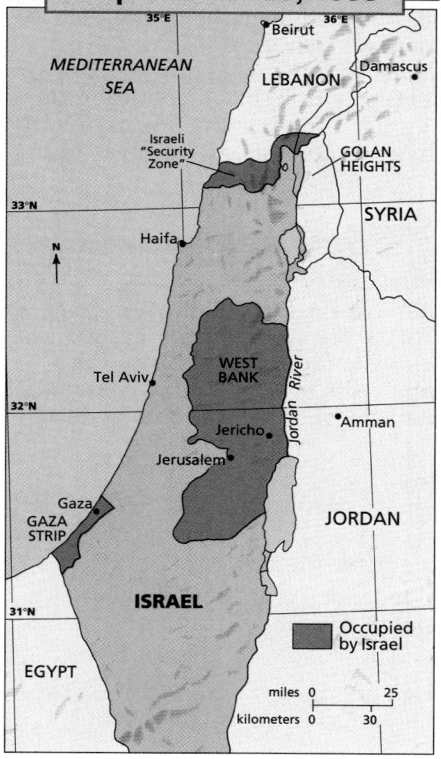

MAP STUDY

PLACE The Gaza Strip lies along the Mediterranean Sea. **About how many miles long is it from its most northern to most southern point?**

L3 **History** Have students research and write a report about the scientific discoveries made that helped the Allied cause during the war. Have them point out developments that had a direct impact on the Allied efforts. Encourage them to share their research with the class.

DID YOU KNOW ??

The five Arab nations that invaded Israel after it was established in 1948 were Egypt, Syria, Lebanon, Trans-Jordan, and Iraq.

LINKING PAST TO PRESENT

The ancient Arabic word *intifada* means "to shake off." This word is today applied to the Palestinian uprising. The Palestinians wish to shake off Israeli occupation of the West Bank and the Gaza Strip. In 1990, Israeli Prime Minister Yitzhak Shamir, unable to stop the violence of the *intifada*, decided to place restrictions on the 120,000 Palestinians from the West Bank and Gaza who work in Israel while preserving Israel's control of Palestinian territory.

MAP STUDY

Answer

about 25 miles (or 40 km)

EXTENDING THE CONTENT

Over the years many attempts to bring about peace between the Arabs and Israelis have been made. One of the most controversial moves took place in 1977, when, at the invitation of the Israeli government, President Anwar el-Sadat of Egypt journeyed to Jerusalem to make a speech before the *Knesset*, the Israeli parliament. Sadat was the first Arab head of state to make an official visit to Israel. About two years later, on March 27, 1979, President Sadat and Israeli Prime Minister Menachem Begin signed the Camp David Accords, the first formal peace treaty between Israel and an Arab country.

INDEPENDENT PRACTICE

L3 **Critical Thinking** Have students read more about apartheid and what it has meant in South Africa. Have them share their findings with the class and lead a discussion to compare and contrast apartheid with the treatment of African Americans in the first half of the twentieth century.

L2 **History** Have students investigate and write a report about the history of the African National Congress. The reports should include the goals and activities of the organization. LEP

DID YOU KNOW ??

Although he was trained to be a chief in the Tembu royal family, Nelson Mandela fled to Johannesburg to study law. While there, he joined the ANC and campaigned against apartheid. In 1960 Mandela, who was the leader of the ANC, formed a military operation to press for change. In 1962 officials charged Mandela with treason and sabotage, and jailed him for life. He was eventually released in 1990.

VIDEODISC

Use the following to enrich Chapter 39.

WH D 51 10319
"Non-Whites Only" bus notice.

WH D 73 10341
Mandela meets with de Klerk.

Photograph of Nelson Mandela

official groups. At that time, other Arab nations also said that they, too, might sign an agreement with Israel.

South Africa South Africa has followed a system of **apartheid** (uh pahr′ tāt), or separation of the races, almost since its beginning. Although blacks made up more than 75 percent of the population, the apartheid system put most of the country's wealth and power in the hands of the white minority. Black South Africans were not allowed to vote in national elections and were not allowed to choose where they lived or worked. The United States set up trade restrictions against South Africa because of this policy.

In 1989 Frederick W. de Klerk became the new president of South Africa. Recognizing the need for change, de Klerk set to work to end apartheid. This caused the turmoil and, in some cases, violence in the country to become worse. He lifted the long-standing ban on the African National Congress, South Africa's leading black political group. In 1990 he released Nelson Mandela, the head of the African National Congress, from prison after 27 years. By 1992 most of the laws that defined apartheid had been thrown out. All South Africans now had the right to vote. An election to choose a new government was scheduled for 1994.

Major opposition to Mandela and the ANC now comes partly from white hard-liners and partly from black political groups vying for power. One such group is the Inkatha Freedom Party led by Zulu chief Mangosuthu Buthelezi (mangō sū thū bu tuh lā′ zē).

Section 2 Review

1. **Identify:** Saddam Hussein, George Bush, Gulf War, Josip Tito, Serbia, Slovenia, Croatia, Bosnia-Herzegovina, Somalia, Mohammed Farah Aidid, Palestine, Gaza Strip, Palestine Liberation Organization (PLO), Yasir Arafat, Frederick W. de Klerk, African National Congress, Nelson Mandela, Inkatha Freedom Party
2. **Define:** *intifada*, apartheid
3. Why did Saddam Hussein invade Kuwait, and how did the United States react?
4. What is the root of the conflict in Yugoslavia?
5. What major change did Frederick W. de Klerk make once he became president of South Africa?

Critical Thinking

6. Would you have supported or opposed military action by other countries to end the conflict in Yugoslavia? Why?

SECTION 2 ANSWERS

1. Gulf War, war against Iraq; Hussein, Iraqi ruler (p. 650); Bush, U.S. President (p. 651); Tito, leader of Yugoslavia; Serbia, Slovenia, Croatia, Bosnia-Herzegovina, Yugoslav republics (p. 652); Somalia, African country (p. 653); Aidid, Somalian clan leader; Palestine, Arab nation; Gaza Strip, part of Israel (p. 654); PLO, Arab nationalists; Arafat, leader of PLO (p. 655); de Klerk, president of South Africa; African National Congress, black political group; Mandela; South African leader; Inkatha Freedom Party, black political party (p. 656)
2. *intifada,* Palestinian uprising (p. 655); apartheid, separation of the races (p. 656)
3. to take over Kuwait's rich oil reserves; a coalition of nations attacked Iraq
4. ethnic conflicts
5. He ended apartheid.
6. Answers will vary.

Assign the Chapter 39 **Section 2 Quiz** in the TCR. Testmaker available.

Reading a Demographic Map

In order to show information about where people live on the earth, mapmakers use **demographic maps.** Among other things, these maps can show population density, or the average number of people per square mile, or square kilometer, of land.

Some parts of the world have many people living in each square mile, or square kilometer. People generally live in areas with good physical environments. Other parts of the world have few people, and there are even some areas in which no people live. These are known as *uninhabited* areas.

For example, on the "World Population" map below, the color green indicates areas, such as Southeast Asia, with more than 250 people per square mile, or 97 people per square kilometer. This is the highest population density shown. The color light brown indicates areas, such as Antarctica, that are uninhabited.

Map Practice

1. What color represents 60-125 people per square mile (25-50 per sq. km)?

2. What areas in South America have densities of 2-60 people per square mile (1-25 per sq. km)?

World Population

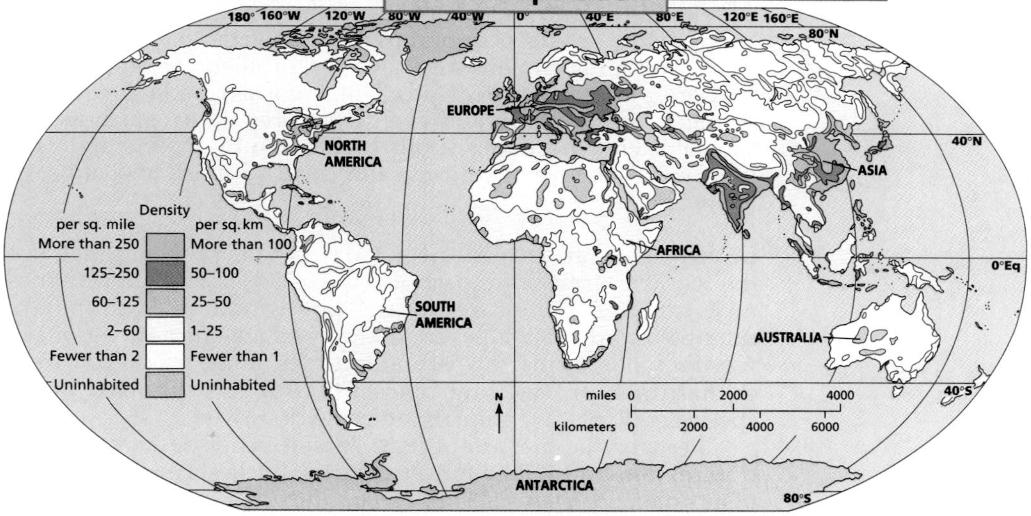

Teaching

MAP SKILLS

Reading a Demographic Map

Instruct the students to read the instructional part of the feature. Ask: Why do mapmakers use demographic maps? *(to show information about where people live on the Earth)* Name one thing that a demographic map can show. *(population density)* What are uninhabited areas? *(places in which no people live)* Direct students to study the map. Ask: What color indicates uninhabited areas? *(gold)* What does the color green indicate on the map? *(more than 250 people per square mile, or 100 people per square kilometer)* What is the approximate population density of the area where you live? *(Answers will vary.)*

Next, have students work in pairs or in small groups to write questions and answers based on the map of World Population densities. Have a spokesperson from each pair or small group ask the rest of the class their questions.

ANSWERS to Map Practice

1. salmon

2. much of the coastal areas

SPOTLIGHT ON: WORLD POPULATION

The population of the world is computed only after a careful census has been taken. These counts must be made in a systematic way to record a *de jur* census, which tallies people according to their legal place of residence, or a *de facto* census, which counts them as residing where they spent the night of the day on which the census was taken. In either case, the census distribution is determined by where people sleep, rather then where they work. Thus, it is a nighttime population measure.

L3 Mathematics Have students investigate the world populations in ten-year increments starting in 1900 and ending with projections for 2010. Have students graph their findings.

L3 Science Have students read more about the work of Gregor Mendel and Norman Borlang. Tell them to write a brief summary of the achievements of each man in the area of agriculture, and conclude with an opinion of which man's work had the most far-reaching effects and why. Have students share their findings with the class.

DID YOU KNOW ??

Desertification of world land is a major problem. Some 22 million acres today are "beyond restoration." Of all the world's desertified land, almost four-fifths is in Africa and Asia.

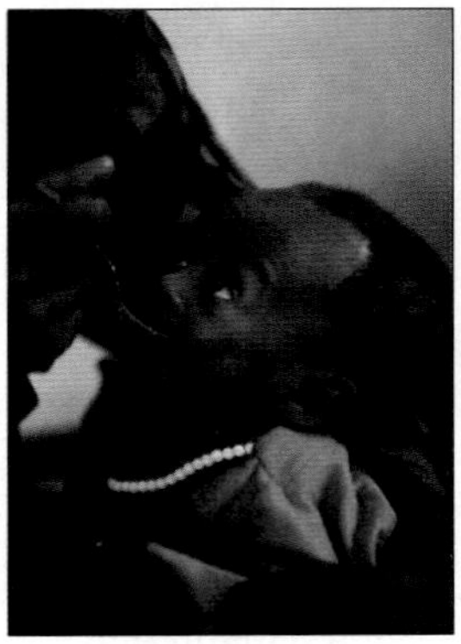

Photograph of Somali Famine Victim

Section 3

THE WORLD TODAY

As the year 2000 approaches, the world faces great challenges in producing enough food, protecting the environment, and improving health care. The future of the world and its quality of life will depend on how these challenges are met by its citizens.

Feeding a Growing Population About one-fifth of the world's population goes to bed hungry each night. Almost 40,000 children under the age of five starve to death each day. Yet the world's population continues to grow. At present, it is about 5.4 billion. Scientists estimate that the population will reach 14 billion by the year 2100.

Producing enough food for the growing population is a problem. Most of the land that can be farmed is already being farmed. In fact, as the Sahara and other deserts spread, the amount of farmland is shrinking. Also, today's farmers must learn to protect resources that future farmers will need. One example is topsoil, which is being rapidly eroded by wind and water. Wise use of water, pesticides, and fertilizers is also needed.

In the 1960s, scientists developed new and more productive kinds of wheat and rice. This was known as the Green Revolution. This development was not as helpful as expected, however. Using the new seeds also meant having to use large amounts of irrigation water and chemical fertilizers. Farmers in developing countries, where the grain was needed, could not afford to buy fertilizers or pumps to bring water to their land.

Developing nations also face the problem of proper food storage and transportation. These countries lack modern warehouses, railroads, and even paved roads. As much as one fifth of their food either spoils or is eaten by insects and rats. Improving facilities would increase food supplies and improve the health of people.

Saving the Environment Many of the problems that face the world's farmers are part of a larger crisis. Human activities now threaten the entire natural environment. Swamps are drained, meadows are paved, and forests are cut down to make way for roads, farms, towns, and factories. In the process, however, **habitats,** or dwelling places, that once supported many species of plants and animals are being destroyed.

Perhaps the most important habitat being destroyed is the tropical rain forest. Rain forests have the thickest concentration of plants on land. Plants absorb carbon dioxide and release oxygen. As rain forests are destroyed, the amount of carbon dioxide in the

SPOTLIGHT ON: NORMAN BORLAUG

Norman Borlaug, an agronomist born in Cresco, Iowa, in 1914, won a Nobel Peace Prize in 1970 for his efforts to eradicate hunger and build international prosperity. In 1944, Borlaug was sent to Mexico by the Rockefeller Foundation to head a team of scientists experimenting with the improvement of grains. His teams developed improved wheat seeds, a new type of higher-yield rice, and more efficient uses of fertilizers. As a result, Mexico's wheat harvest was greatly increased, and food production was improved in other developing nations, such as India and Pakistan.

RAIN FORESTS The Brazilian rain forest shown here was stripped of its valuable wood. Unless replanting takes place, a valuable resource will be lost. **What happens to the Earth's atmosphere when rain forests are destroyed?**

atmosphere increases. Carbon dioxide tends to trap heat from the Earth's surface as a greenhouse does. Scientists believe the **greenhouse effect** is making the earth grow warmer. The warmer temperatures might cause ice caps in the Arctic and Antarctic regions to melt, flooding millions of acres of low-lying coastal areas.

The harmful buildup of carbon dioxide in the atmosphere comes largely from automobiles and factories that burn fossil fuels. Getting rid of such factory wastes, some poisonous, and other community wastes is a growing environmental problem. In the past, sewage and trash, were buried in designated landfills or dumped into rivers and oceans. Landfills, however, are overflowing.

In 1992 delegates from 178 nations gathered in Brazil for a historic meeting called the Earth Summit. They discussed ways to balance economic development with the needs of the environment. The nations pledged to take steps to limit global warming, halt poisonous-waste pollution, preserve the world's forests, and protect endangered species. Richer nations agreed to give poorer nations about $6 billion a year for environmental programs. These agreements, however, must be approved by at least 50 nations before they go into effect. It may be many years before people see any results.

Improving Health Care

The people who live in the industrial nations of the world are generally healthier than the people in developing countries. In industrial nations, many **communicable diseases**, or diseases that are passed along from an infected person or animal to another person or animal, have been

CAPTION ANSWER

The amount of carbon dioxide in the atmosphere increases. This traps heat from the Earth's surface much as a greenhouse does.

L2 **Environment** Have students list ways American people waste resources. Have them read their lists and explain how the wasteful practices might be eliminated.

MAKING CONNECTIONS

➤➤ **Civics** In 1987 a fifth-grade civics class in Closter, New Jersey, took action against McDonald's for the company's excessive use of polystyrene (plastic foam) packaging. The students' concern was based on the fact that polystyrene take decades to decompose and if it is burned, it emits toxic fumes. The students created a letter-writing campaign to change McDonald's packaging material to something biodegradable. In 1990, as a result of the letters, McDonald's began phasing out the plastic foam in favor of paper wrapping materials.

EXTENDING THE CONTENT

Acid rain is a term used to describe precipitation carrying large amounts of dissolved acids, especially sulfuric acid and nitric acid. Many adverse effects are attributable to increased environmental acidity. Lakes and streams, forests, crops, and human health are damaged by acid rain. In 1984, many nations agreed to reduce their sulfur emissions by at least 30 percent by 1993. Several countries, such as Canada and France, set even higher reduction goals. Four of the largest emitters of sulfur have not joined the "30 percent club"—the United States, England, Spain, and Poland.

CAPTION ANSWER

178 nations

L1 **Health** Have students discuss the need for immunizations and whether they think the possible discomfort outweighs the benefits. Then have them write a letter to their local health department requesting a list of suggested immunizations. When students receive this list of information, suggest they put it on a poster to display. LEP

DID YOU KNOW ??

In the early 1990s it was estimated that close to 7 million Africans were already infected with HIV. Governments throughout Africa have initiated programs to educate their people about the disease and to combat and control its spread. The Kenyan government has identified AIDS as the nation's number one health challenge and has taken the lead in educating its citizens about the disease and its prevention.

VIDEODISC

Use the following to enrich Chapter 39.

WC L 71 38726

An offshore oil rig in the Arabian Gulf.

ENVIRONMENT The Earth Summit that met in Brazil wanted to solve environmental problems that people have caused. **How many different countries took part in the meeting?**

wiped out. New medicines and medical procedures have made remarkable progress against non-communicable diseases, such as heart disease.

In developing countries, however, millions of people still die from communicable diseases. One such disease is cholera. Since 1991 cholera epidemics have swept Central America, Colombia, Ecuador, Peru, Bangladesh, and India.

Another widespread communicable disease is malaria. About 100 million people suffer from it, and between one and two million people die from it every year. About eight million people get tuberculosis every year, and about three million of them die. In fact, tuberculosis kills more people than any other communicable disease.

Scientists are also working to find a cure for a new disease—Acquired Immune Deficiency Syndrome, or AIDS. The first cases of AIDS were reported in the late 1970s. HIV, the virus that causes the disease, was identified in 1981 but a cure has not yet been found. It is believed that by the early 1990s, at least 10 million people were infected with HIV but had not developed the disease of AIDS. By the year 2000, according to the World Health Organization, about 40 million people will carry the virus.

Other illness prevention is also needed. For example, diseases such as cholera are caused by bacteria that live in water containing human and animal waste. Providing clean drinking water and better sewage systems in countries where cholera is

COOPERATIVE LEARNING

Divide the class into small groups to simulate a city planning commission meeting to solve environmental problems in their city. One group should act as members of the planning commission, which conducts research on the issues and listens to petitions from the citizens' groups in order to prepare a plan of action. The citizens' groups should deal with these or other urban problems: low-income housing, smog control, water pollution, noise control, urban waste. Each group should gather data about a problem, report its findings to the commission, suggest solutions, and respond to questions from the commissioners. Encourage the use of visuals.

common would greatly improve the health of people. Stricter enforcement of the immunization of children against measles and whooping cough would increase the number of those who live to adulthood.

A Changing World While many areas of the world are breaking up politically, at the same time they are becoming more connected economically. Few nations have the resources to make all the goods their people need and want. As a result, most countries today are part of a network of international trade.

In this new global economy, **multinational companies,** or companies that operate across national boundaries, are playing a growing role. Many countries are banding together to form trading blocs. The European Community (EC), sometimes known as the Common Market, is an economic organization of Western European nations. Its goal is to create greater economic and political cooperation among member nations. The United States, Canada, and Mexico are creating a similar trading bloc through the North American Free Trade Agreement (NAFTA).

A global economy involves global communication. Satellites now link telephones and fax machines around the world. Information is flowing faster as more sophisticated computers are built. A global culture is also developing.

Many people see hope for the future in globalization. After all, many of the world's problems are global and can only be solved with worldwide cooperation.

MULTINATIONAL PIZZA This Moscow restaurant was opened through investment by a U.S. company. Businesses opened by foreign companies help Russia's economy grow. **Why do most nations want to be connected to others economically?**

CAPTION ANSWER

Few nations have the resources to make all the goods their people need and want.

MAKING CONNECTIONS

➤➤ **Economics** While welcoming the benefits of multinational companies, countries frequently resent the loss of control that occurs when business ventures originate beyond their borders. Such economic linkages, however, can have its advantages. Interlocked economic fortunes ensure that the destiny of one country is increasingly tied to those of other countries. Such ties among nations might serve as a deterrent to war.

ASSESS

CHECK FOR UNDERSTANDING

Ask students to summarize the main points of the chapter, orally or in writing. Discuss the answers to the Section and Chapter Review questions.

EVALUATE

Assign the Chapter 39 **Performance Assessment Activity** in the TCR.

Administer the **Chapter 39 Test**. Testmaker available.

EXTENDING THE CONTENT

Controversies over the North American Free Trade Agreement were raised in the United States. For example, some people believed that American jobs would shift to Mexico where labor is cheaper. Others argued that the productivity of labor in the United States is high, and that the loss of jobs would be offset by creating greater demand for exports to Mexico as its level of income rises.

RETEACH

Have students work in pairs to decide on the main points studied in each section of this chapter. Then have the class agree on the main points.

Assign the Chapter 39 **Reteaching Activity** in the TCR.

ENRICH

Have students prepare a proposal to the board of directors of a fast-food company outlining plans to open branches in another country and explaining the benefits and risks of such a venture.

Assign the Chapter 39 **Enrichment Activity** in the TCR.

CLOSE

Have students evaluate the following statement, "The world has become a global village, and no country can be an island unto itself."

MEETING CHAPTER OBJECTIVES

Each objective is tested by the Review questions in parentheses.

1. Discuss Eastern Europe after the collapse of communism. (CU 1, 2, 3; CT 1)

2. Describe how European countries turned toward capitalism. (BV; CT 1)

3. Explain why world tensions developed after the cold war ended. (BV; CU 4, 5, 6, 7; UYJ)

4. Examine the world challenges of the twenty-first century. (BV; CU 9; CT 3, 4; GH; UYJ)

Section 3 Review

1. **Identify:** Green Revolution, Earth Summit, Acquired Immune Deficiency Syndrome (AIDS), European Community (EC), North American Free Trade Agreement (NAFTA)
2. **Define:** habitats, greenhouse effect, communicable diseases, multinational companies
3. Why are scientists afraid that food production will not keep pace with the growing population?
4. Why are scientists concerned over the destruction of the tropical rain forests?
5. What communicable diseases threaten world health?

Critical Thinking

6. In what ways is your area of the world developing a global culture?

Chapter Summary

1. Between 1989 and 1991, communism collapsed in Europe and the cold war came to an end.
2. In 1989, Hungary opened its border with Austria. The Berlin Wall was opened and later torn down.
3. In Poland change came about peacefully as Solidarity gained control of the national legislature. In Romania, dictator Ceausescu was ousted and executed.
4. In the Soviet Union, Mikhail Gorbachev shut down the Communist Party. Later that year the Soviet Union itself dissolved.
5. The unification of East and West Germany has been accompanied by such problems as unemployment and the rise of right-wing political parties supporting Nazism.
6. In the Persian Gulf, Iraq's invasion of Kuwait in 1991 led the United States to attack and defeat Iraq.
7. Since 1991, Yugoslavia's six ethnically mixed republics have been in conflict.
8. In Somalia and Haiti, United Nations peacekeepers tried to protect the people.
9. In the Middle East, negotiations between Israel and the Palestine Liberation Organization have led to a plan providing self-rule for the Palestinian Arabs.
10. In South Africa, the election of Frederick W. de Klerk led to the end of apartheid and to political and economic reforms.
11. The destruction of tropical rain forests, the greenhouse effect, and the disposal of wastes are environmental problems facing the world.
12. In the year 2000, the world faces the challenges of feeding a growing population, protecting the environment, and improving health care.

SECTION 3 ANSWERS

1. Green Revolution, advanced farming (p. 658); Earth Summit, economic environmental meeting (p. 659); AIDS, disease caused by HIV (p. 660); European Community, European trading bloc (p. 661); NAFTA, trading bloc of the U.S., Canada, and Mexico (p. 661)
2. habitats, dwelling places (p. 658); greenhouse effect, warming caused by pollution (p. 659); communicable diseases, diseases that are spread (p. 659); multinational companies, companies operating in other nations (p. 661)
3. Most available land is being farmed and overused.
4. because habitats are being destroyed and the amount of carbon dioxide in the atmosphere is increasing
5. cholera, malaria, tuberculosis, AIDS
6. Answers will vary.

Assign the Chapter 39 **Section 3 Quiz** in the TCR. Testmaker available.

CHAPTER

Review 39

Building Vocabulary

Write an newspaper editorial describing the most important challenges facing the world today. Use the following words in your editorial.

privatize
apartheid
habitats
greenhouse effect
multinational companies
communicable diseases

Check for Understanding

1. Why was the Berlin Wall opened and later taken down?
2. How did communism end in Romania?
3. How does the Commonwealth of Independent States differ from the Soviet Union?
4. What was the outcome of the Gulf War?
5. What was the role of the United Nations in Bosnia-Herzegovina?
6. What was the cause of the crisis in Somalia?
7. What has led to the negotiations for peace in the Middle East?
8. What was life like for black people in South Africa under apartheid?
9. Why was the Green Revolution not successful in solving the food shortage in developing countries?

Critical Thinking

1. Why do you think many of the former Soviet nations are moving toward democracy slowly, rather than quickly?
2. How would you try to solve the crisis in Somalia?
3. How do you think developing nations might solve their health problems?
4. What do you think the following statement means: The world is getting smaller. Do you agree or disagree? Why?

Geography in History

REGIONS Look at the World Population map on page 657. Scientists are predicting great increases in population by the year 2100. In what regions would you expect this growth to occur? Explain.

Using Your Journal

Review the details you have noted about the challenges facing the world. Imagine that you are a world leader attending a global conference in which you are presenting the world problems that you consider to be most important. Choose the three most important problems and write a plan explaining what solutions you would offer.

CHAPTER 39 REVIEW ANSWERS

BUILDING VOCABULARY

Editorials will vary, but students should use all the vocabulary words and support their opinions with reasons.

CHECK FOR UNDERSTANDING

1. when it no longer could keep Berliners in and when communism ended
2. with violence and the execution of the dictator
3. It is an organization of independent nations.
4. Iraq lost and had to leave Kuwait.
5. as peacekeepers and to help protect civilians being killed
6. hunger, poverty, and civil war
7. the *intifada* and the Gulf War
8. They were not allowed to vote, or other basic freeedoms.
9. These countries could not afford the fertilizers and equipment needed.

CRITICAL THINKING

1. Answers will vary, but students might indicate that the nations are overcoming many years of communism.
2. Answers will vary, but students should indicate specifics.
3. Answers will vary but students should give specific examples of preventative measures.
4. Answers will vary.

+ BONUS +

TEST QUESTION

For Chapter 39 Test

Think about the following challenges facing the world today, rank each, and explain your rankings: producing enough food, protecting the environment, and improving health care. *(Answers will vary.)*

USING YOUR JOURNAL

Plans will vary, but students should indicate specific ways that they would solve the problems. Have volunteers share their plans.

GEOGRAPHY IN HISTORY

Answers may vary but should indicate areas already heavy populated to become more heavily populated, such as: Europe, Asia, India, NE United States, West Africa, and the east coast of South America.

EMERGING DEMOCRACY

FOCUS

OBJECTIVES

Locate countries in which recent government reorganizations have taken place. Identify the kinds of recent changes that have taken place in many governments in the Eastern Hemisphere.

BELLRINGER

Ask students to write down the names of the countries in the Eastern Hemisphere that have gone through changes in the last five years.

MOTIVATIONAL ACTIVITY

Have students share the names of the countries they came up with, having a volunteer list them on the chalkboard. Then explain that in this Culture Close-Up they will learn about the dramatic changes in governments in the Eastern Hemisphere during the last quarter of the twentieth century.

UNIT 12 CULTURE CLOSE-UP

Emerging Democracy

"Democracy" and "dramatic change" were the guide words for the Eastern Hemisphere in the last quarter of the twentieth century.

Geography Connection

Across the Eastern Hemisphere, government reorganizations took place that changed the face of world politics forever.

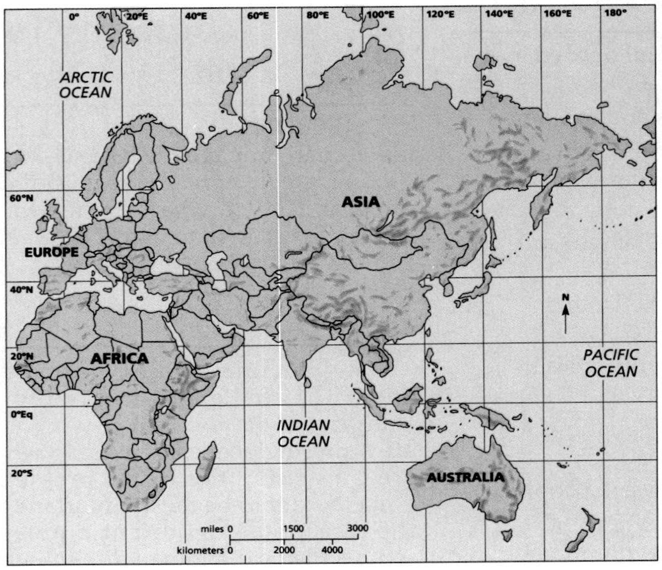

▲ As these Romanians did in 1989, people in one Eastern European nation after another raised their voices demanding the right to govern themselves.

664

MEETING SPECIAL NEEDS

If possible, arrange for a senior citizen of your community, perhaps a member of a student's family, to visit the class and recall political changes that person has witnessed in his or her lifetime. Summarize the major political breakthroughs and changes students expect to see in their lifetimes. This discussion of political changes will help auditory learners recognize the main ideas of the Culture Close-Up.

The communist Soviet Union dissolved into independent states in 1991. Free elections in its former republics, such as Azerbaijan, allowed voting for the first time in decades. ▶

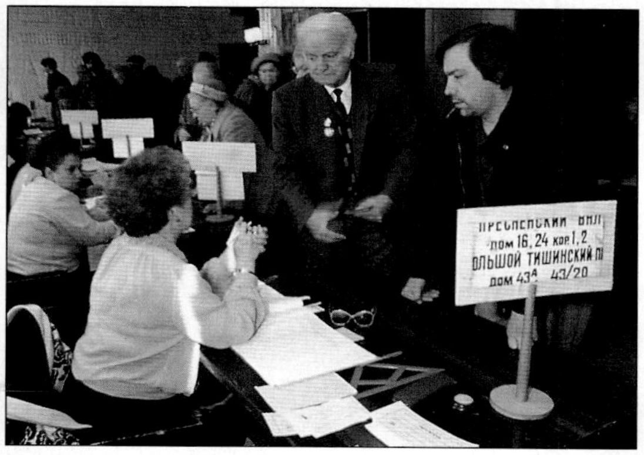

▲ In 1993 Russians voted in a free election for the first time in 75 years.

People in Ukraine also achieved their independence and the right to control their country's government. ▶

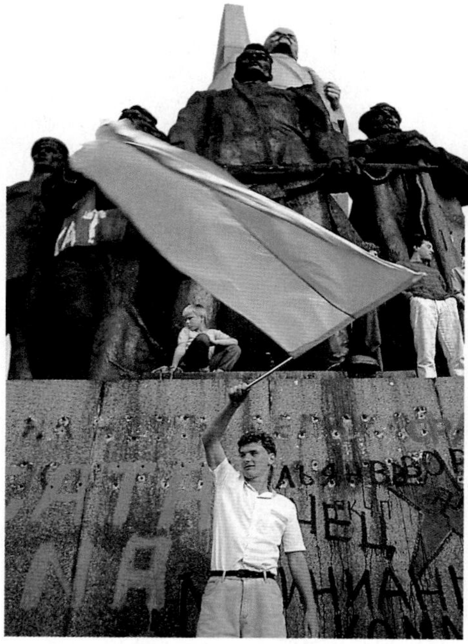

TEACH

L1 **Geography: Location** Ask students to use the map of the Eastern Hemisphere on page 664 to locate the countries discussed in the motivational activity that have taken dramatic steps towards democracy in recent years. LEP

L3 **Critical Thinking** Have students respond to the following question: Based on current trends, what kind of world order do you think might emerge after the year 2000?

EXTENDING THE CONTENT

As president of the Russian republic, Boris Yeltsin negotiated treaties between Russia and other former Soviet republics. He hoped to see his nation become a voluntary commonwealth of equal states. During an interview in late 1990, Yeltsin wondered, "This raises the question, do we need a central government at all?" He cited the European Community as a model, where sovereign states maintain their autonomy, but delegate supranational authority over trade and defense issues to a weaker central bureaucracy in Brussels, Belgium. Yeltsin's words indicated that he knew that the road to political reform is not an easy one: "I belong to those who are prepared to take the route with potholes and have no fear of the risks."

UNIT 12 CULTURE CLOSE-UP

L3 **Critical Thinking** Have students research to find out about the changes in the daily lives of the people in the nations that made up the former Soviet Union, since its dissolution. Students might make charts to compare and contrast the changes in daily life by country since they are diverse. Have students share their charts with the class. LEP

GLOBAL READING FOR STUDENTS

Students in your class may be interested in reading about changes in the governments in Eastern Europe. Suggest *The Commonwealth of Independent States and Central/Eastern Europe: Global Studies* by Milton F. Goldman, Dushkin, 1992. (Challenging/Nonfiction)

In Germany, the breaking down of the Berlin Wall in 1989 brought reaction from all parts of the world. Since that time, a united Federal Republic of Germany has been building a new economy. ▶

◀ Poland held its first free election, since its communist takeover, in June of 1989. The country then moved quickly to establish an economy based on privately-owned business.

These women sorting fresh eggs are part of Hungary's growing free economy. ▶

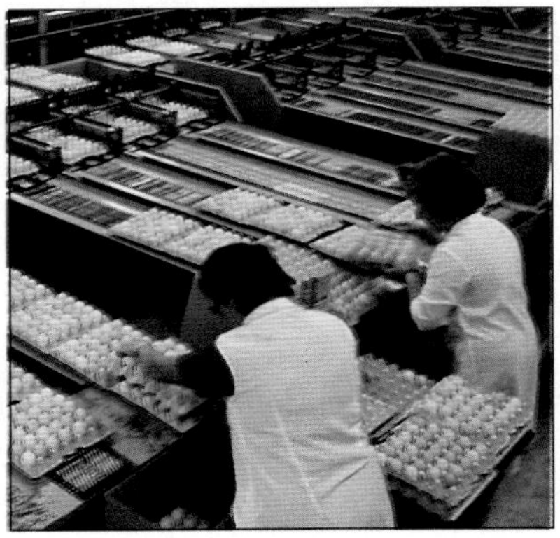

COOPERATIVE LEARNING

Have students work in groups to prepare a video presentation on the countries or regions discussed in this Culture Close-Up, including the nations of the former Soviet Union, Romania, Germany, Poland, Hungary, Eritrea, and China. Each group should research the political changes that have occurred in their area since 1989, prepare a script that explains the changes, and cooperate in filming their segment of the video. When segments have been filmed, have a member from each group serve on a committee that plans and executes the introduction to the video.

CULTURE CLOSE-UP

UNIT 12

▲ Africa also made democratic advances. In 1993 Eritrea achieved its independence from Ethiopia. Then, South Africa held its first election ever in which blacks were allowed to vote.

▲ Human rights are still an issue, however, in China, the largest stronghold of communism left in the Eastern Hemisphere. Many people protested in Tiananmen Square in 1989.

Taking Another Look

1. **What part of Europe was most affected by changing governments?**
2. **What happened to the organization of the Soviet Union in 1991?**
3. **From whom did Eritrea achieve its independence?**

Critical Thinking

4. **Why do you think so many countries in Europe moved toward democracy at the same time?**

ASSESS

CHECK FOR UNDERSTANDING

Have students answer the questions in Taking Another Look on page 667.

ANSWERS to Taking Another Look

1. Eastern Europe
2. It dissolved into independent states.
3. Ethiopia
4. Answers will vary. Students might note that increased interdependence among all nations of the world has helped create changes in governments.

ENRICH

Discuss with students the meaning of the phrase *global citizen* and how it applies to each of them.

CLOSE

Ask students to discuss the possible difficulties that might occur as nations change from communism to democracy.

MEETING SPECIAL NEEDS

The pace of recent political changes has been very fast. Help students visualize these changes by asking them to make a time line on the bulletin board listing the changes discussed in this Culture Close-Up. Encourage them to include visuals.

PHOTO CREDITS

ARTISTS: Barbara White; Sam MacKenzie-Crane.
MAPS: June Barnes; Circle Design/Peter Getz (Locators); Mapping Specialists (Updated); Intergraphics, Maryland Cartographics Inc., R.R. Donnelley & Sons Co.

PHOTOS: American Museum of Natural History: 140, 142. **American Numismatic Society:** 126. **Ancient Art & Architecture Collection:** 203(tr), 204(t), 205(c,b), 310(tr), 311(t) Allan Eaton; 312(tl) B. Norman; 145(b), 205(t), 310(br), 311(bl,br), 312(r), 313, 426(r), 428(bl) Ronald Sheridan. **ARAMCO:** 335(l). **Art Resource, NY:** 86, 383 Borromeo; 262, 484 Bridgeman; 274 D.Y.; 95(t), 361(t,b), 362(t,b), 427(c), 429(c), 538(c), 539(tr) Werner Forman; 138(t) Fotofilms SA; 54, 69, 70(l), 100, 255(l,r), 277(b), 279, 319(b), 364, 402, 440(b), 454, 460, 502, 514, 515, 519(r), 560, 569, 570 Giraudon; 66, 116, 192, 316, 432 Erich Lessing; 138(b) O'Neill; 26, 162, 171(t), 178, 183, 188(b), 208, 218, 224, 227(t), 243(b), 248(b), 252, 267(b), 277(t), 280, 349(t), 386(t), 434(b), 451, 457(r), 458, 519(l) Scala; 76, 188(t), 212, 563(b), 583(r) SEF. **Arxiu Mas:** 491(r). **Dirk Bakker:** 94(t), 95(b), 96(c,b), 97(t,b). **The Bettmann Archive:** 112(t), 154, 158, 164, 166, 197, 295, 385(t), 387, 388, 410, 448, 469, 612, 614, 631(l). **Vladimir Bibic:** 68. **Biblioteca Trivuziana, Milan:** 421. **Black Star:** 628(t) Dennis Brack; 152(b) Dan J. McCoy; 659 Claus Meyer; 480(br) Charles Moore; 666 Christopher Morris; 658 Klaus Reisinger; 649 Daniel Sheehan; 305 Ted Spiegel; 638(l) James Sugar; 611, 632, 665 (t,b) Peter Turnley. **Ira Block:** 28(r); **Bodleian Library, Oxford:** 343, 439. **Ruth Bogart:** 61(t). **E.Bohm Mainz:** 123. **Lee Boltin:** i(l,r), v(c), vi(c), 38, 60, 82, 128, 133, 146(t), 246, 258(br), 259; 260(tr,br), 261, 312(bl), 428(tl), 429(t), 481(b), 539(tl), 540(tr,bl). **Bowdoin College of Art Museum:** 513; **Norma Brenneman:** 371. **The Bridgeman Art Library:** 102. **The British Library, London:** 112(b), 372(r). **The British Museum:** 72, 137, 159, 213(b), 268(r), 301(b), 368(t), 373(b), 490. **Zdenek Buriam:** 34, 42. **Circle Design:** 375 Carol Spengel; **City of Sheffield, England:** 532. **Peter Clayton:** 155(b), 211, 225(t). **Holden Collection/Cleveland Museum of Art:** 437. **Peter Connolly:** 172. **Conoco Inc:** 20(l). **DRK Photo:** 51(t) Melinda Berge; 204(c) Tom Bledsoe; 202(b) Stanley Breeden; 204(b) Fred Bruemmer; 49(tr,bl) John Cancalosi; 203(tl) R.J. Erwin; 48(br) M.P. Kahl; 203(c) Stephen J. Krasemann; 597(t), 599(b) Peter D. Pickford; 48(c) Tom Till; 48(t), 51(b), 203(b) Belinda Wright. **Dumbarton Oaks:** 319(t). **Copyright Reserved to Her Majesty Queen Elizabeth II:** 456(b), 507. **Mary Evans Picture Library:** 180(l), 185(t); 195(t) J. Chapman. **File Photo:** 103(t), 110, 194, 210(b), 272, 278, 285(t), 291, 325, 352, 354, 372(l), 386(b), 393(b), 407(t), 435(l), 471, 474, 509, 535, 575, 606; 443(t) Bob Kellar Collection. **Kevin Fleming:** 157. **Folger Shakespeare Library:** 443(b), 444(r),445(r). **Werner Forman:** 131(t). **FPG International:** 185(b), 613, 615; 563(t) Jules Talon; 620 (inset) US Air Force Photo. **David R. Frazier, Photolibrary:** 7. **Freer Gallery of Art:** 91(l), 336, 338, 342. **Eugene Gilliom:** 153, 175, 199(r), 210(t), 348. **Giraudon, Paris:** 412. **THE GRANGER COLLECTION, New York:** v(b), vi(b), vii(c), 25(r), 50(tr), 64, 118, 120, 131(b), 150, 155(t), 169, 170, 195(b), 220, 223, 229(b), 242, 243(t), 253(t), 285(b), 288, 292(t), 302, 303, 346, 357, 366, 369(t,b), 373(t), 374, 376, 380, 384(l), 398, 401(t,b), 403, 404, 405, 407(b), 413, 415(b), 416, 423, 452, 466, 468, 492, 493, 495, 506(l), 508, 516, 517, 522, 525(t), 526, 528, 530, 542, 546(b), 562, 568, 573, 574, 578, 580, 581, 582, 592, 593, 604, 608, 609, 616, 621, 634(t). **Susan Griggs Agency:** 136 Mike St. Maur Sheil; **Courtesy of Gulf Oil Corp:** 20(r). **Robert Harding Picture Library:** 6, 538(t); 540(tl) Michael Botham; 18 Robert Francis; 276 John Gardey; 132 Geoff Renner; 539(b) Adam Woolfitt. **Hawaii Visitors Bureau:** 591. **Hirmer Fotoarchiv:** 61(b), 63. **Historical Pictures Service, Chicago:** 88, 184, 222(b), 227(b), 266, 268(l), 282, 355, 368(b), 384(r), 389, 419, 445(l), 453, 455, 470, 473, 505, 518, 533, 546(t), 557, 566, 583(l), 584. **Michael Holford:** 122, 167, 171(b), 199(l), 225(b), 248(t), 406, 457(l), 585; 28(l) Gerry Clyde. **The Image Bank/Chicago:** vi(t) Guido Alberto Rossi; 98 Steve Dunwell; 298 Ric Meola. **Imperial War Museum, James Prinsep Beadle:** 602. **Courtesy of Institute of History & Philology, China:** 91(l). **Jeronimos Church, Lisbon:** 488. **Wolfgang Kaehler:** iv(t), 43, 600, 634(b). **Timothy Kendall/Museum of Fine Arts:** 130. **Knudsen Information Center:** 301(t). **Lennart Larsen/Frances Lincoln Publishers:** 300. **Library of Congress:** 441, 444(l), 510(b), 531, 547, 588, 589. **Library of Istanbul Univ:** 393(t). **The Louvre:** 435(r). **Magnum Photos:** 94(br), 480(tr) ; 481(t,c), 482 (c,b), 483(t) Bruno Barbey; 32, 39, 260(l) René Burri; 70(r) Elliott Erwitt; 16 Steve McCurry; 483(b) Inge Morath; 482(t) Marc Riboud; 540(br), 541(t,b) Dennis Stock. **Doug Martin:** 249. **George Matchneer:** 9. **The Metropolitan Museum of Art:** 73(t), 186, 417; 111 Rogers Fund, 1913; 74 Rogers Fund and Edward S. Harkness Gift, 1929. **©Musees Nationaux:** 418. **Museu Paulista, Universite de Sao Paulo:** 556. **N.Y. Convention & Visitors Bureau:** 14(b). **Collection of The New-York Historical Society:** 476. **N.Y. Library/Astor, Lennox & Tilden Foundations:** 497. **National Army Museum:** 605. **National Cowboy Hall of Fame & Western Heritage Center:** 544. **National Gallery of Art:** 236, 250, 253(b), 351(l), 395, 440(t),. **©National Geographic Society, Painting by:** 320 Andre Durenceau; 318, 450 Michael Hampshire; 238 Birney Lettick; 107, 182, 198, 307, 414 Tom Lovell; 392 Robert W. Nicholson. **National Maritime Museum:** 459. **National Museum of Ireland:** 290(t,b). **National Park Service:** 14(t). **National Portrait Gallery:** 456(t). **The National Trust/A.C. Cooper:** 293. **Don Nieman:** 382. **North Wind Picture Archives:** 109, 221, 229(t), 269, 292(b), 415(t), 553. **Robert Frerck/Odyssey:** 640. **Ohio Dept. of Natural Resources/Dept. of Reclamation:** 21(l,r). **Orbis Book Publishing Corp. Ltd./Owen Wood:** 510(t). **Organization of American States:** 552, 554. **Courtesy of The Oriental Institute Museum, The Univ. of Chicago:** 58 photographed by Victor J. Boswell, Jr., National Geographic Society. **Courtesy of Parke Davis & Co:** 79, 339. **Peabody Museum:** 139. **Photo Researchers:** 420 ARCHIV; 124 George Holton; 598(br) Hubertus Kanus; 8(r) Will & Deni McIntyre/The National Audubon Society Collection; 29, 36(t) John Reader/Science Source; 596(r) Mitch Reardon; 8(l) Lawrence Schiller/Science Source; 2 Science Source. **C.M. Dixon/Photo Resources:** 152(t), 213(t), 214, 326. **PHOTOTRI:** 180(r). **Pierpont Morgan Library:** 283(l). **Courtesy of the Pilgrim Society, Plymouth, Massachusetts**: 486. **Enoch Pratt Free Library:** 496(b). **Reuters/Bettman** 624. **H. Armstrong Roberts:** 496(t). **Roger-Viollet:** 36. **Royal Ontario Museum:** 174. **SABA:** 661 Ricki Rosen; 644 Shepard Sherbell. **San Antonio Convention & Visitors Bureau:** 491(l). **Sheridan Photo Library:** 45; 50(tl), 283(r) B. Norman. **George Silk, Life Magazine © Time Warner:** 620. **SIPA Press:** 650 Aral; 667 Robert Papstein; 656 Jacques Witt. **Smithsonian Institution:** 527, 529; 597(b) photograph by FRANKO KHOURY, photographer UNKNOWN 598(l) National Museum of African Art, Eliot Elisofon Archives. **SOVFOTO:** 610. **Stanley Seaberg:** 226. **STOCK MONTAGE:** 264, 390, 571. **Superstock:** 232 S. Barrow; 96 A. Briere; 121 S. Fiore; 206 M Howell; vii Pablo Prints; 314, 330 K. Scholz; 430 Sistine Chapel/Bridgeman Art Library, London; 168 S. Vidler; 361 Courtesy of the Board of Trustees of the Victoria & Albert Museum/Bridgeman Art Library, London. **SYGMA:** 628(b), 651; vii(b) Regis Bossu; 647, 665 Georges De Keerle; 639(b) Paulo Fridman; 666(c) Grochowiak/SAS; 652 Jon Jones; 667 J. Langevin; 664 Orban; 666(b) Photoplus; 653 Patrick Robert; 641 Oscar Sabetta; 627, 654 Les Stone; 660 Allan Tannenbaum; 646 Zadora. **Tass News Agency:** 633. **Tom Stack & Assoc:** 631(r); 548 George Schneegass. **Tony Stone Images/Chicago:** 639(t) Ian Murphy. **Tretyakov Gallery, Moscow:** 349(b). **U.S. Coast Guard Photo–Courtesy of the National Archives:** 618. **Uniphoto:** iv(b), v(t).**UPI/Bettmann:** 626, 630, 636. **Vatican Museum:** 187, 215, 234. **Jean Vertut:** 40. **Victoria & Albert Museum, London:** 534. **Leonardo da Vinci Museum:** 434(t). **Virginia Museum:** 512. **Vision International:** 85, 335(r), 340, 351(r) Pablo Koch; 78 Tetrel Explorer. **Walters Art Gallery, Baltimore:** 267(t). **Wan-Go Weng:** 90. **Westlight:** 23 Comnet; iv(c), 49(tl,br), 50(b), 52, 71, 148, 254, 258(tr) Dallas & John Heaton; 202(t) Brian Vikander. **James Westwater:** 525(b). **Laurie Platt Winfrey, Inc.:** 145(c), 146(c), 427(b), 586; 144, 147 The Avery Brundage Collection; 321 Biblioteca Vaticano; 362, 363 Bibliotheque Nationale, Chinois; 360(b) Bibliotheque Nationale; 461 Chester Beatty Library; 427(t) Fujiwara Takanobu Jingogi, Kyoto; 587 Metropolitan Museum of Art; 428(r) Okura Shukokan Museum, Tokyo; 145(t) 146(b) Seattle Museum; 598(tr) Sterling Memorial Library, Yale University; 147, 429(b) Tokyo National Museum. **Woodfin Camp & Associates:** 333 Robert Azzi; 635 Jehangir Gazdar; 599(t) Piero Guerrini; 12 Mike Maple; 4 Michael S. Yamashita.

APPENDIX

ATLAS 670-680

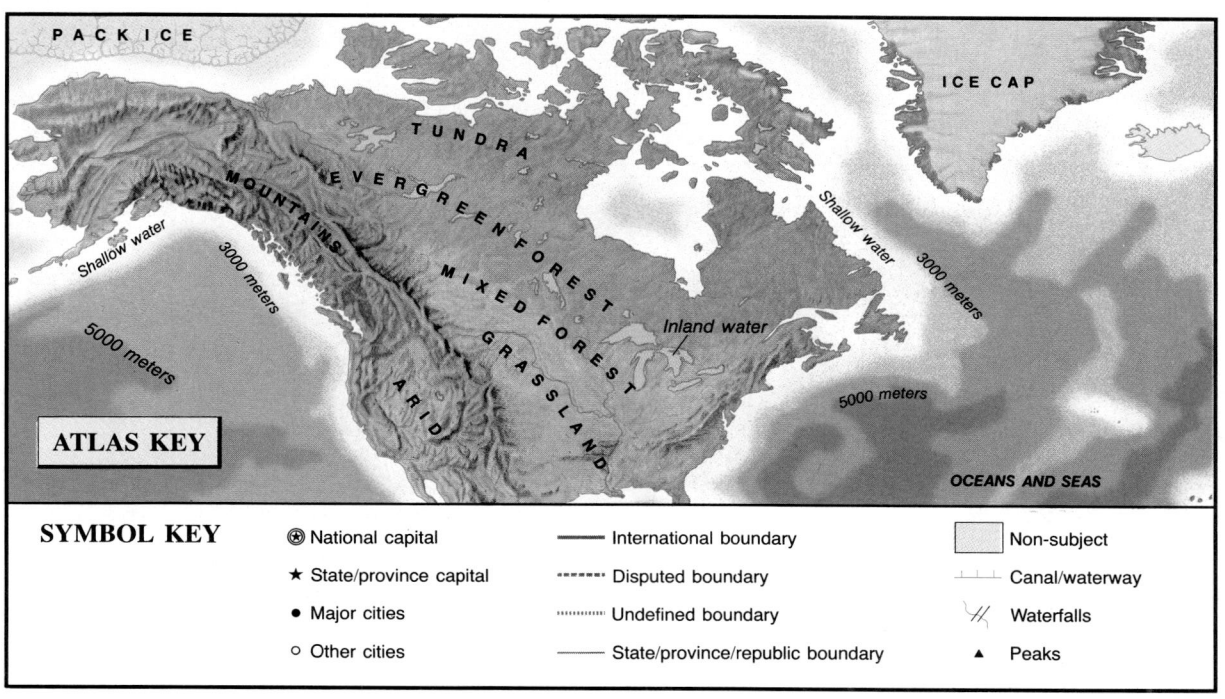

GLOSSARY 681-689

INDEX 690-696

ATLAS KEY

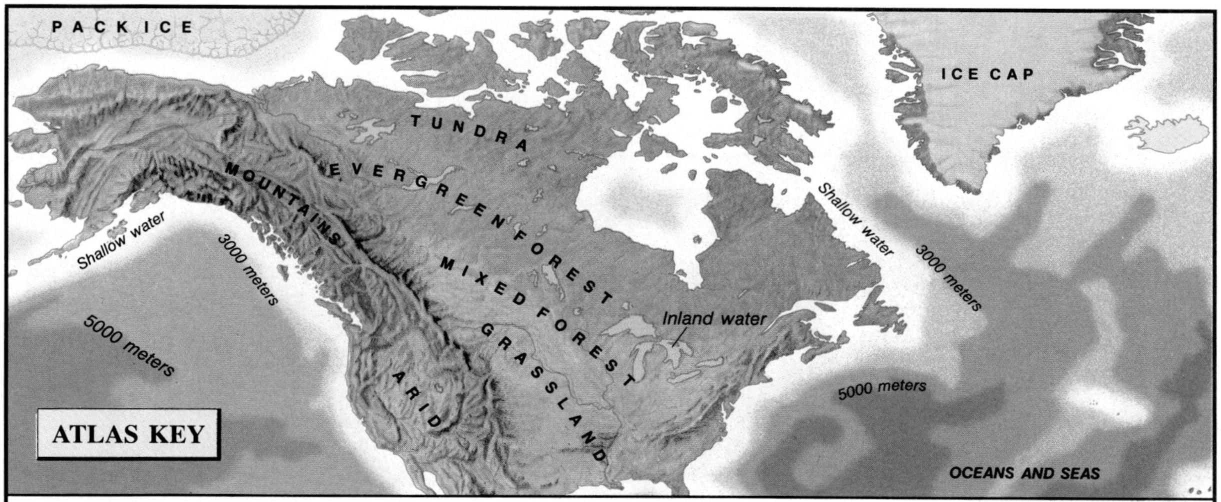

SYMBOL KEY

⊛ National capital	International boundary	Non-subject
★ State/province capital	Disputed boundary	Canal/waterway
● Major cities	Undefined boundary	Waterfalls
○ Other cities	State/province/republic boundary	▲ Peaks

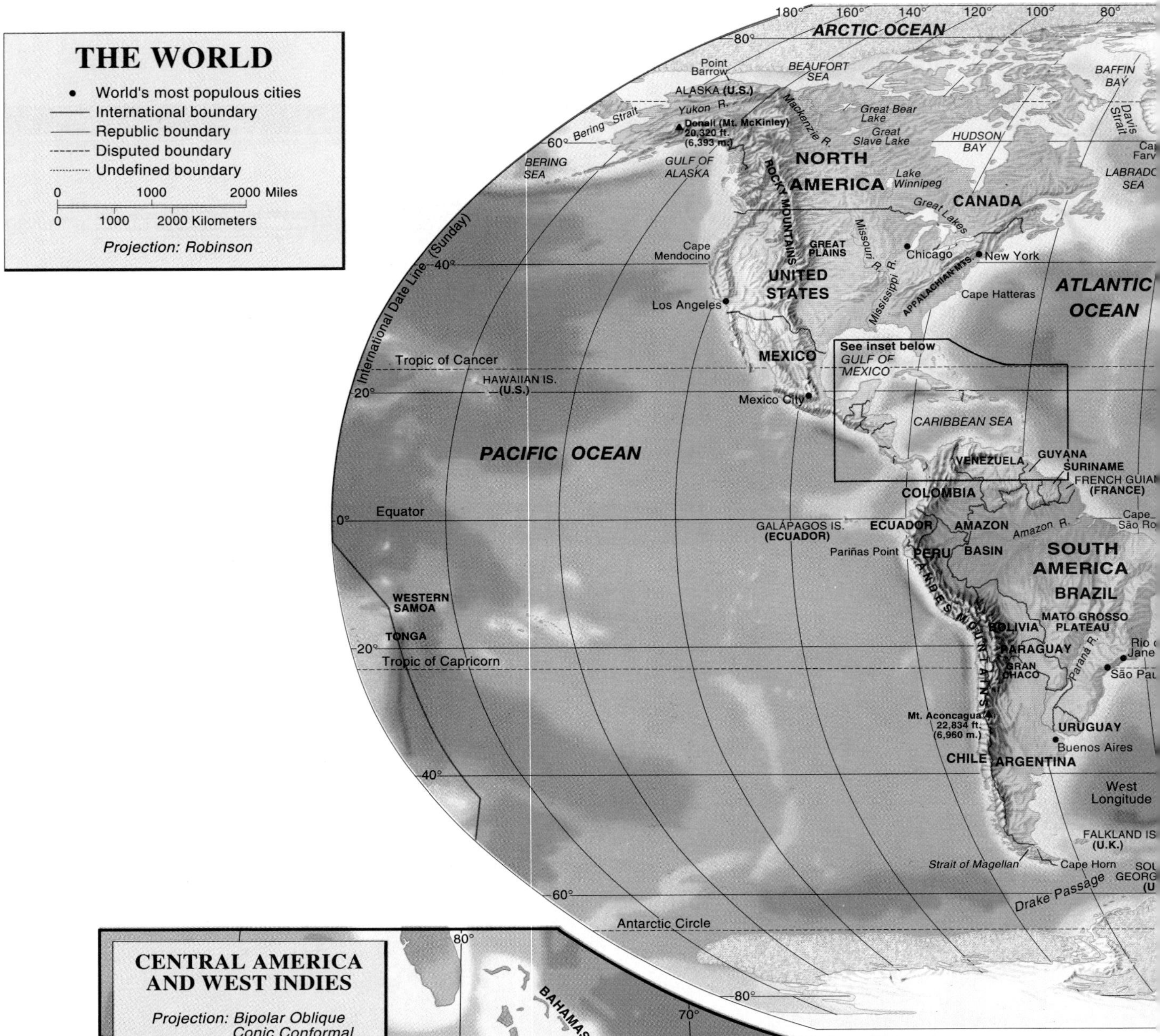
THE WORLD
World's most populous cities
International boundary
Republic boundary
Disputed boundary
Undefined boundary
0 1000 2000 Miles
0 1000 2000 Kilometers
Projection: Robinson
ARCTIC OCEAN
180° 160° 140° 120° 100° 80°
80°
Point Barrow
BEAUFORT SEA
BAFFIN BAY
ALASKA (U.S.)
Yukon R.
Mackenzie R.
Great Bear Lake
Davis Strait
Bering Strait
Denali (Mt. McKinley) 20,320 ft. (6,393 m.)
Great Slave Lake
HUDSON BAY
60°
BERING SEA
GULF OF ALASKA
NORTH AMERICA
ROCKY MOUNTAINS
Lake Winnipeg
LABRADOR SEA
CANADA
Great Lakes
International Date Line (Sunday)
Cape Mendocino
GREAT PLAINS
Missouri R.
Chicago
New York
40°
UNITED STATES
Mississippi R.
APPALACHIAN MTS.
ATLANTIC OCEAN
Los Angeles
Cape Hatteras
MEXICO
See inset below
GULF OF MEXICO
Tropic of Cancer
HAWAIIAN IS. (U.S.)
20°
Mexico City
CARIBBEAN SEA
PACIFIC OCEAN
VENEZUELA
GUYANA
SURINAME
FRENCH GUIANA (FRANCE)
COLOMBIA
Equator
0°
GALÁPAGOS IS. (ECUADOR)
ECUADOR
AMAZON BASIN
Amazon R.
Cape São Roque
Pariñas Point
PERU
SOUTH AMERICA
BRAZIL
ANDES MOUNTAINS
WESTERN SAMOA
MATO GROSSO PLATEAU
BOLIVIA
TONGA
PARAGUAY
Paraná R.
Rio de Janeiro
20°
Tropic of Capricorn
GRAN CHACO
São Paulo
Mt. Aconcagua 22,834 ft. (6,960 m.)
URUGUAY
Buenos Aires
CHILE
ARGENTINA
40°
West Longitude
FALKLAND IS. (U.K.)
Strait of Magellan
Cape Horn
SOUTH GEORGIA (U.K.)
60°
Drake Passage
Antarctic Circle
80°

CENTRAL AMERICA AND WEST INDIES
Projection: Bipolar Oblique Conic Conformal
80°
BAHAMAS
70°
Tropic of Cancer
60°
GULF OF MEXICO
CUBA
TURKS AND CAICOS IS. (U.K.)
ATLANTIC OCEAN
20°
VIRGIN ISLANDS (U.S. AND U.K.)
HAITI
DOMINICAN REPUBLIC
ANTIGUA AND BARBUDA
MEXICO
BELIZE
JAMAICA
PUERTO RICO (U.S.)
ST. KITTS AND NEVIS
GUADELOUPE (FRANCE)
DOMINICA
GUATEMALA
MARTINIQUE (FRANCE)
HONDURAS
CARIBBEAN SEA
N
ST. LUCIA
ST. VINCENT AND THE GRENADINES
EL SALVADOR
BARBADOS
GRENADA
PACIFIC OCEAN
NICARAGUA
ARUBA (NETHERLANDS)
NETHERLANDS ANTILLES (NETHERLANDS)
TRINIDAD AND TOBAGO
10°
COSTA RICA
0 250 500 Miles
0 250 500 Kilometers
VENEZUELA
PANAMA
COLOMBIA
GUYANA
90°
80°

670

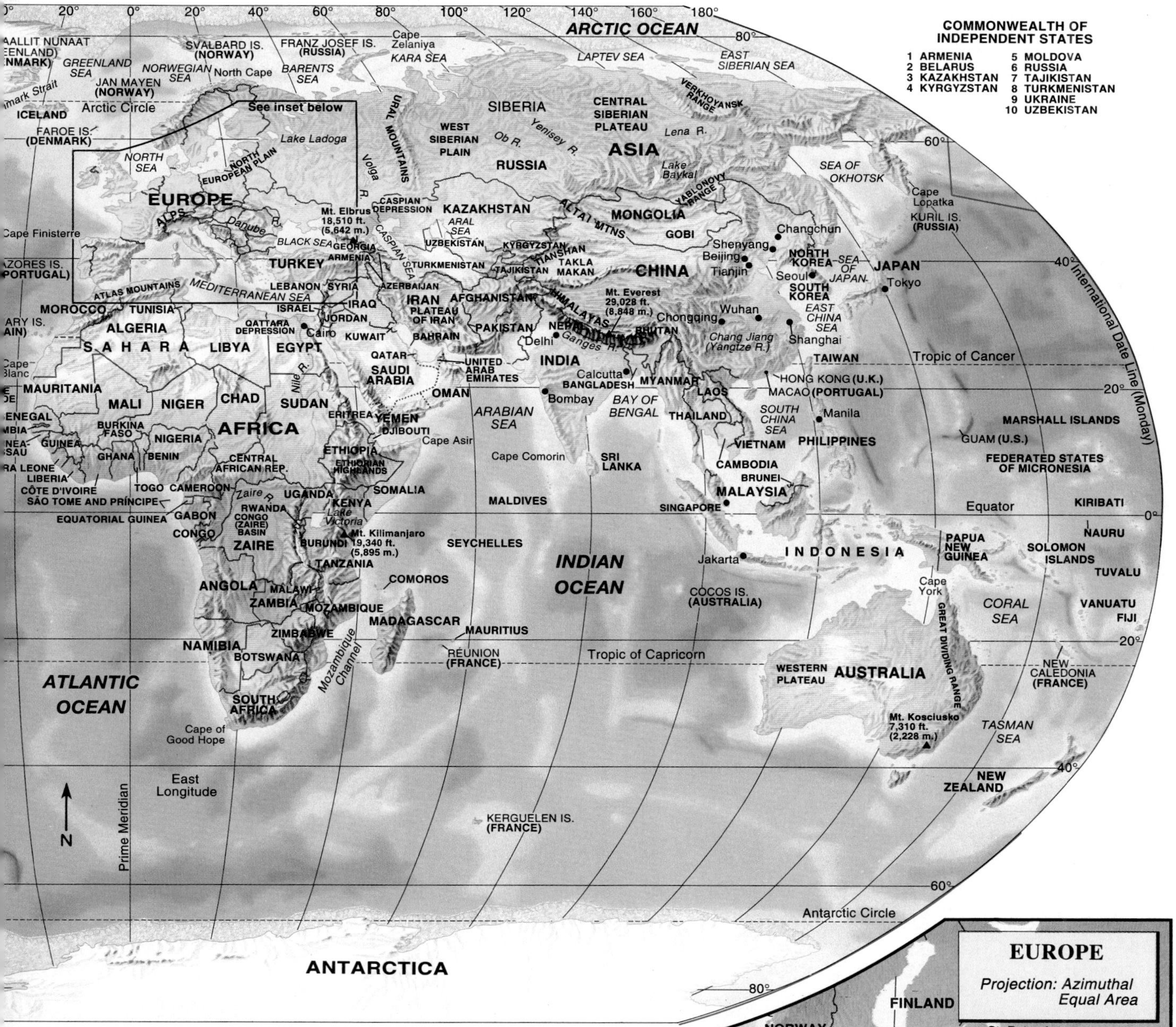

COMMONWEALTH OF INDEPENDENT STATES
1 ARMENIA
2 BELARUS
3 KAZAKHSTAN
4 KYRGYZSTAN
5 MOLDOVA
6 RUSSIA
7 TAJIKISTAN
8 TURKMENISTAN
9 UKRAINE
10 UZBEKISTAN
20°
0°
20°
40°
60°
80°
100°
120°
140°
160°
180°
ARCTIC OCEAN
80°
SVALBARD IS. (NORWAY)
FRANZ JOSEF IS. (RUSSIA)
Cape Zelaniya
KARA SEA
LAPTEV SEA
EAST SIBERIAN SEA
GREENLAND SEA
NORWEGIAN SEA
North Cape
BARENTS SEA
JAN MAYEN (NORWAY)
ICELAND
Arctic Circle
See inset below
FAROE IS. (DENMARK)
Lake Ladoga
URAL MOUNTAINS
SIBERIA
WEST SIBERIAN PLAIN
CENTRAL SIBERIAN PLATEAU
VERKHOYANSK RANGE
Ob R.
Yenisey R.
Lena R.
ASIA
RUSSIA
60°
NORTH SEA
NORTH EUROPEAN PLAIN
Volga R.
Lake Baykal
YABLONOVYY RANGE
SEA OF OKHOTSK
Cape Lopatka
KURIL IS. (RUSSIA)
EUROPE
ALPS
Danube
Mt. Elbrus 18,510 ft. (5,642 m.)
CASPIAN DEPRESSION
KAZAKHSTAN
ARAL SEA
ALTAI MTNS.
MONGOLIA
GOBI
Changchun
Cape Finisterre
BLACK SEA
GEORGIA
ARMENIA
CASPIAN SEA
UZBEKISTAN
KYRGYZSTAN
TIAN SHAN
Shenyang
Beijing
Tianjin
NORTH KOREA
SEA OF JAPAN
JAPAN
AZORES IS. (PORTUGAL)
TURKEY
TURKMENISTAN
TAJIKISTAN
TAKLA MAKAN
CHINA
Seoul
SOUTH KOREA
Tokyo
40°
ATLAS MOUNTAINS
MEDITERRANEAN SEA
LEBANON
SYRIA
AZERBAIJAN
IRAQ
IRAN
AFGHANISTAN
Mt. Everest 29,028 ft. (8,848 m.)
MOROCCO
TUNISIA
ISRAEL
PLATEAU OF IRAN
HIMALAYAS
Chongqing
Wuhan
EAST CHINA SEA
ALGERIA
QATTARA DEPRESSION
Cairo
JORDAN
KUWAIT
BAHRAIN
PAKISTAN
NEPAL
BHUTAN
Chang Jiang (Yangtze R.)
Shanghai
International Date Line (Monday)
SAHARA
LIBYA
EGYPT
QATAR
Delhi
Ganges R.
INDIA
TAIWAN
Tropic of Cancer
Cape Blanc
SAUDI ARABIA
UNITED ARAB EMIRATES
Nile R.
Calcutta
BANGLADESH
MYANMAR
HONG KONG (U.K.)
MACAO (PORTUGAL)
20°
MAURITANIA
OMAN
Bombay
BAY OF BENGAL
LAOS
MALI
NIGER
CHAD
SUDAN
ERITREA
YEMEN
ARABIAN SEA
THAILAND
SOUTH CHINA SEA
Manila
MARSHALL ISLANDS
SENEGAL
BURKINA FASO
AFRICA
DJIBOUTI
Cape Asir
VIETNAM
PHILIPPINES
GUAM (U.S.)
GUINEA
NIGERIA
ETHIOPIA
Cape Comorin
SRI LANKA
FEDERATED STATES OF MICRONESIA
GHANA
BENIN
CENTRAL AFRICAN REP.
ETHIOPIAN HIGHLANDS
CAMBODIA
SIERRA LEONE
LIBERIA
TOGO
CAMEROON
Zaire R.
UGANDA
SOMALIA
BRUNEI
MALAYSIA
CÔTE D'IVOIRE
SÃO TOME AND PRINCIPE
RWANDA
KENYA
MALDIVES
KIRIBATI
EQUATORIAL GUINEA
GABON
CONGO (ZAIRE) BASIN
Lake Victoria
SINGAPORE
Equator
0°
CONGO
ZAIRE
BURUNDI
Mt. Kilimanjaro 19,340 ft. (5,895 m.)
SEYCHELLES
NAURU
PAPUA NEW GUINEA
SOLOMON ISLANDS
TANZANIA
INDIAN OCEAN
Jakarta
INDONESIA
TUVALU
ANGOLA
MALAWI
COMOROS
Cape York
ZAMBIA
MOZAMBIQUE
COCOS IS. (AUSTRALIA)
CORAL SEA
VANUATU
MADAGASCAR
FIJI
ZIMBABWE
MAURITIUS
GREAT DIVIDING RANGE
NAMIBIA
Mozambique Channel
RÉUNION (FRANCE)
20°
BOTSWANA
Tropic of Capricorn
NEW CALEDONIA (FRANCE)
WESTERN PLATEAU
AUSTRALIA
ATLANTIC OCEAN
SOUTH AFRICA
Mt. Kosciusko 7,310 ft. (2,228 m.)
Cape of Good Hope
TASMAN SEA
40°
East Longitude
NEW ZEALAND
N
KERGUELEN IS. (FRANCE)
Prime Meridian
60°
Antarctic Circle
ANTARCTICA
80°

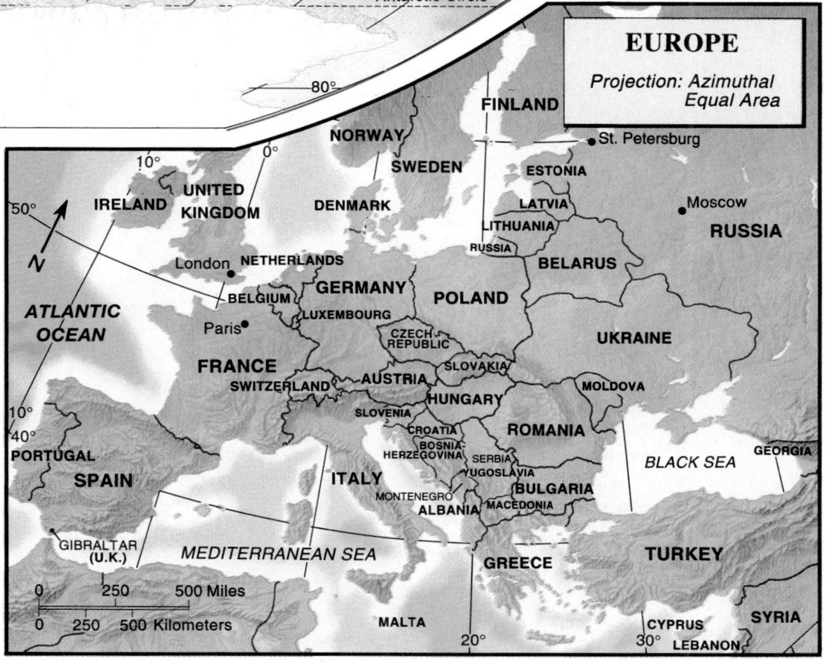

EUROPE
Projection: Azimuthal Equal Area
FINLAND
NORWAY
St. Petersburg
0°
10°
SWEDEN
ESTONIA
UNITED KINGDOM
IRELAND
DENMARK
LATVIA
Moscow
50°
LITHUANIA
RUSSIA
N
London
NETHERLANDS
BELARUS
BELGIUM
GERMANY
POLAND
ATLANTIC OCEAN
Paris
LUXEMBOURG
CZECH REPUBLIC
UKRAINE
FRANCE
SLOVAKIA
SWITZERLAND
AUSTRIA
MOLDOVA
HUNGARY
SLOVENIA
10°
40°
CROATIA
ROMANIA
PORTUGAL
BOSNIA-HERZEGOVINA
SERBIA
BLACK SEA
GEORGIA
YUGOSLAVIA
SPAIN
ITALY
MONTENEGRO
BULGARIA
ALBANIA
MACEDONIA
GIBRALTAR (U.K.)
MEDITERRANEAN SEA
GREECE
TURKEY
0 250 500 Miles
0 250 500 Kilometers
MALTA
CYPRUS
SYRIA
20°
30°
LEBANON

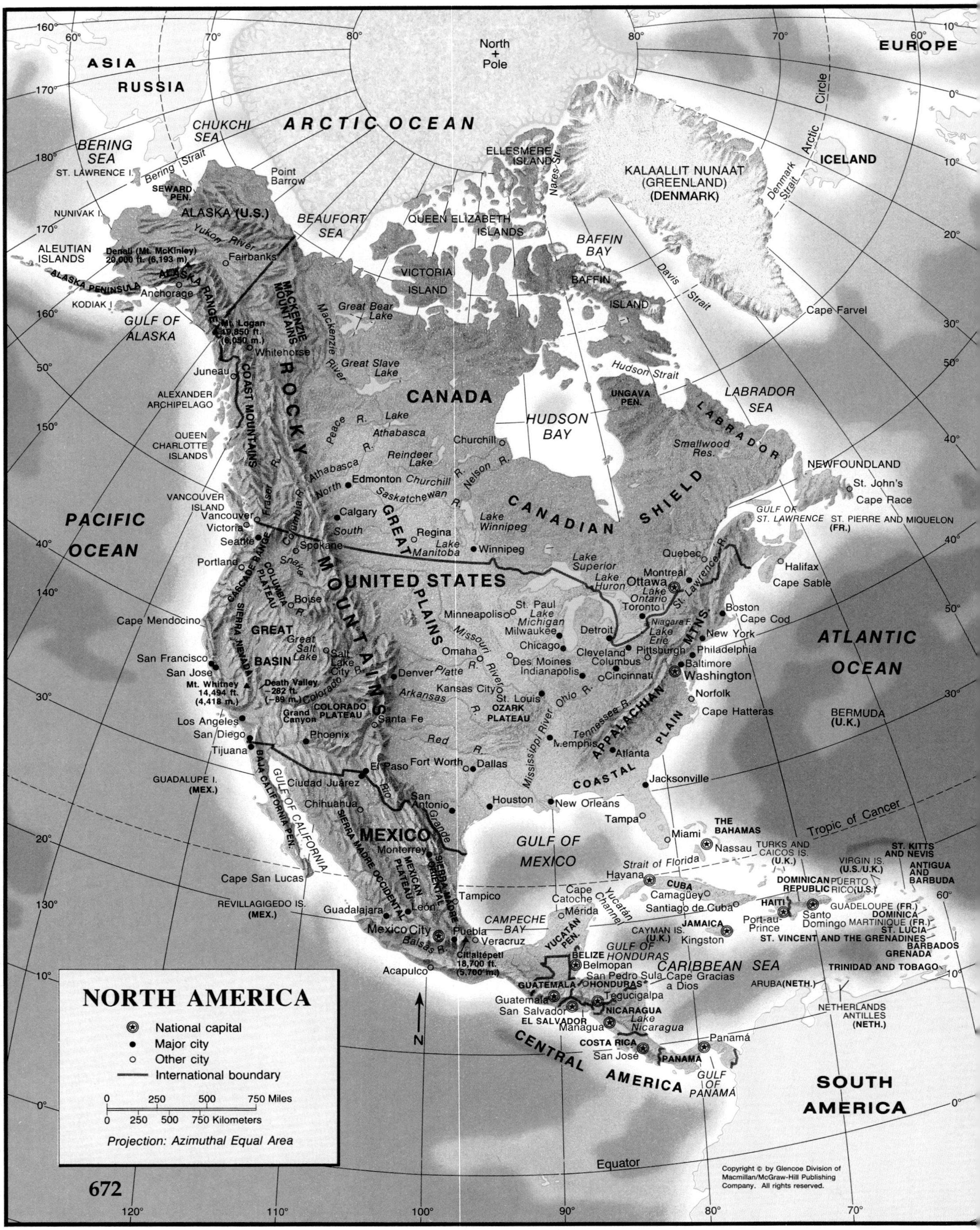
NORTH AMERICA
National capital
Major city
Other city
International boundary
0 250 500 750 Miles
0 250 500 750 Kilometers
Projection: Azimuthal Equal Area
North Pole
ASIA
RUSSIA
EUROPE
ARCTIC OCEAN
CHUKCHI SEA
BERING SEA
Bering Strait
ST. LAWRENCE I.
SEWARD PEN.
Point Barrow
NUNIVAK I.
ALASKA (U.S.)
BEAUFORT SEA
Yukon River
ALEUTIAN ISLANDS
Denali (Mt. McKinley) 20,000 ft. (6,193 m)
Fairbanks
ALASKA PENINSULA
ALASKA RANGE
Anchorage
KODIAK I.
GULF OF ALASKA
Mt. Logan 19,850 ft. (6,050 m.)
Whitehorse
MACKENZIE MOUNTAINS
Mackenzie River
Great Bear Lake
Great Slave Lake
Juneau
COAST MOUNTAINS
ROCKY MOUNTAINS
ALEXANDER ARCHIPELAGO
QUEEN CHARLOTTE ISLANDS
VANCOUVER ISLAND
Vancouver
Victoria
Seattle
Portland
PACIFIC OCEAN
CASCADE RANGE
COLUMBIA PLATEAU
Snake
Boise
Cape Mendocino
SIERRA NEVADA
GREAT BASIN
Great Salt Lake
Salt Lake City
San Francisco
San Jose
Mt. Whitney 14,494 ft. (4,418 m.)
Death Valley -282 ft. (-89 m.)
COLORADO PLATEAU
Grand Canyon
Los Angeles
San Diego
Tijuana
Phoenix
Santa Fe
Denver
BAJA CALIFORNIA PEN.
GULF OF CALIFORNIA
GUADALUPE I. (MEX.)
Ciudad Juárez
El Paso
Chihuahua
Rio Grande
SIERRA MADRE OCCIDENTAL
MEXICO
Monterrey
MEXICAN PLATEAU
SIERRA MADRE ORIENTAL
Cape San Lucas
REVILLAGIGEDO IS. (MEX.)
Guadalajara
León
Tampico
Mexico City
Puebla
Veracruz
Balsas R.
Citlaltépetl 18,700 ft. (5,700 m.)
Acapulco
CAMPECHE BAY
CANADA
Peace R.
Lake Athabasca
Athabasca R.
Reindeer Lake
Churchill
Churchill R.
Nelson R.
North Saskatchewan R.
South
Edmonton
Calgary
Regina
Lake Winnipeg
Lake Manitoba
Winnipeg
GREAT PLAINS
UNITED STATES
CANADIAN SHIELD
HUDSON BAY
QUEEN ELIZABETH ISLANDS
ELLESMERE ISLAND
Nares Str.
VICTORIA ISLAND
BAFFIN BAY
BAFFIN ISLAND
Davis Strait
Hudson Strait
UNGAVA PEN.
LABRADOR SEA
LABRADOR
Smallwood Res.
KALAALLIT NUNAAT (GREENLAND) (DENMARK)
Denmark Strait
ICELAND
Arctic Circle
Cape Farvel
NEWFOUNDLAND
St. John's
Cape Race
GULF OF ST. LAWRENCE
ST. PIERRE AND MIQUELON (FR.)
Halifax
Cape Sable
Quebec
Montreal
Ottawa
St. Lawrence R.
Lake Superior
Lake Huron
Lake Ontario
Toronto
Niagara F.
Lake Erie
Lake Michigan
Minneapolis
St. Paul
Milwaukee
Detroit
Chicago
Cleveland
Pittsburgh
Columbus
Des Moines
Indianapolis
Cincinnati
Omaha
Missouri River
Platte R.
Kansas City
Arkansas R.
St. Louis
OZARK PLATEAU
Ohio R.
Tennessee R.
Mississippi River
Memphis
APPALACHIAN MTNS.
Atlanta
Red R.
Fort Worth
Dallas
San Antonio
Houston
New Orleans
COASTAL PLAIN
Jacksonville
Tampa
Miami
Boston
Cape Cod
New York
Philadelphia
Baltimore
Washington
Norfolk
Cape Hatteras
ATLANTIC OCEAN
BERMUDA (U.K.)
Tropic of Cancer
GULF OF MEXICO
Strait of Florida
THE BAHAMAS
Nassau
TURKS AND CAICOS IS. (U.K.)
Havana
CUBA
Camagüey
Santiago de Cuba
Cape Catoche
Mérida
Yucatán Channel
YUCATAN PEN.
CAYMAN IS. (U.K.)
JAMAICA
Kingston
HAITI
Port-au-Prince
DOMINICAN REPUBLIC
Santo Domingo
PUERTO RICO (U.S.)
VIRGIN IS. (U.S./U.K.)
ST. KITTS AND NEVIS
ANTIGUA AND BARBUDA
GUADELOUPE (FR.)
DOMINICA
MARTINIQUE (FR.)
ST. LUCIA
ST. VINCENT AND THE GRENADINES
BARBADOS
GRENADA
TRINIDAD AND TOBAGO
ARUBA (NETH.)
NETHERLANDS ANTILLES (NETH.)
BELIZE
Belmopan
GULF OF HONDURAS
CARIBBEAN SEA
San Pedro Sula
Cape Gracias a Dios
GUATEMALA
HONDURAS
Guatemala
Tegucigalpa
San Salvador
EL SALVADOR
NICARAGUA
Managua
Lake Nicaragua
COSTA RICA
San José
PANAMA
Panamá
GULF OF PANAMA
CENTRAL AMERICA
SOUTH AMERICA
Equator
Copyright © by Glencoe Division of Macmillan/McGraw-Hill Publishing Company. All rights reserved.
672

LATIN AMERICA
National capitals
Major cities
Other cities
International boundary
0 500 1000 Miles
0 500 1000 Kilometers
Projection: Miller Cylindrical
UNITED STATES
ATLANTIC OCEAN
PACIFIC OCEAN
GULF OF MEXICO
Tropic of Cancer
Equator
Tropic of Capricorn
BERMUDA (U.K.)
Tijuana
Ciudad Juárez
Rio Grande
GULF OF CALIFORNIA
SIERRA MADRE OCCIDENTAL
SIERRA MADRE ORIENTAL
MEXICO
MEXICAN PLATEAU
Monterrey
GUADALUPE I. (MEX.)
Cape San Lucas
Guadalajara
León
Mexico City
Citlalépetl 18,700 ft. (5,700 m.)
REVILLAGIGEDO IS. (MEX.)
CAMPECHE BAY
YUCATÁN PENINSULA
Cape Catoche
Yucatán Channel
Havana
CUBA
THE BAHAMAS
TURKS AND CAICOS IS. (U.K.)
CAYMAN IS. (U.K.)
GREATER ANTILLES
Windward Passage
HAITI
DOMINICAN REPUBLIC
Port-au-Prince
Santo Domingo
San Juan
PUERTO RICO (U.S.)
VIRGIN IS. (U.S. & U.K.)
JAMAICA
Kingston
LESSER ANTILLES
ST. KITTS AND NEVIS
ANTIGUA AND BARBUDA
GUADELOUPE (FR.)
DOMINICA
MARTINIQUE (FR.)
ST. LUCIA
BARBADOS
ST. VINCENT AND THE GRENADINES
GRENADA
Port-of-Spain
TRINIDAD AND TOBAGO
Belmopan
BELIZE
GULF OF HONDURAS
Mt. Tajumulco 13,845 ft. (4,220 m.)
GUATEMALA
Guatemala
HONDURAS
Tegucigalpa
San Salvador
EL SALVADOR
NICARAGUA
Lake Nicaragua
Managua
COSTA RICA
San José
ISTH. OF PANAMÁ
Panamá
PANAMA
GULF OF PANAMÁ
CARIBBEAN SEA
ARUBA (NETH.)
NETHERLANDS ANTILLES (NETH.)
Point Gallinas
Barranquilla
Cartagena
Maracaibo
Lake Maracaibo
Valencia
Caracas
Ciudad Bolívar
Orinoco R.
LLANOS
VENEZUELA
Medellín
Bogotá
Cali
COLOMBIA
Georgetown
GUYANA
Paramaribo
SURINAME
Cayenne
FRENCH GUIANA (FR.)
GUIANA HIGHLANDS
Delta of the Amazon
ECUADOR
Quito
Cotopaxi 19,347 ft. (5,897 m.)
Mt. Chimborazo
Guayaquil
GULF OF GUAYAQUIL
Pariñas Point
GALÁPAGOS IS. (ECUA.)
Iquitos
Negro R.
AMAZON BASIN
Manaus
Amazon R.
Belém
São Luís
Fortaleza
Teresina
Cape São Roque
Natal
Recife
Madeira R.
Tapajós R.
Xingu R.
Tocantins R.
SELVAS
Purus R.
Rio Branco
Chiclayo
PERU
Trujillo
Chimbote
Callao
Lima
Cuzco
ANDES MOUNTAINS
Arequipa
Lake Titicaca
La Paz
BOLIVIA
Cochabamba
Santa Cruz
Sucre
Potosí
BOLIVIAN PLATEAU
Lake Poopó
Guaporé R.
MATO GROSSO PLATEAU
BRAZIL
Brasília
BRAZILIAN HIGHLANDS
São Francisco R.
Sobradinho Reservoir
Salvador
Belo Horizonte
Rio de Janeiro
Cape São Tomé
São Paulo
Santos
Curitiba
Iguazú Falls
Paraguay R.
GRAN CHACO
PARAGUAY
Asunción
Antofagasta
ATACAMA DESERT
Salta
Tucumán
Corrientes
Paraná R.
Uruguay R.
Pôrto Alegre
SAN FÉLIX I. (CHILE)
SAN AMBROSIO I. (CHILE)
JUAN FERNÁNDEZ IS. (CHILE)
Mar Chiquita Lake
Córdoba
Santa Fé
Rosario
Mt. Aconcagua 22,834 ft. (6,960 m.)
Valparaíso
Santiago
Mendoza
Mirim Lake
URUGUAY
Montevideo
Buenos Aires
La Plata
Río de la Plata
Concepción
ARGENTINA
PAMPAS
CHILE
Negro R.
Bahía Blanca
BLANCA BAY
Chiloé I.
GULF OF SAN MATÍAS
VALDÉS PEN.
PATAGONIA
Chubut R.
Comodoro Rivadavia
GULF OF SAN JORGE
Cape Tres Puntas
L. Buenos Aires
L. San Martín
L. Argentina
GRANDE BAY
Stanley
FALKLAND IS. (U.K.)
Strait of Magellan
Punta Arenas
TIERRA DEL FUEGO
Cape Horn
Drake Passage
SOUTH GEORGIA I. (U.K.)
Copyright © by Glencoe Division of Macmillan/McGraw-Hill Publishing Company. All rights reserved.
673
105° 90° 75° 60° 45°
30° 15° 0° 15° 30° 45°

EUROPE
National capital
Major city
Other city
International boundary
Republic boundary
Canal
0 100 200 300 Miles
0 100 200 300 Kilometers
Projection: Azimuthal Equal Area
Reykjavik
ICELAND
Arctic Circle
NORWEGIAN SEA
Prime Meridian
FAROE IS. (DEN.)
SHETLAND IS. (U.K.)
ORKNEY ISLANDS
Cape Wrath
OUTER HEBRIDES IS.
SCOTLAND
NORTHERN IRELAND (U.K.)
Glasgow
Edinburgh
Belfast
PENNINE RANGE
UNITED KINGDOM
IRISH SEA
ISLE OF MAN
Dublin
IRELAND
Cork
Liverpool
Manchester
Leeds
Sheffield
ENGLAND
Birmingham
WALES
Cardiff
Bristol
London
Cape Clear
St. George's Channel
English Channel
Strait of Dover
NORTH SEA
ATLANTIC OCEAN
GUERNSEY I. (U.K.)
JERSEY I. (U.K.)
BRETON PEN.
Le Havre
Seine River
Paris
Marne R.
Nantes
Loire River
FRANCE
BAY OF BISCAY
Bordeaux
Garonne R.
CENTRAL MASSIF
Toulouse
Midi Canal
Montpellier
Marseille
GULF OF LION
Lyon
Rhône R.
Cape Finisterre
CANTABRIAN MTNS.
Bilbao
Ebro River
PYRENEES
Aneto Peak 11,168 ft. (3,404 m.)
ANDORRA
Andorra la Vella
Zaragoza
Barcelona
Porto
Valladolid
Duero River
PORTUGAL
Tagus River
IBERIAN PENINSULA
Madrid
Lisbon
Setúbal
SPAIN
SIERRA MORENA
Guadiana River
Valencia
Cape St. Vincent
Seville
Málaga
Granada
Murcia
Strait of Gibraltar
GIBRALTAR (U.K.)
Palma
BALEARIC IS. (SP.)
MEDITERRANEAN
AFRICA
NORWAY
Trondheim
SCANDINAVIAN HIGHLANDS
Bergen
Goldhöpiggen 8,097 ft. (2,468 m.)
Oslo
SWEDEN
Lake Vänern
Uppsala
Stockholm
Lake Vättern
Skagerrak
Kattegat
Göteborg
JUTLAND
Copenhagen
DENMARK
Malmö
Odense
BORNHOLM I.
ÖLAND I.
GOTLAND
BALTIC SEA
Kiel Canal
Hamburg
Elbe R.
Rostock
Gdańsk
Szczecin
Bremen
Mittelland Canal
Hannover
Berlin
NETHERLANDS
Amsterdam
The Hague
Rotterdam
Antwerp
Essen
Dortmund
Magdeburg
Oder River
Poznań
BELGIUM
Brussels
Cologne
Liège
Bonn
GERMANY
Leipzig
Dresden
Wrocław
LUXEMBOURG
Luxembourg
Frankfurt
Chemnitz
Marne-Rhine Canal
Rhine R.
Strasbourg
Stuttgart
Danube River
Prague
CZECH REPUBLIC
Ostrava
Brno
Munich
Bodensee
LIECHTENSTEIN
Vaduz
Zurich
Bern
Lausanne
Geneva
L. Geneva
SWITZERLAND
ALPS
Mt. Blanc 15,771 ft. (4,807 m.)
Mt. Rosa 15,203 ft. (4,634 m.)
Innsbruck
Salzburg
Linz
Vienna
Bratislava
AUSTRIA
Graz
Budapest
L. Balaton
Ljubljana
SLOVENIA
Zagreb
CROATIA
Sava R.
Pécs
Milan
PO VALLEY
Po R.
Turin
Genoa
Venice
Bologna
Nice
Monaco
MONACO
Florence
SAN MARINO
San Marino
APENNINES
DINARIC ALPS
BOSNIA-HERZEGOVINA
Split
ADRIATIC SEA
CORSICA (FR.)
VATICAN CITY
Rome
ITALY
Naples
Bari
SARDINIA (IT.)
Cagliari
TYRRHENIAN SEA
G. OF TARANTO
IONIAN SEA
Palermo
SICILY
Catania
Strait of Sicily
PANTELLERIA (IT.)
MALTA
Valletta
SEA
60°
30°
20°
10°
0°
70°
40°
50°

BARENTS SEA
Murmansk
KOLA PENINSULA
TIMAN RIDGE
Pechora R.
WHITE SEA
Arkhangel'sk
White Sea-Baltic Waterway
N. Dvina River
Vychegda River
URAL MOUNTAINS
Mt. Konzhakovskiy 5,147 ft. (1,569 m.)
Kama R.
RUSSIA
ASIA
FINLAND
Lake Onega
Sukhona River
Perm
Lake Ladoga
Lake Saimaa
Volga-Baltic Waterway
Helsinki
St. Petersburg
GULF OF FINLAND
Tallinn
ESTONIA
Chudskoye Lake
Rybinsk Reservoir
Kama River
Ufa
Ural River
Kazan
Yaroslavl
Nizhniy Novgorod
Kuybyshev Reservoir
LATVIA
Riga
W. Dvina R.
Volga River
Volga-Baltic Waterway
Moscow
Samara
Orenburg
EUROPEAN PLAIN
Smolensk
Oka R.
Tula
CENTRAL RUSSIAN UPLAND
RUSSIA
VOLGA UPLAND
Volga River
Saratov
Vilnius
Minsk
BELARUS
Don River
Voronezh
Kursk
Volgograd Reservoir
KAZAKHSTAN
Ural River
ARAL SEA
Pripet River
Desna R.
Volgograd
Volga River
DEPRESSION
Kiev
Kremenchug Reservoir
Khar'kov
Lugansk
Tsimlyansk Reservoir
UKRAINE
L'vov
DNIEPER UPLAND
Dniester R.
Dnepropetrovsk
Donetsk
Krivoy Rog
Zaporozhye
Don River
Rostov
Astrakhan
Delta of the Volga
CASPIAN
CARPATHIAN MTNS.
Prut River
MOLDOVA
Chişinău
DNIEPER LOWLAND
Dnieper River
Kakhovka Res.
SEA OF AZOV
Krasnodar
Groznyy
CASPIAN SEA
Cluj-Napoca
ROMANIA
Odessa
CRIMEA
Braşov
CAUCASUS MTNS.
Mt. Elbrus 18,510 ft. (5,642 m.)
WALLACHIA PLAIN
Bucharest
Danube River
Constanţa
BLACK SEA
Ruse
BULGARIA
Varna
Burgas
Sofia
Plovdiv
Musala Peak 9,596 ft. (2,926 m.)
Bosporus
PENINSULA
TURKEY
Salonika
Dardanelles
SEA OF MARMARA
AEGEAN SEA
ASIA
Athens
RHODES
CRETE (GR.)
Iraklion
Copyright © by Glencoe Division of Macmillan/McGraw-Hill Publishing Company. All rights reserved.
675

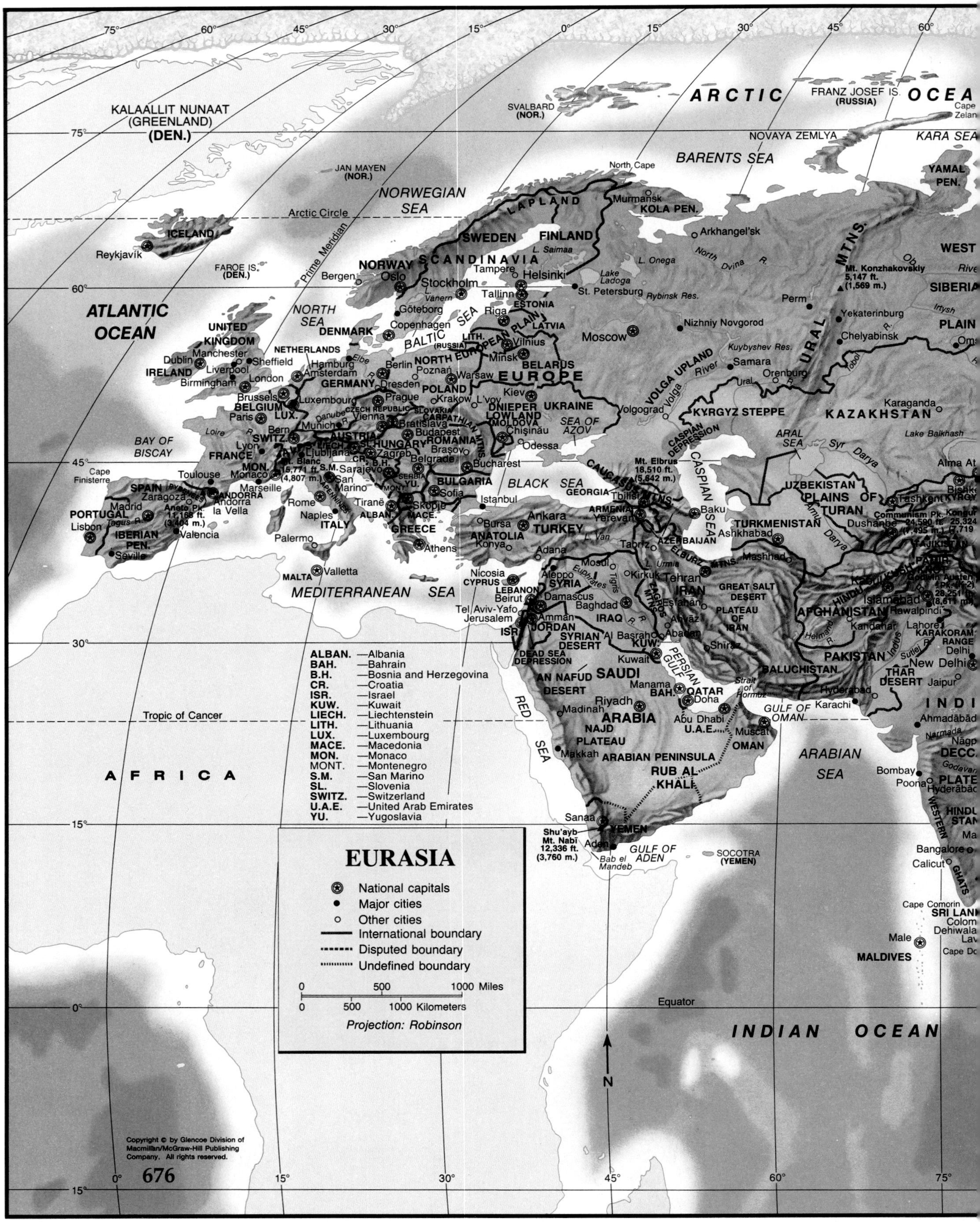

EURASIA
National capitals
Major cities
Other cities
International boundary
Disputed boundary
Undefined boundary
0 500 1000 Miles
0 500 1000 Kilometers
Projection: Robinson
ALBAN. —Albania
BAH. —Bahrain
B.H. —Bosnia and Herzegovina
CR. —Croatia
ISR. —Israel
KUW. —Kuwait
LIECH. —Liechtenstein
LITH. —Lithuania
LUX. —Luxembourg
MACE. —Macedonia
MON. —Monaco
MONT. —Montenegro
S.M. —San Marino
SL. —Slovenia
SWITZ. —Switzerland
U.A.E. —United Arab Emirates
YU. —Yugoslavia
ARCTIC OCEAN
ATLANTIC OCEAN
INDIAN OCEAN
KALAALLIT NUNAAT (GREENLAND) (DEN.)
SVALBARD (NOR.)
FRANZ JOSEF IS. (RUSSIA)
NOVAYA ZEMLYA
BARENTS SEA
KARA SEA
North Cape
JAN MAYEN (NOR.)
NORWEGIAN SEA
Arctic Circle
ICELAND
Reykjavík
FAROE IS. (DEN.)
Prime Meridian
LAPLAND
SWEDEN
FINLAND
NORWAY
SCANDINAVIA
Bergen
Oslo
Stockholm
Helsinki
Tampere
St. Petersburg
Murmansk
KOLA PEN.
Arkhangel'sk
NORTH SEA
BALTIC SEA
UNITED KINGDOM
IRELAND
Dublin
Manchester
Sheffield
Liverpool
Birmingham
London
DENMARK
Copenhagen
Göteborg
Tallinn
ESTONIA
Riga
LATVIA
LITH.
Vilnius
Minsk
BELARUS
Moscow
Nizhniy Novgorod
NORTH EUROPEAN PLAIN
EUROPE
NETHERLANDS
Hamburg
Amsterdam
Berlin
Poznań
Warsaw
POLAND
GERMANY
Dresden
Prague
Krakow
L'vov
Kiev
UKRAINE
DNIEPER LOWLAND
MOLDOVA
Chişinău
SEA OF AZOV
Odessa
BELGIUM
Brussels
LUX.
Luxembourg
CZECH REPUBLIC
SLOVAKIA
Vienna
Bratislava
Budapest
Munich
Paris
FRANCE
Bern
SWITZ.
AUSTRIA
HUNGARY
ROMANIA
Braşov
Bucharest
Lyon
BAY OF BISCAY
Cape Finisterre
Toulouse
Marseille
MON.
Monaco
Mt. Blanc 15,771 ft. (4,807 m.)
Ljubljana
Zagreb
Belgrade
Sarajevo
S.M.
San Marino
SERBIA
YU.
BULGARIA
Sofia
SPAIN
PORTUGAL
Lisbon
Madrid
Zaragoza
ANDORRA
Andorra la Vella
Aneto Pk. 11,168 ft. (3,404 m.)
Valencia
Seville
IBERIAN PEN.
Rome
Naples
ITALY
Tiranë
ALBAN.
Skopje
MACE.
GREECE
Athens
Palermo
MALTA
Valletta
MEDITERRANEAN SEA
BLACK SEA
Istanbul
Bursa
Ankara
TURKEY
ANATOLIA
Konya
Adana
Nicosia
CYPRUS
LEBANON
Beirut
Damascus
SYRIA
Aleppo
Tel Aviv-Yafo
Jerusalem
ISR.
Amman
JORDAN
DEAD SEA DEPRESSION
SYRIAN DESERT
IRAQ
Baghdad
Mosul
Kirkuk
Al Basrah
KUW.
Kuwait
GEORGIA
Tbilisi
ARMENIA
Yerevan
AZERBAIJAN
Baku
CAUCASUS MTS.
Mt. Elbrus 18,510 ft. (5,642 m.)
CASPIAN SEA
CASPIAN DEPRESSION
Volgograd
VOLGA UPLAND
Samara
Orenburg
KYRGYZ STEPPE
KAZAKHSTAN
Karaganda
ARAL SEA
Lake Balkhash
Alma Ata
Tabriz
Tehran
IRAN
ELBURZ MTS.
ZAGROS MTS.
Esfahan
Ahvāz
Abadan
Shiraz
GREAT SALT DESERT
PLATEAU OF IRAN
Mashhad
TURKMENISTAN
Ashkhabad
UZBEKISTAN
PLAINS OF TURAN
Tashkent
Dushanbe
Communism Pk. 24,590 ft. (7,495 m.)
AFGHANISTAN
Kandahar
HINDU KUSH
Islamabad
Rawalpindi
Lahore
KARAKORAM RANGE
PAKISTAN
BALUCHISTAN
Karachi
Hyderabad
New Delhi
Delhi
THAR DESERT
Jaipur
Ahmadabad
Bombay
Poona
Bangalore
Calicut
Cape Comorin
SRI LANKA
Male
MALDIVES
ARABIAN SEA
GULF OF OMAN
Strait of Hormuz
PERSIAN GULF
Manama
BAH.
QATAR
Doha
Abu Dhabi
U.A.E.
Muscat
OMAN
SAUDI ARABIA
AN NAFUD DESERT
Riyadh
Madinah
Makkah
NAJD PLATEAU
ARABIAN PENINSULA
RUB AL KHALI
RED SEA
Sanaa
YEMEN
Aden
Shu'ayb Mt. Nabī 12,336 ft. (3,760 m.)
GULF OF ADEN
Bab el Mandeb
SOCOTRA (YEMEN)
AFRICA
Tropic of Cancer
Equator
Mt. Konzhakovskiy 5,147 ft. (1,569 m.)
URAL MTS.
Perm
Yekaterinburg
Chelyabinsk
WEST SIBERIAN PLAIN
YAMAL PEN.
Copyright © by Glencoe Division of Macmillan/McGraw-Hill Publishing Company. All rights reserved.
676

90° 105° 120° 135° 150° 165° 180° 165° 150° 135°
SEVERNAYA ZEMLYA
TAYMYR PEN.
LAPTEV SEA
NEW SIBERIAN ISLANDS
EAST SIBERIAN SEA
75°
WRANGEL ISLAND
Noril'sk
Yenisey
CENTRAL SIBERIAN
PLATEAU
VERKHOYANSK RANGE
KOLYMA PLAIN
Bering Strait
CHUKOTSK PEN.
Anadyr R.
Lower Tunguska R.
River
LENA PLATEAU
Yakutsk
Lena River
Kolyma R.
KOLYMA RANGE
Cape Navarin
RUSSIA
Angara R.
SIBERIA
Magadan
60°
Mt. Klyuchevsk 15,584 ft. (4,750 m.)
BERING SEA
Krasnoyarsk
Bratsk Res.
STANOVOY RANGE
SEA OF OKHOTSK
KAMCHATKA PEN.
KOMANDORSKIY IS.
Novosibirsk
Novosibirsk Res.
Lake Baykal
YABLONOVY RANGE
SAYAN MTNS.
Amur R.
Komsomol'sk
Cape Lopatka
Semipalatinsk
Lake Zaysan
ALTAI MTS.
MONGOLIA
Ulaanbaatar
DA HINGGAN LING
Khabarovsk
KURIL ISLANDS
DZUNGARIAN BASIN
MONGOLIAN PLATEAU
NORTHEAST
Songhua Jiang
Harbin
(MANCHURIAN)
La Pérouse Strait
L. Khanka
Vladivostok
Sapporo
45°
Ürümqi
TIAN SHAN
GOBI
Changchun
PLAIN
TURFAN DEPRESSION
ASIA
Shenyang
Anshan
TAKLA MAKAN
Huang
Beijing
N. KOREA
SEA OF JAPAN
Tianjin
NORTH CHINA PLAIN
P'yŏngyang
CHINA
JAPAN
Inchon
Seoul
KUNLUN SHAN
BAYAN HAR SHAN
YELLOW SEA
S. KOREA
Taegu
Kawasaki
Tokyo
Kyoto
Wei He
He
Xi'an
Kitakyūshū
Osaka
Yokohama
HIMALAYAS
Annapurna Pk. 26,502 ft. (8,078 m.)
PLATEAU OF TIBET
Nanjing
Lhasa
Mt. Everest 29,028 ft. (8,848 m.)
Mt. Kangchenjunga
Chengdu
Jiang
L. Tai
Shanghai
PACIFIC
Chang
Hangzhou
L. Poyang
EAST CHINA SEA
30°
Changsha
Nanchang
RYUKYU IS. (JAP.)
BHUTAN
Brahmaputra R.
YUNGUI PLATEAU
Guiyang
Fuzhou
OCEAN
Kathmandu
Ganges R.
Varanasi
BANGLADESH
Dhaka
Kunming
Jiang
Guangzhou
Formosa Strait
T'aipei
TAIWAN
Kaohsiung
Tropic of Cancer
Khulna
MYANMAR
Chittagong
Mekong
Calcutta
ANNAMITE MTNS.
Hanoi
Macao
Victoria
Irrawaddy
Mandalay
Haiphong
MACAO (PORT.)
HONG KONG (U.K.)
Luzon Strait
BAY OF BENGAL
Chiang Mai
LAOS
Vientiane
Cape Engaño
PHILIPPINE
Bassein
Rangoon
KHORAT PLATEAU
Savannakhet
SOUTH
LUZON
SEA
Ubon Ratchathani
THAILAND
Da Nang
INDOCHINA
Quezon City
Preparis Channel
15°
Thonburi
Krung Thep (Bangkok)
CAMBODIA
VIETNAM
Manila
Tonle Sap
ANDAMAN IS. (IND.)
CHINA
MINDORO
PHILIPPINES
ANDAMAN SEA
Phnom Penh
Cebu
PALAWAN
Ho Chi Minh City
SEA
MINDANAO
Davao
NICOBAR IS. (IND.)
George Town
MALAY PEN.
Bandar Seri Begawan
BRUNEI
SULU ARCH. (PHIL.)
Point Tinaca
Ipoh
Kuala Lumpur
Medan
Strait of Malacca
MALAYSIA
Singapore
HALMAHERA
SUMATRA
SINGAPORE
BORNEO
Equator
0°
Jambi
Pontianak
BORNEO HIGHLANDS
Cape d'Urville
Jayapura
BARISAN MTNS.
Banjarmasin
CELEBES
Palembang
Jaya Pk. 16,499 ft. (5,029 m.)
JAVA SEA
Jakarta
Ujung Pandang
BANDA SEA
NEW GUINEA
Sunda Str.
Bandung
Semarang
INDONESIA
JAVA
Surabaya
90° 105° 120° 135° 150° 165°
15°
677

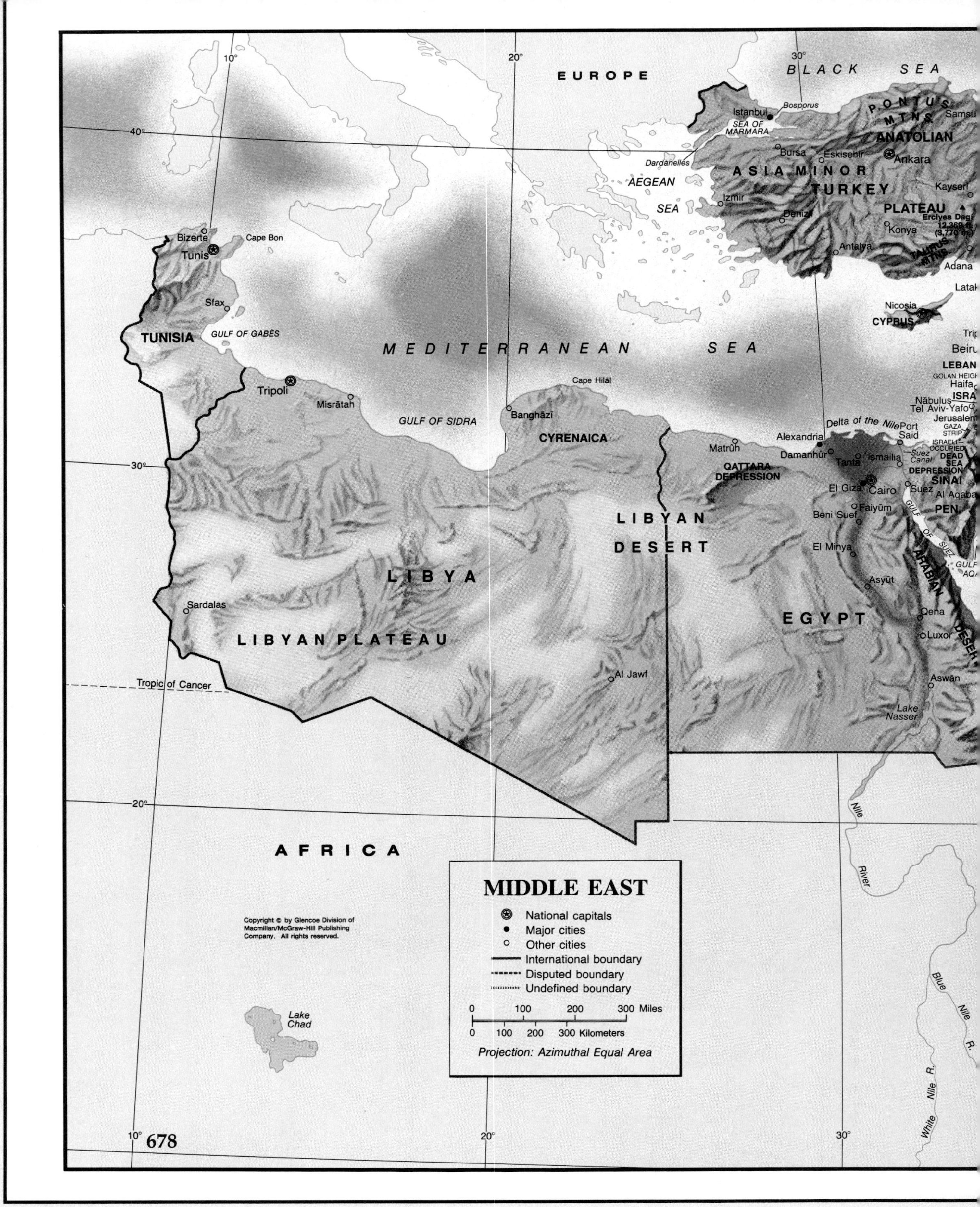

MIDDLE EAST
National capitals
Major cities
Other cities
International boundary
Disputed boundary
Undefined boundary
0 100 200 300 Miles
0 100 200 300 Kilometers
Projection: Azimuthal Equal Area
EUROPE
BLACK SEA
MEDITERRANEAN SEA
AEGEAN SEA
SEA OF MARMARA
Bosporus
Dardanelles
Istanbul
Bursa
Eskisehir
Ankara
Izmir
Denizli
Konya
Antalya
Kayseri
Adana
PONTUS MTNS.
ANATOLIAN PLATEAU
ASIA MINOR
TURKEY
TAURUS MTNS.
Erciyes Dagi 12,369 ft. (3,770 m.)
Nicosia
CYPRUS
Bizerte
Tunis
Cape Bon
Sfax
TUNISIA
GULF OF GABÈS
Tripoli
Misrātah
GULF OF SIDRA
Banghāzī
Cape Hilāl
CYRENAICA
LIBYA
LIBYAN PLATEAU
LIBYAN DESERT
Sardalas
Al Jawf
Tropic of Cancer
Matrūh
QATTARA DEPRESSION
Alexandria
Damanhûr
Tanta
Ismailia
Delta of the Nile
Port Said
Suez Canal
El Giza
Cairo
Suez
Faiyūm
Beni Suef
El Minya
Asyūt
EGYPT
Qena
Luxor
Aswān
Lake Nasser
GULF OF SUEZ
SINAI PEN.
Al Aqaba
DEAD SEA DEPRESSION
Haifa
Nābulus
Tel Aviv-Yafo
Jerusalem
GAZA STRIP
ISRAELI-OCCUPIED
GOLAN HEIGHTS
AFRICA
Lake Chad
Nile River
Blue Nile R.
White Nile R.
Copyright © by Glencoe Division of Macmillan/McGraw-Hill Publishing Company. All rights reserved.
10°
20°
30°
40°
678

ASIA
Trabzon
Erzurum
Mt. Ararat
16,945 ft.
(5,165 m.)
Lake Van
Diyarbakir
Tabriz
Ardabīl
Urmia
Lake Urmia
Rasht
ELBURZ
MTNS.
Qazvīn
Tehran
Mt. Demavend
18,386 ft.
(5,604 m.)
Mashhad
GREAT SALT DESERT
PLATEAU OF IRAN
IRAN
ZAGROS MOUNTAINS
Mosul
Irbīl
Kirkuk
Tigris
Hamadān
Qom
Bākhtarān
Arāk
Eṣfahān
Bīrjand
MESOPOTAMIA
IRAQ
Euphrates R.
Baghdad
Karbalā
Al Hillah
An Najaf
An Nāṣirīyah
Ahvāz
Abadan
Al Baṣrah
Aleppo
Deir-ez-Zor
SYRIA
Hims
Damascus
SYRIAN DESERT
Kermān
Shīrāz
Zāhedān
Būshehr
Bandar 'Abbās
KUWAIT
Kuwait
Hawalli
Al Ahmadī
AN NAFUD DESERT
Ha'il
NAJD PLATEAU
Buraydah
PERSIAN GULF
Ad Dammām
Manama
BAHRAIN
QATAR
Doha
Al Hufūf
Strait of Hormuz
Dubai
Abu Dhabi
GULF OF OMAN
Muscat
Tropic of Cancer
Cape Al Hadd
UNITED ARAB EMIRATES
Riyadh
Madinah
Yanbu al Bahr
TUWAYQ MTNS.
RED SEA
SAUDI ARABIA
ARABIAN PENINSULA
RUB AL KHALI
OMAN
Duqm
Jiddah
Makkah
At Ta'if
ASIR MOUNTAINS
Salālah
Sanaa
Mt. Nabī Shu'ayb
12,336 ft.
(3,760 m.)
YEMEN
Al Ghaydah
Al Mukallā
Al Hudaydah
Ta'izz
Aden
Bab el Mandeb
GULF OF ADEN
ARABIAN SEA
Lake Tana
Cape Asir
SOCOTRA
(YEMEN)
40°
50°
60°
30°
20°
679

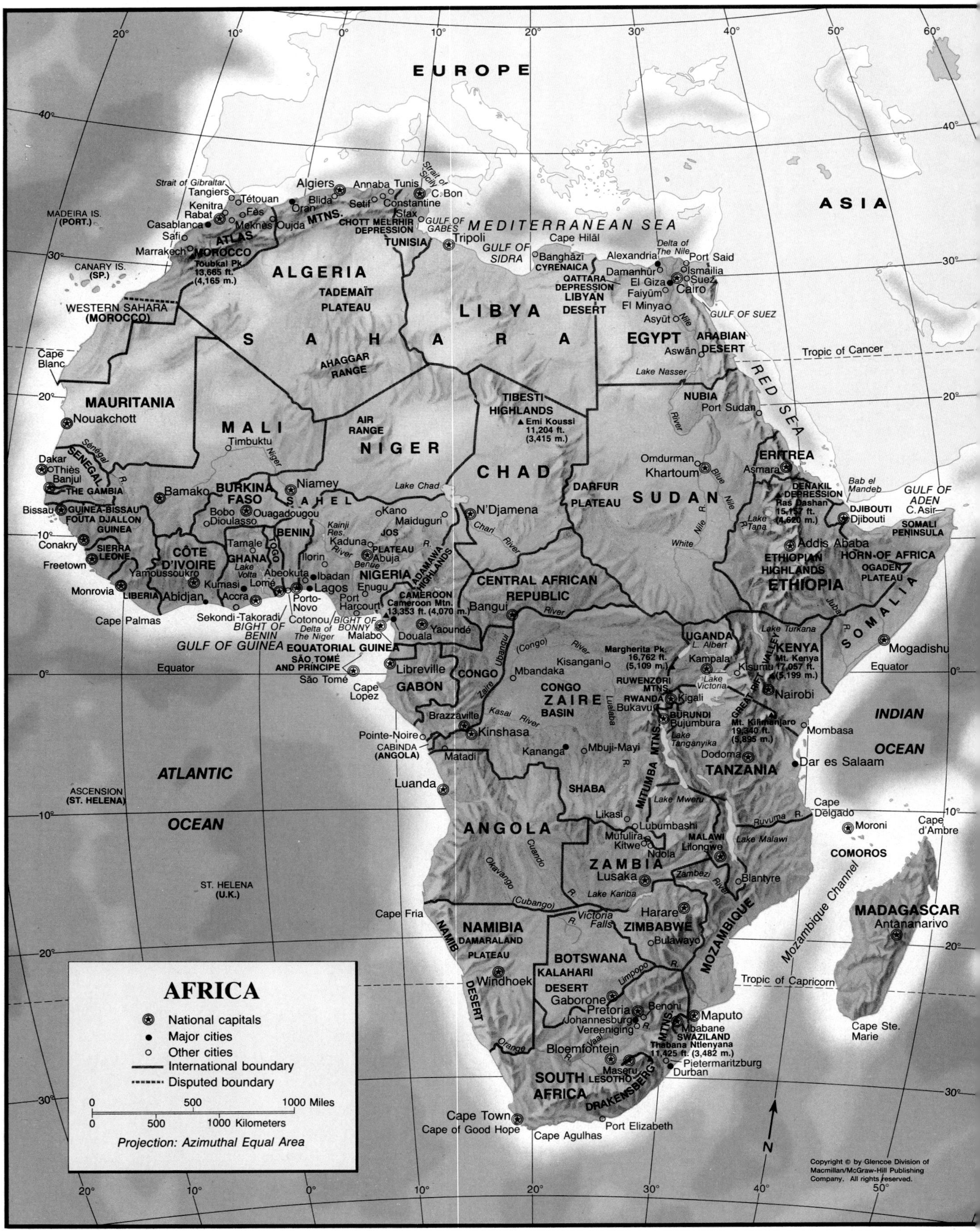
AFRICA
National capitals
Major cities
Other cities
International boundary
Disputed boundary
0 500 1000 Miles
0 500 1000 Kilometers
Projection: Azimuthal Equal Area
EUROPE
ASIA
MEDITERRANEAN SEA
ATLANTIC
OCEAN
INDIAN
OCEAN
GULF OF GUINEA
GULF OF ADEN
RED SEA
Mozambique Channel
Tropic of Cancer
Tropic of Capricorn
Equator
S A H A R A
SAHEL
MADEIRA IS. (PORT.)
CANARY IS. (SP.)
WESTERN SAHARA (MOROCCO)
ASCENSION (ST. HELENA)
ST. HELENA (U.K.)
Strait of Gibraltar
Tangiers
Tétouan
Kenitra
Rabat
Fès
Casablanca
Meknès
Oujda
Safi
Marrakech
MOROCCO
ATLAS MTNS.
Toubkal Pk. 13,665 ft. (4,165 m.)
Algiers
Blida
Oran
Annaba
Tunis
Setif
Constantine
Sfax
C. Bon
Strait of Sicily
CHOTT MELRHIR DEPRESSION
GULF OF GABES
TUNISIA
Tripoli
GULF OF SIDRA
ALGERIA
TADEMAÏT PLATEAU
AHAGGAR RANGE
LIBYA
Cape Hilāl
Banghāzī
CYRENAICA
QATTARA DEPRESSION
LIBYAN DESERT
Alexandria
Delta of The Nile
Port Said
Damanhūr
Ismailia
El Giza
Suez
Cairo
Faiyūm
El Minya
Asyūt
Nile
GULF OF SUEZ
EGYPT
ARABIAN DESERT
Aswān
Lake Nasser
NUBIA
Port Sudan
Cape Blanc
MAURITANIA
Nouakchott
MALI
Timbuktu
Niger
AIR RANGE
NIGER
TIBESTI HIGHLANDS
Emi Koussi 11,204 ft. (3,415 m.)
CHAD
Lake Chad
N'Djamena
Chari River
Dakar
Thiès
SENEGAL
Sénégal R.
Banjul
THE GAMBIA
Bissau
GUINEA-BISSAU
FOUTA DJALLON
GUINEA
Conakry
SIERRA LEONE
Freetown
Monrovia
LIBERIA
Cape Palmas
Bamako
BURKINA FASO
Niamey
Bobo Dioulasso
Ouagadougou
CÔTE D'IVOIRE
Yamoussoukro
Abidjan
GHANA
Tamale
Lake Volta
Kumasi
Accra
Sekondi-Takoradi
TOGO
Lomé
BENIN
Porto-Novo
Cotonou
BIGHT OF BENIN
Abeokuta
Ibadan
Lagos
Ilorin
Kainji Res.
Kaduna
Kano
Maiduguri
JOS PLATEAU
Abuja
NIGERIA
Benue R.
Enugu
Port Harcourt
Delta of The Niger
BIGHT OF BONNY
ADAMAWA HIGHLANDS
CAMEROON
Cameroon Mtn. 13,353 ft. (4,070 m.)
Malabo
Douala
Yaoundé
EQUATORIAL GUINEA
SÃO TOMÉ AND PRÍNCIPE
São Tomé
Libreville
GABON
Cape Lopez
CONGO
Brazzaville
Pointe-Noire
CABINDA (ANGOLA)
Kinshasa
Matadi
Luanda
CENTRAL AFRICAN REPUBLIC
Bangui
Ubangi
Mbandaka
(Congo) River
Kisangani
ZAIRE
CONGO BASIN
Zaire
Kasai River
Kananga
Mbuji-Mayi
Lualaba
SHABA
Likasi
Lubumbashi
MITUMBA MTNS.
Lake Mweru
SUDAN
Omdurman
Khartoum
Blue Nile
White Nile
DARFUR PLATEAU
ERITREA
Asmara
DENAKIL DEPRESSION
Ras Dashan 15,157 ft. (4,620 m.)
Bab el Mandeb
DJIBOUTI
Djibouti
C. Asir
SOMALI PENINSULA
Lake Tana
Addis Ababa
ETHIOPIAN HIGHLANDS
ETHIOPIA
HORN OF AFRICA
OGADEN PLATEAU
SOMALIA
Juba
Mogadishu
Lake Turkana
UGANDA
L. Albert
Kampala
Margherita Pk. 16,762 ft. (5,109 m.)
RUWENZORI MTNS.
KENYA
Mt. Kenya 17,057 ft. (5,199 m.)
GREAT RIFT VALLEY
Kisumu
Lake Victoria
Nairobi
RWANDA
Kigali
Bukavu
BURUNDI
Bujumbura
Lake Tanganyika
Mt. Kilimanjaro 19,340 ft. (5,895 m.)
Mombasa
Dodoma
TANZANIA
Dar es Salaam
Cape Delgado
Ruvuma R.
Moroni
COMOROS
Cape d'Ambre
MADAGASCAR
Antananarivo
Cape Ste. Marie
ANGOLA
Cuando
Okavango
(Cubango)
Cape Fria
Mufulira
Kitwe
Ndola
ZAMBIA
Lusaka
MALAWI
Lilongwe
Lake Malawi
Blantyre
Zambezi River
Lake Kariba
Victoria Falls
Harare
ZIMBABWE
Bulawayo
MOZAMBIQUE
NAMIBIA
DAMARALAND PLATEAU
NAMIB DESERT
Windhoek
BOTSWANA
KALAHARI DESERT
Gaborone
Limpopo R.
Pretoria
Benoni
Johannesburg
Vereeniging
Vaal R.
Maputo
Mbabane
SWAZILAND
Thabana Ntlenyana 11,425 ft. (3,482 m.)
Orange
Bloemfontein
Maseru
LESOTHO
Pietermaritzburg
Durban
SOUTH AFRICA
DRAKENSBERG MTNS.
Cape Town
Cape of Good Hope
Cape Agulhas
Port Elizabeth
N
Copyright © by Glencoe Division of Macmillan/McGraw-Hill Publishing Company. All rights reserved.

GLOSSARY

Pronunciations are indicated in parentheses.

A

abbot (ab′ uht) Monastery head. (p. 255)
abdicate (ab′ duh-kāt) Give up the throne. (p. 565)
absolute location (ab sō lūt lō kā shun) Exact location of a place on the Earth's surface. (p. 5)
acropolis (uh krop′ uh lis) Fortified hill in ancient Greek cities. (p. 163)
act of homage (akt of om′ ij) Ceremony in which a vassal promises loyalty to a lord. (p. 368)
ages (ā′ juhs) Time periods. (p. 27)
agora (ag′ uh ruh) Ancient Greek marketplace. (p. 163)
airlift (ār′ lift) System of carrying supplies into an isolated area by airplane. (p. 626)
alchemists (al′kuh mists) Scientists who try to turn metals into gold and silver. (p. 343)
alliances (uh lī′ uhn siz) Agreements between people or countries. (p. 195)
amendments (uh mend′ muhntz) Law changes. (p. 513)
ancestors (an′ ses terz) Family members from past generations. (p. 89)
annexation (an ek sā shuhn) Incorporating an area into an existing state. (p. 549)
anointed (uh noin′ tuhd) Blessed with holy oil. (p. 279)
anthropologists (an thruh pol′ uh jists) People who study human beings. (p. 24)
apartheid (uh pahr′ tāt) Separation of the races. (p. 656)
apostles (uh pos′ uhls) Men chosen by Jesus to teach his beliefs to others. (p. 253)
appeasement (uh pēz′ muhnt) Giving in to demands. (p. 615)
apprentice (uh pren′ tis) Person who is learning a craft or trade. (p. 406)
archaelogy (ar kē ol′ uh jē) Study of remains of past human cultures. (p. 25)
archaeologists (ar kē ol′ uh jists) People who study ruins and artifacts. (p. 24)
archbishops (arch′ bish uhps) Bishops at the head of churches in large cities. (p. 253)
aristocrats (uh rist′ ō kratz) Members of the upper class. (p. 164)
armada (ar mah′ duh) Fleet of warships. (p. 459)
armaments (ar′ muh muhnts) Military supplies. (p. 605)
armistice (ar′ muh stis) Agreement to stop fighting. (p. 605)
artifacts (ar′ tuh fakts) Products of human skill. (p. 25)
artillery (ar til′ uhr ē) Mounted guns. (p. 604)
artisans (art′ uh zuhnz) Skilled workers. (p. 57)
assembly line (uh sem′ blē līn) Work system in which each worker adds one part to a product until it is assembled. (p. 527)
astrolabe (as′ truh lāb) Navigational instrument used to determine latitude. (p. 468)
astronomers (uh stron′ uh muhrs) People who study the heavenly bodies. (p. 122)
automation (o tuh mā′ shuhn) Process in which machines replace workers. (p. 527)

B

bailiff (bā′ lif) Medieval official who saw that peasants did their work. (p. 375)
balance of power (bal′ uhnts of pau′ uhr) Equal strength among countries. (p. 566)
balance of trade (bal′ uhns of trād) Difference between the amount of goods a country brings in and sends out. (p. 492)
bandeirantes (ban duh ran′ tās) Fortune hunters in colonial Brazil. (p. 488)
bands (bandz) Prehistoric groups that gathered food and lived together. (p. 34)
barbaroi (bar′ buh roi) People who did not follow Greek customs. (p. 197)
barter (bar′ ter) To exchange goods without using money. (p. 241)
berserkers (ber zerk′ erz) Viking warriors. (p. 301)
bishop (bish′ uhp) Diocese head. (p. 253)
blitzkrieg (blits′ krēg) Lightning war. (p. 616)
blockaded (blok′ ād uhd) Closed off. (p. 626)

blood feuds (bluhd fyūds) Longstanding quarrels between families. (p. 268)

bourgeoisie (bur zhwah zē) Middle class. (p. 514)

boyars (bō yahrs′) Members of the wealthy class in czarist Russia. (p. 349)

boycott (boi′ kot) Refuse to pay. (p. 509)

bull leaping (būl lēp′ ēng) Minoan bullfighting. (p. 152)

burgesses (ber′ jis ez) Elected representatives in colonial Virginia. (p. 495)

burghers (ber′ guhrz) Freemen or wealthy merchants who lived in medieval towns. (p. 404)

burgs (bergs) Medieval towns. (p. 403)

C

caliph (kā′ lif) Muslim ruler. (p. 336)

campesinos (kam puh sē′ nōz) Latin American farmers and peasants. (p. 640)

canon laws (kan′ uhn lahs) Church laws. (p. 382)

capitalism (ka pih tuhl izm) An economic system where most production is privately owned. (p. 633)

captaincies (kap′ tuhn sēs) Land in Brazil given to Portuguese nobles. (p. 488)

caravans (kar′ uh vans) Groups who traveled together for safety. (p. 121)

caravel (kar′ uh vel) Portuguese ship. (p. 469)

cash crops (kash krops) Crops sold in the market. (p. 638)

castles (kas′ uhlz) Large, fortified houses. (p. 370)

catacombs (kat′ uh kōmz) Underground cemeteries. (p. 214)

cathedrals (kuh thē′ druhlz) Churches headed by bishops. (p. 386)

caudillo (kau dē′ yō) Latin American military dictator. (p. 556)

census (sen′ suhs) Population count. (p. 234)

chancellor (chan′ suh luhr) English university head. (p. 387); Prime minister. (p. 613)

charters (char′ tuhrz) Documents that enabled towns to control their affairs. (p. 405)

chateaux (sha tōz′) French castles. (p. 440)

chieftain (chēf′ tuhn) Clan leader. (p. 267)

churches (cher′ chez) Groups of people who share the same religious beliefs. (p. 252)

circuit judges (ser′ kit juj′ iz) Judges who travel throughout a country. (p. 415)

citadel (sit′ uh duhl) Fortress. (p. 85)

city-states (sit′ ē stāts) Cities and the surrounding territories. (p. 57)

civil disobedience (siv′ uhl dis uh bē′ dē uhns) Refusal to obey government demands. (p. 634)

civilians (suh vil′ yuhnz) Non-soldiers. (p. 604)

civilization (siv′ uh luh zā shuhn) Society with a developed knowledge of farming, trade, government, art, and science. (p. 33)

civil wars (siv′ uhl wōrz) Wars between citizens of one nation. (p. 159)

clans (klans) Groups based on family ties. (p. 367)

classical writings (klas′ i′ kuhl rī tēngs) Ancient Greek and Roman writings. (p. 433)

clergy (kler′ jē) Religious leaders. (p. 367)

climate (klī′ mit) Average weather condition at a place over a period of years. (p. 14)

code of chivalry (kōd of shiv′ uhl rē) Rules knights had to live by. (p. 373)

cold war (kōld wōr) Non fighting hostility between nations. (p. 625)

collectivization (kuh lek ti vuh zā′ shuhn) Uniting small farms into large ones controlled by the government. (p. 611)

colonies (kol′ uh nēz) Permanent settlements. (p. 105)

colonize (kol′ uh nīz) Permanently settle in an area. (p. 487)

communes (kom′ yūnz) Political groups formed by townspeople in medieval Italy. (p. 405)

communicable diseases (kahmū ni kah bl dis ē zez) Diseases that are passed from an infected person or animal to another person or animal. (p. 660)

compass (kum′ puhs) Instrument used to tell direction. (p. 468)

concentration camps (kon suhn trā shuhn kamps) Prison camps for political enemies. (p. 620)

conquistadores (kon kē stuh dōr′ ēz) Spanish conquerors in the 1500s. (p. 473)

constitution (kon stuh tū′ shuhn) Written laws used to govern a state. (p. 169)

constitutional monarchy (kon stuh tū′ shuh nuhl mon′ uhr kē) Monarchy limited in its powers by a constitution. (p. 518)

consuls (kon′ suhlz) Heads of the ancient Roman Republic. (p. 219)

continental drift (kon tuh nen′ tl drift) Theory that the continents move. (p. 10)

convents (kon′ vents) Communities of nuns. (p. 255)

converted (kuhn ver′ tuhd) Changed. (p. 277)
coracles (kor′ uh kuhls) Small Irish boats. (p. 290)
core (kōr) Central part of the Earth. (p. 10)
corregidores (kō rā hē dō′ rās) Spanish royal officials. (p. 423)
cotton gin (kot′ n jin) Cotton-cleaning machine. (p. 527)
counts (kounts) French law court officials. (p. 281)
cremation ovens (krē mā′ shuhn uh′ vuhns) Furnaces that burn bodies to ashes. (p. 619)
crusades (krū sāds′) Wars fought to regain the Holy Land from Muslims. (p. 388)
crust (krust) Outer layer of the Earth. (p. 10)
culture (kuhl′ chuhr) Way of life. (p. 61)
cuneiform (kyū nē′ uh form) Sumerian writing made up of wedge-shaped signs. (p. 58)
czar (zahr) Russian ruler. (p. 355)

D

dauphin (do′ fuhn) Eldest son of the king of France. (p. 417)
defensive league (di fen′ siv lēg) Protective group formed by Greek city-states. (p. 173)
democratic (dem uh krat′ ik) Favoring the equality of all people. (p. 169)
depression (di presh′ uhn) Economic decline. (p. 607)
descendants (di sen′ duhnts) Offspring. (p. 107)
de-Stalinization (dē stahl uh nuh zā′ shuhn) Attack on Stalin's policies. (p. 633)
developing countries (duh vel′ uh pēng kuhn′ trēs) Countries advancing in production, technology, and standard of living. (p. 634)
dictator (dik′ tā tuhr) Absolute ruler of a state. (p. 228)
dictatorship (dik tā′ tuhr ship) Government ruled by a dictator. (p. 613)
diet (dī′ uht) Formal assembly. (p. 421)
diocese (dī′ uh sis) Area under the control of a bishop. (p. 253)
direct tax (duh rekt′ taks) Tax paid directly to a government. (p. 509)
doge (dōj) Ruler of Renaissance Venice. (p. 440)
domesticated (duh mes′ tuh kāt uhd) Tamed. (p. 42)
domestic system (duh mes′ tik sis′ tuhm) Manufacturing done in workers' cottages. (p. 526)
domus (dō′ muhs) Roman house. (p. 236)
dowry (dow′ rē) Wealth brought by a woman when she marries. (p. 322)
dubbing (dub′ ēng) Ceremony in which a squire is made a knight. (p. 374)
dynasty (dī nuh stē) Series of rulers from the same family. (p. 88)

E

earthquake (erth′ kwāk) Shaking or sliding of a portion of the Earth's crust. (p. 11)
Eddas (ed′ uhz) Written poems based on stories of Viking gods. (p. 303)
elevation (el uh vā′ shuhn) Altitude. (p. 9)
embalming (em bahm′ ēng) Process used to keep dead bodies from decaying. (p. 73)
emigrated (em′ uh grāt ed) Left one's country. (p. 200)
emigrés (em′ uh grāz) French political exiles. (p. 518)
emirs (i miuhrs′) Muslim army leaders. (p. 393)
emperor (em′ phur uhr) Ruler of an empire. (p. 233)
enclosure (en klō′ zuhr) Fencing off common land for individual use. (p. 525)
erosion (i rō′ zuhn) Wearing away by wind, water, and ice. (p. 12)
estates (e stāts′) French social classes. (p. 513)
excavated (ek′ skuh vā tuhd) Uncovered by digging. (p. 27)
excommunicated (ek skuh myū nuh kā ted) Barred as a member of the Roman Catholic Church. (p. 382)
extended families (ek sten′ duhd fam′ uh lēs) Parents, children, and other relatives living together in one house. (p. 639)

F

factories (fak′ tuhr ēz) Buildings where goods are manufactured. (p. 200)
factory system (fak′ tuh rē sis′ tuhm) Workers and machines in one place to make goods. (p. 527)
fairs (fāuhrz) Medieval gatherings for trade. (p. 402)
fasces (fas′ ēz) Rods tied around an ax. (p. 215)
federal (fed′ uhr uhl) National government. (p. 546)
feudalism (fyū′ dl iz uhm) Medieval political system based on the relation of lords to vassals. (p. 367)

fiefs (fēfs) Pieces of land given to vassals by their lords. (p. 368)
flying shuttle (flī′ ēng shut′ l) Weaving device that carries thread quickly back and forth across the piece being woven. (p. 526)
foreign policy (fōr′ uhn pol′ uh sē) Relations with other countries. (p. 507)
Forum (fōr′ uhm) Roman public square. (p. 215)
freemen (frē′ muhn) Peasants who paid the lord for the right to farm their own land. (p. 377)
freedmen (frēd′ muhn) Former slaves. (p. 234)
friars (frī uhrs) Preachers. (p. 385)

G

galleons (gal′ ē uhns) Spanish ships. (p. 459)
garrison (gar′ uh suhn) Military force stationed in an area. (p. 609)
genocide (jen′ uh sīd) Deliberate destruction of an entire people. (p. 620)
gentiles (jen′ tīls) Non-Jews. (p. 249)
geography (jē ahg ruh fē) Study of the Earth and the ways people live and work on it. (p. 5)
glaciers (glā′ shuhrz) Great Ice sheets. (p. 13)
gladiatorial games (glad′ ē uh tōr ē uhl gāmz) Roman games in which gladiators fought. (p. 215)
gladiators (glad′ ē ā tuhrz) Fighters in gladiatorial games. (p. 238)
glasnost (glaz nōst) Russian policy allowing openness. (p. 633)
grand jury (grand jūr′ ē) Jury that examines accusations and advises criminal charges. (p. 415)
Greek fire (grēk fīr) Chemical weapon used by the Byzantines. (p. 324)
greenhouse effect (grēn hows uh fekt) Carbon dioxide traps heat from the Earth's surface. (p. 659)
guerrilla warfare (guh ril′ uh wōr′ fār) Hit-and-run fighting. (p. 573)
guilds (gildz) Medieval craft organizations. (p. 406)
guillotine (gil′ uh tēn) Machine that cuts off a victim's head. (p. 518)

H

habitats (ha buh tats) Dwelling places. (p. 658)
haciendas (ah sē en′ duhz) Large ranches. (p. 640)
hajj (haj) Muslim journey to Makkah. (p. 336)
hard-liners (hahrd līnuhrz) People who stick to their ideas regardless of circumstances. (p. 632)
heavy industry (hev′ ē in′ duhs trē) Industry that manufactures machines. (p. 611)
helots (hel′ uhtz) Spartan slaves. (p. 164)
heresy (her′ uh sē) Religious belief at odds with church doctrine. (p. 253)
heretic (her′ uh tik) Church member who disagrees with official doctrine. (p. 451)
hieroglyphic (hī uhr uh glif′ ik) Egyptian writing system based on pictures. (p. 77)
Holocaust (hol′ uh kahst) Nazi program of genocide against the Jews. (p. 621)
holy of holies (hō′ lē of hō′ lēs) Innermost and most sacred chamber of a temple. (p. 104)
home territory (hōm ter′ uh tōr ē) Area where hunters and food gatherers lived. (p. 35)
hostage (hos′ tij) Person held by another until certain promises are carried out. (p. 193)
humanists (hyū′ muh nists) Philosophers who believe that people are important. (p. 433)
hypothesis (hī poth′ uh sis) Possible explanation for a problem. (p. 188)

I

icons (ī konz) Sacred pictures of Eastern Orthodoxy. (p. 325)
imam (i mam′) Muslim prayer leader. (p. 335)
immigrants (im′ uh gruhnts) People who settle permanently in a different country. (p. 534)
imperialism (im pir′ ē uh liz uhm) Establishing colonies and building empires. (p. 579)
indentured servants (in den′ chuhrd ser′ vuhntz) Settlers who pledged labor for their passage to the Americas. (p. 495)
indulgences (in dul′ juhnt sez) Church pardons that lessen punishment for sins. (p. 450)
industrialized (in dus′ trē uh līzd) Developed industry. (p. 533)
inflation (in flā shuhn) Period when prices go up and money value goes down. (p. 240)
interchangeable parts (in tuhr chān juh buhl parts) Machine parts made to a uniform size so they could be easily replaced. (p. 527)
internal combustion engine (in tuhr′ nuhl kuhm buhs′ chuhn en′ juhn) Engine that is fueled by gasoline. (p. 535)
isolationist (ī sō lā shun ist) A country that stays out of the affairs of other countries. (p. 606)

intifada (in tuh fah duh) A 1987 Palestinian uprising. (p. 655)

J

jarls (yahrlz) Viking military leaders. (p. 301)
journeyman (jer′ nē muhn) Person who works under a master for a daily wage. (p. 406)
joust (jowst) Contest on horseback between two knights. (p. 374)
judge (juj) Hebrew tribe leader. (p. 112)
junker (jung′ kuhr) Rich Prussian landowner. (p. 574)
junta (hun′ tuh) Committee organized to take over a government. (p. 553)
juris prudentes (jū′ ruhs prū′ duhntz) Roman lawyers. (p. 236)

K

kaiser (kī′ zuhr) German emperor. (p. 574)
keep (kēp) Strongest part of a castle. (p. 371)
khan (kahn) Mongol leader. (p. 353)
king's peace (kings pēs) Protection extended to any area an Anglo-Saxon king visited. (p. 295)
knight (nīt) Warrior on horseback. (p. 369)
kremlin (krem′ luhn) Russian fortress. (p. 354)

L

labyrinth (lab′ uh rinth) Maze. (p. 153)
ladies (lā′ dēz) Noblewomen. (p. 372)
landforms (land′ forms) Physical features of the Earth's surface. (p. 9)
latifundias (lat uh fuhn′ dē uhs) Large Roman estates. (p. 225)
latitude (lat′ uh tūd) Imaginary lines that measure distance from the Equator. (p. 14)
legionaries (lē′ juh ner ēz) Roman soldiers. (p. 221)
legions (lē juhnz) Divisions of Roman soldiers. (p. 221)
liberals (lib′ uhr uhls) People who favor political reforms. (p. 566)
limited government (lim′ uh tid guv′ uhrn muhnt) Government has only powers given to it by the people. (p. 513)
lords (lordz) Medieval nobles. (p. 283)

M

macadam road (muh kad′ uhm rōd) Road made of layers of crushed rock. (p. 529)
manifest destiny (man′ uh fest des′ tuh nē) Belief that the United States should extend from coast to coast. (p. 548)
mandate (man′ dāt) Authority to govern. (p. 606)
manors (man′ uhrz) Medieval estates with a lord and tenants. (p. 375)
mantle (man′ tl) Part of the Earth beneath the crust and above the core. (p. 10)
martial law (mar′ shuhl lah) Rule by the army instead of by civil government. (p. 505)
mass (mas) Worship service. (p. 382)
masters (mas′ tuhrz) Experts. (p. 406)
megaron (meg′ uh ron) Square room in the center of a Mycenaean palace. (p. 155)
mercantilism (mer′ kuhn tēl iz uhm) System in which colonies provide wealth to their parent country. (p. 508)
mercenaries (mer′ suh nār ēz) Men hired to be soldiers for a foreign country. (p. 175)
messiah (muh′ sī′ uh) Savior. (p. 248)
mestizos (me stē′ zōz) People of mixed European and Native American Ancestry. (p. 490)
metropolitans (met ruh pol′ uh tuhns) Eastern Orthodox Church officials in charge of large cities. (p. 325)
migrate (mī′ grāt) To move from one place to another. (p. 34)
minerals (min′ uhr uhls) Nonliving substances found beneath the Earth's surface. (p. 19)
ministers (min′ uh stuhrz) Protestant religious leaders. (p. 452)
minstrels (min′ struhlz) Medieval traveling poets and singers. (p. 285)
missionary (mish′ uh ner ē) Person who tries to convert nonbelievers. (p. 250)
mobilize (mō′ buh līz) Prepare troops for action. (p. 604)
monarchies (mon′ uhr kēz) Countries ruled by a king or queen. (p. 411)
monasteries (mon′ uh ster ēz) Places where monks live. (p. 255)
monks (mungks) Men who live in a religious community. (p. 255)
monopoly (muh nop′ uh lē) Total control. (p. 508)
monsoons (mon sūnz) Seasonal winds that change direction. (p. 16)
mosaics (mō zā′ iks) Colorful pictures made of stone or glass. (p. 323)

mosque (mosk) Muslim house of worship. (p. 335)
multinational companies (mul tē na shun ul kum pun ēz) Companies that operate across national boundaries. (p. 661)
mummy (mum ē) Wrapped body of preserved dead person. (p. 73)
mundus (muhn′ duhs) Meeting point of the worlds of the living and the dead for the Romans. (p. 216)
municipal (myū nis′ uh puhl) Relating to a city. (p. 215)
mutiny (myūt′ n ē) Revolt against officers. (p. 472)

N

nationalists (nash′ uh nuhl ists) People in favor of national independence. (p. 566)
national workshops (nash′ uh nuhl wuhrk′ shops) Factories run by workers but paid for by the government. (p. 570)
natural resources (nach′ uhr uhl rē′ sōr sez) Materials found in nature. (p. 19)
necropolis (nek rop′ uh luhs) Etruscan cemetery. (p. 214)
nobles (nō′ buhlz) People having high rank in a kingdom. (p. 90)
nomadic (nō mad′ ik) Wandering. (p. 129)
nonrenewable resources (non ri nū′ uh buhl rē sōr sez) Irreplaceable natural resources. (p. 20)
nuns (nunz) Women belonging to a religious order. (p. 255)

O

oath-helpers (ōth help′ erz) Germans who swore an accused person was telling the truth. (p. 269)
ocean current (ō′ shun kur′ uhnt) Water that flows in the ocean in a steady stream. (p. 16)
oligarchy (ol′ uh gahr kē) Government in which a few people rule. (p. 169)
omens (ō′ muhnz) Signs believed to indicate the future. (p. 214)
open-hearth process (ō′ puhn hahrth prah′ ses) Process that uses a special kind of furnace to make steel inexpensively. (p. 529)
oracles (ōr′ uh kuhlz) Greeks through whom the gods spoke. (p. 179)
oracle bones (ōr′ uh kuhl bōnz) Bones used by the Shang to receive messages from ancestors. (p. 90)
orator (ōr′ uh ter) Public speaker. (p. 195)
ordeal (ōr dēl) Painful test used by the Germans to decide innocence or guilt. (p. 269)
orders (ōr′ duhrs) Groups of friars. (p. 386)

P

page (pāj) Person who helped knights care for their horses and armor. (p. 373)
pancratium (pan krā′ shē uhm) Olympic event that combined boxing and wrestling. (p. 183)
papal line of demarcation (pā′ puhl līn ov dē mahr kā′ shuhn) Line drawn in 1493 dividing Spanish and Portuguese land claims. (p. 473)
papyrus (puh pī′ ruhs) Egyptian paper. (p. 78)
parchment (parch′ muhnt) Material made from thin animal skin used for windows and as paper. (p. 153)
parish (par′ ish) Area assigned to a local church. (p. 253)
patriarchs (pā′ trē arks) Most important bishops in the early Christian church. (p. 253)
patricians (puh trish′ uhnz) Powerful upper-class citizens of ancient Rome. (p. 219)
peninsulares (puh nin sū la′ rās) Colonials born in Spain who later came to the Americas. (p. 490)
pentathlon (pen tath′ luhn) Olympic game made up of five events. (p. 183)
perestroika (pār uhs troi kuh) Russian system of restructuring. (p. 633)
perioeci (pār ē ē′ sī) Merchants and artisans in Spartan villages. (p. 166)
phalanx (fā′ langks) Greek infantry formation. (p. 194)
pharaoh (fār′ ō) Egyptian ruler. (p. 70)
philosophes (fē luh zofs′) French philosophers of the 1700s. (p. 514)
philosophia (fi la sō fē′ ya) The love of wisdom, according to the Greeks. (p. 185)
piazza (pē aht′ suh) Italian city square. (p. 436)
pilgrimage (pil′ gruh mij) Religious journey to a shrine or holy place. (p. 133)
pilgrims (pil′ gruhms) People who travel to a holy place to worship. (p. 332)
pillars of faith (pil′ uhrs of fāth) Five Muslim duties as described in the Quran. (p. 335)
planned communities (pland kuh myū′ nuh tēz) Cities built to a definite plan. (p. 85)
plebeians (pli bē uhnz) Poor and lower-class citizens of ancient Rome. (p. 219)
plebiscite (pleb′ uh sīt) Popular vote. (p. 563)

polar zone (pō′ luhr zōn) Climate zone more than 60° north or south of the Equator. (p. 15)
polis (pah′ lis) Greek city-state. (p. 163)
political parties (puh lit′ uh kuhl par′ tēz) Groups with set ideas about government. (p. 546)
political science (puh lit′ uh kuhl sī′ uhns) Study of government. (p. 187)
popular sovereignty (pop′ yuh luhr sov′ ruhn tē) Idea that government derives its powers from the people. (p. 513)
population (pop ū lā shuhn) Number of living things in a particular area. (p. 42)
population explosion (pop ū lā′ shuhn ek splō′ zhuhn) Sudden growth in the number of people. (p. 136)
precipitation (prē sip uh tā shuhn) Falling moisture such as snow or rain. (p. 16)
prehistory (prē′ his tuh rē) Time before people began to keep written records. (p. 33)
prevailing winds (pri vā′ lēng winds) Winds that blow mostly from one direction. (p. 16)
priest (prēst) Religious leader, usually Roman Catholic or Eastern Orthodox. (p. 253)
priest-king (prēst king) Sumerian governmental and religious leader. (p. 59)
printing press (prin′ tēng pres) Machine for printing books, using movable type. (p. 441)
privatize (prī vuh tīz) Allowing private citizen ownership. (p. 648)
proletariat (pro luh tār′ ē uht) Industrial working class. (p. 568)
prophets (prof′ its) People claiming to have messages from God. (p. 112)
protectorate (pruh tek′ tuhr it) Country that gives up foreign policy to an imperial authority. (p. 582)
provinces (prah′ vins uhs) Political districts. (p. 119)
psalms (sahms) Sacred songs. (p. 112)
publicans (pub′ luh′ kuhnz) Ancient Roman tax collectors. (p. 225)
purges (per′ juhs) Removals of undesirable members. (p. 631)
pyramids (pir′ uh midz) Large Egyptian tombs. (p. 71)

Q

quipus (k′ pūz) Inca counting devices. (p. 142)

R

reformation (ref uhr mā′ shuhn) Change. (p. 449)
reform (rē form) Change that leads to improvement. (p. 61)
reign (rān) Period of power. (p. 63)
relative location (rel uhtiv lō kā shun) Location of place in relation to other places. (p. 6)
relics (rel′ iks) Sacred objects from the past. (p. 319)
relief (ri lēf′) Differences in height between a region's summits and lowlands. (p. 9)
renewable resources (ri nū′ uh buhl rē sōr sez) Replaceable natural resources. (p. 20)
repealed (ri pēld′) Abolished or called back. (p. 507)
representative government (rep ri ent′ uht iv guv′ uhrn muhnt) System of ruling in which officials are elected. (p. 546)
republic (ri pub′ lik) Government in which citizens choose their leaders. (p. 219)
revolution (rev uh lū′ shuhn) Activity designed to overthrow a government. (p. 503)
right of extraterritoriality (rīt ov ek struh ter i tōr ē al′ uh tē) Right of an accused person in a different country to be tried in a court of his or her own nation. (p. 587)
river system (riv′ uhr sis tuhm) River and all streams that flow into it. (p. 14)
rule by divine right (rūl bī duh vīn′ rīt) Rule based on the theory that a monarch's right to rule comes from God. (p. 243)
runes (rūnz) Letters of the Viking alphabet. (p. 303)

S

sabbath (sab′ uhth) Day of the week used for rest and worship. (p. 113)
sans-culottes (san skū′ lahts) French city workers and peasants in the 1700s. (p. 518)
satellite nations (sat′ l īt nā shuhns) Countries controlled by another, stronger country. (p. 626)
scientific method (sī uhn tif′ ik meth′ uhd) Process used by scientists for study. (p. 188)
scorched-earth policy (skōrchd uhrth pahl′ uh sē) Tactic of destruction used by a retreating army. (p. 564)
scribe (skrīb) Sumerian writer. (p. 58)
scriptures (skrip′ churz) Sacred writings. (p. 247)

INDEX

D

E

I

J

K

L